KT-552-402

SOME KIND OF HERO 07

THE REMARKABLE STORY OF
THE JAMES BOND FILMS

MATTHEW FIELD & AJAY CHOWDHURY

The
History
Press

DUDLEY LIBRARIES

000002179165	
Askews & Holts	16-Aug-2018
	£20.00
2DU	

First published 2015

This edition published 2018 by

The History Press
The Mill, Brimscombe Port
Stroud, Gloucestershire, GL5 2QG
www.thehistorypress.co.uk

© SKOH Limited, 2015, 2018

The right of Matthew Field and Ajay Chowdhury to be identified
as the Authors of this work has been asserted in accordance with the
Copyright, Designs and Patents Act 1988.

All rights reserved. No part of this book may be reprinted
or reproduced or utilised in any form or by any electronic,
mechanical or other means, now known or hereafter invented,
including photocopying and recording, or in any information
storage or retrieval system, without the permission in writing
from the Publishers.

British Library Cataloguing in Publication Data.
A catalogue record for this book is available from the British Library.

ISBN 978 0 7509 6977 2

Typesetting and origination by The History Press
Printed and bound in Turkey by Imak

SOME KIND OF HERO 07

000002179165

DEDICATION

Matthew: For my mum and dad, Adrian and Wendy, the two people responsible for introducing me to the world of James Bond. For my wife Philippa, who endured this project with me. And for my children Sophie and William: through their eyes I look forward to experiencing these films all over again. . .

Ajay: For my late father Diljeet and my dear mother Jasprit, who gave their three sons: my older brother Avneet, my twin brother Udey and myself the gift of James Bond. And for Zayn, Emrys, Teya, Cyrus, Ishani and Leeya, and those for whom Bond is yet to come. . .

. . .and to our dear friend – Brian James Smith.

CONTENTS

AUTHORS' NOTE

STUDIO LOGO

This book has been two decades in the writing. It is based on over 120 primary interviews made in person, by telephone and email, as well as hundreds of secondary interviews and articles sourced from newspapers, periodicals, magazines, websites, radio and television shows – published (and unpublished) over the past sixty-two years.

All original interviews were prepared and conducted by both authors but sometimes one or the other asked the actual questions. On those occasions the authors have taken a Lennon and McCartney approach and the interviews are jointly credited.

While every effort has been made to trace copyright holders and secure permissions for all quotes used, if any have been inadvertently overlooked, the publishers will be pleased to acknowledge them in future editions of this book. For any corrections or copyright enquiries please notify the authors by email: somekindofhero007@gmail.com.

In keeping with the tradition started in Raymond Benson's THE JAMES BOND BEDSIDE COMPANION, all book titles mentioned in the text are shown in capitals, e.g. GOLDFINGER and all film titles are italicised, e.g. *Goldfinger*.

INTRODUCTION

GUN BARREL

Ajay Chowdhury: In August 1977 on a rainy holiday in Caernarfon, North Wales I became a James Bond fan. My parents took their three restless sons to the cinema to watch *The Spy Who Loved Me*; when Bond cascaded off a mountain, only to be saved by his Union Jack parachute, I fell with him. From Luxor to the Lotus to the Liparus, I was led into the world of 007. Jaws' first appearance cloaked in shadow was genuinely terrifying. And, to cap it all, Roger Moore as James Bond finally gave me a hero I could respond to – audacious, assured, brilliant and, uniquely, British. Other things struck me, too: Ken Adam's gun-metal genius, Marvin Hamlisch's disco Bond '77 theme and the ingenious gadgets (I have never looked at ordinary objects in the same way since). I was six years old and too young to appreciate the libidinous delights of the film – that came later – but I was thoroughly entertained. Over the next few years I would enjoy *Star Wars*, *Star Trek* and *Superman*, but nobody did it better than Bond, as *Moonraker* proved. My theory is that we become Bond fans after the *second* Bond film we see. This is because we connect the dots and see the similarities between films. The gun barrel, the music, the titles, M, Q, Moneypenny – they all trigger a sense of connectivity, which inspires us to follow the journey of all 007's adventures.

Matthew Field: In July 1987 I went to the cinema for the very first time; the venue was the Poole Arts Centre and the film was *The Living Daylights*. I, too, was six years old and loved every minute of it. Later that year, following minor surgery, I woke to discover a gift at the foot of my hospital bed: Sally Hibbin's THE OFFICIAL JAMES BOND 007 MOVIE POSTER BOOK. I read it from cover to cover and, like every cereal packet reader, even digested the copyright notice. But, it would be an agonising eight years before I got to experience another

007 film in the theatre – what felt like a whole lifetime's wait. When *Licence to Kill* was awarded a 15-rated certificate this eight-year-old was left gazing at the poster outside the cinema, unable to watch it. Finally when *GoldenEye* arrived in 1995 I remember seeing it with ten of my classmates. We were the *GoldenEye* generation. From then on it became a ritual to see the new Bond film at the cinema, except girlfriends and wives now accompany us and on the last occasion, the Odeon Bournemouth was replaced by the Royal Albert Hall, when we attended the premiere of *Skyfall* together.

Field and Chowdhury: Being a James Bond fan is akin to supporting a sports team; when you see a Bond film at the cinema it is like watching your team play a match. However, the game is only part of the fun. Sports fans speculate on players, who will be transferred, whose performance was good or bad. Bond fans speculate on the actors chosen and critique their suitability. Sports fans follow the coaches, the managers and specialist trainers – the behind-the-scenes staff are increasingly under the spotlight. Bond fans follow the filmmakers, directors, writers, designers and stunt teams – noting their influence on the resulting picture. The importance of ownership and investment is reported more these days as sports teams have become huge franchises. For the Bond series, studio shenanigans have similarly affected the spy's performance. Team appreciation is often handed down from one generation to another and the family spirit of Bond has passed through, what in showbusiness terms, are eons. While the Bond team has cherished its star players from Sean Connery to Daniel Craig, we have also cherished our team founder Ian Fleming and our managers from Harry Saltzman and Cubby Broccoli to Michael G. Wilson and Barbara Broccoli. Without these people James Bond would not return.

We started out as James Bond fans and owe a huge debt of gratitude to the Bond community whose work we have admired and, in some cases, with whom we have formed friendships.

We stand on the shoulders of the following James Bond heroes: Ross Hendry, Richard Schenkman and Bob Forlini who founded the earliest James Bond fan clubs. John Pearson, John Brosnan, Steven Jay Rubin, Raymond Benson, Lee Pfeiffer, Philip Lisa, Dave Worrall, Andrew Lycett, Alan Barnes, Marcus Hearn, John Cork, Bruce Scivally and Paul Duncan – the authors of our favourite James Bond bibles.

We would also like to thank the following individuals from the global fan community who have added to our knowledge of 007: Oliver Bayan, Michael van Blaricum, Remmert van Braam, Heiko Baumann, Luc Le Clech, Jeremy

Duns, Brad Frank, Tim Greaves, Markus Hartmann, Charles Helfenstein, Jerome Nicod, Thomas Nixdorf, Edward Coffrini Dell'Orto, Laurent Perriot, Andrew Pilkington, Doug Redenius, David A. Reinhardt, Pierre Rodiac, Graham Rye, Panos Sambrakos, Robert Sellers, Dr. Siegfried Tesche and Wolfgang Thuerauf.

In a professional capacity, we have both become involved in various aspects of the entertainment industry and so began to appreciate the work of the producers in a more professional context. We went from Bond fans to Bond scholars. As we delved deeper into the Bond mythos we realised there were many untold tales from many unsung heroes who played key creative roles in the series. We gained a renewed respect for not only how the series was founded but also how a Rolls Royce standard has been maintained.

This book was written to *accompany* the DVDs and the trove of Bond treasure already in the public domain. We have deliberately refrained from reviewing each film because every fan has their favourites and their guilty pleasures. This book is not a definitive 'making-of volume', but hopefully offers an insight into the reasons behind some of the creative and commercial decisions made. We are huge fans of the Ian Fleming Bond books and continuation novels, and encourage people to read a Bond adventure. However, the literary tale of Bond was not the remit of this volume.

We have sought to accurately cite our sources and provide a contextualised story of events. Over the years so many errors have entered the narrative, which have then been repeated as fact. We hope to rectify some of those myths with this book. Where stories have differed and recollections have been contradictory we have used our judgment to decide the version of events related. Where we have erred we do encourage the reader to contact us with any corrections by email: somekindofhero007@gmail.com.

This manuscript was conceived, in some form, over two decades ago, but the book you are reading is extremely recent. We have deliberately chosen to end our tale at the announcement of the 2015 film, *SPECTRE*. As you read this we hope you have digested the twenty-fourth Eon Bond film, then discussed – or probably argued over – it with friends and family. *SPECTRE* will undoubtedly be another great chapter in the remarkable story of the James Bond films.

In preparing this book many unlikely events occurred. In 2010 we attended the Edinburgh International Film Festival of which Sir Sean Connery was a patron. We found ourselves at a private festival party – a traditional Scottish ceilidh. We spent the evening plotting how to engineer an introduction to our carefully guarded host, Sir Sean. Many ideas were considered, from the sublime to the ridiculous. During our deliberations we were interrupted by an apologetic festival publicist, who politely enquired whether we would mind awfully posing with Sir Sean with a glass of red wine on behalf of the drinks sponsor. Generously we consented; five years later it was time to ask Sir Sean to repay that favour.

After contacting his fellow Bonds we wrote a lengthy plea to Sir Sean requesting an interview for this book. No response. We then sent a personal note to his home in the Bahamas. Nix. We telephoned his team but got nowhere. We planned trips to New York, Scotland and the Bahamas to finesse the interview but all came to naught. Finally, as our deadline approached, we gave it one last try and telephoned Sir Sean's home in Paradise Island. After negotiating with an intermediary, miraculously, we were put through. The world's most famous voice came on the line. A rather bad line. Sir Sean explained, 'I cannot be responsible for the mail in this country because it goes to Jamaica first. We have a phone system and a mail system not to be envied.' Sir Sean excused himself as he had a pressing engagement. He was open to rearranging an interview at a later date. Too late for this book!

SOME KIND OF HERO will return.

Matthew Field & Ajay Chowdhury

London, August 2015

The authors share a glass of wine with 007 – Sean Connery.

PREFACE TO PAPERBACK EDITION

PRE-TITLE SEQUENCE

To take up the analogy in the introduction to the hardback of this book, our James Bond team called *Spectre* has played its match and left the field. The film was the second highest grossing worldwide in the series and carried off an Oscar for Best Original Song to boot. As usual, true Bond fans debate its merits but it now sits comfortably as a Blu-ray, DVD or download in collections around the world. And we wait to see what the team manager and players come up with next for *Bond 25*.

We are pleased to present our account of the making of the 24th Eon 007 film. There was a long tail on this ghost: *Spectre* represents the breadth and depth of the remarkable history of the James Bond films, being the culmination of the rich, contentious backstory of some of the plot elements and characters. We were granted fascinating, fresh interviews for the preparation of the additional chapters in this paperback and are deeply grateful to the following: Daniel Craig, Rory Kinnear, Steve Begg, Chris Corbould, Per Hallberg, Michael Lerman, Daniel Kleinman, John Logan, Callum McDougall, Debbie McWilliams, Gary Powell, Jany Temime, Neal Purvis, Robert Wade and especially to Sam Mendes.

The authors would also like to thank Sir Sean Connery for his input.

We have had the opportunity to clarify, correct and reconfigure the original text of this book and for assisting us with this, we thank the following eagle-eyed readers: Professor James Chapman, Udey Chowdhury, Joanna

Clément (née Harwood), John Grover, Tim Partridge, Steven Saltzman and Alan Stephenson. For additional help we are grateful to: Greg Bechtloff, Daniel Couch, Anders Frejdh, Professor Sheldon Hall, M. David Mullen ASC, Steve Oxenrider, Vipul Patel, Doug Redenius, Mike Smith, Dave Worrall and, for special services, Brian James Smith, Mark Witherspoon and Gareth Owen.

This edition is dedicated to the memory of the late James Bond heroes Peter Janson-Smith, Sir Ken Adam, Lewis Gilbert and Guy Hamilton.

Matthew Field & Ajay Chowdhury
London, May 2018

The authors take their hardback to Pinewood Studios, 2016. (Matthew Field)

THE OTHER FELLA

Ironically, for someone who didn't want to get typecast as James Bond, it's the one thing I always get asked about. It always comes back to 007. Over the years I became the rogue Bond, the guy who turned his back on the most coveted role in cinema. To this day journalists remain fascinated how a male model, who had never stepped on a movie set in his life, convinced two of the most powerful producers in the business that he was the guy to fill Sean Connery's shoes. I guess it is a fascinating tale.

I had no fear when I went up for the role. I nearly died as a kid, and coupled with growing up in a rough Australian suburb, I threw myself 100 per cent into life. When I was cast in 1968, people around me felt that 007 was out of vogue, not current – part of the Establishment. I wasn't a dedicated actor – I just wanted to have a good time: make love, not war.

Discussing my recollections of making *On Her Majesty's Secret Service* for this book stirred many memories; chiefly, what it was like to be at the centre of the James Bond storm. One minute I was standing in Harry Saltzman's office being offered the biggest role in showbusiness and then, eighteen months later, I was back in Australia where I started. I soon got back on my feet, however, and since then have lived so many lives and enjoyed and endured so many rich, life-changing experiences.

This year, I returned to Piz Gloria in Switzerland where I made the film, some forty-five years ago. I was warmed by the generations of people from all around the world who had come to celebrate my Bond film, which has aged like a vintage wine. It has gone on to become a firm favourite amongst 007 connoisseurs.

I've enjoyed contributing to SOME KIND OF HERO and I hope it both informs and entertains you. Matthew and Ajay have done a great job in telling my part of the remarkable story of the James Bond films.

George Lazenby
Los Angeles, August 2015

George Lazenby revisits Piz Gloria in 2015. (Matthew Field)

1

SHOWBIZ IS A GHASTLY BIZ

IAN FLEMING

an Fleming had always wanted his James Bond novels to be filmed. He understood that commercially more books were sold as a result of films being made from them – cinema reached larger audiences than libraries. In an amusing article titled 'How to Write a Thriller' Fleming admitted that he wrote 'unashamedly, for pleasure and money'.[1] The writer elaborated, 'You don't make a great deal of money from royalties and translation rights and so forth and, unless you are very industrious and successful, you could only just about live on these profits, but if you sell the serial rights and film rights, you do very well.'[2]

In correspondence to a friend in October 1952, months before the publication of his debut novel CASINO ROYALE, Fleming stated, 'What I want is not a publisher, but a "factory" that will shift this opus of mine like 'Gone with the Naked and the Dead'. I am not being vain about this book but simply trying to squeeze the last dirty cent out of it.'[3] Fleming's blending of two of the biggest selling novels of the age – GONE WITH THE WIND by Margaret Mitchell and THE NAKED AND THE DEAD by Norman Mailer – was an example of his sly, often overlooked, humour that is to be found throughout his writing. However, it was also a sign of his ambition.

A further indication of Fleming's aspirations was the bespoke typewriter he had specially made before finishing his debut novel: a Royal Quiet Deluxe model, but this one was gold-plated at a 1952 cost of $174.[4] It represented a sizeable investment in his proposed future career and was a perfect example of Fleming's style to complete the manuscript of a first novel with such a luxurious machine in his possession.

Fleming also purchased a small theatrical agency, Glidrose Productions Limited. Named after its principals, John Gliddon and Norman Rose, the company served primarily as a corporate vehicle for Fleming to assign the literary copyright of his novels. If royalties were to run to riches this shrewd act would save Fleming huge sums in taxes. This was in November 1952, five months before publication of his first novel.[5] Undoubtedly this was a writer preparing for success.

Ian Fleming was born on 28 May 1908 at 27 Green Street in London's exclusive Mayfair.[6] His father, Valentine, was the son of Robert Fleming, a native Scot from Dundee, who had started work aged thirteen as an office boy with a local merchant.[7] Robert Fleming went on to make a fortune by investing in the railways of the United States of America.[8] He subsequently founded an eponymous merchant bank, which the Fleming family ran privately for generations to come.[9] Robert's actions certainly spoke louder than words in keeping with the Fleming clan motto – 'Let the Deed Shaw.'[10]

Ian was dealt a severe blow early in life when his father was killed in action during World War I. Valentine's widow, Eve, was left to raise her four sons – Peter (the eldest), Ian, Michael and Richard – on her own. While Valentine had left them financially comfortable it was on the condition that Eve did not remarry, and this branch of the family was effectively disinherited from the banking fortune.

While his eldest brother, Peter, was dutiful and diligent, Ian's disrupted childhood made him more daring and dangerous. Having been educated at Eton and then in Kitzbühel, Austria, Fleming excelled at athletics, winter sports and foreign languages. He formed a deep love of motorcars and an even deeper love of women – his time at the Royal Military Academy, Sandhurst came to a discreet end after he contracted a 'social disease'. After various attempts at a City career Fleming finally found firmer footing as a journalist, a career which allowed him to travel the world and meet extraordinary characters.

During World War II he served as the assistant to the Director of Naval Intelligence, Admiral Sir John Godfrey. Working in the Admiralty's Room 39 in Whitehall Fleming was privy to many secret meetings and events; he gained first-hand experience of weapons and underwent specialist training. Fleming met tough commandos and German spies, and was frequently asked to come up with ingenious intelligence ideas to thwart the enemy.[11]

In particular Fleming had dealings with the Political Warfare Executive run by Denis Sefton Delmer; this unit was responsible for sending black propaganda to the Germans via radio communications. As part of a psychological war programme, the idea was to sap German morale, and Fleming's language skills made him ideally suited for this task.[12]

All these experiences would find their way into his later work; Fleming brushed with the Establishment but was not quite part of it. As a restless, errant second son, Fleming enjoyed living on the edge of life. His Scottish background, his Etonian and Continental upbringing, womanising and observational journalism, as well as his close proximity to the intelligence world would all inform what many saw as his fantasy alterego: James Bond.

Ian Fleming began his book on the morning of 'the third Tuesday in January'[13] in 1952. On this day, he sat down to write what he called 'the spy story to end all spy stories'.[14] Working from Goldeneye, his holiday home in Jamaica, Fleming wrote quickly and with almost no notes. CASINO ROYALE drew upon experiences and extrapolations from his gambling days in Le Touquet and Deauville in France. The nub of the novel was based upon a real-life failed attempt to gamble away Nazi resources in Estoril, Portugal.[15] Fleming's first adventure was more a tone novella – incorporating exciting action on the green baize battlefield, as well as the streets of the fictional French seaside resort of Royale-les-Eaux and its environs. It was a tale of cheating and chance in life, love and death evoking strong sensations and the moral relativism of the Cold War.

Fleming saw James Bond as a modern anti-hero. His very name was a statement about how Fleming viewed his character. In a television interview shot at Goldeneye on 5 February 1964 Fleming recounted:

> When I started to write these books in 1952, I wanted to find a name which wouldn't have any of the romantic overtones, like Perriguine Carruthers. I wanted a really flat, quiet name. One of my bibles out here is James Bond's BIRDS OF THE WEST INDIES and I thought, 'James Bond, well now, that's a pretty quiet name,' so I simply stole it and used it.[16]

By chance, on the same day as that television interview, Fleming met the American ornithologist whose name he had stolen. Fleming inscribed a copy of his latest Bond novel 'To the real James Bond, from the thief of his identity'.[17]

CASINO ROYALE is not strictly an origin story, exploring how James Bond came into being. By the time Bond enters the narrative, he is already a Double-0 (the prefix to his code number designating his licence to kill). Bond is chosen for the mission in the story because he has already displayed a penchant for gambling and high-risk situations. M is set up as the chief of the Secret Service – a stern father figure who happened to have been an admiral. Miss Moneypenny occupies a sentence or two and Q Branch is referred to tangentially in a technical capacity. Bond forms firm friendships with a variety of people, such as philosophical French agent René Mathis, a man from the CIA who resembles a blonde Frank Sinatra, Felix Leiter and, back in London, Bond's best friend in the Service and M's Chief-of-Staff, Bill Tanner. Fleming also offered from the outset a high-toned insider's view of Bond's world: his preferred car, an Amherst Villiers supercharged Bentley, the potent martini – shaken, not stirred – and a beautiful companion, in this case, the hard-nippled Vesper Lynd.

CASINO ROYALE was published in the UK on 13 April 1953 by Jonathan Cape Limited.[18] Not one to miss a trick, Fleming had known the book would be published a couple of months before Queen Elizabeth II's coronation, so had deliberately titled the book to cash in on royal fever and the modest first pressing of 4,750 copies sold out quickly.[19] Meanwhile Fleming set about creating Bond's second adventure, LIVE AND LET DIE, on his golden typewriter. Author and friend Paul Gallico predicted after reading CASINO ROYALE that Bond would be perfect for the silver screen, but it would take some time getting there.[20]

The American agency Curtis Brown fielded initial enquiries about the possibility of adapting the novel for the screen. Normally when a book is adapted to screen any potential adapter first purchases an option. An option is an agreement to lease the rights to that book for a period of time. During this time the producer will try to get certain elements together. These elements could be to hire a writer to pen a workable screenplay, get the commitment of stars and a director and to raise the funds for a production and secure distribution (generally in that order). Once the film goes into production a further, more substantial, sum is usually payable. An option is commonly a smaller percentage for the eventual sum payable if the film gets made. Once the option period has expired, the rights usually lapse and the author keeps any sums paid regardless of whether a film has been made. Throughout the fifties the option price on the Fleming books gradually rose as they increased in sales and visibility.

In 1953 early interest came from a number of parties. Associated British Pictures were interested in Bond, but wanted to only use the character as a springboard on which to base another film.[21] The massive Music Corporation of America (MCA) enquired but this too came to naught.[22]

That same year veteran mogul of the British film industry, Sir Alexander Korda, expressed an interest in LIVE AND LET DIE, which, at that point, was still unpublished. Fleming was flattered by the interest, but Korda subsequently bowed out. This did not prevent Fleming pitching Korda his next, as yet unwritten, Bond novel – MOONRAKER. Fleming kept up the workflow and produced a new James Bond book every year. LIVE AND LET DIE was published in 1954 and MOONRAKER in 1955.

Curtis Brown sold what was effectively a licence to the Columbia Broadcasting System (CBS) to produce a one-off adaptation of CASINO ROYALE for $1,000; it was not an outright sale of the rights. On 21 May 1954 CBS broadcast a live one-hour adaptation of CASINO ROYALE as part of their *Climax!* series, sponsored by the Chrysler Corporation. It starred Barry Nelson as American 'Card Sense' Jimmy Bond who remembered, 'This show was done live at CBS Television City on a budget of about $25,000.'[23] Nelson was not proud of his debut as James Bond, 'It needed rewriting, more time in rehearsal, a bigger budget. It was done in haste, the exotic flavour of the story was totally lost and they just dismantled the character.'[24] Furthermore the female lead playing the first Bond girl, Valerie Mathis – not Vesper Lynd from the book – was not around, 'Linda Christian missed rehearsals – she had just initiated a divorce from Tyrone Power – so that didn't help the teamwork.'[25] That team included noted Hungarian actor Peter Lorre, who played the first Bond villain – Le Chiffre. The live broadcast required last-minute editing to fit the running time, as Nelson remembered, 'They went through and cut three words here, a line there, a half-a-word here, and the script ended up looking like a bad case of tic-tac-toe.'[26] All this last-minute anxiety took its toll, as Nelson explained, 'When some people get nervous, they get a facial twitch. Well, I had a body twitch. It was sheer fear. Peter Lorre saw me shaking and said, "Straighten up, Barry, so I can kill you!"'[27] Apocryphally after he is killed onscreen Lorre gets up and calmly walks off the set in full view of the cameras. Nelson was sanguine about the production years later, '[It was] really, truly funny and that's too bad because it wasn't supposed to be.'[28]

In May 1954 yet another film agent, John Shepridge of Famous Players, brokered a deal. He managed to sell a six-month option for CASINO ROYALE to Gregory Ratoff for $600.[29] In this case, if CASINO ROYALE was filmed, Fleming would pocket a further $6,000. In March 1955 Ratoff decided to purchase the film rights outright. When the Bond novels were eventually sold, this was the reason why CASINO ROYALE could not be included as part of the deal – one book had escaped the net. Ratoff's agent was the powerful Charles K. Feldman, a figure who would later loom large in the world of Bond.[30] Ian Fleming, in a typical show of flair, bought a Ford Thunderbird to celebrate the sale.[31]

In spring 1954 Stanley Meyer, the producer of television's *Dragnet* series at Warner Brothers, was looking for a new venture. He approached Fleming's West Coast agent, 'Swanee' Swanson, for an option on LIVE AND LET DIE and MOONRAKER. Meyer's offer was $500 for an option against $1,000 if the films were made. In what was to become a pattern Fleming held out for more money: he wanted $1,000 for the option against $25,000;[32] the books were not sold.

In November 1955 Swanson fielded an offer for $1,000 for a nine-month option for MOONRAKER from actor/producer John Payne. This option sum would be set off against a payment to Fleming of $10,000 should production go ahead.[33] However, back in England, the Rank Organization (the owners of Pinewood Studios) were interested in the same title. Fleming attempted to play the two parties off against each other, trying to get Rank into an auction with Payne – hoping to bump up the option price to $5,000. Potential legal ramifications clouded the film's horizon with an angry Payne eventually dropping out of the deal. Rank now had an open goal to grab the rights. However, the heat had gone out of the deal and Rank also passed.[34] Fleming claimed to have originally conceived MOONRAKER, his third novel, as a cinematic enterprise.

While the literary copyrights were retained by Glidrose Productions Limited, the film rights to the books were set up in trust for Fleming's son Caspar.[35]

A number of patterns began to emerge which explained why film deals could not be closed despite Fleming's Bond novels selling well. Chiefly, while his UK publishers, Jonathan Cape, were the only people authorised to handle film rights, Fleming had a range of agents informally dealing with his affairs, which complicated matters. Also, Fleming was either too vague about the deal or pitched his asking price too high. The rights situation became confusing for potential purchasers. One can easily see how the complex web of options, timelines and financial risk conspired to prevent a Bond film being made.

In 1956 Ratoff re-emerged and it was announced that a feature film of CASINO ROYALE would be filmed on locations in London and Italy 'using top stars' at a budget of $1.5 million.[36] Intriguingly, according to a US report at the time, Fleming appears to have tried his hand at screenwriting:

> Although the author has written an adaptation, Mr. Ratoff, who is now in Paris, is negotiating with a 'noted scenarist, as well as with two well-known stars to play the leads'. The plan is to film it in CinemaScope and color this summer in England, Estoril in Spain and San Remo. Twentieth Century-Fox is slated to release this feature.[37]

Once again, nothing came of this.

Meanwhile, Fleming continued to write the novels: DIAMONDS ARE FOREVER was published in 1956 and FROM RUSSIA WITH LOVE emerged the next year. Fleming was 'getting very fed up with Bond'[38] and his fifth novel was an attempt to push the literary boundaries. FROM RUSSIA WITH LOVE culminated in a cliffhanger ending in which Bond collapses, seemingly poisoned to death.

In 1956 Fleming went on a wildlife expedition to the island of Inagua in the Bahamas with a party that included his friend Ivar Bryce. This trip formed the basis for Crab Key – the exotic island retreat of Fleming's next villain. The research came in handy when, via Bryce, neophyte film producer Henry Morgenthau III approached Fleming to develop a television project. Aiming to boost the Jamaican tourist industry, Morgenthau came up with an idea ultimately entitled *James Gunn – Secret Agent*.

In August 1956 Fleming wrote a twenty-eight page outline, which Morgenthau III tried to develop into a television programme. Fleming received $1,000 against $2,000 if the pilot was accepted. Ultimately it was not and when the six-month option expired Fleming retained the rights, which he converted into his sixth book – DR. NO.

Published in spring 1958 DR. NO was the first of Fleming's novels to outrage the British Establishment. Critic Paul Johnson dismissed it as 'Sex, Sadism and Snobbery',[39] while sales skyrocketed. When a promising film offer was made for DR. NO Fleming now commanded an option fee of $3,000 against $30,000.[40]

It was at this moment that CBS approached Fleming for both a film and a television project. CBS chief, Bill Paley, was behind a project being prepared for a friend of his to be made in Monte Carlo. Paired with Greek shipping magnate Aristotle Onassis, Paley hired the now higher profile Fleming to develop a film.[41] However, CBS's head of television, Hubell Robinson, had independently approached Fleming for a television series. Now the author saw an even greater deal on the horizon. It was for Hubell that Fleming first wrote a memo describing how he saw James Bond on the screen. Fleming opposed:

> too much stage Englishness. There should, I think, be no monocles, mous-
> taches, bowler hats, bobbies or other 'Limey' gimmicks. There should be
> no blatant English slang, a minimum of public school ties and accents, and
> subsidiary characters should generally speak with a Scots or Irish accent. The
> Secret Service should be presented as a tough, modern organisation.[42]

Bond himself, should be a 'blunt instrument wielded by a government department'.[43] Fleming began developing numerous story outlines for thirty-two episodes.

Fleming suddenly had an embarrassment of film offers. As part of his CBS television deal, he had to stop the putative *Dr. No* film deal in its tracks[44] – at some point Paley had discovered that his television colleague was also working on a Fleming project. In the end the CBS deals cancelled each other out and Fleming was once again back to the drawing board.[45]

In summer 1958 Fleming's friend, American businessman Ned McLaine, set up a meeting for him to meet two London-based American film producers; lunch was arranged at the discreet Les Ambassadeurs Club in Mayfair. Present were Fleming, brothers Ned and Jacque McLaine, Fleming's MCA agent – Bob Fenn and the two American producers. Fenn spoke about the then still live CBS television deal and the sales figures of DR. NO, but only one of the producers seemed to be talking. Fenn suggested that an option for all six books could be purchased for the sum of $50,000. The quieter of the two producers reacted, 'Come on, how can you talk figures like that? I'm sorry gentlemen but these books aren't even television material.'[46] With that the American producer, whose name was Irving Allen, stormed out of the restaurant. He left his embarrassed business partner to apologise to Fleming *et al.* and pay the bill. The name of that business partner was Albert R. Broccoli.[47]

From January to February 1959 Fleming once again wrote up the ideas he had originally conceived for other media. The episodes for the television series became short stories: FROM A VIEW TO A KILL, RISICO, QUANTUM OF SOLACE, THE HILDEBRAND RARITY and the title story of the anthology: FOR YOUR EYES ONLY. They were collectively published the following spring.

It was in this context of false starts that Fleming's childhood friend, the wealthy Ivar Bryce, re-entered the picture. Bryce had facilitated Fleming's purchase of not only his golden typewriter, but also his Goldeneye hideaway. Now he suggested that they produce the first James Bond film themselves with material specifically written for the screen.[48] Their mutual friend, Washington lawyer, Ernie Cuneo gave them the initial idea – gangsters steal an atomic bomb and hold the world to ransom.[49] The friends looked outside the film industry for people to assist in bringing Bond to the screen. This fateful decision had consequences that echoed in cinemas and courtrooms, banks and boardrooms for decades to come.

Ivar Bryce hired a filmmaker whose 1959 feature, *The Boy and the Bridge*, he had financed; Kevin McClory was an Irish maverick who brought with him production experience, having been a veteran of productions like *The African Queen* (1951) and *Around the World in Eighty Days* (1956). McClory remembered how the project started: 'I met Ian Fleming in 1958. At that time, I think he was a little bit dried up. When he met me I'd not read any of his novels. He couldn't understand why no distributor had made a film of his novels.'[50] Fleming was keen for an adaptation of an existing novel. McClory was blunt, 'I said, "I don't want to do any of them." I could see his face drop.' Instead, the Irishman outlined his ideas:

> I was working on an underwater picture for the Bahamas [with John Steinbeck and Burgess Meredith]. I [saw] the potential, I am doing an underwater story, it's set in The Bahamas. The Bahamas is perfect for Bond. It's full of very, very rich individuals who have rather large yachts and large yachts attract nubile attractive young ladies who do not look at the girth of the owner they merely look at the size of the yachts.[51]

McClory had been inspired by something he had heard during World War II,

I read a statement by President Truman, when he was president [during the war], the Secretary of State, General Groves had come to him and said that it was possible that a small country or a group could obtain an atomic weapon and hold the world to ransom. The word "group" stood out.[52]

With a storyline ready, they sought a professional screenwriter. After much deliberation the man they initially chose was Paul Dehn, who had won an Oscar for Best Screenplay for the 1950 film *Seven Days to Noon*. Dehn then met with Fleming to discuss the project. However, in August 1959 the author wrote to Bryce:

Alas, Dehn can't take the job for two excellent reasons. Firstly, he wrote a film in which London was held up by an atomic bomb. And secondly, he says that he is really only interested in the development of character in murderers etc. and this bang, bang, kiss, kiss stuff is not for him.[53]

Eventually, the team chose Jack Whittingham to help write the screenplay.[54]

Fleming had to leave the project, as McClory remembered 'He was offered a job by *The Sunday Times* [to write THRILLING CITIES]. What did I think if he went off, could I complete this?'[55] McClory was confident he could, 'I'm dyslexic. I'm totally visual, screenwriting is a natural for me. He went off to do THRILLING CITIES, and Jack and I soldiered on.'[56]

Cuneo's original idea, via a presidential tale, birthed Ernst Stavro Blofeld. Blofeld became the head of international criminal organisation SPECTRE (Special Executive for Counter-Intelligence, Terrorism, Revenge and Extortion).

At one point Alfred Hitchcock was approached as a director for the film.[57] McClory remembered what happened with the work, 'We wrote all the screenplays between 1959 and 1960.'[58] The film project ultimately fell through.

As he had done with the material that formed his novel DR. NO and his collection of short stories FOR YOUR EYES ONLY, Fleming went back to his desk at Goldeneye and converted the screenplay into another novel – THUNDERBALL. When the book was published in early 1961 Fleming inscribed his gift copy to Ivar Bryce, 'Zeus to this Thunderball'.[59]

Later he would write mournfully to Bryce, 'Showbiz is a ghastly biz and the last thing I want is for you to lose your pin-striped trousers in its grisly maw. Nor of course do I want the first James Bond film to be botched.'[60]

In any event in December 1960 Fleming once again met with another film producer at Les Ambassadeurs.[61] Mindful of his previous disastrous meeting with Allen and Broccoli, Fleming was probably not hopeful. However, it is possible his spirits lifted when he found out who he was meeting: a Canadian producer named Harry Saltzman.

2

A SUBLIME HUSTLER

HARRY SALTZMAN

Harry Saltzman was born Herschel Saltzman on 27 October 1915. Raised in Quebec, his early years were a mystery, even to him. After spending the first seven years of his life in Saint John his father, a horticulturalist, moved to Cleveland with the family. Saltzman later revealed, 'I didn't find out until I was thirty that I'd actually been born in a hospital in Sherbrooke.'[1]

In 1932, aged seventeen, he went to Paris to study political science with economics, but was soon lured away by the smell of greasepaint. His third wife Adriana Saltzman said, 'He was attracted by showbusiness from the age of six.'[2] He began work for a musical theatre producer,[3] 'He told [Harry] a lot of things and that is how he started.'[4] He was sent around travelling circuses and vaudeville houses all over Europe handpicking talent.[5]

At the beginning of World War II Saltzman served in the Royal Canadian Air Force in Vancouver,[6] however, his war career is shrouded in intrigue. In a letter dated September 1943 Robert E. Shepherd, director of operations for the US Office of War Information (OWI) – the department involved with psychological war operations – stated, 'Mr. Saltzman will be assigned to the North African theatre of war to serve on the staff of Mr. C.D. Jenkins, Deputy Director in charge of all Office of War Information operations in North Africa.'[7] A further letter from Shepherd dated December 1943 said, 'Mr. Saltzman's services are more urgently needed in London … to serve at the American Embassy as Assistant Representative of the Overseas Operations Branch of the Office of War Information. Mr. Saltzman's principal function will be to serve as a motion picture distributor.'[8] The letter suggested that Saltzman would be billeted at the Dorchester Hotel. Bond historian and film writer, David Giammarco noted:

> During the war, British intelligence secretly held whole floors of offices at a number of hotels, including the Dorchester and the Landmark. An enlisted man of limited salary could hardly afford to be living in a five-star hotel. But intelligence officers and assets could come and go within these hotels without suspicion.[9]

Giammarco also uncovered Saltzman's Oath Of Allegiance to the United States dated March 1939. It misidentifies Saltzman's place of birth as St. Johns, New Brunswick and the author suggests, 'False birth places are standard procedure in intelligence filing systems'.[10] This could also explain Saltzman's confusion over his birthplace.

The paper trail points to Harry Saltzman being a spy and with his command of foreign languages, as well as his knowledge of Europe, it is likely that he played an active role in US intelligence during World War II. Even more intriguingly Saltzman operated in exactly the same field as Ian Fleming for a period – psychological warfare – and during this time Saltzman and Fleming were both in London. Giammarco spoke to retired intelligence officers who 'seemed to feel that Ian and Harry had a prior relationship well before [their first recorded meeting in] 1961.'[11] It may well have been that Harry Saltzman and Ian Fleming worked together in two fields of espionage: one actual and, later on, one fictional.

In 1945 Saltzman assisted in setting up a film division for the United Nations Educational Scientific and Cultural Organization (UNESCO). The division was primarily established to aid Chinese philosopher Lin Yutang in his work to ease tensions in China, where a civil war between the Nationalists and Communists was still being fought. However, Saltzman was disheartened by the assignment: 'East–West differences seemed so hopeless, I quit.'[12]

Piecing together Saltzman's post-war life is like assembling a mosaic of miscellaneous pieces. In a sign of what was to come Saltzman would, even at this point, have many business and personal interests, which would necessitate him regularly commuting across the Atlantic.[13]

After a brief and unsuccessful marriage, which produced Harry's daughter Merry,[14] Saltzman left his then home in California and ended up in Paris after World War II, living near the Etoile.[15] Amongst other things, Saltzman worked as a production manager on the live television show, *Robert Montgomery Presents* in New York. It was here that he formed a relationship with future best-selling author Judith Krantz. She remembered Harry as 'a wonderful companion, with a fantastic imagination. He resembled a giant panda as much as a human can.'[16] Krantz was further impressed that Harry knew the famous French writer Colette but was warned off a romantic entanglement, 'Harry's much too sophisticated to be interested in a little girl like you. You think you've been around? Well, Harry's a guy who's really been around, not just one quick year in Paris.'[17] Krantz remembered that one of his businesses at the time 'consisted of wooden horses that he rented to carnivals and vacation hotels.'[18] Judith could have been the next Mrs. Saltzman but she refused his proposal of marriage, 'He thought it was because he didn't have any money. "Listen", Harry assured me, "I'm going to make money, I promise. I can make ten thousand a year, twenty, thirty – I could probably make fifty thousand a year!"'[19] They drifted apart, but Harry would more than make good on his dreams.

Soon afterwards Harry had his first success when he went on to produce the hit television show *Captain Gallant of the Foreign Legion* from France. It was around about this time that Harry met a refugee from Romania, Jacqueline Colin, in Paris. She became the love of his life and mother to three more children – Steven, Hilary and Christopher.[20]

Another woman who would play a significant role in Harry's life was Johanna Harwood. Harwood had not previously spoken in detail about her role in the James Bond films until the authors tracked her down to the south of France. Now an elderly widow living in Monte Carlo, Harwood remembered being an ambitious young Scots-Irish girl eager to make a career in the film industry; she would go on to be an important, but unsung figure in the future of 007.

For two years in France Harwood trained in all aspects of film production. As a result, upon returning to Ireland, Harwood was constantly in work.[21] She met Harry Saltzman, after working in continuity for several years:

> I soon realised very few continuity girls do anything else afterwards. I wanted to get out of continuity and go into scriptwriting. I went to work for Famous Artists – the agency. They had a London office and there was just the man who worked for them and me as his assistant. The man I was working for was John Shepridge, who was a friend of Harry Saltzman. And then at one point John Shepridge went to work in Paris for [the Head of Twentieth Century-Fox, Darryl F.]. Zanuck and he let the office to Harry Saltzman. What I hadn't understood at the time he was also letting me with the office. I didn't like this at all and told Harry Saltzman when he turned up assuming I was going to work for him. So he said 'What do you want to do?' and I said 'I want to write scripts.' And he said 'Well you stay on as my assistant and I'll let you write scripts for me.' He had read a script I had written.[22]

Harwood observed Saltzman closely as he flitted between Paris, New York and London for the best part of the next decade.

Hilary Saltzman remembered her father was a 'voracious reader and he loved history and he loved geography, and he loved learning about new things and developing new ideas. He loved the theatre.'[23] Harry's first venture into feature films proved to be the template for his future way of working. Taking critically acclaimed literary material – in this case, a play – he adapted it into colourful entertainment, featuring a big star of the day. The result was *The Iron Petticoat* made in 1956 starring Bob Hope.

Also in 1956 the Royal Court Theatre in Sloane Square, London launched its first season, establishing it as a 'writer's theatre'.[24] New material from contemporary playwrights, eager to make cultural change, was staged there. One such playwright was John Osborne, whose play, *Look Back in Anger*, directed by Tony Richardson, was a startling revelation at the time.

In 1957 the Royal Court presented in New York and got Saltzman involved. Tony Richardson recalled meeting Harry:

> He had a perfect mogul's figure – stocky, tubby – crinkly grey hair and the face of an eager, coarse cherub. He bubbled with plans, and he had great charm. He was a splendid raconteur. By his generosity, in big and small things – he always loved to give – he radiated affluence.'[25]

Richardson was in thrall, 'What Harry was able to exude in abundance was potential. You always knew he would somehow, somewhere, discover the magic carpet that would transport you to riches. His schemes veered wildly.'[26] Richardson recounted some of those schemes, including selling 'Blue Chip Stamps' to exchange for Broadway theatre tickets, thereby cornering the market.[27] 'Harry was a sublime hustler', he concluded.[28]

Saltzman eventually did get backing for the project as Richardson remembered:

> Harry persuaded Warner Brothers to finance the movie. To do it, we formed a company. We called it Woodfall. John and Mary Ure [Woodfall alumni] had rented a little house in Woodfall Street, Chelsea. As we hadn't a name, we just looked out the window, saw the sign and christened our enterprise.[29]

Using his commercial contacts, Harry provided much-needed financial clout to launch the new venture consisting of himself, Osborne and Richardson. Together the energetic producer, the vituperative playwright and the eccentric director formed the film company that would change British cinema in the late fifties.

Saltzman moved to London and Tony Richardson recalled the energy he brought with him:

> He rented a house in the fashionable part of Chelsea – Lowndes Cottage. Harry immediately installed a mini-empire. Secretaries, chauffeurs, multilingual cooks arrived from wherever: international hookers rotated in the guest

rooms. Hollywood stars like Kirk Douglas and Burt Lancaster, producers like Charlie Feldman, were often guests. Harry was totally in charge of the business side. It was great fun. Harry created a wonderful atmosphere and I – and John too – enjoyed every minute of it.[30]

Not everybody understood or enjoyed the constant parties as Johanna Harwood explained:

[Harry] didn't pay the rent on [Lowndes Cottage], it was paid for by Woodfall Productions. Tony Richardson would arrive at what he considered the office and straight into their bedroom. Poor Jacqueline Saltzman used to complain bitterly but she probably didn't realise it was Woodfall Productions paying the rent.[31]

Osborne remembered Saltzman's singular style:

'What do you want to eat tonight?' he'd ask. 'French, German, Italian, Jewish? I know the best Finnish restaurant in town.' One always, rightly, chose the best in town. A week later he might ask the same question. 'Well, that Finnish place was terrific. Why don't we … ' He would cut you off like some blundering toddler. 'Forget it. I know a much better place.' I don't think we ever went back to a best-restaurant-in-town.[32]

Harwood remembered Saltzman 'was a very sociable person in, or on the fringes of, the London jet set.'[33]

On the fringes, Harwood felt, because he did things differently: 'Harry Saltzman had a fearful habit of working breakfasts and he'd call people in for breakfasts. Anytime he needed to get something across me it would be at breakfast time.'[34] She also noted, '[Saltzman's] big fault was that he was tactless. He was always rubbing people up the wrong way because he was saying things, unkind things but he wasn't actually unkind. He never thought this might upset this person.'[35] Despite his quirks, Harwood understood what Saltzman brought to the table, 'He was an extraordinarily good salesman. If he had one really big quality, I would say it was he could sell anything. He could go off with an idea and sell it to anybody. What he couldn't do later was develop the idea.'[36]

Saltzman, Osborne and Richardson would introduce Britain to 'the kitchen sink drama'. As a trio they brought to the screen the critically acclaimed social realism pictures *Look Back in Anger* (1959) starring Richard Burton, *Saturday*

Night and Sunday Morning (1960) starring Albert Finney and *The Entertainer* (1960) starring Laurence Olivier. Saltzman had proven adept at finding regional British actors and making stars of these diamonds in the rough. Osborne and Richardson crafted the films but, as director of photography Oswald Morris recalled, 'Harry tried to get on the floor when we did *Look Back in Anger* and *The Entertainer* but Tony wouldn't have him on the floor.'[37]

Saltzman expressed his vision for Woodfall in an essay written in 1960:

> I believe there is a place in Britain for realistic, hard-hitting films which take chances and show the well trodden paths of stereotyped, purely commercial, film-making. We did not form Woodfall Productions from an arty-crafty point of view. We are extremely commercial-minded and we regard the properties we have as commercial properties. But the most important thing about our company is that we insist on having artistic control of our pictures. We want to make them honestly. In other words, we control the script, the cast, the shooting and the completion of the picture. We won't allow our distributors or the people who back us to tell us how to make a picture. It's a hard road, we're the only people doing this in England and it is a battle all the time.[38]

However, the vanguard of this English 'new wave' soon lost the will to fight. The problem was art was not lucrative. Saltzman had written that he thought, 'these [Woodfall] pictures will export.'[39] An early sign proved ominous as he recounted:

> While I was on honeymoon, I took *Look Back in Anger* to Jack Warner to show him; after all, his company had financed it, so I figured he should see it. Jack and I looked at it and after about seven or eight minutes, Jack said, 'What language are they talking?' 'English,' said I. 'This is America,' said Jack and got up and walked out.[40]

Despite his assertions in *Films and Filming* magazine, Saltzman later admitted, '[*Look Back in Anger*] didn't do much business anywhere in the world. I never made a film that got such good reviews and was seen by so few people.'[41]

Harry's self-confidence remained undimmed. Sometimes he would advise other professionals on their own jobs, like when he criticised a United Artists' executive about the theatre he had chosen to open a film at in Paris. The executive recalled Saltzman admonishing him, '"How could you do such a thing – you're destroying this film by opening in that theatre?"'[42] The executive was Eric Pleskow who worked for United Artists at the time in international distribution. He jokingly responded to Saltzman's criticism, '"Well, actually I'll explain it to you, I'm an underground person and I'm working for Paramount and I'm trying to destroy United Artists, that's why I put it in that theatre."'[43] Pleskow, who would go on to head the studio behind Saltzman's biggest success, was amused by the producer, '[Harry] considered himself an expert on almost everything at that time.'[44]

Towards the end of 1960, Saltzman left Woodfall hoping to find fortune. Osborne was disappointed:

> I had a farewell meeting with Harry, who had decided that it was time to end his association with Woodfall. I had hoped he hadn't regretted it and I don't believe he did. But Tony [Richardson] and I had become like last week's greatest restaurants. I had enjoyed Harry's company when he was at his effervescent best, before marriage tamed his bravado. He had fairground flair and uncanny taste. [Woodfall] saw the light in Harry's bustling brown eyes … without him, [it] would never have got started. He never disowned the rest, although failure to make money was the most damnable sin of his trade.[45]

Michael Deeley, future Oscar-winning film producer of *The Deer Hunter* (1978), worked in production at the time and observed Saltzman and his partners. Deeley's shrewd analysis of the workings of Woodfall was tougher than Osborne's:

> Saltzman's ascerbic attitude led to his early departure from the partnership. Harry was a hard bastard, extremely brusque. If he saw no advantage in having a conversation with you he likely wouldn't reply to 'Good morning'. His lovely wife made up for a lot of her husband's roughness, but there was a vulgarity to Harry that didn't sit well with Richardson or Osborne. These two were both of striking height and each, in his own way, very English. Harry was a short, round, Canadian and had once been a circus barker. Loaded with aggression, he loved to cause an argument.[46]

When Osborne enquired what he was doing after Woodfall, '[Harry] told me, shoulders twitching with excitement, "I've bought the Bond books. All of them."'[47]

Harry Saltzman later remembered his conduit to Fleming, 'I had read the books and my lawyer in London, Brian Lewis, happened to be the same as Ian's lawyer.'[48] Over lunch in Les Ambassadeurs Lewis had encouraged Fleming to do a deal with Saltzman for commercial reasons. Fleming's ill health meant if no rights were sold, the trust value of his estate would be artificially low, based on the price of the Ratoff sale in 1954.[49] Fleming had told Saltzman the last film he had seen was *Gone with the Wind* (1939) and that he considered cinema a low form of art. Saltzman met the challenge, 'Well, I'd like you to see my films,' and proceeded to show Fleming *Saturday Night and Sunday Morning*.[50] Fleming was hardly a kitchen sink fan, but perhaps their respective war histories were exchanged and a rapport formed. For the sum of $50,000 – the amount Irving Allen had baulked at a few years before – Fleming promptly granted Saltzman a six-month option of the film rights to the existing James Bond novels. Fleming told fellow journalist Roderick Mann on a flight after signing the deal, '"What do you think? Two films? Three? That should be about it surely. Then the joke will be over."'[51]

Based on the information that later came to light regarding Saltzman's wartime intelligence career, his daughter Hilary, 'strongly believe[s] that [Fleming] and my father shared some similar experiences. Even though they couldn't publicise it, I really think that Ian felt that this series was safe in my father's hands.'[52]

Saltzman promptly asked Johanna Harwood to write a short synopsis of each of the books, she recalled:

> I'd written several screenplays for Saltzman by this time, of course, none of which he'd made because he didn't get them off the ground. But I'd done a good few. It's always the same – the producer needs a cheap screenplay but until they set up the affair they have no money. So that was why I was so terribly useful to have about because I was unknown and cheap. He wanted the screenplay in a hurry because he had to show it around to people.[53]

Harwood had actually written a short Bond story, 'Some Are Born Great', published in *Nursery World* magazine on 3 September 1959:

> [Fleming] wrote them a letter back, which [they] sent on to me – a very nice little letter which said 'a delicious little poke at James Bond'. I don't think he ever knew it was me. It just sort of amused me, the way he writes, it was something that flashed through my mind and I thought that would be fun. I sent it to *Nursery World* because I thought they would be the most likely to publish it.[54]

She wrote the piece as 'J.M. Harwood' and explained, 'Nobody called me Johanna in those days. I used J.M. because we were still in the days when women writers didn't necessarily want to appear as woman writers.'[55] It is doubly ironic that this intelligent, adventurous and ambitious woman became the first official writer of the James Bond film series.

Two novels could not be included in the sale. CASINO ROYALE had been sold previously to Gregory Ratoff and Fleming's most recent book THUNDERBALL, at this point, had not been published. Indeed, Fleming's ninth book was beset by problems. Kevin McClory had been set to direct a film based on the screenplay written by himself and professional screenwriter Jack Whittingham and author Ian Fleming. McClory had discovered Fleming's novel then used these ideas, but did not credit the team behind them. McClory later recalled, 'Our last screenplay was called "Thunderball". We only saw the book ten days before publication. We knew he was writing a book [but we didn't know that one]. We were friends and fellow co-writers. We took him to court.'[56] Fleming had merely followed his old pattern of converting unused film and television material into the book he was writing. Fleming's literary agent, Peter Janson-Smith recalled, 'Ian was genuinely upset that they thought he deliberately plagiarised them. I think he sort of remembered and he added things. A couple of months or whatever later when Ian was writing his book, he just didn't remember that maybe somebody else had suggested this or suggested that.'[57] McClory and Whittingham had immediately sought an injunction to assert their co-ownership. In spring 1961 the book was eventually published but the legal action had precluded anyone else exploiting THUNDERBALL.

The value of the Ian Fleming novels had leapt due to the 17 March 1961 edition of *Life* magazine in which Fleming's fifth and pivotal Bond novel, FROM RUSSIA WITH LOVE, had been listed as the ninth favourite book of the year by the most powerful man on earth: President Kennedy.[58] President Kennedy's endorsement spread like wildfire across the world. As a personal acquaintance of the president, Fleming could not have been more pleased. To say Bond's stock was rising would be a considerable understatement. Fleming's works became the first global, literary phenomenon, arguably creating a new genre: the spy thriller. The books were selling in the tens of millions and Fleming became an international celebrity – all this without a single film being made.

As spring became summer Saltzman was unable to obtain financing, an agreement with a production company or a distributor for the proposed project. He was essentially an outsider, unknown in film circles, despite his modest success as an independent producer. He was all too aware that Fleming, meanwhile desperate for a film deal, would walk away with the option fee and would still be able to sell what was fast becoming an even more valuable property.[59] Time was ticking. Suddenly he had a change of fortune – Saltzman's friend, the screenwriter Wolf Mankowitz called him with a strange request; Mankowitz wanted him to meet someone – Albert R. Broccoli.

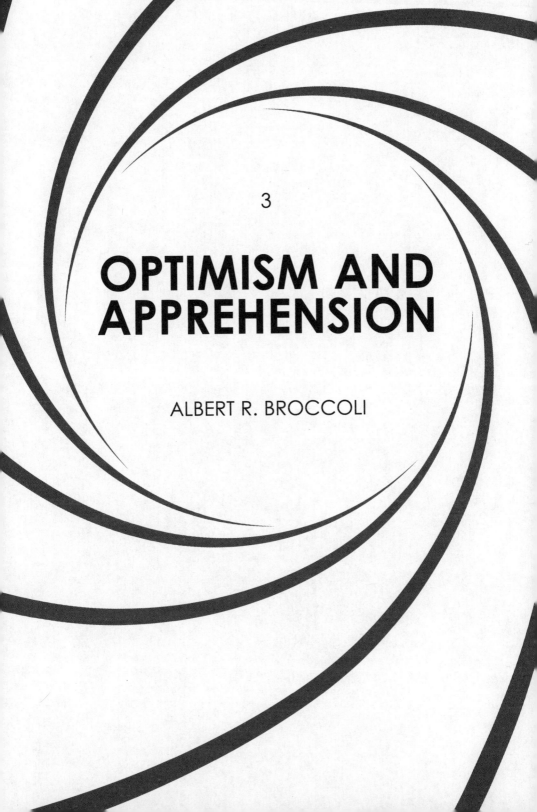

3

OPTIMISM AND APPREHENSION

ALBERT R. BROCCOLI

lbert Romolo Broccoli was born in Queens, New York City on 5 April 1909. Broccoli's family had first cultivated the vegetable bearing their name in Italy centuries before immigrating to the United States. The family were very poor, as Broccoli's third wife, Dana, later recalled, 'before there was any subsidy by the Government and they were sad days and hard days.'[1]

One morning, while working on the family farm before school, Cubby saw the then rare sight of a plane, the *Spirit of St. Louis*, flying overhead. He distinctly remembered being waved to by its pilot Charles Lindbergh. The daring aviator inspired the young farm boy from Long Island to walk a little taller. Cubby later told Dana, that it was 'the first time he really wanted to be something above and beyond what he was.'[2]

Over time Albert earned his nickname Cubby. He recalled:

There was a famous cartoonist, his name was Herschfield and he had a cartoon called Abe Kabibble and in school they likened me to Abe Kabibble. Then they got tired of that and they called me Kabibble. Then that was too much and they called me Cubby. Everybody thinks it was because I was cuddly.[3]

There is, however, another version of how Broccoli got his moniker. According to Dana, 'When he was a very little boy he had a cousin – they were six weeks apart, they're like twins – and his cousin [Pasquale De Cicco] just could not say "Albert" so he called him "Cubby".'[4]

Cubby left the family business in Long Island on the East Coast and went west. The cousin he had grown up with, Pasquale (now calling himself 'Pat'), was working as an agent and producer in Hollywood. Moreover, Pat had married heiress Gloria Vanderbilt in 1941. De Cicco invited his cousin to join him and begin a career away from the family farm.[5]

Future Bond film director Guy Hamilton recalled stories told to him by Cubby from this era:

When he was assistant director, he would be sent to call Errol Flynn or Gable, or whoever it was from the caravan and they'd say, 'Cubby, one dollar that fly on the wall will land before the other one.' 'You're on,' says Cubby. And poor Cubby lost all his wages. They took such pity on him that Cubby was always invited to whatever party was happening this weekend. But whether he wins or loses isn't important, this is the true gambling thing – it is the buzz. It's like taking a drug. Winning, losing not important.[6]

Another time, Cubby was in a bar and was challenged by a stranger to guess the result of a coin flip, Cubby made a wager but repeatedly lost. The stranger, amused by Cubby's resolve, turned out to be film producer, mogul and inventor Howard Hughes.[7] Through him Cubby got a job as an assistant to director Howard Hawks. This led to Cubby working on the infamous 1939 film *The Outlaw* and other films for Hawks and Hughes.[8] Hawks was an early fan of Fleming's, 'I wanted to do the Bond series. The great imagination that the writer had.'[9]

Cubby spent World War II in the US Navy where he served in the Entertainment Division with another future film producer Ray Stark.[10] When he was demobbed, Cubby became a representative at the powerful Charles K. Feldman's Famous Artists Agency. It was here that Cubby learned his trade and earned the admiration of one of his young clients Robert Wagner, who recalled, 'He believed in me. When I was with him, I was his guy. He had a lot of other clients but he had that ability to make everybody feel like they were the only one in his life.'[11] Wagner liked Cubby's chutzpah. After an argument between Feldman and L.B. Mayer of MGM, all Famous Artists agents were banned from the lot. Wagner was horrified when he and Cubby 'got tossed out of the Thalberg building and I thought my career was coming to an end. I said, "Cubby, do you think I'll ever work again?"'[12] Cubby's response was cool under fire, '"Come on kid, let's go to Fox!"'[13]

Eventually Broccoli tired of being an agent. Robert Wagner felt that 'Charlie Feldman was a big influence in his life. Cubby had that ability to recognise good writing and he wanted to go further than just managing people and their careers.'[14] During this period he had a short-lived marriage to starlet Gloria Blondell.[15] In 1946 Cubby worked on 'a smaller kind of nonsense called *Treasury Agent* [also titled *Avalanche*], which I'd made on a six-day schedule and an $80,000 budget, most borrowed from my cousin, Pat De Cicco. My cousin took producer credit, leaving me coming in at the tail-end as production manager.'[16] The film introduced Cubby to the company lawyer Arthur Krim.[17] Krim would be more helpful to Cubby fifteen years later when he was running the studio United Artists. Another key introduction the film made was with its director: Irving Allen. Allen was already an Oscar-nominated director and would actually go on to win an Academy Award a year later for Best Short Subject (Two Reel) for *Climbing the Matterhorn* in 1947.[18]

In 1952 Cubby met up with Irving Allen in New York and they decided to form a production company, so, named after the hotel in which their business partnership was formed, Warwick Film Productions was born. With his recent Academy Award success, Allen was seen as the artistic heavyweight of the duo, yet despite their credentials, their initial attempts to raise financing in the USA faltered. However, Cubby recalled they were attracted by the tax incentives for filmmakers now being offered in Europe and were further induced to leave America by the air of creative freedom away from the McCarthy witch hunts plaguing the film capital of the world. Broccoli remembered later, 'I've never produced a picture in Hollywood. When I tried to make a deal they laughed at me. I wanted to shoot here, but people wouldn't even talk to me.'[19] So, in the year Ian Fleming sat down to write the first James Bond novel, Albert R. Broccoli travelled to England to begin a new life.

During this period there were strict currency controls in place that prevented box office receipts in Europe being sent back to the USA; many European businesses partnered American firms in order to release these frozen funds by making films which could then be shown in the USA, thus generating dollars. As a result film investment boomed – it was effectively a Marshall Plan for the European film industry. In the UK the Eady Levy provided an additional incentive to make films there. The levy (named after Treasury official Sir Wilfred Eady) was effectively a tax on cinema tickets – a proportion of the ticket price was retained by cinemas and a proportion returned to production companies who had made 'British' films, i.e. films made with key British talent. As the size of the rebate was linked to the number of tickets sold, the more successful the picture, the more money the production companies received. Basically popular films were rewarded.[20]

Warwick Films needed to make a big splash with their first production. Director Guy Hamilton later recounted what was required, 'Cubby was really the foundation of their success because they had the scripts but they needed a star for the finance.'[21] Securing a star for a series of independent productions made in England was not easy. Hamilton remembered how Cubby did it:

> The biggest star at that period was Alan Ladd and Irving Allen said, 'You'll never get him' and Cubby said, 'I know his wife – she's really his agent – and if we offer her a million dollars … ' Irving replied, 'Cubby, we haven't got a million dollars.' Cubby countered, 'If we get Alan Ladd, we will. It will be the highest salary that any US star has got and she'll fall for it.' She did. And Warwick took off.[22]

Having secured Ladd, Columbia Pictures agreed to distribute Warwick's pictures. Ladd starred in the Warwick productions *The Red Beret* (1953), *The Black Knight* (1953) and *Hell Below Zero* (1954). Ladd's son, Alan Ladd Jr., recalled, 'I was with my father at the time. [Cubby] was a warm, very lovely man. My father adored him.'[23] Coming full circle, in the 1980s, Ladd Jr. would go on to head the studio that produced the Bond films.

The Red Beret was directed by Terence Young, a history graduate from the University of Cambridge, who was born in Shanghai. During World War II, he had served in the Guards Armoured Division and after the war directed films in the UK, France and Germany.[24] Young would go on to direct *Safari* and *Zarak* (both 1956) and *No Time to Die* (1958) for Warwick. The film was rewritten by screenwriter and playwright Richard Maibaum, a native of Chicago who had written several films for Ladd including an early spy picture, *O.S.S.* (1946) and an adaptation of *The Great Gatsby* (1949). Maibaum remembered being in America when 'Cubby showed up in my living-room. The Ladds had told him they'd like me to script so Cubby signed me up.'[25] Maibaum wrote unpretentious, entertaining screenplays for Warwick that were designed to make British or Commonwealth subjects play in America. Irving Allen later opined that Warwick's deliberate, non-parochial film-making was 'so important in attracting people back to the theatres'.[26]

Warwick's first post-Alan Ladd hit was *Cockleshell Heroes* (1955), directed by and starring José Ferrer about the daring World War II mission, Operation Frankton. In 1956 Warwick negotiated a deal to produce nine films for Columbia Pictures over three years at a cost of £6 million. Warwick later took advantage of an empire development scheme that provided British grants to producers who filmed on location in Commonwealth nations. The company filmed in Kenya for *Safari* and *Odongo* (both, 1956). The films were scripted and cast in five weeks, in order to shoot them back-to-back; they featured the same characters on location to save time and costs. Warwick also filmed in India for *Zarak* (1956).

The majority of Warwick's output was shot by South African Ted Moore. Moore moved to the UK in 1930 and during World War II served as a pilot and as a member of the RAF's Film Unit.[27] He was the camera operator for Cinematographer Jack Cardiff on the arduous location shoot for *The African Queen* (1951).[28] At Warwick, Moore started as a camera operator before progressing through the ranks to become cinematographer on *A Prize Of Gold* (1954), starring Richard Widmark. Moore's output at Warwick showed his skill at working on exotic locations and capturing simple, elegant shots in bright Technicolor (Warwick was the first British independent company to shoot in CinemaScope).[29]

The team at Warwick ensured that they made their tight budgets go a long way and that the production value reached the screen – key to this was the art department whose settings ensured the films had cinematic appeal. At the latter end of their run, Warwick hired Ken Adam to design, as he put it, 'profitable crap'.[30] Adam had arrived in London in 1934 after having to flee from Berlin.[31] During World War II he ended up flying in the RAF, making him the only German émigré to do so.[32] He was urbane and stylish and was influenced by the minimalism of German expressionist cinema. Around this time, Broccoli noted the efficiency of a Warwick stalwart in the art department, Syd Cain, and earmarked him for future development.[33]

Warwick's films often featured action sequences performed by Bob Simmons and many of them had bright title songs. Peter Hunt edited the films and Warwick had a stock company of regular actors, which included: Bernard Lee, Anthony Newley, Anita Ekberg, Francis De Woolf, Walter Gotell, Sydney Tafler, Desmond Llewelyn – all names who would later be connected with the Bond series. The parallels to the future Bonds films were obvious – full-colour features shot on real locations, packed with ambitious action, filmed on a relatively tight budget, starring international actors and often based on a best-selling contemporary novel.

Cubby Broccoli had maintained a good working friendship with Mike Frankovitch, head of production for Columbia in the UK. However, generally relations with Columbia had become strained; Warwick's output had consistently been successful, but they were only as good as their last picture. *Fire Down Below* (1957) had gone over budget with filming in Trinidad and Tobago, and the demands of its mercurial star Rita Hayworth.

Cubby was something of a junior partner under Irving Allen's hefty, Oscar-winning shadow; they had very different management styles. Future Bond production designer, Ken Adam, after pitching a proposal with future Bond alumni, Maurice Binder, remembered being thrown out of the office by Allen, '[Allen was] very explosive and vulgar at times, but a good showman. Cubby used to collect the wreckage and urge you not to take Irving seriously.'[34] Adam summed up his impression of Allen with, 'He had one great asset that he was a very good editor so nobody could pull the wool over his eyes. He was not a very friendly person. I thought that Irving was in many ways a monster.'[35]

This disparity between Allen and Broccoli would soon cost them a vital film project: James Bond. Broccoli had always believed the Fleming novels could lead to a successful series of films; Allen did not. In the summer of 1958 Cubby was distracted because he had to care for his second wife Nedra – who was stricken with cancer, and bring up their children Tony and Tina. It was during this period that Cubby and Irving were also trying to secure the Bond novels. They met with Ian Fleming in a setting that must have, by now, become familiar to the author – Les Ambassadeurs. It was at this meeting that Irving Allen had denounced Bond to Fleming's face, suggesting, 'These books aren't even television material.'[36] Broccoli was not deterred. The CASINO ROYALE rights were still out there, owned by Gregory Ratoff. When Ratoff died from leukaemia in December 1960, Cubby remembered, 'I tried to buy the property from the widow. She wasn't in the mood to sell.'[37] The reason for her reluctance to part with the rights was a case of fate again intervening; she was represented by none other than Cubby's old boss at Famous Artists Agency, Charles K. Feldman. Cubby was rueful, 'Charlie told her "You shouldn't sell it." He was quite intelligent and a rather crafty sort of a chap and he decided that he was going to get that property and purchase it.'[38] That, it seemed, was that.

Nedra succumbed to cancer, adding personal woes to professional ones. Warwick's critically acclaimed *The Trials of Oscar Wilde* (1960), directed by Ken Hughes, had been a box office disappointment. After several disagreements with Columbia Pictures, Warwick Productions effectively ceased trading in 1961. Irving and Cubby formally went their separate ways. Cubby recalled, 'Any time one of us particularly wanted to do something, the other didn't. I was ready to go solo.'[39] Allen and Broccoli continued to share their offices in South Audley Street, in London's salubrious Mayfair district, well into the sixties but as producers, they were on their own.

Things were not all bad for Cubby; he found love again with Dana Wilson. Wilson was a talented writer who had been married to the first screen Batman, Lewis Wilson, and together they had had a son, Michael. Cubby and Dana got married on 21 June 1959 with Cary Grant as their best man;[40] soon they would all be in London together.

Wolf Mankowitz was a veteran writer on the British film scene. He was well connected and well known, having been a co-founder of the famed showbusiness restaurant The White Elephant on Curzon Street. In 1961 Wolf found himself toiling with Cubby Broccoli over a film version of ONE THOUSAND AND ONE ARABIAN NIGHTS when fate came to their aid.[41]

Frustrated at the lack of progress with the *Arabian Nights* project, Cubby still regretted missing the opportunity to secure the Bond film rights. He made enquiries and when he found that the option had been taken out by another producer, he 'was uncertain whether to wait for it to expire or to start talking there and then'.[42] Broccoli's enquiries led to Saltzman who owned the option. It was a stroke of luck as Broccoli knew Mankowitz, who, in turn, knew Saltzman:

> Wolf Mankowitz said, 'I know [Saltzman] … he hasn't been able to make a deal and there are twenty-one days left on his option.' The next day, in came Harry Saltzman. I didn't want another partner after Irving Allen and I had broken up. I told Saltzman I wanted to buy the Bond books, but he dismissed the Bonds as a bit of nonsense, and said, 'I'd like to go into business with you. I've got a property called *Gold in the Streets*. It's about going to New York and getting rich. Then I've got something else about a scarecrow who comes to life.' I told him I was only interested in the Bond books. He finally said, 'Why don't we do them together?' Well, I was afraid that someone else would acquire them and I finally agreed to a 50/50 partnership.[43]

Broccoli first approached his friend Mike Frankovich at Columbia Pictures, hoping their Warwick history would seal the deal. Frankovich took Broccoli very seriously and, armed with Fleming's novels, called a board meeting and got a reader to provide an analysis. There is an apocryphal story that the reader confused Ian with his older brother, Peter, who also wrote books – but non-fiction travel tomes, and reported accordingly. Another story tells how the same script editor thought Bond was a sub-par Mike Hammer (a fictional private investigator) and too English to boot.[44] Eric Pleskow, an executive at United Artists who eventually got the Bond deal, later recounted another version, 'It was a question of the budget for the picture. The difference was £100,000 and they couldn't get together on that so obviously they left.'[45] In a decision as disastrous as Decca passing on the Beatles a year later, Columbia Pictures passed on producing the James Bond pictures in 1961.[46]

Pleskow recounts what happened next, 'In those days, United Artists and Columbia Pictures were in the same building 729, 7th Avenue so since they were in the same building they figured they would go to United Artists.'[47] Unfazed, Broccoli went downstairs to meet with Arthur Krim, the lawyer who had helped him years ago on *Avalanche*. Krim now ran United Artists – the only studio ideally suited to exploit European production. Founded in 1919 UA was famously run by director D.W. Griffiths and actors Douglas Fairbanks, Mary Pickford and Charlie Chaplin. When they took over the studio it was described as, 'the lunatics have taken charge of the asylum'.[48] Indeed, by the early fifties, the lunatics had brought the studio to the verge of bankruptcy. Arthur Krim and Robert Benjamin took over the enterprise and through a combination of granting unparalleled creative freedom to their producers and investing in prudent productions, they set about slowly rebuilding the once giant studio. Aided by not having to maintain contract players and a studio backlot, United Artists became 'the studio without walls'.[49] Over the decade that followed United Artists became a niche purveyor of groundbreaking, quality films.

The studio was enjoying success with popular characters such as Mike Hammer – the American detective featured in a series of hard-boiled novels penned by Mickey Spillane. Fleming was a Spillane fan and the two authors have often been compared, including possibly by Columbia's reviewer. Two Mike Hammer films had been produced by Victor Saville and he, too, had approached United Artists in the late fifties to option the Bond property. For some reason Saville had been rebuffed by the United Artists' executives, although he had been supported by one: Max Youngstein.[50] Another United Artists' executive and early Bond fan was David Picker, who also recalled trying to get the rights:

A cousin of mine was married to [Semon Wolf, a Wall Street broker] who said, 'You should read these books they'd make a great movie.' So I read a couple and had our office make an enquiry but Fleming was just not prepared to sell the rights. It was a few years later when he needed some money the word came out that he might consider making a deal. I went after them [but] they were simply not for sale.[51]

In 1961 United Artists opened a London office. Headed by George 'Bud' Ornstein, the office based at Film House in Wardour Street had a skeleton staff and could not administer more than five films a year.[52] It was not the most fertile ground to plant blockbuster seeds in. Picker remembered:

[Broccoli and Saltzman] spoke to [Ornstein] and said they wanted to come and meet with me and my boss in New York – [they] did not tell him what it was about actually. They told him not to mention it. So we set up the meeting and they came in and met with Arthur Krim and Bob Benjamin and myself.[53]

On 20 June 1961 Broccoli and Saltzman walked downstairs to United Artists, Broccoli approached the meeting with Arthur Krim, Robert Benjamin, Arnold Picker and ten others with 'a mixture of optimism and apprehension'.[54] Also present was David Picker, nephew of Arnold; Krim recalled him saying, 'If David likes the idea, we'll talk.'[55] In a case of nepotism working, the young Picker agreed immediately to go with the project.

While it is a matter of record that Krim relied heavily on David Picker's view of the material, future United Artists' executive, Mike Medavoy later revealed higher powers had been work:

> At that meeting what they didn't know was that Arthur Krim was a close friend of John Kennedy's. John Kennedy had been reading the Bond books and was a fan. He had mentioned it to Arthur Krim. They walked into a situation in which they were really going to receive a favourable ear because the President of the United States had been reading the books.[56]

David Picker had particular insight into Cubby and Harry at this early stage:

> They were very different. Cubby was very comfortable in the business, had been in the business for years. Harry had been involved in the business but hadn't dealt on the level Cubby had. He was a partner in Woodfall, they'd made a few small movies, but he'd never dealt with the American majors and he was far less comfortable than Cubby was. It was all new to him, I'm not sure that he had had the kind of business experience that at the time someone like Cubby would have had. There was an element of trust already established and this was all new to Harry.[57]

Pleskow takes up the story:

> [Saltzman said], 'What do we do now?' So Broccoli said, 'What are you talking about? We have a handshake deal with Arthur Krim.' In those days, we were known for keeping our word, we had a very good reputation, our word was our bond – not James Bond (laughs). Saltzman says, 'That means nothing.' Broccoli was getting very annoyed, finally he picked up the phone and called Arthur and before Cubby could say anything, Krim said, 'I know why you're calling me, you want something on paper' and Krim, having been a lawyer, he was able to dictate the proper letter and it was delivered an hour later to the hotel. So that's how we got the Bond pictures.[58]

The deal with United Artists would not be formalised until 2 April 1962, after the first James Bond film had finished shooting.[59]

Other formal agreements were required. Fleming had spread the film rights across an array of family trusts. Len Deighton recalled:

It was into this snake pit of obligations that Harry and Cubby trod. Harry told me that he and Cubby were determined to keep the various lawyers, family members and representatives apart. To do this, they took over a London hotel. Each title was assigned to a room and occupied by lawyers, trustees and beneficiaries according to who had been empowered to sign the agreement. [Cubby and Harry went] from room to room with the threat that unless there was agreement of all, there would be money for none.[60]

It was yet another example of why, perhaps, the Bond film deals had taken so long to come to fruition.

Broccoli and Saltzman acted quickly. They formed a corporate entity – Danjaq, Société Associés (S.A.) based in Lausanne, Canton of Vaud, Switzerland. Broccoli immediately wrote an advance to Saltzman of $1,000 and after a little haggling, entered into a 50/50 partnership. The company was named after Cubby and Harry's respective wives, Dana and Jacqueline.[61] Johanna Harwood remembered a curious detail, 'they put Mrs. Broccoli first because Cubby had always sort of rather vaguely said "Why do we always put Saltzman and Broccoli?"'[62] According to Steven Saltzman, Harry's son, Danjaq 'was set up with shares that were actually bought privately by Dana and Jacqueline separately with cash they could demonstrate was not linked to their husbands. Private, free money, so that they could actually have shares in it.'[63] The company was administered by Bank Fiduciaire executive Gerald Schlaeppi in Switzerland and into it were vested all the copyrights and future profits of the Bond franchise at a hugely advantageous tax rate.[64]

The producers then formed an English company that actually made the films as an independent entity. This service company was called Eon Productions Limited and was formed in England on 6 July 1961. The name Eon did not mean anything at first but later, as legend took hold, a retronym emerged. The brainchild of two hardened gamblers, EON came to stand for 'Everything or Nothing'.[65]

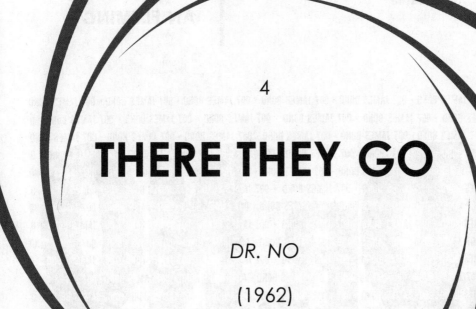

4

THERE THEY GO

DR. NO

(1962)

Shooting **Now** · **on location**

in Jamaica

**THE FIRST
JAMES BOND FILM . . .**

IAN FLEMING'S

007 JAMES BOND · 007 JAMES BOND · 007 JAMES BOND · 007 JAMES BOND · 007 JAMES BOND · 007 JAMES BOND
MES BOND · 007 JAMES BOND · 007 JAMES BOND · 007 JAMES BOND · 007 JAMES BOND · 007 JAMES BOND · 0
007 JAMES BOND · 007 JAMES BOND · 007 JAMES BOND · 007 JAMES BOND · 007 JAMES BOND · 007 JAMES BOND
MES BOND · 007 JAMES BOND · 007 JAMES BOND · 007 JAMES BOND · 007 JAMES BOND · 007 JAMES BOND · 0
007 JAMES BOND · 007 JAMES BOND · 007 JAMES BOND · 007 JAMES BOND · 007 JAMES BOND · 007 JAMES BOND
MES BOND · 007 JAMES BOND · 007 JAMES BOND · 007 JAMES BOND · 007 JAMES BOND · 007 JAMES BOND · 0
007 JAMES BOND · 007 JAMES BOND · 007 JAMES BOND · 007 JAMES BOND · 007 JAMES BOND · 007 JAMES BOND
MES BOND · 007 JAMES BOND · 007 JAMES BOND · 007 JAMES BOND · 007 JAMES BOND · 007 JAMES BOND · 0
007 JAMES BOND · 007 JAMES BOND · 007 JAMES BOND · 007 JAMES BOND · 007 JAMES BOND · 007 JAMES BOND
MES BOND · 007 JAMES BOND · 007 JAMES BOND · 007 JAMES BOND · 007 JAMES BOND · 007 JAMES BOND · 0
007 JAMES BOND · 007 JAMES BOND · 007 JAMES BOND · 007 JAMES BOND · 007 JAMES BOND · 007 JAMES BOND
MES BOND · 007 JAMES BOND · 007 JAMES BOND · 007 JAMES BOND · 007 JAMES BOND · 007 JAMES BOND · 0
007 JAMES BOND · 007 JAMES BOND · 007 JAMES BOND · 007 JAMES BOND · 007 JAMES BOND · 007 JAMES BOND
MES BOND · 007 JAMES BOND · 007 JAMES BOND · 007 JAMES BOND · 007 JAMES BOND · 007 JAMES BOND · 0
007 JAMES BOND · 007 JAMES BOND · 007 JAMES BOND · 007 JAMES BOND · 007 JAMES BOND · 007 JAMES BOND
MES BOND · 007 JAMES BOND · 007 JAMES BOND · 007 JAMES BOND · 007 JAMES BOND · 007 JAMES BOND · 0

DR. NO

AN EON PRODUCTION IN TECHNICOLOR
STARRING SEAN CONNERY AS  **JAMES BOND**

**for release by
UNITED ARTISTS**

PRODUCERS HARRY SALTZMAN AND ALBERT R. BROCCOLI

Since Eon Productions did not own James Bond's first adventure, CASINO ROYALE, the question was which book should they adapt first? Broccoli and Saltzman initially began developing Fleming's most recent best-seller THUNDERBALL published in April 1961. However, this title was tied up in litigation with Kevin McClory. UA executive David Picker remembered the reasons behind the final choice:

> They talked about GOLDFINGER or THUNDERBALL – but for the first movie you had to have a limit on what you could spend and those were more expensive movies to make than *Dr. No*. We agreed that the first one would be *Dr. No* and then hopefully if the series took off we would go on from there.[1]

Picker outlined how the studio gained its artist-friendly reputation:

> United Artists' philosophy was very simple: we were never involved in the production. As a courtesy we might go by and say hello, or have a lunch, but the actual day-to-day nature of the inter-relationship between the crew and the cast – unless there was a problem – we knew nothing about it. That just went on without our involvement on any level. The only time we saw them was when they brought the picture in. They had no obligation to report to us in any way, shape, matter or form if the picture was on budget and on schedule, because under the United Artists' code of business they were free to make their movie as long as they used the script we approved, the cast we approved and the budget we approved.[2]

United Artists had set a budget of $40,000 for the screenplay[3] and Eon set about getting an acceptable blueprint for the first James Bond film.

Having worked on initial outlines to attract finance, Johanna Harwood received the following telegram from Harry Saltzman, 'Have concluded Bond deal with United Artists. Production starting 15 October. Stop. Urgent do screen treatment break down THUNDERBALL. Stop. DR. NO or THUNDERBALL probably first subject. Stop.'[4]

Harwood was under starter's orders, 'I remember getting the telegram saying that we were going to do it and would I please do the script at once in Paris. I wrote *Dr. No* mostly over there, although I went back and forward.'[5] Harwood was not impressed with the novel DR. NO, 'I thought it was one of the less good ones. It was the Americans who chose it. By this time I think Ian Fleming was pushing it a bit.'[6]

When Wolf Mankowitz introduced Cubby Broccoli to Harry Saltzman, he had done so on one condition, 'If I call and ask if he'll do a deal, can I write the screenplay?'[7] Mankowitz was teamed up with Richard Maibaum to develop Harwood's draft. The novel, only recently a bestseller in 1958, already needed updating, as Maibaum explained: 'When Wolf and I began working on the script, we decided that Fleming's Dr. No was the most ludicrous character in the world. He was just Fu Manchu with steel hooks. It was 1961 and we felt that audiences just wouldn't stand for that kind of stuff anymore.' Instead the writers created a new villain with Dr. No becoming 'a little marmoset monkey. We wrote the whole thing, about forty pages. Wolf and I thought it was marvellous and we showed it to Cubby and Harry. Cubby was outraged.'[8]

DR. NO was Ian Fleming's sixth Bond novel published in the UK on 31 March 1958. Based on Fleming's trip to the Bahamian isle of Inagua with Ivar Bryce, Fleming was also inspired by current events – failed early rocket tests had put the USA behind the Soviets in the space race and unrest in the Caribbean seemed to be leading to revolution.

The plot is typical Bond: Fleming's villain is the son of a 'Chinese girl of a good family [and a] German Methodist missionary'. Dr. No is an ex-member of the Chinese gangster association the Hip Sing Tong and, as a result of embezzling from them, has had his hands cut off and replaced with hooks. He has reinvented himself, including his name – 'Julius for my father, No for my rejection of him' – and has built up his base, the island fortress, Crab Key. This fictional isle is home to a rare species of bird, who deposit large amounts of guano (dung), which Dr. No sells lucratively as fertiliser. When a group of ornithologists go missing while on an expedition to the island, the local British Secret Service chief, Strangeways, investigates and is killed. Dr. No does not want anyone snooping around his island in case they discover his real business; he is using radio beams to affect the telemetary of nearby US rocket tests, causing them to fail. It is revealed his backers are the Soviets, seeking supremacy in the early days of the space race. Bond encounters the Three Blind Mice; has a giant, poisonous centipede crawl dangerously up his naked body; and is trained by Quarrel, his Cayman islander friend from LIVE AND LET DIE, prior to his journey to Crab Key. The finale has Bond undergoing a torturous obstacle course observed by Dr. No in some sort of warped experiment in pain. Upon escaping Dr. No's lair Bond is forced to do battle with a giant squid before killing Dr. No by burying him in guano. The film followed the basic story with many of the same events, but liberties were taken with the source material and the characterisation of Bond. Harry Saltzman would later say of Fleming's work, 'The books are larger than life. As a matter of fact, I think we are closer to life-size than the books are.'[9] This would be the first and last occasion that would be true.

Harking back to Broccoli's experience at Warwick producing for a global audience and Harry's nuanced, sophisticated European world-view, the producers were mindful of staying clear of politics. A few years later Cubby Broccoli reflected, 'We try to make entertainment for the man who sits in the seat because he's the critic, he's the judge. The theatres are full of these critics. They like this kind of picture because it's escapism and they identify themselves with what's on the screen. We know this. They don't want to be identified with any political arrangement or any political figures.'[10] In a key change, Dr. No would not be working for the Soviets; his backers would now be SPECTRE, the organisation originally featured in THUNDERBALL (the novel which was still subject to legal dispute). Interestingly, the Bond film plots almost never depended on Cold War allegiances.

United Artists' London chief, Bud Ornstein, wrote to David Picker in New York on reading the first draft of the screenplay, 'I must tell you that personally, I have not been too impressed to date with Maibaum's work and only hope that he will come up with something much better this time as we have had many story conferences with him.'[11] Fleming suggested thriller writer Berkely Mather (the pseudonym of Lieutenant-Colonel John Evan Weston-Davies) perform an uncredited polish and Mather delivered a draft on 28 November 1961.[12] Mather was also the author of THE PASS BEYOND KASHMIR, a film of which Eon would later announce as one of their future productions.[13]

Harwood understood why Mather had been brought in, 'He was supposed to masculinise the dialogue, that's why they got someone with army experience.' Upon reading Mather's draft, 'Harry Saltzman rolled his eyes and said, "This won't do at all". He had them all talking like Chicago hit men.'[14] Harwood claims that when Mather saw a preview of *Dr. No* he changed his mind and wanted a screen credit contradicting his previous feelings about the project.[15]

Harwood did not meet her other collaborators, 'We never wrote it together. I never met Mankowitz, I passed Maibaum a couple of times on the stairs and he always said "Good morning" very pleasantly. But he was a pro.'[16] The final Maibaum and Mankowitz screenplay was dated on 12 December 1961 and it was on this fourth draft that the final budget was calculated.[17]

If finding the right tone was difficult so, too, was finding the right director. United Artists had final approval as Bud Ornstein recalled, 'based on the treatment, directors so far have shied away from the project. I feel that it is important to get the director assigned as soon as possible so that he can adapt the script to his own thinking.'[18] Broccoli and Saltzman allegedly favoured Phil Karlson but his fee of $75,000 was well over the $40,000 budgeted for the director.[19] David Picker also felt, because of the subject matter, 'It was clearly going to a British not an America director.'[20]

Bryan Forbes, Guy Green and Ken Hughes all turned down the film.[21] Guy Hamilton and Terence Young were the frontrunners,[22] but Hamilton declined for personal reasons.[23] In any event, United Artists felt that, despite Young's 'tendency to go over schedule and budget',[24] he was the right choice. Picker explained, 'It was easy to say Terence was the living embodiment of James Bond – his style of dress, his style of life – he could have played James Bond himself.'[25]

Terence Young was the prototypical James Bond. Young appreciated the fine things in life and could match Fleming with urbane superiority:

> I'd met him through his wife, Ann Rothemere. I also met him through Noël Coward. I'd been staying at Noël's house in Jamaica and Ian was there. We met just after I'd been signed to do the picture at some big press show put on by United Artists. He said, 'So they've decided on you to fuck up my work.' I said, 'Well, let me put it this way, Ian, I don't think anything you've written is immortal as yet, whereas the last picture I made won the Grand Prix at Venice. Now, let's start level.[26]

Young went to work immediately on the script with who he called, the 'continuity girl', Johanna Harwood, '[We] took a room at the Dorchester Hotel and we worked day and night.'[27]

Harwood remembered Terence Young's involvement in the script rather differently, 'It was a joke really because what he had done was pretty well copied paragraphs out of the book. There were great big swathes which said "Bond thought hard about what he was going to do next." Things you can't put in a picture at all.'[28] The Young-Harwood draft was dated 8 January 1962, a mere eight days before principal photography was due to begin in Kingston, Jamaica. Upon seeing the finished screenplay Broccoli recalled that Wolf Mankowitz requested his name be removed from the credits of the film.[29]

Previous accounts of the making of the film suggest that Harwood's sole contribution to the writing of the screenplay was the topical joke of having Dr. No behind the recent theft of Goya's portrait of the Duke of Wellington. She recalled, 'I came up with the idea at a script conference at Harry Saltzman's place.'[30]

Over fifty years later, Harwood reflected:

By now of course the whole thing is chewed around the edges as you can imagine – everything has been changed by one person, by two people. It would [have] been nice to go back to the very first script I did. Of course they are not going to admit that's a good idea – because they've just spent thousands paying all these other people. So I do what I can with all the scripts lying around pasting and cutting and rewriting. We are running out of time now more or less. At some point someone says 'What's this little girl doing writing tough dialogue?'[31]

Beyond the obstacles of writing the screenplay and choosing a director, the greatest task was to find the man who would be James Bond. The film had a budget of $140,000 for the entire cast.[32]

Cary Grant was a Bond aficionado but was considered too expensive and, even if he had been affordable, would not sign for more than two films.[33] This was despite having been Cubby's best man at his recent wedding. Fleming was acquainted with another star who might have been suitable for the role: David Niven. The actor recalled bumping into the author at Boodles, the gentleman's club in London during the war, 'we laughed together at the same things for years to come'.[34] However, Broccoli felt Niven was not tough enough for the part.[35]

Before any actor had been cast, Fleming envisaged James Bond should have a background similar to himself. Bond's mother was Swiss and his father was from a Scottish family, but raised in England. Fleming had conceived Bond's Scottish ancestry when researching the Bond family name years before.[36] Fleming thought Bond resembled the golfer Henry Cotton and in CASINO ROYALE Vesper Lynd likens him to one of the great songwriters of the age, Hoagy Carmichael. According to Fleming's stepson, John Morgan, Fleming actually had an actor in mind to play Bond: the little known Edward Underdown.[37]

Broccoli recalled, '[United Artists] were reluctant to make the series using an unknown actor but eventually, after some talk, we did get an understanding that the picture would be done, if it could be done cheaply. In short, a million dollar budget – tops.'[38] United Artists had wanted a big name to play James Bond. However, since Eon Productions had conceived a series of six films, to be released one per year from 1962 onwards, they were unsure whether a star would commit to such a long tenure, and if so, how much for.

An apocryphal story is that Fleming initially thought the then unknown actor Roger Moore would make a good Bond. That Fleming had even heard of Moore is only likely because the British actor was well acquainted with Fleming's best man, Noël Coward. Moore himself was sceptical of the story, 'I wouldn't think so because it was '56 when we worked together.'[39] Broccoli thought Moore 'slightly too young, perhaps a shade too pretty. He had what we called the "Arrow collar" look: too buttoned-down smart.'[40] Another actor purported to have been considered was Patrick McGoohan who had starred in the 1956 Warwick film *Zarak* and was enjoying great success in the television series *Danger Man*.

Harry Saltzman also mentioned McGoohan along with actor Michael Craig.[41] However, it is alleged that McGoohan, a strict Catholic, turned the role down on moral grounds. Saltzman thought his own 'kitchen sink' star Albert Finney could also have been a good fit. Other names mentioned by Broccoli included Trevor Howard and Michael Redgrave, while director Terence Young wanted Richard Johnson to play the role.[42] Young, however, was one of the few directors who had worked with the eventual choice, Sean Connery, who he met when working on *Action of the Tiger* (1957).

Many individuals have taken credit for bringing Connery to the attention of the producers. Lana Turner was the first to introduce Broccoli to the Scotsman on the set of *Another Time, Another Place* in 1958. Cubby's first impressions were, 'He was a handsome, personable guy, projecting a kind of animal virility. He was tall, with a strong physical presence and there was just the right hint of threat behind that hard smile and faint Scottish burr.'[43] Broccoli could see the latent appeal in the actor, 'The movie he was making with Lana was poor, but it revealed other potential in Connery. A flair for wearing stylish clothes and an easy, confident style in front of the cameras. It was this image that persisted in my mind.'[44]

In summer 1961, while at Goldwyn Studios in Los Angeles, Cubby attended an advance screening of the live action Disney musical *Darby O'Gill and the Little People* – one of Connery's first leading roles. Dana Broccoli recalled, '[Cubby] said, "I've just seen an actor and I think he's terrific but I don't know if he has any sex appeal. I was just knocked out by him. I thought he was just incredible."'[45] Peter Hunt, who would eventually edit the first Bond film, recounted how he had known the director and the producers individually before production:

I had been acquainted with the director, Terence Young, since I was sixteen. I later did some special work for Cubby Broccoli and Irving Allen. I also knew Harry Saltzman, and one night we were having dinner. At the time I was working on a film called *On the Fiddle* [1961], with Sean Connery. Harry began talking about how he was going to make these Bond films with Cubby Broccoli. They were discussing who was going to play Bond, and I sent up a couple of reels of Connery. Whether that influenced them or not, I don't know.[46]

Connery was born on 25 August 1930 in Fountainbridge, Edinburgh and left formal schooling aged thirteen. After a number of jobs including delivering milk and coffin polishing, he enlisted in the Royal Navy to travel the world. Unfortunately he only got as far as Portsmouth and was invalided out early due to stomach ulcers. He settled on acting because it offered more longevity than his other career opportunity – a professional footballer for Manchester United. By the time the Bond offer came up Connery had carved a solid career as a working actor on stage, television and film, doing B-movies and the classics.

Just prior to shooting *Dr. No* Connery married his long-time partner, the actress Diane Cilento:

> Sean was given the James Bond books to read and received a callback for an audition. He gave me the book for my opinion. I found the dialogue stilted, the character of Bond relentlessly awful unless he was given a sublime sense of humour, and the violence, or 'license to kill' stuff, could only be brought off if it was accomplished with a lot of ritualistic absurdity and fun.[47]

With this advice ringing in his ears Connery set out his terms at Eon's South Audley Street offices in Mayfair, London:

> Broccoli called and said he had this Fleming film and thought I might fit the part. He asked me over and after we discussed it a bit further I said I would be interested provided they put some more humour into the story. I felt this was essential. He agreed, then said, 'When can you test?' I asked 'What test?' He said 'A film test.' I said, 'Sorry, but I'm not making tests. I'm well past that. Take it or leave it but no test.'[48]

Harry Saltzman recalled Sean's behaviour during the meeting, 'Whenever he wanted to make a point, he'd bang his fist on the table, the desk, or his thigh, and we knew this guy had something. When he left, we watched from the window as he walked down the street and we all said, "He's got it!"'[49] Broccoli remembered, 'One of the things that appealed to us both was the way he moves, he moves like a cat, he moves very well.'[50] Saltzman agreed, 'For a large man he moves extremely well. He had acting ability, he had experience, he was the right age. I might tell you we had a lot of opposition when we picked him from everybody.'[51]

The producers were always adamant they needed a slightly tougher British figure to play Bond to add the requisite level of machismo to the gentleman spy. Saltzman said, 'When we spoke to him, [we] saw he had the masculinity the part needed.'[52] Broccoli noted the misconception about the literary Bond, 'There was a general feeling that he should be the school-tie hero, here in England. And he isn't.'[53] Saltzman agreed that their Bond was a tougher interpretation. 'There was a kind of an idea from the books that he was a very well bred, well educated, very erudite gentleman. Actually in the books, he isn't. He doesn't read. Actually Ian Fleming's picture of him was not as an educated gentleman. Ian Fleming [said he] was a blunt instrument. And we try to keep him in that image.'[54]

Broccoli understood the key to success was to make the unknown actor become Bond. 'If the books were successful, they would make whoever played Bond famous. A star couldn't have been tied up for a series of pictures; and we felt this to be vital. United Artists had failed with Micky Spillane because they used a different star each time and the public got no chance to form an affectionate identification with him.'[55] Associate producer Stanley Sopel remembered:

> I think they always knew from day one that Sean Connery would be Bond. He didn't look like anybody's idea of Bond when we first saw him but there was something there. We did go through the motions of screen-testing some fifteen or twenty hopefuls, of everybody's idea of what Commander Bond should look like: 6' 2", British upper-crust, with the sort of chiselled face. Had a genius come out of that testing, Connery probably wouldn't have gotten the part, but he was it from the beginning.[56]

Eventually the balding 31-year-old actor did screentest, under the guise of auditioning actresses for the role, at Pinewood. Upon receiving the material of Connery in New York, Picker and Krim telegraphed, 'NO. KEEP TRYING.'[57] On 23 August 1961 Cubby reported the words of United Artists' West Coast chief Robert Blumofe to Harry, 'New York did not care for Connery, feels we can do better.'[58] But UA's Bud Ornstein in London supported the producers' choice, 'He is the best we have come up with to date and I do believe he could be James Bond.'[59] Sean Connery was announced as Bond in *The Daily Cinema* on 3 November 1961.[60]

Connery appreciated the opportunity, 'I could see that, properly made, this would be a start – a marvellous opening. It had the ingredients of success: sex, action, and so forth. The only thing lacking, I thought, was humour.'[61]

Finding Connery was only the beginning. Not only did he have to act Bond, he would have to become Bond. Terence Young took Connery on an extensive crash course in all things refined. Various sartorial establishments in London dressed Bond: tailored suits from Anthony Sinclair of Conduit Street, shirts and ties from Turnbull and Asser of Jermyn Street, his trilby hat from Lock and Co., and handmade shoes from Lobb and Co., both of St. James's Street. Young schooled Connery in the background and manners one would expect of Fleming's Eton- and Fettes-educated spy. He advised Connery to sleep in his suit to get comfortable with it, taught the actor to eat with his mouth closed. Young tutored Connery into becoming the refined gentleman spy. Diane Cilento recalled, 'Terence Young had a son called [Shaun], so he called my Sean, "Junior".'[62]

Production buyer on the film Ron Quelch attended Eon's offices at South Audley Street to talk about the character James Bond, 'It was basically a meeting covering all the amenities/aspects of Bond himself. Would he have cufflinks? Would he have a tiepin? What watch would he have? That went on for the best part of a day.'[63]

Connery admitted, '[I'd] only read two Bond books [before filming began]. The thing was, I found Fleming much more interesting than his writing.'[64] Connery shared his feelings further, 'When I first met Fleming there was certainly no dissention between us on how to see Bond. I saw him as a complete sensualist – senses highly tuned, awake to everything, quite amoral. I particularly like him because he thrives on conflict.'[65] Watching Connery as Bond entering his flat after the introductory gaming scene, observing his panther walk gleaned from years working with ballet dancer, Yat Malgrem, and seeing him smell Miss Taro's towel and cooling his silencer after killing Dent – Connery's effortlessness in these scenes belied the training of a professional actor. Wearing a hairpiece for even his first Bond film, Connery's saturnine Bond look was confected by the make-up department of John O'Gorman and Eileen Warwick.

Prior to shooting Connery explained his approach to the character, 'James Bond is very much for breaking the rules. He enjoys freedom that the normal person doesn't get. He likes to eat. He likes to drink. He likes his girls. He is rather cruel, sadistic.'[66] Connery worked with his director to lighten Bond, 'Terence Young, agreed with me that it would be right to give it another flavour, another dimension, by injecting humour, but at the same time to play it absolutely straight and realistically.'[67]

Eon now needed to cast the first Bond girl, Honey Ryder. Martine Beswick, then new to the film industry, was up for the part, 'When I went to meet Terence Young, he took a good look at me and said, "You're too young and you need experience. Go and get some experience. Because I have an idea for you. I want you for my next film.'"[68] Also up for the part was Gabriella Licudi, who, at twenty, was also deemed too young.[69]

Then Broccoli happened to spy a photo of a woman in a wet shirt amongst the hundreds of photos of actresses floating around Eon's offices and thought 'she looked very attractive – wet – like a sea lion.'[70] Broccoli followed this up with a call to casting director Max Arnow, who informed him, 'No photograph can catch the beauty of this girl.'[71] However, Arnow went on to say, 'she has a voice like a Dutch comic.'[72] Broccoli was not put off, but time was running out – they had two weeks before they were to begin shooting.

Ursula Andress remembered her big break, 'I was in Los Angeles at that time. I said, "Ok send the script over." Everybody knows I never really read the scripts because I never really wanted to work.'[73] During a party hosted by Andress and John Derek, Kirk Douglas picked up the script for *Dr. No* sitting unread on the table. Douglas read the script aloud to the party guests. 'We all laughed. He just read a few pages to me and everybody said "Ursula do it. It's Ian Fleming – a writer who is liked all over the world." Douglas said, "You should do it."'[74]

Dr. No established the three-girl Bond formula: an initial, fun dalliance with a sex siren; an intriguing tangle with a femme fatale who works for the enemy; and then a final-reel encounter with the leading lady. In the opening of *Dr. No* audiences meet James Bond across a hazy gaming table as he challenges Sylvia Trench – the first James Bond girl – in a game of *chemin de fer*. Eunice Gayson had starred in Terence Young's 1956 Warwick film *Zarak*. At the time of the making of *Dr. No*, Eunice was starring in the London stage production of *The Sound of Music* and composer Richard Rogers would not release her from a long theatre run. Young suggested that he write a small part for her that could be filmed around her stage schedule (she needed to be in London by the early evening making her unavailable for long filming days). She had known of Sean Connery, having seen him on stage in the Oxford Playhouse. They subsequently became neighbours and he visited her flat to share his incredulity that he had been cast as Bond.[75]

Zena Marshall was the second actress in the structure: the villainess Chinese minx Miss Taro. While having lunch with Terence Young, he had been complaining that they had tested thirty oriental actresses but still could not find their girl. Zena merely suggested, 'What about me?' On 21 December 1961 she found herself opposite Sean Connery in competition against Talitha Pol, Lina Margo and Violet Marceau for the part.[76] The tests were lensed by Geoffrey Unsworth, who would go on to become a legendary cinematographer in his own right.[77]

In the novels Bond has a flirtatious relationship with his own secretary, Loelia Ponsonby, while M's personal assistant – Miss Moneypenny – is cool and distant. The film incarnation of Moneypenny is a blend of both characters. Lois Maxwell won the role of cinema's most famous secretary when her husband – television executive Peter Marriot – became seriously ill in 1961. Maxwell explained her predicament, 'It was on my son's second birthday. Right out of the blue Peter had a double coronary. The doctors didn't expect him to live and I knew I would have to find work to support us all. So I phoned round some of the people I knew in the film business and pleaded for anything they could give me.'[78]

Maxwell had appeared in Young's 1948 production *Corridor of Mirrors*, 'I called Terence Young and Cubby Broccoli – who was a friend of my husband Peter – and said "I need a job as soon as possible."'[79] They offered Maxwell one of two parts – Miss Moneypenny or the aforementioned Sylvia Trench. Lois joked her legs were not her strongest offering and that she 'didn't fancy the idea of being seen in a pyjama top [either]. I thought there might be a chance of playing Moneypenny again if the film was successful – which would, of course, be good for the family finances.'[80] At the wrap party Maxwell recalled meeting Ian Fleming. 'He came up to me after seeing the film – or, rather the rough cut – and said, "When I wrote the part of Miss Moneypenny, I had, in my mind's eye, a tall, elegant woman with the most kissable lips in the world. And you are precisely that."'[81]

Bernard Lee was cast as Bond's Secret Service chief, Sir Miles Messervy, known as 'M'. Lee had been a Warwick regular and had played a series of important roles in key British films including Carol Reed's *The Third Man* (1949). Lee's M would be more of an authoritarian figure for the film Bond to rebel against than the tough father figure of the novels.

Peter Burton played Major Boothroyd – the armourer. The way Bond is handed his Walther PPK with the gun fetishised as a gadget would become a trope of the series with Bond's equipment being explained by the quartermaster, soon to be known simply as 'Q'. The reference to the weapon jamming on his last mission was a nod to the literary Bond, who at the end of FROM RUSSIA WITH LOVE is left for dead.

Ian Fleming had suggested his friend and neighbour in Jamaica, Noël Coward, for the title role. Coward wittily cabled the author, 'Dear Ian, the answer to *Dr. No* is No, No, No, No!'[82] Harry Saltzman had admired Joseph Wiseman as a drug fiend in *Detective Story* (1952) and the noted Canadian stage actor was promptly cast as the Chinese scientist.[83] Made up to look vaguely oriental and dressed in a Mao Tse-Tung tunic, Wiseman's character wore black metal gloves instead of hooks. His cold line readings and economical movements formed the template for future Bond villains. Wiseman later said, 'I had no idea what I was letting myself in for. I had no idea [the film] would achieve the success it did. As far as I was concerned, I thought it might just be another grade B Charlie Chan mystery.'[84] Johanna Harwood remembered a more enthusiastic actor on set, 'He was there at the script conference and I remember going out to Pinewood or coming back from Pinewood in the same car as him once and he chatted very enthusiastically about the script and about the film.'[85] Sean Connery's wife, Diane Cilento, admired Wiseman's 'amazing face and a vulnerable passion that simmered just below the surface.'[86]

Casting was completed with some notable supporting players: Felix Leiter was played by Jack Lord, who would go on to worldwide television fame as Steve McGarrett in CBS's *Hawaii Five-O*. Professor Dent was played by Young's long-time friend Anthony Dawson and Bond's Cayman Islander ally, Quarrel, was personified by American John Kitzmiller – a Fellini alumnus and winner of the 1957 Best Actor award at Cannes.

To create the world of James Bond, Broccoli engaged department heads from his Warwick days: director of photography Ted Moore and production designer Ken Adam, assisted by art director Syd Cain, who put all the money on the screen.

Broccoli enlisted composer Monty Norman early on in production. He recalled, 'I had written a musical called *Belle or the Ballad of Dr. Crippen* (1961). One of the main backers was Cubby Broccoli. It was murdered frankly by the critics. [Cubby] was furious and he said, "One of these days we'll do something together again."'[87]

Years later Broccoli called Norman:

He said "We are doing the James Bond material. Would I like to do the first one?" I was about to say, "Can you give me a while to think about it?" When Harry Saltzman said, "We're doing all the location in Jamaica why don't you come out with your wife all expenses paid" – and that was the clincher!' He continued, laughing, 'Suddenly I found time. My wife [actress Diana Coupland] and I thought, "We don't know if this is going to be a big flop of a film, but at least we'll have sun, sea and sand for a few weeks."'[88]

Dr. No embodied the electronic age and Ken Adam wanted to innovate:

'My previous experience of Pinewood hadn't been that great. I called in all the heads of department – the construction manager, the chief plasterer, the chief painter – and said I wanted to play around with new materials, new technologies, new techniques, anything they could think of. They rose to the challenge. That stimulated my imagination.'[89]

Adam's initial reaction to the screenplay was not great, 'My wife Letitzia read [the script and said] "You can't possibly do this. You would prostitute yourself." I remember being offered a profit participation deal by Cubby and Harry. But because of my reservations about the script, I turned down the offer.'[90]

Adam recalled how the days leading up to principal photography were spent: 'We went down to Florida to look at marsh buggies, [as the basis for the dragon tank used to scare the locals from being too inquisitive] and then to Jamaica, but we didn't have a great deal of time because we had to start shooting. Then Syd Cain, my art director, came out to join us. I supervised the main locations but went back to London to work on the sets.'[91]

On 16 January 1962 *Dr. No* began filming at Palisades Airport, Kingston.[92] Monty Norman recalled that the fun started on the flight to Jamaica, 'Broccoli and Saltzman chartered a plane to take the whole British contingent to Jamaica. They were a motley bunch consisting of technicians, actors, stuntmen and essential film crew. During that long flight they all got to know each other very well and it became like a showbiz party.'[93] The first shot in the can was of Sean Connery in a phone booth staring intently at his chauffeur, played by Reggie Carter, who Bond has just discovered is working for the enemy.[94]

Throughout January and February 1962 the crew flitted all over Jamaica shooting both scenes set on the island and those at the fictional Crab Key. The unit went to Government House where Bond meets Pleydell-Smith and smells the trail of Miss Taro and Professor Dent.[95] They then found themselves at a concrete factory in the Blue Mountains where car action was filmed on a private road in the vicinity.[96] Stuntman Bob Simmons drove both Bond's convertible 1961 Sunbeam Alphine Series II and the ill-fated hearse[97] in which the villains had met their demise chasing Bond.

Ursula Andress arrived on the island in February 1962. It was the first time she had met the producers and Terence Young, having never screentested for the role. Andress's first scene was the closing shot of the picture: Bond casting their boat adrift from Leiter's US Marine gunboat.[98]

During production Ian Fleming, with his wife Ann, journalist Peter Quennell and poet Stephen Spender, visited the unit while they were shooting in Falmouth. Fleming paid particular attention to Andress, 'He always came on the set and we talked and then he invited me to dinner in Ocho Rios at Goldeneye – his house. He was a very interesting man, he was very intelligent, interested in culture. He was James Bond.'[99] Andress had read the Bond novels and considered them, 'Very well written, very fun and very educational in many things.'[100] Ever playful, Fleming wrote the actress into the new Bond book he was currently writing – ON HER MAJESTY'S SECRET SERVICE. Monty Norman was impressed by Fleming, too, 'I also went to his house once – Goldeneye. He was very interested in West Indian music [and] in the idea of doing something for Ursula Andress, as she comes out of the water, some piece of music.'[101] In the novel, Bond sings the calypso, 'Marion'.

Andress described Connery and Young as great mentors, 'I didn't know hardly anything about acting and Terence and Sean were very helpful to me. The thing I remember the most was that we were like a family – Sean, Terence and I – we were like a family together.'[102] Monty Norman mainly socialised with Jack Lord. 'He was a lovely man, and he and his wife and my wife and I used to see quite a lot of each other. What we used to do quite often was have dinner together at one great long table. To be fair to Harry, he was also part of it and Cubby was that kind of man.'[103]

Laughing Water, the estate of Mrs. Minnie Simpson, was the locale of Honey Ryder's entrance from the waves in a stunning bikini complete with hunting knife.[104] In Fleming's novel Honey emerges from the water, completely naked, her hands covering her groin and, endearingly, a broken nose, leaving her breasts on display. No censor was going to pass such a scene for a general 1962 audience. Upon arriving in Jamaica Andress had collaborated with costume designer, Tessa Prendergast, on the making of what was still, in the sixties, a rather risqué piece of clothing. Fashioned from a British Army webbing belt, Andress fitted her ample frame into the most famous bikini in the world. She noted a common misconception about the item of clothing, 'It's not actually white – it's a sort of ivory colour.'[105] Ursula was unsure of the initial design – a traditional Jamaican style:

I didn't like the palm trees or the leaves or the tropical flowers on the print of the fabric. I wanted something very simple. I had a very special idea about how I wanted the bikini. We designed it together. I chose the material, I didn't sew it, but I helped to cut it!

The design also had to be suitable for the action sequences, which required a lot of 'running and falling'.[106]

On 8 February 1962 Ursula Andress emerged from the warm Caribbean water and embedded herself in the imagination of billions of viewers for generations to come.[107] The bikini was sold years later in 2001 at auction for £41,125 – more than twenty-seven times her £1,500 salary for appearing in Dr. No.[108] 'It was a rag. Who wanted it? I was going to throw it away and then a friend of mine said "Oh keep it!" I had it in a box in Los Angeles for years.'[109]

One of the key people Monty Norman met while on location was Chris Blackwell – the son of Fleming's sometime mistress, Blanche Blackwell, and heir to the Crosse and Blackwell food fortune. Blackwell served as a location manager on the film, but was also an unofficial music guide. Norman recalled, 'They were sensible enough to know the Caribbean music, which hadn't been used that much in films was a good idea for that film. Practically all the Caribbean stuff was recorded in Jamaica.'[110] Monty Norman 'had a lot to do with Chris. I suppose he was the man who knew the area'[111] and was full of praise for Byron Lee, who 'was a big band leader in Jamaica and the West Indies.'[112] Vocal duties on the songs by Lee's band, the Dragonnaires, were taken on by Eric 'Monty' Morris.[113]

The crew went next to Reynold's Bauxite Docks to film the exterior of Dr. No's Crab Key hideaway. This site would be recreated in miniature by special effects technician John Stears back at Pinewood Studios. Ultimately the model would be blown up – the first of many explosive finales to the Bond films.

The Vanzie Swamp Salt Marsh was the setting for Bond's, Honey's and Quarrel's – encounter with the dragon tank,[114] used by Dr. No to keep the locals at bay; these scenes were themselves somewhat cursed. Firstly the tank, made in Miami, was delayed due to a freak snowstorm in Florida and upon arrival it was discovered the vehicle had been damaged in transit.[115] The conditions for filming with it were terrible, as the crew were beset by leeches and mosquitoes on the marshes.[116]

The unit left Jamaica on 23 February 1962.[117] Despite harmonious working relationships the location shoot had been plagued by unforeseen problems – local work practices, bad weather, delayed actors and equipment. Many shots had not been captured and the production had gone over budget; work would resume at Pinewood Studios.[118]

Scenes of Bond gambling in the small hours at Le Cercle were inspired by the first time audiences meet 007 in Fleming's debut novel CASINO ROYALE. Terence Young was inspired by the introduction of Paul Muni in the 1939 film *Juarez*[119] – James Bond is seen from behind and in profile, but never fully revealed. Ken Adam's magnificent set had been based on Les Ambassadeurs in London; it was the perfect stage to introduce Bond to cinema audiences. We see

Bond being chased on the *chemin de fer* table by the stunning Sylvia Trench in a striking red dress who prompts his introduction, 'Bond. James Bond'. Young deliberately altered the timing of the scene so that instead of flicking his lighter and uttering the words, Connery paused a beat and then exhaled as he reveals his name, for the first time, through a haze of smoke.[120] Eunice Gayson recalled Connery was nervous before they shot the scene and was asked by Young to help Sean relax. After lunch and a few calming drinks, the scene was captured in posterity for the delight of generations.[121]

Zena Marshall recalled spending days in bed with Sean Connery. She later thought some of what they shot must have been cut out by the censor:

Ian Fleming seemed to think my role was important, this enemy agent making love with Bond, each tacitly knowing the other is out to kill them. There were a few re-takes because Terence wanted us to relax into the mood of lovemaking and we did some sections twice for different markets. In Ireland, for example, they couldn't see my tits, so more covered up [publicity] shots were taken Sean was very rough and raw but his charm was exceptional.[122]

Someone else who would spend days in bed was stuntman Bob Simmons. Sean Connery was terrified of spiders and a plate of glass was placed between him and the arachnid for the scene involving a tarantula crawling up Bond's body. However, reflections could be seen in the glass and Broccoli requested Simmons allow a real tarantula to walk across him.[123]

Andress, too, was subject to exotic creatures. In the novel, part of Dr. No's experiment in torture is to tie up Honey and observe her being devoured by migrating crabs. A version of it was filmed in the studio, but Andress recalled, 'It was cut from the film because the crabs were too frozen – they had been flown in and they had to be de-iced. Terence suggested hot steam – they ended up half cooked so everybody took a crab home for dinner.'[124]

Fleming's James Bond rarely kills in cold blood and reveals he does not like doing so. Young wanted to show Bond's ruthlessness and a scene was written especially for the film: the killing of Professor Dent. Dent empties his gun into a figure he thinks is Bond sleeping. However, Bond has rigged his bed with strategically placed pillows. Knowing Dent has run out of bullets, Bond quips, 'That's a Smith and Wesson and you've had your six' and shoots him at point blank range, even shooting Dent in the back after he has fallen. It is powerful moment and paved the way for other screen heroes to be similarly ruthless. Johanna Harwood remembered, 'There was an awful lot of talk about it for and against. And they shot it both ways in case the censorship objected. I thought it was a mistake. I argued very, very firmly he shouldn't do it. I thought he's going to lose audiences' sympathy.'[125]

The finale in Dr. No's nuclear reactor was filmed on Pinewood's A Stage towards the end of March 1962.[126] Ken Adam had obtained real technology from International Business Machines (IBM) following his own inspection of the atomic facility at Harwell.[127] By this time Adam had blown his design budget and he had to dip into the contingency fund to finish the eerie spider room set, which is the audience's first encounter with the strange world of Dr. No. Cubby joked with Adam that he should keep a low profile as Film Finances, the completion bond company, were inspecting the set that day.[128]

Principal photography officially wrapped on 26 April 1962.[129] The film was over budget and over schedule. The production was actually taken over by Film Finances, who would then oversee post-production duties.[130] Despite the cost overrun, what audiences saw was, in the words of Stanley Sopel, 'a $5 million movie, which we had made for $1.2 [million]'.[131]

Sound designer Norman Wanstall was to become another key player on the Bond team. He had worked his way up the ranks on Sink the Bismarck (1960, directed by Lewis Gilbert), alongside Dr. No editor Peter Hunt. Using quick cutting, sacrificing realism for pacing and style, combined with Wanstall's exaggerated sound effects, the team came up with a new visual language for films.[132] Norman Wanstall remembered:

> Peter looked at the sort of material we were getting and said, 'I think we'd better make this move so fast, people won't have time to analyse it. Let's make it go with a bang, just before people start to analyse whether it's silly or not. Let's move it along and make it exciting and special and macho' – that was a very big decision. I'm sure that if another editor had cut those early Bonds they wouldn't have had the same impact.[133]

Harry Saltzman later opined this was the result of the film not being made by British filmmakers, 'The tempo wouldn't have been there. We've put into the picture a North American tempo.'[134]

Dr. No opens with what would become the classic Bond introduction. A series of white dots appear on a black screen which then becomes the view from the striated inside of a gun barrel. Bond appears and is tracked by the gun. Suddenly, Bond turns and fires and a wash of red blood covers the screen

– Bond has shot his would-be assassin. The evocative sequence was designed by the graphic artist Maurice Binder.[135] Binder dreamed up the gun barrel sequence in less than fifteen minutes:

> I had a meeting with the producers at eleven o'clock, so at nine o'clock I had to do a storyboard for *Dr. No*. I didn't quite know what I was going to do but I did like the idea of gunshots across the screen so I felt if we have gunshots, maybe we could have a gun barrel. I had price tags, those little sticky things and I stuck them down fast – bang, bang, bang – and I drew a circle for the gun. They said it was fine, 'Do it.'[136]

Binder relied on a team he had worked with before. Trevor Bond recalled, 'Maurice Binder came into my life with a storyboard for *The Road to Hong Kong* [1962], the last "Road" film with Bing Crosby and Bob Hope.'[137] Shooting the gun barrel proved problematic, as Trevor recalled:

> It was a Colt .45 – a British service revolver, short-barrelled. We couldn't focus down to get the rifle in. The actual lens just couldn't cope with it. I had an idea – I had been a photographer in the Air Force when I did my National Service – and I had heard about pinhole cameras. So we got a piece of black paper and stuck a pin through it and cog the iris to shut right down and we got a perfect picture of the gun barrel. We had to have a policeman standing by – a British bobby because of the gun laws in England.[138]

The electronic sounds heard as the white dots glide across the screen were somewhat revolutionary at the time. Maurice Binder recalled,

> The film itself had Dr. No working with computers to topple the rocket. I thought we should have computer sounds on the titles. I looked for where I could get the sound effects and they said there was this little old lady in Surrey who had been doing experiments with electronic sound. She sent me a couple of selections, I then wanted to use a big bang to follow the shot.[139]

Binder also used the bebop section of the 'James Bond Theme' with the bold brass movement, eschewing the guitar opening. Monty Norman was not happy initially:

> I had a small row with Binder actually. I wanted the theme to be done exactly as is – from beginning to end – as so many themes are done that way. But

he started moving it. I said, "You're ruining it, you're absolutely ruining it."
I sent him a couple of letters and I protested to Harry and Cubby about it.
But, you know, they were right.'[140]

Binder revealed who the figure seen through the gun barrel was:

The little man you see on the first film is Bob Simmons, the stuntman who
doubles for Sean Connery. At that point, nobody knew Sean Connery and
nobody knew Bob Simmons, so what difference did it make?[141]

Trevor Bond explained the rationale behind the first James Bond title sequence,
which became an innovative artistic triumph of the series, 'It started with the
idea of early computers – lots of lights and blobs – and these dots going bleep,
bleep, bleep which turned into the gun barrel. I wanted to use native dancers
as a visual accompaniment without losing the formularised graphic feeling that
had been established. I got the three blind beggars walking on a tread board –
[and] did it all against a white background.'[142]

The titles were accompanied by the aforementioned 'James Bond Theme',
which must now be the most famous theme in the world. Norman recalled
that its roots lay in a piece of music titled 'Bad Sign, Good Sign', taken from
an abandoned musical he had written in 1959.[143] The show had been set in the
Indian community in Trinidad and was based on:

A House for Mr. Biswas, the V.S. Nipaul book. There was one number in there
that I thought was very good. It had a very Asian quality and if the show had
ever gone it would have been sung by somebody accompanied by a sitar.
I thought, 'I wonder what would happen if I split the notes?' It was quite
remarkable. I was at home [sitting by a piano]. I thought, 'This has to be
the beginning of the theme.' I'm not an orchestrator and a few people had
suggested John Barry because he was getting a few hit band songs. So I got
John Barry to do it.[144]

Norman said, 'I worked with Barry on what I wanted: a rhythmic sustained
sound for the opening four bar figure; low octave guitar for my main melodic
theme; big band for the hard riding middle section, etc. John did a wonderful,
definitive orchestration of the Bond theme.'[145]

If ever there was a case to exemplify the old showbusiness adage that 'where
there's a hit, there's a writ', the composition of the 'James Bond Theme' was it.

In what had been the source of decades of litigation, John Barry alluded to the fact that he composed the theme from scratch with his band, the John Barry Seven.[146] Claiming to have been brought in by United Artists' London music chief Noel Rogers, the theme was said to have its roots in Barry's composition 'Bees Knees'.[147] Vic Flick's distinctive guitar sound graces both tunes, but Norman retained the credit and copyright to the track. In 2001, during a five-day trial, with evidence from all the parties and musicologists, a jury found that Monty Norman had, indeed, composed the 'James Bond Theme'.[148] During the proceedings it was revealed that the track had earned Norman approximately £485,000 from 1976 to 1999.[149] John Barry received a mere £250 fee back in 1962.[150]

As had been the case with the Warwick films, music played an important part in the continuing Bond series. A potential source of huge revenue, United Artists took care to retain all copyright, licensing and synchronisation rights to the music in the films. Danjaq also shared in the revenues and retained a free hand in choosing composers and artists.[151]

Danjaq were restricted by Fleming in a very limited deal regarding licensing. One area Fleming prohibited from being exploited in connection with Bond was toiletries, including soap and deodorants.[152] The producers did seek tie-in deals with a range of companies from purveyors of cigarettes and alcohol to Gossard bikinis, Hathaway shirts and Triumph cars.[153] In keeping with the Fleming device of inserting real brand names in his books, the James Bond films were alive to the publicity benefits of product marketing from the outset.

An enduring marketing element would be the '007' logo used to advertise the film. David Chasman, a creative director at United Artists, gave the job of designing the graphic to a friend, Joseph Caroff, who remembered, 'I wrote "007" and realised the "7" could be the handle of a gun. It just happened. I gave it a little styling and made it look bold. While I only got $300 for the job, it has brought me a great deal of business.'[154]

Maurice Binder was behind the film's unusual trailer campaign. Sean Connery recorded a voiceover, wittily counterpointing the onscreen action, 'I thought it was polite to knock before shooting.' Binder recalled that the first trailer was not well received by United Artists in New York who thought the irony of the commentary was outrageous.

Early omens for the movie were not good, as Harry Saltzman remembered:

When we had a print ready, there were about eight people from United Artists, including Arthur Krim, who came to see it. We started the picture at

10 a.m. and when it was over a few minutes before 12 noon, the lights came up and nobody said anything except a man who was head of the European operation for United Artists. He said, 'The only good thing about the picture is that we can only lose $840,000.' Then they all stood up, and Cubby and I were just shattered.[155]

Dr. No was first screened at Terence Young's club, the Traveller's, in July 1962.[156] Another preview took place in Wimbledon a few months later. Then, on 5 October 1962, the London Pavilion paid host to the worldwide premiere. The first tangible indications of the scale of success were felt at the premiere, as Monty Norman recalled, 'Within no time at all, you could feel the buzz in the place especially the moment he says, "Bond, James Bond" and the music comes in behind him. That was an amazing moment.'[157] Harwood met Fleming for the first time at the after-party, 'He was very urbane and I remember him saying, "There is some very good caviar on the buffet."'[158] Ian Fleming diplomatically said upon seeing the film 'those who have read the book are likely to be disappointed but those who haven't will find it a wonderful movie. Audiences laugh in all the right places.'[159] Saltzman remembered, however, 'Fleming didn't like Sean Connery because he spoke with a Scottish accent. Fleming saw James Bond as himself, high-born, very educated, very English, posh public school accent.'[160]

The film played well in the UK but was only booked into Odeon's flagship cinema at Leicester Square due to the Rank chain needing to make good on their British picture quota policy.[161] Saltzman believed that was why '*Dr. No* got a major commercial shot'.[162] It proved fortuitous for Rank to Saltzman's satisfaction:

> We broke every record known. We made £69,000 the first week, and we held the record for eleven years. We played twenty-four hours a day at £1 per ticket. They never saw such business, and the most surprised was United Artists. To them, it was a B picture. They hated it.[163]

Broccoli was confident, 'We knew we had a good little film and knew it was going to make money – but there was more. This semi-sadistic, unscrupulous man of the law and womaniser fascinated people. Women loved him, men wanted to be like him – the impeccable manners, the flare, the sex appeal.'[164]

Despite the UK success, the US release in May 1963 was badly handled. Broccoli recalled the distributors were 'anxious to get their money back so they schlocked the film out, playing it in drive-ins. *Dr. No* never opened in New York, Chicago or any key city. It opened from the inside.'[165]

During its theatrical life, *Dr. No* has been estimated to have grossed $16,067,035 in North America and $43,500,000 internationally.

Sean Connery became an instant star and preparations were already underway to film the next Ian Fleming thriller. When he first took on the role, Connery was concerned about signing up to a series, 'I wasn't sure I wanted to get involved in that and the contract that would go with it. Contracts choke you, and I wanted to be free.'[166] However, Sean Connery and James Bond were about to become indistinguishable.

5

I MUST RETURN

FROM RUSSIA WITH LOVE

(1963)

EON PRODUCTIONS LTD.

HARRY SALTZMAN

ALBERT BROCCOLI

THE MOST SUCCESSFUL FILM 1962

IAN FLEMING'S

Dr. NO

STARRING

SEAN CONNERY as JAMES BOND

DIRECTED BY TERENCE YOUNG

COMPLETED

BOB HOPE — ANITA EKBERG

CO-STARRING EDIE ADAMS & LIONEL JEFFRIES

CALL ME BWANA

DIRECTED BY GORDON DOUGLAS

STARTS SHOOTING ON LOCATION IN ISTANBUL - MARCH

STARRING
SEAN CONNERY as JAMES BOND

FROM RUSSIA WITH LOVE

the SECOND JAMES BOND FILM

TO BE DIRECTED BY
TERENCE YOUNG

Flushed with the success of *Dr. No* the newly established team at Eon Productions wasted no time in progressing with their next production: *Call Me Bwana*. Now a quirky curiosity, the movie was predominantly a Harry Saltzman initiative.[1] Co-written by *Dr. No*'s Johanna Harwood with Nate Monaster, Mort Lachman and Bill Larkin, *Call Me Bwana* is a Cold War romp involving a space capsule returning from a mission to the moon. Holding vital information, the capsule lands in a fictional African state and the Americans send Matthew Merriwether, played by Bob Hope, a famed (but, in fact, fake) explorer to track down the capsule before the Soviets, who have assigned Luba (played by Anita Ekberg), a respected anthropologist, to get there first. Harwood admitted, 'I'm not sure that I have ever actually seen it because it came out when I was in Paris and I don't think it has been shown since.'[2]

Shot at Pinewood Studios, with second unit material filmed on location in Kenya, the film bills Harry Saltzman as 'executive producer' while it is 'produced by Albert R. Broccoli'. Bob Hope had starred in Saltzman's first film, *The Iron Petticoat* and Anita Ekberg had appeared in the Warwick production *Zarak* for Broccoli.

Director Gordon Douglas was assisted by the core team who had worked on *Dr. No*; cinematography by Ted Moore, editing by Peter Hunt and design by Syd Cain (Adam was already working for Stanley Kubrick on *Dr. Strangelove*, 1964). The picture also features an amusing title sequence by Maurice Binder.

The film contains some amusing moments, including a spoof of the *Dr. No* tarantula scene and a game of golf in the African plains, where famed professional Arnold Palmer turns up as himself, as well as some classic Bob Hope-isms thrown into the mix.

Composer Monty Norman also returned to the Eon fold, but was rueful about the experience:

I never got a contract from Harry at the beginning. I said, "The director's happy, you seem to be happy, everyone's happy, Bob Hope is certainly happy. Isn't it time we talked money?" [Harry] said, "If you wanna talk money, we can't do business!" Harry was a really good film man and also a theatre man for that matter but he was very difficult and most people had trouble with him at one stage or another. There should have been a Harry Saltzman survivors' club.[3]

Prior to production, journalist Donald Zec suggested to Broccoli that Eon's next film should feature a popular new beat combo. Broccoli raised it with Saltzman who said, 'Let me ask you something, Cubby: would you rather make a film with four long-haired schnooks from Liverpool who nobody's ever heard of, when we've got Bob Hope – Bob Hope! All ready to go.'[4] That was the rationale for the Bond producers missing the opportunity to produce the first Beatles film.[5] *Call Me Bwana* remained the only non-Bond Eon Productions feature film until 2014's *The Silent Storm*.

So eager were United Artists to get back into the James Bond 007 business, they immediately approved a production budget of $2 million for the second film. The producers received a larger fee, an increased overhead allowance and personal expenses budget. If both *Dr. No* and the second film recouped their costs together, Danjaq's profit share on subsequent pictures would increase from 50 per cent to 60 per cent.[6] But there was one man who was not happy: Sean Connery. Overnight Connery had become the top-grossing star in England. While *Dr. No* had been unceremoniously dumped in the US drive-in circuit in May 1963, it had still been successful enough for United Artists to double the budget.

Connery now regretted signing a multi-picture deal and, having glimpsed the success that lay ahead, wanted more. His then wife, Diane Cilento, remembered that Cubby and Harry did not want to alter the contract, 'There was a long legal wrangle, which entailed lawyers, agents, flaring tempers, shouting and lots of aggravation.'[7] She understood that Connery's agent, Richard Hatton, was 'bargaining from a position of impregnable strength'[8] and terms were eventually agreed. Connery would get a $100,000 bonus on top of his $54,000 salary.[9] Financial gripes aside, he was still enthused by James Bond. Connery mused, 'I suppose the Walter Mitty in every man makes him admire a man like Bond a little. Ian Fleming told me he studied psychology before the war in Munich. Perhaps that's why he seemed to know such a lot about the hidden yearnings in men and women.'[10] Connery had an interesting thought process, 'I once wondered what Bond thought of Fleming. He would admire him. Admire his well-founded, well-used substance and forthrightness. Admire immensely his brain and his reasoning powers, his villains and his heroines.'[11]

FROM RUSSIA WITH LOVE was chosen as the second Fleming novel to be adapted for the screen. The THUNDERBALL situation was still a legal quagmire. The most recent novel, THE SPY WHO LOVED ME, published on 13 April 1962 was an experimental novella that Fleming had not wanted filmed. Cubby Broccoli considered FROM RUSSIA WITH LOVE 'one of Fleming's best stories [where the] leading characters were well fleshed out. It was a tough straightforward spy adventure and the public was familiar with the title.'[12] This was also the book that President Kennedy had highlighted as one of his favourites a couple of years earlier. Fleming expressed his gratitude:

> I would not know how to go about soliciting such complimentary remarks from high places. I only met President Kennedy once socially when he was still a US Senator and I don't believe I made such a profound impression on him that he would read my books as a result of our meeting. Yes the President has mentioned his fondness for my books on many occasions and I am proud to number him amongst my most ardent fans. In recent years, I have always sent him an autographed copy of each new book as soon as it comes off the presses. I think that is the least I can do.[13]

Like all Bond screenplays, its development went through many hands and processes. Richard Maibaum remembered, 'On *From Russia With Love*, they had Len Deighton start.'[14] Len Deighton was the hot new thriller writer of the day, following in the slipstream of Ian Fleming. His debut novel, THE IPCRESS FILE, featured a nameless hero who was seen as an anti-Establishment retort to Fleming's world: a classless stick to beat the elitist Bond. Deighton was fêted by the press as the brave new hope and had even met Fleming. He met with Saltzman at Pinewood Studios the week *Dr. No* opened in October 1962. The producer wanted to buy the film rights to THE IPCRESS FILE. At subsequent meetings, Deighton was asked if he would like to write the screenplay for *From Russia With Love*. Deighton remembered the offices at South Audley Street: 'A rabbit warren of small rooms served by a dark staircase – no elevator – on which one met all manner of film people.'[15] He dealt mainly with Saltzman on the picture: 'I saw Cubby from time to time but our conversations were just friendly day-to-day comments. I never discussed films with him. His quiet voice and shy manner made it difficult to believe that he had been an agent in Hollywood.'[16] Saltzman suggested a winter trip to Istanbul and Deighton jumped at the chance to escape the cold British winter.[17]

Deighton was unaware of any other writers involved at this stage, 'There were only four of us on the recce and Harry's conversations with the art director gave me the impression that we were starting from scratch. So did the sessions I had with Harry every day over breakfast at the hotel.'[18] Deighton felt Harry understood screenwriting, which, unlike other forms of writing, had the unique opportunity of, 'the chance to tell the audience something the hero does not know.'[19] Deighton was accompanied on the trip to Turkey with designer Syd Cain and director Terence Young.

Deighton recalled, 'From Istanbul I went to spend Christmas in Beirut – a town I knew and liked – and returned to London for New Year. I kept in touch with Harry during the writing – let's say I probably delivered the screenplay in February [1963].'[20] The producers felt it was progressing in the right direction and called in Richard Maibaum, who wrote a treatment dated 28 January 1963.[21] Maibaum thought it the best of the Fleming novels, 'I think we crystallised the kind of thing that the Bond movies should be. That film was the one in which we set the style. In fact, I wrote that script in just six weeks. It still remains my favourite.'[22] Maibaum recalled he got solo screenplay credit, while Johanna Harwood got an adaptation credit because 'she worked some with the director, Terence Young, and made several good suggestions.'[23]

Speaking to the authors in 2012 Harwood remembered things differently. She was asked to start work on *From Russia With Love* 'long before *Dr. No* came out because they were getting the second one, ready to go, to make straight afterwards.'[24] Harwood recalled the effect the success of the first James Bond film had on the second:

[The producers] were absolutely tickled pink. But what happened when we started working on *From Russia With Love* was quite another matter. Nobody knew why [*Dr. No*] had been successful. They were all terrified that the second one wasn't going to be the same. The first draft of *From Russia With Love* was done by this time and it was just torn to pieces because people wanted to get the same effect as *Dr. No* and they didn't know how. It was panic stations.[25]

The problem was, according to Harwood, the James Bond formula had yet to be established, 'Now I suppose you could say [it is] the James Bond girls, the gadgets and so on. I can remember one moment when Harry Saltzman said, "Now what we need here is a scene, you know, like that scene in the Marx Brothers when they are all trapped in a lift."'[26] Harwood considered '[Saltzman] the driving force. I practically never saw Broccoli. I never, for instance, got any feedback to say Cubby Broccoli hadn't liked something – I often wondered if he actually read the stuff. It was always Saltzman who wanted to change things.'[27]

Harwood formed an insightful picture of Sean Connery, 'What struck me most about him on the one or two times that I met him before the shooting – we had lunch out at Pinewood – he was interested in the story, not just his role. I have seen an awful lot of actors who are only interested in their own part.'[28] She was not, however, a fan of Terence Young:

Harry said I should rewrite FROM RUSSIA WITH LOVE with Terence Young. I thought this is going to be agony. We had one afternoon together where I watched Terence Young running his pencil through it rewriting the scenes and saying 'There that's much better isn't it?' I had to bite my tongue because I was thinking 'It's not much better. And he's not going to listen if I tell him.' So I went off and found Harry Saltzman and I said 'I'm leaving. There's no good me sitting there watching Terence Young wreck it even further, you're just paying two people instead of one.' And I left. And he said 'Well we've been together a long time are you sure?' And I said 'Yes I'm perfectly sure.' And that was it.[29]

Harwood's draft was simply a straight, faithful adaptation of Fleming's novel:

I don't know where Maibaum came in. I presume he did the nitty-gritty on that one. Anything that was vaguely like the book was mine. I didn't invent the character of Q. Someone else must have put him in. And I nearly didn't get the screen credit actually. Because I wasn't there any longer, they dropped it but my agent went and got it back.[30]

Maibaum felt Harwood's credit unfair, 'I was a little put out that she was given an adaptation credit because I don't think she deserved it, but there are always politics in these things.'[31] Berkley Mather, developing his novel THE PASS BEYOND KASHMIR as a Sean Connery vehicle for Eon (ultimately never produced), also made an uncredited contribution.[32]

FROM RUSSIA WITH LOVE was Ian Fleming's fifth Bond novel published in the UK on 8 April 1957. While it was the most overtly anti-Soviet of the novels, the backgrounds were gleaned from an appreciation of the country in the early thirties and Fleming's knowledge of the Enigma device used by the Germans during World War II. The novel concerns the Soviet counter-espionage outfit SMERSH targeting Bond in revenge for his successes against them. Lured by the temptation of the SPEKTOR – a Soviet cipher machine proffered by a defecting attractive desk agent, Tatiana Romanova, Bond is sent to Turkey to take delivery of both. In reality the SPEKTOR is booby-trapped and Bond is to be filmed making love to Romanova before both are dispatched by Red Grant. The sex tape is to be leaked causing a stain on Bond and the British Secret Service's reputation. The novel was an experiment in structure as the first third details the planning and rationale behind the assignation attempt as we follow the triptych of villainy – Kronsteen,

Donovan 'Red' Grant and Rosa Klebb about their deadly preparations. Bond only appears in the last two parts of the novel – the lamb to the slaughter.

The producers, again, softened the book's political edge. A Bond film staple was introduced – the 'Siamese fighting fish' analogy – an independent, non-aligned power playing off East and West against each other. In the film, the villain was again SPECTRE (the decoding machine now a Lektor). Seeking revenge against Bond for the death of their previous operative, Dr. No, SPECTRE hope to kill Bond and obtain the cipher machine. By making Bond apolitical, the producers showed foresight at the height of the Cold War. Broccoli recalled, 'We decided to steer 007 and the scripts clear of politics. Bond would have no identifiable political affiliation. None of the protagonists would be the stereotyped Iron Curtain or "inscrutable Oriental" villain. It was old-fashioned and would induce pointless controversy.'[33] Maibaum recalled that *From Russia With Love* was accused of soft-pedalling the then political scene of the day:

> *Commentary* [magazine] held forth that we weren't anti-Russian enough. In fact, I think we were ahead of government policy towards the Russians. We let up on them sooner than the government did. We had Rosa Klebb become a defector from the Russians and attributed all that was going on to Blofeld's bunch, unlike the novel.[34]

Maibaum also recalled that Bond's observation about Red Grant's uncouth drinking habits – 'Red wine with fish! I should have known' – nearly failed to make the film, 'The heated argument that ensued between producers, director and writer might have made an uninformed listener think fisticuffs were inevitable. Cubby's "OK" settled the matter – this time in my favour.'[35]

In the novel when Bond is caught by Red Grant on the *Orient Express*, he relies on the fact that Grant will make good on his taunt that Bond will be shot precisely in his heart. Bond then manoeuvres his gunmetal cigarette case over his heart in the inside pocket of his coat. This case deflects the bullet giving Bond enough time to defeat Grant. The screenwriters play on the fact that the recent best-selling novel would have been absorbed by many in the audience. So, in the film when Red Grant removes Bond's cigarette case, the tension suddenly increases. The subsequent showdown between Grant and Bond is especially taut. Other changes included an extended series of chases after Bond leaves the *Orient Express*. The novel ended with Bond seemingly poisoned by the curare on the tip of Rosa Klebb's boot blade. Here, the twist conceived for THUNDERBALL of having the girl save Bond is used when Tatiana Romanova shoots Klebb.

While the screenplay was being developed, the hunt for the actress to play Tatiana Romanova was gaining momentum. On 28 February 1963, the *Daily Express* ran a story entitled 'Wanted – A Girl for 007' – and over 200 girls auditioned. The tests were filmed at Pinewood with *Dr. No* villain Anthony Dawson playing Klebb.[36] Future *Goldfinger* girl Tania Mallet remembered:

> I did a screentest for *From Russia With Love*. In a studio in Pinewood there was cameraman, there wasn't a director, there wasn't a producer. A cameraman said look right look left. It was very casual in those days. The powers that be thought that I had a far too English accent for the part.[37]

Ironically, the part was eventually dubbed by Barbara Jefford. Broccoli recalled that Polish actress Magda Konopka and Yugoslavian actress Sylvia Koscina were in the running.[38] *Casablanca* star, Ingrid Bergman's daughter, Pia Lindstrom, was also considered.[39] The producers wanted German actress Elga Gimbel Andersen, however, a disgruntled United Artists' studio executive nixed her chances when she refused his advances.[40] Eventually they settled on Daniela Bianchi, a 20-year-old Italian actress who had recently come second in the 1960 Miss Universe competition. While not quite resembling the 'young Greta Garbo' as described by Fleming, she was pretty, pliant and adequate in the role. Bianchi remembered only a dozen reporters attended the press launch at the Connaught Hotel, 'This was the second film so this character of James Bond still wasn't very well known'.[41] Maibaum approved of Bianchi's casting:

> My favourite of all the Bond girls is Daniela Bianchi. She didn't really wanna be an actress. She would sit on the set and read an Italian novel and eat chocolates and when Terence would get peeved he would scream at her, 'You cow!' but she would just shrug and laugh. The great thing about her was, could there be anything more ridiculous than a cipher clerk working for the Russians who sees a picture of Bond and falls in love with him? She made it stand up. She seemed to be the kind of girl who'd do that, and my God, the scene in the stateroom is probably the sexiest scene in the Bonds.[42]

Robert Shaw was selected to play Red Grant, the eerie psychopathic assassin. Shaw was an accomplished playwright and theatre actor and, having been a contemporary of Connery's on the London acting scene, was only too happy to share billing. He also shared Connery's agent, Richard Hatton and the two actors had a friendly rivalry, which helped in their characterisations.[43] Terence Young gave Shaw time before filming to prepare for the role. Shaw underwent an intense gym regime to bulk up and get physically fit.[44] On location, Shaw spent at least two hours a day in the gym, working out with Turkish wrestlers.[45] As Red Grant, Shaw had to convince audiences he could take a knuckleduster to his solar plexus.

Harry Saltzman came up with the first in a long line of inventive casting suggestions, when he suggested singing legend Lotte Lenya to play the witch-like villainess, Rosa Klebb, a Soviet turncoat now working for SPECTRE. With the lesbianism of the novel dialled down low and the scraped bun of hair in place, Lenya was perfect casting, although her benign, real-life self showed how good an actress she was. Married to Kurt Weill, she was the first singer of his jazz standard 'Mack the Knife', written with Bertol Brecht. Only someone with Saltzman's vaudevillian background could have come up with such offbeat casting.[46]

Lenya remembered:

I was working at the Royal Court playing in *Brecht on Brecht* when the call came, 'Miss Lenya, we have a part for you.' The producer, a Mr. Saltzman said, 'It's an Ian Fleming story.' I said, 'I'm very sorry about my ignorance, but I don't know who Ian Fleming is.' So he replied, 'Well, we'll send you a book over in the afternoon. Could you read it and we can talk to you tomorrow?' I said, 'Oh, sure, I'll read it.' On the first page was a description of Rosa Klebb: she weighs 240lbs, her bosom is catholic down to her knee. And that was the description. Saltzman invited me to meet with him, so I went to his office looking very slim then. I said, 'Mr. Saltzman, [I read the book and] Rosa Klebb weighs 240lbs.[47]

Lenya was provided with a fat suit by the costume department but she refused to wear it.[48] Daniela Bianchi remembered the singer fondly, 'Lotte was a very small, very sweet woman. Her role of a tough villain was just totally different from what she was.'[49]

A key character in *From Russia With Love* is Bond's local ally, Kerim Bey – MI6's man in Istanbul. Cubby remembered one of the biggest stars in Mexico, Pedro Armendáriz, and flew out to California to offer him the part.[50] This big colourful man was perfect casting for a big colourful part.

Vladek Sheybal had been in a Polish film, *Kanal* (1957), about Debussy, which had also involved Harry Saltzman. Saltzman suggested Sheybal for Kronsteen, the master planner for SPECTRE. The actor, however, demurred at taking such a small role, but another person from his past was a factor in changing his mind. Sheybal had directed Diane Cilento in a television play and had spent a lot of time with the actress and her then boyfriend, Sean Connery, for whom he had found a small role in the production. Now Diane's husband, Sean Connery, directly asked for and welcomed Sheybal to the set.[51]

Returning cast members were Bernard Lee as M, Lois Maxwell as Moneypenny and Eunice Gayson as Sylvia Trench. However, a new face was to join the regulars and would become the most enduring cast member of the series. Desmond Llewelyn recalled how he got the part of Major Boothroyd, head of Q Branch – and how he fought to play it:

> I did have a very good part in a film called *They Were Not Divided* (1950). I played a Welsh tank driver and it was thanks to that part I was put up for the second Bond film, *From Russia With Love*. Luckily for me the chap who played Boothroyd in *Dr. No* was unavailable. As Terence Young had written and directed *They Were Not Divided*, I got the part. Actually, he wanted me to play the character as a Welshman, but I refused. I had quite a battle with him. I said you mean you want me to play it [adopts a broad, lilting Welsh accent], 'I've got a nice suitcase and knife that pops out here.' Luckily I managed to persuade him against it.[52]

Llewelyn 'played it absolutely straight. At the rehearsals the line introducing the character was, "Miss Moneypenny, ask Major Boothroyd to come in." Well, Terence said we can't do that because it's a different Boothroyd. So it was changed to "Ask the Equipment Officer to come in," and the equipment officer is from Q Branch, and that's how the name Q came about.'[53] Llewelyn enjoyed the courtesy of Cubby Broccoli, personally welcoming him to the set.[54] It was only one day's work – for which he earned £30 – but he did get to meet the creator of James Bond. Ian Fleming joined the cast for drinks, 'I asked him if he recollected a friend of mine being at school at Eton. He said yes, but I don't suppose he did.'[55]

Blofeld was mysteriously credited with just a question mark, but years later, production controller of Eon Productions Reg Berkshire researched the point definitively: 'On examination of contracts and ledgers, it appears that Anthony Dawson played the part and was dubbed by Eric Pohlmann.'[56]

Virtually the same crew who had worked on *Dr. No* and *Call Me Bwana* were hired for *From Russia With Love* with two major exceptions: production designer Ken Adam and composer Monty Norman. Adam was still engaged on Stanley Kubrick's *Dr. Strangelove* and in his stead, as an art director, was Syd Cain – Adam's assistant on the previous Bond.[57] Monty Norman felt his demand for payment on *Call Me Bwana* precluded him from a second Bond film and John Barry, who had steered Monty Norman's 'James Bond Theme' to popular life, took up the musical baton. It was the start of Eon's tactic of promoting from within their own ranks.

As pre-production geared up, Ian Fleming's agent, Peter Janson-Smith, recalled the lively scene at the Mayfair office:

> Some of the early meetings were like scenes out of an American comedy film. I remember one where we were all sitting around, there was Cubby Broccoli, Harry Saltzman and there were several lawyers and a merchandising agent and me, and various people. Every chair had a little table with a phone on it and all these phones were ringing. Harry Saltzman spoke French with a very Canadian accent: he had one phone here and he was speaking in French and this one in English.[58]

Many of the visitors to South Audley Street in those early days recall similar stories of Saltzman on two phone calls at once in two different languages. Hilary Saltzman felt that for her father:

> Communication was so key to him to stay in touch and to be available to all of the people that he was working with and there was never a bad moment to get a hold of him. He always wanted to be available to whomever he was working with. And he was always 100 per cent on whatever he was working on, whether it was the Bond film, or the other films or theatre. He was 100 per cent involved in everything. He wanted to know what the production designer was doing, what the director of photography was doing, how the sets looked. He always had a say in everything and an interest in everything – from the music to the script.[59]

On 1 April 1963 production commenced on B Stage at Pinewood Studios, where M briefed James Bond on his latest mission.[60] Eleven days later the studio gardens were used for the opening sequence in which Red Grant hunts down 'James Bond' on SPECTRE Island who, upon being garrotted by Grant's trick watch, is revealed to be a hapless SPECTRE agent. A re-take was filmed because when the mask was pulled from the assassin's face the actor looked too much like Connery. A moustache was later inserted. Sean Connery played the quarry for Red Grant. The eerie moonlit sequence was the brainchild of Terence Young who was parodying the 1961 Alain Resnais picture, *Last Year at Marienbad*, a film Young described as pretentious.[61] The stalking sequence was supposed to have been set in the dangerous SPECTRE island assault course later seen in the film. The idea of killing Bond in the beginning has been attributed to Saltzman,[62] but it seems the positioning of the sequence, after the gun barrel and before the titles, was the decision of both Peter Hunt and Terence Young when the film was being edited.[63]

On 20 April 1963 the crew flew to Istanbul.[64] According to Broccoli the exotic location was another reason Fleming's fifth novel was chosen as the second film.[65] The Warwick alumni were used to the challenges of shooting in foreign locales and were immediately thrown in at the deep end, when filming in Saint Sophia Mosque. The site could not be closed and the filmmakers shot scenes while real tourists walked around the interior. Syd Cain explained, 'The shooting schedule inside the mosque was sporadic as the Turkish government would only allow us to shoot when it did not interfere with normal tourism activity.'[66]

The location proved difficult with the locals unfamiliar with the disciplines of film-making. At Sirkeci Station, Cain recalled how: 'For three frustrating takes in a row [the train driver] managed to miss the mark, each time ripping out the cables to the generators and plunging the station into darkness. Finally, on the fourth take, the scene was completed.'[67]

As James Bond increased in popularity, the unit drew crowds everywhere they went. One newspaper report painted a vivid picture:

Istanbul: crowds of between 2,000 to 3,000 people have been forming amid the seventy-two-man movie unit each time they set up their cameras on the busy thoroughfare here. The other day director Terence Young faced his biggest challenge, when he staged a scene of Sean Connery … running into the main entrance of the Sirkeci Railroad Station [doubling for Zagreb station] near the Galata Bridge. This sequence drew the biggest crowd ever, all of whom seemed more fascinated with the camera than with the star. After making two takes with a thousand pairs of eyes staring into the lens, Young realised that the crowd had to be distracted by some other spectacle. So after lunch, he sent one of the company stuntmen across the street to hang from a third floor balcony screaming for help. With the assistance of the Istanbul police, he also arranged for a fire engine to arrive, with sirens screaming, to rescue the man from the balcony. Quite understandably the crowd rushed across the street to watch the new action, and Young and his crew, working quickly, got the scene they needed in one fast take.[68]

The boat chase scenes, as Bond heads for Venice with Tatiana at his side, were scheduled to be shot in the Pendik, near the Greek border. Technical problems halted production when the boats were not fast enough and the locals had poured kerosene in the engines by mistake.[69]

While Young sent assistant director David Anderson to shoot plates for the *Orient Express* scenes, he took the principals to the industrial section of the city where they shot the assassination of Bulgarian agent, Krilencu.[70] In the novel he escapes from a trapdoor set within a poster of the Marilyn Monroe film *Niagara* (1953), but here the filmmakers had an even better idea. Syd Cain remembered, 'We had the bright idea to get some maximum publicity for another Eon Production, the forthcoming *Call Me Bwana*. I ensured the entire side of the wall on which the villain would climb down sported a gigantic advert for the film.'[71] It is from Anita Ekberg's mouth that Krilencu escapes before he's satisfyingly shot by Kerim Bey.

Ian Fleming visited the unit while they were shooting in Turkey, associate producer Stanley Sopel remembered, 'He was terribly interested. It wasn't publicity – he just wanted to see what the hell we were up to. He stayed about a week, enjoyed himself, said, "Carry on, fellows" and away he went.'[72] Cubby Broccoli remembered a change in Fleming on location,

> In the London production meetings he would sit there in his detached manner, diffidently suggesting an idea or two. Fleming in Istanbul was in his element. I can picture him now in one of Istanbul's exclusive restaurants, a quivering midriff an inch or two off the end of his Turkish cigarette and his pale blue eyes locked on the dancer's navel.[73]

Broccoli enjoyed Fleming's company:

> I got to know him better when we were doing *From Russia With Love*. We went down to Turkey on the same plane. He loved to order food and later when my wife Dana came down, he took us out to dinner several places. In one case he was rather annoyed because one of our people insisted on ordering food. He wanted to do the ordering. He didn't want somebody going into a Turkish restaurant ordering en masse. So he sulked a bit when

he got there and found out this was all pre-ordained. When they asked what he wanted, he said, 'Well, I'll have a Spanish omelette'. In Turkey! That was his way of getting back, and saying that he didn't approve of the dishes that were ordered.[74]

In his autobiography Broccoli revealed the offending crew member was Saltzman.[75]

Diane Cilento accompanied Connery to Turkey and while in Istanbul, bonded with both Fleming and Armendáriz, as they enjoyed the city's exotic delights in the company of their local bodyguard, Mustapha.[76] Mustapha had organised a wrestling bout between Turkish wrestlers and the English stuntmen. Cilento recalled the hosts outmanoeuvred the tourists in an expert display of nimbleness.[77] She also observed at first hand the competitiveness between her husband and Robert Shaw. The latter had challenged Connery to a race, Connery had nonchalantly accepted but seemed unconcerned while Shaw was seen training for the whole week. On the day of the race the entire crew turned out to spectate. Shaw was kitted out in fine running shoes while Connery turned up wearing heavy-duty boots. The race commenced and Shaw charged ahead seemingly outpacing Connery. But the track was stony and flinty and made running in ordinary sports shoes impossible. Connery, however, in his boots, could withstand the terrain and in due course overtook Shaw and won the race.[78]

Harry Saltzman had a tough, irrascible side to him which annoyed many colleagues. However, Syd Cain recounted a gentler, more sensitive side to the producer on the Turkish set:

A voice boomed out across the store: 'What are you doing Syd?' It was Harry. I explained I was looking for a present to take home for my wife, Angela. 'This is what you should buy her' said Harry, showing me a Harem ring made of rubies and blue-enamelled gold. I told Harry it was out of my reach. That night, I was surprised to see the ring on my bedside table. I explained [to] Harry [that he] had embarrassed me by doing this, that my wife would have immediately known I couldn't have afforded such a present, though I appreciated his wonderful gesture. Harry understood and said, 'This is what you do. Tell your wife it's a present from me, for all the hard work you have done and that she's to come out to the location for a holiday – all on the company, of course.' This was more than generous of Harry and Angela enjoyed a wonderful time in Turkey.[79]

John Barry spent two weeks in Istanbul to pick up local colour and found the place bizarre:

> If ever I walked into a page of Kafka, this was definitely it. One night me and Noel Rogers went into this gorgeous place with a really long bar and a 50-foot brass rail holding it all together. The next thing we knew we leaned on this rail and the whole thing just collapsed on top of us, every nut and bolt. It was a very strange evening. Istanbul's like that. You get in a cab, go half a mile and then three old ladies get in holding chickens.[80]

The production was shadowed by sadness when it was discovered that Pedro Armendáriz was suffering from cancer with only weeks to live. Upon returning to Pinewood, Young arranged for the Mexican to have all his scenes shot first so that he could quit the production and return home, so Syd Cain hastily designed the gypsy camp set in ten days.[81] Young remembered, 'We'd shot all his scenes out of continuity. We did the gypsy encampment scene and as we got the last shot, the rains came. We'd literally got the last shot in the can, I'd said, "Cut, print it. On your way, Pedro, go home and get some sleep."'[82] Armendáriz left the production on 9 June 1963.[83] Young then literally stepped into his shoes, 'I then played the part of Armendáriz with Sean and all the other actors without his being there for the rest of the picture.'[84]

Armendáriz's truncated shoot affected the part played by Nadja Regin, Kerim's girlfriend in the film. 'I should have had a slightly larger part but because of the arrangement, Terence Young had to make sure that Pedro Armendáriz could finish his part, they had cut certain things.'[85] Regin remembered her co-star 'was always courteous but very withdrawn. He hardly spoke to anyone.'[86] On one occasion, however, the ice did break. 'I had seen a Mexican film of his in Yugoslavia. I said, "I saw you in La Perla (1947)." The thought of a Mexican film being so valued in a country like Yugoslavia meant something to him. He was easier with me.'[87]

Young was forced to cut his favourite scene featuring Armendáriz for continuity reasons. A moustachioed Bulgarian spy in a beret tails Bond when he first reaches Turkey; the Bulgarian is killed by Red Grant in the Saint Sophia Mosque. Later in the film, in an attempt to explain how Bond loses his tail en route to his rendezvous with Tatiana, a clever sequence was devised. A Bulgarian agent is prevented from following Bond in an elaborate car crash. Bond transfers into Kerim Bey's Rolls Royce which swishes up alongside the site of the incident. The Bulgarian is unable to follow because of his crashed car. Armendáriz as Bey leans out of his window and admonishes the enemy agent. Tapping off a particularly long ash from his cigarette, he opines, 'That, my friend, is life'.[88] On a preview it was noted that the enemy agent was the same man who played the Bulgar killed earlier by Red Grant in the mosque. Continuity-wise it made no sense. Young was sad to see the scene go, as it showcased Armendáriz to great effect. In light of his health situation it was symbolic of a philosophical attitude to life. Pedro Armendáriz committed suicide a week after completing work on the film.

After she failed to secure the lead in *Dr. No*, Young made good on his idea for Martine Beswick in *From Russia With Love*. Cast as one of the duelling gypsy girls Zora, against Aliza Gur who played Vida, Beswick was thrilled to appear in a Bond film. The fight over the right to marry the Gypsy chief's son was originally to be filmed in Turkey, but according to Gur, 'The weather was against us so we had to do it back at the studio.'[89] Gur felt, 'Terence Young chose me because, like most men, he's intrigued by Israeli girl soldiers.'[90] Beswick recalled, 'We literally rehearsed [for] three weeks. It was like a dance sequence, it was choreographed. Terence wanted to use the hand-held. He needed to be able to come in and shoot really close.'[91] However, Beswick remembered the fight was spiced with rivalry, 'Because I was a really good friend of Terence, [Gur] was furious about that and was very rude saying, "You slept with him." I didn't get on with her. She was difficult, let's put it that way. But we got a really good fight. Both of us probably had to be hurt a little bit.'[92] Beswick sheepishly admitted, 'Terence said, "Really give her one" even though I was known as "Battling Beswick", I really couldn't.'[93]

Another vicious, but less sexy fight was arranged by Peter Perkins, who had taken over from Bob Simmons as stunt co-ordinator. Bond and Red Grant's showdown at the end of the film was to be brutal. Simmons was engaged on Irving Allen's *Genghis Khan* (1965), but returned to double Connery for the train fight, while Jack Cooper doubled Shaw. Cain's *Orient Express* interior was based on a recce the designer had made of the real train in Paris.[94] Two stationary cameras were initially used to shoot the scene but, at editor Peter Hunt's suggestion, a hand-held camera was used.[95] Steven Saltzman, Harry's son, made an interesting observation about this scene:

It was the apex of everything [Harry] felt Bond was about. It was gritty, [Bond] could get hurt, he could get damaged. The fight on the train blew his mind. [In] the rest of the series, as you can see, even the early ones like *Dr. No*, they all have a kind of cartoon inability-to-be-killed quality to the character.

He thought *[From] Russia with Love* was the best of the lot. For him Robert
Shaw was the greatest of all the heavies.[96]

When the Bond films began they were not children's entertainment, they were
aimed at an older audience. The gypsy girl fight, the train combat sequence,
and Bond and Tatiana's honey-trap lovemaking (while secretly being filmed)
troubled the British censor John Trevelyan. However, he justified his lenient
classification of the films:

> Bond is a fantasy figure for the millions who lead dull lives. Our greatest
> problem with these films in my time was the film *From Russia With Love*.
> I could easily argue that the Bond films were more harmful than many
> others; the violence was surreal, and it was treated callously. Our defence was
> this, that obviously audiences did not find the violence realistic or nasty but
> entertaining. In the end we reached agreement [with the producers].[97]

Syd Cain's art direction went for a more realistic feel than *Dr. No*. The initial
chess room scene set in Venice was augmented by a splendid matte painting
by Cliff Culley, as well as other realistic paintings rendered by a particularly
workmanlike Scottish scenic artist. This contrast between craft and high art
came to a head when Cubby escorted a visiting group of journalists around the
set. They stopped to admire the work and gasped in amazement. One journalist
asked if it was in the style of Rubens. The Scottish artist responded gruffly, 'Yes,
it's all tits and arseholes.' Cubby moved them on quickly.[98]

The scene where Bond encounters thousands of rats in the Byzantine cisterns underneath Istanbul could not be filmed with authentic wild rats due to
health and safety restrictions.[99] Instead, tame rats were purchased and painted
in cocoa. However, the rodents would just sit under the hot lights, licking the
chocolate off each other. Syd Cain flew to Madrid where animal husbandry
laws were a little more relaxed. With the help of a local rat-catcher, he populated the set built in a warehouse with hundreds of rats, and the crew were
protected by a glass cage. However, the shot was plagued when the rats over-
ran the place. Cain was outmanoeuvred by his producer, 'Cubby Broccoli was
a man of some considerable girth but he moved like an Olympic runner to
outrace me to a stepladder.'[100]

Bianchi remembered her playful co-star during the pivotal love scene around
which *From Russia With Love* hinged, 'I was very concerned about keeping the
sheet tight around me because underneath I was dressed in a body stocking.

Sean naturally did everything he could to complicate things. Then Terence made us repeat the scene so many times. It was rather comical.'[101]

Things were not always harmonious. Vladek Sheybal, tiring of Saltzman's instructions on his acting, left the set and only returned on an assurance from Young that the producer be banned from the set during the completion of the actor's scenes.[102] Johanna Harwood observed the dynamic between the different producers:

> Cubby Broccoli's great place in the film industry was that he was nice. He was calm. What happened was when Harry Saltzman rubbed someone up the wrong way and there was a real problem on the horizon, Cubby would go in and smooth things down. Cubby did exactly the same thing with Irving Allen who was exactly like Saltzman, brash and tactless.[103]

From Russia With Love came in $200,000 over budget and behind schedule.[104] A number of scenes still had to be captured, including the boat chase abandoned in Pendik. Young was pragmatic and suggested they shoot the sequence at a cove he knew in Crinan on the west coast of Scotland in July 1963.[105] Syd Cain recalled how events unfurled:

> When we arrived on location, I suggested to Terence that another cove up the coast might be more appropriate. He agreed to take a look and climbed into a helicopter with my assistant art director, Michael White. They no sooner took off than a crosswind tipped them on one side and they slipped into the sea. Terence found himself 10 feet under the water but managed to break the canopy and swim clear, suffering a badly cut hand in the process. Michael had thrown himself clear as they hit the water. Terence and Michael went back to work almost immediately, Terence directing with his arm in a sling.[106]

Diane Cilento remembered Cubby Broccoli cheering the crew up by cooking them a lobster dinner on the windy, cold location.[107] Filming eventually wrapped on 23 August 1963.[108]

Post-production benefitted greatly from the increased budget compared to *Dr. No.* Norman Wanstall recalled:

> The gypsy camp sequence was shot with English extras, so it was obviously up to me to give it a totally Turkish (and Russian) atmosphere and bring the whole sequence to life. I needed the appropriate voices to react rowdily to

the belly dancer and the gypsy fighters and to mix with the Russians during the battle sequence. With some trepidation I marched into the production office and said 'Right, I need eighteen Turkish men, a dozen Turkish women and as many Russian blokes as you can find.' To my relief and surprise the manager replied, 'Okay Norm, when do you want them?' From that day on my requests were never questioned. Terence Young was ecstatic when he heard the gypsy tracks.[109]

Wanstall also remembered working on the helicopter scenes, 'We were provided with all the gear, including a couple of young daredevil pilots who only looked about eighteen. They threw those 'copters around the sky like I've never seen before and John Mitchell did a fantastic job with the recordings.'[110]

Wanstall did get an insight at this stage into the difference between the producers:

[Saltzman] was viewing rushes with us and he said to Peter [Hunt], "We're going to need someone that can really do some good sound effects on this." Peter turned and said, "Well you know we've already got somebody?" He didn't even know who I was. Cubby would have known – he was very, very aware of who was doing what.[111]

Warwick Films had a long tradition of title songs so a similar device emerged for the Bond pictures. *From Russia With Love* naturally leant itself to such treatment with a song written by Lionel Bart. Terence Young remembered how Bart got Bond:

Lionel came into my life when I chose a song of his for a film I was making, *Serious Charge* (1959). The song was called "Living Doll" and it's still around today. Harry Saltzman was keen on Lionel Bart and I must say I was too. I liked him very much. I think Harry had committed himself to Lionel Bart and that's why he wrote "From Russia With Love", which was a charming song.[112]

Young's experience with Bart helped pave the way for Barry's involvement, as some were still a little cautious about him, despite his prior reworking of the Bond theme.

After his last-minute work on *Dr. No* John Barry was anxious to score *From Russia With Love* in its entirety. Barry's orchestral booker Sid Margo remembered, 'He was thrilled to pieces. He called me up straight away and said, "I've got the Bond film, Sid! I can't believe it"'[113] Perhaps to supplant Monty Norman's 'James Bond Theme', Barry created a parallel action cue, '007'. Despite having to use Lionel Bart's theme song, Barry was exacting in getting the best from the composition. Margo heard it first hand:

> Recording the 'From Russia With Love' song took up most of the session. Much longer than usual. Normally we'd get several tracks done in a session, but that song took all afternoon. John was very particular to get the strings sounding exactly right. The poor strings players had to play so high at the top of the violin, they were practically picking their noses.[114]

The song was performed by Matt Monro, then managed by Don Black. Monro was disappointed to discover when he later saw the film in Paris that the song had been relegated to the end credits.[115] It is heard as source music on the radio while Bond 'punts' with Sylvia Trench, but it is an instrumental version that was heard over the titles; Monro might have got scant consolation when the song got a nomination for the Best Original Song Golden Globe Award in 1965, the gift of Hollywood Foreign Press Association.[116] The only significant award the film did win was Ted Moore's BAFTA for Best Colour Cinematography in 1963.[117]

Maurice Binder did not return to Bond due to a dispute with Harry Saltzman. This time Eon went to famed advertising graphic designer Robert Brownjohn. Trevor Bond remembered, 'Brownjohn, a graphic designer, had never made a film in his life so they said you'd better have Trevor Bond to help you out because he's done the first one.'[118] Trevor recalled Brownjohn's initial ideas was to create a title sequence around chess pieces inspired by the scene in the film. Ultimately, the titles were projected on the curves of a belly dancer, which was a new technique at the time. The concept was inspired by two things: Brownjohn's wife leaving a screening early and the film being projected on her as she left and by the work of László Moholy-Nagy, who was experimenting with projecting light on clouds.[119] Brownjohn, when pitching the idea, lifted up his shirt and danced in the beam of light saying, 'It'll be just like this except we'll use a pretty girl.'[120] Three girls were used for the sequence, including actress Nadja Regin who played Kerim's girl – the biggest problem was to keep the actress in focus while she undulated.[121]

From Russia With Love received an ecstatic reception at the press screening on 8 October 1963.[122] The premiere was a glitzy affair held at the London Pavilion on 10 October 1963. Fleming attended accompanied by his doctor Jack Beal, as his state of health was perilous at the time.[123] Most of those involved thought the film would come and go. Desmond Llewelyn remembered his feelings at the time, 'I didn't really think any more about the film. None of us, except perhaps Connery, were stars then and the Bond hype hadn't begun.'[124] Not invited to the premiere, Llewelyn watched the film at his local cinema in Hastings.[125]

In Los Angeles Cubby Broccoli took his mother Cristina and his mother-in-law Stella Natol to the Los Angeles premiere at Grauman's Chinese Theatre. He was proud to display his success to this particular audience. However, upon arrival at the cinema it was completely dark. The manager explained there had been a riot and the police had intervened and closed the venue. Unimpressed, Cristina was further aghast when Cubby told her they disposed of all the costumes after shooting was completed.[126]

After officially being released in the US on 8 February 1964 at New York's Astor Theatre, *From Russia With Love* would go to improve upon *Dr. No's* cinematic performance, by eventually grossing $24,800,000 in North America and $54,100,000 throughout the rest of the world.

It was the last complete film that author Ian Fleming would see and the film had a fond place in Cubby's heart because of this association:

> Ian Fleming was a great man, a great storyteller and great company. I enjoyed every minute I spent with him and am glad he lived to see the success of the first two films. If I had to pick one of the films as my favourite it would probably be *From Russia With Love* as I feel it was with this film that the Bond formula and style were perfected.[127]

6

THE MIDAS TOUCH

GOLDFINGER

(1964)

JAMES BOND IS BACK IN ACTION!

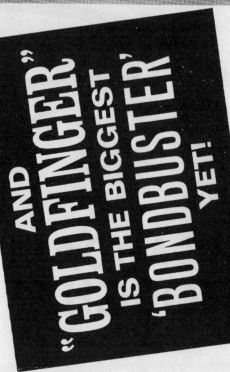

AND "GOLDFINGER" IS THE BIGGEST 'BONDBUSTER' YET!

"GOLDFINGER" now surpasses "From Russia, With Love"—which was the most successful film ever released in Britain in any year! Read these staggering figures!

First Week—Odeon Leicester—Britain's Top Theatre

"GOLDFINGER" BREAKS HOUSE RECORD HELD BY "FROM RUSSIA, WITH LOVE"!

"RUSSIA" $40,678 "GOLDFINGER" $48,515

AND IN LONDON PREMIERE SHOWCASE THEATRES, "GOLDFINGER" NOT ONLY SURPASSES "RUSSIA" FIRST WEEK FIGURES BY 101% BUT HAS BROKEN EVERY EXISTING HOUSE RECORD!

Theatre	"From Russia, With Love"	"Goldfinger"
Bromley	$ 7,694	$ 14,686
Finsbury Park	5,704	17,651
Hammersmith	9,439	28,356
Ilford	11,088	18,116
Streatham	9,117	20,062
Watford	7,717	13,171
Kingston	6,650	16,380
Purley	5,351	11,528
New Victoria	19,247	25,217
Total	**$82,007**	**$165,167**

The U.S. Strikes "GOLD" in December! Stake out your claim now!

ALBERT R. BROCCOLI AND HARRY SALTZMAN PRESENT

SEAN CONNERY

"IAN FLEMING'S "GOLDFINGER"

ALSO STARRING
GERT FROBE · HONOR BLACKMAN · SHIRLEY EATON as PUSSY GALORE

GERT FROBE as GOLDFINGER

TECHNICOLOR

SCREENPLAY BY RICHARD MAIBAUM AND PAUL DEHN · PRODUCED BY HARRY SALTZMAN AND ALBERT R. BROCCOLI · DIRECTED BY GUY HAMILTON

THRU UA

Terence Young was already thinking about the third James Bond film, *Goldfinger*, while *From Russia With Love* was still in production. However following early script development, he declined to direct the picture. Over a decade later, Young explained, 'The idea of going on and making a James Bond film every year for the next ten years … it's just not my bag. I want to do something else.'[1] However, Young admitted the real reason was 'one of those sacred commercial things, the kind one only discusses with one's lawyer.'[2] Young had become increasingly frustrated that he was unable to secure a profit-share deal in light of the success of the first two films. Ironically he had been offered a cut of the action on *Dr. No* but had instead opted for a higher salary.[3]

The producers sought a director they had both courted in their respective pasts: Broccoli had wanted him for *Cockleshell Heroes* (1955) and Saltzman had offered him *The Iron Petticoat* (1956) – the man was Guy Hamilton. The filmmaker had been in the running to direct *Dr. No*. It was a decision he regretted, but Hamilton had to refuse the film due to personal problems that would not allow him to leave the UK for an extended location shoot in Jamaica.[4] Broccoli felt his style, pace and flair for comedy made him an ideal choice for Bond.[5]

Hamilton, the son of an English diplomat, had been raised in France. On joining the film industry he had learnt his craft as an assistant director to filmmakers, such as Carol Reed and John Huston on *The Third Man* and *The African Queen* respectively. Throughout the fifties Hamilton had directed a number of slick genre films and boys' own adventures; he'd come up through the ranks of the British film industry, much like Terence Young. United Artists' executive David Picker thought Guy Hamilton, in contrast to Young, was 'a tall, quiet, deliberate man whose thoughtful demeanour was solid and professional.'[6]

Young and Hamilton were represented by the same agency, MCA. Shortly after Hamilton signed up for *Goldfinger*, there was potentially a conflict of interest. Hamilton recalled Young's agent was:

> sounding the water to coax me to step aside and let Terence back again. But [the producers] had already engaged me. History suggests Terence asked for a percentage and Terence was [now] prepared to back off. But this was Cubby, rule one: there is no way we pay the director a percentage.[7]

Arriving at the discreet headquarters of Eon Productions, Hamilton described the producers' shared office, 'There were two big desks – one was Harry's and one was Cubby's. There were a few chairs around, anybody who came along sat there and you were yelled at or spoken to by the two of them.'[8] Despite huge European success, Hamilton felt the studio 'still put [Bonds] out on the B circuit in America, which meant a limited number of prints.'[9] By the third film, Broccoli and Saltzman decided to bring in their own studio representative and hired Mike Beck, who would become a central cog in the marketing operation.[10] They also hired a publicist, Tom Carlile – a 6ft 6in Texan who had been a *Life* magazine staffer and became 'one of the earliest unsung contributors to the Bond Saga to the press of the nation he was and remained 'Mr. Bond.''[11] With *Goldfinger* set in Miami and Kentucky the producers were:

> pushing United Artists'[12] to break the American market. Before production began David Picker recalled Irving Moskovitz and Norman Tyre (Harry's and Cubby's respective lawyers) negotiating 'a modest adjustment from the 50/50 partnership on the back end, as well as an increase in producing fees.[13]

Connery was at the mint too, '[Bond's] going to make me rich depending on how the tax works out. Rich enough to retire, though, I suppose. I've a contract to do three more Bond movies in the next three-and-a-half years and I'm perfectly happy about it. It gives me security for that time and also leaves me free to make other films for a great deal of money.'[14] Connery received $50,000 for *Goldfinger* plus an undisclosed percentage. However, compared to the $400,000 he received for Hitchcock's *Marnie* (1964), his Bond fee was modest. Connery cried on Hamilton's shoulder, who told him, '"Sean, love, you've got an agent. If your agent isn't tough enough, there are plenty of people who would like to represent you."'[15]

Richard Maibaum began adapting ON HER MAJESTY'S SECRET SERVICE while *From Russia With Love* was still in production and due for release in autumn 1963. The book had been a bestseller that year. In order to meet the slated release date of September 1964, *On Her Majesty's Secret Service* (*OHMSS*) required location shooting in Switzerland in the winter of 1963–64. Coming so close on the heels of the second Bond film there simply was not enough time to prepare the winter scenes in Switzerland. The producers turned to GOLD-FINGER instead and Richard Maibaum delivered a fifty-four page treatment dated 20 May 1963. Maibaum's early draft featured many of the elements which would later form the key moments in the film: a Bentley with *Ben Hur*-inspired wheel blades, the laser room scene and Oddjob with his razor-edged bowler hat. It was Pussy Galore who would be painted gold, performing a burlesque style dance for the gangsters hired by Goldfinger. Following Maibaum's first draft, Berkley Mather, who had contributed to *Dr. No* and *From Russia With Love*, did an uncredited rewrite delivering a second draft in September 1963.

Maibaum felt he needed to play to audiences' growing sophistication, 'We dared to do something seldom done in action pictures: we mixed what was funny with what was serious.'[16] Fleming was not quite so sure, telling the screenwriter, '"The pictures are so much funnier than my books." He was a little bemused and a little obtuse about it, I thought, because he really didn't understand that we were trying to make them funnier.'[17]

Published on 29 March 1959 Ian Fleming's seventh novel was originally titled THE RICHEST MAN IN THE WORLD[18] featuring a villain named after the brutalist Hungarian architect Ernö Goldfinger (renamed Auric for fictional purposes).[19] Bond is sent to investigate Auric Goldfinger for gold smuggling on behalf of the Bank of England. Bond discovers that Auric is an agent of SMERSH, the Soviet counter-intelligence apparat, and soon uncovers Operation Grand Slam – Goldfinger's plan to create havoc to Western economies by poisoning the water supply of Fort Knox and robbing the $15 billion of gold contained in the repository.

In a letter dated 30 April 1963 Maibaum outlined his new approach, 'Whereas DR. NO was a mystery (a man is killed: who did it? – and why?) and [FROM] RUSSIA [WITH LOVE] was a straight suspense story (we know almost all of the plot against Bond and want to see how he foils it); GOLDFINGER is what I call a duel. Bond versus Goldfinger. It is not, I repeat not, a story about a robbery.'[20] Instead, Maibaum has Goldfinger set off an atomic device, which would render the world's largest hoard of gold radioactive for over fifty-seven years. This would increase the value of Goldfinger's own hoard 'considerably', as well as creating economic meltdown in the West. This time the Chinese, not the Soviets, are Goldfinger's backers.

Maibaum took inspiration from *Life* magazine:

I'm dreaming up a machine which utilises the new laser beam. I visualise a demonstration of the beam, showing it cutting through steel, and then used as the buzzsaw was in the book, threatening to cut Bond in half. This out-Flemings Fleming. Using the very latest scientific discovery in the old proven way of scaring the wits out of people[21]

Another variation from the Fleming novel was the opening of the film. Fleming's first chapter, 'Reflections in a Double Bourbon', recounts Bond's regret at having to kill a Mexican *capungo* (bandit) during a mission to stop a drug blackmail plot. Written midway in the Bond cycle GOLDFINGER is the longest novel in the series and marks the point where Bond becomes a more reflective, world-weary agent. However, the pre-title sequence is a perfect example of how elements of the novel were adapted for the screen. The sequence bears no relevance to the rest of the film (other than to set up why Bond is in Miami). The gun barrel opens on a fake seagull – in an earlier draft this was a dead dog[22] – disguising James Bond's scuba gear. Bond casually throws away his seagull headgear before emerging in a dock in an unnamed Latin American country. Bond, still clad in black wetsuit, sneaks, via a hidden door, into a Ken Adam storage facility. Using plastic explosive squeezed from his belt, Bond then booby-traps the warehouse to disrupt Mr. Ramirez's plan of 'using heroin-flavoured bananas to finance revolutions'. His mission complete, Bond removes his wetsuit to reveal a perfectly pressed white dinner jacket underneath. He then inserts a red carnation in his buttonhole. Upon reading the screenplay Connery felt it was too humorous and unbelievable although the clothes-under-the-wetsuit gag was drawn from Dehn's wartime knowledge of a Dutch resistance operation.[23] Bond casually enters a thriving bodega to meet his contact just as the time bomb he planted goes off. As the crowd exit in panic Bond casually saunters backstage to meet Bonita, a dancing girl. She emerges from the bath and embraces him. Her warm body flinches as she touches the cold metal of Bond's gun so he hangs up his shoulder holster near her bath. Just as Bond is about to get down to some unfinished business with her, he catches the reflection of a bandit – named Capungo – in Bonita's eye. Spinning her around so Capungo coshes the poor girl instead, Bond then battles the swarthy bandit, toppling him into Bonita's bath. As Capungo struggles to reach Bond's gun hanging nearby, Bond reacts quickly and tosses an electric heater into the tub, electrocuting his would-be killer. 'Shocking,' Bond quips. 'Positively shocking.' The new-boy director Guy Hamilton had 'a tremendous belief in the necessity of the pre-credits. Now children, if that makes you laugh, please leave your brains under the seat – you'll have more fun.'[24]

Hamilton thought the screenplay was 'too American', citing M's meeting with the Governor of the Bank of England as an example, and required a rewrite.[25] Saltzman suggested Paul Dehn, who had declined the offer to write Bond for Kevin McClory a few years earlier. Dehn was now enthused:

During the war I was an instructor to a band of thugs called the SOE [Special Operations Executive], so I got a pretty good view of what counter-espionage was like. I was offered, by Anthony Asquith, the film *Orders to Kill* [1958] because I'd had this experience during the war and it was about an agent who went out to kill a man and found that he couldn't kill him. This, along with my other experiences, led to *Goldfinger*.[26]

Hamilton felt Dehn's input was such that 'Paul was lucky to share a credit with Maibaum.'[27] Maibaum said of Dehn's 23 December 1963 draft:

> Tends to get very English-y now and then, coy, arch, self-consciously tongue-in-cheek. It's lost the aspect of dead seriousness we had in the other two. It's always fatal if the audience gets the idea that we think we are being funny. Nowhere in *No* or *Russia* does Bond really lose his essential dignity. Here he is just a patsy and a comic one at that. Parts of the script sound as if it were written for Bob Hope and not Sean Connery. Don't forget you hope to make more films after *Goldfinger*, so don't sell Bond short in terms of character.[28]

In February 1964 Maibaum noted Connery's concerns about the broadness of the script; the star favoured a more serious approach with humour injected subtly as in previous Bonds. Further revisions were done by Dehn[29] and Maibaum.[30]

By *Goldfinger*, Connery had slipped comfortably into the role:

> In *Dr. No*, the character was established. By the end of the second film the audience had thoroughly got hold of him. After that the interesting thing was to surprise people who thought they knew how he was going to react to a situation. You'd play the reality, play the humour, have a bit of playful repartee with the audience and do something unexpected.[31]

Hamilton admitted they were:

> helped naturally by what had come before. Terence had understood a lot of things from the audience reaction to *Dr. No*. [Sean] matured rapidly and the difference between *No* and *Russia* is vast. Myself, Sean and the team – we all knew what we were aiming for. Bond was sweetened, I suppose, by the perfection of formula.[32]

Hamilton had known Sean Connery when they 'were nodding acquaintances at Gerry's drinking club opposite the stage door of Her Majesty's [theatre in London].'[33] Hamilton felt his star 'wished that his old friend Terence was there. He was very grateful to Terence. I think he was very sorry that Terence wasn't doing it.'[34]

For the title role an early proposal was the American actor Victor Buono.[35] Harry Saltzman also suggested Theodore Bikel, the American star of *My Fair Lady* (1964), who was flown in from New York for a screentest. Bikel didn't display the menace the character required and Broccoli backed German actor Gert Fröbe. Hamilton recalled Broccoli screening for him *Es Geschah am Hellichten Tag* (*It Happened in Broad Daylight,* 1958), 'He was deliciously evil and wicked'.[36] United Artists' European distribution executive Eric Pleskow remembered Fröbe from years earlier:

> I was a film officer at the end of the war and I ran the studio for the US Army in Munich. I remember him as the thinnest of all the thin people. He was not only a heavy as far as the character was concerned but he also had gotten very heavy as a person.[37]

Oddjob, Goldfinger's admirable manservant, in the novel was a Korean with 'arms like thighs', who came accoutred with a razor-edged bowler. Hamilton had spotted Olympic wrestler Harold Sakata – nicknamed Tosh Togo – on television one Saturday afternoon. 'On Monday morning I went in and said "I've seen Oddjob". He was very happy to be bought out of his wrestling contract to do a film.'[38] Despite no previous acting experience – unless one counted wrestling – Broccoli felt Sakata's 'square head, the quizzical Oriental eyes and the sheer tonnage of the man made him the perfect henchman.'[39]

Maibaum transformed Fleming's lesbian gangster Pussy Galore into Goldfinger's personal pilot and leader of her own all-female flying squad. Honor Blackman had gained attention as judo-fighting, leather-clad Cathy Gayle on television and recalled:

> I was just coming to the end of *The Avengers* but I'd done it for two years. I'm not keen on playing the same character for years; I wanted to move on to something new. I went to see Harry. They'd decided beforehand that I would play her so it was less an audition, but more of a meeting to discuss the part. I learnt afterwards that the original script was altered before they saw me and they put judo into it.[40]

Blackman understood it was a good career move, 'I suppose they'd had two pictures before and that the character Bond was getting a reputation. I'd read

GOLDFINGER obviously. I wanted do a film that was going to be an international success and although I'd been successful it was only in the UK.'[41] Blackman was thirty-eight years old when she filmed *Goldfinger*, several years senior to Connery.

The casting of Goldfinger's ill-fated ward Jill Masterson – Masterton in the novel – also went to an experienced actress, Shirley Eaton, who had already starred in many British films:

> My agent [Richard Stone] sent me for an interview with Harry. All he was interested in was me looking nude in gold paint. I said I would do it if it was done elegantly. The part was small, but I only went to be interviewed because it was a James Bond film.[42]

It was agreed that Eaton would get equal billing with Honor Blackman[43] as she had done far more feature film work than the lead.[44]

The third female part – the character of Tilly Masterson, Jill's sister – was played by Tania Mallet, who had tested for *From Russia With Love*. The successful model explained her nonchalant approach in her initial meeting: 'I lived across the park from Eon's offices, near Marble Arch. On a rainy day, I arrived there with my dog who walked in across their white shag carpet. Harry looked a bit embarrassed and taken aback.'[45] As a top model she dismissed the salary offered: 'That won't keep me in cigarettes.'[46] Eventually, terms were agreed but Mallet 'never signed anything.'[47]

Originally Margaret Nolan was not slated to appear in *Goldfinger*, 'They wanted me to do the titles but I said I wouldn't do them unless I got a part in the film. So they gave me the part of Bond's Miami masseuse, Dink.'[48] Nolan remembered, 'It was Saltzman who was really keen on me. Apparently they wanted me to sign this contract to publicise *Goldfinger* and to tour the world with it. I turned them down. I wanted to be taken seriously as an actress.'[49] She later appeared in the Saltzman production *Toomorrow* (1970).[50]

Prior to his stint as Cato Fong, Inspector Jacques Clouseau's lethal yet bumbling manservant in *A Shot In The Dark* (1964), Burt Kwouk appeared as Red Chinese nuclear fission specialist, Mr. Ling. He would go on to appear as a Chinese general in *Casino Royale* and SPECTRE Number 3 in *You Only Live Twice* (both 1967). Noted British character actor Richard Vernon would make a convincing Governor of the Bank of England whilst Michael Mellinger was the ill-fated Kisch, Goldfinger's lieutentant.

Production designer Ken Adam, after a one-film absence working on Stanley Kubrick's *Dr. Strangelove*, returned to the Eon fold. He remembered the film fondly, 'I think *Goldfinger* was maybe the best example of a Bond film that I designed, where the settings accentuate the dramatic message of the film. I had complete free hand.'[51] However, Adam's arrival meant that Hamilton had to challenge another Eon stalwart: 'In a friendly way, I had to cut him down to size. Ken likes to build things and I like to use stuff that is already there and doesn't cost anything. Ken doesn't like locations because he doesn't get a credit for nature.'[52] Adam recalled: 'Initially I had to prove myself to [Guy]. But once I had done that I had no problems and he used to back me up in discussions with Harry and Cubby.'[53]

The creative team flew out to Louisville to meet the man who ran Fort Knox – Zero Mostel's brother-in-law. Hamilton asked if it was possible to take pictures inside. '"No you cannot," he said. "Even the President is not allowed inside."'[54] Adam also remembered, 'When I walked around the perimeter, there were loudspeaker messages telling me not to go any further. "You are now entering a restricted area."'[55] Hamilton pointed out to Adam that if nobody had ever seen Fort Knox from the inside they could let their imaginations run wild. They originally looked at filming the Fort Knox exteriors in Portugal, 'It looked as much liked Fort Knox as St. Paul's Cathedral so we all retreated and that was the end of the Portuguese story.'[56]

In a case of vehicular irony, Maibaum's screenplay has Bond driving a Bentley – Bond's car of choice in the novels. However, Fleming has 007 tail Goldfinger to Switzerland in an Aston Martin DB Mark III drawn from the Service's car pool. Ken Adam recalled the debate as to what car Bond should be driving in 1964. 'There were E-Type Jaguars, Aston Martins, Italian Ferraris and Alfa Romeos. We decided the Aston Martin [DB5], which was by far the most expensive British sports car, would be the right prop for Bond.'[57] Saltzman called Aston Martin's general manager, Steve Heggie, who showed no interest, 'We had many such requests in those days from film producers and in general it cost Aston Martin more than it was worth.'[58] But Saltzman persisted and eventually the British company agreed to loan the production two DB5s. By committee the production team dreamt up an array of gadgets with which to equip the car. Adam drove an E-Type at the time and recalled, 'In those days it didn't have any forward bumper, so my car was continuously being damaged by other people.'[59] Adam fitted Bond's car with over riders which could also ram cars, 'I got my own back with the DB5. It got rid of all my frustrations.'[60] Hamilton's frustrations were the increasing number of parking tickets he was receiving around London, so his 'ambition was to have a revolving number plate'.[61]

Connery was ambivalent about his four-wheeled co-star: 'I think its setting in the story and in the film gave it a more unique quality than the car actually possessed.'[62]

Special effects wizard John Stears converted the standard DB5 into Bond's gadget-laden super-machine. Crew members would take it for lunch, causing technician Joe Fitt to worry, 'I thought Harry was gonna have a coronary. Here was a £25,000 car, one of a kind, and a crewmember had borrowed it.'[63] Saltzman referred to it as the '$45,000 bag of tricks'.[64]

Inspired by the Fleming books, the Bond movies have become instrumental in partnering brands with films and Aston Martin has since become synonymous with 007. Hamilton remembered that the producers were hungry to strike product placement deals and *Goldfinger* continued the 007 trend to tie in commercial brands with a film. Arriving at Pinewood one morning Hamilton found Saltzman personally dressing the bathroom set of Goldfinger's private jet, 'I catch Harry with a sack full of Fabergé. He was rather embarrassed – but there was Harry at eight o'clock in the morning inventing product placement!'[65]

On 15 January 1964 filming began in Miami, Florida without Sean Connery, as he was still filming *Marnie* for Hitchcock. Guy Hamilton and cinematographer Ted Moore led a small unit to the USA to shoot key material for the opening of the film. During these scenes we first meet Auric Goldfinger who is mysteriously cheating Mr. Simmons, his gin partner, by the pool of the Fontainebleau Hotel. Jack Lord, who had played Felix Leiter in *Dr. No*, was scheduled to reprise the role.[66] Lord had signed a two-picture deal with Broccoli and Saltzman in January 1963[67] but, according to his agent, wanted 'more money and co-star billing'.[68] Lord did not reprise his role as Leiter. Instead Austin Willis was cast as Felix Leiter, while Cec Linder was there to play Mr. Simmons. However, at the last minute, the actors swapped roles. Noted Linder, '[Willis] had a right to be upset. He got a few days on the picture, but I ended up with twelve weeks.'[69] Guy Hamilton used a novel approach to introduce Florida in the picture: 'I hate subtitles. On the recce I had seen, while we were on the beach, a little plane flying along with a banner reading "Welcome to Miami".'[70]

In Miami the body of gangster Mr. Solo is despatched when his Lincoln Continental is destroyed in one of the world's first car-crushing machines. Sean Connery recalled how onlookers were amazed at the production's profligacy, 'It's understandable, I suppose. After all, to own a Lincoln Continental is part of the great American dream. And there we were squashing one flat. "Goddam sadists!" the man shouted!'[71] The gag had been sold to the production for £500 cash[72] by Wolf Mankowitz, who had taken his inspiration from a *Times* newspaper article 'about the Mafia disposing of bodies by sticking them in the boots of cars and getting them trashed'.[73] It turned out to be an expensive idea.

Hamilton was keen to shoot authentic local colour to give the film an American flavour, especially specific details that could not be faked in Europe. The later part of the film was set in Kentucky, but Hamilton found plenty to shoot in Florida. He was particularly proud of one shot of a certain food shop, 'This was too good an opportunity to miss. God is smiling on me. Of course, it's years later that Kentucky Fried Chicken is everywhere!'[74]

On 9 March 1964, Connery joined the set back in England. At this point, Hamilton was surrounded by the key crewmembers, nearly all of whom had previously worked with Terence Young. Stunt arranger Bob Simmons recalled, 'It wasn't easy for him to walk into the James Bond world at that stage. Terence had left behind him a team used to a certain director's style.'[75] Hamilton began as he meant to go on, observing that the crew were 'surprised by the success of *Dr. No* and *Russia* [and] were a bit lazy and arrogant. They thought they were the crème de la crème. It was part of my job to put a big boot up all their arses.'[76] Time was precious; *Goldfinger* was scheduled for worldwide release in September 1964. Hamilton explained, 'I wasn't, for instance, prepared to shoot miles of film and leave half of it on the floor, as had [previously] been the case. [In *Goldfinger*] there were only about twenty shots that never appeared on screen.'[77] Some were from an extended Q Branch scene, which included a Post Office van springing open. The final cut features Bond being briefed by Q with the gadgets displayed in the background.

Hamilton noted that the producers seldom visited the studios during production, 'They were always busy up in [South] Audley Street – they saw rushes up there, so they rarely came to the studio.'[78] However, Saltzman was on the set to ensure that the first day at Pinewood got off to great start:

Harry comes on and he's not technically minded. He's got a bottle of champagne and he says 'This is to wish you all tremendous good fortune with this picture.' And he smashes the bottle of champagne on the camera. He can't understand why no one claps – we were all stunned; there is broken glass everywhere.[79]

Hamilton also remembered when Harry visited he 'would come on with friends and their children and they all stay there waiting for me to say "Action!" I realised for Harry it was a show. It's front row seats at the circus.'[80]

Pinewood Studios and its environs were used ingeniously to simulate other more exotic locations. The Latin American pre-title sequence was shot in the Paddock Tank and the exterior of the huge storage facility was filmed near Staines. The car chase in which Bond tries to escape from Auric Enterprises (Goldfinger's factory) in Switzerland was shot in the alleys of Pinewood Studios[81] – one of which is now named 'Goldfinger Avenue'– and the studio workshops doubled for the factory. The lake featured in Bond's parachute jump at the end of the film is the Pinewood pond. Even the golf clubhouse statue was a specially made figure, rigged to be decapitated by Oddjob's hat, and placed in the Pinewood garden near the mansion house.

While filming the Fontainebleau interiors in April 1964, Hamilton recalled, 'Fleming came down to lunch – [he was then] a very sick man. I was very sorry that I couldn't really talk to him because studios weren't really his scene. He was tired and he couldn't wait to get back.'[82]

While other cast members went to America and Switzerland, Honor Blackman was realistic '[The production] didn't take me to any glamorous locations. It took me to Northolt Airport. I don't think anybody can refer to that as "glamorous." Everything was on the lot at Pinewood as far as I was concerned.'[83]

Blackman's first scenes with Gert Fröbe were fraught:

> It was a nightmare, first off. Gert had to start the scene and I thought 'Jesus, what the hell is he saying?' So I just waited for him to stop speaking and trusted to luck that he'd said the right thing. That was the first scene he'd ever played in English – or supposed English. He had a tutor with him. By the end of the film he'd improved tremendously.[84]

Michael Collins later dubbed the German actor.

Maibaum wrote to Broccoli before production began, 'For God's sake, don't forget to keep Guy sticking a go-fast pill up Fröbe's ass. He may be great but German actors give everything the full treatment – and slow.'[85] Gert Fröbe had been forced to be a member of the Nazi party during World War II and so Hamilton recalled the actor being 'very, very nervous and very upset'[86] by the thought of playing the scene in which Goldfinger orders the American gangsters to be gassed to death.

Richard Maibaum's laser table sequence was shot on an atmospheric Ken Adam set. The laser cutting through metal was actually the flame acetylene torch creeping along to Connery's crotch. 'When it was explained to me, of course, [I] had some reservations about lying there and how effective this

laser really was. It's a vulnerable position, like some gynaecological explora-
tion or something.'[87] Special effects technician Burt Luxford was tasked with
controlling the acetylene torch but, 'As I couldn't really see how far up the
table I was, I had to be told when to stop. As I got nearer and nearer to his
crotch Sean was sweating a bit. I was about 3 inches from his crotch when
I stopped.'[88] Effects maestro John Stears added the laser beam as an optical
image later; it was the first time a laser beam had been realistically portrayed
on screen. The '"Do you expect me to talk?" "No, I expect you to die"'
dialogue exchange – credited to Dehn – has gone on to become one of the
most memorable moments in the Bond series.

In yet another memorable scene, Pussy Galore, using her judo skills, throws
Bond around a hay barn. Blackman appreciated the crew's concern: 'When
I got on the set the prop men were putting straw about the place and they
were piling it up and saying, "Is that alright, Honor?" Well, since I'm used to
the cement floor [on *The Avengers*], I think it's heaven.'[89] Blackman also enjoyed
the scene for other reasons:

> I remember when we got to the end of the throwing and we were both in
> the hay together [director of photography] Ted Moore actually said, 'The next
> scene is a close up and would you mind terribly if I didn't use the stand-ins,
> could you bear staying there while I light it?' Sean and I – he's the sexiest
> devil in the world – there we were very hot in the hay, I must say. And I'm
> sure Moore only did it because he might think it was rather pleasant. There's
> no question there was a great attraction between the two of us. I was married
> at the time so I had to rein in my horses.[90]

Action sequence arranger Bob Simmons choreographed the scene with
Blackman, 'The struggle had to be characterised. It was a question of imagining how Bond would successfully seduce her, and it had to be natural and
convincing despite the overt sexism.'[91] Ironically Connery was unsure about
the tussle thinking it might emasculate 007 – improbably, Bond's roll in the hay
with Pussy changes both her sexuality and her allegiance. Later it is revealed
that Pussy Galore saves the day by switching the poison-gas canisters with fake
ones, which her pilots release harmlessly over Fort Knox.

In the novel Bond only hears of the death of Jill Masterton but does not
see it. In yet another filmic improvement we see the now-renamed Masterson
painted head to toe in gold paint, dead from skin suffocation. Shirley Eaton
thought:

It was a strange thing, I never felt nude. A lovely French make-up man painted me with a biggish sable brush. I just stood in the make-up room with things on my boobs and my little G-string. It was just photographed so well by Guy that I did look completely naked.[92]

Doctors cautioned the filmmakers on how to shoot the scene.[93] Eaton still had time for fun:

It was a closed set. Sean told Graham [the actor Graham Stark, who was shooting a naval film on a neighbouring set] and he poked his head round the make-up room. He had a pure, beautiful white immaculate naval uniform and, because he was being cheeky, I went up and hugged him [covering him in gold paint].[94]

Eaton's appearance proved a boon to the Bond film, 'The photographer took the pictures in the studio. Lovely Tom [Carlile] he looked after me as best he could. He [was] jumping up and down because they'd got me on [the] front of *Life* magazine. In those days, [that] was huge.'[95] When the film's initial marketing failed to grant Eaton her contractual equal billing, her agent Richard Stone sued and an out-of-court settlement was reached,[96] although, for many viewers, her iconic appearance surpassed any billing.

Desmond Llewelyn's Major Boothroyd returned for his second appearance, now named Q for the first time. Llewelyn recalled, 'For Terence, [Q] was a straight ordinary part. Guy gave me this idea of a love/hate relationship I have with Bond. As soon as Hamilton said I don't really like Bond it all fell into place.'[97] Hamilton's rationale for Q's dislike was simple, 'He doesn't treat your gadgets with any respect.'[98] Hamilton's insight set up the relationship for future films.

Lois Maxwell recalled that she was asked to provide her own wardrobe for Miss Moneypenny:

I said to them I didn't have any clothes. It was an utter lie – here everyone was having wardrobes that cost thousands; the designer bought these three outfits for me. I did try to have it put into my contract that the clothes would be given to me at the end of the film. Whereupon Harry Saltzman's wife, who was much shorter than I was, apparently told him that she was going to get my clothes.[99]

The duel on the green between James Bond and Auric Goldfinger was filmed at Stoke Poges golf club in Buckinghamshire. Originally Bud Ornstein (head of United Artists in the UK) had suggested looking at golf courses in Portugal, when the filmmakers had considered shooting some of *Goldfinger* there. For Sean Connery, the sequence sharpened a life-long love affair with the game, 'Within a few years of *Goldfinger*, my golf was good enough to play against professionals in competitions.'[100]

In June 1964 the Fort Knox finale was shot at Pinewood Studios. The exterior was built on the backlot and the interior on A Stage. Ken Adam recalled, '[I] used my theatrical background to experiment. I had seen bank vaults at the Bank of England and I wanted to have the gold 40ft high and make it look like a prison with the gold behind bars.'[101] The impressive set had not daunted the young draftsman whom Ken Adam had employed – Peter Lamont – who would go on to design no less than nine Bond pictures himself and become a key member of the creative team.

Bob Simmons worked closely with Harold Sakata, choreographing the final duel between Bond and Oddjob inside Fort Knox. Simmons remembered, 'Harold agreed to crash face down on the floor without any attempt at a break-fall. He thudded down like a block of granite. It was a tremendous shot.'[102] Connery was injured in the sequence, pulling his shoulder. He recalled another injury at Sakata's hands: 'When he gave me that chop behind the neck at the fridge he put me on the floor. He wasn't quite used to the cinema technique of taking it to the wire and then stopping.'[103] In the film Oddjob's bowler hat instead became steel-rimmed; the only time he ever shows any sign of fear is when Bond attempts to turn the deadly hat on him. The climactic fight was foreshadowed by the pre-title bout in which stuntman Alf Joint played Capungo. Yugoslavian actress Nadja Regin returned to the series to play the hapless Bonita, who gets coshed when Bond sees the threat approaching in the reflection of her eye. Regin found the proximity rather extreme: 'They had to film my eye in a close up and every time they hit the clapperboard it gave off a little bit of dust and it went into my eye [ruining the shot]. It took a little while.'[104]

Both bouts exemplified what was emerging as the Bond style – carefully scripted action in which Bond outwits his opponent, usually using their own devices against them. All the action was shot for real, while Peter Hunt's styl-ised editing and quick cutting covered the stuntmen replacing the actors and ensured a seamless blend between what had actually happened and what the audience saw. Excitement was emphasised by a pounding score and by Norman Wanstall's exaggerated sound effects – an innovation at the time.

On 6 July 1964 the unit moved out to Switzerland to shoot Bond pursuing Goldfinger's Rolls Royce Phantom III through Andermatt in the Swiss
Alps.[105] Upon arrival they discovered that the Aston Martin had been damaged
in transit. A second Aston, which had been transformed into the effects car,
was flown out immediately to replace the road car.[106] Tilly's white Mustang
convertible was the first of its kind to be seen in Europe and – unlike the Aston
Martin – came free, courtesy of the Ford Motor Company. Mallet remembered
the moment, 'They pulled the cover off this beast. It was four blocks long. We
in England had never seen cars that big.'[107] Driving around the Swiss mountain
ravines was precarious, as Mallet explained, 'It had very bad steering. What
I was doing driving it then, I must have been completely off my tree. Guy kept
saying, "Faster, faster, faster." At one point I got down to the bottom and Sean
was green – I nearly pushed him off the edge.'[108]

Tania Mallet did not remember 'one single direction'[109] from Guy Hamilton.
She was grateful for her co-star, 'The most help I got was from Sean. [At rushes
he would say] "Your chin is too high – it looks great in photographs, what you
need in movies is an eyeline. When you turn to me, you need to drop your chin
so we can see your eyes."'[110]

Saltzman's wife, Jacqueline, had made cameo appearances in the previous
films. Hamilton created something special for her in the Swiss location, 'In the
sixties, you wouldn't imagine seeing a lady at a petrol station.'[111] Tania Mallet
recalled, 'She was dressed as a pump attendant [at the garage]. We were all
giggling about it. Harry was going to walk towards the garage without looking at anyone across the background like Hitchcock.'[112] However, there was
opposition from certain quarters as Hamilton revealed, 'I got back to Pinewood
weeks later and Cubby says, "No fucking way. Over my dead fucking body."'[113]
Jacqueline Saltzman's cameo appearance was cut.

Guy Hamilton, aware of the tight delivery deadline, flew back to America
with Broccoli to complete the last leg of principal photography – the aerial
shots of Fort Knox. He recalled:

> As we had to start without Sean we were already tight at that end. Then a lot
> of the aerial stuff at Fort Knox was done by a second unit. Peter [Hunt] had
> been lumbered with some second-rate pick-up crew in America. Politely it
> was agreed that it should be done again.[114]

Hamilton re-shot the material with Ted Moore. The production was assisted
by an ex-US Army colonel named Charles Russhon. Russhon was connected

to the late President Kennedy's famous press secretary Pierre Salinger and as such was able to fix it for the crew to shoot in the air around Fort Knox, as well as for hundreds of soldiers to drop to the floor as if gassed.[115] A sign saying 'Welcome General Russhon' can be seen around the Kentucky airport hangar door; it was placed in the film as a nod to Russhon's 'larger than life [presence] on the set'.[116]

Cubby's stepson Michael G. Wilson joined the shoot, albeit by coincidence:

I graduated and I came over to London. I drove out with Cubby to the airport with my mother and he said, 'Gee, I could really use some help with this film. It's too bad you don't have your passport.' And I had it in my back pocket. So I went with him to New York and we went down to Fort Knox for three weeks, and that was my first taste of working in the film business.[117]

Wilson doubled Sakata in the long shots but could only do so with a key prop, as Hamilton remembered, 'We are ready to shoot and he's forgotten Oddjob's hat at the motel twenty miles away. So he gets a bollocking. I always tease him!'[118]

Broccoli fondly recalled recruiting Pussy Galore's Flying Circus. They hired male pilots from a nearby flying school and kitted them out in black jumpsuits and blonde wigs.[119] Hamilton recalled, 'if you got close you [could see] blonde wigs and cigars!'[120]

With filming complete Sean Connery flew off to Rome to be with his wife Diane Cilento, who was shooting there with Rex Harrison. Ian Fleming died on 12 August 1964; he was fifty-six. When the news reached Connery he was playing golf with Harrison. The actors played an extra eighteen holes with Connery using the Penfold Hearts ball, the brand Fleming had given Bond in his match against Goldfinger in the novel, in tribute to the author. Connery later commented, 'It seemed appropriate. I think Ian would have liked that.'[121] Fleming died before *Goldfinger* was completed.

Back in London Hamilton and his editor Peter Hunt were racing to finish the cut. Hunt was yet another Bond stalwart getting used to working with a new Bond director. Hamilton reflected:

As an editor [Hunt] wasn't used to having somebody looking over his shoulder. But I insisted that I see the rough cut once a week, as it grows. Peter didn't really like being booted up the arse. Peter was always reluctant. 'I'm the editor!' 'Yes, I know you are Peter and you get away with bloody murder because Saltzman and Broccoli wouldn't know a cut from their arseholes.'[122]

Dubbing editor Norman Wanstall, who was close to the scene noted, 'The hierarchy began to look upon Peter as something vital, he had a lot of power and virtually ran the show.'[123] Hamilton completed the picture under pressure:

> Peter Hunt and I were frantically putting it together imagining that the producers in their wisdom would delay the opening date. We run the picture for [Broccoli and Saltzman]. Every five minutes we look at each other and nod because we see a trim. It's awful when you know what would improve it and there were sections where more than a trim was needed. The lights come on and Cubby and Harry say, 'Yeah, we like it. We got a picture.' And we burst into tears as the picture is removed and is run off for [negative] cutting. If only I had had another week.[124]

A variant of the film was released where Bond is fighting to defuse the 'particularly dirty cobalt and iodine bomb' in Fort Knox and manages to do so just in time. 'Three more ticks and Mr. Goldfinger would have hit the jackpot!' Bond remarks regarding his deft timing. This is odd in that the insert shot of the bomb timer reveals the counter on '007'. In some release prints, it was '003'. Some prints of the film announced the next in the series to be *Thunderball*, some said it would be *On Her Majesty's Secret Service*.

Only three weeks before *Goldfinger* was due to be released composer John Barry was still scoring scenes fresh from the cutting room. Hamilton recalled the rush, 'He said to me quite seriously, "There is going to be a premiere and the orchestra will be in the pit and I'll be conducting. After that I don't know what you'll do."'[125] The director gave his own musical suggestion on the title track, 'I did take John up to my flat and played him Lotte Lenya singing "Mack the Knife" in German. That's the sort of sound I liked and he listened patiently.'[126] Barry went to lyricist Anthony Newley 'because we had the same divorce lawyer. Tony said, "Well, what the hell is this about? I can't understand – it's a terribly abstract title." I said, "It's 'Mack the Knife'. It's a song about a villain."'[127] Newley worked with Leslie Bricusse who, when they heard Barry's initial motif, both sung 'Wider than a mile … ', Johnny Mercer's lyric from Henry Mancini's 'Moon River', which they thought the tune was similar to.[128] Barry felt, 'Choosing the singer was like casting a movie; it had to be the right choice. Shirley [Bassey] was great casting for "Goldfinger". Nobody could have sung it like her. She had that great dramatic sense. When it came to the studio, she didn't know what the hell

the song was about but she sang it with such conviction that she convinced
the rest of the world.'[129]

Robert Brownjohn, whose opening credits for *From Russia With Love* had
been projected on a belly dancer, was rehired. Brownjohn felt film titles
were 'just like super book jackets. The problem [is] producers always leave
the titles to the last minute. They see what cash, if any, they've got left and
then decide on the cheapest way to tackle the job! GOOD TITLES ARE
EXPENSIVE.'[130] Brownjohn, known as BJ, was assisted by lighting cameraman David Watkin and editor Hugh Raggett and production manager
Trevor Bond who recalled, 'We were going to project objects on her body
but that was too difficult, it was hard to make them stand out. It was BJ's
idea to project scenes from the film. The golf ball going down the cleavage
is pure BJ. It was brilliant.'[131] David Watkin, who would later win an Oscar
for cinematography for *Out of Africa* (1985), recalled, 'BJ was like an excited
child, taking alternately one colour of pills for up and another for down from
a Georgian silver snuff box. He was continually exhorting the crew to get a
move on.'[132] Margaret Nolan remembered:

I had to be painted all over with a sponge. I had a bikini on. I was never nude.
The whole thing was totally professional. It went on for over a week. Lying
and sitting on this big bench. I couldn't see what they were projecting on
to me at all.[133]

Like Shirley Eaton, Nolan earned everlasting fame as the model on *Goldfinger's*
poster campaign.

Interestingly the Post Office van scene from Q Branch is in the titles, as is
an unseen moment from the previous Bond film where Connery falls to the
ground while being chased by a helicopter.

When Barry saw an early cut of Brownjohn's sequence he felt his song
was not quite working and began writing his melody to the pictures: 'I came
up with that line (the sleazy wah wah wah wah brass line) – and it was like a
common scream but it worked like a bitch.'[134] On hearing the song, Saltzman
was not enthusiastic, according to Barry:

He just kept swearing, saying, 'John, I need to get the kids in the cinemas and
I can't do it with a song like this.' He wanted to get rid of it and was adamant
about it, but in the end he capitulated saying, 'The only reason this song is

staying in the movie is because we don't have time to redo it. The print's wet and it's got to be in the theatres by next week.'[135]

Upon release the record went gold. Co-lyricist Leslie Bricusse, heard of its success later, 'Because our attention was focused elsewhere that summer, we not only didn't see the movie, we didn't even know Shirley Bassey had recorded the song until we returned to New York in October and received a call from United Artists Records to say that they had a couple of framed soundtrack gold records for us waiting to be collected.'[136]

On 17 September 1964 Goldfinger premiered at the Odeon Leicester Square. Sean Connery was unable to attend, instead Honor Blackman stole the limelight wearing a specially designed gold finger jewel on her hand, 'It was terribly grand when one got applauded as one walked down the staircase. I remember my dressmaker making my gear for the night and he was so overexcited. It was the most glamorous night of my life.'[137] Over 5,000 fans were crammed outside the Odeon and Tania Mallet was terrified:

> The police had absolutely no idea of the volume this, the third film, had attracted. They had no idea of crowd control at all. As I was walking into the cinema the crowd broke through the barriers and came behind me and I ran up the stairs in Leicester Square to the left and the crowd came through the plate glass windows. I'd never been subjected to the mob mentality. It's like a tidal wave, there's no reasoning.[138]

On 16 February 1965 Connery attended the French premiere while in France shooting Thunderball. With crowds, six-deep, stretching down the entire length of the Champs Élysées Connery drove the Aston Martin DB5 accompanied by six golden girls on motorcycles to the cinema and at one point was joined by an eager female fan, who dived through the open window into his lap. Bondmania had arrived.

Goldfinger grossed a staggering $46 million on its initial release recouping its negative cost in the UK alone. By early 1965 it had qualified for $1.4 million in Eady money and entered THE GUINNESS BOOK OF RECORDS as the fastest grossing film of all time.

When Goldfinger was ready for release in the USA, the US censor Geoffrey Shurlock threatened to ban the picture because the name Pussy Galore should have been cleared at script level. Blackman remembered Eon's publicity man:

Tom Carlile was so lovely and so protective, it was great being with him. When I was in the USA I discovered they were all so po-faced about my name. The Americans saw a picture on the front page of an English news-paper with me talking to Prince Philip and the headline read, 'The Prince and The Pussy.' They were taken aback but they took that as permission that it was a decent film and decent character otherwise Prince Philip wouldn't be talking to me.[139]

Broccoli flew to the States to talk to the censor and promptly persuaded him by showing the newspaper cuttings of Prince Philip and Blackman. Hamilton was cynical, 'We conned Shurlock in the usual way by inviting him and his wife out to dinner and saying we were very big supporters of the Republican or the Democratic Party. We'd trade a glimpse of tit for something else. Appalling.'[140] Still, the name caused quite a stir when Blackman appeared on the chat show circuit, 'They were so puritanical. So when they would just say "your character" I would always pipe up, "Oh, you mean Pussy Galore?"'[141]

More potential bad publicity hit *Goldfinger*. Eric Pleskow remembered that Gert Fröbe had been 'a Nazi party member who [had been] unable to work once the German film industry had started again.'[142] During the publicity for the film Fröbe's wartime past caught up with him and the film was banned in Israel. However, disaster was averted as it emerged that Fröbe had actually saved the life of one Mario Blumenau and his mother, so the ban was lifted.[143]

Broccoli and Saltzman's wish to break in America was granted through masterful marketing. In December 1964 the Aston Martin DB5 commenced a promotional tour of the USA.[144] Then, 300,000 paperback tie-ins of the Fleming novel were printed.[145] Shirley Bassey's *Goldfinger* theme became a *Billboard* hit peaking at Number 10 and the soundtrack album eventually knocked the Beatles off Number 1 on the US album charts.[146] Maximising the pre-release publicity and controversy, the film opened with the then huge number of 485 prints, reducing the average advertising budget by more than half.[147] In the words of *Variety*, '*Goldfinger* isn't just big. It is, to use the word advisedly, incomparable. In the first fourteen weeks of its domestic release it has racked up rentals for United Artists of $10,374,807 in 1,409 play dates. No other film in the memory of film historians has ever performed with such speed for such a volume.'[148]

Goldfinger broke box office records everywhere. United Artists gave *Goldfinger* the treatment that the producers had been hoping for; in New York the pic-ture ran twenty-four hours a day. Broccoli was so impressed by the queues outside the Grauman's Chinese Theatre in Hollywood that he went out and took photographs.[149]

During its theatrical lifetime, Goldfinger would gross $51,000,000 in North America and $73,800,000 which, inflation adjusted, would make it one of the enduring, all-time money making films.

Goldfinger was innovative in that it was the first blockbuster to marry exaggerated visuals with heightened sound. The audio in the film was not realistic but created a fantastic aural soundscape matching the visual flair. *Goldfinger* was the first James Bond film to be nominated for an Oscar; it was for the Best Sound Effects Editing category. On 5 April 1965 the thirty-seventh Academy Awards was held at Santa Monica Civic Auditorium or 'Santa Monica on Thames' as Bob Hope quipped, referring to the number of nominated Brits. *Goldfinger* was nominated alongside just one other nominee – *The Lively Set* – a film about dragster racing produced by Universal Pictures. Norman Wanstall remembered the adventure:

> My wife and I were looked after like a king and queen. There was a bottle of Scotch on the table in the hotel and people kept ringing up and asking if I was ok. There was a limousine laid on, etc. I remember thinking,'"this is ridiculous. This is a 28- or 29-year-old technician just doing a job. This is something that happens to other people – it belongs in a different world.'[150]

The category was presented by American actress Angie Dickinson, who announced the winner from the envelope and the auditorium was filled with the powerful strains of 'Goldfinger'. Wanstall had just won the first Oscar of the James Bond film series and 'felt 10ft tall.'[151] On the night he simply said, 'I'm a technician so perhaps I'll leave the eloquence to the actors that follow.'

Although he had seen the successful transition of Bond from page to screen, Broccoli regretted that Fleming never saw James Bond become a worldwide phenomenon, 'When he died it was a great loss to us especially because he began to like what we were doing.'[152]

Speculation had already started as to Bond's endurance. The trade press noted, 'How long can James Bond go on in this fashion? Nobody concerned with the pix would care to speculate too freely – it might be bad luck. However, they feel that because of the whammo biz for *Goldfinger* chances are that the upcoming film, *Thunderball*, will be another winner.'[153]

WINNER WHO TAKES ALL

THUNDERBALL

(1965)

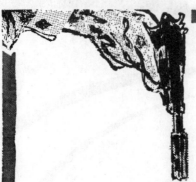

HARRY SALTZMAN & ALBERT R. BROCCOLI
PRESENT

SEAN CONNERY
as
JAMES BOND 007
in
IAN FLEMING'S

Thunderball

Produced by
KEVIN McCLORY

Directed by
TERENCE YOUNG

TECHNICOLOR®

AN EON PRODUCTION
Released thru UNITED ARTISTS

IN PRODUCTION FEBRUARY 1965

Had it not been for the machinations of the English legal system Richard Maibaum's draft screenplay of *Thunderball* dated 18 August 1961 would have become the first James Bond film. However, the long-running copyright dispute between the co-creators of the underlying story prevented the screenplay being filmed. On 26 November 1963 Mr. Justice Ungoed-Thomas, sitting in court room nineteen of the Royal Courts of Justice in London, presided over the agreement between the parties: Ian Fleming and Ivar Bryce – the defendants, and Kevin McClory and Jack Whittingham – the plaintiffs. McClory recalled, 'Under the settlement I got the full copyright in all those screenplays, outlines and treatments. Also the film rights that we'd written and discarded over an eleven-month period. Also the film rights of the novel *Thunderball*.'[1] In addition all future copies of the book had to contain the declaration: 'Based on a screen treatment by KEVIN McCLORY, JACK WHITTINGHAM and IAN FLEMING'. For years the parties had all tried to bring James Bond to the cinema. Now, in the slipstream of the incredible success of the Eon series, McClory was sitting on a potential cinematic goldmine.

In January 1964 McClory hinted to *Variety* that he planned 'to film THUNDERBALL on his own with "the new James Bond", as opposed to the "old James Bond" (Sean Connery).'[2] McClory was then reported to be in Rome looking for local talent for one of his female leads in the film and was 'dickering with several major companies and some indies who want to finance the item.'[3] In February 1964 it was reported that McClory had offered Richard Burton the role of Bond.[4] McClory's old colleague director Guy Hamilton observed, 'I could see that Kevin had understood the way films were made and with his heiress wife [Bobo Sigrist] he now had money to afford lawyers and agents and could put up a good fight.'[5] It was a shrewd observation because McClory was at the same time negotiating with Eon to produce the film under their now-established banner.[6]

Early prints of *Goldfinger* had stated that the next Bond film would be *On Her Majesty's Secret Service*. The title had even been announced in *Variety*[7] while *Goldfinger* was still shooting. Guy Hamilton was keen on the book, 'If I ever did another [Bond film] I'd like to do ON HER MAJESTY'S [SECRET SERVICE] because I think Bond falling in love is reason enough to make it – but seriously.'[8] However, now there was an opportunity to corral one title back into the Eon herd and the producers did not want to waste it. In November 1964 *Variety* sensed a deal appeared to have been done, 'The pic is on the UA [United Artists] sked to be the next Bond film. Terms of the secret settlement are partially indicated by the production billing for the project. It is being produced by McClory in association with Broccoli and Saltzman. This, of course, differs from prior arrangements in which the Eon men produced the pix themselves.'[9]

Eventually Eon made the tactical manoeuvre of engaging McClory. Broccoli rationalised their position:

> We didn't want anyone else to make *Thunderball*. We had the feeling that if anyone else came in and made their own Bond film it would have been bad for our series. After *Goldfinger* we naturally felt we knew more about Bond than anyone else. So I went ahead and made the deal with McClory to ensure that the best of Fleming's stories could be our film.[10]

They made the Irishman an offer he could not refuse: $250,000 cash plus 20 per cent profits on the proviso that McClory could not produce another film from the THUNDERBALL film rights he still retained for ten years from the US release date.[11] The deal was so seemingly amicable that Broccoli even became godfather to McClory's children.[12] *On Her Majesty's Secret Service* was deferred again.

The relationship between Eon Productions and United Artists was running smoothly. David Picker explained:

> Anything that happened during the making of the films was simply a casual friendship relationship. They had no obligation to do anything except bring us the film when it was finished, as long as it stayed on budget and there had been no problems. When you start making these films and they become successful there is a lot more leeway than when you are taking the initial risk.[13]

Eric Pleskow exploited the success of the series, 'The Bond pictures became a weapon for our company [with exhibitors]. With the power of the Bond pictures, I was able to [negotiate] some pretty good things in the foreign area that were unique in the business.'[14] Pleskow remembered his colleague's attitude towards Broccoli and Saltzman, 'David Picker used to negotiate with them from picture to picture. Somehow they always ended up getting a little better deal.'[15] Ever the dealmaker Broccoli dropped hints that Universal Studios were interested in doing a deal with him and his partner saying, 'and, of course, we're interested'.[16] However, he was keen to emphasise, 'UA has been very good to us. I'd like to make a picture [in the States] – it's been a long time since '52.'[17] Therefore, it was a confident United Artists who increased the budget to $5.6 million.[18] *Thunderball* director Terence Young reflected, 'For *Dr. No* I only had

$1 million, for *From Russia With Love* I had $2 million, which was really quite a lot of money in those days – it was a nice figure. When I made *Thunderball* we had so much money we used to throw money out of the window.'[19]

Yet, for Sean Connery the over-identification with Bond was becoming a burden:

> The problem is to get across the fact, without breaking your arse, that one is not Bond, that one was functioning reasonably well before Bond, and that one is going to function reasonably well after Bond. There are a lot of things I did before Bond – like playing the classics on stage – that don't seem to get publicised. So, you see, this Bond image is a problem in a way and a bit of a bore, but one has just got to live with it.[20]

For *Thunderball* his deal had been significantly enhanced and he would receive 5 per cent of the producers' profits.[21] Despite this Connery was cautious about the future of Bond, 'I can't see the cycle going on past [the next film]. But who knows? America seems to lap them up. My only grumble about the Bond films is that they don't tax one as an actor.'[22]

While developing *Thunderball* with Fleming it had always been assumed that Kevin McClory would follow up his 1959 directorial debut *The Boy and the Bridge* with Bond. McClory was an experienced film hand but perhaps not competent enough to handle a film this size. Guy Hamilton was pleased:

> Kevin McClory I knew well because I was an assistant and he was a boom operator. He was a fucking nuisance – always slow getting his shadow out of the way. We were on many pictures [and] also in digs together, just by Shepperton Studios. He and I were poker players – we taught our landlady to play; Kevin and I very rarely paid our rent. I was delighted that he moved on from being a boom operator to being a producer.[23]

A junior in the art department Peter Lamont also knew of McClory's reputation, 'He was [assistant] director on *Moby Dick*. There's always this tale that he was the one who lost the whale.'[24] Dubbing editor Norman Wanstall, who received his Oscar for *Goldfinger* during the filming of *Thunderball*, remembered McClory's presence:

> I was suddenly aware that whenever we had meetings there was a third party. This guy used to sit there in his overcoat and I used to think, 'Well, what's

his role? Why have we got somebody new involved?' Then, of course, it was explained to me, all this business about how he wrote the story. I don't remember him having any great say in procedures. I got the feeling that he was a bit of a loner really – that he was there because he had the right to be – rather than the fact he was heavily involved in the production.[25]

Having completed *Goldfinger* Guy Hamilton was approached to direct a second Bond:

> I was out in LA. Cubby and Harry came out, and they were fussing about because they were going to make *Thunderball* and they wanted me to direct it. Harry was looking around to see what the situation was and I said, 'I don't really want to make another Bond because I have run out of ideas.'[26]

Eon tried to secure Hamilton again when he was on honeymoon in Las Vegas, 'Cubby and Kevin McClory turned up. [*Thunderball*] didn't race my motor. I find all the underwater swimming, slow, slow, slow. As a climax it's very difficult to make work.'[27]

Eon then went back and offered the film to Terence Young. He accepted the task for salary only, despite being offered a piece of the film by Broccoli on the proviso, 'If you want the percentage, then lower the cash.'[28] After Hamilton's success with *Goldfinger* Young felt, 'I think I only agreed to do *Thunderball* because, in a childish way, I wanted to prove that anything you can do, I can do better. It was really childish of me.'[29] Richard Maibaum felt Young had 'not been given the credit he deserves for the style of the films. He's not a meticulous director but he's an inspired one at times. While there are things in his pictures that are sloppy, I think he's the best we've had at doing a romantic scene.'[30] Terence Young was later rueful about his role, 'I said after *Thunderball*, "I think you don't need a director anymore, you want an MIT graduate to handle all the machines."'[31]

Richard Maibaum signed on to revisit the *Thunderball* draft he had first written pre-*Dr. No*:

> In rewriting it four years later I had to remember the proven public delight in jokes, gadgetry and so forth. Now the two [scripts] are completely different because now we know exactly what it is the public love about Bond and how they best like to see the stories treated in the cinema.[32]

THUNDERBALL was published in the UK on 27 March 1961. The novel opens with Bond visiting Shrublands, a health farm (inspired by Fleming's actual stay at the similar Enton Hall), under orders from M. Bond makes enquiries after noticing, by sheer coincidence, a Chinese Tong sign on a certain Count Lippe. Unfortunately for Bond his enquiries become known to Lippe who traps 007 painfully in a spinal traction machine. Bond exacts revenge by locking Lippe in a sauna, causing him severe burns. The two men also joust over the affections of the attractive nurse Patricia Fearing.

Little does Bond know that the injuries he inflicted on Lippe would lead to the count's death at the hands of the sinister group he had pledged allegiance to. It was deemed by this organisation that Lippe's bout with Bond nearly jeopardised a mission to facilitate the theft of two atom bombs. Lippe had been working in cahoots with Giuseppe Petacchi, a NATO pilot and inside man, to hijack a nuclear bomber. Once Petacchi's part in the mission is over, he is killed and the sinister group blackmails the Western governments by threatening to explode the two atomic bombs they have stolen unless their ransom demands are met. Deducing the weapons may be in the Bahamas, Bond travels there and quickly befriends the beautiful Dominetta 'Domino' Vitali. She is the ward of a mysterious new arrival to the island, Emilio Largo, ostensibly there to hunt for sunken treasure. It transpires that Domino's real name is Petacchi and she is the sister of the traitorous Giuseppe. Inveigling himself in Largo's good graces, besting him at the gaming tables and seducing Domino, Bond unravels the plans of the group. With the help of Felix Leiter and the US Navy, Bond tracks down Largo and his team of frogmen and a thrilling underwater fight ensues. The bombs are recovered, but not before Bond's life is saved by Domino when, in a surprise revearsal, she kills Largo – exacting revenge for her brother's death.

Fleming was a keen underwater swimmer in his private cove at his Jamaican home Goldeneye. He had written beautiful underwater scenes in previous novels and co-creator Kevin McClory must have sensed a kindred spirit. This was the first Bond novel in which Fleming did not use the Soviet Union as villains, his attitude having softened towards the supposed 'Evil Empire'. The author reflected, 'I rather liked the Russians, I've worked there twice and they are a very great people and I don't want to rag them too much. There's a tremendous relaxation in Russia, and the West and Russia may get very much closer together. That's my feeling, that's my nose. If that's going to happen, if peace is going to break out, the last thing I want to do is provide any hindrance to the process.'[33]

The creation of SPECTRE was an attempt to progress the Bond novels and the acronym-named terrorist group proved prescient. Fleming noted, 'It's a very difficult thing to do to get these villains to grow on trees.'[34] The head of SPECTRE is Ernst Stavro Blofeld, a Polish-born spy gangster, who founds his private enterprise by stealing ciphers and building wealth. Blofeld is given a fascinating backstory and shares Fleming's birthday. He is a physically large, imposing man, who rules his fellow boardmembers – populated by a who's who of hate organisations – with a sedate iron-fist, while chewing violet-scented breath drops. Bond does not actually meet Blofeld in the story, thus setting things up for a return. Once again Fleming appropriated the name from a real person he went to Eton with, Tom Blofeld – the father of famed cricket commentator Henry Blofeld.

Given that it was a project originally conceived for the screen, it is ironic that the screenplay for *Thunderball* required so much work. Maibaum had had the chance to tell the author before his death about the problems of adapting his novels, 'I said this to Fleming once, "There is an untransferable quality in your writing." It's all very well; Fleming writes two and a half pages describing the fish underwater, the beautiful waving weeds, the colours – but, what the hell, it's just a pretty piece of celluloid when you see it on the screen.'[35] By now, Maibaum had established the Bond formula:

> Hitchcock said to me, 'If I have thirteen bumps I know I have a picture.' By 'bumps' he meant shocks, highpoints, thrills. Mr. Broccoli and Mr. Saltzman and myself have not been content with thirteen 'bumps'. We aim for thirty-nine. Our objective has been to make every foot of film pay off in terms of exciting entertainment.[36]

Maibaum also felt the casting impacted on his writing:

> I must say there have been times when we have not been bright enough to make the villain different and interesting enough from what has gone on before. In *Thunderball* Largo was a disappointment partly because it was played by an actor who I thought was miscast. I had to invent other people to augment his villainy.[37]

Maibaum's screenplay would be given a polish by television writer and playwright John Hopkins, who went on to write *The Offence* (1972) for Sean Connery based on his play *This Story is Yours*.[38]

Following on from their television interview with Ian Fleming, the Canadian Broadcasting Company televised the only known interview of the producers talking together and shot in the library of Broccoli's town house in Green Street. It offered a great insight into Bond. Saltzman noted the screenplays were 'a group effort in the writing, the conception, the adaptation from the book, the creation of the gimmicks and the artwork involved, as well as the direction.'[39] Broccoli agreed:

In the story, in the casting, even in the set designing and the gimmicks, all of the thoughts that go into – for instance the DB5 Aston Martin – Harry and I [are involved]. We, all of us, collectively have huge arguments – all good natured arguments – but they're important so that out of it comes what you see on the screen, good, bad or indifferent.[40]

The producers began the arduous task of testing actresses for roles in the film. A number of those discussed were names that would ultimately make their cinematic mark, just not in *Thunderball*. First there was future sixties icon Julie Christie. Cubby remembered her well:

I marked her name down because she was beautiful and both Dana and I were raving about her acting. So I brought her into the office a few days later to see Terence and Harry. She was very nervous. She came in wearing a pair of jeans and she was terribly dishevelled and didn't look at all like she did on television. I was disappointed in seeing her this way. In fact, I couldn't believe it was the same girl.[41]

Terence Young was sympathetic, 'It wasn't the ideal place for a shy young actress to meet the powers that be. There were a lot of people hanging around Audley Square in those days – mentally undressing every girl who walked in and [I] immediately thought this chick wasn't destined for such an atmosphere. She had class and was more than just a pretty face.'[42] The next girl actually hired was Raquel Welch. However, at the personal request of Twentieth Century-Fox head, Richard Zanuck, Cubby reluctantly released her.[43] Faye Dunaway also tested but chose another part instead.[44] Other girls in the running were Yvonne Monlaur, Maria Buccella,[45] Marisa Menzies and Gloria Paul.[46]

The producers eventually cast the stunning 23-year-old, former Miss France, Claudine Auger:

I was a member of the National Popular Theatre in Paris appearing in all the classic roles. I got a call from London asking if I would like to test for a leading role in a James Bond thriller. The theatre director would not give me the time off to take the test so I arranged to do it in one day. I flew to London in the morning and returned to Paris the same night.[47]

Auger recalled she tested 'in a very sexy bathing suit'[48] on a beach set at Pinewood Studios, 'I heard nothing for two weeks. Then I got a call from Terence Young.'[49] While excited she got the part – 'I couldn't sleep for two or three nights'[50] – the Parisian was calm, too, 'Somehow I always felt I would become Domino. I had read the book about seven times and knew her inside out.'[51] Auger identified with the character, 'I am very much sort of a Domino girl myself. Whatever it is I am doing, I enjoy doing it – loving, driving, riding, travelling, shopping, even cooking. [Fleming's heroines] are essentially feminine, the ultimate in the modern emancipated woman.'[52] In the book the character is Italian, but in the film her name is changed to Derval to reflect the casting, although Auger's French accent meant that yet again a Bond girl was dubbed by Nikki van der Zyl.[53]

Established Italian actress Luciana Paluzzi arrived at Pinewood to screentest only to discover 'there were about 300 girls. I couldn't believe how many people were in the make-up room. I did the test for the leading role and then I went back to Rome. I got a call one day and Terence said, "I have good news and I have bad news."'[54] The bad news was that she was not going to play Domino; the good was she had landed the part of femme fatale Fiona Volpe, who Paluzzi felt was:

Like a female Bond. She lives like he does. She's 100 per cent feminine, but able to do the things he does. In many ways Fiona is similar to the girl I played in *To Trap a Spy* [1964] [when] I tried to kill Napoleon Solo – 'The Man from UNCLE'. But nothing is as good as Bond. Being a Bond girl is like doing five years' worth of work in one. It gives you a special kind of magic. It makes you a demi-goddess.[55]

Perhaps because of this, the producers could afford to pay less. Paluzzi recalled:

Cubby was adorable and Harry was tough like a bulldog, but to me he was very nice. They discussed my salary with my agent. I wasn't happy. I said, 'My God this is nothing.' I went to their office on [South] Audley Street. Both of them were on the phone and I was sitting on a chair waiting for them to finish. They were arguing about salaries and one of them said, 'If your client doesn't want to do it for this price, then tell him I have 3,000 people outside this door who want to do this role.' And slam! They hung up. Then they turned to me and smiled and said, 'Yes, Luciana, what can we do for you?'[56]

In the screenplay and in early promotional material Fiona's last name is Kelly,[57] but, once again, the name was changed to Volpe to reflect the Italian casting.

Molly Peters remembered how she was discovered for the role of Patricia Fearing, 'I used to do so-called glamour modelling. I tested – after I had completed the scene [with Sean's stand-in] there was spontaneous applause.'[58] Young had actually given her 'a cough and a spit'[59] role in his previous film *The Amorous Adventures of Moll Flanders* (1965). Peters thought her character was 'very English and she had to be more efficient, more nurse-like.'[60]

According to *From Russia With Love*'s Martine Beswick, Harry Saltzman was against her making a second appearance in a Bond film. She recalled his philosophy, 'we don't have the same one twice, they're all Kleenex, throw 'em out.'[61] It was her friend Terence Young who wanted her for the part of Paula Caplan, Bond's Bahamian contact, '[He] said "Don't be ridiculous, she's a Jamaican" and he actually fought for me. There I was the original Island girl. The only problem was I had not seen the sun in years – I was grey. And I was thin. When we got to Nassau, I was told to lie in the sun and eat. I had to get a tan.'[62]

Adolfo Celi remembered how he was cast as the villain Emilio Largo:

I was travelling back from Hollywood where I had finished *Von Ryan's Express* [1965] with Frank Sinatra and in New York I purchased the novel THUNDERBALL by Fleming. I hadn't seen *Dr. No* but I had heard about it. Anyway, I read the book on the plane during my flight from New York to Spain, where I had to shoot a film with Jean-Paul Belmondo and I thought, 'How nice it would be acting in a film from this book but probably they will never call me.' I made the film in Spain and then I got to Rome with some money, and decided to go to Paris. I was leaving when my agent told me to go to the Georges Cinq where there was a producer who wanted to see me. The producer turned out to be Saltzman; a bit of discussion took place and we landed it. I got to the hotel attired and with a bit of make-up reminding me of Emilio Largo, as I knew something of the character this was some help.[63]

Felix Leiter was also recast, although not known to international audiences Rik Van Nutter was a known quantity to Eon. His wife, Swedish actress Anita Ekberg, had starred in *Call Me Bwana*. Van Nutter remembered he and Anita were:

> having one of those immense Italian dinners in London with Cubby and Dana, when Cubby suddenly came out and said I looked just like Felix Leiter. Now I'd read all of the Bond books and I knew that Felix had straw-coloured hair, blue eyes and long legs. So I fit the bill physically. I later met with Terence Young who tested me with some Bond girls.[64]

Guy Doleman played Count Lippe, Philip Locke would play the sinister Vargas, Earl Cameron was Pinder, Bond's Bahamian contact, and one of Fleming's previous choices to play Bond, Edward Underdown, had a small role as an RAF officer.[65]

Originally the pre-title sequence was set in a Hong Kong Fan-Tan parlour and featured a girl dressed as a peacock sitting in a cage. Bond follows her into her dressing room and then slugs her, revealing she is in fact a man in drag![66] A late revision to the script – dated 16 January 1965 – moved the action to the funeral of a SPECTRE agent, Jacques Boitier (seemingly pronouced Bouvar). Bond observes the agent's widow and notes that she does not wait for a car door to be opened for her but opens it herself. That tips Bond off and when he offers his sincere condolences – 007 punches the widow to reveal the supposedly dead SPECTRE agent.

The sequence was now set in France and shot at the Chateau D'Anet, near Paris. It was there on 16 February 1965 that filming began on *Thunderball*.[67] This was an opportunistic use of Sean Connery's time in Paris, as he was attending the French premiere of *Goldfinger*.[68] Terence Young was not enamoured by Château D'Anet,[69] but, 'That was very much altered when I got on set and saw what the set was like. It was very much dictated by the décor.'[70] Madame Boitier was played as a widow by Rose Alba and as a man by stuntman Bob Simmons in drag. Once again the action set piece is edited in a stylised fashion by Peter Hunt and amplified by John Barry's wailing score.

The sequence introduced the world to the Bell Aerosystems Rocket Belt – flown by Bond to escape his would-be SPECTRE assassins. This unique piece of equipment had been sourced by Colonel Charles Russhon,[71] in the words of Peter Lamont, Eon's 'Mr. Fixit'.[72] Production manager David Middlemas paid tribute to the technological awareness of his producers, 'Cubby and Harry were always on the lookout for new ideas, e.g. the jet pack in *Thunderball*. They heard about this and wrote it in.'[73] One of the pilots, Bill Suitor, recalled how he became a rocket man:

I began flying at Bell Aerosystems in 1964 at the age of nineteen. The rocket belt had been developed by Bell for the US Army and part of its contract stipulated that it had to train a man of 'draft age' with no previous flying experience. It just so happened that the inventor of the belt, Wendell Moore, was a neighbour. I was an architecture student at the time and not very happy, so when he said, 'Wanna job?' I jumped at the chance. Me and another Bell pilot, Gordon Yeager, shared the flights in *Thunderball*.[74]

And so it was that the rocket belt entered history. 'No well dressed man should be without one,' Bond quips stowing it in the boot of his Aston Martin DB5 – by now the most famous car in the world and another returnee from *Goldfinger*. Harry Saltzman explained the importance of the pre-title sequence, 'We do these openings to make it very evident that it is tongue-in-cheek, that it is larger than life and we're not pushing any political ideology. We are making an entertainment motion picture.'[75]

After his tour de force on *Goldfinger*, Ken Adam was undaunted by the fact that most of *Thunderball* would be shot beneath the waves, 'As a designer it gave me another dimension to work in.'[76] Now promoted to chief draughts-man after his stint on *Goldfinger*, Peter Lamont recalled, 'Ken breezed into the office one morning and said, "OK, we're doing *Thunderball*, you'd better learn to swim underwater." So I had a crash course [and] by the time I got [to the Bahamas] I'd been certified and I could do whatever. Initially I went out there for a couple of weeks. Fourteen weeks later, I was still there.'[77]

The Bond team received incredible cooperation from the RAF's chief of Fighter Command.[78] Peter Lamont went to RAF Waddington to check out a real Vulcan bomber, then at the vanguard of Britain's nuclear arsenal. Lamont was eager to see a real nuclear weapon but security considerations prevented that. However, Lamont remembered, 'One night we were invited to the RAF's [Bomber] Command down at Naphill and our liaison man said, "All the questions that you've ever asked me, are all here, all you've got to do is look for [the answers]."'[79] So tacitly the Bond design team was given access to a nuclear weapon to ensure 'everything that we ever did was pretty accurate.'[80] By this time working on a Bond film opened doors not usually accessible to film productions. However, when the Ministry of Defence requested that the Bond crew share their secrets, the Eon team were unable to reciprocate. When asked about Q's re-breather device, which gave 007 about four minutes of oxygen, Lamont had to reveal that it was just a film prop made up of soda siphon capsules.

In March 1965 the Bond team descended on the Bahamas like an invading army. Martine Beswick remembered the fun started in Britain, 'They chartered a plane to take us all out there. The entire cast and crew on a plane from Heathrow to Nassau. That was the beginning. Champagne flowed, [the] food was fantastic. We were living the Bond style already.'[81] David Middlemas found their new producer helpful, 'Kevin McClory knew the islands better than any of us. [He] was well known, so we had an enormous advantage and got terrific cooperation and the goodwill was tremendous.'[82]

Goodwill was certainly required as the Bond crew requested the island re-stage their annual Christmas junkanoo at Easter. Middlemas remembered, 'lots of meetings with the various people involved to get clearance. We didn't dictate costume or anything, we just asked people to turn up.'[83] Richard Jenkins, the third assistant director, recalled:

Terence planned to film around the parade as it moved through downtown Nassau. He told us that whatever happened we weren't to try to stop it or move it backward. We just had to shoot around it doing the best we could. The parade was something like two miles long, travelling around in a big circle and there were forty companies co-sponsoring the event. To bring the whole thing to a halt might have caused a riot. Whistle, whistle, boom, boom – wild drinking; 45,000 watching it. Terence was sipping some champagne from a paper cup when he said, 'God, this is a rough location, my champagne is warm.'[84]

The Bond sets had become so lavish even Terence Young, a famous bon viveur, learned a thing or two:

A boat comes towards us [with a] gentleman in a white suit. I noticed quickly he had the big cordon of the Legion D'Honneur. He said, 'I've brought you a present' and he took out a big magnum of Dom Perignon, took some glasses out, took some lumps of ice [and] poured champagne all over them. I said, 'No, no, no. No champagne and ice.' He said, 'My friend, I shall never teach you how to direct pictures, you should never teach me to drink wine. I am the Count de Vogue and I own Moët et Chandon who make Dom Perignon. Take the ice out after thirty seconds.[85]

Connery's wife Diane Cilento joined in the fun with a trip in an amphibious vehicle – a DUKW or 'Duck' – with Bahamian property developers Sir Harold Christie and John Huston. Their hosts were Kevin McClory – Huston's former assistant – and his wife, the heiress Bobo Sigrist, who had brought, according to Cilento, 'ridiculous supplies of picnic goodies and champagne on ice'.[86] Beswick felt, 'The luxuries had a lot to do with Terence. Tables set up with table cloths and having proper lunches under the coconut tree.'[87] Luciana Paluzzi agreed, 'Because of Terence Young, we would never be sitting in a dressing room or trailer. No, he would get a yacht for us to change in. If we were shooting on the beach, there would be these beautiful white tents like you see in Morocco.'[88]

Nevertheless, Beswick felt some tension between the incoming Irishman and the established producing duo, 'It was actually a divided camp. I loved my gang: Terence and Kevin and his wife, Bobo. Sean was in with us a lot. They weren't happy with them. Harry and Broccoli, I used to see them around.'[89]

Desmond Llewelyn, Q, was sent to the Bahamas to film his scenes as:

wet-weather cover [to shoot interiors in the event of rain]. If I wanted to go out, I would have to ask a very fussy little production manager for permission. He would look at the weather and if it was sunny say, 'OK'. After I had been out there about three weeks he told me I was going home. Cubby had a fit because it was much cheaper to keep me out there. Eventually I did my scene a couple of weeks later – in the studio.[90]

Many scenes were shot on Paradise Island due to Kevin McClory's connections and friendship with property developer Huntington Hartford. Harford was heir to American and Pacific (A&P) grocery chain, along with his sister Josephine. In a cruel twist of fate Josephine Hartford was married to Ivar Bryce. The wealthy heiress had had to pay for Bryce's failed court case – including writing a cheque for McClory's costs. Naturally her brother's relationship to her legal opponent put distance between the siblings. Cubby Broccoli, benefitting from McClory's contact with her brother Huntington, reached out to Josephine and Ivar Bryce. Bryce had a writer friend whose wife had been ill and incurred expensive medical treatment. Bryce asked Cubby if he could find work for this friend whose name was Roald Dahl and so Dahl was hired to write the screenplay for the next Bond film.[91]

The high-society class of the island was co-opted for a few nights to film scenes at the Café Martinique. Here, Bond dances with Domino in a romantic

sequence at the café after Bond has beaten Largo at *chemin de fer* – the gambling was shot back at Pinewood as the café had no such casino. Over 300 of
the Bahamian elite, including Huntington Hartford and his wife Diane, Sir
Berkeley and Lady Omerod – the parents-in-law of Kevin McClory – turned
out to play themselves.[92] Eon Productions provided free Dom Perignon and
caviar, as well as £1,000 for the best-dressed couple[93] and the Nassau Tourist
Board donated money to the Red Cross.[94]

The shoot was not always so genteel. Memorably Palmyra, Largo's palatial
residence - in actuality, Rock Point - had its own shark pool. In one sequence
Bond is trapped in it; McClory had quipped, '[Sharks] aren't really dangerous
so long as you stay away from their business end.'[95] His theory was about to
be tested. Sean Connery was filmed in the pool separated from the sharks by
a wall of plexiglass. Unbeknownst to the actor there had not been enough of
the transparent material to complete a full wall, leaving a gap that allowed a
real shark to swim towards him. The look of genuine fright on Sean Connery's
face in the film was not an act.[96]

In 1965 the world beneath the ocean had not been exploited in commercial
cinema. The producers chose Lamar Boren to help them; Boren worked at the
Ivan Tors studio in Miami and had experience shooting beneath the waves,
having made the enormously successful television shows – *Flipper* and *Seahunt*.
Boren remembered Cubby Broccoli contacting him when *Thunderball* was
first discussed in 1961,[97] '*Thunderball* was the most ambitious underwater film
in film history. Cubby and Harry were so pleased with our footage that they
kept increasing its importance in the film.'[98]

Boren felt the film's bespoke technology helped it, 'One thing that made the
whole project even more interesting was the creation of so many functional
underwater props and gadgets.'[99] Ken Adam allowed his creativity to run wild
designing underwater bomb carriers and sleds, 'I was so amazed when I found
people who could make my designs work. I was fortunate to contact Jordan
Klein in Miami.'[100]

Like Boren, Jordan Klein was another underwater film-making pioneer. He
invented unique crafts and, for *Thunderball*, constructed a stingray-like bomb
carrier, the Disco Volante hydrofoil and assorted gadgets.[101] He also helped Lamar
Boren with the filming, 'I shot most of the inserts – little crabs on the ocean floor,
dead divers, spear hits, etc. I also ended up on camera, running the bomb carrier.
That's me in the cockpit. I had a gold Rolex on and you can see it.'[102]

Some of the surreal logistics of shooting a Bond film came to play in the
sinking of the Vulcan bomber. Peter Lamont, enjoying his first location shoot,

remembered the hugely problematic stages of dealing with this uniquely Bondian prop. Initially the Vulcan was created in full-scale on dry land 'opposite Potter's Wharf on Paradise Island, in tubular scaffolding'.[103] Now, the 14-ton set had to be taken out to sea.[104] This was problematic.[105] Too heavy for existing equipment, a special crane had to be chartered to lift the dummy plane.[106] The Vulcan was then floated by barge to a place called Golden Keys where it was sunk beneath the waves.[107] Camouflage netting was then placed over the sunken prop.[108] Lamont remembered, 'I flew over it in a helicopter. And I defy anybody to say that it was underwater.'[109] John Stears had to replicate the underwater location in miniature very much like the real location. He would commute to the Bahamas every weekend from Pinewood until he found the ideal site: Rose Island.[110]

To film the treacherous death of the turncoat pilot Petacchi, an Ivan Tors diver, Courtney Brown, actually had his air hose cut. Brown had been supposed to reach for the 'bale-out' bottle of air, hidden out of sight. However, Brown dropped the spare bottle and could not reach it for a dangerous length of time. The delay caused the hapless diver to be hospitalised.[111]

Kevin McClory's dream to shoot a large-scale underwater finale was realised off the coast at Clifton Pier. Here the SPECTRE divers, placing the atom bomb off the coast of Miami, are spectacularly stopped by sticks of aqua-paras, parachuting from the sky and taking the battle to the ocean floor. Colonel Charles Russhon arranged for the production to receive $92,000 of free underwater gear, as well as the Fulton Skyhook seen at the end of the film during which Bond and Domino are unceremoniously hauled from their life raft by a line attached to an aircraft.[112]

The sequence was overseen by yet another veteran underwater filmmaker Ricou Browning. Browning had gained B-movie fame by playing *The Creature from the Black Lagoon* (1954). Now he had a monster of a scene to film, as he recalled, 'We needed sunlight. Then we would rehearse the sequence before we went into the water. Everything was orchestrated underwater with hand signals. If we had a problem we could never correct it underwater. We'd surface, discuss it and go back down to complete the sequence.'[113] The unfortunate Courtney Brown had a second accident – he was injured by an exploding squib[114] – while Ricou Browning accidently shot himself with a harpoon gun.[115]

At the climax of *Thunderball* the navy catches up with Largo as he tries to escape on the Disco Volante. The vessel breaks into two sections: a floating cocoon with a gun emplacement and a high-speed hydrofoil. Ken Adam purchased an old hydrofoil made by Denison Rodriguez in Puerto Rico for

$1,000. Art director Peter Murton spent three months in Florida overseeing the conversion of the wreck into a film-ready craft.[116] Terence Young had initial concerns that it would not work, 'They tried to make it come apart for about five days in a row and it wouldn't come apart, even with men with axes and hammers hitting the goddam thing.'[117] However, Young recalled, '[When we came to shoot] the boat came by and clean as a whistle the front came off, the back remained and that was it. Sean and I went off and played golf.'[118] For Peter Lamont things were less comfortable, 'I remember being in it when we were doing the chase at the end, with the cocoon, and being thrown all over the place.'[119] When the boat exploded the crew used a new form of liquid explosive procured by Charlie Russhon. John Stears, special effects maestro, was sheepish, 'I put the windows out 60 miles away. I was using deviants of rocket fuel and when we blew it I remember looking and there was a hole in the water of some 50ft and the debris came out of the sky some THREE minutes afterwards.'[120]

The island was explosive for other reasons, Peter Lamont recalled:

It was still part of the Commonwealth. They were under British rule, and the Bay Street Boys [the white Bahamian Government] ran it. I remember a frigate came in and the Marines were there because there was kind of a semi-riot when Lynden Pindling [a black lawyer] was possibly going to become the first Prime Minister. If you look at the sea chase at the end the frigate's there.[121]

The location shoot had been testing. Connery noted to a reporter, 'I've had everything here from the trots to leprosy.'[122] The same report also highlighted more personal problems in detail, 'Connery was the eye of this hurricane of activity. [He] was dogged by reporters and photographers from all over the world. [Diane] Cilento indeed later admitted that prior to shooting, they had been separated and felt the location [might] have been a reconciliation for her and Connery.'[123] Cilento had observed a shift in how her husband was handled by the director. Young was 'treating [Sean] very differently, like Russian royalty.'[124] In one incident, a nurse failed to sterilise the re-breather device and was publicly chastised by Young. Connery, uncharacteristically, failed to intervene.[125] Cilento noted, 'In the face of an inflamed emotional scene on set, he had arrived in a state of virtual catatonia. It was a very telling turning point.'[126] Connery put a brave face on it, 'I think one's got to have the constitution of a rugby player to get through all the nineteen-week shooting and if you can get a laugh with it, it makes it twice as easy.'[127]

In summer 1965 the Bond team returned to Pinewood Studios, where Ken Adam's sets awaited them. The designer tried to innovate with SPECTRE's gunmetal meeting chamber, 'I was getting fed up with boardrooms and long tables. So I decided they would just be sitting on armchairs; it was a pretty contemporary design.'[128] For the conference room where the 'oo' agents are assembled, Adam employed Austrian scenic artist Ferdie Bellan, used by Alexander Korda, to create the large tapestries, which ascend to reveal a gigantic map.[129] Careful viewers can spot Colonel Charles Russhon dressed in uniform sitting on the desk by the red phone when it is announced that NATO are to pay SPECTRE the ransom. Molly Peters enjoyed Russhon's presence on set, 'He was with us most of the time in full uniform. He had a great sense of humour.'[130]

One famous publicity still shows Molly Peters in bed with Connery wearing a tartan hat and Terence Young sipping tea at the foot of the bed. Peters remembered, 'England and Scotland were playing football. Connery was in his element saying that the English were going to get slaughtered.'[131] Peters thought Young 'was very patient, very meticulous on how he created his shots. He was a gentleman, he had a good sense of humour. I felt he was fatherly, I would have given him my full trust.'[132]

In the film, Bond blackmails nurse Patricia Fearing into the steam room after his ordeal on the traction table. Molly Peters kept fluffing her line, '"It'll stretch [instead of shrink] you back to size." I fluffed it more than once. Terence did get exasperated with me. Connery didn't show any impatience over it.'[133] Peters noted that Connery was protective of her, after finding her in tears for personal reasons one day he asked her, '"Who said anything to you? I'll go and sort them out."'[134] Her experience as a glamour model left her unperturbed by the nudity of the scene, 'Terence cleared the set. They put sticky plasters over you – that to me is more obscene than anything else.'[135] Peters enjoyed working with Connery, 'I was overawed; he is impressive. Very tall, very much in his prime physically.'[136] She remembered, 'He could be quite funny, waddling like Groucho Marx, mucking about with a hat, a towel around him.'[137]

The exterior of Shrublands was shot on location at Chalfont Park House. Broccoli's silver Rolls Royce can be seen with its distinctive number plate, CUB 1, in the background. When Bond deflects further liaisons with Fearing by saying 'another time, another place' Molly Peters was unaware the line was in fact a reference to Sean Connery's 1958 film starring Lana Turner.[138]

Fiona Volpe's explosive execution of Count Lippe was filmed at Silverstone racetrack as Stears recalled, 'We shot that sequence all for real. Real bike, real rockets and the car was doing 60, 70mph and the bike was doing about a hundred maybe (it had to be going that fast to get clear of the debris).'[139] Bob Simmons, who drove Lippe's car, threw himself clear just as it ran into the ditch and exploded. For a moment Young thought he had lost his key stuntman, but Simmons nonchalantly sidled over to the crew wondering what all the fuss was about.[140]

At Pinewood, Terence Young put Bond back in his element – a game of *chemin de fer* in a Nassau casino – in reality another stage set. In this scene Bond toys with Largo, dropping the word 'spectre' into conversation to provoke a reaction. Largo responds giving the old Mafia hex sign. Celi had no experience of the classic card game:

> I have never been able to play a game of cards and they were compelled to tell me all from the beginning to end. The only reason why I had that cool and detached face was that I didn't care at all. I was completely out of it. As I said, 'Banco!' everybody said, 'Look how that one says "Banco!"'[141]

Celi explained the spell is soon broken, 'Even now when I go near a casino they recognise me. "God, now we will have that one who gambles so well." But as soon as I ask, "Which is the red and which is the black", they understand that I am a totally harmless monster.'[142] Also making Hitchcockian appearances in the same scene are producer Kevin McClory – lying on a couch blowing out cigar smoke as Bond enters the caisse – and McClory's wife, Bobo Sigrist – the blonde Bond dodges as he enters the casino.

During post-production Terence Young realised, 'The underwater does not lend itself to a Bond picture. You cannot move somebody underwater at more than four miles an hour without his mask coming off.'[143] Norman Wanstall, the Oscar-winning sound man, agreed with Young, 'All the underwater stuff was silent. Peter [Hunt] said, "This is going to be terribly tedious." I had all these great sounds. I thought I was really going to make my mark on this film.'[144] Wanstall recalled attending a rough-cut screening with Cubby Broccoli and John Barry:

> I put over the underwater scenes a lot of the stuff I had made. John Barry was there and I remember him saying 'Christ I'm glad I came to this run. I was going to put fifteen trombones over that. I was going to make it all bassy and deep. But you're doing it – we don't want to clash.'[145]

Unfortunately, when the sound was mixed with Barry's score a lot of Norman's tracks were lost, 'His stuff was drowning mine and hours of work mixing underwater sounds never got heard.'[146]

John Barry's immediate reaction when he came to score the picture was that 'Thunderball' would make the worst song title of all time, proclaiming 'What does it mean?' The Italians had christened James Bond 'Mr. Kiss Kiss Bang Bang' and Barry with lyricist Leslie Bricusse took this phrase and used it, 'It's a very sultry song. Dionne Warwick was over here and she said "I'd love to do it."'[147] Later, Shirley Bassey also recorded the song for the film. Barry was disappointed when he learnt from the producers that 'Mr. Kiss Kiss Bang' Bang had been rejected, 'United Artists said we have to go with "Thunderball" as the title. There was always this big argument from United Artists that they loaded on to Cubby and Harry, "Do you know how many millions of dollars of publicity we get every time that title comes across the radio?"'[148] Bassey's company, SVB Ltd, promptly sued the producers and it emerged during the court case that Bassey had recorded the song in October 1965 for a fee of £500.[149] Johnny Cash also submitted a song called 'Thunderball' for consideration but it was not used.[150]

Matt Monro's manager and newly emerging lyricist Don Black was asked to write the title track and, like Barry, was perplexed by it, 'The first thing I did was look Thunderball up in a dictionary and it wasn't there.'[151] The song was eventually recorded by Welsh singer Tom Jones who had just had a big hit with 'What's New Pussycat?' Barry recalled, 'That was a momentous occasion, the recording session for "Thunderball." Tom, I believe, fainted on that last note.'[152]

Title designer Maurice Binder was back after being away from the series, due to 'having a bit of a ruckus at the time with the producers.'[153] The climax of the pre-title sequence inspired him, 'It was an underwater picture. The last scene before the titles had this jet of water coming from Bond's Aston Martin at these guys who were trying to shoot at him. So that filled the screen with water and we segued into our titles.'[154] Binder was inspired in other ways too. While drinking in Raymond's Revue Bar, a gentleman's establishment in London's Soho, he saw two girls swimming in a tank above the bar.[155] In July 1965 Binder shot the title sequence with Micky de Rauch, Billie Bater and Jean McGrath.[156] Using the Pinewood tank to shoot the underwater scenes, Binder remembered filming the girls:

They were underwater swimmers but they balked at being photographed in the nude. I said, 'Go put the make-up on' and suddenly these two black-and-white minstrel girls came out, all nude. I said, 'I thought you didn't want to appear nude' and they said, 'This is not us.' They had so much black paint on they felt they were fully clothed.[157]

Binder shot the girls using black-and-white film against a white background and then shot bubbles against a black background, allowing him to alter the colour at will.[158]

Post-production on the epic film took so long that the premiere at the Odeon Leicester Square, scheduled for 21 October 1965, had to be cancelled.[159]

Kevin McClory's lawyer, Peter Carter-Ruck, remembered a last-minute row between McClory and Broccoli and Saltzman regarding the former's main title credit.[160] *Thunderball* was credited as being produced by Kevin McClory and presented by Harry Saltzman and Albert R. Broccoli. At a preview screening it became a heated argument with Saltzman stating, ironically, 'We must not get emotional'.[161] Joining his wife half-an-hour into the screening, on being told the excitement he had missed, Carter-Ruck replied, 'It was nothing like the excitement which I have been experiencing in Harry Saltzman's office.'[162]

Released initially in Tokyo on 9 December 1965 and in the US on 22 December, *Thunderball* would open lavishly in London on 29 December at two cinemas simultaneously: the Pavilion and the Rialto. Stars who attended both premieres included Claudine Auger, Adolfo Celi, Luciana Paluzzi, Martine Beswick, Guy Doleman and *Goldfinger* Bond girls Tania Mallet and Honor Blackman. Desmond Llewelyn also attended, 'It was thanks to Kevin [McClory] that *Thunderball* was my first premiere which he invited me to.' Again, Sean Connery was not present.

Bondmania was in full force when NBC aired their documentary, *The Incredible World of James Bond*, on 26 December 1965. Anticipation for the next 007 adventure was at an all-time high. The film followed the literary Bond to his Scottish roots in Glencoe and on to London, and looked at the then embryonic Bond marketing phenomenon, as well as featuring footage from the Bahamian set of *Thunderball* and scenes shot at Pinewood. With promotion like this *Thunderball* was a success of phenomenal proportions. Until the release of *Skyfall* (2012) inflation adjusted it remained the highest grossing James Bond film. With a worldwide gross of $141.2 million, James Bond really was everywhere.

On 18 April 1966, at the Santa Monica Civic Auditiorium, John Stears won the Oscar for Best Visual Effects at the thirty-ninth Academy Awards, beating the other nominated film *The Greatest Story Ever Told* (1965). Presented by Dorothy Malone, Ivan Tors collected the award for John Stears and said,

'I accept the award for John Stears with gratitude. In his name I would like to thank those who had assisted him, especially Jordan Klein, the underwater engineer, and the underwater team, Cubby Broccoli and Harry Saltzman for giving them such a fine opportunity to do the fantastic.'[163] Stears later commented, 'Oscars are a thing which if they happen, they happen. I don't think you must ever go into a production saying, "I am going to win an Oscar." But I was very happy.'[164] It was the James Bond films who schooled a generation of effects technicians and designers and laid the foundation for the blockbuster films which were to follow. Indeed Stears won a second Oscar over a decade later for his groundbreaking work on George Lucas's *Star Wars* (1977).

Sean Connery had been absent from the premieres and felt the film was more about the apex of technology. Connery longed for more character:

> We've reached the limit as far as size and gimmicks are concerned. In *Thunderball* we have Bond underwater for about 40 per cent of the time, and there is a love scene underwater, and attacks by aqua-paras from the sky, and two-man submarines under the sea, and Bond is menaced by sharks. Instead of the Aston Martin we have a hydrofoil disguised as a cabin cruiser, and Bond escapes with a self-propelling jet set attached to his back. So all the gimmicks now have been done. And they are expected. What is needed now is a change of course – more attention to character and better dialogue.[165]

At the time of *Thunderball*'s release Connery was rueful about stardom:

> I find that fame tends to turn one from an actor and a human being into a piece of merchandise, a public institution. Well, I don't intend to undergo that metamorphosis. This is why I fight so tenaciously to protect my privacy, to keep interviews like this one to an absolute minimum, to fend off prying photographers who want to follow me around and publicise my every step and breath. The absolute sanctum sanctorum is my home, which is and will continue to be only for me, my wife, my family and my friends. I do not and shall not have business meetings there or acquaintances or journalists. When I work, I work my full stint, but I must insist that my private life remain my own. I don't think that's too much to ask.[166]

Future Bonds for Connery were going to be a chore, 'I make a Bond every fourteen months. You must realise that no one imagined that Bond would take off in such a phenomenal way. What you do is close your eyes and ears a lot and carry on the best you can.'[167] He continued:

> I have only two more Bonds to do. On *Her Majesty's Secret Service* and possibly *You Only Live Twice*. They would like to start *On Her Majesty's Secret Service* in Switzerland in January [1966], but I'm not sure I'll be free in time and I don't want to rush it, although they say the snow will be at its best then. I'm not going to rush anything anymore.'[168]

It was clear Connery was thinking of quitting the mink-lined cage, 'I'd like to see someone else tackle Bond, I must say though I think they'd be crazy to do it.'[169] Connery was aware of what made him happy, 'I can still call the shots. The only thing that counts anyway is your own assessment. The satisfaction it gives you and also how much money you're making because nobody pretends that you're going to eat notices.'[170]

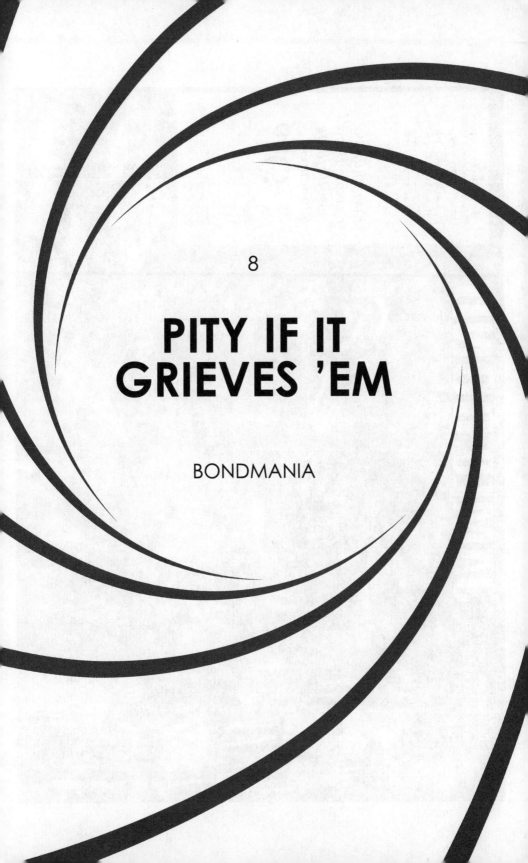

8

PITY IF IT
GRIEVES 'EM

BONDMANIA

Complete set, packed
with action and intrigue

JAMES BOND

and the world of 007

Get a realistic 4-scene stage,
10 lifelike handcolored figures
—plus all these working units:

1. Laser-beam Torture Machine
2. Flame-shooting Dragon Tank
3. M's bulletproof Office Desk
4. Revolving-top Pool Table
5. Customized Aston-Martin Car
6. Two-section Hydrofoil Yacht

*Everything to
recreate Bond's
most thrilling
adventures*

All
this
for
only
$9.99

Help James Bond challenge ruthless villains and their
running gadgets. Every item authentically reproduced from actual settings and characters in 4
great movies: "From Russia with Love," Dr. No,"
"Goldfinger," and his latest—"Thunderball."
With orders from M, head of British counterspies,
007 sees each gun or other device match each
villain's hideout. There he must face fiendish machines. Beat your cleverness lends a hand—and Bond
soon turns the tables on the bad guys (hurray!).
22x25½-in. stage. Plastic units. 3¼-in. figures.
49 N 5980—Shipping wt. 3 lbs. 8 oz . . . Set $9.99

LASER MACHINE
...spring-powered slab
moves Bond towards
the deadly "ray"

DRAGON TANK
...spews out plastic
flames when you
press the turret

M's DESK
bulletproof "glass"
goes up to protect
Britain's top agent

FLIPS

POOL TABLE
...top flips over to control panel
and map of Fort Knox

ASTON-MARTIN CAR
...bullet shield rises, license plate rotates

"DISCO VOLANTE" YACHT
...drops stern section
for fast getaway on hydrofoils

ODDJOB

DR. NO

BOND
IN DINNER
SUIT

SCENE FROM "THUNDERBALL"

"M'S" OFFICE

DR. NO'S LABORATORY

BOND
IN SCUBA
OUTFIT

DOMINO

BOND WITH
SCOPE RIFLE

LARGO

"M"

MISS
MONEY-
PENNY

GOLDFINGER'S LODGE

GOLDFINGER

The phenomenal success of the 007 films by the mid sixties birthed a pop cultural boom dubbed 'Bondmania'. In 1965 British paperback sales of Fleming's James Bond novels peaked at 6,782,000.[1] Eon's film series was the first bona fide marketing juggernaut. The movies now generated significant income away from the theatres as a 1966 report set out:

> Evidently impressed by the more than \$100,000,000 worth of products gar-
> nered by the Licensing Corporation of America on goods linked to industry
> productions – an indication of the industry's changing attitude toward licens-
> ing – once viewed as a mere promotional ploy, like the 'tie-in', with its
> primary value gauged by the box office [success] it stimulated. With the
> take from sales on hard and soft goods soaring, vidseries and features seem
> to be commercials for the products, which once were used to plug the film.
> At present, licensing has grown to such proportions, even actors ask for a
> percentage of the take (007 Sean Connery, a shrewd bargainer, gets a slice of
> the licensing fee derived from the sale of Bond-linked products). 150 Bond
> Items Initiation of licensing as big business came when United Artists' Bond
> films captured the atavistic instincts of the global film-going public. Via an
> arrangement with Saltzman-Broccoli, the twin titans of the Bond lode, and
> United Artists, LCA was able to line up more than 150 products branded
> with the 007 mark. Capitalisation on the Bondmania came relatively late in
> the series, (*Goldfinger* and *Thunderball*), but even so, more than \$50,000,000
> in product links are being mined by the participants.[2]

Harry Saltzman explained, 'There's such a demand and in order to channel the demand, we've had to form companies in association with our distributors, the Ian Fleming Estate, with the various people who have profit participa-tions. But it has been very gratifying that it's a worldwide movement.'[3] Cubby Broccoli was keen to outline, 'Our primary interest in the inception of this was exploitation of the picture. When we went into the merchandising ideas, it did develop bigger than we planned it. It's very beneficial publicity-wise. Less so in a merchandising way for Harry and myself.'[4] Indeed Saltzman felt, 'If we were less creative producers and more businessmen producers we'd probably have had a larger piece.'[5]

Prior to *Dr. No* the spy film had traditionally been linked to wartime exploits. After *Goldfinger* and *Thunderball* a worldwide spy craze began with, at its peak, more than thirty secret agent films being released in the USA during 1966;[6] there were also endless spy spoofs and television series. While there are too many films and products to mention, a few had direct connections to the originators of Bond.

Norman Felton, the successful producer of television hit *Dr. Kildare*, came across Ian Fleming's non-fiction travel articles later collated as THRILLING CITIES.[7] The producer had an idea for a new television programme and in October 1962 met with Fleming in New York. Fleming etched out his ideas on eleven Western Union Telegram blanks, detailing characters and attributes as he set out developing the series. In early 1964 Felton teamed up with Sam Rolfe to announce *Ian Fleming's Solo* – an international spy series set in the thrilling cities of the globe.[8] Eon promptly fired a legal shot claiming it infringed upon their Mr. Solo character from *Goldfinger*. The television producers backed down, renaming their show *The Man from UNCLE*, but retaining the name Fleming had coined for the lead character – Napoleon Solo.[9] The SPECTRE-like acronym 'UNCLE.' stood for United Network Command for Law Enforcement.

MGM produced the very successful television series, which ran from 1964 to 1968. Robert Vaughn played Napoleon Solo who teamed up with Russian agent – Ilya Kuryakin, played by David McCallum. The pair answered to Leo G. Carroll's M-like Alexander Waverley. They were usually pitted against agents of THRUSH (novelised to mean: Technological Hierarchy for the Removal of Undesirables and the Subjugation of Humankind). Several MGM feature films expanded from the television footage were released including *The Spy With My Face* featuring Senta Berger and *To Trap a Spy* with Bond girl Luciana Paluzzi. In 1966 a short-lived television spin-off series *The Girl from UNCLE* starred Stephanie Powers; the character she played was called April Dancer – another Ian Fleming moniker.[10] In 1983 a television film *The Return of the Man from UNCLE* brought the original lead actors back. This time they were joined by none other than George Lazenby, whose character was named J.B. and drove a silver birch Aston Martin DB5 wearing a white tuxedo. In 2015 a feature film titled *The Man from UNCLE* was released, directed by Guy Ritchie; it starred Henry Cavill as Napoleon Solo, the runner-up to Daniel Craig in the 2005 casting call for Bond.

Ian Fleming's other non-fiction work THE DIAMOND SMUGGLERS was also subject to film development. Commissioned by Percy Sillitoe of private security firm, International Diamond Smuggling Organization (IDSO), Fleming wrote a true-ish life account about the illicit gem trade in South Africa and the surrounding region. Based on the activities of IDSO agent John Collard, Fleming would grant another fictional agent the initials J.B. – this time standing for John Blaize. The story was published in book form in 1957 and the film rights were immediately bought by the Rank Organization for £12,500. Producer George Willoughby eventually obtained the rights and set about developing his own film. Willoughby had worked with Cubby Broccoli on *Hell Below Zero* (1954), as well as with director Terence Young on *Action of the Tiger* (1957), which had also starred Sean Connery. At some point, according to Willoughby:

> Fleming himself wrote for the Rank Organization a film treatment on this subject, and, although he used the name of John Blaize for the hero, his treatment had, nevertheless, very little to do with the actual articles he wrote for *The Sunday Times*. Our basic storyline would be based mainly on the treatment written by Ian Fleming himself.[11]

British star Richard Todd partnered in the project and a number of writers became involved. Chief amongst these was Kingsley Amis, an acknowledged Fleming fan and author of the first serious appreciation of Fleming's work THE JAMES BOND DOSSIER (1965), as well as the first published continuation Bond novel COLONEL SUN (1968). Alas, the project has yet to come to fruition.

On 22 April 1966, *The Poppy Is Also A Flower* was televised on ABC in the US. Produced by Euan Lloyd and directed by Terence Young the film was based on an idea by Ian Fleming and concerned the growing problem of the opium trade. The picture was partly funded by the United Nations and therefore a number of international stars including Trevor Howard, Rita Hayworth, Marcello Mastroianni, Anthony Quayle, Omar Sharif and Eli Wallach starred for reduced fees. Harold Sakata also made an appearance.

In 1962 Harry Saltzman optioned the right to make a film of Len Deighton's THE IPCRESS FILE, featuring a chippy spy who is caught up in espionage bureaucracy. The agent was unnamed in the books but for the films was called Harry Palmer (apocryphally after the Bond producer). Presented by Saltzman, but produced by Charles Kasher, three Harry Palmer films were made during the sixties. *The Ipcress File* (1965), directed by Sidney J. Furie, featured the work of Bond alumni: Ken Adam, John Barry and Peter Hunt. *Funeral in Berlin* (1966) was directed by Guy Hamilton and *Billion Dollar Brain* (1967) directed by Ken Russell and featuring opening titles by Maurice Binder. They were produced outside the Eon fold by Saltzman's Lowndes Productions Ltd, which signed emerging star Michael Caine to play Palmer. Steven Saltzman explained the allure Deighton's work had on his father, 'Harry liked the anti-hero. I think there's a very good link between Harry's films with *Look Back in Anger* and the 'kitchen sink' dramas. There was this kind of grit in the throat that he kept going in the sixties with the series of Len Deighton movies.'[12] Author Len Deighton felt there was nothing kitchen sink about Saltzman's life, especially his Mount Street home:

> Not a typical mews, it must have been totally rebuilt for the rooms were quite large and light. Various works of art and paintings in evidence. Adjoining there was the comfortably large dining room. Usually Harry took everyone out for dinner but if he gave dinner at home it was very formal with cut-glass decanters and shiny silverware.[13]

However, exposure to Saltzman convinced Deighton of one thing, film was a producer-led enterprise:

> The producer chose the subject, bought the story rights, briefed the screen-writer, raised the money, employed the director and chose the actors and the technical team. And it was the producer who had to understand the budget estimates and who kept the cost in check by adding or cutting elements of locations and corresponding studio rents. And, not least of the worries, keep-ing peace with the various trade unions.[14]

Steven Saltzman thought for his father:

> it was a complete natural progression, almost like he said, 'Well, this is not glamour business at all.' You're in the trenches, people are employees, they're not paid well and they can be hit and they can be hurt – they're at risk. He didn't ever feel that really came through with Bond. Bond was never going to die and nobody who ever saw a Bond film or read a Bond book ever thought he was really at risk. With Harry Palmer there was risk at every turn, the most personal, emotional risk.[15]

This was borne out for Steven by the performance of Michael Caine:

> I remember being at Pinewood and Michael was showing me the make-up on his wrists that were used when he was attached in the brain-washing scene and he said, 'I can't take a shower, I can't go for a bath, I have to keep this as it is because it's got to be the same in shot after shot after shot.' I remember seeing his wrists and realising that was difference between [Bond and Palmer]. This guy here is at risk.[16]

Caine remembered Saltzman 'talked about my seven-year contract in numbers I could not comprehend.'[17] Steven Saltzman remembered, 'For his birthday Harry gave him his contract, and said, "I have a present for you" and he tore it up.'[18] Decades later, Caine would ressurect Harry Palmer for *Midnight in St. Petersburg* (1995) and *Bullet to Beijing* (1996). These were not produced by Saltzman, who had passed away in 1994, but would co-star Sean Connery's son Jason.

Columbia Pictures, having lost Bond in 1961 to UA, did their best to make up for it. Just as the Bond films inspired hundreds of imitators, the Fleming novels created a demand for a flood of spy literature. These included the Matt Helm books by Donald Hamilton which formed the basis for Columbia's spy franchise. The producer of these films was none other than Cubby's former partner, Irving Allen, who stated, 'Originally we had [the first film] *The Silencers* written as a melodrama but we decided after we had a script that we couldn't copy the Bonds.'[19] Dean Martin was signed to star and got a large participation in the films. The series ran to four films, *The Silencers* and *Murderers' Row* (both 1966), *The Ambushers* (1967) and *The Wrecking Crew* (1969), as well as a weak television series in the mid-seventies. The films were wild romps with no pretence of the seriousness of their source novels with Dean Martin often crooning songs throughout. The initial film was directed by Phil Karlson, United Artists' preferred choice to helm *Dr. No*, and starred Victor Buono – a contender for *Goldfinger* – as the villain. Interestingly, during this period, Allen still had an office at Eon's South Audley Street headquarters and the then art director Peter Lamont remembered, 'We used to have meetings with Cubby up in his office and Irving was always earwigging. When he did those Matt Helm pictures some of the stuff we discussed was then filmed [by Allen].'[20] If James Bond represented The Beatles of the genre, Matt Helm might be considered The Monkees.

Cubby's former boss, Charles K. Feldman, retained the rights to the first James Bond novel CASINO ROYALE. Initially the adaptation was to have been to a serious thriller. However as the spy craze peaked, Charles K. Feldman decided all that was left to do with 007 was a send-up in the style of his 1965 hit *What's New Pussycat?* Five directors were credited: Joe McGrath, Robert Parrish, John Huston, Val Guest and Ken Hughes (Richard Talmadge and Anthony Squire also managed events on set). The film was the concoction of the following screenwriters: Wolf Mankowitz, Michael Sayers, Ben Hecht, Woody Allen, Terry Southern and Billy Wilder. The many stars included Woody Allen, Peter Sellers, Ursula Andress, David Niven, William Holden, Deborah Kerr, Charles Boyer,

John Huston, George Raft, Joanna Pettet, Jacqueline Bisset, Orson Welles, Peter O'Toole and Jean-Paul Belmondo. The film had a score by Burt Bacharach with lyricist Hal David penning the Oscar-nominated classic 'The Look of Love'. Feldman felt his film 'could shatter the "Bond" image, because of the satire we have created [part of which was written by Sellers]. But *Casino Royale* is not just a Bond satire, it is a film on its own. I think it will be a bonanza!'[21] Peter Sellers was hopeful, too, when asked about the similarities to Bond, 'Box office-wise, hopefully, but actually this is completely different – a new kind of aim. The new innovations are in the way it's being shot, colour, technically – and the script. I'm only in one section of the story. It might well be that *Casino Royale* will have a whole new approach to film-making.'[22] The film was perhaps the apex of the spy craze with a variety of surreal scenes, like a flying saucer landing in London's Trafalgar Square; John Huston playing M in a red wig; Deborah Kerr as a mad Scotswoman; and Woody Allen in a dual role as Jimmy Bond and the head of deadly organisation FANG. Broccoli said in response, 'We're very good friends – have been for years. Sure, he's doing a take on. But we don't object to it.'[23] Released on 13 April 1967, months before *You Only Live Twice*, it marked the first 'Battle of the Bonds'. However, the film cost £4,000,000 and flopped, damaging the market for spy films, which began to collapse in on itself. It would be the last film Charles K. Feldman would ever make.

Operation Kid Brother (1967) marked the absolute surrealist height of the spy craze, in some ways topping *Casino Royale*. Directed by Alberto De Martino, this Italian po-faced spoof had the gall to star Sean Connery's younger brother Neil as an international doctor/spy. The picture aped Bond further in its casting: Adolfo Celi, Daniela Bianchi, Bernard Lee, Anthony Dawson and even Miss Moneypenny herself – Lois Maxwell – playing Miss Maxwell. Maxwell recalled Sean was 'furious'[24] with her and Lee, as he thought the picture did nothing more than manipulate the Connery family. 'I told him I was making more money in that one film than I had made in all of the official Bond films put together.'[25]

Neil Connery, a plasterer – who referred to Sean as 'the brother'[26] – was heard on Scottish radio by Terence Young discussing union matters. Realising Neil sounded exactly like his brother he reported it to Italian producer Dario Sabatello, who met Connery in the Caledonian Hotel in Edinburgh. Neil remembered, Sabatello asked him, '"How would you like to act?" I said, "An actor? Wow, I'd look upon it as a challenge." That's the way I do everything.'[27] Eventually Neil's services were secured for $5,000.[28] The film featured a catchy song, sung by Christy and composed by Ennio Morricone called 'Man For Me

(O.K. Connery)'. Neil remembered, 'When I was doing my test they said "OK, Connery, OK", so that's what they called the film in Italy.'[29]

Harry Saltzman was sanguine about such films, 'We have stopped several kind of imitations that were harmful already. We try to protect ourselves. There are nine Italian motion pictures being made, quickies, they're made in ten to twelve days. They don't hurt us – people know they aren't Bond pictures.'[30]

The spy craze eventually dissipated, but all of the merchandising and attention would have a huge impact on one man. After all, Sean Connery was still 007.

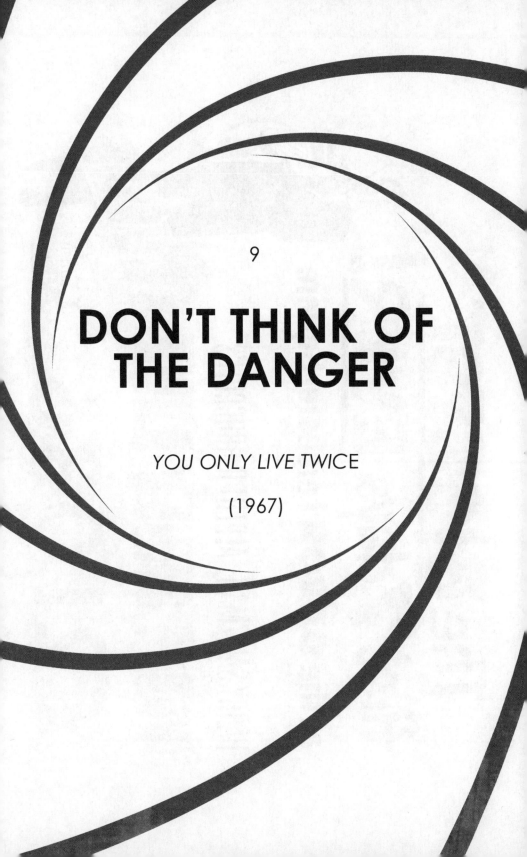

9

DON'T THINK OF THE DANGER

YOU ONLY LIVE TWICE

(1967)

The **BIGGEST** **EVER!**

first **7** days

at the **ODEON** Leicester Square

HARRY SALTZMAN and ALBERT R. BROCCOLI'S

"YOU ONLY LIVE TWICE"

£21,036

RELEASED THROUGH
UNITED ARTISTS
A Transamerica COMPANY

n April 1966, while *Thunderball* was still breaking box office records around the world, *Variety* announced the first signs of fissures in the Eon camp:

> Although many observers have already applied the simple arithmetic of division to the recent behaviour of Harry Saltzman and Albert 'Cubby' Broccoli, the dual titans of Bondism, and deduced that their paths have indeed diverged, details of the as yet unconfirmed arrangement remain clouded in rumor. To clear the air, it's this: separation but not divorce. As described by one source, Saltzman's and Broccoli's parting of the ways is an 'amicable arrangement', by which properties held in concert will be split between them, a process still in negotiation, but the pair will remain partners in their ownership of the Ian Fleming properties and produce Bond pix as a team.[1]

The report acknowledged:

> the complexities of dividing the Bond empire would be too involved, probably requiring a UN council meeting to apportion the proceeds from the four-picture Bond lode, which has, thus far, earned rentals conservatively estimated at $52,755,000 with the final results of 007's latest adventure, *Thunderball*, yet to be tallied. Add to this the estimated yearly gross of more than $50,000,000 in Bond merchandising, which includes more than a hundred separate products from some sixteen manufacturers.[2]

United Artists respected the producing capabilities of Broccoli and Saltzman. They had done more than package the Bond films; they had kept the formula alive and increasingly profitable, while attempting to control costs. They were more than just studio-appointed producers. The pair would constantly renegotiate their deal to reflect this and, by 1967, their fee per picture had risen to $420,000 plus 75 per cent of the profits.[3] Seemingly their separation would not affect production of the Bonds; they would informally be the key producer on alternate films, each one being involved; one having final say.[4] Broccoli took the producing reins for *You Only Live Twice*. He acknowledged the difficulties leading to this moment, 'I knew that Harry Saltzman and I wouldn't be able to conceal our own disagreements much longer. It wasn't just a conflict of personalities, while other partnerships have survived. It was, at least the way I saw it, two totally contrasting attitudes to Bond.'[5]

The results of Bondmania and the spy craze had not gone unnoticed by Sean Connery. By October 1965 the man who was Bond was in full-scale revolt, in *Variety*-speak:

Sean Connery sez he will not report for his next James Bond pic in February. He's contracted to Saltzman-Broccoli for two more but will not return to Bond-age unless the pacts are rewritten to limit the skeds to twelve weeks lensing. (Connery claims the most recent, *Thunderball*, required five months.) 'There's no time for anything else,' he maintains. 'And I spent a session in the hospital between 'em once. I don't intend to do that again.'[6]

By December 1965 it seemed the producers had taken the hint as the trade press reported to the world:

Sean Connery can cancel plans of beefing to Cubby Broccoli and Harry Saltzman about the skedded Feb. start of [*On*] *Her Majesty's Secret Service*, to have been his next James Bond role. He was going to give 'em an ultimatum on the pic, plus shorter working weeks, on his return to England this month. But Broccoli arrived in town yesterday and nonchalantly revealed, 'We have decided to accommodate him and have delayed the film until late next year.'[7]

The producers acknowledged the strain in relations with their star, as Broccoli told the press, '"We have a contract with him for two more films." After those? "It's a big worry," he said, very unworried. "We'll make one-a-year until kingdom come."'[8]

Broccoli was unfazed by Connery's recalcitrance, 'Although we only have Sean Connery for two more films (as of now), we are not going to stop. They'll be continued – like the "Tarzana" – after Edgar Rice Burroughs stopped writing them. We own six more and the rights to do more.'[9] The star was not making things easy, as the industry press noted:

Sean Connery is staging his own private cliffhanger as to whether or not he will sign for Saltzman's and Broccoli's fifth Bond issue. Connery and his lawyers have been pummelling Saltzman and Broccoli to up his current 5 per cent of the profits ante to an 'unspecified' percentage of the gross. This latter bid is a switch from Connery's recently reported demand for 10 per cent of the profits.'[10]

It seemed Connery's campaign had been launched much earlier, 'During the filming of *Thunderball*, he asked to renegotiate his contract after more than half the film was in the can. The exact results of his well-timed demand are not known, but reportedly he settled for a hefty cash settlement.'[11]

The producers were anxious to accommodate their star, at least for the next film. Firstly, they delayed *On Her Majesty's Secret Service* again by choosing to make *You Only Live Twice* beforehand. This meant they did not have to commence shooting in February 1966 in Switzerland and could defer production until later in the summer.[12] Secondly, they agreed to lighten the schedule for Connery, publicly stating he would not be needed for the complete sixteen-week shoot.[13] It was also the producers' intention to make the story more human. In February 1966 Broccoli claimed, 'This one will be less gimmicky and more realistic, since the imitations have gotten so gimmicky. Bond will use his head much more, rather than mechanical things – although there will be some gimmicks.'[14] Connery, for the moment, had been appeased.

In July 1966 halfway through shooting, Connery was released from his contract, in the hope that a new deal could be reached for the next Bond.[15] Despite Connery's public acrimony with Broccoli and Saltzman, for UA's David Picker, 'It was a surprise. My thoughts were this was a bad idea and that's obviously what led to our finally coming to understand what the problem was. We were expecting another film from Sean and he didn't want to do it.'[16]

During the production of *You Only Live Twice*, United Artists also underwent a change of direction. The profitable film company was eventually purchased by the $2.4 billion insurance concern Transamerica Corporation, led by John R. Beckett.[17] United Artists was to be headed by Arnold and David Picker and Max Youngstein; Arthur Krim and Richard Benjamin remained on board and the film company continued with complete creative freedom from its parent.[18] The familiar United Artists' logo was joined by the Transamerica Corporation 'tree' at the start of each new film.[19]

In December 1965 at the Tokyo premiere of *Thunderball*, Broccoli told *Variety* that he would be returning to Japan in January or February 1966 to scout locations for *You Only Live Twice*, which would have a budget 'substantially less'[20] than that spent on *Thunderball*, which had gone over budget and schedule due to the elaborate underwater scenes. He also announced director Lewis Gilbert would helm the picture.[21]

Gilbert was a reliable filmmaker and throughout the fifties and sixties he had directed numerous British pictures, some of which he had also written and produced. Lewis Gilbert's latest film *Alfie* was causing a stir – a year later he, as producer, was nominated for a Best Picture Academy Award. Gilbert had initially declined the challenge of directing the fifth Bond film, 'It would be like Elizabeth Taylor's fifth husband. I'd know what do but I wouldn't know how to make it any different.'[22] Broccoli's response made him think again, '"You're making a mistake. You have the world's biggest audience and it's waiting to see what kind of hash you make of it."'[23] Gilbert understood the benefits Bond could have on his career, 'Directing is very national. You tend to think only in terms of what will go in Britain. You're not practised into thinking what will go in Cambodia and Hong Kong. Cubby and Harry know. They've become experts.'[24]

Gilbert was aware that a James Bond film could place him on the international map. Lewis felt Cubby took the lead on the picture because Harry had reneged on a promise given to Sean, 'If you crossed [Sean] or he suspected that you weren't being straight with him, then you were off his list for good and Harry was definitely off his list.'[25]

With Ted Moore unavailable as he was photographing *A Man For All Seasons* – for which he would win an Academy Award – the producers hired acclaimed director of photography Freddie Young. He had won two Oscars for *Lawrence of Arabia* (1962) and *Doctor Zhivago* (1965) – both directed by David Lean with whom, incidentally, Broccoli had been developing a non-Bond, Boer War project entitled *Rags Of Glory*.[26]

New writers were also involved. In November 1965 Academy Award-nominated US screenwriter Sydney Boehm delivered a treatment closely based on the novel.[27] American Harold Jack Bloom (who in 1955 had written an episode of *Captain Gallant of the Foreign Legion*, a television show produced by Harry Saltzman) then took over writing chores, retaining elements of Boehm's treatment.

YOU ONLY LIVE TWICE – Fleming's twelfth Bond book was published in the UK on 28 March 1964. Bond – mourning his wife of a few hours, Tracy, killed by Blofeld at the end of the previous novel – is in danger of losing the confidence of M. He is sent on a diplomatic mission to secure secret Japanese–American cipher traffic that has been denied to the Service as the UK wanes as a world power. 007 is to be promoted to a four figure number, 7777, if he can obtain the signal intellegence, which is vital to British interests. Bond is to assassinate a wealthy foreign visitor who has set up a toxic 'garden of death' in a castle on the coast. In these killing grounds a foreigner named Dr. Guntram Shatterhand has facilitated the Japanese obsession with suicide. In a powerful moment Shatterhand is revealed to be none other than Ernst Stavro Blofeld, the man responsible for murdering Bond's wife. Bond learns about Japanese culture and goes undercover in an Ama fishing village, befriending Kissy Suzuki, who previously had a brief acting career in Hollywood. She is now a diving girl, accompanied by her pet cormorant named David – after the only man who was good to her in Los Angeles: David Niven. Bond thwarts Blofeld by causing a volcanic explosion, but is knocked out and loses his memory. He stays with Suzuki for some time and she becomes pregnant. But before Bond discovers this he begins to sense he must leave and heads for the Soviet port of Vladivostock.

Broccoli - armed with his new creative team: Lewis Gilbert, Harold Jack Bloom and Freddie Young, alongside regular production designer Ken Adam – embarked on a reconnaissance trip to Japan to scout locations. Adam recalled they were particularly looking for the ancient castle on the coast of Kyushu as described by Fleming in his novel, 'We covered about two-thirds of Japan in three weeks. We didn't find anything that Fleming talked about – poisonous gardens [or] castles.'[28] They flew over Japan in two small helicopters attempting to find what they were looking for. Gilbert recalled how on one occasion he and Freddie Young were greeted by an elderly pilot, 'He laid the map on the table, and as he pointed out our route his hand didn't stop shaking ... Cubby and Ken, enjoying our misery, were struggling not to laugh.'[29] The old man had trained during the war as kamikaze pilot![30]

On the southern island of Kyushu, Adam remembered that 'everybody became excited by this area, like a moonscape, of extinct and some not-so-extinct volcanoes.'[31] The perfect place for a villain's lair, Adam immediately did some thumbnail sketches, 'Cubby said to me "How much do you think it's going to cost? A million dollars?"'[32]

Adam recalled other unusual and exotic discoveries in Japan, 'We'd all experienced a relaxing massage with beautiful Japanese ladies, so they became part of the story, too. We heard about the "Ninjas" – a legendary commando unit, so we dedicated a scene to them as well.'[33] Two hours before they were due to catch their flight back to London, Broccoli was invited to witness a Ninja demonstration. The team cancelled their scheduled flight, only to learn later that the plane had crashed and killed everybody on board. It brought an unsettling new meaning to the title *You Only Live Twice*.[34]

Back in London, Bloom delivered a draft screenplay dated 23 February 1966.[35] Broccoli remembered that the writer 'came up with the idea of having these Ninja-like Japanese characters crawling all over Tokyo, and it just didn't work.'[36] Bloom left the picture and was replaced by popular children's author

Roald Dahl. Dahl had been developing a screenplay with director Robert Altman, *The Bells of Hell go Ting-a-ling-a-ling*, an air force drama for United Artists which was never produced.

Dahl had met Fleming several times and noted, 'There was a great red glow when Ian Fleming came into the room.'[37] He once described Fleming as 'a sparky, witty, caustic companion, full of jokes and also full of obscure bits of knowledge.'[38] Dahl's famous short story, LAMB TO THE SLAUGHTER, had been suggested to him by Fleming and the writers were both hard-drinkers and womanisers. Ironically Dahl was not a fan of YOU ONLY LIVE TWICE, describing it as 'tired, bad, Ian's worst book'.[39]

Dahl felt, 'If you've got enough money to live comfortably, there's no reason in the world to do a screenplay. It's an awful job,'[40] but he later claimed he needed the money and that's why he took the on the assignment. Dahl admitted that when he took the call from Broccoli, he 'really hadn't heard of him. I thought he was joking. After all, a man with the last name of a vegetable?'[41] Shortly after their conversation Dahl met with the producers in South Audley Street, 'Neither of them looked undernourished. Cubby Broccoli and Harry Saltzman were sitting in an enormous room where the telephones never stopped ringing.'[42] Dahl confessed he was not a James Bond fan; he'd only seen *Goldfinger*. '"You better see the others right away,"' one of the producers told Dahl. They added, '"We'll send them out to your house with a projector and someone to work it."'This was the first small hint I was to get of the swift, efficient, expansive way in which the Bond producers operated.'[43]

Broccoli and Saltzman negotiated a deal with Dahl's US representative, one of the most powerful dealmakers in Hollywood, Swifty Lazar. Terms were agreed before Dahl had even left the meeting and he immediately began working with Lewis Gilbert, whose initial response was 'Roald is an interesting writer for a Bond film – he's a bit quirky isn't he? He did have a reputation for not being easy to get on with but I got on very well with him.'[44] Gilbert also recalled that Dahl was handpicked for a specific reason, 'We needed his storytelling skill to strengthen Fleming's plot and his dark humour to complement it.'[45] Dahl enjoyed Gilbert's company, too, 'I've written quite a few films [since then] and he is the only director I ever worked with who is any kind of decent fellow. He not only helped on script conferences but had some good ideas and then left you alone.'[46] Dahl was instructed to deliver a first draft in eight weeks. This was to be followed by 'a second in four more [weeks] and a complete script in twenty weeks.'[47] The writer remembered attending two or three script conferences with the producers and amusingly 'Harry would usually nod off to sleep in the middle'.[48] His first twenty-eight page treatment was dated 20 May 1966.[49]

During 1965 the first astronauts walked in space and they did again in *You Only Live Twice*. Dahl has SPECTRE plotting to cause war between the USA and the Soviet Union by capturing their respective capsules in space. This is to be to the advantage of a 'new power' – essentially China. SPECTRE has devised a capture vehicle capable of being reusable and landing using reverse thrusters in a silo disguised as a volcano. The British Secret Service traces the mysterious craft to Japan and sends James Bond to investigate. As far-fetched as James Bond's latest mission sounded, it was like all Bond films before and after: rooted in reality. While Dahl was writing the screenplay astronauts were walking in space. In January 1966 a US air force bomber went missing off the coast of Spain with two atomic bombs on board, leading to speculation that an unfriendly nation might be at play. Said Broccoli, 'Both stories gave our scripts a strong flavour of authenticity.'[50]

Dahl was also told that the large volcano the production team had discovered in Japan should play a major part in the story. He claimed he never read any of Bloom's material, 'They had probably – and hadn't told me – commissioned a screenplay from him and it hadn't been any good, but had picked out that idea and possibly one or two others, which they had asked me to put in.'[51] Dahl was instructed by Broccoli to begin the film with Bond faking his own death, thereby throwing his enemies off the trail (rather like Jacques Bouvar in *Thunderball*).[52] Bloom was bitterly disappointed to discover his credit would be reduced to 'Additional material by'. Bloom claimed Dahl changed none of the action he had written and that he 'should have been given joint credit at the very least. Had that picture been done here [in Hollywood], I would have been properly credited but [the British] weren't crazy about using American writers. I was very disappointed.' Bloom said he 'made up everything you saw on screen' and until he was hired 'there was no story at all.'[53]

Roald Dahl went away with his family on holiday to Tenby for a week to finish the final screenplay.[54] Upon delivering the script he wrote to his UK agent, Armitage Watkins, announcing that Broccoli and Saltzman were thrilled with the draft but in fact he thought it to be 'the biggest load of bullshit I've ever put my hand to'.[55] Dahl was reluctant, however, to share the credit for this 'bullshit' with Bloom, 'I was told that there would be a share, and I said "Well, there's no way anyone's going to share the full credit." There was a little fight about that and they gave him what you see.'[56]

Meanwhile Connery continued to struggle with the public's perception of him. It became unbearable for him that the cinemagoers failed to differentiate Sean Connery from James Bond. By the time *You Only Live Twice* went into production, Connery was one of the most recognisable faces on the planet. His wife said it had become terrifying living with the public fanaticism, 'Every day, the conviction had become more deeply rooted – we had to have somewhere to get away from the torment of living in such a frenzied fishbowl.'[57] British documentary maker Alan Whicker was on hand throughout production making a documentary for the BBC. Connery expressed his frustrations, 'It's an invasion of one's privacy and I don't believe in any of that rubbish about the price of fame and all that sort of jazz.'[58] Connery didn't have a personal publicist either, 'It was around the same time as the Beatles. The difference was that they had four of them to deal with it.'[59]

When creating Bond's latest sexual conquests Dahl asked the producers, '"He wants a woman doesn't he to chase around and fall in love with?" They said, "Well three would be better!"'[60] By the fifth Bond film the producers had found a Bond girl formula. They told Dahl:

> So, you put in three girls. No more and no less. Girl number one is pro-Bond. She stays around roughly through the first reel of the picture. Then she is bumped off by the enemy, preferably in Bond's arms … Girl number two is anti-Bond. She works for the enemy and stays around throughout the middle third of the picture. She must capture Bond, and Bond must save himself by bowling her over with sheer sexual magnetism. This girl should also be bumped off, preferably in an original fashion. Girl number three is violently pro-Bond. She occupies the final third of the picture and she must on no account be killed. Nor must she permit Bond to take any lecherous liberties with her until the very end of the story. We keep that for the fade-out.[61]

United Artists chief Bud Ornstein flew to the Canary Islands to visit legendary Japanese actor Toshiro Mifune to persuade him to play Tanaka, but the Kurosawa star declined, instead choosing John Frankenheimer's *Grand Prix* (1966).[62] The production team headed back to Japan for a second time in May 1966 to audition actors for the oriental roles.[63] The locations were dependent upon the production using local girls, 'Not girls from Hawaii. Not half-caste girls. Not American-Japanese girls but – Japanese girls.'[64] Gilbert enlisted the translation help of Tetsuro Tamba, an actor who had previously starred in the director's film *The 7th Dawn* (1964).[65] He recommended Japanese actresses who possibly could pick up the language in a relatively short time. The two actresses selected were Akiko Wakabayashi and Mie Hama both contracted to Japanese distributor Toho

Studios.[66] They had previously worked together in *King Kong versus Godzilla* in 1962. Hama had a reputation as the Brigitte Bardot of Japan – one of the most photographed women in the Orient.[67] Gilbert remembered, 'We brought them to England three months before shooting and tried to get them to speak English. We put them with English families and sent them to school in the day.'[68] Tamba landed the part of Tanaka when Mifune declined.[69]

Mie Hama did not learn English well and assistant director William P. Cartlidge recalled:

> They were going to sack her. Tamba said, 'If you do it she is quite likely to commit suicide. Their culture is kind of different. She will be so ashamed she is likely to do herself in.' Cubby said, 'Well it's only a movie. We are not going to take that chance.'[70]

Hama was saved the humiliation by being given the less linguistically taxing role of Kissy Suzuki – later dubbed by the reliable Nikki van der Zyl.[71] Hama was grateful for the kindness shown to her:

> I was simply terrified when I was first given the part – the Bond films are the most popular ever to play in Japan and all my friends told me that the eyes of the world were upon me. Suddenly I'm on my way to England to appear with Sean Connery in utterly strange surroundings. I am grateful to him for his kindness, and although I only understood a few words of what he said I didn't need language to appreciate his charming manner.[72]

Akiko Wakabayashi was offered the larger role of Aki, a creation of the filmmakers, who in an earlier draft had been known as Suki. A resourceful Japanese Secret Service agent, Aki zips about Tokyo in a flashy Toyota sports car. Wakabayashi understood 'how popular the Bond films [were] in Japan [and] how important this picture could be for [my] career.'[73]

The role of SPECTRE agent Helga Brandt – the 'anti-Bond bitch'[74] – was given to established German actress Karin Dor. After testing successfully there were protracted negotiations at the Dorchester, during which Saltzman forced Dor's agent to take her client and leave.[75] Dor remembered, 'Saltzman came running down and took her arm, pulled her out [of the car] and said to me "You have the worst agent I have ever worked with!"'[76]

You Only Live Twice would finally reveal the true identity of SPECTRE head Ernst Stavro Blofeld. Having seen him with his back to camera in *From Russia*

With Love and *Thunderball*, voiced by Eric Pohlmann, the fifth Bond film would bring James Bond face-to-face with his cat-stroking adversary. Gilbert recalled:

> We get a cable from Harry who was in Los Angeles saying 'I've seen the most marvellous Czech actor and am sending him to England. We must start with him on Monday.' He turned up on his first morning and I couldn't believe it – he looked a bit like Father Christmas.[77]

Gilbert worked with Jan Werich for two days in November 1966, before it was decided that the actor was not malevolent enough for Blofeld. British character actor Donald Pleasence, who shared the same agent as Sean Connery, took over at short notice, 'I ended up spending three very, very intensive weeks playing that role to the bolts on the camera instead of another actor. Understandably, it really wasn't an enormously rewarding or fulfilling experience.'[78] Pleasence recalled, 'The producers liked my style, but didn't find me physically imposing.'[79] He suggested they use make-up to give Blofeld a physical defect, a facial scar to appear more menacing.[80] Cartlidge remembered, 'In those days you actually used glue – when it dried, it pinched your skin and made it look like an ugly scar. That's quite painful. He ended up with really severe bruising down his face.'[81] Ernst Stavro Blofeld with his white Persian cat, operating from a hollowed out volcano complete with monorail and a piranha pool for disposing of unwanted SPECTRE agents, became the archetypal James Bond villain, as well as the inspiration for Mike Myers's Dr. Evil three decades later.

The villainy would be completed by Teru Shimada as Mr. Osato and the tall Ronald Rich as the silent Hans who meets the same fishy fate as Helga Brandt.

Filming began at Pinewood Studios on 4 July 1966. Connery filmed his first scene in bed with actress Tsai Chin, shooting the pre-title sequence in which Bond fakes his own death. Chin later appeared as Madame Wu, one of the gamblers in the epic poker game in *Casino Royale* (2006).

One of the first sets on which Gilbert filmed was villain Osato's Japanese office. Adam created a modern space, like one would find at the top of a state-of-the-art skyscraper. Later the set would be ripped apart when Bond brawls with one of Osato's henchmen. Adam prepared for this, 'We had sliding paper screens that could be torn. I also introduced a lot of stainless steel around the bar, a tree, and a gun in the ceiling that follows Bond all the time. A modern version of the traditional Japanese idiom, inside a high-rise building.'[82] Adam had a collection of Japanese antiques imported to dress the set, and made replicas of them so they could become integral to the fight sequence.[83] Incidentally,

Connery shared the scene with the late professional wrestler Peter Maivia, who is the maternal grandfather of Dwayne 'The Rock' Johnson.

While *You Only Live Twice* was in production, the World Cup football tournament was taking place in the UK, which the hosting team ultimately went on to win. Lewis Gilbert and Sean Connery were both football fans, so it was a great delight during production when the England squad took time out to visit the cast and crew at Pinewood Studios on 12 July. The crew arrived in Japan three days before the final between England and Germany. Dor recalled she still had not received her working permit, 'Saltzman said, "If we don't get the working permit in the next day we have to pay you out and pick another actress."'[84] Dor watched the final on a portable television leant to her by Connery, the actor joked to her, '"If the Germans win Karin will never get the working permit!"'[85] The permit came through days later and she joined fellow cast members in Japan. As World Cup victory took the nation by storm, Gilbert recalled how the cast and crew organised their own match while on location, 'Cubby generously sent off for football kit, shirts, shorts and boots.' Broccoli was concerned when Connery fell and injured his ankle pointing out 'he's not insured for that sort of thing'.[86]

Connery's stay in Japan became a nightmare. As his plane touched down in Tokyo he was besieged by the waiting press. Broccoli greeted the paparazzi himself and pleaded with them to allow Connery some privacy. Associate producer Stanley Sopel said, 'When we were actually shooting there could be two or three hundred little chaps with their cameras, which would absolutely interfere with the filming. The Japanese police were completely powerless to control them.'[87] They even followed him into the toilet, 'Coming at me like a firing squad. I've never known it like this before. I knew Bond was popular – but this has been incredible.'[88] Eventually a team of twelve bodyguards was employed to guard Connery and escort him everywhere he went. Gilbert recalled, 'So the first morning we lined up these security men as Sean's car arrived, six on each side. Sean got out of the car and suddenly twelve guards whipped out twelve cameras and all started shooting him. Well, that was the end of the security guards.'[89]

Connery found the attention 'completely swamping. It became a terrible pressure, like living in a goldfish bowl.'[90] To cope with the increasing media interest a press conference was staged at the Tokyo Hilton, which was attended by over 300 journalists:

I'd been an actor since I was twenty-five, but the image that the press put out was that I just fell into this tuxedo and started mixing vodka martinis. And, of course, it was nothing like that at all. I'd done television, theatre, a whole slew of things. But it was more dramatic to present me as someone who had just stepped in off the street.[91]

James Bond had become, as Connery later observed, 'a Frankenstein monster'.[92]

In contrast, Claire Russhon said her husband, Colonel Charles Russhon, enjoyed working on all of the Bond films but one of the ones he found most interesting was *You Only Live Twice* because it required him to return to Japan where he recalled some of his World War II experiences.[93] She explained:

In preparing for the Bond filming, there was a reception for the Japanese officials at which a gentleman greeted Charles and said 'You have gained weight.' It was a Japanese general who explained that he was on the welcoming committee at Atsugi Air Base, when that first plane arrived [after the atomic bombing of Hiroshima and Nagasaki].[94]

In the film when 007 arrives in Tokyo he meets Aki who, in time, takes Bond to Tiger Tanaka, head of the Japanese secret service, in his underground complex. Aki and Bond rendezvous at a sumo-wrestling hall. Filmed at the Kuramae Kokugi-kan (National Sports Dome) Gilbert featured one of the top sumo fighters of the period, Sadoyanama, in a brief cameo role playing himself.[95] The production advertised a free show in order to fill the 12,000 seats with extras. Gilbert recalled Freddie Young invited David Lean, who happened to be passing through Tokyo.' ... He enjoyed himself so much he stayed all day. When he left he expressed his thanks for letting him do so by saying, "I don't get the chance to watch other directors work."'[96]

Ken Adam had originally demurred from using a Toyota motor car in the film due to snobbery towards Japanese brands.[97] Making a splash at the 1965 Tokyo Motorshow, the new Toyota 2000 GT, designed by Toshihiro Okada, was a vehicle fit for a Bond film.[98] The car was so new that the designers were asked to present sketches to Cubby Broccoli on one of his pre-production visits to Tokyo.[99] One of only two convertibles made, 2000 GT was driven by Aki in the film, saving Bond from Osato's hitmen. In reality, Wakabayashi could not drive so stuntmen in drag doubled her.[100] Close-ups purporting to be the Toyota shot back in Pinewood after the location shoot concluded were of a completely different car.[101]

In August 1966 Desmond Llewelyn flew to Japan to reprise the role of Q.[102] Once again, Major Boothroyd was dispatched into the field to brief 007 on his latest toy, an autogyro helicopter called Little Nellie, 'I was demonstrating all the stuff on Little Nellie and I managed to learn it … just. I breathed a sigh of relief that I finished explaining all the various gadgets.'[103] Watching Llewelyn explain the flamethrowers, heat-seeking missiles and machine guns was Little Nellie's real father, pilot Wing Commander Ken Wallis. Once Gilbert had shouted 'Cut!' Wallis remembered, 'Mr. Llewelyn said his lines [perfectly, but] he pointed out all the wrong gadgets!'[104]

Little Nellie had been discovered by Ken Adam while he was shaving one morning. Adam had heard Ken Wallis, an eccentric wing commander, being interviewed about his small one-man helicopter by Tony Scase on the BBC *Today* programme. The film's aviation advisor Hamish Mahaddie called Wallis and invited him to demonstrate the autogyro at Pinewood.[105] Adam was a fighter pilot during World War II so was naturally impressed with Wallis's contraption. Following the Pinewood demonstration on 14 June 1966,[106] Wallis remembered, 'Cubby Broccoli stood looking at it and said "We shall want it in Japan in six weeks' time."'[107] Wallis was in fact scheduled to appear in a James Bond-esque spoof in Brazil when he got the call.[108] Dahl soon found a place in the script for Little Nellie.

Inspired by the gadget-laden Aston Martin DB5, Wallis met with John Stears to discuss the weaponry that could be fitted to his craft, 'There was a thought of having a corkscrew on top of the rotor blades that you screw into the enemy helicopter but I didn't think that was a very good idea.'[109] Ken Adam suggested that it would be interesting to take the gadget further and make the gyrocopter 'a do-it-yourself kit', which enabled Little Nellie to break apart and bolt back together. 'So I came up with the idea of the very chic crocodile suitcases',[110] which were in fact designed by Ken's wife Letizia.[111]

What followed was a spectacular battle between Bond and four SPECTRE helicopters above Blofeld's volcano fortress. Filmed up in the mountains of Kyushu, the sequence was the directorial debut of editor Peter Hunt, 'I was supposed to direct *You Only Live Twice*, but they went with Lewis Gilbert. I got very sulky and said, "I'm not going to work any more for you." They gave me a holiday with pay, and I went around the world.'[112] Hunt met up with his former colleagues while they were shooting in Japan. 'Broccoli said, "Why don't we give Peter the second unit to do?" Eventually I did the second unit, and ended up editing [the film] as well.'[113]

In order to complete the seven and half minutes of action, Ken Wallis spent forty-six hours in the air and made a total of eighty-five flights.[114] Hunt recalled that the sequence was born out of a proposed car chase in the original screen-play, before Ken Wallis and his autogyro were discovered.[115]

The first unit completed a foot chase across the rooftops of Kobe Docks and Kagoshima seaport. The ninja training school sequences in which James Bond trains with the Japanese Secret Service were filmed at Himeji Castle, while the Hotel New Otani stood in for the exterior of Osato Chemicals. On 25 August Sean Connery celebrated his thirty-sixth birthday in Kyushu, wearing thick traditional costume, filming Bond's mock wedding to Kissy. In the small fishing village of Akime, Connery's wife, Diane Cilento, briefly doubled Mie Hama for the diving sequences out at sea. Cilento recalled she was 'taken away by the make-up department and given a black wig and lots of extended eyeliner to turn me into an Oriental. A revealing but oddly cut swimsuit completed the transformation.'[116]

Roald Dahl also visited Japan with his wife, actress Patricia Neal, who was recovering from a stroke. Dahl was impressed by the extravagance of a Bond set, 'It was a very well-oiled machine by then. You also had the feeling they had the money in the bank and they were going to make a fortune. So no money was spared in the making of it. You went everywhere by helicopter.'[117] Upon finding Connery and the crew relaxing in kimonos after a swim, Dahl described them as a strange motley crew.[118] Connery, a committed Scottish Nationalist, made a cultural observation of his own, '"Well, you Roald, look like an English arse-hole in your khaki shorts, or to be precise, a *Norwegian* arsehole."'[119]

Cubby's daughter, Barbara Broccoli had a revelation in Japan, 'I was about seven or eight. What an exciting experience that was. We were at a tea ceremony and the reaction to Sean Connery was so extraordinary. That's when I figured out this was all just playing.'[120]

Locations outside Tokyo were pretty remote. Cameraman Freddie Young remembered the daily trek to the rim of the then dormant volcano of Mount Shinmoe, which was doubling for the exterior of Blofeld's lair. Young remembered that the rim was just wide enough to allow a two-seater helicopter to fly into the crater. The key principals and crew were flown up but ' … many of the crew had to go up on horseback, then on foot, slogging it through the mud. We had just got the last shot in the can when a thick mist descended, making flying impossible.'[121] Instead it was a two-mile scrambling walk down to the plateau where horses awaited. Gilbert recalled how the Eon team spirit came to the fore, 'Everyone carried the equipment down, including Cubby and Sean.'[122] Roald Dahl felt sorry for Hama, who suffered in the heat and while filming up on the crater rim, she 'passed out cold and had to be rushed home by speedboat and helicopter. But she came back for more, and under the sizzling sun, pouring with sweat, she and Bond went into the final clinch and the director said, 'Print it ...'[123]

On 19 September 1966 the first unit headed back to Pinewood, leaving Peter Hunt's second unit to complete the Little Nellie sequence.[124] Disaster struck as aerial cameraman Johnny Jordan lost his foot when one of the SPECTRE helicopter blades sliced through his leg while filming above the village of Ebino. Peter Hunt was sitting in a Jeep directing the action from below. He had been concerned that the Japanese helicopter pilots were too spread out, wary of flying in too close formation, which meant it was difficult to get them all in frame.[125] Freddie Young reported Jordan was leaning out the helicopter to get a better camera angle 'when a gust of wind caught one of the helicopters and dragged it towards him.'[126] He kept filming and even turned the camera onto his injured foot in the hope that the footage might be of use to the surgeons later. Back in England Jordan's foot was amputated. Filming on the sequence was halted and Hunt completed the action over Torremolinos in Spain during December. Bob Simmons remembered that Peter Hunt changed his entire crew 'using French stunt pilots'.[127]

On 19 October, at Pinewood Studios, Gilbert filmed the obligatory scenes with the Secret Service staff. An amusing twist was put on the briefing sequences; after Bond is buried at sea his body is collected from the ocean floor and checked aboard a Navy submarine, to be greeted by M and Miss Moneypenny. During the making of *You Only Live Twice* Lois Maxwell was asked by famed US film critic Roger Ebert what it was like working with Sean Connery, she expressed the extremely bad time the actor had in Japan, 'I think he's trying to eat himself out of the role. And he's grown a Fu Manchu moustache and muttonchop sideburns. He's a Scotsman, you know. Very shy. A tremendous sense of personal privacy.'[128]

On set, Lewis Gilbert recalled Bernard Lee famously struggling with alcohol, 'You had to shoot him in the morning because you wouldn't get him in the afternoon.'[129] Assistant director William Cartlidge remembered, '[Bernard] went off to the pub and crashed the car after lunch. We picked him up and brought him back [to Pinewood]. Bernard was a problem.'[130]

During shooting Connery made a guest contribution – his voice – to a neighbouring film, Charlie Chaplin's *A Countess From Hong Kong*, as a result of Chaplin-Connery camaraderie developed on the Pinewood lot.[131]

Alan Whicker's documentary, *Bond Wants a Woman, They Said ... But Three Would Be Better*, was broadcast in March 1967 on BBC Television. Ken Adam's volcano set, created to shoot the volcano action scenes in, can be seen being built over the old tank where the 007 Stage would be constructed a decade later. The vast set occupied double the footprint and height of what would become the largest soundstage in the world. With construction commencing in May 1966 and costing the entire budget of *Dr. No,* Ken Adam noted the reactions of his producers; 'Harry had quite a shock when Cubby had said yes to a million dollars. Cubby was the gambler, more of a gambler in that sense.'[132]

At roughly 400ft in diameter, 125ft high the construction team waterproofed the free-standing set as best they could. However, Adam was nervous:

> The nightmare comes from suddenly realising you have designed something that has never been done before in films and that is bigger than any set ever used before. You wake up at night wondering whether or not the whole thing will work. You surround yourself with the best possible construction engineers and they can't help. They may be qualified to build the Empire State building or the Eiffel Tower – buildings that follow normal construction techniques but we have built a structure for which there are no previous terms of reference and with which no one has had any experience. But this set is a designer's dream. To be given the freedom to plan such a complicated structure is a challenge no artist could resist. And seeing your drawings and ideas taking shape and becoming reality in steel and concrete is the most satisfying feeling. It is like seeing your own baby grown and become a superman.[133]

Adam took great delight in the enthusiasm the workers had as they watched the volcano take shape, '[On] Sundays they brought their grandmothers and children and grandchildren to see it. Everybody got enthused by it.'[134] Adam even recalled once checking in on the twenty-four-hour construction at 2 a.m.:

> We had been to a party and I felt I had to be there, not the party. So we drove out to Pinewood and we climbed up to the top of the set where the plasterers were working in pretty awful conditions. I had a bottle of brandy with me for them.'[135]

When it was finished the construction was so big it could be seen from three miles away.[136] Norman Wanstall remembered even the most blasé studio workers were excited by it, 'That was our lunch time. The first thing you did was to down tools and go and see the set. No one had ever seen anything like this before. It was a miracle of engineering.'[137]

Peter Lamont, now promoted to set decorator, was required to source equipment and vehicles such as Land Rovers and the Mini Mokes required to dress the volcano. In one of his first ever meetings with the producers, Lamont presented his costings to Harry Saltzman:

> I remember getting into one big argument with him. I remember submitting this list and Harry went absolutely potty. And he said, 'God dammit, can't we get this stuff for free?' I remember, almost in tears, leaving the room and Stanley Sopel, the associate producer, came out and he said, 'Don't argue with him, you know what to do, buy the damn things.'[138]

Later at a lavish opening for the set many of the crewmembers, including Lamont, were required to drive the visiting VIPs into the set using the Mini Mokes 'and who do I pick up but Jacqui and Harry [Saltzman]. I remember he said, "Oh yes, we've got all these things for free!"'[139] Following the press day, in which the cast were photographed together in the crater, Ken Adam was proud to discover 'a photograph of the volcano appeared in nearly every newspaper in the world.'[140]

On 31 October 1966 Lewis Gilbert staged his first shots inside the volcano. Freddie Young joked, 'We'll probably use every lamp we've got – plus all the candles we can find.'[141] Cartlidge recalled the set was 'full of fog and [we had to] spend a fortune with those great big bloody heaters'[142] trying to make everything visible each morning.

Bob Simmons was required to co-ordinate the climatic battle as the Japanese Secret Service infiltrate Blofeld's hideaway, 'Virtually every stuntman in England was called to Pinewood'.[143] Simmons had 120 stuntmen[144] for the sequence with forty sliding down ropes from the crater lid, 120ft into the set. He even had men flying down the rope one-handed, firing a sub-machine gun with the other. He explained, 'Once a stuntman hit the ground he had to move off quickly because of another one coming right down behind him and some of them had to go on the trampolines to intercut with explosive effects.'[145] Working on his first Bond film was stuntman Vic Armstrong, 'I was a ninja, one of Bond's cohorts who slid down the ropes. It was like being in the Albert Hall when you walked in there. It was a phenomenal set, I was absolutely awestruck when I walked in and saw it, stunning.'[146]

Lewis Gilbert described it as one of the most challenging feats he had ever faced as a director. To show off the sheer magnitude of the set and give audiences an enhanced experience, he and Freddie Young had originally proposed to shoot *You Only Live Twice* on Super 70mm.[147] 'No film of my knowledge has ever had a set this large, with so many mechanic devices, with so much to film in one place. Every time I look at the set, I'm left with a feeling of determination not to waste one inch of all that marvellous space.'[148] Sceptics asked why the set could not have been constructed in model form, 'Yes, I suppose it could,' pondered Adam later. 'But we could not have had [so many]stuntmen abseiling down a model. The fact that it was real added an enormous amount to the tension.'[149]

In 1965, The Beatles began to grow dissatisfied after playing the gigantic Shea Stadium in New York. Amidst the cacophony of fans nobody could hear them perform. On 2 December 1966, another weary British icon, Sean Connery, completed what were meant to be his last scenes as James Bond on the Shea-like volcano set: amidst the technology, no one could see him perform. The main unit finished filming on 23 December. While the last details were brought together thereafter; the second unit headed to Scotland for the aerial sequence in which Helga Brandt parachutes to safety leaving Bond trapped aboard her Areo Commander light plane. Gibraltar harbour was used to film Bond's burial at sea aboard HMS *Tenby*; and the beautifully clear water in the Bahamas was used by Lamar Boren, who handled the underwater photography on *Thunderball*, to film Bond's body being picked up from the ocean floor and carried to the safety of M aboard the submarine.

Honoured to be working with such a veteran of the film industry, Broccoli and Saltzman threw Freddie Young a party towards the end of production, inviting over 200 guests to celebrate Freddie's fiftieth anniversary in the film business, a career that had begun, incredibly, in 1917.[150] Even though he had worked with some of the biggest names in Hollywood Freddie Young, too, respected the treatment the Bond producers had bestowed on him:

> At the end of *You Only Live Twice* Cubby Broccoli asked me to go to Hollywood to supervise the colour grading of 600 prints required for crash release. Cubby booked us into a sumptuous suite at the Beverly Wilshire Hotel and arranged for me to be entertained every night and taken to baseball games, Disneyland, and so on. For me it was the product of fifty years' hard slog to receive this VIP treatment.[151]

When Peter Hunt left the Bond fold following his aforementioned disagreements with the producers, Gilbert brought in his own editor, Thelma Connell, to edit *You Only Live Twice*. Recalled dubbing editor Norman Wanstall, 'She was a very experienced editor but Bond editing was a style that was totally Peter's and very, very difficult to immediately adapt to.'[152] Following his second unit debut, Wanstall remembered Hunt was back on side with Broccoli and Saltzman when *You Only Live Twice* entered pre-production. 'When Hunt returned from location, Thelma was in the editor's seat. Peter who had lorded the editing right from the beginning, naturally wanted to be in the hot seat again. Thelma began to lose her confidence and left the picture.'[153] Peter Hunt finished cutting the film.

John Barry's score for *You Only Live Twice* is led by the film's title track: a romantic ballad he wrote with lyricist Leslie Bricusse, who recalled:

> I had been invited down to Palm Springs for the weekend by Kirk and Ann Douglas. I took the music of *You Only Live Twice* with me and, on a glorious autumn Sunday morning, I wrote the lyric in Kirk's study. I remember smugly thinking as I sat there, how good can it get? I was being handsomely paid to spend the weekend in the home of one of my favorite movie stars, writing the title song for a movie of one of my favorite heroes of fiction. I was the house guest of Spartacus, writing for James Bond.[154]

A track was written in late 1966, and later recorded by Julie Rogers, but both Barry and Bricusse felt they could do better and reconvened in Hollywood in January 1967 to start again.[155]

Much to Barry's dismay, Harry Saltzman hired a musical supervisor to oversee the score and immediately there was a dispute over who was going to record the song.[156] Stories vary as to whether it was Barry of the supervisor who rejected another proposed artist: upcoming gospel singer Aretha Franklin. Lewis Gilbert recounted, 'When the movie was all over Cubby told me he was going to America to talk to Frank [Sinatra] – he was a great buddy of Frank Sinatra's – and the next thing I knew Nancy was doing it.'[157] Frank's daughter, Nancy Sinatra, who had enjoyed a hit with 'These Boots are Made for Walking', recalled being 'panic-stricken from the very beginning by the whole procedure. I was twenty-six and really scared.' She said of the experience, 'I'd rather have a root canal than go through that again. "You Only Live Twice" was difficult in a lot of ways – it was quite rangy – I wasn't used to that.'[158] By the end of the recording session there was not one perfect version of Sinatra's rendition. John Barry explained the solution; 'What's now in the movie was made up of about twenty-four takes. It was a real masterpiece of editing. There was just no way that we'd ever have got it in one take.'[159]

On 12 June 1967, Sean Connery attended his supposedly last Bond premiere, at the Odeon Leicester Square, in the presence of Her Majesty Queen Elizabeth II. Even the Queen was intrigued by the news that Connery was quitting and asked him if it really was his last 007 picture. 'I'm afraid so, Ma'am,' he replied. Connery reportedly told the press, 'I will only do things that passionately interest me for the remaining thirty-five years of my life.'[160] 'Sean Connery IS James Bond' screamed the posters. *You Only Live Twice* grossed a respectable $111.6 million worldwide, although it was a diminution on that of *Thunderball*. Perhaps the excesses of Bondmania, the rival Bond film, *Casino Royale*, and Sean Connery's fatigue with the part had taken their toll on James Bond.

10

NOTHING MORE,
NOTHING LESS

ON HER MAJESTY'S SECRET SERVICE

(1969)

NOW IN PRODUCTION... IN SWITZERLAND...
IN LONDON.... IN PORTUGAL AND AT PINEWOOD STUDIOS

ON HER MAJESTY'S SECRET SERVICE

ALBERT R. BROCCOLI AND
HARRY SALTZMAN
presents

JAMES BOND
007

IAN FLEMING'S

ON HER MAJESTY'S
SECRET SERVICE

starring
GEORGE LAZENBY · DIANA RIGG · TELLY SAVALAS

Directed by
PETER HUNT
Screenplay by
RICHARD MAIBAUM
Produced by
ALBERT R. BROCCOLI AND HARRY SALTZMAN
TECHNICOLOR® PANAVISION®   United Artists

n the late sixties, following the 1967 summer of love, the Beatles' *Sgt. Pepper's Lonely Hearts Club Band* and the rise of long-haired men, free love, the birth control pill and psychedelic fashions, popular culture was undergoing a seismic shift. The growing war in South East Asia was making militaristic notions and Establishment ambitions out of vogue. Various institutions were caught up in a period of change and amongst them were the film studios. Journalist Charles Camplin described the journey from films as mass family entertainment to a 'minority art-form, important and newly influential, wildly divergent'.[1]

With their fingers no longer on the pulse of what audiences wanted to see, the film studios started to lose money. Large expensive films, shot in large expensive studios by large expensive crews made film production a very risky business. When *Easy Rider* (1969) grossed significantly more than its budget of $360,000, the shift in taste began to make business sense.

In this environment United Artists was now flush with Transamerica Corporation's cash. In 1968 the studio boasted, 'Albert R. Broccoli and Harry Saltzman made a series of James Bond films with a series of our checks. And a check for the NEW James Bond – *On Her Majesty's Secret Service* in the Swiss Alps. We're pretty free with a buck.'[2] United Artists was with the spirit of the age, 'We don't just make motion pictures. We make tomorrow.'[3] Inevitably, United Artists too began to have a series of expensive flops.[4]

David Picker, at thirty-nine, became president of United Artists. In the words of Transamerica's chief John Beckett, 'Young men, or at least men young in outlook create change and are willing to try new things.'[5] In the past Picker could rely upon a James Bond film to keep his new audience – the Transamerica stockholders – happy. Connery's early release from his contract with Eon Productions had not gone down well, 'Nobody was thrilled. The concern was using a different James Bond. Not a great idea – unless we could get Sean back.'[6]

Connery had been holding out to the Bond producers for 10 per cent of the gross.[7] In February 1968 Saltzman said, 'Connery wants to do it'.[8] Broccoli was chagrined by his star's attitude, 'Has anyone ever asked us if WE would want him to do it? Would you want anyone to do a film if he kept telling everyone he doesn't want to do it? We want a new "Bond".'[9] Saltzman agreed, 'I think it's time for a change. Frankly, I don't have any idea yet who we'll cast for the part. The new one will be much lighter and less gimmicky than the other Bond films, recently, and we have to find a new approach.'[10] Broccoli was confident the character was the star, 'I don't think "Bond" will ever be passé. No more so than "Sherlock Holmes" or "Tarzan".'[11]

Lewis Gilbert declined the offer to direct, 'To me there was nothing in it. I'd done my Bond. It was extremely successful and now I can go back to making my films in my own way.'[12] As would often become the case, Eon Productions promoted from within. For Peter Hunt, it was not a moment too soon, 'By that time I'd worked with Broccoli and Saltzman for eleven years, including on *The Ipcress File* and *Call Me Bwana*.'[13] Associate producer Stanley Sopel felt:

> It was a natural move for Peter to become a director. I suppose one of the problems always is that to move an editor who's at the top of his class to the directing field on a picture that's going to cost between six and nine million dollars is not always the decision of the producer. I'm sure both Harry and Cubby would have given him the break earlier but we had to worry about the money boys. They said, 'It's a big investment; let him cut his teeth on a million dollar movie first.' They were able to persuade United Artists to let Peter do *OHMSS*, particularly with a new actor. If we would have had Sean to do it, it would have been easier for Peter.[14]

David Picker had faith, 'I wasn't concerned about Peter [Hunt] because Peter was a pro – we trusted Peter.'[15]

Peter Hunt had earned the trust of United Artists and the producers. Harking back to both Broccoli's and Saltzman's pre-007 days, Hunt remembered the first time he came across Bond, 'I was editing a film in Hong Kong and an assistant of mine was raving about this new book that had come out. I was a very great fan and friend, and had been since I was about the age of sixteen, of Terence Young.'[16] Hunt felt his time in the editing suite had been good training:

> In the cutting rooms you learn by everybody else's mistakes. You become an editor and you know what you are doing with film. All film is sort of plasticine in a way. Of course you have a basic blueprint or a good script to work from but circumstances are such you have to compromise. There are many situations which, as the director, you are forced into, when you have to make hasty decisions. If you are ingenious enough you can create the illusion. We are creating an entertainment that is going to take people out of themselves for two hours by sheer illusionary methods. I remember a pet phrase of Alexander Korda, 'Do not worry, we can fix it in the cutting rooms.'[17]

Hunt recalled the group discussions regarding the re-casting of James Bond, 'We had a big meeting. When you come down to deciding a new James Bond, it wasn't up to just the producers or myself. You had United Artists involved and they had to agree to it, all their hierarchy were there: Arthur Krim and David Picker.'[18]

They thought about playing to the changing times and modern culture, and Hunt raised the question, 'Do we want to become modern and have a long-haired one? Do you want to change the image and start with something to go on with?'[19] Hunt was relieved when it was agreed to go for 'another Sean Connery type. "Fine, OK, at least now we've got some idea of what we're looking for."'[20]

In October 1967 acting agencies and provincial repertory companies were primed[21] for 'the biggest star search in film history'[22] – the hunt for the new James Bond. Michael Gambon humorously recalled his inappropriateness for the part:

> I was given a smoked salmon sandwich and a glass of champagne. Cubby said, 'We're looking for a new James Bond,' and I started laughing. I said, 'James Bond, me? I'm not the right shape.' He said, 'Teeth, well we can do that in an afternoon. And Sean wears a piece. I'll get a toupé for you.'[23]

Actor Michael Billington, who would later go on to star in many classic British television shows in the seventies and would become a perennial Bond contender, recounted his first 007 near miss, 'Bud Ornstein at United Artists asked me to meet with him at the UA offices. Some weeks later I was called in for a meeting.'[24]

NBC's *Batman* star Adam West also remembered meeting with the Broccolis on a promotional trip to London to discuss the role.[25] Patrick Mower, not yet a leading man on British television, recounted going up for the re-casting of Harry Palmer, but was later informed that the part on offer was really 007. Mower went to a meeting with Broccoli, Saltzman and casting director Dyson Lovell at South Audley Street. In the waiting room was 'Ian Richardson, Michael Gambon, Anthony Valentine and every luminary from the theatre and television world.'[26] Broccoli also considered rising star, Oliver Reed, 'Oliver already had a public image; he was well known and working hard at making himself even better known. We would have had to destroy that image and rebuild Oliver Reed as James Bond – and we just didn't have the time or the money.'[27]

Roger Moore was also in the frame, 'It was first of all, "Would I want to do it?" How it was set up, where it would shoot, we should start thinking about it.

No negotiations were made with lawyers or agents. It was a conversation with Cubby and Harry. It was just talk.'[28] Later, it was reported he was 'busy with two "Saint" features.'[29]

The Lion in Winter (1968) was the critically acclaimed film that introduced the world to classically trained actor Timothy Dalton. The Bond producers came calling and Dalton:

> was absolutely flattered, but I thought Sean was a tremendous Bond – too good, actually. It would have been a very stupid move to try and take over from him. But there was a second, more practical reason. I was only about twenty-four or twenty-five at the time. And Bond can't be that young. He must be a mature man. Basically I considered myself too young and Connery too good.[30]

Ian Richardson, Robert Campbell, Anthony Rogers, and Hans de Vries all got to the final stages[31] of more than 400 actors considered for the role.[32] However, it all came down to one man. When, during the writing of this book, the authors finally spoke with George Lazenby from his property empire in Los Angeles, he was amusing, brightly articulate and still displayed his forthright, uncomplicated charm as he told his extraordinary story.

Born on 5 September 1939 in Goulburn, Australia, Lazenby was not supposed to survive childhood due to his kidneys rotting away. However, Lazenby, even then, defied the odds, 'the doctors were wrong. Maybe that stuck with me – [the idea that] whatever I've got to do I better get on with it.'[33] Lazenby said he 'dropped out of high school before I got an intermediate certificate. I turned fifteen and I was out of there.'[34] He felt school was a 'programming tool, I didn't intellectualise things. I was an instinctual person.'[35] Things appeared to come easy for him, 'Champion darts player, best shot in the army. I didn't show fear.'[36] Living in rural Australia was tough, 'even your best friend will fight you on a Friday night.'[37] Arriving in London, hot on the heels of a woman, he established himself as a top male model, working all around the world for print and television advertisements. Lazenby came to popular attention in a 'Big Fry' television commercial. He was of his time:

> I had more money and more girls before I was James Bond. I'd see something [and] I'd just go get it. I'd walk up to them in the street and say, 'Hey, you and me let's go?' And they'd say, 'Get out of here' or they'd go. It was in the sixties when the pill came out and there was no deadly disease, it was great. It was OK to smoke and OK to drink – nobody looked down on you for anything.[38]

Lazenby did not intend to audition for James Bond:

> A friend of mine's [Ken Gaherity] girlfriend came into town and he said,
> 'You got to help me out, I got a date with an agent, Maggie Abbott. She's on
> a street corner and I can't leave her standing there; my girlfriend's here and
> I can't get there.' So I went on this blind date and she took me to a screening
> [with] the Beatles and the Rolling Stones. I was very impressed – I looked at
> them rather than the movie.[39]

Lazenby went to Paris, where he was tracked down to La Cupole restaurant by
Abbott from London, 'I think you're right for a film they're having trouble for.'[40]
She would not discuss it on the phone and wanted George to return to London.

Back in town, Lazenby had forgotten about the conversation, 'I'd just been
out with this girl three or four days before on a first date.'[41] Gaherity implored
him to visit Abbott and he reluctantly agreed. When she told him the role was
James Bond, 'I nearly fell off my chair.'[42] Abbott warmed to his 'carefree confident
attitude, along with [his] arrogance.'[43] George went to the casting but was thrown
out because he was not in the actors' union. Abbott admonished him, '"No – you
gotta GET it! See Dyson Lovell, he's right up the stairs, first door on the right"'[44]
While in the offices, Lazenby noted the clean-cut look of the actors – he had
long hair and sideburns, and was dressed in the latest French fashions. Lazenby
already had a Rolex watch, but worked quickly on the rest. He went to Sean
Connery's barber, Kurt's, located in the basement of the Dorchester. He asked
for his hair to be cut like Bond. Kurt then sent him in the direction of Connery's
tailor - Anthony Sinclair. No bespoke suit could be readied in time but there was
one Connery had rejected. It fitted Lazenby like a sartorial Excalibur.[45]

Lazenby returned the next day, manoeuvred past the gatekeeper and upstairs
to Lovell's office, where he found him on the phone to Saltzman. He looked
up to see Lazenby in Sean Connery's suit, hair coiffed by Connery's barber, his
arm leaning on the doorframe so his Rolex was in view, purring, 'I heard you're
looking for James Bond'.[46] Lovell told the producer, '"There's a guy here that
really looks the part." Harry said, "Bring him over"',[47] so they went to Saltzman's
Tilney Street offices round the corner. On the way Lovell quizzed him about his
acting background; Lazenby invented a biography. Upon entering the offices,
Saltzman, who was on the phone with his feet on the desk, motioned his guest
to sit down by jerking his upturned shoes. Lazenby was put off by both gestures
and walked over to the window and looked out, 'He told me later this really
impressed him'.[48] When asked to repeat his story, Lazenby motioned to Lovell

and told Harry, "'I just told him, let him tell you." I thought I wouldn't remember – as it was a bunch of lies. I was really afraid. There was a boardroom and these really aggressive people. I'd never met anybody like this before.'[49]

Lazenby was asked to return the next day – Friday – at four o'clock to meet with Peter Hunt. He demurred and said he would be filming in Paris, 'I just wanted to get out of there – I just knew I wouldn't be getting anywhere with these guys.'[50] Saltzman enquired how much Lazenby would be paid, '£500 – half a year's wages to an Englishman.'[51] Lazenby was told to go and see Stanley Sopel to draw the £500. Lazenby related the story to Maggie Abbott from a phone box outside the office and she was incredulous, "'What?! No one's ever heard of anybody getting paid for a call back!'"[52]

That evening Lazenby 'went for an acting lesson to Kevin Duggan who lived across the hallway from me. "Look I'm up for the James Bond film, I'm meeting the director tomorrow." Kevin went, "You want an acting lesson *now* – *for tomorrow?*"'[53] Duggan, a drama teacher, called some friends over and got Lazenby to take part in a role-playing exercise, which involved locating a key. When he could not find the key, despite its obvious placement, Lazenby was told, 'The reason you couldn't see it was because you were wondering what we were thinking about you.' When Lazenby found the key the second time, Duggan said, 'You can act!'[54]

One of Duggan's friends who was called over that evening was Ronan O'Rahilly, who would later become Lazenby's Svengali. The wealthy founder of the hugely popular counter-culture pirate station, Radio Caroline, 'wasn't into money. He was into changing the way people thought about things. He was a Kennedy fan.'[55]

Lazenby met with Peter Hunt the next day, only to find the director was already annoyed with him. On a location scout in Switzerland Hunt was planning a weekend break, but had been called back early to meet with Lazenby. George was scared:

> I don't know what came over me, I said, 'Peter, I've never acted a day in my life. I've modelled but never spoken in front of a camera.' And he's looking at me, 'What? And you say you can't act? You've fooled two of the most ruthless men I've ever met in my life. Stick to your story and I'll make you the next James Bond.'[56]

The first challenge was Saltzman; he was not impressed with Lazenby, his past now revealed, "'Get him out of here. He's a 'clothes peg'. We'll be the laughing stock of the industry if we hire a male model.'''[57] Hunt insisted Lazenby try for the part, but was told he could not be tested at the studio for fear of word getting out that a non-actor was testing for Bond. In secret, tests took place at Woodlands, 'Harry's house out near Pinewood. [Surrounded by] acres and acres. Beautiful old mansion.'[58] The crew had to be discreet, Lazenby remembered Hunt reassuring his producer, 'I'll get Samuelson, the guy who owns the camera company and a couple of guys I know.'[59] At Saltzman's estate Lazenby swam and then rode horses, 'I just got on without the saddle', until they tired, 'That must have impressed them.'[60]

When he was testing for the role, Lazenby would go out alternate nights with Broccoli and Saltzman, 'because the two wives didn't get along.'[61] He observed, 'Europe was Harry's turf. Cubby was the money man.'[56] Lazenby sensed Dana Broccoli was 100 per cent supportive of her husband. One evening, when Cubby asked Lazenby, '"Do you play baccarat? Come upstairs and I'll show you how to play." Cubby lost £60,000 that evening and as he went home in his £10,000 car, Dana agreed with George's observation that Cubby had lost six of the vehicles!'[62] Lazenby used to play with Saltzman's daughter, Hilary, and Broccoli's daughter, Barbara, as children. Hilary recalled, 'I had the biggest crush on him when I was a kid.'[63]

He was then screentested at Pinewood, 'Everyone thought I was the stand-in James Bond for the other actors. I didn't even have a dressing room. Peter Hunt had me out there testing for all the actors playing other roles.'[64] Lazenby had elocution lessons to remove his Australian accent and learned to 'bagpipe the wind in your stomach so when you get nervous, it doesn't show.'[65] Lazenby's gait was also polished, 'I used to sway. On CinemaScope, it would go all over the place so I had to walk like Prince Philip.'[66]

The producers put the putative Bond up in a Grosvenor House apartment and it was here, according to Lazenby, that his sexuality was tested to ensure he was not gay. A male employee brought up girls on separate occasions and stayed while Lazenby made love to them. Years later, the employee revealed himself to be John Daly, who went on to become a producer at the Hemdale Group.[67] Finally, Lazenby's fighting prowess was auditioned in a fight sequence involving a number of stuntmen, one of them being Yuri Borienko, who went on to play the chief henchman in the finished film. Lazenby recalled, 'I only had a twenty minute practice to show me how to stage fight. I'd only been a real fighter before that.'[68] During the test, Lazenby punched Borienko who fell down with a bloody nose, 'That's when Harry stepped over him, grabbed me and says, "We're going with you. Tell anybody and the deal's off. Get out of town."'[69]

On 7 October 1968 the coronation of the new James Bond took place before the world's press at the Dorchester, where it had all begun four months earlier. Lazenby famously said, "'I'm really looking forward to being Bond, for the bread and the birds. It's not that I'm a sex maniac. Forget my ego. I wouldn't even care if they didn't put my name on the marquee.'"[70] Hunt explained the choice:

Sean Connery had 'sexual assurance'. I interviewed hundreds [of] wonderful actors, marvellous people on the stage but they didn't have this quality. They might be able to try to act it but it was not an inherent thing. It was quite by chance we came across George Lazenby. You do look at him if he walks in the street and so do the girls.[71]

A soon-to-be Bond girl in two ways – the lead in the next film and, briefly, Lazenby's companion – Jill St. John concurred, 'Cubby told me when they were interviewing people for the first James Bond, in walked Sean. And when he left, every secretary said, "Who is that?" And he said the only other time it happened again was when George Lazenby walked into the office.'[72]

ON HER MAJESTY'S SECRET SERVICE was first published in the UK on 1 April 1963. Bond hunts down Blofeld after his escape at the end of THUNDERBALL and following the events of THE SPY WHO LOVED ME (where Bond thwarts a SPECTRE attack on a Soviet nuclear defector in Toronto). Fleming's eleventh Bond book starts with a series of flashbacks detailing Bond's courtship of Teresa di Vincenzo – known as Tracy – the wayward daughter of Corsican gangster Draco. The setting for the romance is an autumnal Royale-les-Eaux. There, Bond rescues her twice: paying for her *coup de déshonneur* – an unfunded, losing bet at the casino, and instinctively saving her from a suicide swim to the horizon. When Tracy hints to her father that Bond might be a sort of cure for her woes, Draco implores him to help his daughter, offering the spy a £1 million dowry. It emerges that Bond is frustrated by Operation Bedlam: the seemingly fruitless pursuit of Blofeld. In exchange for Draco's underworld connections locating Blofeld, Bond agrees to see Tracy again. The head of SPECTRE now seeks recognition as the Comte Balthazar de Bleuville, such nobility to be confirmed only by London's College of Arms. This allows 007 to infiltrate Blofeld's mountaintop lair, Piz Gloria, in Switzerland posing as heraldry expert Sir Hillary Bray. Piz Gloria, accessible only by cable car, is a mysterious clinic where, assisted by the matron-like Irma Bunt, Blofeld is seemingly seeking to cure the allergies of a number of beautiful young girls from around the UK. Bond escapes the mountain in a thrilling ski chase, during which a pursuing goon falls into a snowplough train. Back at M's home, Quarterdeck, government boffins deduce that the allergy treatments are actually germ viruses and the girls are Blofeld's method of despatching disease across the Dominion's agricultural base. Bond and Draco launch a commando raid on Piz Gloria to prevent the economic destruction of Britain. Bond chases Blofeld down a bob run, but the villain yet again escapes. Over the course of the novel, Bond falls in love with Tracy and, on New Year's Day, marries her in Munich. Their wedded bliss lasts only hours when, in a shocking finale, Bunt and Blofeld, attempting to machine-gun Bond, kill Tracy instead. Heartbreakingly Bond, in a state of shock, reassures his dead wife, 'We've got all the time in the world'.

Peter Hunt was inspired:

> One of the reasons why I stuck my neck out to do this sixth James Bond film was that [it's] one of the best of the Bond stories. It involves many other facets of Bond as a person, rather than simply Bond as an agent. Here is a James Bond who is going to fall in love. He is going to find himself involved for the first time. Now that to me was tremendous because I had to develop a style, which would give me two stories interwoven. One is a Bond adventure and the other is an emotional relationship which culminates in marriage and this to me was a great challenge.[73]

Richard Maibaum concurred, 'It was the best of Ian Fleming's novels. It had a wonderful relationship between Bond, the girl and her father.'[74] *On Her Majesty's Secret Service* (*OHMSS*) was to have followed *Goldfinger* and *Thunderball*, but was deferred on both occasions. Richard Maibaum penned a series of treatments and screenplays dated June 1964 through to September 1968, including test scenes for the new actors trying for Bond.[75] Had Sean Connery been held to his contract, *OHMSS* could have been very different as ideas and casting suggestions from those screenplays suggest. At one point, Blofeld would have been revealed to be Goldfinger's twin brother, with Gert Fröbe in line to play the part.[76] A later casting suggestion for Blofeld was Max von Sydow.[77] Bond would have rescued Tracy in an Aston Martin capable of driving underwater complete with harpoon device.[78] Alternatively, Bond was to have been equipped with the new Ford Gran Turismo Mk III.[79] All the screenplays pre-1968 are gadget-laden affairs with 007 being fitted out with blowpipe skipoles, skistrap grenades and a 3D television.[80] Bond was to have despatched the villains causing statues to fall on them.[81] Instead of Bond being imprisoned by Blofeld in the cable car wheelhouse, 007 is originally trapped in a chimpanzee cage.[82]

By the time Peter Hunt took on the production, the technology was pared down and the initial French location was changed to Portugal.[83] Maibaum himself thought it vital to visit locations and was inspired by a trip to Mürren to include 'a glass-enclosed telephone booth. Not only was it different from the kinds of glass-enclosed booths that you see elsewhere but it was a very important story point – Bond is anxious to get in touch with London.'[84] Maibaum also discovered 'a collection of antique cowbells,'[85] inspiring the idea for a fight set among them which would make 'sounds like Quasimodo ringing the bells of Notre-Dame' and become more exciting by attracting the attention of those Bond is seeking to hide from.[86] Lazenby recalled meeting Maibaum, 'We never spoke about the writing because he knew I knew nothing about it. He used to study me.'[87] Simon Raven wrote additional dialogue, notably Tracy's poetic verbal joust with Blofeld at Piz Gloria while he holds her captive prior to the helicopter attack.[88]

The leading lady was the most important female character to appear in a Bond film to date. At first, this Bond girl was set to be Gallic for, as Eric Pleskow remembered, 'Harry Saltzman was a Francophile.'[89] They met with top French star Brigitte Bardot, according to Hunt, 'on three occasions. On the third she calmly announced that she had just signed a deal to do *Shalako* [1968] – with Sean Connery.'[90] Another French star Catherine Deneuve was discussed.[91] Like Honor Blackman, the leading lady was sourced from the hit television show *The Avengers*. Enter experienced Shakespearean actress Diana Rigg who would become Mrs. James Bond. Of the part, the Contessa Teresa di Vincenzo (née Draco), Rigg said:

> I suppose she's a bit of a mixed up lady. I think she's much more dimensional than most of the other women who have been in the Bond pictures. Really to a large extent they've been set dressing and therefore the visual titillation or whatever you call it. The thing that attracted me to this part is that it's got many more facets than being attractive. I could not have done it if it was to be attractive.[92]

Hunt had invited his putative co-stars to dinner to test their chemistry. They got on very well and Rigg remarked:

The Broccoli family. *Clockwise from top left*: Cubby Broccoli, Michael Wilson, Dana Broccoli, Tony Broccoli, Barbara Broccoli and Tina Broccoli, London 1963. (Rex Shutterstock)

Left: Everything or Nothing. Harry Saltzman, Ian Fleming and Cubby Broccoli. (Rex Shutterstock)

Danjaq United. *Left to right*: Jacqueline Saltzman, Cubby Broccoli, Harry Saltzman and Dana Broccoli at the *Goldfinger* premiere in September 1964. (Rex Shutterstock)

Sean Connery as James Bond, 1963. (Rex Shutterstock)

Honor Blackman, who starred as Pussy Galore, and director Guy Hamilton on the set of *Goldfinger*. (Rex Shutterstock)

Scotland forever. Director Terence Young, Mollie Peters and Sean Connery on the set of *Thunderball*. (Rex Shutterstock)

Left: Sean Connery on the set of *You Only Live Twice*. (Bernard Vandendriessche)

Below: OHMSS. Diane Cilento, Sean Connery and Queen Elizabeth II at the premiere of *You Only Live Twice*, June 1967. (Rex Shutterstock)

George Lazenby announced as James Bond in October 1968. (Rex Shutterstock)

Early publicity shot of George Lazenby as Bond in London 1968. (Rex Shutterstock)

Mr and Mrs James Bond, George Lazenby and Diana Rigg, on the set of *On Her Majesty's Secret Service*. (Rex Shutterstock)

Clockwise from above: No one Is forever. Harry
Saltzman, Cubby Broccoli and Sean Connery on
the set of *Diamonds Are Forever*. (Rex Shutterstock);
Harry Saltzman and Cubby Broccoli searching for
a new Bond. (Rex Shutterstock); The producer and
M, Mr and Mrs Bernard Lee, with Cubby Broccoli,
1974. (Rex Shutterstock/Bernard Vandendriessche)

Moneypenny and Q, played by
Lois Maxwell and Desmond
Llewelyn respectively, 1983. (Rex
Shutterstock)

The new direction. Roger Moore and director John Glen on the set of *For Your Eyes Only*. (Rex Shutterstock)

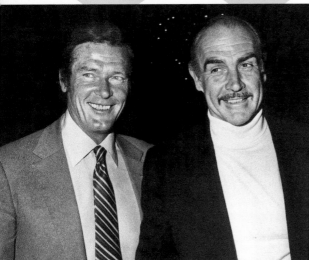

Double 007. Roger Moore and Sean Connery, 1983. (Rex Shutterstock)

Lifetime achievement. Roger Moore congratulates Cubby Broccoli on winning his Irving G. Thalberg award, Los Angeles, 1982. (Rex Shutterstock)

Left: Timothy Dalton as James Bond. (Rex Shutterstock)

Below: Dangerous 007. *Licence to Kill* cast Robert Davi, Caroline Bliss, Timothy Dalton and Talisa Soto. (Rex Shutterstock)

Many people when they find themselves in a completely new world, face problems which they're not prepared for. [George will] get over them because he's resilient, young and very, very good looking. I think he fits [the role] very well, in fact he's got a quality which is exactly right for any person who's going to follow Sean Connery and that is he's casual. He's not trying, he's not earnest and doesn't appear to be very frightened. He's very flip and that's going to be the most successful factor.[93]

Many years later Rigg reflected, 'I know perfectly well why I'd got the job. George Lazenby was ill-equipped. I was there to steer him through and give it some gravitas.'[94]

Donald Pleasence would not return as Blofeld. According to Hunt '[he] is a fine actor but I wanted someone who would play it more realistically. If you look at him you never see him move anywhere. I had to cut his movements, as he just minced everywhere.'[95] Greek-American actor Telly Savalas was chosen to play the new Blofeld. He had been nominated for an Oscar and had just starred with Diana Rigg and Bond contender Oliver Reed in *The Assassination Bureau* (1968). Savalas was a personal friend and gambling buddy of Cubby Broccoli to boot. He described Blofeld as a man with 'flair, he's a cosmopolitan man, he knows his way around, you would imagine he knows the right wine and the right girl and the right time and the right place and, you play that as humanely as you can, you've got a very interesting villain.'[96] Richard Maibaum was not a fan of Savalas's Blofeld, 'He should have had an accent or something but I couldn't convince Peter Hunt to get him to use one.'[97]

Future potential Bond George Baker was cast as Sir Hilary Bray, based on an actual friend of Fleming, Italian actor Gabriele Ferzetti would play Marc-Ange Draco, head of the Corsican mafia, the Union Corse. After testing potential Bonds, Yuri Borienko landed the part of henchman Grunther, James Bree was Gumbold, Blofeld's Swiss lawyer and German actress Ilse Steppat would embody Blofeld's lumpen mistress, Irma Bunt.

It was Peter Hunt's intention right from the start that *On Her Majesty's Secret Service* would look as real as possible and maximise on location shooting rather than in the studio.[98] Ken Adam was unavailable for the film, designing *Goodbye Mr. Chips* (1969) for director Herbert Ross. He had, however, worked on the film when it was being prepped prior to *You Only Live Twice*:

Harry had invited me and my wife to spend Christmas [1965] in Switzerland. He lent me one of his big American cars to look for locations, which was absolutely crazy because it didn't have any chains. I was sliding all over the place. I was also flying in helicopters looking for a big or a hidden fortress on top of the mountains.[99]

Returning for the first time since *From Russia With Love* was production designer Syd Cain. In mid-1968 Harry Saltzman and Cain inspected the Maginot Line, but Cain felt it was cinematically uninteresting and he could do better at Pinewood. They went to another location in St. Moritz but Cain was unenthusiastic about this, too. Frustrated, Saltzman shouted "'Find the bloody thing yourself.'"[100] Cain then discovered the Schilthorn mountain, near Mürren, facing the Eiger, Jungfrau and Mönch mountains. Peter Hunt loved the location but Swiss bureaucrats opposed building a heliport – vital for the crew to ferry equipment – feeling it would mar the beauty. The producers suggested that the heliport would be invaluable for mercy missions and rescues and they would pay for major improvements.[101] The building atop Schilthorn in 1968 was a year old and not yet finished. Italian engineers who had built the Simplon Tunnel worked on the project, and 500 tons of concrete were hauled to the top of the mountain by cable cars and helicopters. Peter Lamont remembered Piz Gloria:

hadn't been finished because I think they ran out of money. They negoti-ated, and they allowed us there to finish, as we put it, the Alpine remixes. We wanted to build on the heliport. Hubert Fröhlich, the production manager, got all the equipment up to the top. They constructed the heliport. They had to take a generator up there in pieces. This was all done at night on the cable pathway. In the meantime we finished off the Alpine run.[102]

Lamont was proud of the work:

Hunt arrived, met by us all. I said, "Peter, you should come to the Alpine room now because you will never ever see it again like it is now." We went up, and it was sensational. It was dressed, all ready. Everything was live, all the drinks, everything. We had so much booze. Of course, from then on, you can imagine with the equipment there, you never ever saw it the same again.'[103]

At a total cost of £125,000,[104] building on the top of a mountain was cheaper than building the inside of a 'volcano'.[105]

Hunt chose a new director of photography – Michael Reed– having used him to shoot the second unit on *Goldfinger* and *Chitty Chitty Bang Bang* (1968). The cinematographer felt the biggest asset his director had was:

communication. He understood the problems and difficulties I was about to face when he told me he wanted to shoot the picture in actual locations. The interiors of Piz Gloria were a nightmare to light, every lamp was reflected in the huge expanse of glass windows and had to be flagged off, and the filters on the windows had to be constantly changed to balance the light inside with the light outside. Peter understood this and gave me the time I needed.[106]

On 21 October 1968, the 120-man crew occupied the tiny village of Mürren and the surrounding area. Things did not start well for Lazenby, who fell out with Hunt on the first day when he was asked by a crewmember to clear the set with a loudspeaker.[107] Those ushered off the set were friends of the director who never forgave the actor. Hunt said, "'Don't forget who got you this job! Never speak to me again. Just speak to the first assistant.'"[108] When Hunt saw Lazenby at a birthday celebration thrown for the director, he left his own party. Saltzman looked at the gift he bought for Hunt and Lazenby remembered him saying, "'I guess this is for you.' It was a mink duffel coat. I used to ride my motorcycle in it.'[109]

Lazenby also fell foul of Diana Rigg who at the start of the shoot had told him, 'You know if you don't fool around with the other girls, maybe something can happen. We'd had a little bit of a kiss and cuddle one night, that's as far as it got.'[110] The actress caught him with a production secretary in the stunt tent.[111] Later at Pinewood Studios, on a press day, Diana Rigg hollered across the commissary that she was having garlic for lunch before a love scene and hoped George was too. The press seized on this in what became known at the 'Garlic Incident'.[112] Rigg subsequently dismissed the gesture as a mere joke[113] and Lazenby, too, felt it got blown out of proportion, 'She had her way of doing things and I had mine. She was more complicated than I was.'[114] Rigg felt her co-star, 'was just difficult. He kind of thought he was a film star immediately.'[115]

Lazenby described Savalas as 'a ruthless son of a gun.'[116] When he noticed Lazenby's per diem cash payments went unspent, Savalas invited the neophyte Bond to join a poker pool. 'Saltzman came up and saw it, he got all my money back and said, "Leave my boy alone."'[117] Lazenby compared himself to his predecessor on these payments when he received £100 week, 'How much did the other fella get? Being Australian, "fella" is common'.[118]

The tension made the small village like a prison for Lazenby. He even had a helicopter fly him to Geneva for trysts with girls.[119] He purchased guns illegally and fired them off around the crew making them nervous.[120] 'I did all my stunts', he remembered, including 'fighting and jumping out of helicopters'.[121] Lazenby enquired of the crew whether the 'other fella' did his own stunts, too. Stuntman Vic Armstrong thought, 'Lazenby was very good, very professional about his job.'[122] The insurance company, however, did prevent Lazenby from skiing, but there was just the man for the job.[123] In 1964 for the Winter Olympics Willy Bogner had made a 35mm documentary shot in CinemaScope:

In the [1964 Winter Olympics] I was a downhill racer. I had developed a technique, never done before, of filming high speeds with a 35mm hand-held Panavision camera. That's how basically I got the job. Cubby Broccoli saw my film and decided to use me for his next Bond. You sometimes had to ski backwards for close-up shots with the actors.[124]

Hunt still had a job to do, 'Of course, in the rushes we got lumps of sky, bits of his bottom and somebody's shoe but then one took all the best pieces and turned them into exciting sequences.'[125]

The isolated conditions led to delays and overruns, which necessitated Hunt bringing in a former colleague and sound editor of his to direct the final bobsleigh sequence and eventually edit the film – John Glen.[126] Glen's editing background allowed him to break down the action:

When you look at such scenes in the rushes, you have to look at them with a trained editor's eye; 70 per cent or more of the shot will be unusable. Taken as a whole the stuff may not look impressive [but] you may be able to extract two feet.[127]

He issued a shot list for every cut in the sequence to every member of the crew.[128]

Returning to that crew was aerial cameraman Johnny Jordan, who had been badly injured on *You Only Live Twice*. Glen thought, 'Johnny was a perfectionist. He always wanted another go. No one could direct Johnny when he was shooting in the sky. You just told him what you wanted and you knew he would come back with some beautiful pictures.'[129] Dangling underneath a helicopter from his parachute rig, Jordan became a legend among the village folk of Mürren; he also made the groundcrew wear white oversuits so they would not be seen in shot.[130] To make up for lost time, the crew did not take rest days and Glen with Hubert Fröhlich, his 'organising wizard', inspired the crew by getting usable material daily.[131] Such leadership would not go unnoticed by Cubby Broccoli.

The cable car stunts proved unexpectedly dangerous when the hooks designed to keep the stuntmen safely secured to the high-altitude cables froze and the stuntmen nearly slid down the entire run of the route. Lazenby's double, George Leech, suffered a dislocated arm.[132] Unfortunately, 1968 was an unexpectedly warm winter and the production employed several local builders to fill trucks with snow and an army of locals to shovel it on the streets for the scene where Bond arrives as Bray in Lauterbrunnen.[133]

Glen was assigned the unenviable task of capturing the bobsleigh sequence as quickly as possible. But first it had to be built. Syd Cain remembered, 'Peter Hunt wanted to utilise an old run in St. Moritz, but it was found to be too old and unsafe. I then found Franz Capose, an ex-bob sled champion, who was able to build a new run for us above Mürren.'[134]

Glen had never met Broccoli until the day the producer arrived on location and insisted that he be allowed to try out the run for himself.[135] The bobsleighs set off with champion Heinz Lau and Olympic skier Robert Zimmerman doubling for Lazenby and Savalas respectively. But the mild weather had made the ice unpredictable and an accident, which left Zimmerman with facial injuries, was captured by pursuing cameraman Willy Bogner Jr and appears in the finished film.[136] The skiers used fibreglass machine guns with light bulbs at the end of the barrel to simulate gunfire.[137]

Meanwhile Anthony Squire was in nearby Lauterbrunnen staging the stock car sequence. Diana Rigg actually drove 'that car around, the poor cameraman was green.'[138] Hunt now had to stage the film's most spectacular and dangerous sequence – the avalanche that engulfs Bond and Tracy. As early as summer 1968 Hunt had had the Swiss Army plant explosive charges in the snow and had patiently waited for the winter snows to completely cover them, ready for the stunt in spring 1969. However, things went slightly awry: while the second unit was filming the bobsleigh sequence, the avalanche triggered naturally, ruining all the preparation. A desperate Glen tried to create a convincing avalanche using a snowplough and even tried setting off the charges anyway to see what would happen. The avalanche seen in the finished film is made up mostly of stock footage combined with a smaller avalanche that Glen was able to rig up in May.[139]

In December 1968 the main unit returned to England to shoot scenes at Pinewood Studios. Of the many sets built there, the Wheel House set was impressive; in the film Bond is trapped here by Blofeld. The giant cogs and wheels were made of oak so that they could be finessed by chisel in case any minor changes to the design were needed; it was created to actually work by John Stears, who returned to the series to guide the special effects.[140]

A sequence partially shot, but never used, involved Bond chasing Phidian (a Blofeld spy) at the College of Arms; Bond chases him down a wall out of the college. The sequence was to end with Phidian dying and the Secret Service putting out a notice of a train accident explaining the death of Phidian and Bond.[141] Lazenby remembered the sequence 'pulled my shoulder out climbing a wall.'[142] Another unused concept were Ken Adam's production sketches of Draco's transportable base assembled from shipping containers, 'It was like a mobile office but quite sophisticated. It was a personal idea.'[143]

In the novel Bond reports to M at his chief's home, Quarterdeck, after his escape from Piz Gloria. During the second week of April 1969, the crew found themselves in Marlow, ten miles from the studio, where the house named Thames Lawn stood in for M's home. George Lazenby remembered Bernard Lee, an alcoholic, would sometimes leave make-up drunk. The crew were at a loss to work out how the Bond veteran snuck drink onto the set; Lazenby discovered Lee would 'hide gin in the big fat German fountain pens'.[144] The actor would have to be steadied on set by prop-master Patrick Weymouth.[145]

Lois Maxwell 'quite liked George [Lazenby]. I mean, I didn't think he was much of an actor, but his escapades amused me immensely; the way he would chase women was a hoot.'[146] She thought the film had 'a little more humanity in it than the others, with Bond's wife being shot and the creation of a situation that everyone in the audience can relate to. And for Moneypenny, of course, it's the end of her dreams. She's just left weeping with her memories.'[147]

While earlier drafts of the screenplay were gadget-laden, in the final story Bond only uses a portable safe-cracker photocopier device in a tense Hitchcockian scene where he breaks into Blofeld's Swiss lawyer Gumbold's office. In the pre-title sequence, Q shows M radioactive lint as a way of keeping tabs on 007. Desmond Llewelyn remembered, 'There was a scene in the original script that had me giving Bond a new Aston Martin but all that was cut out.'[148]

Lazenby recalled he used to ride a motorcycle to work, donated to him by 'Triumph and BSA just because I was James Bond.'[149] The actor was tailed in the car sent to convey him to the studio, the 'chauffeur kind of watching me to make sure I get to work.'[150] Eventually, the producers prevailed upon him to commute by a safer vehicle; he was given an Aston Martin.[151]

The crew's globetrotting resumed at the end of April 1969 when the production headed out to Estoril in northern Portugal with locations at the Palacio Hotel. During these early scenes Bond romances Tracy and they were key to contrast with snowy Switzerland. Just down the coast at Guincho Beach, Lazenby shot his pre-credit fight with the goons trying to abduct Tracy. Hunt needed specific geography:

We needed a flat beach bordered by a road. We found this big long beach, which runs parallel to the road, this was one of the scenes in the book. Most other places in Europe are vacation spots with promenades and that's always a difficulty because they're not isolated. They have tourists around.[152]

The seascape-with-figures image was important for the director, 'I didn't want Mediterranean waves. I had a very dramatic scene and I wanted big, Atlantic waves. What I really wanted was the best of both worlds between the Atlantic and the Mediterranean. Well, I found that in Portugal.'[153]

Also shot in Portugal was Draco's birthday party, which was staged at the Da Vinho estate in Zambujal. Again Hunt sought extra layers:

What I wanted was to put behind our sympathetic character – Draco – some form of farm or cattle. I didn't want to show it obviously, only subliminally when this man is involved in the destruction of Blofeld, there is an added reason. He is also a farmer. What I found was the Da Vinho estate with their own private bullring. In Portugal, they don't kill the bull, they play the bull with horses, it's more horsemanship which I thought was absolutely right for this man's background.[154]

The estate was the setting for Bond's wedding and Lamont remembered the elaborate set dressing:

I'd never ever seen so many flowers in my life. And, of course, the day we went out to shoot it, we had all these garlands up and it poured with rain. I can't tell you. It looked so sad afterwards. Anyway, all these florists, they really got together, they remade all this stuff, and they did an absolutely wonderful job.[155]

Desmond Llewelyn thought, 'It was a very big set up. I think we were out there for a week.'[156] Q is told by Bond, 'This time I've got the gadgets and I know how to use them.' George Lazenby, appropriately enough, 'had very little to do with Llewelyn, but I chased Bernard Lee on horseback and he fell over. He was a good sport about it.'[157] No one else on set was amused.

Diana Rigg enjoyed the opulence:

> I loved doing Bond. Apart from anything else, I had never been in anything so extravagant. The money they spent. I came from subsidised theatre and suddenly I had to look at a watch so what do they do? They send me down to Kensington market and came up with several boxes [for me] and I said, 'That one.'[158]

Portugal was also the location for the most dramatic moment in any Bond film – the shattering climax when Tracy is murdered by Irma Bunt. By this stage in production, Lazenby felt he was 'beginning to learn how to act. I was letting the tears flow. Diana was biting me on the leg and I think she thought she could make me cry or something. I'd read the book, I felt really sad and emotional.'[159] However, Hunt admonished him, 'Get rid of the tears, James Bond doesn't cry.'[160]

Finally, on 23 June 1969 the lengthy and traumatic shoot was over, almost two months past the scheduled end date. But further problems were awaiting the production.

When John Glen began editing, it soon became clear that the film was not going to fit into the usual running time of less than two hours. Glen's first cut came in at 170 minutes and a lot of footage had to be sacrificed to make the film more manageable. Around thirty minutes of footage was discarded but even at 140 minutes, *On Her Majesty's Secret Service* remained the longest 007 film until 2006's *Casino Royale*. Broccoli and Saltzman opted to leave the decision on cutting the film to the manager of the Odeon Leicester Square, so when shown a print he was asked if anything should be removed. Thankfully, forsaking the chance to squeeze in an extra screening each day, the cinema manager suggested that the film be released as it stood.[161]

The score for *On Her Majesty's Secret Service* was again provided by John Barry, 'What I felt was, "Well, we've lost Sean, and we've got this turkey in here instead. And so I have to stick my oar in the musical area double strong to make the audience try and forget that they don't have Sean do Bondian beyond Bondian."'[162] Hunt added, 'I took [John] by the throat and threatened him with his life, and I said, "You had better write me the best Bond score ever." And he did.'[163] Hunt relied upon Barry's instincts, 'I just expected him to know it all. I just said I want the whole film to sound lush, big and beautiful.'[164] Barry had a clear rationale behind his choices:

The reason that we used the instrumental over the titles was because, 'We have all the time in the world' is the last line in Fleming's book. It's the only time that Bond ever gets married for real so to start the movie off with that would have been dramatically inaccurate so I said, 'Let's do the instrumental for the opening and then we bring in the song halfway through the movie as the love theme and go from there.' I harked back to 'September Song' from the film *September Affair* (1950) by Walter Huston; John Huston's father singing about the autumn of his years in a reflective vein.[1645]

However, Hunt had to fight for Barry's vision:

John had this idea to have Satchmo do the song and I thought it was great but someone phoned Harry and said, 'Well we can get him but he's going to cost $5,000 and we can't have the rights.' So, Harry said, 'OK, forget it.' When he told me though I said, 'No way.' I just screamed at him down the phone.[166]

'Satchmo' was, of course, Louis Armstrong, one of the great singers of the Jazz Age. Like Barry, he was also a trumpeter. Barry was moved by the memory of recording with Armstrong:

He was the sweetest man you could ever meet but because he'd been laid up ill for so long, he had very little energy left. He couldn't even play his trumpet but he managed to sing our song, even if it was just one verse at a time. What I couldn't believe though was at the end of the session he came up to me and said, 'Thank you for this job. Thank you for using me.' I couldn't believe it. I should have been thanking him and there he was my hero thanking me.[167]

The poignant song had words by regular Burt Bacharach lyrist Hal David. David wrote two other songs for the film: the contemporary Christmas carol, 'Do you Know How Christmas Trees are Grown' and 'The More Things Change'; the latter remaining unused. Lazenby, however, had his voice to add:

Well, Broccoli and Saltzman never understood music. I offered to get them Blood, Sweat and Tears for the music in *OHMSS* and if you look up the records, in 1969, when the film was released they had five hit records in the Top 10. I had an underground tape with them before they even recorded through my connections in the music industry. As it turns out now, I prefer Louis Armstrong.'[168]

John Barry remembered Lazenby ruefully:

> [He] came down to one of the sessions. He stood at the back and listened to
> the score for one of the scenes. Then he came up to me and said, 'It fits!' as if
> it was the greatest compliment I could ever have hoped for. I thought 'Christ,
> we've got a real brain going here. What do you think I do for a living?'[169]

Maurice Binder's titles featured scenes from previous Bond films to help audiences adjust. Lazenby remembered putting his own twist on the gun barrel, 'I spun around and went on my knee. And they said, "Don't do that, do it standing up."'[170] However, his unique interpretation was used.

Throughout the shoot the producers and Lazenby's agent, Maggie Abbot, tried to get George to sign a contract for further Bond films. Lazenby was paid $50,000 for *OHMSS* but did not feel he was paid a lot compared to Connery. He was due to receive $75,000 for the next film plus a percentage.[171] Lazenby admitted, 'Maggie didn't have any influence over me. She was trying to get me to sign the contract.'[172] However, Lazenby's guru, Ronan O'Rahilly, was, 'Living through me vicariously by upsetting the establishment.'[173] O'Rahilly advised George that Bond was over and that he should be part of the new youth culture movement. Lazenby, with his short, Bond hair and Savile Row suits felt out of sorts with his peers. His refusal to sign the contract caused tension with the producers, but Lazenby felt, 'I was never an actor before and the contract was this thick and it was for seven films. I signed a letter of intent. Ronan O'Rahilly kept sending [the contract] back for amendments for nine months.'[174] Lazenby refused tempting inducements, 'Harry, he was the one who offered me £1 million anywhere in the world to do another Bond film. He was getting into trouble with United Artists because he hadn't got me signed and I'd finished the film.'[175] O'Rahilly countered that the new Bond could earn half a million for a few weeks work on European films, like Clint Eastwood had done, with the benefit of not being typecast. Lazenby admitted, 'Ronan had a hold of my brain.'[176] When O'Rahilly went back to Ireland to attend his brother's funeral, Maggie Abbot tried to get Lazenby to sign. However, when Lazenby called O'Rahilly, the latter exploded, accusing the producers of being unethical by exploiting his bereavement.[177]

No doubt because of the contractual situation, rifts within the Bond team increased. Lazenby recalled Peter Hunt ignoring him on the street prior to the release of the film, '"Hey Peter, it's me," I shouted. "Yes, I know," he replied. At the post-synching, he had someone else speak to me. [I had] not seen the film before the premiere. Peter Hunt wouldn't invite me to see it for sure.'[178]

However, before the release of the film, Peter Hunt was confident, he said, '"I am more convinced than ever now that the picture has been completed that the choice of George Lazenby as Bond was right. We revert to the concept of Bond implicit in Fleming's books."'[179] Hunt took some of the credit:

Many people have said to me, 'How are you going to make him an actor?' There's a great difference between a film star and an actor. With a great knowledge of technical know-how, as well as the human element, the necessary feelings to encourage, coax and bully them, you can get a performance. Films, after all, are made up of small pieces of film and very cleverly edited together; it is sometimes possible to make a performance from anybody. It's the shaping of the film after it is shot that makes the performance.[180]

Lazenby was later nominated for Best New Star of the Year at the Golden Globes.[181]

On 18 December 1969, *On Her Majesty's Secret Service* premiered at the Odeon Leicester Square in the presence of the Duke and Duchess of Kent and in aid of the Newspaper Press Fund.[182] Lazenby had grown 'a beard and long hair so [he] could get laid.'[183] Cubby 'asked me not to come [to the premiere] with a beard. But it was my way of saying "I'm myself – I'm not James Bond" as it were.'[184] Lazenby misinterpreted the power of the final scene, noting the audience 'had a sad look on their face, I thought it was a failure. I thought it wouldn't be a hit.'[185] The after-party was at the Café Royale and was attended by Kevin McClory and Ian Fleming's widow, Anne, and his son, Caspar.[186]

Lazenby noted the changing times, 'People weren't into James Bond. Out of vogue, it wasn't current. Make love not war. [People were] smoking marijuana on the streets in London. Even Wall Street had taken off their ties. I'd go into a restaurant and they'd say, "Waiter!"'[187] Lazenby donated his clothes, 'Three suitcases full of them to the Salvation Army [with labels stating] "Specially made for George Lazenby for *On Her Majesty's Secret Service*."'[188]

The film was a critical and commercial success from the day of release, as contemporary box office records and reviews show. Grossing $87 million worldwide,[189] the film was a drop off from its predecessors, but not a disaster and was still profitable. However, while James Bond would return, the producers could not promote a man as James Bond who would not return and word got out accentuating the negativity surrounding Lazenby, who felt the pair had blackballed him in the business, 'No one would hire me. They thought I was under contract.'[190]

Lazenby's 'tour of America which they had planned for me was cancelled so I went anyway at my own expense.'[191] While promoting the film in New York with O'Rahilly, Lazenby got a call, 'Arnold and David Picker were on the phone. I went to their office. They had rows and rows of books all round the office. "See all these books here. They're all books that we own that we can make into movies. You can take your pick of any one of these books and do one in-between each James Bond film." I looked at Ronan and he said, "Nah, they'll only let you do Bond-type stuff. Because they won't want to ruin the image."'[192] Lazenby again refused.

Lazenby recalled a final attempt, 'They came to me when I was living in LA with Jill St. John. Cubby said, "Will you come back?" I responded, "No Cubby, I'm out of here."'[193] In February 1970 *Variety* ran the headline, 'Lazenby won't be in next Bond film',[194] *Bond 7* which was 'slated to roll next October'.[195]

A last meeting with Broccoli was memorable. It was at the commissary in MGM years later in 1976 with Greg Bautzer, Howard Hughes's lawyer. Cubby said, '"How you doing George? Need any help? We could make a few phone calls." Lazenby replied, "I don't need it. And I got up and walked away."'[196]

Lazenby went on to develop a real estate fortune. He remains in contact with Roger Moore and bumps into Timothy Dalton at British Consulate functions in Los Angeles. In 2002 during the series' fortieth anniversary celebrations, Lazenby attended the premiere of *Die Another Day* screened before Queen Elizabeth II at the Royal Albert Hall, 'I wanted to meet the Queen, like everybody does.'[197] When introduced on stage, Lazenby achieved closure, 'A sprinkling of people started to stand up and then everybody did. I got a standing ovation. That gave me goose bumps.'[198]

Noticeably missing was Sean Connery, another actor estranged from Bond. As Australians about town in London during the sixties, Lazenby had met Connery's wife, Diane Cilento, 'She sent me a note saying, "I feel sorry for you" when I got the job and I thought "That was strange", but then on the other hand she'd spent some time with the other bugger.'[199]

Years later, Lazenby would meet the 'other bugger'. 'I was in a restaurant in Burbank. In walks Sean. He came over and shook my hand and said, "You were good." He looked at me and winked. And I got up and left.'[200]

11

ALL I NEED TO PLEASE ME

DIAMONDS ARE FOREVER

(1971)

UNITED ARTISTS* ANNOUNCES

THE HIGHEST 7-DAY TAKE

IN THE HISTORY OF THE MOVIE INDUSTRY IN THE U.K!

£34,848

(NET)

FIRST 7 DAYS ODEON LEICESTER SQ

HARRY SALTZMAN and ALBERT R. BROCCOLI present

Sean Connery
as
James Bond 007

in IAN FLEMING'S **"Diamonds Are Forever"**

PANAVISION® · TECHNICOLOR®

Directed by GUY HAMILTON

United Artists
Entertainment from Transamerica Corporation

*UA THE HOT COMPANY!

United Artists had sustained significant losses, so much so that the share price of its parent company Transamerica Corporation had fallen nearly four times by the end of 1970.[1] In the beginning of increasing encroachment on the previously independent United Artists, a detailed management guide was issued to all in the Transamerica Group.[2] Transamerica chief John R. Beckett attempted to get the studio to take a more scientific approach to choosing pictures, employing a sociologist, psychologist and anthropologist to appraise trends.[3] Audiences were being lured away from screens by the emergence of television. Arthur Krim returned to run United Artists as a much more selective picture producer.[4]

In January 1970 Broccoli attended a 'huddle with UA executives for two days.'[5] He felt pleased with the Bond films' contribution to cinema, 'It is important to our industry to encourage one another and say, "Well, goddammit, we can make money in this business," to get some spirit in it. We, in our own way with the Bond pictures, have rejuvenated the bloody industry.'[6] While *OHMSS* had been a success, Broccoli felt returns had not been maximised; he disclosed later that although a financial success, 'I have a feeling it would have been more profitable with someone else starring. Like Sean Connery.'[7]

Once again, Eon Productions needed to find a new James Bond. Broccoli had understood there was precedent for new actors in popular roles, 'Well, there were fourteen Tarzans.'[8] George Lazenby was now feeling rueful about his squandered opportunity, 'I was getting bad advice. I learned a lot. I think I could come good now.'[9] Lazenby met Broccoli again, but the producer was careful, '"We'll be in touch George,"' and showed him to the door.[10] Saltzman was keen, 'not to rush into another Lazenby situation.'[11]

Guy Hamilton was signed to direct *Diamonds Are Forever*. His debut Bond, *Goldfinger*, was seen as the gold standard of the series so far and it was felt he could add sparkle to the series after the relatively lacklustre previous entry.[12] He was happy to return to the franchise after a break.

In November 1970 it was announced that the new Bond film would be made in Hollywood. Cubby Broccoli was mournful,

I'm feeling very gloomy about having to go. It makes me sick to see how bad things are in the business. I haven't made a film in America since 1950. I've explained to my friends in the Rank Organization at Pinewood. It was a bit of shock, but they understand.[13]

Broccoli explained, 'We have a geographical problem with the latest Bond. It will be *Diamonds Are Forever*, which is one of the better of the Fleming stories still left to us. Most of it is set in Vegas and there seems to be no way of making it in Britain.'[14] *Diamonds Are Forever* would be based at Universal Studios. Ken Adam, back as production designer, remembered, 'Harry Saltzman had just bought Technicolor and had a very good relationship with Universal.'[15] For Hamilton, it was a victory. He had vowed never to make another picture in Britain, having experienced tough union problems directing *Battle of Britain* (1969).[16]

By November 1970 ten actors had screentested at Pinewood with Broccoli confirming, 'They were all British. We haven't picked anyone yet but we're hoping they will be of British stock.'[17] Guy Hamilton considered the casting process:

> Cubby's and Harry's territory, plus United Artists'. I tested all the junior actors of the period, plus a couple of oddities. None of them had any star quality as far as I was concerned. It was obviously tiresome because if ever Cubby liked one, Harry didn't. If the pair of them did like him, UA didn't.[18]

Associate producer Stanley Sopel acknowledged the producers were trying something unconventional, 'We tested about four American actors. There's some marvellous actors in the United States, but there's no James Bond.'[19] Cubby did discuss the role with an old client, as Robert Wagner recalled, 'The end of the conversation was Bond was an Englishman. He was apologetic about it in a way. I'm so identified as an American.'[20] No one could be more English than explorer Ranulph Fiennes (uncle of actor Ralph Fiennes), who remembered auditioning after 'Sean Connery had retired and his successor, George Lazenby, pensioned off. The interview lasted ten minutes, sufficient for Mr. Broccoli to decide I was too young, most un-Bond-like and facially more like a farmhand than an "English gentleman."'[21]

Guy Hamilton had heard that Roger Moore was in the frame, but was committed to do Sir Lew Grade's television series *The Persuaders*.[22] Others mentioned included British singer Malcolm Roberts,[23] Brett Halsey[24] and John Gavin.[25] John Gavin had previously appeared in Stanley Kubrick's *Spartacus* and Alfred Hitchcock's *Psycho* (both 1960) and Bond spoof, *OSS 117 Double Agent* (1968). Hamilton recalled, 'Dana [Broccoli] was pro-Gavin, hence Cubby was pro-Gavin. I don't really know where Harry stood.'[26] Under their agreement with United Artists, production had to commence in a specified timeframe. A contemporary report stated, 'Pressure to start the picture was now coming from New York. United Artists, a company in troubled waters, needed a vintage Bond quickly.'[27] Broccoli explained, 'Time was getting awfully short. We had to have someone.'[28] With that, Gavin was announced to play James Bond on 29 January 1971.[29]

United Artists had veto rights as to who could play 007 and Hamilton recalled United Artists' president David Picker 'was anti-Gavin'.[30] The studio chief felt:

> We had to get Sean back. I saw Sean, he revealed to me his unhappiness. The only way I could get him back was to make a series of conditions that would enable him to do the film on the terms that he felt comfortable with. Harry and Cubby really were smart enough to realise that the only way to save the series was to have Sean.[31]

Harry Saltzman knew the star 'wouldn't even speak to us'.[32] During the shooting of *You Only Live Twice*, when Saltzman fell ill with Bell's palsy, distorting one side of his face, Connery reportedly said, 'I hope he gets it on the other side.'[33] Hamilton knew, 'You don't bullshit Sean Connery. He likes to know the score.'[34] Broccoli felt, 'He'd talk to Sopel.'[35] Sopel met up with Connery and his agent, Richard Hatton, and over a bottle of Scotch 'went over a lot of old ground. I finally just mentioned a magnificent sum and Sean just laughed.'[36] Sean's favourite Bond girl, Ursula Andress, also reportedly came 'from Paris to London'[37] to persuade him to return to the role.[38]

Then, United Artists made Sean Connery an offer he could not refuse. Picker laid down a salary of $1.25 million plus, reportedly 12.5 per cent[39] of the gross.[40] Additionally, United Artists were prepared to back two projects of Connery's choice.[41] When the deal was announced on 1 March 1971, it was 'unheard of in the present cost-cutting era'[42] and entered the GUINNESS BOOK OF RECORDS for the highest payment to an actor in cinema history. Picker recalled agent Richard Hatton thanked United Artists for getting involved, outlining that the producers had treated his client 'like shit'. Picker noted:

> They renegotiated their own deals with UA, but never addressed what Sean had brought to James Bond. He was simply, in their minds, an actor lucky to get such a break. He felt used and under-appreciated and he didn't like it one bit. A condition of Sean's return was he wouldn't have to talk to either of the producers.'[43]

Connery also laid down demands that the picture must be completed inside eighteen weeks and if the schedule was extended, he would receive an extra $145,000 for every additional week.[44] In the past, Connery had lost work due to overrunning Bond productions: the problematic *From Russia With Love* cost him his role as Irish playwright Sean O'Casey, for director John Ford in the production *Young Cassidy* (1963).[45] Picker was pleased, 'Fortunately, I was able to find out what the problem was, I found a way to solve it and we were able to recreate one more quality film which enabled us to move forward with the rest of the series.'[46]

Connery needed to think about his return to Bond, 'It took a week to make the decision. Why did I come back? Well, the money offered me was tremendous.'[47] Connery would go on to donate his entire fixed fee to his recently founded charity – the Scottish International Education Trust (SIET), which concerned itself with the preservation of new management systems and the retaining of Scottish talent within its borders to prevent a brain drain. In 1967 he had directed *The Bowler and the Bunnet* for Scottish television, this was a documentary on industrial relations in the shipyards of the Clyde. The return to Bond would provide SIET with so much money it would have no excuse to fail and the timing seemed right:

> I've been three years in the process of setting up my own trust. I'm sure that in the film business again there'll never be that opportunity to make that sort of money. Doing the other five [Bond] pictures was a constant conflict to get a better deal. Now, after three years away, the climate has changed and they've come around to agreeing. It's as simple as that.[48]

It is unknown what became of Connery's share of the gross, which would have dwarfed his fee over the lifetime of the film.

Stanley Sopel was in Eon's office on the Universal lot when he first heard that Connery had signed:

> Sean telephoned from London saying he was going to do it. I had this burning secret in me; Cubby rang me the next morning and said, 'Come over and have breakfast, I have some great news for you.' I shot over to his house, and as I drove through the gates he said, 'Sean's gonna do the picture!' I think we had champagne for breakfast to celebrate.[49]

Eon honoured John Gavin's contract and paid his fee in full. Broccoli said, 'It was a business arrangement – with our consent, of course. So we accepted the fact that Sean is Bond – but not that John is not. I think John Gavin will be eligible for the James Bond role when it comes up again.'[50]

DIAMONDS ARE FOREVER was published in the UK on 29 March 1956. Fleming's fourth novel concerns the Service's infiltration of a smuggling operation in a British diamond mine in French Guinea. James Bond takes the place of diamond smuggler Peter Franks, going undercover disguised as a policeman, first to London's diamond district in Hatton Garden. He meets sassy American smuggler, Tiffany Case who leads him, ultimately, to the Spangled Mob gangster outfit headed by Jack and Seraffimo Spang. Bond travels to New York where he meets the next link in the ring, a red-headed hunchback called Shady Tree and also reunites with Felix Leiter, now sporting a hook and false leg after his ordeal at the hands of Mr. Big's goons. Bond travels to the heart of the American racing scene – Saratoga Springs. Here, a fixed horse race results in the death of jockey Tingaling Bell. Hot sulphur mud is poured on the hapless rider's face, burning him to death. The thugs who do this are two tough, gay gangsters – Wint and Kidd. Bond follows the trail to Las Vegas, where more crooked gambling ensues before Bond ends up in Spectreville – a Western ghost town complete with working steam engine. After being tortured by Wint and Kidd, Bond is rescued by Tiffany and they both escape but not before Bond kills Serrafino Spang in a spectacular train chase. Bond and Tiffany return to the UK aboard the steam liner *Queen Elizabeth II*, on which they are attacked by Wint and Kidd; Bond brutally kills them. A coda takes place in the veldt of Sierra Leone, where Jack Spang is tracked down. Attempting to escape by helicopter, Bond shoots Spang down using an anti-aircraft gun. Tiffany ends up moving in to Bond's flat in London.

Broccoli felt, 'Like most of the Ian Fleming stories they need updating to make a film. You can't just take them now, as we were able to in the early days with *Dr. No* and more or less get a script right out of the book.'[51] In late 1969 Richard Maibaum began work on a story about Bond avenging the death of his late wife Tracy.[52] Harry Saltzman suggested inexpensive locations, such as Thailand and India, which would probably release United Artists' funds frozen in the local currency; treks through the jungle and tiger hunts made Broccoli feel it was more like a modern-day *Tarzan* epic.[53]

Borrowing from an early draft of *On Her Majesty's Secret Service*,[54] Maibaum resurrected the idea of Goldfinger's brother appearing – this time as a twin, who was a mad Swedish shipping magnate armed with a laser canon housed in the hull of one of the fleet's supertankers.[55] Maibaum recalled Gert Fröbe was to be cast again, 'This fellow is supposed to say at one point, "Oh, my brother Auric – mother always said he was retarded."'[56] Vegas casinos apparently moored a fleet of exotic boats – Chinese junks and Roman galleys – on nearby Lake Mead. Bond would marshall these to chase the villain, 'because Goldfinger gave the city such a bad name, they wanted to do something patriotic to catch [him].'[57] Bond would paraphrase Nelson, 'Las Vegas expects every man to do his duty.'[58] Hamilton found boats boring and scrapped Maibaum's watery finale.

Cubby Broccoli then had a dream about his friendship with reclusive billionaire inventor, aviator and film mogul Howard Hughes. Cubby's friend never left his Vegas penthouse and only communicated with the world via his personal assistant. Cubby dreamt 'he looked into Hughes's penthouse at the Desert Inn, but when Hughes turned around, it was an imposter.'[59] Maibaum produced a draft dated 8 July 1970.[60]

Scriptwriter Tom Mankiewicz then made his debut in the world of 007. He recalled how the producers found him:

> I wrote the book for the Broadway musical, *Georgy Girl* and [it] closed after three nights. I came back to California with my tail between my legs wondering if it's ever going to happen. My agent called me and said, 'How'd you like to write the next James Bond movie?'[61]

Mankiewicz related what led to his agent's call:

> Cubby said, 'Here's the deal: I need a total rewrite on *Diamonds Are Forever*. I need an American writer and I want him to be young. Most of the picture takes place in Vegas. The Brits don't write people in Vegas well, but I need someone who can write in the British idiom and it's impossible to find someone.' David Picker said, 'I was at a musical two nights ago, *Georgy Girl*, all the characters are British and I thought the book was really terrific. It was written by a Mankiewicz.'[62]

Tom's father was acclaimed director, Joseph L. Mankiewicz and his uncle was *Citizen Kane* (1941) scribe, Herman.

Mankiewicz was thrilled to be working on a Bond, 'They had such confidence in me that they signed me up on a two-week guarantee. Two weeks to turn in the first thirty pages, and the greatest phone call I ever got in my life was from Cubby, "Keep going."'[63] Hamilton admitted:

Sure, it was quite a departure from old Bond, [but] it was larger than life, zany. I said to Tom, 'All that rough American lady language I love, but I can't write it. You are attuned to that. You are also twenty-five and represent younger Hollywood, what's cool and not cool. I will explain Bond to you.' I was a daddy to him.[64]

Hamilton worked daily with Mankiewicz and 'Cubby [who] had a lovely home in Beverly Hills – which he used as his office – would come to the studio when necessary.'[65] Hamilton took inspiration from unlikely sources, 'I saw an ad for Disneyland [and thought what] if all the villains were actually Disney characters and James Bond is in a lot of big trouble fighting Minnie Mouse.'[66] Mankiewicz confirmed it was a conscious decision to make *Diamonds Are Forever* more comedic, more entertaining, so that if Sean rejected the screenplay anyone could have played 007, 'they had John Gavin waiting in the wings, who was going to play Bond if they couldn't get Sean back.'[67] Tone was important and the original ending with Tiffany Case at the mercy of Wint and Kidd was, according to Mankiewicz, 'too S&M; tying her to the bed got a little hot for the censors.'[68]

Mankiewicz was told that:

Sean had said that he was not going to do it unless he got a script he liked. I became a big hero on the Bonds because they sent the first sixty pages [to Sean]. He said he liked it,' "The writer, how old is he?' And they said, 'twenty-six.' And then Sean started calling me 'Boyo – tell the boyo to keep working.' Sean liked it that way too.'[69]

In the pre-title sequence, Bond is hell-bent on finding Blofeld and implicitly extracting revenge for his wife's murder. In a South American clinic, Bond has dispatched a man who he thinks is Blofeld. Professor Metz, an expert in light refraction, is duped by wealthy, reclusive billionaire Willard Whyte to develop a satellite-based laser weapon, which can destroy targets on earth. In order to produce the necessary refraction, large quantities of diamonds are required. A series of sinister deaths signify the smuggling operation is being shut down to prevent detection. Bond is to join the pipeline as Peter Franks and travels to Amsterdam to meet Tiffany Case. Using the digestive tract of Franks's body to hide them, the diamonds are smuggled stateside. After more links in the chain are killed, Bond convinces Tiffany that she is in danger. Bond discovers Whyte's empire has been taken over by Blofeld. The evil villain is parasitically using Whyte's worldwide interests and, as a recluse, Whyte is the perfect kidnap

victim – no one has seen him in years. Rescuing Willard Whyte from house
arrest, the inventor explains that the rogue spacecraft can be controlled by a
simple tape cassette. Deducing Blofeld is probably using an oil rig off Baja,
California as the satellite-control station, Blofeld is revealed to be double-
crossing the idealistic Dr. Metz, who developed his weapon altruistically to
force global disarmament. Now Blofeld begins demonstrating his capabilities
by destroying a US intercontintental ballistic missile silo, a Korean missile
battery and a Red Chinese submarine. With nuclear supremacy up for grabs
to the highest bidder, Bond, with the clumsy help of Tiffany Case, thwarts
global catastrophe as the oil rig comes under attack from helicopter-borne US
forces. In gratitude for their work, Bond and Tiffany return home to the UK
on the cruise ship *Queen Elizabeth II*. here Bond is ambushed by but amusingly
dispatches Wint and Kidd.

Broccoli arbitrated Mankiewicz's wit. The writer remembered his Sherlock
Holmes allusion, '"Alimentary, my dear Leiter." And Cubby says:

> 'What the fuck is this?' 'It's the alimentary canal, Cubby. It means it's stuck up
> his ass.' He said, 'Take it out – no one will know that.' It stayed in the picture.
> In Mann's Chinese [Theatre], out of 1,500 people two guys laughed. Cubby
> looked over to me and said, 'Big deal – two doctors.'[70]

Broccoli also fought the inclusion of Blofeld's taunt to Bond:

> 'As La Rochefoucauld once observed, humility is the worst form of conceit.'
> Cubby said, 'Get it out.' Then, he started calling it 'Nicklaus - is that Nicklaus
> line still in there?' Guy loved it. Years later, Guy says, 'By the way, Cubby,
> I saw *Diamonds* in Paris and La Rochefoucauld got a big laugh,' and Cubby
> answered, 'Paris was the only place we made no fucking money.'[71]

Later, Richard Maibaum contested the screenplay credit and it went to arbitration. He complained to Broccoli in a letter that Mankiewicz 'had all the fun
of second guessing and none of the agony of sweating out the basic story, but
what the hell that's showbusiness.'[72] He also gave Broccoli his thoughts on how
he hoped the finished product would turn out:

> Cubby, you may not like me saying this, but my heart is in the Bond series
> and I hope to hell you have a cutter as good as Peter Hunt. Peter may have
> become a monster as a director and I think he did a hell of a job with an

idiot like Lazenby, but as an editor his contributions to the success of the films can't be over emphasised. He made the films move. Guy's tempo is not particularly fast, and Peter compensated for it, as he did Terence, too. I'm speaking out like this because I still care, whatever I might have said in a fit of momentary frustration.[73]

With Sean Connery back on board, Cubby Broccoli wanted to ensure he now enjoyed the experience. It was important to him that, after this last picture together, they walked away as friends.[74] On set, Connery confided his feelings about wealth, 'However rich you get you never really lose your basic acquisitiveness.'[75] The pressure to perform was solely on the star, 'I feel like I'm at the centre of a huge emotional web. If I'm vulnerable or sick the entire production goes to cock. Nobody seems to realise the strain.'[76]

Universal was still run like a classic studio with an art department employing over 100 assistants. Ken Adam wasn't even allowed to do his own sketches, as there were in-house illustrators. Once Connery was back on board, David Picker calculated that if the film was shot in the UK, Eady Levy payments would almost pay for the star's record-breaking fee. For this reason, it was decided the production should move back to Britain. Having already set up shop at Universal for Ken Adam 'it was a gigantic logistical problem because I had nobody from the British Bond team with me.'[77] Adam called upon Peter Lamont to liaise with the Universal team and set up an art department at Pinewood. Adam was then free to join the unit when location work began in Las Vegas.

Howard Hughes was tremendously helpful to the production, and Hamilton was grateful: 'We were persona (very much) grata in Las Vegas, because it takes special permission to shoot a film there, especially inside the casinos.'[78] Later on, Broccoli would receive indirect requests from Hughes to see the latest Bond picture, and Hamilton recalled, 'I said to Cubby, "Send him the new one, and then halfway through the reel put in an insert shot that says 'Howard Hughes, you prick! Why don't you call me? Love, Cubby.'" And Cubby said, "No, you don't know Howard." We never did get to meet him.'[79]

Broccoli also relied on legendary lawyer Sidney R. Korshak. Allegedly the Chicago mafia's man in Los Angeles, he was one of Hollywood's most influential fixers. An unamed Korshak acquaintance felt 'Cubby Broccoli and Sidney were like brothers.'[80] Hamilton recalled that Korshak was also very helpful in securing working permits for the British contingent, 'There were only four limeys – me, Sean, Ted [Moore – cinematographer] and Ken [Adam]. The rest were U S of A.'[81]

As with *Goldfinger*, *Diamonds Are Forever* featured gangsters. Hamilton remembered, 'They were already in the Fleming books. [DIAMONDS ARE FOR-EVER] which is all about gambling and what have you, that was inevitable if you go to Vegas at that time, it was mob controlled.'[82]

Hamilton had been fascinated by the underworld and cites his innocent upbringing in Paris for his interest, 'It started at Sunday School in Paris, I was about nine or ten, we had an American in the class and he mentioned Chicago. So, instead of getting along with the bible lessons, we all quizzed him about Chicago and Al Capone. That was a very satisfying introduction.'[83] Hamilton retained an enduring fascination with organised crime.

As well as guaranteeing the cooperation of the Vegas teamsters, Korshak asked 'whether a small role could be arranged for actress Jill St. John, a close friend of his.'[84] Jill St. John had also been connected to Henry Kissinger and had briefly courted George Lazenby. St. John was quoted at the time as saying, 'The longest period of celibacy for Jill St. John is the shortest distance between two lovers, I suppose.'[85]

Guy Hamilton described his only argument with Cubby following lunch with Korshak:

[We were] in [Cubby's] red Ferrari – a little two-seater, I said 'Korshak is an impressive character.' And he said 'Yeah, you know Jill St. John? She's a good friend of his. And I thought it would be nice if she played Plenty O'Toole.' I said 'Cubby you're joking.' He said 'No, it's a small part, come on, he does us a favour, we do him a favour.' I said 'But Cubby, Plenty O'Toole – the whole joke is she's got enormous tits. He said 'Jill St. John is gonna play Plenty O'Toole.' I said 'Over my dead body Cubby, I mean it's ridiculous.' He stopped the car and we go at it. This is the only real fight or shouting match that Cubby and I ever had. And I meant it because to me it would fuck the whole thing up. I said 'Jill St. John is a perfectly capable actress. I've seen her in a lot of stuff. She would be fine for the bigger part. But fucking Plenty O'Toole? No fucking way.' Everything cools down. I can see Cubby's brain whirring. And he said 'Yeah. I think it's a good idea.' And of course he is delighted to ring Korshak and say 'Your girlfriend (or whatever the relationship) is up for the lead.' Korshak informs Jill who is then wheeled round that evening for a drink.[86]

Hamilton felt St. John knew 'she had been imposed on me by the strength of Korshak. [In the end] I thought Jill was splendid in the picture.'[87]

Hamilton said of Tiffany Case on location, 'She has to purvey a genuine haughty sex appeal. She has all the complicated sexuality of Scarlett O'Hara.'[88] Broccoli felt, 'There are three actresses in the world who would be great as Tiffany – Faye Dunaway, Jane Fonda and you'll have to think of the third. Could it be Raquel Welch?'[89]

Jill St. John remembered she 'had known the Broccolis. Luckily I didn't have to [screentest]. They had seen some of my former movies and I was thrilled.'[90] She felt a strong connection with the part:

> I rather thought of her as myself. I put a lot of myself into the character. And I loved the name. I did think she was intelligent and I have that conceit. And I did think she could get herself out of most situations, which I have done. But she was outside the norm – she was a diamond smuggler, she was a crook, she was many, many things. And I feel like I've had several lives. I really identified with Tiffany Case.[91]

St John also had input into the look of the character, 'The designer's name was Donfeld and we had lots of fun costumes, some of which I still have. I still have the bikini I wore on the oil rig.'[92]

Plenty O'Toole, a good-time Vegas girl, was played by Lana Wood, younger sister of Natalie:

> I received a call from my agent saying that Cubby Broccoli and Tom Mankiewicz wanted me to come out and chat with them about the new James Bond film. I was delighted because I was an Ian Fleming fan. I then received a call from Tom Mankiewicz, who is a friend and he said, 'Please try to look tall.' He said he was pulling for me. When they started going over the script and discussing casting, he brought my name up immediately. So I went out and shopped for an outfit that would make me look tall![93]

Mankiewicz's joke tipped her to wear high-heeled boots. 'I remember walking in those heels trying desperately to look taller.'[94]

Wood recalled Cubby Broccoli. 'He was a presence. Very charming, very interested in what I had to say. Of course, I felt like I had an ally there because of Tom Mankiewicz, who was such a dear friend of the family. It was not a terribly long interview and there was no [screen]test.'[95] During production Lana would make another friend on set in Connery. 'I had had dinner at his house when he was married to Diane in Putney. I felt very comfortable with him.'[96] Wood remembered only seeing Harry Saltzman once on the film at breakfast, but was advised by Mankiewicz not to disturb him: 'He will get very angry.'[97]

Wood was initially up for the role of Tiffany Case and appeared to have won it. However, she then:

> got a phone call from my agent. They said that Cubby absolutely adored me. They said that they had run into a political situation but Cubby likes me so much, would I consider playing the smaller role of Plenty O'Toole and not the lead? I said, absolutely I'd be delighted just to be a part of it. I didn't really know what role I was interviewing for – I was just going.[98]

Wood remembered Hamilton,:

> Guy was very easy going. The first day I cornered him and said, 'This [is how] I see Plenty … I don't want her to come off as a heavy or someone manipulative, I want to speak in a higher voice, I want to make her very sweet, very honest, very empty headed.' I tried to mimic Leigh Taylor Young and Minnie Mouse. I needed that type of a lilting voice. I wanted her to come off as very ingenuous. It was a choice.[99]

Hamilton gave her free rein. '"Lana," he said, "Do whatever you want."'[100]

Charles Gray was cast as the third consecutive actor to play Ernst Stavro Blofeld. Hamilton admitted it was a villain he 'inherited' and that Gray was 'not ideal casting.'[101] Gray recalled Mankiewicz telling him, 'Blofeld is like Hedda Hopper, the notorious gossip columnist. At one point we even had him dressed in drag, we had him say outrageous lines. He was sophisticated and funny.'[102] Jill St. John remembered her co-star:

> was a little removed. Not aloof, but removed. I remember we made a deal that I would teach him chess if he would teach me bridge – neither one of us completed it. But we tried. I thought he was rather interesting. And I liked that character, he played such an androgynous character – that's not easy to pull off. And I thought he pulled it off beautifully.[103]

Rounding off the predominately American supporting cast, was country and western singer Jimmy Dean as tycoon Willard Whyte, Norman Burton as the fourth Felix Leiter, jazz musician Putter Smith as Mr. Kidd and Bruce Glover as his partner in crime Mr. Wint – lighter and more comedic, but as sinister as their literary counterparts. Bruce Glover, a straight actor, was inspired by his co-star:

> I looked over at Putter Smith and started an inner monologue going – 'So we're gay and gays kiss' – I looked at Putter's snagly moustache, teeth and mouth, and knew I did not want to kiss that mouth. So what about this Putter guy? I looked there he was a musician, I think they all are hearing music all the time he was animated and [had] happy slapping palms. He had no idea how hard acting was. I loved it, what fun he was to look at, he was like a big wind-up toy, just wind the key in his side. There was the relationship; he was *my toy*.[104]

Small roles were also found for old-school Hollywood talent such as Bruce Cabot, star of the original *King Kong* (1933) and Marc Lawrence, both of whom were friends of Cubby's. Hamilton remembered: 'These old actors had, in a way, fallen on hard times. Cubby was delighted to be able to help them out.'[105] Joseph Furst played the misguided professor Dr. Metz.

Production began on 5 April 1971 in the Nevada desert, doubling for South Africa. The first scene in the can was villains Mr. Kidd and Mr. Wint, killing Dr. Tynan by dropping a deadly scorpion down his shirt.[106] Bruce Glover remembered, 'The property master came to me and said, "Bruce come with me, we have to pick out your scorpion."'[107] Mankiewicz remembered:

> I had originally had Mr. Wint and Mr. Kidd put a scorpion down his mouth and the Brits said, 'The kids will not be allowed to see that,' although it's fine with the Americans. Then you saw Lana Wood's breasts for about a quarter of a second and the Americans said, 'No, no, no', and of course that's fine with the Brits because they are healthier about that.[108]

On 12 April 1971 Sean Connery reported for duty as James Bond. Hamilton recalled that Connery was particularly pleased with the screenplay, 'He did suggest alterations, but fundamentally he agreed that Bond must be exaggerated, expanded, after the kind of saturnine presence of *OHMSS*.'[109] Tom Mankiewicz met Sean Connery for the first time when he touched down in Vegas:

> I was surprised by how much homework he had done. He had gone through [the script] very carefully and the thing that was surprising to me was that most of the notes he had were for other parts. For instance, he would say,

'Couldn't she say something better than this to that guy?' Most of the time it had nothing to do with him.'[110]

Mankiewicz's comments echoed of those of fellow Bond writer Johanna Harwood, made a decade earlier. Connery thought it, 'The best [script] they've had, certainly construction-wise with a beginning, middle and an end of a story.'[111] Hamilton also enjoyed the story, feeling that the 'dollies are snappier [and] anything is possible.'[112]

After a two-film hiatus, Hamilton fought to retain the veteran Bond cinematographer, 'I needed Ted Moore. Ted Moore is not a member of the American Society of Cinematographers. [Cubby] said, "Guy, it's taken care of." I said, "Cubby stop bullshitting me." I didn't yet know of Korshak's influence.'[113]

Connery joined the unit shooting the first major action sequence: Bond escaping the Vegas police in a red Ford Mustang Mach 1 along the sidewalks of the famed Freemont Street. The scene was the brainchild of Guy Hamilton, 'We can do a car chase up and down downtown Vegas because that has got the best lighting, all the signposts, the cowboy with the cigarette … it's fantastic.'[114] Mankiewicz recalled Hamilton 'hated American cars, so in any sequence with American cars – and there are a couple in *Diamonds* – the American cars all had to spin out, they were useless, they were these big, flabby, you know, pieces of tin.'[115] Hamilton needed to close busy downtown Vegas for three nights and Broccoli leaned on Korshak to make it happen. The director was ordered to attend a meeting with the Las Vegas Downtown Traders' Association set up by Korshak. '"Now how many people are against this proposition?" You can see fifty people dying to hold their hands up but at the back there is the heavy gang. [Korshak says] "See Mr. Hamilton we're walking you to Vegas."'[116]

Stunt co-ordinator Paul Baxley, who had doubled Steve McQueen and performed the famous motorcycle jump in *The Great Escape*, led a team of twelve drivers, who destroyed twenty-four of the fifty-five cars needed to complete the sequence. Set entirely at night, Hamilton recalled that Ted Moore was 'impressed by the amount of free lighting'[117] supplied by the garish neon.

While the unit was shooting the car chase, Mankiewicz remembered Harry Saltzman appearing in Vegas. Sitting with Sean Connery in his trailer were Hamilton, Jill St. John, Cubby Broccoli and Mankiewicz, 'Just as we were about to do the first shot, there was a knock on the door and Harry walked in, defiantly. Sean stood up and grinned and said, "Harry", and went over and kissed him on the cheek. Harry just stood there immobile, and left the next day.'[118]

Hamilton spent several nights shooting in the casinos. Ken Adam recalled that Broccoli would play baccarat every evening. 'Cubby, who was a big gambler, said I was his lucky mascot and I had to sit next to him and play. Cubby used to give me a thousand dollars to keep on playing.'[119] Wide-eyed, Tom Mankiewicz watched in awe:

Cubby never won or lost less than $50,000. And I remember we were in one of the last mob-owned casinos, the Riviera, when one night Cubby said he wasn't going to gamble anymore – just keno cards from now on. And then he would proceed to buy 10,000 keno cards! It's like the guy who says 'I'm not drinking hard booze anymore,' and then you watch him down twenty-five beers in a row. So, I said, 'Cubby, why don't you just go back to the baccarat table?'[120]

As for Sean Connery, Hamilton recalled the actor barely went near the tables '[He] threw a few dice maybe, tried one-arm bandits. Basically he was there for the job, and his sights were set further away.'[121]

Tiffany Case needs to find out where the real diamonds are after Bond is nearly cremated. She aims to seduce him to find out the information and so a team of goons rudely interrupt Bond's plans with Plenty by throwing her out of the high-rise Vegas hotel window. As the gangster played by Marc Lawrence, drawls, 'I didn't know there was a pool down there,' we see Plenty splash to safety. Lana Wood recalled filming the scene in stages:

I was thrown out of a first floor window onto a mattress. We then changed locations over to the International Hotel and they had built this taller platform near the deep end of the pool and had a stuntman standing on the platform. I climbed on his shoulders and he pushed me upward and moved back so that the fall was accurate, so the last 16ft was me. The only thing that bothered me was that I would be standing on a stuntman's shoulders in a pair of rather transparent light blue panties out in the open, which concerned me. They said, 'No, no, no, it's going to be about two, three in the morning by the time we get to that scene, there won't be anybody around.' Well, I climbed up there and I looked around and there were hundreds of people who were all on the inside of this glass walkway separating them from the pool area and watching. It was a long way to fall and I was not thrilled when I came up and they said, 'OK, we've got to go for another shot.'[122]

Bond is found gambling on the roulette wheel when Plenty O'Toole spies a new conquest. Bond's quip on hearing her name – 'Named after your father, perhaps' – was yet another example of the Mankiewicz wit. Lana Wood, the diminutive actress remembered shooting with 6ft 4in Sean Connery, 'I know they were a little panicky that they couldn't make me look tall enough, so I ended up standing on an apple box for Sean.'[123] Further scenes involving Plenty including a dinner at Vegas eaterie Dome of the Sea – where Bond orders wine and sends it back, foreshadowing the ending – were cut.

Cubby Broccoli requested a cameo be filmed with famed Rat Pack crooner Sammy Davis Jr., which later ended up on the cutting room floor. Hamilton didn't think it was the greatest idea in the world. 'I couldn't think of any shtick. We've got enough problems keeping the picture the right length. He was very sweet and professional. We just chopped it out. And I think Sammy was glad we did because it would not have done him justice.'[124]

The actor was a friend of Lana Wood:

> I was travelling with two cats and one of their nails caught on my cheek, so I had this rather significant cat scratch; I went down into make-up and everybody started getting upset, 'Oh, what are we going to do, what are we going to do?' And I took some eyelash glue and stuck a dot on my cheek and took a piece of hair, cut it and stuck it onto my cheek and said, 'There, now Plenty O'Toole's got a curl on her cheek.' Later that day, Sammy called me up in my room as I was just getting un-Plenty-fied [concerned about my injuries].[125]

Desmond Llewelyn flew into Vegas to film his scenes as Q, this time demonstrating a voice box detector and the one gizmo Llewelyn wished worked in real life – an RPM controller, a small signet ring which ensures the slot machines pay out every time! The actor recalled:

> When I'd finished the scene, I was left there with all this money that I'd won. So, I thought to myself, that I could either stuff it all in my pockets and go back to my hotel or chance my luck on the other machines. I decided on the latter, thinking I might go home rich. I put ever single coin back in and didn't win a bloody sausage. So much for Q's gadgets.[126]

In downtime, Llewelyn took in the sights and sounds of Vegas with Charles Gray and was amazed by the free entertainment such as the flying acrobats in the circus that were wasted on the distracted gamblers below.[127]

Bond's escape from Willard Whyte's Techtronic research centre across the Nevada desert in a moonbuggy was shot during the first week of May.[128] While working on the script in Hollywood, Mankiewicz and Hamilton were amused by America's obsession with, and continued pontification about, the lunar landing. 'I said to Tom, "Come on, James Bond is going on the moon." And he said, "Oh, how do you reckon that?" I said, "They apparently have out in the desert, in Utah, somewhere where they test all this crap that is going to the moon."'[129] What followed was a clever sequence in which Bond escapes from a makeshift moonscape inside Whyte's laboratory, out into the heat of the Nevada desert. Conceptualised by Ken Adam, the one-off lunar machine was built by Dean Jeffries – a custom car designer in California. Adam's brief from Guy Hamilton was simple – 'it should look grotesque'.[130] The final vehicle was fragile and kept breaking at high speed, Hamilton recalled it was 'fine going up and down outside the studio lot but once it got out on to the real [terrain] it had problems.'[131] Interestingly, twenty-two years later, this unique Bond vehicle was restored by Graham Rye, then president of the James Bond International Fan Club. Rescued from a field in Kent, it went on to become an exhibit at Planet Hollywood, Las Vegas.

On 15 May 1971 the unit moved out to Palm Springs; first they shot at Kirk Douglas's property – the same house where Leslie Bricusse had penned the lyrics to 'You Only Live Twice'. Lana Wood remembered the scene, 'The whole thing was I went to [Tiffany's] house, was going to battle her for the man I called Peter Franks and got bored, started trying on her wigs, bad guys break in, think I'm her and tie my ankles together and throw me into the pool.'[132] The scene was ultimately cut, but Wood recalled the danger of playing a drowned corpse:

> They used a block of cement and they tied my ankles to it. It started to slip towards the deep end and there came a time when I would hear the camera stop rolling and would go to reach for the rope to clear my mouth and nose and couldn't. I literally could not clear my face to breathe. So they got a little panicky and jumped in and turned me loose pretty fast.[133]

Ken Adam also used the rather unusual, but architecturally interesting, Elrod House for Willard Whyte's mountain retreat. It was here that Bond had a sparring match with the sultry gymnastic bodyguards Bambi and Thumper. With its vaulted ceilings and exposed rock surfaces, one could be forgiven for thinking the house was actually designed by Ken Adam himself. When he first discovered this outlandish property, Adam's initial enquires proved disappointing. He turned to Cubby, who once again leaned on Sidney Korshak 'and within twenty minutes we had the permission.'[134] Thumper was played by Trina Parks, who was first spotted by the producers on stage at the Flamingo in Las Vegas. Parks was asked if she fancied doing 'a wild scene with Sean Connery'.[135] The credit for the actress playing Bambi was ascribed to Donna Garrett, but years later journalist Tim Greaves revealed that she was only a stunt double; the uncredited actress who actually played Bambi was Lola Larson.

The finale of *Diamonds Are Forever* plays out on Blofeld's oil rig, off the coast of Baja, California when Felix Leiter leads a CIA helicopter attack on Blofeld. Jill St. John remembered her commute to the set, 'It was in Oceanside. You'd have to take a helicopter out to the oil rig and if the weather was windy or bad it was always a bit precarious.'[136] The oil rig was to have been demolished by explosive-bearing frogmen who rehearsed the scene on the surface.[137] Although the frogmen were omitted from the final sequence, this small piece of information may explain why divers can be seen on the film's poster art created by Robert McGinnis.

In June 1971 work continued back at Pinewood. Miss Moneypenny was seen on a rare jaunt out of the office in Dover, where she gives 007 his necessary papers before he embarks on his mission beginning in Amsterdam. Hamilton was 'tired with this hat-throwing routine. Let's get [Moneypenny] out of the office.'[138] Lois Maxwell nearly lost the part when her agent asked for more money. The producers said they'd recast, 'I said, "OK, replace me." Suddenly, the Bond people came through and said that there had been such a furore because they were going to find another Moneypenny that they wanted me to do it.'[139]

Bond's briefing with M and Sir Donald Munger of De Beers was a signature scene for Mankiewicz's wit. Firstly, there are a number of in-jokes: Bernard Lee as M abstaining from alcohol on 'doctor's orders' and reference to Connery/ Bond's abstention from the series – 'We do function in your absence' were nods to real life. The drinkmanship came as a result of Cubby's lawyer Norman Tyre pointing out a mistake, as Mankiewicz recalled:

He was part of the wine jury who gave the stars out to different wines, and he said, 'Would you tell that kid that there is no year on a Sherry bottle, it can't be '61. What they do is take casks and put the worst vintage on top and then the next and the next and then the best vintage is on the bottom, so they all run through the best vintage but there's no year.' So quickly, embarrassed as I was, I changed the scene to reference the original vintage on which the sherry [was] based.[140]

Saltzman thought Vegas and its vulgarities made it 'the home of producers everywhere.'[141] Hamilton noted similar taste in Bond's accommodation:

Caesar's Palace, the presidential suite, fan-fucking-tastic! Anything that wasn't moving was painted gold. There were mirrors everywhere. It was so gloriously vulgar so kitschy, it's unbelievable. And [Ken Adam] said, 'But it's awful!' I said, 'That is the whole point Ken!' He said, 'BUT THEY WILL THINK I HAVE DESIGNED IT!'[142]

Adam later admitted he 'never liked designing those kitschy Las Vegas sets'.[143] Jill St. John enjoyed the camaraderie of the crew at Pinewood:

Bob Simmons was really brilliant. I remember one day at Pinewood he made breakfast for all of us and he made kippers – I had never had kippers – which I thought was the best thing I'd ever had. It was that kind of set where you've got the head stuntman making breakfast for you.[144]

The actress enjoyed living in London too, 'I rented 16 South Audley Street which was owned by Jacqueline Saltzman.'[145]

St John noted Dana Broccoli 'was so wise besides being so warm. If Cubby would win a lot of money somewhere, she would immediately go out and buy a painting – a good one – or a good piece of furniture. Occasionally, a piece of jewellery. It was usually something of lasting value.'[146]

The Broccolis were thoughtful and generous hosts to St. John:

I could walk to their house, they could walk to mine. You'd be there for dinner and you'd meet all these wonderful, fabulous people. I remember I'd never had treacle tart and their cook had made a particularly spectacular one and I raved about it and the next day a treacle tart was delivered to my house in South Audley Street.[147]

By contrast, St. John felt, '[Harry] reminded me a little bit of a grey-haired bulldog. He was very kind. He wasn't as tall as Cubby, he was not a fat man but a stocky man. Those are the guys who are really strong, they're small and compact. I much more gravitated towards Cubby.'[148]

Guy Hamilton admitted he found 'fights boring'[149] and in an attempt to create an exciting punch up for Bond's confrontation with diamond smuggler, (the actual) Peter Franks, he found inspiration in a Victorian lift in a friend's London apartment block. Hamilton thought this was 'a marvellous place for a fight because it's small [and] every time they swing, [an] elbow will break something.'[150] Bond's opponent was former wrestler and Honor Blackman's judo teacher Joe Robinson, 'It was Sean who recommended me to the director because he knew what I looked like and what I could do. I trained him to fight in those scenes and did all the choreography for it.'[151]

On Friday, 13 August 1971 Sean Connery's work was completed, on time, in eighteen weeks. Hamilton recalled, 'I was always careful about keeping to the schedule. And we finished exactly at four o'clock on the last day of [Sean's] contract.'[152] He noted that 'with a limited number of days, one has to clearly perceive the thing. All our problems were worked out before we shot a foot of film.'[153] Connery was vindicated, 'It can be done you see, if there's money at stake. I've been frigged about too much on other Bond pictures.'[154] It was appropriate that the last shot of his schedule was Connery being placed in a coffin and the lid closing – an analogy that closed the lid on his association with Eon Productions.

Barry's score perfectly encapsulated the Bond of the seventies. Hamilton was insistent *Diamonds Are Forever* captured the Vegas vibe:

I have a tendency, that drives John absolutely nuts, to put bits of music on my rough cuts to see how it works. The umpire band in 'Circus, Circus' was absolutely terrible. John had removed that and put on something rather slick. I said, 'You have missed the whole point [it is supposed to be] terrible.' He said, 'But I can't have that music on my LP!'[155]

In an attempt to rekindle the *Goldfinger* success, John Barry composed the title song for Shirley Bassey. The lyrics were written by Don Black, who confessed, 'Seediness was what we wanted. It had to be over-the-top with a dash of vulgarity.'[156] Recalled Barry, 'Shirley would say, "What's it about John?" I said, "I'll tell you what to do: don't sing it about a diamond, sing it about a penis."'[157] Although the lyrics were suggestive Black admitted, 'I certainly didn't think of a penis when I wrote it, I was just thinking of diamonds.'[158] Upon hearing the recording Saltzman had another outburst at his composer. 'He was so impossible to deal with ... I could never deal with Harry.'[159] 'Diamonds Are Forever' became another Bond classic and won an Ivor Novello award for John Barry and Don Black. Additional sonic kudos was earned by Gordon K. McCallum, John W. Mitchell and Al Overton who were were nominated for the 1971 Academy Award for Best Sound.

Maurice Binder's process to design the titles was mercurial as he explained:

I find storyboards are good for sketchy ideas. Many advertising agencies use these storyboards to sell the client on a sketchy idea and then they're stuck with it. I mean, the client remembers the storyboards, and it becomes a hard issue. I like to use storyboards as a reference, because every time I look through the camera, I see new things that I want to capture. My mind changes constantly. I'm certainly not going to just shoot a storyboard, because what you can do on film, you can never reproduce with a sketch. I make some pencil sketches for myself. I tell the production department what I want. The main reason that the titles are filmed last is that the music isn't written until the picture is finished.[160]

Binder also designed the teaser trailers where a Christmas bauble hanging on a tree riffs on the gun barrel sequence with Connery firing at the audience from within it. The emphasis of the campaign was on the return of Sean Connery as James Bond.

Connery sparked press interest when he attended a London screening with his guest Roger Moore. *Diamonds Are Forever* was first shown in West Germany on 14 December 1971. After opening in London on 30 December there was a presentation in Connery's hometown, Edinburgh, at the local Odeon with all proceeds going to Connery's new charity. With a worldwide gross of $116 million, the movie significantly out-performed *OHMSS*. United Artists' gamble had paid off – the public loved the return of Sean Connery as 007 in the series' seventh film.

When asked if Bond had had his day, Connery responded, 'Possibly. I wouldn't know. It's perfectly possible the cycle has ended. I came back for the one, that was the understanding. I've got other things I want to do.'[161] Broccoli said while *Diamonds* was in post-production that in his opinion Connery, 'would be very good for the next [film]. I think that Sean could play quite a few James Bonds. He's mature, he looks great in this picture, better than he's ever looked.'[162]

12

GIVE THE OTHER FELLA HELL

LIVE AND LET DIE

(1973)

XVIIII

THE SUN

VI

THE LOVERS

XIII

DEATH

Academy Award
Nomination
BEST SONG
"LIVE AND LET
DIE"

MUSIC and LYRIC
by
PAUL and LINDA
McCARTNEY

"LIVE AND
LET
DIE"

United Artists

II

THE HIGH PRIESTESS

XX

JUDGMENT

VII

THE CHARIOT

Arthur Krim had returned to more actively oversee United Artists[1] and the sale of film libraries to television was starting to help the diminishing studio coffers. United Artists and Eon agreed to sell the US television rights for the first seven Bond films to ABC for $17.5 million – an estimate based on the purchase price for *Goldfinger* of $2 million.[2]

Steven Saltzman confirmed the worsening state of affairs at his father's company, Eon Productions, '[Broccoli and Saltzman] alternated on films. It didn't mean they weren't both involved but one had final decision and was actually dealing with it on a daily basis. For *Live and Let Die* it was Harry.'[3] Eric Pleskow, soon-to-be president of United Artists taking over from David Picker, remembered, 'In those days, I stayed at Claridges and they came to see me. They were sitting on opposite sides of the room, wouldn't look at each other. It was like [being] in a kindergarten trying to get the children to talk to each other.'[4]

Eon Productions was still run from two offices. Saltzman recruited a personal assistant from Saudi Arabian arms dealer Adnan Khashoggi – Sue Parker. Parker set out how things were:

> I sort of noticed that after the meetings, Guy Hamilton and Tom Mankiewicz and various other production managers – [including] Claude Hudson; they would all disappear and go over to Cubby's office. Tom Mankiewicz said, 'Oh, we're going to have a drink. Harry doesn't have anything in the office. Cubby had got this big bar.' [Harry] said, 'Well, go out and buy some booze.' The difference is that Harry hadn't noticed.[5]

It was no surprise that in this atmosphere, long-time associate producer Stanley Sopel was headhunted by Sean Connery. According to Sopel's son, David, 'He approached a few of the guys at Eon including my dad and said "Come with me, we'll set up a production company and we'll make films."'[6] Ultimately, Connery's Tantallon Films, formed with agent Richard Hatton, produced Sidney Lumet's *The Offence* (1972) – the United Artists' film made under Connery's *Diamonds Are Forever* deal.

Guy Hamilton was reluctant to sign for Bond again, saying, 'I don't want to spend my life making James Bond, that's what you do.'[7] Saltzman had thrown down a gauntlet, which had originally enticed him to helm *Diamonds Are Forever*: 'the challenge [of] making a Bond without Sean'.[8] It remained unmet.

The studio still wanted Connery. Tom Mankiewicz recalled sounding the actor out, '"Boyo, all they can offer me is money." The only two things he ever wanted in his life were to own a golf course and a bank. And he had both.'[9]

United Artists suggested they cast an American, and a star, mentioning names like Steve McQueen and Paul Newman.[10] Clint Eastwood confirmed, 'My lawyer [who also] represented the Broccolis said, "They would love to have you." But to me, well, that was somebody else's gig. That's Sean's deal. It didn't feel right for me to be doing it.'[11] After seeing him on television, Hamilton recommended Burt Reynolds, 'I remember at an after-premiere party Cubby [had] Burt Reynolds as a guest. So obviously there had been mutterings and flutterings of a possibility.'[12] Broccoli, again, thought of John Gavin.[13]

Between 5 and 7 June 1972 screentests took place in London.[14] One contender was future Bond villain Julian Glover, 'I'd just done a series for BBC TV called *Spy Trap* – very loosely, a sort of Bondian thing.'[15] Glover remembered, 'Guy was there. It was at Pinewood – I couldn't work the gun properly. I was very bad [and came] away feeling very ashamed.'[16] Once again, Michael Billington tested for:

> a specially written scene. I think I did well on the test for *Live and Let Die* and liked Guy Hamilton. I heard from my agent's "insider" that there was going to be an offer made. When it was announced that Roger Moore was going to do it, I was stunned.[17]

Roger Moore, whose name had been in and out of the frame, enquired about the role. Saltzman explained to him, '"Basically, the problem is that you made a picture for UA called *Crossplot* [1968], which they weren't too happy with."[18] Saltzman was reassuring, "You're on my mind."'[19] Parker can 'remember very clearly Harry calling Roger, saying "Hang in there. I think it's all going well, we are seeing this person and that person. You'll get it." I don't think Dana [Broccoli] wanted him. I remember Harry saying, "You know, she's trying to put the knockers on it."'[20]

Roger Moore while at Pinewood Studios filming the first series of his Tony Curtis crime-fighting double-act television show *The Persuaders* had interacted with the Bond crew.[21] 'When Sean left the franchise, I knew the role was up for grabs again and declined Lew Grade's offer to make a second series.'[22] Moore, Broccoli and Saltzman would 'sit around the [gambling] tables like real-life James Bonds.'[23] The producers would 'sometimes show me the films in the Audley Street screening room.'[24] Moore remembered, 'We were great social friends and with Harry, we would have a poker school probably once a week or play gin.'[25]

Saltzman called Moore with a breakthrough:

'You mustn't talk about this, but I think Cubby has come round to thinking in terms of you for Bond. But he says you're too fat. David Picker says the last time he saw you your hair was down your back. What are you going to do?' I said, 'I'll take weight off and get my hair cut.' He said, 'Don't discuss this with anybody except your agent.'[26]

Moore received a three-picture deal worth $1 million plus a percentage.[27] His salary for *Live and Let Die* was $180,000, with an increase of $60,000 per picture and a percentage of profits starting at 2.5 per cent rising to 3.25 per cent.[28]

DennisVanThal [was my agent]. Dennis Selinger was a great friend, socially, and he would assist on negotiations but was not taking commission, that was Dennis VanThal. DennisVanThal was London Management and Dennis Selinger was ICM.The relationship was between Harry and Dennis Selinger.[29]

Moore commented:

The money is comforting. I'll make no bones about that. But it was not the God and the goal. I'm happy as long as I can make enough for my children to continue living in good style. Possibly by doing Bond, I will be able to move myself out of fourteen years of television.[30]

Moore met Guy Hamilton at the Fleming haunt – Scotts 'over a dozen oysters and martinis. I confessed to Guy that in reading the script I could only ever hear Sean's voice saying, "My name is Bond." In fact, as I vocalised it to myself I found that I was giving it a Scottish accent.'[31] Hamilton was adamant, '"You don't play Sean. Forget Sean. We've got to. There are lots of things that Sean does very well that you can't do and there are a lot of things you do well that Sean can't do."'[32]

Roger Moore remembered his first encounter with Connery, 'We met at a cocktail party somewhere. Billy Barnes. It would have been '62 or '63.'[33] The two actors grew to be friendly with each other over the ensuing decade. Moore admitted:

It's a tough shake to follow Sean. But I won't give an imitation, I promise you that. Sir John Gielgud has played Hamlet scores of times. But that doesn't stop other actors from having a crack at the role. They bring their own individuality to it. Hopefully, I'll do the same for James Bond. It is inevitable, I suppose, that comparisons will be drawn with Connery. That can't be helped. In any case it is better to go into a vehicle that is successful than something that's not.[34]

'My job is to bring out your strengths and cover your weaknesses,'[35] Hamilton remembered saying to Moore. 'Roger had enough hair to stuff a mattress and we had to get his hair cut which was quite dramatic. He kept popping in at Tilney Street and saying, "How's this Guy?" I said, "No, Roger, it's got to be short back and sides. Proper." And he'd go off again.'[36] Broccoli also told Moore, '"Think like Bond, act like Bond, BE Bond!"'[37]

On 1 August 1972 the Dorchester was host again to the unveiling of a new James Bond.[38] Moore announced:

> I think that I've got an even-money chance to make it. After all, I've been around a long time in this business. I did *The Saint* on television for seven years then *The Persuaders* on television with Tony Curtis. And as a matter of fact, Cubby and Harry tell me that when they first started making the Bonders, I was their first choice for the role. I don't believe them, of course. But that's what they say.[39]

Moore never took Bond seriously, 'My attitude is that he's sort of a ridiculous hero. I mean heroes to me are ridiculous and I have to play them tongue in cheek.'[40] Moore read a few Fleming books but he:

> only found one thing and that was he had a scar on his cheek and looked like Hoagy Carmichael. And the only other key to his character was that he had come back from Mexico where he had eliminated somebody. He didn't particularly like killing but took pride in doing his job well.[41]

He learned the Bondian walk, Moore was told, 'You have to move like a cat, pushing off with the ball of the foot, feeling the earth beneath you. Once you move it's got to look like you could walk through a brick wall if necessary.'[42] *Cosmopolitan* magazine approached Moore for a male centrefold and suggested using a Walther PPK to protect his dignity, 'I said not even with a Thompson sub-machine gun.'[43]

Hamilton had insisted the producers re-hire screenwriter Tom Mankiewicz, 'I said, Maibaum is a very nice man, I had a lot of respect for him, but at this period he'd run out of, to me, freshness. He was basically an old man compared to Tom.'[44] Mankiewicz's agent Robin French asked Saltzman for a fee of $100,000 to write *Live and Let Die*. Saltzman said they could guarantee fifty. French agreed as long as it came with 2 per cent of the profits. After a brief silence Saltzman replied, 'We'll not talk science fiction. Okay, he'll get a hundred.'[45]

LIVE AND LET DIE was published in the UK on 5 April 1954. Fleming's second Bond novel sees 007 set out to New York, Florida and Jamaica to thwart a gold smuggling operation run by Mr. Big – 'Buonaparte Ignace Gallia' – a huge Haitian criminal mastermind. Big employs a mixed bunch: Tee Hee – so known for his cackle, Whisper – lung disease has left him barely audible, and numerous others. Masquerading as Baron Samedi, Voodoo Lord of the Dead, Big plays on the fears of African-American followers whom he uses as an intelligence network. He is actually a Soviet SMERSH agent. Big has discovered gold – from the hoard of seventeenth-century pirate Sir Henry Morgan – off the coast of the Isle of Surprise, near Jamaica. He is recovering the gold and selling it in America to fund Soviet activities there. Big is aided by a beautiful seer, Simone Latrelle, known as Solitaire. Bond is pursued by a network of agents to Harlem. Seeking freedom from her captive life, Solitaire assists Bond and, after planting a limpet mine on Big's yacht, they thwart him just as they themselves are about to be keel-hauled to death. In America Bond also reunites with Felix Leiter, only, later in the action, to discover Leiter's mutilated body and a grim note – 'He disagreed with something that ate him' – the aftermath of being manipulated into a shark pool.

Mankiewicz recalled,:

> Having had the experience of *OHMSS*, United Artists was desperately concerned that the film be, above all, entertaining. David Picker said to me, 'I want to have enough stuff in this picture so that no matter *who* plays Bond, it is a terrific, entertaining evening in the movies, for anybody.'[46]

Broccoli was concerned by the condescending way the book treated racial minorities.[47] By 1972, as the US gradually emerged from years of segregation, there was an increasing cultural awareness amongst its black population. A new genre featuring African Americans in prominent and positive roles was becoming popular in mainstream cinema. When *Shaft* (1972) became a hit with all audiences, the era of the 'Blaxploitation' picture boomed. Cubby Broccoli sampled a couple of these movies while in New Orleans with Hamilton, who recalled, 'It was an experience with an all black audience when you're the only whitey in there.'[48]

Following MGM's success with *Shaft* every studio began developing similar 'black gold'.[49] In an America only recently emerging from segregation, an industry report noted:

> A common sight these days is two lines at a twin theatre, one white and one black each purchasing tickets for 'their' picture. Plotting of *Live and Let Die* indicates the industry's recent efforts to maximise grosses by integrating theatre audiences. The Bonders are naturals for this angling since many of the Blaxploitation pictures resemble Bond in blackface.[50]

Hamilton asked, '"Where should we take Bond this time?" Tom said, "You're a jazz fiend, you would love New Orleans." "What else is there?" "Well, there are jazz funerals." I thought that was terrific.'[51] They needed more:

> [Mankiewicz] said, 'Well, there are bayous.' Immediately my mind went back to the Esther Williams pictures that I adored. There was one where they had girls on top of the skiers – a pyramid and motorboats went up a ramp and jumped. I thought, 'Yeah we can make a motorboat chase out of this.'[52]

The boat sequence was conceived, according to Hamilton, for *Diamonds Are Forever*, 'We were in Vegas [at the] Hoover Dam and I wasn't happy because it was just boats on water. That to me is incredibly dull. Thinking about it, boats crossing roads, jumping over roads, that's the start of a chase that will be fun.'[53]

In the pre-title sequence three British agents are killed. They have been investigating the prime minister of Caribbean island, San Monique – Dr. Kananga, who doubles as a Harlem gangster – Mr. Big. Bond is sent to New York and soon discovers that Big is using voodoo to maintain a vice-like grip on his territories. Bond encounters Big's claw-armed henchman Tee Hee and the virginal Solitaire, Big's personal clairvoyant. 007 follows the trail to New Orleans where he discovers a heroin processing plant. Travelling to San Monique, Bond is met by CIA agent Rosie Carver, who turns out to be a traitor. It is here Bond meets an incarnation of Baron Samedi and where he tricks Solitaire into sleeping with him. With 007 captured, Mr. Big is provoked into revealing himself as Dr. Kananga in order to establish whether Solitaire has lost her virginity – and with it her powers. San Monique is growing vast quantities of poppies and Kananga's diplomatic status makes their processing and distribution by Big's Harlem network easier. Having amassed two tons of heroin, they plan to distribute it for free in the US, significantly increasing demand, which they will then profit from by supplying more at full price. Tracking Kananga down to his underground distribution plant, Bond and Kananga fight to the death, the latter exploding after ingesting an expanding shark pellet. Bond and Solitaire travel back by train only to be assailed by Tee Hee, whose claw-arm is used against him. The film ends with a resurrected Baron Samedi riding the train.

Ken Adam was committed to *Sleuth* (1972) directed by Joseph L. Mankiewicz – Tom's father – so Syd Cain returned as production designer. Hamilton described Cain as 'a straightforward craftsman, very good because we didn't need any huge romantic sets or anything hugely imaginative.'[54] Although *Live and Let Die* was predominantly led by Harry Saltzman, Cubby Broccoli escorted Guy Hamilton, Tom Mankiewicz and Syd Cain on a reconnaissance mission to New Orleans and the West Indies in March 1972. Cain recalled they started in Grenada and went from island to island:

> Martinique, Antigua, Puerto Rico, Haiti. Haiti was a 'must' as many people there practice voodoo and Guy wanted to get the "feel" of the place. Despite the value of seeing actual voodoo practised, it was decided not to film in Haiti due to the unstable political situation and a recent rash of riots that had broken out.[55]

They finally settled on Jamaica.

Initially, Hamilton had reservations about the island, 'Terence had used it in *Dr. No* very efficiently. To hell with *Dr. No* – we don't have beach scenes.'[56] The location would be a stand-in for the fictional island of San Monique. They needed to find something different. Inspired by the coffee plantations on the island, Mankiewicz wrote a scene in which Bond is thrown into an industrial bean grinder.[57] Cain recalled what happened next. 'I saw a big sign on the gate which read TRESPASSERS WILL BE EATEN.'[58] They had discovered a crocodile haven run by a certain Ross Kananga. 'We not only used his farm but we named our villain after him.'[59] In earlier drafts, the character was called Jakata.[60]

The final leg of the location hunting took place in the South where Mankiewicz remembered overt racism was rife:

> The minute you got out of New Orleans into those parishes, you were in another country. We negotiated with the sheriff where the boat chase took place and we were going to spend something unbelievable then, like a million and a half dollars, in his parish in 1972. He said, 'I know you got a lot of Negroes on your crew and in your cast and I don't want Negroes driving

[vehicles] in this parish.' And Cubby said, 'Well sheriff, I guess we'll have to find another parish to drop our million and a half in.' And the sheriff said, 'Now hold on, hold on.' And, of course, we insisted that every vehicle be driven by an African-American.[61]

Mankiewicz found some of Saltzman's ideas absurd:

'Now Bond is asleep in bed and he hears a noise and he looks over and he's in bed with a crocodile.' I would say, 'Harry, why doesn't the crocodile eat him? They've got little feet, how does it get [up there in bed]?' Harry would jump up and down and say, 'You're the writer, God dammit!' Harry's great fantasy – he brought it up on every movie I was on – he had this fixation of Bond walking into a giant spin dryer and they close the door. Harry said, 'I don't know, figure it out.'[62]

Tom Mankiewicz delivered his draft screenplay dated 5 May 1973. Diana Ross, the African-American singer turned actress, was suggested for the role of Solitaire, as Mankiewicz recalled, 'Cubby got in touch with her people. She was a huge star at the time. It was David Picker and the powers that be, who said, "No".'[63] Hamilton was told that, 'UA were concerned if there was kissing between Bond and a black girl'[64] that some towns in the US would refuse to run the picture. Picker told Mankiewicz that if Connery had played Bond he may have taken a chance, but with a new actor he was risking enough.[65] 'He always felt that Bond was a port in this storm, a port where people could go to escape and be entertained. He didn't want to contribute to everything that was going on politically and socially at the time.'[66]

An actress who purportedly turned Solitaire down to have a child was Gayle Hunnicutt. However, Sue Parker remembered, '[Harry] was a bit Mr. Malaprop – he got people's names wrong. Did you hear the one about Gayle Hunnicutt? Well she came in for an audition and he kept called her "Hunnicunt".'[67]

The producers eventually cast 21-year-old British actress Jane Seymour, star of the recent hit television show *The Onedin Line* and daughter-in-law of Richard Attenborough, as Solitaire. When Seymour arrived for her audition in South Audley Street, she noted the increasing strain between Saltzman and Broccoli:

The two of them had this huge argument right in front of me about who spotted me first … Then one of the secretaries pulled me out of there and said, 'I think you better come wait out here.' There were politics involved, as I later found out, and since this was a 'Harry film' I only ever saw Cubby again once, which was when he invited me to his house and gave me my first [glass of] champagne and my first taste of caviar.[68]

Seymour was cast on the spot after Saltzman witnessed Jane removing her hat and watched her long hair tumble down her shoulders. She remembered her feelings on leaving the office, 'I was in total shock about the whole thing. I got into my little Volkswagen Beetle and accidently backed into Harry Saltzman's Rolls Royce.'[69]

CIA double agent Rosie Carver had originally been white but Mankiewicz rewrote the character after Solitaire was switched. 'The story was about black people and we could not pretend that Bond would not be attracted to a black woman. We compromised a bit; they kissed and they obviously made love but you don't see them in bed together.'[70] Hamilton admired the producers for quashing studio concerns, 'Cubby said, "If we lose some dates in Mississippi, we lose some dates in Mississippi."'[71]

Gloria Hendry recalled her entry to the Bond world, 'I got a call from my manager, he said, "The Bond people would like to see you so you need to fly to New York and audition." I said, "Who's paying for this audition?" He said, "You are."'[72] Hendry invested in her career and met Harry Saltzman:

I walked into his office and this wonderful man stands up, white haired with dark eyes, very regal and he points to me to sit down. And he said, 'How was your trip to New York, Madame?' No one's ever called me 'Madame', being a young woman. He said, 'How soon can you get ready to go to New Orleans? I'd like to introduce you to Guy Hamilton and Roger Moore, they're shooting a movie.' I said, 'OK.' – I mean, an actress never refuses. I was picked up in a limousine. I had never been in one before. I get on this flight – first class – I had never flown first class before.[73]

Hendry was immediately in awe on meeting her potential co-star, '"Oh my God, this is The Saint." A week later, I had the part.'[74]

African-American actor Yaphet Kotto was cast as central villain Dr. Kananga a.k.a. Mr. Big, Hamilton later observed:

Yaphet Kotto, I regret bitterly. I did not enjoy working with him at all. Originally it was to be a very distinguished American black actor. Suddenly

Harry Saltzman announced he's out and UA say Yaphet Kotto is really hot property. We were forced into Yaphet Kotto. I'd never met him until he turned up on the set.[75]

Kotto recalled, 'Picker, one of the executives from United Artists, walked up to me in the street and said I had been cast in *Live and Let Die*. I was shocked because it was the first time an executive had come and told me the role was mine.'[76]

When Hamilton first met Kotto on location in Jamaica, the impression was not good:

He starts off thinking he should be playing Bond – quite seriously. He was very badly behaved, he would try and make life difficult. I am tremendously pro-black and I was determined because of having a big black cast that they all be treated properly – it wasn't us – it was the American crews that treated them like shit[77]

Kotto didn't like the script, 'It was just too simple. There were too many [lines like] "Hey baby!" We don't talk like that man, we really don't. I don't know where [Mankiewicz] got that shit from. He overloaded it.'[78] Kotto also felt *Live and Let Die* failed to push the envelope far enough, 'If you are going to do a movie and use black and white characters go the whole way. Was [Kananga] having sexual intercourse with Solitaire or not? Yes he was! Those issues were overlooked. They couldn't make up their mind how far to go with that.'[79]

Roger Moore wrote in his diary on the making of the film: 'When Yaphet Kotto came to New Orleans and gave the Black Power salute there were those who said he had a chip on his shoulder. As a black actor in a predominantly white industry perhaps he believed he had to assert himself.'[80] Asked about Moore's comments by the authors Kotto replied:

I don't think that was fair. [But] I can see how he would have arrived at that opinion because I was very aloof and removed from everyone. I stayed away from everybody. It may have appeared I had a chip on my shoulder because I was quiet. I am not there to socialise. I think method actors are misunderstood. Maybe he wasn't used to method actors. I don't know what his problem was. It didn't bother me then, it doesn't bother me now.[81]

Kotto revealed:

> Broccoli became my father. He was very, very, very, warm and paternal to me. He was concerned about what I ate and how I got along with Saltzman because he wasn't there for the shooting. Harry was tough. Saltzman was like Martin Luther King. I said 'Harry wouldn't it be great if we had black stuntmen?' So for the first time in history, he hired back stunt co-ordinators on the movie. If you look at the movie you'll see all those boats are being driven by black drivers. He was so happy to do it. Saltzman says to me 'Who else would do a thing like this Yaphet?' I said 'Harry you are the greatest.'[82]

Geoffrey Holder not only played Baron Samedi, but also choreographed the voodoo dance sequences. Holder had in fact met Ian Fleming in Harlem during the early sixties, when the author was brought as a guest to a dinner party he was hosting.[83] Holder attended a dance school run by an aunt of Yaphet Kotto. Yaphet recalled:

> I've known him practically all my life. I was eleven years old and one day at my aunt's house, a party was being readied and the guests started coming in. I came out of my room and there was this tall guy, just coming in the door and I heard this laugh. Little did I know that years and years later I would be doing a movie with him![84]

Mankiewicz recalled Holder taking him to a real voodoo ceremony while filming in Jamaica, 'I drank something that I will never know what it was! I really started seeing people coming out of graves that night!'[85] Also present was Jane Seymour who found the entire affair rather freaky:

> all the people were definitely in trances, and I witnessed the sacrificing of chickens and blood flying around. The women were all in white dresses, just completely out there I certainly got the idea of what we were trying to do in the film, so you could say I definitely did my research![86]

The film featured an assortment of African–American actors playing heroes and villains. Roy Stewart was Bond's San Monique help, Quarrel Jr., a call back to *Dr. No*, while Lon Statton played Harold Strutter, 007's New York contact. Earl 'Jolly' Brown was the rotund Whisper and Julius W. Harris was gleeful as he chewed scenery as henchman Tee Hee, deprived of his arm by Good Old

Albert, a hungry crocodile, and now equipped with a mechanical claw. Both the villains were different from their literary counterparts.

Principal photography commenced on 13 October 1972 in New Orleans.[87] Roger Moore also noted how his relationship with Harry Saltzman shifted:

> Harry changed in the sense that I was no longer a friend, I was an employee. Harry could treat the making of Bond rather like owning Hamleys. Chairs would be lined up on the set and he would have his visitors down. There was a more relaxed attitude with Cubby around, a great deal of respect from the crew for him. Cubby wouldn't prioritise guests coming. The picture went ahead and went ahead in an easy fashion.[88]

Moore recalled:

> We arrived at the location we were going to shoot and all the tables were laid up with knives and forks and plates I said, 'Wow, you could tell this was an English production.' And Harry went apoplectic and he screamed at George Crawford the catering manager that too much money was being spent on catering and everything was cut down to a minimum. George Crawford was given a limited amount of money for each meal and so George retaliated by serving rotten chicken. The brothers immediately called an emergency meeting and threatened to strike and we went back to having full rations.[89]

Filming began with the epic boat chase, which took twenty-four days to shoot in the Louisiana lakes and bayous.[90] The sequence involved speedboats flying over roads, skidding across lawns, landing in swimming pools and at one point sliding through a wedding ceremony. Peter Lamont, now promoted to art director, was tasked with prepping the locations around the bayous. Lamont had two weeks to re-find every inch of the sequence, as all the locations spotted on the previous recce were unrecognisable, 'all the vegetation was growing. You couldn't see anything. We gave [the photos] to Mankiewicz and said "Right, write the boat chase."'[91] Mankiewicz recalled:

> For a long time, all I had in the script was, 'And then follows the most amazing boat chase you ever saw.' We were about ten days from shooting when United Artists asked, can you write that 'most amazing boat chase you ever saw'. So Guy sent me to my room to finally write the scene into the script.[92]

During their reconnaissance the filmmakers spotted a sprawling twelve-acre estate with a house in the middle belonging to the Treadway family. The Treadways would become invaluable to the production, providing their estate for the wedding sequence and becoming unofficial location co-ordinators during the shoot.[93] Another local, Doree Schneider, played the bride driven to tears when the boat chase cuts straight through her wedding party. Schneider recalled how friendly the locals became with the crew, 'We would celebrate their birthdays and have cake and candles; Guy Hamilton, Derek Cracknell, Peter Lamont – all have photos with their cakes. I guess we showed them true Southern hospitality.'[94]

Before shooting commenced Lamont also oversaw the preparation of twenty-nine vehicles at the Glastron Boat Company in Austin, Texas for the ambitious sequence; five of these doubled Bond's sleek speedboat.[95] Local stunt driver Jerry Comeaux supervised the boats and stuntman for the bayou jump.

When Roger Moore arrived he was thrown straight into action behind the wheel of the Glastron, which was capable of speeds up to 75mph. The end result was a sequence crowned by Jerry Comeaux, who set a Guinness World Record when, doubling as Bond in the Glastron GT-150, he leapt a distance of 120ft from the water over two cars and back into the bayou. Comeaux spent six weeks preparing the leap, constructing special ramps and made over a hundred practice jumps.

It was fourteen days into production before Roger Moore even uttered his first line of dialogue. Whilst rehearsing with the speed boats the new 007 suffered an accident, which left him with a chipped tooth and an injured knee.[96] The vehicles proved unruly when shooting the wedding stunt, a craft slammed into a Cyprus tree. Lamont recalled, 'the whole side of the boat was wiped out'.[97] Minutes later Comeaux attempted the stunt again and damaged a second boat. A perfect result was achieved on the third take.

Guy Hamilton had driven across the USA on his honeymoon in 1965 and had become fascinated by the corrupt sheriffs to be found in small rural towns:

> I was pulled over. I had to think very clearly because in some states you must freeze with your hands on the wheel. In other states you've got to leap out and spread. And a Sheriff Pepper comes up and says, 'Good evening. You're not from round here are you?'[98]

For light relief, and to break up the lengthy boat chase, Mankiewicz created the Southern redneck Sheriff J. W. Pepper, who is ill-prepared for the havoc Bond and Mr. Big's hoodlums are about to wreak in his parish. He explained:

I love writing dumb sheriffs. When you're writing a screenplay, sometimes characters just take off with you. There was just going to be a sheriff in the boat chase
but the more I was writing with him, the more fun I was having with him. Guy
Hamilton just adored the character so his part just kept getting bigger.[99]

The role was first offered to Slim Pickens, memorable from *Dr Strangelove*,
according to Clifton James, who ultimately played it.[100] Casting director Marion
Dougherty invited him to read for the role in New York, as the late actor
recalled to authors in 2014:

Dougherty knew me from a play I had done – *All the King's Men*. Surprisingly,
I think I was the only one that she called. I guess she figured I could do the
part. I read it in about five minutes; they gave me the part and I flew to New
Orleans the very next day.[101]

Mankiewicz thought James was perfect casting, 'All those Southern sheriffs
down there all looked exactly like Clifton James. Clifton would say, "Hello, boy"
and all these sheriffs would keep laughing and say, "Goddam, you're funny."'[102]
    When regular special effects wizard John Stears was unavailable, Syd Cain
enlisted Derek Meddings,[103] a leading pioneer of miniature special effects, who
had come to the fore on work for Gerry Anderson, most famed for *Thunderbirds'*
'Supermarionation' television show, which itself owed a nod to Bond. Meddings
supervised the boat chase and the car chase with 'Peter Lamont guiding me
because I was the new boy to these fantastic Bond pictures.'[104] Following Bond's
elaborate jump over Sheriff Pepper one of Mr. Big's pursuing speedboats ploughs
into Pepper's parked police vehicle. Meddings made the resultant 'car-boat'.
    The climax of the boat chase was originally to be Hamilton's aforementioned
Esther Williams-inspired sequence which saw Bond racing up the bayou to be
confronted by 'a triangle of men on skis carrying the prettiest girls with little
banners on top. Bond manages to swerve past the triangle but the villains come
along and the whole triangle collapses in front of the audience.'[105] Watching the
rushes back in London, Broccoli told Saltzman, 'This fucking boat chase just
goes on and on,'[106] and put a stop to any further action. Hamilton was disappointed that Saltzman did not defend the stunt 'sufficiently'.[107]
    On 1 November 1972 the unit moved to New Orleans Lakefront Airport[108]
to film a madcap action sequence involving Bond outrunning Mr. Big's cohorts
in a Cessna plane. The sequence was different from the standard chase, in the
fact the plane never even takes to the sky and all the action unfolds on the

ground. Mrs. Bell, who Bond 'borrows' the aircraft from was played by local actress Ruth Kempf, who had never appeared in an international picture but 'had read every single one of the Ian Fleming James Bond 007 books – so my delight to be in one of his books brought to the screen was enormous.'[109]

While at Lakefront Airport, Yaphet Kotto joined Roger Moore and Jane Seymour for a photo call with attending press. Kotto caused a fracas when he began punching the air with a Black Power salute: Moore recalled:

[Publicity director] Derek Coyte pointed out that the pictures would rouse resentment from the rabid whites and would be seen as an endorsement of black power by militant blacks. We are making anything but a political picture, but Derek said the photographs syndicated far and wide would involve us in a controversy, which could do nothing but harm. Yaphet was incensed. At midday he and the black stuntmen lunched together and during the afternoon Derek Coyte was ostracised by blacks [with whom he] had previously been pally.[110]

Kotto was later disappointed to learn he had been left out of key publicity surrounding the film:

Harry was concerned about the image of an African–American bad guy. One day he called me and said, 'Just before anyone tells you, I wanna tell you we had all the press here. They talked to all the actors.' I said, 'Harry they didn't talk to me.' That bothered me. Still bothers me to this day. When the film opened I was in a Harlem bar on 135th Street because I wasn't invited to any of the openings. I was very depressed. I was in bar with my brothers and sisters watching television. I cried a little bit, I got emotional, I was with my people but I wanted to be with [the cast and crew] but the door was closed on my ass.[111]

Despite this sense of ill feeling, Kotto did attend the US premiere.[112]

On 12 November 1972 the crew left New Orleans and headed for Jamaica, the location doubling for the fictitious island of San Monique. Moore remembered his commute to the set:

Harry insisted on driving me to location sometimes [from] where we were staying in Ocho Rios. And Harry drove as though everybody knew that Harry Saltzman was a producer and *they* would be coming round the corner on the wrong side of the road. It was absolutely terrifying – I was absolutely petrified of being driven by him.[113]

Roger Moore visited Ian Fleming's home Goldeneye in Oracabessa and was photographed sitting at the desk where the author wrote the James Bond novels.[114] The ghosts of *Dr. No*'s location shoot in Jamaica were to be found in the Laughing Water set of the Sans Souci Hotel, where Geoffrey Holder first appears as a nightclub dancer.

Jane Seymour joined the production in Jamaica, 'Roger Moore used to call me "Baby Bernhardt" because I'd take things ever so seriously.'[115] Seymour became the subject of much of Hamilton's and Moore's humour:

> We were naughty because she was prissy, she took life very seriously and between takes Roger and I did not take life so seriously. I cannot say anything awful about Jane because she worked very hard and cared very much. Not an easy part for a young white girl to play. It should have been someone older and more sensuous I think.[116]

Gloria Hendry joked at her leading man's expense prior to shooting their love scene, 'I purposefully ate a lot of garlic the night before, [but Moore quipped] "You're lucky, my wife is Italian."'[117] Carver's death scene – shot by a weaponised scarecrow – was not pleasant either, 'On my run when I fell down; they had me on that ground for so damn long. And, of course, the sugarcoated blood that's on me – those ants were having a freaking ball! I wanted to get up so bad.'[118] Her impression of the producers was that 'they had the same flavour, meaning they were very serious men; strong, sturdy and confident. You knew they were in charge. I saw Cubby once or twice on set but this was Harry Saltzman's venture. He was producing this one. Harry was like a teddy bear for me.'[119]

Action shot in Jamaica included James Bond escaping to safety across San Monique behind the wheel of a London bus. The spectacular climax sees Bond racing towards a low bridge shearing clean off the upper deck as he escapes to safety. Syd Cain's art department bought an AEC Routemaster from London Transport and hired bus driver Maurice Patchett to perform the stunt, who also trained Roger Moore to drive the vehicle.[120] Back in London, Moore had undergone a crash course on the skid-pan at Chiswick.[121] The Routemaster had arrived in the traditional London red livery. Cain had it sprayed nlue and green, the colours of the fictitious San Monique transport. Cain recalled that Patchett, who also performed a 180-degree U-turn at high speed, found his brief film-making experience 'a welcome reprieve from driving a bus through the streets of London'.[122]

On *Live and Let Die*, Hamilton and Mankiewicz perfected the 'snake-pit situation'[123] – putting Bond in impossible scenarios and devising inventive ways for him to escape. Their self-imposed challenge was to keep their viewers on the edge of the seats, Hamilton remembered the mantra, "'Audience – you have got thirty seconds to guess." We had some beauties, that we never found a solution for.'[124] One of the most memorable was Bond stranded on an island in a crocodile farm surrounded by hungry reptiles. The resolution was devised and performed by farm owner Ross Kananga. Bond would use the beasts as stepping stones to escape. To perform the stunt, Kananga tied the crocodiles' feet to concrete blocks leaving their heads and tails free. Syd Cain recalled:

> When Ross did it the first time he in fact slipped and fell into the water, and on the fifth take he was actually bitten on the heel of his shoe. Guy Hamilton said, 'OK, chaps that's enough of that, it's getting far too dangerous,' but Ross insisted on doing it once again, of course, now the crocodiles would be expecting him. The moment they felt him running across their backs they made every attempt to snap at him. It was on the sixth take that he managed to do the stunt, and that's the one you see in the finished film.[125]

Moore noted with a smile, 'A little touch that I thought was really evil: [in the scene Bond is wearing] crocodile shoes.'[126]

In December 1972 the unit regrouped at Pinewood Studios.[127] Derek Meddings showcased his skills once more, this time creating a miniature of Mr. Big's poppy fields to be destroyed by multiple explosions. The sequence was originally supposed to be shot on location but having run out of time Hamilton wanted to finish [in Jamaica] and get back to England to proceed with the studio work.[128] Meddings recalled, 'It is extremely difficult to spot that the fields were a miniature, in fact, since Roger Moore and Jane Seymour were seen running around the fields, it seems completely unlikely that they had been miniatures.'[129] Meddings work looked so impressive he would become a regular member of the Bond team.

Syd Cain's flagship set was Dr. Kananga's underground lair complete with monorail and shark pool; the entrance to the base was through a voodoo graveyard. Roger Moore described it as Harry Saltzman's own private side-show, imagining him saying, "'This is all mine, my puppets are over there."'[130] Saltzman's daughter Hilary recalled that she had her eleventh birthday party at the studios, 'My whole class was invited to watch *Live and Let Die* being shot that day. And that was an extraordinary experience. I thought it was awesome so I can't imagine what my class thought!'[131] On one occasion Saltzman, oblivious that the red studio light was on, continued talking to his latest round of guests. First assistant director Derek Cracknell bravely announced, "'Quiet on set everybody! And that includes *you* Mr. Saltzman, sir.'"[132] Cracknell's audacity extended to even the leading star, Hamilton recalled a moment on set:

> Roger is now smoking Havanas. It just so happens that we are now ready to shoot and Roger's just lit up his cigar. And Derek says, 'I'll look after it Rog.' Roger comes back and [Derek] hands him the cigar which is now half-length and he says, 'Well, if you will fluff your lines, it's your fucking fault.' Roger gave Derek a box of Havanas as a passing present.[133]

For the first time since *Dr. No*, *Live and Let Die* took audiences inside Bond's home, created on the B Stage,[134] Syd Cain recalled that Saltzman's first impression of the set was not good, "'Bond is larger than life and the set is too small. I won't let you shoot on it.'"[135] The producer eventually relented, deciding that the situation was so critical that M and Moneypenny must make an emergency visit to Bond's home. Hamilton recalled they wanted to introduce audiences to Roger Moore 'not in M's office which is the classic scene, because there were too many connotations, but in his own home.'[136]

There had been doubts that Bernard Lee would reprise his role as M due to the tragic death of his wife, Gladys Merredew, who had been killed in a fire at their home on 30 January 1972.[137] Moore recalled, 'Kenneth More asked me to tell Harry and Cubby that he would play M, and they could send the fee to Bernard, which is a very gentlemanly gesture. Our co-producers said they will take care of him anyway.'[138] Lee did eventually return.

Lois Maxwell knew Moore; they'd trained together in the same class at RADA back in 1944.[139] Quizzed on the difference between Connery and Moore, Maxwell would reply, 'If Moneypenny had her choice she would have Roger as her husband and Sean as her lover.'[140]

In the film M briefs Bond about a series of assassinations, which have taken place in the pre-title sequence. The presence of M and Moneypenny at Bond's flat serves another function, as they issue Bond with special ordnance: a Rolex watch with a magnetic field capable of deflecting a bullet at long range. Q was mysteriously written out of the film. Desmond Llewelyn was later told, 'Saltzman was getting fed up with gadgets.'[141]

M tells Bond that the Service is also looking for an Italian agent, Miss Caruso, who has temporarily disappeared. She becomes Roger Moore's first 007 conquest and was played by Madeline Smith who remembered:

I was in an episode of *The Persuaders* and I think that [Roger] suggested me for the part because I never auditioned. They'd completed most of the film by then. They were just finishing bits and pieces off. He looked absolutely divine. I can remember an impression of a very empty, Malmost-like aircraft hanger and the sets kind of tucked away in a corner and him busy rehearsing something with a stuntman, also little Jane turning up and sitting quietly on a chair to do some sort of completing shots. It was very much an end-of-film feeling. I never met the producers. It was like doing a little television comedy sketch. The part didn't even have a name when I [shot] it – later they called me Miss Caruso.[142]

In the film, Bond uses his special Rolex to delicately unzip Miss Caruso's dress. Smith recalled, 'It was very unlaborious. They'd put a thread down the back of the dress. Derek Meddings is an absolute master and for him that was a very simple little thing to do.'[143] Moore remembered Derek Cracknell was on the floor 'with his hands up Madeline's skirt pulling a hidden wire attached to the end of a zip, so the floor around our feet was getting pretty crowded.'[144] Smith joked, '"Crackers must have had a nice happy holiday down there!"'[145]

Live and Let Die wrapped in March 1973 with final location shooting in New York. With the picture shooting on the doorstep of United Artists' parent company Transamerica, Hamilton dreaded the daily visits by curious studio executives to watch him shoot an action sequence in which Bond steers an out-of-control taxi from the backseat, through the streets of downtown Manhattan. Hamilton's answer was to offer the studio suits the thrill ride of a lifetime and place them in the middle of the action:

> About three of them got into one of Jerry Chitwood's cars and I told Jerry to get one of the police cars to bang into the car. Then, 'Action' and suddenly a police car comes along and bangs into them. The UA people go bananas and they got out and I never saw them again.[146]

Eon stalwart Charles Russhon arranged for the suspension of traffic 'on FDR drive for a Bond chase scene (and that isn't done in one take).' Roger Moore called him 'Mr. Fixit' because he seemed to be able 'to do or get anything in New York City'.[147] Before Bond's driver is shot by one of Mr. Big's hoodlums, Bond had been on his way to meet CIA buddy Felix Leiter. Again the character was recast, this time played by David Hedison – an actor Roger Moore had known since *The Saint*.[148]

Upon wrapping, Moore joked the schedule had been like a holiday, 'After filming a one-hour show (*The Persuaders*) every ten days, a two-hour movie in twenty-two weeks was easy.'[149]

John Barry's involvement in the stage musical *Billy* meant he was unavailable to score *Live and Let Die*.[150] Roger Moore wrote that originally Cubby wanted to talk to Bond lyricist Leslie Bricusse to pen a lyric.[151] Paul McCartney, had recorded a track at his own expense and submitted it to the producers. Hamilton recalled:

> Harry takes me to the only recording studio in New Orleans. 'I have been sent a tape by George Martin, who is the arranger of all the Beatles numbers.' I said, 'I'm not a Beatles fan but let's hear it.' Well, it's not exactly my music but the Beatles are the Beatles. I said, 'I don't think you should look a gift horse in the mouth.'[152]

Ron Kass, former head of Beatles label Apple Records, was now working for Harry Saltzman.[153] McCartney had wanted to contribute to *Diamonds Are Forever*. Now Kass arranged for the ex-Beatle to go to a screening of *Diamonds Are Forever* in Saltzman's private screening room, which McCartney attended with Ringo Starr.[154] For *Live and Let Die*, McCartney used the Fleming novel as inspiration, 'I read it and thought it was pretty good. And that afternoon I wrote the song.'[155] The songwriting credit, shared with his wife Linda, may have been an attempt to circumvent his publishing obligations to his former Beatles publisher Northern Songs. Any co-writes, other than those with John Lennon, would not, he had argued, fall under the existing agreement.[156]

Long-time Beatles' producer George Martin recalled Saltzman:

> 'stunned me when he said, 'Who shall we get to sing the song?' I said, 'Well, you do have Paul McCartney!' 'What do you think about Thelma Houston?' I said, 'She's very good, but you do have Paul McCartney!' 'How about Aretha Franklin?' He always thought in terms of women.[157]

B.J. Arnau, as a Fillet of Soul nightclub act, performs the song in the film. However, as regards the title track, Martin 'had to diplomatically tell [Saltzman] that if he didn't take Paul McCartney he didn't get the song.'[158]

Mankiewicz remembered Cubby was not too enamoured with the song either:

'Boy didn't we get taken – listen to this!' I said to him, 'Cubby, this is terrific.' Jerry Moss of [A&M] Records was in London at the time [and] listened to it, 'Cubby, I can guarantee you that this record will go platinum and it will become the Number 1 song in the world. If you don't like it, I'll be happy to give you $1 million for your rights to the song right now.' Cubby just stared. Starting the next day, Cubby said, 'We have this great song by Paul.'[159]

Madeline Smith recalled more enthusiasm in other quarters, 'I'm remembering Roger coming in with a cassette player with the music and making us all sit around and listen to it and saying, "Isn't this amazing music by Wings?" And we all concurred and said, "Yes, it's fantastic."'[160]

Later, when Maurice Binder was creating the opening title sequence, McCartney tweaked the track to match the visuals. Binder asked him for several fast sections where he could feature the girls writhing with their hands up and dancing.[161] Binder's favourite moment in the sequence was 'the transition from the eyes of the real face to the eye sockets in the skull.'[162] Gloria Hendry recalled Saltzman 'introduced me to Maurice Binder – he said, "Why don't you marry Maurice Binder?" He wanted to stamp out the race situation, "We all should inter-marry." I went out with Maurice a couple of times but we both knew we weren't fit for each other.'[163]

McCartney received a $15,000 songwriting fee for the title track. With a $25,000 total music budget available that only left $10,000 to complete the score, which wasn't enough to hire a composer in Barry's league.[164] Martin's only other film work had been the Beatles' *Yellow Submarine*. Mankiewicz noted, 'Once you've given away the title song, you couldn't get John Barry or any other well-known film composer to do the score; the main title is where a composer's money comes from and his renown.'[165] The writer felt 'George wrote a wonderful score. A lot of things were intentionally a little different so we didn't handicap poor Roger with things reminiscent of Sean.'[166] Roger Moore went as far as to say, 'It's not last year's music, it's not even this year's music, it's next year's.'[167] The track hit the Top 10 singles charts in both the UK and the US, and was the first Eon James Bond title song to be nominated for an Academy Award.

Roger Moore was understandably anxious to see how his James Bond would be received. He could hardly forget attending a private screening of *On Her Majesty's Secret Service* with Harry Saltzman and producer Robert Goldstein four years earlier. When the lights came up following the downbeat ending as Bond cradles Tracy's body in his arms, Saltzman turned to the group and asked

'"What do you think of my new monster?" Bob Goldstein said, "You made a mistake, Harry. You should have killed him and saved her."'[168]

Before his promotional duties began, the Moore family holidayed in California, staying with the Broccolis in Beverly Hills. Roger Moore was hot property and was asked to present the Best Actor category at the Academy Awards on 27 March 1973. He left the stage still clutching the Oscar – Marlon Brando sent Native American activist Sacheen Littlefeather to decline the award in protest of the depiction of American Indians by Hollywood.

On Sunday, 24 June 1973, *Live and Let Die* had its world premiere at Grauman's Chinese Theatre in Los Angeles.[169] On 5 July 1973 the film opened in the Odeon Leicester Square with a premiere attended by Princess Anne. While travelling to the London press conference, Moore felt his nerves for the first time, 'But I was fairly philosophical. I imagine it's like having a baby, there's nothing you can do to stop it, the baby is going to come out no matter what.'[170]

Live and Let Die performed way above United Artists' and Eon's expectations when it began out-grossing *Diamonds Are Forever*. The film would go on to achieve a worldwide gross of $126.4 million. Roger Moore as James Bond proved there was life in the series. Broccoli and Saltzman were relieved that Bond could survive the departure of Connery, but the question was now was could 007 survive the Danjaq partnership?

13

JUST BEFORE THE KILL

THE MAN WITH THE GOLDEN GUN

(1974)

BOND

"THE MAN WITH THE GOLDEN GUN"

$20,592,437

WORLDWIDE GROSS—3 WEEKS!

ALBERT R BROCCOLI and HARRY SALTZMAN present

ROGER MOORE AS in IAN FLEMING'S **JAMES BOND 007** in

"THE MAN WITH THE GOLDEN GUN"

with CHRISTOPHER LEE · BRITT EKLAND

Produced by ALBERT R BROCCOLI and HARRY SALTZMAN

Screenplay by RICHARD MAIBAUM and TOM MANKIEWICZ

Directed by GUY HAMILTON   Music Score by JOHN BARRY   COLOR

PG

United Artists

Entertainment from
Transamerica Corporation

Arthur Krim considered his steering of United Artists back to profitability in the seventies to be on a par with bringing the company back from bankruptcy in the fifties.[1] He was aided in this by his long-standing business associate Robert Benjamin[2] and new team of executives – including Eric Pleskow, Mike Medavoy, recruited by Pleskow to run the West Coast, and William Bernstein heading business affairs.[3] While *Live and Let Die* was in production, United Artists responded positively to early footage of Roger Moore's debut and wanted to follow it up quickly. Hence, the ninth James Bond film was ushered into production immediately.

In March 1973 *Variety* reported the title of the next James Bond film would be *The Man With the Golden Gun* and that it would be shot in the Far East.[4] The studio's speed was faster than Broccoli would have liked, 'We were on a tight time schedule and I chose to go along with United Artists rather than improve our position story-wise and production-wise.'[5] Broccoli and Saltzman's business relationship was in trouble. Eric Pleskow, now UA President remembered, 'I only knew [Broccoli and Saltzman] were not getting along as a result of the stoppage of production. I had to go over there to get at least an armistice going. Eventually they hated each other.'[6] In his suite in Claridges he had to get the pair 'to continue to work'.[7] Pleskow noted Saltzman's childishness, 'It was like kindergarten. Harry Saltzman was complaining that Cubby always managed to sit next to me and he couldn't and it used drive him crazy because he couldn't – like it was such a big deal to sit next to me.'[8] Harry's son, Steven Saltzman acknowledged, '*Golden Gun* was Cubby. Especially considering Harry's wife, my mother, started becoming sick at that point.'[9] Jacqueline Saltzman would succumb to cancer over the next few years.

In February 1973 Guy Hamilton indicated that he might pass on a fourth Bond on the basis he needed a change of scenery, especially 'after eighteen months on this one, including preparatory work.'[10] The real reason behind Hamilton's reluctance to return was the state of play between Saltzman and Broccoli:

I shuffled out to meet Arthur Krim at UA and I said, 'It's simple: I have equal respect for the pair of them and I can work with either of them but together it's a disaster area.' It slowed everything down and a lot of good ideas went out the window because if Cubby liked it, Harry didn't on principle. So it was arranged diplomatically that the next picture would be Cubby's or Harry's. I think that was the solution Cubby desired. I don't think Harry cared enormously because he had so many other interests.[11]

So diverse and random were his interests that Roger Moore even remembered sitting in Saltzman's Tilney Street office as the producer tried to convince Guy Hamilton to invest in gold bars.[12] In the end Hamilton did return for practical reasons, as he recalled, 'It must have been money. My agent Dennis Van Thal (the same agent as Roger Moore's) made a deal that we were allowed a certain amount of independence.'[13]

THE MAN WITH THE GOLDEN GUN was published in the UK on 1 April 1965, less than eight months after Ian Fleming's death. He had written the manuscript, the previous January and February in Jamaica, but had not been well enough to polish it. Although Kingsley Amis was consulted on the work by the publishers, Jonathan Cape, he did not finish the novel as is often reported. The story continues on from the previous book, YOU ONLY LIVE TWICE, where Bond is left, having lost his memory, in the Japanese village with a hint he should go to Vladivostock in the Soviet Union. GOLDEN GUN begins with Bond trying to assassinate M following a brainwashing exercise by the KGB. After he fails, M, advised by the Service's neurosurgeon, Sir James Molony, sends Bond out on an impossible mission: to kill Francisco 'Pistols' Scaramanga. (Fleming named Scaramanga after a fellow pupil he despised at Eton.) The streetwise and tough hoodlum has killed a number of British agents using a gold-plated .45 Colt, which shoots silver-plated solid gold bullets. Scaramanga, a Cuban, has been running amok in the Caribbean and is suspected of assisting Castro to foment a rebellion in the region by destabilising the sugar crop. Bond ingratiates himself in Scaramanga's gangster organisation, which is attempting to interest investors in a Jamaican real estate project. Bond is aided in his efforts to stop them by his personal secretary – Mary Goodnight, a character established in the previous two novels.

Hamilton was never a fan of the source material, 'We were very much scraping the bottom of the barrel to find Bondian situations in the novel.'[14] While promoting the film, Hamilton said:

Fleming was writing very much about a Commander Bond, Royal Navy which I like to bring back occasionally to remind the audience. The dragons have changed. Fleming was always writing about the Russians as the villains, the Cold War. Life has gone on. To me, the problem these days is to find the dragon. Bond is St. George, a private method of being St. George but ultimately he's killing dragons for the benefit of mankind.[15]

To summon inspiration, the production team thought about locations. For Hamilton it was a process of elimination, 'Where should we take Bond this time? We've done the Caribbean, we've done America, so we think about moving East.'[16] He had seen footage of Ha Long Bay in Vietnam[17] and ' … wanted to go back to Hong Kong and Singapore and all the places I had been. So I went off with Cubby and we searched.'[18] The director drew on his previous adventures:

I'd done the whole of the East with Carol Reed looking for locations for *Outcast of the Islands* (1951); from Cairo to Singapore to Hong Kong, Borneo, Bali. I was in Ho Chi Minh City, then I went up to Hanoi on my own. I thought I was the first person from the Western world who had ever been to Angkor Wat because it was an extraordinary area of temples and these jungles [in Cambodia].[19]

As well as looking at the Far East, the team also considered the Middle East. Hamilton explained:

Barbara Broccoli was at some school in Mayfair and her best friend at that time was the daughter of the ambassador to Lebanon or Iran or something. Obviously the ambassador to Iran was impressed by Bond, so he said, 'If Mr. Broccoli you ever come to Iran you will be welcome with open arms.' So Cubby never looks a gift horse in the mouth and says, 'We are on the way to the Far East, we'll drop in.'[20]

Hamilton dismissed Israel, 'I had worked in Israel with David Niven [*The Best Of Enemies* (1961)] and there wasn't anything particularly Bondian there.'[21] But Broccoli insisted they take a look. 'We stopped in Lebanon. Two things: they have a huge casino about twenty miles outside and a short distance up, you go uphill, woods and there is snow at the top. But you've done Bond with snow and you've done Bond with casinos. So Lebanon no, no.'[22]

They arrived in Iran in summer 1973.[23] Albert Lamorisse's unfinished film, *The Lover's Wind*, featured the ancient citadel of Arg-é Bam, and Cubby and company flew to visit the remote location.[24] After enduring a hair-raising flight across the turbulent desert winds, Cubby had the indignity of being strip-searched when the authorities thought the camera was a gun.[25] It was not a good start. Hamilton recalled, 'There is basically bugger all in Tehran. You couldn't move left or right – everything was army. The Shah was like that. We were there for about ten days and quickly realised Iran is not a place to bring a Bond unit.'[26] The final nail in the coffin was Israel declaring war on Egypt.[27] Conflict caused them to look elsewhere.

Hamilton remembered how he found the eventual locale used in the film, 'I stumbled across it in *National Geographic* magazine, which was great for looking for Bond locations.'[28] He then took a short walk:

> to the Thai embassy which is only five doors up the road from Audley Street.'[29] However, the staff there 'didn't know where it was. Eventually we found out it was called Phuket. Cubby and I went out there and discovered … there was absolutely nothing there apart from a brothel. So we arranged to send the girls off on holiday and parked the unit in Bangkok and it worked very happily.'[30]

Thus the islands of Phang Nga Bay, including Khao Phing Kan and Ko Tapu, soon became a major tourist destination thanks solely to James Bond.

By now, Tom Mankiewicz was acclimatised to the Bond writing process:

> I made up the story, Cubby made up the story, Harry made up the story, Guy made up the story. It's always been a committee in the beginning; there's always been a writer there to make up the story but so many people have ideas and especially when they're old hands at Bond, they know how to write a Bond story correctly. Writing a Bond story correctly is a trick, like riding a unicycle or mixing together a perfect cake; you need this ingredient, that ingredient and people work at it.[31]

Co-art director Peter Lamont remembered Cubby being particularly democratic, 'When we used to go to meetings, his edict was if you've got anything to say, say it, because it could be thrown out as being absolutely ridiculous, but it might be bloody good, so you should listen to everybody.'[32]

Mankiewicz would witness at first hand the sensibilities of both producers:

> Harry is so mercurial. He gets these brainstorms. Now Cubby is more the conscience of the audience. He wants to make sure everyone understands everything. I used to use the example – that never happened – that you could say to the two of them, 'Bond falls off the boat and as he's sinking underwater, he meets an octopus. But it has nine arms.' Harry would say, 'And he's bright red and he's on roller skates and he blows up.' And Cubby would say, 'I still don't understand what's funny about the nine arms.' You'd say, 'But, Cubby,

octopuses usually have eight arms.' And he'd say, 'I know that. But do you think everyone in the audience is going to get that?'[33]

Saltzman, despite taking a backseat, wanted *The Man With the Golden Gun* to feature an elephant stampede, having seen elephants working the teak forests pulling logs in northern Thailand. To do this work the elephants wore leather shoes to protect their feet from the sharp forest undergrowth. Immediately Saltzman requested that production manager Claude Hudson acquire fifty sets of elephant footgear – four for each elephant. The scene was never shot as it was considered too dangerous but months later in Bangkok the production took delivery of 200 elephant shoes![34]

Mankiewicz's original vision for *The Man With the Golden Gun* never made it to the screen. 'I had always envisaged it as a classic shootout; as *Shane* [1953], if you will. There was Jack Palance, who would have made a great Scaramanga. It was going to be Roger versus Jack Palance. . .'[35] Palance had been 'offered the "heavy" in the next James Bonder' in January 1974.[36] Hamilton confirmed, 'Cubby and I had lunch with Palance in LA, but he turned us down.'[37] Hamilton was not 'hugely disappointed. Palance had read something – and he was a strange character – very silent. By the time we get back to the UK we still haven't got a Scaramanga, we still haven't got a script.'[38]

Mankiewicz took inspiration from real-life encounters in Hong Kong:

There was a famous man called Run Run Shaw who ran the Shaw Studios. He was the first Asian ever to be knighted. Run Run could get you heroin, bazookas, tanks or the best suit in Hong Kong. He had three Rolls Royces, all of which had the same licence plate – Run Run. Nobody knew which one he was in because he never wanted people to know where he was. A member of his family had been kidnapped ... the police couldn't find him but they found the kidnappers' bodies hacked to death in the back of Run Run's car. He had a brother in Singapore named Runme. I turned them into characters called Hai Fat and Lo [sic] Fat.[39]

Loh Fat was later excised from the shooting script.

Mankiewicz noted the screenplay 'got mired down in all kinds of story problems.'[40] He also felt his relationship with Hamilton had deteriorated, despite their great friendship and respect for each other. 'We were very short tempered with each other and I resigned from the project after the first draft. It was a lot of personal things and also just the way everything was going at the time.

It was an unhappy time in my life and in his.'[41] Hamilton was in fact preparing to leave the UK and live in Majorca because of Britain's high tax rates,[42] and agreed that his relationship with the young US writer had waned:

> I got on with Tom terribly well on the previous two – *Diamonds Are Forever* and *Live and Let Die*. But I left Tom in London and went off with Cubby to the Far East to find locations. And Tom was left rather on his own in the UK. I saw him next when he came out to join us in Hong Kong. We said, 'We have got this Tom and we have got that Tom.' And I don't think he was a happy boy. And he probably had something up his sleeve in America.[43]

Mankiewicz left the project gracefully, 'I finished the first draft and I went to Cubby, "Cubby, I really think my usefulness is done on this picture." And he said, "OK, if you feel that way."'[44] He was to be replaced by veteran Bond scribe Richard Maibaum, who Mankiewicz remembered in his autobiography, 'Dick was a good deal older than I was. He has more Bond credits than anybody. Somebody said, "Well, maybe Dick's written himself out. This is his tenth." We shared credit, and he gets first credit because it's alphabetical. M-A-I and M-A-N. We shared credit without ever having met.'[45]

Mankiewicz was rueful about the final product, his last Bond as a credited screenwriter, 'Everything just never fell into place. I'm not saying anything against Guy Hamilton but I wanted to make it a little more serious, a little harder than it was.'[46] He was dissatisfied with his own work, 'This was the third in a row I had done and I was feeling like I was writing the same scene over and over again.'[47]

Daily Variety announced Richard Maibaum's return in November 1973.[48] It was the height of the energy crisis. The writer remembered:

> As usual we were looking for a world threat and it came down to either solar power or weather control. Harry Saltzman felt that weather control was not a good idea. He felt that it would just be a lot of special effects and stock footage showing hurricanes and tropical storms. He was right at the time.[49]

Although the Solex Agitator was Maibaum's idea he had his doubts, 'I sort of felt there wasn't enough to keep it going. We felt we had to flesh it out and it just didn't work.'[50]

Hamilton admitted the script process was 'messy. I was concentrating terribly on finding locations and trying to think of Bondian shtick in these locations

– feeding whoever was writing the script.'[51] Hamilton outlined his idea of what a classic Bond story required:

> Bond is as good as his villain. If he's got no opposition then what he does is pretty meaningless. The better the villains are the better Bond is because they make better problems for him. I like a Mr. Big who is as intelligent as Bond. They are always very rich, so that we don't have to go in the back alleys of Marseilles or Southend. If he has an island, it's a private island. If he has an aeroplane, it has a swimming pool in it. They have an evil idea and they want to use their power or their wealth for something which you, the audience, must understand that if they were successful would mean that the price of petrol will go up. Therefore you ask, 'Bond, please do something about it.'[52]

The ninth James Bond film was an eco-thriller. Scaramanga has been employed by wealthy industrialist Hai Fat to obtain a Solex Agitator – a fuel cell that can make a solar energy plant 98 per cent efficient. The Solex has been developed by British scientist Professor Gibson, who is negotiating a safe return to the British after his defection to the Chinese. Scaramanga kills Gibson in a Hong Kong street and his manservant, a midget named Nick Nack, steals the Solex from the scene of the crime. It is this killing that convinces Bond that Scaramanga is not after him. Previously MI6 had received a golden bullet engraved with '007', so Bond was deemed to be a target and as such would jeopardise the hunt for Gibson. Bond is taken off the assignment in order to track down Scaramanga first. Bond travels via Beirut where he picks up a golden bullet used to kill 002 and then on to Macao to visit Lazar – Scaramanga's bespoke armourer.

Following the consignment of bullets, Bond questions Scaramanga's girlfriend Andrea Anders in Hong Kong. She later reveals she sent the golden bullet, hoping that Bond would come after her lover, kill him and free her from sexual slavery. Bond meets up with MI6 agent Mary Goodnight and they go on the mission together. Scaramanga decides he no longer needs Hai Fat and kills him in his palatial home in Thailand; he takes the Solex and installs it in his island energy complex. With plans to franchise the solar technology to the highest bidders or blackmail the oil companies to keep the solar energy off the market, Scaramanga truly has the sun in his pocket. Bond tracks down Scaramanga who has kidnapped Mary Goodnight and taken her to his island retreat. There Bond and Scaramanga confront each other in a duel around the island and Scaramanga's Fun House. During the pre-title sequence we see Scaramanga honing his shooting skills against hapless gangster Rodney in the Fun House. The sequence culminates with Scaramanga revealing his prize target – a wax figure of James Bond. Bond outmanoeuvres the hitman using the prop dummy of himself to kill Scaramanga. Meanwhile, the solar plant is sabotaged unwittingly by Mary Goodnight leading to catastrophic meltdown. The island explodes, but Bond and Goodnight escape on Scaramanga's sailing junk only to be accosted by a revenge-seeking Nick Nack.

Roger Moore was always destined to star in the screen adaptation of *The Man With the Golden Gun*. When Sean Connery initially relinquished the role of 007 in 1967, Moore had been in the frame to take over.[53] At the time there were discussions of setting the film in Cambodia but turmoil in the region near to where the Vietnam War was raging nixed the production.[54] Roger Moore went off to work on other projects, and George Lazenby became the new James Bond in *OHMSS*. Perhaps it was an omen. While shooting *Live and Let Die* in Jamaica, Moore had a psychic reading which predicted he would shortly visit the Far East.[55] Moore was looking forward to again working with Guy Hamilton, who he thought was a 'tremendously efficient, [a] wonderful technician, [with a] very keen eye, typical ex-naval officer. He knew what he wanted. Guy played by the book. Great sense of humour.'[56]

Destiny also had a hand in Christopher Lee's casting as a Bond villain. A step-cousin of Ian Fleming (his divorced mother married Ian's maternal uncle Harcourt), Lee and Bond's creator often played golf together and there was apocryphal talk of Lee being cast as Dr. No. Lee remembered being offered the part of Scaramanga over lunch at The White Elephant by Guy Hamilton. It was a conscious decision to create a 'Contre-Bond'.[57] Lee thought:

> The character in the book is a great ox of a man. He's really just a thug. He has no charm at all. He's extremely unpleasant. He's just a thug who kills with a golden gun and there's nothing more to him than that. In fact, he's one of the least well-written characters of all Fleming's books. The way the character comes out of the script is infinitely superior.[58]

Lee revealed at the time that he felt Hamilton reached hidden depths by deliberately opting for a lighter touch to the part:

> I've known [Guy Hamilton] for many years. [He] got something out of me as an actor, which I've never been able to show on the screen. In his own words,

he got the spook out of me. He got the dracula out of me. He's getting me to do this picture in such a light way that you can hardly believe this man is as lethal as he is. He's getting me to smile. He's getting me to laugh, which I must admit I don't find very easy as an actor. He's getting the lightness of performance out of me, the contrasts. This man isn't just a straight, down-the-middle, conventional heavy. He's got things out of me that no other director has either had to get or wanted to get or even tried to get.[59]

Hamilton remembered it more simply, 'Chris Lee, I think, was a fairly obvious choice and I thought he'd be good company to play opposite Roger.'[60] Writer Richard Maibaum later disagreed with Lee's approach, 'I thought the character in the novel was very unusual. But it was all lost. Lee wanted to play it like a spoiled Guard's Officer. In other words he was trying to outdo Bond and it couldn't be done.'[61]

Following an appearance in the cult horror film *The Wicker Man* (1973), Swedish actress and former Mrs. Peter Sellers Britt Ekland was keen to land a part in the next James Bond film. She explained, 'I'd seen Ursula Andress in *Dr. No* and I'd thought that was the most incredible looking person I'd ever seen, not as much a role model but as a truly fun and exciting kind of woman and I thought that's what I want to do.'[62] Learning that the next film would be *The Man With the Golden Gun*, Ekland read the Fleming novel, dressed accordingly as James Bond's secretary – Mary Goodnight – put her hair in a bun and headed for Cubby Broccoli's office. A secretary was not exactly what the producer was looking for:

He said, 'Well, you know, we only really use the title of the stories on Bonds and we build our stories around the title of the books.' As I was leaving he introduced me to Roger Moore who had just come into his office. I left to go to the USA, to start a movie in Colorado. I was there for six weeks shooting and on the plane back to London I read that a Swedish girl, Maud Adams, was the new Bond girl. I was shattered. I couldn't believe it.[63]

Later Ekland's agent, Maggie Abbott of Creative Management, informed her that Cubby Broccoli wanted to meet with her. 'In my naiveté I thought he wanted to tell me personally that I didn't get the role. When I got to his office he said, "You are Mary Goodnight."'[64] Ekland 'didn't see Harry. He was not on set, [or] on location. He might have flown in and then flown out again. My day-to-day involvement with him was not great.'[65]

Maud Adams also recollected how she got the role of Andrea Anders, Scaramanga's mistress:

> William Morris called me and said they were casting a new Bond movie and would I meet with Cubby Broccoli and the casting people in New York. I don't recall I had to read anything. Cubby Broccoli in the meeting mentioned that we had met before and I laughed and said, 'No, no, I would have known,' and he jogged my memory and said I'd been at Pinewood Studios, which was true with a Swedish friend who ran one of the gambling clubs in New York, where Cubby was a frequent guest. [Our mutual friend] had invited me out to Pinewood Studios to have lunch and then after lunch he said to me. 'Would you like to see the Bond set?' So he took me over there and he showed me around and I remember a couple of people coming up to me and saying hello, just briefly, and apparently one of them was Cubby.[66]

Following the meeting:

> Cubby asked me to meet him at his hotel, which got my antennae up. [I was] a little nervously of course, thinking, "What is this all about?" But it did turn out that what he wanted me to do was meet Dana, his wife. And Dana apparently had quite a lot of influence over Cubby as far as who he picked for his actress.'[67]

It was Guy Hamilton who first spotted Maud Adams when he met her in New York, 'I found her extraordinary elegant, quite different. And the Swedish element, I thought, for a Bond girl, made her a very interesting and pleasant change. She had very limited acting experience but the part didn't demand great weight.'[68] Speaking in 1975, Hamilton revealed the prevailing attitudes of the day:

> One of the tragedies of life is that men motivate things. James Bond is a motivator. He goes to point A and if he meets a girl on the way [she] is to be used for the situation, his mission. It's very difficult to write a good Bond lady's part because they're there as part of the scenery. We try very hard to give them character. I think it's high time that James Bond met Women's Lib and don't think we haven't been playing around in that area.[69]

Throughout shooting Roger Moore referred to Maud and Britt as 'Mud' and 'Burt'. He played many tricks on the pair and told them many jokes, all

X-rated.[70] According to Guy Hamilton on set the girls would natter away in Swedish, earning them the nickname the 'au pair girls'.[71]

Christopher Lee noted that for 'probably the first time in a Bond film the people in this picture are people and not cardboard cutouts or caricatures. They may be a bit bizarre but at least they're believable.'[72] Hamilton set out why:

> I like two villains. Mr. Big says, 'I hate the sight of blood so that now you've discovered my terrible secret, Mr. Bond, you will excuse me while l hand you over to my staff to deal with you.' Now the staff are the heavy gang and the heavy gang can't just be characterless goons, they have to be interesting.[73]

Hamilton reflected, 'I've done Oddjob, let's go the opposite [in size]. And he can be just as dangerous in his way although he is a midget.'[74] So entered the character of Nick Nack, played by diminutive actor Hervé Villechaize. Hamilton recalled the actor's tragic history:

> He was French and his father was a French doctor, who was certain that for his son this was only a temporary thing. He fed him pills and stretched him on a bed every night, convinced he would grow to normal length. He suffered all that as a child but was an amazing character.[75]

Originally named Demi-Tasse in Mankiewicz's draft, Scaramanga's manservant came across as a mini-Oddjob.

Clifton James reprised his role as Sherrif J.W. Pepper. Hamilton was unabashed, 'Well, it was pretty corny. But he was such a lovable character we thought we'll have him again.'[76] James recalled, 'Cubby called me himself on the phone, we didn't go through any agents or anything.'[77] Prior to flying to Thailand, Hamilton contacted James, 'he said, "Go and pick up a couple of Hawaiian shirts!" I went to Macy's and got a couple of shirts and they were made in Bangkok!'[78]

The film was studded with Asian talent in the form of Richard Loo played Hai Fat, Chan Yiu Lam as karate ace Chula, Francoise Therry as naked bather Chew Me, Soon-Taik Oh as Hong Kong Police Lieutenant Hip with his two karate fighting nieces portrayed by Qui Yen and Joie Vejjajiva. Carmen du Sautoy made a brief appearance as Beirut belly dancer Saida, and Sonny Caldinez made an even briefer turn as Kra, the sole technician on Scaramanga's island. Casting was completed by veterans James Coussins as Colthorpe and Marne Maitland as weaponsmith Lazar.

With the cast assembled, most of Hamilton's crew from *Live and Let Die* returned including director of photography Ted Moore. Ken Adam was busy working with Stanley Kubrick on *Barry Lyndon* (1975), for which he would win his first Oscar. Syd Cain was preparing *Gold* (1974) in South Africa and was also unavailable. Hamilton recalled:

> There are an enormous amount of things that bored the arse off Ken. If it was a maid's bedroom, 'My talent is wasted on the maid's bedroom.' "Peter [Murton] do the bloody bedroom.' When Ken was brilliant he was brilliant. When he was awful he could be boring and then he would hand over to the junior mob. Peter Murton, for I don't know how many years, worked for Ken. So Peter was extremely well trained and you couldn't promote a more qualified person because he was familiar with the way Bond works.[79]

Once again Eon promoted from within and after working in various capacities, credited and uncredited, on the Bonds, Peter Murton became the third James Bond production designer.

On 6 November 1973 the crew assembled in Hong Kong harbour to film James Bond jumping aboard the partly submerged *Queen Elizabeth* liner, which in the story was amusingly serving as MI6's secret hideaway. While location scouting Peter Murton recalled how every morning 'we would take the ferry and see the poor hulk of the *Queen Elizabeth* lying on its side at a 45-degree angle and Cubby came up with the idea of using it as M's office. You always look for a link between the real locations and the sets.'[80] Moore himself was doubled for most of the scene and interiors were filmed later at Pinewood as the actor was not due to start work until the following spring.

In April 1974 the crew descended upon Khao Phing Kan island, the beautiful retreat doubling as Scaramanga's island hideaway.[81] The site was only accessible by boat or helicopter and the local accommodation was very basic: a converted bordello and a series of 'jungle houses'.[82] Hamilton took the rough with the smooth, 'When you get there it's tremendously like hard work. The conditions are very, very rough to take 160 people into the middle of nowhere. Very long hours, always problems with the weather, with heat, equipment breaking down – it's no picnic.'[83] Peter Murton did minimal work but again was seeking to meld reality with studio work, 'We found a crevasse and built some steps. That linked to the idea I had to make the villain's den within a rock.'[84]

Peter Lamont remembered preparing the island, 'It was the first recce we went out on. John Graysmark and I were co-art directors. I remember the night before we went Peter Murton said, "Be prepared to stay." I came home seven months later.[85] Challenged by the primitive facilities:

> It was a place that was undeveloped at the time. Believe me, the Bonds have always been first in these places. I was the one who ran everything. Telephones didn't work. Telexes took three days, and a letter – God knows where it went. The accountant used to get off the plane, give us our per diem and get back on the plane again. We were really out there.[86]

Lamont even doubled up as a 'kind of a local doctor. I used to have all these remedies, and it was amazing what you could get.'[87]

Forever taking inspiration from the latest technology, the filmmakers chose a Republic Seabee amphibious seaplane as Bond's mode of transport when travelling to Scaramanga's island. It was an aircraft that could also mount dry land and, if fitted with wheels, travel on land too. This was effectively Q Branch's 'car with wings', which Desmond Llewelyn's Q asserted they had created earlier in the film. Hamilton said, 'I'm bored with little boats, let's have a seaplane.'[88] The Seabee plane was purchased in America and then flown to Thailand; a complex administrative job overseen by Dana Broccoli's son Michael G. Wilson, who was slowly becoming more involved with each film.[89]

When the crew first flew over the archipelago, Peter Murton felt like they had travelled back in time.[90] Bond and the audience were introduced to the extraordinary location of Phang Nga Bay in exhilarating aerial shots captured by first assistant director, Derek 'Crackers' Cracknell. In the story, the Seabee was seen flying low to avoid radar detection approaching Scaramanga's island, Khao Phing Kan.[91]

During the very low approach Colonel Claire, the specialist American pilot doubling for Roger Moore,[92] hit a rock outcrop. This damaged the left-wing float, which meant it had to be removed (which can be seen in the film).[93] When the Seabee made its approach to the island in the water, Colonel Claire did an exceptional job of the amphibious landing, mounting the Seabee by its hull on the beach with only the right float.[94] The seaplane was then stripped of its instruments and spare parts in hours[95] before being blown up by John Stears and his effects crew.[96]

Khao Phing Kan featured in the first shot of the film, the gun barrel opening on Scaramanga's exotic beach where he lazes on a sun lounger with Andrea Anders. Christopher Lee recalled he had 'to take off my clothes which is something I never thought I'd have to do in a film.'[97] Roger Moore recalled his co-star standing under a rudimentary hose at the end of the day's filming to wash off the fake tan applied daily.[98] Script supervisor, Elaine Schreyeck, remembered

Lee, 'saying he didn't really have a wig but he did. And he explained to me at the beginning to look out for it.'[99] Maud Adams was fond of Lee, 'I could hear him in the morning getting ready to go to set. He would start with vocal exercises. He seemed very formidable in the beginning. He was very sweet; he took me to dinner several times. I found out that he spoke Danish, his wife, Gita, is Danish.'[100] The two Bond girls were caught out by Lee:

> Britt and I would sometimes joke about people around us in Swedish. And I think we made a few comments about Christopher Lee a few times in his presence, speaking in Swedish, we [both] thought we had a secret conversation. And it turned out that he understood what we were saying. Fortunately, we hadn't really said anything too damaging.[101]

Adams remembered the location, 'We had our dressing rooms on a boat that we had anchored out there. We went out in small boats. As we're going out we're seeing all these fishing villages and people were living on rafts with roofs over their heads looking.'[102] Ekland was not a fan of the accommodation, 'There were neon lights – it was called Bamboo – the bar with a brothel on top. And being Swedish, I'd never seen these huge cockroaches. They were attracted by lights and I'm just lying there at night looking at these things crawling across the windows being absolutely terrified.'[103] Not only was the location arduous, but it was dangerous as well. Ekland remembered the unit 'brought in their own petrol-driven generators to run all the equipment and, of course, those were stolen continuously.'[104] Pirates plagued the islands.[105]

For the grand finale, skips full of explosives were placed around the tiny land mass at various points to simulate the destructive end to the solar energy complex. Bond and Mary Goodnight were required to run through the explosions to Scaramanga's junk to make their escape. Guy Hamilton remembered Derek Cracknell once again playing mischievous pranks on Roger Moore:

> Roger doesn't like bangs! Derek of course was very naughty because he'd say 'Right, Roger you see there is a bang there, there is a bang there and when you clear the first bang and you reach the second bang, I'll let the first one off. And when you clear that one, I'll let the third one go.' Of course, that's pretty boring. So "ACTION!" and Roger comes running out and Cracknell lets the second one go right in front of Roger and before Roger can pick his brains up, he lets the first one go up behind him and he doesn't know where the fuck to go because he daren't come forward in case the third one goes off.[106]

A bikini-clad Ekland remembered the scene only too well as her hand slipped from Moore's grasp. Heroically, he went to retrieve his leading lady, 'You're very vulnerable when you're half naked. I could feel it and I freaked out. I threw myself on the floor. And you see Roger dragging me up and that was real.'[107]

The crew then moved to Bangkok. Clifton James was invited to suggest ideas as to why J.W. Pepper should find himself in the Far East, 'I suggested that he was taking boy scouts on a trip. Then, of course, Tom Mankiewicz came up with the idea of me being on vacation.'[108] James had some input in his scenes, 'I added a few things. Roger and I would be rehearsing and I would say, "Oh we should say this," and Roger would agree.'[109] Maibaum disagreed with this on-set improvisation:

> I have to admit that *The Man With the Golden Gun* in particular is a weak film. What happens is that they get on the set and try things, which seem like a good idea at the time but they don't consider that the writer has been breaking his head for six months trying to think of things. On a moment's notice they come up with something that's not that great. Sometimes it does work but very rarely.[110]

Bond flees Hai Fat's karate school and then makes for the nearby canals – klongs – where he commandeers a small speedboat to make good his escape. Peter Murton remembered shooting the boat chase in the klongs, 'You have to equate whether it's cheaper to build it into a studio or to use the actual location. In this case we kept it down to a certain number of crossings and therefore we were able to control the location. The locals were very cooperative.'[111] Hamilton set out the challenges of a Bond action sequence:

> If James Bond was on a bicycle and was being chased by a tank, how could he win? Because you start off by saying he's on a hiding to nothing. [The audiences] will say, 'Idiot! You won't get very far.' But then Bond is a genius and will say, 'When *I* am riding a bicycle it's quite a different story.'[112]

The boat chase is capped off by Bond vanquishing his pursuers by cutting their boat in half with his, as only Bond could do.

007 is then spied by Sheriff Pepper, on his vacation, a moment underlined with a *Live and Let Die* musical reference. The boat chase was capped comedically by the sheriff being knocked into the klong by an insulted elephant,

'Guy was very upset he thought I was hurt. I had to go the doctors to get purified because the klong was so dirty there were dead dogs floating around in it.'[113] Such scenes amused the normally stoic cinematographer Ted Moore, whom James remembered with affection, 'I liked Ted a great deal. I could hear him laughing at scenes as we filmed them.'[114]

On location the unit were oblivious to the acrimony going on behind the scenes between Cubby and Harry in London. Broccoli did his best to make everyone happy, dishing out gambling chips to the crew on the floating casino in Macao.[115] Ekland remembered, 'Every weekend there'd be a dinner at his favourite Italian restaurant, half a block down on the same side of the hotel. Even when we were shooting in Bangkok and we were staying at the Oriental we never ate anything but Italian.'[116] In particular, she remembered Cubby's wife, Dana, 'She was a very beautiful, supportive person. She was always there.'[117]

Clifton James described Broccoli simply as 'one of the boys. He was on the set all the time in Bangkok. Cubby was so friendly and part of the company so much you wouldn't think he was a producer.'[118] This feeling extended to the production crew as Peter Lamont explained, 'Didn't matter if it was the sweeper-up, he knew everybody by Christian name. He was a gentleman.'[119]

The Man With the Golden Gun was Cubby's first film as the on-set producer with Roger Moore. Between takes the producer and star would play backgammon beginning a legendary tradition that would continue on every film; a game of high stakes that would more often than not get in the way of shooting. Moore amusingly recalled Broccoli telling an assistant director, 'You can't have him yet – I'm playing him like an old banjo.'[120]

Britt Ekland noted, 'Because Maud had been a model she worked even harder than I did because she felt the need to be accepted as an actress. I was never a model, I always started as an actress. Because I came from acting I didn't feel the pressure.'[121]

Providing a welcome distraction on set was Hervé Villechaize. Hamilton remembered:

Hervé gets us into a fair amount of trouble because we move from Hong Kong to Bangkok, who are quite strict about hookers coming into Bangkok because I think they have got enough of their own. But Hervé is arriving with his own tall Chinese lady from Hong Kong. [Cubby] had to clear her or sign a paper to say she would go again with Hervé. I think Broccoli was as impressed as I was.[122]

Maud Adams was impressed too, 'When we were filming he was always in a good mood, boundless energy. He would spend nights out and come back in the morning with two girls on his arms and a cigar in his mouth and still be ready to go to work that day.'[123]

Hamilton saw Hervé chatting up his co-star, 'Maud Adams is on the bar stool and Hervé said, "I would love to fuck you Maud." And she said, "If you do I shall be very annoyed. And if I ever discover you have I shall be very annoyed."'[124] Adams noted, 'There was a very introspective part of him too. He liked to draw, he was a good artist, and he would make drawings and he would put them under my door in the hotel room. Charcoals, simplistic, not figurative.'[125] Elaine Schreyeck was also charmed, as between takes, Hervé would take over her typewriter and 'write me love letters.'[126]

Hamilton discovered Hervé's secret, when he commissioned a plaster cast of the actor's entire body. 'A few weeks later one of the plasters said, "Guv, he's got a schlong like I've never fucking seen in my fucking life."'[127] Hamilton was not surprised when Hervé would say, 'I am so tired Guy. Please do not use me this morning I was up all bloody night.'[128]

The Man With the Golden Gun was the first significant production to feature a computer-designed stunt – Bond's AMC Hornet hatchback performing the corkscrew spiral jump over the Mae Klong River.[129] Cubby trumpeted to *Variety*'s 'Army' Archerd that the film would 'boast a chase so extraordinary, the gimmick has been copyrighted.'[130] For $300 Raymond J. McHenry rigged up a computer simulation in Cornell University with Jay Milligan. The driver was Loren 'Bumps' Willard.[131] The crew erupted with instantaneous applause when the stunt was finally performed for real. It was a signature moment in the film but Cubby later felt more could have been done, 'The normal thing to do (but we didn't have time) was to have the police cars also try to do the same thing and they go into the river, for added humour and added suspense.'[132]

At the end of June 1974 filming continued at Pinewood.[133] Peter Murton stepped boldly into the Bond design brotherhood:

> With the interior sets on *The Man With the Golden Gun*, I tried to portray our villain, Scaramanga, as a very educated man with great taste. Interestingly, Scaramanga's maze was the set that gave me the most trouble. It took me weeks to figure it out. We were using mirrors and playing with different colours, we had dark areas, and so on. I first built it as a model. We never had a complete set, instead it was a series of little pieces of set. It was all done in editing.[134]

Scaramanga's solar energy plant was built to full scale, but Murton used some creative licence, 'I'm not a scientist I had to do some research; I found references to radioactive pools. Dry ice was used to simulate the helium. We had explosions on the real set but most of the destruction was done using miniatures and orchestrated by John Stears.'[135]

Special effects supervisor John Stears returned to the Eon fold for the first time since *OHMSS*. His greatest challenge was Scaramanga's flying car; based upon the real invention of Henry Smolinski and Hal Blake. The inventors were to have flown their vehicle in the film but unfortunately died in their flying car prior to production.[136] Stears remembered:

> I was working with a full-sized aircraft and I was basing everything on the power specification of an American jet engine. There [were] so many problems with it – it was a prototype – so I had to change everything at the last minute and we just about got away with it.[137]

Returning, after his sterling work on *Live and Let Die*, was effects magician, Derek Meddings. Scaramanga's island was built in miniature on Pinewood's Paddock Tank. Meddings was gifted at blowing models up. It is an art to create debris and dirt to scale and match it on film to real locations. The shelling of Monte Cassino in World War II inspired the destruction of the island. Meddings layered explosive charges when constructing the model so that the explosions really looked as if they were coming from within the bowels of the lair.[138]

After completing location photography in the Far East, cinematographer Ted Moore was suddenly taken ill. A replacement was urgently required. Hamilton remembered:

> This all happened when we got back from Thailand. We started working at Pinewood doing the interiors and Ted Moore suddenly vanished on a Friday and then on Monday there was Ossie [Morris]. It all happened very quickly. We never really got to the bottom of it.[139]

Academy Award-winning cinematographer Oswald Morris, in an interview for this book, just three weeks before he passed away, recounted his memories:

> [Broccoli and Saltzman] were in dead trouble through no fault of their own. Whatever went on out there I do not know. Nobody's ever told me. We never saw Ted again. He never came on the stage. I get the feeling he got off the

plane and went straight home. I had taken several films over and I was fed up with doing this. A phone call came on a Wednesday and it was my agent Dennis Van Thal. 'The Bond film is coming back from the Far East and the cinematographer isn't staying on the film. They want you to take it over.' I said, 'I really don't want to do it.'[140]

Broccoli was insistent and requested Morris meet the Bond team for dinner. 'They couldn't find anybody. "You're the only one," my agent told me.'[141] With sets completed at Pinewood Studios and a non-negotiable release date set for Christmas 1974, the unit was scheduled to continue filming just two days later.[142] Morris admitted he was worried about his reputation if he turned the film down. 'Dennis said, "I think if you don't do it, it would damage your career because they are quite powerful people – the Bond people."'[143] After much persuasion from his wife, Lee, Morris signed on for the six-week shoot. 'Cubby said, "You can have whatever money you want." I deliberately didn't take them to the cleaners because I think that is petty.'[144]

Bernard Lee once again returned as M. Oswald Morris remembered working with the actor on *The Spy Who Came In From the Cold* (1965), '[Lee] didn't hit the bottle as much as he did later. Poor old Bernie. When he was sober he was very good.'[145] During a 1974 chat show appearance, Lois Maxwell complained, when asked about all the exotic locations, 'I'm stuck in the office in Pinewood all the time.'[146] Hamilton amusingly interrupted, 'We can't afford to take you!'[147]

After a one-picture absence Desmond Llewelyn returned to shoot his scenes in August 1974.[148] Upon reading the screenplay Llewelyn questioned that the script featured two separate characters: Boothroyd and Q when, in fact, Major Geoffrey Boothroyd is Q;[149] the secondary character was changed to Colthorpe. Llewelyn's first film with the new Bond set up an ongoing practical joke – Roger Moore had all Desmond's dialogue rewritten as hard-to-learn and harder-to-perform technical gobbledegook.[150]

Although jewellers Colibri are credited with making the golden gun, what they fabricated was unusable and did not have the required look. Production buyer Ron Quelch and Peter Lamont quickly enlisted another jeweller, J. Rose, to make a practical prop. There were two versions of the powerful weapon: a fully assembled and a component gun. Christopher Lee was trained to assemble the gun by Lamont, who practised putting it together in front of the television at night.[151]

Production wrapped the same month. In the last scene, Roger Moore, in a grey silk suit he was going to take home for his own wardrobe was suddenly drenched in wallpaper paste. He looked up to see his producer, Cubby, with an empty bucket on a ladder above him.[152]

Regular composer John Barry returned to score the film but was given only three weeks to complete his work.[153] The time pressure affected Barry's feelings towards the title song, 'It's the least interesting Bond song. It's the one I hate most. It just never happened for me.'[154] Lyricist Don Black felt hampered by the title:

> If we had to do it again, we'd tuck it away in the middle. For a song to actually ignite around the world, there has to be something primal about the idea, something universal. *The Man With the Golden Gun* you're talking about an assassin. You can't imagine Tony Bennett singing it. It's very hard to create a standard with that title.[155]

Nevertheless, Black did his best, 'I just thought, "Try and write provocative, sensual lyrics." They were a bit on the nose, "He has a powerful weapon" – that got your attention straight away. It's a delicious piece of nonsense really, a piece of cartoon hokum.'[156] Lulu, who had been sought to appear in *Casino Royale* back in 1967, was signed to sing the title song.[157] She had previously had a Number 1 hit with another Don Black track, 'To Sir With Love'.[158] Don Black approved, 'She was a great choice, we wanted her.'[159] Lulu was thrilled, 'Of course it was such an honour. Before I'd even heard the thing I was dying to sing it. I really thought it was more of a Shirley Bassey song but I felt I did a really bad impression of Shirley.'[160]

Maurice Binder faced new challenges when he came to create the title sequence:

> There was a dancer – Carolyn Cheshire, who has since developed her muscles and become the Jack LaLanne of England. She was very good and all nude for '[The] Man With the Golden Gun'. I used some rippling water, which covered her body, so we got away with that, but when she danced around sideways, some inappropriate hair stuck out. She wouldn't shave. I said, 'Carolyn, we must do something.' She said, 'Brush it down! Use Vaseline! Do whatever you want to do, but I'm not shaving.' So, I said, 'Give me that brush, and let's try it.' There I was, brushing away, when I suddenly felt something behind me. At that time, they were shooting the film itself on the next stage. Anyhow, I looked around, and there are Cubby Broccoli and Roger Moore. Cubby looked down at me, standing before Carolyn

with my brush, and said, 'Look, I'm the producer of this picture. Are you sure we're paying you for this?'[161]

Binder also designed the teaser trailer, which featured footage of a scene ultimately excised from the final cut. On Scaramanga's island, at the end, Bond was to discover a number of items left on the beach. He quickly contrives a Molotov cocktail with an empty Thermos flask and throws it at Scaramanga. 'The Man With the Golden Gun' shoots it with his supposed single bullet and the flask explodes. The sequence shows that Francisco is cheating and has more than a single shot. Christopher Lee recalled how the scene showed his character was a cheat, 'I see it and I shoot it out of the sky. My last bullet! As Bond supposes. But lo! I have another in my belt buckle. Excellent scene. And they cut it!'[162]

The Man With the Golden Gun received its royal world premiere on 19 December 1974, at the Odeon Leicester Square, attended by Prince Philip and in aid of the Stars Organization for Spastics. The film opened in the USA the following night to a muted reception, both critically and commercially. With only 11.1 million admissions, the second film in Roger Moore's three-picture contract marked a downward trend after such a promising start with *Live and Let Die*. Earning an eventual worldwide gross estimated to be $97.6 million, against a production budget of just $7 million, the film was highly profitable. However, artistically and production-wise, the tensions and inter-company wrangling had left their mark.

14

TWO SCORPIONS IN A BOTTLE

BROCCOLI VS SALTZMAN

HARRY SALTZMAN and ALBERT R. BROCCOLI present

ROGER MOORE AS
JAMES BOND 007

in IAN FLEMING'S

"THE SPY WHO LOVED ME"

Directed by GUY HAMILTON

......FOR 1976 RELEASE

United Artists
Entertainment from
Transamerica Corporation

Hilary Saltzman thought her father 'had the attention span of a gnat. He couldn't be idle. He probably had A.D.D. I think one of the reasons why [Bond] was so successful was because he needed to be entertained and for him to be entertained it had to be a constant, there couldn't be a pause. He just always wanted to go one better, one higher, one longer, one stronger and he had many, many interests.'[1]

Those interests were reflected in the range of international films Saltzman presented. In 1966 there was the French-language curiosity featuring a cameo by Sean Connery – *Un Monde Nouveau,* directed by renowned Italian Vittorio De Sica. In 1967 *Shock Troops* was a Franco-Italian co-production and an early film directed by the soon-to-be celebrated Costa-Gavras. In 1973 Oliver Reed top-lined the film *Fury,* based on the unfinished 1832 novel VADIM by Russian writer Mikhail Lermontov. Saltzman, a committed Zionist, also produced the documentary, *Israel: A Right to Live* (1967) directed by John Schlesinger and with a writing credit by Wolf Mankowitz. The film started as a BBC production but got lost in creative and political struggles and thus has been seldom seen.

Saltzman was also a named producer on a range of international oddities. Two films released in 1965 were the Italian language *E Venne un Uomo* (*And There Came a Man* aka *A Man Named John*) starring Adolfo Celi and the black-and-white Shakespearean opus *Chimes at Midnight* starring and directed by Orson Welles. In 1970 he commenced and abandoned *Nijinsky* (aka *The Dancer*) starring Rudolf Nureyev and directed by his old Woodfall cohort Tony Richardson.

Initially the Harry Palmer films were distributed by other studios: *The Ipcress File* (1965) by Rank and *Funeral in Berlin* (1966) by Paramount. However, the third and final film in the series – *Billion Dollar Brain* (1967) was released by United Artists. The studio also backed Saltzman's other Michael Caine titles of the late sixties: *Play Dirty* (1968) – co-written by Melvyn Bragg and Saltzman's mother-in-law, Lotte Colin, and *Battle of Britain* (1968), in which Caine joined the crème de la crème of the British acting fraternity. All of Saltzman's solo United Artists' pictures lost money to the tune of $15 million.[2]

The only non-Bond solo project Broccoli produced was Ian Fleming's other creation – *Chitty Chitty Bang Bang* (1968). Directed by Ken Hughes, who had helmed *The Trials of Oscar Wilde,* scripted by *You Only Live Twice*'s Roald Dahl and designed by Ken Adam, the film also starred *Goldfinger*'s Gert Fröbe as the baddie Baron Bomburst and Desmond Llewelyn in a minor supporting role. If ever there was such a thing, it was a James Bond adventure for children. The film was made under Broccoli's Warfield banner and released through United

Artists. It went on to lose the studio $8 million.[3] Broccoli felt the failure deeply
and it was reported a few years later, 'He blames the roadshow [hard ticket]
craze of the mid-sixties for its dim returns, "Ticket prices were simply out
of reach for youngsters, the main audience for the film."'[4] Hilary Saltzman
reflected, 'Cubby was the financial brain. Cubby was the person who had to
deal with the studio and he was the person who brought in the financing on
the initial films and the two of them together, their insight together, brought
about the popularity of the [Bond] films.'[5]

In December 1974 *Variety* claimed, 'Broccoli's only complaint is that producing the complicated Bond pictures at a rate of one per year consumes so
much of his time he can't produce other pictures.'[6] However, having produced
a string of varied films to varying success in his Warwick days, Broccoli knew
Bond was a phenomenon worth staying true to.

While the Bond films had been hugely profitable for United Artists, Saltzman
could not offset his losses for his non-Bond productions against his profits for
the Bond films.[7] He had also been given an increasingly generous studio overhead with which to develop other productions.[8] One project Saltzman wanted
to make was the biopic of Canadian Métis resistance leader, Cuthbert Grant,
which would have starred Sean Connery.[9] Saltzman's son, Steven, recalled his
father, 'would read on a voracious level and today, his estate still owns maybe
150 books that have never actually been made into movies.'[10] Then, as now, in
the motion picture business, most films get paid for but never made.

Some of Harry's projects did make it into production, but never reached
audiences. Saltzman teamed up with The Monkees impresario, Don Kirshner,
to make *Toomorrow* (1970), a musical sci-fi starring Olivia Newton-John and
directed by Val Guest.[11] The film was made by another of Saltzman's companies – Sweet Music Productions, based in Switzerland.[12] However, when the
cheques started bouncing Val Guest sued only to find his court victory could
not prise money from the company as the loans had been invalidly secured.[13]

In addition to running up film debts, Saltzman was also engaged in battle
on another front – the boardroom. In 1970 Harry had invested heavily in
Technicolor stock and now began leading a dissident group of stockholders
in a *coup* against the chairman of the company, Patrick J. Frawley, alleging misconduct.[14] However, years of costly wrangling later, Saltzman felt compelled to
sell his controlling stock in 1972.[15] He sued Technicolor claiming that there had
been a conspiracy to force him to divest his shares.[16] Saltzman was effectively
ousted from the board, who claimed he had wrongfully raised money from
Swiss banks to purchase the shares in the first place.[17] Ultimately, Saltzman

ended up encumbered by large liabilities with loans and litigation squeezing in on him.

Steven Saltzman understood how the clash affected Cubby Broccoli and their Swiss company – Danjaq S.A., 'Harry would end up wanting to borrow money and therefore it would be a loan. However, Harry got in the shit with Technicolor and he ran out of money. Cubby then would stop giving Harry permission to pull money out.'[18] Eric Pleskow explained why:

> If one took out then the other would have to do that too. Harry Saltzman bought a number of companies in France and he wanted to take some of that money out. Cubby, who was an American citizen, said, 'I'm not taking any money out because I don't want to pay the taxes.' Slowly, slowly Harry had to eventually sell out because he needed to get the money to pay off whatever he needed to.[19]

Under Swiss law all the corporate actions required approval of all stockholders.[20] They had reached a deadlock.

Pleskow remembered his concerns were 'not about the contract between United Artists and them but it was about each other. I only knew they were not getting along as a result of the stoppage of production.'[21]

Two factors meant a solution needed to be found. Firstly, Saltzman, unbeknownst to Broccoli, had put up his Danjaq shares as collateral against the various loans he had taken out to indulge his creative and corporate fancies. One debtor, Union Bank of Switzerland (UBS) attempted to realise their investment by trying to force the sale of shares in Danjaq and release Saltzman's share of the cash. The lien Saltzman had put on his shares was of dubious legality.

The second pressure point came from United Artists. Broccoli had refused to allow the release of funds from Danjaq, Saltzman refused to allow production of the next Bond film.[22] The Spy Who Loved Me had already been announced and was slated to be the fifth Bond film directed by Guy Hamilton. Under the distribution agreement with United Artists, Danjaq therefore was required to option a new book every eighteen months.[23] At United Arists' discretion, it could force Danjaq to commence principal photography within a specified period of time on a new Bond film. If Danjaq defaulted, United Artists could assign the project to another producing entity.[24] For dividend-hungry stockholders of Transamerica Corporation's most lucrative film asset, the quarterly consciousness meant new 007 product must be in the market to help boost the share price. If Danjaq did not start making a Bond film soon, it would

forfeit the right to make Bond films at all. And Saltzman's veto powers gave
him leverage to prevent production. It was a snake-pit situation worthy of the
best Bond film.

During this period, while developing *The Spy Who Loved Me* for a 1976
release, director Guy Hamilton did not pry, 'I think that its extraordinarily bad
taste if you suddenly say to Cubby, "What's happening between you and Harry?
I understand all is not well."You know the divorce is obviously around.You
obviously [know] there are huge sums of money involved. Keep your nose out
of that. It's just sad.You just wish that they part happily and everybody lives
happily ever after.That's all you can do.'[25]

Such was the antipathy between the partners that they were likened to 'two
scorpions in a bottle.'[26] Saltzman's secretary, Sue Parker felt that the producers
lived very separate social lives:

> They were totally different people. Jacqui used to have these wonder-
> ful lunches at Woodlands. Cubby used to quite like to go gambling at the
> Clermont and Harry wasn't into that.The only time I met them socially was
> when I was going out with Tom [Mankiewicz] and we used to go to Cubby's
> for dinner in Green Street. I can't ever remember going to any function or
> social thing with the Saltzmans and the Broccolis.[27]

However, Steven Saltzman recalled there was a person who kept the scorpions civil, 'Maurice Binder was the back-channel between Harry and Cubby
throughout the entire period when they didn't get along.And they never didn't
get along.'[28] The simplest solution would have been for Harry to have sold to
Cubby. Steven Saltzman remembered, 'Cubby wanted to buy it but I don't
think Jacqui wanted to let him buy it.'[29]

Now a range of potential purchasers were sought to buy into the Bond
business. Parker remembered speaking to her former employer, a multi-mil-
lionaire arms dealer, 'I went to Paris to try and get Khashoggi to buy his half
and he was really interested. Harry needed about $9 million at that point to
get out of trouble. I remember Khashoggi saying, "How much? $9 million?
Yeah that's no problem." And $9 million then was a lot of money. Cubby said,
"No, no, no."'[30] Cubby arranged various suitors of his own: Sir James Hanson
(a gambling pal of his from the exclusive Clermont Club), John Daly (of the
Hemdale Group, Eon's Mayfair neighbours) and talk show host David Frost
(also a media mogul).[31] It is probable that as friends of Cubby's, Saltzman refused
to sell to them.

With no sign of any new Bond film imminent, United Artists were hopeful when Saltzman sought to sell his share to them. It was to be through an intermediary, 'Gee, isn't this great?'[32] UA's Head of Business Affairs Herb Schottenfield thought.[33] 'But Broccoli didn't think it was so great,'[34] Schottenfield added. Broccoli wanted the studio to sit tight in the hope that Saltzman would cave and sell his shares to his partner directly.[35]

United Artists executive Danton Rissner stumbled upon information that changed the situation dramatically, 'I remember being sent over to London while Harry was in receivership. While there I also ran into Alan Hirschfield and Peter Guber [of Columbia Pictures] in Harry's office. I passed on this information to Arthur Krim, Eric Pleskow and Bill Bernstein. Clearly they were attempting to see if Columbia could get involved in acquiring Harry's position in the Bonds.'[36] In November 1975 *Variety* reported on the deliberately leaked Columbia development, 'It was news to Broccoli when contacted here by *Daily Variety*. No surprise in a way, since relations had been on the chilly side, but courteous nonetheless in that they had huddled on joint business only a few days before the news broke. Broccoli said a divorce would require his approval. Whether UA was likewise in the dark on Saltzman's action isn't known, but some insiders wouldn't be surprised if Eric Pleskow and company decide to outbid Col. [Broccoli and Saltzman's] togetherness has been limited to "must" business affairs.'[37]

United Artists could not afford to have half their chief asset sold to a rival studio. Herb Schottenfield remembered we 'made some noises [and] completed the transaction – no longer over the objections of Broccoli – but certainly not with his blessing. We wound up being Broccoli's partner.'[38] Steven Saltzman remembered the incentive for his father, 'When he sold out of Bond he had a few choices. He had an offer on the table from Columbia and he had an offer on the table from United Artists. Well, Columbia was offering stock, United Artists was offering cash. He took the United Artists deal.'[39]

In December 1974 *Variety*, for the first time, set out the full magnificence of 007. The films had achieved $275,000,000 in rentals[40] – rentals being approximately one-third of the gross returned to the studio after distribution and exhibition fees. Each Bond film earned an estimated $2,500,000 from video sales[41] and cumulatively the nine Bonds were positioned to realise close to another $22,500,000 in television earnings.[42] United Artists had averaged a 34 per cent distribution fee, which had earned the studio to date $112,000,000.[43] *Variety's* report said, 'The Bond bonanza is clearly the worldwide record-holding series. Asked how long Bondmania will continue, Broccoli replied, "Until Doomsday."'[44]

It was using figures like these that a valuation was placed on Saltzman's share of the most lucrative film series in history. United Artists came to a figure of $36 million.[45] This consisted of releasing Saltzman from an outstanding debt of $10 million[46] and a cash payment of $26 million,[47] to be spread across five years so the buyout qualified as a tax-free transaction under Swiss law.[48]

Cubby Broccoli painted the scene vividly in his memoir WHEN THE SNOW MELTS.[49] He described armies of lawyers meeting expensively in the Beau Rivage Hotel in Geneva, Switzerland – the legal jurisdiction which governed the fate of Danjaq S.A.. Broccoli was aided by his long-time attorney Norman Tyre and assisting Tyre was Cubby Broccoli's step-son, Michael Wilson – a Stanford engineering graduate and a successful specialist tax lawyer. Wilson had become increasingly involved in the family business like a real-life cross between Tom Hagen and Michael Corleone, the *consigliere* and reluctant son respectively in *The Godfather* saga. They were up against the famed lawyer for the Kennedy clan Sargent Shriver – a symbolic opponent for the staunchly Republican Broccoli.[50]

Sue Parker was with Saltzman when the agreement was finalised:

There was a deal breaker about the car. Harry wanted to keep the Rolls Royce and somebody said, 'No.' I remember Pete Schiller [Harry's lawyer] calling [UA President, Eric] Pleskow and saying. 'For Christ's sake. You're not going to break the deal at three in the morning because of a goddamn car?' So they gave him the car. UA were being petty. This is a huge deal. It's Bond for Christ's sake. I remember that telephone call so clearly. Nobody could believe it. I remember Harry jangling his keys. He didn't come into the room when all the lawyers were talking and I'd be re-drafting the documents and everything. It was signed and Harry went to bed. We are in a suite in the Beau Rivage Hotel. I remember Pete Schiller putting the phone down and saying, 'Done. I think we got a deal.' Harry is back in the room and he's not looking happy. And he thanked everybody and we kind of hugged – all of us – and Pete Schiller and I went into the bar. He was devastated. Jacqui wasn't there. Oh it was awful. Harry went to bed. Harry was sad.[51]

Concluded on 17 December 1975, *Variety* blared 'the sale to UA – important enough to be announced by UA chairman Arthur B. Krim – ends many years of personal conflict between the two producers, as well as providing Saltzman with improved liquidity in his own separate biz affairs.[52]

A reason for Harry Saltzman's fall from grace is proffered by his daughter, Hilary:

[Jacqueline] got sick [in] 1973 and not many people knew she was sick. I think that already sort of removed him somewhat from his ability to focus on what was happening in the Bond films as much as what was happening in his own personal life. My father had a very intense temperament. He would scream and yell and stamp his foot and get what he wanted and he wasn't a quiet man but his ideas, and what he was fighting for, are a large part of what is the Bond legacy today. My mother's illness played a large part in my father's decision making and what he did.[53]

United Artists later reported internally that a 'conservative approach'[54] was taken on determining the price for Saltzman's share: cash, securities, investments residuals on the first nine Bonds and anticipated future income, resulting in UA having 'paid for the cow with its own milk.'[55] A memo stated, 'The advantages to UA are considerable. The actual residuals of the nine Bonds already made, in fact, substantially exceed those which are used in the computation since we left out all reissue values and estimated our remaining network and television syndication residuals at a low figure.'[56] It would not be the last time that the studio behind Bond would so deliberately undervalue its assets.

Steven Saltzman remembered his father 'realised he sold [his Danjaq shares] too cheaply. Harry took seven years to get paid. He then had no stock in Bond, he was in a litigation to try and get his money. He made a mistake. He transferred the ownership before he got paid. It was a real bone of contention.'[57]

Sue Parker reflected on happier times, 'He was a spender, Harry. Jacqui was a spender. Everything with Harry was excessive. He was larger than life. They would go to Fortnum's. He wouldn't buy a bottle of wine he'd buy four cases. He loved his wine and he had a wonderful wine cellar. Jacqui wore beautiful clothes and beautiful jewellery. They indulged the kids; they had every toy known to man.'[58] Parker recalled life at the Saltzman family home Woodlands in Buckinghamshire, 'It was fabulous. The great thing about especially Jacqui, even though I was essentially his PA, his secretary, they never made me feel like that. I was sort of one of the family and became very close to Maurice Binder, too. There was quite a lot of caviar and good wine flowing. And she was a fabulous cook. He loved to entertain. He used to have people down there to play cards. It was lovely. We used to go down for the weekend or go down on Sundays. They were very generous hosts and people used to love going down there, Roger and Luisa [Moore] definitely.'[59]

The Saltzmans now needed to downsize. Steven recalled, 'I remember when money was tight and he had to go to mum to sell her diamonds. I mean, my mum had a 69-carat solitaire diamond and she always said, "Well, I have it here as insurance, [if] we need the money." I remember leaving [Woodlands], I remember the wine cellar being sold, I remember the art being sold [and] Woodlands Park – my father sold it to Adnan Khashoggi.'[60]

During that period the kindness of one star stuck in Steven Saltzman's mind, 'Michael [Caine] was extraordinarily generous with Harry.'[61] Steven surmised that Caine never forgot a significant gesture from his father. As a birthday present to the actor Harry had torn up Michael's film contract to enable him to do [other pictures].[62] 'Michael never, ever, ever forgot Harry. And I know that on a few occasions there were some very dark nights Harry had to talk to Michael.'[63]

As a duo, Broccoli and Saltzman were hugely important in the British film industry. Towards the end of 1974 there were ominous signs afoot in the UK regarding proposed changes for incentives to filmmakers. It was reported that:

> Recent plans over Britain's Eady plan, its film subsidy, Broccoli feels were aimed at Eon, which, because of its enormous box office, benefits hugely from the subsidy (amounts are keyed to box office). 'The Bond pictures', said Broccoli, 'are the biggest contributors to the Eady Fund and limiting its take would not be good.' The implication, not enunciated by Broccoli, is that limiting Eon's Eady take could lead to the latter's departure – further reducing Britain's already slumping film industry.[64]

Steven Saltzman remembered the climate too, 'At the time we were at super-tax and I remember Cubby and Harry went to see the Chancellor of the Exchequer and said, "Look, we probably indirectly provide 6,000 jobs. We know how many people we employ. We are the biggest part of Pinewood." And my father just could not believe it – the Government didn't get it.'[65]

In film-making terms, it was the equivalent of The Beatles splitting. Harry Saltzman was out of the Bond business. He had sold his 50 per cent share of Danjaq to United Artists who were now also the sole distributors for Bond in perpetuity.[66] The studio was now hoping to get a Bond film a year after the stoppage in production. In 1975 it was reported, 'Broccoli assumes sole producer reins beginning with The Spy Who Loved Me rolling next spring. Future slate calls for Moonraker to roll in 1977 and For Your Eyes Only in 1978. The company Danjaq has an exclusive releasing deal with UA and also hold exclusive pic rights to Bond stories generated by the estate of the author Ian

Fleming.'[67] From being one-half of the most successful independent produc-tion duos in film history, Albert R. Broccoli found himself shackled to a huge, corporate behemoth as his business partner. The repercussions would echo for decades to come.

15

SOME KIND OF MAGIC

THE SPY WHO LOVED ME

(1977)

THE JAMES BOND 007™ PHENOMENON CONTINUES...

Albert R. Broccoli
and
United Artists
are pleased to announce
the start of the tenth
James Bond production

"THE SPY
WHO LOVED
ME".

The world's largest stage,
now under construction at Pinewood Studios,
is being built especially for "The Spy Who Loved Me."

United Artists' return to profitability did not seem to help Transamerica Corporation's stock price.[1] The large insurance behemoth needed more cross-company oversight, which negatively impacted upon the soaring film division.[2] United Artists started to amass a film library, obtaining the rights to the MGM catalogue from Kirk Kerkorian.[3] The studio was now producing a string of Oscar-winning successes including *One Flew Over the Cuckoo's Nest* (1975) and the early Woody Allen films. It had also inaugurated *Rocky* and revived *The Pink Panther* film series. Moreover, now they were not just distributors, but partners with Albert R. Broccoli in the James Bond franchise.

THE SPY WHO LOVED ME was published in the UK on 16 April 1962. It was an experiment to try to capture a female readership for Bond. The book is structured in three parts, 'Me', 'Them' and 'Him'; it is the nightmare biography of the fictional Vivienne Michel, whose voice Fleming writes in the first person. 'Me' deals with how Michel, an adventurous Canadian, has arrived at her job minding the Dreamy Pines Motor Court in the Adirondack Mountains. She relates her life in England, her lost virginity leading to a string of doomed love affairs and why she has now returned to her native Canada. 'Them' is set in the present day and introduces Sluggsy Morant and Sol 'Horror' Horowitz, two thugs sent to terrorise Michel. She is brutalised and fights back but eventually is overpowered and about to be killed when James Bond suddenly enters the scene. 'Him' is a more conventional tale where Bond betters the thugs and discovers they have been hired to destroy the motel and frame Michel as part of an insurance scam by Dreamy Pines owner Mr. Sanguinetti. Bond tells Michel a bedtime story about his recent job in Toronto to stop a SPECTRE hit squad killing a Russian defector. Bond vanquishes the villains and then leaves. For Vivienne, James Bond is 'The Spy Who Loved Me'. The experiment was deemed not to have been a success and Fleming initially barred all reprints and paperback editions. The author stipulated that no film should be made from the book.

Cubby Broccoli said at the time, 'The title always interested me – THE SPY WHO LOVED ME – it's a very good Fleming title.'[4] However, Danjaq had to agree not to use the novel in any form.[5] With Saltzman gone, Broccoli now brought step-son Michael G. Wilson formally into the fold as special assistant to the producer. Wilson's first task, remembered Broccoli, was to conduct protracted negotiations 'with the Fleming estate before we obtained final clearance to go ahead and use the title.'[6]

In November 1974 a trade advert announced, 'Harry Saltzman and Albert R. Broccoli present *The Spy Who Loved Me* directed by Guy Hamilton.' The four-time 007 helmer recalled that photographs of nuclear submarines had inspired the initial concept, '[What if] the Russians did know where all the British submarines were?'[7] Hamilton remained director – turning down other films – through a parade of writers until, in November 1975, Alexander Salkind announced that Guy Hamilton was to direct his $20 million production – *Superman*.[8] Hamilton remembered, 'They were offering money – serious money.'[9]

Broccoli was also influenced by Project Azorian – a top secret CIA operation to recover a sunken Soviet submarine from the Pacific Ocean in 1974, fronted by his friend Howard Hughes. 'It was the kind of thing that belongs in a Bond movie.'[10]

Thunderbirds creator Gerry Anderson claimed Saltzman approached him in the early seventies; '"The next Bond film is going to be called *Moonraker*. I want you to write and produce it."'[11] Excited, Anderson wrote an original seventy-page treatment with regular collaborator Anthony Barwick. Anderson eventually declined the £20,000 for the outline, 'The whole reason for writing the treatment for *Moonraker* was that I desperately wanted to produce this Bond picture myself.'[12] Details of Anderson's and Barwick's storyline are vague – 'we had an oil tanker which upended and fired atomic missiles'[13] – but it seemed similarities remained in the final film. Anderson claimed and settled out of court for £3,000. He explained, 'Part of the deal was that I had to hand over the treatment and make sure any copies were destroyed. I accepted.'[14]

It is unclear whether this treatment was the same as that attributed to Barwick, involving a villain named Zodiak, who, with albino henchmen brothers – Tic, Tac and Toe – threatens to destroy a fleet of nuclear submarines if the Western powers fail to surrender their art treasures.[15]

New York comic book writer Cary Bates also developed a submarine-themed story in which Bond teams up with former lover Tatiana Romanova to thwart SPECTRE plans to hijack a nuclear submarine. The script also featured Hugo Drax, from the Fleming novel MOONRAKER, who was to have planned world dominiation from a base under Loch Ness, Scotland.[16] Novelist Ronald Hardy then added a submarine-tracking device in his draft.[17] Derek Marlowe and Academy Award-winner Sterling Silliphant also contributed ideas.[18]

A CLOCKWORK ORANGE author, Anthony Burgess, then entered the fray. Using a typewriter given to him by Hamilton and Broccoli in New York,[19] Burgess remembered the stipulation was for 'a totally original story',[20] but nevertheless resurrected characters from his 1966 novel, TREMOR OF INTENT. The bizarre pre-title sequence finds 007 in Singapore, fighting a Chinese musical Tong society – drowning one gang member in a tub of shark-fin soup – before he is shot. Recuperating, 007 faces a Chinese surgeon who is about to remove the bullet, using a form of acupuncture as an anaesthetic. Bond later witnesses a terrorist attack at Singapore airport and discovers that those responsible are CHAOS: the Consortium for the Hastening of the Annihilation of the Organized Society. The chairman of CHAOS is an 'Orson Welles monster, crippled and confined to a wheelchair.'[21] In a Swiss private clinic, devices are secretly inserted into the bodies of wealthy patients transforming them into human bombs. CHAOS plans to detonate one of these devices at the Sydney Opera House while the British Queen is in the audience. Bond uses his newly acquired acupuncture skills to perform an emergency operation and defuse the bomb.[22] Andrew Biswell, director of the International Anthony Burgess Foundation, described the script as, 'An outrageous medley of sadism, hypnotism, acupuncture and international terrorism.'[23]

United Artists' executive Mike Medavoy brought in emerging talent John Landis. After meeting Broccoli at his home in Beverly Hills, Landis was sent to London.[24] He recalled, 'I was given a beautiful apartment, a 16mm projector and all the James Bond films up until that point.'[25] Landis shared an office with Anthony Burgess, 'I wrote a lot of stuff, [but] never wrote a screenplay. We never worked out the whole story. Our villain was Blofeld – Rosa Klebb's son. We had an underwater base and underwater vehicles,[26] as well as a supertanker that captured submarines and could sink to the bottom of the ocean at anytime.'[27]

Landis sketched one opening, 'James Bond comes into a room and this machine, this robot, which is unbelievably efficient, tries to kill him. Finally at the end you think Bond has been killed and it's revealed it was a training exercise. Cubby liked [it] very much.'[28] Broccoli liked another less well:

We fade up and you are in a central square in some Latin American country. Violently staggering into the shot is James Bond, which is supposed to be Roger. I wanted him to have a deep cut in his forehead with blood running down his face. He's clearly in trouble. He looks and sees the cathedral and dashes up the stairs, opens the big door and goes inside. The troops go up and down every pew searching. They give up. On the altar, is an enormous crucifix and on the back of it, hiding, is James Bond. Cubby went 'NO!' He was really against it. The thing that got Cubby was I wanted to pull people out of the confessional, guns in their face.[29]

With material like this and Burgess writing a treatment about, according to Landis, 'a kidnapping of the Pope',[30] it was no wonder that Broccoli lost faith in his writers.[31] Landis recalled, 'Guy was floating above everything, he was just amused.'[32] Guy *was* amused, taking credit for Landis' crucifix gag, the once Sunday school boy admitted he 'was slightly anti-Catholic'.[33]

Hamilton remembered, 'I went to Hollywood for about a week to work with Dick Maibaum. Maibaum didn't want to work with me and I didn't want to work with Maibaum.'[34]

The veteran Bond scribe began the story with an alliance of the world's deadliest terrorists breaking into SPECTRE's lair. 'They level the place, kick Blofeld out and take over. They are a bunch of young idealists.'[35] The loose affiliation of the Red Brigade, the Baader-Meinhof Gang, the Black September Organization and the Japanese Red Army intends to capture a nuclear submarine and wipe out the world's oil fields.[36] Maibaum undertook a reconnaissance trip to Budapest but 'Cubby thought it was too political. So many young people in the world support those people that we would have scrambled sympathies in the picture.'[37] Dana Broccoli, a writer herself, sat with her husband to try and combine the best of all the story material to date.[38]

Throughout this period, the producers were at odds. Landis observed:

First of all their offices were separate. Sometimes I would pitch it to Harry first and sometimes I would pitch it to Cubby first. They had the same response, 'What did the other one say?' And basically if the other one liked it you were fucked. They were at war.[39]

United Artists' executive Danton Rissner also recollected:

going back and forth between Harry and Cubby's offices, which were across the street. If Cubby wanted Lewis Gilbert to direct, Harry would say, 'No.' If Cubby suggested Tom Mankiewicz to write, Harry said, 'No.' Finally I got tired of going back and forth and suggested, 'Why don't I just holler out the window and get a "No" from Harry?' Pat De Cicco, Cubby's cousin, was there also and suggested he go over to Harry's but it was turned down as the chances were that Pat might throw Harry out the window.[40]

On 18 December 1975, just days before the Broccoli-Saltzman divorce was finalised in Switzerland, it was announced that Lewis Gilbert would direct his second Bond film.[41] His recent *Operation Daybreak* (1975) had been screened by Broccoli to an impressed United Artists.[42] According to Gilbert's trusted associate producer, William P. Cartlidge, the director 'needed something big again in his career.'[43] Gilbert thought the current script lacked humour[44] and his next hire – after Cartlidge – was bawdy comedy novelist Christopher Wood. They had just worked together on the film, *Seven Nights in Japan* (1976), and Wood was asked to fly there to meet the crew on a location hunt at the Expo '75 exhibit in Okinawa.

Back in London, Wood was ensconced in the same Park Lane pied-à-terre that John Landis had occupied a year earlier. 'Good old Eon, they certainly knew how to make you feel important and desirous of giving your best.'[45] Wood recalled reading the most recent Maibaum draft, 'It all took place in Norway then and the villains were hippies. It seemed very weird to me.'[46] He felt it 'bore little resemblance to the traditional Bond movies I had always enjoyed. With director Lewis Gilbert it was back to basics.'[47] When he took the job on, Wood was unaware that he was following in the footsteps of many writers, 'I would have had a heart attack, I could have counted my minutes in Cubby Broccoli's office if I had known that.'[48] Wood worked with Gilbert on a daily basis, 'We would discuss the script in Cubby's office if he wasn't there or sometimes if he was. Ken Adam and Michael Wilson would join us from time to time.'[49] The writer was impressed by Eon's headquarters, which he noted was filled with gadgets and gizmos, which visitors were forbidden to touch, 'This was [Cubby's] nursery and these were his toys.'[50]

Wood developed Maibaum's script incorporating ideas from the previous writers and drafts from the basic story put together by Broccoli. The super-tanker element was an idea Maibaum had originally developed for *Diamonds Are Forever* and the amphibious car was taken from the treatment written by Cary Bates. 'We discussed things with Cubby and Michael Wilson. I then wrote on my own, went back and discussed things with Lewis, and so on. It was like putting together a jigsaw puzzle.'[51]

Screenwriter Vernon Harris, who had a long association with Lewis Gilbert, also contributed uncredited revisions. Harris, according to Wood, had to 'bulk out the screen descriptions to a length that corresponded exactly to the time it took to play the scene on the screen.'[52]

In December 1975 Kevin McClory's ten-year moratorium on producing a film from the THUNDERBALL material he owned had expired. It transpired that he had been developing a new Bond film in partnership with none other than Sean Connery. When he was alerted to copyright infringing elements of *The*

Spy Who Loved Me screenplay, he issued urgent legal proceedings. Connery, as his partner, was required to submit evidence in support of McClory. The Eon script contained many similarities to their own – they too had visited Expo '75 and featured a marine facility. However, after injunctive court proceedings in June 1976, what chiefly emerged was that McClory owned the film rights to Blofeld and SPECTRE. The defeat shocked the Eon team forcing them to remove all mention of Bond's arch-nemesis and his villainous organisation.[53]

In the pre-title sequence of *The Spy Who Loved Me* a British nuclear submarine is endangered. At the same time, so is a similar Soviet vessel. The Soviet's top agent, Triple X, is set on the trail. When the emergency message gets sent Triple X is revealed to be the beautiful Anya Amasova, who is in a relationship with a KGB colleague. Bond is similarly urgently recalled from Austria but not before a Russian hit squad, led by Sergei Barzov, attempts to kill him. 007 dispatches Barzov in a high-speed ski chase but is then seemingly trapped as he is headed off by a precipice. Undeterred Bond skies on towards the void and into it. Bond falls and falls further until a parachute unfurls, sporting the Union Jack.

The main plot centres around wealthy shipping magnate Karl Stromberg, who has funded the development of a submarine-tracking device, conceived by Professor Markovitz and Dr. Bechmann. Stromberg's secretary leaks microfilm plans of the device on to the open market highlighting the vulnerability of their Polaris nuclear fleet to the Royal Navy. One of their ships is missing and unbeknownst to them, so too is a Soviet submarine. Bond is sent to Cairo to track down the vendor of the device. Via his contacts Fekkesh and Max Kalba, he eventually meets up with Amasova, who also is investigating a missing submarine. Narrowly escaping an encounter in Egyptian ruins with the mute giant Jaws, Bond and Amasova are tasked by their superiors – General Alexis Gogol, Head of the Soviet Secret Service, and M – to partner in a mission of détente. Following clues gleaned from the microfilm, the duo travel by train to Sardinia but while on board are attacked by Jaws. In Sardinia they are escorted by Stromberg's aide, Naomi, to her boss's marine-research facility, Atlantis – a massive structure capable of rising and sinking below the sea. While touring Atlantis they notice two things: a model of an underwater city and an oddly shaped bow on a model of the supertanker *Liparus*. A chance observation by Anya reveals that it was Bond who killed her lover Barzov. She turns cold, vowing revenge but only when the mission is over. Frostily they both board the US submarine Ranger only to be caught by the *Liparus* whose bow opens up to reveal it is capable of capturing vessels within its bulk.

In the belly of the supertanker lie the missing British and Soviet submarines. Stromberg is revealed, in SPECTRE-like fashion, to be playing East against West to create nuclear Armageddon. He then plans to repopulate the oceans with cities, the model of which they saw on Atlantis. Anya is taken captive back to Atlantis, but Bond escapes the guards' clutches and frees the submarine crews – Soviet, British and American – who, fighting together, overcome their captors in a huge battle. Upon escaping the *Liparus*, Bond rides to Atlantis on a wetbike, fights Jaws and Stromberg, killing the latter, and rescues Anya. Adrift in an escape pod at sea, Anya holds Bond at gunpoint, threatening revenge, but then relents and falls for Bond's charms. Bond and Anya are caught in bed by their superiors; when asked what he's doing, Bond responds, 'Keeping the British end up!'

Roger Moore bonded quickly with Lewis Gilbert, 'If there was something to trip over, Lewis would trip over it. If there was a queue in an airport for a plane, Lewis would miraculously find himself at the front. Nobody noticed him.'[54] Moore compared his 007 directors, 'Guy was more serious about Bond, whereas Lewis would [say], "Come on dear, it's a bit of fun."'[55] That fun was enhanced by a last-minute script polish by Tom Mankiewicz who recalled, 'I rewrote *The Spy Who Loved Me* at Cubby's house for no credit because they had already given out the credits. I had a typewriter and I was at the cottage down by the pool. Cubby paid me cash under the table to rewrite the picture.'[56] Mankiewicz claimed, 'A lot of the dialogue is mine.'[57] As the rewrites went off to England, Mankiewicz recalled Moore reportedly asked Broccoli, '"When did Mankiewicz get on this picture?" Cubby said, "He's not on the picture, Roger." He said, "Of course he is. He's on every fucking page. Tell him he's doing a good job."'[58] Mankiewicz also had fun with his own name, christening the doctor killed by Stromberg at the beginning of the film, Professor Markovitz.[59]

To play a more accomplished Bond woman of the seventies, Broccoli initially approached several well-known actresses, including Catherine Deneuve, Marthe Keller and Dominique Sanda.[60] However, the producer felt, 'Their agents made things impossible. Everyone scents big money in a Bond film – and starts talking about percentages. If only because there isn't [an actress] who would make the slightest difference to the success of the series.'[61] One of the initial casting ideas for Anya, actress Lois Chiles,[62] was not pursued because, Gilbert recalled, 'we were told by her agent that she had retired'.[63] Broccoli felt any 'high-priced ladies [would] contribute no more than' his new discovery, New Yorker Barbarah Bach, would.'[64] Previously Bach had only appeared in Italian and French films, *The Spy Who Loved Me* was her first English-language role.[65] Broccoli had liked a test she had done for Tony Richardson and the actress then auditioned for Anya.[66] Cast late in pre-production, Bach had in fact secured the role through her then boyfriend, Danton Rissner, who lobbied[67] for a part for her and Gilbert 'began to think she could play the female lead'.[68] Gilbert saw a challenge, 'She did not always like it when I had her do many takes – but I remember I would tell her, believe me, you'll thank me when you see the film at the premiere. And she did.'[69] Editor John Glen was a friend of Rissner:

> Danny felt that if she didn't work he would probably get fired. I ran the first
> sequence where Barbara was acting with Roger – a decent scene – for him.
> Danny was so apprehensive he was huddled down in his seat. As the scene
> evolved, he rose in the seat. He was so pleased.[70]

Having previously cast him in *Ferry to Hong Kong* (1959), Gilbert suggested German actor Curd Jürgens (usually billed as Curt Jurgens) for Bond's nemesis. The villain was renamed Karl (initially Scandinavian, he was called Sigmund) to fit the actor, who felt it was, , 'A good part. A real villain always gives you something to play and I've done lots of them. Producers suffer from a lack of imagination; they always like to cast Germans as villains.'[71] Stromberg had webbed hands and Jürgens recalled the cast and crew christened him 'Fish Fingers'.[72] Jürgens 'loved doing Bond. They make you feel young. They are fun and nobody takes them too seriously.'[73]

In the sole sliver of inspiration from the novel – Sol Horror's metal-filled mouth – Wood credited the creation of Jaws to Richard Maibaum.[74] Now, it was a matter of finding the right actor for what would become a Bond archetype. Native-American actor Will Sampson, fresh from United Artists' Oscar-winning *One Flew Over the Cuckoo's Nest* (1975), was considered,[75] but the director's secretary then spotted Richard Kiel in the US television series *Barbary Coast*.[76] Kiel met Broccoli in The Polo Lounge, Beverly Hills, as had David Prowse (soon to inhabit Darth Vader's cloak). The producer described the part to Kiel:

> We are not quite sure how we want to do this, but they are either going to
> be like tools, pliers, the teeth will be made out of metal and he kills people
> with them.' My first reaction was 'Yuck, this is not what I was hoping for.'
> That was my gut reaction.'[77]

Kiel recalled Gilbert's explanation of why 'we added the bit where Jaws drops the giant rock on his foot. That's clearly when we told the audience: there's an element of fun to the character. The menace was there but there was something almost endearing about him.'[78]

Caroline Munro landed the part of Naomi, Stromberg's personal aide and deadly helicopter pilot: 'I had been involved in a poster campaign with Lamb's Navy Rum. I wore a wetsuit with tousled hair with a knife; it was a very strong image. Cubby had seen one of these along with some of the stuff I'd done.'[79] Munro paid tribute to the casting director, Maude Spector: 'She did every big film at that time. When she liked you, she really liked you. With a Bond film they do it not like a mass casting, they do it very individually which is rather a nice way of doing it.'[80]

Michael Billington, a putative Bond since 1969, appeared as KGB agent Sergei Barzov, who is killed by 007 in the pre-title sequence. It is his death that sets up an interesting sub-plot when his lover is revealed to be agent Triple X, Anya Amasova: 'I knew that if I did it, it might prevent me from doing Bond in the long run; but I thought, "Why not?" A couple of weeks in St. Moritz skiing and Bond was only a picture or two from demise anyway, or so I thought, what did I care?'[81] Gilbert cast Sean Bury – his teenage lead in *Friends* (1971) and the sequel *Paul and Michelle* (1974) – as one of the crewmen when the British submarine is first captured. Sydney Tafler, Gilbert's brother-in-law and Warwick alumni, played the captain of the *Liparus*. Edward de Souza was Bond's Egyptian Cambridge chum Sheik Hosein, who starts Bond on his quest to track down the microfilm. Nadim Sawalha played the ill-fated Aziz Fekkesh and Olga Bisera, his temptress girlfriend, Felicca. Vernon Dobtcheff sneered as Mojaba Club owner Max Kalba while Albert Moses played his bartender. Cyril Chaps and Milo Sperber were the doomed Doctor Bechman and Professor Markovitz respectively who were betrayed by Marilyn Galsworthy as Stromberg's assistant. Strongman Milton Reid, who had appeared briefly in *Dr. No* playing a guard, returned as Jaws' assistant, Sandor. Also returning to the series after his turn in OHMSS was George Baker who now played Royal Naval Captain Benson with Moore's long time friend, Robert Brown as Admiral Hargreaves.

Gilbert approached French cinematographer Claude Renoir, grandson of the great painter Jean, to photograph *The Spy Who Loved Me*. They had worked together successfully on *The Adventurers* (1969) and *Paul and Michelle*. Renoir had had a very distinguished career in France and Brigitte Bardot allegedly wouldn't make a film without him.[82] 'Cartlidge recalled, 'He was a wonderful photographer of people which wasn't always the forte of British cameramen.'[83] The production had extreme difficulty with the Association of Cinematograph Television and Allied Technicians (ACTT) when it was announced that Eon had hired a French director of photography, as Cartlidge related: 'They said "You have to have a British cameraman." We had just joined the Common Market at that point and I pointed out, "Actually with the free movement of labour you can't stop him coming in."'[84] Ultimately donations were made to the right causes. 'That's how we got him in, usual story, a bit of bribery.'[85] Gilbert had campaigned for Renoir because of his efficiency. 'Every single crewmember was amazed at the speed with which Renoir lit these enormous sets. And in Egypt, we were shooting the pyramids and the Sphinx at night and he just used a few lights to do it.'[86]

Of Ken Adam, Broccoli commented, 'I don't say he's indispensable but he's preferable. In my opinion he's one of the big contributors to the film.'[87] Adam, whose previous designs had been linear, was keen to give the Bond movies a new look.[88] 'I let myself really go wild,'[89] Adam later recalled. 'I started by experimenting with new shapes and new form; with Atlantis and the interior of the supertanker.'[90]

The interior of Stromberg's supertanker came complete with gantries, walkways, monorail and a submarine bay to house three 300ft nuclear submarines. Broccoli had investigated using a real tanker, but it was impractical and expensive; the insurance premium was unaffordable.[91] Up to that point, the largest set required for a Bond film had been the volcano in *You Only Live Twice*. 'I had no desire to repeat what had happened on *You Only Live Twice* where I ended up with a workable but ultimately wasteful free-standing set. So I designed the tanker interior in terms of what could remain for use after the film was finished.'[92]

It was decided that a brand new stage would have to be built. Broccoli had hoped that the Rank Organization, who then owned Pinewood Studios, would also co-finance. Instead, 'they decided we could build the stage on the studio lot and we would control it; so we went for it. We did it because of the specific needs of this picture.'[93] Eric Pleskow put United Artists into the real estate business, 'We needed a large studio – I negotiated for that with the Rank people at Pinewood. I built this studio on the property of Pinewood and we financed the building of this studio.'[94] Broccoli outlined the deal, 'United Artists and Eon will rent the 007 Stage through the guidance of Rank. The purpose is to keep it up and make a profit out of it, because I think a stage of this size is important in a studio that is alive like Pinewood.'[95]

Named the 007 Stage, it was officially opened by former Prime Minister Sir Harold Wilson on 5 December 1976. Broccoli's wife Dana broke open the

champagne on the conning tower of the American submarine.[96] After both
the Royal Navy and US Navy refused to assist the production with the open
water shots of the submarines, Adam's models, which he had constructed from
marine ply, were extracted from the supertanker set and photographed out on
to the open sea.[97]

Danton Rissner remembered that Michael Wilson, 'came up with the idea of
using the ski jump.'[98] Wilson had happened upon a *Playboy* magazine advertisement
for Canadian Club Whiskey featuring a daredevil skier leaping off Mount Asgard.
Broccoli loved the shot and thought it perfect for a Bond film, '[Michael Wilson]
found the boy who did it – Rick Sylvester, a Beverly Hills boy. We talked to him
and we brought him over to London, and we asked him if he wanted to do it.'[99]

Sylvester had first performed the stunt for his own amusement off El Capitan
in Yosemite National Park in 1972. He had devised this idea that he christened
a 'skiBASE' jump. 'It was my creation. I didn't see it as a stunt; it was an outdoor mountain adventure. My intention was only to do it once.'[100] However
he repeated it a second time to capture some video footage as a keepsake. The
third jump was a half-aborted attempt for Canada Club, as seen by Michael
Wilson.

Sylvester had grown up in Hollywood. His classroom register had been a
who's who of the film-making community, but he did not come from a film
industry background. When he got the Bond call, Rick was unemployed following the end of his second season as a ski instructor:

> I had just gone on what you guys called the dole and suddenly my phone
> rings, 'This is London calling. I'm Cubby Broccoli the producer of the Bond
> films.' I had never even heard of Eon Productions. I never considered myself
> in a true sense a stuntman. I considered myself a climber, a skier. I have a good
> imagination but I never dreamed of the stunt being in a Bond movie.[101]

John Glen, who eight years earlier had shot the bobsleigh sequence for *OHMSS*,
was asked to repeat his work on *The Spy Who Loved Me* as well as edit the film.
Glen was in Paris with Lewis Gilbert editing *Seven Nights in Japan* when he got
the call:

> Cubby and Lewis met for lunch at the Ritz. Lewis came back and said
> 'Cubby wants you to do something on this film.' I'm sure if Guy had directed
> the film I wouldn't have done it. I certainly wouldn't have edited it and
> maybe the ski parachute would never have been filmed? His [Hamilton's]

second unit directors were mainly cameramen who were sent off to film scenes. I have the feeling that Guy would have wanted to control every little bit himself.[102]

Sylvester met with the filmmakers in London to discuss the stunt.[103] Glen recalled they 'talked about a vertical face in the Lauterbrunnen Valley – a 200ft drop we used in *OHMSS*, but that wasn't enough.'[104] Broccoli recalled that Sylvester suggested they return to the locale of the Canada Club attempt, 'He found the special place where we would do it, which was up in Baffin Island in Canada.'[105] Glen was impressed: 'It was not easy to get there. Mount Asgard was 5,800ft of vertical cliff face.'[106]

Glen and Sylvester travelled to Canada to shoot test footage and undertake a feasibility study. Costing $250,000 it was, in 1976, an expensive sequence for a mere few seconds of screen time:

I presented the budget to Cubby. When he read the bottom line he didn't blink. He took my report and went inside the viewing theatre to join Lewis Gilbert and Danton Rissner. They ran our footage and I nervously waited outside. When Cubby emerged fifteen minutes later he looked me in the eye and simply said 'Do it.'[107]

Sylvester had certain anxieties about the jump, 'Unlike El Capitan, I wasn't familiar with the location. Asgard was more of an unknown quantity. And despite what was depicted in and thus implied by the Canadian Club ad, due to certain interesting circumstances, [I] had not previously skied off.'[108] Recalled Glen, '[Rick] didn't tell us at this stage that he hadn't actually performed the stunt but afterwards Rick confided in me! It was a bit of a gamble really.'[109] Superstitious about this fourth attempt, Sylvester admitted, 'I was really daring the devil. I was thinking: now I'm not just doing it for adventure but I'm doing it for filthy lucre – to be paid. I was actually getting quite worried.'[110]

The crew was based in Pangnirtung, the second largest Inuit settlement on Baffin Island.[111] They spent two weeks waiting for the correct conditions. The first week was devoted to ascertaining camera locations and testing conditions. Sylvester remembered everyone was anxious about the dangers involved:

One didn't want to risk being blown back into the cliff face. René Dupont [production co-ordinator] said something to me which to this day I've regarded as a really gracious thing. 'Rick, if you don't feel good about the thing, if you don't think you can safely do it, then you shouldn't. Forget about the expense of all this. Your life is more important. Just let me know and I'll call it off.' I really appreciated that.'[112]

But then bad weather set in, hampering the chances of capturing the jump. Each morning the crew would take a helicopter from their base up to Asgard to inspect the conditions. Sylvester recalled how the rain continued 'persisting day after day. Each chopper reconnaissance flight returned with a report of "no go". Phone calls started coming in from the Bond production headquarters [in London], "Has he done it yet?"'[113] Glen was getting apprehensive:

I knew I was running out of time. We tried everything. If we didn't get the shot, and the odds were stacked against us, we would have to think of something else to open the movie. If I didn't get it they may have kept me on as the editor, but I don't think I would have been doing any action directing and my career would have been curtailed there and then.[114]

With each day that passed Sylvester's anxiety increased:

I was becoming a drama queen awakening each morning hoping for rain with thoughts that I get to live for another day, that I'd been granted another stay of execution. I felt guilty that my fears were subversive to the entire operation. After all, I'd consented to do it. And now I didn't want to. I was secretly and privately rooting against it.'[115]

Broccoli recalled, 'One day when everyone was getting very discouraged, this twenty-minute break came and they said, "OK, Rick are you ready?"'[116] Sylvester remembered the moment they had the green light, as the word came back from the top of Asgard that conditions were good: 'There were shouts and excitement. "We can do it! We have to hurry! Let's go!" I was stunned. This has been the worst weather since we've been here. What about all of René's concerns for my safety and wellbeing? Where did that go? Boy, he sure changed. The pressure from those phone calls.'[117]

Cameras and cameramen got in position including the helicopter, all of which had been meticulously planned and rehearsed:

I got myself together and got my chute on. I was asked if I was ready. With mixed feelings and unable to come up with any reason not to I answered "yes". Next it was communicated to me that the cameras were rolling. Film's expensive. That was it. I went."[118]

John Glen gave Sylvester one instruction, 'I said, "Don't forget Rick you are James Bond." And shoved the red flag in the snow to indicate to go.'[119]
    Sylvester admitted he:

sort of messed up. I had some delay in getting stable; the position one wants to be in, horizontal, stomach to earth. This may have been due to the suit and heavy-ish ski boots, as opposed to the baggy jumpsuits most common among parachutists. As a result I fell farther than planned, further than everyone expected me to, before deploying the chute. As a result I fell out of range of the camera on the chopper before I got the chute open. The chopper camera was supposed to be the master shot, resulting in the most essential footage.[120]

Of all the camera angles, just one captured the shot perfectly, tracking Sylvester all the way down the mountain.
    When Sylvester safely landed, Broccoli recalled, 'All of sudden the weather turned and snow and sleet came in. They got the crew out by helicopter but most of the equipment was left up there. They got cameras out, but tripods and all the heavy less important equipment was still up there a year later.'[121] The footage was rushed off to the labs in Montreal. Would another jump be necessary? Sylvester remembered the unit taking the call from the lab. The footage from the camera on the cliff's edge was good enough. It would suffice. 'It rained another week before the sun returned. The Bond crew never would have stayed another week. It's incredible the jump happened.'[122]
    Back at Pinewood, Broccoli and Lewis Gilbert were elated with the mate-rial. John Glen remembered the word got around about this amazing footage and before long it became 'the most run sequence ever, before it even got cut into the film. It got the picture off to a fantastic start because we knew we had an epic beginning. '[123] Visitors to the set were treated to a sneak peak including Prince Charles, who, according to Glen, 'saw it three times'.[124] The editor was protective over the piece of film: 'Maurice Binder wanted it and immediately of course he wanted to play around with it.'[125] Assistant editor John Grover remembered their worst nightmare very nearly became a reality, 'Binder took the original negative and accidently put a scratch on it. Technicolor saved the shot by repairing the negative. But it could have been a disaster. I think he ate a lot of humble pie.'[126]

ChristopherWood admitted he got carried away with the pre-title sequence. 'At one stage I became so obsessed. He skis over, the parachute goes pop, he comes down, now what can he do next? What's going to happen when he lands?'[127] Stunt arranger Bob Simmons recalled Bond was to land on a lake behind a speedboat, 'where he fires a grappling iron which hooks on to the boat and turns himself into an instant water skier.'[128] Wood later admitted, 'It would have been too much. It would have become ridiculous, stupid, you wouldn't have believed it.'[129]

Principal photography began at Pinewood Studios a month later on 31 August 1976.[130] Amongst the first scenes to be filmed were those featuring Bernard Lee as M and Lois Maxwell, whose appearance as Miss Moneypenny, was particularly short and forgettable. This time M's secretary can be found hidden away in MI6's temporary headquarters deep inside an Egyptian tomb. Maxwell felt Lewis Gilbert 'never had this feeling between Moneypenny and Bond. We tried to put it in and Lewis would say, "Oh no, cut that, forget about that one." I don't think Lewis ever really liked Moneypenny. I think he just thought of her as a secretary.'[131] Maxwell did read the Fleming novel and described it as 'positively pornographic.'[132]

Q is first seen at the Faslane Naval Base in Scotland to brief Bond on the tracking device that has been used to kidnap the British submarine. Upon reading the script, Llewelyn was delighted at the prospect of visiting Faslane:

> I thought marvellous I'm going to get an extra day's [work]. Ken [Adam] said, 'No, no you are going to do it in the studio.' I said, 'Why? You've got the whole thing up [in Scotland].' He said, "You can't possibly use that, it looks like a broken down boat shed.' Then, of course, you see his most wonderful set.[133]

Llewelyn would get an even better location visit though, when Q would be required to deliver Bond his brand new Lotus Esprit in Sardinia.

The Spy Who Loved Me also introduced two new recurring characters. The first was Sir Frederick Gray, the Minister of Defence played by Geoffrey Keen and the second was General Alexis Gogol, head of the KGB, portrayed by Walter Gotell. In his first of six appearances, Gogol joins forces with M, to solve the mystery of their missing nuclear submarines. The character was an attempt at creating a sympathetic Russian in Western cinema, Gotell explained:

> It must have been the early seventies. A film was being made with Elizabeth Taylor, by George Cukor in Russia. Cukor invited Cubby to visit the

location. Cubby came armed to Russia with a copy of a Bond picture and showed it to them. The Russians rolled about with laughter. They said 'This, is absolutely great. We would love to take your films the only reason why we can't is because you've made it anti-Russian. Why don't you make the films with not a pro-Russian but with something where we are equal villains?' So Cubby turned around and said, 'Let's make a character who is KGB, not a villain, not a hero but who will be acceptable in terms of Russian distribution.' That was the origin of Gogol.[134]

Interestingly, when the 007 Stage was opened at Pinewood, in an attempt to cultivate an ethos of détente, members of the Russian embassy were invited to the opening ceremony to which Barbara Bach was dressed in Anya Amasova's full Russian military regalia. A photo was also staged of Bach in this very costume greeting Sir Harold Wilson.[135]

The first action sequence to be completed was Bond battling Jaws aboard the train. Kiel spent many hours rehearsing the fight with Bob Simmons. It was Kiel's idea to grab Roger Moore by the face, 'Bob Simmons just loved that because my hands are so big.'[136] Kiel later admitted when he saw the completed film and Anya Amasova opens her wardrobe to find Jaws staring back at her, that he forgot Jaws was hiding in there. 'The camera zooms in to a shot of my steel teeth and the train whistle goes, it scared me! I jumped out of my seat.'[137]

In mid-September 1976[138] the motor-cycle/car/helicopter chase began filming on the Italian island of Sardinia. Bond and Anya in a brand-new Lotus Esprit are pursued by a helicopter, flown by Stromberg's deadly pilot Naomi, which strafes their path with machine-gun fire. The scene involved Bond racing around the hairpin bends of the Sardinian countryside. The scene was directed by Ernest Day and the helicopter pilot was Marc Wolff, a Vietnam veteran who would later fly on many future Bonds. Munro recalled that as a pilot, Wolff 'told me a little bit of what would happen. Because it was a Bond film you had to look as if you knew what you were doing. He did [instruct me on the] joystick.'[139]

Naomi did not have much screen time but Munro thought her, 'Evil but fun to match Roger's tongue-in-cheek-ness. We didn't over discuss it.'[140] One character touch did get through, 'I suggested on Naomi's brown boots because it was meant to do with the sea, they had two little gold dolphins on the side.'[141]

It appears Bond is outgunned when his sleek white sports car careens off a jetty and into the sea, only to miraculously transform into a submarine. Ken Adam recalled the filmmakers had decided it was time to update Bond's choice of wheels and give him 'the latest British sports car.'[142] Adam had previously owned a Lotus and thought that apart from it being a fabulous piece of engineering, its shape could make a believable looking submarine.[143] Lotus marketing manager Don McLaughlan recounted how, when he was tipped off a new Bond film was in preparation, he asked his chairman, Colin Chapman, whether he could take the car down to the studio to try to catch the production team's interest. It was left strategically parked so anyone who worked at Pinewood would notice it. The car was carefully moved around the lot so interest could be maintained. It was – the Bond crew called Lotus soon after enquiring about the vehicle.[144]

Art director Peter Lamont visited Lotus to discuss the venture, only to discover they were not prepared to shower the production with free cars. Not because they did not want to, but simply the cars did not exist. There was only one.

> [Lotus] said, 'We're prepared to sell you our car at factory price, we're certainly not giving you one.' I went back a second time and I met a fellow called Don McLaughlin. I said, 'We need another car.' He said, 'Peter! We've only got the one. We only make so many a week!' I said, 'Well, how about the Chairman's? He's got an identical one.'[145]

Before long Chapman's Esprit was on location in Sardinia. Roger Moore recalled the Esprit was problematic. 'During filming, their engines overheated and batteries ran down quickly. Their low driving position made elegant exits from the car an issue, and all this made the action location in Sardinia a little fraught.'[146] As the cars required such high maintenance, Colin Chapman sent mechanics out from London to look after the two cars.[147]

The model unit headed by Derek Meddings shot the car entering the water and transforming into the submersible in the Bahamas. Lotus gave the production the first three body shells off the production line (all had faults) to modify for the various effects needed for the submarine sequences. Meddings was given six fibreglass models by Lotus needed for the conversion from road car into submersible. 'Everything that had to happen – like when the wheels fold up and the wheel arches cover, and then the fins come out – well, we had to have six cars to do all that, because you couldn't get it all into one car.'[148] Michael Wilson, who supervised the underwater unit, revealed that when underwater the shells were manned by divers in wetsuits. The fins were operated with broom handles, the smoke screen was created with 50 gallons of black emulsion and scale bubbles were created by placing an Alka-Seltzer tablet in a model Lotus.[149] One shell was modified by Perry Submarines in Miami so it could be driven underwater, with

divers operating it from the inside.[150] The sequence was photographed by Eon's
regular underwater cinematographer, Lamar Boren.[151]

On 5 October Gilbert shot the scene of Bond's Lotus emerging from the sea
onto the beach at Capriccioli.[152] Richard Kiel, whose son R.J. is the blonde toddler
pointing at Bond's Lotus as it emerges from the water,[153] recalled Cubby sitting
in with a journalist on an early cut and apologising for Roger Moore's gag, in
which he casually drops a fish out of the window as the Lotus drives up the beach
promising it would not be in the final picture.[154] It would become a signature
Moore–Bond moment. Writer Christopher Wood despised this on-set improvisation. 'We are just sending the whole thing up. But you see Lewis Gilbert does have
a sentimental humoristic attitude towards Bond and the movies that I don't.'[155]
Gilbert was confident on his approach. Guy Hamilton had gone to great lengths
to reinvent the Bond character with Roger Moore, but Gilbert felt Moore had
not quite found his stride, 'I said to Cubby "He'll only score on his humour."'[156]

The Lotus Esprit was not the only vehicle that would be an onscreen first.
After Stromberg has escaped the sinking supertanker at the end of the film,
Bond hunts him down to Atlantis, and uses a wetbike to make his way to the
oceanographic laboratory where Stromberg is holding Anya captive. Designed
by Nelson Tyler, the very first wetbike ever built, the prototype, was the one
used for the filming of *The Spy Who Loved Me*.[157] Moore was given time to
practice on the beach at Cala di Volpe in his bathing trunks, but as the actor
amusingly recounted, the scene required him to arrive at Stromberg's lair in full
naval uniform immaculate without a hair out of place.[158] Tyler recalled, 'When
he rode it for the scene he didn't fall once.'[159] Caroline Munro was required to
ride on the back of the bike with Roger for publicity photos and recalled it
drew great attention because 'that was the first time it had ever been seen.'[160]

On 11 October 1976 production continued in Egypt.[161] Filming took place
in Cairo, Luxor, and at the Pyramids. Conditions were so tough, Cartlidge
remembered, the crew said, '"Listen Bill, can we cut the day off and get out
of here as soon as possible?"'[162] When a morale-boosting food shipment from
London failed, Roger Moore remembered, 'Cubby rolled his sleeves up and got
into the kitchen to start cooking. He loved to make a spaghettata for the crew.
He was really caring and worrying about people.'[163] Gilbert remembered this
generosity fondly, Cubby 'in the food tent, in a chef's hat personally cooking
spaghetti for a hundred people. We all lined up and Cubby with a big ladle
served everyone. I told him it was his finest hour.'[164]

One memorable sequence was Bond walking across the desert with Anya
after making their escape from the Karnak temple ruins in full evening dress.

Roger Moore joked in an interview, 'I unfastened my zipper. As we walked off into the sunset my trousers slowly slid down until they were around my ankles. You can imagine the effect it had on the film crew!'[165] John Glen recalled Bach was straightfaced and considered Moore's humour 'schoolboy – they weren't the best of buddies I don't think.'[166]

The Pyramids were later replicated in model form and Charles Gray made his third but un-credited contribution to the Bond series as one part of the *son et lumière* voiceover.

With government censors on set, the gag where Bond quips 'Egyptian builders' had to be handled sensitively. William Cartlidge suggested, "Don't worry tell him to mime it and we'll put it in afterwards." Which is what we did!'[167] Roger Moore later heard it got 'the biggest laugh in Cairo.'[168]

Thankful to have completed such an agonising location, the crew moved back to the comfort of Pinewood Studios. On 2 November the main unit began shooting the Atlantis interiors. Shots of Stromberg's amphibious structure, found off the coast of Sardinia, rising in and out of the ocean, were overseen earlier by Derek Meddings' unit in the Bahamas using a gigantic 8ft tall model.[169] Adam had created this spiderlike design after discarding any reference to the structure they had looked at in Japan:

> It was one of the few times that I really was in a fit of depression. I had more problems designing that than any other set I've ever done. I locked myself into my office at Pinewood and I started designing. And do you think I could come up with something? No. I worked nearly a week before I came up with this tarantula. Once I had the basic idea everything else followed. It was really quite incredible. I was really very excited.'[170]

While shooting the Atlantis interiors, Roger Moore was injured by an explosion during the final confrontation between Bond and Stromberg. 'I was supposed to leap out of the way of a chair which they were blowing up behind me. But they blew it up before I'd moved out which was rather uncomfortable because it peppered my backside with two shilling-sized burns.'[171]

Throughout the scorching summer of 1976, contractors Delta Doric were under pressure with just seven months to build the new stage on the Pinewood lot. While the production was in Egypt, construction had fallen behind, and Broccoli had written sternly to Pinewood's managing director Cyril Howard requesting Rank ensure extra labour was employed to meet their start date. Broccoli stressed in one memo, 'Bond films keep you guys alive and I expect

you to look after my picture while I am away.'[172] Director of photography
Claude Renoir set out the challenges, 'That set is completely closed on top and
we show the ceiling in most of the shots, so the problem is the same as it is in
some real-life locations – no place to put lights, without showing them in the
picture. There is no room for big lamps, so I am using a lot of very small lamps.
Where you cannot put light, it is much better not to put light than to put too
much.'[173] Ken Adam wanted to convey drama:

> On this big set we have a major light change. When the submarine enters the
> set it is in relative darkness, and then the lights go on and expose the whole
> set. To my way of thinking, when Claude kept the set dark it looked more
> dramatic than when all the lights went on. Hopefully, I give cameramen the
> elements to compose on and to create dramatic lighting. I think that's much
> more important than seeing every little detail. In my earlier days as a designer,
> I tried to make it possible to see every detail of the set, and the first person
> who really said I was wrong was Stanley Kubrick. He knows a lot about
> photography and I had to agree with him.[174]

After Kubrick's death, Adam revealed he had asked the director to advise on
lighting the set, 'Stanley [Kubrick] thought I had gone mad. I said, "Stanley
I will organise that you and I are the only people there on a Sunday. All we
do is walk through the stage and if you have any ideas I'll be very grateful."'[175]
Kubrick had not wanted to be seen undermining the cinematographer but
suggested building in floodlights as part of the set.

Kubrick's daughter worked on the film and it was she who designed Jaws'
teeth. Broccoli rejected the initial design by Hollywood make-up and pros-
thetic artist John Chambers.[176] Broccoli recalled Kiel could only keep his dental
fittings in 'for a certain length of time.'[177]

Gilbert admitted that when you walk onto a Ken Adam set you are:

> confronted by problems very few directors have to confront. When I said at
> the opening of the new stage that I loved Ken Adam's set but I hoped I could
> find the actors, I wasn't joking. That's a major problem on all his sets, because
> you have to show faces as well as sets – after all, it's faces which sell pictures,
> not sets.'[178]

Gilbert also pointed out another headache for a director on such a colossal
set was time. 'Not time in shooting, but time in film. You see if you have

someone walking across the set it takes ten seconds. So the cutting has to be nipped faster.'[179]

Moore was not the only one to sustain injury during studio filming. While shooting on the 007 Stage in Stromberg's control room, the giant globe showcasing the submarines' positions caught fire. Made of plastic the giant sphere was lit from inside and Cartlidge recalled it went up in flames and damaged part of the set. Extras were injured when red-hot melted plastic started dripping. 'Some people got light burns [and] seven or eight people ended up in hospital to get treated.'[180]

The exterior of the Liparus was filmed in model form by Derek Meddings in the Bahamas. It was an impressive scale replica, at a cost of £100,000, it weighed 20 tons and was 63ft in length.[181]

Filming was completed in January by Willy Bogner's second unit in St. Moritz, Switzerland filming the ski chase, the precursor to Rick Sylvester's ski-BASE jump shot six months earlier. Other units completed work in Scotland and in the Solent off the coast of Southampton.

John Barry was briefly in the frame to score the film but was unable to due to tax problems.[182] Multi-Oscar winning, 38-year-old American composer Marvin Hamlisch was aware of the precedent set:

A lot of stuff I'm going to write will be reflective of what will have been done already. The only thing that will be different will be the actual theme song which will be more tongue in cheek. It's not about the criminal, like 'Goldfinger', or a title song like 'Live and Let Die' which were pompous, big songs. This is just the opposite. This song is about Bond himself and it is very sexy and soft and all about how fantastic the hero is.[183]

Hamlisch recalled, 'I was very anxious to write a song that I thought was completely different to any of the songs that had been written for the Bond films and I also didn't want it to be quite about the villain. I wanted a song written about Bond.'[184] Hamlisch wrote the chorus first and then consulted his then partner and lyricist Carole Bayer Sager. Hamlisch asked, '"What do you think that could be said about James Bond after all these years?" and she came up with the title, "Nobody Does It Better."'[185] Hamlisch had more time than normal to write the song and returned to the verse about five weeks later. Sager wrote lyrics to reflect Bond's virtues which Hamlisch felt were 'very vain; we decided it was that vain we should have Carly Simon sing it.'[186] Simon had had a recent hit called, 'You're So Vain'. Carol Bayer Sager felt what she 'was writing was a love song to James Bond.'[187] The song which contains the title of the film within the verse, went on to become a huge international hit and recording standard.

Marvin Hamlisch was certainly not hampered by tradition. In the first two reels alone he gives the 'James Bond Theme' a disco makeover, turns to Bach and Mozart for inspiration and amusingly borrows from Maurice Jarre's classic *Lawrence of Arabia*. Gilbert felt his new composer, 'was different. Marvin was much more modern, much more at the fore in that period,'[188] reflected Gilbert. Hamlisch felt his score was of the times, 'It started off with very hot licks and kind of copped the feel of a Bee Gees record'[189] referencing his update of the Monty Norman theme as the disco version, Bond '77.

Maurice Binder originally explored the idea of giving the titles an Egyptian theme. He visited the unit in Luxor and was inspired by images of 'beautiful girls with long fingernails, and beautiful headdresses.'[190] Binder was then hit by the realisation that the first location following the title sequence was a gloomy Royal Navy base in Scotland: 'I said to myself, "I'll have this exotic, beautiful Egyptian title", but Egypt doesn't come in until about two reels later. It would mitigate and take away from the later excitement. So, I decided against it.'[191]

The film premiered at the Odeon Leicester Square on 7 July 1977 – 7.7.77 – in the presence of Princess Anne, her husband Mark Philips and Earl Mountbatten. Gilbert joked, 'I'm sure this is the biggest one. In fact I hope they can get it into this Odeon it's so big!'[192] Broccoli had nothing to worry about. By the time 007 had pulled the cord of his Union Jack parachute, the audiences were cheering. James Bond was back. The Bond team could not have been happier, according to John Glen: 'We all loved Cubby and we wanted the film to succeed, we wanted it to make a big impression.'[193] Roger Moore admitted years later *The Spy Who Loved Me* was his favourite of Bond film, 'I think it was the one where all the elements worked. It had the right balance of locations and humour. I also enjoyed working with Lewis Gilbert tremendously.'[194]

The box office results were staggering. In a year in which Great Britain celebrated the Silver Jubilee of Queen Elizabeth II, patriotism made its way into the cinemas, where a million tickets were sold in the first five weeks in the UK alone.[195]

The Spy Who Loved Me took an incredible worldwide gross of $185m. The film wasn't just showered with financial success, the following spring it was nominated for three Academy Awards. Marvin Hamlisch received nominations for his score and title song. Ken Adam and his art directors Peter Lamont and Hugh Scaife were recognised for production design. Lamont remembered with amusement arriving at the Dorothy Chandler Pavilion for the fiftieth Academy Awards with

Ken Adam, Derek Meddings and Broccoli's two daughters, Tina and Barbara. Walking down the red carpet the crowds excitedly cheered 'and Ken said to Tina "Is that for us?" "No," she said, "John Travolta is following us!"'[196] Unfortunately, *The Spy Who Loved Me* lost out in all three categories. Ken Adam later reflected that although the Bond films were successful, 'to some extent the Motion Picture Academy thought [the Bond films] were rather contrived.'[197]

When interviewed at the premiere, Broccoli revealed that the following week, on 15 July, he was due to have his first meeting about the next Bond picture, *For Your Eyes Only*. 'We start working on the ideas. We don't know where we go we haven't a clue at the moment. Lewis Gilbert again will be directing.'[198]

16

THAT MOONLIGHT TRAIL

MOONRAKER

(1979)

Albert R. Broccoli photographed by Irving Penn

The company we keep

To catch producer Albert R. Broccoli stationary is rare these days. He's a man in motion—Paris, Venice, Mexico and points South (America, that is).

His latest and biggest James Bond saga is taking magnificent shape in all of those locations. "Moonraker" is the title. Lewis Gilbert directs. And Roger Moore is the suave and lethal 007.

It's the eleventh for Broccoli in the screen's most spectacularly successful series. "Moonraker" will be distributed by United Artists—naturally.

Being *the* place for innovative, independent filmmakers like 'Cubby' Broccoli is what UA is all about—and you'll always know us by the company we keep—and the company we're keeping on top.

The interesting place to be **UA** *The place to be interesting*

On 25 January 1978 an open letter appeared in showbusiness bible, *Variety*,[1] addressed to James R. Beckett – seventy of the industry's top filmmakers wrote to Transamerica Corporation voicing their concern at the mass exit of United Artists' top executives – Arthur Krim, Eric Pleskow, Bob Benjamin, Bill Bernstein and Mike Medavoy.[2] The team who had rejuvenated United Artists, critically and commercially, had felt increasingly creatively stifled at the conglomerate, and quit to form Orion Pictures. It sent a shockwave throughout the industry. UA needed to reassure talent they were still the studio to go to. It was important for them to retain the services of recent Oscar-winning director of *The Deer Hunter*, Michael Cimino. United Artists had beaten out strong competition to obtain Cimino's next film, an epic Western, then-entitled *The Johnson County Wars*. Perhaps there was an omen in the feelings of the man who had shared victory for *The Deer Hunter* award, producer Michael Deeley, 'The only flaw I find in my Oscar is that Cimino's name is also engraved on it.'[3]

In February 1978 new studio president Andreas Albeck reassured the industry, 'there is no panic anywhere no demoralisation in the UA family.'[4] He added that the new James Bond picture, *For Your Eyes Only* was 'all go'.[5] Eventually, the film would be titled *Moonraker*. The studio hoped, in the words of their subsequent trade advert for Broccoli, 'The place to be [was] United Artists.'[6]

The place to be for Broccoli was no longer the UK. After more than twenty-five years, the Broccolis left their Green Park town house, relocating to their mansion in Beverly Hills. Broccoli explained, 'I was driven back by the terrible tax conditions [in the UK].'[7] In mid-July 1977 it was already reported 'skedded locations for "*Eyes Only*" include South America as well as Europe.'[8] The same report said Roger Moore was in final negotiations to return as 007, '"If Cubby lets me win a couple of games of backgammon."'[9] Moore's three-picture deal was up but the success of his third Bond ensured United Artists were keen to keep their star.

They were also keen to keep their team, according to director Lewis Gilbert:

Seeing that [it] was a winning one, Cubby asked me to remain. *[It]* was the only one I had a percentage on. A small one. [Broccoli and I] both had the same lawyer [Norman Tyre] and he said I should have something in it because this is the third one I had made. In that 2.5 per cent I know what I've had! They have got twenty-two films with [a large percentage] in every one. It's beyond imagination what it's worth.'[10]

With Gilbert came associate producer William Cartlidge. Meetings took place either around Cubby's pool or in his new offices in the Thalberg Building on the MGM lot from where Broccoli and Robert Wagner had been barred all those years ago – now, UA's West Coast headquarters." That team included UA executive Danton Rissner, Michael G. Wilson, now promoted to executive producer, Ken Adam, and Tom Mankiewicz, hired to turn in a treatment.

MOONRAKER was first published in the UK on 5 April 1955. M requests Bond to assist in a delicate matter. In M's gentlemen's club, Blades, Sir Hugo Drax is suspected of cheating at high-stakes bridge. Drax, who emerged mysteriously from nowhere after World War II, has earned the admiration of a nation, and a knighthood, by seemingly inventing and privately funding the Moonraker, the UK's independent nuclear deterrent. Due to be test-fired in the next few days, adverse publicity could have larger consequences. Bond out-cheats Drax, cauterising ongoing scandal. Awkwardly for Bond, the next day he is sent to the Moonraker launch site on the white cliffs of Dover to investigate a murder/suicide. There he meets Gala Brand, ostensibly a scientist attached to the project, but actually a Special Branch police officer, working undercover. The murder is revealed to be an attempt to halt the revelation that Drax is a Nazi who is now a Soviet agent. He has teamed up with the Soviets, who have assisted with the construction of the Moonraker for an audacious coup. Instead of a dummy warhead fired at a test site in the North Sea, the Moonraker will actually be armed with a real warhead and be re-tasked and aimed at London. Drax will achieve revenge against his nation's victors and the Soviets will achieve a plausibly deniable blow against the West.

After being captured, tortured and left to be incinerated in the blast chamber of the Moonraker, Bond engineers an escape via the exhaust ducts of the launch site. Brand, having assisted with the telemetry of the rocket over months, reconfigures the rocket to the original North Sea test site. Knowing a real nuclear rocket is about to be fired, Bond and Gala listen with bated breath to a radio broadcast commentating on the finale. Drax issues an open speech of coded revenge on his adopted country and boards a submarine which will make good his escape. The rocket hits the test site, and destroys the submarine on its way to Russsia. Now identified as a Soviet vessel, Drax and the treacherous Moonraker team had expected the rocket to destroy London, not them. The nuclear explosion is covered up via huge press intervention while Bond and Gala are honoured by the Queen. Throughout the novel Bond and Gala, while being flirtatious, never consummate their relationship.

Brand's cool reception of him masked her relationship with a fellow police officer, which she had to keep hidden while working undercover. The ending sees Brand receiving the honour the Service has denied Bond, disentangling herself from 007, who walks off alone, described in the book as 'the man who is only a silhouette.'

Whilst publicising *Moonraker*, Broccoli dismissed the novel as being about a 'piddling rocket.'[12] The producer went on to recollect Fleming foreseeing 'at the rate you are making them, the plots will be outdated.'[13] Fleming would urge Broccoli, 'Some day you'll have to step into my shoes, and do your best.'[14] Mankiewicz remembered, 'Cubby asked me to make a start on *Moonraker* because they didn't have any idea how to kick it off. I wrote three or four pages. I was never going to write it. I tried to piece together a barebones story form for Lewis to go and find himself a writer.'[15]

The Bond team visited National Aeronautical and Space Administration (NASA) early on to inspect the then-new space shuttle,[16] a re-usable spacecraft capable of launching and re-entering the Earth's atmosphere. When not in flight, the shuttle was carried on the back of a 747 jet. Broccoli said the production received 'valuable help and advice'.[17]

Tom Mankiewicz's first draft outline was dated 20 March 1978.[18] The story was partially set in the Himalayas and featured a bow-and-arrow wielding heroine called 'The Archer'. Mankiewicz remembered scenes set at the Taj Mahal and Bombay.[19] Cartlidge remembered scouting locations in Nepal and the Kashmir region looking for a monastery for the villain's lair and snow for a ski sequence.[20] The icy locations would also utilise UA's frozen rupees, which could be spent on travel and accommodation for the picture.[21] When it was discovered these two items did not qualify for the use of the funds, the location was abandoned.[22] More locations were scouted including Mexico and an Indian village in Guatemala, which was never used.[23]

Cartlidge recalled, 'Cubby got invited to Rio and courtesy of the government was taken to Iguazu Falls. I remember him coming back saying "We gotta shoot there it's fantastic."'[24] In February 1978, while in Rio, Gilbert and cinematographer Claude Renoir shot documentary footage of the famous carnival, which would provide the backdrop to part of the film.[25]

Mankiewicz delivered a revised treatment dated 8 May 1978, which would subsequently change the title from *For Your Eyes Only* to *Moonraker*.[26] The treatment came with a note suggesting the space shuttle taskforce, which in the outline was known as the Enterprise fleet – the name of the first space shuttle – should be changed to the Moonraker fleet.[27]

Christopher Wood was then hired to pen the shooting script for which he would receive solo credit. He recalled the collaborative nature of writing a Bond screenplay, 'Everyone has a point of view and tugs your sleeve and you are like a putty pencil which people twist into writing whatever they want.'[28] Wood came up with lots of ideas, 'We were going to use a Hawker jump jet at one stage,'[29] as well as utilising the walkways in Venice for a motorbike chase, but 'Cubby was not convinced. To him a motorbike chase was too downmarket for Bond.'[30] Wood recalled, 'At one stage the boat was going to go underwater then Bond comes up in a jet pack. Cubby has a jet pack fixation.'[31] The final screenplay included a scene in the Eiffel Tower restaurant, Bond and Holly being keel-hauled by Drax's yacht in Rio's Guanabara Bay and aerial action above the Amazon using Acrostar jets – set pieces saved for future films.

Wood, a Fleming fan, understood the tonal shift the series was undergoing, 'My James Bond is an earthbound man who wears a suit and tuxedo and punches people on the nose. When you put him in space kit you lose that touch, he disappears behind that mask.'[32] He wanted to keep his Bond dangerous, 'One example: in the glassworks scene, I wanted 007 attacked with a white-hot poker that would be plunged into a padded chair just beside his head. The leather/straw filling would ignite, melt, shrivel, with flames scorching Bond's face as he struggled to twist away.'[33]

Christopher Wood's final screenplay was dated 19 May 1978.[34] Additional script editing was undertaken by Vernon Harris. British writing duo Dick Clement and Ian La Frenais were then hired 'to jazz up some scenes and to write better dialogue. We wrote some scenes improving the glassworks in Venice with Lois Chiles.'[35] They also wrote a scene set in a Brazilian bordello, which was never shot.[36] Clement was struck by a chilling stage direction, 'It just said NOTE: From this moment on everyone is weightless. It was one of those little things that puts millions on the budget in one sentence.'[37] Although their work was minor, La Frenais was hopeful 'maybe next time we will be asked to write a Bond film.'[38] They would meet Mr. Bond again, but it would not be Cubby Broccoli on the other end of the line.

In the pre-title sequence of *Moonraker*, a space shuttle, on loan to the British, carried on a jumbo jet, is skyjacked. Wealthy space pioneer Hugo Drax has privately funded the Moonraker space shuttle programme and has secretly constructed a space station with radar-jamming technologies so it cannot be monitored from Earth. When a fault on one of his shuttles occurs, he re-takes the space shuttle on loan to the British. Sent to Los Angeles to investigate the missing shuttle, Bond meets Drax, who has a liking for Chopin and two Doberman Pinschers in a French chateau brought stone-by-stone from France. Bond then tours the Moonraker facility and meets Dr. Holly Goodhead, ostensibly a NASA scientist attached to the project, but actually a CIA agent, working undercover. Drax appears to have recruited physically perfect specimens from all around the world to train as astronauts. An accident in a centrifuge chamber at the hands of Drax's manservant Chang nearly kills Bond. After Bond sleeps with Drax's aide, Corinne Dufour, she reveals Drax's safe, where Bond discovers specialist work is being done at the Venini glassworks in Venice. Spied on by henchman Chang, the next day Corinne is killed by Drax's Dobermans.

Bond travels to Venice where he uncovers a secret laboratory using the special glassware, which is being shipped to Rio. Phials placed strategically in globes are being filled with what later transpires to be a nerve gas toxin that kills only humans, not animals or plants. Bond steals a sample of the toxin but is accosted by Chang. They fight their way destructively through a glass museum finishing in St. Mark's Clocktower through which Chang is thrown to his doom. Flying down to Rio, Bond partners with Goodhead, who notes Drax Air Freight has been continually flying out of the city many air shipments. Bond and Holly are attacked by Jaws on a cable car above Rio but while the agents outwit the giant, they do not outwit Drax's faux ambulance which captures them. Bond escapes but is separated from Holly. Briefed by M, Q and Moneypenny in a monastery, it transpires the source of the toxin is a rare orchid – Orchidae Nigra – found only in a remote part of the Amazon. Equipped with a gadget-filled Glastron speedboat, Bond travels to the orchid region of the river where he is attacked by Jaws and Drax's goons on boats and forced towards the Iguazu Falls. Exiting the boat by hang glider (Jaws miraculously survives the falls), Bond is lured to an ancient Guatemalan pyramid, now a secret launch site for Drax. Drax reveals he has perfected the poison of the orchids which will now cause death to only humans. Bond is reunited with Goodhead in the blast chamber of Moonraker from which they just manage to escape via the exhaust ducts.

They commandeer Moonraker 6 and discover an entire city in space. Drax reveals Operation Orchid: he will launch fifty globes from space – each capable of killing 100 million people – to annihilate the Earth. From space, his perfect specimens will breed and then repopulate the planet. Bond and Holly disable the radar-jamming device. When a strange object suddenly appears on their maps, the US, after checking with General Gogol, launch marines into orbit to investigate. A space laser battle ensues between Drax's troops and the marines. At a pivotal moment, the giant Jaws, realising he will not be part of Drax's master race, betrays his boss and assists Bond. The marines board the space station, neutralising the globe-launching mechanism. 007 kills Drax but not before three poisonous globes are launched. Bond and Goodhead fly a laser-armed Moonraker and destroy the globes.

Moonraker relied heavily on special effects. With Broccoli now a tax exile, basing the production in LA meant Eon could work closely with one of the growing emergence of high-end visual effects houses. Similar facilities were not yet established in the UK. Cartlidge invited John Dykstra, formerly of George Lucas's company Industrial Light and Magic, to meet the Bond team. The effects house set out their terms; they wanted a large fee, Cartlidge recalled, '$2 million and 2 per cent of the movie.'[39] Broccoli demurred calling in Ken Adam and Derek Meddings, 'We're going to have to do it the old-fashioned way.'[40] If shot in Hollywood, the film would fail to qualify for Eady Levy funds, Cartlidge remembered, 'Although capped at $2 million, it was a lot of money to consider losing.'[41] If based in America, Gilbert was concerned he would be too close to the studio. According to Ken Adam, Gilbert 'felt that Big Brother would be watching. He didn't want that kind of supervision.'[42] Cartlidge remembered another incentive, 'We had just built the 007 Stage – were we going to abandon that and all the investment?'[43]

Prior to making *The Spy Who Loved Me*, Lewis Gilbert and William Cartlidge had produced *Seven Nights in Japan* in Paris, as a Franco-British co-production. They now suggested *Moonraker* be shot in France. There were three studios in Paris – Boulogne Studios, Studios Cinéma and Epernay Studios – which combined, could handle the Bond film. Post-production and effects would be done at Pinewood and on the 007 Stage. Cartlidge explained, 'You got the benefits of both countries – the Eady money and in the case of the French – they've got a subsidy as well. So we got both doses, which cheered UA up enormously.'[44] On 3 July 1978, *Moonraker* became the largest and most expensive film to be made from this dual nationality pact.[45] The co-production deal was set up between Eon Productions and Les Productions Artistes Associés, a French subsidiary of UA.[46]

In 1977 Broccoli said of production designer Ken Adam, 'Nobody is indispensible in this business. We can get someone else to do it. You might want to use John Barry, of *Star Wars*. [Ken Adam] is a very expensive art director, and indulgent with the kind of money I have.'[47] *Moonraker* would prove to be Ken Adam's last Bond film. Across the three Parisian studios Ken Adam built over fifty sets[48] culminating in a three-tier space station.[49] His work was so important to the series it became a selling element, even appearing on the poster campaigns. When asked what is the most expensive aspect of a James Bond film, Cartlidge quipped, 'Ken Adam sitting there with a sheet of blank paper and a charcoal pencil.'[50] Due to French co-production laws Ken Adam could only use art director Charlie Bishop from London while an entirely new team was assembled in France led by French art director Max Douy.[51] Peter Lamont supervised the work in the UK.

Roger Moore's three-picture contract had ended with *The Spy Who Loved Me*.[52] Moore commented, 'The position is that if Broccoli makes another Bond and offers it to me, I'll decide then and there if I want to do it.'[53] Moore signed up for his fourth Bond movie on 5 January 1978.[54] Of *Moonraker*, he said:

> I spend eight months working on [it] and it was back breaking. I only had three days off in that whole time. If you worked a horse like that, you'd be in trouble. On top of that, we had visits from 360 journalists. It got to the point where I had to excuse myself to go and do a scene. Spending eight months being blown up and climbing under waterfalls and struggling through jungles isn't fun. The real problem with the Bond films is they're so physically taxing.[55]

Moore felt the weight on his shoulders, 'I was asked during the making of *Moonraker* when I was next going to make a serious film. I replied that I thought spending around $30,000,000 on one film was pretty serious.'[56]

American actress Lois Chiles was cast as Dr. Holly Goodhead, after the confusion over her availability for the previous film. Broccoli said, 'I've liked Lois for years. I knew that eventually we'd have her as a Bond girl.'[57] When Gilbert found himself sitting next to Chiles on a plane, the actress thought, 'Wouldn't it be a strange twist of fate if that would be my next film?'[58] Chiles had mixed feelings:

> You have to realise this was the seventies and women were very upset about being portrayed as sexual objects. So becoming a Bond girl was not necessarily desirable. Wearing that yellow spacesuit during much of the movie didn't make me very alluring, and some fans were disappointed. But it was their concession to the women's movement.'[59]

Chiles conceded, 'I needed the work, I needed the money and I needed the experience.'[60] Gilbert acknowledged, 'This, of course, has presented us with

the biggest challenge the series has faced so far: portraying intellectual qualities, while presenting Playboy-type visuals.'[61]

Roger Moore remembered early talk of James Mason for the role of Drax,
'I admired him greatly and thought it was terrific casting.'[62] As part of the
co-production deal, certain key on-screen talent had to be French. Michael
Lonsdale felt he was cast 'because I made a picture called *The Day of the Jackal*
[1973] with Fred Zinnemann which was a great success in England. One day
I was in Monte Carlo and was sitting on a coffee terrace and a man came and
said, "I'm pleased to shake your hand and I think we should perhaps be working
in the same film." And that was Roger Moore.'[63] At that point, Lonsdale was
unaware he had been cast.[64] Completing the French requirements was actress
Corinne Cléry.

Broccoli revealed, 'We had thousands of letters from youngsters who asked
us to please bring Jaws back.'[65] Kiel recounted it was Bob Simmons who first
suggested they film an alternative ending to *The Spy Who Loved Me* in which
Jaws survives.[66] Arriving in France, Kiel was disappointed to read the script
and discover Jaws was to be given a girlfriend even taller than his own 7ft 2in
physique. Kiel protested and threatened to walk away from the picture, he had
not yet signed a contract.[67] Early footage of the pre-title freefall was shown
to Kiel, 'The stuntman had done my part and the only thing missing was my
close-up. Cubby said "We're making you into a star!"'[68] Kiel fought against the
giant girlfriend idea, 'I felt strongly that what they had in mind wouldn't work
for me or the audience.'[69] The filmmakers eventually succumbed. When filming the moment where Dolly, played by a very petite French actress, Blanche
Ravalec, meets Jaws, Kiel recalled:

> Cubby Broccoli was sitting with a journalist and very loudly, so he could
> make sure I could hear said, 'Richard and I had quite a falling out about
> this. We wanted to do it in a different way and Richard wanted to do it his
> way, and actually he was absolutely right.' It was his way of letting me know
> he appreciated it, the fact I stood my ground and did something I knew
> would work.'[70]

Kiel recalled it was Lewis Gilbert's grandson who first raised the question,
'Why does Jaws have to be a bad guy?'[71] 'There was certainly some criticism
by the James Bond fans, those that want to take it deadly seriously, but in terms
of general audiences it was accepted very, very well.'[72] Screenwriter Wood felt:

the whole business of Jaws turning into a lovable moral ape was totally against what I wanted. I fought as hard as I could to stop the love interest with this diminutive little apple strudel with the pigtails which I find embarrassing and totally diminished any kind of tension in the story. To me it was just pukesville.'[73]

Michael Lonsdale fondly remembered Kiel, 'He had a baby during the shoot. And the day he came to the studio with that little baby in his hands it was most extraordinary because, you know, the giant looking to that tiny little baby. It was amazing.'[74]

Michael G. Wilson's martial arts teacher Toshiro Suga appeared as the formidable Chang, Emily Bolton was Station VH's Manuela and famed British comedian Alfie Bass appeared humorously as a 'consumptive Italian'.

Days before the picture began shooting in Paris, a key crew change was forced upon the production. During a location recce in Venice, Gilbert had noticed Claude Renoir struggling to read.'[75] The cinematographer revealed, 'I have been preparing the picture for three months and within the last two or three weeks I noticed that my vision was deteriorating and impairing my photographic judgment.'[76] Cartlidge was devastated when Renoir had to resign, 'We'd been in pre-production and taken Claude to South America and done all the recces. Cubby effectively arranged for Claude to go to America to the top eye man.'[77] Renoir declined Broccoli's kind gesture and underwent surgery in France.[78] Optimistically Renoir said, 'Mr. Broccoli has promised me the Bond film after *Moonraker*.'[79] Sadly, Renoir was forced to retire and did not work again. He was replaced by his own recommendation, fellow Frenchman Jean Tournier.[80]

On 11 August 1978 principal photography commenced in Paris, where the main unit would first complete six weeks of studio work. Broccoli threw a launch party at the exclusive Ile-de-France restaurant moored on the River Seine where photographers swarmed to take pictures of Roger Moore and his new leading lady Lois Chiles.[81]

Moonraker begins with Bond on the last leg of an African mission aboard a private jet. Bond is pushed out of the plane and has to skydive to retrieve a parachute from the villainous pilot. Bond then has to grapple with Jaws mid-air. Bond opens his parachute, jerking him away from the giant. Jaws pulls at his parachute chord but rips it off. Flapping his arms, Jaws plummets into a circus below. Fresh from his triumph filming the ski-parachute, second unit director John Glen was assigned to top the previous pre-title sequence. 'It was the first time anyone had attempted an action sequence in freefall.'[82]

Glen recalled the stunt had been the brainchild of Michael Wilson.[83] 'His research was amazing. He would research a subject and find out all kinds of amazing things which one wouldn't normally do.'[84] It was Wilson who discovered B.J. Worth and his team of skydivers.[85] 'They came into the office in California and said they could do this and they could do that and we started to think what we could use them for.'[86] Glen and Wilson worked out an action sequence and with Glen's editing experience sketched out a storyboard. Broccoli was dubious and filming took place three months before principal photography, giving them time to substitute another idea if the sequence proved untenable.[87]

In May 1978 Glen travelled to the small town of Yountville, California where his unit would be based.[88] B.J. Worth and his team camped in tents on the side of the airfield, which was a short drive away.[89] The 6ft 5in member of the US parachute team, Ron Luginbill, doubled Jaws while two-time world champion Jake Lombard, with his remarkable resemblance to Roger Moore, doubled Bond.[90] It was filmed over five weeks and took ninety-two jumps.[91] With each jump Glen:

[could] only really shoot about two seconds of actual footage because by the time everyone gets into position and the cameraman gets into position you are running out of altitude, you are down to about 1,500ft and you need to start thinking about pulling your chute. So it had to be very carefully orchestrated. One shot would just be taking the strap off someone's shoulder then cut! It was very technical in that sense.[92]

Glen recalled their biggest challenge was finding camera equipment to shoot the sequence. Previously, skydiving footage had generally been shot on lightweight 16mm cameras and then blown up. 'We needed to get pristine quality so we needed 35mm.'[93] They required a camera and lens that could be fitted to a helmet, light enough so when the cameraman pulled his chute, it wouldn't break his neck. By chance, Michael Wilson discovered a plastic anamorphic lens in a second-hand camera shop in Paris. 'We got Continental Cameras Systems to adapt the whole thing for a helmet camera, a lightweight camera [which] only had three minutes of film because it was such a small magazine.'[94]

Originally Jaws was to crash through the big top and into the middle of an elaborate trapeze act. The sequence was filmed using the Traber family, the world-famous German circus performers but the scene was later left on the cutting room floor.

In a snake-pit situation inspired by early trips to NASA Bond is nearly killed by dangerous gravitational forces when his centrifuge training session is sabotaged by Chang. A menacing set was built in Paris by Ken Adam. 'I tried to give it an almost claw-like look, with a frightening atmosphere.'[95] It took eight weeks to build and Lewis Gilbert only filmed on it for two days.[96] 'It bruised [Roger's] face quite badly.'[97] Moore explained, 'We did that with air hoses and a lot of acting.'[98]

Filming took place at the magnificent Vaux-le-Vicomte, a seventeenth-century chateau outside of Paris, which doubled for Drax's Californian estate. Lonsdale remembered Drax's dangerous Dobermans:

> The Japanese man came with some meat for the dogs. Throwing some on the carpet but [the dogs] wouldn't move. The man [who was responsible] for the dogs was quite upset. He was, 'Go on, go on, *allons y, allons y.*' They didn't like it: there was too much light and people.[99]

In late September 1978 the main unit departed for Venice.[100] Here, John Glen shot a 60mph gondola chase down the narrow canals and waterways. Venice was a challenging location logistically and all equipment had to be transported around the city on barges. Cartlidge, a nautical scholar, used his knowledge of the Dover Tide Tables to calculate the Venetian tides, 'It was necessary because going under these bridges with our barges the clearance under them would sometimes be less than a foot. So if you tried to move the unit at the wrong time of the day you are in trouble.'[101]

Andy Albeck and Steven Bach from UA were shocked to discover what the entry 'special location facilities' budgeted at $2 million stood for.[102] Cartlidge recalled:

> They kept picking away at me and it went on a while I used every bloody euphemism I could bloody well think of. 'Fuck it – it's for bribes!' Well they nearly fell off the bloody chairs. 'SHIT! BRIBES? It's illegal!' I said, 'First of all it may be illegal in America but it ain't illegal in the UK and this is an Anglo-French co-production. How do you think we shoot some of these sequences? In the script we've got a gondola doing 65–70mph down the Grand Canal. Do you know what the speed limit is there? Six knots.'[103]

The chase climaxes with James Bond turning his modified gondola into a hovercraft, escaping across a crowded St. Mark's Square. The sequence was handled by John Glen.[104] Capturing the shot of the gondola exiting the water proved tricky resulting in Roger Moore being thrown into the water on several occasions to the amusement of the ranks of massed tourists.[105]

Moonraker marked the swansong of series regular Bernard Lee who filmed his final performance as M in Venice alongside Geoffrey Keen reprising his role as the Minister of Defence. John Glen recalled sharing a ride from the lido up the canal with Lee and Keen, 'It was wonderful to eavesdrop on these two old actors sniping away at each other but actually having an awful lot of fun.'[106] Roger Moore recalled Geoffrey Keen became Bernard Lee's keeper in the sense of 'keeping Bernie off the sauce'.[107]

Desmond Llewelyn also filmed his scenes in Italy, 'They were looking for a monastery, but they couldn't find one in South America, so the one you see in the film is in fact in Italy.'[108] The unit filmed in a monastery in the St. Nicolo enclave in Venice, which doubled as the British Secret Service's Brazilian hideaway.[109] This is where Lois Maxwell also joined the production, 'Cubby very kindly gave my daughter a part as an extra. They were filming in Paris, and he looked after her as part of his own family. He used to take her home, cook spaghetti. There weren't many other extras staying with the producers and his wife!'[110]

The sets for both Miss Moneypenny and M's offices were broken down at the end of each Bond film and stored at Pinewood. For *Moonraker* they were flat-packed and shipped to Paris for filming.[111]

Michael Lonsdale recalled Lois Chiles:

> was upset because she tried to make a strong character. Gilbert told her, 'What are you doing?' 'Well, I'm trying to give some character.' So he says, 'Oh, please stop it, you're a beautiful girl, Michael is the horrible man and that's all.' And she started weeping and I went to her [dressing room], 'Yes, you mustn't try to do something extraordinary.'[112]

Richard Kiel thought, 'Roger felt that Lois Chiles was just a little bit too serious. He was kidding with her about it, she got upset, so he was trying to lighten things up a bit.'[113]

Kiel remembered a visual gag which eased the tension on the space station set, 'Suddenly a little Martian creature pops up, in a green outfit, waving, cleaning the Plexiglas. Of course we all start cracking up.'[114] Assembly editor John Grover revealed, 'The camera crew knew that was going to happen so they turned over on it. On *Moonraker*, we were shooting stuff for [the Wanker Film].'[115] Peter Davies, who joined the Bond series as junior editor after having worked with John Glen on *Escape to Athena* (1979), remembered:

when I first got to Paris on *Moonraker* it was toward the end of November. My first full editing job was compiling [the Wanker film] using out-takes and scenes that Roger was always messing about in. And extra footage of crew was secretly filmed so that nobody escaped. It was great fun to do and no expense was spared in the making of it. Anyway we had a full house when showing it just before the Christmas break and it was very well received. Even Prince Charles saw it.[116]

Roger Moore recalled the finale in which Bond and Holly make love in zero gravity in the Moonraker shuttle:

Hanging around on wires is for Peter Pan, not for me, they actually had to make a mould of my body and then cast a metal sheet for me to be encased in. That in turn was attached to the bar of a hidden forklift truck, which moved me up and down. It was highly uncomfortable I can tell you.[117]

Michael Lonsdale was also required for wire work, to film Drax's death scene as Bond dispatches him out of an airlock chamber into outer space. 'It was shot in a very funny way. They made the tunnel where he disappears upwards. I had to be pulled up on a string. I had to go towards the camera and move my arms as if I was flying. It's my first time [doing a stunt].'[118] Scenes of Drax's astronauts in a zero-gravity love chamber were shot but edited out.

After Christmas the unit flew out to Rio de Janeiro for the final leg of production. As the charter was about to leave Paris, Roger Moore was taken ill at the airport with kidney stones. Cartlidge dispatched the flight to Rio and stayed in Paris to await news of Moore's condition.[119] 'While they were in the air I actually sat down in Paris and worked out a new schedule where for five days they could shoot without Roger.'[120] Doctors feared that operating on the star would require a twelve-week recovery period which Cartlidge estimated would cost the production 'in the region of $15–20 million.'[121] Moore recovered in four days and flew straight to Brazil on Concorde. As soon as the aircraft touched down in Rio, hair and make-up jumped aboard. When Bond arrives in Rio in the film, it is actually Moore arriving.[122] Publicist Jerry Juroe informed the gathered press that Moore had passed his kidney stone and Broccoli joked, 'To think the future of my $30 million movie is hanging on a goddam pebble.'[123]

Ernest Day's second unit began shooting at Iguazu Falls. They filmed Bond's Glastron speedboat plummeting over the falls while Bond exits by hand glider – a similar sequence was originally conceived for the finale of *Diamonds Are*

Forever with Blofeld on Lake Mead. Special effects supervisor John Richardson, working on his first Eon-Bond film, was forced to be as daring as Bond. When the Glastron boat was impaled on rocks near the edge of the waterfall, it had to removed for the crew to take clear shots for back projection plates.[124] Richardson dangled from a helicopter to try to shift the boat – a dummy which weighed a ton[125] – by hand:

> Once I got hold of the boat there was no way I was going to let go! So the helicopter is pulling and my arms are getting longer and longer by the second, and suddenly I hear this ping, ping, ping, ping, ping. I thought, "What on Earth is that?" I could hear it quite loudly over the noise of the helicopter, and I suddenly realised it was the stitching on the harness I was wearing – breaking.'[126]

Richardson was forced to let go but providence intervened as the boat was washed over by heavy rains that very night.[127] The fall was completed in miniature by visual effects supervisor Derek Meddings.[128] The rest of the boat chase was shot in Port St. Lucy, a small town in the Florida Everglades.[129] Richardson built a radio-controlled, self-propelled torpedo, which Bond employed to lethal effect.[130] Richardson recalled:

> Explosions in water are always one of the most dangerous situations for us. We have to be very careful in order to avoid accidents because charges can drift and boats don't necessarily follow the right line. We had to make sure that the boats were as close as they could be to the explosions, but not too close.'[131]

William Cartlidge recalled securing the cable car location with two brothers who purportedly owned the business, 'However, the father starts to look through the storyboards and realises his precious cable cars crash. When the film comes out nobody will go on his cable car again. The father who actually owns the company [and] locked us out.'[132] Under Brazilian law, the Bond team were informed, it could take two years to settle.[133] Cartlidge solved the situation with an invitation, '"I'd like to bring you and your family to England to the royal premiere." Do you know what happened? He died. So that's how it resolved itself.'[134]

For the cable car fight neither stuntmen Dickie Graydon nor Martin Grace could wear harnesses, as these would have restricted their movements as they fought in and out of the girders of the cable car.[135] The fight was originally to be shot in two sections with a break where Graydon could then attach himself with a line before going over the edge of the car, 'I was desperately waiting for the word "Cut!" I had no alternative but to go, grab the handrail at the edge of the cable car and hang on for real. I wasn't attached by anything other than just pure terror.'[136] Martin Grace explained, 'The fight area on top was like a large billiard table – that seems small when you are 1,300 feet from the ground.'[137] Gilbert recalled, 'Mishika Scako my assistant kept nudging me saying "Lewis say cut" but I was riveted, watching this incredible scene.'[138] Even Broccoli was impressed, 'It was frightening. The drop was hundreds of feet. But that's the dedication you get from people working on a Bond film.'[139]

As the ambitious Michael Wilson was adept underwater, Glen recalled the producer's step-son was given a chance to direct the sequence where Bond grapples with an anaconda in Drax's pyramid pool. However, despite several attempts to edit the footage to Wilson's satisfaction with assembly editor Alan Strachan, the scene would not work. When Cubby saw the revised version, he was dismissive. Glen remembered Cubby's instruction, '"Put it back the way it was." Cubby was probably harder on his own family than on someone outside the family.'[140]

On 19 February 1979 Broccoli threw a party at Chez Régine to celebrate the end of principal photography.[141] Close-ups and pick-ups were completed in Paris with principal photography completed on 26 February 1979, four weeks over schedule.[142]

Broccoli's mantra was, 'We're closer to science fact in our approach than science fiction.'[143] Renowned space pioneer, Eric Burgess, was hired to back up Broccoli's claims.[144] Creative licence was at times, essential, as Burgess acknowledged, 'Although sound cannot be transmitted through the vacuum of space, action without sound would seem very slow and tedious. It was decided, therefore, to use sound effects as well as a musical soundtrack.'[145] Dubbing editor Colin Miller recalled creating sounds for the laser pistols, 'Each one of those was a very short burst visually. We called in a guy who had his own synthesizer. We then had to fit each one of those laser bursts one by one, there were hundreds and hundreds of them.'[146]

Derek Meddings and his crew took over the 007 Stage for ten months from August 1978.[147] It was swathed in $60,000 of black velvet to enable them to create star fields behind the models and stuntmen.[148] All remaining surfaces were painted black to prevent scattered light.[149] 'I was up to my ears in effects. We were competing with *Star Wars*. I had to come up with a way of doing the effects for *Moonraker* that were of the simplest fashion.'[150]

A major task was to integrate the astronauts hanging on wires with lasers, models and opticals. Cartlidge recalled the 007 Stage was a mass of tram wires hanging from the roof, 'It had never been built to take any weight from the ceiling so all this had to be specially constructed. It was a long and complicated process.'[151] One of the many stuntmen suspended from the roof was future Bond stunt co-ordinator Paul Weston, 'That was tough. Everything was on your crutch. Guys were passing out.'[152] Roger Moore was pleased the 007 Stage was being used, because 'this film was having to pay rent for use of the tank and that money goes back into *The Spy Who Loved Me* profits, of which I have a slice.'[153]

Gilbert recalled, 'We had three basic things: the world, the stars and the shuttle flying well above the Earth. So first of all Derek shot the Earth, then he would rewind and shoot the stars. Two months later he would rewind again and do the scene with the shuttle. My shots would then be put into that, plus adding things like laser beams. It was very complicated and had to be carefully drawn on storyboards before we began.'[154]

UA Executive Steven Bach wrote, 'One very difficult effect which neces-sitated exposing a single strip of negative forty-eight separate times rather than resorting to lab work and optical printers. A mistake or miscalculation in any one of the forty-eight exposures would have destroyed hundreds of costly hours of effort.'[155] Burgess said their work was made harder by the fact live action with the actors was being filmed in Paris while the model and effects were happening in Pinewood and required continuous contact between both units.[156]

On 14 May 1979[157] and after thirty-nine weeks in production, Meddings and his team created the last special effect for *Moonraker*. NASA was so impressed with Meddings's work they requested to use footage from the film to make a television commercial to rekindle interest in the American shuttle.[158] After a ten-month production period Broccoli was relieved to see complete arguably the most arduous Bond production to date. As each scene was completed he would rip the pages from his script; Broccoli concluded, 'The payoff is when all that's left is the covers.'[159]

It was advantageous for John Barry, now a British tax exile, to go to Paris to score and record the music for Moonraker. Editor John Glen recalled, 'When we did the music returns I used to go through with John Barry and [ask him] "Mark the film where it's yours and mark the film with another colour when it's Monty Norman's." We used to have to split up the royalties.'[160] Barry did not want to keep conceding royalties to Monty Norman. A case in point was

Moonraker's pre-title sequence, 'When Bond was in freefall and dives down to accelerate towards the chap with the parachute it had to be the "James Bond Theme". John Barry didn't have that written into the score. There was a big argument. John always kind of resented it in a way and he fought against it.'[161]

For the title song Barry originally collaborated with lyricist Paul Williams on a song proposed for Frank Sinatra.[162] For unknown reasons the crooner who at first appeared enthusiastic, passed on the song. John Barry asked Williams to revamp the lyric for another artist but Williams refused because, 'When Sinatra likes a lyric, it's finished.'[163] Kate Bush also declined the song.[164] John Glen remembered listening to the demo track in the editing room in Paris. 'Certainly Lewis and Cubby both agreed it wasn't what they were looking for, for this movie. Funnily enough in a later film [I directed] he revamped that song.'[165]

It was time to start afresh. Barry approached lyrist Hal David with whom he had written, 'We Have All the Time in the World', a decade earlier:

> It was a very rushed date to get it done. John made a cassette with the melody, I sat down and wrote the lyric. John liked it a lot and we called Broccoli. Cubby came over. Now, I'm sure John plays better today than he did then but he didn't play great piano and he didn't necessarily play in time either. And I sang the lyric, I'm not one of the great singers, and so with John playing and me singing and really not in time, it must have sounded dreadful. At any rate when it was all over, Cubby turned to us and said, 'Oh, that's a peachy song!'[166]

The new title song was first recorded by American singer Johnny Mathis. Barry claimed, 'it just didn't work out.'[167] Fate then intervened, 'Back in LA, I was having lunch in a Beverly Hills hotel when who should walk into the lounge? – none other than Shirley Bassey! We were in a studio within a week.'[168] Bassey admitted years later, 'It was not really my song, it was Johnny's [Mathis]. I did it for John Barry, to help him out.'[169]

The delayed composition affected the titles as Maurice Binder was cutting visuals to Barry's rhythm.[170] This also meant Binder had to take extra care with his nude models so as not to incur censorship problems:

> When they start printing those prints there's no stopping it; it's like a news-paper press. If the censor says, "You've got to take that booby out or cover up that behind," it's big trouble, so I'm very careful. On *Moonraker* I was more careful than I was on some of the previous pictures.'[171]

Assembly editor John Grover recalled Binder's perennially late delivery, 'We had to cut the titles in for the premiere in the theatre.'[172]

Moonraker premiered at the Odeon Leicester Square on 26 June 1979. Sporting a thick un-Bondian beard for his next picture *North Sea Hijack* (1980), Moore hosted a one-hour television special from the event for ITV.

In July 1978 Cubby Broccoli publically thought the eleventh Bond film would cost $15 million.[173] Associate producer William Cartlidge remembered early draft budgets coming in at at least $20 million, whittled down verbally by Cubby to UA executive Danton Rissner to $18 million and by Rissner to $16 million on the phone to boss, Andy Albeck. Cartlidge was incredulous, 'In an afternoon, $4 million has evaporated just like that. Cubby didn't care. He knew they were the games everybody played. He played them himself. He said, "It'll just make them feel better for now."'[174] When ensconced in Paris, Cartlidge calculated a preliminary budget for *Moonraker* at a cool $32 million,[175] prompting UA to force the budget down to $28,498,724.[176] Broccoli was chagrined by the increased cost, 'The forces of nature pushed the budget up. The forces of economy, the forces of inflation, and the incredible cost in Europe.'[177] The use of three Parisian studios was to have saved money, but art director Lamont reflected, 'They all had their own separate staff, because you can't mix them. So you in effect treble what you start with. And the French said, "If you want to work overtime, you haven't got enough people."'[178] The final budget was closer to $33 million.[179] Lewis Gilbert quipped, 'I used to make entire feature films for less than the *Moonraker* telephone bill.'[180]

Ken Adam justified his exacting style, 'While I agree to go to such lengths could be labeled as extreme, the end result to even the untrained eye must be more attractive and exact in its immediate conveyance of the setting than if we had taken less time and effort to create it.'[181] Adam felt the pressure:

It was costing a lot of money because of these such enormous sets: the space station, space corridors, the control room, the great chamber under the waterfalls, the laboratory, the centrifuge – and it was all very ambitious, and people were starting to get very worried about the costs. They started saying I was going over budget.[182]

Cartlidge was circumspect:

There may well have been conversations, not about replacing [Adam], because who could you replace him with? But when we were going through some dramatic days trying to get these sets working in Paris, there could well have been: 'Could we do without him?' Because in that sense all the sets were designed and in the works. But I don't think Cubby would have allowed it.[183]

Danton Rissner at UA had been recovering from heart surgery. Ken Adam felt he needed studio support, 'I wasn't happy and they needed me. I was asking [Rissner] to help me out. And Danny was very outspoken and said, "Fuck you and your bloody film, I'm lying in bed and practically dying." We could have done it cheaper in this country.'[184]

Steven Bach explained the studio's attitude, 'Whatever budget concerns [were] muted by the assumptions everyone, including UA, made regarding *Moonraker.* James Bond couldn't miss.'[185]

Indeed he could not. *Moonraker* grossed a series high of $202.7 million worldwide, topping the record set by *The Spy Who Loved Me*. However, in that decade, production costs had risen fourfold and production costs at this level, for this studio, could not be sustained. James Bond would have to get back down to earth.

17

READ BETWEEN
THE LINES

FOR YOUR EYES ONLY

(1981)

And in the U.S. and Canada...

THE 'EYES'
HAVE IT!

$172,830,071

10 Days—1,086 Theatres

ALBERT R. BROCCOLI presents

ROGER MOORE
as IAN FLEMING'S

JAMES BOND 007™

in FOR YOUR EYES ONLY

Starring CAROLE BOUQUET • TOPOL • LYNN-HOLLY JOHNSON • JULIAN GLOVER

Produced by ALBERT R. BROCCOLI • Directed by JOHN GLEN

Music by BILL CONTI • Executive Producer MICHAEL G. WILSON

Associate Producer TOM PEVSNER • Production Designer PETER LAMONT

Screenplay by RICHARD MAIBAUM and MICHAEL G. WILSON • PANAVISION® TECHNICOLOR®

Title Song Performed by SHEENA EASTON

ORIGINAL MOTION PICTURE SOUNDTRACK
ON LIBERTY RECORDS AND TAPES

PG PARENTAL GUIDANCE SUGGESTED

United Artists
A Transamerica Company

DOLBY STEREO
IN SELECTED THEATRES

COPYRIGHT © MCMLXXXI UNITED ARTISTS CORPORATION
ALL RIGHTS RESERVED

Michael Cimino's film, retitled *Heaven's Gate*, became one of the biggest box office disasters of all time. The effects did not take long to ripple through United Artists and alter their production methods. This financial disaster would change the manner in which the studio produced films. By the time pre-production began on the twelfth James Bond film, things were going to be done differently. A global financial crisis, oil price rises and increased inflation also meant that a 1980 US dollar would go less far than before. The sums spent would be less than that of *Moonraker's* astronomical budget and cash flow would be held tightly in check.[1] An important aspect of that cost was going to be the price of key above-the-line talent: the man who would play Bond.

On the Sugarloaf Mountain set of *Moonraker* noted British film journalist Barry Norman was implored by producer Cubby Broccoli to become a spy himself, 'Ask him if he's gonna make the next one. I have to know.' Norman, whose father had directed Roger Moore in both *The Saint* and *The Persuaders*, was not about to give away vital intelligence. When Cubby asked Norman, 'What did that asshole of an actor have to say?' Norman passed on Moore's non-committal response and Cubby went away cursing.[2]

Roger Moore was in a strong negotiating position. *Moonraker* had become the highest grossing Bond film and with Sean Connery still lurking in the wings developing a rival Bond, Moore seemed to be holding all the aces. However, Cubby was no mean player himself and kept his cards close to his chest stating at the time, 'Peculiarly enough, we have put Roger in the fortuitous position that he is in. I think it is fortuitous being Bond, but having done that we normally get pummelled by the agents to get more money.'[3]

A number of contenders entered the running to become the next James Bond. Michael Jayston, who would later go on to voice Bond in audio books and a 1990 radio production of YOU ONLY LIVE TWICE, was a favourite.[4] Broccoli remembered Timothy Dalton and sounded the actor out again.[5] Dalton recalled, 'I went to see Cubby Broccoli in Los Angeles. At that time they didn't have a script finished. It was never quite clear at that time if Roger was giving it up.'[6]

In July 1980, upon release of *The Sea Wolves*, his third film with director Andrew V. McLaglen, Moore told a press conference 'I don't want to take another six months out of my life playing James Bond again.'[7] Roger by this time had established himself as an international action movie star. A number of his films had been produced by Broccoli's protégé, Euan Lloyd and Michael Klinger. Moore explained his ire:

I'm not competitive by nature and I can usually get a bag of toffees without having to ask. If they hadn't been testing other actors we would at least still be talking. I think they've been rather ill-mannered about it. I have told Cubby that is it and that I'm not available to do the film. Yes, it does mean that I won't do another Bond.[8]

After *Moonraker* Broccoli felt:

We were overcrowding the public on fantasy and outer space. I found it very boring too. It might suit somebody else but it didn't have to be Bond. Everyone keeps on saying, "When are you going to do another *Russia With Love* type of thing?" So we're trying the adventure, Hitchcockian sort of thing, full of suspense, excitement and thrills."[9]

Broccoli's vision for Bond's future coincided with that of the studio, 'We were asked by United Artists, by the distributor to do it, and we felt we wanted to go back to, I can only describe it as more of the *Russia With Love/Goldfinger* type of story. More of the possible, a little less of the probable, more adventure.'[10] With that in mind, Cubby discussed bringing back previous Bond veterans Terence Young, Peter Hunt and Guy Hamilton to direct.[11] Both Lewis Gilbert and Guy Hamilton had received a percentage of the producer's profit for their last Bond pictures so cost may have precluded their return.

John Glen remembered meeting Cubby for lunch with various Bond stalwarts discussing the names of previous Bond directors who could return – a meeting in which the ambitious Derek Meddings volunteered to helm the picture. Later that week, Cubby, Dana and Michael Wilson requested to meet Glen at Pinewood. This time he was alone. They offered the film to him to direct.[12] Glen was hired in early 1980[13] and announced as the director in June of that year.[14] Like Peter Hunt before him, he had never directed a feature film. Once again, Broccoli promoted from within his organisation and gave new talent a chance to flourish. The director was eager to assemble a team to rework James Bond for the eighties.

Glen knew that team would require some changes:

We were becoming increasingly budget conscious. Sometimes Ken [Adam] was probably a little too extravagant in certain areas. Peter [Lamont] was in the wings, working as art director. He was also very well qualified. He was reaching a stage in his career where we were either going to promote him to production designer or he was going to leave the fold and do his own films for someone else because he was that good you couldn't ignore him anymore.[15]

Lamont recalled he had just come back from shooting *Sphinx* (1980) in Egypt and for the first time in years, he had no further work booked. Then the phone rang, 'Reg Berkshire [long-time production controller of the Bond films] said, "Who would you like to work for next? Ken's gone off to America with Herb Ross."' "Why not me?"'[16] Berkshire made a phone call and fifteen minutes later, Lamont had been promoted to production designer. 'My wife said to me "Are you crazy?" I said, "Well, if it doesn't work, I'll go back to be supervising art director and I'll never try it again."'[17]

Lamont understood he was stepping into some big shoes: Ken [Adam] was my mentor. I worked on eleven films with him in all positions. He's a flamboyant character – very talented. He's a different animal to me. I'm not an artist like Ken, he's very flamboyant with his FloMaster and all that.'[18] Lamont 'read the script first and then broke it down into sets, locations.'[19] Lamont's way of working developed:

> I did sketches in those days but my problem is this: it's rather like an illustrator – like the Ralph McQuarries of this world (who are wonderful, don't get me wrong) - but they don't have any concept of how you're going to arrive at what he's done. I prefer models, when you have a model everybody knows what you're going to do.'[20]

Next, Glen brought back the Baffin Island camera crew from his *The Spy Who Loved Me* expedition. Cinematographer Alan Hume remembered the director's loyalty:

> I believe [Glen] had to work hard at convincing Cubby because I was really considered as a "modest budget" filmmaker, as my *Carry On* films had so epitomised. I can imagine Cubby felt a little apprehensive at having a new director and two DoPs [directors of photography] with very little "big film" experience. Full credit to John though, he argued for us and Cubby said OK.'[21]

John Glen obtained the services of a key team member from the ski jump sequence, 'I conned Alec Mills to come on my film as camera operator because I thought Alec was the best.'[22] Mills remembered his first job on the film was to go up to Grimsby to capture establishing shots of the *St. Georges* spy ship.[23]

Glen also brought on board Arthur Wooster – another veteran from his second unit team. Wooster would shoot most of the daring action unit material on *For Your Eyes Only*. However, for a cameraman expected to be nimble in a tight situation, his first meeting with Cubby Broccoli was inauspicious. Unknown for big-budget film work and wearing thick pebble glasses, Wooster tripped up and fell on the floor upon entering Cubby's office in Pinewood Studios. Glen had to work extra hard to convince an already sceptical Cubby to hire Wooster.[24]

Glen was keen to employ the extraordinary ski cameraman he worked with on his first Bond film, 'I used my old friend Willy Bogner to good effect which was a direct leftover from *OHMSS*. When we came to my first movie he was foremost in my mind to use on the [snow] sequence.'[25] Elaborate car stunts involving small, manoeuvrable cars were performed by L'Equipe Rémy Julienne. The French father and sons stunt team had burst to fame realising the kinetically precise car chase involving Minis in *The Italian Job*, a film on which Glen had worked as an assistant sound editor in 1969.

Glen was pleased to have another Bond stalwart on the team, 'Derek [Meddings] was the most marvellous special effects man. He helped me an awful lot on the films I did with Michael Klinger.'[26] Bob Simmons returned as the action sequences arranger. Finally, Al Giddings, was flown in from Los Angeles to oversee the complex underwater filming in the Bahamas which doubled for the Ionian Sea. With all the new and promoted talent assembled, Broccoli hired Tom Pevsner as his associate producer. With a career dating back to the fifties, Pevsner's immense experience helped to guide the production cost effectively.

Glen appreciated he had formed a new team for his Bond and that *For Your Eyes Only* represented a big opportunity for all of them, 'We were people who know our Bonds very well – we'd put our time in – and this was our big opportunity. So we had the nucleus [of] fairly new guys. Cubby had told me he wanted to get back to the Fleming style – more hard-edged.'[27]

Glen was determined to set his stamp on the film. 'There's an awful lot of me in that movie, all of my experiences that I gathered over the years, this thirst for action – I was determined that the action would be fantastic.'[28] Glen had a vision for Bond, even early on:

All the time I was editing the earlier Bonds, all I remember thinking is that, if I ever get a chance to direct, let it be a Bond film, because it was my forte. I have that enthusiasm and knowledge of the characters and the instincts for what it takes to pull one off.'[29]

Michael Wilson, after his attempt at action directing on *Moonraker*, now turned his hand to another expression of creativity, teaming up with Richard Maibaum for the first of five Bond screenplays they would write together. Maibaum described how they worked:

> When we start out, we do a very full treatment, sometimes 50 or 60 pages long. I've done [many films] with Cubby and he likes to know beforehand what it's going to be. We lay it our very carefully and very thoroughly in scripting. Sometimes we sit there and write together. Sometimes Michael will write the first draft or I will write the first draft and we give it to the other fellow and argue about it. There's an awful lot of arguing that goes on. But, you know what they say, if collaborators don't argue, then there's one collaborator too many.[30]

Glen remembered, 'If Cubby ever asked for Dick to remove anything from his scripts, [he] would drop to one knee throwing his arms out and making an impassioned and theatrical plea to preserve the scene.'[31]

Maibaum wrote in long-hand and typed up the screenplays later, while Wilson used a word processor.[32] According to Maibaum, it was 'a close, fruitful collaboration.' Maibaum thought Wilson had 'lots of good ideas. He's a versatile, accomplished man. He's a lawyer, engineer, businessman, writer and, all in all, a solid contributor.'[33] Cubby was proud of his stepson, 'I brought Michael into the Bond pictures. He came in a very eager young man, quite knowledgeable about various aspects of the film business. He learns rapidly and I think he's probably now technically more informed than I am in certain matters.'[34]

Glen recalled working with Maibaum and Wilson in Hollywood. Cubby would advise them to 'Look at earlier films to study their structure – where are the bumps?'[35] The director explained what Cubby meant by bumps, 'What we try to do is put James Bond in a situation from which he *just* gets out and then throw him straight into another and then another and another. I work very closely over a script. I devise a lot of the action stuff.'[36] The challenge with a new Bond screenplay was to strike a fine balance between preserving a tried and tested formula and treading new ground.[37]

Maibaum remembered that coming up with the story is the hardest part of the Bond script, 'It's murder, but once you've got the caper, you're off to the races and the rest is fun.'[38] In the case of *For Your Eyes Only*, in keeping with Cubby's wishes, a serious tale of Cold War espionage was crafted from two of the eponymous collection of five short stories first published as a volume in the UK on 11 April 1960.

FOR YOUR EYES ONLY sees Bond avenge the death of the Havelocks, personal friends of M. The enforced purchase of the Havelocks's Jamaican property, Content, will effectively launder dirty funds of two murderous thugs – a renegade from Cuba's Batista regime, Gonzales and Von Hammerstein, an ex-Nazi. Bond tracks them down to a remote estate in an autumnal valley in Vermont. While reconnoitring the estate, Bond meets Judy Havelock, the daughter of the murdered couple. She is armed with a bow and arrow and is bent on revenge. After a tense vigil, morning arises and Gonzales takes a dive only to be perforated by Havelock's arrow. A furious gunfight ensues in which the villains are vanquished, the sound of the gun fight resounding around the valley. The original title of Fleming's story was 'Death Leaves an Echo'. While retaining Fleming's character Judy – now renamed Melina – Maibaum attempted to do something different with the love story, 'The whole idea was that the great lover, James Bond, can't get to first base with this woman because she's so obsessed with avenging her parents' death.'[39]

RISICO concerns a blood feud between two Italian resistance fighters, Kristatos and Enrico Colombo. One is smuggling heroin for the Soviets and Bond is sent to terminate the pipeline. Set in Rome and off-season Venice, Bond encounters a Lisl Baum, the mistress of the mysterious gangster, the Dove. After posing as a novelist exploring the underworld, Bond is chased across a live mine field before tracking down and shooting the villain in a two handed grip at the top of a mountain.

These two short stories were kept more or less intact and intertwined with a contemporary Cold War story involving the then topical problem of spy ships and Polaris missiles. The MacGuffin, the Automatic Targetting Attack Communicator – ATAC – is a direct throwback to the Lektor decoding machine in *From Russia With Love*. If ATAC falls into the wrong hands, it could retarget and control the West's nuclear arsenal. For the first time in a decade, fealty to Fleming was achieved, something John Glen was keen on, 'I am versed in Fleming and a great admirer of Fleming. I like his style and the way he's written scenes. I've stuck to it as closely as I could.'[40] For this film, the Fleming fan went even further – other unused elements from novels already filmed were included, chiefly the keel-hauling sequence from LIVE AND LET DIE. Glen recalled:

That was a scene that had been in and out of Bond scripts for as long as I can remember. It is a scene which no one really wanted to shoot, except for Cubby. The reason it was rejected by most directors was because it was such a complex sequence to shoot with no guarantees you were going to get it.[41]

Whatever went on between Cubby, Roger and the studio was something Glen kept pretty tight to his chest. 'I wasn't party to the negotiations. All I know was my brief was to find a new Bond.'[42] Glen also sought continuity with the series due to the uncertainty over whether Roger Moore would return. 'We had to be prepared in case the negotiations broke down to break in a new Bond. So the opening in the churchyard was my idea.'[43] The pre-title sequence references the death of Tracy Bond in 1969 where Bond is visiting her grave inscribed 'We Have All the Time in the World'. This mention of Glen's first Bond film, *On Her Majesty's Secret Service*, was perhaps an inauspicious reference for any putative new Bond, considering the fate of that film's 007. Glen remembered:

> The scene that followed with the helicopter that was sent for [007] was quite a good idea. I was walking round the studio with Cubby one Sunday and one of the carpenters brought his son into the studio and he had what was then a novelty – a remote control car.'[44]

In the film Bond is collected by a Jet Ranger helicopter emblazoned with the words 'Universal Exports'. In the novels this was the cover name for the British Secret Service: this touch of Fleming was another element last cited in the films in *OHMSS*. The helicopter ferrying Bond back to his office in an emergency is then revealed to be a remote-controlled vehicle being flown with wild abandon by the villain. This sequence had originally been written to cap the car chase in Spain but it was felt that would be too similar to the helicopter/Lotus action scene in *The Spy Who Loved Me*. Eventually, after some initial reluctance and months looking for another idea, the remote-control flight became the basis for the new pre-title sequence.[45]

Incidentally, the villain is revealed to be a wheelchair-bound, bald-headed avenger with a white cat. A scripted reference to the tenth anniversary of their last meeting – *For Your Eyes Only* was to be released in 1981, ten years after Blofeld's last appearance in 1971 - was nixed due to the legal position with Kevin McClory. The wheelchair-bound character was kept deliberately ambiguous.

Once an initial treatment had been drafted, Glen explained:

> Michael Wilson and Tom Pevsner and I will do a lightning reconnaissance. You wouldn't believe the speed the three of us whizz around at. On *For Your Eyes Only* we were intending to shoot in Athens, around the Acropolis. So we went there and quite frankly didn't like what we saw. It looked impossible and the local co-operation wasn't very good and they're sensitive about

people even walking on the ground and anyway it's not the most attractive place in the world.'[46]

Glen was concerned Athens was so polluted the photography would suffer badly. 'It's like continual haze. You've only got to half close your eyes and realise it wouldn't look good. It's a great shame but it's a fact of life. It was such a busy disorganised place [and logistically difficult].'[47] The Bond crew had better luck further north, in mainland Greece. Broccoli remembered, 'We went on a recce, to see these marvellous monasteries in Kalambaka. We talked to the bishop and the bishop agreed. We paid them a rather substantial sum of money to shoot there.'[48] Glen thought the flexibility of a Bond script was helpful, 'One advantage of sandwiching location surveys with intervals of working closely on the script was the ability to adapt action scenes to fit the locations. Our surveys must have been the shortest on record.'[49]

As the screenplay was being finalised, there was still uncertainty over who would play Bond. One of the would-bes who came close to becoming Bond in For Your Eyes Only was Michael Billington, a historical Bond-in-the-wings, who, in the intervening years, had become close to the Broccoli family. He remembered, 'The troops were gathering to go to Corfu to begin filming but Roger was being "coy". I think the money was an issue. Cubby had me fitted out with wardrobe and flew me to Corfu.'[50] Billington even underwent an in-costume photo shoot.[51] The actor claimed to have been on standby for Moore in case a deal could not be reached.[52] Glen tested many actors,[53] using the execution of Professor Dent scene from Dr. No as well as Bond ordering breakfast and his meeting with Tatiana Romanova in his hotel suite from From Russia With Love.[54]

Moore never discussed financial matters with his producer directly, 'We were playing backgammon and it was Cubby's turn to throw the dice. He picked them up, popped them in the cup and hesitated. "You can tell your agent to shit in his hat."'[55] Eventually his agent agreed terms with Broccoli and Roger Moore resumed the role of 007 for the fifth time. The actor was familiar with John Glen, '[He] knew exactly what a frame of film was worth. [He] knew very much what was needed because he was an editor.'[56]

Maibaum recalled the screenplay could now be written to suit Moore's signature style, 'In the treatment stage of writing a screenplay, Bond is just a character. But when we get down to writing the scenes, we tailor it to Roger. He has a particular personality and the scenes must be written accordingly.'[57]

Joining Eon's regular casting director, Maude Spector, was Debbie McWilliams, who would continue to work on the series for decades to come.[58] Carole Bouquet had auditioned for Holly Goodhead in *Moonraker*[59] and Glen remembered seeing her on set in Paris.[60] Bouquet eventually won the role of Melina Havelock, avenging daughter of Sir Timothy Havelock and her mother, Iona. The French actress later admitted to being a bit po-faced on set:

> I wanted respect at least. I didn't want to be a bimbo. It's a great movie to look at and it's a great movie for special effects but [not] for actors who are trying to act. I was dreaming of Shakespeare which is absurd now but at the time it was important to me.[61]

Bouquet was ambitious, 'I never intended to become just another Bond girl. I'm not simply a plastic doll like the rest of them.'[62] Broccoli recalled that Bouquet's boyfriend had drug problems which caused her to be late to the set.[63] She further compounded the *froideur* by tactlessly saying the 53-year-old Roger Moore reminded her of her father.[64]

Topol recalled he was at a 'Fourth of July party at some American's house in London, and Dana Broccoli said to Cubby, "How about Topol for the part?"'[65] The Israeli actor was promptly cast as the mysterious Colombo. Topol recalled, '[I added] the nuts. I love pistachio nuts. It had that Mediterranean quality that I think I wanted to chew.'[66]

Julian Glover had appeared in *The Saint* including one episode directed by Roger Moore. Glover had been asked to go and see Cubby Broccoli on the strength of his appearance in a 1980 television drama-documentary called *Invasion*, where he played doomed Czech leader, Alexander Dubcek, 'Cubby saw it and he wanted someone tremendously honest to play his villain. Not someone who seemed to be like a villain but someone who has got a really nice track record and is a frightfully nice bloke.'[67] Glover remembered:

> I went on a Sunday morning to the Broccolis' flat in Grosvenor Square, around the corner from the Eon offices in South Audley Street. I just talked with Broccoli and Dana and then [they] went off and the costume bloke, Tiny Nicholls, said 'It's in Dana's hands, Julian.' And indeed they came out with a broad smile and they asked me to do it.[68]

Glover felt Kristatos was a complex character who required much thought:

> [He] didn't reveal himself by being a horrible person. When things started going wrong then he revealed his true colours. John Glen helped me with

my efforts to remain plausible. I said to him 'You must watch out if I ever seem villainous and please don't let me do that.'[69]

Lynn Holly Johnson was cast as Olympic hopeful, Bibi Dahl:

I had already done *Ice Castles* [1980] and had already worked with Bette Davis in London. Michael Wilson wanted to create a character that antagonised Bond and wrote the character of Bibi Dahl. The audition was like no other audition I have ever been on. I went to Cubby's house in Beverly Hills. We didn't really talk about the business too much or the character he just wanted to see what I was like. Next thing I knew I had the part.[70]

As a professional skater, Johnson:

always had costume dresses made by somebody who only did skating competition dresses. In London they took me to [Bermans and Nathans] a place who had never done a skating dress. It's particular because the skirt has to flow in a particular way and I remember thinking this is not going to work, these people have never done a skating dress. But they made a beautiful dress and I still have it.[71]

Bibi's mentor, Jacoba Brink, was played by acclaimed English actress, Jill Bennett. who had a three-way connection with the Bond team. She had once been married to Harry Saltzman's Woodfall partner, the playwright John Osborne, had starred in *Hell Below Zero*, co-produced by Cubby and had attended RADA with Roger Moore.

Rounding out the principal female cast was Australian actress Cassandra Harris who played the ersatz Austrian Countess Lisl von Schlaf.[72] According to Glen, 'Every time [writer Maibaum] created a leading lady for one of his scripts it was always based on [his wife Sylvia], or more specifically, his romantic view of her as a fairytale princess from Austria.'[73]

The film featured an interesting array of villains: Michael Gothard stalked Bond as the sinister Emile Leopold Locque, John Wyman was a henchman of sorts in champion East German skier, Eric Kriegler, Jack Klaff as Apostis and Stefan Kalipha set the story in motion as Cuban hitman Hector Gonzales. John Hollis played an uncredited Blofeld and making an early screen appearance was Charles Dance as Claus. On the side of angels were Jack Hedley and Toby Robins as Sir Timothy and Lady Iona Havelock respectively and John Moreno as Bond's ill-fated Italian contact, Luigi Ferrara. Caroline Cossey, who sizzled in a bikini under her professional name Tula, gained brief notoriety when it was revealed she had been born a man.

On 15 September 1980 principal photography commenced at the Villa Sylvia on Kanoni Island, near Corfu.[74] Alan Hume remembered, 'We'd just set up and were almost ready to shoot when I felt a hand on my shoulder. It was Cubby. "Good luck, Alan," he said as he patted me on the shoulder and I know only too well what he meant – mess it up and you're for it!'[75]

The Greek island was used extensively to double Spain for the resulting car chase shot around the winding roads surrounding Pagi. Bond, seeking a quick getaway, runs to his Lotus Esprit Turbo only to find a guard, played onscreen by stuntman Bob Simmons, has activated the burglar protection facility: a self-destruct system blows the Lotus and the thief up. This was a reversal of what had become a Bond trope: a huge chase sequence with Bond commandeering a gadget-rigged vehicle. It was a signature motif of new writer Michael G. Wilson:

> I don't like the use of gadgets. We've seen too many of them. They're always a cheat. Usually you set up a gadget that can only be used in a very unique situation that wouldn't apply generally. What I like best is when you set up a situation that the gadget is perfect for and Bond really needs it. Just as he takes it out of his pocket, it's knocked from his hand and plummets nine stories down to the ground. Now what's Bond going to do? That's the fun.[76]

Glen mused, 'People have conventions. In Bond movies you have to do the unexpected.'[77] The use of a Citroën Deux Chevaux was due 'partly to the fact we were using French actress, Carole Bouquet, somehow they went together. Derek Meddings came up with the yellow colour – I'd always seen it as a blue one – it was nice because it photographed well.'[78] The resultant chase as Melina and Bond escape the heavies in this underpowered car became a signature sequence of the film. Vehicle stunt arranger Rémy Julienne felt:

> You cannot make a spectacle with Mercedes on these roads, they are too large. Cubby asked, 'What do you think the best cars would be for the villains?' I said something like a Peugeot 405, an average car, something easy to work with. Tom Pevsner said, 'But Cubby, we have a financial agreement with Mercedes.' Cubby said, 'I don't care.'[79]

Julienne doubled the size of the engine in the Citroën, giving the car more power.[80] Six identical yellow 2CVs were donated by Citroën and they were all returned still running, 'despite their bodywork [being] badly in need of surgery.'[81]

This action sequence became Glen's style:

> I developed a technique where I always put the audience in the driver's seat. The way you shoot it, it's from the point of view of the audience, to let them experience it themselves. It's a technique that you can't do with multi-cameras. You have to plan it very, very carefully. The audience really gets into it that way. Because you can only watch car chases for so long; it gets pretty boring seeing cars screech back and forth unless you get inside the car and see it from that perspective.[82]

The sequence impressed Maibaum, 'I think there's no doubt that John Glen is the premier action director in the world today. He is absolutely fantastic. Everyone does a car chase, but there's always something different and unexpected in his action sequences. He's really a genius in that way.'[83] Another aspect of Glen's direction was to shape action with humour. In this chase, he borrowed a trick he'd used for the stock car sequence in *OHMSS*, and inverted the film so it appears as if the chasing black Peugeot is spinning upside down.

Shooting in southern Corfu, on the beach near Lake Korission, where Countess Lisl is killed by a dune buggy, was problematic. The sand kept disrupting the engines and the shoot went days over schedule. Coming at the start of the movie, Glen felt the pressure, especially as this location was attended by cost-conscious executives from UA. He appreciated Cubby's discreet way of protecting his crew from the studio brass and giving advice privately and tactfully.[84]

It was here that Glen first noticed the striking but little-known actor, Pierce Brosnan. Glover remembered, 'He came to visit Cassie and we spent several wonderful evenings together. [At] that time we were all saying he ought to play James Bond!'[85] Brosnan reminisced:

> It was a terribly exciting time for us all, being part of a Bond movie, to go to Corfu. I'd been in the West End theatre for about a year and a half in a play and I was out of work so the job came at a very appropriate time. I remember Roger being extremely cordial – just charming and effervescent really with his kind of bonhomie towards myself and the children and towards my late wife.'[86]

One scene proved to be a point of minor conflict for director and star. Moore felt uneasy kicking Locque's balancing Mercedes over the edge, believing the action too brutal for his interpretation of Bond. He preferred tossing a pin of The Dove – left at the scene of death of his colleague in Cortina earlier in the film – to unbalance the car. Glen argued it was in keeping with the character of Bond, that he be seen to shove the car over in vengeance for the death of his colleague. He felt it was the hard-edged side somewhat missing in previous films.[87]

On 17 October 1980 the crew moved to mainland Greece to shoot at Trinity Rock in Meteora,[88] the location discovered and paid for on Glen's earlier recce. However, the production was to face disruption at the monastery. Broccoli remembered:

> Even though the bishop made the deal, two new monks came in – the only two monks in the entire monastery that wouldn't permit us to come in there. The bishop tried to tell them that we were entitled to access, but no way. These gentle monks hung all kinds of things around: paraphernalia, flags, everything to make the background unusable.[89]

The monks protested at their holy establishment being used in a film promoting sin. The crew solved the problem by building a mock monastery on a neighbouring barren rock for long shots.[90]

Attempting to reach the rendezvous where the ATAC will be exchanged to the Soviets, Bond must climb the sheer cliff face of Meteora. Nearing the top, Bond's pitons are removed by a guard. 007 falls, jerked to a halt by his rope still attached to the mountain. After performing the parachute jump in *The Spy Who Loved Me*, Rick Sylvester had suggested if the Bond films ever did a mountaineering sequence to keep him in mind. When the Bond team contacted him, he suggested the production use an expanding piton device to assist the ascent. Sylvester was disappointed that not more was made of this 'James Bond device'. Indeed, the gadget was the suggestion of Pat Banta, the husband of Cubby's daughter, Tina, who had joined Sylvester's mountaineering crew.[91] Sylvester remembered, 'Climbing is a very exciting thing but it's a very slow thing. When Hollywood thinks of climbing, they think of falling. Now falling is dramatic.'[92] Sylvester liaised with the effects department and devised an ingenious method of making his fall look breathtaking: tying sand-bags to the coiled rope so that as it unspooled, it would slow the rate of his drop.[93]

In November 1980 the crew went to London and back to Pinewood Studios. In the intervening years, the British had elected the Conservative Party back into power. Headed by a forceful and charismatic leader, Britain now had a female Prime Minister for the first time. One of Margaret Thatcher's first initiatives was to lower certain taxes in an effort to encourage the entrepreneurial spirit. This enabled the Bond films to return home after their Parisienne adventure for *Moonraker*.

Pinewood meant continuity with Bond tradition. As did certain cast members, including Bernard Lee who was again hired to play spy chief, M. However, this time, things would turn out, alas, differently. Desmond Llewelyn remembered his co-star was 'brought down to Pinewood but he just couldn't do it, he was very ill.'[94] Glen recalled Lee knew his time was up, 'It was very obvious he wasn't up to it. He admitted that, he accepted that.'[95] Tragically, before he could return to complete his scenes as M, Bernard Lee succumbed to stomach cancer on 16 January 1981 at the age of seventy-three. The producers did not wish to immediately recast the role of M. Instead they introduced the character of Tanner, in the novels Bond's best friend in the service and a contemporary of 007's. The first onscreen Tanner, James Villiers recalled, 'Roger and Broccoli came to a play I was in at the time. They said they wanted me to be in the next Bond film – get down to Pinewood tomorrow, it's urgent.'[96]

Desmond Llewelyn filmed his scenes as Q in a relatively gadget-free adventure. The actor was soon embroiled in an elaborate joke played on him by John Glen and Roger Moore:

> I was sitting in the corner of the set, rehearsing my part, when John came over and said, 'Look, I'd like you to learn these extra lines for this afternoon's shooting,' and handed me a sheet of paper covered in technical gobbledegook. 'I can't possibly learn this in time,' I replied aghast. Whereupon John muttered, 'Of course you can,' and pushed off. Two hours later, he returned with Roger, both grinning broadly. 'Don't worry Q,' they chorused. 'We've decided not to use those lines after all.'[97]

Q's key scene featured a computerised identification database known as the Identigraph, a gadget taken from the GOLDFINGER novel. The scene was problematic despite a professional being brought on to explain it to the actors. Llewelyn remembered that Roger Moore 'did the whole thing a damn sight better than the professional. Roger was brilliant. Not only could he reel off his lines without faltering, but mine too.'[98] Lois Maxwell returned as Moneypenny and John Glen, again, channelled the series' past, with Bond anachronistically, throwing his hat on the hat stand. Glen reinjected Moneypenny's scenes with humour and affection. Maxwell was amused by the offscreen antics, '[Roger] comes through the door at the wrong time, and on my mark is an enormous electrician. Roger places a carnation in his hand and says, "Oh, be still, my bleeding heart."'[99] Geoffrey Keen returned as the Minister of Defence.

Large portions of *For Your Eyes Only* were shot underwater as the sunken wreckage of the St. Georges in the Ionian Sea becomes the centre of attention as it contains the ATAC device. Lamont designed what he called the film's *'pièce de résistance'*: a ruin of an underwater temple complete with Grecian columns. The set was built at Pinewood and put together like a puzzle in 60ft of water near Coral Harbour in the Bahamas. In the evening, the columns had to be laid flat on the seabed to give the surface traffic enough room to manoeuvre.[100] Al Giddings supervised the underwater shoot and once completed, sets and his camera housing and rigging were transported back to Pinewood where the scene was completed in the underwater tank on the 007 Stage. Bouquet had a problem with her inner ear preventing her going underwater. All the shots of the actress and Roger Moore were done dry with wind fans blowing their hair and the film shot at high speed through fish tanks placed in the foreground. To give the impression of being underwater, the footage was slowed down so that the actors appeared to be in buoyant water. From the lessons learned on *Moonraker*, the negative was double exposed, overlaying the actors with actual bubbles shot underwater.

Famed Margaret Thatcher impersonator, Janet Brown, together with John Wells, playing her husband, Denis, were hired to give the movie a comical ending. Unbeknownst to them, the voice at the other end of Bond's Seiko watch was a parrot, Max, played by Chrome, a parrot owned by none other than Mrs. Bond herself – Diana Rigg.

Pinewood's Paddock Tank was host to some amazing Derek Meddings's miniatures: the St. Georges spy ship was sunk and the imperceptible recreation of the Albanian coast later destroyed in spectacular 007 style. Meddings was also involved in the shooting of the pre-credit sequence in Becton Gasworks with the clever use of foreground miniatures.[101]

In November 1980 the pre-title helicopter sequence was shot over the Beckton Gasworks in London. Martin Grace, doubling for Roger Moore, was tasked with climbing out of the helicopter and hanging underneath while it did all kinds of daring manoeuvres to shake Bond off:

Every day was an adrenaline rush, roaring engines first thing each morning being lifted swiftly above chimney tops to 400ft above ground. The chopper would drop like a stone only to recover and make dangerous flights down through rows of pipe work. We had an excellent pilot, Marc Wolff, an American, the best in movie-making and I had complete trust in his ability.'[102]

In late January 1981 the crew moved to Cortina D'Ampezzo, in the Italian Dolomite mountain range for snow sequences set in and around the town which had played host to the 1956 Winter Olympics. Unfortunately, the town experienced the mildest spring for years resulting in the production having to truck snow into the town from nearby mountains. Bond stayed at the Miramonti Hotel and meets his local contact, Luigi Ferrara, at the observation post on Mount Tofana.

The town's Olympic ice rink and ski jump were used effectively for sequences shot by Willy Bogner. Roger Moore recalled the dangers of being Bond, 'On the ice hockey sequence I got banged up quite badly.'[103] The star damaged his shoulder on the penultimate night of shooting in Cortina but he was heroic to the end. Hospitalised, Moore realised, 'We would then be stuck for a week, so I said that I would have a needle and a local anaesthetic and worked the next night.'[104]

Unfortunately for the unit, this ice-bound injury would not be the last. Rémy Julienne recalled:

They asked me to perform as a consultant, to go and find locations in Cortina d'Ampezzo, to give input. They told me they would not hire me to perform the sequence, as they already had a team. I had a lot of experience with motorcycles on snow, on ice, with special nails they used.[105]

While shooting the bob-run scenes in the nearby facility, Rémy Julienne and Willy Bogner worked together to capture amazing shots of a motorbike, a skier and a bobsleigh chasing each other at speeds of 55 miles per hour. Bogner had to be connected to the bobsleigh by wire to keep pace with the action. However, during the shooting of this sequence, a bob overturned trapping stuntman Paolo Rigon underneath. He was dragged to his death leaving a pall over the unit. Principal photography was completed in February 1981.

John Barry was unable to score the film in the UK because he had ongoing problems with the British tax authorities. On his recommendation, Broccoli spoke with Bill Conti, who had been Oscar-nominated for Best Song for *Rocky* in 1976. Cubby put the composer and his family up in London for two months while Conti worked on the score and title song. Conti updated the Bond sound for the eighties, employing brass and synthesizers. Originally, he wanted to use Barbara Streisand to record the song, but then Sheena Easton was suggested to him. Easton had had a transatlantic hit album after being discovered in the BBC talent documentary, *The Big Time*. Conti and Cubby were concerned the album only showcased a thin pop vocal – Cubby cited to Conti 'the big voiced heritage of Bond.'[106] However, after meeting with Easton's producer, Christopher Neil, they were assured she had a powerful voice. Prior to presenting the song, Conti bumped into Maurice Binder who expressed a desire that the title of the film should appear on screen simultaneously with Easton singing it. Conti quickly implored lyricist Michael Leeson to rewrite the song, beginning with the words, 'For Your Eyes Only'.[107]

Easton remembered the recording:

took a long time because I was with Bill and Micky – they called me in from time to time to have me sing parts of it to see how it sounded on the voice. The recording took a couple of days for me to sing it and for the musicians to put it down.[108]

The song went on to become a Top 10 hit either side of the Atlantic and was nominated for an Academy Award.

Maurice Binder, was also taken with the singer:

After I had already shot part of the titles, Cubby showed me a tape of a television show Sheena had done. I was looking for beautiful faces with beautiful eyes to coincide with the title. I told Cubby, 'This girl has a beautiful face. Gee, I could use those eyes.' And Cubby said, 'Why don't you use Sheena in the credits?' We only had a few weeks left for shooting. We were right up to the starting gun.'[109]

Easton noted it was uncomfortable as she had to wear a neck brace to keep her face perfectly still for the camera.[110] Binder felt, 'Sheena was fun to work with, bright and very co-operative. No moods. If we had to do a shot over, we did it. Putting her in the titles did present a problem, the words and the lips must work together, so it becomes like a miniature musical.'[111] Easton became the first and only Bond singer to appear in the opening titles.

Maurice Binder also cut the film's trailer but the new emphasis on character caused problems with the censor. Binder had included the scene in which Bond kicks the Mercedes off the cliff:

'The British censor said, 'No, you can't show that happening.' I said, 'Why?
The guy inside is a vicious assassin who almost killed Bond. And Roger is
just giving the car a little extra kick to send him on his way.' But the censor
still said, 'No, we consider that killing a man in cold blood.'[112]

Binder was also creative when it came to showcasing the female lead, Carole
Bouquet:

Cubby said to me: 'This girl, she doesn't smile. She has a beautiful smile, and
she's not smiling.' I said, 'I do have a take where she does smile.' And he said,
'Well, why don't you use it?' and I said, 'Well, the dialogue went like this – "By
the way, we haven't met, my name is Bond, James Bond. I guess a little fuck
would be out of the question?"' I took the dialogue from the first take and
cut to the smile.[113]

On 24 June 1981 *For Your Eyes Only* received its royal world charity premiere
in London at the Odeon Leicester Square in the presence of Prince Charles
and his fiancé, Lady Diana Spencer. They were to be married that July and
their attendance caused a global stir. Harry Saltzman, whose wife Jacqui had
passsed away earlier in January 1980, attended the premiere with their children,
Steven, Christopher and Hilary. The latter remembered, 'Cubby invited [us].
They hugged each other and were very happy to be in each other's company
and there were no hard feelings.'[114] It was a healing for Cubby and Harry after
many years apart. Pierce Brosnan also had fond memories of the occasion:

I was then working on a show called *Nancy Astor* and I wore the costume
which was a beautiful black tie affair. There is a photograph of Cassie in
the line-up on the red carpet with me standing behind her grinning like a
Cheshire cat with a moustache.[115]

For Your Eyes Only grossed over $194 million worldwide and more than $52
million in North America. The new team assembled to make the film ushered
in a new era of Eon talent who would stay with the series for decades. An
antidote to the bloated budget of *Moonraker*, the inflation-busting ingenuity of
the new Bond team yielded sizeable dividends. The gamble had paid off and
Bond was back to Earth with a bang.

18

TWO OF
A KIND

OCTOPUSSY

(1983)

007 BEGINS SHOOTING TODAY AT CHECKPOINT CHARLIE

Photography begins this week at Checkpoint Charlie in West Berlin, followed by filming at Pinewood Studios, England and other locations in India, Germany, and the U.K.

ALBERT R. BROCCOLI presents

ROGER MOORE as IAN FLEMING'S JAMES BOND 007™ in

OCTOPUSSY

Produced by ALBERT R. BROCCOLI   Directed by JOHN GLEN

Executive Producer MICHAEL G. WILSON

FOR RELEASE JUNE 1983

DISTRIBUTED BY

MGM/UA
ENTERTAINMENT CO

nited Artists went through a period of uncertainty after the financial disaster Michael Cimino's *Heaven's Gate* had wrought upon the company.[1] Andreas Albeck suddenly took 'early retirement'[2] as President on 18 February 1981.[3] He was replaced by Norbert T. Auerbach,[4] who had served as Warwick's general representative in Europe,[5] and Auerbach's shared history with Albert R. Broccoli might have been of comfort to Transamerica Corporation's most reliable producer. Announcing a \$25 million commitment to the next Bond film, Auerbach stated:

> We have no problem accommodating that kind of budget. It's always a risk, but it's a risk we're willing to take. [Broccoli is] an extremely responsible producer who loves to bring them in at fifteen or twenty or twelve or whatever, because he knows the less the picture costs, the more money he and we will make.[6]

The report went on to state that *Octopussy* was 'slated for an early 1982 start and a Christmas release the same year – an update from a previous 1983 projection.'[7] The studio's eagerness to announce that they were bringing the thirteenth Bond film forward was explained less than one month later.

Transamerica sold United Artists to Metro-Goldwyn-Mayer (MGM) for a reported \$380 million,[8] \$100 million more than Wall Street had valued the company at.[9] Another Bond picture on UA's upcoming slate could only raise the studio's value and make them a more attractive purchase.[10] MGM was owned by Kirk Kerkorian, a wealthy Vegas-based billionaire whose chief attorney, Greg Bautzer, was an old family friend of Cubby Broccoli.[11]

By the time *Octopussy* was released, United Artists went through yet another change in management, now comprised of Frank Rothman, Joseph Fischer and the notorious cheque fraudster, David Begelman.[12] Rebranded MGM/UA the two companies would share resources, but UA would still operate independently and separately as a production entity.

For now, Metro-Goldwyn-Mayer's Leo the Lion, would roar with pride over its share in the James Bond franchise. Broccoli mused:

> We continue to make the films unencumbered with United Artists. They don't interfere with our operation other than to ask us what we're going to do and who's going to be in it. But they have been very good with us and I'm sure MGM knows that. It's an operation that has to be operated the way we do it. All we want them to do is provide the cash.'[13]

Veteran Hollywood studio executive Peter Bart, now at MGM/UA, mused that:

> Cubby ran his 'Bond business' as though it were a family farm. He had no
> intention of changing his modus operandi now for some newcomer. Indeed
> when the MGM/UA team blithely suggested its intentions of having more
> input on the next Bond film, the proposal was quickly stonewalled. If MGM/
> UA wanted another Bond picture, Broccoli declared, the studio would have
> to play by the customary rules. This meant advancing as much as $6 million
> before studio executives caught even a glimpse of an outline – forget about
> seeing a script. That was the way it had been done in the past, and that was
> the way it would continue.[14]

Prior to production commencing on *Octopussy*, Albert R. Broccoli was informed
that he would be the recipient of the Irving G. Thalberg Memorial Award from
the Academy of Motion Picture Arts and Sciences. Sporadically given to producers for continued production excellence, Cubby was thrilled to accept the award
at the fifty-fourth Academy Awards on 29 March 1982 at the Dorothy Chandler
Pavilion in Los Angeles. Cubby paid tribute to his team on receiving the award:

> I never dreamed when I came to Hollywood in 1934 that I would be stand-
> ing here to receive an award from a man who was the idol of all of us. This
> is a great moment in my life and I feel a great sense of accomplishment,
> not only for myself but all my colleagues with whom I've worked over the
> years, the actors, the writers, the directors and those exceptionally devoted
> and dedicated technicians at Pinewood Studios in Great Britain and for my
> associates at United Artists.[15]

Cubby thanked his previous business partners Irving Allen and Harry Saltzman,
as well as Arthur Krim. He finished his heartfelt speech by thanking the
Academy 'for allowing a farm boy from Long Island to realise this dream.'[16]
At an early birthday party following the event, Cubby proudly said, 'It was
the greatest honour of my life.'[17] Broccoli had come of age in the town that
had once spurned him. The party at Chasen's restaurant was attended by his
family as well as names from the past including Mike Frankovitch, Cary Grant,
John Gavin, David Hedison, Christopher Lee, as well as Hollywood royalty –
Billy Wilder, Irving 'Swifty' Lazar and Jimmy Stewart.[18] Also in attendance was
Roger Moore, who had presented the Thalberg to Cubby, and Sean Connery.[19]
Cubby was happy to have them there, 'They are both very good friends of mine,

and I've liked working with both of them.'[20] Broccoli had left Hollywood in 1952, so to be embraced by the film community after nearly twenty-one years of phenomenal success must have felt like vindication.

Roger Moore exploited the uncertainty regarding the studio situation. While publicising *For Your Eyes Only* he said, 'There's such a state of change within United Artists and Transamerica. Nobody knows who's going to make the final decision.'[21] Incentivised by the threat of Sean Connery returning as 007 for a reported $5 million, Moore gambled this would not be the right time for Eon to introduce a new James Bond.[22] He rejected the $3 million Cubby had offered him,[23] commenting, 'It's a stalemate.'[24]

US-based casting director Jane Jenkins was hired to come to the UK to cast for an American television pilot whose central character happened to look a lot like James Bond. In reality, they were trawling for a potential replacement for Roger Moore, testing for Bond-ish qualities, 'Basically we had to see how the guy handled a girl, a gun and a martini and how he'd look in a tux.'[25] The operation had to be kept secret with names being fed to them by UK casting chief Debbie McWilliams, who was too well known in Britain to be overtly part of the process. Cubby's daughter, Barbara Broccoli, also participated but acted as Jenkins's assistant when in reality she was the boss, making sure to conspicuously ask, 'Can I get you another cup of tea, Miss Jenkins?'[26]

Lewis Collins, tough guy Bodie in television's *The Professionals*, had portrayed the more sophisticated Peter Skellen in the recent SAS action thriller *Who Dares Wins* (1982). The film was produced by Euan Lloyd, Cubby's former Warwick assistant:

> When Barbara Broccoli saw my finished film she suggested her father should meet [Collins]. I understand Lewis made the fatal mistake of appearing in dress closer to Bodie than to Peter Skellen. Possibly it was overconfidence on Lewis's part. I am sure he would have made an excellent Bond.'[27]

Oliver Tobias, a handsome emerging British leading man, famous for the soft-core porn film *The Stud* (1978), in which he appeared opposite Joan Collins, had reportedly met with Eon. Tobias's agent Al Mitchell said, 'Oliver is being seriously considered for Bond.'[28] In early 1982, when this was put to Cubby, he responded, 'No comment.'[29] Yet again, Michael Billington claimed to have tested for the part when, 'Roger was being "extra coy."'[30] Broccoli was again considering an American actor and let slip, no doubt for Roger Moore's benefit, that the latest actor being tested was James Brolin.[31]

The Man With the Golden Gun actress Maud Adams was asked to stand in for the James Brolin test, 'Obviously they want to keep it secret. I was looking forward to seeing everybody again so I gladly went. James Brolin was very good, but it was unusual to hear an American accent playing James Bond.'[32] Glen conducted a three-day test with the actor and felt, 'Brolin did a great job, a very manly guy.'[33]

The game of brinkmanship continued with Cubby stating, 'I hope Roger does it but if he decides not to, I will understand. These films are really hard work.'[34] By June 1982 the producer explained, 'Roger is asking more than I am prepared to pay. There comes a point where you just have to say no, even to a friend, and Roger is a friend. Roger can't go on doing it. So perhaps this is a good time to launch a new actor.'[35] Broccoli stated he was under no pressure from the studio to sign Moore, 'they leave the choice entirely to me,'[36] but the imminent threat of the return of Connery would probably have precipitated the return of Moore. Eventually, in mid-July 1982, a deal was reached. Moore commented, 'The poker game is over. We both got tired of dealing so we decided to cut for it. I think we are both happy with the outcome.'[37]

Relations between Broccoli and Moore always healed quickly. Cubby's secretary Janine King, remembered Roger Moore could often be found between Bond films at South Audley Street playing backgammon with Cubby. On one occasion Moore even answered the telephone and took a message, 'I couldn't help chuckling because whoever was on the other end of the phone would be so astounded if they knew it was Roger Moore they were leaving a message with. That was what was so lovely about Eon Productions.'[38]

Pleased with director John Glen's debut effort on *For Your Eyes Only*, Broccoli asked him to repeat duties on *Octopussy*:

> I've agreed for several reasons: I've always loved the Bonds, they've always appealed to my rather childish side. I feel I'm very well equipped in terms of experience and knowing the character so well. I'm a great believer in the characterisation of Bond. I think the more of that we show in the future the better we'll be. We'll continue the trend away from push-button technology; get back to the real Bond.'[39]

Octopussy would be, Glen thought, 'a start-from-scratch-situation,'[40] although he added, 'It's important to incorporate Fleming's work into the movie stories, isn't it? Otherwise, you're just using the title and nothing else.'[41]

OCTOPUSSY was first published in the UK on 23 June 1966, initially conprising the title story and another, the Berlin-set THE LIVING DAYLIGHTS. The paperback would also include the story featured in the November 1963 edition of auction house Sotheby's publication, THE IVORY HAMMER, entitled THE PROPERTY OF A LADY.

The title story is the tale of the corruption of Major Dexter Smythe, a British Army officer who, towards the end of the war, steals hidden Nazi gold and kills Hannes Oberhauser, his Austrian guide in the process. Relocating to Jamaica, Smythe slowly lives off his ill-gotten gains and reflects on his life: an empty marriage, increasing ill-health, laundering his gold, swimming in his own private reef and visiting Octopussy, his 'pet' cephalopod. Smythe plans an experiment to feed a poisonous scorpion fish to the octopus. Towards the end of the tale, James Bond enters with evidence of the wartime murder of Oberhauser. Bond implicitly leaves Dexter Smythe with the option of an honourable exit rather than facing a trial in England. Fate intervenes and Dexter Smythe meets his demise when poisoned by the scorpion fish he attempts to feed to Octopussy.

THE PROPERTY OF A LADY is a similarly sedentary episode. Bond tracks MI6 double agent Maria Freudenstein, who is to be paid, surreptitiously by the Soviets, from the proceeds of the sale of an *objet d'art* by Fabergé, through auction at Sotheby's. Bond identifies the KGB agent sent to the auction to push the price up to the requisite payment amount. The agent subsequently faces diplomatic expulsion and Bond strikes a small blow against the Soviet intelligence apparat.

A completely new writer entered the Bond fold to pen the screenplay of the thirteenth official James Bond film: George MacDonald Fraser. The reactionary Scottish scribe, who might have been described as Flemingesque, had written films for producer Alexander Salkind, including *The Musketeers* series and an initial draft of *Superman* (1978). However, it was his series of historical Flashman novels that attracted John Glen, 'He's a great expert on India and that was going to be location for our movie so we thought he could bring his special humour.'[42] However, Fraser felt that he might have been imposed upon Cubby by the notorious MGM executive, David Begelman to settle an outstanding legal matter.[43]

MacDonald Fraser's early ideas included a pre-title sequence set during the Isle of Man's TT motorcycle race with a 'duel-to-the-death sidecar race between Bond and a heavy' as well as '007 trapped in a cage with an angry gorilla.'[44] John Aspinall, a Clermont Club pal of Cubby's, had a private wildlife sanctuary in his home which John Glen visited.[45] The director affirmed a scene involving Bond as a lion-tamer was not included because it could have been perceived as a slight against the logo of UA's new parent company, MGM.[46]

Fraser delivered his screenplay in April 1982. Production designer Peter Lamont recalled:

> The first draft was about 200 pages and everyone panicked. It was a long script, but when you read it, all the stage directions were there. It was almost a shooting script. He'd never been to Udaipur, but he'd done all his research and he knew India like the back of his hand.[47]

The dialogue was completely rewritten, and Fraser's structure and key action sequences were streamlined. Notable elements that were dropped included a super-charged tuk-tuk supplied by Q Branch with a bulletproof shield and other concealed weaponry. Bond was to drive a green Bentley which is destroyed during a fight with a gorilla. Kamal Khan was altered from 'a striking figure in his wine-coloured turban and forked beard', to the 'westernised' character played by Louis Jourdan. Miss Moneypenny was absent, replaced by a Miss Smallbone, and Goldfinger was to make a cameo appearance outside the American airbase in Germany. Fraser attempted to provide a backstory as to how Octopussy had earned her name – October Debussy – she was born in October and her mother liked Debussy.

Broccoli decided the script needed a rewrite. Glen noted, 'I was too close to [the story], I couldn't be objective. What Cubby used to do, he used to keep a little distance from the script so he could be objective. It obviously didn't grab him.'[48] Richard Maibaum returned to revise Fraser's work along with Michael G. Wilson. Richard Maibaum saw events overtake the development of the screenplay:

> When we were writing the plot of *Octopussy* we had little idea that it would be virtually the truth. There is a big scandal in Moscow about the State Circus. [Soviet Premier] Brezhnev's son-in-law was involved in the scandal. The State Circus was being used to smuggle jewellery into Russia. They were taking payment, presumably from the various places they performed, but they didn't take money, they took jewellery.'[49]

Maibaum indicated that the down-to-earth approach adopted in *For Your Eyes Only* would continue:

We're sticking with the format we've come back to using, more or less, *From Russia With Love* for style. We're staying with that straight-down-the-line narrative. We are not cheating. We will not press a button and have a miracle happen. Bond has to do it for real and he might have to suffer.[50]

Michael Wilson concurred, 'The first three Bond films were certainly classics of the cinema. And I have no qualms about being compared to these pictures, I want to see *Octopussy* listed in that league.'[51] Wilson elaborated, '*Octopussy* is a spectacle, it's basically still a fantasy product, but more realistic.'[52]

While Glen strove to retain elements of Fleming, Wilson acknowledged the difficulty of extracting entire plots from the latter short stories, 'The basic material begins to wear thin. We stuck closely to the books in the beginning, but we were finally forced to inject whole new ideas in later movies.'[53] Broccoli confirmed early on, 'We're making Octopussy the name of a girl in our film. She's beautiful and powerful. A semi-villain, who gets redeemed at the end.'[54] It seemed to be a natural move. When National Research Group polled 600 women aged between twelve and forty-nine about the title, *Octopussy*, 37 per cent of them objected to it. However, when the same group were told it was a James Bond movie, only 4 per cent objected.[55] Mindful of the American Pussy Galore embarrassment in 1964, Broccoli trod carefully, 'We don't want a controversy but if they insist on making one, it'll end up only helping the movie.'[56]

The final storyline featured the exiled Afghan Prince Kamal Khan, who has entered into partnership with Octopussy, the fabulously wealthy head of the resurrected Octopussy cult. Though her international business network, Octopussy has established a smuggling ring. Using her travelling circus, a form of entertainment welcomed on both ideological sides, Octopussy can travel from Eastern to Western Europe with ease. Khan has teamed up with radical Soviet General Orlov to smuggle out of the Kremlin repository, real Tsar-era jewellery. These are then replaced by expert fakes, manufactured by curator Lenkin, so nobody misses the actual treasures. The smuggled jewels are sold at auction houses around the world, netting the enterprise huge profits. When 009 infiltrates the Octopussy organisation, he manages to retrieve a fake Fabergé Russian Coronation jewelled egg called 'The Property of a Lady'. However, 009 is mortally wounded by twin knife-throwing act, Mischka and Grischka, after struggling to escape with the fake. His final act is to alert the British. Orlov and Khan are informed by Lenkin that an unscheduled inventory is to be done by the Soviet authorities and, in the absence of the fake, the original jewel needs to be urgently recovered. Kamal Khan attends Sotheby's with his

Sikh bodyguard Gobinda and his beautiful companion Magda. At the auction Bond bids against Khan, pushing up the price of 'The Property of a Lady' – 007 knows Khan has to buy it back. While bidding, Bond switches the original with the fake.

Following Khan to Udaipur, India, Bond is assisted by section head Sadruddin and his tennis-playing agent Vijay. Using the real jewelled egg as collateral, Bond out-cheats Khan in a game of backgammon with loaded dice. To gain the original egg, Sikh warrior Gobinda violently pursues Bond in an Indian tuk-tuk taxi through a crowded bazaar, but Bond finds refuge at Q Branch's makeshift workshop.

Bond confronts Octopussy on her all female-island commune. She explains that Bond gave her father, Major Dexter Smythe, an honourable alternative by committing suicide rather than facing trial for stealing gold during the Korean War in the early fifties.

Bond discovers Khan is in league with Orlov, planning to engineer a nuclear accident at an American airbase in West Germany; the explosion will be interpreted as self-inflicted – not a sign of aggression to be retaliated against. Europe will demand nuclear disarmament, which will leave the Western borders open to the vastly superior Soviet conventional forces. Khan in turn will have the sole proceeds of the cache of Tsarist jewellery. Khan will double-cross Octopussy and Magda, both of whom will perish in the nuclear accident. As Octopussy's train speeds towards the American airbase, it innocently carries the nuclear device, Bond fights with Gobinda and the twins on the train, avenging 009 by killing the brothers. The Russian authorities gun Orlov down at the border. Forced to enter the circus dressed as a clown, 007 defuses the bomb with seconds to spare. Now, convinced of Khan's treachery, Octopussy and Magda lead an attack on the Prince's palace. Khan and Gobinda kidnap Octopussy and escape in a Beechcraft propeller plane. Bond clings on to the aircraft as it takes off. Gobinda and Bond duel outside the plane before 007 hurls him to his death. Bond rescues Octopussy, while Khan crashes fatally. Wounded from their fall, they are later found recuperating on her barge.

Lots of casting suggestions accrued for the title role. Celebrity photographer Terry O'Neill lobbied for his wife, actress Faye Dunaway, 'It suddenly came to me that Faye would be wonderful in this role. I put it to Cubby and he was very interested.'[57] Cubby had sought the actress for *Thunderball*, 'I wanted her then but we weren't able to work it out.'[58] Dunaway herself professed to be a fan, 'I'd love to be able to do this film. I've always admired the expertise of the Bonds. I hope we can work things out.'[59] Director Glen remembered other high-profile actresses were considered, including Sybil Danning and Kathleen Turner.[60] However for a prominent female star, Broccoli did not wish to pay a Hollywood salary, because, he said, 'The film itself is the star.'[61] Michael Billington tested potential actresses Deborah Shelton and Susan Penhaligon.[62] Casting director Jane Jenkins had originally looked to cast Indian actresses Persis Khambatta and Susie Coelho or those who could, in a sign of the times, 'pass for Indian,'[63] including Barbara Parkins.[64] Singer Grace Jones was considered but Glen recalled the production 'couldn't quite arrange it because she was performing on the road.'[65] Glen also wistfully remembered talking to Cybill Shepherd.[66]

After an extensive search, Jane Jenkins remembered Cubby saying, 'You know, *The Man With the Golden Gun* was on television last night. Maud Adams was awfully good in that – let's use her.'[67] Adams, fresh from the James Brolin tests recalled her 'curiosity was piqued when they took the time to change the way I looked. But when I got the part I was really surprised.'[68] Adams admitted, 'The title shocked me [but] once you've used the word a few times, it was part of who she was.'[69]

Cubby Broccoli suggested Louis Jourdan for the role of Afghan Prince Kamal Khan.[70] The French-born actor who had become a classic Hollywood fifties heart-throb, was an old friend of the producer. Jourdan relished the role:

> I think the key is to try to make villainy as attractive as possible since James Bond is perfection about what is good and what is right. I have tried to make my villain what is perfect about what is bad, evil and wrong, but always with humour. Humour is the key to the Bond pictures.'[71]

When questioned why Khan had a French accent, Broccoli reasoned, 'He could always have gone to school in France.'[72]

Kabir Bedi, up for the part of henchman, Gobinda, felt his casting was an attempt:

> to internationlise the franchise even more. The producers of the Bond films don't have to sell their roles too hard because any actor in the business considers it a great privilege to be part of a Bond a film. You know you will get known by a totally different audience.'[73]

George MacDonald Fraser recommended Bedi based on their previous work on *Ashanti* (1979).[74] Bedi felt:

I just had to play on the real silent menace of the character. I did suggest to Michael Wilson, 'Give Gobinda certain supernatural powers, Eastern magic, so Bond has to battle a totally different kind of villain.' He could have been able to levitate, sorcery, do charms, spells, have all things that could have confounded Bond. They said, "No, no we prefer to keep things realistic," which I found ironic.'[75]

Bedi explained Gobinda's heritage, 'I am a Sikh by origin. I can tie a turban. It's like learning to play the violin; it takes years of practice. [Gobinda's turban was] beautifully layered as the professional turban tiers tie it.'[76]

Like other actresses Kristina Wayborn had been on Eon's radar for some-time: 'I actually was contacted by the Broccolis for one of the films prior to *Octopussy*. At the time, I was to play Greta Garbo so we kind of let [it] go. [When] I met with them at MGM, they just offered me the role right there.'[77] Of her character, Wayborn felt, 'It was never really discussed how the character was going to be played. I was athletic and I had a little mystery, that comes across. You really don't know where Magda stands, what she's up to, who she's allied with.'[78] She remembered shooting an energetic love scene, 'John said to me, "I want you to absolutely attack Roger, just devour him." I said, "No problem, that's easy, Roger is a gorgeous man."'[79] The take, together with Bond's quip, 'What I do for England' was deleted from the final film but was used in the theatrical teaser trailer.

After a brief appearance in *The Spy Who Loved Me*, Albert Moses returned to the series to play Sadruddin. However, a problem arose when the role was split into two parts, to allow a non-unionised actor, Indian tennis star Vijay Amritraj, to appear in the film. The producers had to placate actors' union, Equity, to pre-vent production problems.[80] Amritraj remembered the Broccolis were big tennis fans and he met them often at Wimbledon.[81] On one such occasion, Broccoli told Amritraj, '"We've tried a lot of actors for this role we'd love for you to consider doing the screentest." James Brolin [did] the screentest with me at Pinewood.'[82] Amritraj's tennis skill was the reason cited as to why a union actor could not perform the role.[83] Tennis was woven into the part and later into his costume, 'In the backgammon scene, I wore a cravat in the colours of the International Club. I did have tennis racquets on my jacket buttons.'[84] The film opened in London two weeks before the Wimbledon tennis championships and a handful of tennis stars attended the premiere. Amritraj recalled that the Wimbledon qualifying rounds had commenced, so 'When I died in the film, one of the players jumped up in the middle of the theatre and screamed "I'm in, I'm in!"'.[85]

David Meyer, who together with his twin brother, Tony, played Mischka and Grischka respectively, recalled the producers 'saw some French acrobatic, nightclub entertainers in Paris. They found their way into the script.'[86] Meyer remembered the French act 'didn't fancy being killed in the film so we got a call.'[87]

Completing the cast was eccentric theatre actor Steven Berkoff, playing General Orlov. Although he enjoyed the role he felt, 'John Glen curbed some of my excesses.'[88]

Robert Brown was cast as Bernard Lee's replacement as M.[89] Brown had previously appeared in *The Spy Who Loved Me* as Admiral Hargreaves, 'Roger and I go back a long time; we made the *Ivanhoe* series together, and we've been friends ever since. I'm godfather to his eldest. He suggested to Cubby that I may be a replacement.'[90] Brown described his initial meeting with Eon as similar to his entry as a young man into the military, 'You just sat there and you were grilled. It was quite something, but I was fortunate, because that afternoon they said, "Okay."'[91] Richard Maibaum noted, 'We looked for someone with the same background as Bernard Lee.'[92]

After proving their worth on *For Your Eyes Only*, John Glen retained his key crew. Peter Lamont returned to design the film and Alan Hume once again served as cinematographer. Hume felt, 'Glen was much more comfortable. We had longer prep time on this one which obviously helped alleviate some of the pressure.'[93] Glen also assembled his signature team of action specialists: Rémy Julienne for vehicular stunts, B.J. Worth and Rande DeLuca for aerial sequences, and veteran stunt arranger Bob Simmons. Bob Simmons had worked for Broccoli for nearly four decades and outlined his process:

> First, the script is presented to me. I start by broadening out the visual ideas as Cubby and Michael allow me to elaborate. I've never had any opposition from them on anything I do. Everything can be worked out, if you give it plenty of thought. Nothing is left to guesswork. Simple stunts are often the most difficult, and yet you have your own set of rules. Cubby says, 'Look, I can't replace you if I lose you. But I can always get another stuntman.'[94]

Glen was forced to make one change:

> Derek Meddings more or less gave us an ultimatum. 'Either I have autonomy over my budget [or I do another picture].' Tom Pevsner is a very, very good producer and one of his jobs is to make people be disciplined. Derek did

resent that. You sometimes reach a stage with someone in their career where they outgrow the job.'[95]

John Richardson was brought in to head special effects.

In May 1982 second unit and aerial work began on the pre-credit sequence ahead of principal photography. The stand-alone sequence, unconnected to the plot, finds Bond in an unnamed 'banana republic'. Arriving in a Land Rover towing a horsebox, it seems Bond is attending a polo gymkhana set in a military airbase. However, 007 is there to effect his mission to sabotage a spy plane. Just as Bond places a magnetised limpet charge hidden in a briefcase in the nose of the aircraft, he is discovered and the charge is removed. In the filmmakers continued attempt to ground Bond, Wilson explained, 'I feel that any gadget which is used should have a general utility. Sometimes, it's nice to write in one that doesn't work, so Bond must use his wits and his physical courage to get out of trouble.'[96] Bond is captured, but engineers an escape whereupon we discover that the horsebox does in fact contain a mini Acrostar jet. Bond takes to the skies and is forced to outwit a guided missile. Stunt pilot John William 'Corkey' Fornof conceived and executed the sequence, which had originally been planned for *Moonraker*.[97]

The Bond crew returned to Northolt Airbase, first used in *Thunderball*, to shoot the pre-title polo and hanger sequences. The set was dressed with palm trees to give it an authentic South American look. Camera operator Alec Mills recalled press reports incorrectly speculating that the trees were to make Argentinian prisoners of war from the recent Falklands conflict feel at home.[98]

Based in Hurricane Mesa in Utah, the sequence was handled by Philip Wrestler, a director John Glen had known since his editing days in the fifties.[99] Cubby told Fornof, 'These are the shots we need, now you put the magic in them.'[100] Fornof pushed the action as hard as possible recalling one shot in particular, 'From the camera it was a beautiful but we ran it for a test audience one night, and more than half got sick or were nauseous. People felt like they were being sucked into the scene, which I felt was fantastic but didn't play too well.'[101] The sequence culminated with Bond leading the missile through an aircraft hangar, manoeuvring the Acrostar through a narrowing gap the other side, while the missile blows the hangar and the spy plane to smithereens. Fornof offered to fly through the hangar but remembered his producer's wisdom, 'Cubby told me, "Do you know why we hire you? We don't hire you to take risks. We hire you because you are known to eliminate the risks." They hire me to say, "No", when there is no way to get the shot when it's needed.'[102] Effects maestro John

Richardson cleverly integrated foreground miniatures and put a model of the jet on a rotating arm mounted to a rigged Jaguar. The plane was driven at high speed through the hangar, allowing extras to run through the shot, while the jet turned on the rotating arm on the car.[103] Richardson blew up a 5ft tall miniature of the hangar.[104] After performing a victory roll, Bond realises he is out of fuel and must touch down immediately. The idea of landing on a public highway originated from a real-life experience when Fornof was forced to make an emergency landing on a busy North Carolina freeway, miraculously coming to a halt in a gas station.[105] Bond has just enough fuel to reach the United States, landing in a small town where he requests an astonished pump attendant to 'Fill her up, please.'

While in Utah, Wrestler also worked with Jake Lombard and B.J. Worth to film the aerial combat between Bond and Gobinda. Wrestler edited 'all the stuff I shot and then shipped it back to England,'[106] but was disappointed by feedback that said the Beechcraft fight looked too easy.[107] Editor John Grover remembered, 'the material [Wrestler] supplied was terrific.'[108] Wrestler recalled, 'They asked me for a shot of the twin-engine plane doing a loop the loop [but I would] need to be 20 miles away to shoot it.'[109] A model of the plane, loaded with explosives, was to be launched by a rig used for testing ejector seats in the area to capture Khan's death.[110] However, the model drifted out of range of the cameras, dangerously passing over a busy freeway, before crashing unseen.[111] Bond and Octopussy were to have tumbled out of the plane into a raging river. Wrestler storyboarded an elaborate white water rapids sequence that was to follow,[112] but Glen felt the sequence was 'surplus to requirements'.[113]

On 10 August 1982 principal photography commenced at Check Point Charlie.[114] In the middle of September 1982 the crew arrived in Udaipur, India. United Artists had chosen the country partly because they could release their frozen funds, which they had previously attempted to do on *Moonraker*.[115] The unit shot in the exotic Lake Palace Hotel, set in Lake Pichola. As guests of the local Maharajah, the cast and crew were treated like royalty. Peter Lamont cannibalised two abandoned boats he discovered on the banks of the lake to create Octopussy's ceremonial barge.[116]

Glen recalled that Louis Jourdan found the notoriously laidback atmosphere of the Bond set 'difficult to accept'.[117] Kristina Wayborn suggests the actor kept his distance for personal reasons, 'Louis and his wife had suffered the loss of their son within the year of the film.'[118] Bedi observed, 'Louis was very nice, very civil but a very private person. Reserved. I think he opened up more with Roger than anyone else on the set because I think they were friends from before.'[119] Steven Berkoff had his own perspective, 'Louis Jourdan was charming and taught us little word games to play while we were waiting around, like identifying movies through a series of codes in your chat. When we all played these games I knew I had arrived.'[120]

Having worked with both Guy Hamilton and John Glen, Maud Adams described their individual approaches, 'John Glen was more approachable than Guy Hamilton. He was more involved with the actresses.'[121] Paired once again with a fellow Swedish actress, she found Wayborn to be, 'rather a recluse [very different from Britt and I]. Kristina was very much to herself, very focussed, almost distant. Today, we're good friends.'[122] Shooting in Udaipur was intense as Adams recalled, 'When they announced they needed extras for a scene we almost created a riot because so many people showed up and they couldn't take everybody. It was a big problem for the production company.'[123]

Crowds plagued the taxi chase sequence and were amazed by the vehicles taking part. Rémy Julienne had had to soup up the rickety conveyances, 'The tuk-tuks had Honda 250 cross motorcycle chassis with adapted suspension. For every stunt we had a specialised one, at least five or six,'[124] and they were capable of going 70mph.[125] Vijay Amritraj was impressed by his co-star, 'It's hotter than hell. It's one thing to be in a studio with a blue screen behind you, but this was real. And through the heat of Udaipur there is Roger Moore with his tuxedo on looking completely cool and collected and without a drop of sweat.'[126]

Roger Moore once again set out the challenges of being Bond, 'These films are hard work. You should have seen me charging through the jungle in India pursued by a horde of villains on elephants, swinging on a vine across bottomless gorges and running into giant spider webs.'[127] Harry Saltzman's long-desired elephant sequence was eventually filmed, culminating with a cameo of Michael G. Wilson on the tourist boat which rescues Bond.

Vijay Amritraj observed:

Michael [Wilson] was very focussed on a Bond film and I think his ability to write, to be able to create, to be able to develop a character even more so. I think a lot of Michael's thought process came out of Dana. Dana was very focussed. I think they had a lot of internal meetings where Dana's input made a lot of difference to the creation of the script.'[128]

Amritraj elaborated further:

I think Barbara maybe had a little bit more of a global perspective of other films and what needed to be brought in. Barbara, I think, made all the difference to the team. That's why I think they work very well together because they complement each other in so many different ways.'[129]

By October 1982 the production had moved to the Nene Valley Railway museum, a historical private rail network which doubled for the East and West Germany and where complex action in, around and on top of Octopussy's train was filmed. When Moore was asked if he did his own stunts, he replied, 'Of course I do! I also do my own lying.'[130] David Meyer did dangerous work himself:

> When we've got three of you fighting on top of the train, we've got to show somebody's face. Roger Moore's not going to be up there or Kabir. Normally you might have got a stuntman doing that bit. I have to say it was one of the most exciting things I've ever done in my life.'[131]

Despite the professionalism of a Bond set, unfortunately things went wrong. Martin Grace, doubling for Roger Moore recalled, 'Over many days I did shots climbing up, running on and emerging from the bottom of the travelling train. It was in fact like second nature to me.'[132] Director of photography Alan Hume remembered that while the stretch of the track had been checked, the train was not returned to its starting position, which meant they would be going into unknown territory ahead.[133] This would have severe consequences, as Martin Grace outlined:

> The action required us to look through the train windows which meant I could not look ahead. I got hit on the pelvis by a solid wall built parallel with the railway track. The impact was so lightning fast that I only realised that I had hit something when I found I was hanging prone for dear life on the side of the train, my pelvis area numb at first like a gigantic tooth extraction injection.'[134]

Travelling at high speed, Grace suffered acute injuries from the unseen protrusion but managed to hold on to the train.[135] He did recover after a lengthy period but the dangers of doubling 007 for real were apparent.[136]

In November 1982 the Bond team returned to Pinewood Studios causing Broccoli to reflect on twenty-one years of Bond, 'We started off there and they're Bond addicted and dedicated filmmakers. They know what we want and need.'[137] Peter Lamont's sets filled the stages:

Once we had settled in Udaipur and the script was approved, I started researching the interior design for Octopussy's boudoir, consulting reference books on the subject, depicting all of the luxurious architecture. Octopussy's bed is made from polystyrene, covered with red ochre, which we rubbed down to give the impression of wood.'[138]

It was on this exotic set that Maud Adams accidentally injured Moore, 'I did have a mishap with Roger at one point when I kicked him in the groin by accident when he twirls me around, the first time we kissed. It's not something you do to James Bond!'[139]

Lamont also created a War Room where Orlov outlines his radical plans to his fellow comrades:

It's the Kremlin set. I modelled it after the Palace of Congress. We built a hammer and sickle design into the floor and an elliptical table on a moving floor. It was possible to swing it around to face a giant war map, listing all the Eastern bloc tank visions, illuminated via back projection.'[140]

The 007 Stage housed the Monsoon Palace, 'The film demanded a courtyard and helipad. We managed to secure a Russian-built helicopter used for ferrying supplies to oil rigs in the North Sea.'[141]

Early on in the shoot, Kabir Bedi found Roger Moore to be:

quite aloof, quite reserved, quite aristocratic. I didn't get the feeling that he was terribly approachable. But actually in the course of filming, especially in Udaipur and later when we were shooting the sequences in Peterborough, we would go for long walks together, I got to know Roger much better. [I] found him to be an interesting, warm, and a very knowledgeable, intelligent person. A bit of a contrast to the image he seemed to portray in films.[142]

Steven Berkoff thought Moore, 'exceedingly pleasant to work with,'[143] but remembered, 'the day of our "big" scene, the poor man couldn't remember his lines, although up till then he had been very strong on lines. Did I make him feel ill at ease? Eventually we shot it almost a sentence at a time.'[144] If there was any awkwardness, Roger Moore would be the first to try to diffuse it. Maud Adam recalled, 'Love scenes with Roger Moore always turned into a riot, it was hard to be serious.'[145] Editor John Grover recalled Moore would 'send an assistant director to buy hundreds of sweets'[146] to help ease any tensions on the set.

It was on the Monsoon Palace set, just before Christmas 1982, that Desmond Llewelyn experienced his first action scene as Q, flying a hot-air balloon which drops Bond into the fray, 'The studios were freezing: the girls were covered in goose pimples and Roger was fed up with shooting the same thing over and over again. The poor chap wanted to fly home to Switzerland for the holiday.'[147] The actor was pleased, 'It was practically the only time I ever met any Bond girls. They were great fun and I got to know them quite well as I did a promotional tour with them to Australia and America.'[148] Llewelyn was appreciative of the role:

> I take it as a compliment that many people, including some supposedly sophisticated press people, who've interviewed me, actually believe I've had a hand in inventing the devices that Bond uses in the films. I try not to disillusion the public and have always familiarised myself with the workings of all the equipment I supposedly create for Bond's adventures in the field. But the truth is that I'm merely an actor and not particularly mechanical, at that. I sometimes have a dickens of a time trying to get some of the gadgets to work right for me.[149]

Appearing for a second time as Smithers was Jeremy Bulloch, more famous for inhabiting *The Empire Strikes Back*'s (1980) Boba Fett. Llewelyn discounted the significance of the character, 'Smithers was only really an extra. He was an awfully nice chap.'[150]

Lois Maxwell's first inkling that her time behind the typewriter might be coming to an end was when she discovered Moneypenny was to be given a new assistant – Miss Penelope Smallbone – played by writer James Clavell's daughter Michaela. 'I suppose I was jealous of the girl, subconsciously at least.'[151] Maxwell thought:

> Right, this is the push, next will be the shove. I had to introduce her to Roger when he came in as Bond. Perhaps it was the shock of having some new dialogue, but what came out was 'James, may I introduce my assistant Miss Smallbush.' Roger didn't miss a beat. He had these carnations in his hands and he just let them droop as he said, 'Moneypenny! We all know where your mind is at.'[152]

Vijay Amritraj remembered a special moment at Pinewood:

Christopher Reeve was shooting *Superman* [*III*, 1983] on another stage at
the time. And Chris Reeve, in his cape, came down into the commissary at
Pinewood one day when Roger and I were sitting at a corner table and he
sat with us and I almost died – I was completely in awe of these two characters sitting with me at the lunch table. Roger Moore in his black tie and
Christopher Reeve in his cape. How do you beat that? You're having lunch
with James Bond and Superman.[153]

Sean Connery's rival Bond film was being shot in Elstree concurrently. John
Glen was not worried, 'I knew we had a good movie – I hoped they had a good
movie.'[154] On one occasion, the rushes for *Never Say Never Again* were sent to
Pinewood by mistake and Glen remembered the *Octopussy* production paid for
the car to repatriate the film cans, 'The editors were friends of mine.'[155] Roger
Moore remembered commiserating with Connery, 'We were both making a
Bond at the same time. We saw one another a few times. We discussed what
method the producers were using to kill us.'[156]

Principal photography on *Octopussy* was completed on 21 January 1983. John
Barry returned, collaborating with lyricist Tim Rice who 'was surprised and
delighted to be asked by John, "Would you like to write the lyrics for the song
in the next James Bond movie?" I thought, "Well, that's a silly question. Yes!"
He said, "Well, the film's called *Octopussy*."' John Barry was clear, '*Octopussy*
was just a no, no as a title.'[157] Upon hearing the name of the movie, Tim Rice
recalled, 'There was a bit of a silence. "I'm not sure I can come up with a great
lyric called 'Octopussy.'" And [John Barry] said, "Why not choose six titles that
are vaguely Bond-ish. Then they'll choose one of the six, they're bound to like
one of them."'[158] Basing the lyric on the scripted lines, 'We're two of a kind,'
Rice's song was called 'All Time High', a slogan which became integral to the
marketing campaign.[159] Singer Rita Coolidge recounted how she got the gig,
'The story that I heard is that Cubby Broccoli's daughter wanted me to be
the singer and they hadn't chosen the singer yet so she very subliminally put
on Rita Coolidge records. One night [Cubby] heard me singing and he said,
"That's the voice I want for the new film."'[160] With the song not actually ready
on the day of recording and producer Phil Ramone's frustrations manifest in
the studio, Coolidge had uncomfortable memories of the song.[161] 'All Time
High' was not a chart success, but Tim Rice has gone on to state it has become
immensely successful, judging from his royalty statements.[162]

Maurice Binder shot the titles from March to May 1983. He avoided using
a circus motif or India locales, so as not to telegraph the exoticism of the

film which would open on dull East Berlin. Binder's work was innovative at the time:

> We used laser beams [and] projected these images on top of nude girls. I've used computers before, but I wanted to use them for something more than swirls of smoke. Projecting laser beams … gives quite brilliant colors. I shot part of the titles before I had the final song, but I did have the lyrics. Some of the titles illustrate actions which are in the lyrics. For instance, where Rita Coolidge sings, 'I didn't want to waste a waking moment,' I have an image of a girl suddenly opening her eyes. There's another part where the song goes, 'We move as one' and I have a guy and a girl swinging around, with her legs wrapped around him.[163]

Maurice Binder oversaw the trailer campaign which featured Maud Adams introducing audiences to the new Bond adventure. Mindful of Connery's return as 007, trailers and posters declared, 'Nobody does HIM better!' and that 'Roger Moore IS James Bond.' With a heavy emphasis on the 'James Bond Theme' and elements that were traditional to the series, *Octopussy* seemed to be the culmination of what was now being recognised as a James Bond brand. It had been twenty-one years in the making.

On 6 June 1983 *Octopussy* received its royal world charity premiere in London at the Odeon Leicester Square in the presence of Prince Charles and Princess Diana. *Octopussy* grossed over $182 million worldwide and increased its North American take to $62 million.

In his twenty-first year, the cinematic 007 was still a global phenomenon. In a television special, *James Bond: The First 21 Years*, hosted by Roger Moore, a number of global personalities of the time paid tribute to the coming-of-age birthday of Ian Fleming's fictional spy. For the 'farm boy from Long Island', Broccoli's cinematic furrow was now lauded in good-natured jest. Chief of fans was the then President of the United States, Ronald Regan, who contributed:

> I've been asked to state my feelings about a fellow named Bond, James Bond. Well, as I see it, 007, is really a ten. He's our modern-day version of the great heroes who appeared from time to time throughout history. Bond is fearless, skilled, witty, courageous, optimistic and, one other thing, he always gets his girl. James Bond is man of honour. Maybe it sounds old-fashioned, but I believe he's a symbol of real value to the Free World. Of course some critics

might say that Bond is nothing more than an actor in the movies. Well, then, we've all got to start somewhere.[164]

The creative team assembled for the eighties-era Bond were now hitting their stride. With an emphasis redirected from expensive sets and technology to physical action and character, John Glen and his team would continue to give the series renewed creative avenues to explore, mining elements of the Fleming novels and using specialist action teams to create groundbreaking sequences. Now partnered with a studio for whom film-making seemed something of a distraction, Eon also had to be resourceful with budgets and take on increasing competition from those inspired by the 007 legacy. Broccoli noted:

> I get a kick out of seeing the success of other people who make films, like Spielberg and Lucas. I get a kick out of seeing the lines of ticket buyers standing there. Because that's our business and if they didn't have that success with other films, we would *all* deteriorate. They breathe a success into the whole industry which is what we need.'[165]

Cubby was not getting any younger and the franchise was looking to the future. As Barbara Broccoli gained a formal role on the productions, the James Bond legacy needed to be nurtured. It was with this confidence that Albert R. Broccoli's Eon Productions faced the ultimate challenge at the box office that autumn when Sean Connery returned as 007 in *Never Say Never Again*. In what would be termed, 'The Battle of the Bonds', interest in Ian Fleming's hero was never higher.

19

NO MATTER
YOUR ATTITUDE

NEVER SAY NEVER AGAIN

(1983)

SEAN CONNERY
is JAMES BOND in
THE BIGGEST FALL OPENING IN MOTION PICTURE HISTORY
THE BIGGEST BOND OPENING EVER
007 HAS A NEW NUMBER…
$9,725,154
FIRST 3 DAYS
1550 THEATRES
NEVER SAY NEVER AGAIN
JACK SCHWARTZMAN and KEVIN McCLORY Present
A TALIAFILM Production An IRVIN KERSHNER Film
SEAN CONNERY "NEVER SAY NEVER AGAIN"
Also starring
KLAUS MARIA BRANDAUER · MAX VON SYDOW · BARBARA CARRERA · KIM BASINGER · BERNIE CASEY · ALEC McCOWEN and EDWARD FOX as "M"
Director of Photography DOUGLAS SLOCOMBE B.S.C. Music by MICHEL LEGRAND Executive Producer KEVIN McCLORY Screenplay by LORENZO SEMPLE, JR.
Based on an Original Story by KEVIN McCLORY, JACK WHITTINGHAM and IAN FLEMING Directed by IRVIN KERSHNER Produced by JACK SCHWARTZMAN
PG PARENTAL GUIDANCE SUGGESTED
SOME MATERIAL MAY NOT BE SUITABLE FOR CHILDREN
DISTRIBUTED BY WARNER BROS
A WARNER COMMUNICATIONS COMPANY

The moratorium for Kevin McClory not to produce another Bond film based on the THUNDERBALL materials – part of his agreement with Broccoli and Saltzman in 1965 – had elapsed. On 7 January 1976 Kevin McClory placed a one-page advert in *Variety* announcing '*James Bond of the Secret Service*: a Paradise Film Production' to begin shooting later that year in the Bahamas. McClory had shrewdly united best-selling thriller writer Len Deighton with none other than Sean Connery to collaborate on a screenplay.

In September 1975 Connery had visited McClory at his home in County Kildare, Ireland, ostensibly to participate in a charity event, later filmed and called *Circasia* (1975).[1] McClory said, 'I knew Sean didn't want to play Bond again, but he knows more about Bond than anyone else and has a vast number of ideas about what Bond can do.'[2] McClory made the inspired decision to hire Connery to *write* his James Bond film and felt the star 'did not just contribute throwaway lines, he also got involved in the construction of the plot. He made enormous contributions and we got on very well.'[3] Deighton recalled, 'Sean came up to my home in Ireland and I visited him in at his home in Spain. Sean had very useful and explicit ideas about the character of James Bond.'[4] Deighton elaborated:

> Kevin McClory asked me to work with his American lawyers so that I could write a screenplay that could not be described as a sequel. I did exactly that. I produced a wall chart of the events of the existing film and an overlay to show how each sequence of the script was based upon one in the film.'[5]

Broccoli could not prevent McClory remaking *Thunderball*. Connery elaborated on the new story, now entitled *Warhead*:

> Those airplanes that were disappearing over the Bermuda Triangle? We had SPECTRE doing that. There was this fantastic fleet of planes under the sea – a whole world of stuff had been brought down. They were going to attack the financial nerve centre of the United States by going in through the sewers of New York – which you can do – right into Wall Street. They'd have mechanical sharks in the bay and take over the Statue of Liberty, which is quite easy, and have the main line of troops on Ellis Island.[6]

McClory enthusiastically told the industry press that filming would begin in 1977, with locations including Nassau, New York and Japan, 'If you visualise *Star Wars* underwater, you get some idea of our story.'[7]

United Artists Chairman Arthur Krim responded to the announcement:

Danjaq and United Artists are entitled, through the rights granted by Ian
Fleming and the Fleming Estate, to the exclusive use in the future of the
'James Bond-007' character, except for THUNDERBALL. No person, corporation
or entity, other than Danjaq and United Artists can use, or grant rights to use,
the character 'James Bond-007' in any other film which goes beyond the story
of THUNDERBALL, and anybody who proceeds on any other premise does so at
legal peril.[8]

Litigation during the development process would usually kill projects, but
McClory produced a trump card. In 1978 Sean Connery intimated he would
return to the role of James Bond. Connery had found his work with Len
Deighton on the screenplay rewarding, 'I was discussing it with my wife. She
said "Well, if it's going so well why don't you play the part?" And coming from
her I gave it more thought than I normally would I suppose. It seemed quite
a good idea after all these years.'[9] Connery revealed that McClory had at one
point asked him to direct the project.[10] His agent, Dennis Selinger, advised him
otherwise, 'In my own mind, I'm sure he did it out of pique against Broccoli and
Saltzman.'[11] Connery also suggested that he had been persuaded by the financial
rewards, 'I'd own a considerable piece of it and the financial return would be in
ratio to my investment which hasn't been the case before.'[12]

On 28 July 1978 *Variety* announced Paramount had acquired Kevin McClory's
rights and was now working with him to develop the project.[13] McClory revealed,
'Sean Connery will star, together with Orson Welles and Trevor Howard. Our
budget will be $22.5 million.'[14] Connery's fee was reported to be as much as
$10 million.[15] However, a double-pronged attack in the British High Court by
both the Trustees of the Fleming Estate and the collective of United Artists, Eon
Productions Ltd and Danjaq S.A.[16] cowed Paramount, who decided not to proceed with the film. Mystified, McClory said of Paramount's decision, 'The budget
had been agreed and I had a letter of authorisation to pay Sean a certain amount
of money against the gross. I don't know why they decided not to proceed.'[17]
For now, Connery walked away too, 'The new aristocracy, the lawyers and the
accountants got in the middle. I stepped back when they came in. Perhaps some
lawyer will play the part?'[18]

A further two years passed and, after injecting a substantial amount of his
own time and money, McClory's film looked doomed. Or so everyone thought.
Determined he ploughed on, looking for new financial backers.

In 1980 McClory's screenplay found its way to Lorimar, a production company known for television output such as *The Waltons* and *Dallas*.[19] There, the screenplay was shepherded by Lorimar executive Jack Schwartzman. Previously a tax attorney for one of Hollywood's most notable law firms – Greenberg and Grakal – Schwartzman felt qualified to enter the mire: 'My job was to investigate the legal ownership rights and determine if it was something Lorimar should get involved with.'[20] Lorimar never developed the project further.[21]

When Schwartzman left Lorimar, fate reunited him with McClory's project, 'An investment banker friend of mine from New York called and said he represented the gentleman that owned the rights and was I interested in getting involved with it?'[22] Schwartzman was confident of the legal position, 'Kevin McClory has the specific rights that he claims to have in *writing*. There is *no* doubt about it.'[23] Schwartzman was not deterred by the project's tarnished litigious history:

> Money runs away from lawsuits. Broccoli and United Artists alleged a number of causes for legal action. Additionally, in a separate action, the Fleming Estate sued McClory. They never denied he had certain rights, but they alleged that the movie he intended to make was outside the scope of his rights. Consequently, when somebody casts that kind of cloud over a project, it's not an easy matter to obtain the financing required to make a movie of such magnitude.[24]

Nevertheless, Schwartzman was assured, 'Essentially, all the experiences, relationships and tools I have acquired during my entire legal career were brought into play. It's sort of a microcosm of my professional life.'[25] Schwartzman optioned McClory's rights enabling him to make a film independently.[26] McClory received credit as an executive producer, with the rights reverting to him after a period.[27] McClory's role during production was, according to Schwartzman, 'a kind of liaison for its Bahamas location shooting.'[28]

Schwartzman had even suggested a partnership with Danjaq, 'I offered Broccoli the opportunity to present the picture, as he had done with *Thunderball*. He wasn't interested.'[29] Schwartzman later revealed that his opponents wished him well,[30] 'They also said that if I went outside my rights, they would do everything in their power to protect themselves.'[31]

Sean Connery needed reassurance to commit:

> Out of the blue Jack Schwartzman approached me with a view to doing this one. I said, 'Two conditions, one it is totally clean and I have no more dealings

with lawyers and I have total indemnification from yourself." And he provided both of these clauses.'[32]

In October 1981 Connery signed a contract that gave him $5 million up front and an undisclosed share of the gross.[33] Connery was an early client of Creative Artists Agency (CAA) head Michael Ovitz, who promptly leant the star his martial arts tutor, Steven Seagal, to help get fit for the role.[34] Ovitz had also brokered Connery's approval on script, director, principal cast and lighting cameraman.[35] Schwartzman admitted no producer ever liked to give a star such power but, 'It was something he wanted in order to protect himself.'[36] Connery revealed it was his wife, Micheline, who coined the eventual title:

> Warners and everybody came up with reams and reams of titles you cannot believe. She came up with *Never Say Never Again*. She said 'You did say you would never do it again!' Incidentally the producer promised my wife a sable coat for the title. She has never received it!'[37]

Schwartzman worked with Mark Damon of Producers Sales Organization (PSO), to independently finance the production and raised the funds through twenty-six international distributors with Warner Brothers taking the United States, Canada, South America and the UK.[38] Having spent eleven years in senior management at the studio, recently retired John Calley was retained by Warners as an 'exclusive consultant'.[39] Schwartzman now 'went around the world, meeting with distributors in each of the major countries. I made distribution deals with them in their markets. I obtained from them certain guarantees, which I then used as a collateral package to acquire bank financing.'[40] In March 1982 Connery's participation was announced.[41]

Warner Brothers were favoured as the US major because when the film was previously being developed by Kevin McClory, Warners assured themselves of his position having 'done a substantial amount of research into the question of the rights.'[42] According to Schwartzman, the fragmented finance plan meant 'by going the independent route, a number of people would have had to chicken out before *Never Say Never Again* could be terminated.'[43]

Schwartzman did not touch the Deighton/Connery screenplay, 'At the time I made my deal, it was the subject of the litigation, and I didn't want to be tarred with the same brush.'[44] Understanding the legal quagmire, he instead developed a screenplay that stayed as close as possible to Fleming's THUNDERBALL material. Under the banner of Taliafilm, the production company operated by

Schwartzman and his wife Talia Shire (sister of Francis Ford Coppola), they hired Julian Plowden, one of Schwartzman's Lorimar associates, to write a screenplay.[45]

Echoing McClory's inspiration about nuclear terrorism after the war, Schwartzman felt THUNDERBALL's threat was still relevant:

> I remember listening to the Carter-Regan debate on television and when Carter claimed that the next President of the United States would more than likely have to deal with a nuclear hijack, the skin on the back of my neck began to crawl. That's the situation in our film and I don't believe that the idea is pure fantasy anymore.[46]

Next Schwartzman hired Lorenzo Semple Jr., known for his work on the *Batman* television series and *Flash Gordon* (1980), to pen the screenplay, 'The kind of film I was looking for was somewhere "in the middle" of the films Lorenzo had written. On one hand he wrote *Three Days of the Condor* on the other he wrote *Batman*.'[47] Semple considered the legal parameters an interesting challenge:

> Like many people, I fancy myself an amateur attorney. In reading all that material, I was amazed by how much was undefined regarding rights to the property. Although it was set down in writing, there were various interpretations. Part of the fun of doing the screenplay was threading my way through this legal minefield.[48]

Semple recalled that Schwartzman was heavily insured in preparation for further litigation:[49] '

> I remember one day in Los Angeles when Jack pitched the project to lawyers representing the insurance company. They had read the script and were being very difficult. One young guy kept coming up with differences from [*Thunderball*]. Jack silenced him by saying, "Look, we have the rights. You've got the legal papers, read them. We're adapting the novel again."'[50]

Lorenzo Semple wanted to change the Bahamas as a location, 'but Jack and his lawyers were nervous of moving the setting.'[51] As the project developed Semple said the grey area of what they could and could not do became contentious. The lawyers stressed 'if it's too different from the *Thunderball* movie, then you're not doing a remake, you're doing a sequel.'[52] Semple expressed that all involved thought underwater sequences were dull and looked slow on screen but they were required, due to the legal restrictions, 'to have an underwater battle more than we [actually] wanted [to].'[53]

Semple cited the major change to the storyline was putting James Bond in semi-retirement.[54] Bond would now operate in a modern bureaucratic Secret Service which, Connery noted, 'don't approve of uncontrollable operatives.'[55] An original idea was to have Bond dispatched to Scotland, working on a North Sea fishing boat spying on Russian submarines.[56] Much discussion was had as to how Connery should play Bond and what appearance they should give the character, 'We did talk about the possibility of doing it with no hair piece, a moustache, a beard. It created more problems than it solved.'[57] Said Schwartzman, 'Our approach is to have Sean play the character at his age, which is 52, and not go on pretending Bond is still 32.'[58]

From the beginning, Connery was angling to make a film which harked back to his early Bond pictures,[59] 'In *Dr. No* and *From Russia With Love* one had done the character. Then the stories became progressively more involved with hardware and less of the essence of what Fleming had originally written.'[60] He cited *From Russia With Love* as the benchmark, a film he described as having 'marvellous locations, interesting ambience, interesting characters … a detective story with espionage, exotic settings and nice birds … That was what I was more interested in and pushed for.'[61]

Sean Connery responded well to Semple's initial seventy-page treatment.[62] Following a first draft screenplay, the writer joined Connery for several days at his home in Marbella incorporating further thoughts and ideas.[63] 'Sean has a great fondness for James Bond,'[64] noted Semple. Upon delivery of a second draft, the project became more realistic because, as Semple explained, 'for the first time Sean was faced with having to put up or shut up.'[65]

Never Say Never Again largely hews to the *Thunderball* storyline although there are interesting tweaks: an ageing Bond, a more technocratic MI6, a nuclear threat to the world's oil supplies and the topical updates on Bond's passions. However, most of the tropes remain including the double nuclear hijack and Domino's brother and his death being used to turn her against Largo. The finale of Bond being saved by Domino underwater when she kills her ex-lover had survived from the earliest iterations of the project as initiated by Fleming, Bryce and McClory all those years ago.

Connery's first choice to helm *Never Say Never Again* was Richard Donner but the *Superman* director didn't respond well to the script. 'I was quite alarmed by that fact, because when an actor wants a certain director and the director doesn't want the job, everybody becomes terribly insecure,'[66] said Semple. Terence Young and John Guillermin were mooted but as Semple recalled, 'Sean wanted the most "artistic" director he could have.'[67]

Schwartzman and Connery then met with American director Irvin Kershner, who had just had a resounding hit with *The Empire Strikes Back* (1980), the film many consider to be the strongest episode of the *Star Wars* saga. Kershner had also directed Sean Connery in *A Fine Madness* in 1966 and he had been one of Schwartzman's clients at Greenberg and Grakal.[68] Kershner admitted he was 'not exactly fond of many of the James Bond pictures,'[69] but took on the film because not only had it been a personal invitation from Sean Connery, but he had previously never directed anything in this genre.[70]

As pre-production commenced, relationships began turning sour, which ultimately dampened the atmosphere throughout production. Semple and Kershner bickered from the beginning, 'Quite a few people in Hollywood turn white at the very thought of Kersh becoming involved with a project. His habit is to immediately say the script is terrible and start rewriting it himself.'[71] Later Kershner reasoned, 'I think Lorenzo is a terrific writer and very knowledgeable, with a nice sense of form and rhythm. It's just we had a lot of problems, trying to make a film out of this book. I think he didn't quite realise that.'[72] The rapport between director and producer also began to wane. Kershner said later, '[Schwartzman] didn't know production at all, but he sort of assumed he would learn very quickly. I don't think he did.'[73]

Kershner's hiring eventually led to Semple's departure; the writer compared working with Kershner to working with a child.[74] 'He would say,"I've got a sensational idea. Let's do this."Two days later, he would say,"That's terrible. It doesn't work at all."'[75] Scenes were constantly being rewritten, replaced and changed. Now in pre-production in London, Semple recalled that:

> Jack [was] running out of money … so they tell me to cut the script down, cut out some of these big numbers. Then they send the script to Sean Connery and he says "This is not the movie I signed to do. I'm not doing it." So what do they do? They fire me.'[76]

Semple asserted that 'Kersh, Sean, the assistant director and a secretary pasted together another script, restoring material from the earlier drafts … All together.'[77] Schwartzman asked his brother-in-law, Francis Ford Coppola, for his opinion, 'He rewrote a few things here and there. Basically he was acting as "a friend of the court."'[78] As pre-production began at EMI Elstree, Irvin Kershner met British television writers, Dick Clement and Ian La Frenais, who were in the studio working on *Auf Wiedershen, Pet.*[79] When introduced to Kershner they casually asked if he was looking for a rewrite. Months went by and suddenly, at a day's notice, they found themselves in Nice urgently redrafting, three weeks into production.[80] Clement was prepared, 'We were only employed for a week, ten days. The first thing we saw were the rushes that they had [shot] already. There was an awful lot wrong with them. We realised they were in deep shit. We did what we could.'[81] The duo felt it was not explained why James Bond was even in the Bahamas, prompting Kershner, according to Clement, to stroke his rabbinical beard and comment, 'That's true. On the other hand we have a film crew there shooting so you better come up with something!'[82]

The opening sequence appeared to be a seventeenth-century jousting tournament, which is only revealed to be a contemporary setting once Bond takes off his helmet. Clement felt, 'The problem with this is the big asset you've got in this film is the real James Bond, you've got Sean Connery and he's got a tin can on his head throughout this whole sequence.'[83] Clement and La Frenais wrote a war game scenario where Bond attempts to rescue a victim against the clock. The sequence showcased Connery in action plus it could be shot in the Bahamas, thereby maximising the location. Clement thought the sequence, 'was good [until] they put a song over it which completely buggered it up.'[84]

Clement and La Frenais stayed with the picture throughout production fixing the script daily, 'We were in that lovely situation where [we] didn't create this mess but maybe [we] could help out. We were the innocent UN bystanders.'[85] Sean Connery praised the British duo's humour noting, 'Unfortunately, Lorenzo was – is – American; I don't mean that in a disrespecful way, but basically the humour (in Bond films) is very British. And with an American director and an American writer it had a tendency to go towards American humour.'[86] Feeling the story was in much need of light relief, Clement and La Frenais introduced Nigel Small-Fawcett, a foreign office representative who meets 007 upon his arrival in the Bahamas, played by future *Blackadder* star Rowan Atkinson.[87] Clement thought, 'We'd done enough to earn a credit, but that's down to the Guild and we lost the arbitration.'[88] Connery 'begged [the Writers Guild of America (WGA)] to change their minds, but they were adamant.'[89] Semple was awarded sole screenplay credit. He was informed by a WGA insider that Clement and La Frenais did not have Guild contracts,[90] 'Somebody said to me, "All writing belongs to you until another guy signs a Guild contract."'[91] Semple followed Guild rules out of principle,[92] 'I owed it to all writers [and] to stand up for the Guild and the contract. I wrote a letter to the guild for arbitration saying I wanted sole credit and I got sole credit on this extremely legal technical basis.'[93]

Semple's contract entitled him to a $100,000 bonus if he was awarded solo credit. But later, when the completion bond guarantors took over the picture, they maintained that they were obliged to deliver a negative and nothing more.[94] 'We threatened to put Jack on the strike list if he didn't pay up.'[95] Semple got his bonus.[96] When informed of these events by the authors for the first time in 2015, Dick Clement responded, 'That hurts!'[97]

As well as screenplay and director approval, Connery had sign off on principal cast.[98] Austrian actor Klaus Maria Brandauer – whom Connery declared one of the ten best actors in Europe[99] – would play Maximillian Largo. Kershner felt the antagonist should be 'a modern business man without eye patches, or big fangs, or slices across his face.'[100] Wearing some of his own wardrobe in the role,[101] Brandauer strove 'to show a very normal person with a normal appearance. As happens in real life, his bad character is hidden but sometimes bursts out. He stands for a kind of European power and the total perversion of culture and money.'[102]

Former model and *Playboy* pin-up Barbara Carrera was cast as Fatima Blush, a name taken from an early THUNDERBALL treatment.[103] The actress 'decided to play her as Kali, the Hindu goddess of death, and mix that in with a little black widow and a little praying mantis.'[104] Largo's mistress, Domino, was played by an American actress first suggested by Mrs. Connery after a chance encounter in the Grosvenor House Hotel in London: Kim Basinger.[105] Basinger recounted, 'One of the reasons I accepted the Domino role is she's a dancer and so am I. [Domino was] very naïve and vulnerable. She plays at being a grown-up but she's still a child in many ways.'[106]

Valerie Leon, who was the Sardinian hotel receptionist in *The Spy Who Loved Me*, appeared as the statuesque Lady in Bahamas who fished Bond from the sea. *Auf Wiedersehn, Pet* and *Raiders Of The Lost Ark* star Pat Roach, appeared as the formidable Lippe. Irishman Gavan O'Herlihy made a striking Jack Petacchi, Domino's brother. Manning Redwood and Billy J. Mitchell had brief roles in the film and future Eon Bond films. British character actor Ronald Pickup was amusing as Whitehall mandarin Elliot and veteran voiceover actor, Robert Rietty, appeared as an Italian Minister.

Schwartzman's rights entitled him to use the characters M, Miss Moneypenny as well as CIA operative Felix Leiter. Edward Fox was cast as M, whom Connery described as a deliberate contrast to the 'grey-type character Fleming created played by old Bernie [Lee].'[107] The head of the Double-o Section is now a health-obsessed technocrat. It was subtle touches such as these that Connery hoped would bring Bond up to date. He remarked, 'Look at Britain today, the Thatcher government is making all these cutbacks in government services. We've used all that kind of stuff in the script and it's given the film a new edge.'[108] Miss Moneypenny was played by Pamela Salem, who had previously appeared with Connery in *The First Great Train Robbery* (1979). She recalled, 'I had seen Moneypenny before, of course, in the earlier films played by Lois Maxwell, at first they tried to stir things up between us, [but] it was absolute nonsense and Lois did write me a very nice letter.'[109] Bernie Casey was cast as the first black Felix Leiter. Peter Janson–Smith, director of Glidrose Productions Ltd (Ian Fleming's literary copyright holder), expressed his displeasure, 'It's extraordinary to change Leiter's colour. I would like to know how many black men there are with a mop of straw-coloured hair.'[110] Interestingly, stage actor Alec McCowen was cast as Algernon the Armourer – a new spin on Q. Again, playing towards the Zeitgeist, upon seeing Bond in his workshop, the jaded civil servant mutters, 'Good to see you Mr. Bond. I hope we are going to see some gratuitous sex and violence.' Following a brief pause Bond replies, 'I certainly hope so too.'

Irvin Kershner was supported by a seasoned team of British technicians. Like Kershner, cinematographer Douglas Slocombe, had recently completed a George Lucas project: *Raiders of the Lost Ark* (1981). Slocombe was personally chosen by Connery, the actor said he gave *Never Say Never Again* 'prestige and substance.'[111] The late Slocombe recollected that Kershner 'was a nice man to work with but I don't think he himself was very happy on the movie. It may have been to do with his relationship with the production people.'[112] The film was designed by Stephen Grimes, who, ironically, had been commissioned by Kevin McClory when he was working on the original Bond project with Fleming to produce a series of art drawings to raise interest in their proposed Bond script. Displayed at the 1959 Venice Film Festival, Grimes's art was the first visual reference of what a potential James Bond film could look like.[113]

With two James Bond films scheduled to head into production, the international media were ready to play Sean Connery and Roger Moore off each other in the Battle of the Bonds. Connery met with Roger Moore in London while *Never Say Never Again* and *Octopussy* were in production. Connery reflected, 'In a sense though it's a no-win situation, because we both lose because we're both being set up against each other.'[114] Connery joked he could even find a role for Moore in his picture, 'It was going to be the punch [line] at the end. I was going to be coming down Piccadilly with Kim Basinger [and] she was going to react to somebody she passed and I looked round and it would be Roger who would say "Never say never again."'[115] Broccoli scotched speculation that Connery could appear with Moore in *Octopussy* saying, 'That was only a rumour. They are both better actors than most people give them credit for.'[116]

On 27 September 1982 cameras began rolling in the South of France. It was the film that even the official publicity notes described as one 'nobody believed could ever be made'. On the first day of production, Sean Connery arrived on set to a round of applause,[117] slipping himself back into the role of James Bond by filming a typically Bondian scene inside the casino in Monte Carlo.[118] A motorbike chase in which Bond pursues Fatima Blush at high speed was filmed through the tiny fishing towns along the French Riviera while Villa Rothschild served as the interior of Largo's exotic Middle Eastern home, Palmyra.[119] In the harbour of the small fishing village of Villefranche, *Nabila*, the floating palace belonging to billionaire Adnan Khashoggi (who a decade earlier had briefly been in the running to purchase Harry Saltzman's stake in James Bond), served as Largo's yacht, *The Flying Saucer*.[120]

However, almost immediately the screenplay was plagued with problems, according to Connery 'We'd invented stuff to use in the film to the point where the script was wandering all over the place.'[121] Major rewrites were undertaken by Dick Clement and Ian La Frenais who were flown out to Nice three weeks into production.[122] Kershner complained he had no support from Schwartzman, 'In fact he stayed away from the set. He never showed up. It's pretty convenient, because you can't be responsible if you are not around. It's a good tactic.'[123] As the film slipped behind schedule, Schwartzman threatened to ask the representative from the completion bond company to fire Kershner.[124] Connery was furious, 'Schwartzman was totally incompetent, a real ass. In the middle of everything, he moved to the Bahamas with an unlisted number. It was like working in a toilet … I should have killed him.'[125]

According to Dick Clement, Schwartzman was terrified of Connery,[126] 'We were in on all these arguments down in the Bahamas where there were people arguing about the script and Sean saying, "This is such a Mickey Mouse outfit." It was extremely tetchy and extremely tense.'[127] Every time either Connery or Schwartzman entered the room the other would leave.[128] Months later in London, Ian La Frenais witnessed further dramas when, 'One night I had dinner with Sean and Irvin Kershner at Langans. Suddenly Talia [Shire] appeared and said, "Why are you treating my husband like this?" She was very emotional.'[129]

As Kershner prepared to shoot the motorbike chase, the Yamaha that had turned up on set was not finished to the agreed specification. Originally it was to sprout wings when propelled by the rocket launchers,[130] 'The night before they wheel it out of this truck. I said, "show me how the wings work." [They responded] "Well, er, they were cancelled." "What do you mean they were cancelled?" "Well, somebody in the office said don't bother with them. Too expensive." Nobody told me.'[131]

In mid-November 1982 the main unit moved to the Bahamas[132] joining the underwater unit who were already at work. When Kershner viewed early rushes he deemed much of the material with Connery's double unusable. He had requested the production office send photographs of Sean Connery's body to the Bahamas so they could recruit a diver with a similar physique,[133] 'I said, "Wait a minute where is Sean?" They said, "That's him!" I said, "No, no, no, that's a young man with a thin body!" They had shot thousands of feet underwater, I don't know maybe a million dollars worth. I went crazy.'[134] Kershner was dismayed to learn the reference pictures of Connery were from *Thunderball*. He recruited a member of the diving unit who had a likeness to Sean and the material was re-shot.[135]

The underwater sequences were supervised by Ricou Browning, who had worked on *Thunderball* eighteen years earlier. A complex sequence involved Bond being chased through a shipwreck by sharks, attracted by a homing device Fatima has discreetly attached to his scuba tank. The action was filmed just yards from the Vulcan bomber still sitting on the ocean floor after the making of *Thunderball*.[136] Art director Les Dilley supervised the preparation of a 100ft cargo boat that was realistically aged and then sunk half a mile from shore.[137] Filming in confined spaces inside the wreck with 8ft tiger sharks proved dangerous. Although anchored by their tails to keep them at a safe distance from the crew, one attacked the camera and attempted to eat it.[138] Due to the lack of inactivity, a number of sharks died from oxygen deprivation. The handler removed a set of teeth from one shark and gave one each to the crew as a souvenir.[139] Sean Connery joined the unit for two days.[140] He recalled, 'I was very, very nervous about going under. I was getting through twice as much air as everybody else. The place was covered in bubbles because I was panicking all the time. In the film there is a certain note of panic in my eyes.'[141] Later, following a screening of the footage in Nassau, Connery commended Ricou Browning via telegram, congratulating the unit on the shark chase.

The opening training exercise sequence set in a luscious jungle was filmed in the centre of New Providence[142] with future Eon second unit action director Vic Armstrong doubling Sean Connery. Armstrong swung down the side of a building, through Venetian shutters and let out a burst of machine-gun fire. His wife, Wendy Leech, daughter of veteran Bond stuntman George Leech, played the deadly damsel waiting to knife Bond in the heart as he releases her from her captives. Other scenes shot on the island included Bond's first meeting with the fiery Fatima Blush, as she skis out of the water, crashing into Bond as he sips a martini outside the British Colonial Hotel.

Production was completed back at EMI Studios in Elstree where Steven Grimes built an elaborate cavern and exotic temple. However, a significant amount of the film was shot on real locations.

Two distinguished country homes in England rounded off location work. Waddesdon Manor doubled for the interior of the Monte Carlo casino where Largo challenges Bond to a dual beyond the croupier tables with a holographic arcade game called *Domination*. It was Schwartzman's idea that 007 should be introduced to the world of video games, 'By now baccarat and *chemin de fer* were passé in Bond movies; we wanted to update what Fleming had originally conceived.'[143] Initially the filmmakers discussed the concept with game companies, Atari and Mattel, but neither came up with ideas that satisfied Kershner.[144] Relying on 3D holographic images and coloured light patterns projected onto the actor's faces, visual effects supervisor David Dryer 'spent about three solid days fleshing out the premise and embellishing the game,'[145] which transmitted electronic shocks through the joystick to the loser.[146] Dryer wanted the game not to have a futuristic space-age look, but instead used an unobtrusive mahogany gaming table in which the screens and joysticks emerge from hidden compartments. He commented, 'Everything we did in that sequence was to be an extension of Largo's personality.'[147]

Meanwhile Luton Hoo doubled for Shrublands health farm. Actress Prunella Gee, who played Bond's physical therapist, Patricia, recalled that even at this late stage in production the unit seemed always to be in chaos, 'The schedules were up the creek and there were people everywhere. [Connery] was going back to his hotel to work on the script at night.'[148] Later, Connery would find himself returning to the Bahamas to shoot additional material.[149]

Second unit work was completed in Spain, including one crucial shot of Bond and Domino leaping 40ft from the battlements of Largo's Palmyra into the ocean below on horseback. The stunt had been attempted in the Bahamas but the stunt team could not find a harbour deep enough to ensure that the horse would not hit the bottom.[150] Doubling once again for James Bond was Vic Armstrong, who recalled the worst part of the stunt was not the jump but the holidaymakers who booed and hissed at the production unit, protesting at the cruelty of it.[151] He explained, 'The horse was perfectly safe. We'd done all the precautions, given him endurance training so he had enough energy to swim properly.'[152] As Armstrong prepared to take the leap he said, 'I just hope the horse doesn't flip over. I wouldn't like two tons of horse on top of me.'[153] He need not have worried as by the time Armstrong surfaced, the horse was already ashore.[154]

Never Say Never Again was still having screenplay problems in post-production. Dubbing editor Norman Wanstall, who had been lured out of retirement for the film, reflected that there were times when 'we were putting extra lines on the backs of people's heads in an attempt to explain the plot.'[155] Wanstall confessed nobody found the assembled footage spellbinding.[156] When screening it for Clement and La Frenais, Wanstall remembered, 'By the time the lights came up they were asleep.'[157] Connery recalled that they had a lot of material and the first cut came in at three hours, 'That meant losing a lot of stuff and having Ian La Frenais and Dick Clement come in to write "bridges" to the scenes.'[158]

The film was scored by the triple Academy Award-winning French composer Michel Legrand. Schwartzman had originally sought James Horner, but Connery had turned him down in favour of the Frenchman.[159] Kershner recalled that Horner was in fact unavailable and Legrand's name had surfaced during one of his regular dinner dates with Barbra Streisand. The actress had been in London for post-production on *Yentl* (1983) for which Legrand had composed the score. 'She said, "Why don't you talk to him?" I talked to him and he was very eager to do it.'[160] Legrand had written the music for a previous Connery picture, *Robin and Marian* (1976), the story of an ageing Robin Hood co-starring Audrey Hepburn. His soundtrack was thrown out by director Richard Lester at the last minute and replaced with a John Barry score.[161] The composer reflected ruefully, 'Sean knew it and, for me in a certain manner, it was a way of taking revenge on Lester's film.'[162] Legrand pointed out that ironically *Never Say Never Again* shared the same theme as *Robin and Marian*. 'Can myths age?'[163]

A title song was the next task. Legrand collaborated with husband and wife lyricists, Alan and Marilyn Bergman following his collaboration with them on *Yentl* (1983) which ultimately garned them all an Academy Award. The trio had enjoyed an earlier Oscar win for their song 'The Windmills of Your Mind' written for *The Thomas Crown Affair* (1968) starring Steve McQueen. Like Legrand, the Bergmans had a history with Connery, having met him on a 1961 TV special as Alan recalled, 'We had known him for years.'[164] The title track was produced by famed musicians Sergio Mendes and Herb Alpert, who ironically had played a role in the score for the non-Eon Bond film, *Casino Royale* (1967). 'Never Say Never Again' was originally offered to Welsh power rock singer Bonnie Tyler, who had recently had huge transatlantic hits: 'I was so excited to be part of this. And then I listened to it and I was really deflated. There wasn't anything you could do with that song.'[165] After Tyler rejected the smooth jazz-infused track, Alpert turned to his wife, Lani Hall. Ironically, as part of Mendes' group, Brasil '66,

Hall had performed Dusty Springfield's Oscar-nominated song 'The Look Of Love', written by Alpert's friends, Burt Bacharach and Hal David at the 1967 Academy Awards ceremony.[166] Hall had misgivings 'When I saw that opening and I heard my voice, it didn't match for me. I didn't think the music was the right music for that particular opening.'[167] Interestingly, the studio commissioned Stephen Forsyth and Jim Ryan to write and record a song with minor soul act Phyllis Hyman. Forsyth asserted, 'Warner Bros informed our attorney that the song was to be used as the title song in the picture. However, shortly before its release, Warner Bros informed us that the song could not be used because Michel Legrand, who wrote the score, threatened to sue them, claiming that contractually he had the right to the title song.'[168]

In March 1983, after *Never Say Never Again* had wrapped production, the Ian Fleming estate, in a last-ditch attempt to halt the release of the picture, sought an injunction against the distribution of the film. They claimed it was an exploitation beyond the *Thunderball* remake rights. United Artists and Danjaq were reportedly financing the legal fight on behalf of the Fleming Trustees.[169] Broccoli said, 'The opera isn't over until the fat lady sings.'[170] Schwartzman retorted, 'We're just wondering if the fat lady hasn't already finished her aria.'[171] The English High Court refused to prevent the distribution of *Never Say Never Again*, ruling that the application was unduly delayed and it would be wrong to deny the release. The Fleming Trustees appealed but lost again in June.

On 6 October 1983 Mann's National Theater in Los Angeles hosted the world premiere of *Never Say Never Again*. The opening weekend gross of $9,725,154 was touted as the biggest autumn opening in motion picture history and the biggest Bond opening ever.[172] It was a huge critical and commercial success for those who had been waiting for Connery's Bond to return.

The four-month breathing space between the release of *Octopussy* and *Never Say Never Again* had been healthy for both pictures. Connery felt, 'It would have been stupid to bring them out at the same time. It could have dissipated both films.'[173] The star was vocal in the press about Broccoli's continued quest to ban the rival production. When Johnny Carson asked the first cinematic James Bond on his US chat show who had played the first James Bond villain, he jokingly replied, 'Cubby Broccoli'.[174] Sean Connery later reflected:

> There was a time when I had tremendous loathing for [Broccoli and Saltzman].
> But I don't see that much of them now. Cubby and United Artists have been
> quite relentless with the lawyers; they haven't won a round, but there's been an
> enormous amount of money and time spent. The intention really was to stop

the film *coming*. Now that they've had their innings, as it were with *Octopussy*, I can't imagine why they persist.'[175]

On 14 December 1983 *Never Say Never Again* premiered in the UK at Leicester Square's Warner theatre, in the presence of Prince Andrew. Connery attended along with his wife and brother Neil. Former Bond girl Barbara Bach and her husband Ringo Starr were also present. On stage at the National Film Theatre to promote the film's release Sean Connery did not hide his frustration and anger at *Never Say Never Again*'s troubled production:

> I hate parasites. I hate incompetence. There's nothing I like better than a film that really works, providing you don't have to deal with all the shit that comes afterwards in terms of getting what you are entitled to. But when you get into a situation where somebody who is totally incompetent is in charge, a real ass, then everything is a struggle. There was so much incompetence, ineptitude and dissension during the making of *Never Say Never Again* that the film could have disintegrated … What I could have done is just let it bury itself. I could have walked away with an enormous amount of money and the film would never have been finished. But once I was in there, I ended up getting in the middle of every decision. The assistant director and myself really produced the picture.[176]

Basinger championed Connery, 'If Sean Connery hadn't taken over, the film wouldn't have any chance at all. As it is, if it turns out to be great, it will be one of the biggest mistakes in the history of the industry.'[177]

Sean Connery felt the production 'hassles did leave me disillusioned with the industry for a while. I even considered writing a little book on it. But then I thought, "Why stir up all the aggravation again?" It's probably better left alone.'[178] Jack Schwartzman had an option to make further Bond films from Kevin McClory's rights.[179] Unsurprisingly, he declined, 'It was the first film I produced on my own. And I totally underestimated what I was getting into. There were substantial cost overruns – all of which came out of my own pocket – so, in effect, I paid the price for my own shortcomings.'[180]

Never Say Never Again was made for $36 million against *Octopussy*'s $27.5 million. Connery's return grossed $55 million in North America against *Octopussy*'s $67 million. Worldwide the film grossed an eventual $159 million against *Octopussy*'s $182 million. Financially, it is easy to see who won 'The Battle of the Bonds', but culturally both films have had an enduring legacy.

PHOENIX FOR THE FLAME

A VIEW TO A KILL

(1985)

FIGURES TO BE PROUD OF:

...007,

$26,215,319

& 265 HOUSE RECORDS WORLDWIDE.

UNITED KINGDOM
$6,458,290
NETHERLANDS
$2,451,656
SOUTH AFRICA
$1,301,889
SWEDEN
$2,005,059
ARGENTINA
$901,801

JAPAN
$5,950,757
HONG KONG
$2,063,305
TAIWAN
$1,504,019
SINGAPORE/MALAYSIA
$1,431,931
BRAZIL
$795,342

ALBERT R. BROCCOLI Presents
ROGER MOORE
as IAN FLEMING'S
JAMES BOND 007
A VIEW TO A KILL

United Artists

WATCH THE OPENING FIGURES ON GERMANY, FRANCE, AUSTRALIA, ITALY AND SPAIN.

n the two years it took to produce the fourteenth James Bond film Eon would endure two studio regimes. In February 1983 Frank Yablans became Kirk Kerkorian's latest mogul[1] before giving way to Alan Ladd Jr. in January 1985.[2] In an attempt to rewrite the rules of engagement, the former management played hardball with Broccoli over the budget of the next Bond film. John Glen was aghast:

> It progressively got worse. MGM brought some pretty rough characters in. They came over and gave Cubby a hard time. That I really thought was bad. A man that deserved so much respect was treated with so little respect. They were hatchet men – they had a brief to cut us down to size. At the time they were in [a] desperate plight financially. With United Artists, Cubby had carte blanche. We were all responsible people and these people knew that. When MGM came in. I can imagine a conversation where someone would say, 'We're not spending these millions, we've got to cut down.' Ours were really efficient productions and profitable. That was the irony.[3]

When he took over the studio Alan Ladd Jr. recalled, 'Cubby had a deal with UA. I sort of inherited it. I asked all the lawyers to leave and I just dealt with Cubby face-to-face.'[4]

After his Thalberg Award and *Octopussy* marking twenty-one years of continuous production, Cubby Broccoli was proud, 'To be quite honest the thing that gives me the most satisfaction is the financial success, which leads to making more Bond films. They're not looking for us to win any Academy Awards – a Bond audience isn't going to see an Academy Award picture, they're going to see *excitement*.'[5]

In 1985 Cubby celebrated an unsung hero of the Bond films:

> My wife is a writer and very little has ever been said about her contribution to the Bond films because she's never taken a credit of any kind. Dana and I have worked on the stories: when you get ideas at home, you bring them into the office. But she doesn't like to be quoted as being a writer, because there are more writers that contribute the story's final parts. Michael [Wilson] has come into his own now as a Bond writer.[6]

Not only would Wilson co-write the screenplay of the fourteenth James Bond picture, again with Richard Maibaum, but he would also be promoted from executive producer to co-producer.[7]

If any of the Bond films featured the DNA of Cubby Broccoli running through them, none did more so than *A View to a Kill*. The story evolved around his favourite pastime, horse racing. Christopher Walken, who would play the villain Max Zorin, remembered the producer would often discuss his thoroughbreds, 'I remember we were in a restaurant once, the bill came and he said, "You know how you say, 'I can't pay the cheque' in Italian?" and I said, "Ma fundz a lo", he thought that was amusing. He named one of his racehorses, "Ma fundz a lo".[8] Cubby's secretary, Janine King (who had married John Glen) recalled, 'If the Grand National or a big race was on, he would put a bet on for us girls in the office at Eon.'[9] Patrick Macnee who would appear in *A View to a Kill* remembered that his role as Bond's chauffeur, Tibbett, was originally written as a jockey, 'My dad was really quite a famous racehorse trainer, his name was "Shrimp" Macnee. I [first] met Cubby Broccoli at the Del Mar races in California.'[10] Cubby's beloved Rolls Royce Silver Cloud II, better known as CUB 1, would play a starring role in the film. Macnee was dressed identically to Cubby's own chauffeur, Jimmy O'Connell, who drove the Broccoli family around London in CUB 1 for many years.[11]

John Glen was asked to direct his third Bond film while *Octopussy* was in post-production.[12] He was grateful to Cubby for the opportunities given to him and while his fees rose with each film, finance was not his first thought. Glen did not 'wonder how much money am I going to get … but how much fun are we are going to have?'[13] Glen had some initial thoughts about his next Bond, 'We will try to use as much Fleming original material as possible, sequences that were not used for other films.'[14] He elaborated, 'It's a good situation with the short story, a spy ring in France, the motorcycle courier disappears. I'd like to get George MacDonald Fraser again for the script. I like his sense of humour. We'll continue the trend of getting back to the real Bond.'[15]

FROM A VIEW TO A KILL was published in the FOR YOUR EYES ONLY anthology in April 1960. Bond is tracked down in a Paris café by local Station F agent Mary Ann Russell, who drives him frantically through the French capital's traffic for a briefing. It seems motorcycle dispatch riders are being murdered and their secret documentation stolen in the forests near St. Germain. The papers belong to the Supreme Headquarters Allied Powers Europe (SHAPE). Bond investigates the scene and stakes out the location of the last kill. Incredibly, he discovers a Soviet base hidden in the natural surroundings, from which a small cell of assassins are operating, disguised as dispatch riders. Bond sets himself up as bait, and navigates the same path to draw out the cell. Noting he is followed by an identical rider on the deserted route, Bond kills his pursuer. Having observed the coded behaviour of the assassin, he tricks the group to reveal themselves and neutralises the unit, but not before Russell saves his life. The original title of the story – and the collection – was to be THE ROUGH WITH THE SMOOTH.[16]

Contemplating the source material, Michael G. Wilson said, 'For all practical purposes, we've been out of material for the past five films. We will bring in the occasional Fleming element from the books which haven't been used in the films. But that's not much help when you get down to basic plotting.'[17] Richard Maibaum described the Bond formula:

> The pattern of the story is the same. I think that is one of the attractions of the pictures. You have that engine working, the James Bond syndrome – with all the conspicuous consumption, the luxurious locales, the beautiful women, the larger than life villains. We've carried it much further than Fleming. Bond is absolutely devoted to serving Queen and country; he never questions what he does or the morality of it.[18]

Broccoli acknowledged, 'Let's face it, there's a *sameness* about James Bond that you can't escape, and there are certain threads that continue to keep Bond going.'[19] Roger Moore felt this was part of the appeal, 'It's exactly the same as a child wanting to hear a bedtime story and if you change a word or leave out a few lines because you think he's fallen asleep or you're bored and you want to get off to bed yourself, look out. We want the comfort of the sameness.'[20]

Wilson explained the writing process of *A View to a Kill*, 'We began by creating several different kinds of plots, which Dick and I worked on together after discussing them with Cubby. Once we had formulated the character of the principal villain and a plot to go with it, we began writing a treatment.'[21] Wilson drew unused ideas from previous Bond screenplays too, 'We've had stunts ratting in the back of our minds that we never got around to doing because they weren't suitable to the plot. The Eiffel Tower stunt was originally in a draft of *Moonraker*.'[22] In the past Tom Mankiewicz had mentioned a diamond butterfly pin that flies from the lady's chest, poisoning some hapless victim before returning gracefully.[23] It was another concept that was appropriated for the new plot.

Maibaum confessed to being like:

> Walter Mitty. I'm a law-abiding citizen and non-violent. My great kick comes from feeling that I'm a pro, that I know my job and that I have enough experience so that I can write a solid screenplay. Michael [Wilson] is very

receptive. He's the only man I've actually worked with on the Bonds. Other writers have come on before or after me but never with me until Michael. He has lots of ideas and we like each other, which always helps.'[24]

Wilson explained their partnership, 'Dick is very experienced in this field. The actual writing, we do separately, although we work together on revising the material. Sometimes he will lead off and write the first draft and I'll rewrite behind him; sometimes, it's the other way round.'[25] Glen considered Maibaum 'an old time Hollywood writer [who] was very, very good on structure.'[26] Both writers agreed devising the villainous scheme was what, according to Maibaum, 'drives us up the wall. It must be new and contemporary. It can't be small, it has to be of world-shattering proportions. It also must have a kind of underlying, sardonic humour to it.'[27]

Maibaum revealed that originally villain Max Zorin was going to 'manipulate Halley's Comet so it comes crashing down'[28] destroying Silicon Valley. Both were topical elements as the comet was due to be visible from Earth in 1986 and the emerging technology coming out of Silicon Valley was sparking the public's imagination. John Glen remembered, 'We were trying to think of a very unusual event. During our location [scout] in Silicon Valley we spent a lot of time in Berkeley University and at this top secret atomic establishment.'[29] Wilson, himself an electrical engineer, was a stickler for technical credibility, 'Our plots tend to be fairly realistic. We will never be believable though. This is a fantasy film. But within the terms of our genre, the reality we deal in, Zorin's plot is something that could almost happen. Everything from a geological standpoint is absolutely true.'[30] Wilson acknowledged the similarity of the plot with another superhero, 'Somebody told me this sounds like *Superman*. I didn't even remember it.'[31] In August 1984 the film was announced with the shortened title, *A View to a Kill*.[32] Maibaum said, 'All of us like the title, because it promises excitement and something violent.'[33]

In the pre-title sequence Bond retrieves a stolen microchip from the body of 003 in the frozen wastes of Siberia. Back at MI6, the recovered chip is proof that the Soviets have managed to duplicate Western technology designed to withstand an electromagnetic pulse caused by a nuclear explosion in outer space. Now, it is feared that the Soviets could develop other ways to defeat the West's electronic defences. Staunch anti-Communist Max Zorin has recently taken over the company supplying the innovative microchip. Bond attends Ascot Racecourse to observe Zorin and his girlfriend, May Day, whose horses are achieving miraculous victories. Bond then makes contact with trainer Sir

Godfrey Tibbett, who reveals Zorin has come under suspicion following his series of unlikely wins by his thoroughbreds. Bond travels to Paris where, over lunch in the Eiffel Tower, private detective Achille Aubergine is about to reveal how Zorin wins his races. He is abruptly killed by a poisoned prop butterfly wielded by a shrouded assassin. Bond gives chase but the killer – May Day – base jumps off the Eiffel Tower. Despite Bond's destructive pursuit through the Paris traffic, the assassin escapes. Bond in the guise of James St. John Smythe and Sir Godfrey as a chauffeur, visit Zorin's Chantilly chateau, where the industrialist is hosting a thoroughbred auction. There they discover how Zorin is using microchips and steroids to cheat at the races. Entering the story is the mysterious Stacey Sutton, who appears to receive a payoff from Zorin. Bond and Tibbett are then unmasked resulting in the latter's death. General Gogol appears briefly to admonish Zorin for the apparent death of 007. However, Zorin renounces his KGB ties, citing that he is too busy with his own Project Main Strike. In an airship above San Francisco, Main Strike is revealed to be Zorin's desire to head a cartel promising technological supremacy by wiping out the research and development capital of the world, Silicon Valley. Bond arrives in the US and, with the help of local CIA contact Chuck Lee, learns that Zorin is, in fact, a psychotic product of Nazi genetic experimentation. He was created by war criminal Hans Glaub, who, posing as Dr. Carl Mortner, master-minded the horse doping scam. In San Franscisco Bond crosses paths again with Stacey Sutton, who is revealed to be a State geologist. She is locked in corporate combat with Zorin regarding her father's legacy. Sutton had refused to accept Zorin's payoff for her shares in Sutton Oil, which Zorin has now taken control of. She and Bond join together to investigate Zorin and the dangerous pumping of seawater into pipelines near earthquake faultlines. Bond has a brief fling with former KGB flame Pola Ivanova, sent by Gogol to see what Zorin, their ex-agent, is up to. Zorin then frames Bond and Stacey for the death of a local politician but they defy his fiery trap inside City Hall and, after a hair-raising fire engine chase through the city, they travel to Main Strike Mine. Here, Stacey explains to Bond what Zorin is plotting: first, he will flood a series of mines with seawater, then, by causing an explosion large enough to rupture the San Andreas Fault, Silicon Valley will be washed away, seemingly by natural causes. Zorin will then watch the chaos unfold from his airship in the skies above.

After Zorin executes scores of his own workers and double-crosses May Day, she assists Bond to prevent catastrophe. Outraged, Zorin kidnaps Stacey, but not before Bond, clinging to a mooring line on his blimp, stages a rescue. Ensnaring the airship on the Golden Gate Bridge, Bond and Zorin duel to the death on the world famous landmark. Bond is tracked back to Stacey's house, where he and Stacey clean up a few details in a shared shower.

For once, Cubby Broccoli was not locked in a poker game of negotiations with his star. After *Octopussy*, Roger Moore confirmed his decision was quick, 'Yes, I think so, I was going to do the next one.'[34] In December 1983 he was seen to be in talks with Broccoli for his return.[35] Moore recalled negotiations were 'not between Cubby and I, but between agents and lawyers. My agent in America, David Wardlow, became involved and he did the negotiations towards the end.'[36]

Commenting on the heir apparent, Cubby's stepson, Moore observed, 'Michael was very quiet unlike some of the other writers. He obviously knows the character literally. He's been brought up with it from the time that Dana married Cubby.'[37] While Sean Connery's rogue Bond was still in theatres, it became known that Moore would return for a record seventh consecutive outing as 007. Moore still enjoyed the role, 'You can't be bored. You're up there being somebody else. You're James Bond.'[38] Moore's take on the character was unassailable and he later voiced his feelings about *Never Say Never Again*, 'I think the director, not being English, didn't understand what was happening in development of characters in terms of what is English and what is not English. Sean deserved better than that.'[39] Moore did try to effect a reconciliation between Connery and Broccoli:

> Cubby was rather upset that Sean was so – I don't know if 'unforgiving' is the word. Sean wasn't really ready to make friends with Cubby. I got them together – dinner at my house. I overheard Cubby saying, "Did you really say that if my brains were on fire, you wouldn't piss in my ear." And Sean said, "Not true Cubby, I'd piss in your ear any time!"'[40]

In casting Max Zorin, Glen was looking for 'a rather offbeat character.'[41] An initial inquiry went out to David Bowie who affirmed, 'Yes, I was offered that. I think for an actor it's probably an interesting thing to do, but I think for somebody from rock 'n' roll, it's more of a clown performance. And I didn't want to spend five months watching my double fall off mountains.'[42] Glen recalled:

> Sting was [considered]. He came in the office, we had a long talk about it. The trouble with pop stars is so many people depend on them for a living. They take six months off, all those people are going to be spinning their wheels. In the end the pressure counts and it never seems to happen.'[43]

The producers' eventual choice, was the Academy Award winning Christopher Walken, 'I was in [*Hurly Burly*] in New York. They sent me the script, it seemed like a good job. I knew there were lots of good reasons to do it. How many times does an actor get to be in a Bond film? That would be just fun to do that.'[44] Walken was a childhood fan, 'John Kennedy said that he enjoyed reading [the Fleming books]. They were out suddenly in paperback. I, of course, read them. When the first Bond films came, they made an enormous impression on everybody. I was in high school, I guess, when *From Russia With Love* came [out].'[45] While he did not base his appearance on that of Red Grant, Walken was a fan of Robert Shaw, 'I admired him so much anyway as an actor. In fact, I was part of a theatre company once that he was a star of.'[46] The actor understood his role, 'Max Zorin *is* a Bond villain. I was supposed to be some kind of mutant. Some sort of an invention of scientists; a genetically altered villain. So I had strange hair. But I was a Bond villain. That's special. You're certainly on some sort of list.'[47] The actor felt Bond was part of his childhood.[48] He even had another youthful connection with Bond, as he 'was a child performer'[49] and had starred with Roger Moore in the 1953 *Robert Montgomery Presents* episode of *The Wind Cannot Read*.[50]

In April 1984 Elvis Presley's ex-wife, Priscilla, was prevented from becoming a Bond girl due to her commitments to television soap *Dallas*.[51] This paved the way for actress Tanya Roberts:

I'd done a movie called *The Beastmaster [1982]* and I'd done the *Playboy* cover and [Cubby] saw me and he asked me to come over to an interview. I was just going off to Africa to do *Sheena Queen of the Jungle [1984]*. His daughter was there and Cubby was there. It was very short and he was very sweet and he just asked my schedule and said, "Fine" and that was that. It was that easy.'[52]

Afterwards, Roberts was doubtful, 'I thought, "Oh, God, every girl who has ever been in a Bond movie never has a career afterwards." My agent said, "Do it, do it!"'[53] Roberts felt, '[Stacey Sutton] was on her own and trying to protect what she had. She had a lot of chutzpah and I liked that about her.'[54] The actress was in demand, 'I didn't do much preparation because I was doing my other movie. I couldn't even go to the premiere of *Sheena* because I had to go right into the Bond movie.'[55] While Roberts did not discuss Stacey Sutton with the writers, she remembered, 'I discussed lots of other things with Richard Maibaum. He was a great writer. He was very humble, very sweet and very talented and very helpful.'[56]

New Wave singer Grace Jones was first suggested to the producers by Barbara Bach.[57] The singer, cast as May Day, had only recently ventured into acting but Glen felt, 'We always thought she would be a colourful character. To some extent, the part was written with her in mind. We managed to see some of *Conan the Destroyer* [1984] and were very impressed with her.'[58] Jones was closely involved with May Day's look:

It was a collaboration between my personal designer Azzedine Alaia and [costume designer] Emma Porteous. The film company liked my personal wardrobe. The look is something out of Walt Disney. May Day is a fantasy character. When I first did my make-up, I was afraid John [Glen] would think it was too strong but he loved it and even said that I should add more colour.[59]

Patrick Macnee starred as secret agent John Steed in *The Avengers,* a television contemporary of Roger Moore's Simon Templar. The pair would star together as Sherlock Holmes and Dr. Watson in the television film *Sherlock Holmes in New York* (1976). When Macnee met Broccoli at the horse racing in 1984 he recalled:

We knew each other largely from the fact that he'd filched Honor Blackman off us and put her in *Goldfinger* at very short notice, I may say. But I think he must have thought, 'Racecourse. His father was a trainer. Maybe.' Partly through my dear friend Roger Moore, it all worked out. He could get all the way from a jockey to Sir Godfrey – a really perfectly delightful part.[60]

Zorin was surrounded by some interesting minor villains. His chief-of-staff was Scarpine played by Belgian actor Patrick Bauchau. Scarpine is assisted by Jenny Flex, played by rising Irish star Alison Doody and Pan Ho played by Papillon Soo Soo. Willoughby Gray was Zorin's creator Dr. Carl Mortner and Manning Redwood, who had appeared in *Never Say Never Again,* was cast as Texan oilman, Bob Conley. Previous Bond girls Mary Stavin and Carole Ashby appeared as Commander Kimberly Jones in Bond's iceberg craft, and as Dominique the butterfly whistling girl, respectively.

Rounding off the cast was British Chinese actor David Yip. Michael Wilson recalled, 'We originally thought that since we were in the United States, we would use Felix Leiter. But then we thought since we would be in San Francisco, in Chinatown, it would be a good idea to use a Chinese American agent.'[61] Yip had recently starred in *Indiana Jones and the Temple of Doom* (1984) and joked that after Bond, he just needed a role in the next *Superman* film.[62]

John Glen reassembled his stock crew for the third time including director of photography Alan Hume, production designer Peter Lamont, special effects supervisor John Richardson and editor Peter Davies. Glen also used his full complement of action specialists including parachute artist, B.J. Worth, vehicle stunt arranger Rémy Julienne and ski maestro Willy Bogner. Glen, however, remembered having to let one Bond veteran down gently:

> Bob Simmons got to the stage where he was getting a little bit past it in terms of actively doing the stunts. I'd already discussed it with Cubby and Cubby looked at me and said, 'You'll have to tell him.' I'm talking to a legend and that was the hardest thing I'd ever done in my life. He was a wonderful horse-man, so I said, 'I'd like you to look after all the horses on *A View to a Kill*.' He did a fantastic job and he was happy to do it.[63]

Martin Grace was promoted to action sequence arranger and was grateful to be on the film, 'Coming soon after cheating death on *Octopussy* two years earlier. At that time, I was unaware that this highlight would be Roger's and my own swansong on the James Bonds.'[64]

Before production even began, disaster struck. On 27 June 1984 the 007 Stage burnt down following an accident on Ridley Scott's fantasy epic *Legend*. Seeing the smoke bellowing into the sky, Peter Lamont thought, 'Jesus Christ, it's either a big wood fire burning rubbish, or it's the 007 Stage.'[65] Lamont likened the sight to that of the infamous burning airship *Hindenburg*. When the smoke had cleared Lamont had just one question for Cubby, '"Do you or don't you want to rebuild the 007 Stage?" And [Cubby] said, "I do."'[66] Lamont was assisted by construction company Delta Doric and twelve weeks from the site being cleared and flattened, a new stage was built.[67]

That same month, production began on the pre-title sequence involving ski action shot in Iceland and Switzerland. Willy Bogner again came up with something innovative and was pleased:

> when some of the scenes I had written worked out. We used a snowboard – a new sport never used in cinematography. Bond escapes on a snowboard down a slope and across a lake while being chased by Russians, who sank when they hit the water. It was hard to do but came off very well.'[68]

This moment was accompanied by Gidea Park's cover of the Beach Boys' 'California Girls'. One stunt involved Bond escaped Siberian soldiers by leaping down a glacier on skis. Bogner explained:

> [Skier] John Eaves had to jump down a crevasse to get out of the line of fire, not straight down, but crisscrossing back and forth over the chasm. We had to use jackhammers to prepare ledges on each side of the crevasse for Bond to jump to. Our crew worked on it for five weeks, then suddenly a warm spell came and the glacier moved, widening the crevasse, so we had to abandon the idea and move up the mountain where it was colder. On the last day of the shoot, it went beautifully and we got the scene.[69]

On 1 August 1984 principal photography commenced on *A View to a Kill* with location work at Ascot Racecourse. The entire MI6 team, including Robert Brown reprising the role of M, Desmond Llewelyn as Q and Lois Maxwell as Miss Moneypenny were dressed to the hilt. It was widely anticipated to be Roger Moore's last Bond film and ultimately it was a valedictory appearance for Maxwell too, 'Moneypenny was the smallest part I'd ever played, but I looked forward to each film and seeing the same faces in the crew. I was very much the Queen Mum of the Bond set, and thoroughly enjoyed myself. I'm sorry it's all over in lots of ways.'[70] The actress remembered the moment she was told it was over, 'One night Cubby Broccoli phoned me and said, "I'm sorry, Lois, but we won't be using you in the next Bond film. I wanted to tell you myself, and didn't want you to just get a letter or hear about it in the press." That was very kind of him.'[71]

Later that month, the Bond crew moved to Paris. Walken warmed to Moore, 'I remember on the plane going over from London to Paris, Roger said to me, "Where shall we dine?" And I said, "I don't really know Paris." And he said, "Fouquets. We'll go tonight." And he and I went to dinner at Fouquets.'[72] While in the city the second unit shot an elaborate car chase involving Bond stealing a Renault 11 taxi as he pursues May Day. Rémy Julienne was on home territory:

> It was around 15 August, because Paris gets empty around this period. We had permission to shoot from 5am to 3pm, not a minute more, which was very complicated to do, because we had a car going at more or less 117km per hour. James Bond, who is chasing a parachutist who is coming down from the Eiffel Tower, has no place to pass. [Bond drives the stolen taxi up a ramp while] a bus passes underneath, and in perfect synchronisation, the taxi lands on the bus. It

is a really a matter of hundredths of seconds. It was really very, very difficult. To do this, we rented a part of the airport near Coulombiers to do all the tests. When we started to film it my son Michel was the driver. On the first jump he had a bad bounce, fell a little bit to the side, flipped over onto the roof and went sliding for over 80 meters. We had one spare car [and] re-did the stunt. It worked perfectly.[73]

May Day's jump from the Eiffel Tower was not without complications. Broccoli said, 'It was made from a height of only 800ft – which means your parachute has to open first time.'[74]

Concurrent with the Paris sequences, the crew moved to the Chantilly estate. Tanya Roberts considered the horse stables to be 'lovelier than most people's homes.'[75] The location helped Christopher Walken to get in character, 'My house was the chateau of Chantilly. They put you in those marvellous suits. Just walking around pretending to be a billionaire was kind of cute.'[76] Walken was fond of his 'wonderful, sidekick, cohort Grace Jones who was a lot of fun. I like her music. I remember that occasionally I'd go out with her, her hat would be so big, you couldn't really get near her.'[77] John Glen remembered, 'Christopher Walken was easy to work with. The biggest problem was finding him – he had a tendency to wander. We had to get a junior assistant to keep our eye on him all the time so you knew where he was.'[78] Roberts noted Walken 'was just a little offbeat as a character himself. He's a little unusual, without putting any stigma on it.'[79]

On the estate, Bond and Zorin face-off in a brutal, multi-rider steeple-chase. Zorin lends Bond a valuable thoroughbred, Inferno, with the promise if Bond beats him, he keeps the horse for free. However, the course is rigged and Inferno becomes drug-crazed due to Zorin cheating with his microchip-controlled hormones. Walken, did no actual riding, 'I'm not a horseman. I was born in New York City, [in the film] I'm really on this fake horse on a trolley.'[80]

In September 1984 all units moved to San Francisco where Rémy Julienne staged the fire-engine chase, 'The trucks were very special, they could be driven backwards, they had a separate cabin in the back. The truck is so long it can not take a turn very well, so you need to steer the trailer as well. We always filmed at night from 6pm to 6am.'[81] Tanya Roberts was required to drive the fire engine, 'It was a lot of fun. We had to do [bluescreen]. I couldn't drive in the streets.'[82]

Julienne faced unpredictable dangers on the streets of San Francisco, 'One moment, they tell us all to hide, so everybody hides. Afterwards they told us there was a mad American with a gun, who said, "James Bond, nobody can get him, I will!" So the police captured him.'[83]

In one sequence Zorin, May Day and his cohorts frame Bond for the death of Howe, Stacey's boss in City Hall. They then trap the pair in a lift and set fire to the building. Special effects supervisor John Richardson recalled:

> Originally when we started talking about the burning of City Hall in our office back in Pinewood, everybody assumed it would be a foreground model. I said, 'Why not do it for real?' They replied, 'Don't be ridiculous! They'll never let us set fire to City Hall.' 'Well, I can do it if they'll let us.' So we flew out and met with the mayor [Dianne Feinstein] and the city fire department and tried to convince them that I was intelligent and knew what I was doing. Ultimately, they seemed to accept that we could do what we said we could.[84]

By using controlled burners, smoke and gas, Richardson got the desired effect:

> It was one of those situations where we hadn't enough time to all get ready, but somehow we managed to scrape through. When it came time to shoot, we lit up the building and put it out about twenty-five or thirty times over three nights. Once you're rigged, though, it's no big deal to do it again and again. All the fire engines in the scene were real San Francisco Fire Department engines manned with real crews. We just made sure that some of them were actually coupled up to real hydrants so they could really put the fire out if necessary. I'm happy to say they didn't need to, but they had to pretend to put it out and I was forever rushing around screaming, 'Don't put water on the fire! You'll put it out!'[85]

It was no wonder that shooting throughout San Francisco had to be insured for $100 million.[86] Nevertheless, John Glen found normally inaccessible locations would often become available, 'It's a magic name, James Bond. Wherever you go, people's eyes light up.'[87]

By mid-October 1984 the unit returned to Pinewood. The lift fire was shot in the studio and Roberts remembered, 'That was pretty scary because that was real fire. That was pretty wild.'[88] She said of John Glen, 'He just told you where to stand, where your marks were. He wouldn't have discussions about character, he was more technical.'[89]

For her shower scene at the end, Roberts remembered Moore '[was] full of energy, laughing, because it was always more nerve-wracking for the woman than for the man.'[90] Roger Moore was honest about the reality of love scenes:

They always pick the coldest day of the year, and usually a Monday morning when the studio's been shut all weekend and the heat's been turned off, so you're freezing cold. And you've got sixty to a hundred people standing around and electricians up on the rail staring down. There's very little romance. If you can get really excited about doing that, you should be starring in blue movies.'[91]

In one scene Bond is memorably seduced by the muscular May Day. Roberts remembered, '[Grace Jones] brought a big black dildo. [Moore] was a little taken aback.'[92] Roger was not a fan of Jones's sense of humour:

Occasionally, I would have to unplug her cassette recorder. Such loud music. And that mad, hysterical laughter. Oh, I suppose she was a bit nervous of me because she was giving the odd interview where she was trying to point out that Hans, her boyfriend, would be far more suited to playing the role than myself. So presumably she was waiting for the day to arrive when I would read it and throw an axe at her. I had that as a sword of Damocles to hold over her head.[93]

Hans was the real name of Dolph Lundgren who had a small role in the film as KGB man, Venz. Walken remembered, 'They were both into kick boxing. She and I had had a kind of karate section in the movie and he was helpful in choreographing that.'[94]

Throughout, Tanya Roberts observed the young assistant producer, Barbara Broccoli, 'She worked very very hard. She was always keeping things together, organising things. She was really learning how to be a producer. Learning everything from her father, she was very close to her father. You knew she was going places.'[95]

The finale of the movie, Bond's duel with Zorin and his airship atop the Golden Gate Bridge, was one of the first things shot. Taking advantage of the Fuji blimp filming the Los Angeles Olympics in summer 1984, a skeleton crew were sent out to capture the actual airship approach the San Francisco landmark from a distance. Lamont explained that was why the Zorin Industries logo resembled the corporate green and red livery of Fuji.[96] Christopher Walken remembered, 'I've always loved airships, as kid you'd see them in the air. It was fun having my own in the movie.'[97] The final sequence was completed using a combination of stuntmen climbing on the real bridge and studio work consisting of models and Vista Vision plates. Various scale replicas of parts of the bridge were also built on the back lot at Pinewood.[98] Walken remembered it well, 'They had three different scales of that bridge. We were actually on a set doing that.'[99] While shooting the scene with Roger Moore, Walken exchanged notes, 'I fall off the bridge to my death. We were sitting around waiting for them to light it. He said to me, "Do you always die?" And I said, "Pretty much. In movies, I suppose the villain tends to die." And I was playing a lot of villains. I said to him, "You should play a villain, that would be very interesting. It would be so surprising to see you as a villain." He said, "I'd love to but nobody asks me."'[100] Zorin, fell to his death laughing to himself like a psychopath, as Walken explained, 'I was hanging there and I was about to fall off the bridge on to some mattresses. It struck me as funny, that's all. It wasn't so much the character as it was [me] laughing at his situation.'[101]

As filming neared completion at Pinewood, the production ran out of sets which temporarily shutdown the picture.[102] Over the Christmas period the new 007 Stage was readied.[103] Walken had a special vacation, 'I just loved Roger Moore, I still do. There was a Christmas holiday and he invited me to his house in Switzerland. I went and stayed with his family.'[104]

Lamont felt the Main Strike Mine set was compromised by the rebuilding of the stage and the shutdown:

> The whole premise of that set was that it was going to be a huge composite.
> We were actually going to flood it. Everything was in place to do it, but the
> Stage was going slower and slower [and] then they found there were some
> problems with the [water] tank. I remember we literally started moving parts
> of the set we were going to do there onto other stages.[105]

The finished mine chamber consisted of rail lines, streams, bridges, rolling stock, wooden office sheds, a myriad of tunnels and shafts all completely waterproofed to survive multiple floodings, and completed only two weeks behind schedule.[106] The mine itself was nowhere near the San Andreas Fault, but was actually in the Amberley Pit Museum in West Sussex.

On 7 January 1985, at a Pinewood press conference, the new structure was named after the film's producer. Master of Ceremonies, Roger Moore, cut the ribbon with the words, 'I suppose it's nothing to do with Cubby's girth that it is being called the Albert R. Broccoli Stage, it's because of the size of his heart.'[107] Christopher Walken remembered:

> It was enormous. It's probably the biggest soundstage I've ever been on. If
> you see that scene, you'll see me while I'm raking the machine gun around,

I'm laughing. That happened very spontaneously. It just felt absurd, standing there blasting away. It's almost like watching some sort of video game.'[108]

Moore expressed similar reservations about the scene.[109]

On 16 January 1985 Roger Moore completed his last scene as James Bond. He was not sentimental, 'I don't remember the day any more than on any other picture, just what wardrobe I was going to steal.'[110] After a little more than twelve years, Moore happily relinquished the role, knowing it was time for another actor to play Bond. In conversation with the authors in 2015 Roger Moore refuted allegations contained in Broccoli's posthumous biography about him being more difficult than Sean Connery[111] by the end of his reign as 007, 'I don't what tangent [Donald Zec] was wandering off on. No, it was incorrect.'[112]

Peter Davies was promoted to sole editor and John Glen was proud very little footage was wasted. One deleted scene was particularly amusing. When Bond is released from the French jail after 'breaking half of the Napoleonic code' chasing May Day across Paris, he collects his personal effects. These include a watch with a garrotte which Bond quips is 'from Russia with love'.

John Barry returned for scoring duties and by now, nobody did it better, as he explained:

From the outset, certain basic elements in the series became evident to me. The films put forth a kind of simple, almost endearing comic strip-attitude to danger, intrigue and romance. Chases are fundamental to the style of these films. Just as much as the elaborate and exotic locales. And the music *must* serve these elements accordingly. The main thing is to carry it off with style; don't belittle the subject matter or make it cheap, just give it a whole lot of style and make it sound like a million dollars.[113]

John Taylor, bass player in the world's hottest pop band of the period, Duran Duran, said, 'I dig James Bond to the point of obsession.'[114] Taylor proposed his band write the theme song to Cubby Broccoli in famous London eaterie, Langan's. In the words of the band's record label manager, Ray Still, 'John wouldn't have minded playing James Bond himself.'[115] Barbara Broccoli recalled targeting a specific demographic, 'We had a lot of elements in the movie that we thought would attract a youth audience, Grace Jones being one of the main things. Duran Duran were on the crest of a wave.'[116]

Lead singer, Simon Le Bon, recalled working with John Barry:

He didn't really come up with any of the basic musical ideas. He heard what
we came up with and put them into an order. That's why it happened so
quickly, because he was able to separate the good ideas from the bad ones.
And he arranged them. He has a way of working brilliant chord arrangements. Something which really made it work better.'[117]

Taylor recalled the song was written while the band were falling apart. Due to
their acrimony, John Barry got frustrated working with them. Eventually the
song was completed piecemeal in London and New York by famed producer
Bernard Edwards. Upon release, it was a US number 1 – a Bond first – fuelled
by a Bond spoof pop video set on the Eiffel Tower and directed by Godley
and Creme.[118] Christopher Walken was a fan, 'It's a good song. I remember at
the time I was living in London, I remember going to parties. It was a very
busy time. I got to know Duran Duran a little bit.'[119]

Maurice Binder created a fun day-glow on nude, ski-themed title sequence:

I try to do something that is new, different and exciting each time. I have little
sketches I make on a thematic basis. I'll go on the stage with these sketches,
the girls, the stuntmen. I will shoot sections. Sometimes I find if I run the
film backwards or upside down that the shot works better.'[120]

On 22 May 1985 the world premiére of *A View to a Kill* was held at the Palace
of Fine Arts in San Francisco to thank the city for its co-operation.[121] Mayor
Dianne Feinstein declared it to be 'James Bond Day'. The principal members of
the cast attended while B.J. Worth parachuted down to City Hall to present a
cheque for $100,007 to the Mayor's Youth Fund.[122] The after-party was held at
the Hard Rock Café. Throughout the event thousands of 'Durannies' – fans of
the band – screamed for their rock idols.[123] Those same fans made their voices
heard at the European premiére held on 12 June 1985 at London's Odeon
Leicester Square. Prince Charles and Princess Diana were in attendance.

The film was completely of the new earthy adventure style set by the team
in 1981 and the budget had been kept roughly the same for the third picture
running. While the worldwide gross would reach $161 million, a continuing
downward trend for the series, the film and Bond would still remain immensely
profitable – and entertaining – for all concerned. Any artistic clouds on the
horizon were burned away by box office gold.

Christopher Walken had enjoyed his time with James Bond:

It was very well made. The sets, the costumes, there was a lot of very good workmanship on those movies. On that film I was probably involved for longer than I was on most of the other movies that I've made. I had an apartment in London for that time.'[124]

The veteran actor explained, 'Making a movie is very family intimate, close things, you're with people every day, solving problems and so on. And then when a movie's over, everybody goes their own way.'[125] However, for most actors, the world of James Bond was also the world of the producers, 'The Broccolis get [together] a group of people and it works. [Cubby] was, that overused expression, larger than life, a big personality. He was very present, I remember that.'[126] Walken had fond memories, 'I have occasionally seen the Broccolis. Later on after I'd made the movie, I went to Barbara's wedding in Los Angeles in that beautiful home. They had beautiful paintings. And [Dana] was so interesting and beautiful, she wrote books.'[127]

The world of James Bond had, over the years, become the world of Albert R. Broccoli and he was grateful for his lucky streak, 'All producers or directors select a property and they like it. They also like to think that it's going to be a big success. We have plenty of optimism when we make a film, whatever it is.'[128] He remained enthusiastic too, 'I still love looking at the old Bond films. Maybe it's purely out of reminiscence for the nostalgic things you think about. But there were some very good films made. I can't really put my finger on a favourite. They were all good as far as I'm concerned: they helped keep us going.'[129] But Broccoli was always confident James Bond would return, 'As one goes to premiere we start preparing the next Bond.'[130]

Unlike Connery, Moore never felt 'bottled in Bond.'[131] The actor sought to:

get the fun out of it, let the audience know that if they want to scream hysterically, they can. My attitude is that it's completely unreal. Here you've got this secret agent who's recognised by every barman in the world and they know that he takes his vodka martinis shaken and not stirred. It's crazy. What sort of secret agent is that? So you know that it is a spoof already before you start. I don't like to play him as a true-blue hero. There's always a moment of doubt in Bond's mind. I mean, if I save the girl, I may get killed doing it. So I always let that go through my mind and then say, 'Oh, to hell with it, I've read the script. I know I'm going to live.'[132]

Moore wished any new incumbent in the role well. In 1985 he said of contender Pierce Brosnan, 'He'd be splendid, I'm quite sure.'[133] Roger Moore, his
eyebrow starting to rise, gave advice to the new Bond, 'Well, you have to be
prepared to get up early and say your lines and not trip over the furniture. And
you have to be prepared to answer questions with a smile on your face when
you're asked how your Bond compares to Roger Moore's.'[134]

However, Roger Moore's then-wife, Luisa made a very astute and prescient
observation, 'It's been said that any good-looking actor could play James Bond.
That's ridiculous. Roger made it look so easy only because he has the immense
talent and personality to do it. It's much more difficult to be Bond than anyone
can imagine.'[135]

The first Bond girl. Eunice Gayson as Sylvia Trench and Sean Connery as James Bond in *Dr No*. (Rex Shutterstock)

Above: Guy Hamilton, Roger Moore and Harry Saltzman taking a break from shooting *Live And Let Die*. (Bernard Vandendriessche)

Left: Ian Fleming, Shirley Eaton and Sean Connery chatting on the set of *Goldfinger*. (Rex Shutterstock)

Barbara Bach, Cubby Broccoli and Roger Moore on the supertanker set built for *The Spy Who Loved Me*. (Rex Shutterstock)

The Paris press conference announcing *Moonraker*. Cubby Broccoli, Roger Moore, Lois Chiles and Lewis Gilbert, August 1978. (Rex Shutterstock)

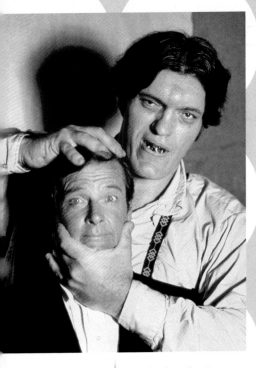

Roger Moore in the grip of Richard Kiel as Jaws during *Moonraker*. (Rex Shutterstock)

Roger Moore and Christopher Walken as Max Zorin share a joke on the set of *A View to a Kill*. (Rex Shutterstock)

Timothy Dalton and Maryam d'Abo at the October 1986 press conference announcing *The Living Daylights*. (Rex Shutterstock)

Cubby Broccoli in July 1988 on the first day of shooting *Licence Revoked*, later released as *Licence to Kill*. (Rex Shutterstock)

Pierce Brosnan announced as James Bond in London, June 1994. (Rex Shutterstock)

Remembering Cubby. Timothy Dalton, Roger Moore and Pierce Brosnan at Broccoli's memorial service in November 1996. (Rex Shutterstock)

hooting *Tomorrow Never Dies*. Pierce Brosnan as Bond and Michelle Yeoh as Wai Lin. (Rex Shutterstock)

Pierce Brosnan, Roger Moore, presenter Michael Parkinson, George Lazenby and Timothy Dalton at the BAFTA 40th anniversary celebration in 2002. (Sir Roger Moore)

Above: Barbara Broccoli and Michael G. Wilson revealing their new James Bond, Daniel Craig, in London, October 2005. (Mark Mawston)

Left: Halle Berry as Jinx in *Die Another Day*. (Rex Shutterstock)

Daniel Craig as James Bond in *Casino Royale*. (Rex Shutterstock)

Above: Daniel Craig presented to Queen Elizabeth II at the *Casino Royale* premiere in London, October 2006. (Rex Shutterstock)

Right: Roger Moore and Daniel Craig at the Ian Fleming Centenary Concert in London, October 2008. (Rex Shutterstock)

Daniel Craig as James Bond looking out over London at the end of *Skyfall*. (Rex Shutterstock)

Skyfall wins big. Bradley Cooper, Robert Wade, Sam Mendes, Barbara Broccoli, Michael G. Wilson, Neal Purvis and Ben Affleck at the BAFTA Film Awards, 2013. (Rex Shutterstock)

SPECTRE announced as the 24th Bond film at Pinewood Studios, December 2014. (Rex Shutterstock)

21

DOWN TO THE WIRE

THE LIVING DAYLIGHTS

(1987)

Licensed to thrill.

007

United Artists is proud to acknowledge its twenty-fifth anniversary with Eon Productions, Ltd.
And to announce principal photography has begun on the fifteenth James Bond Film.

JAMES BOND 007
THE LIVING DAYLIGHTS

Coming next summer from MGM/UA Distribution Co.

Yet again it was musical chairs at the studio. MGM/UA was sold to media mogul Ted Turner and then UA was hived off and sold back to Kirk Kerkorian.[1] In November 1985 independent producer Jerry Weintraub was recruited to head up production.[2] Cubby Broccoli noted wryly how the billionaires were trading vast sums and assets without having any feeling for the film business.[3]

The fifteenth James Bond film was scheduled for worldwide release in the summer of 1987, marking the silver anniversary of the franchise. On 15 September 1985 Richard Maibaum and Michael Wilson sat down to write *The Living Daylights*.

Maibaum recalled the scribes contemplated going back to the beginning:

About [that] time we were wondering whether we were going to have a new James Bond or not. We decided it might be interesting to have a story about James Bond's first mission and how he became the great 007. We wrote a treatment. I and Mike Wilson thought it was quite good. However, Mr. Broccoli, who has an uncanny appreciation of what audiences want, among his other great talents liked it; but he said the audience wasn't interested in Bond as an amateur – as a man learning his trade. They wanted to see James Bond in command of his full professional talents, and Mr. Broccoli said, 'Fellas, we've got to try again.' There was a lot of stuff in that we regretted losing – the whole business about James Bond as a young naval officer, a wild one that couldn't be disciplined, who was reminded by his grandfather that the family motto is The World Is Not Enough. Through a friend of the grandfather, he gets a chance to redeem himself.[4]

THE LIVING DAYLIGHTS was first published with OCTOPUSSY in June 1966. 007 is sent to Berlin to cover the expected escape of Agent 272. The escape has been tipped off to the KGB who will send their top assassin, Trigger, to try to shoot the agent in a narrow window of safety. Bond's mission is simple: to kill the assassin as they attempt to kill 272. Bond liaises with a testy agent, Captain Paul Sender, and waits out a claustrophobic three nights. During this time, Bond takes a shine to a beautiful blonde cellist playing in a female orchestra. On the last night, the escape occurs and Bond zeros his sights on the spot he has identified the KGB sniper will shoot from. Suddenly, Trigger appears and is revealed to be the female cellist. In an instant, Bond adjusts his aim and shoots to wound rather than kill her. This draws the ire of Sender, but Bond feels he has done his job. The wound will have scared 'the living daylights' out of Trigger. The title refers to the fact that the psychological scar left by her near death will end her effectiveness as a killer. Interestingly, Fleming's half-sister, Amaryllis was a famous concert cellist and features in the story as a Fleming in-joke. The story was originally published in the first edition of *The Sunday Times* magazine on 4 February 1962. A working title was TRIGGER FINGER and the story debuted in America as BERLIN ESCAPE.

Maibaum felt the short story was:

> very Bondian – a good springboard. He won't kill a beautiful woman for no reason at all. [But] how to make a good two-hour movie out this story? We had to ask ourselves, "Who is the woman?" One thing led to another and finally the movie's story began to evolve.[5]

By Christmas 1985 director John Glen had been hired to direct his fourth consecutive James Bond film,[6] 'We constrict ourselves to the style we have created. If we did something too different, or wrong, it would end the series.'[7] He added:

> The Bond films tend to have a style which is unique – very fast – moving through a tremendous amount of scenes. Bond action has had its imitators but the unique sense of humour has never managed to be copied. It's something very British, which is why Bond could never be anything other than English, but the films have never really been appreciated in the UK, and during British Film Year, we were never mentioned. We are always looking to film the impossible, and we feel we have to do that.[8]

Glen was keen for the films not to be too parochial, 'The character is so international in scope. We always have actors of various nationalities in the films and try to create plenty of non-verbal communication which makes it more accessible to other countries.'[9]

Michael Wilson reinforced the balance between art and commerce, 'We invariably aim to make stories and situations contemporary, with plenty of jokes. But we try to maintain a degree of subtlety and sophistication. We've tried to stay in tune with the concerns of the time.'[10] Maibaum felt 'that real events were overtaking us. The whole thing suddenly exploded on the front pages with Irangate and we found ourselves with a very hot scenario. Most people, of course, will think we decided on the story after the fact.'[11]

By February 1986 locations were being scouted and a treatment produced.[12] John Glen recounted the influence of his travels:

I had spent a holiday on Gibraltar, many years before with a friend who worked for the war department. I was able to go and see all these fantastic places, which a tourist wouldn't be allowed to see, such as the inside of the rock – which is honeycombed with passages and reservoirs, hospitals and ammunition stores. When we came to make *The Living Daylights* someone suggested we write a sequence involving a NATO exercise that goes wrong. I had been on one of these paint-balling trips so I adapted that idea and developed the sequence with my knowledge of Gibraltar.[13]

Glen also remembered how the Tangier home of billionaire Malcolm Forbes, a friend of Cubby's, inspired the villain, 'He had this beautiful villa, which he kindly allowed us to use. We made Whitaker play war games with toy soldiers because Forbes had all these fantastic toy soldiers and we wrote them into the film.'[14] Peter Lamont recalled, 'Tom Pevsner and I flew out to Munich very early on and went ice yachting in [Weissensee, Austria]. Originally it was going to be an ice yacht chase rather than a car chase.'[15]

The Living Daylights is a complex, topical caper. American Brad Whitaker is in league with Soviet General Georgi Koskov. Koskov is ostensibly negotiating to buy arms for use against the Mujahedin in Afghanistan to secure the Soviet presence there. A down payment of $50 million of Soviet funds is made in secret accounts to Whitaker. The money is intended for use to purchase hi-tech arms from Whitaker but he purchases diamonds instead. These are then smuggled to Afghanistan. The diamonds are used as currency to buy raw opium from unscrupulous Afghan drug lords of the Snow Leopard Brotherhood. This opium is then to be quickly processed into heroin and sold in the West, converting $50 million of Soviet funds to $500 million in drug profits. Part of these proceeds will go to buy the arms for the Soviets pursuant to the original deal. The rest of the profit is shared between Koskov and Whitaker and to fund revolutionaries led by Necros, their junior partner who has an uncanny ability to mimic voices.

Whitaker fronts the money to buy Koskov's girlfriend, innocent cellist Kara Milovy, a Stradivarius cello named The Lady Rose. This big sting is obviously bad news for the West (a huge influx of heroin) and the USSR (leading to a Soviet Irangate of their own). Such an action could destabilise the superpowers drastically. Leonid Pushkin, the new head of the KGB following General Gogol's promotion, is suspicious of Koskov and Whitaker and has started to investigate them. Pushkin has to be stopped. Resurrecting *Smiert Spionam*, 'Death to Spies', an old Beria assassination programme, Koskov uses his KGB contacts to infiltrate an SIS training exercise in Gibraltar, causing mayhem, killing 004 and thus announcing the programme to SIS and embroiling 007. The validity and presence of *Smiert Spionam* has to be made known to the British and in particular their Double-0 Section. Koskov knows James Bond 007 by reputation and specifically requests him to assist in his defection. This takes place in Bratislava and is overseen by the officious Saunders of Section V, Vienna. Hoping Bond will shoot to kill, Koskov sets up his girlfriend Kara Milovy as the KGB counter-defection assassin. Milovy has become excess baggage and can link Whitaker and Koskov and their plans. Her presence will add validity to Koskov's fake defection and her death, at the hands of 007, will tie off loose ends for Koskov. Once Bond has killed Kara, Koskov will brief SIS about *Smiert Spionam* and persuade them to ensure that Pushkin be 'put away'. Koskov will be snatched back (seemingly by the Soviets), adding weight to the imperative to SIS to kill Pushkin. Bond will be licensed to kill Pushkin, and in doing so, thereby stopping *Smiert Spionam* and, conveniently, Pushkin's investigation into Whitaker's and Koskov's misuse of state funds. Upon his return to the Soviet fold, Koskov's defection can be explained as a misinformation initiative of Pushkin's (who will no longer be around to verify this). With no Soviet investigation pending, Koskov and Whitaker can continue, unfettered.

Bond decides in a split second not to kill Koskov's defection-preventing assassin when he targets her. Thus 007 unwittingly unravels Koskov's precariously calculated plan. 007 shoots Kara's gun from her hand in an effort to 'scare the living daylights out of her'. Bond then romances Milovy in Vienna to get her to lead him to Koskov. Tracking him down to Tangier, Bond arranges the fake assassination of Pushkin to provoke the villainous duo's next move. Koskov dupes Milovy into drugging Bond. They are both then taken to Afghanistan to receive Soviet justice. However, Bond and Kara escape the Russian airbase but not before freeing local Mujahedin leader Kamran Shah.

Whilst the film featured one leading lady, there were a number of other interesting female roles. These included Linda, a bored bikini-clad playgirl portrayed by Kell Tyler, Rosika Miklos, Bond's Czech contact filled by rising British TV star Julie T. Wallace, Virginia Hey as Pushkin's companion, Rubavitch, and future supermodel Waris Walsh as a Morrocan girl. Catherine Rabett, former girlfriend of Prince Andrew, and *Grange Hill* star Dulice Liecier played CIA agents Liz and Ava respectively. They assist Felix Leiter, yet again recast, this time essayed by a younger actor, John Terry.

When informed of the plot to use hi-tech arms against his freedom fighters, Shah arranges an assault on the Russian airbase. Bond takes control of a transport aircraft containing the drugs and after a mid-air fight hanging off a cargo net, kills Necros. The essential conceit of the short story remained intact and another Fleming element, *Smiert Spionam* (the motto for Bond's early Soviet opponents SMERSH), is used.

While the screenplay was being written – with no particular actor in mind – the immediate problem was to find a new James Bond. There was no shortage of suggestions to secure the services of diminutive Australian star Mel Gibson. Weintraub suggested a two-picture deal for $10 million,[16] but this was too rich for the Eon pocket.

In early 1986, actress Maryam d'Abo recalled 'feeding lines to the actor Lambert Wilson, who was auditioning for the role [of Bond] at Pinewood Studios.'[17] The scenes used to test actors were the execution of Professor Dent and Bond seducing Tatiana Romanova.[18] The list of hopefuls included Finlay Light, Andrew Clarke and Trevor Eve.[19] Sam Neill, who had played real-life proto Bond, Sidney Reilly, was a favourite among the decision-making team except Cubby Broccoli.[20]

Pierce Brosnan had been the obvious Bond, waiting in the wings. Speaking to the authors from his home in Malibu, three decades later, the actor had a somewhat philosophical recollection of the casting process. Brosnan remembered going down to Pinewood to shoot extensive screentests:

> It was a heady experience, what can I say, it was a great opportunity and one that I revelled in and then to get the role, so to speak, to have this Bond being offered to me was a game changer. As far as I was concerned this was it, I'd been to America, I'd done a television series which had been successful and it seemed just like the logical next step that I should go off and be a movie star and play James Bond. That was my reckoning and thinking. Everything seemed to be in line for that to happen. Unfortunately, [NBC Universal] had me in a contract where they had a sixty-day clause in which they could re-sell the show *Remington Steele*. So during that time, the sixty days, I'd already done the screentest, I'd been accepted. *The Living Daylights* sat on the bedside table and I would open it occasionally and say, 'The name's Bond, James Bond'. But I didn't read it because I thought I'd wait for the ink to dry on the contract before I really started preparing, I didn't want to tempt fate as it were. In those sixty days I did the wardrobe fittings, I met with Cubby, had photographs taken – Cubby and I standing outside the James Bond sound stage, standing before his Rolls Royce. The sixty days rolled on and we were assured I was going to do it and Cubby said to MTM and NBC, 'Look, you can have him for six episodes but no more than six episodes, then he's mine.'

And they said yes and they prevaricated and on Day 58, everything was good. On Day 60 – we were living in Malibu Colony – it was about six o'clock in the evening and I went to the kitchen and I opened up a bottle of Cris Rose champagne, I was walking out with it and my late wife Cassie was sitting on the deck and just as I was walking out the phone rang and it was my agent, Fred Specktor, and he said, 'I'm afraid all bets are off. They want the option of twenty-two episodes and Cubby Broccoli will not go for that.' So in that one phone call and walking out with the bottle of Cris Rose to celebrate, I was no longer James Bond.'[21]

Broccoli did not call to commiserate.[22] Brosnan was deeply affected:

It was such a terrible blow; it was such a shock because your life is going in one direction and in just a phone call it's completely changed around. I went and I did the six episodes of *Remington Steele* and then they cancelled the show. So they got their pound of flesh and you get on with your life. I do remember seeing billboards for Timothy in *The Living Daylights*. It had a delayed reaction, I think, for about six months or so. When Timothy came out in the movie the full impact of it and onslaught of what had happened really came crushing in. One day I was driving down through Beverly Hills and by the time I got to the beach, I had to pull over to the side of the road and scream at the seagulls.[23]

Richard Maibaum felt, 'Pierce would have been more like Roger. But we didn't really make any changes for Roger, either. It's just that he saw Bond in a more humorous fashion than Sean did and was very successful at it as the box office shows.'[24]

Timothy Dalton had been approached to play the role in the past but the approaches had come to naught. It was Dana Broccoli's suggestion to try him again and the Broccolis met Dalton for drinks in the Dorchester.[25] He recollected the most recent approach:

this last spring '86, when it seemed this time that it probably was true that Roger Moore was no longer playing James Bond. Again Mr. Broccoli very kindly said, 'Was I interested?' I couldn't, I was busy, I was doing two plays in the West End with Vanessa Redgrave, *Antony and Cleopatra*, and *The Taming of the Shrew*. The schedules just clashed so that was that. And then at some point later on their schedule got delayed, and I became free.[26]

Dalton tested for the role[27] and remembered the moment when he finally accepted Broccoli's offer as he sat in a departure lounge waiting to catch Concorde to begin filming the television film *Brenda Starr*.

> Without anything to do, I decided to start thinking about whether I really, really should or should not do James Bond. Although obviously we'd moved some way along in that process, I just wasn't set on whether I should do it or shouldn't I do it. But the moment of truth was fast approaching as to whether I'd say yes or no. And that's where I said yes. I picked up the phone from Miami airport and called them and said, 'Yep, you're on. I'll do it.'[28]

When he accepted the part, Michael Wilson offered the actor some counsel at his Hampstead home, warning Dalton of the need to promote the film and the immense publicity whirlwind he was about to enter.[29] It was reported that he would receive £500,000 for his performance.[30] On 6 August 1986 Timothy Dalton was announced to the world as the fourth James Bond. However, he was in Puerto Rico filming *Brenda Starr* and could not attend any press launch. Maibaum approved of the casting, 'I've been feeling for some time that we've been getting a little too far out. I happen to think that Timothy Dalton gives us a new lease of life. We can go back to the more realistic espionage stories rather than the far out fantasy tales.'[31]

Later, Dalton was pragmatic about whether he'd become known, predominantly, for James Bond:

> If I produce another play, it will probably put more bums on seats. I don't think it's a trap, it might be, it could be, but I've found that all the things that I've been asked to do since making this movie, have actually borne no resemblances whatsoever to [Bond].[32]

While promoting his debut Bond film, Dalton conceded:

> I'm probably getting more scripts in through the letterbox and they're terrifically varied in their nature. You know they're not spy stories, there's not one character that's remotely like a James Bond character, so any idea of people asking me to do things that are similar doesn't seem to be the case at the moment.[33]

Dalton was a student of the Bond books:

Fleming was extremely clever, he gave him certain qualities, characteristics, we know a lot of the things he did, but he didn't actually really define the man too much, which of course gave everybody the opportunity of identifying with him on these great sagas that he undertook, fighting off his personal dragons of evil or the world's visions of evil. So I wouldn't really describe him, I'd say I hope I've done that best in the film.[34]

Dalton was anxious to:

Make [Bond] human. He's not a Superman, you can't identify with a Superman. You can always identify with the James Bond of the books, he's very much a man, and a tarnished man really, he's not perfect. I wanted to give him variety. I wanted to capture that occasional sense of vulnerability, and the sense that you could be allowed inside him, but there was something that was in there that you wanted to perceive, that that kind of man must have, and I wanted to capture the spirit of Ian Fleming.[35]

John Glen recalled Dalton had a clear vision of the new James Bond's appearance, suggesting he wear a black leather jacket for certain scenes:

Tim's input began with the first wardrobe meeting: where Bond wasn't wearing the obligatory tux, he wanted a more casual look, perhaps more in keeping with the times. I remember he told me he felt he should also act in a more casual manner and occasionally put his hands in his pockets. I was very much against this ... Tim didn't agree with me, but he respected what I was saying and went along with it for the most part.[36]

Joe Don Baker had been a favourite of the Broccolis since his appearance in acclaimed BBC mini-series, *Edge of Darkness* (1985). He was cast as Brad Whitaker, West Point cheat and self-styled general of his own private army. He described his initial days filming *The Living Daylights*, 'When I first arrived in Tangier, I felt a bit like an outsider – but they're all very nice people and Albert Broccoli is the father of the family, looking after his children.'[37] Baker explained his process, 'My job is to create the character and make him really dangerous but believable. The trick with playing the villain is to sit back and think of all the awful things you could be.'[38]

Jeroen Krabbé, up for the role of villian Koskov, remembered:

I was called to a meeting at Eon Productions. There, behind a table, was Cubby, casting director Debbie McWilliams, Barbara Broccoli and Michael Wilson. It was like appearing in front of a jury. They had seen my first English movie *Turtle Diary* [1985]. Cubby was not really convinced I should get the part so he said 'What else can I see?' 'Just Dutch movies,' I told him. Following the meeting Barbara, Debbie and myself went for lunch. I was so nervous I ate two large portions of wild strawberries. Afterwards I walked back to my agent Jeremy Conway's office and he had just hung up the phone. He said, 'You have the part.' I jumped in the air I was so overwhelmed. I have been a Bond fan ever since they started making the films. When I read the script I thought Koskov was a wonderful role. I said, 'Do you want him to have a strong Russian accent?' [John Glen] said, 'No, no a very light accent.'[39]

Following her screen test duties for potential Bond actors, Maryam d'Abo made a film in Germany, *Laughter in the Dark* (1986), which was never completed. She recalled:

I came back to London in the summer of 1986 and bumped into Barbara Broccoli at a health centre in the West End. She didn't recognise me as I had had my hair cut short. They hadn't cast the leading Bond girl yet. Not long after, my agent said Eon wanted to see me. At this time Pierce Brosnan was supposed to be playing Bond. Coincidently, United Artists had seen material from *Laughter in the Dark* and without knowing Eon had met with me, mentioned to the Broccolis they should consider me for the role of Kara Milovy. I got the part! I always imagined Bond girls being 5ft 10in sirens and I certainly didn't see myself like that. So for me, it was extraordinary that I ended up being in a Bond movie.[40]

d'Abo had first entered the world of Bond in 1984 when she screentested for the role of Pola Ivanova in *A View to a Kill*, but the part eventually went to Fiona Fullerton. 'I remember it involved a seduction scene in a hot tub and I wasn't at all comfortable with that!'[41]

Thomas Wheatley was cast as MI6 agent Saunders, head of Station V in Austria. Wheatley was new to screens as he recalled:

My first piece of television, *Honest, Decent and True*, aired in February 1986 and was seen by Bond casting director Debbie McWilliams. I do recall telling one story to Cubby. After leaving the University of Oxford I had flirted with the idea of a career in intelligence. I had two informal meetings at anonymous and peculiar addresses in London with MI6. On one of those occasions this chap leant forward, looked into my eyes and said, 'Our business Mr. Wheatley is the exploitation of human weakness.' Cubby said, 'We gotta get that line in the film!' I said, 'You can't, you can't, I've signed the Official Secrets Act!' I was offered the role later that afternoon.[42]

With the new James Bond came a new Miss Moneypenny, played by 25-year-old Caroline Bliss, who had portrayed Princess Diana in a television film several years earlier. Following Lois Maxwell's fourteen-film reign in the role Bliss thought:

It crossed my mind that if I did accept this role – I'd be Miss Moneypenny forever. I thought, 'Do I really want to be typecast?' I turned up to the interview and there were many different types of girls there. I met Cubby Broccoli and Michael Wilson, and I think Barbara was there. I sat down and the first thing they said was, 'How do you see the role of Miss Moneypenny now?' I really had to bite my tongue and not say, 'The girl who just walked out of this room!' I got another call a week later asking if I could go to Pinewood Studios to meet the director and Tim Dalton. They were shooting the pipeline scene with Jeroen Krabbé. I saw John Glen walking towards me with Tim Dalton and something in my mind said, 'They just want to see us together, to see if there is chemistry.' Luckily I had seen Tim a few months earlier playing Petruchio in *The Taming of the Shrew*, and we also had a couple of friends in common, so we immediately had things to talk about.[43]

Andreas Wisniewski, an ex-ballet dancer, was cast as Necros. General Gogol was to have investigated the villainous duo but actor Walter Gotell had suffered ill-health so the role of Gogol was reduced. The part of Pushkin was created and John Rhys-Davies, a veteran Welsh actor, played the sympathetic KGB general. Art Malik, a rising British Asian star portrayed the Oxford-educated, Mujahedin leader, Kamran Shah.

Peter Lamont and John Richardson returned to head the design and effects departments respectively. John Glen promoted colleagues through the ranks: camera operator Alec Mills became cinematographer and stuntman Paul Weston co-ordinated the action. Once again, Glen relied on his specialist stunt teams headed by B.J. Worth and Rémy Julienne while John Grover and Peter Davies teamed up to co-edit.

In early September 1986 the pre-title sequence was once again shot ahead of principal photography. Glen sought inspiration from the past, 'I always remember the trouble Peter Hunt took to introduce George Lazenby in *OHMSS*, vague shots of Bond's hands on the wheel, a cigarette; he did everything but show his face. He intrigued the audience and then revealed him in a very exciting way. That is what I wanted to do here with Timothy Dalton as he turns to camera for the first time as the new James Bond.'[44]

John Glen remembered Dalton's late start on the picture:

We wrote the script before we cast Tim, but we adapted the script quite a lot. It was four weeks or so into the film before we knew we had him. It was very awkward because he was already doing [*Brenda Starr*] in America. He arrived off the plane from his last shot and went straight on to our set. In fact I shot round him for a day-and-a-half. When he arrived his hair wasn't the right length to do anything with and he had lost a lot of weight because he had been working so hard. He needed a bit of building up.[45]

The action called for Bond to cling to the top of a burning Land Rover as it careers down the narrow roads of the famous Rock of Gibraltar. Paul Weston talked with Dalton about the stunt action and the actor told him he wanted to make Bond much harder:

If he got a bloody nose he wanted snot running down his nose for two scenes after! He wanted to make it more realistic. When we got up on the rock and looked at the storyboards I said to Timothy 'Look we've got four minutes to make you the new Bond. I can tie you to the top of the jeep and you won't be able to move – but you will be safe.' He said 'Let me do as much of the action as you will allow me to do. I'm strong and I can do it.' I had to really make a snap judgment as to whether I could trust him. Was he an egotist out to just show off? But I quickly realised he could handle it. Timothy wanted the freedom to move along the Land Rover as it was moving. I was on a flat board on the other side and with him all the way down the mountain. He wasn't wired on – these days you would have to be for health and safety![46]

Peter Davies, the co-editor, was on the location:

Arthur Wooster was shooting, basically John gave me responsibility to assist with directing some scenes that were needed of the jeep driving down the rock with the jeep on fire and Bond on top, I can't remember exactly why, but I offered to do the driving! Associate producer Tom Pevsner wasn't too happy about that when he found out, but John defended me and said without me doing it we wouldn't have a sequence.[47]

Cubby Broccoli gave Weston one instruction, 'Look after our leading man!'[48]

Weston appeared in the pre-credit sequence five times himself, 'John Glen said:

'You have to play one of these parts. You can do the soldier at the bottom of the hill.' I'm the one who shouts out, 'Hold on, you're dead!' The crew really took the mickey out of me! When the Land Rover crashes through the market stalls you see me jumping out the way and again just before it hits the wall.[49]

On 29 September 1986 principal photography officially commenced. To begin with, Glen felt Dalton was 'naturally, a bit suspicious of us Bond people. He'd heard all these stories about us. He wasn't going to be railroaded with any sort of a cliché Bond. This sort of spirit was great. Without his realising it, it was exactly what we wanted. We had a real live wire in our midst and he was nobody's fool.'[50] Michael Wilson expected an adjustment, 'The pics changed when Roger Moore came on board, and changed during his tenure, and now Bond is going to alter dramatically with the new guy.'[51]

Glen understood Dalton's reticence:

It was a challenge and hard work initially to get him to believe in us. It must be awful for someone to come in and see that vast experienced crew – all of them having done seven or eight or nine, well, some chaps have been on all fifteen pictures – they are all very experienced. But everyone was aware that he needed encouragement and they gave it.[52]

In October 1986 the crew reached Austria, which also doubled for Czechoslovakia in the film. On 5 October Dalton was unveiled as 007 at an international press conference in Vienna. The actor was self-contained, 'Bond kept his private life secret and I intend to do so too. I've been in international films for some years now and see no reason to change.'[53] d'Abo felt, 'Tim was under a lot of pressure as this was a major change in his life. Here was a man who came from a theatre background, a serious character actor, suddenly launched as a sex symbol all over the world.'[54]

At the press conference Timothy Dalton posed with Maryam d'Abo draped over 007's new Cumberland Grey Aston Martin Volante. Art director Terry Ackland-Snow remembered:

> Cubby Broccoli and Michael Wilson were deciding what car to use. I got Aston Martin to come down to Pinewood with a Volante. Cubby Broccoli sat in it and Michael Wilson drove it. They said, "Can we take it for a spin?" They went to Slough and back. Cubby loved it. The waiting list was two years. Cubby asked them to deliver them in six weeks.[55]

Lamont was amused at the dedication of Aston Martin, 'Tom Pevsner and I had to go up to Newport Pagnell to see Victor Gauntlett who ran Aston Martin at the time. They were all hard tops. The open top in the film was Gauntlett's car. When we wanted his Aston in Vienna he said, "I'll bring it out!" – and he drove it out there for us.'[56]

Bond's Aston Martin Volante is chased by the Czech police across a frozen lake. Bond deploys the vehicle's gadgets, which include lazer hub caps, missiles, outrigger skies, a rocket booster and a self-destruct system. After the latter is used, John Glen suggested a novel way of 007 escaping would be to use Kara's cello case as a makeshift toboggan. His idea was rejected by Cubby. It was only when Glen demonstrated it could work physically, on a music stage at MGM, was it included.[57] D'Abo remembered how difficult the scene was:

> We spent two or three days doing scenes where Bond and Kara escape down the mountain in the cello case. They had placed little explosives under the snow so it looked like they were shooting at us. I have a phobia of big bangs, guns and explosions and during the big explosion scenes in the desert, I would be wearing a Walkman with loud music to block out the loud noise. I was terrified.'[58]

While in Austria the crew filmed at the famed Prater Amusement Park. Thomas Wheatley remembered:

> Originally you were going to see my demise as I'm sliced in two by exploding doors. In the final film we cut to a close up of Bond's face rather than the enormous elaborate special effect which they took ages to film! I remember when filming that special effect that Timothy, upon hearing the Viennese waiter shouting, "Fetch a stretcher," suggested perhaps Bond should look up and say, "You'd better make that two."'[59]

Maryam d'Abo recounted:

We then went to Morocco in November/December 1986. My particular
memory of Tangier is a town buzzing with life and markets. I wasn't needed
until we arrived in Ouarzazate. There the colours of the desert and the skies
were so vivid and the incredible sunrises and sunsets were unforgettable.
Jeroen Krabbé brought out his paints and canvases and did a series of paintings in the desert that were later exhibited here in London. Before we started
shooting we spent a day with Paul Weston and the stuntmen riding on our
horses in the desert by the Atlas mountains. I had this beautiful Arabian white
horse and was the only girl riding with all these men – Tim, Art Malik, Jeroen
and all the stuntmen. I felt like Lawrence of Arabia![60]

Krabbé was spoiled by the production:

While in Morocco we had been eating couscous for a whole month and
everyone was beginning to get a bit fed up of it. So I promised to cook a meal
for about forty people – a nice pasta. The only problem was that we were in
the middle of the desert! Barbara said to me, 'Ok give me your shopping list.'
The next day the products I needed were there. 'You don't want to know
how I got them,' said Barbara. 'I sent a plane … ' I laughed my head off – a
private plane to get some shopping! Only on a Bond film![61]

Peter Lamont noted:

The Moroccan Air Force did make a Hercules available to us and we applied
decals to make it look Russian. Our biggest chore was to build a complete
Hercules interior. We built the cockpit and cargo bay. Even the cargo door
worked. We created terrain on A Stage for the fight! We had all the Red Cross
packages flying out of the net. Red Cross sued us because you are not allowed
to use the Red Cross insignia without permission.[62]

In December 1986 the crew returned to Pinewood Studios. Peter Lamont
remembered, 'For Q's workshop, Philips Electronics supplied us with thousands
of pounds worth of extremely hi-tech computers. The huge video wall of
twelve individual screens was very sophisticated back then. That was the first
time anything like that had been seen on film.'[63] Desmond Llewelyn returned
as Q and enjoyed acting opposite a fellow Welshman, 'In a way it was easier

to work with Timothy because there were no distractions. When you get two stage actors together, there is "something" between them.'[64] Glen recalled:

> Llewelyn's advancing years required them to be inventive, 'Everyone remembered the gas mask scene where Q is demonstrating the stun gas. I always remember Desmond fluffing his lines, because the dialogue was so technical. We loved Desmond so much, so we would always find a way to make life easy for him. I told him we could dub his lines later, that's why Desmond plays the rest of the scene with his gas mask on.'[65]

Robert Brown also reprised his role as M, 'We were all on our toes, it being Timothy's first effort. We needn't have bothered, because he was so consummate. I'd been an admirer of Timothy Dalton's work for quite a few years. I thought his effort in [*The Living Daylights*] was something extraordinary.'[66] Krabbé, was thrilled to be 'confronted by all the old characters that I'd seen in the Bond movies – M and Q. It was marvellous to meet them. I felt like asking Desmond Llewelyn for his autograph because I'd seen him so many times on screen.'[67]

Caroline Bliss made her debut as Moneypenny in Q's workshop:

> In *The Living Daylights* I had very little to do. However what I could do was influence her look. It was my agent who said it would be a good idea to wear glasses, put my hair up and give Miss Moneypenny a glamorous secretarial look. Then in the future we had the option to let her hair down and take her glasses off – so there would be mileage – a journey for the character as they say. When I turned up to film my scenes I found the props man and he had a whole box of old glasses and we picked the least glamorous pair for fun. After the hair stylist put my hair up, I dressed in the pencil skirt and white silk blouse, which I didn't realise was see-through! One of the wardrobe girls said, 'Put this mac on, and then take it off to reveal the whole "look".' I went rushing up to John Glen where he was sitting with Tim, took the mac off and presented to him the new image for Miss Moneypenny. He took one look at me and said, 'Caroline you need to wear a bra!' I don't think he even noticed the glasses![68]

Bliss felt :

> incredibly at home with John Glen. When I began filming I was so nervous, absolutely terrified. John was really lovely and took me aside and said, 'Caroline

take your time – you are the new Miss Moneypenny – we've cast you and we don't want you to be anything but you. Just relax and make it your own.'[69]

Glen regrets not making Bliss's role more memorable, 'Hindsight is a wonderful thing, but we should have given Caroline a specially written scene that established her in the role and then maybe given her a more important part to play in the story. She needed something a little stronger than we gave her.'[70]

On 11 December 1986 Prince Charles and Princess Diana visited Pinewood. Jeroen Krabbé unwittingly became headline news:

We watched a show put on by the stunt guys where they smashed sugar glass bottles over their heads. I was standing in between the royals and I said to Princess Diana, 'You should smash one over your husband's head.' 'Oh I'd love to,' she said. Thomas Wheatley and I were standing behind them and the photo was published the world over.[71]

Wheatley was cynical, 'Looking back on it she probably did it with considerable enthusiasm!'[72]

Co-editor Peter Davies:

loved working with Maurice [Binder], he used to have a cutting room upstairs from us and would always be coming down to share or ask for ideas. We would always be taking the mickey out of him (in a nice way) and I think he quite liked the camaraderie. He did love his girls! He almost spent as long filming the title sequences as John spent shooting the film.[73]

Stills photographer Keith Hamshere described Binder as 'the table hopper [explaining that] in the Pinewood restaurant, he'd suddenly join you, then he'd join someone else. He'd go around the whole restaurant.'[74]

Alan Church was an optical cameraman at General Screen Enterprises as well as a Bond fan.[75] For him working for Maurice Binder was like a dream come true, but it was also a twenty-four hour a day job, 'If you were ill, he'd buy you a Lemsip!'[76] On *The Living Daylights*, a children's paddling pool was used for the ripple effects, a watering can was poured against glass to simulate rain and a revolver was filled with oil to get the required smoke effect when fired. For this last shot, it is Church wearing a black silk stocking glove firing the gun – Binder noticed his assistant had small, delicate hands![77]

Sound editor Colin Miller sourced sonic authenticity:

Using a voice casting director we found a groups of Afghans, they weren't actors, but waiters and domestic servants of some kind. We put twenty of them together in the studio and asked them to do the appropriate shouts throughout that whole fight in the desert. It was quite intimidating for them shouting at a screen but it worked out very well.[78]

The Living Daylights won an award for Best Sound Editing from the Motion Picture Sound Editors Guild (MPSE) in America.[79]

The Living Daylights had many moments filmed which did not make it to final cut. Most famously, Bond escapes the Moroccan bazaar by slinging an ornate rug over the power lines and sliding over them, giving the appearance he was floating on a magic carpet. Bond then swings down a large banner on to the back of a passing motorbike driven by the famous British stunt rider Eddie Kidd and makes his escape, while the bumbling local cop in pursuit of Bond, played by Nadim Sawalha, falls into a vat of paint. Tonally and time-wise, this sequence was not deemed suitable for the new Bond era. Dalton said of the completed film, 'In truth I don't think the audience saw the best film. I think the film was never better than when it was about seven or eight minutes longer. It fact it seemed shorter. It had more little moments and breathing spaces.'[80]

A pirate print of the film leaked in April 1987, including an extended briefing scene with M where the Flemingian term 'accidie' – boredom with life – is mentioned. Also, the Q Branch sequence featured additional gadgets including a ceremonial quill pen that transmits what it writes. The pirate copy caused a major security breach with co-editor John Grover and his assistant, the director's son, Matthew Glen, being under suspicion until it was found a post-production facility had been lax with security. They subsequently went bankrupt.[81]

John Barry returned to work on his twelfth Bond film. Barry started by watching the rough cuts which he preferred to view on a movieola.[82] Usually he had some four weeks to write the forty-five to sixty minutes of score and would then take a further week of studio time to record.[83] Barry accepted:

there are limitations, and after twenty-five years one is working partly to a formula. But you have to write the music with conviction. Bond pictures are real on-the-nose adventures. You have to imagine yourself as a kid on the front row of the stalls and being on the edge of your seat in case the guy on screen is going to cop it or not.[84]

On *The Living Daylights*, Glen recalled:

> We see John Barry conducting the orchestra, which is lovely! John asked me,
> 'Would you get me in the movie? Can I make an appearance?' He'd never
> done that [in a Bond film] before. There was an opportunity of course – who
> is better suited to conduct an orchestra than John Barry?[85]

a-ha's Paul Waaktaar-Savoy worked with John Barry on a title song. Glen
remembered the edict was to sign a current pop group to sing the title song,

> Barbara Broccoli was really in touch with the current music scene and so was
> Cubby Broccoli funny enough! Barbara came up with the idea of a-ha and
> she dragged us to see them at some venue in Croydon. There were all these
> 15-year-old girls screaming – the kids loved them!'[86]

With a video directed by Steve Barron and shot on the 007 Stage, the song
was a European hit but made little impression in the US. Barry did not enjoy
working with the Norwegian pop trio.[87] However, he did enjoy working with
Chrissie Hynde, singer with The Pretenders, who wrote two songs, 'If There
Was a Man' and Necros's theme, 'Where Has Everybody Gone?'[88]

When it came to pre-publicity the team were keen to showcase how Timothy
Dalton brought a sleeker, more dangerous edge to the part. Photographer Keith
Hamshere captured this deadlier 007 while:

> on location at Stonor House. I had Timothy leaning against a pillar. He felt
> very comfortable in this leather jacket and he loved his hair like that – it
> was away from the tradition. He was trying to change the Bond image; he
> was determined to get away from the tux. He wanted a more rough and
> ready look.'[89]

The single image later became the focus of the teaser poster campaign.

On 29 June 1987 the royal world charity premiere of *The Living Daylights*
was staged at the Odeon Leicester Square, renamed James Bond Square for
the day in honour of the series' Silver Jubilee. In attendance once more
were Prince Charles and Princess Diana. Desmond Llewelyn was on hand
to demonstrate Bond's Aston Martin Volante to the royal couple which was
parked in front of the cinema. This time, the square squealed with a-ha fans
who witnessed a stuntman abseil down the front of the theatre to cut in with

Timothy Dalton making his 'entrance' in the televised broadcast later that evening. Timothy Dalton arrived with his Bond girl Maryam d'Abo:

> We arrived late and the police had shut Leicester Square, so wouldn't let our car through. The bobby just didn't believe Timothy was James Bond! Timothy took me by the hand and we had to fight through the crowds. I was tip-toeing in my tightly fitted Ungaro dress. When we arrived at the main entrance, the crowds suddenly parted when they realised we were the two unknown new leads.'[90]

The new direction and the new Bond were certainly a creative shot in the arm for the franchise as worldwide grosses bounced up to $192 million. However, Dalton was cautious about the future:

> It's an uncertain moment for us all, we've all tried very hard to make this the best Bond film for a long, long time, but of course, if I fail, then everybody fails, if I succeed we all succeed. Of course there's danger to it. It's a difficult moment. The film will only reach fulfillment, and we'll only know the answer to that question when an audience sees it. I feel that we've actually done a good job; it seems to me to have developed in a way that I care about. I was given the freedom and the support, for which I am very, very grateful, from John Glen, the director, and Michael Wilson, the co-producer. I was given the freedom to make that character *the* character that I saw, which was essentially to try and capture what I believed Ian Fleming was writing about, to get the spirit of Fleming.[91]

Taking the mantle, Dalton did not think one should take the institution of Bond for granted:

> I don't think there's ever been an intention to make another one, ever. I think they've only been made because the present one has made money, has been successful. And when you are talking about a film that's as expensive as these are, you know we've got to make this one a success first. If it is a success, then I'd be delighted to do another film. What could be a greater pleasure and satisfaction than giving a lot of excitement and enjoyment in a terrific action adventure movie for people all round the world, and doing it again with a different film? I mean success isn't just fame, or notoriety, or money, success is actually achieving your objective. And that's to give people, in this

populist genre, a very thrilling and exciting time in the cinema, and if you've done that, why not take the elements that did it once, and try and do it again? I think that's thrilling, I'd love to.[92]

IAN FLEMING'S
Dr. No
Released thru UNITED ARTISTS

Bernard Lee, Sean Connery and Peter Burton,
11.25 a.m. Monday February 26 1962.

FIRST DAY OF SHOO7ING, PINEWOOD STUDIOS, FEBRUARY 26 1962. THE UNIT HAD RETURNED FROM THE WARMTH OF JAMAICA TO A FREEZING BRITAIN. THE DIRECTOR, CAMERAMAN AND LEADING ARTISTS WERE LATE DUE TO THE WEATHER CONDITIONS. AT 11.25 AM THE FIRST TAKE (SLATE 310) OF DR. NO AT PINEWOOD WAS RECORDED ON D (DAY) STAGE. HISTORY.

SINCE THEN 14 FURTHER INSPIRED CHAPTERS OF THE 007 HEROICS AND ADVENTURES HAVE SPANNED THE WORLD. CUBBY BROCCOLI AND HIS TEAMS, ALONG WITH UNITED ARTISTS, HAVE BEEN HERE AT PINEWOOD FOR EVERY 001 OF THEM. PINEWOOD ESPECIALLY THANKS CUBBY AND HIS CREWS, BUT SO DOES EVERY SEGMENT OF THE BRITISH FILM INDUSTRY. IT IS A PROUD MOMENT IN TIME FOR US. INDELIBLE.

PINEWOOD STUDIOS
Home of Cubby's 25 years of Bond and his word

IN THE BLINK OF AN EYE

LICENCE TO KILL

(1989)

TIMOTHY DALTON IS 007™

"Timothy Dalton brings Bond into the Nineties." — DAILY MAIL

"The best Bond in many summers... Dalton and the Team are capable of taking the Bond phenomenon into the next century." — SCREEN MAGAZINE

"Timothy Dalton is James Bond." — SOR TRONDELAG

$54,603,190

LICENCE TO KILL IS BREAKING
INTERNATIONAL BOX OFFICE AND STILL GOING STRONG
(20 HOUSE RECORDS)

BELGIUM	$762,759	NETHERLANDS	$5,982,486
DENMARK	$2,245,108	NORWAY	$3,154,450
FINLAND	$1,769,797	SINGAPORE/MALAYSIA	$1,966,995
FRANCE	$3,027,504	SPAIN	$2,386,648
GERMANY	$5,270,743	SWEDEN	$5,923,996
HONG KONG	$1,538,829	SWITZERLAND	$1,043,171
ISRAEL	$1,251,741	TAIWAN	$3,277,916
		UNITED KINGDOM	$10,317,763

OPENING IN SEPTEMBER

JAPAN – AUSTRALIA – ITALY – BRAZIL

LICENCE TO KILL

Starring CAREY LOWELL ROBERT DAVI TALISA SOTO ANTHONY ZERBE
ALEC MILLS PETER LAMONT Music by MICHAEL KAMEN
Associate Producers TOM PEVSNER and BARBARA BROCCOLI Written by MICHAEL G. WILSON and RICHARD MAIBAUM
Produced by ALBERT R. BROCCOLI and MICHAEL G. WILSON Directed by JOHN GLEN

PG-13 PARENTS STRONGLY CAUTIONED

Distributed internationally by MGM/UA Through United International Pictures

I n the late eighties the British film industry had changed out of all recognition from its heyday in the sixties. Cinema attendances had fallen to such an all-time low that any monies available for production from the Eady Levy were negligible. High street cinemas had fallen into disrepair and were closing down. In a climate of low admissions, the Eady Levy – effectively a tax on the cinema seat – was seen as an obstacle to the cinema-going public. In 1985 the scheme was abolished. The emphasis was now on rebuilding the nation's cinema stock and the rise of the multiplex began. Linked to box office earnings, the Levy had rewarded producers who made movies the public wanted to see. Now an incentive for large-scale, populist movie making in the UK was removed.[1]

Dwindling cinema attendances stalled production in Britain. The studios could no longer afford to retain a permanent staff of skilled technicians. They went 'four walls' meaning movies booking into a studio would be required to hire their own crews. *Variety* reported, 'The recent no-surprise decision of the Rank Organization to convert its historic Pinewood lot from a full-service to four-wall rental facility underlines the slump in studio-based theatrical production.'[2] By reducing staffing costs, the studio could attract cheaper television work.[3]

Against this backdrop, MGM/UA was going through its usual corporate contortions. Jerry Weintraub had given way to Lee Rich of MGM/UA Communications and Tony Thomopoulos, chairman of United Artists Pictures.[4] Buoyed by their huge library of films, including the Bond pictures, MGM enjoyed a large revenue stream from video-cassette and television.[5] As the James Bond films were financed from America, the exchange rate affected budgets. Unfortunately, the pound was high and this was blamed for the reluctance from US features to shoot in the UK.[6] Additionally the British government's decision to withhold tax on foreign artists' earnings, discouraged A-list talent from working in Great Britain.[7] Charles 'Jerry' Juroe, marketing head of Eon Productions, stated ominously, 'There's a feeling that the general climate in the UK is not conducive to making movies.'[8]

Cubby Broccoli hired director John Glen for a record-breaking fifth consecutive Bond film.[9] Glen was inspired by the possibilities Timothy Dalton in the role of James Bond now gave him.[10] He wanted to push Bond in a harder direction, to compete with the spate of tougher-edged action films like *Lethal Weapon* (1987) and *Die Hard* (1988) that were eclipsing Bond in the North American market.[11]

Richard Maibaum and Michael G. Wilson set about crafting a new adventure that pushed the creative boundaries and reached for a more interesting film.

In the seventies Bond budgets had jumped fourfold, reaching a zenith with *Moonraker*. In an effort to contain costs, ten years later, the Bond team were working with effectively the same budget. Taking into account inflation, Eon had to be more cost-conscious than ever before.[12]

Michael Wilson explained:

When we wrote *The Living Daylights* we didn't know who was going to take over as James Bond. The script was finished and we were well into pre-production before Timothy Dalton was cast, so Tim played Bond as he saw it in our script. This time, having seen his ideas – there's no doubt about it, the films are influenced by the way the actor plays Bond – we saw that Tim has a certain way of doing things.[13]

Wilson concurred with John Glen's vision. 'With Timothy Dalton, we're going back to the basic Ian Fleming character and so coming from that we create a film in the Fleming vein. It's not a comedy and, although it has comic moments, it's much closer to the Fleming idea.'[14]

Towards the end of the eighties the Soviet threat was diminishing with the rise of Mikhail Gorbachev and the thawing of East/West relations. Wilson felt they had to be aware 'of the world situation and what people will accept as a "loosely-based on reality" sort of plot.'[15] John Rhys-Davies, who had played KGB General Pushkin in *The Living Daylights*, recalled he was asked to be involved:

They did ask me to do a couple of scenes. My answer was, 'Well, if the scene was intergral to the story, yes, I'd be happy to. But if not, let's *not*.' I would like to play Pushkin again, and I would like to make him more a central character like he was the last time.'[16]

Pushkin would reappear in Michael France's draft of the *GoldenEye* screenplay.[17]

Richard Maibaum explained that initially the plan was to link the film to *The Living Daylights*, 'We wanted to pick up on a warlord in the Golden Triangle from [the] previous film who was mixed up in drugs and we thought we could incorporate it into a story set in China.'[18] Wilson confirmed, 'We wrote two treatments [one] involved the treasures of China and was quite a different story.'[19]

The Pacific Rim was fast becoming a place of interest, as John Glen recounted:

We did quite a lot of abortive recces. We went on from Japan to China via Hong Kong. Hong Kong always fascinated me. It had been used in a Bond already so we weren't particularly keen to repeat a location. We'd rather a fresh location. China was just opening up to tourism and they'd just discovered the terracotta soldiers in Xian. I was very keen to look at that. We went around for a couple of weeks as guests of the Chinese government. They laid on everything that we needed.[20]

While the British government appeared to be making things harder for film-makers, Glen remembered the production's putative hosts 'had a Chinese naval gunboat put at our disposal for a trip down the Yangtze which is quite a long way from Peking, not Beijing, [as] it was. It was an interesting trip and I was trying to conjure up [ideas]. We'd obviously have to use the Forbidden City, the Great Wall, Xian. Michael and I were swapping notes of what we could do. Things didn't jump at us like they do in certain other places.'[21]

A number of issues stymied Bond shooting in East Asia. Wilson felt, 'There was a question of how expensive and what problems there might be working in China.'[22] Glen felt control was an issue, 'The Chinese said that they would want to vet the script and take out anything they considered was a bit provocative, Cubby said that was impossible and we just didn't go.'[23]

Peter Lamont embarked on an extensive location hunt in the Gulf of Mexico and the Caribbean:

We went out to Los Angeles and looked at various things there. Then we crossed over to Miami, we had the governor's plane take us down to Key West. Then we went to the Bahamas [by private plane] to Martinique, Guadalupe, St. Croix and St. John. The idea was that we would fly over to Mérida and Cancún but unfortunately there was a huge storm so we didn't.[24]

Eventually they arrived in Mexico City and inspected the facilities. Upon returning to London, Lamont was called to see Broccoli in South Audley Street, 'Cubby said, "So, what do you think?" I said, "I think if we go to Mexico City we are mad, the facilities are awful." He looked at me and he said, "If we don't go to Mexico City we're not doing the picture."'[25]

Once the direction of the story was ascertained the production left the UK to set up base at Churubusco Studios in Mexico City. Wilson felt the force of finance:

We had a situation where our movie was set in that part of the world, so
we saved perhaps 15 per cent over what we would have spent in London to
do the same film. Because of the exchange rate with the dollar, Europe has
become a very difficult place to film and our kind of picture is difficult to
make in the United States. So you're really in a quandary. Europe is high-
priced and the US is high-priced.[26]

As a starting point, Maibaum asked, 'Who is the great Satan today?'[27] Wilson
explored the topic, 'In this particular case I thought, "Who are the people that
the Western World consider the bad guys?" When you start looking too deeply
you start eliminating some of them because they're so bad, you don't want to
write about them – just ask Salman Rushdie!'[28]

Maibaum arrived at an answer, 'The drug lord!'[29] Wilson was captivated
by news headlines, stories of narcotics dealers and their extreme world of
violence:

We had a case in the United States last year with a Columbian guy called
Carlos [Lehder] who was one of the 'Big Five' in a drugs consortium.
Apparently the other four didn't have too much contact with him – they
decided he was too violent and crazy to deal with.[30]

Wilson took inspiration from such real-life drug-lords for their central villain, 'I thought there are these guys in Columbia who go down to Miami
and execute whole families just to make a point about a business deal with
someone and this was the sort of person our villain was.'[31]

Wilson mined a creatively rich vein, 'Actually, drug lords are very political.
There are countries where legitimate institutions of democracy are under-
mined by the huge wealth and power of drug lords.'[32] Wilson was inspired by
the international aspect of the crime:

I feel that in the popular cinema, it was an issue that hadn't been addressed.
It's usually people in the United States working with drug dealers and drug
users and what goes on about stopping drugs. This, however, is an effort to
say if you look at what's happening to the countries where drugs are grown
and exported, is it true you're not hurting anyone but yourself when you do
them? Live and Let Die dealt with it in a vague way, but it's really only been
dealt with in journalism and documentaries.[33]

Another news event spurred Wilson. 'Then there was General Noriega, who I thought rather colourful and who was giving the US the two-finger salute over the Panama Canal while harbouring all the drug criminals, dealing in protection and such like.'[34] The writer blended Lehder and Noriega, 'So I thought up this character taking a bit of both of them and thought he would be a colourful character to oppose Bond – hence Franz Sanchez complete with [a] German/Spanish name.'[35]

However the villain was only the beginning. Wilson pondered, 'So you start with James Bond and someone like Sanchez and say, "Right, where do we go from here?" and the story unfolds.'[36] This is the challenge for a Bond producer, as Wilson explained, 'You can't disappoint the audience, but you can't give them what they expect.'[37] Richard Maibaum felt the new story broke new ground, 'What we have is for the first time Bond becoming personally involved to a greater extent than he's ever been before because of the death of Leiter's wife and the maiming of Leiter. This starts him off on a purely personal mission of vengeance.'[38] Wilson acknowledged that vengeance was the subtext in previous films – *Goldfinger* when Jill Masterson dies and the pre-title sequence of *Diamonds Are Forever* in which Bond was bent on revenge for the murder of his wife, 'It wasn't a very developed idea in those films. We never really saw Bond go for revenge before.'[39] He felt their new tale was 'something to make Bond bite'.[40] Wilson explained that the film's 'thrust is that Bond loses his professional objectivity because of his vendetta. In a sense, it's the awakening in him of the realisation that when he loses his objectivity, he begins to make things worse for himself. That makes for a rather impassioned, exciting film.'[41] When Bond goes out on his own for revenge, he becomes professionally compromised, stripped of his licence to kill. This incident gave the film its initial title, *Licence Revoked*.

Again the writers cherry-picked from the works of Ian Fleming. Wilson recounted:

I re-read the Ian Fleming novels from time to time and I remembered THE HILDEBRAND RARITY had this character Milton Krest, a sort of brash American with his ship, the *Wavekrest*. So he's worked into the script, different from Fleming's Krest but the essence is there. And we include a scene from LIVE AND LET DIE which wasn't in the screenplay for that film.[42]

Wilson is referring to Felix Leiter who is maimed by being fed to sharks and left for dead with the macabre note, 'He disagreed with something that ate him.'[43] In addition, *On Her Majesty's Secret Service* was alluded to as Wilson included 'a reference, but very indirect, to Bond being married before. It's sort of bittersweet.'[44]

THE HILDEBRAND RARITY was published in the FOR YOUR EYES ONLY short story collection in 1960. Following a mission in the Seychelles, Bond goes on a cruise with a Humphrey Bogart-esque rich American, Milton Krest and his pliant English wife, Liz. The trip is ostensibly a search for the Hildebrand Rarity, a scarce fish. During the trip, it becomes clear that Liz is in an abusive relationship. Her husband whips her with the tail of a stingray, which he calls 'the Corrector'. Eventually they find the fish, but not before causing a minor ecological disaster. The following morning Bond finds Milton Krest dead with the Hildebrand Rarity shoved in his mouth. He quickly throws the body over-board and clears up any evidence. With no proof of foul play, it will be assumed Krest fell drunkenly overboard and Liz Krest will be a free woman.

Richard Maibaum had been a 'loyal and pioneering member'[45] of the Writers' Guild of America (WGA) and during the development process in 1988, the WGA went on strike. He had worked with Michael Wilson on the story but could not participate in writing the screenplay. Wilson said of Maibaum, 'We've worked a long time together over the years, and I didn't feel I wanted to go through an arbitration. I told him I would be happy to share credit, and he said wonderful. He was put in a difficult spot, and I wasn't prepared to make it more difficult.'[46]

In what became his last 007 assignment, Richard Maibaum reflected on how writing the James Bond films had changed:

The first one was in 1962 and you could be more leisurely. You could have more dialogue scenes and by that happening, you had an opportunity to project a full characterisation of the people. That has slowly begun to tail off, because the action demands that you must move so fast that you haven't got time for leisurely characterisation. It's something I regret, because the only way you can forge a characterisation is by dialogue. There's no time for it today and I think that has gradually happened over the years to *all* action pictures.[47]

The veteran scribe felt:

one thing about the Bonds is that you never know what to expect until you've seen them in front of a packed audience, 25 per cent of which is kids.

Then you get the whole effect. You get the people who talk back to the screen, those who laugh and those who shout. It's really amazing to see Bond pictures in front of that kind of audience and I'm continually surprised by the reaction.[48]

In late November 1988, for the first and only time, the title of a Bond film was changed midway through production. The sixteenth 007 film, *Licence Revoked*, would now be known as *Licence to Kill*, the British spelling of 'Licence' causing comment from American critics when the film was released there. The original title was altered when tests revealed that a large number of people did not know what 'revoked' meant.[49]

The pre-title sequence begins with Bond en route to Felix Leiter's wedding to Della Churchill in Key West, Florida. They receive urgent news that drug lord Franz Sanchez has been lured out of his protective jurisdiction to take back his wayward girlfriend, Lupe Lamora. Bond, Leiter and his colleague, Sharkey, race by DEA helicopter to apprehend Sanchez by fishing him from the skies. Sanchez is then detained in Quantico, but after bribing FBI agent Ed Killifer, is sprung in an elaborate scheme planned by American accomplice Milton Krest. Sanchez, aided by his henchmen Perez, Braun and knife-wielding Dario, exacts brutal revenge for his capture by murdering Della and maiming Leiter. Aided by Sharkey, Bond hunts down Sanchez's inside man, who he discovers is Killifer and kills him. Bond is now forcibly detained by MI6 agents who take him to Ernest Hemmingway's home to face a severe reprimand from M. Bond's activities, including the death of Killifer, have worried his American hosts. M orders 007 to cease his private vendetta, but Bond refuses and his licence to kill is revoked. He eludes his own MI6 minders and continues on his personal vendetta. Bond intercedes on a drug/money exchange between Krest and Sanchez, making off with $5 million of Sanchez's funds. He then meets Leiter's contact, Pam Bouvier, a CIA contract pilot and seasoned agent with huge inside knowledge of Sanchez's operation. They team up and fly to Isthmus City, the fictional Latin American state ostensibly run by President Hector Lopez, but really corrupted by Sanchez with the help of disgraced financial whizz kid Truman-Lodge. Equipped unofficially in the field by Q, who has been tipped off by Moneypenny, Bond attempts to assassinate Sanchez but gets tangled up in a Hong Kong narcotics sting and fails. He manipulates Sanchez into believing he is an ally and slowly sows seeds of doubt into the organisation, turning Sanchez on his own team, resulting in the brutal execution of Krest. Bond discovers Sanchez is planning a vast expansion of his drug empire by using modern marketing methods to sell narcotics franchises to the Far East. Sanchez uses televangelist Professor Joe Butcher to send coded broadcasts allowing criminal customers to communicate the quantity and price of large drug orders. When Bond failed to kill Sanchez, he inadvertently fouled up an attempt by Bouvier to repatriate Stinger missiles which are being used to threaten the skies. Bouvier had been dealing with Heller, Sanchez's head of security, in return for immunity. There are wider consequences at stake than just James Bond's thirst for revenge. He finally confronts Sanchez in his drug laboratory disguised as the headquarters of Butcher's Olimpatec Meditation Institute. Sanchez reveals he can ship vast quantities of cocaine, dissolved in gasoline. An initial convoy of four Kenworth tanker trucks sets off after Bond destroys the drug plant. A fight to the death between Bond and Sanchez takes place on the tankers as they weave through a desolate mountain pass. Bond sets a petrol-soaked Sanchez ablaze with a lighter given to him by Felix Leiter at the wedding.

Timothy Dalton liked the portrayal of Bond in the screenplay, 'The story is based on something personal. He's still the same man, only here he's driven less objectively and professionally than he might be if he was working on a mission or a job. It comes from a personal source, but of course he's still Bond.'[50] Dalton felt:

The film is a different kind of film – more straightforward in its motive. *Daylights* operated on quite a few levels of deception and intrigue. There's a fundamental course for aggression here and lots of blocks to the fulfillment of that. *Licence to Kill* is about vengeance, retribution and setting a wrong – a personal grievance – right, but it broadens, expands and takes on a larger perspective. Ultimately, as in all good Bond films, good does triumph over evil on a better basis than just one of personal revenge. I mean, one's own scope, one's own awareness of how he's behaving is enlarged and is brought back to something that is much more calculating and striving for a good end.[51]

Dalton understood:

The movies themselves had the evolution. You could see the evolution between *Dr. No*, *From Russia With Love* and *Goldfinger*. You could see development, but they were still within a similar area. But even Connery's last film was completely different from, say, *From Russia With Love*. They were two different entities and therefore perhaps required different kinds of performances. The more the films developed into technological extravaganzas and light-hearted comedy spoofs, the more removed they became from the early Bonds. In *Licence to Kill*, too, I hope you see a different Bond.'[52]

Michael Wilson agreed, 'Timothy gives us a different direction to go in, I think the films with Roger emphasised his talents. For Timothy, a gritty, more reality-based piece is the way to go. Giving him one-liners won't play to his strong suit. He plays it fairly straight.'[53] Wilson believed, 'that *Licence to Kill* was tailormade for Timothy Dalton's style.'[54]

Robert Davi, who played drug lord Franz Sanchez, remembered meeting Cubby's oldest daughter Tina, who was a fan of his children's film *The Goonies* (1985).[55] Davi recounted Tina 'knew I was born in Astoria Queens [Cubby's hometown]'[56] and invited Robert to meet her father and the pair hit it off immediately.[57] Davi then appeared as a Palestinian in television film *Terrorist on Trial* (1988). 'Richard Maibaum was watching it and called up Cubby straight away. They called [me] the next day.'[58] The actor felt he had the inside track on the role of the Bond villain, 'I'd done my first film with [Frank] Sinatra. Sinatra was friends with Cubby.'[59] Indeed, for Davi and Cubby, the character's name was an in-joke, 'I used to have lunches with Cubby Broccoli and Sidney Korshak and Frank Sinatra. Franz Sanchez. Frank Sinatra. F. S. That was a cute nod. There was always talk about him being a Bond villain.'[60]

Davi recalled, 'They set up a meeting with Timothy. It was at Cubby's office at MGM in Culver City. They saw that chemistry was going to be interesting between the two of us.'[61] Davi was cast but was warned talent agents with bigger clients would attempt to cloud the choice: 'Of course, there'll be a lot of noise on the street.'[62] Davi researched his character:

> We didn't want a heavy duty accent but a flavour of that world. I got in touch with people from Colombia, Medellin and was inspired by the Columbian music, folk customs, their rhythm and some of the language. I worked on [the lines] in Spanish to distil the accent. I wanted to go authentic [as it] deepens [the portrayal]. Then I took off some of the accent so that it would be more accessible.[63]

Davi added some traits of his own, 'They knew I liked cigars so Sanchez had the Dunhill.'[64]

Carey Lowell played leading lady Pam Bouvier and recalled she was asked to audition for the role of:

A tough CIA agent in a bar. I showed up to the audition in a leather jacket and jeans thinking this is my tough girl image. They took one look at me and said, 'No, that's not what we had in mind. It's a Bond girl remember? You need to go out and find a sexy dress and come back and we'll put you on tape.' So that weekend I went and looked around a mall and I found a hot pink, trashy, stretchy, tight halter dress with a dip from the neck down. I put it on and went in and they were like, 'That's much better.' I met Cubby and Barbara and Michael Wilson. After meeting them, they gave me the thumbs up. I had short hair which sort of threw them. Not a lot of Bond women had short bobbed hair.[65]

Lowell recounted, 'I tried to exercise and be incredibly fit. I have to confess to not doing a bunch of research in terms of CIA agents.'[66]

Actress Talisa Soto remembered her journey to the role of Lupe Lamora, Sanchez's wayward girlfriend. She screentested with key scenes from the movie: Sanchez whipping Lupe, meeting Bond on the Wavekrest and Lupe dealing Bond blackjack hands at Sanchez's casino.[67] Casting directors Janet Hirshenson and Jane Jenkins had compiled a list of girls who tested opposite Davi standing in as 007, 'I got to be James Bond to seventeen of the most beautiful women from around the world, different actresses and models. We had the screentest at Cubby's house.'[68] John Glen saw a freshness in Talisa, 'She had good ideas and responded to direction very well.'[69] Glen noted that initially MGM felt the part was 'a little sketchy, underwritten. We made her the kind of girl that has to have a man around. She's always up to her little tricks. We made her a scheming kind of woman.'[70] Lupe is supposed to be the winner of the Miss Galaxy beauty contest, fixed for her by Sanchez. Soto took inspiration from other areas of her character, 'I really focussed on her being a well-known blackjack dealer. I did some research. I went to Las Vegas and to this one card dealing school. It was a two-hour crash course for blackjack dealers. I was practising every night I can tell you.'[71] Talisa Soto also sought to be original so 'did not go back and do any research on the other Bond girls, because I wanted to create my own character from scratch.'[72]

For the first time in the series' history, an actor reprised the role of Felix Leiter. David Hedison, who had played the part in *Live and Let Die*, 'had a ball for eight weeks jumping out of helicopters, shooting guns.'[73] He was in a unique position to compare Bonds:

Roger was a clown, a lot of fun, always kidding around on set. Tim is much more earnest and serious. Off the set, we got on very well. I found him to be a remarkable person to work with, very caring, very conscious of the scene. He gave a lot to his fellow actors. He was not playing the big star.'[74]

Hedison could also compare directors, 'John [Glen] is very quiet, very unemotional, very caring for his actors, and he has a wonderful even temper. I hardly remember what Guy did. He got it done and did a very good job.'[75]

Benicio Del Toro played Dario, an early role in what would become an Oscar-winning career. He remembered, 'I grew up in San Juan, Puerto Rico. In my room, I had a lobby card of *Thunderball* so I grew up liking James Bond. I met Cubby Broccoli. The experience was fantastic.'[76] Wayne Newton, a famous Las Vegas entertainer gave up a $1 million a week[77] to play corrupt evangelist Professor Joe Butcher for a week in Mexico. According to Michael Wilson, 'he said it was like having a vacation.'[78]

Veteran television actor Anthony Zerbe was cast as Milton Krest:

I try to centre the man in terms of things going on around him. He never really has a happy moment in the film. From the very first appearance of Bond, things go from bad to worse so we are not seeing a man at the height of his powers. We are seeing someone buffeted by the slings and arrows of Mr. Bond. I became a villain because of my eyebrows and my name. I couldn't resist the offer because I'm so often a villain and this is the ultimate villain's movie.[79]

President Hector Lopez of Isthmus City was played by Pedro Armendáriz Jr., marking the first time two generations had starred as significant characters in a Bond film. Armendáriz's father Pedro played Kerim Bey in *From Russia With Love*. Completing this nefarious line-up were Don Stroud as Colonel Heller, Sanchez's head of security, and Anthony Starke as Truman Lodge, a Wall Street whizzkid. Everett McGill was DEA turncoat Ed Killifer, whilst Mexican actors Alejandro Bracho and Guy De Saint Cyr were minor henchmen Braun and Perez respectively. Rising star Cary-Hiroyuki Tagawa was Kwang, a Hong Kong narcotics agent assisted by MI6 agent Fallon, portrayed by Christopher Neame. The then-Governor of Florida, Bob Martinez, made a cameo appearance as a customs official at Key West airport.

By his fourth appearance as M, Robert Brown knew the character well:

He's very much a Royal Navy product but with an uncanny steeliness and resilience to run this business. He's got a personal feeling for his agents,

because although he is a toughie – he'll make decisions that'll appal anybody
– he is still worried about his people. Which is a Royal Naval thing.[80]

Brown enjoyed the rarity of leaving the confines of Pinewood Studios to shoot
his key scene with James Bond on the balcony of Ernest Hemingway's house
in Key West, 'For actors this is a bonus.'[81]

In *Licence to Kill*, Q was given his biggest role yet, coming to Bond's rescue
in Isthmus City. Desmond Llewelyn appreciated he was able to do more with
the character when appearing in longer scenes, 'There are so many times when
there is a pause or a look that needs to be kept in. There are a few scenes which
had that element – the friendship between the two men.'[82] A moment where Q
throws away field equipment – a radio broom – after having admonished Bond
for such ill-treatment of his gadgets was, for Llewelyn, 'just sort of instinctual. It
just felt right.'[83] The role paid off financially too, 'I was on location in Mexico
and for the first time in my life I made some real money out of a Bond film.'[84]

After her debut in *The Living Daylights* Caroline Bliss felt, 'There was definitely an impression that I was now Miss Moneypenny, if I didn't blow it.'[85]
However, her secord turn in the role was brief. Bliss travelled to Mexico for
her one scene, ironically set in London:

> I remember thinking this is really sad, it's only three lines, I can't really do
> anything with her at all. The scene took about a day to film. I wasn't well,
> I immediately came down with flu. I was pretty dosed up. I wasn't happy
> I had gone all the way out there and I wasn't filming at my best.[86]

John Glen once again assembled his core creative team: production designer
Peter Lamont, director of photography Alec Mills, stunt co-ordinator Paul
Weston, an aerial stunt team lead by B.J. Worth and vehicle stunts headed by
Rémy Julienne.

New to Bond was TV's *Miami Vice* costume designer, Jodie Tillen. Dalton
had strong ideas on Bond's look and opted for even more casual apparel for this
film. He fought Tillen's notion of dressing Bond in pastels.[87]

In early 1988 the unit moved into Churubusco Studios in Mexico City. Peter
Lamont remembered the facility had seen better days and spent several weeks
refurbishing and building additional workshops.[88] Even the studio floors had
to be levelled before set construction could begin. Although conditions were
not on a par with Pinewood, Lamont found 'the Mexican construction crews
absolutely wonderful.'[89] As Lamont built the first interior set he witnessed the

craft of the workmen, 'The construction crew had built some louvre doors, which they polished. It was like glass. I said, "We'll leave the doors like that!" I just couldn't paint them white. After that everything that was wood was hand polished.'[90] The 7,500ft altitude and pollution at Churubusco caused health problems among the unit.[91] Tom Pevsner had felt Desmond Llewelyn would not be able to reprise his role due to health risks but Glen allowed the veteran actor to stay.[92]

On 18 July 1988 principal photography began with Cubby Broccoli opening the proceedings with the first take.[93] Lamont recalled that altitude sickness struck again when Cubby was taken ill shortly into production.[94] He later returned to the production in Acapulco.[95]

Among the first scenes shot were Franz Sanchez's entrance to the film where he punishes his errant girlfriend, Lupe Lamora, by whipping her with a stingray tail. Davi recalled, 'They wanted to show tears in her eyes. It was a sexual dance the two of them do all the time. I wanted it to come off much more sensually but they wouldn't allow it.'[96] Behind the scenes, Robert Davi became leader of the gang:

Talisa, me and Benicio hung out. I embodied Sanchez. I looked at Dario almost like a younger brother. When [at the end of the picture] he is getting chewed up in that machine [which processed the cocaine bricks], I remember Benicio and I had a conversation about that moment. I suggested to him, 'Who's the closest person to Dario? Sanchez!'[97]

Del Toro cried Sanchez's name during Dario's death scene.[98]

A practical joke involving actor Anthony Starke and some burnt cork on the make-up table brought Davi to the strict attention of Barbara Broccoli, 'The next thing I know [she is saying], "Davi, what have you done to Anthony Starke?" She was like the Mother Superior. I remember getting scolded for that.'[99]

Lowell, on the other hand, 'mostly hung out with the art department, they were the fun people. They were the people that shot tequila at every meal. It's medicinal in Mexico City to have a shot of tequila.'[100] Davi recalled the said medicine played a large part when he and Dalton were off set, '[Timothy] was surprised that I had a knowledge of the bard. Instead of playing chess, we would hit the tequila, look at the ladies and spew forth the poetry.'[101]

According to Lowell there were some painful incidents, but not for her:

I do remember that one scene where Timothy has got his hands bound and he's hanging over the coke grinder. Benicio reaches over and tries to cut his bindings off to make him fall and he sliced Tim's finger. We had to stop shooting and Tim had to go and get stitches. Benicio felt very badly about it.[102]

Davi's intention was to play Sanchez as humanly as possible, 'When Timothy and I met, we talked about CASINO ROYALE. How Bond and the villain are mirror images of each other. Bond and Sanchez are mirror images of each other. It's a heavyweight title match. Bring Bondian elements to the villain and villainous elements to Bond. You had a shared nuance.'[103] Dalton approved of Davi:

One of my three favourite villains anyway was Gert Fröbe in *Goldfinger*. I thought his performance was magnificent. Davi, too, is moving towards something fairly unique in the Bond films. Davi [is] an actor of a very deep and real power and the work that I've seen him do so far is filled with a sense of danger – it's being played realistically.[104]

Carey Lowell remembered her own preparation, 'I had to go and do a swimsuit test at Cubby's house. Cubby had a gorgeous house with a giant pool. They wanted to see what it looked like when it got wet and they wanted to make sure it wasn't completely see through.'[105] Jodie Tillen also dressed Pam Bouvier in an evening dress inspired by an outfit Talisa Soto had worn to her audition. Dana had spotted it and suggested they use something similar. In the film, Bouvier would remove the bottom half to reveal a hidden Beretta.[106] Lowell had less fond memories of the dress, 'It weighed a ton. At one of my fittings, as I got zipped into it, my skin got caught in the zipper which was excruciatingly painful. They had to cut it off me.'[107]

Lowell's natural short hair was written into the story:

They put me in a wig for the first scene when I go and meet Felix Leiter. And then I go and I transform myself. I go from being Pam Bouvier, the CIA agent, to being Ms Kennedy, Bond's secretary, who has gone for a makeover, which is how they explained that in the film.[108]

The name change referred to Jacqueline Bouvier, the maiden name of President Kennedy's wife.

Lowell observed of Dalton, 'He was a Shakespearean actor who had agreed to star in James Bond. With the kind of theatrical experience he had, [Timothy] made Bond a little bit more serious, more realistic. More of a real person.'[109] Dalton thought at first of the antagonistic relationship between Bond and Bouvier:

> It's faithful to the spirit of Ian Fleming's books. It usually starts with some woman he perhaps doesn't want to be tangled up with, but through the story, getting to know her better and perhaps either endangering himself in order to protect her or finding that she sometimes protects him.'[110]

Lowell remembered their studio-bound moonlit seduction scene on a boat, 'I was so wound up from the scene, I'd just been shot in the back and I was kissing [Timothy] too rapturously. He told me to take it easy.'[111]

Another kiss was more amusing, as Davi recalled, '[Sanchez's pet] iguana didn't like Talisa Soto. Every time she went near it, it would freak out. I said the reason why is it knows she's betraying me. There's a cute little moment that I improvised when I gave it a kiss.'[112]

Other scenes were shot outside Mexico City. For the finale, Joe Butcher's Olimpatec Meditation Institute was a vast concrete construction near Toluca.[113] The location was an Indian ceremonial centre based on the former corn storage silos the Indians used.[114] It was built by the former president of the Indians who lived in the region but it lay untouched for a decade.[115] Lowell thought, 'It was the most bizarre monument in the middle of nowhere. The weirdest place I've ever been. We had to drive for hours to get there.'[116]

The sequence was originally to have been shot in a university amphitheatre complex in Mexico City, but according to Michael Wilson, 'When you wanted to film, the students were having demonstrations – it was right about the time of the elections, so all that fell through.'[117] Davi remembered legendary fixer and attorney Sidney Korshak visiting the set in Mexico, 'There were some issues sometimes and they were working them out with Sid.'[118]

In Acapulco the unit used Arabesque, the magnificent white marble home of the Baron de Portinova, to double for Sanchez's abode. The glare from the marble caused problems with filming.[119] Alec Mills commented on the 'Boy's Own' feel of the piece explaining, 'There is a Bond look. It's the little splash of colour here and there.'[120] Lupe Lamora is seen lounging around Sanchez's home reading. Soto recalled, 'They gave me a flimsy little book. I said, "No, Lupe has things she's working on, things up her sleeve. She wants to take over. Give me something about power."'[121] Key crew members stayed in guest suites around Arabesque and were waited on by sixty staff.[122] It was also the setting for the

film's final moment where Bond jumps from a balcony into a pool, dragging
Bouvier into the water to win back her affections. John Glen recalled tempers
frayed with his leading man during the night shooting of this sequence. It had
been towards the end of an arduous schedule. Glen was tired and suffering
from food poisoning.[123]

The main unit then moved to Key West, Florida at the height of summer
1988. Lamont spent three days with experienced production manager Ned
Kopp, sourcing all the locations bar one:

> We hadn't found Leiter's house. We went to a hotel and had a chat with the
> manager and he said, 'Oh you want so-and-so's house, it's just over there.'
> We went to where this strange fellow lived and it was one of these shotgun
> houses. It was wonderful, it was the part. So we said, 'Would you be interested
> in having James Bond here?' he said, 'Yes, certainly.' We went to the airport,
> picked up John and Michael, and we had found everything.[124]

For the pre-title sequence, Corkey Fornof returned to the Bond fold, 'Cubby
asked me, "Can we take an airplane out of the air?" and I said, "Yes, we can.
I've got a stunt I've been working on for years."'[125] After three weeks' practising
in Miami, Fornof had developed the routine. He worked out how to drop a
person by wire from a US Coast Guard helicopter on to a Cessna aeroplane,
and for that person to loop a cable lasso around the Cessna's tail, so that the
chopper could fly off carrying the plane with the nose pointing down.[126] It
took three weeks to prepare over the skies of Miami and Fornof had to meet
with US Coast Guard chiefs in Washington DC beforehand to obtain the
requisite permissions. The stunt had such potential that members of the CIA
showed up to film the scene too.[127] Fornof 'wrote a test programme, taking our
stuntman out to lower him on to the plane's tail on a wire using sky-diving
skills. We developed a safety measure for me and the helicopter. The most
dangerous part? There was no 'chute on the wire.'[128]

A barefooted waterskier performed the stunt in which Bond escapes Krest's
frogmen after crashing the drug exchange. The seaplane could not take off with
the drag of the barefooted skier, who had to then be equipped with transparent
waterskis.[129]

The final showdown between Bond and Sanchez on a convoy of Kenworth
trucks was shot on 200km of road between Mexicali and Tijuana, the La
Rumorosa mountain pass.[130] The second unit was led by Arthur Wooster, with
the vehicle stunt team headed by Rémy Julienne and action stunts co-ordinated

by Paul Weston. It took over seven weeks to complete the sequence.[131] The crew were spooked by a series of strange incidents on the desolate location including one of the trucks jackknifing and crashing, which delayed the shoot.[132] Another accident occurred when one of the trucks crashed spectacularly into the rockface. John Glen kept the shot in the final film.[133] For one scene, a massive explosion was staged but when the rushes were viewed, a giant flame in the shape of a hand could be seen reaching out.[134]

John Glen recalled the Kenworth truck sequence was 'a scene I'm very proud of because I'd been developing it for eight years. Originally I devised it as a pre-title sequence.'[135] The Kenworth trucks were modified by Rémy Julienne and his team to enable them to perform wheelies and 'high skiing' – the ability to drive on one set of wheels.[136] Each vehicle cost $100,000 and ten were required.[137]

Bouvier pilots a plane to assist 007 during the tanker chase. Lowell was amused, 'Corkey doubled me in the plane with a wig and a dress. It was very funny to see him standing there in my wig and my dress. We were in the middle of nowhere in Mexicali, Mexico.'[138] Warm temperatures meant the air was almost too thin to support the plane while travelling as slowly as the tanker truck, the plane being on the verge of stalling, necessitating multiple takes.[139]

Fornof, in drag, was later assaulted in jest by local Mexican security wielding AK-47 rifles.[140] An angry Barbara Broccoli used the same firmness she had scolded Robert Davi with to dress down Mexican authorities.[141] For all his previous derring-do, Fornof felt that moment 'was the biggest danger in my life.'[142]

Paul Weston doubled Robert Davi for Sanchez's final scene, when, soaked in cocaine-infused petrol, he is set ablaze by Bond disappearing into a fireball. Dressed in two heavy firesuits, with ice cold anti-flame gel, Weston had to use bottled oxygen.[143] He only had three minutes worth of air but, after getting into costume and protective gear, only half that for filming, Weston had to stagger across a carefully worked out path before they extinguished him.[144] Prior to being set ablaze, Weston remembered, 'Timothy, looking at me, a bit white-faced.'[145] Paul Weston eloquently set out the stuntperson's profession:

> We all want to be in the industry because we are creative. A writer creates with his pen, a painter with a paintbrush, but if a nib breaks he gets another pen, if the brush wears out he gets another brush. We create with our bodies and we only get one body. So you have to take care of it and use it as best you can.[146]

Licence To Kill's harder edge had John Glen and Cubby Broccoli locked in a battle with the British censor.[147] Key scenes of controversy included Sanchez whipping Lupe Lamora, the feeding of Leiter to the sharks – performed by a one-legged stuntman[148] – and Sanchez's explosive demise.[149] Unusually, the British Board of Film Classification (BBFC) saw a rough cut of the film as early as February 1989.[150] A series of screenings for the censor continued until June 1989 when it was viewed by the president, James Ferman, six examiners and assorted young people aged fifteen to twenty.[151] Finally the film was passed as a 15 certificate, which meant no one under that age could see it at the cinema. The BBFC held firm and it was reported unanimously 'that 15 is the correct catergory and [there is] no support at all for reclassifying as 12 even with cuts.'[152] It impacted a key demographic for the film and the release was too early for the new 12 classification introduced for *Batman* released in the UK in August 1989.

During the editing process other scenes were excised. When Bond arrives in Isthmus City he watches coverage of Sanchez on television, moodily drinking vodka while retrieving his Walther PPK from a hidden pouch. This latter moment appeared in the teaser trailer for the movie. A sequence of Lupe Lamora depositing Bond on the beach (after helping him escape from Sanchez's home) was also cut. A specially filmed teaser trailer featuring a digital watch counting down to 007 was storyboarded and shot by Billy Manger of Seiniger Advertising Inc. after it was approved by Cubby Broccoli.[153]

John Barry was suffering from ill-health and post-production was delayed in the hope that he would return, but he didn't. In keeping with the recent action trend, Joel Silver's composer Michael Kamen was hired.[154] A musician with one foot in the rock world, Kamen also pitched a title track for the film with Eric Clapton and original James Bond theme guitarist, Vic Flick.[155] Kamen admired Cubby, 'If I wore a hat, I'd take it off [to him]. The Broccoli crowd was very congenial and close. I grew to be friendly with Timothy Dalton.'[156] The actor attended some of Kamen's scoring sessions.[157] Michael Wilson was reticent about the Clapton track, 'We brought together a lot of people and they all worked very hard at it. We didn't really break any new ground.'[158] Other artists, like techno-pop outfit The Art of Noise and funk band Level 42, submitted tracks.[159] MCA, the record label, who would release the soundtrack, secured the deal by impressing the filmmakers with a complete package, including a number of additional songs.[160] A rock track for the Barrelhead Bar, 'Dirty Love', was performed by Tim Feehan and written by Steve Dubin and Jeffrey Pescetto. A calypso, 'Wedding Party', was performed by Ivory and written by Jimmy Duncan and Phillip Brennan. The end title song, 'If You Asked Me To' was written by noted songwriter Diane Warren and performed by soul diva Patti Labelle. The MCA deal was provisional on the company providing a suitable singer for the title track.[161]

'Licence To Kill' would be sung by soul legend Gladys Knight, although Patti Labelle recorded a version of the song too.[162] Barbara Broccoli noted:

> For this movie we decided to go with a female vocalist. The particular song and the particular singer fit this movie best. It's because a) it's a far more serious movie and b) because the female character in the movie is played by Carey Lowell and part of her character development is that she is a tough, strong independent woman who meets up with Bond, is attracted to him and by the end you have a nice relationship and there's another woman who you feel is possibly threatening the relationship, thus the lyric of the song. She has the licence to kill anyone that gets in the way.[163]

Interestingly, the title song was originally credited to Narada Michael Walden, Jeffrey Cohen and Walter Afanasieff. However, later Leslie Bricusse, Anthony Newley and John Barry were added as composers. Commented Barry, 'They ripped off the opening bars to "Goldfinger".'[164]

Maurice Binder's titles were based on images of photography and gambling. The actress in the sequence was Diana Lee-Hsu who also played Loti, a Hong Kong narcotics agent, in the film.[165] The title sequence for *Licence to Kill* begins with a girl holding up an Olympus camera. The designer liked the hands on one take but the face on another. He ended up slightly fogging a rotoscoped image to get the best of both takes.[166] As usual, Binder's work was late but this time back-up titles were prepared by another Binder protégé and end-title artist, Pauline Hume.[167] John Glen also confirmed that a photo-montage of Leiter's wedding as an alternative title sequence was discussed.[168]

On 13 June 1989 the royal world charity premiere of *Licence to Kill* took place at the Odeon Leicester Square, again in the presence of Prince Charles and Princess Diana. All expectations were for a smash performance when it opened in the US one month later. However, the film stalled in America, grossing just $34 million. Worldwide the picture fared much better, grossing $156 million. On a budget of $36 million, the movie was still immensely profitable.

The commercial disappointment of *Licence to Kill* in the States was put down to a web of factors: tough competition for the summer box office, a muddled, inconsistent and poorly funded marketing campaign, as well as reduced box office admissions due to the restrictive rating. It was fair to say that the constant flux at MGM/UA had not helped matters with regard to promoting and funding the roll-out of the film.

Timothy Dalton would remain the Bond of record. In 1990, after the dust had settled, publicist Saul Cooper said, 'We're finding more and more people who feel that if we get the tone of the films right, [Dalton] makes quite an acceptable Bond. Among the many intangibles we're currently facing, he isn't one of them. He will definitely be in the next one and the ones after that.'[169]

23

CHANGE MY
MIND FOREVER

PASSING THE BOND BATON

We are saddened by the passing of

MAURICE BINDER

*A dear friend, a wonderful human being
and a true motion picture visionary*

*Cubby and Dana Broccoli
Michael and Jane Wilson
Barbara Banta
Tina Broccoli
Tony Broccoli*

When interviewed on the Key West location of *Licence to Kill* in late 1988, Timothy Dalton said a curious thing, 'My feeling is this will be the last one. I don't mean my last one. I mean the end of the whole lot. I don't speak with any real authority, but it's sort of a feeling I have.'[1] It was a strange comment to make about a film geared to be a big summer smash hit. While it was true *Licence to Kill* had underperformed, especially in North America, plans for a third Dalton film were set in motion.

Albert R. Broccoli and Michael Wilson were now joined formally by a third producing partner, Cubby's daughter and Michael's half-sister, Barbara Broccoli. Barbara, having worked through the ranks, explained her attraction to production: 'My involvement started because it was about my wanting to spend time with Dad. Growing up, Dad would be getting calls at home all the time, so I used to like to be his secretary.'[2] Graduating from Loyola University, where she majored in motion picture and television communications,[3] Barbara also launched her own production company, Astoria Productions, with Amanda Schiff, to develop her own work.

In what was dubbed a 'bloodless *coup*'[4] Richard Maibaum and John Glen, Bond stalwarts for more than two decades, were let go. The agent for both men, Spiros Skouras, said, 'They had made many pictures together and worked together for a long, long time. It was a great thing for everyone involved.'[5] Richard Maibaum stated:

> I'm not upset about it. It was by mutual consent. Neither Mr. Glen or myself had any commitment beyond *Licence to Kill* and so the company was free to do whatsoever they wanted. I just wish everybody well on the whole enterprise. I've enjoyed working with them and am proud of the work that I've done.[6]

John Glen acknowledged later, 'It happens to us all – my day came when I had to move aside. It's an unfortunate thing. It's a fact of life.'[7] John Glen continued to work successfully in cinema and television into the 2000s. Saul Cooper, long-time publicity head for the Broccoli entities, said, 'I think the feeling is to bring in someone new. The whole trick with Bond is that we are making the seventeenth Bond film. The series has been kept alive for thirty years by the very astute way it has adapted itself to the times.'[8] Danjaq courted new talent and explored new possibilities. Directors such as John Landis,[9] future Bond director Roger Spottiswoode[10] and Ted Kotcheff,[11] who had helmed the Stallone action film *First Blood* (1982), met with Cubby, Michael and Barbara.

As well as new directors, new writers were sought. Eon had discussions with writer-director John Byrum,[12] and husband and wife team Gloria and Willard Huyck,[13] who had penned the ill-fated *Howard the Duck* (1986), but had also worked on *Indiana Jones and the Temple of Doom* (1984).

A new name that entered the fray was Alfonse M. Ruggiero Jr.,[14] a television writer who had penned episodes of action dramas *Miami Vice*, *Airwolf* and *Wiseguy*. Ruggiero was hired to rewrite an original script penned by Michael Wilson.[15] What emerged was an outline for *Bond 17*. The document was prefaced with a note stating the 'robotic devices'[16] in the treatment are 'complex and exotic machines designed for specific tasks'[17] and they would be designed 'especially for the film for maximum and dramatic and visual impact.'[18] Disney was rumoured to be working on the project with Imagineering, their visual effects house, to create 'the most complex anthropomorphic robot ever conceived for the movies.'[19]

The pre-title sequence was set in a fully automated chemical weapons laboratory in Scotland, run by robots. One of the machines runs amok causing a catastrophe, raising questions in the House of Commons. In a changing world, MI6 is now overseen by an officious new broom, Nigel Yupland. M, Q and Moneypenny would return as well as a new Aston Martin. Bond is called in to spy on a hi-tech industrialist, Sir Henry Lee Ching, 'a brilliant and handsome 30-year-old British-Chinese entrepreneur,'[20] who supplies and controls the hi-tech robotic devices used in facilities worldwide. A number of accidents at nuclear plants have been staged including one in Nanking, China. Set in the Pacific Rim, James Bond jets from China to Japan to Hong Kong, encountering the villainous Kohoni Brothers. The seventeen-page treatment played on the concerns of the age: the fate of Hong Kong, computer viruses and an increasing interest in China, a location Eon had sought to use in *Licence to Kill* two years previously. The *Die Hard*-esque finale was set in Sir Henry's hi-tech high rise building, where Bond defeats the nefarious villain with a welding torch.

During 1990 the producers hired British writing duo William Osborne and William Davies to work the treatment up into a feature screenplay. The writers were primarily known for their work on high concept comedy *Twins* (1988). Davies explained how they came to the attention of the Bond producers, 'We knew Barbara Broccoli and her then husband Fred Zollo who was involved in all sorts of classy projects.'[21]

The scribes worked on the project for about one year.[22] Osborne remembered:

> It was all going on during [the build up to] the Gulf War. I do remember having creative meetings [at Eon's offices in Culver City] and CNN would

be on television and we would be watching Saddam Hussein launching scud missiles at Israel. The brief was to try and bring it into the real world as it existed in 1991. There were quite a few jokes in it about cutbacks in intelligence matters. The idea was that Bond was beginning to doubt whether he could still do it.'[23]

Davies remembered everybody knew that the franchise needed to be invigorated somehow:[24] 'It felt like there was a creative impasse. The question was: creatively what can we do something that doesn't throw the baby out with the bath water?'[25] Osborne observed, 'Cubby was still very much in creative meetings. Barbara and Michael were trying to push it, whereas he was more "if it ain't broke why fix it?"'.[26]

Davies recalled:

We began to talk about what was going to be the next Tim Dalton movie. We then sat down with Tim Dalton and we talked to him about it and his point of view. We had this particular take, Bond was now feeling slightly like he was getting too old for it, he was beginning to feel like somebody in his forties. The life he was living, and the action sequences he was getting involved in, were starting to cost him more than they had in they past. We could never make it work sufficiently for Michael. We did two or three drafts and then we came off.[27]

Osborne felt, 'Tim wanted a bit more weight to it, which again was not where we were going creatively because we were slightly riffing on it, winking at the audience.'[28]

The resulting, untitled, screenplay was dated 2 January 1991 and credited to Davies, Osborne, 'Al Ruggiero' and Wilson. The following is a digest of that screenplay.[29]

The pre-title sequence is set in North Africa where, under the guise of taking part in a powerboat race, Bond parascends to a cliff top and it is revealed he is in Libya. There he infiltrates a chemical weapons facility which is guarded by a hi-tech robot. After outwitting his mechanical nemesis and Colonel Al-Sabra of the Libyan State Secret Police, Bond high dives into the water. He is berated by the young intelligence officer sent to evaluate him for failing in his mission to destroy the plant. Just then the plant explodes and the twisted remains of the robot land on the powerboat[30] Bond arrives at MI6 headquarters in London to find Nigel Yupland, a junior defence minister, is wielding the cost-cutting axe.

Moneypenny is engaged to a 'structural engineer from Harrow' and Q Branch is to be shut down. A mournful Q requests that Bond send him a postcard.[31]

The plot centred on a much more cost-effective stealth fighter, the Scimitar, developed by the British and worth billions in arms sales to the economy. The fighter has been stolen while on exercise with the US Navy. Bond is sent to track it down. During his investigations, 007 learns the fighter, with its stealth technology, is to be used to launch an undetectable nuclear attack on China, causing regime change, allowing the hardline General Han to take over. Han will then grant Hong Kong to Sir Henry Ferguson, a ruthless industrialist, as his own private principality. Ferguson has an island retreat in Kowloon. Han has been supplied with hi-tech weapons developed by Ferguson and delivered via Vegas gangsters the Vinelli brothers. When the time comes, Ferguson liquidates the gangsters to cut all ties between the weapons and him. On his mission Bond meets the attractively independent, Connie Webb. She is ostensibly a jewel thief, but there is much more to her. Webb and Bond enjoy a feisty, raunchy and amusing one-upmanship throughout the screenplay.[32]

Set pieces include a monster truck chase, literally, through the streets of Las Vegas, a fight with female body builders, a white water rafting seduction sequence, a fight on a rodeo, a raid on a secret arms depot inside the Hoover Dam, a car chase between Bond's classic gadget-laden Aston Martin DB5 and the villain's similarly equipped vehicle and a full-scale assault on a weaponised building. Bond meets a range of interesting characters including a gay assistant called Jennings, a mysterious, Boba Fett-esque henchperson named Rodin and an old-school avuncular Hong Kong agent called Denholm Crisp.[33] This globetrotting adventure was set in Libya, Vancouver, Vegas, mainland China and Hong Kong.

It is very Bondian and has a lot of Zeitgeistian humour. Replete with splendid one-liners, swearing and a gun barrel in the *middle* of the pre-title sequence, the screenplay would have made a terrific Bond film for Timothy Dalton. Had it been made, it would have secured Dalton's tenure as Bond and perfectly positioned 007 in the post-Cold War age.

In December 1991 *Variety* reported:

Perhaps signaling a narrowing of the rift between the United States and China following the Tiananmen Square massacre, representatives of the China Film Co-Production Corp. are again visiting here in search of servicing or co-production deals for projects to be filmed in China in association with the government-controlled film industry. A major undertaking that may find its way to China is a new James Bond production. A meeting [is] scheduled in Los Angeles with Cubby Broccoli and Michael Wilson, the major domos of the Bond operation.[34]

Production designer Peter Lamont recalled working on *Bond 17* for two days a week for nine months with associate producer Tom Pevsner at Pinewood Studios.

Hanging over the development of the new Bond film was a surprise announcement in August 1990.[35] A bombshell was dropped on the entertainment industry when it was revealed that Cubby Broccoli was exploring selling Danjaq, the company that owned the Bond rights.[36] Control of Eon Productions was ceded to Michael G. Wilson and Barbara Broccoli.[37] The report into the sale suggested that MGM/UA had baulked at the asking price, valued at $166 million but probably worth much more.[38]

The putative sale was linked to Danjaq having to sue MGM/UA.[39] The studio had been taken over by Pathé Communications and the dealmaker behind the corporate trading was Giancarlo Parretti.[40] Parretti had sold the foreign television rights to the James Bond films at cut-rate prices.[41] He had used the sale of these rights to help fund his purchase of the studio with loans from French bank Crédit Lyonnais.[42] This had deprived Danjaq of significant television revenue, prompting Broccoli, after consulting with his long-standing lawyer Norman Tyre, to sue the studio. When Parretti's financial dealings eventually imploded, the French bank was left with temporary ownership of the studio.[43] The litigation was eventually settled in December 1993, when MGM reportedly paid $13.5 million in cash and made other concessions to Broccoli.[44] Once again, it was not the box office that prevented Bond reaching the screen but the tangled corporate ownership of the rights, a legacy of Saltzman's sale to the studio.

Throughout the litigation, it was a strange period of flux for the Bond team. In 1991 they announced *James Bond Jr.*, an animated television show. The central character was Bond's nephew, a modern teenager who attends a high-security English school for the children of diplomats and secret agents. CIA contact Felix Leiter's son, Gordo, is a classmate and there is a tech boffin named IQ. Throughout sixty-five planned half-hour animated episodes, Bond Jr. would battle famous Bond villains in a child-friendly manner. Financed by MGM, at a cost of about $300,000 per episode, the series was produced by Warfield Productions, the US production arm of Danjaq.[45]

During this hiatus Eon took stock of its legacy. In 1990 Graham Rye, then-president of the James Bond International Fan Club (JBIFC), set about archiving a huge range of props and items from the film series stored at

Pinewood Studios.[46] The largest collection of James Bond props ever assembled was unveiled at the JBIFC convention held at the studios in September 1990. It marked the start of the preservation of Bond artefacts that continues to this day. Bond unit photographer Keith Hamshere, acting under veteran Bond publicist, Charles 'Jerry' Juroe, also began archiving the millions of stills from the Bond films, scanning and collating the images which would be enjoyed by generations to come.[47] Before the end of the decade, Eon had catalogued their entire archive of props, costumes, artwork, ephemera and publicity material, overseen by Meg Simmonds who still curates the collection. The archive would form the basis of many exhibitions around the world.

In 1992 Danjaq became incorporated in America and the Swiss entity was dissolved. Eon transferred from their South Audley Street headquarters to equally impressive accommodation at the Hyde Park-end of Piccadilly.

When the litigation with MGM was settled, a number of Bond treatments were commissioned. Screenwriters Richard Smith and John Cork were announced to have been hired to develop films beyond *Bond 17*.[48] John Cork, writer of the Whoopi Goldberg Civil Rights drama, *The Long Walk Home* (1990), remembered his involvement, 'I had met Barbara socially at a screening of *The Long Walk Home* in Los Angeles with Timothy Dalton.'[49] Cork was on the board of recently formed US registered charity, the Ian Fleming Foundation which preserved the legacy of Ian Fleming and James Bond. Cork's encyclopaedic knowledge of the subject was of great assistance:

> What became clear, I think, to [Eon] was that I knew Bond. I knew the cinematic Bond. I knew how the Bond films were made, and I knew the literary Bond, and I knew this at a level that virtually no other writer who would have been pitching to them could have possibly known.[50]

Cork continued:

> I was hired to write a treatment for a 'future' Bond film. I got the feeling that much of the creative energy of the company was focused on developing what would become *GoldenEye* with Michael France. When I went in for my first meeting, they told me they hired me because they liked my vision for Bond, but that my story idea was too close to the idea that they were developing with France, which also had to do with satellites. Thus began the long journey into pitching Bond stories. I must have pitched twenty to thirty. Each one required oodles of research and mapping out characters. None of them went

anywhere! Most of my meetings were with Michael and Barbara, but often Cubby was there, too. John Claflin, the development person for Danjaq at the time, was a constant presence, working to try to get us all on the same page.[51]

Cork's involvement then took a different turn:

At John Claflin's urging, and partially out of frustration at not feeling like we were getting anywhere on a story, I wrote up a document entitled 'James Bond in the '90s.' That, I think, excited everyone. It was somewhat of a character bible that went back to the novels as well as the films and pulled little quotes that helped define Bond's character, that alluded to his past, that gave us a launching point to discuss who this kind of man would be in the 1990s. The document also covered the role of women in the films, the role of the villains in the movies, who M was, who was Q, Moneypenny, Loelia Ponsonby, Bill Tanner, Felix Leiter – all the usual suspects. The document also talked about Bond's 'burden', or what drives him as a character: from losing his parents at a young age to the role of the loss of Vesper in his life. As well as his literary declaration in CASINO ROYALE that he wanted to pursue the threat behind the spies, not just the agents themselves. I wanted to emphasise that Bond was a man who saw the big picture, whose arrogance and disregard for rules and conventions was because he was on a larger mission, a mission that went beyond any single assignment. That character bible was my sole contribution to the creative process. It wasn't a rule book *per se*, but an informed dossier on the key elements of what made Bond films tick. It certainly wasn't a road map for screenwriters, and it was probably of limited use in many ways. But I think it helped everyone focus on what they felt made Bond unique. Occasionally, I would run into someone who had read it (usually a writer) and they would mention something from the document.[52]

John Cork would go on to become the pre-eminent James Bond scholar and chart the James Bond legacy in books and through a series of documentaries and DVD extras.

Throughout the six-year period Bond was off screen, a number of Bond veterans passed away. Richard Maibaum, Maurice Binder and UA Executive Mike Beck all died in 1991. Terence Young passed away in 1994.

The last in this sad list was the man who met Ian Fleming and secured the rights to James Bond, Cubby Broccoli's partner on the first nine Bond movies, Harry Saltzman, who died in 1994. He had continued to work sporadically in film, but in his latter years he focused his attentions back on his first love: theatre. His daughter Hilary remembered, 'My father moved to Paris and had a series of strokes, the first being in 1982. He was still sort of running [theatrical company] H.M. Tennent. After having a couple of strokes, [he] retired.'[53] Upon the death of his wife Jacqueline, Saltzman had got remarried to Adriana Ghinsberg whom he had met in 1981.[54] She described his final years, 'He watched the new Bond films as they were released but they were not his style.'[55] Harry lived with Adriana's family and was still 'interested in everything. He read a lot.'[56] She recalled, 'It was a quite a difficult time because his youngest son [Christopher] died [in 1990] and after that he was extremely sad. It was a shock for him. It was a tragedy for him.'[57]

On 28 September 1994, Harry Saltzman too went to that circus in the sky. Adriana remembered her husband's last moments, 'In the afternoon he was positively well and in the morning it was finished. They called me from the hospital at 3am telling me he wasn't feeling so well and I went there but it was finished. He had a heart attack.'[58]

With the passing of Harry Saltzman, it was the end of an era. A number of heroes behind the Bond films had gone. However, their legacy would live on in the remarkable films they helped create. The heirs of the tradition would ensure that the baton of Bond would be passed on.

24

FROM THE SHADOWS AS A CHILD

GOLDENEYE

(1995)

YOU KNOW THE NAME
$26,205,007™
(FIRST THREE DAYS)
(NOW YOU KNOW THE NUMBER)
LARGEST OPENING IN BOND HISTORY
LARGEST OPENING IN MGM/UA HISTORY

n August 1993 MGM/UA chairman Frank Mancuso appointed veteran studio executive John Calley as the new president of United Artists.[1] A decade earlier Calley had been a key executive at Warner Brothers, the distributor behind *Never Say Never Again*. Production Vice-President Jeff Kleeman was brought on board as the ailing studio looked to revive the James Bond franchise. However, early research was not positive, as Kleeman recalled:

> The reasons were primarily that most teenage boys did not know who James Bond was, or if they did, they knew him as, "that guy my father likes." From MGM/UA's perspective, Bond was a relic of its past that people loved but didn't know what to do with. Frank Mancuso fully empowered John Calley, "Whether it makes sense to me or not, I trust you creatively."[2]

Kleeman remembered the United Artists' analysis, 'The worst that could happen is it loses a little bit of money. On home video, nicely packaged with the other Bond movies it'll be okay. The name of the game internally at the studio was how cheaply can you make the movie?'[3]

In 1993, when MGM/UA announced a seventeenth Bond was in development, co-chairman Alan Ladd Jr. said they were looking for 'an important director to give it a different look.'[4] British directors Michael Caton-Jones[5] and Peter Medak[6] were amongst the few considered.[7] New Zealand-born Martin Campbell had helmed high-end television programmes including two series that were influential on previous Eon productions: *Reilly Ace of Spies* (1983) and the BBC's *Edge of Darkness* (1985), both were written by Troy Kennedy Martin. His 1994 feature impressed the studio as Campbell recalled, '[Calley] said, "I saw *No Escape* and I think you would be very good to do the next Bond film."'[8] Kleeman provided the rationale:

> He'd made it for about $20 million and it was a big sci-fi action movie that looked like it cost more than $20 million. We knew he had never had a breakout successful movie, but we believed he was a genuinely talented director who knew how to work within a budget, who we knew was capable of putting all the money on screen.[9]

Growing up, the director had read the Ian Fleming books and was a fan of the early films[10] and from their first meeting Kleeman felt Campbell 'was very articulate, very interesting and really had a strong point of view about Bond and how to do it.'[11]

In the four years since *Licence to Kill*, Michael G. Wilson noted 'the collapse of the Soviet Union and of the system it upheld means that there are literally thousands of specially trained agents looking around for work. Weapons of mass destruction are just sitting around waiting to be offered to the highest bidder. This is a world in which Bond is needed more than ever!'[12] Any new Bond writer would have to re-position Bond for the nineties.

Michael France, whose Sylvester Stallone hit *Cliffhanger* (1993) had been described as '*Die Hard* on a Mountain', fought hard to get the Bond gig, 'When I was a kid I wanted to be Richard Maibaum, not Bond.'[13] In January 1993 France remembered a lunch with the producers:

> As soon as I showed up they started quizzing me, what my attitude to the character was, what I knew about 007, what I could bring to a new film to make it fresh and different from the blizzard of action movies in recent years. They liked the fact that I knew the movies.'[14]

France felt he convinced Cubby 'that I would take an approach they would like, that would take the characters seriously but still have fun with them.'[15] For several months he met regularly with Michael, Barbara, Cubby and Dana.[16] Screenwriter John Cork remembered running into Michael France and Barbara Broccoli at the Danjaq offices in Santa Monica:

> I mentioned how the inmates were taking over the asylum – me being editor of the Ian Fleming Foundation publication *Goldeneye* at the time and him having published a couple of issues of the [obscure] fanzine *Mr. Kiss Kiss Bang Bang* back in the seventies. He went white as a sheet. Barbara looked at him with this perfectly timed withering look (which if you know her is often only reserved for those she likes) and said, 'Oh, Michael, we know all about that!' To say the blood drained out of his face would be an understatement.[17]

France travelled to Moscow and St. Petersburg and interviewed KGB agents, visited nuclear research laboratories,[18] and openly photographed the KGB headquarters, 'probably the stupidest thing I did in Russia.'[19] During this time Michael Wilson suggested the Arecibo Observatory in Puerto Rico, the world's largest single-dish radio telescope, as a setting for the finale.[20]

Timothy Dalton was the 'the Bond of record'[21] and France wrote 'a lot of physical action [and] some emotional intensity'[22] with him in mind. France noted, 'By the same token, they didn't want to be as serious as *Licence to Kill.* *Goldfinger* was considered the model Bond.'[23]

Michael France's screenplay featured an older villain named Augustus Trevelyan and the electromagnetic pulse (EMP) weapon named GoldenEye. The pre-title sequence was set at a wine auction on a high-speed train. The villainous sommelier gives himself away by serving Bond, a man, before the ladies. The scene culminates with 007 driving his Aston Martin from the car bay of the train to the top of the carriages and down the sleek nose cone. *GoldenEye's* initial draft screenplay featured many sequences used in later Bond films: helicopters with saw-blades, a parachute jump into a sinkhole and a snake-pit situation in a nuclear blast chamber.

United Artists felt further drafts were needed.[24] The producers turned to future Academy Award-nominee Jeffrey Caine, who had previously worked with Barbara Broccoli on an adaptation of his own novel, THE HOMING, as well as an original screenplay about the Navajo code talkers.[25] Caine began a page one rewrite and asserted, 'One of my strengths in screenwriting is that I'm a "structuralist." Barbara was worried the Michael France screenplay didn't have a very well-defined structure.'[26] Caine was not afraid to stand his ground,

> Wilson started from the premise that a James Bond film was largely about big, big stunts. I dug my heels in and said "No." Stunts are desirable and the audience expects to see them but you don't construct a story around preconceived stunts. You find your story and then you find a stunt that will work within it.'[27]

The story featured the internet, which Caine recalled 'had to be explained to me by Michael Wilson as to what it was and what it could do,'[28] and a computer hacker was hired to further explain the capabilities of the World Wide Web.[29] As with Osborne and Davies' *Bond 17* screenplay, *GoldenEye* begins in a chemical weapons facility. Working out of Danjaq's Culver City offices,[30] Caine devised a pre-title sequence to 'establish a mission that 006 and 007 had done together so you knew who 006 was when he turns out to be the bad guy later.'[31] Caine made Trevelyan younger to 'be able to take on Bond in hand-to-hand combat.'[32] He also gave Trevelyan his Lienz Cossack history and had Zukovsky force Bond to play Russian roulette. Coolly picking up the gun, Bond puts the weapon to his head, quickly pulling the trigger, whereupon the Russian chortled, 'Bond, you are the only man I know who can tell the difference between a Walther PPK with one bullet in the chamber and a Walther PPK with no bullet in the chamber, just by the weight.'[33] Caine would later 'grieve for'[34] this lost idea.

GoldenEye was a breakthrough in Jeffrey Caine's screenwriting career. However, he remembered it with mixed emotions. He had shared the experience throughout with his wife Lorna, who tragically passed away just weeks before the film premiered. He recalled, 'She died the day the film poster arrived. I unrolled it and showed it to her. It seemed to have a certain significance that it had arrived within the last minutes of her life.'[35]

GoldenEye's release date was delayed from summer to US Thanksgiving in 1995 for further revisions.[36] Playwright and screenwriter Kevin Wade, a friend of both Barbara and her then husband Fred Zollo,[37] was asked to improve the Bond character.[38] Wade observed, 'Fleming's Bond hews much closer to the archetypal Private Eye of American crime fiction.'[39] Wade took inspiration from 'one Raymond Chandler quote in particular, "Down these mean streets a man must go who is not himself mean, who is neither tarnished nor afraid. He is the hero; he is everything. He must be a complete man and a common man and yet an unusual man." Probably a specious comparison but it guided me in writing the screenplay.'[40] Wade streamlined the plot, reducing a long sequence in a St. Petersburg arms bazaar to a single scene.[41] 'I worked fairly closely with Campbell who was storyboarding those sequences. I was really taking my cues from going upstairs and sitting with him and more or less putting down in words what he had storyboarded.'[42] Wade did not expect credit, 'I did three weeks on a movie that was literally a two-year aggregate for all those other writers.'[43] However, he did donate his name to Bond's CIA contact in St. Petersburg.[44]

Kleeman felt that Caine and Wade had provided a road map for the film, but that a further rewrite was required.[45] Another acquaintance of Barbara Broccoli and Fred Zollo was Bruce Feirstein,[46] known for his best-selling book REAL MEN DON'T EAT QUICHE. Barbara had read some of his spec scripts and Feirstein's wife, a former MGM executive, was an acquaintance of Martin Campbell. An experienced journalist, Feirstein was a regular contributor to *Vanity Fair*, but was still an unknown quantity as a screenwriter, 'I had lots of movies get to the point of almost being green lit but not being made.'[47] In September 1994 Feirstein met with Broccoli, Wilson and Campbell to discuss *GoldenEye*.[48] Working closely with Martin Campbell and Michael Wilson, Feirstein felt, 'The world had changed and Bond hadn't, which went on to inform the whole rewrite.'[49] Jeff Kleeman was a fan, 'Bruce ended up restructuring and rethinking and rewriting far more than we'd ever initially planned. His ideas were just so strong.'[50]

Feirstein remembered a pivotal day, 'One morning about 6.30am we were talking about what we should do with the M character. I said, "It's just a bunch of guys sitting in a room talking." And Martin said, "Why don't you try it as a woman?"'[51] In 1992 Stella Rimington was made Director General of the British internal security service, MI5, so the suggestion was apposite. Feirstein also noted that Barbara Broccoli enjoyed the odd bourbon and occasionally teased that Bond was a sexist and a dinosaur.[52] Rewritten thirty times,[53] the scene penned that morning was the one shot verbatim 'with one word changed'.[54] Bruce Feirstein finished work and left for Los Angeles, 'Martin Campbell wanted to have the script done, nailed and closed before one frame of the film was shot. He said his one goal was to know the script better than anyone on the production, and I believe he did.'[55]

The writing credits were arrived at through an arbitration process: *GoldenEye* was based on a story by Michael France and a screenplay by Jeffrey Caine and Bruce Feirstein. Feirstein's contribution to the finished work impressed the producers so much that he became a key creative voice for the Bond franchise in the nineties and beyond. Feirstein would go on to write two more Bond films and be a scribe for other areas of the 007 world. Firstly, he penned the 'James Bond: A Licence to Thrill' ride which ran from 1998 to 2002 in various US theme parks and briefly in London. After the huge success of the Nintendo 64 *GoldenEye* computer game, Feirstein would shape four further games: *007: Everything or Nothing* (2004) – written with Danny Bilson and Paul Demeo, *James Bond 007: From Russia With Love* (2005) – which featured the return of Sean Connery to an official Eon Bond product, *James Bond 007: Bloodstone* (2010) and finally the 2010 update of the *GoldenEye* game which featured, incongruously, Craig as Bond and a score by David Arnold.

The pre-title sequence of *GoldenEye* begins with a mission in the Soviet Union in which 007 teams up with 006, Alec Trevelyan, to sabotage a chemical weapons facility. Bungee-jumping down a dam to access the plant, Trevelyan is supposedly executed by hardliner Colonel Arkady Grigorovich Ourumov. Bond makes an escape by driving a motorbike off the runway servicing the facility and catches up with a pilotless plane, as the explosive charges he placed destroy the factory. Nine years later, while being psychologically evaluated in the South of France, Bond meets Xenia Onatopp, a pilot for Russian Mafia organisation, the Janus Syndicate. Xenia crushes a Canadian admiral between her thighs, achieving an orgasm. She then uses his credentials to steal the new Tiger Eurocopter – innovatively shielded against electromagnetic blasts. Xenia pilots the helicopter to the Severnaya Space Control Facility in Siberia, where it is revealed she is in cahoots with General Ourumov, who is now commander of Russia's Space Division. Together they steal the control key – the GoldenEye – to a top secret Soviet-era EMP weapon. Setting off one of the satellite-based weapons, it covers all trace of their theft and destroys the facility, but not before programmer Natalya Simonova escapes, unaware that her colleague Boris Grishenko has also survived. The EMP blast alerts MI6 and Bond is summoned to headquarters, where he meets the new, female, M. Unimpressed by his Cold War past, M tasks 007 with tracking down what analysts had previously thought was an unfeasible weapon, which could now threaten the world. Meanwhile Defence Minister Dimitri Mishkin seeks an explanation from General Ourumov as to how the Severnaya facility – under his control – was compromised. Natalya, now a valuable witness to the Severnaya massacre, is captured by Grishenko, who is revealed to be in league with Janus. Bond arrives in St. Petersburg and meets CIA contact Jack Wade who takes him to Russian Mafia contact Valentin Zukovsky, a professional foe from Bond's past. Zukovsky gives Bond information which ultimately leads him – via Xenia – to the head of the Janus Syndicate in an old statue park filled with crumbling Soviet-era icons. Janus is none other than Alec Trevelyan – 006. Trevelyan is a Lienz Cossack, a group who were refused safe haven by Churchill and brutally purged by Stalin after World War II, thus orphaning Alec.

Bond and Natalya are trapped in the stolen Tiger helicopter, set to be destroyed, but they escape just in time only to be taken by Mishkin to a KGB prison. Here, Mishkin is killed by Ourumov who is revealed to be a cohort of Trevelyan. Bond and Natalya try to get free but Natalya is caught, while Bond breaks free by commandeering a tank through the streets of St. Petersburg. Tracking down Trevelyan's private train, Bond parks the tank on the tracks but Trevelyan rams his train into the stationary vehicle. Emerging from the crash, Bond confronts Trevelyan, Xenia and Ourumov. Trevelyan and Xenia manage to elude 007, who kills Ouromov. Bond and Natalya are imprisoned on a booby-trapped train carriage. Natalya uses Grishenko's internet trail against him and works out that they have gone to Cuba. Using the laser on his gadget-filled Omega watch, Bond and Natalya flee from the train carriage before it explodes.

Bond and Natalya reconnoitre Cuban air space looking for a likely satellite control dish. Their light aircraft is attacked and Xenia goes in for the kill only to be hoisted, literally, by her own petard and crushed to death. The Cuban satellite centre is revealed to be beneath a drainable lake. Bond confronts Trevelyan, who now reveals his plan. After electronically hacking into the

Bank of England, he intends to steal the UK's reserves. Then by detonating the remaining GoldenEye EMP satellite over London, the financial heart of the West will be destroyed, causing economic havoc. Thus the depleted hardline Soviet-era generals in Russia will regain power. The weapon will also cover the tracks of Trevelyan's multi-billion dollar theft. Sabotaging the GoldenEye control room, Bond fights Trevelyan on the radar antenna high above the dish and after a brutal struggle in the gear room, coldly releases his former colleague to fall to his death. Grishenko is killed, frozen by liquid nitrogen. Bond is rescued from the exploding dish by a helicopter hijacked by Natalya. They meet up with camouflaged US Marines led by Jack Wade in Cuban territory.

Jeff Kleeman articulated why UA was not prepared to develop a new Bond film with the incumbent actor:

> The Dalton Bonds had not performed significantly well at the box office. We were trying to grapple with the fact that the Dalton movies were not the most beloved of Bond films. We were trying to introduce Bond to a new audience. It seemed counterintuitive to what we were trying to accomplish, to continue on with Timothy at that point.'[56]

Alan Ladd Jr., co-chairman of the studio and friend to Cubby Broccoli, echoed those thoughts, 'I didn't think that [Timothy Dalton] was the appropriate man for it. I thought they could do better.'[57]

Kleeman recalled, 'Barbara, Michael and Cubby made the case for Timothy. They did genuinely love him and for good reason. I'm sure they were disappointed we didn't want to make it with Timothy.'[58] The Broccolis conceded and informed Dalton of MGM/UA's decision.[59] On 12 April 1994 Dalton issued a carefully worded statement, 'Even though the Broccolis have always made it clear to me that they want me to resume my role in their next James Bond feature I have now made this difficult decision. The Broccolis have been good to me as producers. They have been more special as friends.'[60] Dalton was 'very proud of the Bond films I've made. I'm not saying they are without faults but I am very happy to have done them. It has certainly enhanced my worldwide knowledge and fame and it has definitely enhanced my commercial viability. I loved making them.'[61] Eon released their own statement, 'We have never thought of anyone but Timothy as the star of the seventeenth James Bond film. We understand his reasons and will honour his decision.'[62] Calley said, 'we are proceeding with the project as planned and will meet our targeted summer 1995 release date.'[63]

In May 1994 Martin Campbell remembered going 'around the world inter-viewing [potential Bonds],'[64] and recalled meeting Ralph Fiennes socially at Cubby Broccoli's house.[65] Fiennes later revealed, 'there was a conversation that was great and a meeting with Cubby Broccoli that was terrific. It didn't lead to anything on both sides.'[66] Liam Neeson also acknowledged he was 'heavily courted.'[67] Casting director Debbie McWilliams confirmed they did test ten British actors.[68] For MGM/UA, however, they had set their sights on one man: Pierce Brosnan.[69]

Having lost out on the role in 1986, Brosnan managed his expectations:

> My agent said, 'Be prepared. The Broccolis are in town and they are interested in you.' I was very once bitten, twice shy, so to speak. We had lunch at the Peninsula Hotel – Barbara and Michael, John Calley and Jeff Kleeman – that was our first encounter. Then I went and met with John Calley a while later and he said, 'It looks like this is going to happen.' I said to my agent, 'I'd love to do this but I don't want to be dicked around again, I don't want to be waiting at the altar and she not show up.' I did not want to dare to hope in case the whole thing crashed down around my ears again. It happened very quickly after that.[70]

As with Roger Moore, prior to his Bond casting, Brosnan was most famous for a television show, *Remington Steele*. Since the series had been cancelled, Brosnan had worked consistently but not as the lead in major studio produc-tions. However, MGM/UA could not have afforded an established leading man.[71] Kleeman explained, 'Our hope was that *GoldenEye* was going to be successful, the first of many more new Bond films, which meant that we needed an actor who financially and logistically would be available to make a whole series of Bond movies.'[72]

Brosnan confirms he did not shoot a screentest this time around.[73] Matthew Glen, son of director John and an assistant editor on the Bond films, received a request to locate screentests John had shot previously, '[Pierce] got the job again with the same tests I'd made years before.'[74]

Kleeman was at the fateful meeting, 'Cubby who had been sitting very, very quietly, tapped his cane on the floor, not in a super-dramatic way, but just gave it a single tap. Everybody stopped talking and all turned to him. He very simply said, "We should go with Pierce."'[75]

On 1 June 1994 Pierce Brosnan received a call from his agent:

I was standing in the kitchen and I had [Fred Specktor] on the line saying, 'You are James Bond. They want you for the role. It's called *GoldenEye*. You're in, you cannot tell anyone, it's a big secret.' Keeley, my wife-to-be, was standing there beside me. I was giving thumbs up, doing the James Bond gun signal. I put the phone down and I gave my wife-to-be the biggest kiss. We opened a bottle of champagne and I went out and had my photograph taken with a huge shit-eating grin on my face.[76]

Brosnan recalled practising the line 'Bond, James Bond' while brushing his teeth for months before filming began, 'It's quite funny, really just a breath away from parody.'[77]

On 8 June 1994 the international media were invited to the drawing room at London's Regent Hotel to meet the new 007:

It was a baptism by fire. I had no idea what was going to happen. Martin Campbell, Barbara, Michael Wilson – everyone was terribly nervous. I was completely ignorant of what I was about to *really* step in to. Geoff Freeman, the publicist, said, 'Right, Pierce when you hear the ['James Bond Theme'] you just go out here and round the corner.' On came the music, I walked out and I turned the corner into this blitzkrieg of world press, sat on a dais with Martin, Barbara and Michael and realised why they were so terrified.[78]

Sporting long hair and a beard – grown for his upcoming role as Robinson Crusoe – Brosnan, described Bond for the nineties, 'He has to go back to being a more kind of flinty character, more humour's got to come in – and I think also it's time to really try and peel back certain layers of his character and see what lies beneath this man – see what demons might be there.'[79] Following his first exposure to the world press, Brosnan pondered what he had let himself in for:

I got all the newspapers the next morning and I went to a little place I knew on the King's Road – the 'Chelsea Kitchen' – to have breakfast. I opened up the press and there was my life, spread out on the page of every newspaper. Girlfriends, where I'd been, who I was, what I'd done, and so began my world as James Bond. I was catching a plane that night to Papua New Guinea and I remember thinking, 'Well, at least nobody will know me in Papua New Guinea, but two days later I'm jogging through the bush and these kids were going: 'James Bond, James Bond!'[80]

Polish actress Izabella Scorupco was cast as computer programmer Natalya Fyodorovna Simonova. It was casting director Debbie McWilliams who discovered Scorupco in Sweden at the eleventh hour.[81] The actress remembered, 'They had combed Russia and Yugoslavia to find Natalya and ended up, in desperation, at a Swedish casting director's office.'[82] At the time Scorupco was filming *Petri Tears* (1995), a medieval drama in which she spent part of the film dressed as a man – it was this footage that was screened for McWilliams.[83] Her Polish upbringing – with a Russian nanny – helped with the dialect, 'It's almost the same language, Polish and Russian, but it's a little bit softer.'[84]

Famke Janssen, cast as the lethal assassin, Xenia Onatopp, came to the attention of the filmmakers when they saw rushes from UA's supernatural thriller *Lord of Illusions* (1995).[85] Campbell recalled, 'This tall, sort of rather slim, lanky girl came in, she gave a great reading, she was unusual.'[86] Janssen tested opposite Brosnan, reading the casino scene and knew she was ideal for the role the minute she met the producers, 'It was written all over their faces.'[87] Janssen thought Onatopp was 'sick and perverted, really, and that's precisely what I wanted to make her – one sick bitch.'[88]

Sean Bean, best known for his leading role in the television series *Sharpe*, was cast as double agent Alec Trevelyan (006). Bean felt, 'They [Trevelyan and Bond] are a good match – each knowing that the other can be a totally professional, ruthless killer when he wants to be.'[89] Scottish actor Alan Cumming, playing the turncoat, cyberpunk Boris Ivanovich Grishenko 'tried to combine a Russian dourness and American computer-geek awareness.'[90]

Debbie McWilliams's fine casting eye secured Turkish-born French actor, Tchéky Karyo as Russian Defence Minister Dimitri Mishkin and the German Gottfried John as General Ourumov. British television star Robbie Coltrane played former KGB agent, turned arms dealer, Valentin Zukovsky. Initial publicity for the film had Coltrane touted as the bad guy to disguise Trevelyan's treachery. Coltrane was the title star of television's dark psychologist thriller, *Cracker* – an Eon favourite. On reading the script he reflected on its focus on 'organised crime in post-Soviet Russia. There are some rogue nationals and some real mean weapons in the world, and this script made sense to me.'[91] Joe Don Baker returned to the franchise as good guy, CIA contact Jack Wade, two films after his villainous turn in *The Living Daylights*. Baker based his character on Darius, the Texan CIA agent he had played in Martin Campbell's *Edge of Darkness*.[92]

The film would be an early role for Minnie Driver, who played Irina, Zukovsky's flame and awful nightclub singer. Kate Gayson also made a fleeting appearance in the casino scenes: she was the daughter of actress Eunice, the first James Bond girl Sylvia Trench.

Campbell remembered John Calley saying, "'If you're going to get a female M, get a star, get Judi Dench.'"[93] Although other actresses were tested,[94] Martin Campbell wrote to her and offered her the part.[95] One of Britain's most esteemed stage actresses, Dench had made her television debut opposite Bernard Lee in *Family on Trial* (1959).[96] Having just turned sixty, Dench recalled, 'It took me just a second to say yes. I was thrilled and fearful at the same time. It was only three days' work but it was a huge film. I didn't want to fall flat on my face.'[97]

Dench was joined by a new Miss Moneypenny, the aptly named Samantha Bond, 'Nobody was going to knock me playing Moneypenny if Jude was playing M. She raised the credibility for everyone. What more of a party line do you want than to say, "I have a small part in the new James Bond movie?"'[98] Bond had to be diplomatic, 'Caroline Bliss is a good friend of mine. I knew, that she knew, that she wasn't up for it. They were starting fresh. I said to my agent, "Don't say anything to anyone until I've spoken to Caroline."'[99] Both actresses had known each since they attended grammar school and the Bristol Old Vic Theatre School together. Remembered Bliss, 'When [Samantha] got the role she avoided me for a few weeks but eventually she called me. "I'm so sorry darling. I'm so sorry," she said. I burst out laughing. I said, "Look, I'm hoping to become a mum and I'm thrilled it's gone to one of my best friends."'[100] Interestingly, Samantha had been asked to audition for *The Living Daylights* in 1986, but her agent had discouraged her.[101]

Amidst the changes, Desmond Llewelyn reprised his role as Q for the fifteenth time, 'I was ecstatic and very honoured having been the only one asked to return from the eighties era.'[102] Llewelyn told Feirstein, 'I know Q is beloved. But for God's sake, don't make him into some kind of sentimental grandfather – that's what I am in real life.'[103]

Wilson and Broccoli were supported on their first solo Bond with many of the trusted team who had worked on the earlier pictures. *GoldenEye* was production designer Peter Lamont's fifteenth consecutive Bond film, 'I thought Allan Cameron would probably get it because he'd worked with Martin on a picture before. Martin said, "Sweetie come and talk to me. What was your last film?" I said, "*True Lies*." He went white. He said, "My idol is James Cameron." So I was in.'[104]

Phil Méheux had lensed every one of Martin Campbell's feature films prior to *GoldenEye*. Having viewed all the previous Bond movies with Campbell,

Méheux concluded the recent pictures had lacked a distinct look.[105] He stressed to the producers, 'I'm only interested if we can really make it our own and shoot it the way we want to shoot it. We got that confirmation.'[106] Méheux was struck by the style Ted Moore had given the early pictures. He described them as having 'a glossy, worldwide feel, they didn't look like British films. They did look like cosmopolitan, American films – they travelled the world.'[107] For *GoldenEye* 'there was a Martin Campbell-Phil Méheux look, not necessarily a Bond look.'[108]

Barbara Broccoli had noticed costume designer Lindy Hemming's work in the period London gangster film *The Krays* (1990)[109] and was hired to dress Bond for the nineties:

> I thought that it was time for a smart sophisticated elegant Bond again. It seemed that this Bond would have to slip effortlessly among businessmen, bankers and politicians of the world while pursuing his spying career, so I dressed him in the kind of tailoring aspired to by those people at that time. I chose the tailor, Brioni, who made suits for all the world's leading politicians. They gave it their all: wonderful clothes, beautifully tailored. Pierce said that when he put on his suits, it was as though he was stepping into Bond's skin. In a way, a suit is the equivalent of a fine suit of armour, it protects you and, if perfectly fitted, makes you both very confident and, in a strange way, invisible.[110]

An October 1994 start date was set, with a summer 1995 release. Bond's traditional home, Pinewood Studios was 'double-booked',[111] and the production looked all over Europe for studio space.[112] Eventually, Leavesden Aerodrome, an empty factory near Watford, where Rolls Royce had built aircraft during World War II was deemed perfect.[113] Associate producer Anthony Waye felt the task was just starting, 'Now all we had to do was to convert it into a studio capable of housing a multi-million-dollar movie.'[114] Méheux recounted, 'We knew that the runway was very useful. We needed to put in acres of electricity, a dining area, a special effects place where they could build their toys, a costume area, a lighting store for lights.'[115] Méheux was unfazed by the seemingly mammoth task, 'We were professionals; most of us work on location a lot.'[116] Peter Lamont, who had overseen the infrastructure at Churubusco Studios in Mexico on *Licence to Kill*, completed the task 'in about 8 weeks'[117] using Delta Doric, the company who rebuilt the 007 Stage after the fire in 1984.[118] Named Eon Studios and christened 'Cubbywood' by the crew,[119] the facility was later used to film *Star Wars Episode I: The Phantom Menace* and *Sleepy Hollow* (both 1999) and then, Méheux noted, 'Warners turned it into a proper studio [for] the *Harry Potters* and the rest is history.'[120]

Brosnan loved Leavesden, 'There's no ghosts for me to have to contend with. No Sean, no Roger roaming the corridors. If we were back in Pinewood Studios, everyone in the commissary would be nudging and pointing at me saying, "There's the new Bond." I've had to face none of that at Leavesden.'[121]

On Sunday 22 January 1995 Pierce Brosnan introduced the cast of *GoldenEye* to the world's press and remembered the pressure, 'It was palpable. You could, within a mile, feel the energy emanating from the studio – what was at stake. It had all been quiet on the Western Front. Here we were, coming back with *GoldenEye*. The title alone had an allure to it; it felt lucky. *Goldfinger, GoldenEye*.'[122]

Principal photography had commenced on 16 January 1995 with the Severnaya control room scenes starring Izabella Scorupco and Alan Cumming.[123] Two days later Pierce Brosnan shot his first scene as 007 where Bond is reunited with his old foe Valentin Zukovsky.[124]

In late January[125] the main unit headed for Puerto Rico but were restricted on what they could film at the Arecibo Observatory. Lamont recalled, 'They allowed us to go up there to get a couple of shots. We did an awful lot of work back in the studio both full scale and model.'[126] A skeleton crew had filmed wide and aerial shots of the dish the previous November.[127] A scene filmed on the beach at Cibuco Farm was rewritten by Feirstein to to add some depth to Natalya's character, 'Martin thought it would be a great idea to get some input on it from Izabella, which I did in-between takes where she was running from gunfire and explosions. She was surprisingly coherent, given that this was all punctuated by weapon fire. It was one of those times when I got lucky and the words just came to me.'[128]

On 7 February 1995[129] Judi Dench reported for duty, 'I was told M was meant to smoke but my hands were shaking so badly I couldn't make the lighter work. Martin Campbell was terribly understanding and told me not to bother with the smoking.'[130] Brosnan remembered:

She and I sat around an oil heater with blankets on our legs. I remember Martin wanted her to have a cup of tea [in the scene] and she said, 'No, no, a cup and saucer is going to rattle, give me a nice scotch.' She clung on to a glass of scotch and I clung on to the chair and we set forth as James Bond and M.[131]

Costume designer Lindy Hemming 'had looked carefully at Stella Rimington and I knew Judi Dench well. I didn't want to make her look too masculine or frumpy, so I chose Sonya Rykiel and Armani and kept everything soft. I thought she looked beautiful and strong.'[132] Vauxhall Cross, the Terry Farrell-designed real-life headquarters for MI6, inspired Peter Lamont, 'Looking at the exterior I had to decide where M's office would be. We asked to look at MI6's offices, but they didn't allow us, so it's all based on supposition.'[133]

Samantha Bond's one brief scene as Miss Moneypenny was completed in two hours.[134] She was impressed by the eveningwear Hemming dressed Moneypenny in – who returns urgently to the office from a theatre date – but noted, 'That was the year of those funny push 'em up bras, which I had never worn. I got onto the set and it was terribly exposing. Of course, everyone on the set is male, so I wouldn't take my coat off for the rehearsals because I was so embarrassed!'[135]

Three days later[136] Desmond Llewelyn was on set and was full of praise for Martin Campbell, 'We had more rehearsal time than I'd ever had in my life and Judi said the same. If we didn't get something right in the scene, he'd re-shoot it completely. Most of my other directors would cut around and insert, but not him.'[137] None other than Michael Wilson was holding the prompt cards for Llewelyn's lines.[138]

The scene introduced the world to Bond's Atlanta Metallic Blue BMW Z3, the company's first mass-market roadster. A pre-production model of the car was only made available to the filmmakers late into the shooting schedule, so although Q identified many gadgets on the car, few could be paid off in suitable action sequences. The car is only seen fleetingly in Puerto Rico where Bond is briefed by Wade. While Bond and Fleming had often driven non-British cars, the move from Aston Martin was controversial.[139] BMW's product placement was part of *GoldenEye's* innovative marketing strategy led by MGM/UA head of worldwide promotions Karen Sortito, who negotiated with high-end onscreen partners to synchronise their major advertising spend in line with the release of the film, thus reducing the studio's publicity outlay.[140] BMW's $15 million promotional spend allowed the studio to reduce its advertising budget to nearly half that of a similar profile film.[141] Kleeman explained the BMW deal, 'It was a substantial amount of money both in helping the production but also in promoting the movie. We also loved that it was introducing a car that nobody had seen before.'[142] The strategy worked, 7,000 pre-orders for the car came within two weeks of the film opening and showroom traffic was up 70 per cent – the car would not actually be available until 1996.[143] *GoldenEye* was the first time a car manufacturer had a fully fledged promotional tie-in with a theatrical feature.[144]

In late February 1995 Barbara Broccoli led an action unit to Greolieres in France[145] to shoot the cat and mouse car chase between Bond's classic Aston Martin DB5 and Xenia Onatopp's red Ferrari 355. New to the Bond team was second unit director Ian Sharp, recommended to the producers by Martin Campbell who thought, along with Méheux, 'he had the ability to direct a Bond film. [Possibly] he would get to do the next one.'[146] Stunt driver Rémy Julienne explained, 'Although the DB5 is an old wonderful lady it has very low performance, an engine that is not very powerful and uncertain road holding.'[147] Julienne's team modified both cars to make them perform equally.[148] The Aston Martin and Ferrari were involved in a minor collision, resulting in both cars having to be restored overnight.[149] Brosnan himself caused further injury to the classic Bond car while filming in front of the Hotel de Paris in Monte Carlo itself, 'I drove it backwards and forwards all night and I thought, "What is this dreadful burning smell?" I realised I'd been driving with the handbrake on. I made a nifty retreat from the set because the owner was standing glowering and lovingly looking at his car.'[150]

Ian Sharp's second unit spent two weeks preparing the pre-title stunt[151] at the Contra Dam near Locarno, Switzerland.[152] On 11 March 1995 the 900ft[153] bungee jump was performed twice by Wayne Michaels who remembered seeing the dam for the first time when he arrived to film the stunt, 'It was the most extraordinary picture. You kept looking up and up and up and never seemed to get to the top. It was the most enormous, gigantic piece of engineering, quite awe-inspiring. A lot of really burly tough riggers looked at it and said, "Fuck that!"'[154] The University of Oxford bungee jump team had been consulted as Michaels recalled the unique nature of the stunt, 'The dam was a concave design. The way the wind blew up into the dam caused a vortex so we had a real problem making sure I could keep away from the wall and not hit it.'[155] When a sophisticated dummy for testing the stunt failed to arrive, a tree trunk was used instead, as Michaels recalled, 'The ropes snapped and the tree smashed into the wall.'[156] After numerous tests, the perfect day with the correct weather conditions arrived, 'There is this thrill and excitement going into this zone. Literally, just before I was ready to go, I caught out the corner of my eye this little Italian crane driver who did the sign of the crucifix, head to chest and across the chest.'[157] A stuntman, Michaels also had to act:

It was quite a vicious drop, more vicious on me physically than it looked in the film. But a stunt without a performance is never any good. Martin Campbell was adamant that I had to get this gun out of a holster before I went out of shot. Martin was absolutely thrilled because it edited into the next shot perfectly.[158]

For the finale of the pre-title sequence, Bond escapes the Arkangel chemical plant by speeding down a runway on an Italian Cagiva motorcycle, chasing a pilotless Pilatus plane as it sails off a snowy precipice. Bond lets go of the motorbike and free falls after the plane before pulling himself inside the open door and flying to safety. It was filmed in two halves at the Eiger Peak in Switzerland.[159] Jacques Malnuit performed the motorcycle stunt, flying off a 180ft constructed wooden runway at 65 mph.[160] Later, Bond regular B.J. Worth performed the sky-diving element undertaking twenty-five jumps.[161] Phil Méheux remembered that Worth's team rehearsed in America, but when they arrived in Switzerland the plane was a slightly different model and did not have a reverse thrust engine:[162]

It never worked. We all sat in a room and decided the only way we can do this is to support Pierce on wires, on a green screen with a big fan on him and have him slowly winched into the cockpit and make it look as if he caught the plane up. I never felt it was 100 per cent believable, I just thought it was a bit hokey. But at the same time I thought, 'Well, it is hokey, but it is James Bond' and all the opening scenes of James Bond have that little touch of circus world about them.[163]

In May 1995 Pierce Brosnan and Sean Bean staged the final showdown between Bond and Trevelyan. Campbell wanted to pay homage to the Connery-Shaw punch up in *From Russia With Love*.[164] He wanted to make it as visceral as possible but admitted, 'One punch can cover your face in blood,'[165] and that was forbidden on a Bond film. 'When Trevelyan hits the deck, there's a lot of blood, I did an alternative take, thank God, because the American censors went nuts.'[166] The fight begins in a small confined engine room. Méheux recalled, 'The set was a black box, with a black floor. I thought, "Aargh, I've got two actors dressed in black, both wearing black shoes."'[167] Suggesting they paint the floor white to bounce light, Méheux was faced with a protest from the art department.[168] He requested they take the ventilation window from Ourumov's armoured train and build it into the set to allow light to seep through to give more atmosphere.[169]

The central location for *GoldenEye* was St. Petersburg, where the filmmakers were to stage an ambitious tank chase through the centre of the city. After an initial recce, Peter Lamont was concerned by the restrictions placed upon them by the Russian authorities, 'We couldn't run a tank more than 30 km. If we crushed sewers and drains they had to be put right. United Artists were keen that we didn't go to Russia because you are really over a barrel, the Mafia is not like the Italian mafia, you get bloody killed.'[170]

Instead, Lamont suggested that they take advantage of the vast outdoor space available to them at Leavesden and build a section of the city on the runway at the makeshift studio, meaning the first unit would not even have to visit St. Petersburg.[171] Campbell's concern was whether they could replicate other Russian locations beyond those needed for the tank chase. Lamont sourced alternative spots all over London including the Saint Sofia Greek Orthodox Church in Bayswater and Somerset House on the Strand. Campbell said to Lamont, 'Sell it to the producers.'[172] The £1 million cost to build the St. Petersburg set was approved by United Artists and Lamont built the set in just over six weeks.[173]

Barbara Broccoli headed to Russia for ten days to shoot essential action footage. The key images required involved wide shots of the tank chasing armoured jeeps along the canal before they crash through the balustrades and into the water. Even with a reduced unit, Broccoli still encountered problems. Closing the streets for four days suddenly made the locals nervous. She had to demonstrate that everything they were destroying had in fact been replicated by the art department.[174] 'We were shooting in a very sensitive part of town. We were shut down. They thought we were actually damaging the city.'[175]

Stunt co-ordinator Simon Crane recalled that even though they were now shooting the action in a controlled environment, the tank was a highly dangerous vehicle and he carried out three months of tests before filming began.[176] Ian Sharp stressed that 'even with the experience of the many members of the crew nobody had ever done a tank chase before.'[177] Each day presented unforeseen challenges. On one occasion, the tank, instead of sliding down an alleyway, flattened a Panavision camera.[178]

The sequence featured a spectacular shot of the 36-ton monster, nicknamed 'Metal Mickey',[179] bursting through a concrete wall as Bond begins his pursuit through the streets of St. Petersburg after General Ourumov. Driven by future Bond stunt co-ordinator Gary Powell, many stood on set in anticipation, including screenwriter Michael France.[180] Another stunt saw the tank careering into an articulated lorry transporting thousands of cans of Perrier water.

In April 1995 the tank sequence was concluded at the heritage railway site, Nene Valley. The same stretch of railway which had doubled for East Germany in *Octopussy* now doubled for Russia, where Trevelyan's train rams Bond's tank in explosive fashion. To create the Russian locomotive, Lamont's art department dressed a Deltic diesel engine belonging to record producer Pete Waterman.[181] Due to the distinctive cowling, it was nicknamed the 'Darth Train'.[182]

On 1 June 1995 Brosnan's final shot, a close-up behind the controls of the tank, was filmed and principal photography officially wrapped five days later.[183] Brosnan had barely survived his director's fierce focus, 'There was so much pressure on the both of us. [Martin] wanted it so badly and Day 105 was just as intense as Day 1. There was a relentless pressure day in and day out and he was a ferocious, passionate driving force behind the film.'[184] Brosnan felt that he had been kept in the dark about his 007 debut, 'No one said a word to me. No one said, "Brilliant, great." Nothing. One was fairly isolated. I marched to my own drum beat.'[185] Brosnan's fears were soon assuaged, 'I was sitting in the house one day and the phone rang. It was John Calley, "We've been watching all your work and it's absolutely brilliant, we love what you're doing as James Bond."'[186] Roger Moore visited the set to see his youngest son Christian who, alongside Brosnan's son, Christopher, were both working on the film. Impressed with the footage he'd seen, nevertheless Moore senior joked with Brosnan senior, 'They sent for me – I'm back on the job.'[187]

In the days before computer-generated imagery (CGI) was commonplace, miniature effects wizard, Derek Meddings, returned to Bond after having last worked on *For Your Eyes Only* (1981). Director Martin Campbell needed reassurance, but Meddings remembered, 'Once he saw the first few weeks of shots we'd done, he was so excited that I no longer had to convince him.'[188] For *GoldenEye*, Meddings built miniatures of Trevelyan's hidden Cuban GoldenEye satellite control centre as well as its sister site, Severnaya, set in Siberia. Méheux recalled:

[Derek Meddings] knew exactly how he wanted to do everything he did, so he would tell us how to do it. When you think there's hardly any CGI in that film – almost everything was done in camera. When Boris [Grishenko] comes out to get a cigarette and the helicopter lands in front of him, the dish and everything behind him is forced perspective, it looks like it's a quarter of a mile away but it's 12ft behind him. On the screen it looks perfectly real. Derek was a man of great experience and he'd been doing it for years. He was terrific. As was his director of photography, Paul Wilson.[189]

Meddings died suddenly from a heart attack during post-production,[190] but he was posthumously nominated for a BAFTA. Campbell reflected, 'We could never have done the film without him. The tragedy was he never saw the final result.'[191] The edit credits read, 'To the memory of Derek Meddings.'

John Barry rejected the chance to score *GoldenEye*,[192] 'I had commitments, two projects I was really keen on, and I just had a newly born son, so I wanted to have time with him and enjoy that side of my life.'[193] Luc Besson's regular composer, Eric Serra, fresh from scoring *Leon* (1994) was suggested by Campbell, 'I got it into my head that we are in the nineties, we've got to update this musically.'[194] Serra visited Leavesden and noted eighty per cent of the temp track on the rough cut was his *Leon* score, 'proving that they really were fans of my work.'[195] However, due to album commitments, Serra declined.[196] Barbara Broccoli would not take no for an answer, 'She told me I would have the end title song and that I could choose the record company. I couldn't say no anymore!'[197] Beginning work in summer 1995 Serra was given, 'carte blanche'.[198] Serra felt he captured all the musical moods within the first twelve minutes of score which he played early for the filmmakers:

> I wanted feedback, I needed to know if I was going in the right direction. For the whole time Martin Campbell and the editor were kind of talking about their own work, clearly they were not really listening. At the end they turned to me, 'It's great Eric. We love it, it's fantastic. Keep going.' And they left.'[199]

Later, editor Terry Rawlings had reservations, 'When we came to big scenes, like the tank chase, I asked Barbara and Michael and Martin to come over. "We cannot mix with the music he has given us because it doesn't work."'[200] Serra was chagrined, 'C'mon, if you want to do something completely new and modern, you don't let a 65-year-old guy [Rawlings] be the master of it.'[201] The cue in question, a version of the 'James Bond Theme' entitled 'A Pleasant Drive In St. Petersburg' was for Serra 'completely new, completely modern, every half-second there was something effectively synched between the image and the music.'[202] Following an alternative tradition established by George Martin, Marvin Hamlisch and Bill Conti, Eric Serra updated Monty Norman's theme for a new decade – Bond '95, if you will. Serra felt, 'You could have taken all the foleys and the sound effects out' and the music would have perfectly punctuated the action.[203] However, for Campbell *that* was the problem, 'The tank and the rumble of the synths were all in the same tonal range.'[204] The French composer declined the request to re-score, but, with his approval, Serra's orchestrator, John

Altman, conducted a more traditional version of the 'James Bond Theme' for the sequence.[205] This was at Cubby Broccoli's request only one week before the final print was completed and screened.[206]

Serra was extremely disappointed with the sound mix when he saw *GoldenEye* for the first time at the premiere.[207] Voicing his frustrations to Michael Wilson, while on a press tour in Japan, Serra remembered the response, 'He was looking at me almost like I was talking Chinese. He said, "Eric, you are on the Number 1 movie at the box office on the planet and you're not happy?" I was talking to him about an artistic wound that I was feeling.'[208]

The Rolling Stones turned down the opportunity to pen a song for the film.[209] Subsequently, Tina Turner was signed and then set about sifting through about ten songs.[210] Eric Serra's producer, Rupert Hine, who had helped resuscitate Tina Turner's recent career, teamed with the composer and they pitched a song to the singer.[211] However, when Bono and The Edge got involved, Serra recollected he felt like he was racing against 'Usain Bolt'.[212] This half of pop band U2 were Turner's neighbours in the South of France. Of the track, 'GoldenEye', Turner recalled, 'Bono wanted to write the song because he spent his honeymoon at Ian Fleming's house in Jamaica.'[213] True to Barbara Broccoli's initial promise, Hine wrote lyrics for a Serra cue from the *Leon* soundtrack, 'The Game is Over', which became 'The Experience of Love'.[214]

With Maurice Binder's passing four years earlier, the producers remembered music video director Daniel Kleinman's Binder-esque promo for Gladys Knight's 'Licence to Kill'.[215] Kleinman recalled, 'Michael Wilson asking me whether I thought it was a good idea to have naked silhouettes of girls and guns. I remember saying, "Absolutely yes!" Because that is what James Bond is all about, that's the language. It's a bit like saying we want to redesign the Union Jack.'[216] Kleinman graphically told the demise of communism with Binder-esque girls in the titles to signify the passage of time, 'It amused me that you could see the Soviet era being toppled by ladies in lingerie, which is kind of not far from the truth!'[217] Kleinman remembered Michael Wilson questioned the image of a gun emerging from the mouth of a girl, 'It was a little surreal for him!'[218] Kleinman updated the gun barrel, 'I used early computer animation and gave it a three-dimensional move. It kept the spirit of the original but just updated it.'[219] Pierce Brosnan shooting the signature motif remembered it as 'just a giggle. I felt a proper Charlie 'cos, I felt, I'm doing it, I'm walking the walk.'[220]

Before release, Barbara admitted, 'Although I have fallen in love with this movie, until the film is shown to an audience, you never know. It is like bringing home a boyfriend you love and introducing him to your parents. Every woman knows what I mean.'[221] On 19 July 1995, in Wimbledon, the reports from the first test screening of *GoldenEye* were excellent.[222] Ultimately the man she was hoping to impress was, of course, Cubby. By November 1995 Cubby was very sick. He had been preparing his memoirs and managed to write, 'I saw the rushes on *GoldenEye* every day and I liked what I saw.'[223]

On 13 November 1995 *GoldenEye* premiered at a lavish event at Radio City Music Hall in New York. Director of photograhy Phil Méheux remembered his feelings about the 'hokey' pre-title; the acceptance of the scene was key to whether the film would be a hit or not. He recalled the reaction inside the 5,000-seater New York venue, 'My heart was in my mouth – this is the reinvention of Bond, the place is packed to capacity and I thought, "If they laugh at this, then we've had it." But they didn't. There was a huge roar of approval and applause. I thought, "That's it!" That was such a relief.'[224] The producers were also relieved.[225] On 22 November 1995 the film received its European premiere at the Odeon Leicester Square, in the presence of Prince Charles.

The team behind *GoldenEye* had been raised with Bond. *Goldfinger* was the first film Brosnan had seen when he arrived in London at the age of eleven.[226] Martin Campbell recalled watching *Dr. No* with his mother in his native New Zealand. Title designer Daniel Kleinman recalled his die-cast Aston Martin DB5 and his collection of James Bond bubble-gum cards from the mid-sixties.[227] Bruce Feirstein described seeing *Goldfinger* for the first time with his parents at a drive-in in New Jersey.[228] Famke Janssen remembered that with each new Bond film, 'the entire family would go to see it en masse' in Holland,[229] and Robbie Coltrane revealed how, as a child, he would 'imagine having an Aston Martin DB5 and going to a casino and knowing what to do.'[230]

However, Kleeman recalled industry expectation for *GoldenEye* was not high:[231]

> We were making a movie based on a character who, as we said, all market research indicated young male audiences were barely aware of. We were using a director who had never directed a commercially successful feature. We were using an actor who was known for a television series that was now off the air. We were spending, compared to other action movies, very little money.'[232]

United Artists first realised the film's potential following the positive reaction to the teaser trailer directed by Joe Nimziki.[233] To the beats of a modern rendition of the 'James Bond Theme', composed by husband and wife team Jeff Eden Fair and Starr Parodi, Brosnan strode across the screen before turning to camera and asking, 'You were expecting someone else?' James Bond was back.

GoldenEye was released in the US in 2,667 theaters and garnered a US domestic opening weekend gross of $26,205,007 – a record for Bond. The film would go on to break other Bond box office records: achieving a North American gross of $106,429,941 and a worldwide gross of $352,194,034. Pierce Brosnan as James Bond was universally welcomed by critics and public alike. United Artists chief John Calley was proud, 'Getting the Bond franchise reactivated in a big way was thrilling. It means that we have something that is a very durable concept with enormous staying power. We feel we can count on Bond every two years.'[234]

Reacting to the success, Brosnan said he had wanted his 007 debut to be great for Cubby and only for him, 'I missed him on GoldenEye. And I will miss him throughout the making of Bond 18.'[235]

25

NOT THE ONLY
SPY OUT THERE

TOMORROW NEVER DIES

(1997)

ALBERT R. BROCCOLI

APRIL 5, 1909 – JUNE 27, 1996

FROM *DR. NO* TO *GOLDENEYE*,

CUBBY BROCCOLI

IS A FOUNDATION

OF OUR PAST AND REMAINS

AN INSPIRATION

FOR OUR FUTURE.

HE HAS MADE

AN INDELIBLE MARK

ON FILM HISTORY.

HIS LEGACY WILL LIVE FOREVER.

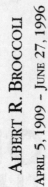

Metro-Goldwyn-Mayer

UNITED ARTISTS

©1996 Metro-Goldwyn-Mayer Inc. All Rights Reserved.

On the evening of 27 June 1996 Albert R. Broccoli passed away peacefully at his home in Beverly Hills.[1] He was 87.

Condolences came from around the world. Roger Moore commented on the tenacity of the man:

The last few years of Cubby's life were not easy for him. He underwent a great deal of fairly drastic surgery. For me it was terrible to see a man who was so vital in every aspect suffering. But his family were always there, particularly Dana. He adored her and she him. I treasure the memory of Dana holding Cubby's hand, and giving that sort of lopsided grin. I miss that grin.[2]

Sean Connery telephoned condolences, later stating, 'My previous differences with Cubby Broccoli were well known, but I recently took the opportunity to make my peace with him.'[3]

On 1 July 1996 Cubby's funeral was held at the Church of the Good Shepherd in Beverly Hills.[4] Timothy Dalton served as a pallbearer and John Barry selected the music.[5] Those whose lives Cubby had touched were there including Jill St John, Maryam d'Abo and Desmond Llewelyn, who felt it was 'an incredibly moving occasion, accentuated by a perfect summer's day and the distinguished actor Gregory Peck who spoke eloquently. I was particularly touched when Barbara included me in the family dinner the night before the funeral.'[6]

In November 1996 at a memorial service held, appropriately enough, at the Odeon Leicester Square, a number of old Eonians and members of the public paid tribute. Recently retired executive producer Tom Pevsner observed, 'Cubby was not only giving employment to thousands of people in this country over the years, he was running alongside that, at Eon, a training academy for British technicians for which we owe him a huge debt of gratitude, and some of the alumni are very, very distinguished.'[7] Norman Tyre, Cubby's attorney, was pleased his friend had:

had the unique satisfaction of living long enough to 'pass the baton', the production of future Bonds, to his children. By his 'presenting' and Michael and Barbara, his children, 'producing', *GoldenEye* – the most successful of all the Bonds – he lived to achieve his goal. Few men have enjoyed a like accomplishment.[8]

Cubby's stepson, Michael Wilson, who had helped steer the Bond films for over two decades would miss Cubby's presence, 'In our office we sat across from each other … He was my mentor and my dearest friend.'[9] In keeping with Cubby's wishes, Wilson vowed James Bond would return:

> Barbara and myself had to view our working life after his death as a new beginning. We have inherited what legions of fans around the world think as something of a Holy Grail. We also have the pressure that goes with it. Cubby never cut back on budgets, skimped on the set or first-class action sequences. He always had high production values. Barbara and I have pledged to produce the films in the same way.[10]

Wilson never took Bond for granted:

> There may be people who can do it better, but the way it would probably go, there's more opportunity for it to be done worse. And I think all you have to do is look at some of the great writers we bring in and listen to what they pitch us. With the ideas they pitch, believe me, it would be very easy for this thing to go off the rails.[11]

In October 1996 John Calley left United Artists to join Sony.[12] He was replaced by Lindsay Doran,[13] who thought:

> Barbara was probably happy to have a woman in charge but she is like the child of a mother who has had twelve husbands. Every time a new husband comes in she thinks 'Okay, I'm going to be nice to you for a while, but you won't be here in three years, so I'm not going to take it all that seriously.' I couldn't blame her for that attitude – Eon had been through so many studio heads by that point.[14]

In May 1995 *Bond 18* was green lit.[15] UA Senior Vice-President Jeff Kleeman[16] noted the initial American reaction to *GoldenEye* was positive and the teaser trailer was playing well,[17] prompting Kleeman to seek 'stories and writers. Our feeling was that although *GoldenEye* was not released across the world until December 1995, it was worth spending $200,000 to get a script moving.'[18] Reaching a new generation with the phenomenal success of Nintendo's tie-in video game, Kleeman saw the 'tremendous awareness of Bond. We had to make the next movie very quickly.'[19]

Crédit Lyonnais, the French bank behind the ill-fated Paretti takeover of MGM, were required under American law, to offload the studio by the end of

1997. Another Bond film generating revenue would only raise the price of the enforced sale. Kleeman understood, 'It was important to show the buyers that Bond was a franchise that could be put into theatres with some degree of regularity and consistency, a genuine on-going concern that you can count on.'[20]

The franchise had previously sought initial ideas from established novelists such as Roald Dahl and Anthony Burgess. They did so again with noted author Donald E. Westlake. In August 1995 he turned in a thirty-five page treatment and a second five-page treatment in October.[21] Both remained unused. Jeff Kleeman remembered the ideas 'ranged from an amazing mega-plot to flood Hong Kong to a pre-title sequence in Transylvania.'[22]

Throughout early 1996 Barbara Broccoli was co-executive producer (with Amanda Schiff) for an HBO TV movie, *Crime of the Century*, under her Astoria Productions banner. Michael Wilson concurrently developed the new Bond with Bruce Feirstein. In March 1996 Bruce Feirstein visited an ailing Cubby Broccoli, 'Clearly he had seen [*GoldenEye*]. I went to pitch him the story for *Bond 18* – a movie about a media mogul – and he liked it.'[23] Feirstein elaborated:

> I was watching Sky TV do a story about the Middle East and then I flicked over to CNN and it was the same event told from two completely different points of view. This wasn't surprising to me as a journalist because having written for magazines and newspapers for years, of course, there are two ways you can tell a story. I had worked for all the prototypes of this character. I had written for magazines owned by Rupert Murdoch, I had been on CNN.'[24]

Like Westlake, Feirstein was drawn to Hong Kong as a setting. In 1995 the transfer of the sovereignty back to China was a hot topic. 'It was in the Zeitgeist. Some people insist that [Westlake's] treatment inspired *Tomorrow Never Dies*, or was an early template, when, in fact, it had nothing to do with it. We're all swimming in the same culture; we're all exposed to the same stuff. It's the execution that counts,'[25] explained Feirstein, who had spent time in Hong Kong during his advertising days in the 1980s.[26] Venice was also discussed as a possible locale following Michael Wilson's suggestion of using the historic Venice Carnival as a backdrop, with Bond evading the enemy disguised in mask and costume.[27]

Feirstein outlined a topical story about media tycoon, Elliot Harmsway, who, enraged by Britain's cowardice in returning Hong Kong to China, intends to destroy the colony before the handover, while his media empire will benefit from worldwide coverage of the disaster.[28] Harmsway was based upon notorious newspaper baron Robert Maxwell, who mysteriously disappeared at sea in 1991. Feirstein explained, 'Everyone thinks I was writing about Murdoch. The proof of that is in the final movie when M turns to Miss Moneypenny and says, "Put in the press release he drowned off his yacht."'[29]

Feirstein titled the script *Tomorrow Never Lies* inspired by the Beatles track 'Tomorrow Never Knows'.[30] As UA prepared a press release to announce the title, Jeff Kleeman recalled that a publicist mistakenly typed, 'Tomorrow Never Dies', but 'we thought that was the better title. All thanks to a typo in a press release.'[31]

Martin Campbell was asked to direct Pierce Brosnan's second Bond film. Instead, he chose to make the swashbuckler *The Mask of Zorro* (1998), 'I felt after I'd done *GoldenEye*, maybe mistakenly, I didn't want to repeat it.'[32] Campbell admitted that Barbara and Michael offered him every subsequent Brosnan picture but he declined every time.[33] Nicholas Meyer was mentioned as a contender.[34]

In September 1996 the producers signed experienced British-Canadian director Roger Spottiswoode.[35] The veteran's innovative work as an editor for Sam Peckinpah had inspired the then hot action director import John Woo. Spottiswoode had handled large studio action, notably with *Air America* (1988). Sounded out to direct a possible early nineties Bond,[36] Spottiswoode 'really didn't know how to do it with Dalton. I like things edgy, not sombre.'[37] Spottiswoode knew 'Peter Hunt. I'd met several of the other [Bond] directors, I'd seen them being made – I worked in Pinewood and you kind of wander on the sets a little bit.'[38] He had served as assistant editor on Harry Saltzman's *Funeral in Berlin*,[39] seeing both Harry and Cubby in their South Audley Street heyday.[40] He admired *GoldenEye*, 'It had a brilliant opening and the tank chase was fantastic.'[41]

United Artists sent the script to consulting agency, Kissinger Associates,[42] who Kleeman noted, 'Ensure the production are aware of any cultural or political issues, so you don't have a situation like we had on *GoldenEye* where we are a few days into shooting in Russia and the Militsiya comes out and we have to go back to London.'[43] Kissinger advised against the Hong Kong handover theme, as Spottiswoode remembered, 'Nobody really knew whether it would be a peaceful handover. To come up with a fantasied version of an event that was only a few months old, did not seem a very wise choice.'[44]

Aware of the ticking clock, Spottiswoode suggested they assemble a writer's think tank to brainstorm fresh ideas.[45] Jeff Kleeman flew six Hollywood scribes to London for a week: Robert Collector (*Memoirs of an Invisible Man*, 1992), David Campbell Wilson (*The Perfect Weapon*, 1991), Tom Ropelewski (*Look Who's Talking Now*, 1993), Kurt Wimmer (*Relative Fear*, 1994), Leslie Dixon (*Mrs. Doubtfire*, 1993) and Nicholas Meyer (*Star Trek II: The Wrath of Khan*, 1982).

Kleeman felt, 'We needed to throw everything we could at the script as fast as we could in order to generate the best possible version within the really meagre time frame we had.'[46]

Kurt Wimmer felt the group was 'pretty diverse consisting of both men and women [who asked], "What are the stakes?"'[47] David Campbell Wilson joked, 'The people in the Eon offices nicknamed us the wank tank!'[48] The team were issued with the Bond bible, an internal document written by John Cork, which detailed every facet of Bond's character.[49] Ropelewski described Michael Wilson as their 'guiding light. He had a strong sense of what Bond should and shouldn't do.'[50]

Their task was to devise key action sequences that the production could begin preparing in advance.[51] A short film featuring stunt riders performing parkour on motorcycles became the genesis for a set-piece across the rooftops of a Vietnamese shantytown.[52] It was also suggested that a motorbike chase could unfold along the Great Wall of China.[53] Another idea was a helicopter chopping up a Vietnamese market.[54] A scene with Bond in drag was rejected by everybody.[55] *Razor Kiss* was a suggested title.[56] Wimmer commented that a comparison of the final film did not resemble what they devised that week but 'certain scenes, elements and set pieces were cherrypicked from ideas that were generated in that room.'[57]

Feirstein wrote a further draft before he was replaced. Nicolas Meyer offered an alternative motive for the media mogul: war between India and China as a form of population control.[58] 'There was a jaw-dropping silence as I concluded this amazing presentation.'[59] Next Daniel Petrie Jr. (*Beverly Hills Cop,* 1984) contributed the German assassin called Dr. Kaufman.[60] Both writers had been enlisted by the eventual director, Roger Spottiswoode.

Petrie Jr.'s draft, dated 13 March 1996, came with a disclaimer on its title page, 'Please note this is the final shooting script. That does not mean there will be no further changes. *Au contraire.* It means that this will be the last draft printed on white paper. Hereafter, changes will be issued on colour paper.'[61]

However, Pierce Brosnan was far from impressed with the results,[62] 'It was not articulate or cohesive enough. I spoke to Barbara and Michael and said that it was inappropriate that at this stage of filming we should be in such a fragile state. It was just a joke.'[63] Brosnan warned the producers they were in danger of 'throwing the baby out with the bathwater.'[64]

At the eleventh hour Barbara and Michael turned back to Bruce Feirstein. Kleeman said they felt Feirstein had the deepest understanding of the new Bond era,[65] 'Bruce had really taken ownership of *GoldenEye,* the 'voice' of Bond, the fine detail of how Pierce's Bond talks and navigates the world.'[66]

The unstoppable schedule to meet the studio shareholders' expectation of a
new Bond film had put pressure on Feirstein. He explained the politics surrounding the writers' weekend:

> When I went to work on *GoldenEye*, I wasn't Eon's writer or Martin
> Campbell's writer. I was an unaligned nation. I was the writer they all agreed
> on. But when Roger Spottiswoode came to work on *Tomorrow Never Dies*, I
> was no longer an unaligned participant: I was Michael and Barbara's writer.
> And if there was one thing that directors always did back then, in order to
> put their 'vision' on a movie, it was to bring in their own writer. Or writers.
> It wasn't personal, and it wasn't about me. It's just the way things are. Now,
> ordinarily, there was nothing at all unusual about that writers' meeting. I go
> to them all the time on big movies. You bring in a bunch of people to spitball
> ideas. The only difference, in this case, was that the writers were given first-
> class tickets to London. I also knew that some of the people at that meeting
> – the writers that Roger had worked with before – were also going to be
> auditioning for my job. So I was in this weird position of being welcoming
> and collegial with my fellow writers, but at the same time knowing that I
> was most likely going to be fired. It was sort of like sitting down to your last
> dinner to share some wine and laughs with your executioners.[67]

Ultimately, and perhaps naturally, Feirstein felt precious time had been wasted:

> At the end of the weekend, I remember sitting there with what was essentially
> my script – the media mogul, the stealth boat, the self-driving car, the original
> opening sequence – and being given thirty days to fix it, including changing
> things we had discussed before the meeting, like changing the Bond girl to
> a Chinese female agent and moving the action from Hong Kong to Ho Chi
> Minh City. This became my 'second draft' that no one has ever seen, but pretty
> much outlines a lot – but not everything – that you see in the final film.[68]

Feirstein received sole credit for the screenplay.

By the time Bruce Feirstein had finished his final draft, dated 18 August 1997,
three weeks before the end of production, only three white pages remained. It
was christened the rainbow script.[69] 'I was writing in a tent outside the Bond
stage, sending in pages as we were shooting, where Pierce was standing on the
deck of the stealth boat, asking "Which way do I go? Do I turn left or do I turn
right?" The answer was, 'Wait. We'll have the pages in a minute.'[70]

In the pre-title sequence Bond prevents a nuclear catastrophe in an arms bazaar in the Khyber Pass. At that same sale, techno terrorist, Henry Gupta obtains a stolen GPS device. Gupta is working for news baron, Elliot Carver, head of the Carver Media Group Network. Using the GPS device and a news media satellite, Carver manipulates a British naval frigate into Chinese territorial waters. Carver then sinks the British vessel using his stealth barge and destroys a patrolling Chinese MIG fighter, framing each side for each other's hostilities. Carver recovers nuclear ordnance from the sunken British frigate. The Carver Media Group Network stokes the fire on both sides with misinformation. When the Carver newspaper, *Tomorrow*, details the incident impossibly early, M sends Bond to Hamburg to investigate the press baron. Carver is in Germany to launch his broadcast capability to reach across the world – except China. At the media launch, Bond meets Chinese agent Wai Lin and reacquaints himself with Carver's wife, Paris, an old flame from his past. After a night of passion, Paris reveals the whereabouts of a secret lab where Bond discovers the stolen GPS tracking device. Bond returns to find Paris dead at the hands of forensic killer Dr. Kaufman. Bond outwits the doctor and eludes Carver's henchman Stamper by using Q's remote control BMW.

Recalibrating the GPS device to correct the deliberate error, Bond finds the wreck of the frigate only to discover nuclear munitions have been stolen. Bond learns that Wai Lin is on the same case working for the Chinese. Together they are captured and taken to Carver's Vietnamese headquarters. Here, they discover what Carver is planning. By inciting hostilities between the UK and China, Carver intends to instigate a naval battle between the nations. He will then fire the stolen British nuclear missile at Beijing. Such a launch will be untraceable from Carver's stealth barge so the Chinese will assume it is has come from the British flotilla in the area. Carver is in league with renegade hardline Chinese General Chang who, in the nuclear confusion, will take control of his country and sue for peace. When the dust settles, Chang, now in power, will grant Carver the long denied and lucrative broadcast rights in his country. Bond and Wai Lin infiltrate the stealth barge and prevent the missile launch, killing Carver and Stamper in the process.

Feirstein thought Albert Finney 'the physical prototype'[71] of the villain but he was never offered the role. Anthony Hopkins responded enthusiastically to Feirstein's summer 1996 draft,[72] but passed to star in Martin Campbell's *The Mask of Zorro*. The role eventually went to thespian Jonathan Pryce. Barbara Broccoli had been an admirer of his work but previously he had not been available.[73] He recalled, 'My children absolutely adored *GoldenEye* and their response to that probably had a lot to do with me accepting the role.'[74] Pryce was attracted to Carver's dangerously real agenda:

It's common knowledge that CNN as a news network was virtually bankrupt before the Gulf War and they happened to have this guy Wolf Blitzer in place – extraordinary name, he sounds like a Bond character – to get those reports on the spot. That turned round CNN's fortunes and this is what Carver is trying to do.[75]

Malaysian actress Michelle Yeoh was cast as Colonel Wai Lin. Feirstein had originally written Lin as a British character called Sydney Winch, whose father was going to have been an associate of Harmsway, the original villain.[76] As the story developed and the Hong Kong handover plot was discarded, the character became redundant. 'Roger [Spottiswoode] thought that if we were going to do the movie in Asia wouldn't it be interesting if Bond's equal and opposite was a female Chinese agent,'[77] recalled Feirstein.

Michelle Yeoh, an established actress in the world of Asian martial arts cinema, was recommended to Spottiswoode by his nephew.[78] Yeoh tested opposite Brosnan,[79] 'I had to prove to the backers that Pierce and I did, indeed, have the right chemistry on screen.'[80] Yeoh was to play Yin Pow but she suggested they change her name,[81] 'Pow, in Chinese, means "bun", one of those typical Bond names like Pussy Galore or Xenia Onatopp. So I came up with Wai Lin with a couple of girlfriends one night in Hong Kong. Wai means "patriotic for the country", that I didn't mind.'[82] Once Yeoh was cast, Wai Lin was rewritten to take advantage of her martial art skills. Feirstein noted, 'Obviously, a Bond film isn't a Jackie Chan film; it had to be slightly more real.'[83]

For the role of Paris, Brosnan tested with Monica Bellucci – he 'championed her'[84] – but the studio wanted an American.[85] Teri Hatcher, star of the hit television show *Lois and Clark: The New Adventures of Superman*, won the part.

The villainy would be completed by noted magician Ricky Jay as corrupt hippie Henry Gupta, famed character actor Vincent Schiavelli as the sinister Dr. Kaufman and Götz Otto as Kaufman's disciple Stamper, who is impervious to pain. Cecilie Thomsen would play Bond's Oxford language tutor Professor Inga Bergstrom, and the film would see early roles for Gerard Butler and Hugh Bonneville, both as Royal Navy personnel. Julian Fellowes, who played Noël Coward in the Fleming TV biopic, *Goldeneye* (1989) and later created *Downton Abbey*, appeared as a stuffy Minister of Defence.

The veteran Bond production designer, Peter Lamont, was unable to commit to *Tomorrow Never Dies*, following overruns on James Cameron's *Titanic* in Mexico.[86] Allan Cameron jumped at the chance simply because 'there are things in a Bond picture that you don't get to design on other films.'[87]

Cinematographer Phil Méheux regretfully declined the offer to return, favouring an ultimately aborted Martin Campbell project.[88] Instead, Robert Elswit became the first American cinematographer to light a Bond film. Seasoned action unit director Vic Armstrong would oversee three major set pieces.

With Leavesden, Pinewood and Shepperton fully booked, executive producer Anthony Waye discovered a former warehouse in St. Albans, Hertfordshire. At a cost of £2 million, location manager Richard Sharkey was given eight weeks to transform it into a studio. By early January 1997 Frogmore Studios was ready for Bond.

In January 1997 Vic Armstrong began filming the pre-title sequence in Peyragudes, the French Pyrenees. Armstrong felt, 'rather than do some mediocre gag we decided to have the biggest shoot 'em up we could, put everything plus the kitchen sink into it.'[89] Production designer Allan Cameron admired the power of a Bond production to gain equipment and permissions usually denied to others, managing to bring a decommissioned Russian rocket launcher 'across Europe to our location'.[90] Armstrong shot for two weeks and used up to nine cameras on the biggest and most explosive set-ups.[91]

Feirstein envisaged the gunbarrel opening on 'a huge vista, I described it as the end of the world, somewhere in the Himalayas. You push in and you push in on this tiny little dot and it's Bond climbing an ice wall. Then he would ski down to where the movie now begins.'[92] However, Spottiswoode felt it was too dangerous to shoot.[93]

Desmond Llewelyn was flown to Hamburg airport in March 1997 to shoot a brief scene in the terminal building, taking advantage of Brosnan's schedule while he was in the city promoting *Dante's Peak*.[94] Continuing *GoldenEye*'s successful partnership with BMW, Q delivers 007 his new BMW 750i. The executive saloon was the biggest model in the BMW fleet. Spottiswoode said, 'I wanted a big imposing car, big enough for Bond.'[95] Refused the luxury of his usual prompt boards, Llewelyn warned his director, 'It would take hours – and it did.'[96]

Originally, Feirstein had written Q out of the story, explaining he had now retired:[97]

Between January and September of 1996 there were conversations about Desmond. We all came to the agreement that we would introduce a new Q. We were going to do something where Bond jumps onto some yacht in the South China Sea and there is Desmond fully retired with three gorgeous women. Bond was going to say, 'You're doing well in your retirement,' and Desmond was going to look at him and say, 'They are my granddaughters!'[98]

Ultimately, the producers weren't willing to say goodbye to Llewelyn just yet and at the age of eighty-three, he reprised his role for the sixteenth time.

Principal photography officially began on 1 April 1997 with insert shots of Pierce Brosnan to be woven in with the action Vic Armstrong had filmed in the Pyrenees three months earlier. Brosnan felt, 'The script wasn't ready. It just wasn't articulate. There didn't seem to be any cohesion to the working days. There seemed to be little fires everywhere. There seemed to be a lot of confusion about the story. They jumped into it with too much alacrity.'[99] Early reports suggested the atmosphere on set was tense.[100]

The ever-changing script was understandably frustrating for the actors. Jonathan Pryce said he had never encountered a production where the screenplay had changed so radically, 'I will make sure in future that it is written in the contract that the script I agree to will be the script we use.'[101]

Judi Dench was handed revised pages when she arrived at Frogmore Studios on 4 April 1997.[102] She complained to Spottiswoode, 'You know, it was very off-putting indeed to have learnt the script, and at a quarter to ten the night before to get a loud knocking on the door by the courier with a new script. That's not fair.'[103] Later in post-production, Dench had another altercation with Spottiswoode during Automatic Dialogue Replacement (ADR) sessions. Arriving late, due to gridlocked traffic, Dench recounted the director standing in the doorway calling to her to hurry as she briskly walked through Soho, 'I simply couldn't shake hands with him. So I said, "Did you see me the other day in Streatham?" "Did I?" "You know you did, I nearly ran you over." At that minute Barbara Broccoli came out of the back and said, "Pity you didn't accelerate and do the job for us."'[104]

In *Tomorrow Never Dies*, M joined the action in the situation room, where she follows Bond's mission with a live commentary as he escapes the arms bazaar in the Khyber Pass. Designer Allan Cameron commented, 'I like the fact that we start with the snow in the Pyrenees and its very bright and light, then you cut to the situation room, which has a bunker feel – quite moody and high tech. I just kept those rhythms going throughout the whole film.'[105]

Samantha Bond returned as Miss Moneypenny in a slighlty expanded role, 'I suddenly felt like part of this Bond family.'[106] M was also joined by her new right-hand man, Charles Robinson, played by British actor Colin Salmon.

Cameron cleverly reused elements of the MI6 situation room set, 'I revamped it into the Hamburg media room, which is part of Carver's empire, and then I revamped it a third time into the Ho Chi Minh City media command centre.'[107] He revealed that Carver's Vietnamese HQ was inspired by Hitler's underground base in Berlin,[108] 'I wanted it to have a slight bunker feeling.'[109]

On 23 April 1997, Teri Hatcher arrived at Stoke Poges, the famed golf club where Bond had played Auric Goldfinger thirty-five years before. It was reported that there were difficulties between Brosnan and the-then pregnant Hatcher.[110] Kleeman played the situation down:

> I do remember the difficulties Pierce and Teri had with each other. [When] you're on a tight schedule emotions get very raw. There was friction on *GoldenEye*. I remember a moment where there was one particular cast member who refused to come out of their trailer because they thought somebody else was getting more attention in a particular scene. It happens on every movie.'[111]

Walking into Bond's hotel room, Paris finds a mournful 007 alone, sipping vodka. Having studied Brosnan's performance in *GoldenEye*, Feirstein used this scene to specifically write to Pierce's strengths:

> He's handsome, he's witty, he's charming – but there's something just below the surface that's darker, and deeper. He kept talking about the way we needed to 'peel back the layers of the onion', to get deeper into the character, which is what I was attempting to do here. A man who can't commit, and is pained by it, remorseful about his relationship with Paris. When Paris says, 'I used to get up every day and look for your obituary in the paper', his reaction is brilliant. And the line works on so many levels – caring about him, angry at him, in love with him, wanting him dead.[112]

At first Brosnan had a hankering to smoke in the scene,:

> It's very moody, and the tux is off, the shirt is undone, the tie is off, the Walther PPK and vodka bottle are there and the scene just cried out for a cigarette. But I just *couldn't* do it. If I smoke, it's moody for the scene and it looks great and sexy, but I have a responsibility to kids and you have to look at that.'[113]

The second half of *Tomorrow Never Dies* takes place in Vietnam as Bond tracks Carver's stealth ship to the South China Seas where he is orchestrating a conflict between China and Britain. The production was set to shoot in Hanoi becoming the first US film to shoot there since the Vietnam War.[114] Spottiswoode and Armstrong with key production crew travelled to the country several times before making the decision to shoot there. 'It had a wonderful look and it was very different. The [Vietnamese Government] were very positive and we got complete permission to do it. They had some concerns about capitalism and a big modern film coming in but we finally ended up with a signed contract and permission from the prime minister's office,'[115] remembered Spottiswoode.

Three weeks before the unit were due to start shooting, Spottiswoode and key department heads were sitting in the departure lounge at Heathrow about to board a plane to Ho Chi Minh City for a final technical scout, when Spottiswoode received disastrous news from Anthony Waye. The director recalled:

> The prime minister had rescinded our permission to go there or film there. They completely turned around and tore up the agreement we had made. The real generals in charge of Vietnam thought they were not properly consulted. We had spent a lot of money, probably a million or more. It was awful. We were stuck at the airport with sixty people and we were supposed to start shooting in three weeks. A third of the movie was on locations we no longer had.[116]

Anthony Waye remembered one theory as to why the Vietnamese government rescinded the permits was because 'it was thought the opening title sequence of *GoldenEye*, featured semi-naked ladies smashing up hammer-and-sickle emblems with sledgehammers, illustrated the fall of communism. We did hear words such as we had "degraded communism". Whether that is true or not, I don't know.'[117] Mused Spottiswoode, 'Vietnam, I must confess was my suggestion, a bad one. Everyone was very gracious not to hang that one around my neck, but I had suggested Vietnam would be a good place to go.'[118]

Vic Armstrong was to shoot a dramatic motorbike chase through and over the streets of Ho Chi Minh City, as Bond and Wai Lin, handcuffed together, escape on a BMW R1200 C motorcycle from Carver's heavies. Spottiswoode said the challenge had been to better the tank chase in *GoldenEye*,[119]

> The idea of a little person bringing down a huge person was a great metaphor for acting against power. It seemed to me a motorcycle chase with the other people in helicopters above you was a wonderful way of doing that. And in the end Bond brings it down with a sling-shot which is the same ending as David and Goliath.'[120]

Construction had started on building a street set in Ho Chi Minh City when permissions were withdrawn.[121] Spottiswoode, Allan Cameron and Vic Armstrong all had experience working in Bangkok, having made *Air America* (1990) together there seven years previously. Eon had shot *The Man With the Golden Gun* in Phuket, which could double for the scenes originally scheduled for Ha Long Bay. Spottiswoode was unfazed, 'Between us all, sitting at Heathrow, we said this is the only way to keep the film going, make our dates and keep moving. We literally went to the desk and switched tickets.'[122] Within three days they had found and replaced all their locations in Thailand.

As soon as they landed in Bangkok, Armstrong studied the skyline looking for suitable rooftops for the bike chase, 'We saw these two big tenement blocks. We went up on the roof and they were absolutely perfect. We did 75 per cent of the sequence on location. We then built replica rooftops on top of the street set we had built at [Frogmore] for what we couldn't do in Bangkok.'[123]

Armstrong admitted, 'My heart sank when I first saw the bike, it was huge.'[124] However, in the end it made the sequence original, 'It was all wrong for the job, not the sort of machine usually associated with chases or stunts.'[125] Doubling Pierce Brosnan and Michelle Yeoh was Frenchman Jean-Pierre Goy and Armstrong's wife Wendy Leech. Armstrong remembered, 'My brother Andy recommended Jean-Pierre Goy. He is one of the best motorcyclists out there and actually did shows with BMW. He came over and roadtested the bike and within ten minutes he was doing wheelies so I knew we were in great shape.'[126]

In Bangkok the heat and long working hours in order to complete the film on time caused further friction among the crew.[127] Brosnan was vocal about the atmosphere, 'Welcome to the arsehole of the world', he said greeting one visiting journalist.[128] Kleeman recalled temperatures became so unbearable for the crew in Bangkok, people's shoes were actually melting, 'The tops of those roofs were asphalt and metal they would heat up well beyond 110 degrees.'[129] Michelle Yeoh found all the chaos rather normal, 'Hong Kong films are known for being very haphazard. The scripts are never ready. New lines get handed to you on set. They are always changing things. It's chaos. So I have felt right at home from the moment I started on *Tomorrow Never Dies*.'[130]

For Allan Cameron the challenge in Thailand was dressing the streets and the extras to resemble the neighbouring capital, 'Bangkok is a thriving, almost westernised city. Hanoi and Ho Chi Minh City in Vietnam have a totally different feel - it's really a calmer lifestyle. There are people on bicycles everywhere, wearing the reed hats.'[131] Cameron changed street and shop signage and put false fronts over buildings to give them a Vietnamese feel. He also re-created the

streets of Ho Chi Minh City on the Frogmore backlot, in a similar way to how
Peter Lamont had built St. Petersburg at Leavesden for *GoldenEye*. One visiting
journalist noted, 'The illusion is complete in every detail. There's a birdcage on
a third floor balcony and a faded *Peanuts* T-shirt flaps from a washing line. Only
the smell of boiled rice and open drains is missing.'[132]

The sequence culminated with Bond and Wai Lin on the BMW bike driving
through a third-floor balcony, over the top of a rotating helicopter and lands on
the second floor balcony the other side. A similar stunt had been achieved in
Terminator 2: Judgment Day (1991) with the bike on wires. Goy was offered the
same technique but declined.[133] Over 200 people gathered on the Frogmore
backlot to watch this spectacular stunt.[134]

In Bangkok, the unit also shot Bond and Wai Lin's escape from Carver's headquarters, sliding down a gigantic banner pinned to the side of a tower block.[135]
Vic Armstrong recalled that the Petronas Twin Towers in Kuala Lumpur were to
have been the original setting when the city was discussed as a possible location.
Armstrong had conceived the idea when he saw a skyscraper under construction
in Hong Kong, 'They put nets around it to stop the debris falling on the pedes-
trians. Those nets are used as hoardings, temporary advertising space. I came up
with the idea of the banner ripping, an old gag they used to use in the circus.'[136]

By the beginning of June, Spottiswoode was overseeing multiple units
working simultaneously around the globe. Bond veteran John Richardson was
supervising a model unit in Mexico, filming the sinking of the HMS *Devonshire*
at Baja Studios.[137] In Florida, Bond sky-diving stalwart B.J. Worth was shooting
a HALO (High altitude, low opening) jump in which Bond must drop into the
ocean under radar to examine the wreck of the HMS *Devonshire*. Feirstein was
kept busy, 'There would be some days when I would get four or five call sheets
for the next day – the underwater stage at Pinewood, the backlot at Frogmore,
the jump by B.J. Worth in Florida, Vic in Bangkok and Roger in London. I can't
believe the way Michael, Barbara and Tony Waye managed it.'[138]

From 9 June 1997 the first and second units spent three weeks filming in
Brent Cross, North London, shooting a car chase, inside a multi-storey car park
in which Bond escapes Elliot Carver's heavies in his gadget-laden BMW 750i,
using a remote control function on his Sony Ericsson mobile from the back
seat. Spottiswoode remembered that when the sequence was first discussed,
Brosnan wasn't convinced:

> he didn't get it because it read like any other car chase … I told him, this is a
> real character scene, as Bond finds a great deal of humour within the action.

We drove him around the car park in the back seat, with his feet out of the rear window, and went so fast he couldn't position himself properly. His head got wedged between the two front seats, he tumbled everywhere and he suddenly saw how funny the scene could be.[139]

Seventeen Aspen Silver BMW's were prepared for the sequence, including four built by BMW engineers in Munich to be driven remotely.[140] Kleeman felt, 'BMWs rules around how we used the car initially hampered us.'[141] In the beginning of the scene, Carver's henchmen were to smash the windscreen with a sledgehammer. The car giant forbade such an action asserting their screens were much tougher and it did not portray the brand in a positive light.[142] 'It was pretty comical, because BMW would say no to everything we would suggest. Finally we said, "Would a ground to air missile break one of your windshields?"'[143] This led to the scene where Stamper and the heavies are slamming the BMW with a sledgehammer but the screen just won't break! Roger Spottiswoode and Vic Armstrong devised the sequence on a bus while location hunting, 'We came up with all these gags like a rocket blasting the car backwards like a shotgun, Peckinpah type stuff. I explained it in one hit to Barbara and she said, "You are absolutely mad."'[144]

At Pinewood Studios, Spottiswoode raced to complete *Tomorrow Never Dies*, shooting an action-packed finale aboard Carver's stealth barge, which Allan Cameron had built on the 007 Stage. Inspired by the shape, colours and sculptural aspects of the US stealth bombers,[145] Cameron created a set which he described as 'very sleek, very secret looking'.[146] Cameron's approach to production design differed from that of Peter Lamont, 'I don't try to create reality. I think it is a huge waste of money and effort to try and create reality for the eye. I like creating atmosphere rather than having every moulding, every little detail right.'[147] Brosnan was thrilled to be working inside the 007 Stage, 'A little bit of Bond history in the making there, it's the first time I've set foot inside it.'[148]

On 18 July 1997 the unit headed to Hamburg for the final leg of location work. Originally the producers had looked at setting the European part of the film in Seville, Spain, but Hamburg served the filmmakers better. The day before the unit travelled to Germany, another disaster threatened the picture, when Brosnan cut his face on the rim of a stuntman's helmet during a fight sequence on the 007 Stage.[149] Eight stitches were needed before he flew to Hamburg, 'I could see the funny side of it. There was a doctor suddenly confronted with James Bond lying on a bed, covered in blood and movie executives talking on mobile phones on how the injury could affect the movie.'[150]

As production wound down in late August 1997, Barbara Broccoli learned her childhood friend Dodi Fayed had been killed along with Princess Diana in a car crash in Paris, 'I met him through friends at the American School in London. Dodi, who loved the cinema, used to visit my father's film sets. We became part of his family and he became part of ours.'[151] Fayed and the Princess of Wales were expected to visit Barbara at Pinewood Studios in early September during the final week of production.[152]

After twenty-three seven-day weeks, shooting sixteen hours a day, *Tomorrow Never Dies* wrapped on 5 September 1997.[153] Spottiswoode faced a very short editing period:

> It has been the most horrendous post-production schedule. Normally I'd have liked four months to fine-tune it, condense, focus and perhaps find it anew in the cutting room. It hasn't been possible here, but I knew that going in. I've just had to grin and bear it. I'm certain when I see it in theatres this Christmas I'll know how to polish it further but won't be able to.'[154]

In order to meet the deadline two editors worked concurrently. Spottiswoode had worked with husband and wife team Michel Arcand and Dominique Fortin previously in Canada. *Tomorrow Never Dies* was the first Bond to be edited digitally, which allowed sequences to be worked on by two editors at the same time. He explained, 'This is so common now but it wasn't back then, to have three [editing suites] looking at footage. We brutalised the post-production time. I think it was two or three weeks from the end of shooting to the preview.'[155]

Spottiswoode was insistent that the final cut came in no longer than two hours.[156] He felt *GoldenEye* had been drawn out, 'I have a thing about long films. You need one ending, not four, and you figure out how to tell it in two hours, better still a little less.'[157] Michael Wilson commended Spottiswoode for completing the picture in such a tight time frame, 'It's been a miracle that he brought it off.'[158]

United Artists' Lindsay Doran recalled *Tomorrow Never Dies* underwent the scrutiny of a test audience in Slough just weeks before release:

> There was just this one little opportunity for human beings to see this movie before it came out. I remember Roger [Spottiswoode] standing up at the front and saying, 'I'm showing this to you, it's my only chance to show it to an audience. I want you to tell me what you *really* think. This is not the time to be nice.'[159]

Spottiswoode remembered:

It was without doubt the worst preview. I had never previewed in England, I had done all my films in America. Everyone seemed to be asleep, not a single laugh, not a titter, not a gasp. I thought we were at a funeral. [MGM] said it was a terrific preview. I was absolutely shocked. We didn't change very much.[160]

After what was described at the time as a tumultuous production, nearly twenty years on Bruce Feirstein reflected on the experience differently:

You were in the heat of it back then and you think this has never happened to anybody before in the whole world. It was a movie that was rushed into production. We all had guns to our heads and there was a lot of tension. We were under tremendous pressure. The truth is, this happens on a lot of movies. Michael and Barbara never panicked. Twenty years ago, I would have used the over-wrought description that it was like 'changing engines on a Concorde mid-flight' but since then I've been on a number of movies that have been exactly the same.[161]

Spottiswoode agreed, 'We had arguments. You want people to be invested in what they are doing, right? People who don't really give a damn are easy to find but they are not very useful. The people you value, are the ones who will fight for what they believe in. I expect to have arguments, I do it with my editors, I've had the same editors for twenty years and we argue like nobody's business. I always think that's part of the process.'[162] Kleeman observed diplomatically, 'Roger's particular weakness is he is incredibly good at intuiting what buttons you can push that will really rile somebody up. And when he realises what button that is, he can't resist pushing it.'[163]

In November 1996 Michael Wilson intimated in a lecture at the Institute of Contemporary Arts in London, that John Barry was set to score *Bond 18*.[164] However, the composer passed after they failed to reach an agreement. Barry's fee at the time was reportedly $1 million but he was willing to take a significant reduction to do the picture. The deal was to involve a contract for $850,000 of which Barry would pay a chunk back to the filmmakers. The reason for this bizarre deal was Barry's agent could not be seen to be letting Barry's price slip.[165] Ultimately, the deal breaker was MGM/UA who were not willing to allow Barry to write the title song. He said in December 1997, 'There were several areas that were non-negotiable. I wasn't going to regress.'[166]

Eon proceeded with arguably John Barry's biggest fan, David Arnold, who had first discussed Bond with MGM shortly before the release of *GoldenEye* while scoring *Stargate* (1994), 'At that point they had already signed Eric Serra so I knew I wasn't going to be doing that. But I said, "If John [Barry] is not going to be involved then I would love to do it."'[167]

Arnold had several theories as to how he landed *Tomorrow Never Dies*. 'I'd heard that [John Barry] suggested to Michael and Barbara that I might be a person they could trust.'[168] He had recently completed an album of Bond covers, *Shaken and Stirred: The David Arnold James Bond Project*, 'Barbara and Michael had heard the record and they were using 'On Her Majesty's Secret Service' – the version I did with the Propellerheads for their car park chase as the temp.'[169]

Barbara Broccoli has since told Arnold that she was in a record shop buying scores to lay up against an early cut of *Tomorrow Never Dies*, when the shop assistant recommended she take a listen to Arnold, 'If it is true, there is a shop assistant somewhere that I owe a very large drink or a very small house!'[170] But ultimately the fact that '*Independence Day* [1996] did a huge amount of business and I won a Grammy for the score'[171] was probably a major factor. 'All of a sudden I went from being the next John Williams to the next John Barry because I was doing a Bond film.'[172]

Before Arnold had met with the producers he had written a spec title song, 'Surrender', inspired by the screenplay, 'I thought I've got nothing to lose! The possibility of me scoring a Bond movie got me hugely excited. I am a bit old school because I love the way songs and score are interpolated and related and it felt that the DNA of the score was in the song itself.'[173] The deal for the title song had already been completed with Sheryl Crow when Arnold was hired and he quashes rumours his song, written with Don Black and acclaimed singer-songwriter David McAlmont, and performed by k.d. lang, was ever considered for the opening titles, 'Because of the success they had with Bono and The Edge and Tina Turner for *GoldenEye*, they were approaching people to write the song independently of the score.'[174] 'Surrender' was ultimately used over the closing credits, 'I was lucky they let me, they were actually being very kind to me, they didn't have to.'[175]

Arnold recalled the brief from UA was to 'get the Bond theme back in a little more upfront and centre.'[176] He approached *Tomorrow Never Dies* by splitting the score into three sections:

The opening third I wanted the music to be more back-to-basics James Bond. When he gets to Hamburg everything gets a bit more technical so I thought we'd move into an electronic realm. And then when we meet Wai

Lin, I wanted it to represent where we were going, the South China Seas, more ethnically driven in its instrumentation.[177]

Following Eric Serra's experimental score for *GoldenEye*, David Arnold's music was a return to more traditional fare and delighted the producers, 'We finished recording the last session and Michael Wilson came up to me and said "Don't do anything in two years' time." I took that as an invitation to do the next one.'[178]

Daniel Kleinman's reinvention of the Bond title sequence on *GoldenEye* ensured his return. The sequence begins with the cinema screen shattered to smithereens by the afterburner of Bond's fighter jet. Kleinman then takes us into a fantasy vision of cyberspace with a ''90s collage of hi-tech imagery.'[179] He used the Bond iconography of guns and girls made from electronic circuitry and x-rays as 'a reflection of modern-day media on one level, and on another, it is about seeing beneath the surface of things.'[180] Kleinman revealed he 'didn't get much help from Roger. He was a sort of bombastic man who liked to think he was some sort of Caesar.'[181] Kleinman felt that the director did not like his work,[182] so much so, 'he didn't want his name on the sequence.'[183] Spottiswoode's credit appeared after the main titles had faded to black and over the first frames of the feature.

Just weeks before *Tomorrow Never Dies* hit theatres, United Artists were dealt an unexpected blow. On 14 October 1997 former UA chief John Calley announced that Sony Pictures Entertainment division, Columbia Pictures, were planning to activate a James Bond motion picture franchise, based on the story rights owned by Kevin McClory.[184] Calley said that although there was not a completed script nor director or star attached, Sony planned to launch their Bond franchise in 1999 with McClory as producer.[185] Calley knew McClory's rights well having been a key production executive at Warner Brothers when *Never Say Never Again* was made over a decade earlier.

MGM president Frank Mancuso responded tersely:

Any claim that [McClory] can create a James Bond franchise is delusional. We hope that Sony has not been duped by Mr. McClory's deception. Today, more than ever, we will vigorously pursue all means to protect this valued franchise that United Artists and the Broccoli family have nurtured for more than three decades.[186]

The announcement could not have come at a worse time for MGM, who were on the cusp of launching a $250 million public offering in the studio, as Crédit Lyonnais prepared to sell MGM. Lindsay Doran reflected:

John was impish. He loved creating mischief. It really felt like a really violent act towards the studio, especially as it coincided with stock IPO But he denied it. He pretended that this was something he wasn't even aware of. Clearly he was, he had the business channel on in his office all the time. He knew what he was doing.[187]

Before his departure from UA, Calley had publicly congratulated the Broccolis in an open letter published in *Variety*, 'Frank Mancuso and I –and all of your extended family here at the studio – congratulate you on this historic achievement with *GoldenEye*. James Bond is thirty-four years old and still setting new records.'[188]

In November 1997 MGM filed a $25 million lawsuit against Sony Pictures Entertainment and John Calley.[189] Represented by Pierce O'Donnell, of law firm O'Donnell & Shaeffer, the attorney told *Variety*, 'This case is about the specious efforts of a global media empire and a disgruntled former executive (Calley) of United Artists Pictures Inc. to lay claim to the most successful and enduring motion picture franchise in history.'[190] O'Donnell said the $25 million in damages were charged in connection with MGM's public stock offering,[191] 'They calculated the timing to inflict maximum injury to MGM/UA.'[192] The lawsuit targeted Calley personally too, 'During his tenure at United Artists Pictures, Calley acquired highly valuable proprietary information about the optimal ways to develop and exploit the franchise and bring it into the twenty-first century.'[193] Confidently, O'Donnell said of both Sony and McClory, 'I don't think they can make a martini that's shaken, not stirred.'[194]

In a move that MGM considered another 'patch in the quilt of ownership,'[195] they purchased the distribution rights to *Never Say Never Again* from Taliafilm. Lindsay Doran said in a statement:

We have taken this definitive action to underscore the point that the Bond franchise has one, and only one, home – with the collective family of United Artists, MGM and Danjaq. We want to make it undeniably clear to any and all encroachers that MGM will do everything to protect what has been established over thirty-five years to be the most valuable film franchise in history.[196]

Jeff Kleeman was unfazed:

None of us took it as a threat to our franchise. We had a great James Bond in Pierce; we had a really strong director in Martin and now another really strong director with Roger Spottiswoode. We felt we had decades' deep knowledge of how to make these movies with Barbara and Michael. We had a studio that wanted to throw everything at it and we knew that at best Sony could make one movie. You actually *couldn't* franchise Bond the way we were franchising Bond when you were limited to essentially making a one-off that was going to be very expensive and feel like the second-hand version of a much more expansive series that was already in the cinema. That's what really baffled me about the deal. I was very surprised when John [Calley], who is one of the smartest people I've ever met in my life, made a deal with Kevin McClory.[197]

On a personal note Kleeman felt disappointed, 'John had been a part of the team, a member of the family, and such a good leader on *GoldenEye*.'[198]

As Michael Wilson contemplated yet another round in the courts, he wearily asked himself, 'Is this a vendetta between the studios? I guess when you have a success you have many imitators and many people who would like to duplicate the success.'[199]

As well as facing the lawsuit, Lindsay Doran was preparing to launch *Tomorrow Never Dies* against the biggest film of the year – *Titanic* – when Twentieth-Century Fox rescheduled its summer release. On 9 December 1997 *Tomorrow Never Dies* had its world charity premiere at the Odeon Leicester Square – unusually - with no royal presence. In America, the film was scheduled to release exactly the same day as James Cameron's $200 million blockbuster on 19 December 1997. Doran was nervous, 'It was very, very scary. If your mandate is: don't screw up the Bond franchise and the first James Bond movie you make is overwhelmed by another movie that's terrifying. We won Friday night. Saturday night it was clear that [*Titanic*] was going to be a problem. By Sunday night it seemed like it was going to be a big problem.'[200] *Tomorrow Never Dies* achieved a North American opening weekend gross of $25,143,007 going on to make $125,304,276 domestically. The worldwide take was $333,011,068 – after *GoldenEye*, the second highest Bond gross ever.

As the final scene faded to black, the end credits of *Tomorrow Never Dies* began with the tribute, 'In loving memory of Albert R. (Cubby) Broccoli'. Barbara and Michael could take comfort in the fact that they had shepherded their father's legacy successfully to a new and increasingly committed generation of James Bond fans.

KNOW HOW TO SURVIVE

THE WORLD IS NOT ENOUGH

(1999)

MGM and Danjaq
Congratulate

Pierce Brosnan

"Our Billion Dollar Bond"

$1,046,000,007

Box Office Gross to Date

Goldeneye   Tomorrow Never Dies
The World is Not Enough

007

Since MGM had purchased the outfit from Transamerica in 1981,[1] United Artists had limped along. In June 1999 MGM, under the new administration of Alex Yemenidjian, Chris McGurk and Kirk Kerkorian announced it was restructuring UA on the eve of its eightieth birthday. All content would be absorbed under the MGM umbrella. MGM's new vice-chairman and chief operating officer, McGurk:

> saw that United Artists and MGM were both doing the exact same type of movies, competing for projects with each other in the open market. I didn't think that was the right thing to do so I came up with the idea of turning United Artists into a specialty film label and having MGM as the big studio release label. As part of that we took the Bond movies and made them part of MGM with the MGM logo. [2]

Lindsay Doran, who would soon leave United Artists, 'understood it from a business point of view but it made me incredibly sad. The Bond films had been United Artists' movies for all those years.'[3]

Jeff Kleeman became part of the new MGM team and continued production executive on the Bond franchise. Said Michael G. Wilson, 'Every time you make a film you are faced with a new group of executives. You know how it is – they have to make a point for being there.'[4] McGurk understood that what Eon:

> really cared about was making sure that they had a studio partner that basically advised and consulted but let them run the show creatively and a studio partner that was there to spend a lot of money, producing and marketing the movie so that their franchise could be competitive with other franchises.'[5]

Wilson did not miss penning Bond films, 'When you're a producer supervising writers, you get your oar in the water. There's enough going on to satisfy that.'[6] He and Barbara Broccoli were impressed by the work of a young British screenwriting duo, Neal Purvis and Robert Wade, after Danjaq's development executive, Simon Mathew, passed them a draft of their most recent screenplay *Plunket and Macleane* (1999).[7]

In late 1997 Purvis and Wade went to Eon headquarters at 138 Piccadilly – 'a Bond villain's lair with 18ft ceilings'[8] – and were asked by Michael and Barbara, '"So what do you think James Bond should do next?"'[9] Both writers were Bond fans and together in the early 1980s had written a spec script set in Northern England about two guys obsessed about James Bond.[10]

Across a number of subsequent meetings, the pair suggested a slew of ideas including a 'villain who wants to play Russian roulette with the earth by blowing up the moon to see where the pieces will land,'[11] a topical plot involving French nuclear weapons testing and a genetically targeted virus that would kill one in ten people.[12] Purvis and Wade viewed all the previous Bond films courtesy of Dana Broccoli's personal 35mm prints.[13]

Barbara then saw an episode of Ted Koppel's current affairs series *Nightline*, which focused on Baku, the capital of Azerbaijan, and how it had become the centre of an oil boom since the break-up of the USSR some years earlier.[14] Interestingly, Robert Wade had also read a similar article in *The Economist* and had bookmarked it as a discussion point.[15] The writers proposed a female villain, inspired by heiress Patty Hearst, who as a kidnap victim became infatuated with her kidnappers, in what was later to be termed Stockholm syndrome.[16] Mythological Greek tragedy also informed the draft, according to Purvis, 'Barbara said, "Bond thinks Elektra is Tracy from *On Her Majesty's Secret Service*, but she turns out to be Blofeld."'[17] The writers suggested a pre-credit chase down the Thames with 007 pursuing the villain down the river on a jet pack.[18]

When Martin Campbell again declined Eon's offer to direct,[19] the producers began talks with Mexican filmmaker Alfonso Cuarón, who would later helm the third *Harry Potter* film.[20] Robert Wade recalled:

> They were genuinely interested in him directing it and this well before he did *Harry Potter*. I'm not sure whether he quite got the Britishness of Bond because we had this boat chase on the Thames and he said, 'Why can't we make that the Hudson River?' It's not quite the iconography is it?[21]

Kleeman confirmed an official offer was put to Cuarón, 'My understanding is that he seriously considered it but ultimately he decided it wasn't for him. He would have been that rare director that was not UK or Commonwealth.'[22]

Michael Apted was hired in August 1998,[23] 'When I was asked if I was interested I thought it was a joke because I had never done anything like it.'[24] Michael Wilson recalled Apted stating at their first meeting, '"I'm not an action director" and we said, "Good, we didn't want one." We wanted someone who was a good storyteller.'[25] Apted met with United Artists and finally with Pierce Brosnan,[26] 'It was clearly for them to meet me and talk to me and to see if it could work. They were taking a certain amount of risk with me so I didn't mind it at all.'[27] Brosnan was impressed by Apted, 'He had a very dry sense of humour, a droll sense of humour, and I really appreciated that. He was very affable and had a vision.'[28]

It was true Apted had never directed anything remotely like a James Bond film. His background lay in dramas such as *The Coal Miner's Daughter* (1980) and *Gorillas in the Mist* (1988) and documentaries, most famously his sociological *Up* series. Apted explained, 'What they were really looking for was a director who had some experience in directing women. When I discovered that, there was something I could offer them, of course the whole thing became a bit more real to me. I was scared shitless going in.'[29] Wilson assured him, 'We could handle all the action elements within our own team we needed someone who could work with the actors and tell this story.'[30] The experience would be an education for Apted, 'The film business is very ageist. At my age, to learn the dynamics of such a huge international action blockbuster was very exciting.'[31]

He was not a Bond fan, 'Frankly, in the sixties when they started, I was more likely to be looking at Fellini or Bergman or Godard and all that sort of stuff, rather than seeing a Bond film.'[32]

After their second draft Purvis and Wade were let go.[33] Barbara and Michael expressed that they had enjoyed one of their most fruitful relationships since working with Richard Maibaum. However, Michael Apted now wanted to bring in his wife, writer Dana Stevens.[34] Purvis reflected, 'It's difficult when it's taken away from you, it's not an enjoyable situation but then that's the nature of the job.'[35] However, the producers also invited them to write the next film.[36] Wade wryly noted, 'It's kind of like a kick in the teeth and then they sort of pick you up and give you a handkerchief.'[37]

Dana Stevens was known to MGM, having recently written the fantasy drama *City of Angels* (1998):

'On every movie that Michael made while I was married to him, there was a sinking feeling from the writers, "Oh no, Michael Apted might bring his wife on to do some work!" I was never credited on any of them. Once Neal and Rob could see I wasn't going to try to get credit, there was no resentment.[38]

Remembered Kleeman, 'It was really nice to have a female screenwriter come in and give her point of view and version of a Bond movie, as we were evolving Bond and surrounding him in late twentieth- and early twenty-first-century society, women and cultural values.'[39] Based at Pinewood Studios, Stevens worked on the script for three weeks,[40] 'It was very surgical, I didn't do any changes to the plot, I really worked on the female characters and dialogue.'[41] In particular Stevens strengthened Elektra's relationships between Bond and M and re-wrote M's motives within the story, 'My recollection is that there was some argument about whether to put Judi so firmly into the story, having [Bond's] superior be in danger.'[42] It was important to Apted that audiences did not immediately guess Elektra King was the villain.[43]

Apted recalled, 'Intellectually everybody wanted there to be some more femininity in the story but when it came to the reality of it, Michael [Wilson] was a little nervous of it.'[44] Stevens remembered her suggestions could often divide opinion in daily script meetings:

> I can remember Michael Wilson scoffing at some of the things I wanted to do with Sophie's character as silly or ridiculous. Barbara and I would say "No, they are not." I can remember at one point I went back to my office and cried because I was feeling like I didn't fit into the Bond ethos. I can see as the Bond franchise moved forward, especially with Daniel Craig, that Barbara's vision is bearing out.[45]

Apted observed that the producers were particularly protective of the James Bond character. In one sequence Elektra asks Bond if he has ever lost anyone he loved, 'I was thinking "Okay, this is a romantic sequence, in romantic sequences people reveal themselves." And Michael and Barbara interceded. Bond never reveals anything about himself.'[46]

Following the Stevens draft, it was now Pierce Brosnan who was unhappy with the screenplay.[47] 'Pierce didn't really like Dana's writing very much because he felt he was being short changed by it,'[48] suggested Apted, 'Bond was second banana here and Elektra and M were taking over the film.'[49] In November 1998 the producers turned back to Bruce Feirstein to work on Bond's character, 'I remember my brief was: Bond needs to drive the story more. I was given Dana's draft and told to fix Bond's role, clarify the story and flesh out some of the characters.'[50] Feirstein was to add some signature Bond humour, although a favoured exchange was ultimately cut:

> It was a line I always wanted to use. M says, 'Contrary to what you believe 007, the world is not populated by madmen who can hollow out a volcano, fill it with big breasted women and threaten the world with nuclear annihilation.' To which Bond looks at her and says, 'It only takes one.' It was shot and I remember sitting next to Barbara watching rushes at Pinewood and her saying, 'Forget it, that's not going to make the movie.'[51]

Feirstein had always wanted to convey how Bond felt about his profession.[52] He achieved this with Brosnan's steely delivery as he grabs Renard by the scruff of his neck in a nuclear weapons bunker and says, 'I usually hate killing an unarmed man. Cold-blooded murder is a filthy business.'

Apted recalled that they tweaked the script all the way through production with even Michael Wilson rewriting sections,[53] 'We were always fiddling with it, it was never a complete script until we finished [the film].'[54] Purvis and Wade welcomed the producer's input, 'Michael was a mentor to us really.'[55]

Purvis and Wade had titled early outlines, *Elektra*.[56] They explored Fleming chapter titles considering *A Whisper of Love, A Whisper of Hate* before settling on a line from their own script – *The World Is Not Enough*. Noted Wilson; 'It's more intriguing and more personal. It refers to the spiritual and moral sides of Bond's character actually transcending the material.'[57] The title was taken from Ian Fleming's ON HER MAJESTY'S SECRET SERVICE in which Bond visits the Royal College of Arms in London and learns of his family motto.

Neal Purvis and Robert Wade created a Bond adventure as overwrought as a Shakespearean tragedy. The history, motivation and interaction between the principal characters underpin the entire story. Elektra King believes her father, Sir Robert King, conned her mother's family out of their oil wealth. Elektra was a wild, wayward, spoiled and sexually mature young lady, who always had power over men. When kidnapped by Victor Zokas a.k.a. Renard and held for $5,000,000 ransom, it was assumed that Elektra suffered from Stockholm syndrome. Sir Robert delays paying the ransom and seeks counsel from his university friend and now head of MI6, M. During that time, Elektra is forced to seduce and turn Renard – while suffering at his hands – to gain her own freedom. M sent 009 to kill Renard but the bullet is lodged in the kidnapper's brain and will not kill him immediately. As a result, Renard has lost all feeling and will die eventually but not before he gains increased physical strength. Elektra then plots her revenge. She pointedly lures MI6 into her plan by using exactly the same amount of cash as the sum sought for her ransom. Bond is duped into bringing back this cash – a refund for payment of a stolen oil-pipeline threat report – from Swiss bankers in Bilbao. However, the money has been booby-trapped. When Sir Robert sets off the bomb that kills him inside MI6's HQ, Elektra takes control of her father's oil business, King Industries.

She then plans to gain control of the world's oil supplies by irradiating the Bosphorus. The vital waterway is required by oil tankers to ship oil from pipelines to the north of the region. Elektra's pipeline is the only one that goes south, avoiding the need to ship her oil by water to Istanbul. She arranges for Renard to steal some weapons grade plutonium, half of which he will use on a suicide mission to contaminate the Bosphorus by staging an accident with an ageing Russian nuclear submarine. The vessel is purchased by a rigged bet at a casino in Baku, now run by Bond's old contact, Valentin Zukovsky. The other half is used to detonate her own pipeline to throw the authorities off her scent and also make it seem all the stolen plutonium has been used. Bond is sent by M to protect Elektra from a perceived threat but is seduced by the heiress and caught up in her treachery. Elektra then kidnaps M to exact revenge for when the Secret Service chief advised her father to delay paying her ransom.

Bond teams up with nuclear physicist Dr. Christmas Jones to overcome the plutonic threat. At the film's finale, King taunts Bond about his supposed inability to kill her, but he does so with ruthless efficiency. He outwits Renard in the nuclear submarine's reactor before the terrorist can cause the meltdown.

Wilson pointed out that at the time, seventy per cent of the Bond box office came from the international markets so it was important to pepper the supporting cast with international faces rather than just Hollywood names, 'We have to be sensitive to world demands, but you try putting that across to Hollywood executives.'[58]

A number of actresses were tested for the role of Elektra King, including the then unknown, Vera Farmiga.[59] Brosnan confirmed Sharon Stone's name was discussed, 'but nothing came to fruition.'[60] Apted had his sights set on Sophie Marceau after seeing her in William Nicholson's *Firelight* (1997).[61] Marceau tested, reading the scenes in which Elektra tortures Bond at the end of the film.[62] Michael Apted recalled, 'I had to fight for her because I think she was quite expensive and cost more money than they would have wanted to pay.'[63] Dana Stevens remembered, 'I think they were concerned not just about money but her being French, her being not a known commodity. Once she did the screentest there was no question it had to be her.'[64]

Following Mel Gibson's *Braveheart* (1995), *The World Is Not Enough* was only Marceau's second English-language film. 'Elektra is supposed to be half English/ half Turkish so that bi-cultural aspect made the part even richer and harder,'[65] commented Marceau during production. Brosnan confessed he did not get to know his co-star all that well, 'She was quite distant and aloof and French. I think that was just her way of working [but] I thought she was a magnificent actress.'[66] Given that Elektra was such a complex character, costume designer Lindy Hemming felt that, 'Her costumes needed to show her progression from a Western society girl with plenty of money, and change gradually, visually, to a mad and vindictive woman controlled by a terrorist and looking more and more reminiscent of her ethnic background.'[67]

United Artists' Lindsay Doran insisted the second female character, Dr. Christmas Jones, be American, 'Sophie Marceau was clearly somebody for European audiences and very important to the movie overseas and the overseas aspect of a Bond movie is huge. It made sense to have somebody in the other part who was more known in America.'[68] With Elektra King, Apted recalled there was a concern from the studio that they were moving too far away from the archetypal Bond girl.[69] Purvis and Wade were asked to rewrite Christmas Jones to make her more American and 'sassy'.[70] Rising Hollywood sex symbol Denise Richards fitted the bill.

Christmas Jones was named after Christmas Humphreys – the prosecutor in the Craig/Bentley case, the real-life story behind Purvis and Wade's debut screenplay *Let Him Have It* (1991).[71] The character was originally written as a French-Polynesian girl working as an insurance investigative agent for Lloyd's of London.[72] UA asked if her profession could be altered, as they had just green lit Pierce Brosnan in *The Thomas Crown Affair* (1999), in which his love interest was also to be an insurance investigator.[73] Purvis recalled; 'We'd originally thought of her as Thandie Newton.'[74] Christmas Jones briefly became a bounty hunter before they settled on a nuclear physicist.[75] There was an attempt during Stevens's rewrite to make Jones more convincing as a nuclear physicist, but in retrospect Stevens felt the character was still not entirely believable.[76] Denise Richards was new to the world of 007,'I didn't grow up watching James Bond movies. I never realised how big internationally the James Bond series was until I was cast.'[77]

Javier Bardem, who over a decade later would win critical acclaim playing Raoul Silva in *Skyfall*, had been in the frame to play international terrorist and Elektra's kidnapper and lover, Renard.[78] A serious contender had also been French actor Jean Reno, who had to decline the role due to personal problems.[79] Finally the part was offered to Scottish actor Robert Carlyle. Best known for his roles in *Trainspotting* (1996) and *The Full Monty* (1997), Michael Wilson first thought Carlyle perfect for the role after seeing him portray a psychopath in British television drama, *Cracker*.[80]

Carlyle imagined the character, Renard, to be of Bosnian decent, a villain from the recent Yugoslavian conflict in Eastern Europe,[81] 'I told an actor friend I was thinking of doing this and he introduced me to a Bosnian actor – Velibor Topic. He told me incredible stories and I started to think about someone from a military background in a similar situation being confronted with the horrors of war.'[82]

During production Robert Carlyle was awarded an OBE. At the honours ceremony the Queen asked him what he was doing at the moment, Carlyle replied, 'I've spent the whole day trying to kill James Bond.'[83]

Robbie Coltrane reprised his role from *GoldenEye*, as the Russian arms dealer Valentin Zukovsky. Coltrane explained that since audiences last saw Bond's lovable foe he has entered the caviar business as a way of laundering funds, 'Before he was buying and selling second-hand grenades on street corners in Moscow. Now he owns a caviar factory which is every Russian hooligan's dream.'[84]

Judi Dench was delighted to discover M was to play a bigger role in the story, 'I had three days on *GoldenEye*, five on *Tomorrow Never Dies* and fourteen or fifteen days on this one.'[85] The actress joked she had yet to travel to exotic locales with the Bond pictures, 'This time they said they were going to take me to Scotland and to Turkey. The nearest I got to either was a painted backdrop of Loch Lomond.'[86] Following her difficult relationship with Roger Spottiswoode, Dench praised Michael Apted as an 'actor's director. No matter what he decides to do there is flexibility for you.'[87]

Desmond Llewelyn returned for his seventeenth appearance as Q but the film-makers decided it was finally time he should be given an assistant. Monty Python star John Cleese revealed, 'The idea is for me to appear in the next two or three movies with the intention of eventually taking over the role of Q when Desmond, who is eighty-four, decides to retire. So it looks as though I may become part of the Bond family, and I couldn't be happier about it.'[88] Cleese knew Apted from years earlier, 'He was an exact contemporary of mine at the same college in Cambridge – we were both at Downing College. We both went there in October 1960.'[89]

The villainy would be augmented by Maria Grazia Cucinotta as the leather clad Cigar Girl, who meets her demise over the Millenium Dome, dance musician and DJ Goldie as the gold teethed Mr. Bullion, Zukovsky's treacherous henchman, professional wrestler John Seru as Gabor, and Danish Dogme star, Ulrich Thomsen as Davidov, Elektra's body guard and assistant respectively. The cast would be completed by Kristen Scott Thomas' younger sister, Serena as Dr. Molly Warmflash and noted stage actor David Calder as King's father, Sir Robert.

Apart from cinematographer Adrian Biddle and editor Jim Clark, 'two key people who would help execute my vision',[90] Apted relied on Eon's regular team to assist him in the production of *The World Is Not Enough*. Approaching seventy Peter Lamont was enjoying the best years of his career. His work on James Cameron's *Titanic* (1997) had recently been crowned with an Oscar win. Returing to the Eon fold, Lamont had been designing Bond longer than his mentor Ken Adam. The producers considered him a crucial member of their team as Wilson affirmed, 'The first thing we do when we start working on the script and we're thinking about locations and whether we can do this or that, is we call up Peter Lamont.'[91]

The producers also turned once more to second unit director Vic Armstrong to assist Michael Apted with key action sequences, which were to include the boat chase down the Thames, a parahawk ski sequence set in the Caucasus mountains and an action-packed helicopter attack off the coast of Baku.

Michael Apted and Peter Lamont hit it off immediately.[92] With Lamont most at home recreating realism,[93] his style dovetailed nicely with Apted's documentary eye. As pre-production began Apted admitted:

> I could see my documentary antennae in a selective way working. The first thing I did when I got the film was to cart them all out to Azerbaijan to see the real [oil] operation around the Caspian and what was going on. That gave us a lot of terrific ideas and a lot of terrific images. I suppose my whole faith in documentaries is that the truth is stranger than fiction.[94]

Lamont remembered the trip, 'Azerbaijan is part of the old Soviet Union, the whole place has been locked up for years and nobody really knew what went on there.'[95] Apted immediately fell in love with the landscape, 'You are always looking for new visual grammar in Bond. Here seemed to be an entirely original location, oil fields all going to rack and ruin left by the Russians. I just thought photographically it was staggering. It was one of the most thrilling parts of the scout for me.'[96] Upon inspection it became apparent that the oil construction complex was not suitable to shoot a feature film on, 'We flew over these derelict platforms, all falling into the sea. You got this stench of petrol and oil. There were trucks isolated where the super-structure had fallen away.'[97]

On Monday 11 January 1999 *The World Is Not Enough* began filming at Pinewood Studios. For Brosnan, it was his first Bond movie to be based at the series' ancestral home; 'They've finally let me in the doors, so to be here, with people who have worked on Bond for so many years, is like no other film.'[98]

Some of the first scenes to be shot were with the MI6 regulars: Judi Dench, Samantha Bond and, returning from *GoldenEye*, Michael Kitchen as Bill Tanner, as well as from *Tomorrow Never Dies*, Colin Salmon as Charles Robinson. These actors gathered in the poplar-lined avenue at Stowe public school, where Apted filmed Sir Robert King's funeral. In a scene deleted from the final film, Bond, following his injury on the Millennium Dome in the pre-title sequence, was to be driven to the ceremony by Miss Moneypenny in his Aston Martin DB5. Samantha Bond thought, 'I've got Mr. Brosnan next to me in this quarter-of-a-million-pound car. He's sitting beside me saying "Faster Bond, speed it up." It's not a girl's car at all, it's very, very heavy. There was no point [to the scene], it was just fun.'[99]

On 28 January[100] Apted filmed with the principals on the city of walkways set, as Bond, Valentin and Christmas Jones are attacked by Elektra's deadly helicopter chainsaws, which carve Zukovsky's caviar factory to pieces. The wooden structure, the first of two major sets Lamont constructed for the film, was built over the

Paddock Tank at Pinewood. As the entire sequence takes place at night, the set was surrounded by a huge backing, into which Lamont inserted 'several thousand fibre optics to give the impression of distance. When all the lights are on at night it appears they twinkle in the distance as if you are there.'[101]

Michael Wilson had wanted to feature these unique helicopters in a previous Bond.[102] B.J. Worth had shown him footage of giant saw blades dangling from helicopters used in large plantations across America and Canada years earlier.[103] The concept had appeared in the screenplay for *GoldenEye* and special effects supervisor Chris Corbould had spent two months on it before the idea was scrapped.[104] Purvis and Wade were shown the *GoldenEye* storyboards and asked if the sequence could be incorporated into *The World Is Not Enough*.[105]

Towards the end of production, Vic Armstrong took over the walkways set to shoot key action. Originally the scene was to feature an elaborate car chase around the wooden walkways with Bond behind the wheel of his new BMW Z8, which according to Lamont, 'was going to be a stealth car, but we didn't shoot it.'[106] This in turn was an idea that would be recycled in *Die Another Day*. Instead, just as Bond leaps into the Z8 and the audience are gearing up for a car chase, 007 jumps straight back out again, as the helicopter saw blade slices the two-seater in half. The moment was based on a Laurel and Hardy gag in which the comedy duo's Model T Ford is split in two.[107] Armstrong wanted shots of real helicopters hovering over the walkways, not just the models hanging from cranes. Due to health and safety at Pinewood, a large proportion of the set was dismantled and rebuilt in Aldershot on an army training ground.[108]

Next, Michael Apted moved the main unit over to Peter Lamont's second major construction, an underground nuclear bunker, a vast cavernous interior built on the 007 Stage. Again, a great deal of action was to unfold. The drama begins when Bond catches Renard red-handed stealing a nuclear weapon, as a team of American scientists led by Dr. Christmas Jones are closing the former Soviet plant in Kazakhstan.

Emerging from the 007 Stage one evening Brosnan was to have a chance encounter with a hero of his own, 'I throw my bags in the car and as I close the trunk there's Sean Connery standing there and he just said, "Are they paying you enough money?" That was my only encounter with Sean. Quite memorable and a very funny line.'[109] Earlier, Connery had wandered unannounced onto the 007 Stage, where he was met by a startled Michael Apted:

I heard this voice behind me say something quite ordinary. I thought, 'Shit' and I turned around and it was Sean. I nearly passed out. I had no idea he was there. It was almost like a dream in many ways: I'm talking to Pierce over the intercom and I've got Sean standing behind me, sat on my shoulder watching the monitor. It was kind of thrilling and scary. I thought he was going to give me some notes![110]

On 21 January 1999[111] Vic Armstrong began shooting the second set-piece action sequence in Chamonix, France. The ski resort was doubling for the Caucasus mountains where Bond and Elektra are chased by parahawks (propellor-driven snowmobiles that fly through the air on paragliding parachutes). At one point Bond thinks he has disposed of a pursuer as they disappear over a precipice, only for a second chute to open. Armstrong suggested, 'My idea was to have a black parachute with a red hammer and sickle on it; a homage to the scene in *The Spy Who Loved Me*. The producers didn't go for it.'[112] Originally envisaged as a ski chase, when stunt co-ordinator Simon Crane saw some old-fashioned paragliders on holiday, the sequence was reconfigured. Armstrong's unit ceased filming when an avalanche blasted through the mountain range where the unit were shooting.[113] The Bond crew gave up their emergency services crew and helicopters for the rescue mission; the disaster claimed several families. The Bond crew were to have filmed a real avalanche, but Armstrong 'felt it was a bit insensitive to shoot it where a lot of people on the crew lost friends and relatives so we recreated it on the stage.'[114] The producers had concerns as to how Armstrong's second unit material shot in Chamonix would cut in with Apted's main unit work. Editor Jim Clark 'worked with an excellent storyboard artist to plug holes in the narrative. After discussions with Michael Wilson, these new images were spliced into the existing material.'[115] Apted and Armstrong could now see how their respective units would marry up once Brosnan and Marceau got to the slopes later in production.

In mid-February 1999 the main unit travelled to Bilbao, Spain, to shoot the opening scene near the Guggenheim Museum where Bond makes a daring leap from a fourth-floor balcony.[116] Brosnan's appeal as 007 was noted by Dana Stevens:

> Pierce was staying in the penthouse suite above our room. All night long the square in front of the hotel was full of people shouting for Pierce 'James Bond' to come out of his room. Eventually, quite late at night, he came out onto his balcony and the crowd cheered as he waved. It brought home to me how internationally successful the Bond films are.[117]

Brosnan could only compare it to Beatlemania. 'It's like a time warp back in the sixties. This has been gobstoppingly wonderful.'[118]

Problems arose when shooting in Istanbul had to be shelved, due to unrest with Kurdish separatist group PKK. Apted had scouted the region quite laboriously, 'We had all the locations but we had to dump them. We went in with a very small unit to shoot some of the stuff on the Bosphorus which we couldn't possibly match.'[119] In early April, unbeknownst to virtually the entire production, Eon sent in an undercover unit to shoot some establishing shots for a film titled *Destiny*.[120] Apted was concerned, 'We were too frightened to take Pierce into Istanbul, because he was a big fat ripe avocado waiting to be kidnapped.'[121] However, Brosnan and Marceau did briefly travel to Azerbaijan to shoot establishing shots at the Bibi-Heybat oil field near Baku, doubling as the King oil field.[122] Apted was forced to compromise, 'We had to then replace it with stuff in Spain so that was pretty tricky because it was a late decision. I was disappointed we couldn't shoot more in Turkey because they have really interesting places there that haven't been seen before.'[123]

In the longest pre-title sequence to date, Bond pursues a mysterious female assassin in a high-speed boat chase down the Thames. Beginning in the stretch of water outside Parliament, the climax of the sequence takes place by Canary Wharf. Apted witnessed the sheer power of Bond:

> It was kind of bizarre. No one had ever been given that kind of permission. If you knock on the door and say you are doing a Bond film people let you do anything, because it is Bond, everybody goes weak at the knees and says, 'Certainly, come in.' And we took full advantage of it.[124]

Location manager Richard Sharkey was faced with securing access for boats to race down the river at 40 knots where ordinary speed limits are 8–10 knots[125] for a sequence that would take six weeks to film.[126] Special effects supervisor Chris Corbould, 'spent many, many weeks liaising with the authorities, showing them that we weren't going to blow up half of London for a film.'[127] However, the unit did run into problems with Parliament. Vic Armstrong recalled, 'MPs were complaining about our jet boats. Jack Straw [the Home Secretary] stood up and said "Look, guys this is a huge advertising campaign for England, for London especially, and the film brings in huge revenues so just put up with it.'[128]

When the sequence was first pitched to Armstrong he was concerned as to how they were going to make it original:

> I looked at *Face Off* (1997) and hundreds of other boat pictures. They all seemed pretty similar. So Simon Crane and myself every Sunday would get a boat and go up and down the Thames looking for all the little places where incidents could happen, picking them out and writing incidents around those areas.'[129]

The most dangerous stunt was the Q-boat performing a 360-degree barrel roll. Simon Crane and Gary Powell spent weeks perfecting it.[130] Armstrong noted, 'It's a very brave thing to do. You are doing 70 mph, if he had gone upside down his head would have come off.'[131] Brosnan shot close-ups on The Thames impressing Armstrong, 'We put him in the boat and he scared the life out of me. He was great and you can see it in his face, he is having a blast.'[132]

In June 1999 as production neared conclusion, a scene was filmed which would become tragically poignant: Q's workshop. Bruce Feirstein gave it careful consideration, 'From the first time I met Desmond he was talking about having himself written out, it was a running joke. Somewhere in my files I have an eleven-page scene he wrote on yellow-lined paper.'[133] For Feirstein it was Arthur bidding farewell to Merlin, 'I remember Barbara didn't want to do it. Barbara did not want to write him out of the movies. "He's going to be with us forever." He was a great uncle to all of us.'[134]

Q leaves Bond with some Arthurian advice, '"First, never let them see you bleed." "And the second?" seeks Bond. "Always have an escape plan."' Then, Q gently disappears as a snooker table parts in two, lowering him out of shot. Feirstein was satisfied, '[Desmond and I] talked about it in the commissary at Pinewood and he was happy with it. In the original version I had Q disappear behind a puff of smoke.'[135]

Lindy Hemming felt Q had been so iconic that, unlike the characters around him, his look needed no updating:

> He could really have worn his own clothes for the part, as he owned so many things that would have been perfect for the character. We had a lovely Harris tweed suit made for him, which even though it got broken down and aged, it never looked as comfortable on him as his own. I asked Desmond if I could swap ours for his. We did and it was a much better costume.'[136]

On 19 December 1999 soon after *The World Is Not Enough* premiered in Los Angeles, Desmond Llewelyn was killed in a car accident. The sprightly 85-year-old had told the press during the publicity tour, he had every intention of continuing in the role, 'just as long Eon wants me and the Almighty doesn't.'[137] Unfortunately, the latter won out. Brosnan paid tribute to him:

> I loved his work as Q. He was the mainstay of the character and being Welsh and me being Irish there was a lovely connection there of the hearts and the minds. He was a father figure in some respects, and I just had a deep love for the

man. He was at a ripe old age when he was doing the films with me so the lines didn't come too readily. It made it very funny, in fact, and he would get himself kind of agitated so I spent a lot of time just calming him down and saying don't worry about it, we'll just make it up as we go along, and he kind of did. He was a delightful man. He was a great talisman for me because he'd been through so many of the films.[138]

Following his highly praised music for *Tomorrow Never Dies*, David Arnold was asked to reprise his work and he admitted, 'There is an element of repetition because it's the same person writing about the same character. You need to find a different way of orchestrating it.'[139] Arnold drew much of his inspiration from Elektra King, which gave his score 'a bittersweet'[140] sound. The character was manipulative and evoked vulnerability, innocence, revenge and seduction – themes Arnold could articulate through his score,[141] 'To write something beautiful and honest was very interesting for me, especially for a Bond movie.'[142]

Arnold had the task of composing the title song, which he wrote with veteran Bond lyricist Don Black:

I had a lot of discussions with Don about it. The song was from the perspective of Elektra trying to seduce the hero – 'if you joined me on this side we could have it all.' It's very seductive in that way but it's not talking about James Bond being a dangerous stranger like so many of them.'[143]

'The World Is Not Enough' was recorded by contemporary rock band Garbage. Michael Apted was an acquaintance of David Stewart of the band Eurythmics and was also developing a future project with Mick Jagger, both of whom the director recalled were discussed fleetingly.[144]

Shirley Manson, lead singer of Garbage, was a Bond fan, 'As soon as I knew we were doing it, I ran out and bought a compilation album and listened to a few of the classics but I got so spooked I had to stop. But then I remembered – and realised I was covered. At least, I wouldn't go down in history as the worst Bond theme ever.'[145] Arnold recalled the track was never officially offered to anyone else. The composer describes looking for an artist to sing a Bond title song is no different to casting:

A lot of people want to do it. A lot of actors want to play James Bond. You look for an artist who can bring something to the film and could almost be in the film. You could easily imagine Shirley Manson in a Bond movie. For me there is something about these people that represents the world of the film we are about to go into.[146]

Arnold and Black wrote a second song, 'Only Myself to Blame', to accompany the end credits. This sombre yet romantic track Arnold commented was, 'cut from the same cloth as 'We Have all The Time in the World'.'[147] The song is about James Bond in thirty years' time, now retired and looking back with regret. Don Black coaxed legendary sixties singer Scott Walker out of retirement to sing it.[148] Arnold understood why the vocal was not used:

[Apted] really liked the song but when we put it over [the end credits], it felt a bit of a downer. You want to send the audiences out on a bit of a high. You have just watched a Bond movie you want to go out excited, ready for the next one. It was a last minute decision to replace it with an upbeat version of the 'James Bond Theme'.[149]

Daniel Kleinman, back for a third Bond title sequence found that 'liaising with David Arnold really made things a lot easier. I could phone him up and say, "give me some lyrics at least."'[150] Arnold sympathised:

It felt that [Danny] and I were in a similar position, we were in the dark, we can't really do what we do until you see the film. When I had a demo I would send it to him almost the day after I had sent it to Barbara and Michael and the studio to give him something to start visualising.[151]

Kleinman explained that his process begins by generating ideas that relate to the storyline and, if possible, the mood and lyrics of the title song.[152] The final sequence for *The World Is Not Enough* was themed around images of girls dripping in oil, floating dreamily through space balanced on planets, juxtaposed with rusting nodding donkeys and other industrial oil trade machinery. He descibed how:

Very thin coats of oil and petrol on puddles give you an amazing refraction of colour. In the studio I photographed petrol on the surface of water and then used that footage to wrap around images of worlds and planets. I felt sorry for these poor girls. We poured fake oil over them as I wanted the oil to define the shape of the models.[153]

Four years on from his first James Bond title sequence, technology had improved greatly:

I'm conscious of trying to push the boundaries of the technology which is some-
thing Maurice always did. If lasers were the latest thing, he'd stick some lasers in.
[*The World Is Not Enough*] is probably one of the more effects-driven sequences.
It maybe felt a bit over-produced, almost *too* digital.[154]

On 3 August 1999 Apted screened *The World Is Not Enough* in a multiplex just
outside of Reading.[155] The director was relieved, 'Staggeringly we previewed the
film five weeks after we finished shooting.'[156] Editor Jim Clark said the reaction was
underwhelming, 'Although there were no walkouts we felt a distinct hostility.'[157]
Clark said the feedback was 'somewhat lower than most Bond movies,'[158] which was
odd considering the film scored 78 per cent.[159] Apted learnt a lot from the screening:

> I'm very glad we did preview it, we completely transformed the beginning of the
> film as a result. We had a very short beginning in fact, which was just the Bilbao
> sequence. And I realised [this] wasn't strong enough to be a pre-title sequence,
> I then had to join it on to the Thames sequence and make that the opening of
> the film.[160]

Brosnan was disappointed by certain cuts enforced upon the love scenes by the
censors:

> We couldn't show any nipples, but that's *all* that kept showing. And it was on the
> same day that the Columbine school massacre took place. So here are all these
> kids buying guns and killing their schoolmates, and here we are on the Bond
> movie worrying about a *nipple* showing. The censorship is pathetic.[161]

On 8 November 1999 *The World Is Not Enough* premiered in Los Angeles at Mann's
Village Theater in Westwood. The European charity premiere took place two weeks
later on 22 November at the Odeon Leicester Square. Brosnan's third Bond had a
North American opening weekend gross of $35,519,007 and continued an upward
trend. Achieving a final domestic gross of $126,943,684 and a worldwide gross of
$361,832,400 the movie surpassed *GoldenEye*.

Brosnan was satisfied with the finished film:

> We came out of the gate with *GoldenEye*, and now looking back, it seems like
> I was just a baby then. My assuredness within the role and my confidence has
> grown a lot. And, quite frankly, I wouldn't have expected anything less of myself.
> And I think the same could be said of Connery: if you look at him in *Dr. No* in

1962 and then his third time in *Goldfinger*, there was this whole mystique about the third Bond, when the actor really gets into his stride.[162]

The World Is Not Enough marked the end of the star's initial three-picture contract. 'If he's game for another we certainly are. It is certainly in all our minds at the moment,'[163] Wilson said enthusiastically. In May 2000 MGM and Danjaq took out a two-page advertisement in *Screen International* congratulating Pierce Brosnan – 'our billion dollar Bond,'[164] referencing the combined box office gross of all three of his Bond pictures.

Throughout the making of *The World Is Not Enough*, Barbara and Michael faced the ongoing dispute with Sony over their proposed plans to launch their own franchise based on Kevin McClory's limited rights. In February 1998 Sony claimed McClory was in fact the joint owner of the 'cinematic' Bond character, and his origins lay in the original *Thunderball* material. It was a high-risk claim, which simply put, was a kidnap attempt to prize 007 away from MGM. Sony were suing for an estimated $3 billion dollars.[165] Pierce O'Donnell, the legal representative for Danjaq and MGM, said, 'This claim is extraterritorial. It makes *Alice in Wonderland* look like a book of logic.'[166] MGM argued that if McClory believed he was entitled to claim, then why had he failed to sue in over thirty-five years?[167]

While legal disputes continued, Sony began developing their proposed Bond film. In May 1998 MGM filed a further injunction proposing that Sony cease all activity, claiming they did not have legal clearance to continue.[168] McClory did not file an opposition until 14 July 1998, blaming health problems for the delay.[169] Now aged seventy-four, the producer told *Variety*, 'My concern has been the statements from Pierce O'Donnell. I think people like O'Donnell should temper their rhetoric. He referred to me as Rip Van Winkle. He should remember that Rip Van Winkle woke up.'[170]

The first chink in Sony's armour appeared on 29 July when Judge Edward Rafeedie granted MGM's injunction preventing Sony from preparing a script, hiring talent or entering into any agreement to produce a Bond film based on the rights it obtained from Kevin McClory.[171] Rafeedie concluded that McClory was not a joint author with Fleming of the Bond character, but the owner of the derivative work.[172] Sony appealed and lost a second time on 20 November.[173] However, Sony did successfully push back the trial, provisionally dated 15 December 1998, to the following year.[174]

On 12 March 1999 Rafeedie dismissed claims by MGM of alleged misconduct by John Calley.[175] An eleventh-hour settlement was made on 29 March when Sony declared themselves out of the Bond business, compensating MGM with

$5 million to settle outside of court.[176] Additionally, MGM obtained the rights to CASINO ROYALE, owned by Sony's subsidiary Columbia Pictures.[177] This news left Kevin McClory out in the cold. He vowed to persue his claim that he was owed profits for creating the cinematic James Bond independently.[178] Unwilling to accept defeat, McClory took out an advertisement in *Variety* a week later proclaiming his next production: *Warhead 2001* was scheduled to be produced in Australia.[179] However, nothing came to fruition.

On 31 March 2000 Kevin McClory's forty-year James Bond adventure neared its end, when Rafeedie ruled that McClory had delayed for too long his allegation that he was the co-creator of the cinematic Bond with Fleming. Rafeedie pointed out there had been three high-profile court cases since he was awarded the rights in 1963 and never before had he contested ownership.[180] McClory appealed and his case was heard for a second time in 2001 with a three-judge panel coming to the same conclusion.[181] Judge M. Margaret McKeown wrote in her judgement, 'So like our hero James Bond, exhausted after a long adventure, we reach the end of our story. Every so often, the law shakes off its cobwebs to produce a story far too improbable even for the silver screen, too fabulous even for the world of Agent 007.'[182] McKeown also commented in her introduction, 'The case before us has it all. A hero seeking to redeem his stolen fortune. The villainous organisation that stands in his way. Mystery. International intrigue … '[183]

Jeff Kleeman noted that Eon's production schedule had been relentless since 1994:[184]

> We had got a movie into the theatres every other year, we were essentially making one movie on top of the other without any break. We were in pre-production, production or post. There was no down time. I don't know of another franchise in Hollywood that had the kind of production schedule that we had. Everyone was a little tired.[185]

Brosnan was also hinting that he was tiring of Bond, 'I don't want to go as quickly off the mark with another as we have the last three. Once this is finished I'd like to take time out, maybe three years, and concentrate on something else.'[186]

It was time to take stock. The next Bond film would not appear until 2002. Noted Brosnan, 'The studio has wanted these three Bond movies quite fast because MGM/UA have not been in the greatest of financial shape. If I believe what I read in the press all they have is us! So they want them at regular intervals and that has been difficult.'[187] Looking to the future, Jeff Kleeman, who was to head to pastures new following the studio shake-up, noted the Broccolis were feeling, 'A culmination of exhaustion and possibility.'[188]

BREAK THE CYCLE

DIE ANOTHER DAY

(2002)

Eon Productions began developing the twentieth James Bond film with MGM in the summer of 2000.[1] Chris McGurk, now firmly established as MGM's executive overseeing the Bond franchise, outlined what the studio wanted from the next Bond:

Collectively, we thought [*The World Is Not Enough*] was a little more plot driven and a little darker than some of the other Bond movies. We wanted to open it up: a little bigger on spectacle and action sequences. We were trying to position the Bond movies in the new age of Hollywood.[2]

McGurk described his view of MGM's partnership with Eon:

It was always a testy relationship. Michael Wilson used to say it was like brother and sister fighting with each other. What we tried to do was to assist them in every way possible to make the right decisions, put the right choices in front of them. Michael was very cerebral, very thoughtful, very wedded to the tradition of the Bond movies. He comes at things from more of an intellectual standpoint. Barbara is more visceral and fiery and emotional about things. Dealing with studio executives, Michael can be the voice of reason and Barbara can be the voice of outrage and despair when she needs to be. That's always a powerful one-two punch when dealing with a lot of these studio executives who, I admit, just don't get it sometimes. All those things make them an incredibly effective producing pair. They almost always get their own way.[3]

MGM were prepared to significantly increase the budget, as McGurk recalled:

Both from a casting standpoint and in terms of production values we really felt we had to step up and spend more money in order to be competitive. We realised even though we were the smallest of the major studios and didn't have as much production capital at our disposal, we had to spend in order to protect and build the franchise.'[4]

As *Bond 20* developed, Eon Productions were also preparing their first foray into the world of musical theatre – with a West End production of *Chitty Chitty Bang Bang*. Spearheaded by Dana Broccoli, Michael, Barbara and her-then husband Fred Zollo, the project reunited Eon with songwriting duo Robert and Richard Sherman, who had written the music for the original film over thirty years earlier. As production commenced on Bond, Barbara and Michael would find themselves splitting time between Pinewood Studios and the London Palladium Theatre where the play was in rehearsal.

As the fourtieth anniversary of the cinematic 007 loomed, the producers were reflective. Barbara Broccoli stated, 'We are very different and have different interests.'[5] Whilst an engineering background kept him focused on the technicalities of the screenplays, Michael G. Wilson cited his half sister's strengths, 'Barbara worked her way up through the various departments, so she knows the nuts and bolts and all about scheduling and budgeting.'[6] Looking back on their partnership Pierce Brosnan commented:

Barbara is the one that is more present, she's become the mother of it all and she's taken on the mantle of her father and her mother, to take care of people and nurture people and create a company of actors and a company of technicians. Michael is more behind the scenes. He's not so accessible. But the combination of the two is a very potent unity and it's very hard to say who really steers the ship. I could never really figure that one out; and I didn't try to.[7]

Michael Wilson's son Gregg was invited to join the producers and the writers in early story discussions. He recalled, 'At that stage I was just taking notes at the story meetings between [Purvis and Wade], Dad and Barbara. Eventually I built a bit of confidence to interject an idea here and there.'[8] Gregg was credited on *Die Another Day* as development executive, which, he said, gave him a broad overview of the entire workings of how a Bond film is put together.[9] Sharp-eyed viewers will spot he is the author of the in-flight magazine article that Bond is seen reading as he is served a martini by an air hostess played by Roger Moore's daughter, Deborah.

Broccoli and Wilson asked director Michael Apted to return and he gladly accepted:

Then the new management [at MGM] un-invited me and I had this very difficult meeting with the Broccolis where they said they had to un-invite me. [MGM] thought, 'We can do better than him. We want to put our mark on it. We can get Tony Scott or John Woo and they couldn't. They came back to me but by that time I had got another job. So that was unfortunate because I would have loved to have done another one.[10]

McGurk remembered: '[Barbara and Michael] loved Apted and we all respected him. We were looking to up the game and do something different. Probably the studio's perspective was that Apted, great director though he was, wasn't the guy to do that.'[11]

The *Rush Hour* franchise director Brett Ratner had brief discussions:

The studio [MGM] wants me, and Pierce Brosnan wants me, but the Broccolis don't want me. It's 'cause I'm American. I'd be the only American director ever to direct a Bond. Also, I'm not fifty years old, and I have a mind of my own, and I'm a strong personality.[12]

McGurk confirmed MGM did talk to Ratner.[13] *The Hollywood Reporter* also noted Stephen Hopkins and Stuart Baird (future *Casino Royale* and *Skyfall* editor) were considered.[14] While McGurk was pushing for an A-lister, Eon were hesitant, 'Barbara and Michael were not confident enough to let a director of that level come in and direct the movie. It's their franchise, it's their golden goose, and they want a lot of control.'[15]

Michael Wilson said:

I think that the studios would choose by the numbers, which director has grossed the most. But we said, 'Take somebody like Martin Campbell, who isn't necessarily the type of person they would choose, but we saw something there when we met him.' We give an opportunity for people to shine.[16]

Broccoli and Wilson made a left-field choice and hired New Zealander, Lee Tamahori, best known for his raw and hard-hitting independent picture *Once Were Warriors* (1994).

Over a decade later Tamahori told the authors:

I was doing another hard-edged, visceral movie in LA which had just fallen apart. First, I wanted to do a movie that my kids could watch because the rest are all R-18. Second, I wanted to move out of the US for a while and I thought it would be nice to make a film in Europe. Third, I felt I was getting pigeonholed. People thought of me as that director from New Zealand who makes films about wife beaters and is only good at tough movies with hard-edged dramatics.[17]

Tamahori admitted it would be interesting to make a studio film outside of these parameters, 'I thought of Bond as the great last gasp of British film-making. And it's the duty of a good ex-colonial to come and take the job of a local British director!'[18]

The studio had doubts about Tamahori, as McGurk explained:

Barbara and Michael were always looking for these quality British directors
to lend a hand on these movies. They didn't exactly have the chops, at least at
that point in their career, that said on paper that they could do these movies.
[Lee Tamahori] did a lot of personal lobbying about what he was going to
do with the movie. The Broccoli organisation with their line producers and
everybody that's been involved forever, almost ensures you're not going to
get a product that's a complete wipeout. It limits the downside. That enabled
us to go with a director who maybe didn't have the kind of experience that
says he's going to nail a Bond movie. [Lee's] a very persuasive guy, he had a
vision for the movie and that's why we went with it.[19]

Tamahori admitted:

To be fair to MGM, I wouldn't have wanted me either. Barbara and Michael
were very much in my camp because they just liked my ideas and to their
credit, hung in there. It took months and months to convince MGM. I was
ready to leave, I thought, 'I can't handle this' and they said 'Hang on,' and I
just wore them down.[20]

Wilson recalled it was vital they had support from Pierce Brosnan in their selection, 'Any problems Pierce had in the past has always been down to the director.
He was quizzical of our choice at first.'[21] Early reports suggested the relationship between Brosnan and Tamahori had been frosty. Brosnan explained, 'It
was trusting this guy. I had done three, he's coming in, and it was really on my
behalf, wondering if he was paying enough attention to what I was doing.'[22]
Brosnan admitted Tamahori took a bit of getting used to 'having worked with
someone like Martin Campbell who is so precise. One has to have patience
because he doesn't come with all the shots lined up and polished.'[23] One night
they thrashed out their differences.[24] Tamahori said, '"I can't have you freaking out because you think I'm shooting a different picture to you. You have
to find a way to trust that I'm looking after your best interests," which he did
and we settled into it.'[25] Brosnan's respect for his director was cemented when
shooting in Spain:

We were standing around waiting for him to work out where he was going to
put the camera. I thought we were wasting too much time so I told him that

and he said, 'Pierce, you've got to understand that camera placement often boils down to half an inch genius or half an inch stupidity.' That shut me up and I went to have another coffee.[26]

Over a decade later, Brosnan descibed Tamahori as 'a wildcard, a wildcard indeed. He was tough, he had an edge to him which was quite brittle and crazy, but we got on all right.'[27]

Scribes Neal Purvis and Robert Wade, invited back to pen their second Bond script, began thinking about ideas in July 2000.[28] Wade recalled, 'We definitely wanted to do an espionage, Cold War movie.'[29] Tamahori, who would join the production a year later, agreed:

> I always loved the hard-edged espionage thriller of the sixties – *The Ipcress File* (1965), *The Spy Who Came in From the Cold* (1965). We wanted all those elements of sixties' Cold War thrillers rather than what was floundering around in the twenty-first century when espionage had become a bit passé.[30]

Barbara encouraged story discussions to 'start off with the topical aspect. What is the world worried about, now or in the next couple of years? And what is James Bond's position in that arena?'[31] Inspiration was drawn from US president, Bill Clinton, who described the 38TH Parallel, the strip of land dividing North and South Korea, better known as the Demilitarized Zone (DMZ) as the 'the scariest place on earth.'[32] Remembered Wade, 'We were all feeling the same about North Korea. It was a hot point in the world, the kind of country you don't go into. It was a breeding ground for terrorists. Michael [Wilson] knew more about it than we did.'[33] The North Korean setting fitted perfectly with the atmosphere they wanted to create, as Wade observed, 'It's the last Iron Curtain.'[34] Purvis liked the idea of a thriller in which Bond, captured at the beginning of the story, spends the rest of the film trying to get home, but he admitted, 'that isn't a Bond movie.'[35]

Purvis and Wade set out to create a 007 epic.[36] 'We wanted to do a *You Only Live Twice* but keeping it realistic and not comic book-y.'[37] They read about a satellite the Russians had put in space, a giant reflective mirror, which had been an attempt to provide Siberia with cheap street lighting.[38] Purvis explained in the wrong hands it would be a fantastic weapon, 'focussing the mirror so that it burns is the Bond element.'[39]

Intrigued by the ice hotel built in Sweden each year, Barbara and Michael sent Peter Lamont to investigate. Recalled Broccoli, 'When he came back, he had so much information about it – photographs, notes and observations. So when we met with the writers, Peter came in and told us all a lot of stuff, and it went into the script.'[40] As the story developed Purvis and Wade read about an indoor beach resort in Japan, complete with wave machine and sliding roof, which they made the villain's lair and the setting for the climax of the screenplay.[41] Peter Lamont visited the Seagaia Ocean Dome in Miyazaki but as Purvis recalled, on inspection 'it was bit tacky and run down'[42] and would have to be built in the studio. Lamont was even set to brave a trip to Korea, 'to go to the frontier, the 38TH Parallel, to see what it was like. On the South there is a viewing platform of the Parallel,'[43] but the trip was cancelled.

The writers also took inspiration from Fleming. Sir Gustav Graves became a modern-day version of Sir Hugo Drax. In Bond's first meeting with M on a British naval vessel, the glass partition between them was inspired by a similar device which slides down to protect the MI6 chief from a brainwashed 007 in THE MAN WITH THE GOLDEN GUN.[44]

When Lee Tamahori joined the picture, the 'bare bones of it stayed the same,'[45] but the screenplay received an overhaul. 'I thought the script had fantastic moments, but also some inherent weaknesses. It got lost in some very labyrinth complexities, where I thought the audience would just head for popcorn.'[46] Purvis felt that Tamahori had a different stylistic vision, 'There is a more realistic version of [Die Another Day] that you could make that would be the same story. I don't think he'd disagree, Lee wanted to do a more comic book type movie.'[47] Reflected McGurk:

> Lee was more focussed on the spectacle of the movie. We were caught up in this idea that Bond had to be competitive with these other big event movies in terms of action and CGI. We were probably all guilty of that. If people criticise the movie that it became too cartoony, it wasn't meant to be.[48]

During production the director admitted, 'We are jumping into stuff that's quasi sci-fi. We've looked at some of our dailies and went, "Wow this is straight out of science fiction."'[49] Wade observed, 'What Barbara and Michael do, once they bring a director on board, they support his vision. And that's the job of the writer as well.'[50] Tamahori recalled he was given the 'freedom to come up with outrageous and outlandish ideas, some of them were embraced, some of them were rejected.'[51] Reflected Wade, wryly, 'It was clear he had suddenly got the biggest toy box in the world.'[52] Wilson justified the sci-fi elements:

[Bond's] world is a blend of the 'science fact authentic', the slightly futuristic, the theoretically possible and the discreetly fanciful. As long as James Bond remains the iconic focus and has had a character journey audiences can respond to, I do feel we can push the action envelope in new and exciting ways.[53]

However supportive the writers were, Purvis and Wade felt the invisible Aston Martin Vanquish was a Q gadget too far. Tamahori said defensively, 'I know everyone laughs at the invisible car but it's based on an idea that is still being developed and works today. We just pushed it to the limit and it became a slightly more ludicrous idea.'[54] The stealth car idea had been mooted for *The World Is Not Enough*. Having been inspired by technology the military were developing for tanks, Wade stated, 'We didn't want it to be actually invisible, we just wanted it to be hard to see, camouflaged in a desert background or an icy background.'[55] Purvis was chagrined, 'It was a bit of a surprise to us that it had become invisible.'[56]

Four weeks into production Tamahori abandoned the finale in the Japanese indoor beach, instead he suggested an airborne finale over the Korean DMZ. He admitted that a major script change at this stage was 'somewhat dangerous but [the Bond films] are so well-oiled that they can embrace a gigantic shift like that in mid-stream.'[57] Tamahori felt another ground-based lair blowing up was not original enough, 'Why don't we go airborne, on the world's largest aircraft?'[58]

Hong Kong features fleetingly at the beginning of the movie, but originally the city was to play a bigger role in the story, with a cameo from *Tomorrow Never Dies*' Michelle Yeoh returning as Wai Lin.[59] Tamahori met with the actress but due to 'contractual problems, things didn't work out.'[60] Bond was to get attacked by a cadre of kung fu fighters on two rising glass elevators that were going up and down a thirty-storey building. Wade recalled it was, 'Gravity defying, *Matrix*-style stuff, done for real because in a confined space, you can actually run around the walls.'[61] Eventually it was decided the sequence was not advancing the story and was dropped.[62]

On 11 September 2001 the creative team was in a script meeting at 138 Piccadilly when news reached them of the terrorist attacks taking place in America.[63] Tamahori was 'affected quite profoundly. Like everyone who was making films at that period we had an uneasy feeling about what we were watching. It looked like something we might have done.'[64] Ironically, in the draft they were discussing, New York was involved in an explosive finale.[65] Wade was sombre, 'The mirror in space was going to attack Manhattan, if you could believe that. We weren't going to do that anymore.'[66] Tamahori recalled their solution was to move the action away from a city environment, 'we pulled the destruction out into the countryside, minefields and the Demilitarized Zone.'[67]

Tamahori wanted to celebrate Bond's ruby anniversary with self-referential nods to the franchise peppered throughout the film. Most striking was Halle Berry emerging from the sea in a bikini complete with belt and hunting knife *à la* Ursula Andress. Another was Q's workshop filled with many of Bond's previous gadgets. Tamahori justified these reminiscences, 'They're only there for fans of the Bond genre.'[68]

The pre-title sequence sees Bond intercepting a weapons deal with Colonel Moon and Zao in the DMZ on the 38TH Parallel separating North and South Korea. Arms are being funded by a trade in African conflict diamonds and the deal is being made possible by hovercraft which float over the minefield in the DMZ. Bond is betrayed and tries to escape but not before exploding the booby-trapped cache of diamonds into Zao's face and battling Colonel Moon. Moon seemingly dies after a vicious hovercraft chase and battle. Bond is captured and tortured at the hands of the North Koreans. After eighteen months in captivity, Western intelligence assets are being betrayed to North Korea. Bond is released by prisoner exchange to find he has been traded for Zao. When M debriefs 007 on a British frigate in Hong Kong harbour, it is revealed that Damian Falco, head of the US National Security Agency (NSA) believes Bond has cracked under torture. 007's licence to kill is rescinded and he is to be quarantined in the Falklands. Breaking out of the frigate, 007 goes on the run. He believes Zao has the answers as to who is framing him for betrayals he is innocent of. Following a tip-off from Chinese Intelligence, Bond travels to Cuba where he tracks down Zao to a gene therapy clinic. Here he meets Giacinta Johnson – Jinx to her friends – on an independent investigation of her own. Bond discovers Zao may be funded by Gustav Graves as conflict diamonds used in the North Korean arms deal seem chemically identical to those emanating from Grave's rich new diamond strike at his Icelandic mine.

Returning to London, Bond meets Gustav Graves and his assistant, Miranda Frost. Graves is to receive a knighthood for using his own immense diamond wealth to fund the Icarus Project. He invites Bond to the unveiling of Icarus in Iceland. Bond is then requested to report back to the Secret Service, for M is suspicious of Graves. Frost is a deep cover agent for MI6, who has infiltrated the Graves organisation. With the source of Grave's money clouded in intrigue, questions over the doubtful funding could cause a shadow just as Icarus is being unveiled. M wants Miranda Frost to shadow Bond while in Iceland.

Bond travels to the frozen tundra in his Q Branch Aston Martin, issued by the new quartermaster. At a specially constructed ice palace, Graves has gathered the world's press to announce his Icarus Project. Jinx is there at the behest of the NSA. Icarus is revealed to be a space-based solar sail capable of redirecting the sun's waves to fall benignly on the parts of the planet most in need of them. However, Bond discovers the evil lurking in plain sight. Icarus can also focus the sun's rays to become a solar weapon. Graves is exposed as Colonel Moon – the product of gene therapy makeover. He has stored conflict diamonds from arms deals to fund the space device. Now Graves will use Icarus to destroy the minefield on the DMZ, which divides the Korean peninsular. Hardline forces in the North, loyal to Graves/Moon will then invade the South. Icarus will give them an unbeatable military advantage, capable of destroying any form of retaliation. Once Korea is united, Graves will continue to use his military advantage against other nations in the area for global domination. Another double cross is then revealed. Miranda Frost is actually working for Graves/Moon and it was she who was haemorrhaging names to the North Koreans, framing Bond. Bond kills Zao in an Aston Martin versus Jaguar chase on a frozen lake and through the ice palace. Now tasked to neutralise Graves, Jinx and 007 team up. After a daring assault on an Antanov cargo plane in North Korean airspace, Bond and Jinx defeat Graves and Frost. Escaping the doomed aircraft, Bond and Jinx end up in bed in a Korean temple.

When the cast was unveiled at the start of principal photography during a press conference in January 2002, the film had not officially been titled. Known only as 'Bond XX', Brosnan joked that they were open to suggestions. Several ideas had been suggested including *Parallel 38*[69] and according to Purvis, 'We also came up with *Double Cross*. Get it? XX? *Bond 20*?'[70] *Double Cross* was a title steeped in secret intelligence as it had been the code name for a high-profile intelligence operation in World War II.[71] David Arnold proffered *Darker Than the Sun*.[72] 'There is the odd dichotomy [with Bond titles], *You Only Live Twice* when it should be once. And I thought it would be a good lyric.'[73]

Bond 20 finally became *Die Another Day*. Asked where it came from Tamahori joked, 'God knows probably off a scrabble board.'[74] In fact, it had been mentioned in passing during a story meeting. Robert Wade said, 'Bond lives to die another day.' 'Barbara looked up and said, "That could be the title!"'[75] Ultimately, the title was a decision made between the producers and MGM.[76] It derived from a poem by A.E. Housman, "But since the man that runs away/Lives to die another day.' Michael Wilson offered that it was 'a cynical twist on that old expression that is very Fleming.'[77] Tamahori was not convinced, 'Personally I felt it sounded like many others. It doesn't really stand out like *Goldfinger*.'[78]

Portraying the gentleman spy for the fourth time, Pierce Brosnan declared, 'Bond is mine now and a sure maturity has come with that in body, mind and soul.'[79] However, it was evident that Brosnan was becoming frustrated by the direction the films were taking, 'In the beginning they were made for adults. Now they're made for kids. It would be great to see some stronger killing.'[80] Wade recalled throughout the making of *Die Another Day* that Brosnan would be a regular visitor to the writers' room at Pinewood, 'He wanted it to be as steeped in Fleming as it could be.'[81] Brosnan admitted later, 'I was never really at home with the one-liners and the humour. I always found them to be rather clunky.'[82] It was Brosnan's idea for Bond to emerge bedraggled with long hair and a beard following 007's imprisonment in North Korea.[83]

By now Brosnan had the confidence to suggest some creative changes. He criticised Eon for 'not wanting to push the envelope. John McTiernan would love to do one. John Woo would love to have done one. Ang Lee would have loved to have done one. Barbara and Michael … Ah, it's an old story.'[84] Brosnan had wanted Martin Scorsese and had even discussed the possibility with him when they met on a flight.[85] Hollywood director Tony Scott revealed he had brief discussions about *Bond 20*, 'but there was a concern it would shift too far away from the marketplace.'[86] Scott may have been alluding to the fact he had suggested Quentin Tarantino should write the screenplay. Michael Wilson denied they spoke with Scott, 'It might have been someone at the studio.'[87]

Halle Berry became the most high-profile actress to be cast in a Bond movie. It was Tamahori who suggested the American actress play the sassy NSA agent Giacinta 'Jinx' Johnson.[88] The character was named after a girl Purvis and Wade knew from the early eighties clubbing scene in London.[89] Wade described the concept behind Jinx, 'If Bond walked into your world he would have a danger-ous presence. She's like Bond and I know that's been said before about other characters but in her case she really is. We're seeing this woman from Bond's point of view. She uses her sexuality to get what she wants.'[90] Tamahori felt the film called for 'the classic Latin spitfire,'[91] and he screentested dozens of actresses before casting the net a little wider. Colin Salmon, who played Bond in these tests, revealed Saffron Burrows, Salma Hayek and Sophie Ellis Bextor, had tried for various roles in the film. The seemingly endless stream of information appearing in the press led casting director Debbie McWilliams to joke that someone must have been going through her rubbish. Tamahori opined, 'They had done Asian with Michelle Yeoh. It was time to head off into some other ethnicity. Almost like a lottery, I think.'[92] The director had seen Halle Berry in *Swordfish* (2001) and realised 'that she'd crack this action genre wide open.'[93] When cast, Berry was causing a stir with her performance in Marc Forster's highly acclaimed *Monster's Ball* (2001). Tamahori was inspired, 'MGM did love the idea of an American actress being in it. To my mind's eye she was my Modesty Blaise.'[94]

Michael Wilson reflected in 2006 that he felt by *Die Another Day* they were naturally attracting a higher calibre of actress, 'Certainly twenty years ago it was difficult to attract leading ladies. It was difficult to get top-notch people. We've steadily been able to develop those roles and raise the level of casting, so I think it was comfortable for Halle to come on board.'[95] The world of Bond certainly did appeal to Berry, 'After doing a movie like *Monster's Ball*, which was very serious and emotionally raw. I thought it would be really fun to do a cool character like Jinx, who's essentially the female equivalent of Bond.'[96] Halle Berry described working on a Bond film had a '"mom 'n' pop" feel to it. Barbara Broccoli is a formidable businesswoman, but she'll also show up at your house when you're sick and play nurse to you. That would never happen in Hollywood.'[97]

During production, Berry won the Best Actress Oscar for her role in *Monster's Ball*. Interestingly, Judi Dench was nominated in the same category for her portrayal of Iris Murdoch. Following the Academy Awards ceremony, Berry immediately returned to Pinewood to resume work on Bond. Pierce warmed to Halle, 'I remember this wonderful, beautiful woman just celebrating her success of the Oscar. We got on extremely well. She was brilliant in the role I thought.'[98] Neal Purvis remembered they were conscious that they were now penning dialogue for the world's hottest actress and the first scenes she filmed upon her return involved Jinx simply standing around a control centre with nothing to say, 'We gave her a couple of lines because you just thought she's got to say something!'[99] Tamahori explained the power of Berry's win on the film, 'Barbara and Michael and MGM realised the marketing power of actually having not just Pierce on the poster but Halle as well.'[100]

While Wade had enjoyed the film version of *Moonraker*, 'it hadn't tracked the book and there was more to the character of Drax, the idea he is a cheat but a kind of hero in the British world.'[101] Moon/Grave's backstory hewed to that of Fleming's for Drax. The writers modelled Moon 'on Uday Hussein, son of Saddam'[102] and there were parallels with Richard Branson. An unknown actor was sought to make the gene therapy transition as credible as possible'[103] and Wilson found Britain to have the advantage of a great pool of classically trained, undiscovered actors working on the London stage.[104] It was in a West End play, *The Royal Family*, appearing opposite Judi Dench, that the producers noticed

Toby Stephens, son of Dame Maggie Smith. Colin Salmon once again stood in as Bond for screentesting duties opposite Stephens. Salmon recounted to Robert Wade that Stephens played various degrees of menace, describing one read as 'really fucking scary but Lee preferred the bigger snarly [approach].'[105] Stephens said, 'I was disappointed that I never got to say, "Goodbye, Mr. Bond." Most Bond villains get to say that. I actually said it in my screentest. I felt that even if I didn't get the part, at least I got to say that line.'[106]

Originally the script was to feature Fleming's Gala Brand, an undercover agent embedded in Drax's organisation in MOONRAKER. Brand was a character Purvis and Wade had attempted to include in a number of their Bond screenplays.[107] She was later changed to Miranda Frost, when her character became treacherous. Frost was played by 23-year-old newcomer, Rosamund Pike. Remembered Tamahori, 'She had just come straight off the boards at Oxford. Not only had she never been on a film set, she was thrust onto a Bond set, so she really was thrown in the deep end.'[108] Like every Bond actress before her, Pike declared her Bond girl of the moment:

> Barbara has definitely had an influence on the way women appear in the films. Bond is contemporary, but it still smells of something old school. It has a very specific breed of glamour, and while the rest of the world is all about blatant sex, this is fun and sophisticated.[109]

Die Another Day embraced the bizzare with a henchman disfigured by diamonds and partly racially modified by gene therapy. Rick Yune, known for his role in the *Fast and Furious* franchise, was cast as Zao, 'My father loved Bond movies and he passed that on to me. When I was a kid we had a James Bond club at my school and we used to do stunts, like break into the school after hours and steal 'valuable information' – a teacher's book or something.'[110]

Once again an assortment of interesting faces essayed minor villainy in the film. Simon Andreu was slimy gene therapist Dr Alvarez, and Mark Dymond played his loud South African patient, Van Bierk. Sarilya was the beautiful but not-quite-deadly Scorpion Girl, Micheal Gorevoy had fun as Grave's technician, Vlad whilst the henchman Mr. Kil was played by Maori actor, Lawrence Makoare. Bond's allies were played by similarly notable choices including Kenneth Tsang as General Moon, Emilio Echevarria as Cuban sleeper agent, Raoul, *Blake's 7* star Paul Darrow as a battleship doctor and Rachel Grant as the fragrant Peaceful Fountains of Desire, while equestrian showjumper Oliver Skeete was the dreadlocked Blades concierge.

Lee Tamahori understood Eon's Bond machine and did not request key personnel of his own,[111] 'I was in Britain and I thought I probably best fall on those who do the job best and right. [Barbara and Michael] said you don't have to hire these people but they are very useful and could be very resourceful to you too.'[112] Peter Lamont, who had undertaken preliminary recces, particularly impressed Tamahori, by his sheer breath of knowledge and experience. Vic Armstrong once again took care of key second unit action, while Bond newcomer David Tattersall served as cinematographer, who explained:

> When you come aboard a Bond film, the initial urge is to push the envelope. There's a cinematographic trend at the moment for desaturating colour and adding grain, kind of dirtying up the image, but those sorts of treatments wouldn't have been appropriate for Bond. We're not talking *cinéma vérité* here – it's full-on gloss, high-key and colourful.[113]

On 11 January 2002 Pierce Brosnan strode onto E Stage at Pinewood Studios, where a gleaming Aston Martin Vanquish and the world's press awaited him. The opening shot of the movie, Bond surfing his way into North Korea had been shot earlier on Christmas Day 2001, off the coast of Maui in Hawaii and was filmed with ace surfing champion Laird Hamilton doubling Bond. Three black-clad surfers waited to catch Jaws, one of the biggest waves in the world, working with Tamahori's storyboard wish list.

Principal photography officially began with the M, Q and Moneypenny scenes. Tamahori enjoyed it, 'When other people have set them up as characters it's great to drop in and play with them.'[114]

Samantha Bond returned for what would be her final appearance as Miss Moneypenny. In a show-stealer she became the first and only Miss Moneypenny to share a kiss with Bond (albeit in virtual reality). Tamahori recalled this had been a late change to the screenplay, 'We knew when we cut it that it worked!'[115] The actress was modest, 'Even if you rolled all four films into one, it's still the smallest part I've ever played. It's the character that's iconic rather than anything I did with it.'[116] Talking several years later Bond said, 'There is a natural life to these things. I didn't want to turn into Auntie Moneypenny. I have huge respect for Lois Maxwell but there's a moment in the films when she turns into that. And besides, I got my kiss!'[117]

In her fourth outing as M, Dench had by now constructed an interesting backstory for her, 'I see her married to this man with grown-up children, two girls. The man is either a writer or a professor or a literary agent – a strong, rather quiet, dusty kind of man who doesn't like going out.'[118]

Following the death of Desmond Llewelyn, *Die Another Day* saw John Cleese take on an iconic role. After Llewelyn's thirty-six-year tenure, Wade recalled they were careful how they introduced a new Q, 'Bond doesn't want to call him Q, he calls him Quartermaster. By the end of the scene, when he's realised he can trust him, that he's a worthy successor, he calls him Q.'[119] Cleese said the hope was he would share the screen with Llewelyn for another two or three films, 'Sadly, that was not to be.'[120] Cleese found he and Llewelyn shared similar feelings on technology:

> I also have terrible trouble learning the lines, dealing with high-tech gadgetry. I've always thought anybody seriously interested in technology has something wrong with them, something missing in the emotional part of them. The funny thing about learning gobbledygook is that some bits come very easily and others not so. I couldn't get 'target seeking shotguns' out clearly – maybe it's a tongue twister – but 'tiny cameras on all sides project the image onto a light-emitting polymer film' – that was quite simple.[121]

Q's workshop could now be found in an abandoned London tube station. The writers had read about Down Street station near Eon's offices in Piccadilly, and Wade explained, 'They had closed that station down in the twenties and it was here where Churchill would have secret meetings. Again, we were trying to go old-world espionage.'[122] In one of Tamahori's fortieth anniversary nods to the series, it is in Q's workshop that Bond rediscovers the jet pack from *Thunderball*, the Acrostar jet from *Octopussy* and the attaché case from *From Russia With Love*, among many other gadgets. Lamont recalled that they delved into Eon's vast archive to see what props were available and several items, including the jet pack, had to be remade.[123]

Throughout the film M is challenged by her CIA counterpart, Damian Falco, played by Michael Madsen. Falco's name was borrowed from Tony Curtis's character, Sidney Falco, in one of Purvis and Wade's favourite films *Sweet Smell of Success* (1957).

The pre-title hovercraft chase was filmed in Aldershot by Vic Armstrong:

> We went down to a hovercraft museum in Hampshire and picked out the models we wanted and saw them tested. We had about eighteen of them. Hovercrafts are difficult things to steer and it was hard to get them to hit their

mark and crash into things on cue. They are a bit like balloons, you bat them in a room and they go all over the place.[124]

The sequence was shot on the tank-testing course in 3ft of mud[125] and completed at Pinewood Studios where Brosnan sustained a knee injury, 'It was a cold February morning I had to do a 200-yard dash with 500 extras, six cameras, explosions and the knee just went.'[126] Brosnan flew to the US for a small operation before filming could continue. 'We have never on a Bond stopped shooting ever. We stopped shooting for seven days,'[127] remembered executive producer Anthony Waye. Brosnan's eagerness to return to work was described by Wilson as 'not too dissimilar to a super-athlete getting hurt.'[128]

A product placement deal with Ford, owners of the Aston Martin marque meant Bond abandoned BMW. Piece Brosnan was thrilled, 'I had to wait three movies before I drove the Aston Martin!'[129] The car chase emerged after location visits to Iceland. Vaunting the visuals of Vatnajokull, a lagoon which, when frozen, traps the icebergs in the inlet, Tamahori said, 'My God has anybody ever raced cars on here? The only thing anybody had ever done was place a car on there for a commercial. Why don't we race these cars and have a chase on the ice?'[130]

The production searched the world for a location suitable for the sequence. According to Armstrong, 'Everywhere had frozen lakes but you got to them and they were covered in 3ft of snow.'[131] The production was to shoot in Hofn, Iceland but the weather and the thickness of the ice could not be guaranteed as Armstrong explained, 'Ten inches was the minimum we were allowed to work on. We bit the bullet and went up there. The sun came out as I arrived, it was all frozen solid with this beautiful, blue ice. It was stunning.'[132]

Meanwhile the special effects department spent months heavily modifying four Aston Martin Vanquish and Jaguar XJR vehicles with four wheel drive so they could operate on the ice and at the sub-zero temperatures.[133] Armstrong wanted them to perform like rally cars, 'We got on the ice and they were just beautiful they could do power slides, long drifts. One of the Astons overcooked it on a corner and hit an iceberg and we realised how solid the ice was, the car just ricocheted off like a pinball machine.'[134] Armstrong described the sensation as the cars whizzed past camera, 'It was like standing on a trampoline bed, the whole lake surface bounced up and down. It was nerve-wracking to think you were standing over a 1,000ft [of] ice cold water.'[135] Back at Pinewood Purvis remembered viewing the rushes, 'What you were seeing was like a David Lean movie – just long shots of cars hurtling across a lake – beautiful.'[136]

The film's central set was Gustav Graves' ice palace. Lamont admitted across the nine Bond films he designed, the palace was the set that pushed his imagination the furthest into the realms of fantasy.[137] Tamahori felt Lamont's masterpiece was not being used to maximum affect. The set had already begun construction on the 007 Stage when Tamahori proposed they reconfigure it to house the climax of the car chase, 'In classic Peter Lamont style he said, "Well, I'd have to do some calculations overnight." The cost increase was massive, millions of pounds maybe £1.5 to £2 million beyond what was already budgeted to build the existing ice palace. But [Barbara and Michael] immediately jumped on board and thought it was a great idea and so did MGM.'[138]

Lamont also built the fictitious club, Blades, inspired by Ian Fleming's MOON-RAKER, to stage a brutal fencing duel between Bond and Graves. The entrance to London's Reform Club was used, according to the production designer, to take advantage of 'its spectacular, great atrium, with the columns and the staircase.'[139] Brosnan, Stephens and Pike rehearsed épée fencing for two months with sword master Bob Anderson.[140] Stephens had experience of fighting on stage but for film found it more complicated. 'For stage fighting, you make very flat, buoyant moves because people are sitting way back in the theatre. For films, you've got to make very small moves, and you're actually aiming to hit someone.'[141]

At the beginning of April 2002, the main unit headed for Spain, doubling for Cuba. Tamahori, Lamont and key personnel had undertaken a research trip to Havana but were prohibited under US law from shooting there.[142] Sequences set in Cuba and the fictional Isla Los Organos were filmed at La Caleta, Spain. In Cadiz, Halle Berry as Jinx homaged Ursula Andress as Honey Ryder. Brosnan beamed, 'Oh boy, I remember her coming out of the water in Cadiz and half of Spain was on the shoreline observing this beautiful lady in her fluorescent orange bikini.'[143]

Bond observes Jinx saunter up to him as he cooly draws on a Havana cigar and orders a cocktail. Wade remembered, 'Pierce said, "Can't I say mojito? Canchanchara sounds like dog food."'[144] Purvis mused, 'We said that it was very Fleming-like, it's obscure, it's exotic.'[145] Mojito won out, but the props department did not have a recipe for the cocktail. Coincidently, Tamahori had been wearing a T-shirt with a mojito recipe on the day before. It was quickly retrieved from the laundry and the drink was swiftly mixed on set.[146]

Die Another Day has become infamous for one action sequence, Bond kite surfing a tidal wave, completed entirely using CGI. Tamahori admitted it was his idea.[147] The producers were nervous about adopting a technique alien to them as Wilson noted, 'Bond films like to do things for real and not go CGI.'[148]

Tamahori said, '[Barbara and Michael] had to question whether we were betraying a fundamental part of the Bond myth. But my argument is that CGI is just another tool and you'll have to embrace it sooner or later or you'll be overtaken by other action movies.'[149] Brosnan had his doubts, 'There's a certain frustration where you just feel rather foolish, hanging on wires or attempting to do some kind of stunt which just seems absolutely ludicrous, and, of course, consequently turns out to be rather silly.'[150] MGM's Chris McGurk conceded that the studio was less than impressed:

> We were all convinced by Lee and by the effects house that they could do it in a way that it wasn't going to look stupid. When I went to the first screening, I remember telling Barbara Broccoli that I thought it looked like Gidget goes to Malibu on a surfboard. Like right out of the fifties, that's how horrible it looked. We were stunned because we'd spent a ton of money on that sequence and we had heard everybody telling us, 'Don't worry.' We repaired it to a huge extent after that, but everybody was let down by what was delivered.[151]

It was not budget constraints that let the sequence down according to Tamahori:

> In 2001/02 we didn't have what we have now in terms of CGI and the elements were never as good as we wanted them to be. It would have required research and development for several years to get it to work. I'm aware that it is less than spectacular. I will take responsibility for that.[152]

'Die Another Day', a techo dance track, performed by Madonna, which she co-wrote with French-based Mirwais Amadzaï, syncopated well with the spiky title sequence. Kleinman commented, 'It's quite staccato, not your kind of usual Bond sweeping, glorious, velvety epic but you work with what you have. You try and make the two things be sympatico. The two things have to meld.'[153] Madonna adapted a pre-existing track she had in the works and re-engineered it for the film.[154] She thought carefully before accepting the assignment, 'Everybody wants to do the theme song of a James Bond movie, and I never liked to do what everybody else likes to do. It's just some perverse thing in me. But then I thought about it and I said, "You know what? James Bond needs to get techno."'[155]

In a series first, the title song artist played a cameo role in the movie opposite Bond. Schedules were reworked and on the last day of principal photography

Madonna filmed her one scene as Miranda Frost's fencing instructor, Verity. The sometime actress and producer insisted her own writer pen the dialogue for the scene. Wade recalled, 'I didn't want to be there because it was all rather embarrassing, she had a guy who'd done album notes or something.'[156] Rosamund Pike recalled, 'It was strange and exhilarating. She made jokes and didn't hang around. I was like, "If I reach out now, I can touch Madonna."'[157]

Composer David Arnold had begun by writing his own theme song, 'I Will Return':

Always, at the end of every Bond movie [the credits announce] James Bond will return. So I thought it might be interesting to write a song about James Bond warning people that whatever they are thinking of doing they better be careful because he is going to be back. I did a verse and a bridge, but I was cautious about finishing it because I knew Madonna was in talks and I knew she would be writing her own thing. The main melody of it is in the 'Peaceful Fountains of Desire' cue.[158]

Arnold subsequently reused some of the lyrics for a song he wrote for Shirley Bassey, 'No Good About Goodbye'.[159]

Arnold's inspiration for *Die Another Day* was drawn from *Moonraker*, 'Conceptually there were some hugely over-the-top moments in it. *Die Another Day* was fantasy.'[160] Arnold was also led by Christian Wagner's editing style, 'Visually it was quite aggressive as a film, he had a very contemporary style.' He described the score as a hybrid of 'electronic, orchestral synthetic and cut-up audio samples.'[161]

In the final scene of the film, a sweeping aerial shot of the Korean coast, settles on a hut where we find Bond and Jinx in an embrace. Tamahori wanted to pay homage to John Barry, 'If you listen to it, it is a thinly disguised John Barry piece from *You Only Live Twice*. I actually wanted to use the [actual] score but everyone was a bit nervous about it, they just felt it was not the right thing to do, to use someone else's music.'[162] Arnold demurred, 'I would have disallowed it simply because when you are trying to create an identity for a film why would you evoke another? It disengages you from the film.'[163] Tamahori relented, 'David said, "Just let me tinker with it and I will John Barry-esque it and make it sound the same."'[164]

In a Bond first, Daniel Kleinman's opening titles featured 007's torture at the hands of the North Koreans. Tamahori explained, 'I wanted to pursue the story through the titles, rather than stop dead and just have a flashy sequence.'[165]

When Kleinman read the script it was unusual to have a theme already mapped out. 'The sequence had to say that he'd been in prison for a long time. You had to suggest he'd been brutally tortured.'[166] Violent images of Bond being hooded, water boarded and beaten were stylised for the censors.[167] Kleinman expanded, 'I showed some of those images through ice or layered with other things to take the edge off a little – slightly more psychological and a little less literal.'[168]

On 18 November 2002, The Royal Albert Hall was transformed into an ice palace for the royal world premiere. The annual Royal Film Performance lured stars from past and present to the biggest Bond premiere ever to mark the series' fortieth anniversary. Among the previous cast members and Bond alumni attending were Shirley Eaton, Richard Kiel, Lois Chiles, Maud Adams, Maryam d'Abo, Fiona Fullerton and Shirley Bassey. As well as the cast of *Die Another Day*, on hand to meet Her Majesty, Queen Elizabeth II were previous Bonds George Lazenby, Sir Roger Moore and Timothy Dalton. Pierce Brosnan remembered his last Bond premiere fondly:

> It was spectacular. It was truly an absolutely and outrageously brilliant night. I remember standing on the side of the stage with all the guys and joking and laughing. I mean, Roger was as gracious as ever. Tim was fantastic. And George, well … I think the least said about George the better.[169]

The critical reception to *Die Another Day* was mixed with many long-time fans expressing disappointment at the outlandish turns the film took after the otherwise well-received first reel. Yet again, the film set a Bond opening weekend record, grossing $47,072,040 in North America. *Die Another Day* went on to achieve a global take of $431,971,116 – the highest grossing Bond film to date by a significant margin.

The question every journalist asked was: is Pierce Brosnan returning for a fifth film? The actor said, 'I'm honouring my contract by doing this fourth film.'[170] He told one reporter, 'The producers have told me that the role is mine as long as I like,'[171] and elaborated further in another interview that 'I would like to do another one, sure. Connery did six. Six would be a number and then never come back.'[172] Brosnan compared the production process of a new James Bond film:

> I think they used to be much more fun. Someone I was working with recently said, 'My God, I used to work on Roger Moore's films – it was a good old laugh!' He said, 'This is fearsome work.' And that's because of the

big bucks and the competition that's out there. They're Leviathans now, these movies. They're monsters.[173]

Tamahori reflected that Martin Campbell had given the series the biggest 'jolt' since the sixties. 'I think Roger Spottiswoode, Michael Apted and, to some degree, myself have been marking time with Martin's style. None of us have been able to make the quantum leap he did. When the next person comes along someone will have the opportunity to push it to the next level.'[174] Tamahori had attended a screening of *The Bourne Identity* (2002) with Barbara and Michael in the summer of 2002.[175] 'I said, "Look, this game's changing fast. You're going to have to rethink this." The writing was on the wall for the end of the franchise as it was then.'[176] In fact when interviewed during the post-production of *Die Another Day* Tamahori was prescient:

> I think it's going to evolve when Pierce gives up and someone else comes along. I don't think it should just be an update of the character, I think it should be a radical reinvention of what the Bond character is and what MI6 is. If he's going to be an agent with a '00' licence to kill people, what does that actually mean? And how can you adapt that to the modern world? All they've ever done is update it. Now you've got to really reinvigorate it.[177]

Tamahori even told one journalist during the publicity for *Die Another Day*, 'I don't care if I never see him in a tux again.'[178]

THROUGH HARDER MEN

CASINO ROYALE

(2006)

Sony Pictures Entertainment

thanks the British Academy of Film and Television Arts
and proudly congratulates our nominees for

CASINO
ROYALE

9 BAFTA AWARD NOMINATIONS

THE ALEXANDER KORDA AWARD FOR THE
OUTSTANDING BRITISH FILM OF THE YEAR
MICHAEL G WILSON, BARBARA BROCCOLI, MARTIN CAMPBELL,
NEAL PURVIS & ROBERT WADE AND PAUL HAGGIS

ADAPTED SCREENPLAY
NEAL PURVIS & ROBERT WADE AND PAUL HAGGIS

ACTOR IN A LEADING ROLE
DANIEL CRAIG

THE ANTHONY ASQUITH AWARD
FOR ACHIEVEMENT IN FILM MUSIC
DAVID ARNOLD

CINEMATOGRAPHY
PHIL MEHEUX BSC

EDITING
STUART BAIRD ACE

PRODUCTION DESIGN
PETER LAMONT, LEE SANDALES, SIMON WAKEFIELD

SOUND
CHRIS MUNRO, EDDY JOSEPH, MIKE PRESTWOOD SMITH,
MARTIN CANTWELL, MARK TAYLOR

ACHIEVEMENT IN SPECIAL VISUAL EFFECTS
STEVE BEGG, CHRIS CORBOULD,
JOHN PAUL DOCHERTY, DITCH DOY
AND

THE ORANGE RISING STAR AWARD
EVA GREEN

On 29 February 2004, at the age of 82, Dana Broccoli passed away. Undoubtedly the matriarch of the James Bond family, her influence on the films had gone largely uncredited. In May 2000 Dana Broccoli explained, 'I was a dark horse because I was very happy taking care of Cubby and I didn't want to be That Wife, pushing herself on the creative team, because there might be resentment.'[1] Dana, who was influential on the casting of the Bond actors, brought a female perspective to the creation of Bond:

> I have a woman's instinct about people. We women don't fall for pretty faces, we want masculine men who are going to protect us forever. James Bond is not politically correct – he's far from that. He has a magnetism, sophistication and earthiness; most women are looking for that all their lives.[2]

Dana revealed steely resolve beneath a velvet exterior, 'I don't have the gift of forgiveness like Cubby did. I'm half Irish and half-Italian – not a good combination. I'm just bloody-minded.'[3] Following Cubby's passing she admitted:

> [He] was irreplaceable. We went through so much together, ups and downs, but it has been a fabulous journey. Nothing has been bigger than Bond. I've got a wonderful family which helps tremendously. That was a large part of our success, the big extended family is very Irish as well as Italian. We all carry Cubby's life with us. I'm the chairman of the board now – Michael and Barbara have kicked me upstairs. They just come to me and say, 'What do you think?'[4]

Just over fifteen months earlier, Albert R. Broccoli's Eon Productions were exploring different paths. In December 2002, coincident with the release of *Die Another Day*, the first official James Bond spin-off film was announced.[5] Studio chief Chris McGurk needed to maximise MGM's one steady asset suggesting a young Bond, 'like *Smallville*'.[6] Instead, capitalising on the success of the highest grossing 007 feature to date as well as the box office and critical clout of Halle Berry, MGM progressed with an idea of a stand-alone Jinx film. This was a concept that was originally mooted for Michelle Yeoh's Wai Lin from *Tomorrow Never Dies*.[7]

Neal Purvis remembered discussing the key aspects of the *Jinx* screenplay in LA with Halle Berry at Barbara Broccoli's house:[8] Giacinta Johnson worked for a think-tank, rode a motorbike, did odd jobs for [NSA chief] Falco and had a lover called Javier, 'who we wanted to be Javier Bardem.'[9] The script featured a shoot-out in a Moroccan tannery and was a 'down and dirtier version of a Bond movie.'[10] Wade described *Jinx* as 'a very atmospheric, Euro thriller, a Bourne-type movie.'[11] *Die Another Day* director, Lee Tamahori, was enthusiastic about the character and showed interest in directing the film.[12] The project was offered to Stephen Frears, as Purvis recalled, 'He loved Halle.'[13] McGurk met with the director, 'At that point we weren't sure Stephen Frears was the right guy to direct *Jinx*. It was like an $80–90 million budget.'[14] Purvis remembered, 'We spent two months on it. Halle Berry was very happy, Stephen and the producers were happy and we were happy.'[15]

However, McGurk recalled MGM got cold feet due to the budget and that recent female-led action films had flopped at the box office, 'The studio ended up killing the movie because we were just too nervous that a) it wasn't going to work and b) it would have a very negative impact on the franchise if it didn't work.'[16] Axing *Jinx* caused consternation with the producers, 'Barbara was really outraged that I had led her down the primrose path and wasted a lot of effort.'[17] In October 2003 *Variety* reported, 'MGM told Eon to put the project on ice. "There were creative differences," says a spokesperson acidly.'[18] Eon was keen to 'press ahead instead with *Bond 21*.'[19] Neal Purvis had thought *Jinx* 'was a pretty good script,' describing it as the bridge to what eventually would become *Casino Royale*.[20]

To begin with Michael G. Wilson felt *Die Another Day* had put them in a quandry, 'When we actually had to sit down and write the next film, it became abundantly clear that we had nowhere to go without being frankly science fiction. And that being the case, it became harder and harder to come up with a plot, and situations in that vein.'[21]

Robert Wade remembered, 'Michael said it's time to read CASINO ROYALE.'[22] In May 2004 Purvis confided, 'As far as we understand it, Pierce Brosnan is Bond.'[23] The Irish actor felt it was fated: 'When I did my first Bond movie Barbara sent me a signed first edition of CASINO ROYALE, saying, 'this is the blue-print for Bond, and we should do this.'[24] Wade explained that their approach in adapting Fleming's first novel as Brosnan's fifth Bond film was simply to involve James Bond in a relationship that mattered to him:

His dealings with women have been sort of as consumable objects, but no one to form an attachment with. [In] the Pierce movies nothing affects him. We tried with *The World Is Not Enough* – he does fall for Elektra and then with *Die Another Day* it's another journey where people have lost faith in him.[25]

In 2004 Pierce Brosnan was looking forward to his return, 'We were all set to make the movie and the deal was being done.'[26] The incumbent 007 had ideas as to how to approach *Casino Royale*, 'I was looking forward to making it edgier and grittier. I thought I'd made some good inroads with the character and felt a sense of ownership after having played him four times, it was a sense of ease and confidence.'[27] McGurk echoed, 'Pierce thought he was 90 per cent of the way to signing a deal for the film.'[28] However, things were about to take a dramatic turn.

Speaking to the authors a decade later, Brosnan remembered:

I was in the Bahamas, working on a movie called *After the Sunset* [2004] and my agents called me up and said, 'Negotiations have stopped. [Barbara and Michael] are not quite sure what they want to do. They'll call you next Thursday.' I sat in Richard Harris's house in the Bahamas, in this old, faded mansion and Barbara was on the line and Michael was on the line and they said, 'We're so sorry.' She was crying, Michael was stoic and he said, 'You were a great James Bond. Thank you very much,' and I said, 'Thank you very much. Goodbye.' That was it.[29]

McGurk was full of praise for Brosnan, 'He had done four movies in the franchise and taken it to another level [but] the Broccolis weren't going to move forward with him as Bond. They blamed his salary demands.'[30] Brosnan would later refute this, 'There have been preposterous ideas that I was asking for $40 million and $30 million, which is not true.'[31] McGurk felt, 'increasing an actor's salary by $5–6 million from *Die Another Day* that was generating a couple of hundred million dollars in profit, the studio didn't think it was a big deal. Pierce knew I wanted him to do *Casino Royale*.'[32] It was speculated Brosnan's new agent was asking for $25 million plus 5 per cent of the gross.[33]

Brosnan had lunch with the producers in a Santa Monica restaurant to pitch his case for his price and also to hear 'their detailed rationale for why they didn't think he should do one more.'[34] McGurk heard that Brosnan 'got up and walked out of the restaurant because they basically said, "No." There was no appeal.'[35] Brosnan recalled he 'was utterly shocked and just kicked to the kerb with the way it went down.'[36] Brosnan held out for the possibility of a return, prior to a new actor being announced, 'Would I go back if they asked me back? Sure I'd go back. No question; it's unfinished business.'[37]

There was uncertainty, yet again, over the fate of MGM. Months of speculation as to whether the studio would be sold and who to ended when Sony Pictures put an offer on the table that was at least a dollar per share higher than their rival Warner Brothers.[38] McGurk felt complications over the sale slowed the development of *Casino Royale* down, but ultimately he thought the movie benefitted from Sony's takeover. An extra year in development meant many more creative eyes took a look at it. Even more importantly, Sony could spend far more supporting the film than MGM who simply 'didn't have the money.'[39]

Sony started off as the brainchild of Japanese innovator Akio Morita, who coined the company name from the Latin word for sound – Sonus.[40] SFrom the fifties to the seventies, Sony slowly grew into a huge Japanese electronics giant – supplying product to the Bond films – before purchasing Columbia Pictures in September 1989.[41] In September 2004 they led a consortium to pay over $5 billion for MGM.[42] McGurk said Sony knew the potential value of Bond in signing the deal, 'That was the one big franchise. It was probably the most profitable franchise out there because of all the ancillary.'[43]

In 1967 Columbia Pictures had backed Charles K. Feldman's bloated *Casino Royale*. They had held on to the rights, which had become Sony's property in the 1989 purchase. It was these rights that were parlayed to MGM and Danjaq as part of the McClory settlement in 1999. It was perhaps destiny that Columbia Pictures would end up behind the long elusive Eon version of Ian Fleming's first novel. Barbara said Cubby had always wanted to make the book, 'He just accepted that it probably wasn't going to happen. I like to think I'm doing it for him.'[44]

Michael G. Wilson praised the new Sony chiefs, 'Amy [Pascal] and her team are very good, experienced filmmakers and executives, and they're very supportive of us.'[45] As vice-chairman and chief operating officer of MGM, it was Chris McGurk's duty to introduce Barbara and Michael to their new studio partners at Sony:

We set up a meeting at Michael Wilson's club in Mayfair. I was there representing MGM and from Sony there was Amy Pascal, Michael Lynton, Howard Stringer and Jeff Blake. It was kind of an awkward meeting. After dinner Amy Pascal decided to ask Barbara what she thought of studio executives. And Barbara said, 'Well, you know what, some are good, some aren't so good but what I don't like are assholes like John Calley.' John Calley had been at Sony and was Amy Pascal's mentor. [Barbara] just started railing at John Calley and how he tried to destroy the Bond franchise and how he was dishonest and had no integrity to the point where Amy put her fingers in her ears, 'I don't want to hear this.' That was Barbara throwing down the gauntlet with the new studio executives she was going to have to deal with.

Michael Wilson interceded and basically calmed her down and straightened the whole thing out. I think she knew she was going to do that when she went in there that evening.[46]

It was brave for the studio to back the new direction: Barbara Broccoli painted an amusing scene:

'OK, what do you want?' asked Pascal. 'Well, we want to go back – to the original book,' replied Broccoli. 'But isn't that like a card game? And doesn't the girl die in the end?' 'That's right.' 'But we'll have fun [with] Q, Miss Moneypenny?' 'No, we won't. And we won't have Pierce. And we want to shoot the opening in black and white.' It was almost like one of those Orange commericials. [47]

She also expressed, 'We were so lucky with Amy Pascal. I think it's something to do with being a woman – it is all about making it work.'[48]

Ian Fleming's CASINO ROYALE is, as we have said, not an origin story. Bond is chosen for the mission because he has already displayed a penchant for gambling. A previous assignment had seen Bond unravelling a Romanian cheating syndicate in Monte Carlo, who were using invisible ink and special glasses to mark cards. By the time Bond enters the piece, he is already a Double-0: the prefix to his code number designating his licence to kill. As an agent, 007 has earned this licence by undertaking two murders: one hot-blooded, one cold. With a cold, steely assassin's eye, he eliminated a Japanese cipher expert in the Rockefeller Centre, New York with a high-powered rifle. In Norway, he kills a Norwegian traitor with a knife.

The story has Bond travel to Northern France to the fictional Royale-les-Eaux, to out gamble Soviet agent, Le Chiffre. Having embezzled French Communist party funds, Le Chiffre must now win high stakes baccarat to replenish the funds. Bond is assisted by junior MI6 staffer Vesper Lynd, French Deuxième Bureau contact, René Mathis, and the laconic, blonde-haired Texan CIA agent Felix Leiter. After a series of card games – in which Le Chiffre's goons try to kill Bond by an elaborate bomb ruse and using a silenced walking-cane gun – Bond loses everything, seemingly wiped out of funds. However, the CIA stake Bond with a massive surprise donation, enabling him to win in a final game against Le Chiffre. In the night of celebration, Lynd is kidnapped and Bond goes chasing after her in his supercharged Bentley. However, a road trap causes Bond to crash spectacularly. 007 is stripped naked and tied to a chair, and his genitals are assaulted by Le Chiffre using a carpet beater. Le Chiffre wants Bond to reveal where he has hidden the winnings. However, at the close of Bond's torture, a Soviet agent intervenes and executes Le Chiffre for embezzling the funds. The Soviet agent then carves a Cyrilic 'M' on Bond's hand, marking him as an enemy agent. The symbol represents SMERSH – the brutal Soviet counter-espionage unit with its motto 'Death to Spies'. Bond undergoes a long recuperation, tended to by Vesper Lynd, not knowing if he can ever be sexually active again. During this time, Bond falls in love with Vesper and they have an affair in the seaside resorts of Northern France as Bond rediscovers his manhood. One evening, he notices a man with a black eye-patch, who precipitates a change in Vesper's behaviour. Their relationship takes a downturn. One morning, Bond finds Vesper's body in bed – she has poisoned herself. Her suicide note is a confession. Her lover has been kidnapped by the Soviets and Vesper has been forced to turn traitor to save him. She had been working in league with the Soviet Secret Service against Bond. However, in the recent holiday, she had refused orders to betray Bond. She tips him off that the man with the eye-patch is an enemy agent. 007 is distraught and vows to go after every SMERSH spy. He calls London to report Vesper's treachery and fate. The novel ends with his final words, 'The bitch is dead now'.

Michael Wilson expressed how they simply went back to basics, 'We took the philosophy that we would make it as though there had never been a Bond film made before. It was the first Fleming book, and it was the one that defines the character of Bond.'[49] In 1986 Wilson and Maibaum had charted out a story featuring a young James Bond before he joined the Service. However, for this screenplay, Wilson 'really didn't rely much upon the work that I'd done with Richard Maibaum. This film [is] pretty much the ideas [of] Purvis and Wade.'[50]

Neal Purvis described early story ideas, 'It started at the Burj Al Arab. Essentially we were trying to update the idea of Le Chiffre losing the money. Then you were trying to maintain the expectations of a Bond movie. Is he going to buy something unpleasant or set up training centres?'[51] Robert Wade felt 'the first big idea was we'll substitute financing of terrorists by bankers for SMERSH in the novel.'[52]

While they had originally begun writing a version for Pierce Brosnan, as the script evolved Wade recalled that all parties realised the story would work better for a young man, 'Showing the two kills that led to him getting his 00 status is definitely what makes it a reboot.'[53]

Purvis and Wade had many ideas when exploring the concept of an origins story. Wade detailed one in which we first meet Bond backpacking in Madagascar, 'He's playing chess with an old drunkard guy called Two Fingers who may or may not be Lord Lucan.'[54]

Purvis was inspired by a sports commerical his wife, Tracy, had produced featuring free-running,[55] and that became the basis for a pre-title sequence.[56] Purvis continued, 'For a long time THE HILDEBRAND RARITY story was in there. We had envisaged Dimitrios [a minor villain] being Milton Krest and the wife being Liz Krest. Bond helps her and 'stuffs a fish down his throat.'[57] Wade recollected that they were also influenced by the little known Fleming short story, 007 IN NEW YORK. The writers borrowed the character Solange, an ex-Secret Service female employee Bond has been sent to meet in New York City, and used her to name the first Bond girl in *Casino Royale* whom Bond encounters on the beach in Nassau riding a white horse. In 007 IN NEW YORK Bond was to meet Solange outside the (fictional) reptile house in Central Park Zoo. Inspired, the writers used this exotic location as the setting of Bond's first kill in an early draft of the screenplay.[58] Other unused ideas included 'a fight in Venice in a butcher's and Bond riding a horse through Venice.'[59] The sequence involving the sabotage of the new Skyfleet airliner was originally going to feature the hijack of a cruise ship in Cape Town, South Africa. The opening being in black-and-white had always been in their minds, but the idea of the sinking house, while not in their treatment came to them when they were writing the script. Purvis and Wade's original ending, true to Fleming's novel, had Bond discovering Vesper's dead body. Bond watches her filmed confession of her betrayal where she reveals the Gettler rendezvous at the bank, which then leads to the finale where Bond chases Gettler into the sinking house.[60]

As the screenplay developed, a director was sought. Chris McGurk suggested Matthew Vaughn, director of the recent *Layer Cake* (2004), but Broccoli and Wilson thought he lacked the requisite experience.[61] In autumn 2004, *Notting Hill* (1999) director Roger Michell recalled, 'I was sent *Casino Royale* as a book just after I'd finished [*Enduring Love* (2004)] with Daniel Craig. I read the book and then they sent me a script. I very quickly said, "This one isn't for me, thank you very much."'[62] No actor had been cast to play Bond at the time.[63]

Eventually, *GoldenEye*'s Martin Campbell was lured back because:

They said they wanted to completely reboot the franchise. In reading the book there was none of the fantastic Bond action and so forth. It had its feet well and truly based firmly on the ground. When you read CASINO ROYALE,

Bond was a very flawed character; he drank too much, he smoked too much, he kind of had attitude. That's really what got me excited about it.[64]

Working with the writers further, Purvis recalled Campbell dismantled the entire script, 'He asked a lot of questions but the whole thing gradually was put back together again. He needed convincing that you should have a half-hour card game … there was a fear that people wouldn't understand it.'[65] Campbell did not play the game and Purvis remembered that regular poker nights took placat Eon's Picadilly HQ, 'Michael [Wilson's] quite an expert. The final hand [played by Bond in the film] was a game that we played with Michael.'[66]

Campbell felt the Purvis and Wade draft needed a rewrite. 'I suggested Paul Haggis should write it, to make it much more gritty, more realistic and make Bond basically a more interesting character.'[67]

Wade was sanguine, 'I think [Martin] just suspected me and Neal because we kind of represented Barbara and Michael's camp, he was always going to make sure we got fired.'[68] After winning awards for *Million Dollar Baby* (2004) and then *Crash* (2004), Paul Haggis was on a well-earned family holiday in Umbria, Italy, when he was visited by Martin Campbell and Barbara Broccoli.[69] Upon reading the draft Haggis advised, 'You don't have an Act III. Would you like one?'[70] Purvis and Wade's original ending had Bond discovering Vesper's dead body. Bond then watches her filmed confession of her betrayal, before giving away Gettler's rendezvous at the bank.[71] Haggis stated:

Here's what I know. Vesper has to be in that sinking house. Everything in him, all the worst in Bond has to come out at that moment. He finally opened up to this woman and she betrayed him. He'll chase them all into this sinking house. There will be a big battle with the villain, he will kill the villain and then he will try to rescue her. She won't allow him to do so and she'll drown. He won't get to save her. And that'll be the end.[72]

Casino Royale is comprised of two halves, the first foreshadowing the elements in the second. Both feature duels between Bond and a European villain in a classical Bondian setting, a pivotal high-stakes card game and a dalliance with a stunningly beautiful woman caught up in the maelstrom of the world. However, whereas in the first half, Bond starts out as a blunt instrument, by the second half we follow his evolution into a more refined and more human secret agent. Neal Purvis, Robert Wade and Paul Haggis improved upon the novel by finessing some of its weaknesses. First, the huge chance aspect is addressed by the fact that poker is literally a battle of wits: Bond plays the opponent and not his cards. Second, they have planted the seed that Le Chiffre is a hunted man. Steve Obanno's scary machete-wielding visit to Le Chiffre and the delectable Valenka sets up Mr. White's 'rescue' of Bond from torture. Third, Vesper Lynd's role is satisfyingly beefed up as she effectively holds the purse strings to the whole operation – her judgement determines Bond's actions – a position of significance when her true allegiance is revealed. The updating of the novel has Le Chiffre playing the market, by using terrorism to affect stock prices. There are other little touches of zeitgeist in the script: the pre-title toilet fight is meant to be set in a Pakistani cricket ground (notice the pictures on the wall) and the opening scene introduces Obanno implicitly as a Ugandan Lord's Resistance Army warlord, complete with child soldiers. This is the new asymmetric enemy – the international terrorist. As usual, Bond films are careful politically, while the date of Mollaka's planned Skyfleet outrage may be significant (the surveillance disk for the day prior is 6 July), M tells us that 'he wasn't even a true believer.' Throughout, we are are asked to look at 'the bigger picture', although M succinctly, yet ascerbically, comments on the state of the reputation of SIS in the current geopolitical climate. This is particularly interesting when Le Chiffre correctly taunts Bond at the end, that he will still be useful to Bond's allies even if he dispatches 007.

In February 2005 Martin Campbell was announced as the director of *Casino Royale*.[73] The situation was still opaque as who would play James Bond because that same month, Eon's Publicity Manager Katherine McCormack, stated:

> For now, Pierce Brosnan is our James Bond. We haven't made any statement to say he isn't our James Bond. It's so difficult to comment when we don't have a script or even a start date. He signed an initial three-contract deal with us and from then on it's on a film-by-film basis. So he hasn't signed one yet.[74]

Casting directors Janet Hirshenson and Jane Jenkins remembered meeting Alex O'Loughlin, Julian McMahon, Karl Urban, Sam Worthington and Ewan McGregor.[75] Campbell tested eight actors[76] including Goran Visnjic, Rupert Friend, Antony Starr and Daniel Craig.[77] 'When they test a Bond, they test them thoroughly, so each had a day of tests. It wasn't like they wheel six people in on one day.'[78] David Arnold recalled that the James Bond screentests had high production values; they were treated 'like it's a sequence from the movie'.[79] Peter Lamont built sets, Phil Méheux lit them[80] and Arnold scored the edited footage.[81] Purvis and Wade's pre-credit sequence set in Dryden's office in Prague was one of the scenes used. Campbell said, 'Pierce was so sculptured to the previous Bond incarnation, very much in the traditional Bond mode. We didn't have anyone obvious this time. So that's why we tested all these people.'[82] Neal Purvis remembered, 'Henry Cavill was very good and went right down to the wire.' But Cavill was only twenty-two at the time and the concern was should Bond be that young?[83]

Chris McGurk recalled he had spotted Daniel Craig in *Layer Cake* and told the Bond producers, '"There's this character actor in there who'd be a great Bond villain." Following a screening, Barbara said, "I'm in love with Daniel Craig, he's going to be our next Bond."'[84] Martin Campbell felt Craig in his test was not on his A-game, 'Poor Daniel was on a film called *The Invasion* (2007), he had to fly across from America. He was exhausted when he came in. He literally got off the plane and had to come and do his test. I wasn't totally convinced.'[85] However, Barbara Broccoli was Craig's champion. According to Campbell, 'Barbara never waivered one inch, she always said this is the man to play Bond.'[86]

When the producers had first approached Craig months earlier he was sceptical:

> I was reluctant to commit. But they said, 'We want to do *Casino Royale*, we want to take it back. We want to depict a more emotional Bond; we want to discover who he is.' But until I saw a script I could make no commitment. I had a couple of meetings with them and I was very honoured, I mean it was incredible – you get taken in to the offices and get to talk about playing James Bond – I suppose it was fantastic. I didn't say no I just said, 'Look I will read the script when you've got through it.' And Barbara being as [canny] as she is, went, 'Oh yes, I will see you in a little while.'[87]

Michael Wilson remembered:

> For us, it was pretty clear that Daniel was the frontrunner. We weren't prepared to give him a draft until it had gone quite a way towards what we thought would be the final. And that being the case, we had eighteen months to two years of uncertainty where we were looking for a back-up, and that's why we did look at a lot of people and tested a few.[88]

Craig remained unconcerned with the speculation, 'I had to get on with my life and in fact I went off and shot *Munich* (2005). When I am up for a role, I never consider who else is up for it because you either get it or you don't get it and I never consider it above or beyond that.'[89] During the period, Daniel Craig was questioned regularly by the press. In January 2005 Craig said, 'My gut feeling about it is that it is something I'd have no comprehension of because I'm an actor, and that (role) is about being more than an actor. To turn down Bond could be a decision that haunts you the rest of your life.'[90] In May 2005 Craig stated, 'It's kind of out of my hands. There are a couple of names going around. It's a high-class problem to have. I don't know. That's the truth of it, I really don't know. I know Barbara Broccoli; I've known her for years. There's nothing to say on that level. But I do know them and I have talked to them, but there's no decision made as yet.'[91]

In the meantime, Paul Haggis was frantically polishing the screenplay, 'Each act took me two weeks to do. So it was six weeks straight through. I believe it was August 2005. I think I finished in mid-September. They sent it to Daniel Craig and that's how they got him.'[92] Craig responded well to the draft, feeling Broccoli was 'very persuasive and said, "Look, come on, just read the script." And I mean honestly I got it and I genuinely didn't want to like it. The script was just great. It's a great story and it was just too much of a challenge for me to turn down.'[93] Amy Pascal of Sony Pictures and Dan Taylor of MGM supported Daniel Craig's casting.[94]

On 14 October 2005 a press conference was held at HMS President, a Royal Naval training facility near the Tower of London. Speeding up the Thames with Royal Marines was Daniel Craig. He faced a barrage from the world's press, which included questions about his private life and his hair, currently long and died blonde for his role in *The Invasion*. While his performance at the huge press event was not exactly assured, most James Bond fans were pleased with the choice. One website, however, garnered a disproportionate amount of media attention skewing the general public's view. There has been speculation about the motives of this website which was connected to a professional PR firm, who may have had links to Craig's disgruntled former representation. After being named the new 007, Craig had signed with Creative Artists Agency (CAA).[95] Between the rumours and a deal being made, Craig had been represented in the US by the William Morris Agency.[96] At the time of signing for Bond, Craig may not have been formally represented and therefore, legitimately, would not have had to pay any commissions.[97] The vocal anti-Craig campaign was not an accurate reflection of the true fan reaction.

According to the official press release, Wilson and Broccoli said, 'It has been a long time ambition for us to film the first book in the series, CASINO ROYALE, which defined the complex character of James Bond. We are thrilled Daniel

Craig will play the character of 007. Daniel is a superb actor who has all the qualities needed to bring a contemporary edge to the role.'[98]

Craig outlined his approach to James Bond:

I think what's been set down with all the other movies is very important. I would ignore that at my peril because that's what's defined him over the years. But I did suggest that we'd got to meet somebody who can make mistakes, who can bleed. Who is feeling fallible and therefore can fall in love. Because without that, you wouldn't believe the love story. I just started attempting to do what I did and they kind of didn't stop me, so I just carried on.[99]

Mads Mikkelsen recalled the Bond team had seen his previous, Danish language work, *Open Hearts* (2002) and the *Pusher* trilogy:

They called me for an audition. I was shooting a film in Prague and I couldn't make it. They called me back again and I couldn't make it and they called me a third time, and they were ready to pay for my travel. Barbara was there and Michael. Daniel was there dressed up in a tuxedo and looked like Bond.[100]

Mikkelsen tested with the torture scene, 'But at that time they had made up their mind and they had seen my films.'[101] The Danish actor was promptly cast as Le Chiffre, the mysterious financial wizard. Mikkelsen created a little backstory:

I always do that for the characters I've done. I think he is probably an orphan. He's a street kid probably from Montenegro somewhere. And as he's a small guy, he has to be smart and slick. And when he starts hustling the cards, hustling with backgammon, he finds himself a real talent, then it goes on from there and he meets some really serious people.[102]

The casting of Vesper Lynd had been narrowed down to Eva Green and Olivia Wilde.[103] Other actresses rumoured to be up for the role were Rachel McAdams and Thandie Newton.[104] There was studio pressure to think about A-listers Angelina Jolie and Charlize Theron.[105] Barbara outlined the difficulties of finding the right actress, 'Vesper – she's in Bond lore. She's the female icon – she's the one that has the largest impact on Bond's character.'[106] Casting director Debbie McWilliams confirmed the latter two were:

'strongly considered. The [casting of a star like] Halle Berry was quite odd in itself. Everybody thinks there was a precedent set by that. You'll see that most of the girls we have chosen haven't been well known at all. We did talk about Audrey Tautou, [but then we] didn't want *The Da Vinci Code* girl. I met Cécile de France, too, but her English wasn't really up to scratch.'[107]

Eva Green was unaware how she appeared on the producers' radar, 'I know [director] Martin Campbell loves Ridley Scott,' she said, in reference to her lead role in *Kingdom of Heaven* (2005). Broccoli felt Eva Green had all the right qualities, 'but it took us months and months to get her to read the script.'[108] Green admitted she had reservations about appearing in a Bond film, 'I was scared I'd be perceived as just another sexy girl in a bikini. But when I read the script, I could see that it was more like a classic love story than a big action movie.'[109] Green described the witty dialogue as a 'poker game between Bond and Vesper … fast talking like the Tracy-Hepburn movies.'[110] Green remembered:

> The first audition was in a very cosy room with Barbara Broccoli, Michael Wilson and Daniel Craig in Prague. We did the train scene. It went OK. After that I went to New York and they said, 'Can you please take a plane and come back to Prague and audition again, because they're not completely satisfied.' It was quite awful, because they said you'll really have to work on your English. It was very formal the second time, costumes and [Sony] were there, it was on set and it was just crazy. I was not very good. I was better, I thought, the first time.[111]

Italian actress Caterina Murino was cast as Solange, the beautiful yet unhappy wife of one of Le Chiffre's villainous associates, who succumbs to Bond's charms. Prior to her audition, Murino fell off a horse and broke a rib. She attended the audition 'completely under morphine.'[112] Upon being cast, Caterina practised horse riding every day for a month to overcome her fear,[113] as her first day on set in the Bahamas required her to ride a horse along a beach.

Judi Dench was not expecting to reprise her role as M: 'Sam Bond and Colin Salmon and all the people in the office weren't in this one so I just stayed schtum and waited and then I found that I was. And then even better they said, "what's more you are going to Prague and Nassau."'[114] Campbell explained casting Dench in obstensibly a prequel 'made no sense on one hand, because she would obviously be much younger than she is in the previous Bonds. But the truth of the matter is, you've simply got to forget all that and say, "Who better than Judi Dench?" It's a different relationship.'[115] Craig was pleased and explained how Bond and M's relationship would explore new ground:

> At the beginning of the film, she is kind of the only human being that he cares about. And she obviously cares about him and by the end of the movie, I think she slightly regrets having put him on this road. It kind of allows him to sort of misbehave. In fact, as long as he has this sort of female figure in his life that controls him then he can be as bad as he is. I am personally very thrilled that I got the chance to work with Judi Dench. She is one of the best actresses around.[116]

Casino Royale revealed more about M, we discover where she lives and learn she has a partner. Dench loved 'the flat Peter Lamont has designed for M … this gorgeous apartment in Canary Wharf.'[117] Said Campbell, 'What kind of home do you imagine M has? An old Georgian house in an elegant London square? No, this woman is full of surprises, so we've gone for a modern penthouse on the river.'[118] Ironically, it was a town house in an elegant London square where we would find M living just two films later.

African-American actor Jeffrey Wright would become the seventh Eon Felix Leiter, although *Never Say Never Again* had been the first to change the race of the character. Giancarlo Gianinni would play an Italianate René Mathis. Other cast members included Tsai Chin (who had appeared as Bond's lover Ling in the pre-titles of *You Only Live Twice*) as Madame Wu, Le Chiffre's travelling gambling companion, and Helena Bonham-Carter's cousin, Crispin, played a hot room doctor. Tobias Menzies played M's assistant, Villiers, named after James Villiers (Tanner in *For Your Eyes Only*), a previous pupil at Robert Wade's school, Wellington College, and for Amherst Villiers, inventor of Bond's supercharger in his Bentley from the Fleming books.[119] Jesper Christensen played Mr. White, the man from the mysterious organisation who has backed Le Chiffre. Ludger Pistor was Mendel, an amused Swiss banker and Joseph Millson was Carter, the fellow rookie agent with Bond in Madagascar.

The film once again featured an interesting array of minor villains including Simon Abkarian as Alex Dimitrios, Solange's cruel husband, Claudio Santamaria as Carlos, Dimitrios' putative Skyfleet saboteur, Isaach de Bankolé as Steven Obanno, disgruntled investor and Lord's Resistance Army chieftain, Clemens Schick as Kratt, Le Chiffre's stiletto-wielding bodyguard and Ivana Miličević as Valenka, Le Chiffre's loyal girlfriend. Richard Sammel was sinister as Gettler, the one-eyed puppet-master of Vesper's treachery in Venice, expanded from the novel.

Working with Martin Campbell was virtually the entire team of department heads who had made *GoldenEye* such a success a decade earlier. Campbell's ever-faithful cinematographer, Phil Méheux, recalled that Campbell wanted to do the film because of the challenge of a new Bond.[120] He also made a brief appearance as the treasury official in M's office wanting his money back! Phil Méheux understood the irrascible director and was somewhat of an agony uncle to the crew:

Martin doesn't take fools kindly. If he starts badmouthing you loudly, it's because he likes you a lot. He would say, 'Come here, you idiot cameraman!' He was a humane person, if he liked you, you were in. When something went wrong that shouldn't have gone wrong, he would let loose.[121]

Also returning was Eon stalwart, production designer Peter Lamont, who would bow out with *Casino Royale*, following a forty-two year association with the James Bond franchise. Lamont had begun as a draftsman on *Goldfinger* and risen through the ranks to design a record nine Bond films.

Costume designer Lindy Hemming, another *GoldenEye* veteran, adjusted the Bond look for Daniel Craig:

He still had to have the tailoring and the sophisticated taste. His character, however, had changed from the old-fashioned British public-school spy to a much more 'tough guy' hands-on approach. Someone who had actually been fighting in a real war, of which there were plenty in the year 2000. He was a much more physical Bond and his tailoring and wardrobe reflected this. He also wore much more 'street' type, fashionable clothing.[122]

While production commenced on 27 January 2006[123] the first official slate was struck three days later on 30 January in Modrany Studios in the Czech Republic.[124] Principal photography took place in Barrandov and Modrany Studios, Prague after the film was forced to leave the UK due to the strength of the pound sterling and the dismal UK tax incentives for production. However, *Casino Royale* would still make use of facilities at Pinewood Studios and shoot at substituted locations in the UK. *Casino Royale* was officially a UK-US-German-Czech production, thereby qualifying for various regional incentives to encourage film investment in Europe.

The first scenes shot were the interiors of the embassy of the fictional state of Nambutu, where Bond confronts and captures bomb-maker Mollaka after a thrilling parkour chase. Peter Lamont noted:

It was complicated – Bond moves through the embassy pursuing and capturing Mollaka – running along corridors, into offices and jumping out of a
window into the compound where he sets off a huge explosion. The beginning of that scene was shot later in the Bahamas, where he follows Mollaka
to the embassy from the building site.[125]

Martin Campbell and the new second unit director, Alexander Witt, had Daniel
Craig begin his tenure as 007 by shooting his way through the embassy in
an exhausting action sequence. Campbell barked directions loudly, imparting
energy to the performances. Craig had invested the time since his announcement as Bond building his body for the role. He then prepared further with
stunt co-ordinator Gary Powell and stunt double Ben Cooke.[126] Craig said, 'Of
course, I didn't do all the stunts, it's impossible. I mean the insurance companies
won't let me. But at a certain stage in every stunt you see it is me, so that was
my kind of ambition.'[127]

Lamont created over forty sets for the film. The interiors included the Casino
Royale Salon Privé, the compound of the Nambutu Embassy, the interior of Le
Chiffre's yacht and the interior of the sanatorium where Bond recuperates in
Italy. Lamont considered, 'Barrandov Studios in Prague a good base of operations, with a great workforce and excellent sound stages.'[128] Shooting continued
at Modrany Studios until the middle of February 2006 and then moved to the
main studio, Barrandov.[129]

Danube House, a new office building on the banks of the Vltava, doubled for
the office in which Bond confronts MI6 traitor Dryden at the beginning of the
film.[130] The startling pre-title sequence was deliberately devised to make audiences understand this was a different take on the franchise. Méheux noted: 'If
you want to do something different and turn everyone around, do something
in black-and-white.'[131] He explained the sequence was also a deliberate nod to
the Cold War classics, in particular, the first of the Harry Palmer films, which
had been produced by Harry Saltzman:

In *The Ipcress File* there's a shot where the table lamp is huge in the frame and
a man's face is in the top right-hand corner. I really like that look. Part of the
dialogue in the opening sequence was done with very carefully controlled
shots that have huge things in the foreground and faces pushed to the corner
of the frame.[132]

Prague also stood in for other locations, becoming variously Miami, London and Montenegro. The marble Vitkov Monument (a mausoleum) became the interior of Gunther von Hagens's Body Worlds exhibition, which in the film is set in the Miami Science Centre. Vaclav Havel Airport doubled for Miami International Airport with these scenes being shot in the thick of winter. Costume designer Lindy Hemming recalled, 'The extras arrived in fur boots and big parkas. We had to strip them off and make them wear shorts, sandals and T-shirts to look like Miami tourists. They thought we were torturing them. That's the magic of Bond films – transforming somewhere into somewhere else. We seem to do that every day.'[133] Virgin Airlines tycoon Richard Branson and his son, Sam, made cameo appearances walking through the airport security scanner.

Originally, the African sequences were to be shot in South Africa,[134] but the production then decided to use the varying locales of the Bahamas to double not only as Madagascar but also as the Italian Riviera. This was because in March, the water in this region is warmer and bluer than in the Mediterranean.[135] Wilson explained the benefits to both the production and the Bahamas:

> The Bahamas is ideal for filming because of its close proximity to the United States, where equipment can be readily purchased. Bahamians speak English and are familiar with film units, so there's a certain amount of support available here. It's also a major tourist destination, so you can get high-quality hotels and restaurants for the crew while they are working here. And, of course, the weather. We normally spend about US $1.74 million a week, in addition to location costs.'[136]

Shooting continued on 23 February 2006 at the 200-year-old Buena Vista Hotel in Nassau, which doubled as the Nambutan embassy on Madagascar.[137] Peter Lamont converted a disused motel into a Madagascan shanty town where Bond is observing a snake and mongoose fight at the beginning of the film. It is interesting to note that the mongoose's snarl and snake fangs were added in digitally during post-production.[138]

An abandoned hotel complex, now a Royal Bahamian Air Force base, at Coral Harbor on New Providence Island was dressed to resemble a building site – the setting for the innovative parkour chase. Eon had used the same locale during the making of *Thunderball* and *The Spy Who Loved Me*.

This highly original free-running chase was the brainchild of Sébastien Foucan, the co-creator and one of the foremost practitioners in the art of parkour:

It's about adapting yourself within your environment to overcome barriers to your physical progress. It's all about free-flowing movement. My character's skill is that he can move swiftly to escape from Bond, so we tried to find a way to move quickly and efficiently rather than do stunt tricks.[139]

The highlight of this intense sequence was Bond and Mollaka climbing amongst the girders of a crane before jumping from its arm to another crane below. Foucan explained, 'There were security systems in place, but all the action is real. There was no point pretending the chase around the girders wasn't going to be dangerous – it was.'[140] Stunt co-ordinator Gary Powell allowed Daniel Craig to partake in the action on top of the crane:

He was 90ft up in the air running across an 8-inch-wide girder. He was on a safety cable but it is still very unnerving to be at that sort of height with the wind whistling around you. Believe me, it's not easy for stunt people and that height is intimidating. He did it, and he did a fantastic job.[141]

Executive producer Anthony Waye recalled it was a headache finding such a location with such specific requirements:

We had looked in several cities including London and Cape Town. We needed seven weeks where we could have total control, but of course no construction company is going to stop work for that length of time and allow you to use their site. It was by chance, at the end of a day's location scouting in the Bahamas, that we found an abandoned, half-finished hotel, now derelict.[142]

Negotiating with the commodore, Waye made four trips to the Bahamas in a month to talk with the government before permission was finally granted:

Then one of those problems you don't think about happened right as we started our construction schedule. Katrina, a very strong hurricane, hit New Orleans. To assist with the massive clean-up that followed, all available cranes in the US went down there, so we had to ship the two 100ft cranes and a large mobile crane over from the UK. A major logistical nightmare.[143]

The Bahamas was also a setting in itself. Wilson noted: 'It's important that a Bond film has glamorous and exotic locations.'[144] Bond's arrival by seaplane was shot at Paradise Island, home to Sol Kerzner's The One and Only Club, which doubled as the Ocean Club where Bond beats Dimitrios at poker. Top Kerzner executive, Jerry Inzerillo, makes a cameo appearance as a player at the table. Also in this scene is Diane Hartford. She was previously the uncredited girl Bond speaks to at the Kiss Kiss Club in 1965's *Thunderball*, a production which received the local assistance of her husband, the wealthy property developer, Huntingdon Hartford.

Golfers Tiger Woods and Ernie Els own the secluded Albany House estate on the West Coast of New Providence Island that served as Dimitrios's beachfront mansion, where Bond famously emerges from the sea in his blue trunks. Barbara Broccoli said eight years later, 'We didn't sit there thinking, "Oh, we're going to have this iconic moment." It didn't happen that way at all. We were just in the Bahamas and there was a scene where he was coming out of the sea and it struck us when it happened, "Oh my God this is an iconic moment."'[145] Craig noted that when he got the role, 'I just said, "Ok, let's get fit, let's do it, let's get into shape." And thank God I did because I don't think I would have lasted if I hadn't pulled that together. And I kind of wanted, when he took his shirt off, I wanted it to look like he could do the things that I was attempting to do.'[146]

Bahamian Bond soon became Bohemian Bond. Michael Wilson noted:

> The setting for the Casino Royale in the novel is Royale-Les-Eaux in France, but the production moved the location to an unnamed town in Montenegro. We needed somewhere that seemed to be out of the reach of the international banking authorities in order for Le Chiffre to feel safe enough to come out of hiding.[147]

The Casino Royale itself was difficult to find in just one location. The production scouted around Trieste and then along the coast of Croatia. Peter Lamont explained:

> We could find the broad tree-lined boulevards we wanted, but no grand hotels exist there yet, and we needed imposing buildings for the Casino Royale and the Hotel Splendide exteriors. Karlovy Vary was the first place we looked in the Czech Republic and that's where we ended up shooting the Hotel Splendide exterior and lobby, and the Casino Royale exterior and public gambling room, with the Salon Privé and hotel bedrooms being built at Barrandov Studios.[148]

In the Fleming novel, the card game played was baccarat but Wilson explained, 'That game is no longer popular and there are very few people who understand

it, whereas poker is now recognised throughout the world, with poker tourna-
ments on television and online gaming at an all-time high.'[149] The producer
amusingly described himself as a 'recovering poker addict.'[150] Wilson outlined the difficulties of capturing the gaming scenes, 'The problem was that
we hired nine people to play against Bond at the table and they came with
varying degrees of experience, so we had to educate all the actors so they
looked like they are poker pros. We brought in Thomas Sanbrook as our poker
expert.'[151] Together with screenwriters, Neal Purvis, Robert Wade and Martin
Campbell, Wilson designed and supervised the games played at the Casino
Royale tournament.[152]

The other challenge was how to make the gaming scenes interesting for anyone
who is not a poker aficionado. Director of photography Phil Méheux said:

Betting itself is pretty boring. So you have to deal with the drama between the
characters. It's all about looks, so you never really want to be too wide, but you
also don't want just a bunch of close-ups. We had a whole day of rehearsal with
all the actors playing their cards and then we worked out where best to seat
everyone and how to shoot it. We tried to approach it with as many variations
as we could within those limitations. We did one card game that was all filmed
with a static camera and we did another where the camera was constantly
moving around the table. Then we did one game where the camera starts pretty
far back and slowly closes in on Bond and Le Chiffre ... You can fly a camera
down a wire as two people are having a conversation ... and it can be a fun
moment but you very quickly start to diffuse the drama if you're just moving
around them. I try to avoid movement for movement's sake.[153]

Casino Royale is a 'new money' gambling palace and the costumes of the other
poker players reflect this. During production, Lindy Hemming admitted she
loved casino scenes:

With the clothing worn by the card players around the gambling table in
Casino Royale I wanted to show what the very richest people could have
tailored as eveningwear. Infante, the African dictator, is wearing an African
version of a gambling evening suit, the Russian has a mink collar and the
Argentinian has a suit with real gold threads running through it. Even
Veruschka, who plays the German heiress, is dressed by Brioni, as they started
a new woman's wear company this year.[154]

Martin Campbell commented on the infamous torture scene:

> I transferred the whole thing to an empty barge, somehow the metal and the
> drips and the chains all suited it better. The key to that scene was the psycho-
> logical confrontation between them both. Bond clearly wins that. Despite Le
> Chiffre having him tied to the chair naked, Bond wins.[155]

Towards the end of May 2006 the production moved to Lake Como, Italy,
where the private estate Villa La Gaeta was used for the film's ending, in which
Bond 'introduces' himself to Mr. White. The grounds of Villa del Balbianello
became the sanatorium where Bond recuperates from his torture.[156]

Eon Productions then went back to familiar territory: Venice. Anthony Waye
noted the unique beauty of the city but said, 'It does take some getting used to,
where all your equipment is moored on barges or wheeled in small barrows
through the city.'[157] Waye explained the challenges, 'You've got to first of all train
the crew how to get to their location each day. Very complicated. We've had maps
drawn of how to get to the location. But I think they make things even more
complicated.'[158] The location inspired Lindy Hemming to design 'the red dress
[Vesper] wears when Bond follows her. We made sure that none of the extras
wore any red, so that we could see her as Bond catches glimpses of her through
the crowds in Venice. It's a small homage to *Don't Look Now* (1973).'[159] Lamont
amusingly recalled his work being too realistic:

> In St. Mark's Square (Piazza San Marco) we were allowed to use an empty
> building as [Basel] bank where Bond looks for Vesper. Of course, it is one of
> the busiest tourist destinations in the world, and as soon as we had completed
> the work and opened the door, we were inundated with tourists trying to
> change money. This also happened to us at Prague airport, where we were
> shooting interiors for Miami airport. We set up an exchange booth and had
> lots of potential customers, some of whom couldn't understand why we had
> no currency for them.[160]

Permission was granted to allow Bond's and Vesper's yacht (the *Spirit '54*) to
sail along the Grand Canal between the Academia and Rialto bridges, the first
time a yacht had sailed the Grand Canal for many years. On 27 May 2006, skip-
per Mick Newman (doubling Craig) and his wife, Wiss (doubling Eva Green
complete with dark wig and Versace sunglasses), arrived in Venice off the coast
of St. Mark's Square. Marc Wolff, Vietnam veteran and seasoned Bond aerial

camera pilot, captured the stunning establishing shot of the floating city. The
ensuing days were spent filming the boat on the canals. Bond moors outside
the luxurious Cipriani Hotel on Guidecca. Newman recalled:

> One of the scenes has Bond sitting on the bow of the yacht typing on a laptop
> … suffice to say when he's finished he throws the laptop into the water. The
> two rehearsals were done with a rubber fake laptop. The next five takes were
> done with brand new, top of the range, Sony laptops! About £1,500 a pop!
> The reason, I was told, was that if the laptop spun in the air and the audience
> could see it was not showing what our Mr. Bond had typed, their belief
> would be gone. The laptops were retrieved by a diver, wiped with a towel
> and by the time the shot was in the can there was a bizarre washing line with
> laptops dripping in the sun![161]

The exterior of the collapsing house was situated on the Grand Canal opposite
the Rialto market, where the Venetian authorities were persuaded to permit the
production to sink compression pipes into the canal to simulate water spouting as
the house sank, and to stop normal canal traffic for short intervals of time.[162] Phil
Méheux explained the background of the location-specific climax to the film:

> For a long time people were afraid that Venice was sinking and it turned
> out what was making Venice sink was the fact that houses were drawing
> water from wells under their foundations, and when the water went out, the
> foundations were sinking into the empty gap. They've stopped doing that
> and Venice isn't sinking anymore. But with that in mind, we fabricated this
> idea that this old-fashioned villa might be kept on the water line with fixed
> industrial balloons while it was being renovated.[163]

The real work of capturing the scene, however, would take place on the 007
Stage at Pinewood Studios.

The Bond production team finally wrapped principal photography in the
UK in July 2006. A scene cut from the pre-title sequence established the traitor
killed in the toilet fight being tracked by Bond to a cricket match in Pakistan.
This was shot at the famed Eton College public school and the grounds were
dressed with palm trees to add the appropriate Eastern flavour to a quintes-
sentially English location.[164] In early July the production moved to Black Park
near Pinewood Studios to film the rebel camp in Uganda where Mr. White
introduces Le Chiffre to Steven Obanno.

Casino Royale has Bond behind the wheel of an Aston Martin DBS. The car was developed prior to production starting and the Bond team inspected the process at the Aston Martin factory in October 2005 because, in the words of the car makers' design director, Marek Reichman, 'there was curiosity on both sides. We wanted to meet the new Bond and work out whether it was even a good association for us. But Daniel's a very cool guy.'[165] The car was given a bespoke colour, 'Casino Ice' and was the victim of a spectacular crash sequence shot at the hill circuit in Millbrook in Bedfordshire. It was shot by a nitrogen cannon and rolled seven times, earning a Guinness World Record.[166]

Throughout June and July 2006 the first and second units continued at Dunsfold, spending a total of ten weeks filming the Miami airport chase. Bond and Carlos commandeer a petrol tanker, a vehicle Chris Corbold had useful previous experience with on *Licence to Kill*.[167] The film sees Bond crashing into various vehicles, including a bendy bus and the belly of an aircraft although this latter sequence was cut from the final film.[168] The action tears onto a runway, with Bond being chased by the Miami police in cars while avoiding a near miss with a landing jet. The plane barely avoids the road traffic but gets close enough for its massive engines to blast a cop car off its wheels. This effect was achieved by a combination of literally yanking back a real car by cable[169] and the use of digital and model effects including a toy car – purchased from Hamleys[170] – filled with salt to replicate broken glass spilling out.[171] The landing jet, background plates and extended surroundings of Miami airport were added digitally in post-production. Martin Campbell and second unit director Alexander Witt were keen to capture the look of an airport at night, as seen at the climax of the Michael Mann thriller, *Heat* (1995).[172]

Carlos aims to explosively sabotage the (fictional) Skyfleet prototype, the world's largest airliner. Although Peter Lamont met with aircraft manufacturers, he had to design an original plane. He remembered:

They keep their new models under wraps and probably wouldn't want to be associated with a storyline such as this so we had to come up with an original design. We could use the body of [an old 747 at the location] to save us the huge expense of building something of that bulk. The plane had no engines, but it was in fairly good condition. I looked at many references of airplane construction and decided our Skyfleet should look like the B-52, with pairs of tandem engines, and an altered cockpit profile. I don't know if my design would fly, but the B-52s managed![173]

The plane was also filmed as a miniature with background and human activity in the hangar being shot separately and added in digitally. Visual effects supervisor John Paul Docherty said, 'The cockpit reveal was a very conscious homage to *2001: A Space Odyssey* (1968).'[174]

The last three weeks of July 2006 were spent at Pinewood. An exterior, one-third scale model of the collapsing Venetian villa was shot on the Paddock Tank. The model was filmed at the same angle to the sun as the actual location for a more seamless match. The destruction was made realistic by the fact that the model was made of thousands of little bricks, which were then pneumatically released.[175]

The interiors were shot on the Albert R. Broccoli 007 Stage and proved to be among the most challenging on the film. Peter Lamont remembered:

> During the building process at Pinewood, the whole thing became more complicated, as the decision was taken that the house would not just sink vertically, but would need another axis to move the building from side to side as it sank. Chris Corbould and his special effects team built a fantastic rig for us.[176]

Chris Corbould recalled:

> The rig was massive – 90 tons, marrying together electronics and hydraulics. I was anxious to get really fast movement, to sell the fact that the house is sinking. The hydraulic valves were controlled by computer because there was so much movement in the system – it moved up and down and tilted through two axes. It would have been easy to bottom out on the tank or hit the roof, so we needed to have a lot of safety features.[177]

The rig could be immersed in 19ft of water. Corbould continued:

> I reckon I spent around eight hours a day in the water on that set, of which around two were spent under the water, just fixing problems. We had huge banks of compressors outside the tanks, pushing water up as the house falls down, so all of that had to be kept in working order. As shooting progressed, and the house sank, debris and dust started to fall into the water, so the visibility decreased and we ended up feeling our way around. There was definitely a learning curve. It was the biggest rig the crew and I have ever put together, and a complicated set as well. I remember when we started on the film and

they said, 'There will be no gadgets or gizmos,' and then they threw this one at us. But, in the end, I think the audience likes to see someone take a risk. Rather than watch what they know is a blue screen, they appreciate the feat of bravery and the effort that goes into the real thing. I think we are heading for a revival of special effects over visual effects.[178]

However, no special effects could match the dramatic events of 30 July 2006, when, in a case of history repeating, Pinewood's largest soundstage caught fire. Twenty-two years earlier, prior to the filming of *A View to a Kill*, an accidental blaze claimed the 007 Stage. Luckily filming had been completed on *Casino Royale*, sets were being dismantled and no one was hurt.[179]

David Arnold returned and to introduce a new 007 took an innovative approach with this score by withholding the use of Monty Norman's 'James Bond Theme':

My argument was he hadn't become James Bond yet so if we start playing it now in its entirety then we kind of get ahead of the film. Sony were concerned this was an intellectual exercise which an audience wouldn't understand. I went back and re-did a few cues where I thought it would be a legitimate point to start planting the seeds of the Bond theme; he wins the Aston Martin in a game of cards at the hotel; he puts the tuxedo on for the first time; those things which you kind of associate very much with Bond iconography.[180]

Campbell agreeed: 'At the end of the movie it sounds so much better because you haven't had it. It was like an orgasm.'[181] The orchestra even clapped when they finally got to play it in the scoring session.[182]

Chris Cornell performing a Bond theme song was the suggestion of Lia Vollack, head of music at Sony.[183] On 26 July 2006 it was announced that Chris Cornell had written, with David Arnold, the main title track, 'You Know My Name'.[184]

Arnold approved: 'You try and find someone that sounds like the character. Chris obviously had a voice that could kick a wall down, something that Daniel could physically do, so it felt like that was an interesting match.'[185] The composer wanted to create a more anthemic piece:

We were thinking about the idea of masculinity in music. Having been on the set and watched Daniel Craig, I always knew right from the start it should be much more of an aggressive piece. I think we've had enough of the kind of glorious velvet curtain, 'You're a dangerous stranger' kind of song. It needed to be something much more muscular, which made me start thinking about the idea of who in contemporary music is the vocal equivalent of that kind of man?[186]

Chris Cornell prepared by reading Ian Fleming's source novel and viewing a rough edit of the film.[187] Cornell was a huge Beatles fan: 'The song "Live and Let Die" had a big impact on me as a kid, as did Sean Connery's James Bond.'[188] However, Cornell was not limited by the past, 'The brief was to think outside the box, go do whatever you want.'[189] Cornell wanted his song to:

> live in the film. I ended up speaking with David Arnold for a long time. I loved the idea that if I came up with a melody that's in the first few minutes of the movie and that reverberates throughout the rest of the film. That's an impact on a film that people will see forever. Which led me to want to work with David.[190]

Title designer Daniel Kleinman was inspired by Ian Fleming's playing card design for the dust jacket of the first edition of the 1953 novel, 'I definitely looked back at that original cover – it was a really great cover – and the fact that he actually physically designed it, I thought that was great, I'll use that.'[191] Kleinman extrapolated the concept:

> The idea was based around the graphic nature of playing cards and roulette tables so it kind of felt logical. The patterns on money, I didn't want it to be too simplistic, but it also didn't feel right to have figuratively filmed people so it was a change. It's within the Bond language. It's still the kind of genre.[192]

Like the content of this Bond reboot, the titles had to forego some Bond staple ingredients. Kleinman recalled it was Martin Campbell's idea:

> not to have the girls in the titles sequence. He felt it wasn't appropriate to the story and I think he's absolutely right. He did have ideas, but he'd be so busy any input he had was just of a very general nature. He trusted me to get on with it.[193]

Casino Royale received its royal world charity premiere on Tuesday, 17 November 2006. The beneficiary was the Cinema and Television Benevolent

Fund (CTBF). The Bond film was shown simultaneously in all three major Leicester Square cinemas: the Odeon, the Odeon West End and the Empire. Daniel Craig had strong support, 'Pierce Brosnan and Sean Connery have both wished me well. But what matters most to me is if the public believe in this. It is great that the film critics are coming out for me in force, but hearing those cheers just now has touched me.'[194] The cast and crew would be presented to the patron of the charity, HRH Queen Elizabeth II.

Barbara Broccoli and Michael Wilson waited nervously to see how the world would respond to their radical overhaul. Broccoli pointed out that:

> There was a lot of controversy when Sean Connery was first decided upon because he was not what people were expecting and there's something really exciting about that. I think Daniel is the sort of actor who will always surprise people because he will find something that no one else could find in a role. He just absolutely got under the skin of the character and from the minute you see him on the screen in the role, you forget everyone who's come before, which is a pretty remarkable thing.[195]

Barbara had concerns not only about how Craig would be received, but also about the new positioning of Bond, 'The last four films have been suitable for little children. This film isn't … it's too tough for kids. That's been the biggest challenge preparing people for the fact that it is darker.'[196] Eon's gamble paid off spectacularly. With a final worldwide gross of $594 million and with all-time high US and UK grosses of $167 million and $105 million respectively, Bond showed an upward trend never before matched in franchise history.

Casino Royale garnered an unprecedented nine British Academy of Film and Television Arts (BAFTA) nominations. These included the Alexander Korda Award for the Outstanding British Film of the Year – Michael G. Wilson, Barbara Broccoli, Martin Campbell, Neal Purvis and Robert Wade with Paul Haggis; Best Adapted Screenplay – Neal Purvis and Robert Wade with Paul Haggis; Best Actor in a Leading Role – Daniel Craig; The Anthony Asquith Award for Achievement in Film Music – David Arnold; Best Cinematography – Phil Méheux BSC; Best Editing – Stuart Baird ACE; Best Production Design – Peter Lamont, Lee Sandales and Simon Wakefield; and Best Achievement in Special Visual Effects – Steve Begg, Chris Corbould, John Paul Docherty and Ditch Doy; Best Sound – Chris Munro, Eddy Joseph, Mike Prestwood Smith, Martin Cantwell and Mark

Taylor; and the Orange Rising Star Award – Eva Green. On 11 February 2007 the *Casino Royale* crew won the latter two awards and the James Bond franchise entered a new age.

Neal Purvis felt that Michael Wilson and Barbara Broccoli:

> want to stimulate themselves. Making the same film over and over is not what they want to do. They want to be challenged and so to put themselves outside of their comfort zone is exactly what they wanted and they also know in the grand scheme of things what *Casino Royale* meant in so many ways.[197]

SLICK TRIGGER FINGER

QUANTUM OF SOLACE

(2008)

Barbara Broccoli and Michael Wilson's creative gamble had paid off in spades. Sony Pictures' Amy Pascal was a fan, 'What we found is that you can strip away a lot of the bells and whistles, but it still feels uniquely like a Bond film. Throughout the story of the franchise, the actors, tone and style of the films have changed, but the fundamental essence of what makes Bond endures.'[1] Bond seemed to fit well at the new studio. Eon Productions received an upfront fee and the full budget costs of making the film.[2] The producers also had their usual gross points and had immense creative freedom.[3] Wilson described the relationship as 'collegial. We're all headed in the same direction. The idea that someone throws down the gauntlet – it never comes to that.'[4] Michael and Barbara proudly congratulated Amy Pascal and Michael Lynton of Sony Pictures for winning the *Variety* 2007 Showmen of the Year Award, 'We cannot think of two more deserving people.'[5] The studio was anxious to get another Bond underway – and quickly. Prior to *Casino Royale* even being completed, a release date for the follow-up was set: 2 May 2008.[6]

Broccoli stated the tough position they now found themselves in, 'The good news is *Casino Royale* did so fantastically well. The bad news is, "Oh my God, what do we do now?"'[7] Added Wilson, 'There was a sense that *Casino Royale* left Bond hanging in a really dark place. We needed to get past that.'[8] Barbara attempted to explain the state of Bond's mind, as they began to explore where to take him next:

Casino Royale was his coming of age. He started off as one thing – a soldier with a certain point of view. And through the course of that film, his emotional life took over and he was betrayed. And at the end, he let his guard down and so now he feels that he can never do that again. He shuts down entirely emotionally, or refuses to let any emotion out, and this film is about the conflict within him, his desire for revenge and his desire not to allow his emotions to take over his judgement.[9]

Casino Royale had always been envisaged as a two-part story. Wilson explained that 'there were so many unanswered questions at the end of *Casino Royale* and we think our audiences will be interested in the answers.'[10]

A screenplay had been in development prior to *Casino Royale* even going into production. In October 2005, at the press conference announcing Daniel Craig as James Bond, Michael Wilson had said, 'Purvis and Wade are also starting on the next Bond script.'[11] In October 2006 the producer reiterated, 'We've been working and exploring different ideas, and so far all those ideas are about continuing where this film left off.'[12]

Neal Purvis recollected, 'We wrote [the film] as a direct sequel to *Casino* and we were trying to do the same thing again. I don't know whether we were being perhaps too self-indulgent or too ambitious because we were allowed to do whatever we wanted in a sense.'[13] Robert Wade continued:

> Vesper had this boyfriend. In the novel CASINO ROYALE he'd been captured by the Russians and so she's being blackmailed in that way. Our big idea was the boyfriend who is being held in Algeria was never a prisoner. It was just blackmail. She's been ensnared. It gives Bond a target. Her life has been ruined and he goes after this guy.[14]

Wade outlined the initial story for *Bond 22*, 'Our version starts where the movie starts. Bond's got Mr. White in the boot of the car.'[15] Mr. White is handed over to the CIA for questioning. Bond, unbeknownst to Mr. White, allows him to escape, only to follow him and be led to White's ultimate employers. White goes to the Palio in Siena – a passion of his – knowing he is to be killed by his own organisation. Bond turns up and witnesses White duly being shot by his own outfit. Bond pursues the killer across the Palio, ending in a vertiginous rope fight where 007 kills the hitman. M reprimands Bond as a vital lead is now dead. The money that Mr. White had collected at the end of *Casino Royale* is being used by a new, mysterious organisation, Quantum, which is hiding in plain sight at OPEC. The villain, named Dante, is in league with the boyfriend of Vesper, Yusef Kabira. Bond infiltrates the organisation and takes on the next job of the assassin he killed in Siena: a woman in Libya who is trading trafficked antiquities that have been looted from Iraq.

Wade identified a key moment in their story: Bond captures and tortures Yusef over a prolonged period, extracting information from him but also out of rage for Vesper.[16] The writers sought gritty ruthlessness for these scenes and were influenced by the John Boorman film *Point Blank* (1967).[17] Bond goes rogue from both MI6 and the CIA.[18] Wade remembered various drafts resurrected Moneypenny, but also killed M.

Director Roger Michell, who most famously helmed *Notting Hill* as well as two independent dramas starring Daniel Craig, had read an early draft of *Casino Royale* but was unimpressed. A year later, in early 2006, he was asked by Barbara Broccoli to read the shooting script:

What I read was a really marvellous script. [Barbara said,] 'If you'd read that script, would you have said yes to directing *Casino Royale?*' and I said, 'Yes, I would.' So she said, 'Well why don't you do the next one?' This is 2006. They wanted a 007 film in 2007.[19]

Again, not keen on the story in development, Michell proposed an outline of his own and told Broccoli and Wilson, 'If you think it's got potential I'd like to bring on an American writer.'[20] *Ocean's Eleven* (2001) scribe Ted Griffin briefly collaborated on the project.[21] Michell wrote a ten-page outline which he thought was a really crisp sequel to *Casino Royale*. He felt his story went:

… through the hymn sheet of a Bond film. It was a multi-city quest – Bombay, Berlin, Istanbul – with a great bad guy who had figured out a way to bring the internet down. Planes would have fallen out of the sky, nuclear reactors would have stopped reacting and the world would have gone into meltdown. It started off with Bond drunk, driving through Rome with somebody in his boot. I typed this up and presented it to the Brocs. I could see it wasn't overwhelming them.[22]

Michell visited the set of *Casino Royale* at Pinewood and discussed the sequel with Martin Campbell, 'We spent a long evening having dinner together where he was really, really useful and gave me the heads up about how the whole thing works. He couldn't have been a better predecessor.'[23]

Michell remembered the speed of events:

I drove to Pinewood and I couldn't find anywhere to park. Eventually, miles away I found a scruffy little gap. Then I walked to the Bond offices and there was a parking space with my name hand painted on a bloody sign. This is unofficially my first day on the project. Barbara said, 'I know this might seem a little odd but would you mind taking a meeting now with the people who are designing a video game of the next film. So I sat down and went through the motions with these very enthusiastic young Americans who are about to start designing a video game for a film that hasn't yet been scripted.[24]

Michell was out of his comfort zone, 'We just started running out of road. I started to realise that we were going to have to start to go into prep on this film without a script. And I suddenly started to absolutely see a world of pain ahead for me as a director.'[25] Robert Wade remembered, 'I think he got really nervous about it. He himself said the biggest action sequence he'd filmed prior to any of that was when in something he did a book falls off a table.'[26]

Michell made a difficult decision, 'I went into the office [and said], "I'm terribly sorry I'm not going to do this." I hadn't signed a contract, I wasn't breaking any deals, but everybody's expectation was that I was going to do it.'[27]

Upon Michell's departure, the film was delayed to a November 2008 release.[28] The director was rueful, 'If they'd said to me, don't panic, we'll wait until we've got a decent script then I would have stayed on it.'[29]

In the Purvis and Wade draft, the coda took place at the floating stage of the Bregenz opera, where Quantum are using earpieces and hiding in plain sight to have secret meetings within meetings. Bond catches up with Dante, only to find he has already been killed by Quantum, leaving Bond to chase further up the Quantum hierarchy.[30] Purvis remembered a symbolic ending with Bond walking in front of a giant eye 'and he's just a silhouette again.'[31]

Purvis and Wade delivered a draft in May 2007.[32] Wade was positive, 'They were really excited about it and we started working with Roger Michell very quickly.'[33] Michell's departure meant a director was sought who would also help develop the screenplay.

Casino Royale screenwriter Paul Haggis recalled, 'I had a lunch with Amy [Pascal] in which she asked if I would ever direct a Bond film. I said, "I don't think so." But I was never approached to direct it.'[34] After Michell left the project, experienced adventure helmer Tony Scott, and up-and-coming action directors Jonathan Mostow (*Terminator 3: Rise of the Machines*, 2003) and Alex Proyas (*I, Robot*, 2004) were mentioned.[35] However, one name stood out from the pack: Marc Forster.

Forster, a Schweizer-Deutsch director who had studied in New York, had made a name as a highbrow director of quality but quirky productions, including *Stranger Than Fiction* (2006) and *The Kite Runner* (2007). Robert Wade remembered meeting the director at a birthday dinner Halle Berry had thrown during *Die Another Day*.[36] Marc Forster had directed Berry's Oscar-winning performance in *Monster's Ball* (2001). Forster remembered:

I met Barbara briefly at that dinner while I was shooting *Finding Neverland* and they were shooting with Halle on *Die Another Day* in London. Instantly, I felt incredibly welcomed and got such warmth from [Barbara], even though I was the only one present who was not working on her film. I didn't see her for a few years after that until I got a call from my agent to see if I wanted to meet with her and Michael Wilson to chat.[37]

But Forster had no interest in directing a Bond picture, 'I really didn't see any upsides. I was at a place in my career that I felt, within the $20–$40 million range, I could do any film I wanted and with complete creative control.'[38] Studio chief Amy Pascal had worked with Forster on the offbeat comedy *Stranger Than Fiction* and coaxed him to meet Eon.[39]

Forster had read a couple of Fleming novels, CASINO ROYALE and FROM RUSSIA WITH LOVE, 'James Bond's mother is Swiss,'[40] he pointed out with enthusiasm. However, he had not been brought up on the Bond films and admitted to only catching up with classics such as *Dr. No*, *From Russia With Love* and *Goldfinger* as part of his own film education.[41] Forster was surprised when he was offered the job and had 'to think hard about whether I wanted to do it. I'm not sure I could have found a way into Bond before Daniel Craig reinvented him.'[42] When he mentioned the prospect to his frequent editor, Matt Chesse, and cinematographer, Roberto Schaefer, he said Barbara Broccoli had told him, 'You know you're the first non-Commonwealth director, the youngest on top of it.'[43] Forster, who had shown flair for handling British subjects in *Finding Neverland*, felt, 'Ultimately, nationality doesn't matter.'[44]

Forster was intrigued by Bond's motivation, 'It's the first time you really see this character in a truly vulnerable, almost fragile place. He has lost probably the only woman he has ever truly cared about and it broke him. He feels betrayed and angry, and is motivated by revenge, which is such a precarious motivation.'[45] He wanted to develop the initial Purvis and Wade draft, 'the themes in the original script didn't really speak to me,'[46] and he brought back Paul Haggis to develop the story. Haggis was reluctant this time, 'I remember getting the call and I was in Los Angeles and they said, "Would you like to do the sequel?" I said, "No." I don't think I can do a better job than *Casino Royale*. But they were insistent and they offered me a lovely deal.'[47]

Marc Forster 'was always interested in the concept of water and natural resources.'[48] Haggis did 'some research. In fact, I think it's the Bush family who own quite a bit of land in Bolivia and, or so it's rumoured, it happens to be on top one of the great aquifers where there's a huge resource of underground water.'[49] Haggis took inspiration from the Bechtel water scandal in Bolivia where water was privatised with disastrous results. Barbara Broccoli liked the idea, 'Although these are not political films, we like to get the atmosphere of the world situation … a relevant and more realistic story.'[50] Haggis injected some of his own personal political views, 'my natural sentiments about the American government [is] whenever they truly get involved in something it's often for corporate reasons, so that came from my years of demonstrating against various actions – American foreign policy around the world.'[51] Forster felt, 'It's important even if you make a commercial film to personalise it.'[52] He underlined the message in the piece, 'There is something incredibly poignant about leaving a man in the desert with a can of oil. I loved the metaphor of the scene, the desert, the oil. No matter how much you fight for it and sacrifice for it, oil will never be able to keep you alive.'[53]

Haggis suggested a startling ending which the filmmakers rejected:

What Bond wants to know when he's interrogating [Greene is], 'Where is she?' He gives him the information he wants, which is strictly personal. We find Bond in Albania at an old Soviet-type orphanage. It's run by a religious order and he goes back there and he finds that there's a child and he takes the money and he hands it over to the nuns. 'Take care of her', and walks away, realising Vesper had betrayed him because there was a child. She had a child with this man she was in love with. We know that she was in love and this man betrayed her in *Casino Royale*. But then I thought that was not a strong enough reason to betray Bond. If there was a child involved that they'd taken from her and were holding, then that's a compelling reason to betray someone. We expect Bond to come and keep the child but he doesn't. Bond realises he's just trying to give this child the best life he possibly can and walks away. And that's where M meets him, out front, afterwards, in Albania when he's walking away from the orphanage.[54]

Haggis had a title for the film, *Sleep of the Dead*:

because that's what it was all about – allowing the dead to sleep. And in the case of [the heroine, Camille] she's trying to avenge a situation. Bond, too, is completely driven by the dead, figuring Vesper couldn't sleep until she knew that everything was fine with the child. So it was *Sleep of the Dead* that I had. *Quantum of Solace* was a title that Barbara chose later.[55]

Haggis 'did two drafts and a couple of polishes and then it was right down to the deadline. It was a week before and the writers' strike was going to go.'[56] The 2007–08 Writers Guild of America strike slowed down feature film and television development in Hollywood, when it disallowed all 12,000 Guild members to work following a dispute with the larger studios in a bid to secure increased funds for writers. Marc Forster felt the dispute impacted the movie, 'We were headed in an interesting direction but, unfortunately, because of the writers' strike, Paul and I were never able to actually complete it. That then led us into shooting only a partially completed script, one that would have needed more time and development.'[57] An uncredited rewrite was performed by Joshua Zetumer but in the end it came down to Daniel Craig thrashing it out with Foster, who remarked. 'There was a very intense relationship between us while we were doing that.'[58] Daniel Craig remembered it rather more dramatically:

> We were fucked. We had the bare bones of a script. Me and the director were the ones allowed to [rewrite it]. The rules were that you couldn't employ anyone as a writer, but the actor and director could work on scenes together. I say to myself, 'Never again,' but who knows? There was me trying to rewrite scenes – and a writer I am not.[59]

QUANTUM OF SOLACE was a short story first published in the US edition of *Cosmopolitan* magazine in May 1959.[60] It subsequently appeared in the FOR YOUR EYES ONLY anthology, published a year later. The tale unfolds as Bond listens to the governor in Nassau telling a torrid story of colonial marriage gone wrong and is introduced to the theory of the quantum of solace: the amount of comfort in any relationship that makes it worth continuing. In the words of Michael Wilson, 'It's uncharacteristic of most of Fleming's work. It's a character study that doesn't involve any plots or anything with spies, but we thought it was an intriguing title and referenced what's happened to Bond and what happens to Bond in this film.'[61]

The pre-title sequence of *Quantum of Solace* begins directly where *Casino Royale* ended. Bond drives a maimed Mr. White in his Aston Martin to a safe house in Siena, Italy. Unknown forces try to apprehend Bond in a car chase by a lake in Northern Italy and through the quarries of Carrara. Deep in the Siena safe house, Mr. White is to be questioned, when suddenly, an MI6 operative, Craig Mitchell, turns traitor and effects White's escape. Bond gives chase through the Palio but ends up killing the turncoat. Back at MI6 headquarters, analysis of marked funds laundered by Le Chiffre lead Bond to Haiti. Bond infiltrates the organisation as an assassin, Mr. Edmund Slate, who is set to kill Camille Montes. She has been tracking a brutal Bolivian, General Medrano, who appears to be in league with Dominic Greene, head of Greene Planet, ostensibly an environmental protection organisation. Greene is fronting a private organisation that is planning a coup in the region, the first of many. Greene is keeping the CIA's South American station chief, Greg Beam, notified. America will turn a blind eye to the coup, provided it is granted oil rights under the new regime. Bond follows Greene to the floating opera at Bregenz, Austria where he insinuates himself into a meeting of Quantum (a sinister organisation with tentacles in governments worldwide) – randomly seated in the audience, connected by earpieces. Bond ascertains that Quantum's most important operation is the Tiera Project, which seeks to control the world's most precious resource. Bond is chased by Greene's men but escapes, not before being framed for killing the bodyguard of senior British politician, Guy Haines. As a result, 007 is disavowed by M.

In Italy, Bond meets up with René Mathis, who after being falsely accused of treachery in *Casino Royale*, has been compensated with a beautiful villa. Persuading Mathis to help him investigate Quantum, they fly to Bolivia and meet local agent, Strawberry Fields. After meeting with Camille again, Bond realises they are both seeking revenge: she for her family's death at the hands of Medrano, he for those who forced Vesper to betray him. Bond uncovers a conspiracy involving the toppling of the Bolivian government and the domino effect of Quantum's influence in South America by controlling its natural resources. Quantum, with the aid of sexed-up CIA dossiers and a poodle-like British Government, will inadvertently impose the exiled dictator General Medrano upon the people for the promise of oil, which they have been deliberately led to believe exists as a result of the deep mining project, Tiera. Bond is framed for Mathis's death by corrupt Bolivian police who, dying, reveals he was working undercover under a false name.

Searching for the signs of project Tiera, Bond and Camille reconnoitre the area by plane but are attacked by local fighters. Forced to parachute into a sinkhole, they discover what Quantum is up to: they have not discovered oil, they have discovered water and are creating a series of underground dams to cause an artificial drought. Bond returns to his hotel to discover Fields has been symbolically drowned in crude oil: another piece of misdirection. M is under pressure to assist the CIA but allows 007 to follow his hunch. Greg Beam issues a capture-or-kill order against Bond who, tipped off by Felix Leiter, escapes and follows Greene to the hotel La Perla de las Dunas, where he discovers the setting for the deal between General Medrano and Quantum – a facility in the Atacama Desert. Bond and Camille raid the complex, which is destroyed by fire. Camille finally gains vengeance for her family by killing Medrano. Greene is dragged into the desert by Bond where he divulges information about Quantum. 007 leaves Greene with just a can of motor oil to drink. Bond and Camille part in Bolivia where she, having killed Modrano, has finally achieved her quantum of solace. Bond then tracks Vesper's treacherous lover, Yusef Kabira, to Russia. Kabira is attempting to ensnare a Canadian agent, but Bond intervenes. However, instead of killing him, 007 allows M and MI6 to take over questioning of the Quantum agent. Having learnt to look for the bigger picture, and by finally allowing the ghost of Vesper to rest, he too achieves his quantum of solace. Bond is welcomed back to the Service.

Forster's original ending, which he filmed but discarded, was Bond coming back to assassinate Mr. White:

> Ultimately, it wasn't necessary to the story. I didn't feel it served the story to bookend it with Mr. White in the car trunk and then again being assassinated. Also keeping Mr. White alive, not having Bond shoot him, keeps the mystery of the organisation alive and I felt that was more interesting than tying up every loose end.[62]

In his second appearance as James Bond, Craig was keen the film had the same impact as his debut, 'We have got expectation on us now which can be double-edged. People always talked about the fact *Casino Royale* was a departure for Bond and this has to be a departure again.'[63] Craig wanted his Bond pictures to stand the test of time, 'It's important that we make the best movies possible, so I can hopefully sit back in semi-retirement at some point and look back and think they were wonderful movies.'[64] Again, the part required intense physical fitness, 'Bond used to do ten press-ups and smoke fifty cigarettes and drink a bottle of something and pop a pill. So it doesn't sound very Bond-like to talk about fitness regimes.'[65] Forster was inspired by the actor, 'Once I met Daniel, I wanted to do the film. I felt he had the same goal, that we both felt like working together, making personalised stories about the character.'[66]

Noted French actor, Mathieu Amalric, was hired to play Dominic Greene. He sought advice from his predecessors, 'I talked with Max von Sydow, who was in *The Diving Bell and the Butterfly* (2007), and who was a villain in a James Bond film. And in *Munich* I played opposite Michael Lonsdale, who was also a villain.'[67] Worried about the impact a Bond film would have on his art house career, Lonsdale advised him, 'the pleasure is to be where you're not supposed to be.'[68] Forster had noticed Amalric in *The Diving Bell and the Butterfly* and *Heartbeat Detector* (2007), 'In the old Bond films, it was clear who were the good guys and who were the bad guys. Today, it's not so clear. I feel like Mathieu looks so sympathetic and normal, the type you can't see right away is the villain.'[69] Amalric took inspiration from reality, 'Greene has the smile of Blair and the craziness of Sarkozy.'[70] Amalric was surprised by the freedom afforded him, 'There's no storyboard so things can change [during] rehearsals or we bring things. I have never been to [drama] school. I never learned to be an actor.'[71]

Olga Kurylenko played Bolivian Secret Service agent, Camille Montes. Kurylenko remembered how she got the part, 'First I went for general casting in Paris, then I got invited for an audition in London, then I did the final audition with Daniel [Craig].'[72] She discovered she had won the role on Christmas Eve, 'It was the best Christmas present.'[73] The Russian actress worked non-stop with a dialogue coach because she was to speak with a Bolivian accent.[74] Forster saw Montes as:

> … the mirror image to Bond. They aren't capable of connecting with another human by opening their heart to them. Because of that, they see through each other and are unable to physically be with one another. In regards to not over explaining everything, I find it's much more interesting for the audience to draw their own conclusions. Whatever you come up with in your own brain is going to be more compelling to you. It's better when there are some loose ends.[75]

British actress Gemma Arterton played the ill-fated Agent Fields whose first name, Strawberry – a tip to the famous Beatles song and area in Liverpool – is only revealed in the 'concrete poetry'[76] of Pauline Hume's end credits. Arterton recalled she went 'to two auditions. I was in a play at the Globe in London and the casting directors came to see me in it. They asked me in for an audition. Then I got a second audition where I met the director and everyone, then I had a screentest which was petrifying.'[77] Arterton remembered the test:

> I had to do a scene from this Bond. I hadn't read the script so I didn't know anything about anything. You go in and have all your hair and make-up done, and I was so scared. They make you look as great as they can and then you go on set and there were literally about sixty people looking at you and thinking, 'Could she be a Bond girl?'[78]

Arterton was filming in Gibraltar when she heard she had the part:

I got a phone call from my agent singing the 'James Bond Theme' tune down the phone. I'll never forget it, my colleague turned to me with tears in his eyes and said, 'This is such a big moment in your life, your life has just changed forever and I was here to see it happen.' Thinking about it now, on the way to my audition, 'Nobody Does It Better' was playing on my car radio so I think it was meant to be.[79]

Giancarlo Giannini reprised his role as René Mathis, 'Compared to Martin Campbell who specialises in action scenes, Marc Forster is different. He works a lot with an actor's ability to act. We talk a lot. He knows my films well.'[80] Forster felt the scenes between Bond and Mathis were pivotal to the film:

[There is a dynamic] between the two of them and their emotions. I think Bond is a mystery. There is this hard shell and Bond is not someone who talks about his emotional state – because he shouldn't. You don't want Bond to say these things. What's much more interesting is his reactions and actions towards other people.[81]

Judi Dench returned as M but she did not take the role for granted:

Every one of them, and this is the sixth I've done, have been very, very different. It's just that I get more to do in this one, which is terrific. I'm just as frightened as I was with all the others! But, I've learned to use a few more gadgets and look like I'm running MI6, I hope.[82]

Dench felt M was a complex character:

In all of us, there are things that are admirable and things that are reprehensible. If you are going to make up a person to be as real as you can possibly make them, then they must be made up of both of those sides of a character. I don't know whether I'd have her over for dinner. It would depend on whom else she was with![83]

Forster saw the M/Bond relationship in unique terms:

Ultimately this is a mother/son relationship. One that needs to be rebuilt – not because of something that M did necessarily, but because he is so

broken because of [Vesper] his trust for the sex is gone. He is shut down.
I wanted to juxtapose that with the need to be loved, which is something
I think every human experiences. We all want to be loved and known – and
if that is ripped away from you, you can become a shadow or a shell of a
person. Bond is a shadow when we meet him in this story. I think psychologically it is interesting because M is an older woman and an authority
figure. How do you trust someone who is in charge of you when you
feel they will betray you or leave you at any moment? He learns to trust
again and ultimately finds his way back through her guidance. A beautiful
moment is when M says to him at the end, 'I need you back' and he replies,
casually and in true Bond fashion, 'I never left.'[84]

Purvis and Wade had originally intended Vesper Lynd to reappear in the film.
They had Bond 'imagining her, seeing her, he's haunted by her in our version.
And also I think there were some flashbacks as to how she got caught up in it
all.'[85] At the release of *Casino Royale*, Barbara Broccoli had hinted to Eva Green
about a possible reappearance, 'She explained to me some things about the
Algerian boyfriend. Vesper's just naïve and she thought she was in love with
him, but then she meets Bond and it's really, real, real love.'[86] Ultimately, Eva
Green spent a day on the production for the photograph of her with Yusef
Kabira, played by Simon Kassianides, to be taken.

Appearing for the first time was Rory Kinnear as Tanner, while Jeffrey Wright
returned as Felix Leiter, as did Jesper Christensen, who again played Mr. White,
now revealed to be working for the villainous organisation Quantum. David
Harbour played the oily CIA station chief, Gregg Beam, and Joaquín Cosío
played General Medrano. Neil Jackson played bogus geologist Mr. Edmund
Slate, Lucrezia Lante della Rovere was feisty as Mathis' girlfriend, Gemma and
Stana Katic briefly appeared as Kabira's next target, Canadian intelligence agent
Corinne. Charlie Chaplin's granddaughter, Oona, played a hotel receptionist,
Tim Pigott-Smith played an ethically slumbering British Foreign Secretary
while the voice talents of directors Alfonse Cuaron (a one-time potential Bond
helmer) and Guillermo del Toro were used for the dogfight sequence.

Marc Forster brought some changes to the Bond production team. He
explained:

I believe very much in that family structure. In my own movies I have my
own family and when I accepted this, I said to Barbara and Michael, 'I have
to bring my own family along, you have your family, but I have to bring my

own because that's the way I work best and I need that to support me and to work in the most efficient way.[87]

Forster brought in a new production designer, Dennis Gassner who had won an Oscar for *Bugsy* (1991). A Coen Brothers alumus, Forster was inspired by Gassner's work, 'He has such a good sense of design and style that I felt would match the earlier Bond movies done by Ken Adam. He had the same spirit.'[88] Gassner similarly felt Forster was:

a kindred spirit. I go with my instincts on every aspect of how I design films, it's all emotional response to things. I viewed the film as a blank canvas. I was asking Marc for something to hold on to, we needed to find something, a touchstone. When it occurred to me, it was so obvious, it was Daniel. He is our James Bond ... that great face; it is angular and chiselled, he has great textures to his face and, of course, his piercing blue eyes. From that moment we started to create the language and it built up from there.[89]

Forster also brought in his long-term director of photography Roberto Schaefer and editor Matt Chesse (working here with Richard Pearson). Schaefer said they persuaded Forster to take the film, 'When Marc told me he had been offered this movie, my response was, "How could you not do a Bond film?" I told him that to be part of a Bond film is every boy's dream. Our editor, Matt Chesse, said exactly the same thing.'[90] Schaefer liked working with Gassner:

Dennis is really collaborative, maybe more so than anyone I've ever worked with. So often on films, there are incredible sets, but [shots] end up being fairly close and you don't really see them. When I see beautiful architecture, I want to show it off; without being gratuitous, I like to find a way to work good sets into a film.[91]

Also new to both the Bond and Forster families was George Clooney and Steven Soderbergh's then preferred costume designer Louise Frogley:

I wanted something that was beautiful and elegant that would remind us of the type of suit Sean Connery wore in the early Bond films. I wanted to use "mohair tonic" for the suits. It is a very strange material but it films beautifully, it's just lovely. Not only did we want a very rare material but we needed a huge quantity because we had to make so many suits. Tom Ford found it for us.[92]

Ford gave Bond a new look:

> These suits don't have belts, they have side adjusters and they are higher on the waist, the trousers are narrow and there are no pleats. The jackets are single-breasted, two-buttoned with a narrow lapel and as narrow a shoulder as possible for a man that is as muscular as Daniel. They give a lovely silhouette.[93]

Forster brought the style of Jason Bourne to James Bond by hiring that series' innovative second unit director Dan Bradley. Craig addressed the competition:

> I don't think it's like Bourne at all. Dan's here to do exactly what he's good at doing. He's just come off *Indiana Jones* – are we going to be more like *Indiana Jones?* We're applying Dan's talents to the movie. Sorry to be political about it, but I'm certainly not getting into a pissing competition with the Bourne fans.[94]

Bradley likes to script his own action sequences:

> So the first thing I asked Marc is if he minded me taking a pass at the action in the script. Fortunately, he really liked what I dreamt up. Through this process we quickly found we were on the same page concerning the action in the film.[95]

Early material of the Palio horse race in Siena, Italy was filmed by a splinter unit in August 2007.[96] The world-famous Palio festival, featuring the medieval horse race, was filmed by fourteen cameras set up at strategic points of the race. The filmmakers were under an obligation to adhere to strict conditions and treat the event with full respect.[97] The idea to feature the race had been discussed much earlier, during the production of *Casino Royale*. Prospective director Roger Michell had attended the Palio with Neal Purvis and Robert Wade in 2006. It was one of the few times the writers attended a location scout and Wade described it as 'everything that a Bond recce should be.'[98] Executive producer Anthony Waye recalled shooting the Palio was a logistical nightmare:

> In the original [screenplay] Bond got in the race [on a horse] but [the authorities] wouldn't allow that and we couldn't have recreated it. One of

the trickiest things was to meet the management committee. Some of them were very loath to [allow filming]. I don't know whether they felt they were cheapening the event by allowing it in a film. They agreed in the end but we had some fairly hefty meetings with that mob.'[99]

Principal photography began at Pinewood Studios on 3 January 2008. Fourteen different sets were built on five sound stages during January including the art gallery rope fight and the new hi-tech MI6 headquarters. Gassner designed and built a state-of-the-art Secret Service nerve centre full of light and glass:

> I pushed the notion to modernise MI6. The feeling I had with *Casino* was that Judi was at a place that was a bridge between the older M's world and Bond's world and I wanted to get her up to speed, I wanted her on a computer. Her voice is the signature of MI6, her voice is the ultimate command. I decided she should have a smart wall and her voice should activate anything she needs to command and control her world.[100]

Gassner also built the interior of the Andean Grand Hotel where Agent Fields would be suffocated in oil in homage to Jill Masterson in *Goldfinger*. Gemma Arterton found the scene uncomfortable, 'I couldn't move, I couldn't see, I couldn't breathe or hear because the oil went into my ears. It was unpleasant, but it's something I'll always remember and it will be an iconic part of the film.'[101]

Filming also took place at Bruneval Barracks, Montgomery Lines in Aldershot to replicate the Russian sequence at the finale of the film where 007 tracks down Yusef, the Algerian Quantum agent who ensnared Vesper. The Sculpture Garden in the Barbican Centre in the City of London played host to the new exterior of the MI6 building.[102] Commented Craig, 'It's one of those very special London places. There was some opposition to us shooting there but it works. We don't have "London, England" at the bottom of the screen, but it's still obviously London – probably because it's pissing with rain.'[103]

Bodyflight, the UK's first and world's largest skydiving wind tunnel in Bedford, was used by the visual effects department to film James Bond and Camille during their freefall from the DC-3 plane in Bolivia.[104] Daniel Craig and Olga Kurylenko trained with Gary Powell and his stunt team for several weeks before filming at the site for one day. The scene where Mathis tries to ease Bond's pain on a plane to Bolivia, still hurting after a flotilla of Vesper martinis, was shot at a mock-up lounge built at 'The Base', Virgin Atlantic's newest state-of-the-art training facility near Crawley.[105]

The Reform Club in Pall Mall, London was used as the government building where the foreign secretary reprimands M. In 2002, Eon had used the same location in *Die Another Day*, in which it had doubled, in part, for the interior of Blades.[106]

In early February 2008 shooting moved to Panama City. Forster highlighted the importance of the locations, 'We were working with a script that wasn't completely developed, and in light of that I felt I needed to supplement the story with visuals and subtext in order to really drive the action. All of these locations lend themselves as characters and props throughout.'[107] *Quantum of Solace* had many locations and Forster saw this as an opportunity:

> Each of the locations comes with it's own challenges and difficulties, but also it's own gold mine of possibility. Ultimately, because the [Eon] team is so well versed in making movies in every country all over the world for decades, it feels more secure. The rooftops in Italy for the opening sequence become magnificent tools and weapons in the first chase scene and fight sequence. The desert in Chile, where Bond leaves Mr. Greene, is its own character – ultimately Mr. Greene's executioner.[108]

The Inac Building in the Old Town, Casco Viejo, doubled for the Andean Grand Hotel, where Bond chooses to blow his supposed lottery winnings. The art department gave the impressive building (usually the government's working offices of the Instituto Nacional de Cultural – Institute of Culture) a full makeover with new awnings, polished floors and a full paint job inside and out. The locals were very helpful as 700 Panamanian extras were engaged and the local officials 'offered full cooperation, helping to manage traffic, isolate the area of cars and people'.[109] Barbara Broccoli recalled:

> They don't have a big film infrastructure in [Panama] so there were a lot of challenges to make it possible to shoot. But the community there were very helpful to us – we had to displace quite a few people for a period of time and they were very co-operative with us.[110]

Michael Wilson was pleasantly surprised, 'We expected Colón to be more difficult than it was. It was logistically difficult but the filming went very smoothly considering we were in a part of the world that is a little remote.'[111] A third action unit joined the main unit in Colón to shoot a boat chase, supposedly in Haiti, where Bond rescues Camille from the clutches of General Medrano.

Meanwhile, during January and February 2008[112] in Mexico, a crew of sixty-six, led by second unit director Dan Bradley, filmed for seventeen days from a small airport near the town of San Felipe. In the sequence, Bond flies a vintage 1939 DC-3 plane and is attacked by an acrobatic Marchetti armed with machine guns and a Huey helicopter. For environmental and safety reasons no practical effects could be filmed on location, so all gunfire and smoke was added later as a visual effect. Two ground camera crews covered the action from the mountains. The locations were so remote that the crew and equipment had to be ferried there by helicopter each day.[113]

On 24 March 2008 Daniel Craig flew by private jet to the Chilean city of Antofagasta.[114] The barren open landscapes of northern Chile were to double for water-starved Bolivia. The crew travelled for up to two hours each morning to reach the ESO Paranal (the European Organization for Astronomical Research in the Southern Hemisphere) used to shoot the exterior scenes set at La Perla de las Dunas. Set at an altitude of 6,000ft, the observatory is built into the crest of a mountain bordering the southern extremity of the Atacama Desert and provides astronomers with an environment remote of any dust or light sources – a perfect atmosphere for studying the stars. The hotel is usually occupied by no more than twenty astronomers. ESO welcomed the 300-strong crew as Bond and Camille raced across the roof of the building in pursuit of their nemeses.[115] This was production designer Dennis Gassner's favourite:

> It is the furthest location we travelled to and it came to me in a very serendipitous fashion. We were looking for deserts in the world and the Atacama came up in conversation, so I went online. The first web page on the Atacama had a very, very small photograph of the ESO hotel and it just jumped right out at me. I was here in London, Marc was in LA at his computer and within five minutes he called and said, 'We have it, this is it!'[116]

On 1 April 2008 a fracas was caused in this last location by the ire of one Carlos Lopez, the suspended mayor of Sierra Gorda, who disapproved of Chile being used to duplicate Bolivia and tried to disrupt the set. Marketing director for Eon Productions, Anne Bennett commented, it was 'a small incident that took no more than five minutes to clear up.'[117] April fool, indeed! Filming concluded in Chile in the Atacama Desert on 3 April.[118]

Production then returned to Siena to shoot the rooftop chase to intercut with the Palio sequence. When Eon had filmed the colourful footage of the horse race a year earlier, Forster was unsure how the sequence would work.

Then he discovered the city's underground Roman tunnels and cisterns, so he formulated the idea of intercutting the foot chase through the sewers and rooftops of the city with the Palio.[119] Action director Dan Bradley was impressed with the way Craig threw himself into the action, 'There were several leaps across streets and alleyways from four- or five-storey rooftops and Daniel did them all. He even jumped out of a window and dropped 20ft toward the roof of a speeding bus.'[120] An initial idea of filming inside the Duomo di Siena cathedral was nixed because it was deemed the scene would be disrespectful to the sacred monument. As an alternative, Bond emerged from the *bottini* (the network of tangled underground tunnels) at the fountain of Piazza del Campo during the Palio di Siena.

From April to May 2008 the action continued at Lake Garda in Northern Italy, shooting the pre-title Aston Martin versus Alfa Romeo car chase. It was shot on a number of locations including the Gardesana, a famous and beautiful road around the lake between Limone and Tremosine, and the 2,000-year-old Canalgrande and Fantiscritti marble quarries, as well as the Miseglia tunnel. Seven Aston Martin DBSs were used for the short sequence.[121] Anthony Waye recalled it was a logistical nightmare:

> We were closing off the roads and tunnels for twelve hours a day and only re-opening for an hour during lunch. As these were the only available access routes to the small towns and villages, we had to work with the local police and council and make sure our plans for each day were publicised so people knew when to travel. We laid on a boat that would take people and school children from one village to another.[122]

Bradley explained:

> I love the bit where Bond loses the driver's door of the Aston Martin. I have never before seen that in a car chase. In the middle of the chase, Bond's door is ripped off, now it's like, every car that comes past him, every shot that is fired at him, the potential for Bond's demise withers from every moment. I love that, I love what it gives us in terms of storytelling and the threat to Bond.[123]

The chase climaxed with Bond careering through the marble quarry in Carrara. Stunt co-ordinator Gary Powell remembered, 'There's lots of skidding around hairpin bends, stuff the Astons aren't really designed to do. There are foot-deep potholes all over the place, and we smashed the car to pieces. Daniel Craig spent ages training on the *Top Gear* track.'[124] Waye described Carrara as spectacular but very dangerous: 'We were originally going to shoot part of the sequence inside the mountains where, from years of extracting large blocks of marble, giant caves had been created.'[125]

Capturing on film such dangerous stunt sequences, performed for real, was not achieved without incident. On 19 April 2008 an Aston Martin engineer, Fraser Dunn, lost control of one of the DBS cars as he was delivering it to a press event and it went spinning into Lake Garda. More seriously, on 23 April an accident occurred at Limone sul Garda near Brescia, hospitalising Greek stuntman Aris Comninos, who sustained critical injuries. Another stunt driver, Italian Bruno Verdirosi, suffered minor injuries.[126] Naturally, such serious accidents affected the whole team. Barbara Broccoli later commented:

> The nature of what we do is challenging and dangerous and so obviously we hire the most expert people and we rehearse and we do everything we can to make it as safe as possible and we have all the safety measures put in place in the event that something goes wrong and unfortunately something did go wrong. It is like a family and when one of your team gets hurt, we all feel it deeply and it was very, very distressing.[127]

In late April the unit commenced two weeks of night shoots at the Bregenz Festival House in Austria, where James Bond eavesdrops on Quantum. The floating stage wih a striking set in the form of a giant eye was built for the 2007/8 production of Puccini's *Tosca*. It is here Bond infiltrates Quantum's meeting in plain sight and then evades capture in a scene artfully intercut with scenes from the opera. Over 1,000 extras were dressed in black tie and evening dress to fill part of the massive amphitheatre.[128]

Finally the team returned to Pinewood in May 2008. The backlot was utilised to build the exterior of La Perla de las Dunas while the interior of the desert hotel was built on the recently rebuilt Albert R. Broccoli 007 Stage. The faciltiy had burned down a second time on 30 June 2006, just after *Casino Royale* had finished filming. The sound stage was fitted with over fifty explosives to film Bond's violent confrontation with Greene.[129] As usual, the Bond film ended with a bang. Filming was completed by the end of June 2008.

Michael Wilson was happy, 'We finished on time, 103 days, which is fantastic. Which is short actually, it's usually 109 and more. But this time it was 103 and it didn't go over. Second unit had weather problems and different things, but it was good.'[130]

Editors Matt Chesse and Richard Pearson had five or six weeks to edit the whole film. Forster felt this was too little time:

Normally, I've had fourteen weeks for any of my films so far. Six weeks for this film is crazy. I wish we would have more time to craft the film properly. For instance, with *The Dark Knight*, Christopher Nolan had a year to cut his movie, to work on the visual effects, to reflect. I don't have that time and so compromises have to be made.[131]

Although a lot of key Bond personnel had been replaced, David Arnold remained. Forster felt, 'He is such a talented musician. I wanted to just do slight variations on the original score – to keep the traditional ideas alive with a little bit of an updated spin.'[132] Arnold recalled the assignment:

It was a much shorter film with much less music, quite different in a lot of ways. What was unusual was that Marc Forster sent me cut sequences – actually assembled sequences – of characters. He sent me Greene – Mathieu Amalric's character – so I could write something that felt like it belonged to him. He sent me stuff about the actual organisation – about Quantum – so I was able to write a sort of Quantum theme, which became 'Night at the Opera'. So it was interesting coming up with music away from the movie which I probably wouldn't have done before.[133]

Arnold had originally begun work on a title song with Mark Ronson and Amy Winehouse:

I'd sketched out an idea musically, but I didn't want to do a lyric because I thought [Amy's] got to sing it so it would be a good idea for her to write it. She had notes and bits and pieces. Mark actually put together a rough track with a couple of layers. His love for Barry, the period and obviously with Amy's style, it was coming out as a contemporary post-sixties piece. It was all the more upsetting when she couldn't finish it because I think it would have been something really special. Her voice was just out of this world. Sadly it wasn't to be.[134]

Instead, Jack White was hired and wrote a theme titled, 'Another Way to Die', performed, for the first time in a Bond film, as a duet with Alicia Keys. Arnold commented, 'It was kind of short notice. Lia Vollack at Sony, who was a brilliant collaborator and knew her stuff about music and got [Jack White].'[135] According to White, 'After a couple of years of wanting to collaborate with Alicia, it took James Bond himself to finally make it happen.'[136] The basic track was written and recorded by White in his Nashville studio, with Keys adding piano and vocals, 'Alicia put some electric energy into her breath that cemented itself into the magnetic tape. Very inspiring to watch. You're definitely taking on a responsibility. There's a tradition of powerful music in all these films. But that's why I'm involved creatively with music, for challenges like this.'[137]

Absent from the film was title designer Daniel Kleinman. Instead, rounding out the Forster family, was the work of design committee MK12. James Bond moves through a desert landscape firing his PPK, while silhouetted nudes form patterns around him and a naked girl emerges from beneath the sands of time. MK12 partner and creative director Ben Radatz described the Bond title sequences as:

> the definition of a successful marriage between craft and technique, and – if that weren't enough – the Broccolis have always had a knack of finding the right people for the job. Binder, Brownjohn, Kleinman – all visionary graphic directors, were able to weave abstract narrative, high technology, and high design into a single graceful statement that defined the franchise as much as 007 himself.[138]

Radatz described MK12's first week on the job, 'We felt like kid astronauts with keys to an actual shuttle, like someone was going to call our bluff at any minute.'[139] MK12's initial creative brief was to explore the element at the heart of the film – water:

> We learned that we'd been thinking about the film from an opposite perspective than that of Marc and the producers: where we saw water as the central theme, they saw the lack of water as Bond and Greene's motivation. Our initial concept set Bond in a landscape made of backlit female forms submerged in water. After mulling over random ideas for a few days, it occurred to us that the same technique could be transplanted to a desert scenario, with the female forms instead becoming sand dunes.[140]

MK12 decided to reintroduce the familiar naked women from past Bond title sequences that were missing in *Casino Royale*:

We didn't want to be as exploitative as in past sequences; instead, we approached it from a fine arts angle, looking to a lot of renaissance nudes and early experimental photography. We were really inspired by the photographic nudes of Karen Rosenthal and Man Ray – specifically, their eye for distorting and decontextualising the human figure.[141]

MK12 also contributed to the creative title cards announcing the location of each chapter in the film in unique fonts as well as creating the interfaces within MI6.

Quantum of Solace received its royal world charity premiere simultaneously in the Odeon and the Empire cinemas in Leicester Square, London on 29 October 2008 in the presence of Princes William and Harry. With an eventual world-wide gross of $586 million ($168 million in North America, $80 million in the UK), just under that of *Casino Royale*, the experimental direction and artistic ambition of the new Bond era was being strengthened and maintained.

30

STAND TALL TOGETHER

SKYFALL

(2012)

**FOR YOUR CONSIDERATION
IN ALL CATEGORIES**

INCLUDING

BEST PICTURE

BEST ACTOR
DANIEL CRAIG

BEST SUPPORTING ACTRESS
JUDI DENCH

BEST SUPPORTING ACTOR
JAVIER BARDEM

SKYFALL
007

"...nobody does it better than Daniel Craig."
KATE MUIR, THE TIMES

"The distinction of 'Skyfall' lies in the elegance of
its sensationally entertaining villain, Silva, played by
Javier Bardem...He does this not with physical weaponry
but with an actor's arsenal of skill and daring."
JOE MORGENSTERN, THE WALL STREET JOURNAL

"Bardem is sneeringly fiendish as Silva,
Judi Dench is an intriguing blend of stern
Machiavellian matriarch and honest vulnerability."
CLAUDIA PUIG, USA TODAY

MGM   SonyPictures.com/Awards   COLUMBIA PICTURES

Barbara Broccoli said of the release of *Skyfall* in 2012, '[it] was important to us, for the Bond fans, that they can celebrate the fifty years.'[1]
Michael Wilson reflected: 'no one really thought that we were going
to get to fifty years of Bond, let alone twenty-three pictures. No one
contemplated this kind of success and it's really down to the public. They are
the people who keep on supporting us.'[2]

However, the future of the Bond franchise was, yet again, in jeopardy.
Development had begun on a new Bond film in 2009, but after several months
working on a screenplay, Eon Productions found themselves once again para-
lysed by complications with MGM. In 2004 a consortium led by Sony had
purchased part of the studio. However, MGM still controlled assets including
the rights to the James Bond films, which were shared by Danjaq LLC and
Sony's Columbia Pictures Industries, Inc. For this reason, development of a
Bond film was stymied when MGM accrued debts of more than $4 billion.[3]
Executives came and went as Barbara and Michael sought answers.[4] In August
2009 MGM was put up for sale with a $2 billion minimum asking price.[5]

In early April 2010, Eon enquired with prospective buyers, Sony and Warner
Brothers, to ascertain if they could realistically proceed with *Bond 23*; they
only had weeks left before they would have to exercise an option they had on
director Sam Mendes.[6] A sale was not imminent. On 19 April 2010 Barbara and
Michael had little choice but to announce, 'Due to the continuing uncertainty
surrounding the future of MGM and the failure to close a sale of the studio
we have suspended development of *Bond 23* indefinitely. We do not know
when development will resume.'[7] Said Barbara, 'We were gutted. We thought,
"Here we go again,"'[8] mindful of the previous hiatus between *Licence to Kill*
and *GoldenEye*.

Daniel Craig was sanguine but knew if the delay lasted his future as James
Bond may come under threat.[9] The producers kept Craig fully informed as
the situation developed:

> I count them as close friends. I probably know a bit more than I should.
> There is a lot of tension going on. Barbara and Michael involve me so I get
> to know the good stuff and the shit stuff. I probably involved myself in the
> politics a little bit too much.[10]

At the end of 2010 MGM emerged from bankruptcy. The new co-chairmen,
Gary Barber and Roger Birnbaum, raised $500 million of credit to ressurect
the studio, while Amy Pascal at Sony agreed a complex distribution deal that

Sony would co-fund *Skyfall* with a stake also in *Bond 24*.[11] As Barber explained, getting Bond back in action was a vital step in reviving MGM, 'When you have something of that ilk, it's one of your most significant assets. [Bond] is the crown jewels of the company. When you look at the Lion and you look at James Bond, it's synonymous with the company.'[12]

Michael Wilson's youngest son Gregg, now promoted to associate producer, suggested:

> *Skyfall* would have been a very different, and not as good a movie, if we had to shoot it a year earlier. Essentially, there was a whole different movie that we eventually threw away, because we just felt it wasn't quite right. If the calendar was different we would have just had to make that movie.[13]

As they waited for the outcome of MGM's financial woes, Barbara and Michael continued their foray into the world of theatre, producing their first Broadway play, *A Steady Rain*, a two-hander starring Daniel Craig and Hugh Jackman, which opened in September 2009.

The following month, at Jackman's birthday party, Craig remembered meeting his *Road to Perdition* (2002) director Sam Mendes.[14] Craig recalled, 'talking about what I felt the future was for the series, and how it had been really tricky with *Quantum of Solace* and how I was keen to do something extra special with the next one.'[15] A by-now drunk Craig propositioned Mendes, '"How do you fancy directing a Bond?" and he kind of looked at me, and he went, "Yeah!" And it snowballed from there.'[16]

Craig sheepishly called Barbara and Michael the following morning, telling them of his offer to Mendes, 'I was writing cheques I didn't have the money for.'[17] Barbara Broccoli was amused, 'I think it kept Daniel up all night. He said, "Are you going to kill me?" We were like, "My God, no!" And then we said "Is he really interested?"'[18] Mendes certainly was. He was a Bond fan. As a child Mendes vividly remembered seeing *Live and Let Die*, 'The voodoo stuff scared me and the boat chase thrilled me.'[19]

Mendes found early success in the theatre, directing Judi Dench in the West End aged twenty-four. Appointed Artistic Director of the renowned Donmar Warehouse in London's Covent Garden, Mendes spent a decade working up to directing his first feature film. *American Beauty* (1999) won Mendes an Oscar for Best Director. Recent films had been well received but not commercially successful. Mendes needed a hit film and the Bond series had their first Oscar-winner at the helm. On meeting the producers in New York, Mendes 'was very honest about *Casino Royale* and *Quantum of Solace*. Michael did say at one point, "Why would an auteur or somebody who has had a career in serious pictures want to do a Bond movie?" I said, "Bond is a serious movie." And I stuck to that throughout.'[20] Mendes thought Christopher Nolan's *The Dark Knight* (2008) made it 'a lot easier for big action adventure movies to deal with dark, complex issues. The landscape changed after that film.'[21] *Casino Royale*, Mendes felt, 'woke me up to the possibilities of Bond.'[22]

Mendes had no desire to be a cog within a well-oiled machine,[23] 'There's obviously a risk involved in giving me that amount of input and control.'[24] Barbara Broccoli set out the parameters, 'When we start working on development with a director, we make sure we're all making the same movie; that we all have a clear vision. We're very collaborative but you don't want to hire Sam Mendes and then handcuff him.'[25]

Neal Purvis and Robert Wade returned to write their fifth consecutive James Bond film. This time, however, they were teamed with Academy Award-nominated playwright and screenwriter Peter Morgan to collaborate on a treatment. Purvis and Wade would draft a screenplay, which Morgan would then polish.[26] It was unusual to request an established writing duo to write with a another scribe but Purvis felt the producers wanted to 'see what comes out of this little experiment'.[27] Wade remembered: 'Neal and I are pretty well steeped in Fleming, I think Peter was more interested in Le Carré. It just didn't work.'[28] Morgan only made one brief comment about his involvement, 'It's a shocking story.'[29]

The treatment, titled *Once Upon a Spy*, started during the Cold War. M had been an MI6 agent stationed in Berlin, where she had an affair with a KGB spy. Thirty years later, following M's lover's death, his unscrupulous son, a corrupt Russian oligarch, blackmails M, casting a dark shadow over her career. She sends Bond on a mission to make a payoff. Morgan's idea was Bond would be forced to kill M at the end of the film. Wade recounted, 'We always found that really, really difficult to make credible or satisfying. It was very dark and frankly I don't think it really worked. The only thing that really remained was M's past comes back to haunt her and she dies at the end.'[30]

Director Sam Mendes did not like *Once Upon a Spy*,[31] 'I said to Barbara and Michael, "would you consider retaining the idea of M's death?" And they said yes. From that moment on we knew what we were building towards the whole time.'[32] Barbara described Bond's relationship with M as 'the most significant relationship he has in his life. M is the only person who represents authority to him. You have two extraordinary actors, and we just thought – let's go all the way.'[33]

Purvis and Wade worked on a new outline drawing from Fleming's YOU
ONLY LIVE TWICE and THE MAN WITH THE GOLDEN GUN, where a dishevelled
Bond returns to MI6 after he is presumed dead. Commented Wade, 'The interesting thing about [those Fleming novels] is that at the beginning, Britain's
prestige is very low. M's very pissed off with Bond [and asking], "Is Bond a
basket case?" Those elements were very much there in *Skyfall*. She sends Bond
on a suicide mission against [Silva].'[34] Wade explained M had been made even
more of an outcast in the first draft, 'Judi has a scene on a park bench with
Leiter and it's laid on the line, "We're not giving you our intelligence anymore
because you're not trustworthy, you can't keep secrets and you fuck up." It was
much more explicit.'[35]

The arc between the novels was retained: Bond's high fall leading to
amnesia, his reported death and M's obituary, and his careful readmission
into the Service. Bond's life in a small Turkish fishing village, being cared for
by a beautiful young doctor named Lily, was based on Bond's relationship
with Kissy Suzuki. Lily is secretly pregnant with Bond's child and follows
him to London. However, M intercedes before Lily has a chance to inform
Bond, feeling this news will jeopardise 007's professional commitment. Wade
recalled, 'Everyone was interested in exploring the idea because it has its
antecedent in Fleming.'[36]

Mendes noted, 'There's some pretty heavy stuff going on in YOU ONLY LIVE
TWICE and THE MAN WITH THE GOLDEN GUN. The franchise at the time wasn't
able to embrace all the truly dark notes from those novels. They were a focal
point for us.'[37] Mendes felt the material perfect for a modern audience, 'If
you've got a big franchise movie without a fucked up character, it's not worth
doing.'[38] Barbara thought Fleming was contemporary again, 'It feels like we are
in the right groove for what he had to say about how real villainy is coming
from individuals – not just political states. Individuals who are wielding all sorts
of treacherous plans on the Earth.'[39]

The writers met with Mendes and Craig in New York to discuss the script.[40]
Wade recalled, 'Bond needed to "die" at the start and be cast into the wilder-
ness and then come back and has got to prove himself. We also wanted Javier
Bardem to be the villain.'[41] The scribes wanted to give Craig a worthy, Bondian
adversary. Purvis remembered that they took inspiration from Francisco 'Pistols'
Scaramanga from THE MAN WITH THE GOLDEN GUN,:

He was going to be the man who knocked Bond off the train during the
fight in the pre-titles. Bond recovers, tracks him down to a bar and from there

into the Andes. A HEART OF DARKNESS feel. When he discovers him they're both attacked. So they team up to find who did it. This is a case where you try many ideas before you find the one that fits the story best.[42]

They had not been working on the screenplay for long when MGM was plunged into bankruptcy, so pre-production on the film ceased. Mendes rememberes: '[Barbara and Michael] had to find a way of keeping me officially on without announcing me as a director, so I became a consultant,'[43] During the hiatus he continued to work with Broccoli and Wilson, as well as Purvis and Wade developing the screenplay. Mendes used the extra time to his advantage, 'It made such a difference to the script to have time to go down certain roads that turn out to be blind alleys, as you often do.'[44] Craig recalled both he and Mendes used the time to re-read the Fleming novels, 'We started emailing each other, "What about this?" "What about that?" That's how it snowballed really.'[45]

Wade remarked that they worked with Mendes for nearly a year.[46] They were under pressure to deliver a draft as Gary Barber and Roger Birnbaum needed a script on the table by 8 December 2010[47] to demonstrate to financiers that the future of James Bond was alive and well to attract re-financing. The writers delivered a draft in November 2010 titled *Nothing Is Forever*.[48] The villain, previously actually named Javier Bardem, was now called Raoul Silva, who, seeking revenge against M, plants a bomb in the Barcelona subway, steering her to a safe house where he plans to kill her. A bureaucrat named Mallender becomes her successor.[49]

Purvis and Wade were never happy with the third act. Two weeks before the MGM deadline, they devised the idea of Bond kidnapping M and taking her to safety, to his ancestral home in the remote highlands of Scotland. Wade felt, '[Bond] doesn't think anyone else could protect her and takes her back to the terrain he knows and can control. He was taking his mother figure back to where he was orphaned and it suddenly gives you more thematic depth to the whole film.'[50] Their inspiration was taken from Geoffrey Household's 1939 thriller ROGUE MALE.[51] Mendes liked the concept, as did the producers, and told them to run with it.[52]

Purvis and Wade worked 'like dogs'[53] restructuring the script moving the Spanish subway train scenes to London and creating a completely new climax in Scotland. Purvis remembered: 'Somehow we got it done, cobbled it all together, it wasn't perfect but it was in very good shape.'[54] Wade recollected that those two weeks virtually shaped the future of the film, 'We changed its destiny and I think without that it didn't have a depth to it that it really needed. We knew that when we handed it in, that it was probably the end of our involvement.'[55] However, the writers made one final contribution the night before they delivered the draft by naming Bond's home Skyfall. In looking for an evocative name they took inspiration from author John Buchan, a favourite of Ian Fleming, who named one of his novels – GREENMANTLE.[56] Before Skyfall, many titles had been suggested: Silver Bullet,[57] Magic 44,[58] A Killing Moon[59] and the aforementioned Nothing Is Forever.[60]

Reflected Craig, 'Neal and Robert wrote a great, solid plot that they do so well. They gave us a foundation of a good script that we [could] carry on with.'[61] In January 2011 Academy Award-winner John Logan was hired to rewrite Skyfall. He explained, 'Sam Mendes and I have known each other for fifteen years from theatre circles.'[62] The writer, who had worked with some of Hollywood's greatest contemporary filmmakers – Martin Scorsese, Ridley Scott, Tim Burton – said:

> Coming from the world of theatre, for me, it has always been about character and dialogue. When you look over the vast panoply of Bond films, things tend to emerge, like a lightning bolt: great moments of dialogue, great moments of character interaction – whether it's Bond and Goldfinger, Bond and Blofeld, or Bond and Vesper Lynd. Those are the amazing scenes that just stop your heart because they're unexpected in what's considered a genre movie.[63]

Logan praised the existing script as a 'great machine'[64] and cited his role was 'not so much about cataloging changes as bringing a certain sensibility to the material.'[65] Mendes credited Logan for giving the screenplay 'a distinct flavour and making it not feel like it's the work of a committee.'[66]

Logan said of Craig; 'Dan has a very sensitive ear for dialogue. His response to the words Bond says, even the number of syllables in a line, is instinctively correct. He plays it hard, he plays it real, he plays it with a consequence.'[67] Logan had clear ideas on developing Bond's foe Raoul Silva:

> He's a very theatrical character, he likes to make an entrance, he likes to make an exit, the same way as our first Bond cinema villain fifty years ago, Dr. No, loved to do. [Silva] was always a larger than life character and Javier brought so much to it in his performance. He is a character who speaks in arias.'[68]

Logan wrote the 'two rats in a barrel speech' for when Silva meets 007 for the first time.

Mendes suggested to the producers they reintroduce Q and Miss Moneypenny.[69] Logan created a younger quartermaster, conceiving the scene in which Bond meets Q in London's National Gallery in front of a Turner painting, 'There's initial suspicion of "Who's this kid with spots and why is he telling me about my job?" But they quickly develop a mutual respect.'[70] In the Purvis and Wade draft Q had been a more 'shabby' character potentially to be played by Simon Russell Beale.[71] Bond was to meet Q in a far less salubrious location – a greasy spoon café in the east end of London.[72] Recalled Wade, 'Sam's got a view that Bond can't be seen in anywhere that's sort of on a human scale, it always has to be big which is fair enough, but I actually wouldn't mind seeing Bond in a greasy spoon.'[73] Borrowing from Fleming's short story, 007 IN NEW YORK, where Bond tips off a fellow agent that her lover is an enemy spy, Purvis and Wade introduced Miss Moneypenny by Bond informing her that her boyfriend is a traitor.[74] Eventually she became integral to the beginning of the story and was involved in the action.

Skyfall was a James Bond film that not only marked the franchise's fiftieth anniversary, but was released in a year that coincided with Her Majesty, Elizabeth II's Diamond Jubilee and the Olympic Games hosted by the UK. Like *The Spy Who Loved Me* thirty-five years before it was no accident, commented Logan, that the film was 'tied completely with the iconography of England and the flag.'[75] Craig said following conversations with Mendes they consciously 'wanted to make *Skyfall* ingrained with core British values. Making this movie unmistakably British was a dream of ours.'[76] British playwright and screenwriter Jez Butterworth also consulted and performed minor rewrites.[77]

The pre-title sequence of *Skyfall* begins in Turkey. Silent killer, Patrice, has stolen an MI6 hard drive containing the names and deep cover details of NATO agents embedded in terrorist organisations around the world. Hot on his trail is 007, assisted by field agent Eve. They are in communication with MI6 headquarters as they chase the assassin through Istanbul and continue their pursuit on top of a moving train. In the event that Bond is unsuccessful in eliminating Patrice, Eve has a rifle uncertainly trained on the target while Bond is fighting him. As Bond is running out of time, Eve is ordered to shoot Patrice by M. She, however, misses Patrice but instead hits Bond who falls from the train into a river below. With 007 missing, presumed dead, M writes his obituary. M is sanctioned by Chairman of the Intelligence and Security Committee, Gareth Mallory, for losing the list of agents and is on the brink of being forced into retirement, pending an inquiry.

When a gas explosion at MI6's headquarters at Vauxhall Cross is found to be the result of cyber hacking, M is astonished to be personally taunted. The MI6 attack prompts 007 to return to the fold – he had been hiding out with his lover in a remote spot near the South China Sea. After a series of evaluations – where the word 'Skyfall' causes Bond to leave an interrogation – 007 is readmitted into the Service. Although it is later revealed that he was not deemed fit to return to active service and M has ignored the evaluation report. Bond, equipped by a boyish yet disdainful Q, is sent to hunt Patrice.

Traced by his own specialised munitions, the assassin is tracked down to Shanghai, where 007 kills him. Bond then heads to Macao, following a clue found among Patrice's equipment. Joined by Eve, Bond attends a floating casino where, after cashing in Patrice's high-value chip, Bond is led to the mysterious Severine. After a battle with casino goons in a Komodo dragon pit, Bond seduces Severine on her yacht. By design, she leads him to a deserted island inhabited by Raoul Silva, the cyber hacker behind the MI6 explosion and the theft of the hard drive. Silva, a former MI6 spy, mocks Bond's fealty to Queen and country and intimates Bond has been used callously by M, just like he was. Silva operates according to his own private dictates, free from orders. After a dueling competition with antique pistols – in which Silva kills Severine – Bond outwits his captors and captures Silva.

Back in London, in a secure underground prison, Silva is revealed to be Tiago Rodriguez, a disgruntled Hong Kong-based agent, given up to the Chinese by M when he went rogue and tried to sabotage the 1997 handover. Imprisoned and tortured, Silva was horribly mutilated as a result of his suicide capsule failing to kill him. A long-planned mission of vengeance to humiliate and kill M is now set in motion. Silva's laptop, when analysed by Q, releases a virus, which overrides security measures allowing Silva to escape. After outwitting Bond on the London Underground – nearly killing 007 by causing a train crash – Silva tracks M down to the inquiry. Fortunately, 007's intervention narrowly foils Silva's plot to kill M, but Mallory is wounded.

007 decides to take his chief off the electronic grid. Bond's long-unused Aston Martin DB5, hidden in a south London garage, transports them both north to Bond's ancestral home, Skyfall, in Glencoe, Scotland. Working in concert with Tanner and Q and, from the sidelines, Mallory, Bond hopes to lure Silva to the abode and use his home-ground advantage. Skyfall's housekeeper, Kincade, is surprised to see Bond back, but together they make preparations for the predicted attack. Silva sends a wave of men but they are fended off by Kincade, M and Bond with his Aston Martin. Now, Silva himself flies in by

helicopter and proceeds to destroy Skyfall. However, using an old priest hole, Bond, Kincade and M escape the destruction. Silva tracks Bond and M down to a remote church. There Bond kills Silva but then notices M has been mortally wounded in the battle for Skyfall. Helpless to save her, M dies in Bond's arms. Back in London, Bond is in a reflective mood as Eve is revealed to be Miss Moneypenny. He is sent to meet the new M, Gareth Mallory, in his wood-pannelled office, no longer at Vauxhall Cross but again in the heart of Whitehall. They both agree there is lots of work to be done.

Daniel Craig felt James Bond had changed since 2006, 'In *Casino Royale*, Bond gets described as a blunt instrument, and that is how I played it. This time around, in my grand plan, Bond can start having fun.'[78]

Barbara Broccoli admitted writing M out 'was incredibly bittersweet for all of us. We have been working with [Judi Dench] for seventeen years, she has become an important part of the series and a dear friend; she has brought so much to the character. It was heartbreaking but I think it was right.'[79] Mendes recalled meeting Dench for lunch. 'She arrived at the restaurant and said, "Here I am. Tear-stained and livid!" with a big smile on her face.'[80] Dench reflected, 'Was I peeved? No I don't think I was. I think I've had a fair share.'[81] Wilson felt Dench's last appearance 'wasn't perfunctory; it was central to the whole story.'[82] Dench observed:

> Over the series of seven films she has changed, become a more rounded person and in *Skyfall,* of course, you found out she is fallible and made mis-takes. She started off sort of the same age as Pierce Brosnan, now she's ended up as Daniel Craig's grandmother practically. I might come back as a ghost and give Ralph Fiennes a very, very hard time![83]

Purvis and Wade had named the Silva character Javier Bardem in the original screenplay.[84] The Spanish star had been in talks to play a previous Bond vil-lain, 'but I don't want to say the name of the movie for respect of the actor. But I would say that I was not ready linguistically.'[85] Bardem had first been approached by Daniel Craig at a party at Paul Haggis's house.[86] Bardem thought Silva was, 'An angel of death – a very clean-shaven person who happens to be rotten on the inside.'[87] Mendes suggested to Bardem the key word behind Silva: uncomfortable. 'The physicality, the behaviour, the sense of humour – every-thing has to be kind of uncomfortable, that will be [Silva's] tool.'[88]

Robert Wade described Severine simply as a survivor, 'Like many of the women in the Fleming books, she's toughened herself up because she knows what it is to have been abused at the hands of men.'[89] On her eleventh Bond film, casting director Debbie McWilliams felt it was 'my job to go out and find those special actors that people may not have heard of before. Submissions were received from all over the world and casting sessions took place in locations as diverse as Shanghai, Stockholm, Madrid, Sarajevo, Athens, Istanbul, Beijing and beyond.'[90] French-Cambodian actress Bérénice Marlohe was eventually discovered by McWilliams in Paris,[91] 'She auditioned me on the casino scenes [from *Skyfall*]. I was called back to Pinewood Studios and I was auditioned by Sam on the two same scenes and then the third audition was [with] Daniel and Sam and I got to meet with Barbara Broccoli and Michael Wilson.'[92] Marlohe described her approach to Severine, 'I felt I could use my own personality and imagination to create my character's style – I had the freedom, knowing that this kind of movie allowed me that space.'[93]

Skyfall reintroduced Miss Moneypenny, this time as a field agent, played by Naomie Harris, 'I didn't realise when I signed on to do it how hard action was. I now have a huge respect for action heroes, it was exhilarating and fun but it was tough.'[94] Harris's part as the world's most famous PA was not revealed during the film's theatrical marketing campaign. Harris said when promoting the home entertainment release, 'I had to keep everything a secret for ages. Even when I'd just got given the role I was told that I couldn't tell anyone, so it's nice now to be free of all [the secrecy] and just say, "Yes, I am Miss Moneypenny!"'[95]

Ralph Fiennes was cast as Gareth Mallory, chairman of the intelligence and security committee, who later, becomes the new M. Versed in Fleming, and a one-time candidate for Bond, Fiennes said, 'I got into [the books] when I was about twelve or thirteen, and for a while I was obsessed by them; I knew all the plots and all the characters inside out.'[96] Returning for his second Bond film was Rory Kinnear reprising his role as Bill Tanner, M's reliable chief of staff.

The 31-year-old British thespian Ben Whishaw became the fourth Eon Q. Whishaw was offered the role without auditioning after Mendes saw him in *Bright Star* (2009).[97] Michael Wilson explained, 'The question was how would the character be different to Desmond [Llewelyn]? So, we've gone younger, and made him more of a technical nerd.'[98] Whishaw was aware of the character's legacy and deliberately avoided looking at past Bond pictures. Asked on positioning Q for a new audience, Whishaw explained he had been inspired by '[Mark] Zuckerberg and that whole generation of people who are so powerful in the world. A lot of the conflict in *Skyfall* comes from the new world and the old world rubbing up against each other and Bond is having to adapt to the way the world is now.'[99] Whishaw considered power is 'the knowledge of the cyber world.'[100] Said Mendes:

> There are a couple of things I just couldn't resist Q saying like, 'Were you expecting an exploding pen? We don't go in for that anymore.' Well, I thought, 'You've got to say it.' We've got to come clean. It's a world where every gadget you could possibly imagine is available in the Apple store.[101]

A Woodfall Films veteran, Albert Finney, was cast as Kincade, the Scottish retainer at Skyfall Lodge, who taught young Bond how to shoot. Barbara Broccoli was thrilled, 'Cubby desperately wanted to work with him, and of course, I've wanted to work with him. He is a legend, a fantastic actor and just funny, charming, extraordinary and dead sexy. Be still my beating heart!'[102] In early drafts Kincade had been known as Monroe;[103] potentially a role for Sean Connery. Purvis remembered, 'It was genuinely considered. I think it was probably the right thing that it wasn't Connery. But it's just a nice thing to imagine.'[104] Wade recalled the producers were not so sure, 'they were worried it would overshadow the movie.'[105]

Having collaborated with him on *Jarhead* (2009) and *Revolutionary Road* (2008), Mendes felt Roger Deakins was 'one of the best cinematographers in the world.'[106] Prior to shooting, they 'went through the script together, talking not just about the visuals, but also about character development. It was great to be involved in that interchange of ideas, because those discussions affected how the script developed.'[107] Mendes:

> was very clear from the beginning that this wasn't going to be a Bond movie where we threw seven cameras up and did a sort of pseudo-Bourne job on it. I want it to be very still, classical. Even in the action sequences we used crane and dolly much more than we used jerky hand-held. I feel it has become so cheapened, mostly by television over using it.[108]

Returning to Bond for a second time was production designer Dennis Gassner. *Skyfall* marked his third collaboration with Sam Mendes and seventh with Roger Deakins. Gassner explained, 'Throughout the process of *Skyfall* I considered Bond's emotional journey and how each environment affects him and vice versa.'[109] Gassner designed and built thirty-one sets for the film. MI6's new underground headquarters was an idea based on the historical Churchill bunker, where during World War II many government offices were relocated for protection. Said Gassner, 'The Old Vic locations were a pleasure to work in and our recces of usually red-taped underground London inspired the sets that we built back at Pinewood. This is the great fusion between locations and set build, one informs the other and they become a unit.'[110] Other notable sets included the interior and exterior of Skyfall Lodge, 'It was a harsh place against the elements. What does Bond do to fight back? He goes home, back to his deepest instincts. It's a privilege for us to see it.'[111] Gassner also built Silva's derelict island on the lot at Pinewood, an imaginary location inspired by the Japanese island of Hashima, used by Gassner to 'mine lots of visual ideas. We even pulled the effigy of the leader down in the town square.'[112]

It was in the real Old Vic tunnels that *Skyfall* began shooting on 7 November 2011. The now traditional press conference had been held at the Corinthia Hotel on 3 November 2011, with Michael Wilson confirming 'London's worst kept secret'[113] the title – *Skyfall*.

Javier Bardem filmed his first scenes opposite Daniel Craig and Judi Dench in his underground cell. Working with Dench, Bardem felt, was like standing in front of a water cannon:

> When she opens her mouth and looks you in the eyes you're like, 'Wow! This is a big deal.' You feel a force of nature against your chest. I looked at them both and forgot the lines. There was a silence and Sam said, 'Cut, what's wrong?' and I said, 'Sorry man, I just realised I'm in a James Bond movie and M and James Bond are looking at me.'[114]

Filming was then interrupted, this time by Judi Dench's mobile phone. Her ring tone? The 'James Bond Theme'.[115]

For ten weeks London was used in ways it had never been seen on screen before. Mendes tried to give his hometown 'mood and atmosphere and a sense of a threat. We've shot in some of the expected places, but done it in unexpected ways.'[116] The power of James Bond unlocked parts of the town not usually granted to film production, Craig noted: 'We actually managed to close Parliament Square. We used subterranean London.'[117] The main street of government in the capital, Whitehall, was locked off one Sunday, as Gary Powell recounted, 'We have so many hundred cars and so many hundred extras and all the crew there. To get that operation approved and executed was impressive.'[118]

Temple underground station was built by Dennis Gassner at Pinewood Studios, but Bond's spectacular leap down the central escalator was shot at Charing Cross station. Over the course of four weekends, the production was given access to an out-of-service line.[119] Special effects supervisor Chris Corbould recalled, 'I came up with the idea for the tube train crash, which Sam liked a lot, but then I started to realise the enormity of what I'd dreamt up.'[120] Corbould built a full-scale replica tube train and the stunt was executed on the 007 Stage. Mendes shot the sequence using eleven remote cameras, 'It was a one-shot deal. If it hadn't worked out, it would have been two million quid to re-shoot. That was pretty nerve-wracking.'[121]

Other London locations utilised by the production included Room 34 of the National Gallery where Bond meets Q. One of the film's closing scenes as Bond and Moneypenny gaze out over the London skyline was shot on the roof of the DECC (Department for Energy and Climate Change) and, in tribute to the late composer John Barry, his former house in Cadogan Square, Chelsea, served as M's home.[122]

Budget limitations restricted the main unit filming extensively in China.[123] An ultra modern stadium at Ascot racecourse stood in for Pudong Airport; the Shanghai office block where Bond tails Patrice to was in reality a Bishopsgate office block in London; the actual silhouette fight took place on a set at Pinewood; and the Virgin Active gym in Canary Wharf became Bond's Shanghai hotel swimming pool. However, Alexander Witt and his second unit travelled to Shanghai to shoot exhilarating establishing shots. Veteran Bond aerial pilot, Marc Wolff, was granted rare access to the skies above the city to shoot from a helicopter on loan from the Chinese government.[124] Shanghai, according to Logan, was 'so unlike the world that [Bond] grew up in, the world that he functions in. In a way we were trying to find places for Bond to be uncomfortable.'[125] On shooting Bond's silhouette fight with Patrice atop a Shanghai skyscraper, Deakins recalled they undertook tests weeks earlier using stock footage of floating jellyfish to screen on the electronic billboards, 'It looked interesting, and it was a really deep blue, and we wanted this whole Shanghai section to feel quite cold.'[126]

Dennis Gassner built the Floating Dragon casino at Pinewood Studios on the Paddock Tank. The set was lit by 300 floating lanterns and two 30ft high dragonheads. Twelve artisans were flown in from China to ensure the dragons looked as authentic as possible.[127] The inclusion of two sinister komodo dragons roaming around a pit beneath the casino, from which Bond would make a narrow escape, was the brainchild of Sam Mendes inspired by the stepping stone crocodile jump in *Live and Let Die*. The scene was created entirely using CGI with two Komodo dragons at London Zoo photographed from every angle for the visual effect artists to work with.[128]

In February 2012 the crew spent two days shooting in Glencoe in the Scottish Highlands. Bond's obituary in YOU ONLY LIVE TWICE mentions his father was from the area and now in *Skyfall* it was to be the location of their ancestral home. In reality, Skyfall Lodge was not in Scotland at all but built on Hankley Common in Surrey with its interiors filmed at Pinewood Studios.

The landscape of Glencoe served as a rugged and eerie backdrop for Bond's and M's escape to safety in the classic Aston Martin DB5. Judi Dench recalled shooting the beginning of their escape through the city of London, 'We filmed the entire night of my birthday down the Old Kent Road. A lot of that was cut [but] it was terribly exciting to be in that car.'[129] John Logan said of the DB5:

> When you think of Bond, you think of certain things very clearly and one of them is that particular car. It is Bond's essential car and in a movie about reorienting Bond to his past and to his future, we just had to use it – beyond the fact it's completely cool.[130]

Earlier, Purvis and Wade had positioned the DB5's appearance slightly differently, 'Our concept is Bond opens up the lock-up garage and there's the DB5, but it's the one from *Casino Royale*, it wasn't the one from *Goldfinger*,'[131] said Wade referring to the DB5 Bond won during a card game in the Bahamas in *Casino Royale*. Although the car's appearance was cheered and lauded by fans and critics, Purvis noted, 'it didn't make sense but I understand why they did it.'[132]

One of the DB5s used in the film was from Eon's own archive, the same car that was driven by Pierce Brosnan in *GoldenEye*. Stunt co-ordinator Gary Powell took the incumbent 007 out on the open road the day it arrived at Pinewood Studios, 'People were looking and going, "That looks like Daniel Craig driving the Aston Martin!" It was a chuckle at myself moment.'[133]

In early drafts M was to die in a fire in a whisky distillery. Said Dench of filming her final scenes, 'I was emotional when they said, "Cut. That's it, thanks very much." We all had a drink and a big cake. That was the emotional bit.'[134]

Skyfall's major international location was Turkey, the setting for a pre-title sequence in which Bond pursues Patrice through a crowded market, before jumping on a motorbike and then a frantic fight on top of a train as it hurtles out of Istanbul and into the countryside. Mendes's concept was 'a series of Russian dolls, you think it's this type of action sequence and then it becomes something else and then it becomes something else again.'[135] The original idea was a motorbike chase along the top of a train, suggested by Sam Mendes's eight-year-old son Joe.[136] The filmmakers had first considered shooting the chase in Mumbai, India. Mendes suggested the change was due to the logistical impracticalities of shutting down the centre of a major Indian city, 'We tried to make it work and to embrace the chaos, but in the end there were too many dangers.'[137] Mendes looked at Cape Town, before discovering the possibilities of Istanbul. The Grand Bazaar immediately appealed to the director, as did the opportunity to shoot the motorbike chase across the city's rooftops.

The action begins with a car chase, as Bond and Moneypenny, in a Land Rover Defender, pursue Patrice's Audi through the crowded city. A fleet of twelve Land Rovers and sixteen Audi A5s were modified and reinforced for the sequence. Two of the Defenders had driving 'pods' mounted to the roof, allowing stunt driver Ben Collins to control the car at speeds of 50 mph while Naomie Harris concentrated on delivering dialogue below. When the chase hits a busy market, Bond and Patrice transfer to motorcycles. Supervising art director Chris Lowe recalled, 'We had two guys on Honda CRF250R motocross bikes hurtling at 60 mph across the roofs. At one point a bike broke a jewellery shop window. The owner wasn't happy but I think he used it as a marketing tool: "Bond broke my window."'[138] Stunt co-ordinator Gary Powell had Coca Cola sprayed across the streets to prevent the bikes from sliding.[139]

Finally Bond and Patrice battle it out on top of a freight train. The sequence was shot along six miles of track in Adana, Southern Turkey. Wilson expressed their intention was always to keep the action real, 'If it's CGI, it's just to help out, as opposed to creating the scene.'[140] Barbara added:

> I had my heart in my mouth the whole time; [Daniel] and Ola [Rapace, playing Patrice] were fighting on the roof of a moving train and the moves that they were doing were just heart stopping. Daniel's the reason why the action works as well as it does because he sells it, he's up there and I think audiences know that.[141]

Craig recalled there was an art to working on top of the moving train, 'My first day on the train was just about learning to stand up … it's not the speed that matters, it's the side to side motion. Then when we go over this bridge … they all said, "Don't look down!" And I tried not to.'[142] The fight comes to a climax as Moneypenny accidentally shoots Bond as the train is travelling over a narrow viaduct, sending 007 off the train and 400ft into a river below. It was shot on the Varda Viaduct. Dennis Gassner was very specific when looking for a location:

I looked at so many bridges in nine countries, trying to find the right one and the right feeling. And I remember getting on this bridge in Turkey and standing in the centre by myself and I said, 'I want Daniel to be here right now.' It seemed so iconically perfect [with its stone arch structure] to play a scene where you knew if he went off that bridge something was going to happen. He's going into another world and he comes up in a place that is his own parallel universe.[143]

Craig's double, Andy Lister, performed the stunt following ten weeks of intense rehearsals,[144] 'I've studied how Daniel runs, how he walks, how he fights. But they'll still need to do a face replacement in post-production to make me look exactly like Bond.'[145]

Sam Mendes saw how the title track, co-written by its singer Adele with producer Paul Epworth, was shaped:

With having read the script and trying to set the whole thing up in that context, where it happens in the film, there was really only one thing it could be. It was interesting to want to do something that was simultaneously dark and final, like a funeral, and to try and turn it into something that was not final. A sense of death and rebirth.[146]

Mendes requested he use his regular composer, Thomas Newman, who had scored all five of his previous pictures. The producers were at first unsure. 'He has never done a movie like this,'[147] admitted Mendes who felt the introduction of a new composer was a distinct way of keeping *Skyfall* fresh. 'David Arnold did a fantastic job for all those years, but a change is as good as a rest.'[148] Newman admitted he was not a Bond fan but understood:

there's obviously a huge amount of expectation in terms of what a James Bond score is. I really didn't feel an obligation to meet up to those expectations. Or if I was going to defy them, I wanted to defy them in a way that was pleasing and compelling as opposed to making people feel that I was doing something different for it's own sake.[149]

Michael Wilson requested that Newman subtly weave Adele's title song into the score.[150] Mendes was keen to organically weave flavours of the 'James Bond Theme' into the music too, 'I said the same to Paul Epworth and Adele [and] wherever possible we wove it in.'[151]

Adele recalled she:

> … was a little hesitant at first to be involved with the theme song for *Skyfall*.
> There's a lot of instant spotlight and pressure when it comes to a Bond song.
> But I fell in love with the script and Paul had some great ideas for the track
> and it ended up being a bit of a no-brainer to do it in the end. It was also a lot
> of fun writing to a brief, something I've never done which made it exciting.
> When we recorded the strings, it was one of the proudest moments of my
> life. I'll be back combing my hair when I'm sixty telling people I was a Bond
> girl back in the day, I'm sure![152]

Recorded at Abbey Road Studios in London, 'Skyfall' features the lush accompaniment of a seventy-seven piece orchestra.[153]

Daniel Kleinman returned to main title duties following his absence on
Quantum of Solace. He described his relationship with Sam Mendes as the
most collaborative of all the Bond directors he has worked with.[154] Kleinman's
original idea featured 'girls as caryatids, like columns, people appearing and
disappearing behind them but that didn't really float Sam's boat.'[155] Mendes
approached Kleinman with his own concept:

> Bond goes underwater, down into the underworld, down and down and
> down, like Alice going down the rabbit hole. I wanted it to be Bond's point
> of view – what he sees in the moment of death. He goes back in time, Skyfall
> is in there through the eyes of him as a kid.[156]

Kleinman developed Mendes's idea further so the audience steps 'inside
[Bond's] head. You're seeing the world from his viewpoint and it's his life
flashing in front of him as he thinks he's dying from a gunshot.'[157] Kleinman
described how Mendes would reguarly feedback throughout the process. The
director was unsure of Kleinman's first visuals for Skyfall Lodge, which he had
made 'a little more childish, a little more fairy tale'[158] to signify this was a place
associated with Bond's childhood. 'It's really useful to have another pair of eyes
of someone you trust to bounce ideas off.'[159]

Like Marc Forster, Mendes chose to place the gun barrel sequence at the
end of the movie but he confessed not without much deliberation, 'I was
fully planning to have it at the beginning because for me the gun barrel is
the Christmas Eve of a Bond movie. Christmas Day is never quite as good.'[160]

The first shot of *Skyfall* sees Bond walking towards camera before raising his PPK into frame. Mendes placed the gun barrel sequence at the beginning but 'it looked ridiculous and it killed the first shot of the film.'[161] He even tried cutting from the gun barrel to an establisher of Istanbul, but 'that felt so old fashioned.'[162] He also thought it had more significance placed at the end of the picture, 'You can feel people thinking when M dies, "How the hell are they going to get out of this? You've only got two minutes left?" When the [gun barrel] comes in you're like "YES!" It's uplifting and makes you feel like, "I'm ready for another part of the saga."'[163]

In the lead-up to *Skyfall's* release, Danny Boyle, director of the opening cere-mony for the 2012 London Olympic Games, suggested James Bond accompany Her Majesty the Queen to the Olympic Stadium. Unbelievably, the Queen made herself available to shoot the short film titled *Happy and Glorious* oppo-site Daniel Craig. The segment began with a tuxedo-clad 007 entering Her Majesty's drawing room in Buckingham Palace. 'Good evening Mr. Bond,' she says before Bond escorts her to a helicopter, which was then intercut to the live ceremony in which stuntmen doubling both the Queen and Craig skydived into the stadium to the strains of the 'James Bond Theme'. The world could not quite believe what they had just seen. Daniel Craig said of the extraordinary experience, 'It was quite surreal to be in the palace with the Queen. I am a big fan of Danny Boyle and he did an amazing job … I was proud to be a small part of it.'[164] The opening ceremony, held on 27 July 2012 at London's Olympic Stadium in Stratford, was watched by a global audience of 900 million. This was publicity the *Skyfall* team could never have dreamed of and Mendes was appreciative, 'It was so delightful that the BBC chose to open its highlights every night with, "Good evening Mr. Bond." That was brilliant.'[165] The fiftieth anniversary celebrations also gave *Skyfall* an extra publicity boost, with high-profile exhibitions and the theatrical release of a documentary *Everything or Nothing: The Untold Story of 007*, directed by Stevan Riley who co-wrote it with Peter Ettudgui. The documentary was released on what had been designated Global James Bond Day: 5 October 2012. Fifty years to the day since *Dr. No* had debuted in London. Adele's title track was dropped at 0:07 BST on this date.

Skyfall premiered on 23 October 2012 at the Royal Albert Hall in London in the presence of the Prince of Wales and the Duchess of Cornwall. The glamor-ous affair prompted Craig to comment that it was 'the most memorable night of my career. I just feel honoured and it just shows you what Bond means to everyone.'[166]

Skyfall went on to break a number of Bond box office records. The film became Bond's largest opening weekend in North America, earning over $88 million; it would go on to gross $304 million in the territory. In the UK, *Skyfall* became the highest grossing film in history, garnering a staggering $161 million. Ultimately, the film achieved a global gross of $1.1 billion – a record for the studio, Sony Pictures.

Critically, the reviews had never been better. *Skyfall* was nominated for a total of five Oscars, winning two, one for Adele's classic title song and a second for Per Hallberg and Karen Baker Landers, who were awarded Best Achievement in Sound Editing. Roger Deakins and Thomas Newman missed out, as did the sound mixing team. Adele performed the song live at the Oscars on 24 February 2013, during a ceremony which paid homage to Bond's fiftieth anniversary, including an appearance from Shirley Bassey singing *Goldfinger*. *Skyfall* was nominated for eight BAFTA awards, winning Best British Film and Best Score. Adele's title track also won a Grammy and a Golden Globe. Bondmania once again conquered the world.

In late 2012, Craig confirmed he had signed up for Bonds 24 and 25:

> but I know this is the film business, and we'll take it a picture at a time. I'd love to continue beyond that. What I love about [*Skyfall*] is, we have set things up now, and all we need is to find a good story and produce something as good as this.[167]

Asked about the direction Bond should go next Craig said, 'I don't want to do ludicrous, we've got to keep it in reality, but Christ almighty the world is fucking weird. And, if Blofeld suddenly turned up again, it wouldn't be a bad thing. We've got an outline for a script but it's very loose.'[168]

31

BEEN HERE BEFORE

SPECTRE

(2015)

BEST ORIGINAL SCORE
THOMAS NEWMAN

BEST ORIGINAL SONG
"WRITING'S ON THE WALL"
Music & Lyrics by
SAM SMITH & JIMMY NAPES

FOR YOUR CONSIDERATION

SPECTRE

007

MGM   SonyPicturesAwards.com

When *Skyfall* passed $1.1 billion at the worldwide box office, it became the eighth highest-grossing film ever made. For a franchise twenty-three films old this was a monumental achievement. Sam Mendes reflected:

> Frankly my overriding feeling was one of relief that people were not disappointed in it and had accepted some fairly daring strokes which I had felt nervous about: killing M, taking Bond back to his childhood home, turning him into a much more vulnerable figure than he had been in previous movies, and re-introducing Q, Moneypenny and the new M. Any one of those things could have been wholeheartedly rejected by the audience. And they were all accepted. So that was very pleasing.[1]

For *Bond 24*, MGM and Sony wanted more of the same, and Mendes would be a key component in attempting to repeat *Skyfall*'s success. Barbara Broccoli admitted, 'Everybody seemed to love *Skyfall* and that's what we are going for.'[2] Mendes had had casual discussions with the producers during the making of *Skyfall*:

> Barbara and Michael had made it fairly clear that they were keen for me to do another one. These discussions happen in the heat of battle, you don't want to break up that gang, that family. However, every idea that I ever had about Bond had gone into *Skyfall*. It's like I had cashed in all my chips. I felt like we'd played a lot of cards and what other cards were there left for me to play?'[3]

In February 2013, *Skyfall* won Oustanding British Film at the BAFTA awards and backstage Mendes discussed his possible return, 'We would want to make a better movie next time around, and if we thought we could do that, they might let me have another go.'[4] However, merely weeks later, the director announced:

> It has been a very difficult decision not to accept Michael's and Barbara's very generous offer to direct the next Bond movie but I have theatre and other commitments, including productions of *Charlie and the Chocolate Factory* and *King Lear*, that need my complete focus over the next year and beyond.[5]

Barbara and Michael said in a joint statement, 'We would have loved to have made the next film with him but completely respect his decision and hope to have the opportunity to collaborate with him again.'[6] Mendes would also find himself busy producing the Showtime horror TV series, *Penny Dreadful*, created by John Logan and starring Eva Green, Rory Kinnear and Timothy Dalton.

Barbara and Michael also turned their hands to other projects. Within a year, Eon presented the stage shows *Once* and *Chariots of Fire*, both based on the original hit films, and the play *Strangers on a Train,* an adaptation of Patricia Highsmith's 1950 novel. *Once* won eight Tony awards for its 2012 Broadway run before transferring to London's West End, where *Chariots of Fire* and *Strangers on a Train* had played in 2012 and 2013, respectively.

As well as theatrical productions, Eon were also developing non-Bond feature films. In May 2014, Sony Pictures announced that it was backing a story about NSA intelligence analyst/whistleblower Edward Snowden based on Pulitzer-winning journalist Glenn Greenwald's upcoming book NO PLACE TO HIDE: EDWARD SNOWDEN, THE NSA, AND THE U.S. SURVEILLANCE STATE.[7]

Whilst the Snowden project never came to fruition, Eon Productions first non-Bond feature film since *Call Me Bwana* in 1963, finally got underway in the summer of 2013. A remote Scottish island provided the backdrop for *The Silent Storm*, a taut drama about a stormy marriage between an authoritarian minister and his mysterious wife whose lives are shaken by the unexpected arrival of a delinquent in their home. Directed by Corinna Villari-McFarlane, *The Silent Storm* starred Andrea Riseborough, Ross Anderson and Damian Lewis and premiered at the BFI London Film Festival in October 2014.

However, Barbara and Michael would soon revert to Bond, and they began pursuing Sam Mendes once again. In order to secure him, they were prepared to wait for their director. Mendes recalled, 'It took MGM and Eon accepting that the movie wasn't going to come out in the summer of '15. I said I can't do it that fast.'[8] In July 2013 it was announced that Mendes would helm *Bond 24* due to hit cinemas in October 2015 with a screenplay by John Logan. Barbara said, 'He is a fantastic director and getting him back was a huge relief to us.'[9]

Mendes drew from childhood memories:

Daniel and I both remembered *Live and Let Die* as our first Bond movie. I wanted to make a film that was more flamboyant, more fun, with more adventure and more romance, a bit like the early Roger Moore movies. I felt like there was a different kind of Bond movie that I'd like to try and make.'[10]

Estrella (Stephanie Sigman) escorts Bond at the Day of the Dead festival in *Spectre*. (Rex Shutterstock)

Day of the Dead festival staged in Mexico City for the pre-title sequence. (Rex Shutterstock)

Spectre began with an ambitious single shot culminating on a Mexico City rooftop. (Rex Shutterstock)

Ralph Fiennes as Gareth Mallory, M. (Rex Shutterstock)

Monica Bellucci as Donna Lucia Sciarra in Rome. (Rex Shutterstock)

Christoph Waltz (left) directed by Sam Mendes (right). (Rex Shutterstock)

Bond escapes through ancient Rome in his Aston Martin DB10. (Rex Shutterstock)

Daniel Craig (left), Léa Seydoux (middle) and Dave Bautista at the Sölden press conference. (Rex Shutterstock

Sam Mendes (left) directs Léa Seydoux (right) at Pinewood Studios. (Rex Shutterstock)

Spectacular Alpine action in Obertilliach, Austria. (Rex Shutterstock)

Bond battles Mr. Hinx with the help of Dr. Swann. (Rex Shutterstock)

Bond and Swann escape Blofeld's crater. (Rex Shutterstock)

The Whitehall Brigade in London. Left to right: Tanner (Rory Kinnear), Eve Moneypenny (Naomie Harris) and Q (Ben Whishaw)

Andrew Scott as Max Denbigh (C). (Rex Shutterstock)

Daniel Craig arrives at the Royal World Charity Premiere at the Royal Albert Hall. (Rex Shutterstock)

The Duke of Cambridge meets Daniel Craig at the premiere. (Rex Shutterstock)

Sam Smith and Jimmy Napes collect Oscars for 'Writing's On The Wall'. (Rex Shutterstock)

Logan felt the influence of *Live and Let Die* too

> It's a perverse, strange movie. We talked about the incredibly strong use of
> macabre iconography, Geoffrey Holder as Baron Samedi, the tarot cards. I'm
> sure that's one of the influences which obviously lead to our Day of the Dead
> sequence. We all responded really favourably to that.[11]

Mendes' second Bond film was a reaction to his first:

> *Skyfall* was an entirely reactive movie as far as Bond was concerned. He is one
> step behind Silva. At the end, you could argue he has failed. He has not kept
> M alive. With *Spectre*, I wanted to make Bond more proactive, to give him a
> chance of redemption, and of escape.[12]

Regular Bond writers Neal Purvis and Robert Wade were on to pastures new.
In November 2012, three weeks after the release of *Skyfall*, Wade said during a
master class at the Doha Tribeca Film Festival, 'We're very happy to have done five
Bond movies, I think we've gotten it to a good place. I know that John Logan and
Sam Mendes have come up with a plot for another one, which takes the pressure
off because these films take up a lot of time.[13] Purvis added, 'We were going to
stop with *Quantum of Solace*, but it's good to go out on a high with *Skyfall*.'[14] The
writers had begun working with legendary spy scribe Len Deighton, adapting
his novel SS-GB for UK television. They were also collaborating with maverick
Danish film director Nicolas Winding Refn on numerous projects, including an
adaptation of *Barbarella*. In short, Purvis and Wade were in demand.

John Logan wanted his second Bond film as a co-writer 'to build on what
we did on *Skyfall*, but make it its own unique animal. The themes, ideas and
the characters can obviously continue on, because it is a franchise, and it is an
ongoing story.'[15]

Even before the release of *Skyfall* Logan expressed the view that, 'James
Bond should always fight Blofeld.'[16] Said Barbara, 'SPECTRE has, in the whole
history of Bond, played an important role. We thought, "OK, now's the time
to explore that again in a new and exciting and different way." We wouldn't
be attempting to go there unless we knew we had a good way of doing it.'[17]

Since the settlement in 1999, Kevin McClory continued his attempts to set
up a Bond project. In 2001 he announced production of *Warhead 2001*.[18] His
representative, Marian van de Veen, revealed from McClory's Amsterdam office
that the new film hoped to snare Marlon Brando as Ernst Stavro Blofeld.[19]

His attempt to make another 007 project after *Never Say Never Again* would again fail. Kevin McClory passed away peacefully on 20 November 2006, aged eighty.[20] In November 2013 Danjaq and MGM announced they had purchased all remaining character and story rights from McClory's estate.[21] William Kane of Baker-Hostetler LLP, who represented the McClory family, said:

> We were pleased in bringing to resolution this lengthy and contentious copyright dispute over the James Bond franchise. The fifty-year intellectual property row involving James Bond was settled because of a great deal of hard work by the attorneys for the estate of Kevin McClory, MGM, and Danjaq and will benefit James Bond film fans throughout the world.[22]

SPECTRE and Blofeld were introduced by Ian Fleming in his 1961 novel, THUNDERBALL. In the salubrious Boulevard Haussmann in Paris, the organisation works under the cover FIRCO (Fraternité International de la Résistance Contre l'Oppression), reuniting individuals displaced during World War II. FIRCO's head is revealed to be Ernst Stavro Blofeld, born on 28 May 1908 (Ian Fleming's own birthday) of a Polish father and Greek mother in Gdynia, Poland. After studying economics and political history at the University of Warsaw, Blofeld specialised in engineering and radionics at the Warsaw Technical Institute. He got a job in the Central Post Office and set about accumulating vast amounts of signal traffic and intelligence from both Allied and Axis powers. He gradually parlayed this intelligence into a well-funded private apolitical organisation made up of the elements of the former Nazi SS, various US and European mafia and ex-Soviet intelligence operatives. The group is dubbed SPECTRE: the Special Executive for Counter-Intelligence, Terrorism, Revenge and Extortion. Bond historian John Cork, an expert witness for Danjaq in the McClory dispute, posited that since previous Bond novels had featured a ghost town called Spectreville and a cipher machine named SPEKTOR, it is likely that it was Fleming, not his co-writers Kevin McClory and Jack Whittingham, who coined the acronym.[23] SPECTRE is led with iron discipline by Blofeld who, in Fleming's book, is a large, tall, dark-haired figure who is partial to violet-scented cachous and well-cut suits. He is not bald, does not have a scar, does not wear tunics or own a white cat.[24] Former US president Bill Clinton later applauded Fleming's prescience: 'He had this inkling that non-state actors could one day destablise the world.'[25]

Sam Mendes wanted to refresh the history, 'We are not adhering to any previous version of the SPECTRE story. We are creating our own version. Our film is a way of rediscovering SPECTRE and the super villain, setting him up again for the next generation.'[26]

Logan's first treatment had been developed independent of Sam Mendes, who now came to the project with fresh eyes:

> There had been an idea of shooting two movies at the same time. I felt it didn't work because part one felt like part one. A Bond movie has to feel like it has a beginning, a middle and an end. The audience demands a full meal. And tonally it didn't feel right. Barbara and Michael agreed. I asked, 'Would you allow me to work with John on a new treatment?' and they said, 'Yes of course."[27]

Logan's two-part story took Bond to Central Africa:

> It was a vast, sweeping idea. Neither had a title. It involved modern commu-nication, gold pan mining and the guilt therein. We always walk a tightrope because we want to be relevant but we can't be distasteful. It's not agitprop, it's not propaganda, it's not a documentary – it's an adventure movie.[28]

Logan recalled that early on 'there were many circumlocutions of the Blofeld character and his relationship with Bond. The real meat and potatoes of Blofeld came when Sam and I started working together.'[29] Logan's working title was a chapter from Ian Fleming's YOU ONLY LIVE TWICE: 'The Death Collector':

> In Fleming's world Blofeld was an international gangster who earned his stripes in communications. We looked at it very elliptically – where he could fit in the modern world. All of us feared the Austin Powers effect. How could you truly do a super-villain in such a way to be believable and to be Bondian?[30]

There was a notion to put a twist on the arch-nemesis:

> Sam said, 'What if it's Tilda Swinton?' It was so unexpected and non-tradi-tional. It allowed a *frisson* of sexual energy between Bond and Blofeld and immediately took it away from Donald Pleasence and Austin Powers. We played around with an ending in a volcano as if the *You Only Live Twice* lair existed. It was a paramilitary assault from outside where Blofeld's armour manufacturing plant was.[31]

Logan wanted to mine unused Fleming material,

> I always loved Bond's sea-based adventures and wanted to explore that world
> in detail with Dan Craig's Bond. THE HILDEBRAND RARITY is one of my
> favourite Fleming stories. Bond reunited with, and then tried to save, his lost
> love: the woman who broke his heart in the past. She was in danger due to
> her sadistic lover/husband/brother in a way that hints at the plot of the short
> story. Eventually Bond joins them on a super-yacht, the *Disco Volante*, which
> goes to polar regions and jeopardy ensues. At heart it was a dark love story
> which remains the thread that runs through *Spectre*.[32]

Mendes continued working with Logan on many ideas, 'We went down blind
alleys, we tried things that didn't work. We messed up.'[33] Mendes finally decided
upon Mexico's Day of the Dead festival as the backdrop for the pre-title.
Even then the sequence morphed extensively over months. Assistant director
Michael Lerman remembered, 'At first it was set in Cuba at another type of
festival. There was a car chase and Bond's car went off the side of a dock and
landed on a yacht with a beautiful woman lying there. It had more of a comedic
ending.'[34] In an early draft Bond was to stumble into a weird schoolroom where
he discovers a message that is being given to an unknown terrorist by a shady
figure who we later learn is Blofeld. Bond is rescued by a British Embassy
figure, 'a sweaty linen-suited Brit, written with actor Toby Jones in mind'.[35]

Mendes sent Logan research material concerning smartblood, cutting-edge
technology that could be used for tracking people and transmuting information, 'The hook in my version was that a traitor, who was Tanner, downloaded
all the files of MI6 and all the NATO powers into Bond's smartblood. Blofeld
[was to capture] Bond and drain his blood.'[36] A Logan draft involved MI6
vs CIA in which Felix Leiter played 'a major part'.[37] Another attempt had
Moneypenny 'very badly wounded [in the pre-title sequence]. The rest of the
movie is about her recovering and figuring out Tanner is a traitor.'[38]

At one time the finale involved 'a conference gathering of intelligence personnel targeted by a ship of toxic waste with a bomb on board sailing up the
Thames.'[39] Logan devised an ending which included 'a debate in the Houses
of Parliament, a lot of gun play outside which eventually ended in the tower
of Big Ben. It was very British.'[40] Logan had to leave the film due to his commitment to the TV show *Penny Dreadful*, co-produced by Sam Mendes, who
understood the situation: 'we hit a wall, it was very late in the process'.[41]

Barbara and Michael turned back to the talents of Neal Purvis and Robert

Wade, who were hired for a record-breaking sixth consecutive James Bond assignment. Wade remembered the turn of events:

> We were approached in May 2014 regarding our availability. Fortunately, we were just finishing another movie so were available. It was very interesting coming in halfway through the process, a new experience for us and somehow less pressurised, though a lot is riding on you coming up with the goods.[42]

Purvis recounted, 'We got the call, "we need your expertise." We very quickly read the drafts and could see where they were at. They had a structure and a root and they had locations they were thinking of using. They were pretty well prepared for what they were going to do and had most of the characters.'[43] Wade was appreciative: 'The best thing John had created was the relationship between Bond and Madeleine. That the only person who understands and can cure Bond is the daughter of a hitman is a very nice conceit.'[44]

Purvis recalled, 'There was a feeling that it just needed to be made a bit more Bondian. Bond didn't feel like he was driving the story. The engine we brought was the suggestion of M's message from beyond the grave. That gave Bond the opportunity to be driving the whole plot with his own private agenda.'[45] Wade elaborated, 'Bond makes Q do things against his loyalty to Mallory, he makes Moneypenny his own spy within MI6 – and neither of them know it; Bond is the ringmaster.'[46]

Purvis felt that Logan's idea of including the Whitehall brigade, all unified in the action, 'was straying into Mission Impossible territory'.[47] Q was to be kidnapped in Austria, enticing Bond out to Blofeld's lair in the desert to rescue him.[48] Q helps Bond escape a solar furnace and is forced to kill a man causing Bond to quip, 'Sometimes a trigger has to be pulled'[49] – echoing Q's putdown to 007 in *Skyfall*. According to Wade, 'We didn't think it was appropriate for Q to be involved with that much action.'[50] Mendes also objected, feeling it transformed Q, dramatically, into the 'Bond girl'.[51]

Wade thought:

> It was interesting for Moneypenny not to be in the field. At one stage we had her going down into the paper archives, a very tense scene where she's going to find a file which connects C and Oberhauser. It was a nice scene because everything in the movie is about digital and modernity but actually the secrets are still hidden in these paper files. Originally, the scene when Bond

asks Moneypenny to work against Ralph's orders took place in Highgate Cemetery by Judi's grave. As Moneypenny leaves, Bond says, 'Do you think she'd have liked the irony?' Moneypenny asks, 'What irony?' Bond says, 'Her ending up to the left of Karl Marx."'[52]

Marx is famously buried in Highgate Cemetery. Mendes felt Bond 'trusts Moneypenny with information he would trust no-one else with'.[53]

Mallory was also a thematic factor in the story, as Wade outlined, 'We wanted the film to be about him gaining respect. His moral position is strong. He accepts that you need to have surveillance but it's how you handle it that's the important thing. Giving him real issues and having to fight his corner, not helped by Bond going rogue.'[54]

Wade explained how the events surrounding Edward Snowden – on whom Eon were developing a movie – had an impact on the screenplay, 'Barbara and Michael followed that news story very closely. They handed us information two inches thick. The idea was that if you control Big Data, you control everything.'[55] The surveillance theme also played out in a previously scripted moment in the SPECTRE boardroom in which a bucketful of recently extracted eyeballs is poured onto the conference table as the chairman chastises those gathered to keep watch, see everything.[56]

Not only was the literary heritage of Bond mined for *Spectre* but so were the biographical details of Ian Fleming. Wade explained:

Neal and I thought the snow sequence in Austria should be set in Kitzbühel, where Fleming spent a lot of his adolescence. It's where he wrote his earliest stories. He was sent to go and live with Ernan Forbes-Dennis and Phyliss Bottome and their family who provided therapy for those permanently in a negative contest with their siblings, a condition called *Gegenspieler* – which, of course, is in a way what troubles Oberhauser/Blofeld.[57]

In 1960, Fleming wrote to Phyliss Bottome, 'My life with you both is one of my most cherished memories, and heaven knows where I should be today without Ernan.'[58] Fleming's time in Kitzbühel, almost certainly influenced his short story OCTOPUSSY, which involves Bond's ski instructor, Hannes Oberhauser, of whom the spy poignantly says, 'He was like a father to me when I happened to need one.'[59]

It was this line that inspired Mendes:

Bond's parents died and he had been brought up by his aunt and he was sent for a period to stay with this man in the Alps. It was actually Michael Wilson's idea: what if this guy had a real son and Bond came in, a cuckoo in the nest and ousted this less glamorous, less handsome, less heroic figure. We should have really used that piece of information better in the movie but it's very difficult to drop exposition about Bond's childhood into the middle of a tense action narrative.[60]

Spectre would be the first 007 film overtly to include elements from a non-Fleming Bond novel. COLONEL SUN by Kingsley Amis (using the pseudonym Robert Markham) was first published in the UK on 28 March 1968. The plot sees M being kidnapped, which leads Bond on a trail to Athens and ultimately to a Greek island where he confronts the evil Chinese villain, Colonel Sun Liang-Tan. Once captured in Greece, Bond will be tortured by Sun, who leaves his and M's bodies, framing them for a terrorist attack on a Soviet intelligence conference nearby. Wade recalled that the producers had been obligated to explore the rights to the novel in 1998 as *The World Is Not Enough* also featured M's kidnap, although in a different context.[61] In the novel, Colonel Sun inserts metal skewers by hand into orifices of Bond's head to stimulate his pain senses. Sun described having once deprived a man of his eyes in a previous gory torture. Wade thought it suitable, 'I always remember that scene in that book, it was so horrible. I sent an extract of that to Sam and he responded very strongly to it.'[62] Mendes particularly liked 'the idea of testing someone's pain threshold. The emotional disconnect between Blofeld and Bond. Blofeld has zero empathy, zero interest in human suffering.'[63] Originally Bond and Blofeld were to play a childhood card game in an oak-panelled study, with hazelnuts as chips, which young Bond had consistently won. 'It was very Fleming-like but it wasn't frightening, it wasn't violent and it felt like it was too urbane.'[64] Mendes liked the notion of the clinical setting for the torture, inspired in particular by Colonel Gadaffi's compound in Tripoli, Libya, which had been stormed by rebels in 2011. "Gadaffi had a fully functioning operating theatre for his plastic surgeries. They trashed it very quickly so there's no photo evidence.'[65] The torture device was updated for the twenty-first century with a high-tech contraption designed by Mendes and the art department.[66]

Purvis and Wade had created their own backstory for the SPECTRE organisation. Blofeld, Mr. White and C had served in a unit together in the French Foreign Legion which had become a criminal operation in the desert.[67] Purvis elaborated, 'They needed to survive so they killed everyone else in their unit

and ate them. That's how these three men became this horrible triumvirate.'[68]
The ruins of an old French Foreign Legion fort were once to have been a setting.[69] Mendes felt, 'Large quantities of exposition tend to be like lead weights
in action movies. I thought there was plenty of backstory already for Mr. White
and Blofeld's prior relationship with Bond.'[70]

Initially actor Chiwetel Ejiofor was considered to play C in what was originally a much more expanded role in the story.[71] However, the part was reduced
and eventually played by Andrew Scott. Purvis stated, 'When C became a
younger man, you couldn't really build a connection between him and Mr.
White any more.'[72]

Resurrecting Blofeld was always going to be tricky for Mendes: 'Those
early Bond movies are on the edge of parody and then *Austin Powers* pushed
them over the edge. The big discussion was how to bring Blofeld back without
immediately knowing who it was.'[73] Wade felt, 'Sam had a very clear view.
The point is you don't grandstand, you don't make big threats or have him
speak in any kind of sinister way.'[74] Purvis recalled, 'The white cat came in and
out several times. At one point it walked down the middle of the table at the
SPECTRE meeting.'[75]

The Blofeld character in previous drafts was named Heinrich Stockman[76]
and then Ernst Serban.[77] Purvis explained, 'In the scripts that were handed
out he wasn't called Blofeld for security reasons. They didn't want the secret
getting out there.'[78]

In the traditional Eon way, stockpiled script and set-piece ideas were resur-
rected. The notion of 007 purloining an Aston Martin not yet battle-ready
and escaping via the ejector seat was originally written for the putative third
Timothy Dalton Bond film and survived relocated but virtually intact in
Spectre.[79] Another recycled scene was the death of Mr. White, originally conceived by Purvis and Wade in their first draft of *Quantum of Solace* in which
White committed suicide during the Palio in Sienna.[80] Purvis recalled that
White's original death was inspired by the real-life radioactive poisoning of
Russian dissident Alexander Litvinenko, 'That was in the Millennium Hotel
round the corner from the Eon office.'[81] In *Spectre*, Mr. White's mobile phone
is contaminated by radioactive thallium, causing his inexorable demise.

Purvis and Wade's working titles included 'Stone Ghost' and 'Something
Beginning with M'.[82] Mendes explained the rationale behind the final title: 'When
we decided that Blofeld was going to return, *Spectre* became the obvious title. The
word Spectre, if you don't spell it in capitals so it's not an acronym, is perfect. Here
is a figure from Bond's past who is returning so it had a nice double meaning.'[83]

Jez Butterworth, who had performed an uncredited polish on *Skyfall*, returned for *Spectre*. The playwright thought in this franchise actions speak louder than words, 'Bond shoots other men – he doesn't sit around chatting to them.'[84] Purvis remembered:

> The cuckoo expression was Jez. He did write a backstory more to do with that. He also concentrated on the crater material and the third act for a while. It was dialogue that he was concerning himself with. Sam combined what he wanted from Jez and what he wanted from us into a draft.[85]

Daniel Craig contributed his own ideas. Purvis recalled, 'He has a very good understanding of Bond. It's an advantage having him in the room and having him so focused on it.'[86]

Craig was more realistic,

> I'm not a writer. I've sometimes got a few good ideas but putting it down on paper is a whole different ballgame. No one's a bigger fan of writers than I am. Skilled writers are what make a movie. With John, he writes the script and we get a shape and a form. You're just fiddling with tiny bits you're not rewriting whole scenes. [Rob and Neal] have been involved in all of them that I've made and their input is invaluable. And having someone as talented as Jez around is useful.[87]

Purvis acknowledged another unsung presence, 'Sam's script editor, Jane-Anne Tenggren, was there all the time and it probably wouldn't have got done if she wasn't doing the work she did.'[88]

Sam Mendes explained eloquently the writing process of a James Bond movie:

> Everyone involved was remarkably understanding. Just getting the basic story is so difficult on these films. A big movie very rarely has one writer. Everyone remained friends throughout that process. John Logan did the heavy lifting but hit a wall at a certain point. It was bruising for John to be taken off because he felt he brought *Skyfall* home, so he felt that he should be able to bring this entire movie home with a sole writing credit. We ended up with Rob and Neal and then Jez riding to the rescue. When you're the director of a Bond movie and you have writers, it's a little bit like being the manager of a Premiership football team. After seventy minutes, a couple of your players

are just bloody knackered. It's not their fault, they're just tired. You need to able to take Theo Walcott off and put Olivier Giroud on without offending Theo Walcott and without offending Olivier Giroud that he wasn't picked in the first place! You need to choose who you're bringing on as a sub. You've got the mid-field generals of Rob and Neal who tend to have a real overview, very experienced, they're the sort of Tony Adams: they've been around the block, they know their Bond history but then you also have to bring on Jez who's more like Sanchez up front, he's got fast footwork and he can add that bit of magic. Jez did significantly more work on *Spectre*. Both sets of writers had to work simultaneously and they were fully aware of each other's presence. They managed brilliantly.[89]

The pre-title sequence of *Spectre* begins with Bond and local girl Estrella in Mexico City during an elaborate Day of the Dead parade. Soon after M's demise, 007 had received a video message from her suggesting he track down Mafia hitman Marco Sciarra, kill him and attend the funeral. Aware there may be an infiltrator in MI6, Bond has been roaming the world trying to track down Sciarra. In Mexico, Bond spies Sciarra introducing himself with a special ring and discussing his next target, the Pale King. 007 thwarts Sciarra's plan to bomb a nearby stadium and then stalks Sciarra through the parade. Eventually Bond and Sciarra grapple on the latter's getaway helicopter, which has landed in the middle of the teaming Zócalo Square. 007 kicks the Mafioso to his death mid-flight but not before relieving him of his ring, etched with an octopus symbol.

Back in London, Mallory is on the losing side of a turf war with his rival, Max Denbigh, code-named C, the head of the new Centre for National Security (CNS). Determined to abolish the Double-o programme, preferring drones and satellites to human agents, C has managed to obtain private funding for a new headquarters which will soon have the capability of unlimited mass surveillance. Bond's recent unauthorised escapade in Mexico City plays right into C's hands and M grounds 007.

Moneypenny visits Bond's home, where he reveals to her the message from their late boss. Bond leverages this to turn Moneypenny into 007's mole in the suspect MI6. Bond ponders on a mysterious photo rescued from the smouldering remains of his childhood home, an image of himself as a boy, an older mountaineer and an unidentifiable third person.

Bond travels by boat with Tanner to Q's new Thames-side workshop, opposite the old MI6 Vauxhall Cross HQ, now set for demolition after being wrecked by Silva's gas explosion in *Skyfall*. Bond is injected with smartblood to allow M to monitor his movements. After being given a new Omega watch, Bond colludes with Q to loosen the surveillance shackles long enough for him to purloin the brand-new Aston Martin DB10 designated for 009.

Bond drives the DB10 to Rome, attends Marco Sciarra's funeral and meets his widow, Lucia. While she was married, it was assumed she would keep silent about her late husband's dealings but now she is considered a threat and will inevitably be killed. Resigned to her fate, Lucia is saved and seduced by Bond. In return, Lucia tips him off about her spouse's membership of a secretive sect. Using Sciarra's octopus ring, Bond infiltrates the organisation and witnesses Mr. Hinx take the position of Sciarra on the board by gouging out the eyes of his rival with steel thumbnails. At this point, the chairman reveals himself to Bond as Franz Oberhauser, a figure from Bond's past but believed to have been dead for many years.

Bond is forced to escape in the DB10 pursued hotly by Mr. Hinx in a Jaguar CX75 through the night streets of the ancient capital. Eluding Hinx with the aid of an ejector seat, Bond with Moneypenny's help, deduces that the Pale King is none other than Mr. White, now believed to be in Austria. White was ostensibly connected to the villainous organisation Quantum which Bond holds responsible for the death of Vesper Lynd.

Meanwhile, C and M attend a security conference in Tokyo, a gathering of nine intelligence agencies – Nine Eyes – who plan to pool the results of their omnipresent surveillance. However, when put to vote, the South Africans veto the motion.

In Austria, at Mr. White's remote lakeside bolthole, Bond understands why he was Sciarra's next target. Rejecting his organisation's escalation of indiscriminate violence – a train bombing in Hamburg, an industrial explosion in Tunisia – White seeks redemption. He is near death due to his mobile phone having been laced with radioactive thallium. Bond gains White's trust with the protection of his daughter, who, White tells 007, will lead him to L'Americain, a key clue behind those responsible for the increasing global mayhem. White then kills himself with Bond's gun and the act is caught on CCTV.

Bond visits White's daughter, Dr. Madeleine Swann, working in obscurity as a psychiatrist in the discreet Höffner Klinik high in the Austrian Alps. However, Hinx has tracked down Swann too and snatches her. Bond commandeers a plane, crashing it into the convoy which has kidnapped Swann, thereby rescuing her. Whilst eluding enemy agents, Q performs diagnostics on Sciarra's ring. Toxicology reports show it contains an extremely rare element, also present in the autopsies of Marco Sciarra, Le Chiffre, Dominic Greene, Raoul Silva

– Bond's previous foes – and has DNA traces which prove Franz Oberhauser could not have been dead. Meanwhile, they watch news reports of an atrocity in South Africa – a response against that nation's Nine Eyes veto by Mr. White's former organisation, which Madeleine confides is called SPECTRE.

Madeleine travels with Bond to Tangier and takes him to L'Americain, her father's Moroccan safe house from where he logged information on SPECTRE's activities, including a set of mysterious co-ordinates in the desert. They travel by train to this destination. During the journey, Madeleine suggests Bond is trapped in the life of an assassin and 007 begins to understand there could be solace beyond espionage. Mr. Hinx suddenly appears and a vicious fight ensues between compartments. With Madeleine's help, Bond outwits Hinx.

Bond and Madeleine are received at the remote train stop by a 1948 Rolls-Royce Silver Wraith which chauffeurs them to the Kartenhoff meteorite crater; Oberhauser's lair. They discover Franz to be a person from their respective pasts who has also acted like a puppeteer, influencing Bond's previous missions. Oberhauser is behind the huge investment in CNS and with direct access to the intelligence streams of nine agencies, SPECTRE will have the ability to control global events. This includes the resignation of M from MI6, having lost his turf war with C. Oberhauser shows Swann that Bond facilitated her father's suicide with the leaked CCTV footage. However, Madeleine is unmoved and stays loyal to Bond. In a clinical chamber, 007 is then tortured by insertions into his skull which threaten to disable him permanently. Here Oberhauser reveals he thought of Bond as a cuckoo, easing him out of his father, Hannes Oberhauser's heart, when Bond spent time with the family after he was orphaned. Hurt by parental rejection, Oberhauser contrived his father's death and faked his own. Now, he has taken a name from his mother's line: Ernst Stavro Blofeld. Madeleine helps Bond escape using Q's exploding watch and together they cause the massive desert complex to explode.

They return to London and reunite with M, Moneypenny, Q and Tanner at Hildebrand, a central London safe house. M confronts C in the brand-new CNS HQ while Q hacks into the mainframe to prevent the data stream going online. C attacks M but in the altercation, Denbigh falls to his death. Bond is apprehended and taken to the bombed-out interior of the old MI6 HQ, wired for demolition. Here, Blofeld, scarred by Bond's escape, gives 007 a choice of saving himself or saving a loved one. Instinctively, Bond searches for Madeleine, who was kidnapped by Blofeld when she left Hildebrand. 007 conjures an ingenious escape just as the former riverside HQ implodes by controlled explosions.

Bond and Madeleine chase Blofeld's fleeing helicopter by powerboat down the Thames. 007's crack marksmanship downs the helicopter on Westminster Bridge, leaving Blofeld injured and at Her Majesty's mercy. Spurred by earlier thoughts of turning his back on life as an assassin, 007 does not kill Blofeld. Instead, he throws his Walther PPK into the Thames and seems to walk away from his profession. A coda shows Bond visiting Q's workshop to retrieve equipment. Bond and Madeleine, in a newly refurbished Aston Martin DB5, roar down Whitehall as a new dawn rises.

Mendes reflected on the final story:

> *Skyfall* was a post-Julian Assange movie and *Spectre* is a post-Edward Snowden movie. The political landscape that we were trying to reflect was very recent. The fears that haunted *Skyfall* were to do with hacking and the fears that haunted *Spectre* were to do with surveillance. Neither of them have gone away. Those were things that provided the fuel that drove the antagonist.[90]

In November 2014 Eon Productions became a high-profile victim of the cyber-attack by suspected North Korean hackers on Sony in protest at Seth Rogen's North Korean political satire *The Interview*.[91] Early drafts of the *Spectre* screenplay were stolen and published online, and exchanges between the studio and Eon indicated that a spiralling budget of $300 million was causing friction between the producers and Sony.[92] The chairman and CEO of MGM, Gary Barber, was quoted as saying, 'We don't comment on budgets but I can assure you it's substantially less.'[93] Wilson was rueful, 'The worst thing was they put our script on the [web]. We got it taken down immediately, but that was an out-of-date script, luckily, so it wasn't what we shot, but that was an impact.'[94] Barbara was realistic, 'The stuff about us having fights about the budget, well, what's new? We want to put all the money on the screen. We want to deliver the best film we can. We fight for as much money as we can to make the film. And that's no secret.'[95] Amy Pascal was eventually to lose her job over the scandal.[96] Mendes was sorry, 'She was very good in the crucial moments: script, first preview, marketing, where you want your head of studio to kick in, she kicked in. Otherwise, Barbara and Michael always protected me from studio politics.'[97]

On 3 December 2014 Eon Productions announced key details concerning *Bond 24* at a press conference held on the 007 Stage at Pinewood Studios. Welcoming journalists to the place 'where budgets go to die',[98] Mendes, joined by Barbara Broccoli, revealed the title was officially *Spectre*.

Daniel Craig relished the shift in Bond's character. Said Mendes:

If you look at *Casino Royale, Quantum* and *Skyfall* he's in various forms of crisis. There was an angsty aspect to the character which he played brilliantly but I think he was tiring of it. I think he thought "Can I do a Bond film where I get to have some funny lines, I get the girl and make something that is more like pure entertainment?"[99]

Craig mused, 'You have to make it fun. We're making a Bond movie. I want the celebration of all that back in.'[100] Craig was thrilled to be given a co-producer credit:

It's one of the proudest moments in my career. I've been as involved as I possibly could on every single movie I've made and it was very generous of the producers to say we want you as part of this team. I've been involved with this from the conception, from the first meeting [in which] Sam and I sat down together and [said] 'What are we going to do?'[101]

How they were going to do what they were going to do would be devised by a now veteran Bond crew. Returning for their third consecutive Bond were production designer Dennis Gassner and first assistant director Michael Lerman. Costume designer Jany Temime and composer Thomas Newman returned for their respective second Bond films. Embarking on his fourteenth Bond was Chris Corbould, credited as special effects and miniature effects supervisor as well as splinter second unit director. He was reunited with visual effects supervisor Steve Begg. Both worked closely with Gary Powell, stunt co-ordinator on all the Craig Bonds with a deep family history connected to the series. Returning too were *Skyfall* Oscar-winning sound editors Per Hallberg and Karen Baker Landers.

New to Bond and both fresh from Christopher Nolan's *Interstellar* (2014), were director of photography Hoyte van Hoytema and editor Lee Smith. Mendes was given a preview of the film by his friend Christopher Nolan:

I couldn't just drop a newcomer in to fill Roger [Deakin's]'s shoes. Hoyte comes from the European tradition, but he understands American filmmaking. He has his own very unusual and very particular aesthetic. He's very sharp with clichés, very quick to pick up things that he feels are too well trodden, but he also understands classic filmmaking.[102]

Having shot *Skyfall* digitally, Hoytema suggested *Spectre* be shot on 35mm film and there were even initial discussions to shoot segments of the movie in IMAX.[103] Mendes understood his cinematographer:

> I love digital. I felt the Alexa was very potent and beautiful in the night time scenes of *Skyfall*, particularly in Shanghai, in the office building and the night time casino, two sequences which were brilliantly shot and lit by Roger. But digital felt less romantic, less textured in many of the exteriors. And under bright light I felt it was difficult to control, harsh on actors, less forgiving. Film is difficult, it's imprecise, but that's also the glory of it. It had romance, a slight nostalgia, and that's not inappropriate when dealing with a classic Bond movie.[104]

For such a complex film, *Spectre* had an extremely short post-production schedule. In order to overcome any difficulties arising from this, a detailed heads of department meeting preceded the preparation of the shoot.[105] Filming and planning was overseen by executive producer Callum McDougall, who joined the Bond movies with *The Living Daylights* in 1986.

Eon Productions once again hired casting director Debbie McWilliams, who has more than thirty years' experience with the franchise: 'For each part we build up a dossier on who's around, who's interesting. Because we don't have the finished script until pretty much the day before we start shooting some actors find it quite hard to sign up because they're not quite sure what they're signing up to.'[106] Case in point was two-time Best Supporting Actor Oscar-winner Christoph Waltz, cast as Franz Oberhauser. Mendes explained, 'If he's the son of an Austrian, he should be Austrian.'[107] The director visited Waltz in LA:

> I talked Christoph through the story as it existed. He said, 'Well, that's not on the page.' I said, 'Correct, and it may not be on the page for a while.' Christoph was put in quite a tricky situation because he had to film the first scenes of the character, not knowing where the latter scenes were going to be. Any actor wants to know where they're building towards and he didn't. But he managed magnificently.[108]

Impressed by the recent Bond movies, Waltz felt the role could be artistically fulfilling, 'These films with Daniel Craig have shifted the tone. I consider Bond movies to be an extension of popular theatre, a kind of modern mythology. You see the same sort of action in Punch and Judy, or in the folk theatre of various cultures, like Grand Guignol.'[109] Waltz was inspired by a Teutonic predecessor, 'Gert Fröbe in *Goldfinger* was a German theatre actor propelled into this situation.'[110] He felt a connection with Mendes, 'Sam is a theatre animal. You can feel that in the work between actors.'[111]

Mendes' initial casting thoughts for Madeleine Swann were that she should be representative of her onscreen father, the assassin Mr. White played by Danish actor Jesper Christensen. Therefore, a casting call was put out for 'a blonde Scandinavian actress'.[112] McWilliams 'met a lot of lovely girls – but nobody who really grabbed [Sam]'.[113] As Mendes developed the story, the casting brief changed, 'Debbie is a beat behind the writing process. She was out in Scandinavia auditioning Scandinavian women and suddenly our idea of Blofeld and Austria comes in from left field. We could then broaden the net, we could look at French and German actresses too.'[114] For McWilliams, 'Paris is very fertile soil. I spent two days meeting girls every fifteen minutes.'[115] Michael Wilson gave an insight into the Proust-ian character: '[Madeleine Swann] changes his life, and so you have to get someone who is convincing, like Eva Green was in *Casino Royale*.'[116]

Mendes settled upon French actress Léa Seydoux, who had set pulses racing in *La Vie d'Adèle* (*Blue is the Warmest Colour* – 2013). Seydoux auditioned with three other contenders, reading scenes from both *Casino Royale* and *Quantum of Solace*.[117] The actress later confessed, 'I was very nervous when I did the casting so I had a beer. I don't think it was a very good idea.'[118] McWilliams was forgiving, 'Léa did the train scene from *Casino Royale* but felt she'd let herself down.'[119] Seydoux tested a second time at Pinewood for Sam Mendes, who 'put her in a dressing room and gave her the script. She flew over in the morning, she's French, she's reading English, it's not her language. I knocked on the door two hours later and she's fast asleep in this overheated dressing room, in this enormous coat. I asked, "How's the script?" and she said, "It's great!" She was on page three.' Mendes was aware of Bond publicity lore, 'I always hate the line that is trotted out in the junket that the Bond girl is as tough as Bond which generally means they get in a couple of fights, which doesn't necessarily mean as human beings they match.'[120]

Crucially, Craig admired Seydoux, having seen her performance alongside his wife Rachel Weisz in *The Lobster*.[121] Seydoux was offered the part in April 2014. 'I especially identified with Eva Green as Vesper Lynd in *Casino Royale*. It impressed me that a French actress was playing a Bond girl. But there's no way

I could have imagined myself playing a Bond girl nearly ten years later. For me, that dream was too big.'[122] On Swann, Seydoux reflected:

> Psychology is a big aspect of how my character seduces Bond with her mind and intelligence. I have no background in medicine or psychology, but I read psychology books all the time and have been to see psychiatrists myself. The power to understand the mind is fascinating and, from my experience, therapy really works.[123]

In casting Mafia widow Lucia Sciarra, McWilliams drew from Bond history, 'I've always liked Monica Bellucci, it was an ambition of mine at some time or another to get her in a Bond movie. She came and tested for [Roger Spottiswoode in *Tomorrow Never Dies*].'[124] Pierce Brosnan had campaigned passionately for her when she auditioned for Paris Carver.[125] Bellucci appreciated Spottiswoode sending her 'a beautiful letter when I didn't do the film'.[126] The Italian star had powerful support from Barbara Broccoli: 'I was really afraid that she was going to be the one that got away.'[127] Mendes explained that casting her was not without challenge, 'Initially the studio was resistant to having a fifty-year-old play that part.'[128] Bellucci was surprised, 'I assumed they wanted me to play the new M.'[129] But her self-deprecation belied the serious intent behind the casting:

> My first thought was: 'How can I be a Bond girl at fifty?' After my audition Sam Mendes told me that, for almost the first time in history, he wanted a woman of a similar age to the actor playing Bond, I'd prefer to be called a Bond woman or perhaps a Bond lady'[130]

Neal Purvis admitted, 'Lucia was never written for someone as big as Monica. We'd have written more if we'd known she was going to be in it.'[131]

Spectre reintroduced the classic Bond henchperson in the guise of Mr. Hinx. John Logan initially created 'a henchwoman named Charlotte, a bad CIA agent. We were juggling between if Blofeld was going to be a man or a woman so we didn't want to make it the Amazonian brigade against Bond so the sex shifted back and forth.'[132] McWilliams did 'research all over the world from Russia to China for great big strong guys, we came up with some extraordinary people.'[133] Dave Bautista, a former World Wrestling Entertainment (WWE) wrestler, had made a name for himself in Marvel's *Guardians of the Galaxy*. Two young fans who lobbied for him were Mendes' and Craig's sons.[134] Bautista recalled, 'When

I came over to meet Sam, I only asked two questions. I asked him if Mr. Hinx was a badass. He said, "Yes he's a badass." I said, "Well, is Mr. Hinx intelligent?" He said, "Very."'[135] Robert Wade revealed, 'my German master in school was a man called Pedro Hinks. In Spanish, Hinx means hench as in a horseman, the origin of henchman. It actually means Mr. Hench.'[136]

Max Denbigh, code-named C, was a key character according to Andrew Scott:

> C has the opinion that one man in the field, even someone like Bond, cannot really compete with the huge technological advances that we've made in the 21st century. The idea of people losing control of their digital ghost and their online legacy is central to the storyline – our privacy and how much information we feel is right to keep to ourselves and how much we need to be protected.[137]

The 'home team, Whitehall brigade'[138] introduced in *Skyfall* returned. Ralph Fiennes felt *Spectre* provided a good arc for M: 'For a moment he's out of a job and he finds his way back. He has to bond with Bond so to speak.'[139] M is backed by his quartermaster, Ben Whishaw, who thought this time, 'Q's arc is one of exasperation with Bond. Everybody's loyalty to Bond is challenged but then reaffirmed and Q ends up with the realisation that Bond is operating on a whole different level.'[140] Mendes felt Q assisting Bond in the field upped the drama: 'I really enjoyed the banter and the relationship between Daniel's Bond and Ben's Q in *Skyfall* and I felt we could take that further. I wanted to see someone who obsessively doesn't like to fly putting himself on the line to help Bond.'[141] Rory Kinnear considered Tanner to have progressed, 'Now Judi has gone, he's moved off into his own office and now he's got his own department to look after. His professional career has grown through the three films.'[142] Eve Moneypenny for Naomie Harris was 'now part of a pack [but] with that shroud of mystery. Her relationship with Bond [is] very different – there's a respect between them.'[143] In hindsight Mendes noted, 'Narratively, the Moneypenny story is kind of treading water in *Spectre*. You can't move all these stories forward in a two-and-a-half-hour movie. In terms of the franchise she is waiting there to be used again as something more than a personal assistant to M.'[144]

Jesper Christensen as Mr. White was vital to retrofit a Bond cinematic universe in *Spectre*. Michael and Gregg Wilson appear briefly as intelligence apparatchiks, and Moneypenny's unnamed partner is portrayed by Tam Williams, the step-son of Lucy Williams, Ian Fleming's niece.

Judi Dench returned for one last appearance, to film her message from beyond the grave. For Mendes, it was a good omen:

> Originally, we were working on the idea that she left Bond a letter. But I felt the audience needed to be reminded of Judi so it turned into a visual message. She came in for the morning and it was lovely to see her. We did it before we started principal photography. It felt a very appropriate way to start the new movie, to begin with the person around whom the last movie revolved.[145]

Shooting commenced at Pinewood Studios and around London during December 2014. Mendes requested autonomy from the producers on the studio floor, as he had done on *Skyfall*:

> I need to be alone with the monitor screen. I become very self-conscious. You can have your monitor screen twenty feet away and whenever you have a note, just come over and say, 'Are you sure about this?' But that was new to [Barbara and Michael], I think they had traditionally sat by the director. It's not a comment on them. It doesn't matter whether you're Scott Rudin or Dick Zanuck, I don't have any producers next to me at the monitor screen.[146]

Spectre marked the first time audiences had seen the inside of Bond's London flat since *Live and Let Die*. The undisclosed location was Stanley Gardens in chic Notting Hill. Dennis Gassner felt the spartan set showed 007 'is always going to be on the move and this is just a place to put the few things that he has. I don't think we ever want to see him comfortable. He is an adventurer. That is the life of an agent. If you get too settled you get too soft.'[147]

For Gassner, it was about progression for Q:

> We wanted to say that his laboratory here was more about his inventing side rather than the tactical side. We were still in the Churchill bunker kind of environment but coming off the river this time. That was a fun shift from the old Q to the more studied Q and that translates into the workshop.[148]

Bond's boat ride with Tanner to Q's new laboratory was shot in Camden Lock. For Rory Kinnear, shooting in public was a novel experience, 'We had all the offices overlooking us. They were more excited to see Daniel than me. By the time I got home, someone had given me a copy of the *Evening Standard* with us on the front of it.'[149]

In January 2015, filming continued in Altaussee, Austria, for Bond's approach via boat to Mr. White's safe house, which for Dennis Gassner was 'a real location that was exactly the way I would have wanted it designed, if I'd had to build a classic, isolated, lonely safe house'.[150] First assistant director Michael Lerman recalled that the weather determined the action: 'If it froze over, [Bond would] walk the lake, if not, he arrived by boat.'[151]

The unit then moved to Sölden, where exteriors of the Höffner Klinik were shot at the ice Q hotel, 'an ice jewel',[152] according to Gassner. The interiors were completed at Pinewood, at Callum McDougall's suggestion, much to Mendes' reluctance.[153] Lit expertly by van Hoytema, 'It's such a wonderful feeling to have actors walk onto a set and start settling in as if they're really in a location.'[154] The Pevsner, Q's hotel, another Pinewood interior, was a nod to long-time Bond executive producer Tom Pevsner, who passed away in 2015.[155]

The snowbound location would host a central action sequence. Wilson recalled, 'We were very conscious of what we've done in all these films. That meant we wanted to do something different from being in bobsleighs or using any of the usual winter sports.'[156] At conception stage a ski sequence was considered which was, according to John Logan, 'much more elaborate, a little more *OHMSS*'.[157] This later developed into a skidoo chase.[158]

Mendes elaborated:

> Bond in macro and in micro is a job of reverse engineering. You have a big idea and then you work backwards to see if it makes sense. You find a way to do it within the capabilities of a) the actor b) the filmmaker c) the franchise and the history of the franchise and d) whether it's been done in any Bond pastiche movies. I wanted a snow sequence, Daniel hadn't done one. Daniel says to me, 'Well, I can't ski.'[159]

Ultimately the filmmakers came up with something original. Bond would commandeer a prop-driven 1960s Britten-Norman BN-2 Islander plane to chase Mr. Hinx, who has kidnapped Madeleine Swann. Bond deliberately crash-lands the plane, clipping its wings off before ploughing the now-skidding-on-snow fuselage through a barn and into the villainous convoy of Land Rover Defenders led by Hinx in a Range Rover Sport SVR. Gary Powell explained that for Bond it had to be more than 'just cars driving along in the snow and crashing; other films do that. But as soon as the wings come off the plane and it landed on its belly and it's still going along, then it's a James Bond chase.'[160]

Throughout January and February 2015 the sequence was completed in Kartitsch and Obertilliach. The second unit stayed longer to complete effects shots, which were sent to Mendes for approval. Corbould found fun in the exacting work, 'I have a joke with Sam – every time I cut material together I always put The Who on it because we are both Who fans.'[161] The lack of snow helped working conditions but snow had to be digitally inserted later for continuity purposes.[162]

The train fight was filmed in segments over a period of time. Being Bond can be dangerous, as Craig recalled:

> We're doing this big fight in the [train] with Dave Bautista and we rehearsed it for six weeks. I did a scene with him where he picked me up and threw me against a wall and I said, 'That's great Dave but do it a bit more.' I went one way and my knee went the other. I'd got a physio on set constantly and my work out became twice as long. The alternative was to stop shooting for six months.[163]

Due to Craig's injury, the action scene had to be shot in small sections on stages at Pinewood and a portable set on location.[164] Gary Powell had to alter the fight to calibrate for the size difference between the two actors.[165] Powell praised not only Craig's physical agility but also his attention to character, noting that during the fight, '[Bond] walks between places, he doesn't run.'[166] Mendes was amused at Bautista's hardiness, 'Daniel just hit him square on the nose and there was this crack and Daniel said, "Oh fuck I've broken his nose." There was a lot of blood. [Dave] just reset it, blew the blood out of his nose and carried on.'[167] For Per Hallberg, 'the sound effects needed to be the music. The sound and the rhythm starts slowly but gets faster and faster and faster as the scene gets more and more intense.'[168]

In mid-February 2015, the crew moved to the Italian capital. Mendes wanted 'a night-time Rome, Mussolini-influenced. There was a way of shooting Rome that is golden and terracotta and dappled. I wanted something much more austere and frightening and cold. Rome was not a charming place like Florence or Venice. It was the seat of an Empire – you feel it.'[169] Gassner concurred, 'There was a sense of scale that was massive and Rome really has a sense of that power. We were limited by how big we could make the SPECTRE meeting room on the stages that were available [at Pinewood].'[170] Mendes felt the introduction to the villainous chief was 'very like the opening of *King Lear* – it has a blinding in it.'[171] Hoyte van Hoytema was:

afraid it would feel very contrived if he came into and out of the light like Marlon Brando in *Apocalypse Now*. My idea was to have a big source behind the monumental door so that light streamed as the door opens, and Christoph would be silhouetted by this light behind him.[172]

Per Hallberg had prepared a sparse soundtrack but at Mendes' behest pared the sound down further for maximum sonic impact.[173]

The production worked with Rome's traffic police and municipal officials by encouraging overtime bonus payments to clean the city and clear graffiti, handing out hot meals to the homeless near the Vatican and spending up to $1 million in location fees.[174] Working off detailed storyboards, Michael Lerman recalled getting full permission and an almost presidential escort from the Italian police.[175] It helped the logistics that the car chase was set at night, as by day Roman streets are extremely manic, by night, they are virtually deserted.[176]

Gary Powell explained, 'We had two very fast cars but although Sam wanted it to be spectacular he didn't want it to be *Fast and Furious*. He didn't want cars flipping through the air. So what you basically saw was fast driving.'[177] *Spectre* continued the fifty-year tradition of Bond driving Aston Martins. Chris Corbould worked closely with the manufacturer: 'It's the first time an Aston Martin has been designed for a film. They only made 10. They weren't really road worthy.'[178] Mendes was thrilled, 'I don't know whether it was Aston's brilliance at making me feel very involved or whether I genuinely was. I wanted a car that had clean, clear lines – no unnecessary details – something classic. The car felt like it was born anywhere between the early '70s and now.'[179] Corbould and his team would add gadgetry but recalled, 'There was a big debate on whether we could call it a DB10 or not but they finally relented.'[180]

Gary Powell knew exactly the vehicle he wanted to pit the DB10 against: the Jaguar CX75 concept car, 'I'd seen it a few years before at a car show.'[181] Powell took the technicians from Jaguar and Aston Martin around Rome and showed them what he intended do with the supercars, 'The Jaguar technicians' face went white.'[182] Stunt driver Mark Harbour pursued his colleague Mark Higgins at speeds of over 120 miles per hour and Powell admitted, 'We actually outran the camera helicopter.'[183] As the cars slalomed through the ancient architecture, Powell was advised by the local film commissioner, 'If you hit that [building], get to the airport as quick as you can.'[184]

A spectacular jump at an intersection adorned by four recently and expensively restored sixteenth-century statues was refused by the authorities.[185] According to cultural heritage official Federica Galloni, 'We have not given permission for the sequence at the Quattro Fontane because the site is too delicate from an architectural point of view.'[186] Gary Powell tried his best to sway the decision, 'We showed them the physics of it but couldn't convince them.'[187]

However, permission was granted for the cars to careen down the ancient steps leading to the River Tiber but the filmmakers were under strict instructions to protect them.[188] Barbara Broccoli was especially nervous, warning Powell, 'If you scrape those steps!'[189] To launch the DB10 into the Tiber, a restraining cable was attached to the car to prevent it hitting the fifteenth-century Ponte Sisto.[190]

Mendes had originally wanted to use a classic 1960s Fiat Cinquecento to amusingly bring Bond's Aston Martin to a halt in the middle of the chase.[191] However he was forced to use the contemporary model when he decided he wanted the gag to involve the Fiat's airbag inflating – an additional extra not found on the original.[192]

Neal Purvis visited the set in Rome and was in awe: 'I've never seen so many trucks on one film, as far as the eye could see. So many Italian police, so many roads being closed off, so many Aston Martins all lined up – phenomenal.'[193] Incidentally, the car chase began in the UK, on location at Blenheim Palace, Winston Churchill's family seat.

The filmmakers had wanted to shoot Marco Sciarra's funeral at the Verano cemetery, a 2,000-year-old site built in the ruins of an ancient necropolis but permission was refused.[194] The scene was filmed instead at the Museum of Roman Civilisation.[195] This was the moment the audience was introduced to Sciarra's widow, Donna Lucia. Jany Temime saw her as 'a Cinecittà star. I wanted to have all the characteristics of woman's sensuality [like] Sophia Loren.'[196]

Villa Fiorano, located in the old Appian Way, became the home for Donna Sciarra, where she is first saved and then seduced by Bond. Robert Wade elaborated, 'She recognises the kind of kindred spirit in Bond and he does the great thing of saving her life and giving her a way out. We thought it was so Bondian that he kills the husband and then he fucks the widow.'[197] Bellucci enjoyed 'this moment of passion and fight with Daniel. I had to express so many things in not a lot of time. Four strong scenes. She starts in the cemetery and she finishes in the bed.'[198] For Mendes, the character showcased Bellucci's strengths, 'She makes us feel like there's a history and a longing. One of my personal favourite moments is when she pours herself a drink and she knows she's going to die.'[199] The moment Bond slams the two champagne flutes to the floor was a surprise appreciated by Mendes, 'Daniel did that in rehearsals.'[200]

By mid-March 2015, the Bond unit travelled to Mexico to shoot the pre-title sequence involving a Día de Muertos – Day of the Dead – parade in the capital. Michael Wilson stated, 'This is the biggest opening sequence we've ever done, maybe the biggest [of any] sequence we've ever done.'[201] Initially Mendes wanted to invoke the extended single take from Orson Welles' Mexico-set thriller, *Touch of Evil* (1958):[202] 'I felt that there is a kind of cockiness about Bond at the beginning of the movie, before anything goes wrong, that was implied by not cutting.'[203] His original concept was even more ambitious – to shoot the entire pre-title sequence in one take: 'I decided that would be self-serving, a bit of a showoff. And, in fact, it was better for dramatic reasons to go into more conventional storytelling and start cutting.'[204] Michael Lerman considered recreating the location on the Pinewood backlot in order to facilitate such a complicated set-piece but after scouting Mexico City concluded, 'How could you not shoot it here?'[205]

For Dennis Gassner, authenticity was paramount:

> I live in California and have been part of that culture for a long time because of the tremendous Mexican population in Los Angeles. Everything comes out of research through documentation and through videos we've watched, so really it came from the Mexicans themselves once we'd decided to collaborate and do the big adventure with them.[206]

Lerman oversaw 1,500 extras processed through costume and make-up in under two hours every day.[207] Make-up supervisor Naomi Donne worked with local artists to create individual and distinctly macabre looks for each supporting artiste. For Temime it was an enormous task: 'I went to Mexico and did my research for Day of the Dead. I picked ten shapes to do with death which looked folkloric. We got all the fabric in London and it took us from October until March to complete all the costumes.'[208] In what must have been quite surreal, the choreography and music had been demonstrated and approved by Mendes in the icy surrounds of Austria months earlier.[209] Chris Corbould was on hand to ensure the 'barely drivable [floats] at least got us through the shots'.[210] Lerman communicated to the extras via 'a series of speakers connected to a central microphone:"the God mic"'.[211] It was via this that the experienced first assistant director tried 'to keep everybody standing around for ten to twelve hours a day happy by singing the Bond theme'.[212]

Spectre opens with a glamorous couple cutting their way through the crowded festivities. The man dressed in top hat, tails and skeletal fancy dress is revealed to be James Bond. Mendes felt a connection to his pivotal first Bond experience, *Live and Let Die*: 'You see the skull face and you're like "Oh, it's Baron Samedi." It's actually quite different, but there are echoes. Part of the joy of Bond is riffing on the iconography – I was very aware of all the homages that were being paid.'[213]

In mid-April 2015 production shut down whilst Daniel Craig underwent knee surgery for the injury sustained earlier in production. The actor saw the silver lining, 'We got two weeks off in the middle. It allowed Sam to get into the editing room and look at the movie, which he would never normally get to see until right at the end. He got to look at some rough cuts and he could get an overview.'[214] During recovery, Craig recalled, 'it slowed me down a bit but it didn't actually stop me doing what I wanted to do. So I had to protect myself a bit more. It's movie making. You fake it and you fake it as best you can.'[215] With Craig restricted from running, the opening sequence was revised to justify why Bond and Marco Sciarra suddenly start walking mid-way through chase. The solution was to line the parade with police from whom Sciarra did not want to draw attention. Lerman sourced sixty policemen to line the route, 'We grabbed a lot of real police securing the roads.'[216]

It was Alexander Witt who first discovered a YouTube clip of aerial stunt pilot Chuck Aaron performing a barrel roll with the specially adapted Messerschmitt-Bölkow Blohm BO-105 Red Bull helicopter, something never featured in a movie before.[217] The stunt was to have been showcased later into the film, when Bond escapes Blofeld's Moroccan base, but it was deemed more impactful in the pre-title sequence.[218] Aaron requested they keep the branding in the film but McDougall remembered Barbara Broccoli saying, 'We're not having any helicopter covered in Red Bull logos.'[219] The sound effect during the barrel roll was inserted by Per Hallberg using the actual noise the helicopter makes whilst performing the manoeuvre: 'it has a very different kind of a "Thwack" from any other sound, as if it's hitting something very hard.'[220]

The element of danger came when the copter was required to hover above the teaming crowds in Zócalo Square.[221] Gary Powell was full of admiration for Aaron, who skilfully flew the rotocraft below the building line in very low altitude while landing it perfectly: 'We did have an area cordoned off that if there was an engine failure he could get down. At thirty, forty foot, you haven't got a lot of time to think. You could be the perfect pilot but the piece of machinery can go wrong.'[222] Impressed with the footage of Bond and Sciarra fighting outside the helicopter as it loses control above the crowds, Powell said ruefully, 'We should have made the fight bigger.'[223] In actuality, the most dangerous stunts were filmed over an airfield in Palenque, a hundred miles south of Zócalo Square at sea level, which made flying safer.[224] These scenes as well as crowds enhanced by CGI were melded to those shot in Mexico City in post-production.[225]

In the twenty-seven years since Eon had utilised a smoggy Mexico City and ramshackle Churusbusco Studios for *Licence to Kill*, Callum McDougall was pleasantly surprised by the huge improvements in both air quality and moviemaking infrastructure.[226] Indeed, Bond shared the same art nouveau stained-glass lift in the Gran Hotel Giudad de México: then with Pam Bouvier and now, for *Spectre*, with Estrella.[227] Bond breaks off his seduction in the hotel room, a Pinewood set, and then saunters outside on the rooftops to spy on Sciarra. According to visual effects supervisor Steve Begg:

> The opening continuous shot was blended together from six or seven individual sequences. It was difficult and required most of my attention. Unusually for a scene like this there weren't action shots where you whip panned off them and you could hide things. It was very slow moving, you couldn't lose Daniel Craig at all.[228]

The Mexico shoot was underwritten by tax incentives to a tune of approximately $14 million.[229] There were certain cultural stipulations that the film adhered to: the inclusion of a Mexican Bond girl, a non-Mexican villain, the target of assassination was to be a local governor and not an ambassador, and the shoot should showcase the city's modern skyline.[230] Lerman found the Mexican film authorities 'very supportive and it was very helpful for tourism how much exposure they got from the film'.[231] Bond was good for business, for in 2016, Mexico City staged its first Day of the Dead parade inspired directly by its fictional inclusion in *Spectre*.[232]

In mid-April 2015, the main unit returned to London. Mendes felt, 'The challenge was to try and find a way of shooting London that felt fresh and new and yet a continuation of *Skyfall*.'[233] An example of this was the unique way Trafalgar Square was captured on film, with the old Drummonds Bank doubling for the Hildebrand safe house. The interior of City Hall was used to represent the new CNS building as well as the Nine Eyes conference room in Tokyo. Dennis Gassner liked 'the interior space that has an interesting staircase and something that provided another view across the river from MI6 that was less fortress-like.'[234] Rory Kinnear remembered preparing a sequence with Tanner disguised as a security guard hiding behind a newspaper as Denbigh enters the building but agreed with Mendes' decision not to shoot it as it felt a bit too '*Pink Panther*-y'.[235]

Lerman paid tribute to location manager Emma Pill, who had secured the circular courtyard which is part of the Treasury Building in Whitehall as well as Foreign and Commonwealth Office buildings.[236] Supervising art director Christopher Lowe gave himself a cheeky KBE and included his and Pill's names, along with those of other art department personnel, on the graffiti'd MI6 memorial wall.[237] Opposite the bombed-out HQ, Blofeld was to have pulled up to his helicopter in a contemporary Rolls-Royce Phantom. This short scene was filmed with veteran Bond stuntman Paul Weston playing Blofeld's chauffeur, in Riverside Gardens, Tate Britain, but ultimately was cut.[238]

In late May the denouement on Westminster Bridge was filmed. Callum McDougall explained the challenge was lighting the Thames at night, 'If you look from the Houses of Parliament, the centre of the river is near enough completely dark. Hoyte said, "It's going to need a huge lighting rig," and he was absolutely right. We had eighty electricians a night purely just lighting the river.'[239] With London on high terrorist alert, the pedigree of a Bond production gave *Spectre* permission other films would not be granted.[240] Chris Corbould was restricted from setting any props on fire on Westminster Bridge.[241] The sequence was therefore completed on the 007 Stage at Pinewood involving a full-scale prop helicopter flown on wires crashing onto a partial set.[242] Steve Begg used CG in all scenes with the principals and to remove foliage on the trees, to match footage shot earlier in December 2014.[243] The destruction of the MI6 building began as a miniature shot but was ultimately achieved digitally.[244]

In late June 2015, *Spectre* reached the final leg of production in Morocco. For Mendes, this last locale reflected the evolution of Bond and Madeleine's relationship, 'That story between them gradually warms up as they go to warmer climates.'[245] Gassner concurred, 'Tangier is a romantic image, it being the place of [Madeleine's] parents' honeymoon even though it is faded love.'[246] Hallberg explained the layers of sound were important in this quiet scene, informed by where the room was in relation to the city, conveying the feeling of safety as well as specific details, including distant Vespa mopeds, voices, traffic horns, a call to prayer recorded on location.[247] As in Mexico, Callum McDougall recalls the location was familiar territory for Eon Productions '[In Tangier] there was a picture in the hotel of Cubby Broccoli when we were doing *The Living Daylights*: we shot in near enough the same streets.'[248]

Mendes cited one of his favourite scenes in *Spectre* as the one that takes place at the L'Americain retreat when Bond and Madeleine discover Mr. White's secret room. 'She sees the photographs on her father's wall of her as a young child and realises the man who she's painted as a bad parent, in actual fact, loved her more than anything. That is done in silence with just a reaction shot from Léa. She could convey a lot with very little.'[249]

The train sequence was based on the Oriental Desert Express which travelled from Ouijda to Bouarfa.[250] For Mendes, the sequence helped:

> develop Madeleine into a three-dimensional character to provide Bond with a reason to walk away. Her story on the train about killing a man is a similar tale of learning about the dark part of the human soul too young and that bonds them psychically. In *Skyfall,* I tried to tell the story of how a lonely, orphaned child becomes an assassin. Or in her case, how does the daughter of an assassin end up drawn back to the source of her pain?[251]

To augment the romanticism, Jany Temime dressed Madeleine Swann in a shimmering emerald dress: 'something simple with a 1930s feeling, like *Casablanca*'.[252] To match that theme, Temime tailored Bond in a white tuxedo, invoking images of Humphrey Bogart.[253] The costume designer remembered the blessing and curse of Craig's improvisation: 'The red carnation was on the table, it was a prop. Then Daniel took the flower and put it in his buttonhole and I thought, "Oh my God, that is so perfect." Then I thought "Oh shit, there will be an endless problem with continuity."'[254]

In early July, the production travelled to Erfoud: Mendes wanted to create a sense of 'falling off the grid. They would travel into the north of the Sahara where it's still a barren landscape.'[255] When Bond and Madeleine journey to Blofeld's hideaway, Gassner thought, 'this volcanic kind of space was magical and strange.'[256] The location did have hazards, with the set regularly plagued by sandstorms.[257] Despite the challenges of what had become a long, arduous shoot, Léa enjoyed a moment of levity when during strenuous action in the desert, Craig's 'pants tore in two'.[258]

Gara Medeour, an extinct volcano, doubled as the crater created by the fictional Kartenhoff meteor. For Gassner, Blofeld's base housed within it was a:

> contemporary, slightly futuristic information-gathering centre and an observatory. And the information is about the stars and the planets and it's pulling in the satellite dish information. It is exactly what you would expect a Bond villain to have – access to everything. Information is power, wielding it like a magic sword.[259]

The stolen Modigliani painting *Lady with a Fan* from *Skyfall* can be glimpsed in the room where Swann is held captive.

Steve Begg recalled:

Originally the SPECTRE base was to be underneath this massive crater out in the desert and at the climax of that particular action sequence the whole place exploded and then imploded downwards into this subterranean base. That was written out after Sam felt that was a bit too like a Marvel comic piece of action.[260]

Corbould was quick with a solution, 'I got hold of Sam one day and I said I know you are not keen on this collapsing [crater idea] but I can do an explosion which I can guarantee you'll be blown away with.'[261] On the day the set was rigged to go up in flames, Corbould talked Daniel Craig and Léa Seydoux, through the scene, 'This is going to be a great explosion but I've got to press the button half way through your line so don't fuck your lines up!' Daniel said, "You're kiddng me."'[262] Guinness World Records listed the moment as the 'Largest Film Stunt Explosion' ever.[263] Corbould wryly observed, 'The weird thing was we had an amount of [explosive] left over. We don't just buy the exact quantity we need. We had to destroy it before we left there. The explosion we did to destroy what we had left was three times bigger than the one we had in the film.'[264]

Spectre celebrated completion of principal photography with a wrap party at the Tower of London on 5 July 2015.[265] For Mendes it had been a particularly arduous production:

I had one day off in eight months of shooting and nine months of prep. It's one of those movies that was really hard until halfway. It was particularly tough, physically grueling – a lot of injuries, illness. We hit the wall, halfway, then broke through it. By the end, we were, I won't say sprinting exactly, but we weren't staggering over the line.[266]

Mendes, however, was encouraged

I felt on *Skyfall* a certain amount of 'Can he really do this?' On *Spectre,* the crew all came with their *Skyfall* jackets on, 'What can we do for you guv'nor? We believe in you and we believe in this.' That makes a big difference. You feel like you've got three or four hundred people lifting you on their shoulders every day.[267]

Post-production began in earnest. Visual effects supervisor Steve Begg set out the challenge, 'It was a ridiculously tight post-production schedule. We had to do 1,500 shots. Every day, every hour counts.'[268] Whilst other big effects films normally have nearly a year to complete special effects, the Bond films have an unusually short post-production schedule. To ameliorate the problem, Begg established a relationship with key heads of department at the start of shooting because ideas would change, 'A lot of movies nowadays are organic, they evolve as they go along. When I get into post-production I can second guess solutions because I've already established a bit of a rapport with colleagues.'[269]

Begg was keen to work with legendary effects house Industrial Light and Magic (ILM), founded by George Lucas and John Dykstra. It was from the latter that Cubby Broccoli had been given an exorbitant quote for effects work on *Moonraker* in 1978.[270] Having recently set up a London arm to work on *Star Wars: The Force Awakens,* ILM's key task was to insert the buildings, shot elsewhere in Morocco into Blofeld's crater. 'It was turned around incredibly fast and was so photorealistic that people thought we had shot in a factory and wrapped a digital crater around it.'[271]

Mendes had also requested complete autonomy 'in the cutting room'.[272] Lee Smith presented cut scenes in keeping with the director's sensibilities, an efficient process for the tight sixteen weeks from production wrap to final cut: 'We really had to be editing the movie as we shot.'[273] A notable scene lost in the edit was M challenging Moneypenny for helping Bond, questioning her sympathies, to which she retorted, 'It wasn't love. It was loyalty'.[274]

Mendes tweaked the film further following an early preview, 'I'm from the theatre, previews are normal.'[275] Mendes cited a moment in the Austrian hotel room where Q asks Bond who links 007's former adversaries, to which he responds, 'Me.' The exchange featured in the regular trailer but during the edit Mendes realised 'This scene gives us the wrong spin on that piece of information. So we changed not only the graphic but the line.'[276] Pacing was also an issue, with audiences thinking the film was over after Bond destroys and escapes Blofeld's crater. With a title card and soundtrack change, film-goers were now prepared for the final act in London.[277]

Sound editors Per Hallberg and Karen Baker Landers, like Steve Begg, benefitted from detailed pre-production meetings which helped them complete their task in a much tighter time schedule than *Skyfall*.[278] Hallberg felt sound:

> is one of those subliminal things that affects the audience but they shouldn't really think about it and they don't. But they feel it. It's a lot of intricate work.

There is a thread that needed to be woven from the beginning to the end. You don't want to step on the thread with sound effects to bring the audience out of that mood.[279]

Mendes noted the confidence in his favoured composer, Thomas Newman, as he approached his second Bond soundtrack, 'On *Skyfall* he was a bodybuilder who was three quarters of the way through his full course. When he stepped in on *Spectre* I felt he'd been living in that body for two years, completely confident.'[280] Lee Smith had created a guide score using the *Skyfall* soundtrack: 'I know that would have been hard for [Newman], because it's already his score. I kept saying to him, "But it's so good!" I can't put other composers' scores on this movie!'[281] To complete the task on time, Newman worked hard 'for three-and-a-half months solid. Seven days a week, morning til night'.[282] Newman arranged the source music played by Mexican band Tambuco for the opening sequence.[283] During the car chase, Hallberg felt Newman's score was so good, he dialled down the sound effects.[284] This scene includes the instrumental introduction of John Kander and Fred Ebb's classic, 'New York, New York' from a previously recorded cover version performed by 2006 UK X-Factor runner-up, Ray Quinn. Neal Purvis actually scripted another track, 'I remember meeting Rob in Soho and told him I put Dusty Springfield's "Spooky" in the chase. I thought that made a nice counterpoint to the action. And at that moment it came on in the café we were sitting in.'[285] The work of muzak conductor Geoff Love, who in the 1970s produced a revered instrumental Bond covers album, features as source music when Bond leaves Lucia with Felix Leiter's number.

Mendes talked briefly with Newman about writing the opening song, 'The truth of it is, to write a song, you need a few weeks, to get in the room together, to start throwing ideas around. I was very adamant that we should approach songwriters for the song much earlier than they traditionally have in the past.[286]

The past loomed large for Barbara Broccoli, 'We had such a tremendous success with Adele last time on *Skyfall* so it was a bit daunting trying to come up with a really great, exciting, fresh new idea.'[287] As usual, speculation was wild as to who would perform the track, and Broccoli and company went to great lengths to preserve the secret, 'You can imagine how many conversations go on between the record company and film company and also the studio. We insisted that throughout all of those emails and phone conversations we just referred to "The Artist" in every communication.'[288]

Finally, on 8 September 2015, it was revealed that the multi-Grammy Award-winning vocalist and songwriter Sam Smith would be performing the Bond song.[289] Titled, 'Writing's on the Wall', the track was written by Smith and his long-time collaborator and producer, James Napier, known as Jimmy Napes. Mendes gave them the script, saying, 'Try to give us a key that unlocks the door of the movie and lets us take the first step in.'[290] Smith was appreciative, 'Sam Mendes really worked with us, lyrically. Because I write in a very vulnerable way and Bond isn't necessarily a vulnerable gay man, I had to change certain lyrics so that he sounded stronger.'[291] Napes was also thrilled, 'Growing up I was a massive Bond fan. I kind of dreamt of doing it. Playing piano sometimes I played chords that sounded Bond-y. I had the chords for this song before we were even asked to do it.'[292] Mendes found Smith easy to work with, 'He's someone you can pick up the phone to and talk to as opposed to going through an entourage or seventeen managers and that makes collaboration easier. They did the song in good time and they were able to respond to notes.'[293]

Barbara Broccoli revealed, 'We do get approaches from all kinds of fabulous people and sometimes we've already selected someone and we have to let them down or in other cases it doesn't work out.'[294] Sam Mendes and Daniel Craig were huge fans of the band Radiohead, who, it later emerged, did write a song for *Spectre*.[295] Mendes reflected,

> I absolutely loved their song but when it came in, I felt it was too melancholic to be a Bond title song and Barbara agreed with me. I had said to [Radiohead producer] Nigel Goodrich and [lead singer] Thom Yorke, 'Look I don't think it is a natural fit for a title track, would you mind if I used it in the movie in its entirety?' And they said 'Great, we'd just like to see where you're using it.' The problem was lyrically, it's alive with meaning and uses the word 'Spectre' and in the scene that I used it, you could feel an audience trying to hear what was being said in the song and that was confusing. It felt stylistically out of character with the rest of the film, so try as I might, I couldn't get it to work. The first time Barbara and Michael saw the movie it had the Radiohead song in it and we had a long discussion about it.[296]

Ultimately the song remained unused in the film. Radiohead made their track, entitled 'Spectre', available as a free download on Christmas Day 2015, stating, 'Last year we were asked to write a theme tune for the Bond movie *Spectre*. Yes we were. It didn't work out, but became something of our own, which we love very much.'[297] Band member and co-songwriter Johnny Greenwood later explained, 'I guess there's lots of people interested in who does [the Bond theme]. There's a lot riding on it and the song we did was just too dark or whatever, so that's fine.'[298]

Mendes turned once more to veteran 007 title designer Daniel Kleinman to create the signature Bond sequence. Mendes' conceptional idea was for 'all the various strands in Bond's past coming together in one story – the tentacles of the octopus'.[299] The titles featured Raoul Silva, Vesper Lynd, Le Chiffre and Judi Dench's M. Kleinman recalled, 'the aspiration was to get the actors [from the previous movies] and re-film them.'[300] When this proved unfeasible, the designer did try to access the rushes of the previous films but could not use them for contractual reasons.[301]

Kleinman revealed it was Daniel Craig himself who suggested the sequence should begin with 007:

in a classic Bond way, looking hard, stripped to the waist, surrounded by women. I don't think he took his shirt off in the film. He thought there had to be one moment [of] the sexy potent Bond. I'd be foolish if I didn't take on his take on it. It's not the sort of thing I would normally put in because it's a bit retro and it speaks to Bond of old, the misogynist Bond, harking back to the 60s films. But in this case I rationalised it and I could see it had a narrative intent – you see he is a womanising character and it's not a very healthy relationship he has with women. [Later in the sequence] I suggest that there is one that he gets more entangled with and you see him connect in a more emotional way.[302]

Kleinman researched real footage of octopi but opted for something more stylised, 'It's an octopus of nightmares rather than an octopus of David Attenborough.'[303] Some ideas were too strong, 'At the end of the *ménage à trois* with Bond, a woman and an octopus, I wanted the woman's tongue to come out and be an octopus's tentacle going into Bond's mouth. When everyone saw it moving they thought it was a little bit too much so that came out.'[304] The sequence was shot digitally but was then treated to match the rest of the movie shot on 35mm film.[305]

Kleinman slowed down the pace of the sequence after hearing Sam Smith's track. The words also provided inspiration, 'I like to link the images to the lyrics occasionally, "A million shards of glass" seemed like fractured memories and definitely fits in with the idea that Sam had wanted.'[306]

For *Spectre*, Sam Mendes studied all the previous gun barrel sequences, 'It was fascinating watching how they developed.'[307] He preferred the earlier interpretations, 'the wobbly gun barrel, seeping blood'.[308] Kleinman recalled, 'Sam shot Daniel Craig walking the gun barrel with Hoyte. I did oversee it in post [and] made it more true to the original – an optical effect.'[309] The iconic motif did not open out on the first shot of the film, as had been tradition, because Mendes felt, 'It's all about rhythm. You need the music to die and then you have a moment where you hold your breath and there's the first big beat of the drum. You need time to gather yourself.'[310]

On 26 October 2016, the Royal Albert Hall in London, once again played host to the royal world charity premiere of the Bond movie. *Spectre* was selected as the annual Royal Film Performance, and the Duke and Duchess of Cambridge, William and Kate, and Prince Harry were in attendance.

In autumn 2016, Sam Mendes reflected with the authors in his boutique Covent Garden office:

Walking on the red carpet at the Albert Hall is a little bit like being England football manager and suddenly walking out at Wembley Stadium and thinking, 'Oh my God, there's so many people here.' Of course there are, you're doing something people care about very much and it's owned by the fans and by the public, not by you. When you're locked in your bubble making the movie the job is really to cut out the feelings of everybody else and everyone else's expectations.[311]

The Albert Hall was decked out in the Day of the Dead regalia, as was the British Museum, where the after party was held. The event benefitted the Cinema and Television Benevolent Fund. *Spectre* benefitted studio coffers to the tune just over $880 million worldwide with the North American gross amounting to $200 million and the UK gross totalling $124 million.

On 28 February 2016, at the 88th Academy Awards held in the Dolby Theatre in Los Angeles, comedian Sarah Silverman introduced Sam Smith, who performed his theme song to Hollywood. Later that evening rap star Common and musician John Legend presented the singer and Jimmy Napes with the series' fifth Oscar and 007's second consecutive award for Best Song for 'Writing's on the Wall'. Costume designer Jany Temime proudly observed that presenter Chris Rock had worn a white dinner jacket: 'it has since become fashionable again. I think it's because of James Bond.'[312]

As Sony's highest worldwide grossing film of 2015, *Spectre* showed the 007 brand was at a commercial and critical high. There was no question that James Bond would return – it would just be a question of when.

FUTURES TRICKED BY THE PAST

THE ROAD TO BOND 25

Albert R. Broccoli
wishes to thank
The Academy of Motion Picture
Arts and Sciences,
its Officials
and
the Board of Governors
for having honored him
with
The Irving G. Thalberg
Memorial Award

Sony's deal with Metro-Goldwyn-Mayer to co-finance and distribute the James Bond films concluded with the release of *Spectre*.[1] Danjaq were once again faced with the prospect of yet another corporate partner. Michael Wilson was unperturbed: 'Sometimes they're great and sometimes they're terrible, and you have to deal with them accordingly. All we want to do is make a good film for a reasonable amount of money. We put all the money on the screen. So anyone who helps us to do that makes a good studio executive.'[2]

The key decision-makers in searching for a new distributor would be MGM co-chairmen and chief executive officers Gary Barber and Roger Birnbaum. It appeared MGM had shown Danjaq the courtesy of allowing them to meet their putative business partners. Wilson was sanguine: 'The three people they're considering, all of them are more than suitable with us.'[3] Wilson acknowledged for Danjaq, 'It's not primarily our decision. We're one picture, we will consult with them and they'll make sure we're happy, but [MGM will] have to [decide]. It's their responsibility, because it's for their whole slate. It isn't just for us.'[4]

The Bond operation remains a singular entity in the film world as Wilson elaborated, 'It's almost impossible for us to evaluate it except on the basis of their past successes or failures. Until you work with people you can't evaluate their marketing executives or their publicity people. We pretty much run the marketing anyway ourselves. We create it and they execute it.'[5] Amy Pascal's successor, Tom Rothman at Sony was philosophical, 'The reality is that Sony's had a fantastic run with the Bonds. Sure we're going to compete for (the rights), but let's be honest, so is everybody in the business.'[6]

By late 2016, no distributor had been announced and thus, no screenplay, title, director or cast could have been announced.[7] *Bond 25* lay dormant although a company named B25 Limited was incorporated in England on 6 May 2015.[8]

Barbara and Michael have been steadily working beyond Bond. In 2014, Eon backed *Radiator* (2014), the last film to feature Richard Johnson, Terence Young's initial preference for James Bond.[9] The film was directed by Tom Browne and also starred Gemma Jones and Daniel Cerqueria. In addition to his string of fleeting cameos in the Bond films, Michael G. Wilson played a 'distinguished doctor' alongside stop-motion pioneer Ray Harryhausen in *Burke And Hare* (2010) directed by John Landis and had a speaking part as Lance Armstrong's doctor in Stephen Frears' *The Program* (2015).

In 2016, under the Eon Productions banner, Barbara co-produced, with Colin Vaines and Andrew Noble, *Film Stars Don't Die In Liverpool*. With a screenplay written by Matt Greenhaigh, the story was based on the memoir by British actor Peter Turner and follows the playful but passionate relationship between Turner and the eccentric Academy Award-winning actress Gloria Grahame. What starts as a vibrant affair between a legendary femme fatale and her young lover grows into a deeper relationship. The film was directed by Paul McGuigan and starred Annette Benning, Julie Walters and Jamie Bell, and was released in late 2017. It would garner BAFTA nominations for Best Actress, Best Actor and Best Adapted Screenplay.

Michael and Barbara would also go on to produce *The Rhythm Section*. Blake Lively stars as Stephanie Patrick, a woman on a path of self-destruction after her family dies in a plane crash. After being told by a journalist that the crash was an act of terror covered up by intelligence agencies, Patrick is set on a mission to fill the void between what she knows and what she is told. Based on the work of British novelist Mark Burnell, who wrote the script, the film was shot in Ireland directed by Reed Morano. Paramount, which is backing the production, hopes for a lucrative female-led espionage franchise.[10]

Broccoli had previously expressed her attraction to the theatre was 'the immediacy of it that you are sitting in a dark space and the curtain goes up. It's a magic show.'[11] In December 2016, Broccoli also produced William Shakespeare's *Othello* directed by Sam Gold and staged at the New York Theatre Workshop. The play starred British actor David Oyelowo in the title role. Oyelowo has previously 'played' Bond when he read the audiobook of the 2015 continuation Bond novel TRIGGER MORTIS by Anthony Horowitz. Perhaps he had received advice from his theatrical co-star and the person playing Iago: Daniel Craig.

Early 2017 would see London's Royal Court Theatre staging a production of producer Robert Evans' Hollywood memoir, THE KID STAYS IN THE PICTURE, also co-produced by Barbara Broccoli.

Not content with just film and theatre, Eon Productions also announced a creative alliance with Cove Pictures, a joint venture with Smuggler Inc. and Red Arrow Entertainment, to develop a number of television shows for the international market.[12]

Barbara Broccoli was a key participant in Guiding Lights, the UK film industry's leading mentoring programme. The Eon Production *A Silent Storm* (2014), directed by Corinna Villari-McFarlane, had been a beneficiary of the scheme. The film's producer Nicky Bentham was appreciative: 'Barbara was excited about getting more involved in independent film and new voices. She said she'd help us do whatever it took to make it happen.'[13]

In April 2016, Barbara Broccoli was appointed BAFTA's Vice President for Film, 'I am passionate about BAFTA's role in educating, inspiring and celebrating generations of British film-makers.'[14] She had been kept busy as a Trustee of Into Film, a film education charity working with young people aged 5-19. She is also Patron of the Cinema and Television Benevolent Fund, an Honorary Fellow of the National Film and Television School and an Honorary Member of Women in Film and Television UK, a Patron for Spinal Research and supports many of Oxfam's fundraising efforts. Broccoli also sits on the Board of Governors for BAFTA Los Angeles. The Albert R. Broccoli Britannia Award for Worldwide Contribution to Filmed Entertainment is named after Eon's legendary co-founder.[15]

In 1998 Wilson opened the Wilson Centre for Photography, a study centre boasting one of the largest private collections of photographs, and was the chairman of the board of trustees at the National Media Museum which is based in Bradford, West Yorkshire. In 2013, he won an award for Outstanding Services to Photography from the Royal Photographic Society (RPS).

In July 2015, towards the end of *Spectre*'s arduous eight-month shoot in which the then 47-year-old current 007 incumbent severely damaged his knee, Daniel Craig was asked if he'd like to return as Bond. 'Now? I'd rather break this glass and slash my wrists. No, not at the moment. Not at all. I'm over it at the moment. All I want to do is move on.'[16]

In the interview, embargoed until the film's UK release later that October, Craig went on to say,

> I haven't given it any thought. For at least a year or two, I just don't want to think about it. I don't know what the next step is. I've no idea. Not because I'm trying to be cagey. Who the fuck knows? At the moment, we've done it. I'm not in discussion with anybody about anything. If I did another Bond movie, it would only be for the money.'[17]

The distribution deal between MGM seemingly still not finalised prevented any substantive work on *Bond 25* commencing. Craig's comments caught on like wildfire fuelling rampant press speculation in the news vacuum since *Spectre* had been released. This was reportedly much to the ire of MGM co-chief Gary Barber.[18]

However, during the release of *Spectre*, Craig had told the authors:

> I love the process of making these films. In spite of what's been written and what's been in the press about it. It's a massive collaborative process. The rest of it is just hard work. The best things are. Sometimes I say things like I did

in the press when I was asked two days after I just finished shooting for eight months, 'Would I do another one?' and I said what was on my mind. That's the way I've always spoken, that's why I'm straight. But as I've said I reserve the right to change my mind.[19]

For Eon Productions, the position was clear. In September 2016, executive producer, Callum McDougall, said at the eightieth anniversary celebration for Pinewood Studios, 'We would love Daniel to return as Bond. Without any question he is absolutely Michael G. Wilson and Barbara Broccoli's first choice. I know they're hoping for him to come back.'[20] Despite the opaque contractual situation, Wilson was positive, 'We hope to have Daniel. My sister is more persuasive than I am.'[21]

Hope would spring eternal. In October 2016, at an event appropriately titled 'Beyond Bond', Daniel Craig told a live audience in New York his feelings about playing 007: 'I love this job, I get a massive kick out of it. And if I can keep getting a kick out of it, I will [continue]. Were I to stop doing it, I'd miss it terribly.'[22]

Matters progressed and on 24 July 2017, MGM and Eon Productions announced the US release date of *Bond 25* was confirmed for 8 November 2019.[23] Strangely, no mention was made of the distributor, director, or Daniel Craig's future in the role. Less than a month later, while promoting *Logan Lucky* (2017), Craig finally confirmed he had signed for a fifth Bond picture, during an interview with Stephen Colbert on the US chat show *The Late Show*. Standing up to shake Colbert's hand Craig said; 'I always wanted to. I needed a break.'[24] Just hours earlier in a press junket he had still denied his involvement, 'I know they're desperate to get going and I would in theory love to do it, but there is no decision just yet.'[25] Craig admitted to Colbert, 'I have to apologise to all the people I did interviews with today … But I wanted to tell you.'[26] The live audience was ecstatic. At the end of the show Craig was asked if this was his last Bond movie: 'I think this is it. This is it. I just want to go out on a high note. I can't wait.'[27]

In February 2017, whilst promoting their TV adaptation of Len Deighton's ss-GB, Neal Purvis and Robert Wade were asked if they would return to the incredible world of 007. Wade responded, 'Never say never. But for sure, *Spectre* felt like it closed off a certain way of doing Bond. And I think whatever happens next will be quite different.'[28] Purvis commented on the political climate:

With people like Trump, the Bond villain has become a reality. So when they do another one, it will be interesting to see how they deal with the fact that the world has become a fantasy. Each time, you've got to say something about Bond's place in the world, which is Britain's place in the world … But things are moving so quickly now, that becomes tricky. I'm just not sure how you would go about writing a James Bond film now.[29]

Neal Purvis summarised the situation to the authors:

If you'd have written a screenplay only a few years ago painting what has now happened in the world it would have been considered a fantasy or science fiction, and that's not Bond. But I think we've come to realize that in such uncertain and scary times, there is one man we all need more than ever; a man you can rely on, who'll stick to his guns, and slay the dragon. We still need James Bond.[30]

On 24 July 2017, it was confirmed that Purvis and Wade had been hired to write a record-breaking seventh consecutive James Bond film.

Neal Purvis shared some insight into how development on each new James Bond film usually begins when they first meet with the producers:

We talk about things that are happening in the world, things that might be scary. Barbara or Michael or Gregg might suggest something. Then Rob and I go away and begin writing so that we can bring back material that we can all read and discuss. Sometimes we get the basic story quite quickly and sometimes not. Rob and I will put together a detailed treatment for the studio. Then we get their notes and those get incorporated. Things aren't fixed in stone just because everyone's agreed upon them. Rob and I would to a pub and discuss things. One of us might type something up from that and send it to the other. We'll talk on the phone a lot and there will lots of emails during the day. The collaborative-ness of it all is part of it. These things get changed and revised so much you really do lose any perspective on what I wrote or what Rob wrote. You're just pleased something good's been done even if wasn't you. It's all about getting to the end so that it can be changed again. Just from experience you know that you should pace yourself because the amount of work is phenomenal.[31]

In April 2017, The *New York Times* broke the news that MGM and Eon Productions had started:

> attending dog and pony shows put on by studios that want the rights. Leaders at Sony spent an hour making their case. Kazuo Hirai, the chief executive, helped give the pitch, which emphasized the studio's deep knowledge of Bond and its ideas for expanding the franchise's reach. In true Hollywood fashion, Sony gave its presentation inside a sound stage on a recreated set from *Dr. No*. Also vying for the Bond deal are Warner Bros., Universal Pictures, 20th Century Fox and Annapurna, an ambitious upstart financed and led by the Oracle heiress Megan Ellison.[32]

The report went on to say,:

> MGM and Eon are only offering a one-film contract. The expired Sony deal was for four movies. MGM, which is owned by private equity firms, including Anchorage Capital Partners, probably wants to keep its options open as it considers a sale or public offering.[33]

In late March 2018, in a surprise move, MGM chief Gary Barber was ousted as the studio went into another state of flux.[34] The Bond franchise, now valued between $1–$3 billion, was again an artistic kite flying in a corporate hurricane.[35]

However, the road to *Bond 25* would take an interesting turn. In late February 2018, *Variety*'s Justin Kroll scooped an exclusive, breaking the news that Oscar-winning British director Danny Boyle was in the lead position to direct *Bond 25*.[36] Having previously helmed Daniel Craig in the extraordinary 2012 London Olympic 007 short, *Happy And Glorious*, co-starring Queen Elizabeth II, Boyle was seemingly back for Bond. Trade observer Mike Fleming Jr developed the story further:

> Boyle had an idea for a very specific 007 movie, and he and his *Trainspotting* [1996] partner John Hodge have teamed up to work out the beats. Hodge is writing that version and if it all works out, that would be the 007 film that Boyle would helm. Hodge won't be done for a couple of months, but when he turns in the script, one of two things will happen. MGM and the producers will like it enough to shelve the movie they were contemplating – the listed writers are Neal Purvis and Robert Wade – and they will instead make

the version that was cooked up by the *Trainspotting* team. Otherwise, Boyle won't direct the film and it will be back to the other script.[37]

Ace show business reporter, Baz Bamigboye, then entered the fray, quoting his unusually well-informed sources:

> They took the idea to Barbara, never believing for a minute she would go for it. But she's excited by the concept – and so is her producing partner Michael. But the most important cheerleader in the meeting was Daniel, and he was pushing for Danny to direct. He loves the fact that it's something completely different. He has not signed up for more of the same old Bond. The seed of Danny and John's Bond was planted when Danny directed that incredible short film – featuring Daniel Craig, the Queen and her corgis – for the opening of the 2012 London Olympics. That's where the bond, for want of a better word, was formed, I'd be shot if I told you the story idea they've come up with, but it's pure movie gold. It's high-stakes British movie producing of the highest order. Your Queen should give them all medals if they pull it off![38]

On 14 March 2018, Danny Boyle confirmed some kind of involvement with *Bond 25*:

> John Hodge – the screenwriter – and I have got this idea, and John is writing it at the moment. And it all depends on how it turns out. It would be foolish of me to give any of it away. We are working on a script which we hope they'll like. And it all depends on that, really. Bond would be right at the end of the year.[39]

On 25 May 2018 it was confirmed that Danny Boyle would indeed helm Bond 25 from a screenplay by John Hodge. North American distribution would be handled by an MGM/Annapura joint venture whilst the film will be released internationally by Universal Pictures. Daniel Craig's fifth 007 feature begins shooting at Pinewood Studios on 3 December 2018.[40]

Through Michael and Barbara's continued producing partnership, the legacies of Harry Saltzman and Albert R. Broccoli have never been in healthier commercial and critical shape. They have proven nepotism only goes so far, but talent goes a lot further. Barbara described their relationship as 'two halves of the same brain. We work together extremely well. It's just evolved over the years.'[41]

By 2018, Michael Wilson had been in the James Bond business longer than Cubby Broccoli. Barbara described her sibling's many talents:

> Michael had many careers before the film one. He has an engineering background, and he has a scientific background and he's also good writer, so he's good on construction, on making things work. Michael has a tremendous amount of knowledge, he's a renaissance man. He has the brains of a scientist and the heart of an artist.[42]

Wilson has never tired of his life in James Bondage:

> Writing and producing Bond films – I am so thankful, how many other people have this chance? The big thing you get out of it is that for a rather small contribution to society we have a huge public awareness and interest and that's rather odd. There are lots of people, doctors, lawyers, research scientists, that have absolutely no recognition in life, yet are doing so much that is really important. Here we are doing something that's a matter of giving people a great experience for a couple of hours in life and we take on tremendous media interest. So how can anyone in my position complain?[43]

Quizzed on her personal success Barbara said:

> [Cubby] gave me great confidence. I spent an awful lot of time with him. He was fifty-one when I was born so he was an older father and I think I was always aware that I wanted to spend as much time with him as possible. So I learned from him. He was very great about sharing his knowledge and passion.'[44]

For Barbara it did not matter what profession Cubby had taught her: 'If my father had been running a pizzeria, I'd be making pizzas.'[45]

Asked how long they think the Bond films will continue, Barbara replied, 'As long as the audience wants to see the films they will be made by us, or by some version of our descendants.'[46]

The third generation of the Broccoli family is in the wings, being groomed to follow. *Spectre* marked Michael's son, Gregg Wilson's second Bond film as associate producer. 'And my other son, David, is on the top floor, working on independent projects and the video games. My niece Heather, Tina's daughter, [works in publicity]. So we have a good representation of the family here.'[47]

Barbara also has a daughter, Angelica: 'She has asked me a couple of times, "Am I supposed to take over from you guys?" And I've said, "You do what you want, girl!"'[48]

For now though, how long do Barbara and Michael plan to stay at the helm? Wilson chuckled as he told the authors of this book, 'There is still life in Barbara!'[49] She interjected quickly, 'Where are you going?'[50] Gregg Wilson is in no hurry to take over the empire: 'I have mentors in Dad and Barbara who I hope won't be leaving any time soon.'[51]

Michael, now in his mid-seventies contemplated, 'Bond will go on. Who is to say who will be making the movies? He's a fictitious character that is part of the culture, so he's like Sherlock Holmes or Batman. There will always be a Bond.'[52]

In an era when franchises have sold out to major studios like Star Wars has with Disney, Cubby would have been proud that, under his heirs, his James Bond 007 empire shows no signs of diminishing.

Albert R. Broccoli's Eon Productions will return.

Cubby's heirs: Barbara Broccoli and Michael G. Wilson in 2008. (Brian James Smith)

EPILOGUE

FAR BEHIND US

IT ALL
BEGAN ON
JAN. 5, 1962
WHEN

IAN FLEMING'S
Dr. No

WENT
INTO
PRODUCTION

since then James Bond films
have been seen by nearly

A BILLION PEOPLE

and have become the
most successful attractions
in entertainment history!

Prior to the initial publication of this book, the authors attempted to interview Sir Sean Connery. In October 2016, just days after Hurricane Matthew swept through the Bahamas, they spoke briefly with him again.

Sir Sean, then 86 years old, admitted, 'It's been a while actually. I haven't kept up with any [of the Bond crew].'[1] Recalling figures from the past, the first cinematic James Bond still admired his character's creator, Ian Fleming: 'He was obviously quite clever.'[2] He described his mentor Terence Young, director of *Dr. No, From Russia with Love* and *Thunderball* fondly, 'Very, very good, excellent director.'[3] The helmer of *Goldfinger* and *Diamonds Are Forever*, Guy Hamilton passed away at the age of ninety-three in April 2016. Connery was sad to hear this: 'I didn't know he died. He was a good guy.'[4] He was pleased to hear his *You Only Live Twice* director was still alive in his mid-nineties, 'Oh, Lewis [Gilbert], yes.'[5]

However, for the octogenarian, his days as James Bond 007 were in the past: 'It was a long, long time ago.'[6]

BY HEAVEN ABOVE ME

SIR ROGER MOORE REMEMBERED

O n 23 May 2017 it was announced via Sir Roger Moore's official Twitter account that he had died in Switzerland following a short battle with cancer. He was 89. Although not entirely unexpected, it was a pivotal moment in Bond history – the first of the Eon James Bond actors had left us. A statement, from his children read; 'Thank you Pops for being you, and being so very special to so many people. We are all devastated.'[1] Gareth Owen, Moore's biographer and personal assistant for more than fifteen years recalled the events leading up to his death:

Roger had been back and forth to Switzerland for several months undergoing tests. Towards the end of April, he went in for a scan and we were all hoping for positive news. His daughter Deborah phoned me and said she had been with her father when the doctor came in and she could tell by his face that it wasn't good news. Roger didn't want to know and said, 'Don't tell me.' The doctor spoke to Deborah and informed her Roger had three weeks. So from then on it was about making him comfortable and making him as happy as he could be. He was falling in and out of sleep most of the time. In the last few weeks he had come to terms with dying, he just didn't want to be in any pain. He faced it very bravely with great dignity. He knew his time was ending. Barbara Broccoli called everyday to see how he was. Around 18-19 May, Roger's son Christian phoned me, 'We've been told it is a matter of hours.' Then for the last few days he slept and didn't really wake up. At 2.34 p.m. on 23 May, Roger passed away in Sion Hospital.[2]

Fellow Bond actors were quick to pay tribute. Sir Sean Connery said in a statement; 'We had an unusually long relationship, by Hollywood standards, that was filled with jokes and laughter. I will miss him.'[3] George Lazenby's release read, 'I liked Roger, he was a genuine fellow, a really good guy.'[4] Both Timothy Dalton and Daniel Craig released messages via the official James Bond Twitter account. Dalton posted, 'I knew Roger as a kind and generous man. He was a wonderfully engaging and successful actor. My thoughts are with his family.'[5] Craig's tribute, 'Nobody Does it Better – love Daniel'[6] was accompanied by a picture of the two actors together backstage at the London Palladium theatre as part of Ian Fleming's centenary celebrations. Pierce Brosnan wrote a heartfelt tribute in *Variety*:

Only on reflection do I see how much of an influence Roger Moore had on me as a young Irish immigrant lad from the banks of the River Boyne. I guess the combination of Bond and The Saint ignited a flame for fame in my heart of innocent wonder. I wanted to be up there. Roger as The Saint made me believe in his world. And before I knew it, the man who was The Saint transformed into James Bond, an even greater hero to me as a boy. Never forgetting the audience, never letting the begrudgers in, Sir Roger enthralled the world for many years as Bond. Sir Roger played it to the end with impeccable good manners and a wicked sense of irony that was born of years upon the stage. He saved our world, for heaven's sake, with his movies as James Bond. He is the only actor I ever asked for an autograph. I was 12 years old, and my mom and dad had taken me to Battersea Park. I lined up by the Ferris wheel and waited my turn to get his autograph. I wanted to be somebody like him. Maybe that's why I waited. Little did I know my time would come to someday enter onto the stage as 007.[7]

Sir Roger's funeral took place at Saint Paul's Anglican Church in Monaco on 10 June 2017. Gareth Owen recalled the service was intimate and personal;

There were about 50 people there. It was a Saturday nobody really knew about it, there was no media there. Roger's sons Geoffrey and Christian, Prince Albert of Monaco, and Leslie Bricusse all spoke. David Walliams read Roger's favourite poem, 'If' by Rudyard Kipling. Hymns included 'Morning Has Broken', 'The Lord's Prayer' and 'My Eyes Have Seen the Glory'. The service celebrated the man rather than the actor. Afterwards we went to the Hotel de Paris for a little glass of champagne in his honour.[8]

Sir Roger's ashes were interred in Monaco. Later, his favourite Bond director Lewis Gilbert's ashes were buried next to him.

On 15 October 2017, family, friends, colleagues and admirers gathered at Pinewood Studios for a celebration of Sir Roger's life and work. It was a fitting date, for the day prior would have been his 90th birthday. Gareth Owen explained:

Pinewood is a very special studio because Roger first came here in 1946 to audition for a film called *The Blue Lagoon*. He didn't get it. But over the years he made 15 movies here, 24 episodes of *The Persuaders* and a few very well paid commercials. In 1971 he opened an office here so Pinewood became his second home. This is where he would base his operations, this is where he would quip, "I'm off to Pinewood to do a little bit of light dusting and Hoovering." Pinewood [are] commemorating him by ensuring his name lives on forever. They're unveiling one of their largest and newest stages in his honour.'

Her Royal Highness, Sophie, Countess of Wessex then unveiled The Roger Moore Stage, a new facility on Pinewood's East Wing. Dame Joan Collins and Sir Michael

Caine eulogised their late friend and then Barbara Broccoli and Michael G Wilson took to the stage. Wilson explained Sir Roger's impact beyond Bond:

> Roger was the essence of a true gentleman and he was a true hero, a hero on screen to millions of his fans and a hero, for the last thirty-six years, bettering the lives of millions, as an ambassador of goodwill for UNICEF. He was a great man and a great friend of our families.'

Clearly moved, Wilson concluded. 'We love you Roger and we miss you.'

Ajay Chowdhury: In June 2009, a selection of Warwick and Bond films were screened at BFI Southbank to celebrate the centenary of the birth of Albert R. 'Cubby' Broccoli. After enjoying Park Circus's pristine prints of the first seven Bond films, we came to the eighth, *Live And Let Die.* Once the film had ended, Matthew turned to me and said, 'Talk about a reboot!' In 1973, that might have meant a trip to Lobb & Co., but in the twenty-first century, the term was apt for what Roger Moore had done for the series.

Between 1973 and 1985, over the course of seven films Bond films, Roger Moore not only changed the public perception of who Bond was but also who he should be. As his adventures varied in tone and size, Roger Moore's performances was consistent and considered. He found an unexplored space to develop 007's screen persona, weaponising wit against the sets and stunts and scale. Sir Roger was always the perfect projection of the role which defined him.

As the definitive Englishman, with his rich, oak-y voice, Moore was an instruction manual in urbanity. He unified diverse Bond fans who secretly emulated his unique brand of Cool Britannia before the term had been invented: a raised eyebrow, a smutty quip, ordering champagne, gambling nonchalantly, making quiche … Well, he was certainly some kind of hero for this young Englishman of Indian heritage: as a 6 year old, it was my viewing of *The Spy Who Loved Me* with my parents which made me a Bond fan. A global icon of Her Majesty's government, through the 1977 Silver Jubilee and years of national renewal in the early eighties Roger Moore as James Bond really did keep the British end up.

My era of Bond fans always also enjoyed his other seventies adventure films and so Sir Roger encapsulated our 'Boy's Own' childhoods. As such, we were collectively sad to hear of his passing as with him died part of all our yesterdays. And Sir Roger's passing evoked memories my later father, who introduced me to Bond and, for the briefest of moments when similarly dressed in slacks and a green suede cardigan, reminded me that James Bond is a cultural heirloom, passed from one generation to another.

Matthew Field: I first encountered Roger Moore's 007 on TV in *The Spy Who Loved Me* on Boxing Day 1986. I was 5. The rest remained a mystery, but my imagination ran wild having spent hours leafing through the pages of Sally Hibbin's THE OFFICIAL JAMES BOND MOVIE POSTER BOOK. Moore's likeness was the centre image of seven movie posters bursting with colour, excitement and adventure. I studied every little illustration and detail and spent an age trying to fathom how a speedboat could emerge from the mouth of a crocodile. This oversized book seemed even bigger back then and I can remember losing myself in Dan Goozee's purplish-pink art of Roger Moore casually clinging to the Eiffel Tower in full black tie, his Walther PPK in hand and the city of Paris beneath him. I still have this book, its spine hanging together by Sellotape.

Viewing the Bond films in a post *Casino Royale* era requires a fresh evaluation. While the critics fondly remember Roger Moore's Bond simply as suave and debonair, there are scenes peppered amongst all seven of his Bonders, which showcase the skill of Roger Moore the actor. Ajay is right, that screening of *Live and Let Die* was an epiphany for us. Moore's debut had a fresh youthful confidence that did everything but sail in the wake left by Sean Connery.

In the weeks leading up to Sir Roger's death I had been screening these movies for my two young children. Carefully edited with the fast-forward button, my two-year old son was just as delighted as I had been by Roger Moore's Bond movies. They are firm family favourites and if the reaction of Sophie and William is anything to go by they will continue to entertain generations to come.

I had the pleasure of meeting Sir Roger for the first time in 2000. I remember standing in line as he exchanged stories with fellow Bond veteran Geoffrey Keen. My hero was exactly how I hoped he would be in person. Ajay and I later had the privilege of interviewing him for this book and spent a wonderful Sunday morning on the phone with him as he regaled us with tales of James Bondage from his home in Monaco.

Moore was the perfect raconteur and his sold out tours around the UK said just as much. Ajay and I attended his last performance at the Royal Festival Hall in November 2016. As always he brought the house down with tales of Tinseltown, his tongue firmly in his cheek throughout. But there was a deep, gentle caring soul behind the façade. His UNICEF work was obviously very close to his heart. Before leaving the stage for the final time Sir Roger quoted Sam Levenson's poem, 'Time Tested Beauty Tips', now freighted with extra poignancy, his reading ending: 'As you grow older, you will discover that you have two hands; one for helping yourself, and the other for helping others.' Moore exited stage to a standing ovation, leaving the glow from the stage lights resting upon a Union Flag cushion, which sat on his empty chair. The perfect ending for a quintessential British hero.

ACKNOWLEDGEMENTS

CRAWL, END CRAWL ...

W e would like to thank the following individuals who took the time to share their memories with us …

James Bond 007s: Sir Sean Connery, George Lazenby, Sir Roger Moore, Pierce Brosnan and Daniel Craig.

The Bond Girls: Ursula Andress, Martine Beswick, Nadja Regin, Honor Blackman, Shirley Eaton, Margaret Nolan, Mollie Peters, Karin Dor, Jill St. John, Lana Wood, Gloria Hendry, Madeline Smith, Maud Adams, Britt Ekland, Caroline Munro, Lynn Holly Johnson, Kristina Wayborn, Tanya Roberts, Maryam d'Abo, Carey Lowell, Eva Green, Caterina Murino and Bérénice Lim Marlohe.

The Villains: Bruce Glover, Yaphet Kotto, Richard Kiel, Michael Lonsdale, Julian Glover, Kabir Bedi, David Meyer, Tony Meyer, Christopher Walken, Jeroen Krabbé, Robert Davi, Mads Mikkelsen and Javier Bardem.

The Whitehall Brigade: Desmond Llewelyn, Vijay Amritraj, Thomas Wheatley, Caroline Bliss, Samantha Bond, Rory Kinnear, Naomie Harris and Dame Judi Dench.

And Sheriff J. W. Pepper: Clifton James.

Directors: Guy Hamilton, Lewis Gilbert, John Glen, Irvin Kershner, Martin Campbell, Roger Spottiswoode, Michael Apted, Lee Tamahori, Marc Forster and Sam Mendes.

Screenwriters: Johanna Clément (née Harwood), Len Deighton, John Landis, Ian La Frenais and Dick Clement, Michael G. Wilson, John Cork, William Osborne and William Davies, Jeffrey Caine, Bruce Feirstein, Kevin Wade, Leslie Dixon, Nicholas Meyer, Tom Ropelewski, David Campbell Wilson, Kurt Wimmer, Dana Stevens, Paul Haggis, John Logan, Neal Purvis and Robert Wade.

Designers: Sir Ken Adam, Terry Ackland-Snow and Peter Lamont.

Cinematographers: Oswald Morris, Douglas Slocombe and Phil Méheux.

Action Men: Vic Armstrong, Rick Sylvester, Paul Weston, Wayne Michaels, Gary Powell and Rémy Julienne.

Musicians: Monty Norman, Eric Serra, David Arnold and Chris Cornell.

Studio Executives: Eric Pleskow, David Picker, Mike Medavoy, Danton Rissner, Alan Ladd Jr., Jeff Kleeman, Lindsay Doran and Chris McGurk.

Crew and Associates: Robert Wagner, Ron Quelch, David Sopel, Norman Wanstall, Trevor Bond, William P. Cartlidge, Elaine Schreyeck, Sue St. Johns (née Parker), Colin Miller, Peter Davies, Anthony Waye, Keith Hamshere, Janine Glen (née King), John Grover, Philip Wrestler, Alan Church, Chris Corbould, Pauline Hume, Lindy Hemming, Daniel Kleinman, Terry Rawlings, Debbie McWilliams, Steve Begg, Michael Lerman, Callum McDougall, Jany Temime, Per Hallberg and Roger Michell.

The following members of Harry Saltzman's family: Mrs. Adriana Saltzman, Hilary Saltzman and Steven Saltzman.

The following members of Albert R. Broccoli's family: Michael G. Wilson and Barbara Broccoli.

THIS BOOK HAS NOT BEEN AUTHORISED BY ANY JAMES BOND COPYRIGHT HOLDER

We are grateful to those who have provided support on many levels over the last two decades:

Stephanie Wenborn, Meg Simmonds, Katherine McCormack, Rosie Moutrie and Anne Bennett of Eon Productions Limited; Anna Whelan and Zoe Morley at Sony Pictures Entertainment; David Black, Charles Black and Cathy Bowman of The James Bond International Fan Club (www.007.info); Lee Pfeiffer and Dave Worrall of *Cinema Retro* (www.cinemaretro.com); Gareth Owen and Andy Boyle (www.bondstars.com); Vipul Patel and James Page of *MI6 Confidential* (www.mi6-hq.com); Anders Frejdh of From Sweden With Love (www.jamesbond007.se) and Luc Le Clech, Pierre Fabry, Eric Saussine and Philippe Lombard of James Bond Club France (www.jamesbond007.net).

Jon Auty, Tina Balio, Chuck Binder, Andrew Biswell, Raymond Benson, Steve Boneham, Graham Broadbent, Tim Browne, Dharmesh Chauhan, Joe Colbourne, Nick Cooke, John Cox, Nathalie Cloet, Leigh Debbage, Michael and Ruth Deeley, Gary J. Firuta, Julian Friedman, Anthony R. Gould, Dr. Sheldon Hall, Paul Harris, Roland Hasler, Phil Hazell, Sandy Lieberson, Andrew Lycett, George Martin, David Mason, Mark Mawston, M. David Mullen ASC, Lancelot Narayan, Mark O'Connell, John Ormerod, Tim Partridge, Panos Sambrakos, Paul Scrabo and George Ann Muller, John Royal, Mike Smith, Keerthi Suresh, Dr. Siegfried Tesche, Richard Toogood, Makoto Wakamatsu and Paul Witherspoon.

For assistance above and beyond the call of duty: Varuj Arakelian, Greg Bechtloff, Jeremy Duns, Anders Frejdh, Tim Greaves, Ross Lancaster, Steven Oxenrider, Gareth Owen, Brian James Smith, Bernard Vandendriessche, Mark Witherspoon and Dave Worrall.

Thanks to our indulgent publishers, The History Press: our editors Jo de Vries and Lauren Newby, and especially to our M, Mark Beynon.

And heartfelt thanks to our friends and family …

From Matthew to: Andrew, Natalie, Olivia and Henry Field, Sue Martin, Barbara Spreadbury, Chris, Karen, Isabelle and Lawrence Warner, Woody, Ally, Bailey and Poppy Smallwoods, Michael, Keri, Olivia and Aidan Spreadbury, Harry Neal, Nicholas Cowle and Dipali Patel, David Sillett, Nick Bayliss and Sue Sillett, Nigel, Melissa, Recce and Holly Sillett, Robin, Lynda and Luke Sillett, Steven and Victoria Wrench, Neil and Jessica Spreadbury, Mark and Tamasin Laycock,

Glen and Charlie Beardwood, Robert Way, Alex and Jenny May, Carl and Abby May, Darren and Juanita May, Jason and Liz May, Matthew Smith and Yvonne Roy, Richard Moran, Colette McFadden, Louise McFadden, Courtney Dolliver, Gordon Dale, Albert Sharpe and Iain Ovenden.

From Ajay to: Sonia, Raveena, Karneet, Sharan, Rajneet, Bul Bul, Hardeep, Manjeet, Nirmal, Ravneet, Maira, Lavanya, Sanjeev and Elizabeth Chowdhury, Tejneet and Amarbir Selhi, Emily, Harry, Jasmin and Annabel Baumann, Manveen, Alok, Harveen, Raihan and Sanvir Bal, the late Tejinder Bal, Amarjit, Gurman, Devinder, Noor, Amaanat, Shami, Rommel, Agamjot and Armaan Bal, Aneet, Ashish, Anisa and Alena Sareen, Mrs Amarjit "Papu" Singh, *bhuas* Malika and Jasmine, Rajpal, Tajpaul, Mohindra, Simran, Samantha and Navin Chowdhry, Sudeep Singh, Rasneet Kaur, Mr. Gurtej Singh and Mrs Bani Kaur, Dr Pushpinder Chowdhry MBE, Lindsay Fursland, Bobby Hallen, Ross Cameron and Miles Hendry, Jean Watt, Glenn Warren, William Hinshelwood, Trevor Willsmer, *De koningen en koninginnen van Keizerstraat*, Silvia Schikhof, Trine Yates, the late Vijay Malhotra, Steve Fairburn, Chris Jones, James Lightfoot, John Sapsford, Chris Beasley, Neil McEwan, Neville Raschid, Marios Pattihis, Dan Wise, Robin Lim, Patricia Hare, Kiri Kkoshi, Henry Hadaway MBE, Farah Shaikh, Richard Onslow, Darren Riley, Radford Goodman, Barry Halper and Matthew Robinson.

BIBLIOGRAPHY

THANK YOU, MONEYPENNY

Adam, Ken, and Christopher Frayling, *Ken Adam Designs the Movies: James Bond and Beyond*, Thames & Hudson, 2008

Archer, Simon, and Stan Nicholls, *Gerry Anderson: The Authorised Biography*, Legend, 1996

Armstrong, Vic, with Robert Sellers, *The True Adventures of the World's Greatest Stuntman*, Titan Books, 2011

Bach, Stephen, *Final Cut: Dreams and Disaster in the Making of Heaven's Gate*, Faber and Faber Limited, 1986

Balio, Tino, *United Artists: The Company Built By the Stars*, The University of Wisconsin Press, 1976

—, *United Artists: The Company That Changed the Film Industry*, The University of Wisconsin Press, 1987

Barnes, Alan, and Marcus Hearn, *Kiss Kiss Bang! Bang!: The Unofficial James Bond Film Companion*, Revised and updated second edition, B.T. Batsford – a memmber of the Chrysalis Group Plc, 2000

Bart, Peter, *Fade Out: The Calamitous Final Days of MGM*, William Morrow, 1990

Batey, Mavis, *From Bletchley With Love*, Bletchley Park Trust, 2008

Bennett, Tony, and Janet Woollacott, *Bond and Beyond: The Political Career of a Popular Hero*, Macmillan Education, 1987

Benson, Raymond, *The James Bond Bedside Companion*, Boxtree Limited, 1988

Berkoff, Steven, *Free Association: An Autobiography*, Faber and Faber Limited, 1996

Bond, Mary Wickham, *How 007 Got His Name*, Collins, 1966

Bouzereau, Laurent, *The Art of Bond*, Boxtree – an imprint of Pan Macmillan Publishers Ltd, 2006

Bricusse, Leslie, *The Music Man*, Metro Publishing, 2006

Broccoli, Cubby, with Donald Zec, *When the Snow Melts*, Boxtree – an imprint of Macmillan Publishers Ltd, 1998

Bryce, Ivar, *You Only Live Once: Memories of Ian Fleming*, Weidenfeld & Nicolson,

1975

Burgess, Anthony, *You've Had Your Time: Being the Second Part of the Confessions of Anthony Burgess*, Heinemann, 1990

Burlingame, Jon, *The Music of James Bond*, Oxford University Press, 2012

Cain, Syd, *Not Forgetting James Bond: The Autobiography of Syd Cain*, GBU Publishing, 2002

Carter-Ruck, Peter, *Memoirs of a Libel Lawyer*, Weidenfeld & Nicolson, 1990

Chancellor, Henry, *James Bond: The Man and His World*, John Murray, 2005

Chapman, James, *Licence to Thrill: A Cultural History of the James Bond Films*, I.B. Taurus & Co. Ltd, 2nd Edition, 2007

Cilento, Diane, *My Nine Lives*, Michael Joseph Ltd, 2006

Clark, Jim, with John H. Myers, *Dream Repairman: Adventures in Film Editing*, LandMarc Press, 2010

Connery, Sean, and Murray Grigor, *Being a Scot*, Weidenfeld & Nicolson, 2008

Cork, John, and Bruce Scivally, *James Bond: The Legacy*, Boxtree – an imprint of Pan Macmillan Publishers Ltd, 2002

d'Abo, Maryam, and John Cork, *Bond Girls Are Forever: The Women of James Bond*, Boxtree – an imprint of Pan Macmillan Publishers Ltd, 2003

de Winter, Helen, *What I Really Want To Do Is Produce*, Faber and Faber Limited, 2006

Deeley, Michael, with Matthew Field, *Blade Runners, Deer Hunters & Blowing the Bloody Doors Off: My Life In Cult Movies*, Faber and Faber Limited, 2008

Dench, Judi as told to John Millar, *And Furthermore*, Weidenfeld & Nicolson, 2010

Desowitz, Bill, *James Bond Unmasked*, Spies LLC, 2012

Donovan, Paul, *Roger Moore*, W.H. Allen, 1983

Doyle, Tom, *Man on the Run: Paul McCartney in the 1970s*, Birlinn, 2014

Drazin, Charles, *A Bond For Bond*, Film Finances Ltd, 2011

Duncan, Paul (ed.), *The James Bond Archives*, Taschen, 2012

Eaton, Shirley, *Golden Girl*, B.T. Batsford Ltd, 1999

Farneth, David, *Lenya: The Legend*, Thames & Hudson, 1998

Feeney Callan, Michael, *Sean Connery*, Virgin Books, 2002

Fiegel, Eddi, *John Barry: A Sixties Theme – From James Bond to Midnight Cowboy*, Constable, 1998

Field, Matthew, *Michael Caine 'You're A Big Man … '*, B.T. Batsford – An imprint of Chrysalis Books Group plc, 2003

Fiennes, Ranulph, *Living Dangerously*, Macmillan, 1987

Fraser, George MacDonald, *The Light's On At Signpost*, HarperCollins Publishers, 2003

Frayling, Christopher, *Ken Adam: The Art of Production Design*, Faber and Faber Limited, 2005

Freedland, Michael, *Sean Connery: A Biography*, Weidenfeld & Nicolson, 1994

French, John, *Robert Shaw: The Price of Success*, Nick Hern Books, 1993

Giammarco, David, *For Your Eyes Only: Behind the Scenes of the James Bond Films*, ECW Press, 2002

Giblin, Gary, *James Bond's London*, Daleon Enterprises, 2001

Gilbert, Lewis, with Peter Rankin, *All My Flashbacks*, Reynolds & Hearn, 2010

Glen, John, with Marcus Hearn, *For My Eyes Only*, B.T. Batsford – a member of the Chrysalis Group plc, 2001

Goldberg, Fred, *Motion Picture Marketing and Distribution*, Focal Press, 1991

Goodwin, Cliff, *Evil Spirits: The Life of Oliver Reed*, Virgin, 2000

Greaves, Tim, *The Bond Women 007 Style*, 1-Shot Publications, 2002

Guest, Val, *So You Want To Be In Pictures*, Reynolds & Hearn, 2001

Haining, Peter, *James Bond: A Celebration*, W.H Allen/Planet, 1987

Halpenny, Bruce Barrymore, *Little Nellie 007*, Casdec Limited, 1991

Helfenstein, Charles, *The Making of On Her Majesty's Secret Service*, Spies LLC, 2009

Hernu, Sandy, *Q: The Biography of Desmond Llewelyn*, S.B. Publications, 1999

Hibbin, Sally, *The Making of Licence to Kill*, Hamlyn, 1989

Hilburn, Robert, *Johnny Cash: The Life*, Weidenfeld & Nicolson, 2013

Hirshenson, Janet, and Jane Jenkins with Rachel Kranz, *A Star Is Found: Our Adventures Casting Some of Hollywood's Biggest Movies*, Harcourt Inc., 2006

Hume, Alan, with Gareth Owen, *A Life Through the Lens*, McFarland & Company, 2004

Hunter, John, *Great Scot: The Life of Sean Connery*, Bloomsbury, 1993

Inverne, James, *Wrestling With Elephants: The Authorised Biography of Don Black*, Sanctuary Publishing, 2003

Johnstone, Iain, *The World Is Not Enough: A Companion*, Boxtree - an imprint of Macmillan Publishers Ltd, 1999

Krantz, Judith, *Sex and Shopping: The Confessions of a Nice Jewish Girl*, St. Martin's Press, 2000

Lamberti, Edward (ed.), *Behind the Scenes at the BBFC*, Palgrave Macmillan, 2012

Lane, Sheldon (ed.), *For Bond Lovers Only*, Panther, 1965

Leonard, Geoff, Pete Walker and Gareth Bramley, *John Barry: A Life in Music*, Sansom & Company, 1998

—, *John Barry: The Man With the Midas Touch*, Redcliffe Press, 2008

Lindner, Christoph (ed.), *The James Bond Phenomenon: A Critical Reader*, Manchester University Press, 2003

Luxford, Albert J., with Gareth Owen, *Albert J. Luxford, the Gimmick Man: Memoir of a Special Effects Maestro*, McFarland & Company, 2002

Lycett, Andrew, *Ian Fleming*, Weidenfeld & Nicolson, 1995

Mankiewicz, Tom, and Robert Crane, *My Life as a Mankiewicz: An Insider's Journey Through Hollywood*, University Press of Kentucky, 2012

McGilligan, Pat (ed.), *Backstory: Interviews with Screenwriters of Hollywood's Golden Age*, Ewing/The University of California Press, 1986

Mills, Alec, *Shooting 007 and Other Celluloid Adventures*, The History Press, 2014

Monro, Michelle, *The Singer's Singer: The Life and Music of Matt Monro*, Collins, 2010

Moore, Roger, *Roger Moore as James Bond*, Pan Books, 1973

—, *Roger Moore's James Bond Diary*, (US Ed.), Fawcett Publications, 1973

Moore, Roger, with Gareth Owen, *Bond On Bond*, Michael O'Mara Books, 2012

—, *My Word Is My Bond*, Michael O'Mara Books, 2008

Moseley, Roy, with Philip and Martin Masheter, *Roger Moore: A Biography*, New English Library, 1985

Mower, Patrick, *Patrick Mower: My Story*, John Blake, 2007

Niven, David, *The Moon's a Balloon*, Hamish Hamilton, 1971

Norman, Barry, *And Why Not? Memoirs of a Film Lover*, Simon and Schuster, 2002

O'Connell, Mark, *Catching Bullets: Memoirs of a Bond Fan*, Splendid Books, 2012

Osborne, John, *Looking Back: Never Explain, Never Apologise*, Faber and Faber Limited, 1999

Owen, Alistair (ed.), *Story and Character: Interviews with British Screenwriters*, Bloomsbury,

2003

Owen, Gareth, and Oliver Bayan, *Roger Moore: His Films and Career*, Robert Hale Limited, 2002

Owen, Gareth, with Brian Burford, *The Pinewood Story: The Authorised History of the World's Most Famous Film Studio*, Reynolds & Hearn, 2000

Pearce, Garth, *The Making of GoldenEye*, Boxtree Limited, 1995

—, *The Making of Tomorrow Never Dies*, Boxtree – an imprint of Macmillan Publishers Ltd, 1997

Pearson, John, *The Life of Ian Fleming*, Aurum Press Ltd, Revised Edition, 2003

Pfeiffer, Lee and Lisa, Philip, *The Incredible World of 007: An Authorized Celebration of James Bond*, Updated Edition, Boxtree Limited, 1995

Picker, David, *Musts, Maybes and Nevers*, CreateSpace, 2013

Rankin (curated by), *Blood, Sweat and Bond: Behind the Scenes of Spectre*, Dorling Kindersley, 2015

Richardson, Tony, *Long Distance Runner: A Memoir*, Faber and Faber Limited, 1993

Rubin, Steven Jay, *The Complete James Bond Movie Encyclopedia*, Contemporary Books, Newly Revised Edition, 2003

—, *The James Bond Films: A Behind the Scenes History*, Arlington House Inc., 1983

Russo, Gus, *Supermob: How Sidney Korshak and His Criminal Associates Became America's Hidden Power Brokers*, Bloomsbury, 2006

Sellers, Robert, *The Battle For Bond: The Genesis of Cinema's Greatest Hero*, Tomahawk Press, First edition, 2008

Shubrook, Martin, *Special Effects Superman: The Art and Effects of Derek Meddings*, Shubrook Bros Publications, 2008

Simmons, Bob, with Kenneth Passingham, *Nobody Does It Better: My 25 Years with James Bond and Other Stars*, Javelin Books, 1987

Slater, Robert, *Ovitz: The Inside Story Of Hollywood's Most Powerful Power Broker*, McGraw-Hill, 1997

Smith, Bill, *Robert Fleming 1845–1933*, Whittinghame House, 2000

Soter, Tom, *Bond and Beyond: 007 and Other Special Agents*, Image Publishing, 1993

Sterling, Martin, and Gary Morecambe, *Martinis, Girls and Guns: 50 Years of 007*, Robson Books, 2003

Sturrock, Donald, *Storyteller: The Life of Roald Dahl*, HarperPress, 2010

Swan, Steve (contributor), *Moonraker Special*, World & Whitman, 1979

Sylvester, David (ed.), *Moonraker, Strangelove and Other Celluloid Dreams: The Visionary Art of Ken Adam*, Serpentine Gallery, 1999

Taylor, John, *In the Pleasure Groove: Love, Death and Duran Duran*, Sphere, 2012

Treglown, Jeremy, *Roald Dahl: A Biography*, Faber and Faber Limited 1994

Trevelyan, John, *What the Censor Saw*, Michael Joseph Ltd, 1973

Turner, Adrian, *Adrian Turner on Goldfinger: Bloomsbury Movie Guide No. 2*, Bloomsbury, 1998

van der Zyl, Nikki, *For Your Ears Only: The Voice of the Stars*, Indepenpress, 2013

Walker, Alexander, *Hollywood, England*, Michael Joseph Ltd, 1974

Warburton, Nigel, *Ernö Goldfinger: The Life of an Architect*, Routledge, 2003

Watkin, David, *Why Is There Only One Word For Thesaurus?*, The Trouser Press, 1998

Wood, Christopher, *James Bond: The Spy I Loved*, Twenty-First-Century Publishers, 2006

Woodhead, Colin (ed.), *Dressed To Kill: James Bond the Suited Hero*, Flammarion, 1996

Worrall, Dave, *The Most Famous Car in the World: The Complete History of the James Bond*

Aston Martin DB5, Solo Publishing, 1991

Young, Freddie, *Seventy Light Years: A Life in the Movies*, Faber and Faber Limited, 1999

Yule, Andrew, *Sean Connery: Neither Shaken, Nor Stirred*, Little Brown and Company, 1992

Zec, Donald, *Put the Knife in Gently: Memoirs of a Life With Legends*, Robson Books, 2003

EBOOKS

Deighton, Len, *James Bond: My Long and Eventful Search for His Father*, Kindle Single, 2012

Duns, Jeremy, *Duns on Bond: An Omnibus of Journalism on Ian Fleming and James Bond*, CreateSpace, 2014

Scivally, Bruce, *Booze, Bullets and Broads: The Story of Matt Helm, Superspy of the Mad Men Era*, Henry Gray Publishing, 2013

NOTES

BETTER THAN A COMPUTER

All box office figures (unless otherwise stated) courtesy of Boxofficemojo.com

Chapter 1 Ian Fleming

1   Ian Fleming, 'How to Write a Thriller' *Show: The Magazine of the Arts*, Vol. II No. 8, August 1962

2   Ian Fleming, 'How to Write a Thriller' *Show: The Magazine of the Arts*, Vol. II No. 8, August 1962

3   Ivar Bryce, *You Only Live Once Memories of Ian Fleming*, Weidenfeld and Nicolson, 1975 p. 103

4   Andrew Lycett, *Ian Fleming*, Phoenix, 1996, p. 225

5   Andrew Lycett, *Ian Fleming*, Phoenix, 1996, p. 232

6   Andrew Lycett, *Ian Fleming*, Phoenix, 1996, p. 5

7   Bill Smith, *Robert Fleming 1845–1933*, Whittinghame House, 2000, p. 10

8   Bill Smith, *Robert Fleming 1845–1933*, Whittinghame House, 2000, p. 110–111

9   Bill Smith, *Robert Fleming 1845–1933*, Whittinghame House, 2000, p. 112–114

10   Bill Smith, *Robert Fleming 1845–1933*, Whittinghame House, 2000, p. 116

11   Mavis Batey, *From Bletchley With Love,* Bletchley Park Trust, August 2008, pp. 24–25

12   Mavis Batey, *From Bletchley With Love*, Bletchley Park Trust, August 2008, pp. 24–25

13   John Pearson, *The Life of Ian Fleming*, Aurum Press Ltd, Revised Edition, 2003, p. 223

14   Andrew Lycett, *Ian Fleming*, Phoenix, 1996, p. 154

15   Ian Fleming interviewed by Munroe Scott, *The Sixties*, Canadian Broadcasting Company, 05.02.1964

16   Ian Fleming interviewed by Munroe Scott, *The Sixties*, Canadian Broadcasting Company, 05.02.1964

17   Mrs James Bond, *How 007 Got His Name*, Collins, 1966 p. 40

18   Andrew Lycett, *Ian Fleming*, Phoenix, 1996, p. 241

19   Andrew Lycett, *Ian Fleming*, Phoenix, 1996, p. 244

20   Andrew Lycett, *Ian Fleming*, Phoenix, 1996, pp. 232–33

21   Andrew Lycett, *Ian Fleming*, Phoenix, 1996, pp. 249–50

22   Andrew Lycett, *Ian Fleming*, Phoenix, 1996, pp. 249–50

23   'Barry Nelson: The First James Bond' by Lee Goldberg, *Starlog* #75, October 1983

24   'Shaky, Not Stirred' by Dermot Purgote, *The Mail On Sunday, You Magazine*, 10.05.1992

25   'Shaky, Not Stirred' by Dermot Purgote, *The Mail On Sunday, You Magazine*, 10.05.1992

26   'Barry Nelson: The First James Bond' by Lee Goldberg, *Starlog* #75, October 1983

27   'Barry Nelson: The First James Bond' by Lee Goldberg, *Starlog* #75, October 1983

28   'Barry Nelson: The First James Bond' by Lee Goldberg, *Starlog* #75, October 1983

29   Andrew Lycett, *Ian Fleming*, Phoenix, 1996, p. 264

30   Albert R. Broccoli with Donald Zec, *When the*

Snow Melts, Boxtree, 1998, p. 130

31 Andrew Lycett, *Ian Fleming*, Phoenix, 1996, p. 268

32 Andrew Lycett, *Ian Fleming*, Phoenix, 1996, p. 265

33 Andrew Lycett, *Ian Fleming*, Phoenix, 1996, pp. 275–76

34 Andrew Lycett, *Ian Fleming*, Phoenix, 1996, p. 276

35 Andrew Lycett, *Ian Fleming*, Phoenix, 1996, p. 276

36 *Daily Variety*, 15.02.1956

37 'By Way of Report' by A.H. Weiler, *The New York Times*, 08.01.1956

38 Andrew Lycett, *Ian Fleming*, Phoenix, 1996, p. 291

39 'Sex, Snobbery and Sadism' by Paul Johnson, *New Statesman*, 05.04.1958

40 Andrew Lycett, *Ian Fleming*, Phoenix, 1996, p. 336

41 Andrew Lycett, *Ian Fleming*, Phoenix, 1996, p. 336

42 Andrew Lycett, *Ian Fleming*, Phoenix, 1996, p. 337

43 Andrew Lycett, *Ian Fleming*, Phoenix, 1996, p. 337

44 Andrew Lycett, *Ian Fleming*, Phoenix, 1996, p. 337

45 Andrew Lycett, *Ian Fleming*, Phoenix, 1996, p. 338

46 Steven Jay Rubin, *The Complete James Bond Movie Encyclopaedia*, Contemporary Books, Newly Revised Edition, 2003, pp. 57–58

47 Steven Jay Rubin, *The Complete James Bond Movie Encyclopaedia*, Contemporary Books, Newly Revised Edition, 2003, pp. 57–58

48 Ivar Bryce, *You Only Live Once Memories of Ian Fleming*, Weidenfeld and Nicolson, 1975, p. 123

49 Ivar Bryce, *You Only Live Once Memories of Ian Fleming*, Weidenfeld and Nicolson, 1975, p. 124

50 'How He Came Upon the Rights' Kevin McClory Interview by Morgan Fullam, www.kevinmclory.com, December 1999

51 'How He Came Upon the Rights' Kevin McClory Interview by Morgan Fullam, www.kevinmclory.com, December 1999

52 'How He Came Upon the Rights' Kevin McClory Interview by Morgan Fullam, www.kevinmclory.com, December 1999

53 Robert Sellers, *The Battle For Bond: The Genesis of Cinema's Greatest Hero*, Tomahawk Press, First edition, 2008, p. 29

54 Ivar Bryce, *You Only Live Once Memories of Ian Fleming*, Weidenfeld and Nicolson, 1975, p. 123

55 'How He Came Upon the Rights' Kevin McClory Interview by Morgan Fullam, www.kevinmclory.com, December 1999

56 'How He Came Upon the Rights' Kevin McClory Interview by Morgan Fullam, www.kevinmclory.com, December 1999

57 Robert Sellers, *The Battle For Bond: The Genesis of Cinema's Greatest Hero*, Tomahawk Press, First edition, 2008, p. 30

58 'How He Came Upon the Rights' Kevin McClory Interview by Morgan Fullam, www.kevinmclory.com, December 1999

59 Ivar Bryce, *You Only Live Once Memories of Ian Fleming*, Weidenfeld and Nicolson, 1975, p. 142

60 Ivar Bryce, *You Only Live Once Memories of Ian Fleming*, Weidenfeld and Nicolson, 1975, p. 139

61 Steven Jay Rubin, *The Complete James Bond Movie Encyclopaedia*, Contemporary Books, Newly Revised Edition, 2003, p. 360

Chapter 2 Harry Saltzman

1 'The Man Who Got Bond Going' by Pearl Sheffy, *Calgary Sun Herald*, 29.01.1966

2 Adriana Saltzman: Authors' interview, 14.09.2014

3 Adriana Saltzman: Authors' interview, 14.09.2014

4 Adriana Saltzman: Authors' interview, 14.09.2014

5 'The Man Who Got Bond Going' by Pearl Sheffy, *Calgary Sun Herald*, 29.01.1966

6 'The Man Who Got Bond Going' by Pearl Sheffy, *Calgary Sun Herald*, 29.01.1966

7 'Harry the Spy: the Secret Pre–History of a James Bond Producer' by David Kamp with document commentary by David Giammarco, *Vanity Fair*, 18.09.2012

8 'Harry the Spy: the Secret Pre–History of a James Bond Producer' by David Kamp with document commentary by David Giammarco, *Vanity Fair*, 18.09.2012

9 'Harry the Spy: The Secret Pre–History of a James Bond Producer' by David Kamp with document commentary by David Giammarco, *Vanity Fair*, 18.09.2012

10 'Harry the Spy: the Secret Pre–History of a James Bond Producer' by David Kamp with document commentary by David Giammarco, *Vanity Fair*, 18.09.2012

11 'The Man Who Got Bond Going' by Pearl Sheffy, *Calgary Sun Herald*, 29.01.1966

12 'The Man Who Got Bond Going' by Pearl Sheffy, *Calgary Sun Herald*, 29.01.1966

13 'The Man Who Got Bond Going' by Pearl Sheffy, *Calgary Sun Herald*, 29.01.1966

14 Steven Saltzman: Authors' interview, 26.08.2015

15 Len Deighton, *James Bond: My Long and Eventful Search for His Father*, Kindle Single, 2012

16 Judith Krantz, *Sex and Shopping, The Confessions of a Nice Jewish Girl: An Autobiography*, St. Martin's Press, 2000, p. 134

17 Judith Krantz, *Sex and Shopping, The Confessions of a Nice Jewish Girl: An Autobiography*, St. Martin's Press, 2000, p. 134

18 Judith Krantz, *Sex and Shopping, The Confessions of a Nice Jewish Girl: An Autobiography*, St. Martin's Press, 2000, p. 134

19 Judith Krantz, *Sex and Shopping, The Confessions of a Nice Jewish Girl: An Autobiography*, St. Martin's Press, 2000, p. 134

20 'The Man Who Got Bond Going' by Pearl Sheffy, *Calgary Sun Herald*, 29.01.1966

21 Johanna Clément (née Harwood): Authors' interview, 22.08.2012

22 Johanna Clément (née Harwood): Authors' interview, 22.08.2012

23 Hilary Saltzman: Authors' interview, 29.11.2011

24 Alexander Walker, *Hollywood, England*, Michael Joseph Ltd, 1974, p. 58

25 Tony Richardson, *Long Distance Runner: A Memoir*, Faber and Faber Limited, 1993, p. 95

26 Tony Richardson, *Long Distance Runner: A Memoir*, Faber and Faber Limited, 1993, p. 96

27 Tony Richardson, *Long Distance Runner: A Memoir*, Faber and Faber Limited, 1993, p. 96

28 Tony Richardson, *Long Distance Runner: A Memoir*, Faber and Faber Limited, 1993, p. 96

29 Tony Richardson, *Long Distance Runner: A Memoir*, Faber and Faber Limited, 1993, p. 97

30 Tony Richardson, *Long Distance Runner: A Memoir*, Faber and Faber Limited, 1993, p. 97

31 Johanna Clément (née Harwood): Authors' interview, 22.08.2012

32 John Osborne, *Looking Back Never Explain, Never Apologise*, Faber and Faber Limited, 1999, p. 351–52

33 Johanna Clément (née Harwood): Authors' interview, 22.08.2012

34 Johanna Clément (née Harwood): Authors' interview, 22.08.2012

35 Johanna Clément (née Harwood): Authors' interview, 22.08.2012

36 Johanna Clément (née Harwood): Authors' interview, 22.08.2012

37 Oswald Morris: Authors' interview, 18.01.2014

38 'New Wave Hits British Films' by Harry Saltzman, *Films and Filming*, April 1960

39 'New Wave Hits British Films' by Harry Saltzman, *Films and Filming*, April 1960

40 Alexander Walker, *Hollywood, England*, Michael Joseph Ltd, 1974, p. 56

41 Alexander Walker, *Hollywood, England*, Michael Joseph Ltd, 1974, p. 58

42 Eric Pleskow: Authors' interview, 28.05.2015

43 Eric Pleskow: Authors' interview, 28.05.2015

44 Eric Pleskow: Authors' interview, 28.05.2015

45 John Osborne, *Looking Back Never Explain, Never Apologise*, Faber and Faber Limited, 1999, p. 459

46 Michael Deeley with Matthew Field, *Blade Runners, Deer Hunters and Blowing the Bloody Doors Off: My Life in Cult Movies*, Faber and Faber Limited, 2008, p. 26

47 John Osborne, *Looking Back Never Explain, Never Apologise*, Faber and Faber Limited, 1999

48 'Harry Saltzman Recalls Early Coolness to Bond Features' by Todd McCarthy, *Daily Variety*, 13.05.1987

49 Steven Jay Rubin, *The Complete James Bond Movie Encyclopaedia*, Contemporary Books, Newly Revised Edition, 2003, p. 360

50 Tino Balio, *United Artists: The Company That Changed The Film Industry*, University of Wisconsin Press, 1987, p. 255

51 'Roger Moore Bonded to 007' by Roderick Mann, *Los Angeles Times*, 12.05.1985

52 'Harry the Spy: the Secret Pre–History of a James Bond Producer' by David Kamp with document commentary by David Giammarco, *Vanity Fair*, 18.09.2012

53 Johanna Clément (née Harwood): Authors' interview, 22.08.2012

54 Johanna Clément (née Harwood): Authors' interview, 22.08.2012

55 Johanna Clément (née Harwood): Authors' interview, 22.08.2012

56 'How He Came Upon the Rights' Kevin McClory Interview by Morgan Fullam, www.kevinmclory.com, December 1999

57 Peter Janson-Smith: unpublished interview with Dr. Siegfried Tesche, 19.08.2005

58 Andrew Lycett, *Ian Fleming*, Phoenix, 1996, p. 244

59 Tino Balio, *United Artists: The Company That Changed The Film Industry*, University of Wisconsin Press, 1987, p. 255

Chapter 3   Albert R. Broccoli

1 Cubby and Dana Broccoli interviewed by Paul Ryan, Los Angeles cable TV, 1979

2 Cubby and Dana Broccoli interviewed by Paul Ryan, Los Angeles cable TV, 1979

3 Cubby and Dana Broccoli interviewed by Paul Ryan, Los Angeles cable TV, 1979

4 Cubby and Dana Broccoli interviewed by Paul Ryan, Los Angeles cable TV, 1979

5 Cubby and Dana Broccoli interviewed by Paul Ryan, Los Angeles cable TV, 1979

6 Guy Hamilton: Authors' interview, 01.08.2013

7 Albert R. Broccoli with Donald Zec, *When the Snow Melts*, Boxtree, 1998, p. 42

8 Albert R. Broccoli with Donald Zec, *When the Snow Melts*, Boxtree, 1998, p. 60

9 Joseph McBride, *Hawks on Hawks*, University of California Press, 2nd Edition, 1982, p. 34

10 Albert R. Broccoli with Donald Zec, *When the Snow Melts*, Boxtree, 1998, p. 70

11 Robert Wagner: Authors' interview, 05.05.2015

12 Robert Wagner: Authors' interview, 05.05.2015

13 Robert Wagner: 'Celebrating the Life and Work of Cubby Broccoli' Odeon Leicester Square, London, 17.11.1996

14 Robert Wagner: Authors' interview, 05.05.2015

15 Albert R. Broccoli with Donald Zec, *When the Snow Melts*, Boxtree, 1998, p. 73

16 Alexander Walker, *Hollywood, England*, Michael Joseph Ltd, 1974, p. 182

17 Alexander Walker, *Hollywood, England*, Michael Joseph Ltd, 1974, p. 182

18 *Daily Variety*, 22.03.1948

19 'Just for *Variety*' by Army Archerd, *Daily Variety*, 12.09.1966

20 Tino Balio, *United Artists: The Company that Changed the Film Industry*, University of Wisconsin Press, 1987, p. 236

21 Guy Hamilton: Authors' interview, 04.05.2015

22 Guy Hamilton: Authors' interview, 04.05.2015

23 Alan Ladd Jr.: Authors' interview, 22.05.2015

24 United Artists press release: 'Terence Young, Dr. No's Widely Travelled Director Offers Good Advice' 1962

25 Pat McGilligan (ed.), *Backstory: Interviews with Screenwriters of Hollywood's Golden Age*, University of California Press, 1986, p. 283

26 *Daily Variety*, 06.01.1954

27 'Wrap Shot: *Dr. No*' by Ray Zone, *American Cinematographer*, November 2002

28 'Wrap Shot: *Dr. No*' by Ray Zone, *American Cinematographer*, November 2002

29 'Warwick Will Lense 2 Films In C'Scope' *Daily Variety*, 16.12.1953

30 'Ken Adam and *Dr. No*' by Sir Christopher Frayling, *Movie Classics Cinema Retro #4*, 2012

31 Sir Christopher Frayling, *Ken Adam: The Art of Production Design*, Faber and Faber Limited, 2005, p. 12

32 Sir Christopher Frayling, *Ken Adam: The Art of Production Design*, Faber and Faber Limited, 2005, p. 24

33 Syd Cain, *Not Forgetting James Bond: The Autobiography of Syd Cain*, GBU Publishing Ltd, 2002, p. 11

34 Sir Christopher Frayling, *Ken Adam: The Art of Production Design*, Faber and Faber Limited, 2005, pp. 93–94

35 Ken Adam: Authors' interview, 26.01.2015

36 Steven Jay Rubin, *The Complete James Bond Movie Encyclopaedia*, Contemporary Books, Newly Revised Edition, 2003, pp. 57–58

37 Cubby and Dana Broccoli interviewed by Paul Ryan, Los Angeles cable TV, 1979

38 Cubby and Dana Broccoli interviewed by Paul Ryan, Los Angeles cable TV, 1979

39 Alexander Walker, *Hollywood, England*, Michael Joseph Ltd, 1974, p. 181

40 Albert R. Broccoli with Donald Zec, *When the Snow Melts*, Boxtree, 1998, p. 141

41 Alexander Walker, *Hollywood, England*, Michael Joseph Ltd, 1974, p. 181

42 Alexander Walker, *Hollywood, England*, Michael Joseph Ltd, 1974, p. 183

43 Lee Pfeiffer and Philip Lisa, *The Incredible World of 007: An Authorized Celebration of James Bond*, Updated Edition, Boxtree, 1995, p. 190

44 Steven Jay Rubin, *The Complete James Bond Movie Encyclopaedia*, Contemporary Books, Newly Revised Edition, 2002, p. 58

45 Eric Pleskow: Authors' interview, 28.05.2015

46 Steven Jay Rubin, *The Complete James Bond Movie Encyclopaedia*, Contemporary Books, Newly Revised Edition, 2003, p. 58

47 Eric Pleskow: Authors' interview, 28.05.2015

48 Tino Balio, *United Artists: The Company Built by the Stars*, University of Wisconsin Press, 1976, p. 14

49 Tino Balio, *United Artists: The Company that Changed the Film Industry*, University of Wisconsin Press, 1987, p. 161

50 James Chapman, *Licence to Thrill*, I.B. Taurus and Co. Ltd, 2nd Edition, 2007, p. 41

51 David Picker: Authors' interview, 24.02.2014

52 Alexander Walker, *Hollywood, England*, Michael Joseph Ltd, 1974, p. 185

53 David Picker: Authors' interview, 24.02.2014

54 Tino Balio, *United Artists: The Company That Changed the Film Industry*, University of Wisconsin Press, 1987, p. 259

55 Tino Balio, *United Artists: The Company That Changed the Film Industry*, University of Wisconsin Press, 1987, p. 259

56 Mike Medavoy: Authors' interview, 30.10.2014

57 David Picker: Authors' interview, 24.02.2014

58 Eric Pleskow: Authors' interview, 28.05.2015

59 Tino Balio, *United Artists: The Company That Changed the Film Industry*, University of Wisconsin Press, 1987, p. 259

60 Len Deighton, *James Bond: My Long and Eventful Search For His Father*, Kindle Single, 2012

61 Lee Pfeiffer and Philip Lisa, *The Incredible World*

of 007: An Authorized Celebration of James Bond, Updated Edition, Boxtree, 1995, p. 190

62   Johanna Clément (née Harwood): Authors' interview, 22.08.2012

63   Steven Saltzman: Authors' interview, 16.11.2011

64   Steven Saltzman: Authors' interview, 16.11.2011

65   Steven Jay Rubin, *The James Bond Films: A Behind the Scenes History*, Arlington House Inc., 2nd Edition, 1983, p. VII

Chapter 4 Dr. No

1   David Picker: Authors' interview, 24.02.2014

2   David Picker: Authors' interview, 22.02.2014

3   Tino Balio, *United Artists: The Company That Changed the Film Industry*, University of Wisconsin Press, 1987, p. 255

4   *Hollywood UK: British Cinema in the Sixties – A Very British Picture*, Prod: Charles Chabot & Rosemary Wilton, BBC 2, 19.09.1993

5   Johanna Clément (née Harwood): Authors' interview, 22.08.2012

6   Johanna Clément (née Harwood): Authors' interview, 22.08.2012

7   Alexander Walker, *Hollywood, England*, 1974, Harrap Ltd, 1974, p. 183

8   Albert R. Broccoli with Donald Zec, *When the Snow Melts*, Boxtree, 1998, p. 158

9   *Telescope: 'Licensed to Make a Killing'* Canadian Broadcasting Company, 09.12.1965

10   *Telescope: 'Licensed to Make a Killing'* Canadian Broadcasting Company, 09.12.1965

11   Tino Balio, *United Artists: The Company That Changed the Film Industry*, University of Wisconsin Press, 1987, p. 258

12   Alan Barnes and Marcus Hearn, *Kiss Kiss Bang! Bang! The Unofficial James Bond Film Companion*, B.T. Batsford, 2nd Edition, 2000, p. 11

13   *Daily Variety*, 18.11.1963

14   Johanna Clément (née Harwood): Authors' interview, 22.08.2012

15   Johanna Clément (née Harwood): Authors' interview, 22.08.2012

16   Johanna Clément (née Harwood): Authors' interview, 22.08.2012

17   Charles Drazin, *A Bond for a Bond*, Film Finances Ltd, 2011, p. 38

18   Tino Balio, *United Artists: The Company That Changed the Film Industry*, University of Wisconsin Press, 1987, p. 258

19   Tino Balio, *United Artists: The Company That Changed the Film Industry*, University of Wisconsin Press, 1987, p. 255

20   David Picker: Authors' interview, 22.02.2014

21   Tino Balio, *United Artists: The Company That Changed the Film Industry*, University of Wisconsin Press, 1987, p. 258

22   David Picker: Authors' interview, 22.02.2014

23   Guy Hamilton: Authors' interview, 01.08.2013

24   Tino Balio, *United Artists: The Company That Changed the Film Industry*, University of Wisconsin Press, 1987, p. 258

25   David Picker: Authors' interview, 22.02.2014

26   'Q&A with Terence Young' by Richard Schenkman, *Bondage #10*, The James Bond 007 Fan Club, 1981

27   'Q&A with Terence Young' by Richard Schenkman, *Bondage #10*, The James Bond 007 Fan Club, 1981

28   Johanna Clément (née Harwood): Authors' interview, 22.08.2012

29   Albert R. Broccoli with Donald Zec, *When the Snow Melts*, Boxtree, 1998, pp. 162–163

30   Johanna Clément (née Harwood): Authors' interview, 22.08.2012

31   Johanna Clément (née Harwood): Authors' interview, 22.08.2012

32   Tino Balio, *United Artists: The Company That Changed the Film Industry*, University of Wisconsin Press, 1987, p. 255

33   Albert R. Broccoli with Donald Zec, *When the Snow Melts*, Boxtree, 1998, p. 164

34   David Niven, *The Moon's a Balloon*, Coronet Books/Hodder Paperbacks Ltd, 1971, p. 214

35   Albert R. Broccoli with Donald Zec, *When the Snow Melts*, Boxtree, 1998, p. 165

36   Charles Helfenstein, *The Making of On Her Majesty's Secret Service*, Spies LLC, 2009, p. 22

37   Martin Sterling and Gary Morecambe, *Martinis, Girls and Guns: 50 Years of 007*, Robson Books Ltd, 2002, p. 317

38   Alexander Walker, *Hollywood, England*, Michael Joseph Ltd, 1974, p. 185

39   Roger Moore: Authors' interview, 26.04.215

40   Albert R. Broccoli with Donald Zec, *When the Snow Melts*, Boxtree, 1998, p. 165

41   Alan Barnes and Marcus Hearn, *Kiss Kiss Bang! Bang! The Unofficial James Bond Film Companion*, B.T. Batsford, 2nd Edition, 2000, p. 9

42   Albert R. Broccoli with Donald Zec, *When the Snow Melts*, Boxtree, 1998, p. 169

43   Albert R. Broccoli with Donald Zec, *When the Snow Melts*, Boxtree, 1998, p. 165

44   Albert R. Broccoli with Donald Zec, *When the Snow Melts*, Boxtree, 1998, p. 165

45   Cubby and Dana Broccoli interviewed by Paul Ryan, Los Angeles cable TV, 1979

46   Alexander Walker, *Hollywood, England*, Michael Joseph Ltd, 1974, p. 181

47   Diane Cilento, *My Nine Lives*, Michael Joseph

Ltd, 2006, p. 183

48 Sheldon Lane (ed.), *For Bond Lovers Only*, Panther Books Ltd, 1965, p. 161

49 'Bottled in Bond: Sean Connery' by Pete Hamill, *The Saturday Evening Post*, 6.6.1964

50 *Telescope: 'Licensed to Make a Killing'* Canadian Broadcasting Company, 09.12.1965

51 *Telescope: 'Licensed to Make a Killing'* Canadian Broadcasting Company, 09.12.1965

52 'Bottled in Bond: Sean Connery' by Pete Hamill, *The Saturday Evening Post*, 6.6.1964

53 *Telescope: 'Licensed to Make a Killing'* Canadian Broadcasting Company, 09.12.1965

54 *Telescope: 'Licensed to Make a Killing'* Canadian Broadcasting Company, 09.12.1965

55 Alexander Walker, *Hollywood, England*, Michael Joseph Ltd, 1974, p. 184

56 'Interview with Stanley Sopel' by Richard Schenkman, *Bondage* #10, The James Bond 007 Fan Club, 1981

57 Albert R. Broccoli with Donald Zec, *When the Snow Melts*, Boxtree, 1998, p. 170

58 Albert R. Broccoli with Donald Zec, *When the Snow Melts*, Boxtree, 1998, illustration

59 Tino Balio, *United Artists: The Company That Changed the Film Industry*, University of Wisconsin Press, 1987, p. 258

60 Alan Barnes and Marcus Hearn, *Kiss Kiss Bang! Bang! The Unofficial James Bond Film Companion*, B.T. Batsford, 2nd Edition, 2000, p. 9

61 'The *Playboy* Interview: Sean Connery' by David Lewin, *Playboy*, November 1965

62 Diane Cilento, *My Nine Lives*, Michael Joseph Ltd, 2006, p. 209

63 Sheldon Lane (ed), *For Bond Lovers Only*, Panther Books Ltd, 1965 p. 30

64 'Back in Bondage' by Tom Hutchinson, *The Guardian*, 28.12.1971

65 Sheldon Lane (ed), *For Bond Lovers Only*, Panther Books Ltd, 1965 p. 30

66 Sheldon Lane, (ed), *For Bond Lovers Only*, Panther Books Ltd, 1965 p. 30

67 'The *Playboy* Interview: Sean Connery' by David Lewin, *Playboy*, November 1965

68 Martine Beswick: Authors' interview, 06.04.2015

69 Charles Drazin, *A Bond For Bond*, Film Finances Ltd, 2011, p. 38

70 Alexander Walker, *Hollywood, England*, 1974, Michael Joseph Ltd, 1974, p. 188

71 Albert R. Broccoli with Donald Zec, *When the Snow Melts*, Boxtree, 1998, p. 173

72 Albert R. Broccoli with Donald Zec, *When the Snow Melts*, Boxtree, 1998, p. 173

73 Ursula Andress: Authors' interview, 14.09.2012

74 Ursula Andress: Authors' interview, 14.09.2012

75 Eunice Gayson in conversation with Gareth Owen, *Bond Girls Are Forever*, Pinewood

76 Charles Drazin, *A Bond For Bond*, Film Finances Ltd, 2011, p. 38

77 Charles Drazin, *A Bond For Bond*, Film Finances Ltd, 2011, p. 39

78 Peter Haining, *James Bond: A Celebration*, W.H. Allen/Planet, 1987, pp. 193–96

79 Lee Pfeiffer and Philip Lisa, *The Incredible World of 007: An Authorized Celebration of James Bond*, Updated Edition, Boxtree, 1995, pp. 207–08

80 Peter Haining, *James Bond: A Celebration*, W.H. Allen/Planet, 1987, pp. 193–96

81 'The Lois Maxwell Interview' by Mark Greenberg, *Bondage* #12, The James Bond 007 Fan Club, 1983

82 Steven Jay Rubin, *The James Bond Films: A Behind The Scenes History*, Arlington House Inc., 2nd Edition, 1983, p. 20

83 Steven Jay Rubin, *The Complete James Bond Movie Encyclopaedia*, Contemporary Books, Newly Revised Edition, 2003, p. 457

84 John Cork and Bruce Scivally, *James Bond: The Legacy*, Boxtree, 2002, p. 46

85 Johanna Clément (née Harwood): Authors' interview, 22.08.2012

86 Diane Cilento, *My Nine Lives*, Michael Joseph Ltd, 2006, p. 207

87 Monty Norman: Authors' interview, 03.08.2012

88 Monty Norman: Authors' interview, 03.08.2012

89 Christopher Frayling, *Ken Adam: The Art of Production Design*, Faber and Faber Limited, 2005, p. 96

90 'Ken Adam and *Dr. No*' by Christopher Frayling, *Movie Classics Cinema Retro* #4, 2012

91 Christopher Frayling, *Ken Adam: The Art of Production Design*, Faber and Faber Limited, 2005, p. 95

92 Charles Drazin, *A Bond For Bond*, Film Finances Ltd, 2011, p. 54

93 www.montynorman.com

94 Steven Jay Rubin, *The James Bond Films: A Behind The Scenes History*, Arlington House, 2nd Edition, 1983, p. 18

95 Charles Drazin, *A Bond For Bond*, Film Finances Ltd, 2011, p. 48

96 Bob Simmons with Kenneth Passingham, *Nobody Does It Better: My 25 Years with James Bond and Other Stars*, Javelin Books, 1987, p. 39

97 Bob Simmons with Kenneth Passingham, *Nobody Does It Better: My 25 Years with James Bond and Other Stars*, Javelin Books, 1987, p. 39

98 Charles Drazin, *A Bond For Bond*, Film Finances Ltd, 2011, p. 46–47

99 Ursula Andress: Authors' interview, 14.09.2012

100 Ursula Andress: Authors' interview, 14.09.2012

101 Monty Norman: Authors' interview, 03.08.2012

102 Ursula Andress: Authors' interview, 14.09.2012

103 Monty Norman: Authors' interview, 03.08.2012

76 Studios, Bondstars.com, 02.07.2006

104 Steven Jay Rubin, *The James Bond Films: A Behind The Scenes History*, Arlington House Inc., 2nd Edition, 1983, p. 18

105 Ursula Andress: Authors' interview, 14.09.2012

106 Ursula Andress: Authors' interview, 14.09.2012

107 Charles Drazin, *A Bond For Bond*, Film Finances Ltd, 2011, p. 48

108 Lot 291, Sale 9017, Christie's Auction House, South Kensington, London, 14.02.2001

109 Ursula Andress: Authors' interview, 14.09.2012

110 Monty Norman: Authors' interview, 03.08.2012

111 Monty Norman: Authors' interview, 03.08.2012

112 Monty Norman: Authors' interview, 03.08.2012

113 Monty Norman: Authors' interview, 03.08.2012

114 Syd Cain, *Not Forgetting James Bond: The Autobiography of Syd Cain*, GBU Publishing Ltd, 2002, p. 56

115 Syd Cain, *Not Forgetting James Bond: The Autobiography of Syd Cain*, GBU Publishing Ltd, 2002, p. 56

116 Syd Cain, *Not Forgetting James Bond: The Autobiography of Syd Cain*, GBU Publishing Ltd, 2002, p. 56

117 Charles Drazin, *A Bond For Bond*, Film Finances Ltd, 2011, p. 48

118 Charles Drazin, *A Bond For Bond*, Film Finances Ltd, 2011, p. 48

119 Steven Jay Rubin, *The James Bond Films: A Behind The Scenes History*, Arlington House Inc., 2nd Edition, 1983, pp. 20–21

120 Steven Jay Rubin, *The James Bond Films: A Behind The Scenes History*, Arlington House Inc., 2nd Edition, 1983, pp. 20–21

121 Eunice Gayson in conversation with Gareth Owen, *Bond Girls Are Forever*, Pinewood Studios, Bondstars.com, 02.07.2006

122 Zena Marshall in conversation with Gareth Owen, *Bond Girls Are Forever* event at Pinewood Studios, Bondstars.com, 02.07.2006

123 Bob Simmons with Kenneth Passingham, *Nobody Does It Better: My 25 Years with James Bond and Other Stars*, Javelin Books, 1987, p. 39

124 Ursula Andress: Authors' interview, 14.09.2012

125 Johanna Clément (née Harwood): Authors' interview, 22.08.2012

126 Steven Jay Rubin, *The James Bond Films: A Behind The Scenes History*, Arlington House Inc., 2nd Edition, 1983, p. 21

127 'Ken Adam and *Dr. No*' by Christopher Frayling, *Cinema Retro Movie Classics Special #4*, 2012

128 Ken Adam interviewed by Christopher Frayling, *British Design and Art Direction President's Lectures,* Logan Hall, London, 02.12.1999

129 Charles Drazin, *A Bond For Bond*, Film Finances Ltd, 2011, p. 78

130 Charles Drazin, *A Bond For Bond*, Film

Finances Ltd, 2011, p. 78

131 Charles Drazin, *A Bond For Bond*, Film Finances Ltd, 2011, p. 83

132 Lee Pfeiffer and Philip Lisa, *The Incredible World of 007: An Authorized Celebration of James Bond*, Updated Edition, Boxtree, 1995, p. 204

133 Norman Wanstall: Authors' interview, 27.11.2000

134 *Telescope: 'Licensed to Make a Killing'* Canadian Broadcasting Company, 09.12.1965

135 'Maurice Binder at the Museum of Modern Art' by Richard Schenkman, *Bondage #10*, The James Bond 007 Fan Club, 1981

136 'Maurice Binder at the Museum of Modern Art' by Richard Schenkman, *Bondage #10*, The James Bond 007 Fan Club, 1981

137 Trevor Bond: Authors' interview, 30.07.2012

138 Trevor Bond: Authors' interview, 30.07.2012

139 Lee Pfeiffer and Philip Lisa, *The Incredible World of 007: An Authorized Celebration of James Bond*, Updated Edition, Boxtree, 1995, p. 201

140 Monty Norman: Authors' interview, 03.08.2012

141 'Maurice Binder at the Museum of Modern Art' by Richard Schenkman, *Bondage #10*, The James Bond 007 Fan Club, 1981

142 Trevor Bond: Authors' interview, 30.07.2012

143 Monty Norman: Authors' interview, 03.08.2012

144 Monty Norman: Authors' interview, 03.08.2012

145 Christopher Lindner (ed.), *The James Bond Phenomenon: A Critical Reader,* 'Creating a Bond Market' by Jeff Smith, Manchester University Press, 2nd Edition, 2009, p. 141

146 Christopher Lindner (ed.), *The James Bond Phenomenon: A Critical Reader,* 'Creating a Bond Market' by Jeff Smith, Manchester University Press, 2nd Edition, 2009, p. 141

147 Christopher Lindner (ed.), *The James Bond Phenomenon: A Critical Reader,* 'Creating a Bond Market' by Jeff Smith, Manchester University Press, 2nd Edition, 2009, p. 141

148 Monty Norman vs. *The Sunday Times*, Royal Courts of Justice, The John Barry Resource, www.jollinger.com, March 2001

149 Monty Norman vs. *The Sunday Times*, Royal Courts of Justice, The John Barry Resource, www.jollinger.com, March 2001

150 Monty Norman vs. *The Sunday Times*, Royal Courts of Justice, The John Barry Resource, www.jollinger.com, March 2001

151 Christopher Lindner (ed.), *The James Bond Phenomenon: A Critical Reader,* 'Creating a Bond Market' by Jeff Smith, Manchester University Press, 2nd Edition, 2009, p. 138

152 Christopher Lindner (ed.), *The James Bond Phenomenon: A Critical Reader,* 'Creating a Bond Market' by Jeff Smith, Manchester University Press, 2nd Edition, 2009, p. 138

153 Christopher Lindner (ed.), *The James Bond*

Phenomenon: A Critical Reader, 'Creating a Bond Market' by Jeff Smith, Manchester University Press, 2nd Edition, 2009, p. 139

154 'Joseph Caroff: The Man Who Created the 007 Logo' by Lee Pfeiffer and Mark Cerulli , *Cinema Retro Movie Classics Special #4,* 2012

155 'Harry Saltzman Recalls Early Coolness to Bond Features' by Todd McCarthy, *Daily Variety,* 13.05.1987

156 Alan Barnes and Marcus Hearn, *Kiss Kiss Bang! Bang! The Unofficial James Bond Film Companion,* B.T. Batsford, 2nd Edition, 2000, p. 18

157 Monty Norman: Authors' interview, 03.08.2012

158 Johanna Clément (née Harwood): Authors' interview, 22.08.2012

159 Alan Barnes and Marcus Hearn, *Kiss Kiss Bang! Bang! The Unofficial James Bond Film Companion,* B.T. Batsford, 2nd Edition, 2000, p. 18

160 'Harry Saltzman Recalls Early Coolness to Bond Features' by Todd McCarthy, *Daily Variety,* 13.05.1987

161 'Harry Saltzman Recalls Early Coolness to Bond Features' by Todd McCarthy, *Daily Variety,* 13.05.1987

162 'Harry Saltzman Recalls Early Coolness to Bond Features' by Todd McCarthy, *Daily Variety,* 13.05.1987

163 'Harry Saltzman Recalls Early Coolness to Bond Features' by Todd McCarthy, *Daily Variety,* 13.05.1987

164 'The Man Who Makes 007 Run' by Lee Grant, *Los Angeles Times,* 13.05.1987

165 'The Man Who Makes 007 Run' by Lee Grant, *Los Angeles Times,* 13.05.1987

166 'The *Playboy* Interview: Sean Connery' by David Lewin, *Playboy,* November 1965

Chapter 5 From Russia With Love

1 Albert R. Broccoli with Donald Zec, *When the Snow Melts,* Boxtree, 1998, pp. 180–1

2 Johanna Clément (née Harwood): Authors' interview, 22.08.2012

3 Monty Norman: Authors' interview, 03.08.2012

4 Donald Zec, *Put the Knife in Gently: Memoirs of a Life With Legends,* Robson Books, 2003, p. 201

5 Albert R. Broccoli with Donald Zec, *When the Snow Melts,* Boxtree, 1998, p. 180–1

6 Tino Balio, *United Artists: The Company that Changed the Film Industry,* University of Wisconsin Press, 1987, p. 260

7 Diane Cilento, *My Nine Lives,* Michael Joseph Ltd, 2006, p. 209

8 Diane Cilento, *My Nine Lives,* Michael Joseph Ltd, 2006, p. 209

9 Tino Balio, *United Artists: The Company that Changed the Film Industry,* University of Wisconsin Press, 1987, p. 260

10 Sheldon Lane (ed.), *For Bond Lovers Only,* Panther, 1965, p. 30

11 Sheldon Lane (ed.), *For Bond Lovers Only,* Panther, 1965, p. 31

12 Albert R. Broccoli with Donald Zec, *When the Snow Melts,* Boxtree, 1998, p. 164

13 *From Russia With Love* production Notes, United Artists, 01.05.1963

14 Pat McGilligan (ed.), *Backstory: Interviews with Screenwriters of Hollywood's Golden Age,* University of California Press, 1986, p. 284

15 Len Deighton: Authors' interview, 11.04.2015

16 Len Deighton: Authors' interview, 11.04.2015

17 Len Deighton, *James Bond: My Long and Eventful Search For His Father,* Kindle Single, 2012

18 Len Deighton: Authors' interview, 11.04.2015

19 Len Deighton, *James Bond: My Long and Eventful Search For His Father,* Kindle Single, 2012

20 Len Deighton: Authors' interview, 11.04.2015

21 Box 22, Papers of Richard Maibaum, University Of Iowa

22 Peter Haining, *James Bond: A Celebration,* W.H. Allen/Planet, 1987, p. 106

23 Pat McGilligan (ed.), *Backstory: Interviews with Screenwriters of Hollywood's Golden Age,* University of California Press, 1986, p. 284

24 Johanna Clément (née Harwood): Authors' interview, 22.08.2012

25 Johanna Clément (née Harwood): Authors' interview, 22.08.2012

26 Johanna Clément (née Harwood): Authors' interview, 22.08.2012

27 Johanna Clément (née Harwood): Authors' interview, 22.08.2012

28 Johanna Clément (née Harwood): Authors' interview, 22.08.2012

29 Johanna Clément (née Harwood): Authors' interview, 22.08.2012

30 Johanna Clément (née Harwood): Authors' interview, 22.08.2012

31 Pat McGilligan (ed.), *Backstory: Interviews with Screenwriters of Hollywood's Golden Age,* 1986, p. 284

32 Alan Barnes and Marcus Hearn, *Kiss Kiss Bang! Bang! The Unofficial James Bond Film Companion,* B.T. Batsford, 2nd Edition, 2000, p. 21

33 Albert R. Broccoli with Donald Zec, *When the Snow Melts,* Boxtree, 1998, p. 183

34 'Writing Bond' by Mark A. Altman, *Cinemafantastique,* Vol. 19 No. 5, July 1989

35   'Cheers, 007' by Richard Maibaum,
     Hollywood Reporter James Bond 25th
     Anniversary, 14.07.1987

36   'From the Archive' *007 Magazine* #33, The
     James Bond 007 International Fan Club, 1998

37   Tania Mallet: Authors' interview, 03.04.2015

38   Albert R. Broccoli with Donald Zec, *When the
     Snow Melts*, Boxtree, 1998, p. 184

39   Alan Barnes and Marcus Hearn, *Kiss Kiss Bang!
     Bang! The Unofficial James Bond Film Companion*,
     B.T. Batsford, 2nd Edition, 2000, p. 21

40   Steven Jay Rubin, *The James Bond Films: A
     Behind The Scenes History*, Arlington House Inc.,
     2nd Edition, 1983, p. 25

41   Maryam d'Abo and John Cork, *Bond Girls Are
     Forever*, Boxtree, 2003, p. 159

42   'James Bond – 27 Years and Still Licensed To
     Kill: An Annotated 007 Filmography' by Mark
     A. Altman, *Cinemafantastique*, Vol. 19 No. 5, July
     1989

43   John French, *Robert Shaw: The Price of Success*,
     Nick Hern Books, 1993, p. 34

44   Steven Jay Rubin, *The James Bond Films: A
     Behind The Scenes History*, Arlington House Inc.,
     2nd Edition, 1983, p. 26

45   *From Russia With Love* production notes,
     United Artists, 20.08.1963

46   Steven Jay Rubin, *The James Bond Films: A
     Behind The Scenes History*, Arlington House Inc.,
     2nd Edition, 1983, p. 25

47   David Farneth, *Lenya: The Legend*, Overlook
     Press, 1998, p. 58

48   David Farneth, *Lenya: The Legend*, Overlook
     Press, 1998, p. 58

49   Maryam d'Abo and John Cork, *Bond Girls Are
     Forever*, Boxtree, 2003, p. 33

50   Albert R. Broccoli with Donald Zec, *When the
     Snow Melts*, Boxtree, 1998, p. 186

51   'The Fab Interview – Vladek Sheybal' by Tim
     Mallett and Glenn Pearce, *Fab* #8, Fanderson,
     December 1992

52   Desmond Llewelyn: Authors' interview,
     14.04.1999

53   Desmond Llewelyn: Authors' interview,
     14.04.1999

54   Sandy Hernu, *Q: The Biography of Desmond
     Llewelyn*, S.B. Publications, 1999, p. 77

55   Sandy Hernu, *Q: The Biography of Desmond
     Llewelyn*, S.B. Publications, 1999, p. 78

56   Richard Schenkman, *Bondage* #5, The James
     Bond 007 Fan Club, 1978

57   Syd Cain, *Not Forgetting James Bond: The
     Autobiography of Syd Cain*, GBU Publishing Ltd,
     2002, p. 64

58   Peter Janson-Smith: Unpublished interview
     with Dr. Siegfried Tesche, 19.08.2005

59   Hilary Saltzman: Authors' interview, 29.11.2011

60   Alan Barnes and Marcus Hearn, *Kiss Kiss Bang!*

     Bang! The Unofficial James Bond Film Companion,
     B.T. Batsford, 2nd Edition, 2000, p. 11

61   Steven Jay Rubin, *The James Bond Films: A
     Behind The Scenes History*, Arlington House Inc.,
     2nd Edition, 1983, p. 25

62   Steven Jay Rubin, *The James Bond Films: A
     Behind The Scenes History*, Arlington House Inc.,
     2nd Edition, 1983, p. 25

63   Alan Barnes and Marcus Hearn, *Kiss Kiss Bang!
     Bang! The Unofficial James Bond Film Companion*,
     B.T. Batsford, 2nd Edition, 2000, p. 11

64   Alan Barnes and Marcus Hearn, *Kiss Kiss Bang!
     Bang! The Unofficial James Bond Film Companion*,
     B.T. Batsford, 2nd Edition, 2000, p. 11

65   Albert R. Broccoli with Donald Zec, *When the
     Snow Melts*, Boxtree, 1998, p. 164

66   Syd Cain, *Not Forgetting James Bond: The
     Autobiography of Syd Cain*, GBU Publishing Ltd,
     2002, p. 66

67   Syd Cain, *Not Forgetting James Bond: The
     Autobiography of Syd Cain*, GBU Publishing Ltd,
     2002, p. 67

68   *The New York Morning Telegraph*, 15.05.1963

69   Steven Jay Rubin, *The James Bond Films: A
     Behind The Scenes History*, Arlington House Inc.,
     2nd Edition, 1983, p. 25

70   Steven Jay Rubin, *The James Bond Films: A
     Behind The Scenes History*, Arlington House Inc.,
     2nd Edition, 1983, p. 25

71   Syd Cain, *Not Forgetting James Bond: The
     Autobiography of Syd Cain*, GBU Publishing Ltd,
     2002, p. 67

72   'Stanley Sopel' by Richard Schenkman,
     Bondage #10, The James Bond 007 Fan Club,
     1981

73   Albert R. Broccoli with Donald Zec, *When the
     Snow Melts*, Boxtree, 1998, p. 164

74   Cubby and Dana Broccoli interviewed by Paul
     Ryan, Los Angeles cable TV, 1979

75   Albert R. Broccoli with Donald Zec, *When the
     Snow Melts*, Boxtree, 1998, p. 164

76   Diane Cilento, *My Nine Lives*, Michael Joseph
     Ltd, 2006, p. 185

77   Diane Cilento, *My Nine Lives*, Michael Joseph
     Ltd, 2006, p. 185

78   Diane Cilento, *My Nine Lives*, Michael Joseph
     Ltd, 2006, p. 185

79   Syd Cain, *Not Forgetting James Bond: The
     Autobiography of Syd Cain*, GBU Publishing Ltd,
     2002, pp. 66–67

80   Eddi Fiegel, *John Barry: A Sixties Theme*,
     Constable and Company Ltd, 1998, p. 106

81   Syd Cain, *Not Forgetting James Bond: The
     Autobiography of Syd Cain*, GBU Publishing Ltd,
     2002, p. 66

82   'Q&A with Terence Young' by Richard
     Schenkman, *Bondage* #10, The James Bond 007
     Fan Club, 1981

83 Alan Barnes and Marcus Hearn, *Kiss Kiss Bang! Bang! The Unofficial James Bond Film Companion*, B.T. Batsford, 2nd Edition, 2000, p. 11

84 'Q&A with Terence Young' by Richard Schenkman, *Bondage* #10, The James Bond 007 Fan Club, 1981

85 Nadja Regin: Authors' interview, 03.04.2015

86 Nadja Regin: Authors' interview, 03.04.2015

87 Nadja Regin: Authors' interview, 03.04.2015

88 'Q&A with Terence Young' by Richard Schenkman, *Bondage* #10, The James Bond 007 Fan Club, 1981

89 Tim Greaves, *The Bond Women 007 Style*, 1–Shot Publications, 2002, p. 12

90 Tim Greaves, *The Bond Women 007 Style*, 1–Shot Publications, 2002, p. 12

91 Martine Beswick: Authors' interview, 06.04.2015

92 Martine Beswick: Authors' interview, 06.04.2015

93 Martine Beswick: Authors' interview, 06.04.2015

94 Syd Cain, *Not Forgetting James Bond: The Autobiography of Syd Cain*, GBU Publishing Ltd, 2002, p. 67

95 Steven Jay Rubin, *The James Bond Films: A Behind The Scenes History*, Arlington House Inc., 2nd Edition, 1983, p. 25

96 Steven Saltzman: Authors' interview, 16.11.2011

97 John Trevelyan, *What the Censor Saw*, Michael Joseph Ltd, 1973, p. 158

98 Syd Cain, *Not Forgetting James Bond: The Autobiography of Syd Cain*, GBU Publishing Ltd, 2002, p. 64

99 Syd Cain, *Not Forgetting James Bond: The Autobiography of Syd Cain*, GBU Publishing Ltd, 2002, p. 68

100 Syd Cain, *Not Forgetting James Bond: The Autobiography of Syd Cain*, GBU Publishing Ltd, 2002, p. 68

101 Maryam d'Abo and John Cork, *Bond Girls Are Forever*, Boxtree, 2003, p. 146

102 'The Fab Interview – Vladek Sheybal' by Tim Mallett and Glenn Pearce, *Fab* #8, Fanderson, December 1992

103 Johanna Clément (née Harwood): Authors' interview, 22.08.2012

104 Alan Barnes and Marcus Hearn, *Kiss Kiss Bang! Bang! The Unofficial James Bond Film Companion*, B.T. Batsford, 2nd Edition, 2000, p. 11

105 Steven Jay Rubin, *The James Bond Films: A Behind The Scenes History*, Arlington House Inc., 2nd Edition, 1983, p. 25

106 Syd Cain, *Not Forgetting James Bond: The Autobiography of Syd Cain*, GBU Publishing Ltd, 2002, p. 69

107 Diane Cilento, *My Nine Lives*, Michael Joseph Ltd, 2006, p. 214

108 Alan Barnes and Marcus Hearn, *Kiss Kiss Bang! Bang! The Unofficial James Bond Film Companion*, B.T. Batsford, 2nd Edition, 2000, p. 11

109 Norman Wanstall: Authors' interview, 27.11.2000

110 Norman Wanstall: Authors' interview, 27.11.2000

111 Norman Wanstall: Authors' interview, 27.11.2000

112 Gareth Bramley, Geoff Leonard and Peter Walker, *John Barry: The Man With the Midas Touch*, Radcliffe Press Ltd, 2nd Edition, 2008, p. 81

113 Eddi Fiegel, *John Barry: A Sixties Theme*, Constable and Company Ltd, 1998, p. 106

114 Eddi Fiegel, *John Barry: A Sixties Theme*, Constable and Company Ltd, 1998, pp. 106–107

115 Michele Monro, *Matt Monro – The Singer's Singer: The Life and Music of Matt Monro*, Titan Books, 2010, pp. 205-206

116 www.goldenglobes.org

117 www.bafta.org

118 Trevor Bond: Authors' interview, 30.07.2012

119 Emily King, *Robert Brownjohn: Sex and Typography*, Laurence King Publishing Ltd, 2005 p. 205

120 Emily King, *Robert Brownjohn: Sex and Typography*, Laurence King Publishing Ltd, 2005 p. 204

121 Emily King, *Robert Brownjohn: Sex and Typography*, Laurence King Publishing Ltd, 2005 p. 204

122 Alan Barnes and Marcus Hearn, *Kiss Kiss Bang! Bang! The Unofficial James Bond Film Companion*, B.T. Batsford, 2nd Edition, 2000, p. 11

123 Andrew Lycett, *Ian Fleming*, Phoenix, 1996, p. 232

124 Sandy Hernu, *Q: The Biography of Desmond Llewelyn*, S.B. Publications, 1999, p. 78

125 Sandy Hernu, *Q: The Biography of Desmond Llewelyn*, S.B. Publications, 1999, p. 78

126 Albert R. Broccoli with Donald Zec, *When the Snow Melts*, Boxtree, 1998, p. 201

127 Colin Woodhead (ed.) *Dressed To Kill, James Bond: The Suited Hero*, 'Introducing James Bond' by Albert R. Broccoli, Flammarion, 1996, p. 9

Chapter 6 Goldfinger

1 'The Terence Young Interview' by Richard Schenkman, *Bondage* #10, The James Bond Fan Club, 1981

2 'Breaking Away From His Bondage to Bond' by George Gent, *The New York Times*, 16.01.1966

3 Albert R. Broccoli with Donald Zec, *When the Snow Melts*, Boxtree, 1998, p. 162

4 Guy Hamilton: Authors' interview, 02.08.2013

5 Albert R. Broccoli with Donald Zec, *When the Snow Melts*, Boxtree, 1998, p. 190

6 David Picker, *Musts, Maybes and Nevers*, CreateSpace Independent Publishing Platform, 2013, p. 50

7 Guy Hamilton: Authors' interview, 01.08.2013

8 Guy Hamilton: Authors' interview, 01.08.2013

9 Guy Hamilton: Authors' interview, 01.08.2013

10 'Hand-Picked Bond Marketeers Keep 007 Under Spotlight' by Hy Hollinger, *Weekly Variety*, 13.05.1987

11 'Hand-Picked Bond Marketeers Keep 007 Under Spotlight' by By Hy Hollinger, *Weekly Variety*, 13.05.1987

12 Guy Hamilton: Authors' interview, 01.08.2013

13 David Picker, *Musts, Maybes and Nevers*, CreateSpace Independent Publishing, 2013, p. 50

14 Andrew Yule, *Sean Connery: Neither Shaken, Nor Stirred*, Little Brown and Company, 1992, p. 100

15 Guy Hamilton: Authors' interview, 01.08.2013

16 'Richard Maibaum: 007's Puppetmaster' by Lee Goldberg, *Starlog* #68, March 1983

17 Pat McGilligan (ed.), *Backstory: Interviews with Screenwriters of Hollywood's Golden Age*, University of California Press, 1986, p. 286

18 Raymond Benson, *The James Bond Bedside Companion*, Boxtree, 1988, p. 17

19 Andrew Lycett, *Ian Fleming*, Phoenix, 1996, p. 328

20 Adrian Turner, *Goldfinger, Bloomsbury Movie Guide 2*, Bloomsbury, 1998, p. 188

21 Adrian Turner, *Goldfinger, Bloomsbury Movie Guide 2*, Bloomsbury, 1998, p. 190

22 Guy Hamilton: Authors' interview, 01.08.2013

23 Adrian Turner, *Goldfinger, Bloomsbury Movie Guide 2*, Bloomsbury, 1998, p. 188

24 Guy Hamilton: Authors' interview, 01.08.2013

25 Guy Hamilton: Authors' interview, 01.08.2013

26 Jeremy Duns, *Duns on Bond*, 'Black Tie Spy' Kindle EBook, 2015

27 Guy Hamilton: Authors' interview, 01.08.2013

28 Adrian Turner, *Goldfinger, Bloomsbury Movie Guide 2*, Bloomsbury, 1998, p. 204

29 Adrian Turner, *Goldfinger, Bloomsbury Movie Guide 2*, Bloomsbury, 1998, p. 207

30 Adrian Turner, *Goldfinger, Bloomsbury Movie Guide 2*, Bloomsbury, 1998, p. 207

31 Michael Freedland, *Sean Connery: A Biography*, Weidensfield and Nicolson, 1994, p. 126

32 Michael Feeney Callan, *Sean Connery*, Virgin Books, 2002, p. 129

33 Guy Hamilton: Authors' interview, 01.08.2013

34 Guy Hamilton: Authors' interview, 01.08.2013

35 'Just for Variety' by Army Archerd, *Daily Variety*, 03.05.1963

36 Adrian Turner, *Goldfinger, Bloomsbury Movie Guide 2*, Bloomsbury, 1998 p. 204

37 Eric Pleskow: Authors' interview, 28.05.2015

38 Guy Hamilton: Authors' interview, 01.08.2013

39 Albert R. Broccoli with Donald Zec, *When the Snow Melts*, Boxtree, 1998, p. 191

40 Honor Blackman: Authors' interview, 30.05.2015

41 Honor Blackman: Authors' interview, 30.05.2015

42 Shirley Eaton: Authors' interview, 21.04.2015

43 Shirley Eaton, *Golden Girl*, B.T. Batsford, 1999, p. 16

44 Shirley Eaton: Authors' interview, 21.04.2015

45 Tania Mallet: Authors' interview, 03.04.2015

46 Tania Mallet: Authors' interview, 03.04.2015

47 Tania Mallet: Authors' interview, 03.04.2015

48 Margaret Nolan: Authors' interview, 03.04.2015

49 Margaret Nolan: Authors' interview, 03.04.2015

50 Margaret Nolan: Authors' interview, 03.04.2015

51 Christopher Frayling, *Ken Adam: The Art of Production Design*, Faber and Faber Limited, 2005, p. 139

52 Guy Hamilton: Authors' interview, 01.08.2013

53 Ken Adam: Authors' interview, 26.01.2015

54 Christopher Frayling, *Ken Adam: The Art of Production Design*, Faber & Faber Limited, 2005, p. 139

55 Ken Adam: Authors' interview, 26.01.2015

56 Guy Hamilton: Authors' interview, 01.08.2013

57 Christopher Frayling, *Ken Adam: The Art of Production Design*, Faber and Faber Limited, 2005, p. 139

58 Dave Worrall, *The Most Famous Car in the World*, Solo, 1991, p. 69

59 Christopher Frayling, *Ken Adam: The Art of Production Design*, Faber and Faber Limited, 2005, p. 139

60 Christopher Frayling, *Ken Adam: The Art of Production Design*, Faber and Faber Limited, 2005, p. 139

61 *The Making of Goldfinger*, dir: John Cork, T.W.I.N.E Entertainment, *Goldfinger Deluxe Collector's Edition Laserdisc*, MGM/UA Home Video, 1995

62 *30 Years of James Bond*, dir: Lorna Dickinson & Alasdair Macmillan, London Weekend

Television, 03.10.1992

63 Dave Worrall, *The Most Famous Car in the World*, Solo, 1991, p. 69

64 Dave Worrall, *The Most Famous Car in the World*, Solo, 1991, p. 69

65 Guy Hamilton: Authors' interview, 01.08.2013

66 'Just for Variety' by Army Archerd, *Daily Variety*, 26.02.1963

67 'Broccoli, Saltzman Pact Jack Lord For 2 pix' *Daily Variety*, 09.01.1963

68 'Bond 3: *Goldfinger*' by Tony Crawley, www.crawleyscastingcalls.com

69 Steven Jay Rubin, *The Complete James Bond Movie Encyclopaedia*, Contemporary Books, Newly Revised Edition, 2002, p. 238

70 Guy Hamilton: Authors' interview, 01.08.2013

71 Sheldon Lane (ed), *For Bond Lovers Only*, Panther Books Ltd, 1965 p. 32

72 Alan Barnes and Marcus Hearn, *Kiss Kiss Bang! Bang! The Unofficial James Bond Film Companion*, B.T. Batsford, 2nd Edition, 2000, p. 32

73 Alan Barnes and Marcus Hearn, *Kiss Kiss Bang! Bang! The Unofficial James Bond Film Companion*, B.T. Batsford, 2nd Edition, 2000, p. 32

74 Guy Hamilton: Authors' interview, 01.08.2013

75 Bob Simmons with Kenneth Passingham, *Nobody Does It Better: My 25 Years with James Bond and Other Stars*, Javelin Books, 1987, p. 65

76 Adrian Turner, *Goldfinger, Bloomsbury Movie Guide 2*, Bloomsbury, 1998, p. 96

77 Michael Feeney Callan, *Sean Connery*, Virgin Books, 2002, p. 131

78 Guy Hamilton: Authors' interview, 01.08.2013

79 Guy Hamilton: Authors' interview, 01.08.2013

80 Guy Hamilton: Authors' interview, 01.08.2013

81 Dave Worrall, *The Most Famous Car in the World*, Solo, 1991 p. 69

82 Guy Hamilton: Authors' interview, 01.08.2013

83 Honor Blackman: Authors' interview, 30.05.2015

84 Honor Blackman: Authors' interview, 30.05.2015

85 Adrian Turner, *Goldfinger, Bloomsbury Movie Guide 2*, Bloomsbury, 1998, p. 208

86 Adrian Turner, *Goldfinger, Bloomsbury Movie Guide 2*, Bloomsbury, 1998, p. 64

87 *30 Years of James Bond,* dir: Lorna Dickinson & Alasdair Macmillan, London Weekend Television, 03.10.1992

88 Albert J. Luxford with Gareth Owen, *The Gimmick Man: Memoir of a Special Effects Maestro*, McFarland and Company, Inc., 2002, p. 46

89 Honor Blackman: Authors' interview, 30.05.2015

90 Honor Blackman: Authors' interview, 30.05.2015

91 Bob Simmons with Kenneth Passingham, *Nobody Does It Better: My 25 Years with James*

Bond and Other Stars, Javelin Books, 1987, p. 65

92 Shirley Eaton: Authors' interview, 21.04.2015

93 Shirley Eaton, *Golden Girl*, B.T. Batsford, 1999, p. 12

94 Shirley Eaton: Authors' interview, 21.04.2015

95 Shirley Eaton: Authors' interview, 21.04.2015

96 Shirley Eaton, *Golden Girl*, B.T. Batsford, 1999 p. 16

97 Desmond Llewelyn: Authors' interview, 14.04.1999

98 Desmond Llewelyn: Authors' interview, 14.04.1999

99 'The Lois Maxwell Interview' by Mark Greenberg, *Bondage* #12, The James Bond 007 Fan Club, 1983

100 Sean Connery, *Being a Scot*, Weidenfeld and Nicolson, 2008, p. 294

101 Sir Ken Adam in conversation with Sir Christopher Frayling at the Museum of Design, London, 06.10.2004

102 Bob Simmons with Kenneth Passingham, *Nobody Does It Better: My 25 Years with James Bond and Other Stars*, Javelin Books, 1987, p. 67

103 *The Making of Goldfinger*, dir: John Cork, T.W.I.N.E Entertainment, *Goldfinger Deluxe Collector's Edition Laserdisc*, MGM/UA Home Video, 1995

104 Nadja Regin: Authors' interview, 03.04.2015

105 Steven Jay Rubin, *The James Bond Films: A Behind The Scenes History*, 2nd Edition, Arlington House Inc., 1983

106 Dave Worrall, *The Most Famous Car in the World*, Solo, 1991 p. 76

107 Tania Mallet: Authors' interview, 03.04.2015

108 Tania Mallet: Authors' interview, 03.04.2015

109 Tania Mallet: Authors' interview, 03.04.2015

110 Tania Mallet: Authors' interview, 03.04.2015

111 Guy Hamilton: Authors' interview, 01.08.2013

112 Tania Mallet: Authors' interview, 03.04.2015

113 Guy Hamilton: Authors' interview, 01.08.2013

114 Guy Hamilton: Authors' interview, 01.08.2013

115 Steven Jay Rubin, *The Complete James Bond Movie Encyclopaedia*, Contemporary Books, Newly Revised Edition, 2002, p. 354

116 'Through Airman's Eyes: The Airman and James Bond' by Rachel Arroyo, www.af.mil, 19.01.2013

117 'The Name's Wilson, Michael Wilson' by Liz Jobey, *FT Weekend Magazine*, 13-14 October 2012

118 Guy Hamilton: Authors' interview, 01.08.2013

119 Albert R. Broccoli with Donald Zec, *When the Snow Melts*, Boxtree, 1998 p. 192

120 Guy Hamilton: Authors' interview, 01.08.2013

121 Michael Feeney Callan, *Sean Connery*, Virgin Books, 2002 p. 134

122 Guy Hamilton: Authors' interview, 01.08.2013

123 Norman Wanstall: Authors' interview,

27.11.2000

124 Guy Hamilton: Authors' interview, 01.08.2013

125 Guy Hamilton: Authors' interview, 01.08.2013

126 Guy Hamilton: Authors' interview, 01.08.2013

127 'License to Score' by Tom Soter, *Starlog* #199, February 1994

128 Leslie Bricusse, *The Music Man*, Metro Publishing, 2006, p. 148

129 Eddi Fiegel, *John Barry: A Sixties Theme*, Constable and Company Ltd, 1998, p. 136

130 'Meet the Man Who Gets the Bond Films Off to a Sizzling Start' by Tony Crawley, *Showtime Magazine*, October 1964

131 Emily King, *Robert Brownjohn: Sex and Typography*, Laurence King Publishing, 2005, p. 68

132 David Watkins, *Why Is There Only One Word For Thesaurus*, The Trouser Press, 1998, p. 91

133 Margaret Nolan: Authors' interview, 03.04.2015

134 Eddi Fiegel, *John Barry: A Sixties Theme*, Constable and Company Ltd, 1998, p. 137

135 Eddi Fiegel, *John Barry: A Sixties Theme*, Constable and Company Ltd, 1998, p. 141

136 Leslie Bricusse, *The Music Man*, Metro Publishing, 2006, p. 148

137 Honor Blackman: Authors' interview, 30.05.2015

138 Tania Mallet: Authors' interview, 03.04.2015

139 Honor Blackman: Authors' interview,

140 Adrian Turner, *Goldfinger, Bloomsbury Movie Guide 2*, Bloomsbury, 1998, p. 93

141 Honor Blackman: Author's interview, 30.05.2015

142 Eric Pleskow: Authors' interview, 28.05.2015

143 'Gert Fröbe, 75, Portrayed *Goldfinger* in Bond Movie' Obituary, *Los Angeles Times*, 07.09.1988

144 'Film Plugs and Pluggers' *Weekly Variety*, 23.12.1964

145 *Weekly Variety*, 16.12.1964

146 *Billboard*, 27.03.1965

147 'United Artists' Fort Knox' by Vincent Canby, *Weekly Variety*, 31.03.1965

148 'United Artists' Fort Knox' by Vincent Canby, *Weekly Variety*, 31.03.1965

149 John Cork and Bruce Scivally, *James Bond: The Legacy*, Boxtree, 2002, p. 18

150 Norman Wanstall: Authors' interview, 27.11.2000

151 Norman Wanstall: Authors' interview, 27.11.2000

152 Jeff Rovin (ed.), *The Official Moonraker Magazine*, 'Albert R. Broccoli interviewed!' by Richard Meyers, Warren Publishing Company, 1979

153 'United Artists' Fort Knox' by Vincent Canby, *Weekly Variety*, 31.03.1965

Chapter 7 Thunderball

1   'How He Came Upon the Rights' by Morgan Fullam, www.kevinmclory.com, December 1999

2   'New York Sound Track' *Weekly Variety*, 01.01.1964

3   'Bond Bounces to McClory' *Daily Variety*, 21.01.1964

4   'Offer "*Thunderball*" to Richard Burton' *Daily Variety*, 21.02.1964

5   Guy Hamilton: Authors' interview, 01.08.2013

6   'Bond Bounces to McClory' *Daily Variety*, 21.01.1964

7   '"Secret Service" UA's 4th James Bond Pic' *Daily Variety*, 12.06.1964

8   Guy Hamilton: Authors' interview, 01.08.2013

9   'Feldman Can Shoot His Way In Controls 'Casino Royale' But Sean Connery Unavailable as 'Bond' *Weekly Variety*, 11.11.1964

10   Steven Jay Rubin, *The Complete James Bond Movie Encyclopaedia*, Newly Revised Edition, Contemporary Books, 2003, p. 258

11   Tino Balio, *United Artists: The Company that Changed the Film Industry*, University of Wisconsin Press, 1987, pp. 266–67

12   'Q&A with Kevin McClory' by Richard

Schenkman, *Bondage* #7, The James Bond 007 Fan Club, 1979

13   David Picker: Authors' interview 22.02.2014

14   Eric Pleskow: Authors' interview, 28.05.2015

15   Eric Pleskow: Authors' interview, 28.05.2015

16   'Just for *Variety*' by Army Archerd, *Daily Variety*, 04.01.1965

17   'Just for *Variety*' by Army Archerd, *Daily Variety*, 04.01.1965

18   Alan Barnes and Marcus Hearn, *Kiss Kiss Bang! Bang! The Unofficial James Bond Film Companion*, 2nd Edition, B.T. Batsford, 2000, pp. 43–44

19   *Hollywood UK: British Cinema In The Sixties – A Very British Picture*, Producers: Charles Chabot & Rosemary Wilton, BBC 2, 19.09.1993

20   'The *Playboy* Interview: Sean Connery' by David Lewin, *Playboy*, November 1965

21   Tino Balio, *United Artists: The Company that Changed the Film Industry*, University of Wisconsin Press, 1987, p. 263

22   Alan Barnes & Marcus Hearn, *Kiss Kiss Bang! Bang! The Unofficial James Bond Film Companion*, B.T. Batsford, 2nd Ed., 2000, p. 45

23   Guy Hamilton: Authors' interview, 01.08.2013

24   Peter Lamont: Authors' interview, 06.10.2000

25 Norman Wanstall: Authors' interview, 27.11.2000

26 Guy Hamilton: Authors' interview, 01.08.2013

27 Guy Hamilton: Authors' interview, 01.08.2013

28 Albert R. Broccoli with Donald Zec, *When the Snow Melts*, Boxtree, 1998, p. 198

29 'Breaking Away From His Bondage to Bond' by George Gent, *The New York Times*, 16.01.1966

30 'Q&A with Terence Young' by Richard Schenkman, *Bondage* #10, The James Bond 007 Fan Club, 1981

31 'James Bond – 27 Years and Still Licensed To Kill: An Annotated 007 Filmography' by Mark A. Altman, *Cinemafantastique*, Vol. 19, No. 5, July 1989

32 Peter Tipthorp (ed.), *James Bond in Thunderball*, 'Writing the Bond Films' by Richard Maibaum, Sackville Publishing Ltd, 1965

33 Ian Fleming interviewed by Munroe Scott, *The Sixties*, Canadian Broadcasting Company, 05.02.1964

34 Ian Fleming interviewed by Munroe Scott, *The Sixties*, Canadian Broadcasting Company, 05.02.1964

35 Pat McGilligan (ed.), *Backstory: Interviews with Screenwriters of Hollywood's Golden Age*, University of California Press, 1986, p. 286

36 'James Bond's 39 Bumps' by Richard Maibaum, *The New York Times*, 01.12.1964

37 'Richard Maibaum 007's Puppetmaster' by Lee Goldberg, *Starlog* #68, March 1983

38 Alan Barnes and Marcus Hearn, *Kiss Kiss Bang! Bang! The Unofficial James Bond Film Companion*, 2nd Edition, B.T. Batsford, 2000, pp. 43–44

39 *Telescope: Licensed to Make a Killing*, Canadian Broadcasting Company, 09.12.1965

40 *Telescope: Licensed to Make a Killing*, Canadian Broadcasting Company, 09.12.1965

41 Steven Jay Rubin, *The Complete James Bond Movie Encyclopaedia*, Newly Revised Edition, Contemporary Books, 2003, p. 78

42 Steven Jay Rubin, *The Complete James Bond Movie Encyclopaedia*, Newly Revised Edition, Contemporary Books, 2003, p. 78

43 Albert R. Broccoli with Donald Zec, *When the Snow Melts*, Boxtree, 1998, p. 203

44 Diane Cilento, *My Nine Lives*, Michael Joseph Ltd, 2006, p. 248

45 Albert R. Broccoli with Donald Zec, *When the Snow Melts*, Boxtree, 1998, p. 203

46 Alan Barnes and Marcus Hearn, *Kiss Kiss Bang! Bang! The Unofficial James Bond Film Companion*, 2nd Edition, B.T. Batsford, 2000, p. 43

47 Tim Greaves, *The Bond Women 007 Style*, 1-Shot Publications, 2002, p. 20

48 *Thunderball* Open End Interviews 1965 as reproduced in *Bondage* #10, The James Bond 007 Fan Club, 1981

49 Tim Greaves, *The Bond Women 007 Style*, 1-Shot Publications, p. 20

50 *Thunderball* Open End Interviews 1965 as reproduced *Bondage* #10, The James Bond 007 Fan Club, 1981

51 Peter Tipthorp (ed.), *James Bond in Thunderball*, Sackville Publishing Ltd, 1965

52 Peter Tipthorp (ed.), *James Bond in Thunderball*, Sackville Publishing Ltd, 1965

53 Alan Barnes and Marcus Hearn, *Kiss Kiss Bang! Bang! The Unofficial James Bond Film Companion*, 2nd Edition, B.T. Batsford, 2000, p. 43

54 Maryam d'Abo and John Cork, *Bond Girls Are Forever*, Boxtree, 2003, p. 128

55 Peter Tipthorp (ed.), *James Bond in Thunderball*, Sackville Publishing Ltd, 1965

56 'The Luciana Paluzzi Interview Part II' by Lee Pfeiffer and Dave Worrall, *Cinema Retro* #9, September 2007

57 *Thunderball* Open End Interviews 1965 as reproduced in *Bondage* #10, The James Bond 007 Fan Club, 1981

58 Mollie Peters: Authors' interview, 23.05.2015

59 Mollie Peters: Authors' interview, 23.05.2015

60 Mollie Peters: Authors' interview, 23.05.2015

61 Martine Beswick: Authors' interview, 06.04.2015

62 Martine Beswick: Authors' interview, 06.04.2015

63 'The Adolfo Celi Interview' by Piero Corsini, *Bondage* #13, The James Bond 007 Fan Club, 1984

64 Steven Jay Rubin, *The Complete James Bond Movie Encyclopaedia*, Newly Revised Edition, Contemporary Books, 2003, p. 432

65 Martin Sterling and Gary Morecambe, *Martinis, Girls and Guns: 50 Years of 007*, Robson Books Ltd, 2002, p. 317

66 Steven Jay Rubin, *The Complete James Bond Movie Encyclopaedia*, Newly Revised Edition, Contemporary Books, 2003, p. 129

67 Alan Barnes and Marcus Hearn, *Kiss Kiss Bang! Bang! The Unofficial James Bond Film Companion*, B.T. Batsford, 2nd Edition, 2000, p. 45

68 Alan Barnes and Marcus Hearn, *Kiss Kiss Bang! Bang! The Unofficial James Bond Film Companion*, B.T. Batsford, 2nd Edition, 2000, p. 46

69 'Q&A with Terence Young' by Richard Schenkman, *Bondage* #10, The James Bond 007 Fan Club, 1981

70 'Q&A with Terence Young' by Richard Schenkman, *Bondage* #10, The James Bond 007 Fan Club, 1981

71 'Through Airman's Eyes: The Airman and James Bond' by Rachel Arroyo, www.af.mil Official Website Of the U. S. Air Force, 19.01.2013

72 Peter Lamont: Authors' interview, 06.10.2000

73 'David Middlemas Interview' by Ross Hendry, *007 Magazine* #13, The James Bond British Fan Club, June 1983

74 'Marks, Jet Pack, Go!' by Gavin Newsham, *GQ*, 03.08.2012

75 *Telescope: Licensed to Make a Killing*, Canadian Broadcasting Company, 09.12.1965

76 Christopher Frayling, *Ken Adam: The Art of Production Design*, Faber and Faber Limited, 2005, p. 149

77 Peter Lamont: Authors' interview, 06.10.2000

78 Christopher Frayling, *Ken Adam: The Art of Production Design*, Faber and Faber Limited, 2005, p. 151

79 Peter Lamont: Authors' interview, 06.10.2000

80 Peter Lamont: Authors' interview, 06.10.2000

81 Martine Beswick: Authors' interview, 06.04.2015

82 'David Middlemas Interview' by Ross Hendry, *007 Magazine* #13, The James Bond British Fan Club, June 1983

83 'David Middlemas Interview' by Ross Hendry, *007 Magazine* #13, The James Bond British Fan Club, June 1983

84 Steven Jay Rubin, *The Complete James Bond Movie Encyclopaedia,* Newly Revised Edition, Contemporary Books, 2003, p. 202

85 'Q&A with Terence Young' by Richard Schenkman, *Bondage* #10, The James Bond 007 Fan Club, 1981

86 Diane Cilento, *My Nine Lives*, Michael Joseph Ltd, 2006, p. 250

87 Martine Beswick: Authors' interview, 06.04.2015

88 'The Luciana Paluzzi Interview Part II' by Lee Pfeiffer and Dave Worrall, *Cinema Retro* #9, September 2007

89 Martine Beswick: Authors' interview, 06.04.2015

90 Desmond Llewelyn: Authors' interview 14.04.1999

91 *Ian Fleming: The Secret Road To Paradise*, dir: John Cork, *Casino Royale Blu Ray Deluxe Edition*, 2008

92 Peter Tipthorp (ed.), *James Bond in Thunderball*, Sackville Publishing Ltd, 1965

93 Peter Tipthorp (ed.), *James Bond in Thunderball*, Sackville Publishing Ltd, 1965

94 Steven Jay Rubin, *The Complete James Bond Movie Encyclopaedia,* Newly Revised Edition, Contemporary Books, 2003, p. 64

95 Peter Tipthorp (ed.), *James Bond in Thunderball*, Sackville Publishing Ltd, 1965

96 Christopher Frayling, *Ken Adam: The Art of Production Design*, Faber and Faber Limited, 2005, p. 152

97 Steven Jay Rubin, *The Complete James Bond Movie Encyclopaedia,* Newly Revised Edition, Contemporary Books, 2003, p. 47

98 Steven Jay Rubin, *The Complete James Bond Movie Encyclopaedia*, Newly Revised Edition, Contemporary Books, 2003, p. 488

99 Steven Jay Rubin, *The Complete James Bond Movie Encyclopaedia*, Newly Revised Edition, Contemporary Books, 2003, p. 488

100 Christopher Frayling, *Ken Adam: The Art of Production Design*, Faber and Faber Limited, 2005, p. 149

101 Steven Jay Rubin, *The Complete James Bond Movie Encyclopaedia*, Newly Revised Edition, Contemporary Books, 2003

102 Steven Jay Rubin, *The Complete James Bond Movie Encyclopaedia*, Newly Revised Edition, Contemporary Books, 2003

103 Peter Lamont: Authors' interview, 06.10.2000

104 Peter Lamont: Authors' interview, 06.10.2000

105 Peter Lamont: Authors' interview, 06.10.2000

106 Peter Lamont: Authors' interview, 06.10.2000

107 Peter Lamont: Authors' interview, 06.10.2000

108 Peter Lamont: Authors' interview, 06.10.2000

109 Peter Lamont: Authors' interview, 06.10.2000

110 'John Stears Interview' by Andrew Pilkington, *007 Magazine* #13, The James Bond British Fan Club, June 1983

111 Steven Jay Rubin, *The Complete James Bond Movie Encyclopaedia,* Newly Revised Edition, Contemporary Books, 2003, p. 332

112 Steven Jay Rubin, *The Complete James Bond Movie Encyclopaedia,* Newly Revised Edition, Contemporary Books, 2003, p. 354

113 Steven Jay Rubin, *The Complete James Bond Movie Encyclopaedia,* Newly Revised Edition, Contemporary Books, 2003, p. 59

114 Steven Jay Rubin, *The Complete James Bond Movie Encyclopaedia,* Newly Revised Edition, Contemporary Books, 2003, p. 332

115 Steven Jay Rubin, *The Complete James Bond Movie Encyclopaedia,* Newly Revised Edition, Contemporary Books, 2003 p. 332

116 Christopher Frayling, *Ken Adam: The Art of Production Design*, Faber and Faber Limited, 2005, p. 175

117 'Q&A with Terence Young' by Richard Schenkman, *Bondage* #10, The James Bond 007 Fan Club, 1981

118 'Q&A with Terence Young' by Richard Schenkman, *Bondage* #10, The James Bond 007 Fan Club, 1981

119 Peter Lamont: Authors' interview, 06.10.2000

120 'John Stears Interview' by Andrew Pilkington, *007 Magazine* #13, The James Bond British Fan Club, June 1983

121 Peter Lamont: Authors' interview, 06.10.2000

122 *Look*, 13 July 1965

123 Diane Cilento, *My Nine Lives*, Michael Joseph

124 Diane Cilento, *My Nine Lives*, Michael Joseph Ltd, 2006, p. 248

124 Diane Cilento, *My Nine Lives*, Michael Joseph Ltd, 2006, p. 248

125 Diane Cilento, *My Nine Lives*, Michael Joseph Ltd, 2006, p. 248

126 Diane Cilento, *My Nine Lives*, Michael Joseph Ltd, 2006, p. 249

127 *Thunderball* Open End Interviews 1965 as reproduced *Bondage* #10, The James Bond 007 Fan Club, 1981

128 Christopher Frayling, *Ken Adam: The Art of Production Design*, Faber and Faber Limited, 2005, p. 175

129 Christopher Frayling, *Ken Adam: The Art of Production Design*, Faber and Faber Limited, 2005, p. 175

130 Mollie Peters: Authors' interview, 23.05.2015

131 Mollie Peters: Authors' interview, 23.05.2015

132 Mollie Peters: Authors' interview, 23.05.2015

133 Mollie Peters: Authors' interview, 23.05.2015

134 Mollie Peters: Authors' interview, 23.05.2015

135 Molly Peters: Authors' interview, 23.05.2015

136 Molly Peters: Authors' interview, 23.05.2015

137 Molly Peters: Authors' interview, 23.05.2015

138 Molly Peters: Authors' interview, 23.05.2015

139 'John Stears Interview' by Andrew Pilkington, *007 Magazine #13*, The James Bond British Fan Club, June 1983

140 Bob Simmons with Kenneth Passingham, *Nobody Does It Better. My 25 Years with James Bond and Other Stars,* Javelin Books, 1987 pp. 9–10

141 'The Adolfo Celi Interview' by Piero Corsini, *Bondage* #13, The James Bond 007 Fan Club, 1984

142 'The Adolfo Celi Interview' by Piero Corsini, *Bondage* #13, The James Bond 007 Fan Club, 1984

143 'Q&A with Terence Young' by Richard Schenkman, *Bondage* #10, The James Bond 007 Fan Club, 1981

144 Norman Wanstall: Authors' interview, 27.11.2000

145 Norman Wanstall: Authors' interview, 27.11.2000

146 'New Bond Pic Due In London Dec. 29' *Weekly Variety*, 11.03.1965

147 *The Real John Barry* written and produced by Stuart Grundy, Unique Broadcasting, BBC Radio 2, 26.01.2001

148 *The Real John Barry* written and produced by Stuart Grundy, Unique Broadcasting, BBC Radio 2, 26.01.2001

149 'New Bond Pic Due In London Dec. 29' *Weekly Variety*, 11.03.1965

150 Robert Hilburn, *Johnny Cash: The Life*, Weidenfeld and Nicolson, 2013, p. 272

151 'Too Late Now' Law Report, *The Times*, 22.11.1965

152 *The Real John Barry* written and produced by Stuart Grundy, Unique Broadcasting, BBC Radio 2, 26.01.2001

153 'Maurice Binder Sighting Down a Gun Barrel At 007' by Don McGregor, *Starlog #74*, September 1983

154 'Maurice Binder Sighting Down a Gun Barrel At 007' by Don McGregor, *Starlog #74*, September 1983

155 Maurice Binder lecture, National Film Theatre London, August 1990

156 Steven Jay Rubin, *The Complete James Bond Movie Encyclopaedia,* Newly Revised Edition, Contemporary Books, 2003, p. 416

157 Maurice Binder interviewed by Ross Hendry, *The James Bond British Fan Club Convention*, 24-25.04.1982

158 Maurice Binder interviewed by Ross Hendry, *The James Bond British Fan Club Convention*, 24-25.04.1982

159 'New Bond Pic Due In London Dec. 29', *Weekly Variety*, 11.03.1965

160 Peter Carter Ruck, *Memoirs of a Libel Lawyer*, Weidenfield and Nicholson Ltd, 1990, pp. 157–158

161 Peter Carter Ruck, *Memoirs of a Libel Lawyer*, Weidenfield and Nicholson Ltd, 1990, p. 158

162 Peter Carter Ruck, *Memoirs of a Libel Lawyer*, Weidenfield and Nicholson Ltd, 1990, p. 158

163 AMPAS Broadcast, ABC Television, 18.04.1966

164 'John Stears Interview' by Andrew Pilkington, *007 Magazine #13*, The James Bond British Fan Club, June 1983

165 'The *Playboy* Interview: Sean Connery' by David Lewin, *Playboy*, November 1965

166 'The *Playboy* Interview: Sean Connery' by David Lewin, *Playboy*, November 1965

167 *Look*, 13 July 1965

168 *Look*, 13 July 1965

169 *Look*, 13 July 1965

170 *Look*, 13 July 1965

Chapter 8 Bondmania

1 Tony Bennett and Janet Woollacott, *Bond and Beyond: The Political Career of a Popular Hero*, Palgrave Macmillan, 1987, p. 26

2 'Set Up 20th-Fox Licensing Corp.; Further Evidence of Film Distribs Esteem for Commercial By-Products' *Weekly Variety*, 15.06.1966

3 *Telescope: Licensed to Make a Killing*, Canadian

Broadcasting Company, 09.12.1965

4   *Telescope: Licensed to Make a Killing*, Canadian
    Broadcasting Company, 09.12.1965

5   *Telescope: Licensed to Make a Killing*, Canadian
    Broadcasting Company, 09.12.1965

6   'Broccoli Bonds Spawned Imitators' by
    Lawrence Cohn, *Weekly Variety*, 13.05.1987

7   'Ian Fleming's Other Spy' by Jon Heitland,
    Bondage #17, The James Bond 007 Fan Club,
    Summer 1989

8   'Ian Fleming's Other Spy' by Jon Heitland,
    Bondage #17, The James Bond 007 Fan Club,
    1989

9   'Ian Fleming's Other Spy' by Jon Heitland,
    Bondage #17, The James Bond 007 Fan Club,
    1989

10 'Ian Fleming's Other Spy' by Jon Heitland,
    Bondage #17, The James Bond 007 Fan Club,
    1989

11 'Ian Fleming's Other Spy' by Jon Heitland,
    Bondage #17, The James Bond 007 Fan Club,
    1989

12 Steven Saltzman: Authors' interview, 16.11.2011

13 Len Deighton: Authors' interview, 11.04.2015

14 Len Deighton, *James Bond: My Long and
    Eventful Search For His Father*, Kindle Single,
    2012

15 Steven Saltzman: Authors' interview, 16.11.2011

16 Steven Saltzman: Authors' interview, 16.11.2011

17 Matthew Field, *Michael Caine You're a Big Man*,
    B.T. Batsford, 2003, p. 23

18 Steven Saltzman: Authors' interview, 16.11.2011

19 Bruce Scivally, *Booze, Bullets and Broads: The
    Story of Matt Helm*, Henry Graw Publishing,
    Ebook, 2013

20 Peter Lamont: Authors' interview, 03.01.2014

21 'Just for *Variety*' by Army Archerd, *Daily Variety*,
    28.01.1966

22 'Just for *Variety*' by Army Archerd, *Daily Variety*,
    28.01.1966

23 'Just for *Variety*' by Army Archerd, *Daily Variety*,
    28.01.1966

24 'Moneypenny talks' by Anwar Brett, *Film
    Review Special #21*, 1997

25 'Moneypenny talks' by Anwar Brett, *Film
    Review Special #21*, 1997

26 'Bond Of Brothers' by Brian Smith, *Cinema
    Retro #12*, September 2008

27 'Bond Of Brothers' by Brian Smith, *Cinema
    Retro #12*, September 2008

28 'Bond Of Brothers' by Brian Smith, *Cinema
    Retro #12*, September 2008

29 'Bond Of Brothers' by Brian Smith, *Cinema
    Retro #12*, September 2008

30 *Telescope: Licensed to Make a Killing,* Canadian
    Broadcasting Company, 09.12.1965

Chapter 9 You Only Live Twice

1   'Saltzman and Broccoli Solo But UA 'Bonds'
    Still Bind 'Em' by Richard Albarino, *Daily
    Variety*, 13.04.1966

2   'Saltzman and Broccoli Solo But UA 'Bonds'
    Still Bind 'Em' by Richard Albarino, *Daily
    Variety*, 13.04.1966

3   Tino Balio, *United Artists: The Company that
    Changed the Film Industry*, University of
    Wisconsin Press, 1987, p. 270

4   Tino Balio, *United Artists: The Company that
    Changed the Film Industry*, University of
    Wisconsin Press, 1987, p. 271

5   Albert R. Broccoli with Donald Zec, *When the
    Snow Melts*, Boxtree, 1998, p. 205

6   'Just for *Variety*' by Army Archerd, *Daily Variety*,
    26.10.1965

7   'Just for *Variety*' by Army Archerd, *Daily Variety*,
    14.12.1965

8   'Just for *Variety*' by Army Archerd, *Daily Variety*,
    14.12.1965

9   'Just for *Variety*' by Army Archerd, *Daily Variety*,
    28.01.1966

10 'Sean Connery Pans for Added Gold Beyond
    Present 5% of 007 Loot' *Weekly Variety*,
    02.03.1966

11 'Sean Connery Pans for Added Gold Beyond
    Present 5% of 007 Loot' *Weekly Variety*,
    02.03.1966

12 'Just for *Variety*' by Army Archerd, *Daily Variety*,
    14.12.1965

13 'Just for *Variety*' by Army Archerd, *Daily Variety*,
    14.12.1965

14 'In Tokyo with Dave Jampel' *Daily Variety*,
    24.02.1966

15 Steven Jay Rubin, *The James Bond Films:
    A Behind The Scenes History*, 2nd Edition,
    Arlington House Inc., 1983, p. 74

16 David Picker: Authors' interview, 22.02.2014

17 Tino Balio, *United Artists: The Company that
    Changed the Film Industry*, University of
    Wisconsin Press, 1987, p. 305

18 Tino Balio, *United Artists: The Company that
    Changed the Film Industry*, University of
    Wisconsin Press, 1987, p. 307

19 Tino Balio, *United Artists: The Company that
    Changed the Film Industry*, University of
    Wisconsin Press, 1987, p. 308

20 'Film Bond Film Mainly in Japan' *Daily Variety*,
    29.12.1965

21 'Film Bond Film Mainly in Japan' *Daily Variety*,
    29.12.1965

22 Lewis Gilbert: Authors' interview, 22.05.2010

23 Lewis Gilbert with Peter Rankin, *All My Flashbacks*, Reynolds and Hearn, 2010, p. 263

24 'You Only Live Twice Special part 2' *007 Magazine #36*, The James Bond International Fan Club, July 2000

25 Lewis Gilbert with Peter Rankin, *All My Flashbacks*, Reynolds and Hearn, 2010 , p. 264

26 'Just for *Variety*' by Army Archerd, *Daily Variety*, 11.11.1966

27 Paul Duncan (ed.), *The James Bond Archives*, 'Techincally Perfect and Inventive' by Paul Duncan, Taschen, 2012, p. 150

28 Ken Adam: Authors' interview, 26.01.2015

29 Lewis Gilbert with Peter Rankin, *All My Flashbacks*, Reynolds and Hearn, 2010, p. 268

30 Ken Adam: Authors' interview, 26.01.2015

31 Ken Adam: Authors' interview, 26.01.2015

32 Ken Adam: Authors' interview, 26.01.2015

33 Christopher Frayling, *Ken Adam: The Art of Production Design*, Faber and Faber Limited, 2005, p. 160

34 Albert R. Broccoli with Donald Zec, *When the Snow Melts*, Boxtree, 1998, p. 211

35 Paul Duncan (ed.), *The James Bond Archives*, 'Techincally Perfect and Inventive' by Paul Duncan, Taschen, 2012, p. 150

36 'A Panelled Discussion with Broccoli, Gilbert and Adam, Museum of Modern Art' 29.06.1979, *Bondage #9*, The James Bond 007 Fan Club, 1980

37 John Pearson, *The Life of Ian Fleming*, Jonathan Cape, 1966, p. 231

38 Donald Sturrock, *Storyteller: The Life of Roald Dahl*, Harper Press, 2011, p. 434

39 Donald Sturrock, *Storyteller: The Life of Roald Dahl*, Harper Press, 2011, p. 434

40 'He Only Lived Twice' by Tom Soter, *Starlog*, #169, August 1991

41 Steven Jay Rubin, *The Complete James Bond Movie Encyclopaedia*, Contemporary Books Inc, Newly revised edition, 2003, p. 96

42 '007's Oriental Eyefuls' by Roald Dahl, *Playboy*, June 1967

43 '007's Oriental Eyefuls' by Roald Dahl, *Playboy*, June 1967

44 Lewis Gilbert: Authors' interview, 22.05.2010

45 Lewis Gilbert with Peter Rankin, *All My Flashbacks*, Reynolds and Hearn, 2010, p. 270

46 'He Only Lived Twice' by Tom Soter, *Starlog* #169, August 1991

47 'He Only Lived Twice' by Tom Soter, *Starlog* #169, August 1991

48 'He Only Lived Twice' by Tom Soter, *Starlog* #169, August 1991

49 Paul Duncan (ed.), *The James Bond Archives*, 'Techincally Perfect and Inventive' by Paul Duncan, Taschen, 2012, p. 152

50 Albert R. Broccoli with Donald Zec, *When the Snow Melts*, Boxtree, 1998, p. 208

51 'He Only Lived Twice' by Tom Soter, *Starlog* #169, August 1991

52 'He Only Lived Twice' by Tom Soter, *Starlog* #169, August 1991

53 Jeremy Treglown, *Roald Dahl: A Biography*, Faber and Faber Limited, 1994 p. 164

54 Donald Sturrock, *Storyteller: The Life of Roald Dahl*, Harper Press, 2011, p. 434

55 Donald Sturrock, *Storyteller: The Life of Roald Dahl*, Harper Press, 2011, p. 435

56 Tom Soter, *Bond and Beyond: 007 and Other Special Agents*, Image Publishing, 1993, p. 82

57 Diane Cilento, *My Nine Lives*, Michael Joseph Ltd, 2006, p. 240

58 *Wickers World – 'Bond Wants a Woman They Said … But Three Would Be Better'* dir: Fred Burnley, BBC1, 25.03.1967

59 *Sean Connery: Close Up*, dir. Michael Tobias, Louise Krakower Productions, 1996

60 *Wickers World – 'Bond Wants a Woman They Said … But Three Would Be Better'* dir: Fred Burnley, BBC1, 25.03.1967

61 '007's Oriental Eyefuls' by Roald Dahl, *Playboy*, June 1967

62 'Toshiro Mifune Claims 2 Bids From U.S. Prods' *Weekly Variety*, 16.02.1966

63 Alan Barnes and Marcus Hearn, *Kiss Kiss Bang! Bang! The Unofficial James Bond Film Companion*, B.T. Batsford, 2nd Edition, 2000, p. 72

64 'You Only Live Twice Special part 1' *007 Magazine #35*, The James Bond 007 International Fan Club, August 1999

65 Lewis Gilbert with Peter Rankin, *All My Flashbacks*, Reynolds and Hearn, 2010, p. 267

66 Alan Barnes and Marcus Hearn, *Kiss Kiss Bang! Bang! The Unofficial James Bond Film Companion*, B.T. Batsford, 2nd Edition, 2000, p. 72

67 '007's Oriental Eyefuls' by Roald Dahl, *Playboy*, June 1967

68 'You Only Live Twice Special part 2' *007 Magazine #36*, The James Bond 007 International Fan Club, July 2000

69 Lewis Gilbert with Peter Rankin, *All My Flashbacks*, Reynolds and Hearn, 2010, p. 267

70 William P. Cartlidge: Authors' interview, 24.10.2014

71 Nikki Van Der Zyl, *For Your Ears Only*, IndePenPress, 2013, p. 63

72 Tim Greaves, *The Bond Women: 007 Style*, 1 Shot Publications, 2002, p. 25

73 Tim Greaves, *The Bond Women: 007 Style*, 1 Shot Publications, 2002, p. 25

74 '007's Oriental Eyefuls' by Roald Dahl, *Playboy*, June 1967

75 Karin Dor: Authors' interview, 07.03.2015

76 Karin Dor: Authors' interview, 07.03.2015

77 'You Only Live Twice Special part 1'

007 *Magazine* #35, The James Bond 007
International Fan Club, August 1999

78 'Pleasance Dreams' by Sam Maronie, *Starlog*
#215, June 1995

79 'Pleasance Dreams' by Sam Maronie, *Starlog*
#215, June 1995

80 William P. Cartlidge: Authors' interview,
24.10.2014

81 William P. Cartlidge: Authors' interview,
24.10.2014

82 Ken Adam and Christopher Frayling, *Ken Adam
Designs the Movies*, Thames and Hudson, 2008,
p. 79

83 Paul Duncan (ed.), *The James Bond Archives*,
'Techincally Perfect and Inventive' by Paul
Duncan, Taschen, 2012, p. 150

84 Karin Dor: Authors' interview, 07.03.2015

85 Karin Dor: Authors' interview, 07.03.2015

86 Lewis Gilbert with Peter Rankin, *All My
Flashbacks*, Reynolds and Hearn, 2010, p. 266

87 'Stanley Sopel Interview' by Richard
Schenkman, *Bondage* #10, The James Bond 007
Fan Club, 1981

88 'Bond in Japan' by William Hall, *Photoplay*,
December 1966

89 'Bond in Japan' by William Hall, *Photoplay*,
December 1966

90 'A Secretive Person' by Gordon Gow, *Films and
Filming*, March 1974

91 'Great Scot' by Kurt Loder, *Rolling Stone* #407,
27.10.1983

92 'Great Scot' by Kurt Loder, *Rolling Stone* #407,
27.10.1983

93 'Through Airman's Eyes: The Airman and
James Bond' by Rachel Arroyo, www.af.mil,
19.01.2013

94 'Through Airman's Eyes: The Airman and
James Bond' by Rachel Arroyo, www.af.mil,
19.01.2013

95 Steven Jay Rubin, *The Complete James Bond
Movie Encyclopaedia*, Newly Revised Edition,
Contemporary Books, 2003, p. 356

96 'You Only Live Twice Special Part 1'
007 *Magazine* #35, The James Bond 007
International Fan Club, August 1999

97 'You Only Live Twice Special Part 1'
007 *Magazine* #35, The James Bond 007
International Fan Club, July 1999

98 'It Only Lived Twice' by Peter Nunn, *Classic
and Sportscar Magazine*, November 1999

99 'It Only Lived Twice' by Peter Nunn, *Classic
and Sportscar Magazine*, November 1999

100 'It Only Lived Twice' by Peter Nunn, *Classic
and Sportscar Magazine*, November 1999

101 'It Only Lived Twice' by Peter Nunn, *Classic
and Sportscar Magazine*, November 1999

102 Paul Duncan (ed.), *The James Bond Archives*,
'Techincally Perfect and Inventive' by Paul

Duncan, Taschen, 2012, p. 154

103 Desmond Llewelyn in conversation with
Graham Rye, *The James Bond 007 International
Fan Club 6th Annual Christmas Lunch,*
Pinewood Studios, 21.11.1998

104 Sandy Hernu, *Q: The Biography of Desmond
Llewelyn*, S.B. Publications, 1999, p. 91

105 Bruce Barrymore Halpenny, *Little Nellie 007*,
Casdec Limited, 1991, p. 16

106 Paul Duncan (ed.), *The James Bond Archives*,
'Techincally Perfect and Inventive', by Paul
Duncan, Taschen, 2012, p. 152

107 Ken Wallis in conversation with Graham Rye,
*The James Bond 007 International Fan Club 6th
Annual Christmas Lunch*, Pinewood Studios,
21.11.1998

108 Ken Wallis in conversation with Graham Rye,
*The James Bond 007 International Fan Club 6th
Annual Christmas Lunch*, Pinewood Studios,
21.11.1998

109 Desmond Llewelyn in conversation with
Graham Rye, *The James Bond 007 International
Fan Club 6th Annual Christmas Lunch*, Pinewood
Studios, 21.11.1998

110 Ken Adam in conversation with Graham Rye,
*The James Bond 007 International Fan Club 6th
Annual Christmas Lunch,* Pinewood Studios,
21.11.1998

111 Ken Adam and Christopher Frayling, *Ken Adam
Designs the Movies*, Thames and Hudson, 2008,
p. 75

112 Lee Pfeiffer and Philip Lisa, *The Incredible World
of 007: An Authorized Celebration of James Bond*,
Updated Edition, Boxtree, 1995, p. 204

113 Lee Pfeiffer and Philip Lisa, *The Incredible World
of 007: An Authorized Celebration of James Bond*,
Updated Edition, Boxtree, 1995, p. 204

114 Bruce Barrymore, *Halfpenny, Little Nellie 007*,
Casdec Ltd, 1991, p. 18

115 Lee Pfeiffer and Philip Lisa, *The Incredible World
of 007: An Authorized Celebration of James Bond*,
Updated Edition, Boxtree, 1995, p. 205

116 Diane Cilento, *My Nine Lives*, Michael Joseph
Ltd, 2006, p. 240

117 Tom Soter, *Bond and Beyond: 007 and Other
Special Agents*, Image Publishing, 1993, p. 86

118 Albert R. Broccoli with Donald Zec, *When the
Snow Melts*, Boxtree, 1998, p. 209

119 Albert R. Broccoli with Donald Zec, *When the
Snow Melts*, Boxtree, 1998, p. 209

120 Barbara Broccoli interviewed by Jenni Murray,
Woman's Hour, BBC Radio 4, 13.11.2006

121 Freddie Young, *Seventy Light Years: A Life in the
Movies*, Faber and Faber Limited, 1999, p. 118

122 'You Only Live Twice Special part 2'
007 *Magazine* #36, The James Bond 007
International Fan Club, July 2000

123 '007's Oriental Eyefuls' by Roald Dahl, *Playboy*,

June 1967

124 Paul Duncan (ed.), *The James Bond Archives*, 'Techincally Perfect and Inventive' by Paul Duncan, Taschen, 2012, p. 150

125 Bob Simmons with Kenneth Passingham, *Nobody Does It Better: My 25 Years with James Bond and Other Stars,* Javelin, 1987, p. 97

126 Freddie Young, *Seventy Light Years: A Life in the Movies*, Faber and Faber Limited, 1999, p. 118

127 Bob Simmons with Kenneth Passingham, *Nobody Does It Better: My 25 Years with James Bond and Other Stars*, Javelin, 1987, p. 94

128 'Interview with Lois Maxwell' by Roger Ebert, 18.06.1967

129 Lewis Gilbert: Authors' interview, 22.05.2010

130 William P. Cartlidge: Authors' interview, 24.10.2014

131 'Just for *Variety*' by Army Archerd, *Daily Variety*, 02.11.1966

132 'You Only Live Twice Special part 2' *007 Magazine* #36, The James Bond 007 International Fan Club, July 2000

133 'The Wonderful World Of Pinewood Studios' by Herb A. Lightman, *American Cinematographer* Vol 48, No. 3, March 1967

134 Ken Adam: Authors' interview, 26.01.2015

135 Ken Adam: Authors' interview, 26.01.2015

136 Bob Simmons with Kenneth Passingham, *Nobody Does It Better: My 25 Years with James Bond and Other Stars*, Javelin, 1987, p. 94

137 Norman Wanstall: Authors' interview, 27.11.2000

138 Peter Lamont: Authors' interview, 06.10.2000

139 Peter Lamont: Authors' interview, 06.10.2000

140 Christopher Frayling, *Ken Adam: The Art of Production Design*, Faber and Faber Limited, 2005, p164

141 'The Wonderful World Of Pinewood Studios' by Herb A. Lightman, *American Cinematographer* Vol 48, No. 3, March 1967

142 William P. Cartlidge: Authors' interview, 24.10.2014

143 Bob Simmons with Kenneth Passingham, *Nobody Does It Better: My 25 Years with James Bond and Other Stars*, Javelin, 1987, p. 95

144 Bob Simmons with Kenneth Passingham, *Nobody Does It Better: My 25 Years with James Bond and Other Stars*, Javelin, 1987, p. 95

145 Bob Simmons with Kenneth Passingham, *Nobody Does It Better: My 25 Years with James Bond and Other Stars*, Javelin, 1987, p. 95

146 Vic Armstrong: Authors' interview, 04.06.2015

147 'You Only Live Twice Special part 2' *007 Magazine* #36, The James Bond 007 International Fan Club, July 2000

148 'The Wonderful World Of Pinewood Studios' by Herb A. Lightman, *American Cinematographer* Vol 48, No. 3, March 1967

149 Christopher Frayling, *Ken Adam: The Art of Production Design*, Faber and Faber Limited, 2005 p. 164

150 Freddie Young, *Seventy Light Years: A Life in the Movies*, Faber and Faber Limited, 1999, p. 122

151 Freddie Young, *Seventy Light Years: A Life in the Movies*, Faber and Faber Limited, 1999, p. 122

152 Norman Wanstall: Authors' interview, 27.11.2000

153 Norman Wanstall: Authors' interview, 27.11.2000

154 Leslie Bricusse, *The Music Man*, Metro, 2006, p. 186

155 Jon Burlingame, *The Music of James Bond*, Oxford University Press, 2012, p. 74

156 Eddi Fiegel, *John Barry: A Sixties Theme*, Constable and Company Ltd, 1998, p. 201

157 'You Only Live Twice Special part 2' *007 Magazine* #36, The James Bond 007 International Fan Club, July 2000

158 *James Bond's Greatest Hits*, dir: Stephen Franklin, North One, Channel 4, 18.11.2006

159 Eddi Fiegel, *John Barry: A Sixties Theme*, Constable and Company Ltd, 1998, p. 201

160 Albert R. Broccoli with Donald Zec, *When the Snow Melts*, Boxtree, 199 p. 204

Chapter 10 On Her Majesty's Secret Service

1 'The 1960s: A Revolution In Movie Audiences' by Charles Camplin, *Los Angeles Calendar*, 18.01.1970

2 United Artists Trade Advert, *Weekly Variety*, 28.05.1969

3 United Artists Trade Advert, *Weekly Variety*, 28.05.1969

4 Tino Balio, *United Artists: The Company that Changed the Film Industry*, University of Wisconsin Press, 1987, p. 313

5 Tino Balio, *United Artists: The Company that Changed the Film Industry*, University of

Wisconsin Press, 1987, p. 310

6 David Picker: Authors' interview, 22.02.2014

7 'Sean Connery Pans for Added Gold Beyond Present 5% of 007 Loot' *Weekly Variety*, 02.03.1966

8 'Saltzman (Bond) and Kirshner (Disks) Plot With-It Pics For 18–24 Crowd' by Lee Beaupre, *Weekly Variety*, 14.02.1968

9 'Just for *Variety*' by Army Archerd, *Daily Variety*, 26.07.1968

10 'Saltzman (Bond) and Kirshner (Disks) Plot With-It Pics For 18–24 Crowd' by Lee

Beaupre, *Weekly Variety*, 14.02.1968

11   'Just for *Variety*' by Army Archerd, *Daily Variety*, 26.07.1968

12   Lewis Gilbert: Authors' interview, 22.05.2010

13   Lee Pfeiffer and Philip Lisa, *The Incredible World of 007: An Authorized Celebration of James Bond*, Updated Edition, Boxtree, 1995, p. 204

14   'Stanley Sopel' by Richard Schenkman, *Bondage #10*, The James Bond 007 Fan Club, 1981

15   David Picker: Authors' interview, 22.02.2014

16   'Directing the New 007' by Herb A. Lightman, *American Cinematographer* Vol. 51, No. 3, March 1970

17   'Directing the New 007' by Herb A. Lightman, *American Cinematographer* Vol. 51, No. 3, March 1970

18   'The Making of On Her Majesty's Secret Service' by Philip Masheter, *Movie Collector* Vol 2 #2, March 1995

19   'The Making of On Her Majesty's Secret Service' by Philip Masheter, *Movie Collector* Vol 2 #2, March 1995

20   'The Making of On Her Majesty's vSecret Service' by Philip Masheter, *Movie Collector* ol 2 #2, March 1995

21   Alan Barnes and Marcus Hearn, *Kiss Kiss Bang! Bang! The Unofficial James Bond Film Companion*, B.T. Batsford, 2nd Edition, 2000, p. 82

22   Eon Productions press release, 7 October 1968

23   'Behind the Scenes' by Geraldine Bedell, *The Observer*, 29.02. 2004

24   Michael Billington: Interviewed by Philippe Lombard, February 2003

25   Adam West, *Back To The Batcave*, Titan, 1992, p. 186

26   Patrick Mower, *Patrick Mower: My Story*, John Blake Publishing Ltd, 2007, p. 131

27   Cliff Goodwin, *Evil Spirits The Life Of Oliver Reed*, Virgin Books Ltd, 2001, p. 131

28   Roger Moore: Authors' interview, 26.04.2015

29   'Just for *Variety*' by Army Archerd, *Daily Variety*, 26.07.1968

30   David Giammarco, *For Your Eyes Only Behind The Scenes Of The James Bond Films*, ECW Press, 2002, pp. 197 – 198

31   '400 Candidates: Which man would you pick as the new James Bond?' *Life*, 11.10.1968

32   Eon Productions press release, 07.10.1968

33   George Lazenby: Authors' interview, 15.05.2015

34   George Lazenby: Authors' interview, 15.05.2015

35   George Lazenby: Authors' interview, 15.05.2015

36   George Lazenby: Authors' interview, 15.05.2015

37   George Lazenby: Authors' interview, 15.05.2015

38   George Lazenby: Authors' interview, 15.05.2015

39   George Lazenby: Authors' interview, 15.05.2015

40   George Lazenby: Authors' interview, 15.05.2015

41   George Lazenby: Authors' interview, 15.05.2015

42   George Lazenby: Authors' interview, 15.05.2015

43   George Lazenby: Authors' interview, 15.05.2015

44   George Lazenby: Authors' interview, 15.05.2015

45   George Lazenby: Authors' interview, 15.05.2015

46   George Lazenby: Authors' interview, 15.05.2015

47   George Lazenby: Authors' interview, 15.05.2015

48   George Lazenby: Authors' interview, 15.05.2015

49   George Lazenby: Authors' interview, 15.05.2015

50   George Lazenby: Authors' interview, 15.05.2015

51   George Lazenby: Authors' interview, 15.05.2015

52   George Lazenby: Authors' interview, 15.05.2015

53   George Lazenby: Authors' interview, 15.05.2015

54   George Lazenby: Authors' interview, 15.05.2015

55   George Lazenby: Authors' interview, 15.05.2015

56   George Lazenby: Authors' interview, 15.05.2015

57   George Lazenby: Authors' interview, 15.05.2015

58   George Lazenby: Authors' interview, 15.05.2015

59   George Lazenby: Authors' interview, 15.05.2015

60   George Lazenby: Authors' interview, 15.05.2015

61   George Lazenby: Authors' interview, 15.05.2015

62   George Lazenby: Authors' interview, 15.05.2015

63   Hilary Saltzman: Authors' interview, 29.11.2011

64   George Lazenby: Authors' interview, 15.05.2015

65   George Lazenby: Authors' interview, 15.05.2015

66   George Lazenby: Authors' interview, 15.05.2015

67   George Lazenby: Authors' interview, 15.05.2015

68   George Lazenby: Authors' interview, 15.05.2015

69   George Lazenby: Authors' interview, 15.05.2015

70   '400 Candidates: Which man would you pick as the new James Bond?' *Life*, 11.10.1968

71   'Directing the New 007' by Herb A. Lightman, *American Cinematographer* Vol. 51, No. 3, March 1970

72   Jill St. John: Authors' interview, 05.05.2015

73   'Directing the New 007' by Herb A. Lightman, *American Cinematographer* Vol. 51, No. 3, March 1970

74   'Licensed to Thrill' by Edward Gross, *Starlog Yearbook*, Vol. 5, 1989

75   Boxes 28 and 29, Papers of Richard Maibaum, University of Iowa

76   Charles Helfenstein, *The Making of On Her Majesty's Secret Service*, Spies LLC, 2009, pp. 38–39

77   Charles Helfenstein, *The Making of On Her Majesty's Secret Service*, Spies LLC, 2009, pp. 38 – 39

78   Charles Helfenstein, *The Making of On Her Majesty's Secret Service*, Spies LLC, 2009, pp. 38 – 39

79   Charles Helfenstein, *The Making of On Her Majesty's Secret Service*, Spies LLC, 2009, pp. 38 – 39

80   Charles Helfenstein, *The Making of On Her Majesty's Secret Service*, Spies LLC, 2009, pp. 38–39

81   Charles Helfenstein, *The Making of On Her Majesty's Secret Service*, Spies LLC, 2009,

pp. 38–39

82 Charles Helfenstein, *The Making of On Her Majesty's Secret Service*, Spies LLC, 2009, p. 37

83 Charles Helfenstein, *The Making of On Her Majesty's Secret Service*, Spies LLC, 2009, pp. 38–39

84 Charles Helfenstein, *The Making of On Her Majesty's Secret Service*, Spies LLC, 2009, p. 34

85 Charles Helfenstein, *The Making of On Her Majesty's Secret Service*, Spies LLC, 2009, p. 34

86 Charles Helfenstein, *The Making of On Her Majesty's Secret Service*, Spies LLC, 2009, p. 34

87 George Lazenby: Authors' interview, 15.05.2015

88 Charles Helfenstein, *The Making of On Her Majesty's Secret Service*, Spies LLC, 2009, p. 36

89 Eric Pleskow: Authors' interview, 28.05.2015

90 'The Making of On Her Majesty's Secret Service' by Philip Masheter, *Movie Collector* Vol 2 #2, March 1995

91 'The Making of On Her Majesty's Secret Service' by Philip Masheter, *Movie Collector* Vol 2 #2, March 1995

92 Diana Rigg interviewed by Dick Prout, Radio Record interview, December 1968

93 Diana Rigg interviewed by Dick Prout, Radio Record interview, December 1968

94 *Mark Lawson Talks to … Diana Rigg*, Dir: Louise Bourner, BBC 4, 27.09.2001

95 Peter Hunt interviewed by Ross Hendry, *The James Bond British Fan Club Convention*, March 24-25.04.1982

96 Telly Savalas interviewed by Dick Prout, Radio Record interview, December 1968

97 'Licensed To Thrill' by Edward Gross, *Starlog Yearbook*, Vol. 5, 1989

98 Syd Cain, *Not Forgetting James Bond: The Autobiography of Syd Cain*, GBU Publishing Ltd, 2002, p. 88

99 Ken Adam: Authors' interview, 26.01.2015

100 Syd Cain, *Not Forgetting James Bond: The Autobiography of Syd Cain*, GBU Publishing Ltd, 2002, p. 84

101 Syd Cain, *Not Forgetting James Bond: The Autobiography of Syd Cain*, GBU Publishing Ltd, 2002, p. 84

102 Peter Lamont: Authors' interview, 06.10.2000

103 Peter Lamont: Authors' interview, 06.10.2000

104 Syd Cain, *Not Forgetting James Bond: The Autobiography of Syd Cain*, GBU Publishing Ltd, 2002, p. 84

105 Syd Cain, *Not Forgetting James Bond: The Autobiography of Syd Cain*, GBU Publishing Ltd, 2002

106 Charles Helfenstein, *The Making of On Her*

Majesty's Secret Service, Spies LLC, 2009, p. 182

107 George Lazenby: Authors' interview, 15.05.2015

108 George Lazenby: Authors' interview, 15.05.2015

109 George Lazenby: Authors' interview, 15.05.2015

110 George Lazenby: Authors' interview, 15.05.2015

111 George Lazenby: Authors' interview, 15.05.2015

112 George Lazenby: Authors' interview, 15.05.2015

113 *Mark Lawson Talks to … Diana Rigg,* Dir: Louise Bourner, BBC 4, 27.09.2001

114 George Lazenby: Authors' interview, 15.05.2015

115 *Mark Lawson Talks To … Diana Rigg*, Dir: Louise Bourner, BBC 4, 27.09.2001

116 George Lazenby: Authors' interview, 15.05.2015

117 George Lazenby: Authors' interview, 15.05.2015

118 George Lazenby: Authors' interview, 15.05.2015

119 George Lazenby: Authors' interview, 15.05.2015

120 George Lazenby: Authors' interview, 15.05.2015

121 George Lazenby: Authors' interview, 15.05.2015

122 Vic Armstrong with Robert Sellers, *The True Adventures Of The World's Greatest Stuntman*, Titan Books, 2011, p. 46

123 George Lazenby: Authors' interview, 15.05.2015

124 'Bognor Makes Bond Fly On Skies' James Bond 25 Years, *Weekly Variety*, 13.05.1987

125 'Directing the New 007' by Herb A. Lightman, *American Cinematographer* Vol. 51, No. 3, March 1970

126 'Filming the Thrills, Chills and Spills Of 007' by John Glen, *American Cinematographer* Vol. 51, No. 3, March 1970

127 'Filming the Thrills, Chills and Spills Of 007' by John Glen, *American Cinematographer* Vol. 51, No. 3, March 1970

128 'Filming the Thrills, Chills and Spills Of 007' by John Glen, *American Cinematographer* Vol. 51, No. 3, March 1970

129 'Behind the Cameras Trained Upon 007' by Herb A. Lightman, *American Cinematographer* Vol. 51, No. 3, March 1970

130 'Filming the Thrills, Chills and Spills Of 007' by John Glen, *American Cinematographer* Vol. 51, No. 3, March 1970

131 'Filming the Thrills, Chills and Spills Of 007' by John Glen, *American Cinematographer* Vol. 51, No. 3, March 1970

132 Steven Jay Rubin, *The Complete James Bond Movie Encyclopaedia*, Contemporary Books, Newly Revised Edition, 2003, p. 63

133 Syd Cain, *Not Forgetting James Bond: The Autobiography of Syd Cain*, GBU Publishing Ltd, 2002, p. 47

134 Syd Cain, *Not Forgetting James Bond: The Autobiography of Syd Cain*, GBU Publishing Ltd, 2002, p. 85

135 John Glen: Authors' interview, 11.04.2001

136 John Glen with Marcus Hearn, *For My Eyes Only*, B.T. Batsford, 2001, pp. 52–3

137 Syd Cain, *Not Forgetting James Bond: The*

Autobiography of Syd Cain, GBU Publishing Ltd, 2002, p. 87

138 *Mark Lawson Talks To ... Diana Rigg*, Dir: Louise Bourner, BBC 4, 27.09.2001

139 John Glen with Marcus Hearn, *For My Eyes Only*, B.T. Batsford, 2001, p. 62

140 Syd Cain, *Not Forgetting James Bond: The Autobiography of Syd Cain*, GBU Publishing Ltd, 2002, p. 87

141 Charles Helfenstein, *The Making of On Her Majesty's Secret Service*, Spies LLC, 2009, p. 37

142 George Lazenby: Authors' interview, 15.05.2015

143 Ken Adam: Authors' interview, 26.01.2015

144 George Lazenby: Authors' interview, 15.05.2015

145 George Lazenby: Authors' interview, 15.05.2015

146 'The Lois Maxwell Interview' by Mark Greenberg, *Bondage #12*, The James Bond 007 Fan Club, 1983

147 Peter Haining, *James Bond: A Celebration*, W.H. Allen/Planet, 1987, pp. 193–96

148 Desmond Llewelyn: Authors' interview 14.04.1999

149 George Lazenby: Authors' interview, 15.05.2015

150 George Lazenby: Authors' interview, 15.05.2015

151 George Lazenby: Authors' interview, 15.05.2015

152 'Directing the New 007' by Herb A. Lightman, *American Cinematographer* Vol. 51, No. 3, March 1970

153 'Directing the New 007' by Herb A. Lightman, *American Cinematographer,* Vol. 51, No. 3, March 1970

154 'Directing the New 007' by Herb A. Lightman, *American Cinematographer,* Vol. 51, No. 3, March 1970

155 Peter Lamont: Authors' interview, 06.10.2000

156 Desmond Llewelyn: Authors' interview 14.04.1999

157 George Lazenby: Authors' interview, 15.05.2015

158 Diana Rigg, *No Turn Unstoned*, Assembly Checkpoint, Edinburgh, 16.08.2014

159 George Lazenby: Authors' interview, 15.05.2015

160 George Lazenby: Authors' interview, 15.05.2015

161 John Glen, *For My Eyes Only*, B.T. Batsford, 2001, p. 65

162 Eddi Fiegel, *John Barry: A Sixties Theme*, Constable and Company Ltd, 1998, p. 219

163 Eddi Fiegel, *John Barry: A Sixties Theme*, Constable and Company Ltd, 1998, pp. 218–219

164 Eddi Fiegel, *John Barry: A Sixties Theme*, Constable and Company Ltd, 1998, p. 222

165 Eddi Fiegel, *John Barry: A Sixties Theme*, Constable and Company Ltd, 1998, p. 222

166 Eddi Fiegel, *John Barry: A Sixties Theme*, Constable and Company Ltd, 1998, p. 222

167 Eddi Fiegel, *John Barry: A Sixties Theme*, Constable and Company Ltd, 1998, p. 221

168 'The George Lazenby Interview' by Paul Riddell, *007 Magazine #9*, The James Bond British Fan Club, 1981

169 Eddi Fiegel, *John Barry: A Sixties Theme*, Constable and Company Ltd, 1998, p. 222

170 George Lazenby: Authors' interview, 15.05.2015

171 George Lazenby: Authors' interview, 15.05.2015

172 George Lazenby: Authors' interview, 15.05.2015

173 George Lazenby: Authors' interview, 15.05.2015

174 George Lazenby: Authors' interview, 15.05.2015

175 George Lazenby: Authors' interview, 15.05.2015

176 George Lazenby: Authors' interview, 15.05.2015

177 George Lazenby: Authors' interview, 15.05.2015

178 George Lazenby: Authors' interview, 15.05.2015

179 'The Cinemagic Of 007' by Herb A. Lightman, *American Cinematographer* Vol. 51, No. 3, March 1970

180 'Directing the New 007' by Herb A. Lightman, *American Cinematographer* Vol. 51, No. 3, March 1970

181 www.goldenglobes.org

182 Charles Helfenstein, *The Making of On Her Majesty's Secret Service*, Spies LLC, 2009, pp. 232–33

183 George Lazenby: Authors' interview, 15.05.2015

184 'The George Lazenby Interview' by Paul Riddell, *007 Magazine #9*, The James Bond British Fan Club, 1981

185 George Lazenby: Authors' interview, 15.05.2015

186 Charles Helfenstein, *The Making of On Her Majesty's Secret Service*, Spies LLC, 2009, pp. 232–33

187 George Lazenby: Authors' interview, 15.05.2015

188 George Lazenby: Authors' interview, 15.05.2015

189 Charles Helfenstein, *The Making of On Her Majesty's Secret Service*, Spies LLC, 2009, p. 255

190 George Lazenby: Authors' interview, 15.05.2015

191 'George Lazenby Ten Years Later' by Richard Schenkman, *Bondage #6*, The James Bond 007 Fan Club, 1978

192 George Lazenby: Authors' interview, 15.05.2015

193 George Lazenby: Authors' interview, 15.05.2015

194 'Lazenby Won't Be In Next Bond Film' *Daily Variety*, 27.02.1970

195 'Lazenby Won't Be In Next Bond Film' *Daily Variety*, 27.02.1970

196 George Lazenby: Authors' interview, 15.05.2015

197 George Lazenby: Authors' interview, 15.05.2015

198 George Lazenby: Authors' interview, 15.05.2015

199 George Lazenby: Authors' interview, 15.05.2015

200 George Lazenby: Authors' interview, 15.05.2015

Chapter 11 Diamonds Are Forever

1 Tino Balio, *United Artists: The Company that Changed the Film Industry*, University of Wisconsin Press, 1987, p. 318

2 Tino Balio, *United Artists: The Company that Changed the Film Industry*, University of Wisconsin Press, 1987, p. 319

3 Tino Balio, *United Artists: The Company that Changed the Film Industry*, University of Wisconsin Press, 1987, pp. 318 – 19

4 Tino Balio, *United Artists: The Company that Changed the Film Industry*, University of Wisconsin Press, 1987, p. 320

5 'Broccoli Uses Fast Pay Beat High Interest Rates' by William Tusher, *Hollywood Reporter*, 12.01.1970

6 'Broccoli Uses Fast Pay Beat High Interest Rates' by William Tusher, *Hollywood Reporter*, 12.01.1970

7 Jeff Rovin (ed.), *The Official Moonraker Magazine,* 'Albert R. Broccoli interviewed!' by Richard Meyers, Warren Publishing Company, 1979

8 John Glen with Marcus Hearn, *For My Eyes Only*, B.T. Batsford, 2001, p. 66

9 'First Find The Ladies' by Peter Evans, *Sunday Mirror*, 30.05.1971

10 'First Find The Ladies' by Peter Evans, *Sunday Mirror*, 30.05.1971

11 'First Find The Ladies' by Peter Evans, *Sunday Mirror*, 30.05.1971

12 Charles Helfenstein, *The Making of On Her Majesty's Secret Service*, Spies LLC, 2009, p 260

13 'Shock – as America captures James Bond' by Victor Davis, *Daily Express*, 11.11.1970

14 'Shock – as America captures James Bond' by Victor Davis, *Daily Express*, 11.11.1970

15 David Sylvester, *Moonraker, Strangelove and Other Celluloid Dreams: The Visionary Art of Ken Adam*, Serpentine Gallery, 1999, p. 92

16 Guy Hamilton: Authors' interview, 02.08.2013

17 'Shock – as America Captures James Bond' by Victor Davis, *Daily Express*, 11.11.1970

18 Guy Hamilton: Authors' interview, 02.08.2013

19 John Cork and Bruce Scivally, *James Bond: The Legacy*, Boxtree, 1998, p. 128

20 Robert Wagner: Authors' interview, 05.05.2015

21 Ranulph Fiennes, *Living Dangerously: An Autobiography*, Futura Books, 1987, p. 257

22 Guy Hamilton: Authors' interview, 02.08.2013

23 'Just for *Variety*' by Army Archerd, *Daily Variety*, 08.01.1971

24 'Just for *Variety*' by Army Archerd, *Daily Variety*, 04.01.1971

25 'Just for *Variety*' by Army Archerd, *Daily Variety*, 04.01.1971

26 Guy Hamilton: Authors' interview, 02.08.2013

27 'First Find The Ladies' by Peter Evans, *Sunday Mirror*, 30.05.1971

28 'First Find The Ladies' by Peter Evans, *Sunday Mirror*, 30.05.1971

29 Paul Duncan (ed.), *The James Bond Archives*, 'A Cross, A Privilege' by James Russell, Taschen, 2012, p. 196

30 Guy Hamilton: Authors' interview, 02.08.2013

31 David Picker: Authors' interview, 22.02.2014

32 'First Find The Ladies' by Peter Evans, *Sunday Mirror*, 30.05.1971

33 Lewis Gilbert with Peter Rankin, *All My Flashbacks*, Reynolds and Hearn, 2010, p. 264

34 '007 Leads With His Double Chin' by Peter Evans, *Sunday Mirror*, 06.06.1971

35 'First Find The Ladies' by Peter Evans, *Sunday Mirror*, 30.05.1971

36 'First Find The Ladies' by Peter Evans, *Sunday Mirror*, 30.05.1971

37 John Cork and Bruce Scivally, *James Bond: The Legacy*, Boxtree, 1998, p. 131

38 John Cork and Bruce Scivally, *James Bond: The Legacy*, Boxtree, 1998, p. 131

39 Tino Balio, *United Artists: The Company that Changed the Film Industry*, University of Wisconsin Press, 1987, p. 264

40 Tino Balio, *United Artists: The Company that Changed the Film Industry*, University of Wisconsin Press, 1987, p. 264

41 David Picker, *Musts, Maybes and Nevers*, CreateSpace Independent Publishers, 2013, p. 54

42 '$1 Mil–Plus UA Deal For Connery' *Daily Variety*, 01.03.1971

43 David Picker, *Musts, Maybes and Nevers*, CreateSpace Independent Publishers, 2013, p. 54

44 John Cork and Bruce Scivally, *James Bond: The Legacy*, Boxtree, 2002, p. 131

45 'MGM To Biopic Sean O'Casey; Ford Directs' *Daily Variety*, 09.03.1963

46 David Picker: Authors' interview, 24.02.2014

47 Peter Tipthorp (ed.), *Diamonds Are Forever Official Souvenir Brochure*, 'Sean Is Back As Bond' by John Willis, Sackville Publishing, 1971

48 'On The Set of *Diamonds Are Forever*' by Danny Biederman, *Bondage* #13, The James Bond 007 Fan Club, 1984

49 'On The Set of *Diamonds Are Forever*' by Danny Biederman, *Bondage* #13, The James Bond 007 Fan Club, 1984

50 'Just for *Variety*' by Army Archerd, *Daily Variety*, 16.03.1971

51 Albert R. Broccoli: Interviewed by Stan McMann, circa 1971

52 Charles Helfenstein, *The Making of On Her*

Majesty's Secret Service, Spies LLC, 2009, p. 260

53   Steven Jay Rubin, *The James Bond Films: A Behind The Scenes History*, 2nd Edition, Arlington House Inc., 1983, p. 102

54   Charles Helfenstein, *The Making of On Her Majesty's Secret Service*, Spies LLC, 2009, pp. 38–39

55   Steven Jay Rubin, *The James Bond Films: A Behind The Scenes History*, 2nd Edition, Arlington House Inc., 1983, p. 101

56   'Richard Maibaum – 007's Puppetmaster' by Lee Goldberg, *Starlog* #68, March 1983

57   'Richard Maibaum – 007's Puppetmaster' by Lee Goldberg, *Starlog* #68, March 1983

58   'Richard Maibaum – 007's Puppetmaster' by Lee Goldberg, *Starlog* #68, March 1983

59   'Richard Maibaum – 007's Puppetmaster' by Lee Goldberg, *Starlog* #68, March 1983

60   Paul Duncan (ed.), *The James Bond Archives*, 'A Cross, A Privilege' by James Russell, Taschen, 2012, p. 196

61   Tom Mankiewicz: Interviewed by Dharmesh Chauhan, 20.10.2006

62   Tom Mankiewicz: Interviewed by Dharmesh Chauhan, 20.10.2006

63   Tom Mankiewicz: Interviewed by Dharmesh Chauhan, 20.10.2006

64   Guy Hamilton: Authors' interview, 02.08.2013

65   Guy Hamilton: Authors' interview, 02.08.2013

66   Guy Hamilton: Authors' interview, 02.08.2013

67   Tom Mankiewicz: Interviewed by Dharmesh Chauhan, 20.10.2006

68   Tom Mankiewicz: Interviewed by Dharmesh Chauhan, 20.10.2006

69   Tom Mankiewicz: Interviewed by Dharmesh Chauhan, 20.10.2006

70   Tom Mankiewicz: Interviewed by Dharmesh Chauhan, 20.10.2006

71   Tom Mankiewicz: Interviewed by Dharmesh Chauhan, 20.10.2006

72   Charles Helfenstein, *The Making of On Her Majesty's Secret Service*, Spies LLC, 2009, p. 262

73   Charles Helfenstein, *The Making of On Her Majesty's Secret Service*, Spies LLC, 2009, p. 262

74   Albert R. Broccoli with Donald Zec, *When the Snow Melts*, Boxtree, 1998 p. 224

75   '007 Leads With His Double Chin' by Peter Evans, *Sunday Mirror*, 06.06.1971

76   '007 Leads With His Double Chin' by Peter Evans, *Sunday Mirror*, 06.06.1971

77   Christopher Frayling, *Ken Adam: The Art of Production Design*, Faber and Faber Limited, 2005, p. 173

78   David Giammarco, *For Your Eyes Only: Behind The Scenes of the James Bond Films*, 2002, ECW, p. 91

79   David Giammarco, *For Your Eyes Only: Behind*

The Scenes of the James Bond Films, 2002, ECW, p. 91

80   Gus Russo, *Supermob: How Sidney Korshak and His Criminal Associates Became America's Hidden Power Brokers*, Bloomsbury USA, 2006, p. 399

81   Guy Hamilton: Authors' interview, 02.08.2013

82   Guy Hamilton: Authors' interview, 04.05.2015

83   Guy Hamilton: Authors' interview, 04.05.2015

84   'Has Time Banked the Fires of Sexy Agent 007?' by Peter Evans, *Calendar*, 25.07.1971

85   '007 Leads With His Double Chin' by Peter Evans, *Sunday Mirror*, 06.06.1971

86   Guy Hamilton: Authors' interview, 02.08.2013

87   Guy Hamilton: Authors' interview, 02.08.2013

88   'First Find The Ladies' by Peter Evans, *Sunday Mirror*, 30.05.1971

89   'First Find The Ladies' by Peter Evans, *Sunday Mirror*, 30.05.1971

90   Jill St. John: Authors' interview, 05.05.2015

91   Jill St. John: Authors' interview, 05.05.2015

92   Jill St. John: Authors' interview, 05.05.2015

93   Lana Wood: Authors' interview, 01.05.2015

94   Lana Wood: Authors' interview, 01.05.2015

95   Lana Wood: Authors' interview, 01.05.2015

96   Lana Wood: Authors' interview, 01.05.2015

97   Lana Wood: Authors' interview, 01.05.2015

98   Lana Wood: Authors' interview, 01.05.2015

99   Lana Wood: Authors' interview, 01.05.2015

100   Lana Wood: Authors' interview, 01.05.2015

101   Guy Hamilton: Authors' interview, 02.08.2013

102   Laurent Bouzereau, *The Art of Bond*, Boxtree, 2006, p. 167

103   Jill St. John: Authors' interview, 05.05.2015

104   Bruce Glover: Authors' interview, 24.05.2015

105   Guy Hamilton: Authors' interview, 03.08.2013

106   Albert R. Broccoli: Interviewed by Stan McMann, circa 1971

107   Bruce Glover: Authors' interview, 24.05.2015

108   Tom Mankiewicz: Interviewed by Dharmesh Chauhan, 20.10.2006

109   Michael Feeney Callan, *Sean Connery*, Virgin Books, 2002, p. 166

110   'An Interview With James Bond Screenwriter Tom Mankiewicz' By Tom Soter, *New York Voice*, 22.08.1987

111   Sean Connery interviewed by Sheridan Morley, *Film Night*, BBC 2, 31.07.1971

112   Guy Hamilton: Authors' interview, 02.08.2013

113   Guy Hamilton: Authors' interview, 02.08.2013

114   Guy Hamilton: Authors' interview, 02.08.2013

115   John Cork and Bruce Scivally, *James Bond: The Legacy*, Boxtree, 2002, p. 131

116   Guy Hamilton: Authors' interview, 02.08.2013

117   Guy Hamilton: Authors' interview, 02.08.2013

118   Tom Mankiewicz and Robert Crane, *My Life as a Mankiewicz*, University Press of Kentucky, 2012, p. 136

119 Christopher Frayling, *Ken Adam: The Art of Production Design*, Faber and Faber Limited, 2005, p. 175

120 David Giammarco, *For Your Eyes Only: Behind the Scenes of the James Bond Films*, 2002, ECW, p. 82

121 Michael Feeney Callan, *Sean Connery*, Virgin Books, 2002, p. 168

122 Lana Wood: Authors' interview, 01.05.2015

123 Lana Wood: Authors' interview, 01.05.2015

124 Guy Hamilton: Authors' interview, 02.08.2013

125 Lana Wood: Authors' interview, 01.05.2015

126 'Q-Quips with Desmond Llewelyn' *The Bondmanian News* #12, The Bondmanian Society, February 1997

127 Desmond Llewelyn: Authors' interview, 23.04.1999

128 Alan Barnes and Marcus Hearn, *Kiss Kiss Bang! Bang! The Unofficial James Bond Film Companion:*, B.T. Batsford, 2nd Edition, 2000, p. 199

129 Guy Hamilton: Authors' interview, 02.08.2013

130 Christopher Frayling, *Ken Adam: The Art of Production Design*, Faber and Faber Limited, 2005, p. 174

131 Guy Hamilton: Authors' interview, 02.08.2013

132 Lana Wood: Authors' interview, 01.05.2015

133 Lana Wood: Authors' interview, 01.05.2015

134 Christopher Frayling, *Ken Adam: The Art of Production Design*, Faber and Faber Limited, 2005, p. 173

135 'Kicking Bond Where it Hurts' *The Windsor Star*, 11.12.1971

136 Jill St. John: Authors' interview, 05.05.2015

137 'On the set of *Diamonds Are Forever*' by Robert Short, *Bondage* #8, The James Bond 007 Fan Club, 1980

138 Guy Hamilton: Authors' interview, 02.08.2013

139 'The Lois Maxwell Interview' by Mark Greenberg, *Bondage* #12, The James Bond 007 Fan Club, 1983

140 Tom Mankiewicz: Interviewed by Dharmesh Chauhan, 20.10.2006

141 'First Find The Ladies' by Peter Evans, *Sunday Mirror*, 30.05.1971

142 Guy Hamilton: Authors' interview, 02.08.2014

143 Christopher Frayling, *Ken Adam: The Art of Production Design*, Faber and Faber Limited, 2005, p. 176

144 Jill St. John: Authors' interview, 05.05.2015

145 Jill St. John: Authors' interview, 05.05.2015

146 Jill St. John: Authors' interview, 05.05.2015

147 Jill St. John: Authors' interview, 05.05.2015

148 Jill St. John: Authors' interview, 05.05.2015

149 Guy Hamilton: Authors' interview, 02.08.2013

150 Guy Hamilton: Authors' interview, 02.08.2013

151 'Joe Robinson Interview' by Mitya Underwood, *Newcastle Chronicle*, 12.07.2007

152 David Giammarco, *For Your Eyes Only: Behind The Scenes of the James Bond Films*, 2002, ECW, p. 88

153 Michael Feeney Callan, *Sean Connery*, Virgin Books, 2002, pp. 167-168

154 'Back in Bondage' by Tom Hutchinson, *The Guardian*, 28.12.1971

155 Guy Hamilton: Authors' interview, 02.08.2013

156 James Inverne, *Wrestling With Elephants: The Authorized Biography of Don Black*, Sanctuary Publishing Limited, 2003, p. 73

157 *James Bond's Greatest Hits*, dir: Stephen Franklin, North One, Channel 4 18.11.2006

158 *James Bond's Greatest Hits*, dir: Stephen Franklin, North One, Channel 4 18.11.2006

159 *James Bond's Greatest Hits*, dir: Stephen Franklin, North One, Channel 4 18.11.2006

160 'Maurice Binder Sighting Down a Gun Barrel At 007' by Don McGregor, *Starlog* #74, September 19833

161 Sean Connery interviewed by Sheridan Morley, *Film Night*, BBC 2, 31.07.1971

162 Albert R. Broccoli: Interviewed by Stan McMann, circa 1971

Chapter 12 Live and Let Die

1 Tino Balio, *United Artists: The Company that Changed the Film Industry*, University of Wisconsin Press, 1987, p. 320

2 'ABC Bottled In Bond (James): 7 Pix, Big Payout' *Weekly Variety*, 05.07.1972

3 Steven Saltzman: Authors' interview, 16.11.2011

4 Eric Pleskow: Authors' interview, 28.05.2015

5 Sue St. Johns (née Parker): Authors' interview, 07.10.2013

6 David Sopel: Authors' interview, 16.07.2012

7 Guy Hamilton: Authors' interview, 03.08.2013

8 Guy Hamilton: Authors' interview, 03.08.2013

9 'An Interview With James Bond Screenwriter Tom Mankiewicz' by Tom Soter, *New York Voice*, 22 August 1987

10 Guy Hamilton: Authors' interview, 03.08.2013

11 'Clint Eastwood as Superman or James Bond?' by Geoff Boucher, *LA Times* 07.09.2010

12 Guy Hamilton: Authors' interview, 03.08.2013

13 Roger Moore, *Roger Moore's James Bond Diary*, US Ed, Fawcett Publications Inc., 1973, p. 2

14 Paul Duncan (ed.), *The James Bond Archives*, 'More of an Edge' by Howard Hughes, Taschen, 2012, p. 221

15 Julian Glover: Unpublished interview by Richard Toogood, 20.10.1999

16   Julian Glover: Authors' interview, 27.04.2015

17   Michael Billington: Interviewed by Philippe
     Lombard, February 2003

18   Roger Moore, *Roger Moore's James Bond Diary*,
     US Ed, Fawcett Publications Inc., 1973 p. 1

19   Roger Moore, *Roger Moore's James Bond Diary*,
     US Ed, Fawcett Publications Inc., 1973 p. 2

20   Sue St. Johns (née Parker): Authors' interview,
     07.10.2013

21   Roger Moore with Gareth Owen, *My Word is
     My Bond*, Michael O'Mara Books, 2008, p. 173

22   Roger Moore with Gareth Owen, *My Word is
     My Bond*, Michael O'Mara Books, 2008, p. 173

23   Lee Pfeiffer and Philip Lisa, *The Incredible World
     of 007: An Authorized Celebration of James Bond*,
     Updated Edition, Boxtree, 1995, p. 194

24   Lee Pfeiffer and Philip Lisa, *The Incredible World
     of 007: An Authorized Celebration of James Bond*,
     Updated Edition, Boxtree, 1995, p. 194

25   Roger Moore: Authors' interview, 26.04.2015

26   Roger Moore, *Roger Moore's James Bond Diary*,
     US Ed, Fawcett Publications Inc., 1973, p. 1

27   Gareth Owen and Oliver Bayan, *Roger Moore:
     His Films and Career*, Robert Hale Limited,
     2002, p. 70

28   Tino Balio, *United Artists: The Company That
     Changed The Film industry*, The University of
     Wisconsin Press, 1987, p. 266

29   Roger Moore: Authors' interview, 26.04.2015

30   'Search Over Roger Moore The New James
     Bond' by Thomas Wood, *Los Angeles Times*,
     26.11.1972

31   Roger Moore, *Roger Moore as James Bond*, Pan,
     1973, p. 11

32   Guy Hamilton: Authors' interview, 03.08.2013

33   Roger Moore: Authors' interview, 26.04.2015

34   'Search Over Roger Moore The New James
     Bond' by Thomas Wood, *Los Angeles Times*,
     26.11.1972

35   Guy Hamilton: Authors' interview, 03.08.2013

36   Guy Hamilton: Authors' interview, 03.08.2013

37   'The Moore Bonds the Merrier' by Lisa
     Dewson, *007*, Argus Specialist Publications Ltd,
     1983

38   Gareth Owen and Oliver Bayan, *Roger Moore:
     His Films and Career*, Robert Hale Ltd, 2002,
     p70

39   'The New James Bond' *Parade*, 01.07.1973

40   'For Your Eyes Only Press Conference' Warwick
     Hotel, New York, by Richard Schenkman,
     Bondage #11, The James Bond 007 Fan Club,
     1981

41   'For Your Eyes Only Press Conference' Warwick
     Hotel, New York, by Richard Schenkman,
     Bondage #11, The James Bond 007 Fan Club,
     1981

42   'The Moore Bonds the Merrier' by Lisa
     Dewson, *007*, Argus Specialist Publications Ltd,
     1983

43   Gareth Owen and Oliver Bayan, *Roger Moore:
     His Films and Career*, Robert Hale Ltd, 2002, p.
     70

44   Guy Hamilton: Authors' interview 03.08.2013

45   Tom Mankiewicz and Robert Crane: *My Life
     as a Mankiewicz*, University Press of Kentucky,
     2012, p. 148

46   'The Tom Mankiewicz Interview' by Richard
     Schenkman, *Bondage #8*, The James Bond 007
     Fan Club, 1980

47   Albert R. Broccoli with Donald Zec, *When the
     Snow Melts*, Boxtree, 1998, p. 230

48   Guy Hamilton: Authors' interview 03.08.2013

49   'Updating Agent 007, Next for UA Will Build
     in Black Melo Values' *Variety*, 07.03.1973

50   'Updating Agent 007, Next for UA Will Build
     in Black Melo Values' *Variety*, 07.03.1973

51   Guy Hamilton: Authors' interview, 03.08.2013

52   Guy Hamilton: Authors' interview, 03.08.2013

53   Guy Hamilton interviewed by Mary Parkinson,
     Afternoon Plus, Thames TV, 13.01.1975

54   Guy Hamilton: Authors' interview, 03.08.2013

55   Syd Cain, *Not Forgetting James Bond: The
     Autobiography of Syd Cain*, GBU Publisging Ltd,
     2002, p. 101

56   Guy Hamilton: Authors' interview, 03.08.2013

57   'The Tom Mankiewicz Interview' by Richard
     Schenkman, *Bondage #8*, The James Bond 007
     Fan Club, 1980

58   'Praising Cain' by Terry Adlam, *007 Magazine*
     #22, The James Bond British Fan Club, Spring
     1990

59   Laurent Bouzerau, *The Art of Bond*, Boxtree,
     2006, p. 95

60   Paul Duncan (ed.), *The James Bond Archives*,
     'More of an Edge' by Howard Hughes, Taschen,
     2012, p. 222

61   Tom Mankiewicz interviewed by Lee Pfeiffer,
     *Licence to Learn About Bond: Bond, James
     Bond: The World of 007*, Hofstra University
     Symposium, 06–08.11.2007

62   Tom Mankiewicz interviewed by Lee Pfeiffer,
     *Licence to Learn About Bond: Bond, James
     Bond: The World of 007*, Hofstra University
     Symposium, 06–08.11.2007

63   Tom Mankiewicz interviewed by Lee Pfeiffer,
     *Licence to Learn About Bond: Bond, James
     Bond: The World of 007*, Hofstra University
     Symposium, 06–08.11.2007

64   Guy Hamilton: Authors' interview, 03.08.2013

65   Tom Mankiewicz interviewed by Lee Pfeiffer,
     *Licence to Learn About Bond: Bond, James
     Bond: The World of 007*, Hofstra University
     Symposium, 06–08.11.2007

66   David Gimmarco, *For Your Eyes Only: Behind the
     Scenes of the James Bond Films*, ECW Press, 2002,
     p. 135

67   Sue St. Johns (née Parker): Authors' interview, 07.10.2013

68   David Gimmarco, *For Your Eyes Only: Behind the Scenes of the James Bond Films*, ECW Press, 2002, p. 135

69   'Jane Seymour interview' by Ceri Thomas, *Total Film*, #71, December 2002

70   Laurent Bouzerau, *The Art of Bond*, Boxtree, 2006, p. 153

71   Guy Hamilton: Authors' interview, 03.08.2013

72   Gloria Hendry: Authors' interview, 26.05.2015

73   Gloria Hendry: Authors' interview, 26.05.2015

74   Gloria Hendry: Authors' interview, 26.05.2015

75   Guy Hamilton: Authors' interview, 03.08.2013

76   Yaphet Kotto: Authors' interview, 02.03.2015

77   Guy Hamilton: Authors' interview, 03.08.2013

78   Yaphet Kotto: Authors' interview, 02.03.2015

79   Yaphet Kotto: Authors' interview, 02.03.2015

80   Roger Moore, *Roger Moore's James Bond Diary*, US Ed, Fawcett Publications Inc., 1973, p.135

81   Yaphet Kotto: Authors' interview, 02.03.2015

82   Yaphet Kotto: Authors' interview, 02.03.2015

83   'Live And Let Die and Race' by John Cork, *Goldeneye* #5, The Ian Fleming Foundation, Summer 1997

84   Yaphet Kotto: Authors' interview, 02.03.2015

85   David Gimmarco, *For Your Eyes Only: Behind the Scenes of the James Bond Films*, ECW Press, 2002, p. 136

86   David Gimmarco, *For Your Eyes Only: Behind the Scenes of the James Bond Films*, ECW Press, 2002, p. 136

87   Paul Duncan (ed.), *The James Bond Archives*, 'More of an Edge' by Howard Hughes, Taschen, 2012, p. 225

88   Roger Moore: Authors' interview, 26.04.2015

89   Roger Moore: Authors' interview, 26.04.2015

90   'Leaps and Bonds: 24 Days on the Bayou with Live And Let Die' by Steve Oxenrider, *007 Magazine: Live And Let Die – Archive File #1*, March 2011

91   Peter Lamont: Authors' interview, 06.10.2000

92   Laurent Bouzerau, *The Art of Bond*, Boxtree, 2006, p. 95

93   'In Deep Water' by Peter Lamont, *MI6 Confidential*, #23, December 2013

94   'Leaps and Bonds: 24 Days on the Bayou with Live And Let Die' by Steve Oxenrider, *007 Magazine: Live And Let Die – Archive File #1*, March 2015

95   Peter Lamont: Authors' interview, 06.10.2000

96   Roger Moore, *Roger Moore's James Bond Diary*, US Ed, Fawcett Publications Inc., 1973, p. 6

97   *30 Years of James Bond*, dir: Lorna Dickinson & Alasdair Macmillan, London Weekend Television, 03.10.1992

98   Guy Hamilton: Authors' interview, 03.08.2013

99   Tom Mankiewicz interviewed by Lee Pfeiffer,

Licence to Learn About Bond: Bond, James Bond: The World of 007, Hofstra University Symposium, 06–08.11.2007

100 Clifton James: Authors' interview, 12.01.2014

101 Clifton James: Authors' interview, 12.01.2014

102 Tom Mankiewicz interviewed by Lee Pfeiffer, *Licence to Learn About Bond: Bond, James Bond: The World of 007*, Hofstra University Symposium, 06–08.11.2007

103 'The Derek Meddings interview' by Richard Schenkman *Bondage* #9, The James Bond 007 Fan Club, 1980

104 'A Panelled Discussion with Broccoli, Gilbert and Adam, Museum of Modern Art' 29.06.1979, *Bondage* #9, The James Bond 007 Fan Club, 1980

105 Guy Hamilton: Authors' interview, 03.08.2013

106 Guy Hamilton: Authors' interview, 03.08.2013

107 Guy Hamilton: Authors' interview, 03.08.2013

108 Paul Duncan (ed.), *The James Bond Archives*, 'More of an Edge' by Howard Hughes, Taschen, 2012, p. 226

109 'Same Time Tomorrow, Mrs. Bell?' by Steve Oxenrider, *007 Magazine, Live And Let Die – Archive File #1*, March 2011

110 Roger Moore, *Roger Moore's James Bond Diary*, US Ed, Fawcett Publications Inc., 1973, p. 44

111 Yaphet Kotto: Authors' interview, 02.03.2015

112 'Just for *Variety*' by Army Archerd, *Daily Variety*, 26.06.1973

113 Roger Moore: Authors' interview, 26.04.2015

114 Colin Woodhead (ed.), *Dressed To Kill: James Bond the Suited Hero*, Flammarion, 1996, p. 84

115 Tim Greaves, *The Bond Women 007 Style*, 1 Shot, p. 41, 2002

116 Guy Hamilton: Authors' interview, 03.08.2013

117 Gloria Hendry: Authors' interview, 26.05.2015

118 Gloria Hendry: Authors' interview, 26.05.2015

119 Gloria Hendry: Authors' interview, 26.05.2015

120 Syd Cain, *Not Forgetting James Bond: The Autobiography of Syd Cain*, GBU Publishing Ltd, 2002, p. 108

121 Alan Barnes and Marcus Hearn, *Kiss Kiss Bang! Bang!: The Unofficial James Bond Film Companion*, B.T. Batsford, 2nd Edition, 2000, p 199

122 Syd Cain, *Not Forgetting James Bond: The Autobiography of Syd Cain*, GBU Publishing Ltd, 2002, p. 108

123 Guy Hamilton: Authors' interview, 03.08.2013

124 Guy Hamilton: Authors' interview, 03.08.2013

125 'Praising Cain' by Terry Adlam, *007 Magazine* #22, The James Bond British Fan Club, Spring 1990

126 *30 Years of James Bond*, dir: Lorna Dickinson & Alasdair Macmillan, London Weekend Television, 03.10.1992

127 Paul Duncan (ed.), *The James Bond Archives*, 'More of an Edge' by Howard Hughes, Taschen,

22.03.1973

128 'The Derek Meddings interview' by Richard Schenkman, *Bondage* #9, The James Bond 007 Fan Club, 1980

129 'The Derek Meddings interview' by Richard Schenkman, *Bondage* #9, The James Bond 007 Fan Club, 1980

130 Roger Moore with Gareth Owen, *My Word is My Bond*, Michael O'Mara Books, 2008, p. 182

131 Hilary Saltzman: Authors' interview, 29.11.2011

132 Roger Moore with Gareth Owen, *My Word is My Bond*, Michael O'Mara Books, 2008, p. 182

133 Guy Hamilton: Authors' interview, 03.08.2013

134 Roger Moore, *Roger Moore's James Bond Diary*, US Ed, Fawcett Publications Inc., 1973, p. 1

135 'Praising Cain' by Terry Adlam, *007 Magazine* #22, The James Bond 007 Fan Club, Spring 1990

136 'The Moore Bonds the Merrier' by Lisa Dewson, *007*, Argus Specialist Publications Ltd, 1983

137 'Cottage Fire Kills Wife of Actor Bernard Lee' by Norman Luck, *The Daily Express*, 31.01.1972

138 Roger Moore, *Roger Moore's James Bond Diary*, US Ed, Fawcett Publications Inc., 1973, p. 34

139 'Britain's Last Line of Defence' by Graham Rye, *007 Magazine* #14, The James Bond British Fan Club, 1984

140 'Britain's Last Line of Defence' by Graham Rye, *007 Magazine* #14, The James Bond British Fan Club, 1984

141 Desmond Llewelyn: Authors' interview, 23.04.1999

142 Madeline Smith: Authors' interview, 04.03.2015

143 Madeline Smith: Authors' interview, 04.03.2015

144 Roger Moore, *Roger Moore's James Bond Diary*, US Ed, Fawcett Publications Inc., 1973, p.165

145 Madeline Smith: Authors' interview, 04.03.2015

146 Guy Hamilton: Authors' interview, 03.08.2013

147 'Through Airmen's Eyes: The Airman and James Bond' by Rachel Arroyo, www.af.mil 19.01.2013

148 Roy Mosley with Philip and Martin Masheter, *Roger Moore: A Biography*, New English Library, 1985 p. 165

149 Army Archerd, 'Just for *Variety*' *Daily Variety*,

150 Geoff Leonard, Pete Walker and Gareth Bramley, *John Barry: A Life In Music,* Sansom and Company, 1998, p. 100

151 Roger Moore, *Roger Moore as James Bond*, Pan, 1973, p. 25

152 Guy Hamilton: Authors' interview 03.08.2013

153 *Billboard* 04.09.1971

154 'Just for *Variety*' by Army Archerd, *Variety*, 27.01.1972

155 *For Your Ears Only*, presented by Lois Maxwell, BBC Radio 2, 07.12.1995

156 Tom Doyle, *Man On The Run*, Birlinn Ltd, 2014, p. 48

157 *James Bond's Greatest Hits*, dir: Stephen Franklin, North One, Channel 4, 18.11.2006

158 *James Bond's Greatest Hits*, dir: Stephen Franklin, North One, Channel 4, 18.11.2006

159 Tom Mankiewicz: Interviewed by Dharmesh Chauhan, 20.10.2006

160 Madeline Smith: Authors' interview, 04.03.2015

161 Lee Pfeiffer and Philip Lisa, *The Incredible World of 007: An Authorized Celebration of James Bond*, Updated Edition, Boxtree, 1995, p. 201

162 Lee Pfeiffer and Philip Lisa, *The Incredible World of 007: An Authorized Celebration of James Bond*, Updated Edition, Boxtree, 1995, p. 201

163 Gloria Hendry: Authors' interview, 26.05.2015

164 Christoph Lindner (ed.), *The James Bond Phenomenon,* 'Creating a Bond Market: Selling John Barry's Soundtracks and Theme Songs' by Jeff Smith, Manchester University Press, 2003, p. 130

165 Tom Soter, *Bond and Beyond: 007 and Other Special Agents*, Image Publishing, 1993 p. 117

166 Tom Soter, *Bond and Beyond: 007 and Other Special Agents*, Image Publishing, 1993 p. 117

167 Roger Moore, *Roger Moore as James Bond*, Pan, 1973, p. 154

168 Roger Moore, *Roger Moore's James Bond Diary*, US Ed, Fawcett Publications Inc., 1973 p. 1

169 'Just for *Variety*' by Army Archerd, *Daily Variety,* 26.06.1973

170 Roger Moore with Gareth Owen, *My Word is My Bond*, Michael O'Mara Books, 2008 p. 182

Chapter 13 The Man With the Golden Gun

1 Tino Balio, *United Artists: The Company that Changed the Film Industry*, University of Wisconsin Press, 1987, p. 320

2 Tino Balio, *United Artists: The Company that Changed the Film Industry*, University of Wisconsin Press, 1987, p. 320

3 Tino Balio, *United Artists: The Company that Changed the Film Industry*, University of

Wisconsin Press, 1987, p. 324

4 Army Archerd, 'Just for *Variety*' *Daily Variety*, 22.03.1973

5 'The Albert R. Broccoli Interview' by Richard Schenkman, *Bondage* #5, The James Bond 007 Fan Club, 1978

6 Eric Pleskow: Authors' interview, 28.05.2015

7 Eric Pleskow: Authors' interview, 28.05.2015

8   Eric Pleskow: Authors' interview, 28.05.2015

9   Steven Saltzman: Authors' interview, 16.11.2011

10 'Moore, As New James Bond, Other Fresh Angles To Mark UA's 'Live'' by Jack Pittman, *Weekly Variety,* 28.02.1973

11 Guy Hamilton: Authors' interview, 03.11.2014

12 Roger Moore with Gareth Owen, *My Word is My Bond,* Michael O'Mara Books Ltd, 2008, p. 188

13 Guy Hamilton: Authors' interview, 03.08.2013

14 Gareth Owen and Oliver Bayan, *Roger Moore: His Films and Career,* Robert Hale Limited, 2002, p. 75

15 Guy Hamilton interviewed by Mary Parkinson, *Afternoon Plus,* Thames TV, 13.01.1975

16 Guy Hamilton: Authors' interview, 26.10.2013

17 John Cork and Bruce Scivally, *James Bond: The Legacy,* Boxtree, 2002, p. 151

18 Guy Hamilton: Authors' interview, 26.10.2013

19 Guy Hamilton: Authors' interview, 02.08.2013

20 Guy Hamilton: Authors' interview, 02.08.2013

21 Guy Hamilton: Authors' interview, 02.08.2013

22 Guy Hamilton: Authors' interview, 02.08.2013

23 John Cork and Bruce Scivally, *The James Bond Legacy,* 2002, p. 149

24 John Cork and Bruce Scivally, *James Bond: The Legacy,* Boxtree, 2002, p. 149

25 John Cork and Bruce Scivally, *James Bond: The Legacy,* Boxtree, 2002, p. 150

26 Guy Hamilton: Authors' interview, 02.08.2014

27 John Cork and Bruce Scivally, *James Bond: The Legacy,* Boxtree, 2002, p. 151

28 John Cork and Bruce Scivally, *James Bond: The Legacy,* Boxtree, 2002, p. 151

29 Guy Hamilton: Authors' interview, 02.08.2013

30 Guy Hamilton: Authors' interview, 26.10.2013

31 'The Tom Mankiewicz Interview' by Richard Schenkman, *Bondage* #8, The James Bond 007 Fan Club, 1980

32 Peter Lamont: Authors' interview, 06.10.2000

33 'An Interview With James Bond Screenwriter Tom Mankiewicz' by Tom Soter, *The New York Voice,* 22.08.1987

34 Tom Mankiewicz with Robert Crane, *My Life as a Mankiewicz An Insider's Journey Through Hollywood,* University Press of Kentucky, 2012, pp. 161–2

35 'The Tom Mankiewicz Interview' by Richard Schenkman, *Bondage* #8, The James Bond 007 Fan Club, 1980

36 *Daily Variety* 22.01.1974

37 Guy Hamilton: Authors' interview, 02.08.2013

38 Guy Hamilton: Authors' interview, 02.08.2013

39 Tom Mankiewicz with Robert Crane, *My Life as a Mankiewicz An Insider's Journey Through Hollywood,* University Press of Kentucky, 2012, p. 161

40 'The Tom Mankiewicz Interview' by Richard Schenkman, *Bondage* #8, The James Bond 007 Fan Club, 1980

41 Tom Mankiewicz interview by Dharmesh Chauhan, 20.10.2006

42 Guy Hamilton: Authors' interview, 02.08.2013

43 Guy Hamilton: Authors' interview, 26.10.2013

44 Tom Mankiewicz: Interviewed by Dharmesh Chauhan, 20.10.2006

45 Tom Mankiewicz with Robert Crane, *My Life as a Mankiewicz An Insider's Journey Through Hollywood,* University Press of Kentucky, 2012, p. 147

46 'The Tom Mankiewicz Interview' by Richard Schenkman, *Bondage* #8, The James Bond 007 Fan Club, 1980

47 John Cork and Bruce Scivally, *James Bond: The Legacy,* Boxtree, 2002, p. 152

48 *Daily Variety,* 13.11.1973

49 Steven Jay Rubin, *The Complete James Bond Movie Encyclopaedia,* Contemporary Books, Newly Revised Edition, 2002, p. 383

50 'James Bond – 27 Years and Still Licensed To Kill: An Annotated 007 Filmography' by Mark A. Altman, *Cinemafantastique* Vol. 19 No. 5, July 1989

51 Guy Hamilton: Authors' interview, 02.08.2013

52 Guy Hamilton interviewed by Mary Parkinson, *Afternoon Plus,* Thames TV, 13.01.1975

53 Roger Moore with Gareth Owen, *My Word is My Bond,* Michael O'Mara Books Ltd, 2008, p. 172

54 John Cork and Bruce Scivally, *James Bond: The Legacy,* Boxtree, 2002, p. 149

55 Roger Moore, *Roger Moore's James Bond Diary,* US Ed, Fawcett Publications Inc., 1973, p. 76

56 Roger Moore: Authors' interview, 26.04.2015

57 'The Vampire With The Golden Gun' by Chris Knight, *Cinemafantastique* Vol. 4, Number 1, 1975

58 'The Vampire With The Golden Gun' by Chris Knight, *Cinemafantastique* Vol. 4, Number 1, 1975

59 'The Vampire With The Golden Gun' by Chris Knight, *Cinemafantastique* Vol. 4, Number 1, 1975

60 Guy Hamilton: Authors' interview, 03.08.2013

61 'Licensed To Thrill' by Edward Gross, *Starlog* Yearbook, Vol. 5, 1989

62 Britt Ekland: Authors' interview, 20.06.2010

63 Britt Ekland: Authors' interview, 20.06.2010

64 Britt Ekland: Authors' interview, 20.06.2010

65 Britt Ekland: Authors' interview, 20.06.2010

66 Maud Adams: Authors' interview, 12.04.2015

67 Maud Adams: Authors' interview, 12.04.2015

68 Guy Hamilton: Authors' interview, 03.08.2013

69 Guy Hamilton interviewed by Mary Parkinson, *Afternoon Plus,* Thames TV, 13.01.1975

70 Maud Adams: Authors' interview, 12.04.2015

71 Guy Hamilton: Authors' interview, 02.08.2013

72 'The Vampire with the Golden Gun' by Chris Knight, *Cinemafantastique* Vol. 4, Number 1, 1975

73 Guy Hamilton interviewed by Mary Parkinson, *Afternoon Plus*, Thames TV, 13.01.1975

74 Guy Hamilton: Authors' interview, 02.08.2013

75 Guy Hamilton: Authors' interview, 02.08.2013

76 Guy Hamilton: Authors' interview, 03.08.2013

77 Clifton James: Authors' interview, 12.01.2014

78 Clifton James: Authors' interview, 12.01.2014

79 Guy Hamilton: Authors' interview, 02.08.2013

80 Laurent Bouzerau, *The Art of Bond*, Boxtree, 2006, p. 98

81 John Cork and Bruce Scivally, *James Bond: The Legacy*, Boxtree, 2002, p. 157

82 Gareth Owen and Oliver Bayan, *Roger Moore: His Films and Career*, Robert Hale Limited, 2002, pp. 76–7

83 Guy Hamilton interviewed by Mary Parkinson, *Afternoon Plus*, Thames TV, 13.01.1975

84 Laurent Bouzerau, *The Art of Bond*, Boxtree, 2006, p. 98

85 Peter Lamont: Authors' interview, 06.10.2000

86 Peter Lamont: Authors' interview, 06.10.2000

87 Peter Lamont: Authors' interview, 06.10.2000

88 Guy Hamilton: Authors' interview, 02.08.2013

89 Paul Duncan (ed.), *The James Bond Archives*, 'Smooth Diamond' by Howard Hughes, Taschen, 2012, p. 244

90 Steven Jay Rubin, *The James Bond Films A Behind The Scenes History*, Arlington House Inc., 2nd Edition, 1983, p. 128

91 Paul Duncan (ed.), *The James Bond Archives*, 'Smooth Diamond' by Howard Hughes, Taschen, 2012, p. 244

92 www.seabee.info

93 www.seabee.info

94 www.seabee.info

95 www.seabee.info

96 www.seabee.info

97 'The Vampire With The Golden Gun' by Chris Knight, *Cinemafantastique* Vol. 4 Number 1, 1975

98 Roger Moore with Gareth Owen, *My Word is My Bond*, Michael O'Mara Books Ltd, 2008, p. 192

99 Elaine Schreyeck: Authors' interview, 26.01.2015

100 Maud Adams: Authors' interview, 12.04.2015

101 Maud Adams: Authors' interview, 12.04.2015

102 Maud Adams: Authors' interview, 12.04.2015

103 Britt Ekland: Authors' interview, 20.06.2010

104 Britt Ekland: Authors' interview, 20.06.2010

105 Roger Moore with Gareth Owen, *My Word is My Bond* by, Michael O'Mara Books Ltd, 2008, p. 192

106 Guy Hamilton: Authors' interview, 02.08.2014

107 Maryam d'Abo and John Cork, *Bond Girls Are Forever*, Boxtree, 2003, p. 144

108 Clifton James: Authors' interview, 12.01.2014

109 Clifton James: Authors' interview, 12.01.2014

110 'Licensed To Thrill' by Edward Gross, *Starlog Yearbook*, Vol. 5, 1989

111 Laurent Bouzerau, *The Art of Bond*, Boxtree, 2006, p. 98

112 Guy Hamilton interviewed by Mary Parkinson, *Afternoon Plus*, Thames TV, 13.01.1975

113 Clifton James: Authors' interview, 12.01.2014

114 Clifton James: Authors' interview, 12.01.2014

115 Roger Moore with Gareth Owen, *My Word is My Bond*, Michael O'Mara Books Ltd, 2008, p. 190

116 Britt Ekland: Authors' interview, 20.06.2010

117 Britt Ekland: Authors' interview, 20.06.2010

118 Clifton James: Authors' interview, 12.01.2014

119 Peter Lamont: Authors' interview, 06.10.2000

120 Roger Moore with Gareth Owen, *My Word is My Bond*, Michael O'Mara Books Ltd, 2008, p. 189

121 Britt Ekland: Authors' interview, 20.06.2010

122 Guy Hamilton: Authors' interview, 02.08.2014

123 Maud Adams: Authors' interview, 12.04.2015

124 Guy Hamilton: Authors' interview, 02.08.2014

125 Maud Adams: Authors' interview, 12.04.2015

126 Elaine Schreyeck: Authors' interview, 26.01.2015

127 Guy Hamilton: Authors' interview, 02.08.2014

128 Guy Hamilton: Authors' interview, 02.08.2014

129 'Film Car Chases and Stunts 7 True Stories' by Rebecca Hawkes, *The Daily Telegraph*, 03.05.2015

130 'Just for *Variety*' by Army Archerd, *Daily Variety*, 28.02.1974

131 John Cork and Bruce Scivally, *James Bond: The Legacy*, Boxtree, 2002, p. 155

132 'The Albert R. Broccoli Interview' by Richard Schenkman, *Bondage #5*, The James Bond 007 Fan Club, 1978

133 'New York Sound Track' *Weekly Variety*, 03.07.1974

134 Laurent Bouzerau, *The Art of Bond*, Boxtree, 2006, p. 71

135 Laurent Bouzerau, *The Art of Bond*, Boxtree, 2006, p. 71

136 John Cork and Bruce Scivally, *James Bond: The Legacy*, Boxtree, 2002, p. 156

137 'John Stears Interview' by Andrew Pilkington, *007 Magazine #13*, The James Bond British Fan Club, June 1983

138 *Derek Meddings – The Bond Years* dir: Paul Scrabo and George Ann Muller, 2000

139 Guy Hamilton: Authors' interview, 02.08.2013

140 Oswald Morris: Authors' interview, 18.01.2014

141 Oswald Morris: Authors' interview, 18.01.2014
142 Oswald Morris: Authors' interview, 18.01.2014
143 Oswald Morris: Authors' interview, 18.01.2014
144 Oswald Morris: Authors' interview, 18.01.2014
145 Oswald Morris: Authors' interview, 18.01.2014
146 Lois Maxwell interviewed by Mary Parkinson, *Afternoon Plus*, Thames TV, 13.01.1975
147 Guy Hamilton interviewed by Mary Parkinson, *Afternoon Plus*, Thames TV, 13.01.1975
148 Sandy Hernu, *Q: The Biography of Desmond Llewelyn*, S.B. Publications, 1999, p. 102
149 Desmond Llewelyn: Authors' interview, 14.04.1999
150 Roger Moore with Gareth Owen, *My Word is My Bond*, Michael O'Mara Books Ltd, 2008, p. 188
151 Gary Giblin, *James Bond's London*, Daleon Enterprises Inc, 2001, p. 25 – 6
152 Roger Moore with Gareth Owen, *My Word is My Bond*, Michael O'Mara Books Ltd, 2008, pp. 193
153 Gareth Bramley, Geoff Leonard and Peter Walker, *John Barry: The Man With the Midas Touch*, Radcliffe Press Ltd, 2nd Edition, 2008, p. 81

154 *James Bond's Greatest Hits*, dir: Stephen Franklin, North One, Channel 4, 18.11.2006
155 *For Your Ears Only*, presented by Honor Blackman, Prod: Sara Baker, BBC Radio 2, 27.11.1999
156 *James Bond's Greatest Hits*, dir: Stephen Franklin, North One, Channel 4, 18.11.2006
157 John Burlingame, *The Music Of James Bond*, Oxford University Press, 2012, p. 61
158 John Burlingame, *The Music Of James Bond*, Oxford University Press, 2012, p. 120
159 *For Your Ears Only*, presented by Honor Blackman, Prod: Sara Baker, BBC Radio 2, 27.11.1999
160 'Maurice Binder Sighting Down a Gun Barrel At 007' by Don McGregor, *Starlog* #74, September 1983l 4, 18.11.2006
161 'Maurice Binder' by Don McGregor, *Starlog* #74, September 1983
162 Christopher Lee, *Lord Of Misrule: The Autobiography of Christopher Lee*, Orion Books Ltd, 2003, p. 234

Chapter 14 Broccoli vs Saltzman

1 Hilary Saltzman: Authors' interview, 29.11.2011
2 Tino Balio, *United Artists: The Company that Changed the Film Industry*, University of Wisconsin Press, 1987, p. 272
3 Tino Balio, *United Artists: The Company that Changed the Film Industry*, University of Wisconsin Press, 1987, p. 272
4 'Bond Film–Rental Bonanza Over $275 Mil To Date For UA; Now Aiming 'Golden Gun'' by Richard Albarino, *Daily Variety* 05.12.1974
5 Hilary Saltzman: Authors' interview, 29.11.2011
6 'Bond Film–Rental Bonanza Over $275 Mil To Date For UA; Now Aiming 'Golden Gun'' by Richard Albarino, *Daily Variety* 05.12.1974
7 Tino Balio, *United Artists: The Company that Changed the Film Industry*, University of Wisconsin Press, 1987, p. 259
8 Tino Balio, *United Artists: The Company that Changed the Film Industry*, University of Wisconsin Press, 1987, p. 258
9 'The Man who got the Bond Going' by Pearl Sheffy, *Calgary Sun Herald*, 29.01.1966
10 Steven Saltzman: Authors' interview, 16.11.2011
11 Val Guest, *So You Want To Be In Pictures*, Reynolds and Hearn Ltd, 2001, p. 163
12 Val Guest, *So You Want To Be In Pictures*, Reynolds and Hearn Ltd, 2001, p. 163
13 Val Guest, *So You Want To Be In Pictures*, Reynolds and Hearn Ltd, 2001, pp. 163–4
14 'Technicolor Counterattacks Saltzman's Dissident Group' *Daily Variety*, 16.06.1970
15 'Saltzman Sells 370,500 Shares Of Technicolor' *Daily Variety*, 06.07.1972
16 'Saltzman Files 2 Suits Versus Technicolor' *Daily Variety*, 31.07.1972
17 'Saltzman Trying To Head Off His Techni Ouster' *Daily Variety*, 03.08.1972
18 Steven Saltzman: Authors' interview, 16.11.2011
19 Eric Pleskow: Authors' interview, 28.05.2015
20 Tino Balio, *United Artists: The Company that Changed the Film Industry*, University of Wisconsin Press, 1987, p. 271
21 Eric Pleskow: Authors' interview, 28.05.2015
22 Tino Balio, *United Artists: The Company that Changed the Film Industry*, University of Wisconsin Press, 1987, p. 273
23 Tino Balio, *United Artists: The Company that Changed the Film Industry*, University of Wisconsin Press, 1987, p. 259
24 Tino Balio, *United Artists: The Company that Changed the Film Industry*, University of Wisconsin Press, 1987, p. 259
25 Guy Hamilton: Authors' interview, 02.08.2014
26 Tino Balio, *United Artists: The Company that Changed the Film Industry*, University of Wisconsin Press, 1987, p. 273
27 Sue St. Johns (née Parker): Authors' interview, 07.10.2013
28 Steven Saltzman: Authors' interview, 16.11.2011
29 Steven Saltzman: Authors' interview, 16.11.2011

30   Sue St. Johns (née Parker): Authors' interview,
     07.10.2013
31   Albert R. Broccoli with Donald Zec, *When the
     Snow Melts*, Boxtree, 1998, p. 241
32   Tino Balio, *United Artists: The Company that
     Changed the Film Industry*, University of
     Wisconsin Press, 1987, p. 273
33   Tino Balio, *United Artists: The Company that
     Changed the Film Industry*, University of
     Wisconsin Press, 1987, p. 273
34   Tino Balio, *United Artists: The Company that
     Changed the Film Industry*, University of
     Wisconsin Press, 1987, p. 273
35   Tino Balio, *United Artists: The Company that
     Changed the Film Industry*, University of
     Wisconsin Press, 1987, p. 273
36   Danton Rissner: Authors' interview, 04.06.2015
37   'Harry Saltzman Negotiating To Send His
     Half-Interest In 'Bond' Marriage Col's Way'
     Daily Variety, 14.11.1975
38   Tino Balio, *United Artists: The Company that
     Changed the Film Industry*, University of
     Wisconsin Press, 1987, p. 273
39   Steven Saltzman: Authors' interview, 16.11.2011
40   'Bond Film-Rental Bonanza Over $275 Mil To
     Date For UA; Now Aiming 'Golden Gun'' by
     Richard Albarino, *Daily Variety* 05.12.1974
41   'Bond Film-Rental Bonanza Over $275 Mil To
     Date For UA; Now Aiming 'Golden Gun'' by
     Richard Albarino, *Daily Variety*, 05.12.1974
42   'Bond Film-Rental Bonanza Over $275 Mil To
     Date For UA; Now Aiming 'Golden Gun'' by
     Richard Albarino, *Daily Variety*, 05.12.1974
43   'Bond Film-Rental Bonanza Over $275 Mil To
     Date For UA; Now Aiming 'Golden Gun'' by
     Richard Albarino, *Daily Variety*, 05.12.1974
44   'Bond Film-Rental Bonanza Over $275 Mil To
     Date For UA; Now Aiming 'Golden Gun'' by
     Richard Albarino, *Daily Variety*, 05.12.1974
45   Tino Balio, *United Artists: The Company that
     Changed the Film Industry*, University of
     Wisconsin Press, 1987, p. 273
46   Tino Balio, *United Artists: The Company that
     Changed the Film Industry*, University of

47   Tino Balio, *United Artists: The Company that
     Changed the Film Industry*, University of
     Wisconsin Press, 1987, p. 273
48   Tino Balio, *United Artists: The Company that
     Changed the Film Industry*, University of
     Wisconsin Press, 1987, p. 273
49   Albert R. Broccoli with Donald Zec, *When the
     Snow Melts*, Boxtree, 1998, pp. 164–5
50   Albert R. Broccoli with Donald Zec, *When the
     Snow Melts*, Boxtree, 1998, pp. 164–5
51   Sue St. Johns (née Parker): Authors' interview,
     07.10.2013
52   'Saltzman Sells Danjaq Interest To United
     Artists' *Daily Variety*, 18.12.1975
53   Hilary Saltzman: Authors' interview, 29.11.2011
54   Tino Balio, *United Artists: The Company that
     Changed the Film Industry*, University of
     Wisconsin Press, 1987, p. 273
55   Tino Balio, *United Artists: The Company that
     Changed the Film Industry*, University of
     Wisconsin Press, 1987, p. 273
56   Tino Balio, *United Artists: The Company that
     Changed the Film Industry*, University of
     Wisconsin Press, 1987, p. 273
57   Steven Saltzman: Authors' interview, 16.11.2011
58   Sue St. Johns (née Parker): Authors' interview,
     07.10.2013
59   Sue St. Johns (née Parker): Authors' interview,
     07.10.2013
60   Steven Saltzman: Authors' interview, 16.11.2011
61   Steven Saltzman: Authors' interview, 16.11.2011
62   Steven Saltzman: Authors' interview, 16.11.2011
63   Steven Saltzman: Authors' interview, 16.11.2011
65   'Bond Film-Rental Bonanza Over $275 Mil To
     Date For UA; Now Aiming 'Golden Gun'' by
     Richard Albarino, *Daily Variety*, 05.12.1974
65   Steven Saltzman: Authors' interview, 16.11.2011
66   Tino Balio, *United Artists: The Company that
     Changed the Film Industry*, University of
     Wisconsin Press, 1987, p. 274
67   'Saltzman Sells Danjaq Interest To United
     Artists' *Daily Variety*, 18.12.1975

Chapter 15 The Spy Who Loved Me

1   Tino Balio, *United Artists: The Company that
     Changed the Film Industry*, University of
     Wisconsin Press, 1987, pp. 322–23
2   Tino Balio, *United Artists: The Company that
     Changed the Film Industry*, University of
     Wisconsin Press, 1987, pp. 320–21
3   Tino Balio, *United Artists: The Company that
     Changed the Film Industry*, University of
     Wisconsin Press, 1987, p. 325
4   *The Spy Who Loved Me: Producing*, Producer:

     Victor Lockwood, Open University, BBC2,
     17.07.1977
5   John Cork and Bruce Scivally, *James Bond: The
     Legacy*, Boxtree, 2002, p.165
6   Albert R. Broccoli with Donald Zec, *When the
     Snow Melts*, Boxtree, 1998, p. 245
7   Guy Hamilton: Authors' interview, 03.08.2013
8   *Daily Variety*, 7.11.1975
9   Guy Hamilton: Authors' interview, 02.11.2014
10   Tom Soter, *Bond and Beyond: 007 and Other*

Special Agents, Image Publishing, 1993, p. 128

11 Simon Archer and Stan Nicholls: *Gerry Anderson: The Biography*, Legend, 1996, p. 149

12 Simon Archer and Stan Nicholls: *Gerry Anderson: The Biography*, Legend, 1996, p. 150

13 Simon Archer and Stan Nicholls: *Gerry Anderson: The Biography*, Legend, 1996, p. 150

14 Simon Archer and Stan Nicholls: *Gerry Anderson: The Biography*, Legend, 1996, 150

15 Steven Jay Rubin, *The Complete James Bond Movie Encyclopaedia*, Newly Revised Edition, Contemporary Books, 2003, p. 391

16 Steven Jay Rubin, *The James Bond Films: A Behind The Scenes History*, 2nd Edition, Arlington House Inc., 1983, p.138

17 Steven Jay Rubin, *The James Bond Films: A Behind The Scenes History*, 2nd Edition, Arlington House Inc., 1983, p. 138

18 Steven Jay Rubin, *The James Bond Films: A Behind The Scenes History*, 2nd Edition, Arlington House Inc., 1983, p. 139

19 Anthony Burgess, *You've Had Your Time: The Second Part of My Confessions*, Grove Weidenfeld, 1990, p. 313

20 Anthony Burgess, *You've Had Your Time: The Second Part of My Confessions*, Grove Weidenfeld, 1990, p. 313

21 Anthony Burgess, *You've Had Your Time: The Second Part of My Confessions*, Grove Weidenfeld, 1990, p. 314

22 'Anthony Burgess' 007 Obsession' by Andrew Biswell, *New Statesman*, 9.04.2013

23 'Anthony Burgess' 007 Obsession' by Andrew Biswell, *New Statesman*, 09.04.2013

24 John Landis: Authors' interview, 28.10.2014

25 John Landis: Authors' interview, 28.10.2014

26 John Landis: Authors' interview, 28.10.2014

27 John Landis: Authors' interview, 28.10.2014

28 John Landis: Authors' interview, 28.10.2014

29 John Landis: Authors' interview, 28.10.2014

30 John Landis: Authors' interview, 28.10.2014

31 John Landis: Authors' inteview, 28.10.2014

32 John Landis: Authors' interview, 28.10.2014

33 Guy Hamilton: Authors' interview, 02.11.2014

34 Guy Hamilton: Authors' interview, 02.08.2013

35 'Richard Maibaum: 007's Puppetmaster' *Starlog* #68, March 1983

36 'Richard Maibaum: 007's Puppetmaster' *Starlog* #68, March 1983

37 'Richard Maibaum: 007's Puppetmaster' *Starlog* #68, March 1983

38 Albert R. Broccoli with Donald Zec, *When the Snow Melts*, Boxtree, 1998, p. 244

39 John Landis: Authors' interview, 28.10.2014

40 Danton Rissner: Authors' interview, 04.06.2015

41 'In London' by Fabienne Lewis, *Daily Variety*, 18.12.1975

42 Lewis Gilbert: Authors' interview, 22.05.2010

43 William P. Cartlidge: Authors' interview, 24.10.2014

44 Lewis Gilbert with Peter Rankin, *All My Flashbacks*, Reynolds and Hearn, 2010, p 317

45 Christopher Wood: *The Spy I Loved*, Twenty First CenturyPublishers, 2006, p 30

46 Christopher Wood in conversation with Ross Hendry, *The James Bond British Fan Club Convention*, Wembley Conference Centre, 25.04.1982

47 'How To Write the Perfect Bond Movie' by Christopher Wood, *SFX* #227, November 2012

48 Christopher Wood in conversation with Ross Hendry, *The James Bond British Fan Club Convention*, Wembley Conference Centre, 25.04.1982

49 Christopher Wood: *The Spy I Loved*, Twenty First CenturyPublishers, 2006, p 32

50 Christopher Wood: *The Spy I Loved*, Twenty First CenturyPublishers, 2006, p 33

51 Christopher Wood in conversation with Ross Hendry, *The James Bond British Fan Club Convention*, Wembley Conference Centre, 25.04.1982

52 Christopher Wood: *The Spy I Loved*, Twenty First CenturyPublishers, 2006, p 60

53 Peter Carter Ruck, *Memoirs of a Libel Lawyer*, Weidenfeld and Nicholson Ltd, 1990, pp. 215–6

54 Roger Moore: Authors' interview, 26.04.2015

55 Roger Moore: Authors' interview, 26.04.2015

56 Tom Mankiewicz: Interviewed by Dharmesh Chauhan 20.10.2006

57 Tom Mankiewicz: Interviewed by Dharmesh Chauhan 20.10.2006

58 Tom Mankiewicz and Robert Crane, *My Life as a Mankiewicz*, The University Press of Kentucky, 2012, p 163

59 Tom Mankiewicz: Interviewed by Dharmesh Chauhan 20.10.2006

60 'Brobdingnagian Bond Film Amid The Pyramids' by Roderick Mann, *Los Angeles Times*, 05.12.1976

61 'Brobdingnagian Bond Film Amid The Pyramids' by Roderick Mann, *Los Angeles Times*, 05.12.1976

62 'Why 007 Must Keep His New Film a Secret' by Roderick Mann, *The Sunday Express*, 15.10.1978

63 'Why 007 Must Keep His New Film a Secret' by Roderick Mann, *The Sunday Express*, 15.10.1978

64 Tony Bennett and Janet Woolacott, *Bond and Beyond: The Political Career of a Popular Hero*, Methuen Inc, New York, 1987, p 196

65 *The Spy Who Loved Me: Also Starring*, Producer: Victor Lockwood, Open University, BBC2, 14.08.1977

66 *The Spy Who Loved Me: Also Starring*, Producer: Victor Lockwood, Open University BBC2, 14.08.1977

67 *The Spy Who Loved Me: Also Starring*, Producer: Victor Lockwood, Open University, BBC2, 14.08.1977

68 Lewis Gilbert with Peter Rankin: *All My Flashbacks*, Reynolds and Hearn, 2010, p 318

69 Lewis Gilbert: Authors' interview, 22.05.2010

70 John Glen: Authors' interview, 06.05.2014

71 'The Marrying Kindness of Curt Jurgens' by Jane Ennis, TV Times, 27.03.1982

72 'The Marrying Kindness of Curt Jurgens' by Jane Ennis, TV Times, 27.03.1982

73 'The Marrying Kindness of Curt Jurgens' by Jane Ennis, TV Times, 27.03.1982

74 Christopher Wood in conversation with Ross Hendry, *The James Bond British Fan Club Convention*, Wembley Conference Centre, 25.04.1982

75 Richard Kiel: Authors' interview, 10.06.2001

76 Richard Kiel: Authors' interview, 10.06.2001

77 Richard Kiel: Authors' interview, 10.06.2001

78 Richard Kiel: Authors' interview, 10.06.2001

79 Caroline Munro: Authors' interview, 29.05.2015

80 Caroline Munro: Authors' interview, 29.05.2015

81 Michael Billington interviewed by Philippe Lombard, February 2003

82 William P. Cartlidge: Authors' interview, 10.01.2015

83 William P. Cartlidge: Authors' interview, 10.01.2015

84 William P. Cartlidge: Authors' interview, 10.01.2015

85 William P. Cartlidge: Authors' interview, 10.01.2015

86 'The Man Who's Ensured 007 Has Kept Up With The Times' by Sue Summers, *Screen International*, 26.02.1977

87 *The Spy Who Loved Me: Designing*, Producer: Victor Lockwood, Open University, BBC2, 31.07.1977

88 Ken Adam: Interviewed by Peter Murray, *The Spy Who Loved Me premiere* (unbroadcast), Odeon Leicester Square, 07.07.1977

89 Ken Adam: Authors' interview, 26.01.2015

90 Lee Pfeiffer and Philip Lisa, *The Incredible World of 007: An Authorized Celebration of James Bond*, Updated Edition, Boxtree, 1995, p. 197

91 Christopher Frayling: *Ken Adam: The Art of Production Design*, Faber and Faber Limited, 2005, p. 181

92 Peter Haining, *James Bond: A Celebration*, W.H Allen/Planet, 1987, p. 133

93 'Behind the Scenes of The Spy Who Loved Me' by David Samuelson, *American Cinematographer*, May 1977

94 Eric Pleskow: Authors' interview, 28.05.2015

95 'Behind the Scenes of The Spy Who Loved Me' by David Samuelson, *American Cinematographer*, May 1977

96 Gareth Owen with Brian Burford, *The Pinewood Story: The Authorised History of the World's Most Famous Film Studio*, Reynolds and Hearn Ltd, 2001, p 119

97 Ken Adam in conversation with Graham Rye, *The James Bond 007 International Fan Club 6th Annual Christmas Lunch*, Pinewood Studios, 21.11.1998

98 Danton Rissner: Authors' interview, 04.06.2015

99 Cubby and Dana Broccoli interviewed by Paul Ryan, Los Angeles cable TV, 1979

100 Rick Sylvester: Authors' interview, 09.03.2015

101 Rick Sylvester: Authors' interview, 09.03.2015

102 John Glen: Authors' interview, 11.04.2001

103 John Glen: Authors' interview, 11.04.2001

104 John Glen: Authors' interview, 11.04.2001

105 Cubby and Dana Broccoli interviewed by Paul Ryan, Los Angeles cable TV, 1979

106 John Glen: Authors' interview, 11.04.2001

107 John Glen with Marcus Hearn: *For My Eyes Only*, B.T Batsford, 2001, p. 13

108 Rick Sylvester: Authors' interview, 08.03.2015

109 John Glen: Authors' interview, 11.04.2001

110 Rick Sylvester: Authors' interview, 09.03.2015

111 Rick Sylvester: Authors' interview, 08.03.2015

112 Rick Sylvester: Authors' interview, 08.03.2015

113 Rick Sylvester: Authors' interview, 08.03.2015

114 John Glen: Authors' interview, 11.04.2001

115 Rick Sylvester: Authors' interview, 08.03.2015

116 Cubby and Dana Broccoli interviewed by Paul Ryan, Los Angeles cable TV, 1979

117 Rick Sylvester: Authors' interview, 08.03.2015

118 Rick Sylvester: Authors' interview, 09.03.2015

119 John Glen: Authors' interview, 11.04.2001

120 Rick Sylvester: Authors' interview, 08.03.2015

121 Cubby and Dana Broccoli interviewed by Paul Ryan, Los Angeles cable TV, 1979

122 Rick Sylvester: Authors' interview, 08.03.2015

123 John Glen: Authors' interview, 11.04.2001

124 John Glen: Authors' interview, 11.04.2001

125 John Glen: Authors' interview, 11.04.2001

126 John Grover: Authors' interview, 12.02.2014

127 Christopher Wood in conversation with Ross Hendry, *The James Bond British Fan Club Convention*, Wembley Conference Centre, 25.04.1982

128 Bob Simmons with Kenneth Passingham, *Nobody Does It Better: My 25 Years with James Bond and Other Stars*, Javelin, 1987, p 118

129 Christopher Wood in conversation with Ross Hendry, *The James Bond British Fan Club Convention*, Wembley Conference Centre, 25.04.1982

130 *The Spy Who Loved Me* production notes, United Artists, 1977

131 'The Lois Maxwell Interview' by Mark Greenberg, *Bondage #12*, The James Bond 007 Fan Club, 1983

132 'Britain's Last Line of Defense' by Graham Rye, *007 Magazine #14*, The James Bond British Fan Club, January 1984

133 Desmond Llewelyn in conversation with Graham Rye, *The James Bond 007 International Fan Club, 6th Annual Christmas Lunch*, 21.11.1998

134 Walter Gotell in conversation with Ross Hendry, *The James Bond British Fan Club Convention*, Westemoreland Hotel, 28-29.03.1981

135 Tony Bennett and Janet Woolacott, *Bond and Beyond: The Political Career of a Popular Hero*, Methuen Inc, New York, 1987, p. 192

136 Richard Kiel: Authors' interview, 10.06.2001

137 Richard Kiel: Authors' interview, 10.06.2001

138 *The Spy Who Loved Me* production notes, United Artists, 1977

139 Caroline Munro: Authors' interview, 29.05.2015

140 Caroline Munro: Authors' interview, 29.05.2015

141 Caroline Munro: Authors' interview, 29.05.2015

142 *James Bond's Cars: 5th Gear Special*, dir: Graham Sherrington, Chrysalis Entertainment, Channel 5, 18.11.2002

143 Christopher Frayling: *Ken Adam: The Art of Production Design*, Faber and Faber Limited, 2005, p. 183

144 Don McCaughlin interviewed by Ross Hendry, *The James Bond British Fan Club Convention*, Westemoreland Hotel, London, 28-29.03.1981

145 Peter Lamont: Authors' interview, 06.10.2000

146 Roger Moore with Gareth Owen, *Bond on Bond*, Michael O'Mara Books Limited, 2012, p. 98

147 Peter Lamont: Authors' interview, 06.10.2000

148 'The Derek Meddings Interview' by Richard Schenkman, *Bondage #9*, The James Bond 007 Fan Club, 1980

149 Michael G. Wilson: *Bond and Beyond: The Movie Magic of Derek Meddings*, The National Museum of Film, Photography & Television, Bradford, 28.05.2000

150 Steven Jay Rubin, *The James Bond Films: A Behind The Scenes History*, 2nd Edition, Arlington House Inc., 1983, p. 142

151 Steven Jay Rubin, *The Complete James Bond Movie Encyclopaedia*, Newly Revised Edition, Contemporary Books, 2003, p. 47

152 Paul Duncan (ed.), *The James Bond Archives*, 'The Pure Essence of James Bond' by Jamie Russell, Taschen, 2012, p. 269

153 Richard Kiel: Authors' interview, 10.06.2001

154 Richard Kiel: Authors' interview, 10.06.2001

155 Christopher Wood in conversation with Ross

156 Lewis Gilbert: Authors' interview, 22.05.2010

157 'Tyler Spy Wetbike donated to IFF' by John Cork, *Goldeneye #1*, The Ian Fleming Foundation, Fall 1992

158 Roger Moore with Gareth Owen, *Bond on Bond*, Michael O'Mara Books Limited, 2012, p. 98

159 'Tyler Spy Wetbike donated to IFF' by John Cork, *Goldeneye #1*, The Ian Fleming Foundation, Fall 1992

160 Tim Greeves, *The Bond Women: 007 Style*, 1 Shot Publications, 2002, p. 50

161 *The Spy Who Loved Me* production notes, United Artists, 1977

162 William P. Cartlidge: Authors' interview, 10.01.2015

163 Roger Moore: Authors' interview, 26.04.2015

164 Lewis Gilbert: *A Celebration of the Life and Work of Cubby Broccoli*, Odeon Leicester Square, 17.11.1996

165 'The Moore Bonds the Merrier' by Lisa Dewson, *007*, Argus Specialist Publications Ltd, 1983

166 John Glen: Authors' interview, 06.05.2014

167 William P. Cartlidge: Authors' interview 29.12.2014

168 Bill Desowitz, *James Bond Unmasked*, Spies LLC, 2012, p. 166

169 Martin Shubrook, *Special Effects Superman: The Art and Effects of Derek Meddings*, Shubrook Bros Publications, 2008, p. 53

170 Ken Adam: Authors' interview, 26.01.2015

171 'This is the Noisiest Bond Ever' by Roy Pickard, *Photoplay*, April 1977

172 Telex from Albert R. Broccoli and Danton Rissner to Cyril Howard, Managing Director of Pinewood Studios, 12.10.1976

173 'Behind the Scenes of The Spy Who Loved Me' by David Samuelson, *American Cinematographer*, May 1977

174 'Behind the Scenes of The Spy Who Loved Me' by David Samuelson, *American Cinematographer*, May 1977

175 Ken Adam: Authors' interview, 26.01.2015

176 Richard Kiel: Authors' interview, 10.06.2001

177 Cubby and Dana Broccoli interviewed by Paul Ryan, Los Angeles cable TV, 1979

178 'The Man Who's Ensured 007 Has Kept Up With The Times' by Sue Summers, *Screen International*, 26.02.1977

179 Peter Haining, *James Bond A Celebration*, W.H Allen/Planet, 1987, p. 122

180 William P. Cartlidge: Authors' interview 29.12.2014

181 Chris Bentley, *Bond and Beyond: The Movie*

Magic of Derek Meddings, National Museum of Photography, Film and Television in association with Fanderson and The James Bond Collectors Club, 27–28th May 2000

182 Jon Burlingame, *The Music of James Bond,* Oxford University Press, 2012, p. 123

183 'James Bond's New Music Man' by Glenys Roberts, *The Times,* 28.03.1977

184 *The Spy Who Loved Me: Also Starring,* Producer: Victor Lockwood, Open University, BBC 2, 14.08.1977

185 *The Spy Who Loved Me: Also Starring,* Producer: Victor Lockwood, Open University, BBC 2, 14.08.1977

186 *The Spy Who Loved Me: Also Starring,* Producer: Victor Lockwood, Open University, BBC 2, 14.08.1977

187 Lewis Gilbert: Authors' interview, 22.05.2010

188 Lewis Gilbert: Authors' interview, 22.05.2010

189 *James Bond's Greatest Hits,* dir: Stephen Franklin, North One, Channel 4, 18.11.2006

190 'Maurice Binder Interview Part 2' by Don McGregor, *Starlog #75,* October 1983

191 'Maurice Binder Interview Part 2' by Don McGregor, *Starlog #75,* October 1983

192 Lewis Gilbert: Interviewed by Peter Murray, *The Spy Who Loved Me premiere* (unbroadcast), Odeon Leicester Square, 07.07.1977

193 John Glen: Authors' interview, 11.04.2001

194 Lee Pfeiffer and Philip Lisa, *The Incredible World of 007: An Authorized Celebration of James Bond,* Updated Edition, Boxtree, 1995, p. 211

195 John Cork and Bruce Scivally, *James Bond: The Legacy,* Boxtree, 2002, p. 174

196 Peter Lamont: Authors' interview, 03.01.2014

197 Sir Ken Adam in conversation with Sir Christopher Frayling at the Museum of Design, London, 06.10.2004

198 Albert R. Broccoli: Interviewed by Peter Murray, *The Spy Who Loved Me premiere* (unbroadcast), Odeon Leicester Square, 07.07.1977

Chapter 16 Moonraker

1 *Weekly Variety,* 25.01.1978

2 *Weekly Variety,* 25.01.1978

3 Michael Deeley with Matthew Field, *Blade Runners, Deer Hunters and Blowing The Bloody Doors Off: My Life In Cult Movies,* Faber and Faber Limited, 2008, p. 5

4 'New Prez Albeck, High On Company's Future, Says He's Eyeing Nippon Prod'n Funds' by Harlan Jacobson, *Daily Variety,* 23.02.1978

5 'New Prez Albeck, High On Company's Future, Says He's Eyeing Nippon Prod'n Funds' by Harlan Jacobson, *Daily Variety,* 23.02.1978

6 United Artists Trade Advert, *Daily Variety,* 01.12.1979

7 'The Man Who Makes 007 Run' by Lee Grant, *Los Angeles Times,* 05.06.1978

8 'Just for *Variety*' by Army Archerd, *Daily Variety,* 18.07.1977

9 'Just for *Variety*' by Army Archerd, *Daily Variety,* 18.07.1977

10 Lewis Gilbert: Authors' interview, 22.05.2010

11 William P. Cartlidge: Authors' interview, 10.01.2015

12 Cubby and Dana Broccoli interviewed by Paul Ryan, Los Angeles cable TV, 1979

13 Cubby and Dana Broccoli interviewed by Paul Ryan, Los Angeles cable TV, 1979

14 'A Panelled Discussion with Broccoli, Gilbert and Adam, Museum of Modern Art' 29.06.1979, *Bondage #9,* The James Bond 007 Fan Club, 1980

15 Tom Mankiewicz: Interviewed by Dharmesh Chauhan, 20.10.2006

16 'The Tom Mankiewicz Interview' by Richard Schenkman, *Bondage #8,* The James Bond 007 Fan Club, 1980

17 'Moonraker Comes At Right Time for Ailing French Studios' by Ted Clark, *Daily Variety,* 18.10.1978

18 Paul Duncan (ed.), *The James Bond Archives,* 'Bigger and Better' by Colin Odell & Michelle Le Blanc, Taschen, 2012, p. 262

19 The Tom Mankiewicz Interview' by Richard Schenkman, *Bondage #8,* The James Bond 007 Fan Club, 1980

20 William P. Cartlidge: Authors' interview, 29.12.2014

21 William P. Cartlidge: Authors' interview, 29.12.2014

22 William P. Cartlidge: Authors' interview, 29.12.2014

23 Christopher Frayling, *Ken Adam: The Art of Production Design,* Faber and Faber Limited, 2005 p. 185

24 William P. Cartlidge: Authors' interview, 29.12.2014

25 Lewis Gilbert: Authors' interview, 22.05.2010

26 Paul Duncan (ed.), *The James Bond Archives,* 'Bigger and Better' by Colin Odell & Michelle Le Blanc, Taschen, 2012, p. 262

27 Paul Duncan (ed.), *The James Bond Archives,* 'Bigger and Better' by Colin Odell & Michelle Le Blanc, Taschen, 2012, p. 284

28 Christopher Wood in conversation with Ross Hendry, *The James Bond British Fan Club Convention,* Wembley Conference Centre,

29 Christopher Wood in conversation with Ross Hendry, *The James Bond British Fan Club Convention*, Wembley Conference Centre, 25.04.1982

30 Christopher Wood, *The Spy I Loved*, Twenty First Century Publishers, 2006, p. 131

31 Christopher Wood in conversation with Ross Hendry, *The James Bond British Fan Club Convention*, Wembley Conference Centre, 25.04.1982

32 Christopher Wood in conversation with Ross Hendry, *The James Bond British Fan Club Convention*, Wembley Conference Centre, 25.04.1982

33 Christopher Wood in conversation with Ross Hendry, *The James Bond British Fan Club Convention*, Wembley Conference Centre, 25.04.1982

34 Paul Duncan (ed.), *The James Bond Archives*, 'Bigger and Better' by Colin Odell & Michelle Le Blanc, Taschen, 2012, p. 284

35 Dick Clement and Ian La Frenais: Authors' interview, 09.04.2015

36 Dick Clement and Ian La Frenais: Authors' interview, 09.04.2015

37 Dick Clement and Ian La Frenais: Authors' interview, 09.04.2015

38 Dick Clement and Ian La Frenais: Authors' interview, 09.04.2015

39 William P. Cartlidge: Authors' interview, 24.10.2014

40 William P. Cartlidge: Authors' interview, 24.10.2014

41 William P. Cartlidge: Authors' interview, 24.10.2014

42 Christopher Frayling, *Ken Adam: The Art of Production Design*, Faber and Faber Limited, 2005, p. 184

43 William P. Cartlidge: Authors' interview, 24.10.2014

44 William P. Cartlidge: Authors' interview, 24.10.2014

45 'Moonraker Comes At Right Time for ailing French Studios' by Ted Clark, *Daily Variety*, 18.10.1978

46 William P. Cartlidge: Authors' interview, 24.10.2014

47 'The Albert R. Broccoli Interview' by Richard Schenkman, *Bondage #5:*, The James Bond Fan Club, Winter 1978

48 Steven Swan (ed.), *Moonraker Official Souvenir Brochure*, 'Production Notes' by Steven Swan, Fenited Publishing Corp, 1979

49 Steven Swan (ed.), *Moonraker Official Souvenir Brochure*, 'Space–Age Bond' by Steven Swan, Fenited Publishing Corp, 1979

50 William P. Cartlidge: Authors' interview 10.01.2015

51 Christopher Frayling, *Ken Adam: The Art of Production Design*, Faber and Faber Limited, 2005, p. 185

52 Roger Moore with Gareth Owen, *My Word is My Bond*, Michael O'Mara, 2008, p. 222

53 'Moore Defies The Gravity Of It All' by Roderick Mann, *Los Angeles Times*, 01.07.1979

54 Paul Duncan (ed.), *The James Bond Archives*, 'Bigger and Better' by Colin Odell & Michelle Le Blanc, Taschen, 2012, p. 284

55 'Moore Defies The Gravity Of It All' by Roderick Mann, *Los Angeles Times*, 01.07.1979

56 *Moonraker Annual*, World and Whitman, 1979, p. 20

57 'Over The Moon' by Alan Markfield, *Daily Mirror*, 27.06.1979

58 'Over The Moon' by Alan Markfield, *Daily Mirror*, 27.06.1979

59 'Her Turn With James Bond Resounds' by Peter Lattman, *The New York Times*, 08.11.2012

60 '007 Faces a Foxy Feminist: Lois Chiles' by Peter Lester, *People Weekly*, 13.08.1979

61 'Bond Meets His Match' by Colin Dangaard, *Daily Express*, 15.06.1979

62 Roger Moore with Gareth Owen, *Bond On Bond*, Michael O'Mara Books Limited, 2012, p. 43

63 Michael Lonsdale: Authors' interview, 22.04.2015

64 Michael Lonsdale: Authors' interview, 22.04.2015

65 'A Panelled Discussion with Broccoli, Gilbert and Adam, Museum of Modern Art' 29.06.1979, *Bondage #9*, The James Bond 007 Fan Club, 1980

66 Richard Kiel: Authors' interview, 17.06.2001

67 Richard Kiel: Authors' interview, 17.06.2001

68 Richard Kiel: Authors' interview, 17.06.2001

69 Richard Kiel: Authors' interview, 17.06.2001

70 Richard Kiel: Authors' interview, 10.06.2001

71 Richard Kiel: Authors' interview, 17.06.2001

72 Richard Kiel: Authors' interview, 17.06.2001

73 Christopher Wood in conversation with Ross Hendry, *The James Bond British Fan Club Convention*, Wembley Conference Centre, 25.04.1982

74 Michael Lonsdale: Authors' interview, 22.04.2015

75 Lewis Gilbert: Authors' interview, 22.05.2010

76 'Vision Problems Cause Renoir To Exit Moonraker' *Daily Variety*, 14.08.1978

77 William P. Cartlidge: Authors' interview, 10.01.2015

78 William P. Cartlidge: Authors' interview, 10.01.2015

79 'Vision Problems Cause Renoir To Exit Moonraker' *Daily Variety*, 14.08.1978

80   William P. Cartlidge: Authors' interview, 10.01.2015

81   *Moonraker* production notes, United Artists, 1979

82   John Glen: Authors' interview, 06.05.2014

83   John Glen: Authors' interview, 06.05.2014

84   John Glen: Authors' interview, 06.05.2014

85   John Glen: Authors' interview, 06.05.2014

86   John Glen: Authors' interview, 06.05.2014

87   John Glen with Marcus Hearn, *For My Eyes Only*, B.T. Batsford, 2001, p. 101

88   John Glen with Marcus Hearn, *For My Eyes Only*, B.T. Batsford, 2001, p. 101

89   John Glen: Authors' interview, 06.05.2014

90   'Developing A Special Bond Between Fall–Guy And Camera – a unique shooting challenge for all' by B.J.Worth, *GBCT News* Vol. 1 No.12, June 1979

91   'Developing A Special Bond Between Fall–Guy And Camera – a unique shooting challenge for all' by B J.Worth, *GBCT News* Vol. 1 No.12, June 1979

92   John Glen: Authors' interview, 06.05.2014

93   John Glen: Authors' interview, 06.05.2014

94   John Glen: Authors' interview, 06.05.2014

95   Jeff Rovin (ed.), *The Official Moonraker Magazine,* 'Moonraker: Sets and Special effects' Warren Publishing Company, 1979

96   Jeff Rovin (ed.), *The Official Moonraker Magazine,* 'Moonraker: Sets and Special effects' Warren Publishing Company, 1979

97   William P. Cartlidge: Authors' interview, 10.01.2015

98   'The Roger Moore Interview' by David Giamarco, *007 Magazine #15,* The James Bond British Fan Club, 1984

99   Michael Lonsdale: Authors' interview 22.04.2015

100   Paul Duncan (ed.), *The James Bond Archives,* 'Bigger and Better' by Colin Odell & Michelle Le Blanc, Taschen, 2012, p. 262

101   William P. Cartlidge: Authors' interview, 10.01.2015

102   William P. Cartlidge: Authors' interview, 10.01.2015

103   William P. Cartlidge: Authors' interview, 10.01.2015

104   John Glen with Marcus Hearn, *For My Eyes Only*, B.T. Batsford, 2000, p. 105

105   Christopher Wood, *The Spy I Loved,* Twenty First Century Publishers, 2006, p. 132

106   John Glen with Marcus Hearn, *For My Eyes Only*, B.T. Batsford, 2000, p. 125

107   Roger Moore with Gareth Owen, *My Word is My Bond,* Michael O'Mara, 2008, p. 225

108   Desmond Llewelyn: Authors' interview, 23.04.1999

109   *Moonraker Annual,* World and Whitman, 1979, p. 32

110   'Secrets of 007' by Jonathan Margolis, *The Sydney Morning Herald,* 31.08.1986

111   John Glen: Authors' interview, 11.04.2001

112   Michael Lonsdale: Authors' interview, 22.04.2015

113   Richard Kiel: Authors' interview, 16.06.2001

114   Richard Kiel: Authors' interview, 16.06.2001

115   John Grover: Authors' interview, 12.02.2014

116   Peter Davies: Authors' interview, 03.06.2005

117   'Moore Defies the Gravity of it All' by Roderick Mann, *Los Angeles Times,* 01.07.1979

118   Michael Lonsdale: Authors' interview, 22.04.2015

119   William P. Cartlidge: Authors' interview, 10.01.2015

120   William P. Cartlidge: Authors' interview, 10.01.2015

121   William P. Cartlidge: Authors' interview, 10.01.2015

122   William P. Cartlidge: Authors' interview, 10.01.2015

123   'Tough At The Top' by Victor Davis, *Daily Express,* 19.02.1979

124   '007 x 4: John Richardson' by Nora Lee, *Cinefex* #33, February 1988

125   '007 x 4: John Richardson' by Nora Lee, *Cinefex* #33, February 1988

126   '007 x 4: John Richardson' by Nora Lee, *Cinefex* #33, February 1988

127   '007 x 4: John Richardson' by Nora Lee, *Cinefex* #33, February 1988

128   '007 x 4: John Richardson' by Nora Lee, *Cinefex* #33, February 1988

129   '007 x 4: John Richardson' by Nora Lee, *Cinefex* 3#3, February 1988

130   '007 x 4: John Richardson' by Nora Lee, *Cinefex* #33, February 1988

131   '007 x 4: John Richardson' by Nora Lee, *Cinefex* #33, February 1988

132   William P. Cartlidge: Authors' interview, 10.01.2015

133   William P. Cartlidge: Authors' interview, 10.01.2015

134   William P. Cartlidge: Authors' interview, 10.01.2015

135   *30 Years of James Bond,* dir: Lorna Dickinson & Alasdair Macmillan, London Weekend Television, 03.10.1992

136   *30 Years of James Bond,* dir: Lorna Dickinson & Alasdair Macmillan, London Weekend Television, 03.10.1992

137   Martin Grace: Interviewed by Anders Frejdh, October 2009

138   Lewis Gilbert: Authors' interview, 22.05.2010

139   Lem Pitkin and Joseph Kay (ed.), *The Official*

Moonraker Movie Poster Book, Starlog, 1979

140 John Glen: Authors' interview, 11.04.2001

141 Steven Swan (ed.), *Moonraker Official Souvenir Brochure*, Fenited Publishing Corp, 1979

142 Paul Duncan (ed.), *The James Bond Archives*, 'Bigger and Better' by Colin Odell & Michelle Le Blanc, Taschen, 2012, p. 298

143 Jeff Rovin (ed.), *The Official Moonraker Magazine*, 'Albert R. Broccoli Interviewed' by Richard Meyers, Warren Publishing Company, 1979

144 Steven Swan (ed.), *Moonraker Official Souvenir Brochure*, 'Space–Age Bond' by Steven Swan, Fenited Publishing Corp, 1979

145 Jeff Rovin (ed.), *The Official Moonraker Magazine*, 'Moonraker: Sets and Special Effects' Warren Publishing Company, 1979

146 Colin Miller: Authors' interview, 07.05.2014

147 Paul Duncan (ed.), *The James Bond Archives*, 'Bigger and Better' by Colin Odell & Michelle Le Blanc, Taschen, 2012, p. 298

148 Jeff Rovin (ed.), *The Official Moonraker Magazine*, 'Moonraker: Sets and Special Effects' Warren Publishing Company, 1979

149 Jeff Rovin (ed.), *The Official Moonraker Magazine*, 'Moonraker: Sets and Special effects' Warren Publishing Company, 1979

150 'Derek Meddings: The Man Who Creates The Magic For James Bond' by Don McGregor, *Starlog* #49, February 1981

151 William P. Cartlidge: Authors' interview, 24.10.2014

152 Paul Weston: Authors' interview, 08.04.2014

153 'Moore Defies the Gravity of it All' by Roderick Mann, *Los Angeles Times*, 01.07.1979

154 Peter Haining, *James Bond A Celebration*, W.H Allen/Planet Books, 1987, p. 134

155 Steven Bach, *Final Cut: Dreams and Disaster in the Making of Heaven's Gate*, Faber and Faber, 1986 p. 193

156 Jeff Rovin (ed.), *The Official Moonraker Magazine*, 'Moonraker: Sets and Special effects' Warren Publishing Company, 1979

157 Paul Duncan (ed.), *The James Bond Archives*, 'Bigger and Better' by Colin Odell & Michelle Le Blanc, Taschen, 2012, p. 299

158 'The Derek Meddings Interview' by Richard Schenkman, *Bondage* #9, The James Bond 007 Fan Club, 1980

159 Steven Swan (ed.), *Moonraker Official Souvenir Brochure*, Fenited Publishing Corp, 1979

160 John Glen: Authors' interview, 06.05.2014

161 John Glen: Authors' interview, 06.05.2014

162 John Burlingame, *The Music of James Bond*,

163 John Burlingame, *The Music of James Bond*, Oxford University Press, 2012, p. 137

164 'Kate's No to 007' by Garth Pearce, *Daily Express*, 23.05.1979

165 John Glen: Authors' interview, 11.04.2001

166 *The Real John Barry* written and produced by Stuart Grundy, Unique Broadcasting, BBC Radio 2, 26.01.2001

167 Geoff Leonard, Pete Walker, Gareth Bramley, *John Barry: The Man with the Midas Touch*, Redcliffe Press Ltd, 2008, p. 90

168 Geoff Leonard, Pete Walker, Gareth Bramley, *John Barry: The Man with the Midas Touch*, Redcliffe Press Ltd, 2008 p. 90

169 *James Bond's Greatest Hits*, dir: Stephen Franklin, North One, Channel 4, 18.11.2006

170 'Maurice Binder at the Museum of Modern Art' *Bondage* #10, The James Bond 007 Fan Club, 1981

171 'Maurice Binder at the Museum of Modern Art' *Bondage* #10, The James Bond 007 Fan Club, 1981

172 John Grover: Authors' interview, 12.02.2014

173 'At The Movies' by Tom Buckley, *The New York Times*, 14.01.1978

174 William P. Cartlidge: Authors' interview, 24.10.2014

175 William P. Cartlidge: Authors' interview, 08.04.2014

176 William P. Cartlidge: Authors' interview, 08.04.2015

177 Jeff Rovin (ed.), *The Official Moonraker Magazine*, 'Albert R. Broccoli Interviewed' by Richard Meyers, Warren Publishing Company, 1979

178 Peter Lamont: Authors' interview, 03.01.2014

179 Cubby and Dana Broccoli interviewed by Paul Ryan, Los Angeles cable TV, 1979

180 *Moonraker Annual*, World and Whitman, 1979, p. 20

181 'Adventures with the Bond Set' by Steve Swan, *Moonraker Annual*, World and Whitman, 1979, p 16

182 David Giammarco, *For Your Eyes Only: Behind The Scenes of the James Bond Films*, ECW, 2002, p. 167

183 William P. Cartlidge: Authors' interview, 10.01.2015

184 Ken Adam: Authors' interview, 26.01.2015

185 Steven Bach, *Final Cut: Dreams and Disaster in the Making of Heaven's Gate*, Faber and Faber, 1986, p. 193

Chapter 17 For Your Eyes Only

1   John Cork and Bruce Scivally, *James Bond: The Legacy*, Boxtree, 2002, p. 186

2   Barry Norman, *and why not (as I never did say)? Memoirs Of A Film Lover*, Simon and Schuster Ltd, 2002, p. 259

3   Roy Moseley with Philip and Martin Masheter, *Roger Moore: A Biography*, New English Library, 1985, p. 259

4   Alan Barnes and Marcus Hearn, *Kiss Kiss Bang! Bang! The Unofficial James Bond Film Companion*, B.T. Batsford, 2nd Edition, 2000, p. 135

5   Albert R. Broccoli with Donald Zec, *When the Snow Melts*, Boxtree, 1998, pp. 280–1

6   David Giammarco, *For Your Eyes Only Behind The Scenes Of The James Bond Films*, ECW Press, 2002, p. 198

7   Martin Sterling and Gary Morecambe, *Martinis, Girls and Guns: 50 Years of 007*, Robson Books Ltd, 2002, p. 236

8   Paul Donovan, *Roger Moore*, W. H. Allen, 1983, p. 162

9   'For Your Eyes Only Press Conference' Warwick Hotel, New York, by Richard Schenkman, *Bondage #11*, The James Bond 007 Fan Club, 1981

10 'For Your Eyes Only Press Conference' Warwick Hotel, New York, by Richard Schenkman, *Bondage #11*, The James Bond 007 Fan Club, 1981

11 John Cork and Bruce Scivally, *James Bond: The Legacy*, Boxtree, 2002, p. 186

12 John Glen with Marcus Hearn, *For My Eyes Only*, B.T. Batsford, 2001, p. 109

13 John Glen with Marcus Hearn, *For My Eyes Only*, B.T. Batsford, 2001, p. 110

14 'John Glen Signed To Direct Next James Bond Pic' *Daily Variety*, 25.06.1980

15 John Glen: Authors' interview, 11.04.2001

16 Peter Lamont: Authors' interview, 03.01.2014

17 Peter Lamont: Authors' interview, 03.01.2014

18 Peter Lamont: Authors' interview, 03.01.2014

19 Peter Lamont: Authors' interview, 03.01.2014

20 Peter Lamont: Authors' interview, 03.01.2014

21 Alan Hume with Gareth Owen, *A Life Through The Lens*, MacFarland and Company Inc. Publishers, 2004, p. 117

22 Peter Lamont: Authors' interview, 11.04.2001

23 Alec Mills, *Shooting 007 And Other Celluloid Adventures*, The History Press, 2014, p. 169

24 John Glen with Marcus Hearn, *For My Eyes Only*, B.T. Batsford, 2001, p. 117

25 John Glen: Authors' interview, 11.04.2001

26 John Glen: Authors' interview, 11.04.2001

27 John Glen: Authors' interview, 11.04.2001

28 John Glen: Authors' interview, 11.04.2001

29 David Giammarco, *For Your Eyes Only Behind*

     The Scenes Of The James Bond Films, ECW Press, 2002, p. 175

30 'Richard Maibaum Veteran Screenwriter For A Brand New Bond' *Starlog #120*, July 1987

31 John Glen with Marcus Hearn, *For My Eyes Only*, B.T. Batsford, 2001, p. 111

32 'Richard Maibaum Veteran Screenwriter For A Brand New Bond' *Starlog #120*, July 1987

33 'Richard Maibaum Veteran Screenwriter For A Brand New Bond' *Starlog #120*, July 1987

34 'Albert R. Broccoli' by Adam Pirani, *Starlog #99*, October 1985

35 John Glen with Marcus Hearn, *For My Eyes Only*, B.T. Batsford, 2001, p. 110

36 'James Bond Returns Director John Glen' by Stephen Payne and Gary Russell, *Starburst*, #107, July 1987

37 John Glen with Marcus Hearn, *For My Eyes Only*, B.T. Batsford, 2001, p. 111

38 'Richard Maibaum Veteran Screenwriter For A Brand New Bond' *Starlog #120*, July 1987

39 'Richard Maibaum 007's Puppetmaster' by Lee Goldberg, *Starlog #68*, March 1983

40 'The John Glen Interview' by Richard Schenkman and Tom Sciacca, *Bondage #12*, The James Bond 007 Fan Club, 1983

41 'The John Glen Interview' by Richard Schenkman and Tom Sciacca, *Bondage #12*, The James Bond 007 Fan Club, 1983

42 John Glen: Authors' interview, 11.04.2001

43 'The John Glen Interview' by Richard Schenkman and Tom Sciacca, *Bondage #12*, The James Bond 007 Fan Club, 1983

44 John Glen: Authors' interview, 11.04.2001

45 'The John Glen Interview' by Richard Schenkman and Tom Sciacca, *Bondage #12*, The James Bond 007 Fan Club, 1983

46 'James Bond Returns Director John Glen' by Stephen Payne and Gary Russell, *Starburst*, #107, July 1987

47 John Glen: Authors' interview, 11.04.2001

48 'For Your Eyes Only Press Conference' Warwick Hotel, New York, by Richard Schenkman, *Bondage #11*, The James Bond 007 Fan Club, 1981

49 John Glen: Authors' interview, 11.04.2001

50 Michael Billington: Interviewed by Philippe Lombard, February 2003

51 Michael Billington: Interviewed by Philippe Lombard, February 2003

52 Michael Billington: Interviewed by Philippe Lombard, February 2003

53 Alan Hume with Gareth Owen, *A Life Through The Lens*, MacFarland and Company Inc. Publishers, 2004, p. 117

54 Alan Hume with Gareth Owen, *A Life Through*

The Lens, MacFarland and Company Inc. Publishers, 2004, p. 117

55 Roger Moore with Gareth Owen, *My Word is My Bond*, Michael O'Mara Books Ltd, 2008, p. 295

56 Roger Moore: Authors' interview, 26.04.2015

57 'On Location with A View To A Kill' by Lee Goldberg, *Starlog #92*, March 1985

58 Debbie McWilliams: Authors' interview, 28.09.2016

59 Tim Greaves, *The Bond Women 007 Style*, 1–Shot Publications, 2002, p. 60

60 John Glen with Marcus Hearn, *For My Eyes Only*, B.T. Batsford, 2001, p. 112

61 Tim Greaves, *The Bond Women 007 Style*, 1–Shot Publications, 2002, p. 60

62 Tim Greaves, *The Bond Women 007 Style*, 1–Shot Publications, 2002, p. 60

63 Albert R. Broccoli with Donald Zec, *When the Snow Melts*, Boxtree, 1998, p. 255

64 Albert R. Broccoli with Donald Zec, *When the Snow Melts*, Boxtree, 1998, p. 255

65 'For Your Eyes Only Press Conference' Warwick Hotel, New York, by Richard Schenkman, *Bondage #11*, The James Bond 007 Fan Club, 1981

66 'For Your Eyes Only Press Conference' Warwick Hotel, New York, by Richard Schenkman, *Bondage #11*, The James Bond 007 Fan Club, 1981

67 Julian Glover: Unpublished interview by Richard Toogood, 20.10.1999

68 Julian Glover: Authors' interview, 27.04.2015

69 Julian Glover: Authors' interview, 27.04.2015

70 Lynn Holly Johnson: Authors' interview, 30.05.2015

71 Lynn Holly Johnson: Authors' interview, 30.05.2015

72 Tim Greaves, *The Bond Women 007 Style*, 1–Shot Publications, 2002, p. 12

73 John Glen with Marcus Hearn, *For My Eyes Only*, B.T. Batsford, 2001, p. 112

74 *For Your Eyes Only* production notes, United Artists, 1981

75 Alan Hume with Gareth Owen, *A Life Through The Lens*, MacFarland and Company Inc. Publishers, 2004, p. 117

76 'On Location with A View To A Kill' by Lee Goldberg, *Starlog #92*, March 1985

77 John Glen: Authors' interview, 11.04.2001

78 John Glen: Authors' interview, 11.04.2001

79 Rémy Julienne: Authors' interview, 21.10.2008

80 Rémy Julienne: Authors' interview, 21.10.2008

81 'The Citroën Interview: John Glen A Sense Of Direction' by Anne Gregg, *Citroën Magazine #6*, June 1981

82 David Giammarco, *For Your Eyes Only Behind The Scenes Of The James Bond Films*, ECW

Press, 2002, p. 175

83 'Licensed To Thrill' by Edward Gross, *Starlog Yearbook*, Vol. 5, 1989

84 John Glen with Marcus Hearn, *For My Eyes Only*, B.T. Batsford, 2001, p. 118

85 Julian Glover: Authors' interview, 27.04.2015

86 Pierce Brosnan: Authors' interview, 23.05.2015

87 John Glen: Authors' interview, 11.04.2001

88 John Cork and Bruce Scivally, *James Bond: The Legacy*, Boxtree, 2002, p. 190

89 'For Your Eyes Only Press Conference' Warwick Hotel, New York, by Richard Schenkman, *Bondage #11*, The James Bond 007 Fan Club, 1981

90 John Cork and Bruce Scivally, *James Bond: The Legacy*, Boxtree, 2002, p. 190

91 Rick Sylvester: Authors' interview, 09.03.2015

92 Rick Sylvester: Authors' interview, 09.03.2015

93 Rick Sylvester: Authors' interview, 09.03.2015

94 Desmond Llewelyn: Authors' interview, 23.04.1999

95 John Glen: Authors' interview, 11.04.2001

96 Alan Barnes and Marcus Hearn, *Kiss Kiss Bang! Bang! The Unofficial James Bond Film Companion*, B.T. Batsford, 2nd Edition, 2000, p. 13

97 Sandy Hernu, *Q: The Biography of Desmond Llewelyn*, S.B. Publications, 1999, p. 112

98 Sandy Hernu, *Q: The Biography of Desmond Llewelyn*, S.B. Publications, 1999, p. 112

99 'Moneypenny Talks' by Anwar Brett, *Film Review Special #21*, 1997

100 *For Your Eyes Only: The Royal Premiere*, dir: Steve Minchin, Thames Television, 24.06.1981

101 'For Your Eyes Only and It's Special Effects' by David Samuelson, *American Cinematographer*, Vol.62 No. 8, August 1981

102 Martin Grace: Interview with Anders Frejdh, October 2009

103 'For Your Eyes Only Press Conference' Warwick Hotel, New York, by Richard Schenkman, *Bondage #11*, The James Bond 007 Fan Club, 1981

104 'For Your Eyes Only Press Conference' Warwick Hotel, New York, by Richard Schenkman, *Bondage #11*, The James Bond 007 Fan Club, 1981

105 Rémy Julienne: Authors' interview, 21.10.2008

106 Bill Conti: *The Monday Movie Hour*, Producer Andy Wilson introduced by John Benson, BBC Radio 2, 23.03.1987

107 Bill Conti: *The Monday Movie Hour*, Producer Andy Wilson introduced by John Benson, BBC Radio 2, 23.03.198

108 'For Your Eyes Only Press Conference' Warwick Hotel, New York, by Richard Schenkman, *Bondage #11*, The James Bond 007 Fan Club, 1981

109 'Maurice Binder' by Don McGregor, *Starlog*

#75, October 1983

110 'For Your Eyes Only Press Conference' Warwick Hotel, New York, by Richard Schenkman, Bondage #11, The James Bond 007 Fan Club, 1981

111 'Maurice Binder, Part Two' by Don McGregor, Starlog #75, October 1983

112 'Maurice Binder Sighting Down a Gun Barrel At 007' by Don McGregor, Starlog #74, September 1983

113 'Maurice Binder, Part Two' by Don McGregor, Starlog #75, October 1983

114 Hilary Saltzman: Authors' interview, 29.11.2011

115 Pierce Brosnan: Authors' interview, 23.05.2015

Chapter 18 Octopussy

1 Stephen Bach, Final Cut Dreams and Disaster in the Making of Heaven's Gate, Faber and Faber Ltd, 1986, pp. 386–87

2 'Norbert Auerbach Assumes UA Chief Exec Officer Slot; Albeck In Consultant Role' by Will Turner, Daily Variety, 19.02.1981

3 'Norbert Auerbach Assumes UA Chief Exec Officer Slot; Albeck In Consultant Role by Will Turner, Daily Variety, 19.02.1981

4 'Norbert Auerbach Assumes UA Chief Exec Officer Slot; Albeck In Consultant Role by Will Turner, Daily Variety, 19.02.1981

5 'In London with Earnie Player' Daily Variety, 13.10.1960

6 'UA OK $25 Mil Budget for Next Bond: "Octopussy"' Daily Variety, 16.04.1981

7 'UA OK $25 Mil Budget for Next Bond: "Octopussy"' Daily Variety, 16.04.1981

8 'Boards Approve UA Sale to MGM' Daily Variety, 22.05.1981

9 Stephen Bach, Final Cut Dreams and Disaster in the Making of Heaven's Gate, Faber and Faber Ltd, 1986, pp. 386–87

10 Stephen Bach, Final Cut Dreams and Disaster in the Making of Heaven's Gate, Faber and Faber Ltd, 1986, pp. 386–87

11 Stephen Bach, Final Cut Dreams and Disaster in the Making of Heaven's Gate, Faber and Faber Ltd, 1986, pp. 386–87

12 'Begelman Takes Over Top UA Spot' by Will Tusher, Daily Variety, 02.10.1981

13 'For Your Eyes Only press conference' by Richard Schenkman, Bondage #11, The James Bond 007 Fan Club, 1981

14 Peter Bart, Fade Out The Calamitous Final Days of MGM, William Morrow and Company Inc., 1990, p. 68

15 54th Academy Awards, 29th March 1982, Dorothy Chandler Pavilion, Los Angeles

16 54th Academy Awards, 29th March 1982, Dorothy Chandler Pavilion, Los Angeles

17 'A Happy Birthday for Cubby Broccoli' by Jody Jacobs, Los Angeles Times, 06.04.1982

18 'A Happy Birthday for Cubby Broccoli' by Jody Jacobs, Los Angeles Times, 06.04.1982

19 'A Happy Birthday for Cubby Broccoli' by Jody Jacobs, Los Angeles Times, 06.04.1982

20 'Controversy Over Bond Title Can Only Help Film, Broccoli Says' by Robert Osborne, The Hollywood Reporter, 12.04.1982

21 'For Your Eyes Only Press Conference' Warwick Hotel, New York, by Richard Schenkman, Bondage #11, The James Bond 007 Fan Club, 1981

22 'American Actor as Next 007?' by Roderick Mann, Los Angeles Times, 29.06.1982

23 'Broccoli and Moore: Still No Bond' by Roderick Mann, Los Angeles Times, 15.06.1982

24 'Broccoli and Moore: Still No Bond' by Roderick Mann, Los Angeles Times, 15.06.1982

25 Janet Hirshenson and Jane Jenkins with Rachel Kranz, A Star Is Found, Harcourt Inc., 2007, p. 37

26 Janet Hirshenson and Jane Jenkins with Rachel Kranz, A Star Is Found, Harcourt Inc., 2007, p. 37

27 'He Who Dared' by Mac McSharry and Terry Hine, Cinema Retro #4, 2006

28 'Now The Stud Is In Line To Take Over as 007' by Judith Simons, Daily Express, 21.05.1982

29 'Broccoli and Moore: Still No Bond' by Roderick Mann, Los Angeles Times, 15.06.1982

30 Michael Billington interviewed by Philippe Lombard, February 2003

31 'American Actor as Next 007?' by Roderick Mann, Los Angeles Times, 29.06.1982

32 Maud Adams: Authors' interview, 12.04.2015

33 John Glen: Authors' interview, 11.04.2001

34 'Moore Still Ponders New Bond Role' by Roderick Mann, Los Angeles Times, 27.04.1982

35 'Broccoli and Moore: Still No Bond' by Roderick Mann, Los Angeles Times, 15.06.1982

36 'Broccoli and Moore: Still No Bond' by Roderick Mann, Los Angeles Times, 15.06.1982

37 'Roger Moore Back On As James Bond' Daily Variety, 13.07.1982

38 Janine Glen (née King): Authors' interview, 07.05.2015

39 'The John Glen Interview' by Richard Schenkman and Tom Sciacca, Bondage #12, The James Bond 007 Fan Club, 1983

40 'The John Glen Interview' by Richard Schenkman and Tom Sciacca, Bondage #12, The James Bond 007 Fan Club, 1983

41 Howard Zimmerman (ed.), *The Official Octopussy Movie Magazine*, Starlog, 1983

42 John Glen: Authors' interview, 11.04.2001

43 George MacDonald Fraser, *The Light's On At Signpost*, Harper Collins Publishers, 2003, p. 236

44 George MacDonald Fraser, *The Light's On At Signpost*, Harper Collins Publishers, 2003, p. 242

45 John Glen: Authors' interview, 11.04.2001

46 John Glen: Authors' interview, 11.04.2001

47 'Peter Lamont interview' *MI6 Confidential #21*, July 2013

48 John Glen: Authors' interview, 11.04.2001

49 'Richard Maibaum 007's Puppetmaster' by Lee Goldberg, *Starlog #68*, March 1983

50 'Richard Maibaum 007's Puppetmaster' by Lee Goldberg, *Starlog #68*, March 1983

51 'On the Set of Octopussy' by Richard Holliss, *Starlog #71*, June 1983

52 'On the Set of Octopussy' by Richard Holliss, *Starlog #71*, June 1983

53 'On the Set of Octopussy' by Richard Holliss, *Starlog #71*, June 1983

54 'Controversy Over Bond Title Can Only Help Film, Broccoli Says' by Robert Osborne, *The Hollywood Reporter*, 12.04.1982

55 'Controversy Over Bond Title Can Only Help Film, Broccoli Says' by Robert Osborne, *The Hollywood Reporter*, 12.04.1982

56 'Controversy Over Bond Title Can Only Help Film, Broccoli Says' by Robert Osborne, *The Hollywood Reporter*, 12.04.1982

57 'Moore Still Ponders New Bond Role' by Roderick Mann, *Los Angeles Times*, 27.04.1982

58 'Moore Still Ponders New Bond Role' by Roderick Mann, *Los Angeles Times*, 27.04.1982

59 'Moore Still Ponders New Bond Role' by Roderick Mann, *Los Angeles Times*, 27.04.1982

60 John Glen: Authors' interview, 11.04.2001

61 'Moore Still Ponders New Bond Role' by Roderick Mann, *Los Angeles Times*, 27.04.1982

62 Michael Billington interviewed by Philippe Lombard, February 2003

63 Janet Hirshenson and Jane Jenkins with Rachel Kranz, *A Star Is Found*, Harcourt Inc., 2007, p. 36

64 Janet Hirshenson and Jane Jenkins with Rachel Kranz, *A Star Is Found*, Harcourt Inc., 2007, p. 36

65 'On Location with A View To A Kill' by Lee Goldberg, *Starlog #92*, March 1985

66 John Glen: Authors' interview, 11.04.2001

67 Janet Hirshenson and Jane Jenkins with Rachel Kranz, *A Star Is Found*, Harcourt Inc., 2007, p. 36

68 Maud Adams: Authors' interview, 12.04.2015

69 Maud Adams: Authors' interview, 12.04.2015

70 John Glen: Authors' interview, 11.04.2001

71 *Octopussy The Royal Premiere*, dir: Jim Pople, Thames Television, 06.06.1983

72 'Moore Still Ponders New Bond Role' by Roderick Mann, *Los Angeles Times*, 27.04.1982

73 Kabir Bedi: Authors' interview, 06.05.2015

74 George MacDonald Fraser, *The Light's On At Signpost*, Harper Collins Publishers, 2003, p. 242

75 Kabir Bedi: Authors' interview, 06.05.2015

76 Kabir Bedi: Authors' interview, 06.05.2015

77 Kristina Wayborn: Authors' interview, 07.05.2015

78 Kristina Wayborn: Authors' interview, 07.05.2015

79 Kristina Wayborn: Authors' interview, 07.05.2015

80 Vijay Amritraj: Authors' interview, 08.06.2015

81 Vijay Amritraj: Authors' interview, 08.06.2015

82 Vijay Amritraj: Authors' interview, 08.06.2015

83 Vijay Amritraj: Authors' interview, 08.06.2015

84 Vijay Amritraj: Authors' interview, 08.06.2015

85 Vijay Amritraj: Authors' interview, 08.06.2015

86 David Meyer: Authors' interview, 08.05.2015

87 David Meyer: Authors' interview, 08.05.2015

88 Steven Berkoff, *Free Association: An Autobiography*, Faber and Faber Limited, 1996, p. 332

89 Roger Moore with Gareth Owen, *My Word is My Bond*, Michael O'Mara Books Ltd, 2008, p. 305

90 'Reporting From the Set of Licence To Kill' by Richard Schenkman, *Bondage #16*, The James Bond Fan 007 Fan Club, Winter 1989

91 'Reporting From the Set of Licence To Kill,' by Richard Schenkman, *Bondage #16*, The James Bond Fan 007 Fan Club, Winter 1989

92 'Richard Maibaum 007's Puppetmaster' by Lee Goldberg, *Starlog #68*, March 1983

93 John Glen: Authors' interview, 11.04.2001

94 John Glen: Authors' interview, 11.04.2001

95 John Glen: Authors' interview, 11.04.2001

96 'On the Set of Octopussy' by Richard Holliss, *Starlog #71*, June 1983

97 'James Bond doesn't do CGI: Inside 007's amazing real–world action' by Gavin Clarke, www.theregister.co.uk, 25.10.2015

98 Alec Mills, *Shooting 007 And Other Celluloid Adventures*, The History Press, 2014, p. 184

99 Philip Wrestler: Authors' interview, 06.09.1999

100 'James Bond doesn't do CGI: Inside 007's amazing real–world action' by Gavin Clarke, www.theregister.co.uk, 25.10.2015

101 'James Bond doesn't do CGI: Inside 007's amazing real–world action' by Gavin Clarke, www.theregister.co.uk, 25.10.2015

102 'James Bond doesn't do CGI: Inside 007's amazing real–world action' by Gavin Clarke,

www.theregister.co.uk, 25.10.2015

103 '007 x 4: John Richardson' by Nora Lee, *Cinefex* #33, February 1988

104 '007 x 4: John Richardson' by Nora Lee, *Cinefex* #33, February 1988

105 'James Bond doesn't do CGI: Inside 007's amazing real–world action' by Gavin Clarke, www.theregister.co.uk, 25.10.2015

106 Philip Wrestler: Authors' interview, 06.09.1999

107 Philip Wrestler: Authors' interview, 06.09.1999

108 John Grover: Authors' interview, 12.02.2014

109 Philip Wrestler: Authors' interview, 06.09.1999

110 Philip Wrestler: Authors' interview, 06.09.1999

111 John Glen: Authors' interview, 11.04.2001

112 Philip Wrestler: Authors' interview, 06.09.1999

113 John Glen: Authors' interview, 11.04.2001

114 Trade Advert, Daily *Variety*, 10.08.1982

115 John Glen with Marcus Hearn, *For My Eyes Only*, B.T. Batsford, 2001, p. 149

116 Peter Lamont: Authors' interview, 03.01.2014

117 John Glen: Authors' interview, 11.04.2001

118 Kristina Wayborn: Authors' interview, 07.05.2015

119 Kabir Bedi: Authors' interview, 06.05.2015

120 Steven Berkoff, *Free Association: An Autobiography*, Faber and Faber Limited, 1996, p. 332

121 Maud Adams: Authors' interview, 12.04.2015

122 Maud Adams: Authors' interview, 12.04.2015

123 Maud Adams: Authors' interview, 12.04.2015

124 Rémy Julienne: Authors' interview, 21.10.2008

125 Howard Zimmerman (ed.), *The Official Octopussy Movie Magazine*, Starlog, 1983

126 Vijay Amritraj: Authors' interview, 08.06.2015

127 'Roger Moore is Agent 007' by Charles Bogle, *Starlog* #72, July 1983

128 Vijay Amritraj: Authors' interview, 08.06.2015

129 Vijay Amritraj: Authors' interview, 08.06.2015

130 'Roger Moore is Agent 007' by Charles Bogle, *Starlog* #72, July 1983

131 David Meyer: Authors' interview, 08.05.2015

132 Martin Grace: Interviewed by Anders Frejdh, October 2009

133 Alan Hume with Gareth Owen, *A Life Through The Lens*, MacFarland and Company Inc. Publishers, 2004, p. 124

134 Martin Grace: Interviewed by Anders Frejdh, October 2009

135 Martin Grace: Interviewed by Anders Frejdh, October 2009

136 Martin Grace: Interviewed by Anders Frejdh, October 2009

137 'Controversy Over Bond Title Can Only Help Film, Broccoli Says' by Robert Osborne, *The Hollywood Reporter*, 12.04.1982

138 'On the Set of Octopussy' by Richard Holliss, *Starlog* #71, June 1983

139 Maud Adams: Authors' interview, 12.04.2015

140 'On the Set of Octopussy' by Richard Holliss, *Starlog* #71, June 1983

141 'On the Set of Octopussy' by Richard Holliss, *Starlog* #71, June 1983

142 Kabir Bedi: Authors' interview, 06.05.2015

143 Steven Berkoff, *Free Association: An Autobiography*, Faber and Faber Limited, 1996, p. 332

144 Steven Berkoff, *Free Association: An Autobiography*, Faber and Faber Limited, 1996, p. 332

145 Maud Adams: Authors' interview, 12.04.2015

146 John Grover: Authors' interview, 12.02.2014

147 Sandy Hernu, *Q: The Biography of Desmond Llewelyn*, S.B. Publications, 1999, p. 118

148 Desmond Llewelyn: Authors' interview, 23.04.1999

149 'The Man Called Q' by Charles Bogle, *Starlog* #72, July 1983

150 Desmond Llewelyn: Authors' interview, 23.04.1999

151 'Secrets of 007' by Jonathan Margolis, *Mail On Sunday*, 10.08.1986

152 Vijay Amritraj: Authors' interview, 08.06.2015

153 Vijay Amritraj: Authors' interview, 08.06.2015

154 John Glen: Authors' interview, 11.04.2001

155 John Glen: Authors' interview, 11.04.2001

156 Roger Moore: Authors' interview, 26.04.2015

157 *James Bond's Greatest Hits*, dir: Stephen Franklin, North One, Channel 4, 18.11.2006

158 *The Real John Barry* written and produced by Stuart Grundy, Unique Broadcasting, BBC Radio 2, 26.01.2001

159 *The Real John Barry* written and produced by Stuart Grundy, Unique Broadcasting, BBC Radio 2, 26.01.2001

160 *James Bond's Greatest Hits*, dir: Stephen Franklin, North One, Channel 4, 18.11.2006

161 *James Bond's Greatest Hits*, dir: Stephen Franklin, North One, Channel 4, 18.11.2006

162 *Tim Rice: A Life In Song,* Royal Festival Hall, Southbank Centre, London 08.07.2014

163 'Maurice Binder, Part Two' by Don McGregor, *Starlog* #75, October 1983

164 *James Bond: The First 21 Years*, dir: John Longley, London Weekend Television, 27.05.1983

165 'Albert R. Broccoli' by Adam Pirani, *Starlog* #99, October 1985

Chapter 19 Never Say Never Again

1   Robert Sellers, *The Battle For Bond: The Genesis of Cinema's Greatest Hero*, Tomahawk Press, First edition, 2008, p 181

2   'They're Playing Chess with James Bond as the Pawn' by David Lewin, *Daily Mail*, 28.04.1976

3   Robert Sellers, *The Battle For Bond: The Genesis of Cinema's Greatest Hero*, Tomahawk Press, First edition, 2008, p 173

4   Len Deighton: Authors' interview, 11.04.2015

5   'Lost Warhead production drawing sells at Christie's for £3,500!' by Graham Rye, *007 Magazine* #52, 2009

6   'Great Scot' by Kurt Loader, *Rolling Stone* #407, 27.10.1983

7   'The Snag That Could Kill Off A New Bond Film' by Roderick Mann, *The Sunday Express*, 11.03.1976

8   'Krim: '007' Soley UA's With Limited '*Thunderball*' Angle' by Arthur B. Krim, *Weekly Variety* 30.06.1976

9   *Film 83* Special with Barry Norman, dir: Jonathan Dent, BBC 1, 12.12.1983

10   'The Snag That Could Kill Off A New Bond Film' by Roderick Mann, *The Sunday Express*, 11.03.1979

11   Michael Freedland, *Sean Connery: A Biography*, Weidenfeld and Nicolson, 1994, p. 225

12   'The Battle of the Bonds' by Alan Markfield, *Woman*, 05.05.1979

13   'Par had rights to Bond script' *Daily Variety*, 28.07.1978

14   'Warhead Back Again With 007' by Roderick Mann, *Los Angeles Times*, 08.05.1979

15   'Warhead Back Again With 007' by Roderick Mann, *Los Angeles Times*, 08.05.1979

16   'British Writs Block McClory and Paramount On Bond Caper' *Weekly Variety*, 08.11.1979

17   'Warhead Back Again With 007' by Roderick Mann, *Los Angeles Times*, 08.05.1979

18   Sean Connery interviewed on *LBC Radio*, 1979

19   Steven Jay Rubin, *The James Bond Films A Behind The Scenes History*, Arlington House Inc., 2nd Edition, 1983, p. 173

20   'Producer Jack Schwartzman Brings 007 Back in the Grand Old Fashion' by Jack Ferguson, *Fantastic Films* #36, November 1983

21   'Producer Jack Schwartzman Brings 007 Back in the Grand Old Fashion' by Jack Ferguson, *Fantastic Films* #36, November 1983

22   'Producer Jack Schwartzman Brings 007 Back in the Grand Old Fashion' by Jack Ferguson, *Fantastic Films* #36, November 1983

23   'Bond Vs. Bond' by Hugh James, *CFQ,* May 1984

24   'Producing "Never Say Never Again" Jack Schwartzman, by Steve Swires, *Starlog* #71, June 1983

25   'Producing "Never Say Never Again" Jack Schwartzman' by Steve Swires, *Starlog* #71, June 1983

26   'Producer Jack Schwartzman Brings 007 Back in the Grand Old Fashion' by Jack Ferguson, *Fantastic Films* #36, November 19833

27   'Producer Jack Schwartzman Brings 007 Back in the Grand Old Fashion' by Jack Ferguson, *Fantastic Films* #36, November 1983

28   'Bond VS. Bond' by Hugh James, *CFQ,* May 1984

29   'Producing "Never Say Never Again" Jack Schwartzman' by Steve Swires, *Starlog* #71, June 1983

30   'Muckraker' by Roger Parsons, *Time Out,* no. 668, (London), 10.06.1983

31   'Muckraker' by Roger Parsons, *Time Out,* no. 668, (London), 10.06.198

32   Sean Connery interviewed by Jim Brown, *The Today Show,* NBC, 1983.

33   'Muckraker' by Roger Parsons, *Time Out,* no. 668, (London), 10.06.198

34   Robert Slater, *Ovitz: The Inside Story Of Hollywood's Most Powerful Power Broker,* McGraw Hill, 1997, p. 181

35   Sean Connery interviewed by Marjorie Bilbow, *Starsound*, BBC Radio 2, 15.12.1983

36   'Producer Jack Schwartzman Brings 007 Back in the Grand Old Fashion' by Jack Ferguson, *Fantastic Films* #36, November 19833

37   *Film 83* Special with Barry Norman, dir: Jonathan Dent, BBC 1, 12.12.1983

38   'Bond Vs. Bond' by Hugh James, *CFQ,* May 1984

39   'Warners Shuffles The Top' *Weekly Variety*, 14.01.1981

40   'Producing "Never Say Never Again" Jack Schwartzman' by Steve Swires, *Starlog* #71, June 1983

41   'PSO Souding Out O'Seas Bond Release' *Daily Variety*, 15.03.1982

42   'Producer Jack Schwartzman Brings 007 Back in the Grand Old Fashion' by Jack Ferguson, *Fantastic Films* #36, November 1983

43   'Bond Vs. Bond' by Hugh James, CFQ, May 1984

44   'Producing "Never Say Never Again" Jack Schwartzman' by Steve Swires, *Starlog* #71, June 1983

45   Steven Jay Rubin, *The Complete James Bond Movie Encyclopaedia*, Contemporary Books, Newly Revised Edition, 2003, p. 367

46   *Never Say Never Again* production notes, Warner Brothers, 1983

47   'Producer Jack Schwartzman Brings 007 Back in the Grand Old Fashion' by Jack Ferguson, *Fantastic Films* #36, November 19833

48   'Lorenzo Semple, Jr.: Having Fun with James Bond in "Never Say Never Again"' by Steve Swires, *Starlog* #74, September 1980

49   'Lorenzo Semple, Jr.: Having Fun with James Bond in "Never Say Never Again"' by Steve Swires, *Starlog* #74, September 1980

50   'Lorenzo Semple, Jr.: Having Fun with James Bond in "Never Say Never Again"' by Steve Swires, *Starlog* #74, September 1980

51   'Lorenzo Semple, Jr.: Having Fun with James Bond in "Never Say Never Again"' by Steve Swires, *Starlog* #74, September 1980

52   'Lorenzo Semple, Jr.: Having Fun with James Bond in "Never Say Never Again"' by Steve Swires, *Starlog* #74, September 1980

53   'Bond Vs. Bond' by Lee Goldberg, *CFQ*, April–May 1983

54   'Lorenzo Semple, Jr.: Having fun with James Bond in "Never Say Never Again"' by Steve Swires, *Starlog* #74, September 1980

55   'Bond Vs. Bond' by Lee Goldberg, *CFQ*, April–May 1983

56   'Bond Vs. Bond' by Lee Goldberg, *CFQ*, April–May 1983

57   Sean Connery interviewed by David Hartman, *Good Morning America*, ABC, 1983

58   'Connery and Moore Are Back As Bond In '83" by Jon Nordheimer, *The New York Times*, 20.01.1983

59   *Film 83* Special with Barry Norman, dir: Jonathan Dent, BBC 1, 12.12.1983

60   *Film 83* Special with Barry Norman, dir: Jonathan Dent, BBC 1, 12.12.1983

61   *Film 83* Special with Barry Norman, dir: Jonathan Dent, BBC 1, 12.12.1983

62   'Lorenzo Semple, Jr.: Having Fun with James Bond in "Never Say Never Again"' by Steve Swires, *Starlog* #74, September 1980

63   'Lorenzo Semple, Jr.: Having Fun with James Bond in "Never Say Never Again"' by Steve Swires, *Starlog* #74, September 1980

64   'Lorenzo Semple, Jr.: Having Fun with James Bond in "Never Say Never Again"' by Steve Swires, *Starlog* #74, September 1980

65   'Lorenzo Semple, Jr.: Having Fun with James Bond in "Never Say Never Again"' by Steve Swires, *Starlog* #74, September 1980

66   'Lorenzo Semple, Jr.: Having Fun with James Bond in "Never Say Never Again"' by Steve Swires, *Starlog* #74, September 1980

67   'Lorenzo Semple, Jr.: Having Fun with James Bond in "Never Say Never Again"' by Steve Swires, *Starlog* #74, September 1980

68   'Producer Jack Schwartzman Brings 007 Back in the Grand Old Fashion' by Jack Ferguson, *Fantastic Films* #36, November 19833

69   Irvin Kershner: Authors' interview, 29.08.2001

70   Irvin Kershner: Authors' interview, 29.08.2001

71   'Lorenzo Semple, Jr.: Having Fun with James Bond in "Never Say Never Again"' by Steve Swires, *Starlog* #74, September 1980

72   Irvin Kershner: Authors' interview, 29.08.2001

73   Irvin Kershner: Authors' interview, 29.08.2001

74   'Lorenzo Semple, Jr.: Having Fun with James Bond in "Never Say Never Again"' by Steve Swires, *Starlog* #74, September 1980

75   'Lorenzo Semple, Jr.: Having Fun with James Bond in "Never Say Never Again"' by Steve Swires, *Starlog* #74, September 1980

76   'The Writer Speaks: Lorenzo Semple' Writers Guild Foundation, www.wgfoundation.org, 07.08.2013

77   'Lorenzo Semple, Jr.: Having Fun with James Bond in "Never Say Never Again"' by Steve Swires, *Starlog* #74, September 1980

78   'Producer Jack Schwartzman Brings 007 Back in the Grand Old Fashion' by Jack Ferguson, *Fantastic Films* #36, November 1983

79   Dick Clement and Ian La Frenais: Authors' interview, 09.04.2015

80   Dick Clement and Ian La Frenais: Authors' interview, 09.04.2015

81   Dick Clement and Ian La Frenais: Authors' interview, 09.04.2015

82   Dick Clement and Ian La Frenais: Authors' interview, 09.04.2015

83   Dick Clement and Ian La Frenais: Authors' interview, 09.04.2015

84   Dick Clement and Ian La Frenais: Authors' interview, 09.04.2015

85   Dick Clement and Ian La Frenais: Authors' interview, 09.04.2015

86   Sean Connery talks to Iain Johnstone, *The Guardian Lectures*, National Film Theatre, London, 13.12.1983

87   Dick Clement and Ian La Frenais: Authors' interview, 09.04.2015

88   Dick Clement and Ian La Frenais: Authors' interview, 09.04.2015

89   'My Secret Battle for Bond' By Margaret Hinxman, *The Daily Mail*, 17.10.1983

90   'The Writer Speaks: Lorenzo Semple' Writers Guild Foundation, www.wgfoundation.org, 07.08.2013

91   'The Writer Speaks: Lorenzo Semple' Writers Guild Foundation, www.wgfoundation.org, 07.08.2013

92   'The Writer Speaks: Lorenzo Semple' Writers Guild Foundation, www.wgfoundation.org, 07.08.2013

93   'The Writer Speaks: Lorenzo Semple' Writers Guild Foundation, www.wgfoundation.org, 07.08.2013

94 'The Writer Speaks: Lorenzo Semple' Writers Guild Foundation, www.wgfoundation.org, 07.08.2013

95 'The Writer Speaks: Lorenzo Semple' Writers Guild Foundation, www.wgfoundation.org, 07.08.2013

96 'The Writer Speaks: Lorenzo Semple' Writers Guild Foundation, www.wgfoundation.org, 07.08.2013

97 Dick Clement and Ian La Frenais: Authors' interview, 09.04.2015

98 'Producer Jack Schwartzman Brings 007 Back in the Grand Old Fashion' by Jack Ferguson, *Fantastic Films* #36, November 1983

99 *Film 83* Special with Barry Norman, dir: Jonathan Dent, BBC1, 12.12.1983

100 Dick Clement and Ian La Frenais: Authors' interview, 09.04.2015

101 *Never Say Never Again* production notes, Warner Brothers, 1983

102 *Never Say Never Again* production notes, Warner Brothers, 1983

103 Alan Barnes and Marcus Hearn, *Kiss Kiss Bang! Bang! The Unofficial James Bond Film Companion*, 2nd Edition, B.T. Batsford, 2000, p. 159

104 'Premium Bond Women' by Bart Mills, *You Magazine, The Mail on Sunday,* December 1983

105 Alan Barnes and Marcus Hearn, *Kiss Kiss Bang! Bang! The Unofficial James Bond Film Companion*, 2nd Edition, B.T. Batsford, 2000, p. 159

106 *Never Say Never Again* production notes, Warner Brothers, 1983

107 John Hunter, *Great Scot: The Life of Sean Connery*, Bloomsbury Publishing, 1993, p. 137

108 'Connery and Moore Are Back As Bond In '83" by Jon Nordheimer, *The New York Times*, 20.01.1983

109 'I Think You're Back in Business James' by Graham Rye, *007 Magazine* #15, The James Bond British Fan Club, 1984

110 'Oh! Oh! 007 Is Blacked' by John Mcshane, *Sunday Mirror,* 28.11.1982

111 Sean Connery interviewed by Marjorie Bilbow, *Starsound*, BBC Radio 2, 15.12.1983

112 Douglas Slocombe: Authors' interview, 06.08.2015

113 Robert Sellers, *The Battle For Bond: The Genesis of Cinema's Greatest Hero*, Tomahawk Press, First edition, 2008, p. 35

114 Andrew Yule, *Sean Connery: Neither Shaken, Nor Stirred*, Little Brown and Company, 1992, p. 254

115 *Film 83* Special with Barry Norman, dir: Jonathan Dent, BBC1, 12.12.1983

116 'Controversy Over Bond Title Can Only Help Film, Broccoli Says' by Robert Osborne, *The Hollywood Reporter*, 12.04.1982

117 Robert Sellers, *The Battle For Bond: The Genesis of Cinema's Greatest Hero*, Tomahawk Press, First

118 *Never Say Never Again* production notes, Warner Brothers, 1983

119 *Never Say Never Again* production notes, Warner Brothers, 1983

120 *Never Say Never Again* production notes, Warner Brothers, 1983

121 'Connery Is Back On The Bond Wagon' by Roderick Mann, *Los Angeles Times*, 02.10.1983

122 Dick Clement and Ian La Frenais: Authors' interview, 09.04.2015

123 Irvin Kershner: Authors' interview, 29.08.2001

124 Irvin Kershner: Authors' interview, 29.08.2001

125 'All Together, Now: Sean Connery Is an Icon' by Diane K. Shah, *GQ*, July 1989

126 Dick Clement and Ian La Frenais: Authors' interview, 09.04.2015

127 Dick Clement and Ian La Frenais: Authors' interview, 09.04.2015

128 Dick Clement and Ian La Frenais: Authors' interview, 09.04.2015

129 Dick Clement and Ian La Frenais: Authors' interview, 09.04.2015

130 Irvin Kershner: Authors' interview, 29.08.2001

131 Irvin Kershner: Authors' interview, 29.08.2001

132 *Never Say Never Again* production notes, Warner Brothers, 1983

133 Irvin Kershner: Authors' interview, 29.08.2001

134 Irvin Kershner: Authors' interview, 29.08.2001

135 Irvin Kershner: Authors' interview, 29.08.2001

136 'Underwater for Never Say Never Again' by Robert Steadman, *American Cinematographer*, October 1983

137 *Never Say Never Again* production notes, Warner Brothers, 1983

138 'Underwater for Never Say Never Again' by Robert Steadman, *American Cinematographer*, October 1983

139 'Underwater for Never Say Never Again' by Robert Steadman, *American Cinematographer*, October 1983

140 'Underwater for Never Say Never Again' by Robert Steadman, *American Cinematographer*, October 1983

141 *The Tonight Show Starring Johnny Carson*, NBC, 05.10.1983

142 *Never Say Never Again* production notes, Warner Brothers, 1983

143 Steven Jay Rubin, *The Complete James Bond Move Encyclopedia*, Newly revised edition, Contemporary Books, 2003, p. 369

144 'David Dryer: Never Say Never Again' by Don Shay, *Cinefex* #15, January 1984

145 'David Dryer: Never Say Never Again' by Don Shay, *Cinefex* #15, January 1984

146 'David Dryer: Never Say Never Again' by Don Shay, *Cinefex* #15, January 1984

147 'David Dryer: Never Say Never Again' by Don

Shay, *Cinefex* #15, January 1984

148 'I thought I'd surprise you James' by Kevin Harper, *007 Magazine* #15, The James Bond British Fan Club, 1984

149 'Connery Is Back On The Bond Wagon' by Roderick Mann, *Los Angeles Times*, 02.10.1983

150 Vic Armstrong with Robert Sellers, *The True Adventures of the World's Greatest Stuntman*, Titan Books, 2011, p. 156

151 Vic Armstrong: Authors' interview, 24.06.2015

152 Vic Armstrong: Authors' interview, 24.06.2015

153 Vic Armstrong: Authors' interview, 24.06.2015

154 Vic Armstrong: Authors' interview, 24.06.2015

155 Norman Wanstall: Authors' interview, 27.11.2000

156 Norman Wanstall: Authors' interview, 27.11.2000

157 Norman Wanstall: Authors' interview, 27.11.2000

158 'Producer Jack Schwartzman Brings 007 Back in the Grand Old Fashion' by Jack Ferguson, *Fantastic Films* #36, November 1983

159 Steven Jay Rubin, *The Complete James Bond Movie Encyclopaedia*, Contemporary Books, Newly Revised Edition, 2002, p. 368

160 Irvin Kershner: Authors' interview, 29.08.2001

161 Jon Burlingame, *The Music of James Bond*, Oxford University Press, 2012, p. 166

162 Jon Burlingame, *The Music of James Bond*, Oxford University Press, 2012, p. 166

163 Jon Burlingame, *The Music of James Bond*, Oxford University Press, 2012, p. 166

164 Jon Burlingame, *The Music Of James Bond*, Oxford University Press, 2012, p. 167

165 *James Bond's Greatest Hits*, dir: Stephen Franklin,

North One, Channel 4, 18.11.2006

166 Jon Burlingame, *The Music Of James Bond*, Oxford University Press, 2012, p. 169

167 *James Bond's Greatest Hits*, dir: Stephen Franklin, North One, Channel 4, 18.11.2006

168 The Bond Song You Never Heard' by Tim Lucas, videowatchdog.blogspot.co.uk, 21.04.2008

169 'Brit Bench Won't Ban 'Never' Release' *Weekly Variety*, 01.06.1983

170 'Bond Vs. Bond' by Hugh James, *CFQ* May 1984

171 'Bond Vs. Bond' by Hugh James, *CFQ* May 1984

1672 Trade Advert, *Weekly Variety*, 12.10.1983

173 *The Tonight Show Starring Johnny Carson*, 05.10.1983

174 *The Tonight Show Starring Johnny Carson*, 05.10.1983

175 'Great Scot' by Kurt Loder, *Rolling Stone*, #407, 27.10.1983

176 Andrew Yule, *Sean Connery: Neither Shaken, Nor Stirred*, Little Brown and Company, 1992, p. 258

177 'Premium Bond Women' by Bart Mills, *You Magazine, The Mail on Sunday*, December 1983

178 John Hunter, *Great Scot: The Life of Sean Connery*, Bloomsbury Publishing Ltd, 1993, p. 135

179 'Producer Jack Schwartzman Brings 007 Back in the Grand Old Fashion' by Jack Ferguson, *Fantastic Films* #36, November 1983

180 Steven Jay Rubin, *The Complete James Bond Movie Encyclopaedia*, Contemporary Books, Newly Revised Edition, 2003, p. 368

Chapter 20   A View to a Kill

1 'Frank Yablans MGM/UA's Mr. No. 2' by Roy Loynd, *Daily Variety*, 07.02.1983

2 'MGM, UA Back To Square One' by Ray Loynd, *Daily Variety*, 22.01.1985

3 John Glen: Authors' interview, 11.04.2001

4 Alan Ladd Jnr: Authors' interview, 22.05.2015

5 'Albert R. Broccoli' by Adam Pirani, *Starlog* #99, October 1985

6 'Albert R. Broccoli' by Adam Pirani, *Starlog* #99, October 1985

7 'Wilson To Co-Produce New James Bond Pic' *Daily Variety*, 21.03.1985

8 Christopher Walken: Authors' interview, 15.05.2015

9 Janine Glen (née King): Authors' interview, 07.05.2015

10 *Starsound Cinema*, BBC Radio 2, 20.06.1985

11 Mark O'Connell, *Catching Bullets: Memoirs of a Bond Fan*, Splendid Books, 2012 p. 25

12 John Glen with Marcus Hearn, *For My Eyes Only*, B.T. Batsford, 2001, p. 157

13 John Glen with Marcus Hearn, *For My Eyes Only*, B.T. Batsford, 2001, p. 157

14 *Bondage Quarterly*, Vol. 4 No.2, The James Bond 007 Fan Club, September 1983

15 'Flying High with Bond' by Tom Sciacca, *007 Magazine* #17, The James Bond British Fan Club, January 1984

16 Henry Chancellor, *James Bond The Man And His World*, John Murray, 2005, p. 146

17 David McDonnell (ed.), *A View To A Kill Official Movie Magazine*, Starlog, 1985

18 Pat McGilligan (ed.), *Backstory: Interviews with Screenwriters of Hollywood's Golden Age*, University of California Press, 1986, p. 286

19 'Albert R. Broccoli' by Adam Pirani, *Starlog* #99, October 1985

20 'He Works Hard At Being James Bond'

by Maureen Dowd, *The New York Times*, 26.05.1985

21 *A View To A Kill* production notes, MGM/UA 01.05.1985

22 David McDonnell (ed.), *A View To A Kill Official Movie Magazine*, Starlog, 1985

23 *Bondage Quarterly*, Vol. 4 No.2, The James Bond 007 Fan Club, September 1983

24 David McDonnell (ed.), *A View To A Kill Official Movie Magazine*, Starlog, 1985

25 David McDonnell (ed.), *A View To A Kill Official Movie Magazine*, Starlog, 1985

26 John Glen: Authors' interview, 11.04.2001

27 David McDonnell (ed.), *A View To A Kill Official Movie Magazine*, Starlog, 1985

28 David McDonnell (ed.), *A View To A Kill Official Movie Magazine*, Starlog, 1985

29 John Glen: Authors' interview, 11.04.2001

30 David McDonnell (ed.), *A View To A Kill Official Movie Magazine*, Starlog, 1985

31 'On Location with A View To A Kill' by Lee Goldberg, *Starlog #92*, March 1985

32 'Newest Bond Pic Rolls At Pinewood' *Weekly Variety*, 08.08.1984

33 *A View To A Kill* production notes, MGM/UA, 01.05.1985

34 Roger Moore: Authors' interview, 26.04.2015

35 'Hollywood Soundtrack' *Weekly Variety*, 14.12.1983

36 Roger Moore: Authors' interview, 26.04.2015

37 Roger Moore: Authors' interview, 26.04.2015

38 'He Works Hard At Being James Bond' by Maureen Dowd, *The New York Times*, 26.05.1985

39 'He Works Hard At Being James Bond' by Maureen Dowd, *The New York Times*, 26.05.1985

40 Roger Moore: Authors' interview, 26.04.2015

41 John Glen: Authors' interview, 11.04.2001

42 'Sermon From the Savoy' by Charles Shaar Murray, *New Musical Express*, 24.09.1984

43 John Glen: Authors' interview, 11.04.2001

44 Christopher Walken: Authors' interview, 15.05.2015

45 Christopher Walken: Authors' interview, 15.05.2015

46 Christopher Walken: Authors' interview, 15.05.2015

47 Christopher Walken: Authors' interview, 15.05.2015

48 Christopher Walken: Authors' interview, 15.05.2015

49 Christopher Walken: Authors' interview, 15.05.2015

50 Christopher Walken: Authors' interview, 15.05.2015

51 'Hollywood Soundtrack' *Weekly Variety*, 25.04.1984

52 Tanya Roberts: Authors' interview, 15.05.2015

53 Tanya Roberts: Authors' interview, 15.05.2015

54 Tanya Roberts: Authors' interview, 15.05.2015

55 Tanya Roberts: Authors' interview, 15.05.2015

56 Tanya Roberts: Authors' interview, 15.05.2015

57 'On Location with A View To A Kill' by Lee Goldberg, *Starlog #92*, March 1985

58 'On Location with A View To A Kill' by Lee Goldberg, *Starlog #92*, March 1985

59 *A View To A Kill* production notes, MGM/UA, 01.05.1985

60 *Starsound Cinema*, BBC Radio 2, 20.06.1985

61 David McDonnell (ed.), *A View To A Kill Official Movie Magazine*, Starlog, 1985

62 David McDonnell (ed.), *A View To A Kill Official Movie Magazine*, Starlog, 1985

63 John Glen: Authors' interview, 11.04.2001

64 Martin Grace: Interviewed by Anders Frejdh, October 2009

65 Peter Lamont: Authors' interview, 06.10.2000

66 Peter Lamont: Authors' interview, 06.10.2000

67 Peter Lamont: Authors' interview, 06.10.2000

68 'Bognor Makes Bond Fly On Skies' James Bond 25 Years, *Weekly Variety*, 13.05.1987

69 'Bognor Makes Bond Fly On Skies' James Bond 25 Years, *Weekly Variety*, 13.05.1987

70 'Moneypenny Talks' by Anwar Brett, *Film Review Special*, #21, 1997

71 Lee Pfeiffer and Philip Lisa, *The Incredible World of 007: An Authorized Celebration of James Bond*, Updated Edition, Boxtree, 1995, pp. 207–208

72 Christopher Walken: Authors' interview, 15.05.2015

73 Rémy Julienne: Authors' interview, 21.10.2008

74 *A View To A Kill* production notes, MGM/UA 01.05.1985

75 Tanya Roberts: Authors' interview, 15.05.2015

76 Christopher Walken: Authors' interview, 15.05.2015

77 Christopher Walken: Authors' interview, 15.05.2015

78 John Glen: Authors' interview, 11.04.2001

79 Tanya Roberts: Authors' interview, 15.05.2015

80 Christopher Walken: Authors' interview, 15.05.2015

81 Rémy Julienne: Authors' interview, 21.10.2008

82 Tanya Roberts: Authors' interview, 15.05.2015

83 Rémy Julienne: Authors' interview, 21.10.2008

84 '007 x 4: John Richardson' by Nora Lee, *Cinefex #33*, February 1988

85 '007 x 4: John Richardson' by Nora Lee, *Cinefex #33*, February 1988

86 'On Location with A View To A Kill' by Lee Goldberg, *Starlog #92*, March 1985

87 John Glen: Authors' interview, 11.04.2001

88 Tanya Roberts: Authors' interview, 15.05.2015

89 Tanya Roberts: Authors' interview, 15.05.2015

90 Tanya Roberts: Authors' interview, 15.05.2015

91   'He Works Hard At Being James Bond'
     by Maureen Dowd, *The New York Times*,
     26.05.1985

92   Tanya Roberts: Authors' interview, 15.05.2015

93   'He Works Hard At Being James Bond'
     by Maureen Dowd, *The New York Times*,
     26.05.1985

94   Christopher Walken: Authors' interview,
     15.05.2015

95   Tanya Roberts: Authors' interview, 15.05.2015

96   Peter Lamont: Authors' interview, 06.10.2000

97   Christopher Walken: Authors' interview,
     15.05.2015

98   '007 x 4: John Richardson' by Nora Lee,
     Cinefex #33, February 1988

99   Christopher Walken: Authors' interview,
     15.05.2015

100 Christopher Walken: Authors' interview,
     15.05.2015

101 Christopher Walken: Authors' interview,
     15.05.2015

102 Peter Lamont: Authors' interview, 06.10.2000

103 Peter Lamont: Authors' interview, 06.10.2000

104 Christopher Walken: Authors' interview,
     15.05.2015

105 Peter Lamont: Authors' interview, 06.10.2000

106 *A View To A Kill* production notes, MGM/UA
     01.05.1985

107 *Southeast at Six*, BBC1, 07.01.1985

108 Christopher Walken: Authors' interview,
     15.05.2015

109 Roger Moore: Authors' interview, 26.04.2015

110 Roger Moore: Authors' interview, 26.04.2015

111 Albert R. Broccoli with Donald Zec, *When the
     Snow Melts*, Boxtree, 1998, p. 270

112 Roger Moore: Authors' interview, 26.04.2015

113 David McDonnell (ed.), *A View To A Kill
     Official Movie Magazine*, Starlog, 1985

114 David McDonnell (ed.), *A View To A Kill
     Official Movie Magazine*, Starlog, 1985

115 '*For Your Ears Only*' by Chris Heath, *Empire* #1,
     June/July 1989

116 '*For Your Ears Only*' by Chris Heath, *Empire* #1,
     June/July 1989

117 '*For Your Ears Only*' by Chris Heath, *Empire* #1,
     June/July 1989

118 John Taylor with Tom Sykes, *In The Pleasure

119 Christopher Walken: Authors' interview,
     15.05.2015

120 David McDonnell (ed.), *A View To A Kill
     Official Movie Magazine*, Starlog, 1985

121 'San Francisco Premiere: From A View To A
     Kill' by Alan Stephenson, *Bondage Quarterly*, Vol.
     4, No. 4, The James Bond 007 Fan Club, June
     1986

122 'San Francisco Premiere: From A View To A
     Kill' by Alan Stephenson, *Bondage Quarterly*, Vol.
     4, No. 4, The James Bond 007 Fan Club, June
     1986

123 'San Francisco Premiere: From A View To A
     Kill' by Alan Stephenson, *Bondage Quarterly*, Vol.
     4, No. 4, The James Bond 007 Fan Club, June
     1986

124 Christopher Walken: Authors' interview,
     15.05.2015

125 Christopher Walken: Authors' interview,
     15.05.2015

126 Christopher Walken: Authors' interview,
     15.05.2015

127 Christopher Walken: Authors' interview,
     15.05.2015

128 'Albert R. Broccoli' by Adam Pirani, *Starlog
     #99*, October 1985

129 'Albert R. Broccoli' by Adam Pirani, *Starlog
     #99*, October 1985

130 'Albert R. Broccoli' by Adam Pirani, *Starlog
     #99*, October 1985

131 'He Works Hard At Being James Bond'
     by Maureen Dowd, *The New York Times*,
     26.05.1985

132 'He Works Hard At Being James Bond'
     by Maureen Dowd, *The New York Times*,
     26.05.1985

133 'He Works Hard At Being James Bond'
     by Maureen Dowd, *The New York Times*,
     26.05.1985

134 'He Works Hard At Being James Bond'
     by Maureen Dowd, *The New York Times*,
     26.05.1985

135 'The Moore Bonds The Merrier' by Lisa
     Dewson, *007*, Argus Specialist Publications
     Limited, 1983

Chapter 21 The Living Daylights

1   Albert R. Broccoli with Donald Zec, *When the
    Snow Melts*, Boxtree, 1998, p. 278

2   'Breakup Of MGM/UA Get Underway' by
    Jane Galbraith, *Daily Variety*, 12.11.1985

3   Albert R. Broccoli with Donald Zec, *When the
    Snow Melts*, Boxtree, 1998, p. 279

4   'At The Movies' by Lawrence van Gelder, *The

    New York Times*, 31.07.1987

5   'Richard Maibaum Veteran Screenwriter For A
    Brand New Bond' *Starlog* #120, July 1987

6   'After Helming 4 In A Row, Glen Knows
    Bonds Don't Come Cheap' James Bond 25
    Years, *Weekly Variety*, 13.05.1987

7   'After Helming 4 In A Row, Glen Knows

Bonds Don't Come Cheap' James Bond 25
Years, *Weekly Variety*, 13.05.1987

8   'After Helming 4 In A Row, Glen Knows
     Bonds Don't Come Cheap' James Bond 25
     Years, *Weekly Variety*, 13.05.1987

9   'After Helming 4 In A Row, Glen Knows
     Bonds Don't Come Cheap' James Bond 25
     Years, *Weekly Variety*, 13.05.1987

10   'After Helming 4 In A Row, Glen Knows
     Bonds Don't Come Cheap' James Bond 25
     Years, *Weekly Variety*, 13.05.1987

11   'Richard Maibaum Veteran Screenwriter For A
     Brand New Bond' *Starlog #120*, July 1987

12   'Bonds Turn Up Every Two Years But
     Nevertheless The Producers Are 'Constantly
     Running Scared" by Mark Adams, James Bond
     25 Years, *Weekly Variety*, 13.05.1987

13   John Glen: Authors' interview, 06.05.2014

14   John Glen: Authors' interview, 06.05.2014

15   Peter Lamont: Authors' interview, 13.05.2014

16   Albert R. Broccoli with Donald Zec, *When the
     Snow Melts*, Boxtree, 1998, p. 279

17   Pierce Brosnan: Authors' interview, 23.05.2015

18   Pierce Brosnan: Authors' interview, 23.05.2015

19   Pierce Brosnan: Authors' interview, 23.05.2015

20   'Richard Maibaum Veteran Screenwriter For A
     Brand New Bond, *Starlog #120*, July 1987

21   Maryam d'Abo: Authors' interview, 14.04.2014

22   John Glen: Authors' interview, 11.04.2001

23   John Glen with Marcus Hearn, *For My Eyes
     Only*, B.T. Batsford, 2001, p. 175

24   John Glen: Authors' interview, 11.04.2001

25   Albert R. Broccoli with Donald Zec, *When the
     Snow Melts*, Boxtree, 1998, p. 281

26   *The Living Daylights* Electronic Press Kit,
     MGM/UA, 1987

27   Albert R. Broccoli with Donald Zec, *When the
     Snow Melts*, Boxtree, 1998, p. 281

28   'Timothy Dalton on Penny Dreadful,
     serenading Mae West, and being James Bond'
     by Will Harris, www.avclub.com, 09.05.2014

29   Albert R. Broccoli with Donald Zec, *When the
     Snow Melts*, Boxtree, 1998, p. 283

30   'New Bond Keeps Love Life Secret' by Garth
     Pearce, *Daily Express*, 06.10.1986

31   'Richard Maibaum Veteran Screenwriter For A
     Brand New Bond' *Starlog #120*, July 1987

32   *The Living Daylights* Electronic Press Kit,
     MGM/UA, 1987

33   *The Living Daylights* Electronic Press Kit,
     MGM/UA, 1987

34   *The Living Daylights* Electronic Press Kit,
     MGM/UA, 1987

35   *The Living Daylights* Electronic Press Kit,
     MGM/UA, 1987

36   John Glen: Authors' interview, 06.04.2015

37   David O'Donnell and Carr D'Angelo
     (ed.), *The Living Daylights: The Official Poster
     Magazine*, Starlog, 1987

38   David O'Donnell and Carr D'Angelo
     (ed.), *The Living Daylights: The Official Poster
     Magazine*, Starlog, 1987

39   Jeroen Krabbé: Authors' interview, 03.05.2014

40   Maryam d'Abo: Authors' interview, 14.04.2014

41   Maryam d'Abo: Authors' interview, 14.04.2014

42   Thomas Wheatley: Authors' interview, 04.02.2014

43   Caroline Bliss: Authors' interview, 19.04.2014

44   John Glen: Authors' interview, 06.05.2014

45   'John Glen has long Bond history' by Nora
     Lee, *American Cinematographer*, July 1987

46   Paul Weston: Authors' interview, 08.04.2014

47   Peter Davies: Authors' interview, 03.06.2015

48   Paul Weston: Authors' interview, 08.04.2014

49   Paul Weston: Authors' interview, 08.04.2014

50   'John Glen has long Bond history' by Nora
     Lee, *American Cinematographer*, July 1987

51   'Bonds Turn Up Every Two Years But
     Nevertheless The Producers Are 'Constantly
     Running Scared" by Mark Adams, James Bond
     25 Years, *Weekly Variety*, 13.05.1987

52   'John Glen has long Bond history' by Nora
     Lee, *American Cinematographer*, July 1987

53   'New Bond Keeps Love Life Secret' by Garth
     Pearce, *Daily Express*, 06.10.1986

54   Maryam d'Abo: Authors' interview, 14.04.2014

55   Terry Ackland–Snow: Authors' interview,
     11.06.2014

56   Peter Lamont: Authors' interview, 30.01.2014

57   John Glen: Authors' interview, 06.05.2014

58   Maryam d'Abo: Authors' interview, 14.04.2014

59   Thomas Wheatley: Authors' interview,
     04.02.2014

60   John Glen: Authors' interview, 11.04.2001

61   Jeroen Krabbé: Authors' interview, 03.05.2014

62   Peter Lamont: Authors' interview, 13.05.2014

63   Peter Lamont: Authors' interview, 13.05.2014

64   Desmond Llewelyn: Authors' interview,
     23.04.1999

65   John Glen: Authors' interview, 11.04.2001

66   'Report From the Set of Licence To Kill' by
     Richard Schenkman, *Bondage #16*, The James
     Bond 007 Fan Club, Winter 1989

67   Jeroen Krabbé: Authors' interview, 03.05.2014

68   Caroline Bliss: Authors' interview, 19.04.2014

69   Caroline Bliss: Authors' interview, 19.04.2014

70   John Glen: Authors' interview, 06.05.2014

71   Jeroen Krabbé: Authors' interview, 03.05.2014

72   Thomas Wheatley: Authors' interview,
     04.02.2014

73   Peter Davies: Authors' interview, 03.06.2015

74   Keith Hamshere: Authors' interview, 11.03.2014

75   Alan Church: Authors' interview, 02.07.2006

76   Alan Church: Authors' interview, 02.07.2006

77   Alan Church: Authors' interview, 02.07.2006

78   Peter Davies: Authors' interview, 03.06.2015

79   Peter Davies: Authors' interview, 03.06.2015

80 'Repor From The Set Of Licence To Kill' by Richard Schenkman, *Bondage* #16, The James Bond 007 Fan Club, Winter 1989

81 John Grover: Authors' interview, 12.02.2014

82 John Glen: Authors' interview, 11.04.2001

83 'Tunesmith Barry Keeps In Mind The Kid On The Edge Of His Seat' James Bond 25 Years, *Weekly Variety*, 13.05.1987

84 'Tunesmith Barry Keeps In Mind The Kid On The Edge Of His Seat' James Bond 25 Years, *Weekly Variety*, 13.05.1987

85 John Glen: Authors' interview, 06.05.2014

86 John Glen: Authors' interview, 06.04.2014

87 *James Bond's Greatest Hits*, dir: Stephen Franklin, North One, Channel 4, 18.11.2006

88 Jon Burlinghame, *The Music Of James Bond*, Oxford University Press, 2012, pp. 188–189

89 Keith Hampshire: Authors' interview, 04.03.2014

90 Maryam d'Abo: Authors' interview, 14.04.2014

91 *The Living Daylights* Electronic Press Kit, MGM/UA, 1987

92 *The Living Daylights* Electronic Press Kit, MGM/UA, 1987

Chapter 22 Licence to Kill

1 David Puttnam with Neil Watson, *The Undeclared War*, Harper Collins Publishers, 1997, p. 312

2 'New 4–Wall Tactic At Pinewood Puts U.K. Lots On Guard' *Weekly Variety*, 06.05.1987

3 'New 4–Wall Tactic At Pinewood Puts U.K. Lots On Guard' *Weekly Variety*, 06.05.1987

4 'MGM/UA Officially Separate Again' by Jane Galbraith, *Daily Variety*, 12.07.1988

5 'MGM/UA Officially Separate Again' by Jane Galbraith, *Daily Variety*, 12.07.1988

6 'New Tax, Pound Weigh Heavily on UK Lensing' by Don Groves, *Daily Variety*, 09.03.1988

7 'New Tax, Pound Weigh Heavily on UK Lensing' by Don Groves, *Daily Variety*, 09.03.1988

8 'New Tax, Pound Weigh Heavily on UK Lensing' by Don Groves, *Daily Variety*, 09.03.1988

9 John Glen with Marcus Hearn, *For My Eyes Only*, B.T. Batsford, 2001, p. 189

10 John Glen with Marcus Hearn, *For My Eyes Only*, B.T. Batsford, 2001, p. 189

11 John Glen: Authors' interview, 06.05.2014

12 John Glen with Marcus Hearn, *For My Eyes Only*, B.T. Batsford, 2001, p. 191

13 'Serious Bondage' by Gary Russell, *Starburst* #131, July 1989

14 'Serious Bondage' by Gary Russell, *Starburst* #131, July 1989

15 'James Bond's Final Mission?' by Lee Goldberg, *Starlog* #146, September 1989

16 'The Laughing Vulcan' by Marc Shapiro, *Starlog* #146, August 1989

17 *GoldenEye* screenplay by Michael France, 1–94, First Draft

18 'James Bond 007 Licence To Kill' by Mark A. Altman, *Cinemafantastique* Vol. 19 No. 5, July 1989

19 'James Bond 007 Licence To Kill' by Mark A. Altman, *Cinemafantastique* Vol. 19 No. 5, July 1989

20 John Glen: Authors' interview, 11.04.2001

21 John Glen: Authors' interview, 11.04.2001

22 'James Bond 007 Licence To Kill' by Mark A. Altman, *Cinemafantastique* Vol. 19 No. 5, July 1989

23 John Glen: Authors' interview, 11.04.2001

24 Peter Lamont: Authors' interview, 06.10.2000

25 Peter Lamont: Authors' interview, 06.10.2000

26 'James Bond 007 Licence To Kill' by Mark A. Altman, *Cinemafantastique* Vol. 19 No. 5, July 1989

27 'James Bond 007 Licence To Kill' by Mark A. Altman, *Cinemafantastique* Vol. 19 No. 5, July 1989

28 'Serious Bondage' by Gary Russell, *Starburst* #131, July 1989

29 'James Bond 007 Licence To Kill' by Mark A. Altman, *Cinemafantastique* Vol. 19 No. 5, July 1989

30 'Serious Bondage' by Gary Russell, *Starburst* #131, July 1989

31 'Serious Bondage' by Gary Russell, *Starburst* #131, July 1989

32 'James Bond's Final Mission?' by Lee Goldberg, *Starlog* #146, September 1989

33 'James Bond 007 Licence To Kill' by Mark A. Altman, *Cinemafantastique* Vol. 19 No. 5, July 1989

34 'Serious Bondage' by Gary Russell, *Starburst* #131, July 1989

35 'Serious Bondage' by Gary Russell, *Starburst* #131, July 1989

36 'Serious Bondage' by Gary Russell, *Starburst* #131, July 1989

37 'James Bond's Final Mission?' by Lee Goldberg, *Starlog* #146, September 1989

38 'James Bond 007 Licence To Kill' by Mark A. Altman, *Cinemafantastique* Vol. 19 No. 5, July 1989

39 'James Bond's Final Mission?' by Lee Goldberg, *Starlog* #146, September 1989

40 'Serious Bondage' by Gary Russell, *Starburst* #131, July 1989

41 'James Bond's Final Mission?' by Lee Goldberg, *Starlog* #146, September 1989

42 'Serious Bondage' by Gary Russell, *Starburst* #131, July 1989

43 'Serious Bondage' by Gary Russell, *Starburst* #131, July 1989

44 'James Bond's Final Mission?' by Lee Goldberg, *Starlog* #146, September 1989

45 John Glen with Marcus Hearn, *For My Eyes Only*, B.T. Batsford, 2001, p. 189

46 'James Bond's Final Mission?' by Lee Goldberg, *Starlog* #146, September 1989

47 'Licensed To Thrill' by Edward Gross, *Starlog Yearbook*, Vol. 5, 1989

48 'Licensed To Thrill' by Edward Gross, *Starlog Yearbook*, Vol. 5, 1989

49 Sally Hibbin, *The Making of Licence to Kill*, Hamlyn, 1989, p. 7

50 'The Private Bond' by Dan Yakir, *Starlog* #145, August 1989

51 'The Private Bond' by Dan Yakir, *Starlog* #145, August 1989

52 'The Private Bond' by Dan Yakir, *Starlog* #145, August 1989

53 'James Bond's Final Mission?' by Lee Goldberg, *Starlog* #146, September 1989

54 'Serious Bondage' by Gary Russell, *Starburst* #131, July 1989

55 Robert Davi: Authors' interview, 01.05.2015

56 Robert Davi: Authors' interview, 01.05.2015

57 Robert Davi: Authors' interview, 01.05.2015

58 Robert Davi: Authors' interview, 01.05.2015

59 Robert Davi: Authors' interview, 01.05.2015

60 Robert Davi: Authors' interview, 01.05.2015

61 Robert Davi: Authors' interview, 01.05.2015

62 Robert Davi: Authors' interview, 01.05.2015

63 Robert Davi: Authors' interview, 01.05.2015

64 Robert Davi: Authors' interview, 01.05.2015

65 Carey Lowell: Authors' interview, 26.05.2015

66 Carey Lowell: Authors' interview, 26.05.2015

67 'Chatting At The Plaza' by Richard Schenkman, *Bondage* #17, The James Bond 007 Fan Club, Summer 1989

68 Robert Davi: Authors' interview, 01.05.2015

69 'Chatting At The Plaza' by Richard Schenkman, *Bondage* #17, The James Bond 007 Fan Club, Summer 1989

70 'Chatting At The Plaza' by Richard Schenkman, *Bondage* #17, The James Bond 007 Fan Club, Summer 1989

71 'Chatting At The Plaza' by Richard Schenkman, *Bondage* #17, The James Bond 007 Fan Club, Summer 1989

72 'Chatting At The Plaza' by Richard Schenkman, *Bondage* #17, The James Bond 007 Fan Club, Summer 1989

73 'Licensed To Die?' by Lee Goldberg, *Starlog* #146, August 1989

74 'Licensed To Die?' by Lee Goldberg, *Starlog* #146, August 1989

75 'Benicio Del Toro on Savages and Licence to Kill' www.craveonline.co.uk, 16.11.2012

76 'A Visit To The James Bond Classroom' by Raymond Benson, *Bondage* #17, The James Bond 007 Fan Club, Summer 1989

77 'Chatting At The Plaza' by Richard Schenkman, *Bondage* #17, The James Bond 007 Fan Club, Summer 1989

78 Sally Hibbin, *The Making Of Licence To Kill*, Hamlyn, 1989. p. 39

79 'Report From The Set Of Licence To Kill' by Richard Schenkman, *Bondage* #16, The James Bond 007 Fan Club, Winter 1989

80 'Report From The Set Of Licence To Kill' by Richard Schenkman, *Bondage* #16, The James Bond 007 Fan Club, Winter 1989

81 Desmond Llewelyn: Authors' interview, 04.1999

82 Desmond Llewelyn: Authors' interview, 04.1999

83 Alan Barnes and Marcus Hearn, *Kiss Kiss Bang! Bang! The Unofficial James Bond Film Companion*, B.T. Batsford, 2nd Edition, 2000, p. 178

84 Caroline Bliss: Authors' interview, 19.04.2014

85 Caroline Bliss: Authors' interview, 19.04.2014

86 Peter Lamont: Authors' interview, 06.10.2000

87 Peter Lamont: Authors' interview, 06.10.2000

88 Peter Lamont: Authors' interview, 06.10.2000

89 Peter Lamont: Authors' interview, 06.10.2000

90 'Production Design For That Bond Look' by Nora Lee, *American Cinematographer* Vol. 7 No. 8, August 1989

91 Peter Lamont: Authors' interview, 06.10.2000

92 John Glen with Marcus Hearn, *For My Eyes Only*, B.T. Batsford, 2001, p. 196

93 Sally Hibbin, *The Making Of Licence To Kill*, Hamlyn, 1989. p. 7

94 Peter Lamont: Authors' interview, 06.10.2000

95 Peter Lamont: Authors' interview, 06.10.2000

96 Robert Davi: Authors' interview, 01.05.2015

97 Robert Davi: Authors' interview, 01.05.2015

98 Robert Davi: Authors' interview, 01.05.2015

99 Robert Davi: Authors' interview, 01.05.2015

100 Carey Lowell: Authors' interview, 26.05.2015

101 Robert Davi: Authors' interview, 01.05.2015

102 Carey Lowell: Authors' interview, 26.05.2015

103 Robert Davi: Authors' interview, 01.05.2015

104 'The Private Bond' by Dan Yakir, *Starlog* #146, August 1989

105 Carey Lowell: Authors' interview, 26.05.2015

106 Carey Lowell: Authors' interview, 26.05.2015

107 Carey Lowell: Authors' interview, 26.05.2015

108 Carey Lowell: Authors' interview, 26.05.2015

109 Carey Lowell: Authors' interview, 26.05.2015

110 'The Private Bond' by Dan Yakir, *Starlog* #146, August 1989

111 Carey Lowell: Authors' interview, 26.05.2015

112 Robert Davi: Authors' interview, 01.05.2015

113 John Glen with Marcus Hearn, *For My Eyes Only*, B.T. Batsford, 2001, p. 201

114 'A Visit To The James Bond Classroom' by Raymond Benson, *Bondage* #17, The James Bond 007 Fan Club, Summer 1989

115 'A Visit To The James Bond Classroom' by Raymond Benson, *Bondage* #17, The James Bond 007 Fan Club, Summer 1989

116 Carey Lowell: Authors' interview, 26.05.2015

117 'A Visit To The James Bond Classroom' by Raymond Benson, *Bondage* #17, The James Bond 007 Fan Club, Summer 1989

118 Robert Davi: Authors' interview, 01.05.2015

119 'Licence To Kill – No.16 and Counting' by Nora Lee, *American Cinematographer* Vol. 7 No. 8, August 1989

120 'Licence To Kill – No.16 and Counting' by Nora Lee, *American Cinematographer* Vol. 7 No. 8, August 1989

121 'Chatting At The Plaza' by Richard Schenkman, *Bondage* #17, The James Bond 007 Fan Club, Summer 1989

122 John Glen with Marcus Hearn, *For My Eyes Only*, B.T. Batsford, 2001, p. 189

123 John Glen: Authors' interview, 11.04.2001

124 Peter Lamont: Authors' interview, 06.10.2000

125 'James Bond doesn't do CGI: Inside 007's amazing real–world action' by Gavin Clarke, www.theregister.co.uk, 25.10.215

126 'James Bond doesn't do CGI: Inside 007's amazing real–world action' by Gavin Clarke, www.theregister.co.uk, 25.10.215

127 'James Bond doesn't do CGI: Inside 007's amazing real–world action' by Gavin Clarke, www.theregister.co.uk, 25.10.215

128 'James Bond doesn't do CGI: Inside 007's amazing real–world action' by Gavin Clarke, www.theregister.co.uk, 25.10.215

129 'Incident at La Rumorosa' by Kevin Desmond, *Eyepiece*, Vol. 10 No. 4, June 1989

130 'Incident at La Rumorosa' by Kevin Desmond, *Eyepiece*, Vol. 10 No. 4, June 1989

131 'Incident at La Rumorosa' by Kevin Desmond, *Eyepiece*, Vol. 10 No. 4, June 1989

132 'Incident at La Rumorosa' by Kevin Desmond, *Eyepiece*, Vol. 10 No. 4, June 1989

133 'Incident at La Rumorosa' by Kevin Desmond, *Eyepiece*, Vol. 10 No. 4, June 1989

134 'Incident at La Rumorosa' by Kevin Desmond, *Eyepiece*, Vol. 10 No. 4, June 1989

135 'Chatting At The Plaza' by Richard Schenkman, *Bondage* #17, The James Bond 007 Fan Club, Summer 1989

136 Paul Weston: Authors' interview, 08.04.2015

137 'Chatting At The Plaza' by Richard Schenkman, *Bondage* #17, The James Bond 007 Fan Club, Summer 1989

138 Carey Lowell: Authors' interview, 26.05.2015

139 'James Bond doesn't do CGI: Inside 007's amazing real–world action' by Gavin Clarke, www.theregister.co.uk, 25.10.215

140 Paul Weston: Authors' interview, 08.04.2015

141 Paul Weston: Authors' interview, 08.04.2015

142 Paul Weston: Authors' interview, 08.04.2015

143 Paul Weston: Authors' interview, 08.04.2015

144 Paul Weston: Authors' interview, 08.04.2015

145 Paul Weston: Authors' interview, 08.04.2015

146 Paul Weston: Authors' interview, 08.04.2015

147 John Glen: Authors' interview, 06.05.2014

148 John Glen: Authors' interview, 06.05.2014

149 John Glen: Authors' interview, 06.05.2014

150 Edward Lamberti (ed.), *Behind The Scenes At The BBFC*, 'Case Study: Licence To Kill' by Edward Lamberti, Palgrave Macmillan, 2012, pp. 125 – 126

151 Edward Lamberti (ed.), *Behind The Scenes At The BBFC*, 'Case Study: Licence To Kill' by Edward Lamberti, Palgrave Macmillan, 2012, pp. 125 – 126

152 Edward Lamberti (ed.), *Behind The Scenes At The BBFC*, 'Case Study: Licence To Kill' by Edward Lamberti, Palgrave Macmillan, 2012, pp. 125 – 126

153 'For Your Ears Only' by Chris Heath, *Empire* #1, June/July 1989

154 'For Your Ears Only' by Chris Heath, *Empire* #1, June/July 1989

155 Jon Burlingame, *The Music of James Bond*, Oxford University Press, 2012, pp. 194 – 195

156 Jon Burlingame, *The Music of James Bond*, Oxford University Press, 2012, p. 193

157 Jon Burlingame, *The Music of James Bond*, Oxford University Press, 2012, p. 193

158 'For Your Ears Only' by Chris Heath, *Empire* #1, June/July 1989

159 'For Your Ears Only' by Chris Heath, *Empire* #1, June/July 1989

160 'For Your Ears Only' by Chris Heath, *Empire* #1, June/July 1989

161 'For Your Ears Only' by Chris Heath, *Empire* #1, June/July 1989

162 Alan Church: Authors' interview, 02.07.2006

163 Alan Church: Authors' interview, 02.07.2006

164 'Licensed To Score' by Tom Soter, *Starlog* #199, February 1994

165 Alan Church: Authors' interview, 02.07.2006

166 Alan Church: Authors' interview, 02.07.2006

167 Pauline Hume: Authors' interview, 07.05.2015

168 John Glen: Authors' interview, 11.04.2001

169 'Bond Bombshell: 007 Goes On The Block' by Charles Fleming, *Weekly Variety*, 08.08.1990

Chapter 23   Passing the Bond Baton

1   'Report From The Set Of Licence To Kill' by Richard Schenkman, *Bondage* #16, The James Bond 007 Fan Club, Winter 1989

2   Helen De Winter, *What I Really Want To Do Is Produce*, Faber and Faber Limited, 2006, p. 29

3   *GoldenEye* production notes, United Artists, 1995

4   'Bond Bombshell: 007 Goes On The Block' by Charles Fleming, *Weekly Variety*, 08.08.1990

5   'Bond Bombshell: 007 Goes On The Block' by Charles Fleming, *Weekly Variety*, 08.08.1990

6   'James Bond: Selling The 007 Franchise' by Mark A. Altman, *Cinefantastique* Vol. 21, No. 4, February 1991

7   John Glen: Authors' interview, 11.04.2001

8   'James Bond: Selling The 007 Franchise' by Mark A. Altman, *Cinefantastique* Vol. 21, No. 4, February 1991

9   John Landis: Authors' interview, 28.10.2014

10   'Head of Operations' by Alan Jones, *Film Review Special* #21, 1997

11   'Bond Bombshell: 007 Goes On The Block' by Charles Fleming, *Weekly Variety*, 08.08.1990

12   'Bond Bombshell: 007 Goes On The Block' by Charles Fleming, *Weekly Variety*, 08.08.1990

13   'Bond Bombshell: 007 Goes On The Block' by Charles Fleming, *Weekly Variety*, 08.08.1990

14   'Bond Bombshell: 007 Goes On The Block' by Charles Fleming, *Weekly Variety*, 08.08.1990

15   'Bond Bombshell: 007 Goes On The Block' by Charles Fleming, *Weekly Variety*, 08.08.1990

16   Bond XVII treatment by Michael G Wilson and Alfonse Ruggiero Jnr

17   Bond XVII treatment by Michael G Wilson and Alfonse Ruggiero Jnr

18   Bond XVII treatment by Michael G Wilson and Alfonse Ruggiero Jnr

19   'James Bond: Selling The 007 Franchise' by Mark A. Altman, *Cinefantastique* Vol. 21, No. 4, February 1991

20   Bond XVII treatment by Michael G Wilson and Alfonse Ruggiero Jnr

21   William Davies: Authors' interview, 22.02.2015

22   William Davies: Authors' interview, 22.02.2015

23   William Osborne: Authors' interview, 27.02.2015

24   William Davies: Authors' interview, 22.02.2015

25   William Davies: Authors' interview, 22.02.2015

26   William Osborne: Authors' interview, 27.02.2015

27   William Davies: Authors' interview, 22.02.2015

28   William Osborne: Authors' interview, 27.02.2015

29   Untitled First Draft Screenplay by William Davies, William Osborne, Al Ruggiero and Michael Wilson, 02.01.1991

30   Untitled First Draft Screenplay by William Davies, William Osborne, Al Ruggiero and Michael Wilson, 02.01.1991

31   Untitled First Draft Screenplay by William Davies, William Osborne, Al Ruggiero and Michael Wilson, 02.01.1991

32   Untitled First Draft Screenplay by William Davies, William Osborne, Al Ruggiero and Michael Wilson, 02.01.1991

33   Untitled First Draft Screenplay by William Davies, William Osborne, Al Ruggiero and Michael Wilson, 02.01.1991

34   'Chinese Industry Reps On Visit To U.S. In Search Of Pic Deals' by Hy Hollinger, *Daily Variety*, 06.12.1991

35   'Bond Bombshell: 007 Goes On The Block' by Charles Fleming, *Weekly Variety*, 08.08.1990

36   'Bond Bombshell: 007 Goes On The Block' by Charles Fleming, *Weekly Variety*, 08.08.1990

37   'Bond Bombshell: 007 Goes On The Block' by Charles Fleming, *Weekly Variety*, 08.08.1990

38   'Bond Bombshell: 007 Goes On The Block' by Charles Fleming, *Weekly Variety*, 08.08.1990

39   Albert R. Broccoli with Donald Zec, *When the Snow Melts*, Boxtree, 1998, pp. 297 – 299

40   Albert R. Broccoli with Donald Zec, *When the Snow Melts*, Boxtree, 1998, pp. 297 – 299

41   Albert R. Broccoli with Donald Zec, *When the Snow Melts*, Boxtree, 1998, pp. 297 – 299

42   Albert R. Broccoli with Donald Zec, *When the Snow Melts*, Boxtree, 1998, pp. 297 – 299

43   Albert R. Broccoli with Donald Zec, *When the Snow Melts*, Boxtree, 1998, pp. 297 – 299

44   'Bond set for 0017th' by Suzan Ayscough, *Daily Variety*, 13.05.1993

45   'Bond Waits In Wings As Junior Hits Small Screen' by Terry Ilott, *Weekly Variety*, 22.04.1991

46   'Adventures In The Fan Trade – Part 1' by Graham Rye, *007 Magazine* #43, The James Bond International Fan Club, July 2004

47   Keith Hamshere: Authors' interview, 04.03.2014

48   'Bond Set For 0017th' by Suzan Ayscough, *Daily Variety*, 13.05.1993

49   John Cork: Authors' interview, 22.02.2015

50   John Cork: Authors' interview, 22.02.2015

51   John Cork: Authors' interview, 22.02.2015

52   John Cork: Authors' interview, 22.02.2015

53   Hilary Saltzman: Authors' interview, 29.11.2011

54   Adriana Saltzman: Authors' interview, 16.09.2014

55   Adriana Saltzman: Authors' interview, 16.09.2014

56   Adriana Saltzman: Authors' interview, 16.09.2014

57   Adriana Saltzman: Authors' interview, 16.09.2014

58   Adriana Saltzman: Authors' interview, 16.09.2014

Chapter 24 GoldenEye

1 'Lion Tamers Enter Ring' by Judy Brennan and Andy Marx, *Weekly Variety*, 06.09.1993

2 Jeff Kleeman: Authors' interview, 18.05.2015

3 Jeff Kleeman: Authors' interview, 18.05.2015

4 'Bond Set For 0017th' by Suzan Ayscough, *Daily Variety*, 13.05.1993

5 'Bond Set For 0017th' by Suzan Ayscough, *Daily Variety*, 13.05.1993

6 Jeffrey Caine: Authors' interview, 16.05.2015

7 Jeff Kleeman: Authors' interview, 18.05.2015

8 Martin Campbell: Authors' interview, 19.03.2015

9 Jeff Kleeman: Authors' interview, 18.05.2015

10 Laurent Bouzereau, *The Art of Bond*, Boxtree, 2006, p. 132

11 Jeff Kleeman: Authors' interview, 18.05.2015

12 David Barraclough and John Freeman (ed.), *The Official GoldenEye Movie Souvenir Magazine*, 'Michael Wilson – Producer' by Justin Keay, Titan, 1995

13 Steven Jay Rubin, *The Complete James Bond Move Encyclopedia*, Newly revised edition, Contemporary Books, 2003, pp. 493-494

14 Steven Jay Rubin, *The Complete James Bond Move Encyclopedia*, Newly revised edition, Contemporary Books, 2003, p. 493

15 'Flexing His Writer's Muscle' by Steve Persall, *St. Petersburg Times*, 20.06.2003

16 Steven Jay Rubin *The Complete James Bond Move Encyclopedia*, 2nd Edition, Contemporary Books, 1995, p. 478

17 John Cork: Authors' interview, 22.02.2015

18 Garth Pearce, *The Making of GoldenEye*, Boxtree, 1995, p. 7

19 'Mike France, "How To Write A James Bond Movie"' by John Cork, *Goldeneye #5*, The Ian Fleming Foundation, Summer 1997

20 'Mike France, "How To Write A James Bond Movie"' by John Cork, *Goldeneye #5*, The Ian Fleming Foundation, Summer 1997

21 'Danjaq On Bond Wagon With Two Script Deals' by Suzan Ayscough, *Daily Variety*, 26.05.1993

22 'Mike France, "How To Write A James Bond Movie"' by John Cork, *Goldeneye #5*, The Ian Fleming Foundation, Summer 1997

23 Steven Jay Rubin, *The Complete James Bond Move Encyclopedia*, Newly revised edition, Contemporary Books, 2003, p. 494

24 Jeff Kleeman: Authors' interview, 18.05.2015

25 Jeffrey Caine: Authors' interview, 10.05.2015

26 Jeffrey Caine: Authors' interview, 10.05.2015

27 Jeffrey Caine: Authors' interview, 10.05.2015

28 Jeffrey Caine: Authors' interview, 10.05.2015

29 Jeffrey Caine: Authors' interview, 10.05.2015

30 Jeffrey Caine: Authors' interview, 10.05.2015

31 Jeffrey Caine: Authors' interview, 15.05.2015

32 Jeffrey Caine: Authors' interview, 15.05.2015

33 Jeffrey Caine: Authors' interview, 10.05.2015

34 Jeffrey Caine: Authors' interview, 10.05.2015

35 Jeffrey Caine: Authors' interview, 10.05.2015

36 'Golden Boy' by Corie Brown, *Premiere*, US Ed, April 1996

37 Kevin Wade: Authors' interview, 24.05.2015

38 Kevin Wade: Authors' interview, 24.05.2015

39 Kevin Wade: Authors' interview, 24.05.2015

40 Kevin Wade: Authors' interview, 24.05.2015

41 Kevin Wade: Authors' interview, 24.05.2015

42 Kevin Wade: Authors' interview, 24.05.2015

43 Kevin Wade: Authors' interview, 24.05.2015

44 Kevin Wade: Authors' interview, 24.05.2015

45 Jeff Kleeman: Authors' interview, 18.05.2015

46 Bruce Feirstein: Authors' interview, 14.02.2015

47 Bruce Feirstein: Authors' interview, 14.02.2015

48 Bruce Feirstein: Authors' interview, 14.02.2015

49 Bruce Feirstein: Authors' interview, 14.02.2015

50 Jeff Kleeman: Authors' interview, 18.05.2015

51 Bruce Feirstein: Authors' interview, 14.02.2015

52 'The Road to GoldenEye' by John Cork, *Goldeneye #4*, The Ian Fleming Foundation, Spring 1996

53 'The Road to GoldenEye' by John Cork, *Goldeneye #4*, The Ian Fleming Foundation, Spring 1996

54 Bruce Feirstein: Authors' interview, 14.02.2015

55 Bruce Feirstein: Authors' interview, 14.02.2015

56 Jeff Kleeman: Authors' interview, 18.05.2015

57 Alan Ladd Jr: Authors' interview, 22.05.2015

58 Jeff Kleeman: Authors' interview, 18.05.2015

59 Jeff Kleeman: Authors' interview, 18.05.2015

60 Timothy Dalton press release, 12.04.1994

61 *LBC Radio*, 12.04.1994

62 Danjaq Inc. press release, 12.04.1994

63 'Dalton Bails Out as Bond' by Dan Cox, *Daily Variety*, 12.04.1994

64 Martin Campbell: Authors' interview, 19.03.2015

65 Martin Campbell: Authors' interview, 19.03.2015

66 'The 007 That Never Was: Ralph Fiennes Comes Clean On Bond' by Claire Duffin, *The Telegraph*, 01.03.2014

67 'Non-Stop Star Liam Neeson: "I Was Asked To Be James Bond But Chose Marriage Instead"' *Hull Daily Mail*, 28.02.2014

68 Garth Pearce, *The Making of GoldenEye*, Boxtree, 1995, p. 10

69 Jeff Kleeman: Authors' interview, 18.05.2015

70 Pierce Brosnan: Authors' interview, 23.05.2015

71 Jeff Kleeman: Authors' interview, 18.05.2015

72 Jeff Kleeman: Authors' interview, 18.05.2015

73 Pierce Brosnan: Authors' interview, 23.05.2015

74 John Glen: Authors' interview, 06.05.2014

75 Jeff Kleeman: Authors' interview, 04.06.2015

76 Pierce Brosnan: Authors' interview, 23.05.2015

77 David Barraclough and John Freeman (ed.), *The Official GoldenEye Movie Souvenir Magazine*, 'Pierce Brosnan interview' Titan, 1995

78 Pierce Brosnan: Authors' interview, 23.05.2015

79 'Meet The New James Bond' *GoldenEye* press conference, Regent Hotel, London, 13.06.1994, by Graham Rye, *007 Extra* #13/14 double issue, The James Bond 007 Fan Club, October 1994

80 Pierce Brosnan: Authors' interview, 23.05.2015

81 Martin Campbell: Authors' interview, 19.03.2015

82 'GoldenEye Girl Izabella Scorupco' by Alan Jones, *Femme Fatales* Vol. 4, no. 5, January 1996

83 'GoldenEye Girl Izabella Scorupco' by Alan Jones, *Femme Fatales* Vol 4, no. 5, January 1996

84 *007: The Return*, dir: Bob Cousins, Carlton UK Productions, ITV, 27.11.1995

85 'GoldenEye Girl Famke Janssen' by Alan Jones, *Femme Fatales* Vol 4, no 5, January 1996

86 Martin Campbell: Authors' interview, 19.03.2015

87 'GoldenEye Girl Famke Janssen' by Alan Jones, *Femme Fatales* Vol 4, no 5, January 1996

88 'GoldenEye Girl Famke Janssen' by Alan Jones, *Femme Fatales* Vol 4, no 5, January 1996

89 *GoldenEye* production notes, United Artists, 1995

90 Garth Pearce, *The Making of GoldenEye*, Boxtree, 1995, p. 68

91 David Barraclough and John Freeman (ed.), *The Official GoldenEye Movie Souvenir Magazine*, 'Robbie Coltrane Interview' by Ed Gross, Titan, 1995

92 'Joe Don Baker – Walking Tall With 007' *GoldenEye* press junket, Beverly Hills Four Seasons Hotel, 27.10.1995, by John Cork, *Goldeneye* #4, The Ian Fleming Foundation, 1996

93 Martin Campbell: Authors' interview, 19.03.2015

94 Samantha Bond: Authors' interview, 04.04.2001

95 Garth Pearce, *The Making of GoldenEye*, Boxtree, 1995, p.71

96 Judi Dench as told to John Millar, *And Furthermore*, Weidenfeld and Nicolson, 2010, p. 158

97 'The Day Dame Judi Was Shaken and Stirred by James Bond' by Pauline Wallin, *Today*, 02.03.1995

98 Samantha Bond: Authors' interview, 04.04.2001

99 Samantha Bond: Authors' interview, 04.04.2001

100 Caroline Bliss: Authors' interview, 19.04.2014

101 Samantha Bond: Authors' interview, 04.04.2001

102 Sandy Hernu, *Q: The Biography of Desmond Llewelyn*, SB Publications, 1999, p. 138

103 'Desmond Llewelyn' by Bruce Feirstein, www.salon.com, 23.12.1999

104 Peter Lamont: Authors' interview, 03.01.2014

105 Phil Méheux: Authors' interview, 09.03.2015

106 Phil Méheux: Authors' interview, 09.03.2015

107 Phil Méheux: Authors' interview, 09.03.2015

108 Phil Méheux: Authors' interview, 09.03.2015

109 Lindy Hemming: Authors' interview, 31.05.2015

110 Lindy Hemming: Authors' interview, 31.05.2015

111 Anthony Waye: Authors' interview, 03.01.2014

112 David Barraclough and John Freeman (ed.), *The Official GoldenEye Movie Souvenir Magazine*, 'Michael Wilson – Producer' by Justin Keay, Titan, 1995

113 Anthony Waye: Authors' interview, 03.01.2014

114 Anthony Waye: Authors' interview, 03.01.2014

115 Phil Méheux: Authors' interview, 09.03.2015

116 Phil Méheux: Authors' interview, 09.03.2015

117 'Peter Lamont interview' by Graham Rye, *007 Magazine* #29, The James Bond International Fan Club, 1995

118 Peter Lamont: Authors' interview, 03.01.2014

119 *GoldenEye: The Secret Files*, dir: Jim Sturgeon, The Creative Partnership, ITV, 26.12.1995

120 Phil Méheux: Authors' interview, 09.03.2015

121 'Back on Her Majesty's Secret Service' by Alan Jones, *Cinefantastique* Vol. 27, No. 3, December 1995

122 Pierce Brosnan: Authors' interview, 23.05.2015

123 Paul Duncan (ed.), *The James Bond Archives*, 'Hard and Fast' by Jamie Russell, Taschen, 2012, p. 428

124 Pierce Brosnan: Authors' interview, 23.05.2015

125 Paul Duncan (ed.), *The James Bond Archives*, 'Hard and Fast' by Jamie Russell, Taschen, 2012, p. 431

126 Peter Lamont: Authors' interview, 26.05.2015

127 'The Road to GoldenEye' by John Cork, *Goldeneye* #4, The Ian Fleming Foundation, Spring 1996

128 Bruce Feirstein: Authors' interview, 15.05.2015

129 Paul Duncan (ed.), *The James Bond Archives*, 'Hard and Fast' by Jamie Russell, Taschen, 2012, p. 431

130 'The Day Dame Judi Was Shaken and Stirred by James Bond' by Pauline Wallin, *Today*, 02.03.1995

131 Pierce Brosnan: Authors' interview, 23.05.2015

132 Lindy Hemming: Authors' interview, 31.05.2015

133 'Production Design' by Alan Jones, *Cinefantastique* Vol. 27, No. 3, December 1995

134 Samantha Bond: Authors' interview, 04.04.2001

135 Samantha Bond: Authors' interview, 04.04.2001

136 Paul Duncan (ed.), *The James Bond Archives*, 'Hard and Fast' by Jamie Russell, Taschen, 2012, p. 431

137 'Q–Quips' by Desmond Llewelyn, *The Bondmanian News* #10, The Bondmanian

Society, September 1995

138 'The Making of GoldenEye' by John Cork, *Goldeneye* #4, The Ian Fleming Foundation, Spring 1996

139 'Golden Boy' by Corie Brown, *Premiere*, US Ed, April 1996

140 'James Bond Branding Guru Karen Sortito Dies at 49' by Mike Barnes, *The Hollywood Reporter*, 14.12.2010

141 'Golden Boy' by Corie Brown, *Premiere*, US Ed, April 1996

142 Jeff Kleeman: Authors' interview, 18.05.2015

143 'Toying With Success; Tie–ins Wrap Up Big $' by Gary Levin, *Weekly Variety*, 11.12.1995

144 'Karen Sortito Dies at 49; Marketing Exec Negotiated Product Tie–ins to Bond Movies' by Valerie J Nelson, *Los Angeles Times*, 15.12.2010

145 Paul Duncan (ed.), *The James Bond Archives*, 'Hard and Fast' by Jamie Russell, Taschen, 2012, p. 432

146 Phil Méheux: Authors' interview, 09.03.2015

147 'Rémy and Dominique Julienne interview' by Jerome Nicod and Laurent Perriot, *Bondmag* #11, Club James Bond, June 1995

148 'Rémy and Dominique Julienne interview' by Jerome Nicod and Laurent Perriot, *Bondmag* #11, Club James Bond, June 1995'

149 'Bond's New Wheels' by Dave Worrall, *Classic and Sportscar*, December 1995

150 Pierce Brosnan: Authors' interview, 23.05.2015

151 Wayne Michaels: Authors' interview, 09.06.2015

152 *GoldenEye* production notes, United Artists, 1995

153 Wayne Michaels: Authors' interview, 09.06.2015

154 Wayne Michaels: Authors' interview, 09.06.2015

155 Wayne Michaels: Authors' interview, 09.06.2015

156 Wayne Michaels: Authors' interview, 09.06.2015

157 Wayne Michaels: Authors' interview, 09.06.2015

158 Wayne Michaels: Authors' interview, 09.06.2015

159 *Hollywood's Greatest Stunts: James Bond Special*, ITV, 1996

160 *Hollywood's Greatest Stunts: James Bond Special*, ITV, 1996

161 *Hollywood's Greatest Stunts: James Bond Special*, ITV, 1996

162 Phil Méheux: Authors' interview, 09.03.2015

163 Phil Méheux: Authors' interview, 09.03.2015

164 'Martin Campbell: Ace Director of Spies' *GoldenEye* press junket, Beverly Hills Four Seasons Hotel, 27.10.1995, by John Cork, *Goldeneye* #4, The Ian Fleming Foundation, 1996

165 'Martin Campbell: Ace Director of Spies' *GoldenEye* press junket, Beverly Hills Four Seasons Hotel, 27.10.1995, by John Cork, *Goldeneye* #4, The Ian Fleming Foundation, 1996

166 'Martin Campbell: Ace Director of Spies' *GoldenEye* press junket, Beverly Hills Four Seasons Hotel, 27.10.1995, by John Cork, *Goldeneye* #4, The Ian Fleming Foundation, 1996

167 Phil Méheux: Authors' interview, 09.03.2015

168 Phil Méheux: Authors' interview, 09.03.2015

169 Phil Méheux: Authors' interview, 09.03.2015

170 Peter Lamont: Authors' interview, 26.05.2015

171 Peter Lamont: Authors' interview, 03.01.2014

172 Peter Lamont: Authors' interview, 03.01.2014

173 Peter Lamont: Authors' interview, 26.05.2015

174 'Michael Wilson and Barbara Broccoli interview' *GoldenEye* press junket, Beverly Hills Four Seasons Hotel, 27.10.1995, by John Cork, *Goldeneye* #4, The Ian Fleming Foundation, 1996

175 'Michael Wilson and Barbara Broccoli interview' *GoldenEye* press junket, Beverly Hills Four Seasons Hotel, 27.10.1995, by John Cork, *Goldeneye* #4, The Ian Fleming Foundation, 1996

176 'Simon Crane interview' by Graham Rye, *007 Magazine* #29, The James Bond 007 Fan Club, 1995

177 *GoldenEye: The Secret Files*, dir: Jim Sturgeon, The Creative Partnership, ITV, 26.12.1995

178 *GoldenEye: The Secret Files*, dir: Jim Sturgeon, The Creative Partnership, ITV, 26.12.1995

179 'Reintroducing Bond … James Bond' by David E. Williams, *American Cinematographer*, December 1995

180 'Danger – Tank On The Loose' by Graham Rye, *007 Magazine* #29, The James Bond 007 Fan Club, 1995

181 Peter Lamont: Authors' interview, 26.05.2015

182 Paul Duncan (ed.), *The James Bond Archives*, 'Hard and Fast' by Jamie Russell, Taschen, 2012, p. 436

183 Paul Duncan (ed.), *The James Bond Archives*, 'Hard and Fast' by Jamie Russell, Taschen, 2012, p. 443

184 Pierce Brosnan: Authors' interview, 23.05.2015

185 Pierce Brosnan: Authors' interview, 23.05.2015

186 Pierce Brosnan: Authors' interview, 23.05.2015

187 Garth Pearce *The Making of GoldenEye*, Boxtree, 1995, p. 60

188 'Reintroducing Bond … James Bond' by David E. Williams, *American Cinematographer*, December 1995

189 Phil Méheux: Authors' interview, 09.03.2015

190 *Bond and Beyond: The Movie Magic of Derek Meddings*, National Museum of Photography, Film and Television in association with Fanderson and The James Bond Collectors Club, 27–28th May 2000

191 'Martin Campbell: Ace Director of Spies' *GoldenEye* press junket, Beverly Hills Four

Seasons Hotel, 27.10.1995, by John Cork, *Goldeneye* #4, The Ian Fleming Foundation, 1996

192 Martin Campbell: Authors' interview, 09.03.2015

193 'John Barry interview' by Daniel Mangolt, *Soundtrack!* #58, 1996

194 Martin Campbell: Authors' interview, 09.03.2015

195 Eric Serra: Authors' interview, 12.05.2015

196 Eric Serra: Authors' interview, 12.05.2015

197 Eric Serra: Authors' interview, 12.05.2015

198 Eric Serra: Authors' interview, 12.05.2015

199 Eric Serra: Authors' interview, 12.05.2015

200 Terry Rawlings: Authors' interview, 18.02.2015

201 Eric Serra: Authors' interview, 12.05.2015

202 Eric Serra: Authors' interview, 12.05.2015

203 Eric Serra: Authors' interview, 12.05.2015

204 Martin Campbell: Authors' interview, 09.03.2015

205 Eric Serra: Authors' interview, 12.05.2015

206 'The Making of GoldenEye' by John Cork, *Goldeneye* #4, The Ian Fleming Foundation, Spring 1996

207 Eric Serra: Authors' interview, 12.05.2015

208 Eric Serra: Authors' interview, 12.05.2015

209 John Burlingame, *The Music of James Bond*, Oxford University Press, 2012, p. 201

210 *007 The Return*, dir: Bob Cousins, Carlton UK Productions, ITV, 27.11.1995

211 Eric Serra: Authors' interview, 12.05.2015

212 Eric Serra: Authors' interview, 12.05.2015

213 *Entertainment Weekly*, 03.12.1999

214 Eric Serra: Authors' interview, 12.05.2015

215 Daniel Kleinman: Authors' interview, 14.05.2015

216 Daniel Kleinman: Authors' interview, 14.05.2015

217 Daniel Kleinman: Authors' interview, 14.05.2015

218 Daniel Kleinman: Authors' interview, 14.05.2015

219 Daniel Kleinman: Authors' interview, 14.05.2015

220 'Of Human *Bondage*' by Richard Rayner, *Esquire*, December 1995

221 Garth Pearce *The Making of GoldenEye*, Boxtree, 1995, p. 97

222 'Directing Bond' by Alan Jones, *Cinefantastique* Vol. 27, No. 3, December 1995 p. 22

223 Albert R. Broccoli and Donald Zec, *When the Snow Melts*, Boxtree, 1998, p. 320

224 Phil Méheux: Authors' interview, 09.03.2015

225 John Cork and Bruce Scivally, *James Bond: The Legacy*, Boxtree, 2002, p. 257

226 'The 5th Man' by Neil McCormick, *GQ*, October 1995

227 Daniel Kleinman in conversation with Matthew Field, *James Bond: A Legacy of Excellence,* Promax UK Conference, Mermaid Theatre, London, 03.11.2006

228 'How To Re-Write a James Bond Movie' by John Cork, *Goldeneye* #4, The Ian Fleming Foundation, Spring 1996.

229 David Barraclough and John Freeman (ed.), *The Official GoldenEye Movie Souvenir Magazine* 'Famke Janssen Interview' Titan, 1995

230 David Barraclough and John Freeman (ed.), *The Official GoldenEye Movie Souvenir Magazine* 'Robbie Coltrane Interview' Titan, 1995

231 Jeff Kleeman: Authors' interview, 18.05.2015

232 Jeff Kleeman: Authors' interview, 18.05.2015

233 Jeff Kleeman: Authors' interview, 18.05.2015

234 'MGM Boasts Boffo B.O Year' *Daily Variety*, 04.01.1996

235 Pierce Brosnan: 'A Celebration of the Life and Work of Cubby Broccoli' Odeon Leicester Square, 17.11.1996

Chapter 25 Tomorrow Never Dies

1 'The Life of Albert R. Broccoli' by John Cork, *Goldeneye Magazine: Cubby Broccoli Special Tribute Issue,* The Ian Fleming Foundation, 1997

2 Roger Moore: *Celebrating the Life and Work of Cubby Broccoli*, Odeon Leicester Square, 17.11.1996

3 'James Bond Movie Producer Albert "Cubby" Broccoli Dies at 87' by Jeff Wilson, *Associated Press*, 28.06.1996.

4 Albert R. Broccoli with Donald Zec, *When the Snow Melts*, Boxtree, 1998, p. 324

5 Albert R. Broccoli with Donald Zec, *When the Snow Melts*, Boxtree, 1998, p. 325

6 Sandy Hernu, *Q: The Biography of Desmond Llewelyn*, S.B Publications, 1999 p. 144

7 Tom Pevsner: *Celebrating the Life and Work of Cubby Broccoli*, Odeon Leicester Square, 17.11.1996

8 Norman Tyre: *Celebrating the Life and Work of Cubby Broccoli*, Odeon Leicester Square, 17.11.1996

9 'Heir to the Legacy' by David Giammarco, *Cinefantastique* Vol. 29, No. 9, January 1998

10 Garth Pearce, *The Making of Tomorrow Never Dies*, Boxtree, 1997, p. 13

11 'Heir to the Legacy' by David Giammarco, *Cinefantastique* Vol. 29, No. 9, January 1998

12 'Sony's Rankled, Levine's Ankled' by Dan Cox and Anita M. Busch, *Daily Variety*, 03.10.1996

13 'Re–United Artists' by Anita M Busch, *Daily*

Variety, 07.11.1996

14   Lindsay Doran: Authors' interview, 04.06.2015

15   Garth Pearce, *The Making of Tomorrow Never Dies,* Boxtree, 1997 p. 18

16   Lindsay Doran: Authors' interview, 04.06.2015

17   Jeff Kleeman: Authors' interview, 18.05.2015

18   Garth Pearce, *The Making of Tomorrow Never Dies,* Boxtree, 1997 p. 18

19   Jeff Kleeman: Authors' interview, 02.06.2015

20   Jeff Kleeman: Authors' interview, 02.06.2015

21   Paul Duncan (ed.), *The James Bond Archives,* 'Further to Fall' by Danny Graydon, Taschen, 2012, p. 448

22   Jeff Kleeman: Authors' interview, 18.05.2015

23   Bruce Feirstein: Authors' interview, 14.02.2015

24   Bruce Feirstein: Authors' interview, 14.02.2015

25   Bruce Feirstein: Authors' interview, 24.05.2015

26   Bruce Feirstein: Authors' interview, 24.05.2015

27   Bruce Feirstein: Authors' interview, 24.05.2015

28   Bruce Feirstein: Authors' interview, 14.02.2015

29   Bruce Feirstein: Authors' interview, 14.02.2015

30   Bruce Feirstein: Authors' interview, 14.02.2015

31   Jeff Kleeman: Authors' interview, 09.06.2015

32   Martin Campbell: Authors' interview, 09.03.2015

33   Martin Campbell: Authors' interview, 09.03.2015

34   'Tomorrow Never Dies Roars Into Production' by John Cork, *Goldeneye* #5, The Ian Fleming Foundation, Summer 1997

35   Paul Duncan (ed.), *The James Bond Archives,* 'Further to Fall' by Danny Graydon, Taschen, 2012, p. 451

36   Roger Spottiswoode: Authors' interview, 21.02.2015

37   'Head of Operations' by Alan Jones, *Film Review Special* #21, 1997

38   Roger Spottiswoode: Authors' interview, 21.02.2015

39   Roger Spottiswoode: Authors' interview, 21.02.2015

40   Roger Spottiswoode: Authors' interview, 21.02.2015

41   Roger Spottiswoode: Authors' interview, 21.02.2015 32

42   Roger Spottiswoode: Authors' interview, 20.02.2015

43   Jeff Kleeman: Authors' interview, 09.06.2015

44   Roger Spottiswoode: Authors' interview, 20.02.2015

45   Roger Spottiswoode: Authors' interview, 20.02.2015

46   Jeff Kleeman: Authors' interview, 18.05.2015

47   Kurt Wimmer: Authors' interview, 22.05.2015

48   David Campbell Wilson: Authors' interview, 04.06.2015

49   David Campbell Wilson: Authors' interview, 04.06.2015

50   Tom Ropelewski: Authors' interview, 08.06.2015

51   Roger Spottiswoode: Authors' interview, 20.02.2015

52   David Campbell Wilson: Authors' interview, 04.06.2015

53   Tom Ropelewski: Authors' interview, 08.06.2015

54   Kurt Wimmer: Authors' interview, 22.05.2015

55   Tom Ropelewski: Authors' interview, 08.06.2015

56   Tom Ropelewski: Authors' interview, 08.06.2015

57   Kurt Wimmer: Authors' interview, 22.05.2015

58   Nicholas Meyer: Authors' interview, 22.04.2015

59   Nicholas Meyer: Authors' interview, 22.04.2015

60   Jeff Kleeman: Authors' interview, 02.06.2015

61   Garth Pearce, *The Making of Tomorrow Never Dies,* Boxtree, 1997, p. 25

62   Pierce Brosnan: Authors' interview, 23.05.2015

63   'First of the International Playboys' by Rupert Howe, *Neon,* January 1998

64   'Oh, Oh … So Compassionate' by Martyn Palmer, *The Times,* 11.12.1997

65   Jeff Kleeman: Authors' interview, 02.06.2015

66   Jeff Kleeman: Authors' interview, 02.06.2015

67   Bruce Feirstein: Authors' interview, 08.06.2015

68   Bruce Feirstein: Authors' interview, 08.06.2015

69   Paul Duncan (ed.), *The James Bond Archives,* 'Further to Fall' by Danny Graydon, Taschen, 2012, p. 462

70   Bruce Feirstein: Authors' interview, 08.06.2015

71   Bruce Feirstein: Authors' interview, 14.02.2015

72   'MGM's Completion Bond' by Rex Weiner and Adam Dawtey, *Daily Variety,* 31.12.1996

73   'Jonathan Pryce on Bond Villainy' by Alan Jones, *Cinefantastique* Vol. 29, No. 9, January 1998

74   'Jonathan Pryce on Bond Villainy' by Alan Jones, *Cinefantastique* Vol. 29, No. 9, January 1998

75   David Bailey (ed.), *Tomorrow Never Dies: The Official Souvenir Magazine,* 'Charming or Ruthless' by Richard Vine, Titan, 1997

76   Bruce Feirstein: Authors' interview, 14.02.2015

77   Bruce Feirstein: Authors' interview, 14.02.2015

78   Roger Spottiswoode: Authors' interview, 21.02.2015

79   'Tomorrow's Femme Michelle Yeoh' by Alan Jones, *Femme Fatales* Vol 6, no 8, February 1998

80   'Tomorrow's Femme Michelle Yeoh' by Alan Jones, *Femme Fatales* Vol 6, no 8, February 1998

81   'Tomorrow's Femme Michelle Yeoh' by Alan Jones, *Femme Fatales* Vol 6, no 8, February 1998

82   'Tomorrow's Femme Michelle Yeoh' by Alan Jones, *Femme Fatales* Vol 6, no 8, February 1998

83   'Bruce Feirstein Interview' by John Cork, *Goldeneye* #6, The Ian Fleming Foundation,

1998

84 Pierce Brosnan: Authors' interview, 23.05.2015

85 Bruce Feirstein: Authors' interview, 14.02.2015

86 Peter Lamont: Authors' interview, 26.05.2015

87 David McConnell (ed.), *The Official James Bond 007 Technical Journal,* 'Designing 007' by Joe Nazzaro, Starlog Communications International, 1997

88 Phil Méheux: Authors' interview, 09.03.2015

89 Vic Armstrong: Authors' interview, 24.06.2015

90 Laurent Bouzereau, *The Art of Bond,* Boxtree, 2006, p. 171

91 Vic Armstrong: Authors' interview, 24.06.2015

92 Bruce Feirstein: Authors' interview, 14.02.2015

93 Roger Spottiswoode: Authors' interview, 20.02.2015

94 'Tomorrow Never Dies Roars Into Production' by John Cork, *Goldeneye* #5, The Ian Fleming Foundation, Summer 1997

95 'Tomorrow Never Dies' by Peter Hooley, *BMW Magazine,* April 1997

96 Sandy Hernu, *Q: The Biography of Desmond Llewelyn,* S.B Publications, 1999, p. 145

97 Bruce Feirstein: Authors' interview, 14.02.2015

98 Bruce Feirstein: Authors' interview, 14.02.2015

99 Pierce Brosnan: Authors' interview, 23.05.2015

100 'Bond Never Dies' by Garth Pearce, *Total Film,* #12, January 1998

101 'Shaken Not Deterred' by Garth Pearce, *The Sunday Times,* 30.11.1997

102 Judi Dench as told to John Millar, *And Furthermore,* Weidenfeld and Nicolson, 2010, p. 160

103 Judi Dench as told to John Millar, *And Furthermore,* Weidenfeld and Nicolson, 2010, p. 160

104 Judi Dench as told to John Millar, *And Furthermore,* Weidenfeld and Nicolson, 2010, p. 160

105 David McConnell (ed.), *The Official James Bond 007 Technical Journal,* 'Designing 007' by Joe Nazzaro, Starlog Communications International, 1997

106 David McConnell (ed.), *The Official James Bond 007 Technical Journal,* 'Samantha Bond' by Joe Nazzaro, Starlog Communications International, 1997

107 'David McConnell (ed.), *The Official James Bond 007 Technical Journal,* 'Designing 007' by Joe Nazzaro, Starlog Communications International, 1997

108 David McConnell (ed.), *The Official James Bond 007 Technical Journal,* 'Designing 007' by Joe Nazzaro, Starlog Communications International, 1997

109 David McConnell (ed.), *The Official James Bond 007 Technical Journal,* 'Designing 007' by Joe Nazzaro, Starlog Communications

International, 1997

110 'Bond Never Dies' by Garth Pearce, *Total Film,* #12, January 1998

111 Jeff Kleeman: Authors' interview, 04.06.2015

112 Bruce Feirstein: Authors' interview, 04.06.2015

113 David McConnell (ed.), *The Official James Bond 007 Technical Journal,* 'Pierce Brosnan: James Bond' by Joe Nazzaro, Starlog Communications International, 1997

114 'Trails of the Unexpected' by Louise Tutt, *Screen International,* 05.12.1997

115 Roger Spottiswoode: Authors' interview, 20.02.2015

116 Anthony Waye: Authors' interview, 03.01.2014

117 Anthony Waye: Authors' interview, 03.01.2014

118 Roger Spottiswoode: Authors' interview, 20.02.2015

119 David Giammarco, *For Your Eyes Only: Behind the Scenes of the James Bond Films,* ECW, 2002 p. 305

120 Roger Spottiswoode: Authors' interview, 20.02.2015

121 Vic Armstrong: Authors' interview, 24.06.2015

122 Roger Spottiswoode: Authors' interview, 20.02.2015

123 Vic Armstrong: Authors' interview, 24.06.2015

124 Vic Armstrong: Authors' interview, 24.06.2015

125 'Tomorrow Never Dies' by Peter Hooley, *BMW Magazine,* April 1997

126 Vic Armstrong: Authors' interview, 24.06.2015

127 Garth Pearce, *The Making of Tomorrow Never Dies,* Boxtree, 1997, p. 78

128 'Bond Never Dies' by Garth Pearce, *Total Film* #12, January 1998

129 Jeff Kleeman: Authors' interview, 09.06.2015

130 'First of the International Playboys' by Rupert Howe, *Neon,* January 1998

131 David McConnell (ed.), *The Official James Bond 007 Technical Journal,* 'Designing 007' by Joe Nazzaro, Starlog Communications International, 1997

132 'Tomorrow Never Dies' by Peter Hooley, *BMW Magazine,* April 1997

133 'Tomorrow Never Dies' by Peter Hooley, *BMW Magazine,* April 1997

134 'Tomorrow Never Dies' by Peter Hooley, *BMW Magazine,* April 1997

135 Vic Armstrong: Authors' interview, 24.06.2015

136 Vic Armstrong: Authors' interview, 24.06.2015

137 Paul Duncan (ed.), *The James Bond Archives,* 'Further to Fall' by Danny Graydon, Taschen, 2012, p. 454

138 'Bruce Feirstein Interview' by John Cork, *Goldeneye* #6, The Ian Fleming Foundation, 1998

139 'Roger Spottiswoode, Nobody Directs It Better' by Alan Jones, *Cinefantastique* Vol. 29, No. 9, January 1998.

140 'Tomorrow Never Dies' by Peter Hooley, *BMW Magazine*, April 1997

141 Jeff Kleeman: Authors' interview, 09.06.2015

142 Jeff Kleeman: Authors' interview, 09.06.2015

143 Jeff Kleeman: Authors' interview, 09.06.2015

144 Vic Armstrong: Authors' interview, 24.06.2015

145 David Bailey (ed.), *Tomorrow Never Dies: The Official Souvenir Magazine,* 'Bigger, More Grand, More Lavish' by James Swallow, Titan, 1997

146 Garth Pearce, *The Making of Tomorrow Never Dies*, Boxtree, 1997 p. 52

147 David McConnell (ed.), *The Official James Bond 007 Technical Journal*, 'Designing 007' by Joe Nazzaro, Starlog Communications International, 1997

148 'Pierce Brosnan Interview' by Alan Jones, *Cinefantastique* Vol. 29, No. 9, January 1998

149 Paul Duncan (ed.), *The James Bond Archives*, 'Further to Fall' by Danny Graydon, Taschen, 2012, p. 461

150 Garth Pearce, *The Making of Tomorrow Never Dies*, Boxtree, 1997 p. 96

151 'He Would Have Loved Her Well' by Bridget Harrison, *The Times*, 11.09.1997

152 Garth Pearce, *The Making of Tomorrow Never Dies*, Boxtree, 1997 p. 118

153 Paul Duncan (ed.), *The James Bond Archives*, 'Further to Fall' by Danny Graydon, Taschen, 2012, p. 462

154 'Roger Spottiswoode, Nobody Directs It Better' by Alan Jones, *Cinefantastique* Vol. 29, No. 9, January 1998

155 Roger Spottiswoode: Authors' interview, 15.02.2015

156 Roger Spottiswoode: Authors' interview, 15.02.2015

157 Roger Spottiswoode: Authors' interview, 15.02.2015

158 'Tomorrow Never Dies: The Lost Interviews' by Edward Gross, *Retro Vision*, #6, 1999

159 Lindsay Doran: Authors' interview, 04.06.2015

160 Roger Spottiswoode: Authors' interview, 15.02.2015

161 Bruce Feirstein: Authors' interview, 14.02.2015

162 Roger Spottiswoode: Authors' interview, 15.02.2015

163 Jeff Kleeman: Authors' interview, 09.06.2015

164 Michael G. Wilson, *Beyond Bond,* part of *Bond, James Bond*, Institute of Contemporary Arts (ICA), London, 26.10.1996

165 'Tomorrow Never Dies Roars Into Production' by John Cork, *Goldeneye* #5, The Ian Fleming Foundation, Summer 1997

166 John Burlingame, *The Music of James Bond*, Oxford University Press, 2012, p. 209

167 David Arnold: Authors' interview, 23.06.2015

168 David Arnold: Authors' interview, 23.06.2015

169 David Arnold: Authors' interview, 23.06.2015

170 David Arnold: Authors' interview, 23.06.2015

171 David Arnold: Authors' interview, 23.06.2015

172 David Arnold: Authors' interview, 23.06.2015

173 David Arnold: Authors' interview, 23.06.2015

174 David Arnold: Authors' interview, 23.06.2015

175 David Arnold: Authors' interview, 23.06.2015

176 David Arnold: Authors' interview, 23.06.2015

177 David Arnold: Authors' interview, 23.06.2015

178 'The New Sound of 007' by Greg Bechtloff, *007 Magazine* #39, The James Bond 007 International Fan Club, May 2001

179 'You Only Lead Thrice', by Louise Tutt, *Screen International*, 05.12.1997

180 'You Only Lead Thrice' by Louise Tutt, *Screen International*, 05.12.1997

181 Daniel Kleinman: Authors' interview, 14.05.2015

182 Daniel Kleinman: Authors' interview, 14.05.2015

183 Daniel Kleinman: Authors' interview, 14.05.2015

184 'Sony Splits Bond Market' by Rex Weiner, *Daily Variety*, 14.10.1997

185 'Sony Splits Bond Market' by Rex Weiner, *Daily Variety*, 14.10.1997

186 'Sony Splits Bond Market' by Rex Weiner, *Daily Variety*, 14.10.1997

187 Lindsay Doran: Authors' interview, 04.06.2015

188 *Daily Variety* 28.05.1996

189 '007 Faces Legal Shoot Out' by Paul Karon and Rex Weiner, *Daily Variety*, 18.11.1997

191 '007 Faces Legal Shoot Out' by Paul Karon and Rex Weiner, *Daily Variety*, 18.11.1997

192 '007 Faces Legal Shoot Out' by Paul Karon and Rex Weiner, *Daily Variety*, 18.11.1997

193 '007 Faces Legal Shoot Out' by Paul Karon and Rex Weiner, *Daily Variety*, 18.11.1997

194 '007 Faces Legal Shoot Out' by Paul Karon and Rex Weiner, *Daily Variety*, 18.11.1997

195 '007 Faces Legal Shoot Out' by Paul Karon and Rex Weiner, *Daily Variety*, 18.11.1997

196 'MGM Nabs Never' by Paul Karon, *Daily Variety*, 03.12.1997

197 'MGM Nabs Never' by Paul Karon, *Daily Variety*, 03.12.1997

198 Jeff Kleeman: Authors' interview, 04.06.2015

199 Jeff Kleeman: Authors' interview, 04.06.2015

200 'Tomorrow Never Dies: The Lost Interviews' by Edward Gross, *Retro Vision* #6, 1999

202 Lindsay Doran: Authors' interview, 06.06.2015

Chapter 26 The World is Not Enough

1 'UA for Lion's Niche' by Bill Higgins and Chris Petrikin, *Daily Variety*, 08.06.1999

2 Chris McGurk: Authors' interview, 25.06.2015

3 Lindsay Doran: Authors' interview, 04.06.2015

4 'Michael G. Wilson' by Alan Jones, *Cinefantastique* Vol. 31, No. 9, December 1999

5 Chris McGurk: Authors' interview, 25.06.2015

6 'The World Is Not Enough press junket' by Gregg Bechtloff, Four Seasons Hotel Beverly Hills, 05.11.1999, *007 Magazine #37*, The James Bond 007 International Fan Club, 2000

7 Neal Purvis: Authors' interview, 06.03.2015

8 Neal Purvis and Robert Wade in conversation with Matthew Field, *The Martin Cahill Memorial Lecture*, presented by The Lunch Club, London, 24.07.2013

9 Neal Purvis: Authors' interview, 06.03.2015

10 Neal Purvis and Robert Wade in conversation with Matthew Field, *The Martin Cahill Memorial Lecture*, presented by The Lunch Club, London, 24.07.2013

11 Robert Wade: Authors' interview, 10.06.2015

12 Robert Wade: Authors' interview, 26.05.2015

13 Neal Purvis: Authors' interview, 06.03.2015

14 Iain Johnstone, *The World Is Not Enough: A Companion*, Boxtree, 1999, p. 28

15 Robert Wade: Authors' interview, 26.05.2015

16 Robert Wade: Authors' interview,: 26.05.2015

17 Alistair Owen (ed.), *Story and Character: Interviews with British Screenwriters*, Bloomsbury, 2003, p. 167

18 Robert Wade: Authors' interview, 10.06.2015

19 Martin Campbell: Authors' interview, 19.03.2015

20 Jeff Kleeman: Authors' interview, 09.06.2015

21 Robert Wade: Authors' interview, 12.04.2015

22 Jeff Kleeman: Authors' interview, 09.06.2015

23 'A Dramatic Departure' *Screen International*, 26.11.1999

24 Michael Apted: Authors' interview, 28.10.2014

25 'Michael G. Wilson' by Alan Jones, *Cinefantastique* Vol. 31, No. 9, December 1999

26 Michael Apted: Authors' interview, 28.10.2014

27 Michael Apted: Authors' interview, 28.10.2014

28 Pierce Brosnan: Authors' interview, 23.05.2015

29 Michael Apted: Authors' interview, 28.10.2014

30 *The World Is Not Enough* production notes, written and compiled by Geoff Freeman, MGM, 1999

31 'Michael Apted' by Alan Jones, *Cinefantastique* Vol. 31, No. 9, December 1999

32 'The World Is Not Enough press junket' by Gregg Bechtloff, Four Seasons Hotel Beverly Hills, 05.11.1999, *007 Magazine #37*, The James Bond 007 International Fan Club, 2000

33 Robert Wade: Authors' interview, 26.05.2015

34 Robert Wade: Authors' interview, 26.05.2015

35 Neal Purvis: Authors' interview, 06.03.2015

36 Robert Wade: Authors' interview, 26.05.2015

37 Robert Wade: Authors' interview, 26.05.2015

38 Dana Stevens: Authors' interview, 26.04.2015

39 Jeff Kleeman: Authors' interview, 09.06.2015

40 Dana Stevens: Authors' interview, 26.04.2015

41 Dana Stevens: Authors' interview, 26.04.2015

42 Dana Stevens: Authors' interview, 26.04.2015

43 Dana Stevens: Authors' interview, 26.04.2015

44 Michael Apted: Authors' interview, 25.06.2015

45 Dana Stevens: Authors' interview, 26.04.2015

46 'A Dramatic Departure' *Screen International*, 26.11.1999

47 Michael Apted: Authors' interview, 28.10.2014

48 Iain Johnstone, *The World Is Not Enough: A Companion*, Boxtree, 1999, p. 136

49 Iain Johnstone, *The World Is Not Enough: A Companion*, Boxtree, 1999, p. 24

50 Bruce Feirstein: Authors' interview, 14.02.2015

51 Bruce Feirstein: Authors' interview, 14.02.2015

52 Bruce Feirstein: Authors' interview, 05.06.2015

53 Iain Johnstone, *The World Is Not Enough: A Companion*, Boxtree, 1999, p. 136

54 Michael Apted: Authors' interview, 28.10.2014

55 Neal Purvis: Authors' interview, 06.03.2015

56 Robert Wade: Authors' interview, 26.05.2015

57 'Never Enough' by Alan Jones, *Film Review*, December 1999

58 'Michael G. Wilson interview' by Alan Jones, *Cinefantastique* Vol. 31, No. 9, December 1999

59 Dana Stevens: Authors' interview, 26.04.2015

60 Pierce Brosnan: Authors' interview, 23.05.2015

61 'Sophie Marceau interview' by Alan Jones, *Femme Fatales* Vol. 8 no 9, December 1999

62 Iain Johnstone, *The World Is Not Enough: A Companion*, Boxtree, 1999, p. 71

63 Michael Apted: Authors' interview, 28.10.2014

64 Dana Stevens: Authors' interview, 26.04.2015

65 'Sophie Marceau interview' by Alan Jones, *Femme Fatales* Vol. 8 no 9, December 1999

66 Pierce Brosnan: Authors' interview, 23.05.2015

67 Lindy Hemming: Authors' interview, 21.06.2015

68 Lindsay Doran: Authors' interview, 04.06.2015

69 Michael Apted: Authors' interview, 28.10.2014

70 *Making A Blockbuster: Episode 1: Pre–Production*, Dir: Jane Dickson, Film Education, Channel 4, 15.11.1999

71 Robert Wade: Authors' interview, 26.05.2015

72 Neal Purvis: Authors' interview, 06.03.2015

73 Iain Johnstone, *The World Is Not Enough: A Companion*, Boxtree, 1999, p. 32

74 Neal Purvis: Authors' interview, 06.03.2015

75 Iain Johnstone, *The World Is Not Enough: A Companion*, Boxtree, 1999, p. 32

76   Dana Stevens: Authors' interview, 26.04.2015

77   *The World Is Not Enough* production notes, written and compiled by Geoff Freeman, MGM, 1999

78   Robert Wade: Authors' interview, 26.05.2015

79   Robert Wade: Authors' interview, 26.05.2015

80   *The World Is Not Enough* production notes, written and compiled by Geoff Freeman, MGM, 1999

81   Iain Johnstone, *The World Is Not Enough: A Companion*, Boxtree, 1999, p. 90

82   Iain Johnstone, *The World Is Not Enough: A Companion*, Boxtree, 1999, p. 90

83   'Robert Carlyle Interview' by Tom Henwood, *Flicks*, December 1999

84   'The World Is Not Enough Press Junket' by Gregg Bechtloff, Four Seasons Hotel Beverly Hills, 05.11.1999, *007 Magazine #37*, The James Bond 007 International Fan Club, 2000

85   *The World Is Not Enough* production notes, written and compiled by Geoff Freeman, MGM, 1999

86   Judi Dench as told to John Millar, *And Furthermore*, Weidenfeld and Nicolson, 2010, p. 195

87   *The World Is Not Enough* production notes, written and compiled by Geoff Freeman, MGM, 1999

88   *The World Is Not Enough* production notes, written and compiled by Geoff Freeman, MGM, 1999

89   David McDonnell, *The World Is Not Enough: The Official Movie Magazine,* 'John Cleese interview' by Kim Howard Johnson, Starlog, 1999

90   Michael Apted: Authors' interview, 28.10.2014

91   Helen De Winter, *What I Really Want To Do Is Produce*, Faber and Faber Limited, 2006, p. 31

92   Peter Lamont: Authors' interview, 13.05.2014

93   'Behind the Scenes of Bond' by Alan Jones, *Cinefantastique* Vol. 31, No. 9, December 1999

94   'The World Is Not Enough press junket' by Gregg Bechtloff, Four Seasons Hotel Beverly Hills, 05.11.1999, *007 Magazine #37*, The James Bond 007 International Fan Club, 2000

95   *The World Is Not Enough* production notes, written and compiled by Geoff Freeman, MGM, 1999

96   Michael Apted: Authors' interview, 25.06.2015

97   Peter Lamont: Authors' interview, 03.01.2014

98   'Bond Finds New Buzz' by Chris Manly, *Australian Sunday Telegraph*, 18.04.1999

99   Samantha Bond: Authors' interview, 04.04.2001

100   Paul Duncan (ed.), *The James Bond Archives*, 'Fantasy in a Real World' by Howard Hughes, Taschen, 2012, p. 478

101   *The World Is Not Enough* production notes, written and compiled by Geoff Freeman, MGM, 1999

102   Iain Johnstone, *The World Is Not Enough: A Companion*, Boxtree, 1999, p. 131

103   Iain Johnstone, *The World Is Not Enough: A Companion*, Boxtree, 1999, p. 131

104   Iain Johnstone, *The World Is Not Enough: A Companion*, Boxtree, 1999, p. 131

105   Neal Purvis: Authors' interview, 06.03.2015

106   Peter Lamont: Authors' interview, 06.10.2000

107   Robert Wade: Authors' interview, 26.05.2015

108   Vic Armstrong: Authors' interview, 24.06.2015

109   Pierce Brosnan: Authors' interview, 23.05.2015

110   Michael Apted: Authors' interview, 25.06.2015

111   'Paul Duncan (ed.), *The James Bond Archives*, 'Fantasy in a Real World' by Howard Hughes, Taschen, 2012, p. 478

112   Vic Armstrong: Authors' interview, 24.06.2015

113   Vic Armstrong: Authors' interview, 24.06.2015

114   'Action Man' by Anthony C Ferrante, *Dreamwatch*, December 1999

115   Jim Clark with John H Myers, *Dream Repairman*, LandMarc Press, 2010, p. 269

116   'Paul Duncan (ed.), *The James Bond Archives*, 'Fantasy in a Real World' by Howard Hughes, Taschen, 2012, p. 481

117   Dana Stevens: Authors' interview, 26.04.2015

118   David McDonnell (ed.), *The World Is Not Enough: The Official Movie Magazine,* 'Pierce Brosnan interview' by Kim Howard Johnson, Starlog, 1999

119   Michael Apted: Authors' interview, 26.06.2015

120   Iain Johnstone, *The World Is Not Enough: A Companion*, Boxtree, 1999, p. 137

121   Michael Apted: Authors' interview, 28.10.2014

122   Paul Duncan (ed.), *The James Bond Archives*, 'Fantasy in a Real World' by Howard Hughes, Taschen, 2012, p. 481

123   Michael Apted: Authors' interview, 26.06.2015

124   Michael Apted: Authors' interview, 26.06.2015

125   'Bonded Goods' by Peter Hooley, *Elements: BMW Magazine* in association with *The Daily Telegraph*, 1999

126   Helen De Winter, *What I Really Want To Do Is Produce*, Faber and Faber Limited, 2006, p. 40

127   'We've Been Expecting You Mr. Bond' by Nick Setchfield, *SFX #59*, Christmas 1999

128   Vic Armstrong: Authors' interview, 24.06.2015

129   Vic Armstrong: Authors' interview, 24.06.2015

130   Vic Armstrong: Authors' interview, 24.06.2015

131   Vic Armstrong: Authors' interview, 24.06.2015

132   Vic Armstrong: Authors' interview, 24.06.2015

133   Bruce Feirstein: Authors' interview, 14.02.2015

134   Bruce Feirstein: Authors' interview, 14.02.2015

135   Bruce Feirstein: Authors' interview, 14.02.2015

136   Lindy Hemming: Authors' interview, 21.06.2015

137   Desmond Llewelyn: Authors' interview, 23.04.1999

138   Pierce Brosnan: Authors' interview, 23.05.2015
139   David Arnold: Authors' interview, 23.06.2015
140   David Arnold: Authors' interview, 23.06.2015
141   David Arnold: Authors' interview, 23.06.2015
142   David Arnold: Authors' interview, 23.06.2015
143   David Arnold: Authors' interview, 23.06.2015
144   'The New Sound of 007' by Greg Bechtloff,
      007 Magazine #39, The James Bond 007
      International Fan Club, May 2001
145   'Bond Ambition' by Mark Edwards, *Culture
      Magazine: The Sunday Times,* 10.10.1999
146   David Arnold: Authors' interview, 23.06.2015
147   David Arnold: Authors' interview, 23.06.2015
148   David Arnold: Authors' interview, 23.06.2015
149   David Arnold: Authors' interview, 23.06.2015
150   Daniel Kleinman: Authors' interview,
      13.06.2015
151   David Arnold: Authors' interview, 23.06.2015
152   Daniel Kleinman: Authors' interview,
      13.06.2015
153   Daniel Kleinman: Authors' interview,
      13.06.2015
154   Daniel Kleinman: Authors' interview,
      13.06.2015
155   Jim Clark with John H. Myers, *Dream
      Repairman: Adventures in Film Editing,* LandMarc
      Press, 2010, p. 270
156   Michael Apted: Authors' interview, 28.10.2014
157   Jim Clark with John H. Myers, *Dream
      Repairman: Adventures in Film Editing,* LandMarc
      Press, 2010, p. 270
158   Jim Clark with John H. Myers, *Dream
      Repairman: Adventures in Film Editing,* LandMarc
      Press, 2010, p. 270
159   Jim Clark with John H. Myers, *Dream
      Repairman: Adventures in Film Editing,* LandMarc
      Press, 2010, p. 270
160   Michael Apted: Authors' interview, 28.10.2014
161   David Giammarco, *For Your Eyes Only: Behind
      the Scenes of the James Bond Films,* ECW, 2002, p.
      348
162   David Giammarco, *For Your Eyes Only: Behind
      the Scenes of the James Bond Films,* ECW, 2002, p.
      355
163   'Michael G Wilson' by Alan Jones,
      Cinefantastique Vol. 31, No. 9, December 1999
164   *Screen International* 12.05.2000
165   'Sony Raises Stakes in Studios' Bond Battle'
      Weekly Variety, 23.02.1998
166   'Sony Raises Stakes in Studios' Bond Battle'
      Weekly Variety, 23.02.1998
167   'MGM Aims to Nix Sony's Bond Claim' *Daily
      Variety,* 15.04.1998
168   'MGM Seeks Block on Sony Bond Pic' *Daily
      Variety,* 29.05.1998
169   'McClory Makes Official Claims to Bond
      Rights' by Eric Boehm and Paul Karon, *Daily
      Variety,* 17.07.1998
170   'McClory Makes Official Claims to Bond
      Rights' by Eric Boehm and Paul Karon, *Daily
      Variety,* 17.07.1998
171   'MGM Wins 007 Round' by Janet Shprintz,
      Daily Variety, 30.07.1998
172   'MGM Wins 007 Round' by Janet Shprintz,
      Daily Variety, 30.07.1998
173   'Court Backs MGM on Bond' by Janet
      Shprintz, *Daily Variety,* 23.11.1998
174   'Sony Scores Small Win in Bond Case' by Janet
      Shprintz, *Daily Variety,* 18.09.1998
175   'Judge Stands by Bond Rulings' by Janet
      Shprintz, *Daily Variety,* 15.03.1999
176   'MGM Victory Bonds Fanchise' by Janet
      Shprintz, *Weekly Variety,* 05.04.1999
177   'MGM victory Bonds Franchise' by Janet
      Shprintz, *Weekly Variety,* 05.04.1999
178   'MGM Victory Bonds Franchise' by Janet
      Shprintz, *Weekly Variety,* 05.04.1999
179   *Weekly Variety* 05.04.1999
180   'Judge Rejects Scribe's Claims to 007
      Franchise' *Daily Variety,* 03.04.2000
181   'McClory Loses His Bond Retry' by Lindsay
      Chaney, *Daily Variety,* 28.08.2001
182   'U.S Court Rejects Claim to James Bond' by
      Meg James, *Los Angeles Times,* 28.08.2001
183   'U.S Court Rejects Claim to James Bond' by
      Meg James, *Los Angeles Times,* 28.08.2001
184   Jeff Kleeman: Authors' interview, 09.06.2015
185   Jeff Kleeman: Authors' interview, 09.06.2015
186   'James Bond: Pierce Brosnan' by Alan Jones,
      Cinefantastique Vol. 31, No. 9, December 1999
187   'James Bond: Pierce Brosnan' by Alan Jones,
      Cinefantastique Vol. 31, No. 9, December 1999
188   Jeff Kleeman: Authors' interview, 09.06.2015

Chapter 27 Die Another Day

1   'Plotting Against Bond' by Jason Caro, *Film
     Review Special* #45, 2003
2   Chris McGurk: Authors' interview, 25.06.2015
3   Chris McGurk: Authors' interview, 25.06.2015
4   Chris McGurk: Authors' interview, 25.06.2015
5   Helen De Winter, *What I Really Want To Do Is
     Produce,* Faber and Faber Limited, 2006, p. 32
6   Helen De Winter, *What I Really Want To Do Is
     Produce,* Faber and Faber Limited, 2006, p. 32
7   Pierce Brosnan: Authors' interview, 23.05.2015
8   'All In The Family' *MI6 Confidential,* #19, 2013
9   'All In The Family' *MI6 Confidential,* #19, 2013
10   Michael Apted: Authors' interview, 28.10.2014
11   Chris McGurk: Authors' interview, 25.06.2015

12 *The Hollywood Reporter*, 27.06.2001

13 Chris McGurk: Authors' interview, 25.06.2015

14 The *Hollywood Reporter*, 27.06.2001

15 Chris McGurk: Authors' interview, 25.06.2015

16 'The Real M' by David Richardson, *Film Review Special* #45, 2003

17 'Premium Bond' by Edward Lawrenson, *Sight and Sound*, November 2002

18 'Premium Bond' by Edward Lawrenson, *Sight and Sound*, November 2002

19 Chris McGurk: Authors' interview, 25.06.2015

20 Lee Tamahori: Authors' interview, 02.05.2015

21 'Bond Is Mine Now' by Alan Jones, *Film Review*, November 2002

22 'To Die For' by Mark Salisbury, *Premiere*, US Ed, November 2002

23 'Numero Uno' by Ian Nathan, *Empire* #162, December 2002

24 'To Die For' by Mark Salisbury, *Premiere*, US Ed, November 2002

25 'To Die For' by Mark Salisbury, *Premiere*, US Ed, November 2002

26 'Bond Is Mine Now' by Alan Jones, *Film Review*, November 2002

27 Pierce Brosnan: Authors' interview, 23.05.2015

28 'Plotting Against Bond' by Jason Caro, *Film Review Special* #45, 2003

29 Robert Wade: Authors' interview, 06.06.2015

30 Lee Tamahori: Authors' interview, 02.05.2015

31 *Die Another Day* production notes, Twentieth Century Fox, 2002

32 'Plotting Against Bond' by Jason Caro, *Film Review Special* #45, 2003

33 Robert Wade: Authors' interview, 06.06.2015

34 Robert Wade: Authors' interview, 06.06.2015

35 Neal Purvis: Authors' interview, 06.03.2015

36 Neal Purvis: Authors' interview, 06.03.2015

37 Neal Purvis: Authors' interview, 06.03.2015

38 Robert Wade: Authors' interview, 06.06.2015

39 Neal Purvis: Authors' interview, 06.03.2015

40 Helen De Winter, *What I Really Want To Do Is Produce*, Faber and Faber Limited, 2006, p. 32

41 Robert Wade: Authors' interview, 06.06.2015

42 Neal Purvis: Authors' interview, 06.03.2015

43 Peter Lamont: Authors' interview, 21.06.2015

44 'Plotting Against Bond' by Jason Caro, *Film Review Special* #45, 2003

45 Lee Tamahori: Authors' interview, 02.05.2015

46 'Nobody Does It Better' by Andrew Osmond, *Cinescape*, Nov/Dec 2002

47 Neal Purvis: Authors' interview, 06.03.2015

48 Chris McGurk: Authors' interview, 25.06.2015

49 'Bond Ambition' by David Richardson, *Starburst* #290, October 2002

50 Robert Wade: Authors' interview, 06.06.2015

51 Lee Tamahori: Authors' interview, 02.05.2015

52 Robert Wade: Authors' interview, 06.06.2015

53 'Bond Is Mine Now' by Alan Jones, *Film Review*, November 2002

54 Lee Tamahori: Authors' interview, 02.05.2015

55 Robert Wade: Authors' interview, 06.06.2015

56 Neal Purvis: Authors' interview, 06.03.2015

57 Lee Tamahori: Authors' interview, 02.05.2015

58 Lee Tamahori: Authors' interview, 02.05.2015

59 Lee Tamahori: Authors' interview, 02.05.2015

60 Lee Tamahori: Authors' interview, 02.05.2015

61 'Bigger, Better, Bolder, Badder, Bond' by Ian Freer, *Empire* #162, December 2002

62 Lee Tamahori: Authors' interview, 02.05.2015

63 Lee Tamahori: Authors' interview, 02.05.2015

64 Lee Tamahori: Authors' interview, 02.05.2015

65 Robert Wade: Authors' interview, 06.06.2015

66 Robert Wade: Authors' interview, 06.06.2015

67 Lee Tamahori: Authors' interview, 02.05.2015

68 Lee Tamahori: Authors' interview, 02.05.2015

69 Robert Wade: Authors' interview, 06.06.2015

70 Neal Purvis: Authors' interview, 06.03.2015

71 Robert Wade: Authors' interview, 06.06.2015

72 Robert Wade: Authors' interview, 06.06.2015

73 David Arnold: Authors' interview, 23.06.2015

74 Lee Tamahori: Authors' interview, 02.05.2015

75 Robert Wade: Authors' interview, 06.06.2015

76 Robert Wade: Authors' interview, 06.06.2015

77 'Bigger, Better, Bolder, Badder, Bond' by Ian Freer, *Empire* #162, December 2002

78 Lee Tamahori: Authors' interview, 02.05.2015

79 'Bond Is Mine Now' by Alan Jones, *Film Review*, November 2002

80 'To Die For' by Mark Salisbury, *Premiere*, US Ed, November 2002

81 Robert Wade: Authors' interview, 06.06.2015

82 Pierce Brosnan: Authors' interview, 23.05.2015

83 Lee Tamahori: Authors' interview, 02.05.2015

84 'To Die For' by Mark Salisbury, *Premiere*, US Ed, November 2002

85 Pierce Brosnan: Authors' interview, 23.05.2015

86 'To Die For' by Mark Salisbury, *Premiere*, US Ed, November 2002

87 'To Die For' by Mark Salisbury, *Premiere*, US Ed, November 2002

88 Lee Tamahori: Authors' interview, 02.05.2015

89 Robert Wade: Authors' interview, 06.06.2015

90 Robert Wade: Authors' interview, 06.06.2015

91 'Solid Gold' by Jonathan Van Meter' *Vogue*, US Ed, December 2002

92 'Solid Gold' by Jonathan Van Meter' *Vogue*, US Ed, December 2002

93 'Solid Gold' by Jonathan Van Meter' *Vogue*, US Ed, December 2002

94 Lee Tamahori: Authors' interview, 02.05.2015

95 Helen De Winter, *What I Really Want To Do Is Produce*, Faber and Faber Limited, 2006, p. 37

96 'Halle Berry: Undercover Cop' by William Thomas, *Empire* #162, December 2002

97 'Bonded' by Patrick Demarchelier, *Marie Claire*, UK Ed, December 2002

98 Pierce Brosnan: Authors' interview, 23.05.2015

99 Neal Purvis: Authors' interview, 06.03.2015

100 Lee Tamahori: Authors' interview, 02.05.2015

101 Robert Wade: Authors' interview, 06.06.2015

102 Robert Wade: Authors' interview, 06.06.2015

103 Lee Tamahori: Authors' interview, 02.05.2015

104 'The Real M' by David Richardson, *Film Review Special #45*, 2003

105 Robert Wade: Authors' interview, 06.06.2015

106 *Die Another Day* production notes, Twentieth Century Fox, 2002

107 Neal Purvis: Authors' interview, 06.03.2015

108 Lee Tamahori: Authors' interview, 02.05.2015

109 'Nobody Does It Better' by Karen Kay, *The Times Magazine, The Times,* 26.10.2002

110 'Sinning Ways' by Kathy Brewis, *The Sunday Times*, 20.10.2002

111 Lee Tamahori: Authors' interview, 02.05.2015

112 Lee Tamahori: Authors' interview, 02.05.2015

113 'No Holes Barred' by John Pavlus, *American Cinematographer*, November 2002

114 Lee Tamahori: Authors' interview, 02.05.2015

115 Lee Tamahori: Authors' interview, 02.05.2015

116 'Samantha Bond: Don't Call Me Miss Moneypenny' by Carole Cadwalladr, *The Observer*, 14.11.2010

117 'Samantha Bond: Don't Call Me Miss Moneypenny' by Carole Cadwalladr, *The Observer*, 14.11.2010

118 'The Name's Dench. Judi Dench' by Matt Wolf, *The Times*, 22.11.1999

119 Robert Wade: Authors' interview, 06.06.2015

120 *Die Another Day* production notes, Twentieth Century Fox, 2002

121 *Die Another Day* production notes, Twentieth Century Fox, 2002

122 Robert Wade: Authors' interview, 06.06.2015

123 Peter Lamont: Authors' interview, 21.06.2015

124 Vic Armstrong: Authors' interview, 24.06.2015

125 Vic Armstrong: Authors' interview, 24.06.2015

126 Pierce Brosnan: Authors' interview, 23.05.2015

127 *Die Another Day: From Script To Screen*, dir: Rob Done, Special Treats Production Company, ITV, 20.11.2002

128 Helen De Winter, *What I Really Want To Do Is Produce*, Faber and Faber Limited, 2006, p. 40

129 Pierce Brosnan: Authors' interview, 23.05.2015

130 Lee Tamahori: Authors' interview, 02.05.2015

131 Vic Armstrong: Authors' interview, 24.06.2015

132 Vic Armstrong: Authors' interview, 24.06.2015

133 Vic Armstrong: Authors' interview, 24.06.2015

134 Vic Armstrong: Authors' interview, 24.06.2015

135 Vic Armstrong: Authors' interview, 24.06.2015

136 Neal Purvis: Authors' interview, 06.03.2015

137 Peter Lamont: Authors' interview, 21.06.2015

138 Lee Tamahori: Authors' interview, 02.05.2015

139 Peter Lamont: Authors' interview, 21.06.2015

140 *Die Another Day* production notes, Twentieth Century Fox, 2002

141 *Die Another Day* production notes, Twentieth Century Fox, 2002

142 Peter Lamont: Authors' interview, 21.06.2015

143 Pierce Brosnan: Authors' interview, 23.05.2015

144 Robert Wade: Authors' interview, 06.06.2015

145 Neal Purvis: Authors' interview, 06.03.2015

146 Neal Purvis: Authors' interview, 06.03.2015

147 Lee Tamahori: Authors' interview, 02.05.2015

148 Lee Tamahori: Authors' interview, 02.05.2015

149 'Premium Bond' by Edward Lawrenson, *Sight and Sound*, November 2002

150 Pierce Brosnan: Authors' interview, 23.05.2015

151 Chris McGurk: Authors' interview, 25.06.2015

152 Lee Tamahori: Authors' interview, 02.05.2015

153 Daniel Kleinman: Authors' interview, 14.05.2015

154 Lee Tamahori: Authors' interview, 02.05.2015

155 *Larry King Live*, CNN, 10.10.2002

156 Robert Wade: Authors' interview, 06.06.2015

157 'Rosamund Pike: Undercover Agent' by Ian Freer, *Empire*, December 2002

158 David Arnold: Authors' interview, 23.06.2015

159 David Arnold: Authors' interview, 23.06.2015

160 David Arnold: Authors' interview, 23.06.2015

161 David Arnold: Authors' interview, 23.06.2015

162 Lee Tamahori: Authors' interview, 02.05.2015

163 David Arnold: Authors' interview, 23.06.2015

164 Lee Tamahori: Authors' intervie *Empire* #162, 05.2015

165 Lee Tamahori: Authors' interview, 02.05.2015

166 Daniel Kleinman: Authors' interview, 14.05.2015

167 Daniel Kleinman: Authors' interview, 14.05.2015

168 Daniel Kleinman: Authors' interview, 14.05.2015

169 Pierce Brosnan: Authors' interview, 23.05.2015

170 'The Bond Identity' by Andrew Osmond, *Cinescape*, Nov/Dec 2002

171 'Premium Bond' by Richard McClure, *TV and Satellite Week*, 26.10.2002

172 'Numero Uno' by Ian Nathan, *Empire*, December 2002

173 'Deeply Bonded' by Vicky Woods, *Vogue*, US Ed, December 2002

174 'Premium Bond' by Edward Lawrenson, *Sight and Sound*, November 2002

175 Lee Tamahori: Authors' interview, 02.05.2015

176 Lee Tamahori: Authors' interview, 02.05.2015

177 'Licence Renewed' by Nick Setchfield, *SFX* #98, December 2002

178 'Licence Renewed' by Nick Setchfield, *SFX* #98, December 2002

Chapter 28 Casino Royale

1   'I said:"Cubby He's Fabulous"' by Maureen Paton, *The Daily Telegraph*, 09.05.2000

2   'I said:"Cubby He's Fabulous"' by Maureen Paton, *The Daily Telegraph*, 09.05.2000

3   'I said:"Cubby He's Fabulous"' by Maureen Paton, *The Daily Telegraph*, 09.05.2000

4   'I said:"Cubby He's Fabulous"' by Maureen Paton, *The Daily Telegraph*, 09.05.2000

5   'MGM High Jinx for Bond's Berry' by Marc Graser, *Daily Variety*, 12.11.2002

6   Chris McGurk: Authors' interview, 25.06.2015

7   Jeff Kleeman: Authors' interview, 11.07.2015

8   Neal Purvis: Authors' interview, 06.03.2015

9   Neal Purvis: Authors' interview, 06.03.2015

10   Neal Purvis: Authors' interview, 06.03.2015

11   Robert Wade: Authors' interview, 12.04.2015

12   Lee Tamahori: Authors' interview, 02.05.2015

13   Neal Purvis: Authors' interview, 06.03.2015

14   Chris McGurk: Authors' interview, 25.06.2015

15   Neal Purvis and Robert Wade in conversation with Peter Florence, *The Orange Word: Screenwriters Season 2004*, The British Library, London, 08.03.2004

16   Chris McGurk: Authors' interview, 25.06.2015

17   Chris McGurk: Authors' interview, 25.06.2015

18   'Jinx Nixed by MGM' by Adam Dawtrey, *Weekly Variety*, 27.10.2003

19   'Jinx Nixed by MGM' by Adam Dawtrey, *Weekly Variety*, 27.10.2003

20   Neal Purvis: Authors' interview, 06.03.2015

21   Michael G. Wilson: Authors' interview, 13.11.2006

22   Robert Wade: Authors' interview, 12.04.2015

23   Neal Purvis and Robert Wade in conversation with Peter Florence, *The Orange Word: Screenwriters Season 2004*, The British Library, London, 08.03.2004

24   Pierce Brosnan: Authors' interview, 23.05.2015

25   Robert Wade: Authors' interview, 12.04.2015

26   Pierce Brosnan: Authors' interview, 23.05.2015

27   'Battle Royale' by G. Allen Johnson, *San Francisco Chronicle*, 07.10.2005

28   Chris McGurk: Authors' interview, 25.06.2015

29   Pierce Brosnan: Authors' interview, 23.05.2015

30   Chris McGurk: Authors' interview, 25.06.2015

31   'Battle Royale' by G. Allen Johnson, *San Francisco Chronicle*, 07.10.2005

32   Chris McGurk: Authors' interview, 25.06.2015

33   'Bond Ambition: 007 Gets Face Lift' by Nicola Laporte with Ben Fritz, *Variety*, 06.03.2006

34   Chris McGurk: Authors' interview, 25.06.2015

35   Chris McGurk: Authors' interview, 25.06.2015

36   Pierce Brosnan: Authors' interview, 23.05.2015

37   'Battle Royale' by G. Allen Johnson, *San Francisco Chronicle*, 07.10.2005

38   Chris McGurk: Authors' interview, 25.06.2015

39   Chris McGurk: Authors' interview, 25.06.2015

40   Nancy Griffith and Kim Masters, *Hit and Run*, Touchstone, 1996, p. 192

41   Nancy Griffith and Kim Masters, *Hit and Run*, Touchstone, 1996, p. 7

42   'Leo Caught In Cagey Deal' by Michael Learmonth and Jill Goldsmith, *Weekly Variety*, 20.09.2004

43   Chris McGurk: Authors' interview, 25.06.2015

44   'Spy Game' by Damon Wise, *DVD Review*, April 2007

45   Michael G. Wilson: Authors' interview, 13.11.2006

46   Chris McGurk: Authors' interview, 25.06.2015

47   'Quantum's Leap' by Ian Nathan, *Empire* #232, October 2008

48   'Quantum's Leap' by Ian Nathan, *Empire* #232, October 2008

49   Michael G. Wilson: Authors' interview, 13.11.2006

50   Michael G. Wilson: Authors' interview, 13.11.2006

51   Neal Purvis: Authors' interview, 06.03.2015

52   Robert Wade: Authors' interview, 12.04.2015

53   Robert Wade: Authors' interview, 12.04.2015

54   Robert Wade: Authors' interview, 12.04.2015

55   Neal Purvis: Authors' interview, 06.03.2015

56   Robert Wade: Authors' interview, 12.04.2015

57   Neal Purvis: Authors' interview, 06.03.2015

58   Robert Wade: Authors' interview, 12.04.2015

59   Neal Purvis: Authors' interview, 06.03.2015

60   Martin Campbell: Authors' interview, 19.03.2015

61   Chris McGurk: Authors' interview, 25.06.2015

62   Roger Michell: Authors' interview, 05.11.2014

63   Roger Michell: Authors' interview, 05.11.2014

64   Martin Campbell: Authors' interview, 19.03.2015

65   Neal Purvis: Authors' interview, 06.03.2015

66   Neal Purvis: Authors' interview, 06.03.2015

67   Martin Campbell: Authors' interview, 19.03.2015

68   Robert Wade: Authors' interview, 12.04.2015

69   Paul Haggis: Authors' interview, 18.04.2015

70   Paul Haggis: Authors' interview, 18.04.2015

71   Paul Haggis: Authors' interview, 18.04.2015

72   Paul Haggis: Authors' interview, 18.04.2015

73   Press release, Eon Productions Ltd, 03.02.2005

74   www.empireonline.co.uk, 16.02.2005

75   Janet Hirshenson and Jane Jenkins with Rachel Kranz, *A Star Is Found*, Harcourt Inc., 2006, pp. 39 – 41

76   Martin Campbell: Authors' interview, 19.03.2015

77   Sony Pictures Screen Test Footage, 2005

78   Martin Campbell: Authors' interview,

19.03.2015

79 David Arnold: Authors' interview, 23.06.2015

80 Phil Méheux: Authors' interview, 09.03.2015

81 David Arnold: Authors' interview, 23.06.2015

82 Martin Campbell: Authors' interview, 19.03.2015

83 Neal Purvis: Authors' interview, 06.03.2015

84 Chris McGurk: Authors' interview, 25.06.2015

85 Martin Campbell: Authors' interview, 19.03.2015

86 Martin Campbell: Authors' interview, 19.03.2015

87 Daniel Craig: Authors' interview, 13.11.2006

88 Michael G. Wilson: Authors' interview, 13.11.2006

89 Daniel Craig: Authors' interview, 13.11.2006

90 'Gangster Film Raises Bond Question' by Duane Dudek, *Journal Sentinel,* jsonline.com, 26.01.2005

91 'I Spy the Next James Bond' by Louise B. Parks, *Houston Chronicle,* 05.05.2005

92 Paul Haggis: Authors' interview, 18.04.2015

93 Daniel Craig: Authors' interview, 13.11.2006

94 Press release, Eon Productions, MGM and Sony Pictures Entertainment (SPE), 14.10.2005

95 'New Bond Spied at CAA' by Michael Fleming, *Daily Variety,* 14.12.2005

96 'New Bond Spied at CAA' by Michael Fleming, *Daily Variety,* 14.12.2005

97 'New Bond Spied at CAA' by Michael Fleming, *Daily Variety,* 14.12.2005

98 Press release, Eon Productions, MGM and SPE, 14.10.2005

99 Daniel Craig: Authors' interview, 13.11.2006

100 Mads Mikkelsen: Authors' interview, 13.11.2006

101 Mads Mikkelsen: Authors' interview, 13.11.2006

102 Mads Mikkelsen: Authors' interview, 13.11.2006

103 'Bond Pic Casts Baddie Mikkelsen Confirmed for "Casino"' by Will Tizard, *Daily Variety,* 15.02.2006

104 '"Royale" Pain: New Bond Girl Villain Missing' by Tatiana Siegel and Borys Kit, *The Hollywood Reporter,* 01.02.2006

105 'Bond Ambition: 007 Gets Face Lift' by Nicola Laporte with Ben Fritz, *Variety,* 06.03.2006

106 'Spy Game' by Damon Wise, *DVD Review,* April 2007

107 'The New Bond Girls' by Edward Douglas, ComingSoon.net, 07.07.2006

108 'Spy Game' by Damon Wise, *DVD Review,* April 2007

109 'Once, Twice, Three Times a Bond Girl' by James Mitchell, *The Mail on Sunday,* 29.10.2006

110 'A Shot In The Dark, by Jonathan Crocker, *Total Film* #122, December 2006

111 Eva Green: Authors' interview, 13.11.2006

112 Caterina Murino: Authors' interview, 13.11.2006

113 Caterina Murino: Authors' interview, 13.11.2006

114 *Casino Royale* production notes, SPE, 2006

115 'Spy Game' by Damon Wise, *DVD Review,* April 2007

116 Daniel Craig: Authors' interview, 13.11.2006

117 'No More Mr. Nice Spy' by Damon Wise, *Empire* #210, December 2006

118 *Casino Royale* production notes, SPE, 2006

119 Robert Wade: Authors' interview, 12.04.2015

120 Phil Méheux: Authors' interview, 09.03.2015

121 Phil Méheux: Authors' interview, 09.03.2015

122 Lindy Hemming: Authors' interview, 06.07.2015

123 '"Royale" Pain: New Bond girl, villain missing' by Tatiana Siegel and Borys Kit, *The Hollywood Reporter,* 01.02.2006

124 www.casinoroyale–movie.co.uk

125 *Casino Royale* production notes, SPE, 2006

126 *Becoming Bond,* dir: Rob Done, Special Treats Production Company, ITV, 07.11.2006

127 Daniel Craig: Authors' interview, 13.11.2006

128 *Casino Royale* production notes, SPE, 2006

129 'James Bond Public Enemy No. 1' Ananova. com 03.02.2006

130 *Casino Royale* production notes, SPE, 2006

131 'High Stakes For 007' by Jon Silberg, *American Cinematographer,* December 2006

132 'High Stakes For 007' by Jon Silberg, *American Cinematographer,* December 2006

133 *Casino Royale* production notes, SPE, 2006

134 '007's Producer Renews Bond with Alma Mater' by David Allen, *Dailybulletin.com,* 17.05.2005

135 'True Spirit of Bond' by Mick Newman, *Yachting World,* December 2006

136 'Bond In The Bahamas' by Betty Vedrine, *The Nassau Guardian* 06.03.2006

137 'The Name's Bond, Broke Bond' by Grant Hodgson, *The Sunday Mirror* 19.02.2006

138 'Back To Basics' by Joe Fordham, *Cinefex* #108, January 2007

139 *Casino Royale* production notes, SPE, 2006

140 'Fights, Camera, Action!' by Rob Waugh, *The Mail on Sunday,* 29.10.2006

141 *Casino Royale* production notes, SPE, 2006

142 Anthony Waye: Authors' interview, 03.01.2014

143 Anthony Waye: Authors' interview, 03.01.2014

144 *Casino Royale* production notes, SPE, 2006

145 Barbara Broccoli interviewed by Jenni Murray, *Woman's Hour,* BBC Radio 4, 13.11.2006

146 Daniel Craig: Authors' interview, 13.11.2006

147 *Casino Royale* production notes, SPE, 2006

148 *Casino Royale* production notes, SPE, 2006

149 *Casino Royale* production notes, SPE, 2006

150 *Casino Royale* production notes, SPE, 2006

151 'The Poker' by Yarborough, www.casinoroyale–movie.co.uk, 29.08.2006

152   *Casino Royale* production notes, SPE, 2006
153   'High Stakes For 007' by Jon Silberg, *American Cinematographer*, December 2006
154   *Casino Royale* production notes, SPE, 2006
155   Martin Campbell: Authors' interview, 13.11.2006
156   *Casino Royale* production notes, SPE, 2006
157   'New Bond Revisits Venice' by Peter Debruge, *Variety*, 28.08.2006
158   'Arriving In Venice' by Yarborough, www.casinoroyale–movie.co.uk, 26.09.2006
159   *Casino Royale* production notes, SPE, 2006
160   *Casino Royale* production notes, SPE, 2006
161   'True Spirit of Bond' by Mick Newman, *Yachting World*, December 2006
162   *Casino Royale* production notes, SPE, 2006
163   'High Stakes for 007' by Jon Silberg, *American Cinematographer*, December 2006
164   'Pandora: Ousted but Not Stirred' by Henry Deedes, *The Independent*, 19.06.2006
165   'Lights Camera Aston' by Jason Barlow, *Car*, June 2006
166   *James Bond For Real*, dir: Rob Done, Special Treats Productions, ITV2, 10.11.2006
167   *Casino Royale* production notes, SPE, 2006
168   *Film 2006*, BBC1, 13.11.2006
169   *James Bond For Real*, dir: Rob Done, Special Treats Productions, ITV2, 10.11.2006
170   Steve Begg: Authors' interview, 24.113.2014
171   'Back To Basics' by Joe Fordham, *Cinefex* #108, January 2007
172   'High Stakes For 007' by Jon Silberg, *American Cinematographer*, December 2006
173   *Casino Royale* production notes, SPE, 2006
174   'Back To Basics' by Joe Fordham, *Cinefex* #108, January 2007
175   'Back To Basics' by Joe Fordham, *Cinefex* #108,

January 2007
176   *Casino Royale* production notes, SPE, 2006
177   *Casino Royale* production notes, SPE, 2006
178   *Casino Royale* production notes, SPE, 2006
179   'James Bond Film Set in Ruins after Massive Blaze' by Jeevan Vasagar, The *Guardian*, 31.07.2006
180   David Arnold: Authors' interview, 23.06.2015
181   Martin Campbell: Authors' interview, 13.11.2006
182   Martin Campbell: Authors' interview, 13.11.2006
183   David Arnold: Authors' interview, 23.06.2015
184   Eon/Columbia/MGM press release, 26.07.2006
185   David Arnold: Authors' interview, 23.06.2015
186   David Arnold in conversation with Matthew Field, *James Bond: A Legacy of Excellence*, Promax UK Conference, Mermaid Theatre, London, 3.11.2006
187   Chris Cornell: Authors' interview, 13.11.2006
188   Chris Cornell: Authors' interview, 13.11.2006
189   Chris Cornell: Authors' interview, 13.11.2006
190   Chris Cornell: Authors' interview, 13.11.2006
191   Daniel Kleinman: Authors' interview, 14.05.2015
192   Daniel Kleinman: Authors' interview, 14.05.2015
193   Daniel Kleinman: Authors' interview, 14.05.2015
194   'The Queen Is All Smiles For Her New 007' by Elisa Roche, *Daily Express*, 15.11.2006
195   'The Eve Of Release' by Yarborough, www.casinoroyale–movie.co.uk, 07.11.2006
196   'Spy Game' by Damon Wise, *DVD Review*, April 2007
197   Neal Purvis: Authors' interview, 06.03.2015

Chapter 29   Quantum of Solace

1   'New Face, New Depths' by Danny Graydon, *Weekly Variety*, 10.09.2007
2   'Bond Ambition: 007 Gets Face Lift' by Nicole LaPorte, *Weekly Variety*, 06.03.2006
3   'Bond Ambition: 007 Gets Face Lift' by Nicole LaPorte, *Weekly Variety*, 06.03.2006
4   'Bond Ambition: 007 Gets Face Lift' by Nicole LaPorte, *Weekly Variety*, 06.03.2006
5   Trade Advert, *Weekly Variety*, 10.09.2007
6   'Bond Looking For A Director … Again' by Nicole LaPorte and Michael Fleming, *Daily Variety*, 10.08.2006
7   'The Road To Revenge' by Matt Mueller, *Total Film* #147, November 2008
8   'Quantum's Leap' by Ian Nathan, *Empire* #232, October 2008
9   'Bond's Keeper: Barbara Broccoli' by Martyn

Palmer, *Radio Times*, 18.10.2008
10   *Quantum of Solace* production notes, Sony Pictures Entertainment, 25.08.2008
11   *Casino Royale* press conference, 14.10.2005
12   Michael G. Wilson: Authors' interview, 13.11.2006
13   Neal Purvis and Robert Wade in conversation with Matthew Field, *The Martin Cahill Memorial Lecture*, presented by The Lunch Club, London, 24.07.2013
14   Robert Wade: Authors' interview, 12.04.2015
15   Robert Wade: Authors' interview, 12.04.2015
16   Robert Wade: Authors' interview, 12.04.2015
17   Neal Purvis: Authors' interview, 06.03.2015
18   Robert Wade: Authors' interview, 12.04.2015
19   Roger Michell: Authors' interview, 05.11.2014
20   Roger Michell: Authors' interview, 05.11.2014

21 'Haggis Has Bond's Number – Again' by Jay A. Fernandez, *Los Angeles Times*, 23.05.2007

22 Roger Michell: Authors' interview, 05.11.2014

23 Roger Michell: Authors' interview, 05.11.2014

24 Roger Michell: Authors' interview, 05.11.2014

25 Roger Michell: Authors' interview, 05.11.2014

26 Robert Wade: Authors' interview, 12.04.2015

27 Roger Michell: Authors' interview, 05.11.2014

28 'Bond Looking For A Director … Again' by Nicole LaPorte and Michael Fleming, *Daily Variety*, 10.08.2006

29 Roger Michell: Authors' interview, 05.11.2014

30 Robert Wade: Authors' interview, 12.04.2015

31 Neal Purvis: Authors' interview, 06.03.2015

32 Robert Wade: Authors' interview, 12.04.2015

33 Robert Wade: Authors' interview, 12.04.2015

34 Paul Haggis: Authors' interview, 18.04.2015

35 'Haggis Has Bond's Number – Again' by Jay A. Fernandez, *Los Angeles Times*, 23.05.2007

36 Robert Wade: Authors' interview, 12.04.2015

37 Marc Forster: Authors' interview, 01.07.2015

38 'Quantum's Leap' by Ian Nathan, *Empire* #232, October 2008

39 'Helmer Gives Bond the Cerebral Touch' by Anne Thompson, *Weekly Variety*, 27.10.2008

40 'A License to Pursue the Inner Bond' by Terrence Rafferty, *The New York Times*, 09.12.2007

41 'Helmer Gives Bond the Cerebral Touch' by Anne Thompson, *Weekly Variety*, 27.10.2008

42 'A License to Pursue the Inner Bond' by Terrence Rafferty, *The New York Times*, 09.12.2007

43 Marc Forster: Authors' interview, 01.07.2015

44 Marc Forster: Authors' interview, 01.07.2015

Marc Forster: Authors' interview, 01.07.2015

46 Marc Forster: Authors' interview, 01.07.2015

47 Paul Haggis: Authors' interview, 18.04.2015

48 Marc Forster: Authors' interview, 01.07.2015

49 Paul Haggis: Authors' interview, 18.04.2015

50 'What's Bond To Happen Next' by Devin Faraci, www.chud.com, 07.11.2006

51 Paul Haggis: Authors' interview, 18.04.2015

52 Marc Forster: Authors' interview, 01.07.2015

53 Marc Forster: Authors' interview, 01.07.2015

54 Paul Haggis: Authors' interview, 18.04.2015

55 Paul Haggis: Authors' interview, 18.04.2015

56 Paul Haggis: Authors' interview, 18.04.2015

57 Marc Forster: Authors' interview, 01.07.2015

58 'The Road To Revenge' by Matt Mueller, *Total Film* #147, November 2008

59 'The Greatest Asset to an Actor is Their Ego' by Dave Calhoun, *Time Out*, n.o 2155, London Ed, 08.12.2011

60 Henry Chancellor, *James Bond The Man And His World*, John Murray, 2005, p. 147

61 *Quantum Of Solace* press conference, Pinewood Studios, 24.01.2008

62 Marc Forster: Authors' interview, 01.07.2015

63 *Quantum of Solace* production notes, SPE, 25.08.2008

64 'I'll be Bond Until My Joints Go' by Grant Rollings, *The Sun*, 05.04.2008

65 'I'll be Bond Until My Joints Go' by Grant Rollings, *The Sun*, 05.04.2008

66 Marc Forster: Authors' interview, 01.07.2015

67 'Mathieu Amalric Q&A' by Chris Tilly, www.uk.ign.com, 30.01.2008

68 'Mathieu Amalric Q&A' by Chris Tilly, www.uk.ign.com, 30.01.2008

69 'The Greatest Asset to an Actor is Their Ego' by Dave Calhoun, *Time Out*, n.o 2155, London Ed, 08.12.2011

70 'The Villains' *Live*, *The Mail on Sunday*, 05.10.2008

71 'At the Heart of The Matter: Mathieu Amalric on Being the 'Bond 22' Villain' by Karl Rozemeyer, www.premiere.com, 18.03.2008

72 'Olga Kurylenko Q&A' by Chris Tilly, www.uk.ign.com, 30.01.2008

73 'Olga Kurylenko Q&A' by Chris Tilly, www.uk.ign.com, 30.01.2008

74 'Olga Kurylenko Q&A' by Chris Tilly, www.uk.ign.com, 30.01.2008

75 Marc Forster: Authors' interview, 01.07.2015

76 Pauline Hume: Authors' interview, 07.05.2015

77 'Gemma Arterton Q&A' by Chris Tilly, www.uk.ign.com, 30.01.2008

78 'Gemma Arterton Q&A' by Chris Tilly, www.uk.ign.com, 30.01.2008

79 *Quantum of Solace* production notes, SPE, 25.08.2008

80 'Giancarlo Giannini in New Bond Movie' www.corrieretandem.com, 09.03.2008

81 Marc Forster: Authors' interview, 01.07.2015

82 *Quantum Of Solace* press conference, Pinewood Studios, 24.01.2008

83 *Quantum Of Solace* press conference, Pinewood Studios, 24.01.2008

84 Marc Forster: Authors' interview, 01.07.2015

85 Neal Purvis: Authors' interview, 06.03.2015

86 Eva Green: Authors' interview, 13.11.2006

87 Marc Forster: Authors' interview, 01.07.2015

88 Marc Forster: Authors' interview, 01.07.2015

89 *Quantum of Solace* production notes, SPE, 25.08.2008

90 'Forging A Bond' by Mark Hope Jones, *American Cinematographer*, November 2008

91 'Forging A Bond' by Mark Hope Jones, *American Cinematographer*, November 2008

92 *Quantum of Solace* production notes, SPE, 25.08.2008

93 *Quantum of Solace* production notes, SPE, 25.08.2008

94 'Quantum's Leap' by Ian Nathan, *Empire* #232, October 2008

95   *Quantum of Solace* production notes, SPE, 25.08.2008

96   *Quantum of Solace* production notes, SPE, 25.08.2008

97   'Bond Has Activists On His Tail Over New Film's "brutal" Horse Race Finale' by Richard Owen, *The Times*, 13.08.2007

98   Robert Wade: Authors' interview, 12.04.2015

99   Anthony Waye: Authors' interview, 03.01.2014

100 *Quantum of Solace* production notes, SPE, 25.08.2008

101 'The Homage' *Live*, *The Mail on Sunday*, 05.10.2008

102 'The Christmas Message No One Watched' by Martin Waller, *The Times*, 28.12.2007

103 'Let's Bond' by Dave Calhoun, *Time Out,* n.o 1992, London Ed, 23.10.2008

104 *Quantum of Solace* production notes, SPE, 25.08.2008

105 *Quantum of Solace* production notes, SPE, 25.08.2008

106 *Quantum of Solace* production notes, SPE, 25.08.2008

107 Marc Forster: Authors' interview, 01.07.2015

108 Marc Forster: Authors' interview, 01.07.2015

109 *Associated Press*, 09.01.2008

110 SPE press release, 28.04.2008

111 SPE press release, 28.04.2008

112 SPE press release, 28.04.2008

113 *Quantum of Solace* production notes, SPE, 25.08.2008

114 'James Bond Expected In Chile March 24 For Next Film' www.mercopress.com, 18.03.2008

115 *Quantum of Solace* production notes, SPE, 25.08.2008

116 *Quantum of Solace* production notes, SPE, 25.08.2008

117 'Mayor Protests on Chile 007 Set' bbc.co.uk/ news, 02.04.2008

118 El Mercurio Online, www.emol.com.

119 'Helmer Gives Bond the Cerebral Touch' by Anne Thompson, *Weekly Variety*, 27.10.2008

120 *Quantum of Solace* production notes, SPE, 25.08.2008

121 'The Garage' *Live*, *The Mail on Sunday*, 05.10.2008

122 Anthony Waye: Authors' interview, 03.01.2014

123 *Quantum of Solace* production notes 25.08.2008

124 'The Car' *Live*, *The Mail on Sunday*, 05.10.2008

125 Anthony Waye: Authors' interview, 03.01.2014

126 'Bond Stuntman Fights For Life' *The Sun*, 24.04.2008

127 SPE press release, 28.04.2008

128 *Quantum of Solace* production notes, SPE, 25.08.2008

129 *Quantum of Solace* production notes, SPE, 25.08.2008

130 SPE press release, 28.04.2008

131 'Director Marc Forster on *Quantum of Solace*' by Dave Calhourn, *Time Out* London, 11.08.2008

132 Marc Forster: Authors' interview, 01.07.2015

133 David Arnold: Authors' interview, 23.06.2015

134 David Arnold: Authors' interview, 23.06.2015

135 David Arnold: Authors' interview, 23.06.2015

136 'Quantum of Solace: Jack White Helps Alicia Keys Put a Bomb Under James Bond' by Neil McCormack, *The Daily Telegraph*, 24.09.2008

137 'Quantum of Solace: Jack White Helps Alicia Keys Put a Bomb Under James Bond' by Neil McCormack, *The Daily Telegraph*, 24.09.2008

138 'Quantum of Solace' by Alexander Ulloa, www.artofthetitle.com, 24.01.2011

139 'Quantum of Solace' by Alexander Ulloa, www.artofthetitle.com, 24.01.2011

140 'Quantum of Solace' by Alexander Ulloa, www.artofthetitle.com, 24.01.2011

141 'Quantum of Solace' by Alexander Ulloa, www.artofthetitle.com, 24.01.2011

Chapter 30 Skyfall

1   'Mission Statements' by Nick Setchfield, *SFX* #227, November 2012

2   *Skyfall* press conference, Corinthia Hotel, London, 03.11.2011

3   'Bond helped rescue MGM' by David S. Cohen, *Daily Variety*, 11.05.2012

4   'Killing 007 Aint Easy' by Stephen Galloway, *The Hollywood Reporter*, 16.11.2012

5   'Killing 007 Ain't Easy' by Stephen Galloway, *The Hollywood Reporter*, 16.11.2012

6   'Killing 007 Ain't Easy' by Stephen Galloway, *The Hollywood Reporter*, 16.11.2012

7   Eon Productions press release, 19.04.2010

8   'Killing 007 Ain't Easy' by Stephen Galloway,

     The Hollywood Reporter 16.11.2012

9   'Double OMG' by Chris Nashawaty, *Entertainment Weekly*, 02.11.2012

10   Daniel Craig: Authors' interview, 21.10.2015

11   'Killing 007 Ain't Easy' by Stephen Galloway, *The Hollywood Reporter,* 16.11.2012

12   'Bond helped rescue MGM' by David S. Cohen, *Daily Variety*, 11.05.2012

13   'All In The Family' *MI6 Confidential* #19, 2013

14   'Bond With Bells On' by Alex Bilmes, *Esquire*, October 2012

15   'Double OMG' by Chris Nashawaty, *Entertainment Weekly*, 02.11.2012

16   'Bond With Bells On' by Alex Bilmes, *Esquire*,

October 2012

17 'Double OMG' by Chris Nashawaty, *Entertainment Weekly*, 02.11.2012

18 'Double OMG' by Chris Nashawaty, *Entertainment Weekly*, 02.11.2012

19 *Sam Mendes: Licence To Thrill - A Culture Show Special*, dir: Luke McMahon, hosted by Mark Kermode, BBC2, 26.10.2012

20 'Killing 007 Ain't Easy' by Stephen Galloway, *The Hollywood Reporter*, 16.11.2012

21 *Skyfall* press conference, Dorchester Hotel, London, 21.10.2012

22 'Defense of the Realm' by Dan Jolin, *Empire* #276, June 2012

23 'Defense of the Realm' by Dan Jolin, *Empire* #276, June 2012

24 'Defense of the Realm' by Dan Jolin, *Empire* #276, June 2012

25 Barbara Broccoli: Authors' interview, 21.10.2012

26 Robert Wade: Authors' interview, 12.04.2015

27 Neal Purvis: Authors' interview, 06.03.2015

28 Neal Purvis: Authors' interview, 06.03.2015

29 'Der Mann, der James Bond neu erfindet' by Hannes Uhl, *Kurier*, 19.12.2009

30 Robert Wade: Authors' interview, 09.07.2015

31 Sam Mendes: Authors' interview, 21.10.2015

32 Sam Mendes: Authors' interview, 21.10.2015

33 *Skyfall* production notes, Sony Pictures Entertainment (SPE), October 2012

34 Robert Wade: Authors' interview, 09.07.2015

35 Robert Wade: Authors' interview, 12.04.2015

36 Robert Wade: Authors' interview, 09.07.2015

37 *Skyfall* press conference, Dorchester Hotel, 21.10.2012

38 'The Thinking Man's Bond Director' by Dave Calhoun, *Time Out*, n.o 2200, London Ed, 16.10.2012

39 'Barbara Broccoli: "I Thought James Bond Was a Real Person Until I Was Seven"' by Liz Hoggard, *Evening Standard*, 16.08.2012

40 Neal Purvis: Authors' interview, 06.03.2015

41 Robert Wade: Authors' interview, 12.04.2015

42 Neal Purvis: Authors' interview, 11.07.2015

43 Sam Mendes: Authors' interview, 21.10.2015

44 Sam Mendes: Authors' interview, 21.10.2015

45 *Skyfall* press conference, Istanbul, 29.04.2012

46 Robert Wade: Authors' interview, 12.04.2015

47 Robert Wade: Authors' interview, 12.04.2015

48 Robert Wade: Authors' interview, 09.07.2015

49 Robert Wade: Authors' interview, 09.07.2015

50 Robert Wade: Authors' interview, 12.04.2015

51 Robert Wade: Authors' interview, 12.04.2015

52 Robert Wade: Authors' interview, 12.04.2015

53 Robert Wade: Authors' interview, 12.04.2015

54 Neal Purvis: Authors' interview, 06.03.2015

55 Robert Wade: Authors' interview, 12.04.2015

56 Robert Wade: Authors' interview, 12.04.2015

57 Neal Purvis: Authors' interview, 06.03.2015

58 Robert Wade: Authors' interview, 12.04.2015

59 'Killing 007 Ain't Easy' by Stephen Galloway, *The Hollywood Reporter*, 16.11.2012

60 Paul Duncan (ed.), *The James Bond Archives*, 'Death and Resurrection' by Paul Duncan, Taschen, 2012, p. 560

61 Daniel Craig: Authors' interview, 21.10.2012

62 'John Logan interview' www.collider.com, 20.11.2011

63 *Skyfall* production notes, SPE, October 2012

64 'Killing 007 Ain't Easy' by Stephen Galloway, *The Hollywood Reporter*, 16.11.2012

65 'Killing 007 Ain't Easy' by Stephen Galloway, *The Hollywood Reporter*, 16.11.2012

66 *Skyfall* press conference, Istanbul, 29.04.2012

67 'James Bond Gets Real' by Mark Salisbury, *The Daily Telegraph*, 13.12.2015

68 'James Bond Gets Real' by Mark Salisbury, *The Daily Telegraph* 13.12.2015

69 'Killing 007 Ain't Easy' by Stephen Galloway, *The Hollywood Reporter*, 16.11.2012

70 *Skyfall* production notes, SPE, October 2012

71 Neal Purvis: Authors' interview, 06.03.2015

72 Neal Purvis: Authors' interview, 06.03.2015

73 Robert Wade: Authors' interview, 12.04.2015

74 Robert Wade: Authors' interview, 12.04.2015

75 'James Bond Gets Real' by Mark Salisbury, *The Daily Telegraph* 13.12.2015

76 *Skyfall* production notes, SPE, October 2012

77 'All or Nothing' by Emma Brockes, *The New Yorker*, 10.11.2014

78 'Daniel Craig: Debriefed' by Stephen Galloway, *The Hollywood Reporter*, 16.11.2012

79 Barbara Broccoli: Authors' interview, 21.10.2012

80 Sam Mendes: Authors' interview, 21.10.2012

81 Judi Dench: Authors' interview, 24.01.2013

82 Michael G. Wilson: Authors' interview, 21.10.2012

83 Judi Dench: Authors' interview, 24.01.2013

84 Neal Purvis: Authors' interview, 06.03.2015

85 Javier Bardem: Authors' interview, 21.10.2012

86 'Killing 007 Ain't Easy' by Stephen Galloway, *The Hollywood Reporter*, 16.11.2012

87 *Skyfall* production notes, SPE, October 2012

88 Javier Bardem: Authors' interview, 21.10.2012

89 *Skyfall* production notes, SPE, October 2012

90 *Skyfall* production notes, SPE, October 2012

91 Bérénice Lim Marlohe: Authors' interview, 21.10.2012

92 Bérénice Lim Marlohe: Authors' interview, 21.10.2012

93 Bérénice Lim Marlohe: Authors' interview, 21.10.2012

94 '*Skyfall* Naomie Harris Interview: "I can finally say I'm Miss Moneypenny"' by Simon Reynolds and Tom Mansell, www.digitalspy.co.uk, 19.02.2013

95 '*Skyfall* Naomie Harris Interview: "I can

finally say I'm Miss Moneypenny'" by Simon Reynolds and Tom Mansell, www.digitalspy.co.uk, 19.02.2013

96   'Ralph Fiennes interview' by Gabrielle Donnelly, *Saga Magazine*, October 2012

97   Sam Mendes: Authors' interview, 21.10.2012

98   'Mission Statements' by Nick Setchfield, *SFX* #227, November 2012

99   'Ben Whishaw: On the QT with Q' by James Graham, *Total Film* #194, November 2012

100   'The New Q' by Jon Wilde, *The Mail on Sunday*, 30.09.2012

101   Sam Mendes: Authors' interview, 21.10.2012

102   *Skyfall* production notes, SPE, October 2012

103   Robert Wade: Authors' interview, 12.04.2015

104   Neal Purvis: Authors' interview, 06.03.2015

105   Robert Wade: Authors' interview, 12.04.2015

106   Robert Wade: Authors' interview, 12.04.2015

107   'MI6 under Siege' by Mark Hope–Jones, *American Cinematographer*, December 2012

108   Sam Mendes: Authors' interview, 21.10.2012

109   *Skyfall* production notes, SPE, October 2012

110   *Skyfall* production notes, SPE, October 2012

111   'Dennis Gassner Talks *Skyfall*' by Bill Desowitz, www.indiewore.com, 28.12.2012

112   'Dennis Gassner Talks *Skyfall*' by Bill Desowitz, www.indiewore.com 28.12.2012

113   *Skyfall* press conference, Corinthia Hotel London, 03.11.2011

114   'Sinister? Me?' by Emma Brockes, *Guardian Weekend*, 13.10.2012

115   Javier Bardem: Authors' interview, 21.10.2012

116   *Skyfall* production notes, SPE, October 2012

117   'Steely Dan' by Alexi Duggins, *Time Out,* n.o 2200, London Ed, 16.10.2012

118   'Gary Powell interview' *MI6 Confidential* #17, 2012

119   *Skyfall* production notes, SPE, October 2012

120   'Old Dog, New Tricks' by Joe Fordham, *Cinefex*, #133, April 2013

121   'Killing 007 Ain't Easy' by Stephen Galloway, *The Hollywood Reporter,* 16.11.2012

122   *Skyfall* production notes, SPE, October 2012

123   'Killing 007 Ain't Easy' by Stephen Galloway, *The Hollywood Reporter,* 16.11.2012

124   *Skyfall* production notes, SPE, October 2012

125   *Skyfall* production notes, SPE, October 2012

126   'MI6 Under Siege' by Mark Hope–Jones, *American Cinematographer*, December 2012

127   *Skyfall* production notes, SPE, October 2012

128   'Here Be Dragons' *MI6 Confidential* #20, March 2013

129   Judi Dench: Authors' interview, 24.01.2013

130   *Skyfall* production notes, SPE, October 2012

131   Robert Wade: Authors' interview, 12.04.2015

132   Neal Purvis: Authors' interview, 06.03.2015

133   'Skyfall: The Cars, the Stunts and the Drivers' by K.S Wang, www.motortrend.com, 07.11.2012

134   *The Andrew Marr Show*, BBC1, 10.02.2013

135   *Sam Mendes: Licence To Thrill - A Culture Show Special*, dir: Luke McMahon, hosted by Mark Kermode, BBC1, 26.10.2012

136   Robert Wade: Authors' interview, 08.07.2015

137   'Killing 007 Ain't Easy' by Stephen Galloway, *The Hollywood Reporter,* 16.11.2012

138   'Stig and the Stuntmen' by Martyn Palmer, *Mail on Sunday*, 30.09.2012

139   *Skyfall* production notes, SPE, October 2012

140   *Skyfall* production notes, SPE, October 2012

141   *Skyfall* production notes, SPE, October 2012

142   'Daniel Craig: Debriefed' by Stephen Galloway, *The Hollywood Reporter,* 16.11.2012

143   'Dennis Gassner Talks Skyfall' by Bill Desowitz, www.indiewore.com, 28.12.2012

144   'Daniel's Stunt Double' by Martyn Palmer, *The Mail on Sunday*, 30.09.2012

145   'Daniel's Stunt Double' by Martyn Palmer, *The Mail on Sunday*, 30.09.2012

146   'Paul Epworth Interview' by Matt Patches, www.hollywood.com, 13.12.2012

147   Sam Mendes: Authors' interview, 21.10.2012

148   Sam Mendes: Authors' interview, 21.10.2012

149   'Thomas Newman Interview' by Daniel Schweiger, *Film Music Magazine,* www.filmmusicmag.com, 05.11.2012

150   'Thomas Newman interview' by Daniel Schweiger, *Film Music Magazine*, www.filmmusicmag.com, 05.11.2012

151   Sam Mendes: Authors' interview, 21.10.2012

152   'Adele's 'Skyfall' is Every Inch a Classic Bond Theme' by Seth Abramovitch, *The Hollywood Reporter*, 04.10.2012

153   'Adele's 'Skyfall' is Every Inch a Classic Bond Theme' by Seth Abramovitch, *The Hollywood Reporter*, 04.10.2012

154   Daniel Kleinman: Authors' interview, 14.05.2015

155   Daniel Kleinman: Authors' interview, 14.05.2015

156   Sam Mendes: Authors' interview, 21.10.2012

157   Daniel Kleinman: Authors' interview, 14.05.2015

158   Daniel Kleinman: Authors' interview, 14.05.2015

159   Daniel Kleinman: Authors' interview, 14.05.2015

160   Sam Mendes: Authors' interview, 21.10.2012

161   Sam Mendes: Authors' interview, 21.10.2012

162   Sam Mendes: Authors' interview, 21.10.2012

163   Sam Mendes: Authors' interview, 21.10.2012

164   'I'll Be Too Old to Play Bond at 44 ¾' by Grant Rollings, *The Sun*, 23.10.2013

165   'Locked and Loaded' by Vicki Read, *Telegraph Magazine*, 20.10.2012

166   'Most Memorable Night of Career, Says 007 Craig' by Alistair Foster, *Evening Standard*, 24.10.2012

167   'Daniel Craig: Debriefed' by Stephen Galloway, *The Hollywood Reporter,* 16.11.2012

168   Daniel Craig: Authors' interview, 21.10.2012

Chapter 31 Spectre

1 Sam Mendes: Authors' interview, 29.09.2016

2 'Bond Is Back SPECTRE' by Chris Hewitt and Phil De Semlyen, *Empire*, April 2015

3 Sam Mendes: Authors' interview, 29.09.2016

4 'Skyfall Picks Up BAFTA' by David Churchill, www.thesundaytimes.co.uk, 10.02.2013

5 'Sam Mendes Won't Direct Bond 24' by Phil de Semlyen, www.empireonline.com, 06.03.2013

6 Eon Productions press release, 06.03.2013

7 'Snowden Book "No Place to Hide" for James Bond producers' www.deadline.com, 14.05.2014

8 Sam Mendes: Authors' interview, 29.09.2016

9 Barbara Broccoli interviewed by Jenni Murray, *Woman's Hour*, BBC Radio 4, 13.11.2006

10 Sam Mendes: Authors' interview, 29.09.2016

11 John Logan: Authors' interview, 03.11.2016

12 *Spectre* production notes, Sony Pictures Entertainment (SPE), 2015

13 Press release, Doha Tribeca Film Festival, 19.11.2012

14 Press release, Doha Tribeca Film Festival, 19.11.2012

15 'Screenwriter John Logan on Bond 24' by Phil de Semlyen, www.empireonline.com, 20.01.2014

16 *John Logan: BAFTA Screenwriting Lecture*, British Film Institute, Southbank, London, 20.09.2011

17 'Bond Is Back: SPECTRE' by Chris Hewitt and Phil De Semlyen, *Empire*, April 2015

18 'Return of the Senchai' by Brian Smith, *Bond Magazine* #7, November 1999

19 'Return of the Senchai' by Brian Smith, *Bond Magazine* #7, November 1999

20 'Kevin McClory Obituary' by Graham Rye, *The Independent*, 07.12.2006

21 'MGM, Danjaq Settle 50-Plus Year Legal Fight Over James Bond Rights' by Eriq Gardner, *The Hollywood Reporter*, 15.11.2013

22 'MGM, James Bond Producer End Decades-Long War Over 007' by Ted Johnson, www.variety.com, 15.11.2013

23 'Inside Thunderball' by John Cork, *Goldeneye* #3, The Ian Fleming Foundation, Spring 1994

24 Ian Fleming, THUNDERBALL, chapter 5 'Spectre' and chapter 6 'Violet-Scented Breath' Jonathan Cape Ltd, 1961

25 *Everything or Nothing: The Untold Story of 007*, dir. Stephen Riley, SPE, 2012

26 *Spectre* production notes, SPE, 2015

27 Sam Mendes: Authors' interview, 29.09.2016

28 John Logan: Authors' interview, 03.11.2016

29 John Logan: Authors' interview, 03.11.2016

30 John Logan: Authors' interview, 03.11.2016

31 John Logan: Authors' interview, 03.11.2016

32 John Logan: Authors' interview, 18.11.2016

33 Sam Mendes: Authors' interview, 29.09.2016

34 Michael Lerman: Authors' interview, 06.10.2016

35 Sam Mendes: Authors' interview, 29.09.2016

36 John Logan: Authors' interview, 03.11.2016

37 John Logan: Authors' interview, 03.11.2016

38 John Logan: Authors' interview, 03.11.2016

39 Robert Wade: Authors' interview, 23.09.2016

40 John Logan: Authors' interview, 03.11.2016

41 Sam Mendes: Authors' interview, 29.09.2016

42 Robert Wade: Authors' interview, 13.07.2015

43 Neal Purvis: Authors' interview, 23.09.2016

44 Robert Wade: Authors' interview, 23.09.2016

45 Neal Purvis: Authors' interview, 23.09.2016

46 Robert Wade: Authors' interview, 23.09.2016

47 Neal Purvis: Authors' interview, 23.09.2016

48 Neal Purvis: Authors' interview, 23.09.2016

49 Untitled B24 screenplay by John Logan, revisions by Neal Purvis and Robert Wade, 17.10.2014

50 Neal Purvis: Authors' interview, 23.09.2016

51 Sam Mendes: Authors' interview, 05.10.2016

52 Robert Wade: Authors' interview, 23.09.2016

53 Sam Mendes: Authors' interview, 05.10.2016

54 Robert Wade: Authors' interview, 23.09.2016

55 Robert Wade: Authors' interview, 23.09.2016

56 Untitled B24 screenplay by John Logan, revisions by Neal Purvis and Robert Wade, 17.10.2014

57 Robert Wade: Authors' interview, 23.09.2016

58 John Pearson, *The Life of Ian Fleming*, Aurum Press Ltd, revised edition, 2003, p. 39

59 Ian Fleming, OCTOPUSSY, Jonathan Cape Ltd, 1966

60 Sam Mendes: Authors' interview, 29.09.2016

61 Robert Wade: Authors' interview, 23.09.2016

62 Robert Wade: Authors' interview, 23.09.2016

63 Sam Mendes: Authors' interview, 29.09.2016

64 Sam Mendes: Authors' interview, 29.09.2016

65 Sam Mendes: Authors' interview, 29.09.2016

66 Neal Purvis: Authors' interview, 23.09.2016

67 Robert Wade: Authors' interview, 23.09.2016

68 Neal Purvis: Authors' interview, 23.09.2016

69 Robert Wade: Authors' interview, 23.09.2016

70 Sam Mendes: Authors' interview, 05.10.2016

71 Debbie McWilliams: Authors' interview, 28.09.2016

72 Robert Wade: Authors' interview, 23.09.2016

73 Sam Mendes: Authors' interview, 29.09.2016

74 Robert Wade: Authors' interview, 23.09.2016

75 Neal Purvis: Authors' interview, 23.09.2016

76 Untitled B24 screenplay by John Logan, revisions by Neal Purvis and Robert Wade, 17.10.2014

77 Untitled B24 screenplay by John Logan, revisions by Neal Purvis and Robert Wade,

01.12.2014

78   Neal Purvis: Authors' interview, 23.09.2016

79   Untitled first draft screenplay by William Davies, William Osborne, Al Ruggiero and Michael Wilson, 02.01.1991

80   Robert Wade: Authors' interview, 23.09.2016

81   Neal Purvis: Authors' interview, 23.09.2016

82   Robert Wade: Authors' interview, 23.09.2016

83   Sam Mendes: Authors' interview, 29.09.2016

84   'All Or Nothing' by Emma Brockes, *The New Yorker*, 10.11.2014

85   Neal Purvis: Authors' interview, 23.09.2016

86   Neal Purvis: Authors' interview, 23.09.2016

87   Daniel Craig: Authors' interview, 22.10.2015

88   Neal Purvis: Authors' interview, 23.09.2016

89   Sam Mendes: Authors' interview, 29.09.2016

90   Sam Mendes: Authors' interview, 05.10.2016

91   'MGM Allegedly Battled To Cut James Bond's $300 Million Plus Budget' by Lee Barraclough, www.variety.com, 11.12.2014

92   'MGM Allegedly Battled To Cut James Bond's $300 Million Plus Budget' by Lee Barraclough, www.variety.com, 11.12.2014

93   'Spectre Of Death' by Chris Lee, *Entertainment Weekly* #1387, 30.10.2015

94   '*Spectre* Producer Expects Daniel Craig To Return For Another Bond Movie' by Stephen Galloway, www.hollywood reporter.com, 06.11.2015

95   'Licence Renewed' by Jane Crowther, *SFX Magazine* #267, December 2015

96   'Amy Pascal Stepping Down as Sony Co-Chairman, Sony Confirms – Update' by Mike Fleming Jr., www.deadline.com, 05.02.2015

97   Sam Mendes: Authors' interview, 29.09.2016

98   *Spectre* press conference, Pinewood Studios, 03.12.2014

99   Sam Mendes: Authors' interview, 29.09.2016

100   Daniel Craig: Authors' interview, 22.10.2015

101   Daniel Craig: Authors' interview, 22.10.2015

102   '*Spectre*: Interview with Sam Mendes' by Benjamin B, *American Cinematographer*, www.asc.com/blog, 30.10.2015

103   Michael Lerman: Authors' interview, 06.10.2016

104   '*Spectre*: Interview with Sam Mendes' by Benjamin B, *American Cinematographer*, www.asc.com/blog, 30.10.2015

105   Per Hallberg: Authors' interview, 10.11.2016

106   Debbie McWilliams: Authors' interview, 28.09.2016

107   Sam Mendes: Authors' interview, 29.09.2016

108   Sam Mendes: Authors' interview, 29.09.2016

109   'Coolest Bond Villain Ever' by Robert Chalmers, *GQ*, May 2015

110   'Monica Bellucci interview' by Ricky Camillieri, *AOL Build*, 18.10.2015

111   'Monica Bellucci interview' by Ricky Camillieri, *AOL Build*, 18.10.2015

112   Sam Mendes: Authors' interview, 29.09.2016

113   Debbie McWilliams: Authors' interview, 28.09.2016

114   Sam Mendes: Authors' interview, 29.09.2016

115   Debbie McWilliams: Authors' interview, 28.09.2016

116   '*Spectre* Producer Expects Daniel Craig To Return For Another Bond Movie' by Stephen Galloway, www.hollywood reporter.com, 06.11.2015

117   'Bond's Bombshells' by Jon Wilde, *Mail on Sunday*, 22.02.2015

118   'Léa Seydoux Interview' by Ricky Camillieri, *AOL Build*, 18.10.2015

119   Debbie McWilliams: Authors' interview, 28.09.2016

120   Sam Mendes: Authors' interview, 29.09.2016

121   Sam Mendes: Authors' interview, 29.09.2016

122   'Bond's Bombshells' by Jon Wilde, *Mail on Sunday*, 22.02.2015

123   'I Am So Lucky. Every Girl Wants To Be In A Film With Daniel Craig' by Charlotte Pearson Methven, *You Magazine, Mail on Sunday*, 18.10.2015

124   Debbie McWilliams: Authors' interview, 28.09.2016

125   Pierce Brosnan: Authors' interview, 23.05.2015

126   'Monica Bellucci aka Lucia Sciarra' by Chris Hewitt and Phil De Semlyen, *Empire*, April 2015

127   'Monica Bellucci aka Lucia Sciarra' by Chris Hewitt and Phil De Semlyen, *Empire*, April 2015

128   Sam Mendes: Authors' interview, 29.09.2016

129   'Monica Bellucci On How To Seduce Bond at 51: "Eat Well, Drink Well, Have Good Sex"' by Celia Walden, *The Telegraph*, 18.10.2015

130   'Bond's Bombshells' by Jon Wilde, *Mail on Sunday*, 22.02.2015

131   Neal Purvis: Authors' interview, 23.09.2016

132   John Logan: Authors' interview, 03.11.2016

133   Debbie McWilliams: Authors' interview, 28.09.2016

134   Debbie McWilliams: Authors' interview, 28.09.2016

135   'Bond is back: SPECTRE' by Chris Hewitt and Phil De Semlyen, *Empire*, April 2015

136   Robert Wade: Authors' interview, 23.09.2016

137   *Spectre* production notes, SPE, 2015

138   *Spectre* press conference, Pinewood Studios, 03.12.2014

139   'Mission Control M Head of MI6 Ralph Fiennes' by Ian Nathan, *Empire*, November 2015

140   'Mission Control Q MI6 Quartermaster Ben Whishaw' by Neil Alcock, *Empire*, November

141 Sam Mendes: Authors' interview, 05.10.2016
142 Rory Kinnear: Authors' interview, 18.10.2016
143 'Mission Control Moneypenny M's personal Assistant Naomie Harris' by Chris Hewitt, *Empire*, November 2015
144 Sam Mendes: Authors' interview, 05.10.2016
145 Sam Mendes: Authors' interview, 05.10.2016
146 Sam Mendes: Authors' interview, 29.09.2016
147 'SPECTRE: Dennis Gassner interview "production design"' by Emanual Levy, *Back to the Movies*, www.bttm.com, 16.02.2015
148 'SPECTRE: Dennis Gassner interview "production design"' by Emanual Levy, *Back to the Movies*, www.bttm.com, 16.02.2015
149 Rory Kinnear: Authors' interview, 18.10.2016
150 'SPECTRE: Dennis Gassner interview "Production Design"' by Emanual Levy, *Back to the Movies*, www.bttm.com, 16.02.2015
151 Michael Lerman: Authors' interview, 06.10.2016
152 'A Chat with Dennis Gassner, SPECTRE Production Designer' by Alton Williams, www.battleroyalewithcheese.com, 21.02.2016
153 Callum McDougall: Authors' interview, 20.11.2016
154 'Hoyte van Hoytema, ASC, FSF, NSC: Lighting *Spectre*' by Benjamin B, *American Cinematographer*, www.asc.com/blog, 11.12.2015
155 Callum McDougall: Authors' interview, 20.11.2016
156 *Spectre* production notes, SPE, 2015
157 John Logan: Authors' interview, 03.11.2016
158 Sam Mendes: Authors' interview, 05.10.2016
159 Sam Mendes: Authors' interview, 29.09.2016
160 Gary Powell: Authors' interview, 04.10.2016
161 Chris Corbould: Authors' interview, 04.10.2016
162 Steve Begg: Authors' interview, 09.11.2016
163 'Daniel Craig Interview' by Chris Hardwick and Matt Grosinger, Nerdist podcast, www.nerdist.com, 18.10.2015
164 Sam Mendes: Authors' interview, 29.09.2016
165 Gary Powell: Authors' interview, 04.10.2016
166 Gary Powell: Authors' interview, 04.10.2016
167 Sam Mendes: Authors' interview, 29.09.2016
168 Per Hallberg: Authors' interview, 10.11.2016
169 Sam Mendes: Authors' interview, 05.10.2016
170 '*Spectre*: Dennis Gassner interview "Production Design"' by Emanual Levy, *Back to the Movies*, www.bttm.com, 16.02.2015
171 'Sam Mendes *Spectre*' Interview' by David Poland, *DP30: The Oral History of Hollywood*, 06.11.2015
172 'Hoyte van Hoytema, ASC, FSF, NSC: Lighting *Spectre*' by Benjamin B, *American Cinematographer*, www.asc.com/blog, 11.12.2015
173 Per Hallberg: Authors' interview, 10.11.2016
174 'James Bond Film Crew Clean Up Rome On

175 Michael Lerman: Authors' interview, 06.10.2016
176 Michael Lerman: Authors' interview, 06.10.2016
177 Chris Corbould: Authors' interview, 04.10.2016
178 Chris Corbould: Authors' interview, 04.10.2016
179 *Spectre* production notes, SPE, 2015
180 Chris Corbould: Authors' interview, 04.10.2016
181 Gary Powell: Authors' interview, 04.10.2016
182 Gary Powell: Authors' interview, 04.10.2016
183 Gary Powell: Authors' interview, 04.10.2016
184 Gary Powell: Authors' interview, 04.10.2016
185 Gary Powell: Authors' interview, 04.10.2016
186 'James Bond Film Scene "Too Risky For Baroque Fountain"' by Nick Squires, *The Telegraph*, 08.01.2015
187 Gary Powell: Authors' interview, 04.10.2016
188 Gary Powell: Authors' interview, 04.10.2016
189 Gary Powell: Authors' interview, 04.10.2016
190 Chris Corbould: Authors' interview, 04.10.2016
191 Sam Mendes: Authors' interview, 05.10.2016
192 Sam Mendes: Authors' interview, 05.10.2016
193 Neal Purvis: Authors' interview, 23.09.2016
194 Callum McDougall: Authors' interview, 20.11.2016
195 Callum McDougall: Authors' interview, 20.11.2016
196 Jany Temime: Authors' interview, 05.09.2016
197 Robert Wade: Authors' interview, 23.09.2016
198 'Monica Bellucci Interview' by Ricky Camilleri, *AOL Build*, 18.10.2015
199 Sam Mendes: Authors' interview, 05.10.2016
200 Sam Mendes: Authors' interview, 05.10.2016
201 'Mexican Rave' by Neil Alcock, *Empire*, November 2015
202 John Logan: Authors' interview, 03.11.2016
203 '*Spectre*: Interview With Sam Mendes' by Benjamin B, *American Cinematographer*, www.asc.com/blog, 30.10.2015
204 '*Spectre*: Interview With Sam Mendes' by Benjamin B, *American Cinematographer*, www.asc.com/blog, 30.10.2015
205 Michael Lerman: Authors' interview, 06.10.2016
206 '*Spectre*: Dennis Gassner Interview "Production Design"' by Emanual Levy, *Back to the Movies*, www.bttm.com, 16.02.2015
207 Michael Lerman: Authors' interview, 06.10.2016
208 Jany Temime: Authors' interview, 05.09.2016
209 Michael Lerman: Authors' interview, 06.10.2016
210 Chris Corbould: Authors' interview, 04.10.2016
211 Michael Lerman: Authors' interview, 06.10.2016
212 Michael Lerman: Authors' interview,

Spectre Shoot' by Lee Marshall, *The Telegraph*, 12.03.2015

06.10.2016

213 'Licence Renewed' by Jane Crowther, *SFX Magazine* #267, December 2015

214 Daniel Craig: Authors' interview, 22.10.2015

215 Daniel Craig: Authors' interview, 22.10.2015

216 Michael Lerman: Authors' interview, 06.10.2016

217 Gary Powell: Authors' interview, 04.10.2016

218 Gary Powell: Authors' interview, 04.10.2016

219 Callum McDougall: Authors' interview, 20.11.2016

220 Per Hallberg: Authors' interview, 10.11.2016

221 Michael Lerman: Authors' interview, 06.10.2016

222 Gary Powell: Authors' interview, 04.10.2016

223 Gary Powell: Authors' interview, 04.10.2016

224 Callum McDougall: Authors' interview, 20.11.2016

225 Steve Begg: Authors' interview, 09.11.2016

226 Callum McDougall: Authors' interview, 20.11.2016

227 Callum McDougall: Authors' interview, 20.11.2016

228 Steve Begg: Authors' interview, 09.11.2016

229 'From Mexico With Love: How Sony Got Millions In Incentives To Rewrite 007 film' by Brian Bardwell, www.taxanalysts.org, 03.03.2015

230 'From Mexico With Love: How Sony Got Millions In Incentives To Rewrite 007 Film' by Brian Bardwell, www.taxanalysts.org, 03.03.2015

231 Michael Lerman: Authors' interview, 06.10.2016

232 'Bond Brings Day Of The Dead To Mexico City' by Matt Sandy, *The Times*, 31.10.2016

233 *Spectre* production notes, SPE, 2015

234 'A chat with Dennis Gassner, SPECTRE production designer' by Alton Williams, www.battleroyalewithcheese.com, 21.02.2016

235 Rory Kinnear: Authors' interview, 18.10.2016

236 Michael Lerman: Authors' interview, 06.10.2016

237 Callum McDougall: Authors' interview, 20.11.2016

238 Paul Weston: Authors' interview, 27.11.2016

239 Callum McDougall: Authors' interview, 20.11.2016

240 Callum McDougall: Authors' interview, 20.11.2016

241 Chris Corbould: Authors' interview, 04.10.2016

242 Steve Begg: Authors' interview, 09.11.2016

243 Steve Begg: Authors' interview, 09.11.2016

244 Steve Begg: Authors' interview, 09.11.2016

245 Sam Mendes: Authors' interview, 05.10.2016

246 'A Chat With Dennis Gassner, SPECTRE Production Designer' by Alton Williams, www.battleroyalewithcheese.com, 21.02.2016

247 Per Hallberg: Authors' interview, 10.11.2016

248 Callum McDougall: Authors' interview, 20.11.2016

249 Sam Mendes: Authors' interview, 05.10.2016

250 Callum McDougall: Authors' interview, 20.11.2016

251 Sam Mendes: Authors' interview, 05.10.2016

252 Jany Temime: Authors' interview, 05.09.2016

253 Jany Temime: Authors' interview, 05.09.2016

254 Jany Temime: Authors' interview, 05.09.2016

255 Sam Mendes: Authors' interview, 05.10.2016

256 'A Chat With Dennis Gassner, SPECTRE Production Designer' by Alton Williams, www.battleroyalewithcheese.com, 21.02.2016

257 Michael Lerman: Authors' interview, 06.10.2016

258 'Léa Seydoux Interview' by Ricky Camillieri *AOL Build*, 18.10.2015

259 'A Chat With Dennis Gassner, SPECTRE Production Designer' by Alton Williams, www.battleroyalewithcheese.com, 21.02.2016

260 Steve Begg: Authors' interview, 09.11.2016

261 Chris Corbould: Authors' interview, 04.10.2016

262 Chris Corbould: Authors' interview, 04.10.2016

263 'Latest Bond Adventure *Spectre* Sets Record For Largest Film Stunt Explosion Ever' by Rachel Swatman, www.guinnessworldrecords.com, 10.11.2015

264 Chris Corbould: Authors' interview, 04.10.2016

265 Michael Lerman: Authors' interview, 06.10.2016

266 'Licence Renewed' by Jane Crowther, *SFX Magazine* #267, December 2015

267 Sam Mendes: Authors' interview, 23.12.2016

268 Steve Begg: Authors' interview, 09.11.2016

269 Steve Begg: Authors' interview, 09.11.2016

270 Steve Begg: Authors' interview, 09.11.2016

271 Steve Begg: Authors' interview, 09.11.2016

272 Sam Mendes: Authors' interview, 29.09.2016

273 'Art Of The Cut With Lee Smith On Cutting 007's "SPECTRE"' by Steve Hullfish, *Art of the Cut*, 01.03.2016

274 Untitled B24 screenplay by John Logan, revisions by Neal Purvis and Robert Wade, 01.12.2014

275 Sam Mendes: Authors' interview, 29.09.2016

276 Sam Mendes: Authors' interview, 29.09.2016

277 Sam Mendes: Authors' interview, 29.09.2016

278 Per Hallberg: Authors' interview, 10.11.2016

279 Per Hallberg: Authors' interview, 10.11.2016

280 Sam Mendes: Authors' interview, 29.09.2016

281 'Art Of The Cut With Lee Smith On Cutting 007's "SPECTRE"' by Steve Hullfish, *Art of the Cut*, 01.03.2016

282 *In Tune* presented by Sean Rafferty, BBC Radio 3, 15.10.2015

283 Sam Mendes: Authors' interview, 29.09.2016

284 Per Hallberg: Authors' interview, 10.11.2016

285 Neal Purvis: Authors' interview, 23.09.2016

286 Sam Mendes: Authors' interview, 29.09.2016

287 *The Story of the Bond Song* presented by Nick Grimshaw, BBC Radio 1, 10.11.2015

288 *The Story of the Bond Song* presented by Nick Grimshaw, BBC Radio 1, 10.11.2015

289 Press release, SPE, 08.09.2015

290 Sam Mendes: Authors' interview, 29.09.2016

291 *The Story of the Bond Song* presented by Nick Grimshaw, BBC Radio 1, 10.11.2015

292 *The Story of the Bond Song* presented by Nick Grimshaw, BBC Radio 1, 10.11.2015

293 Sam Mendes: Authors' interview, 29.09.2016

294 *The Story of the Bond Song* presented by Nick Grimshaw, BBC Radio 1, 10.11.2015

295 Sam Mendes: Authors' interview, 29.09.2016

296 Sam Mendes: Authors' interview, 29.09.2016

297 Radiohead, Soundcloud.com, 25.12.2015

298 *The First Time with Johnny Greenwood* presented by Matt Everitt, BBC Radio 6, 19.06.2016

299 Sam Mendes: Authors' interview, 05.10.2016

300 Daniel Kleinman: Authors' interview, 28.09.2016

301 Daniel Kleinman: Authors' interview, 28.09.2016

302 Daniel Kleinman: Authors' interview, 28.09.2016

303 Daniel Kleinman: Authors' interview, 28.09.2016

304 Daniel Kleinman: Authors' interview, 28.09.2016

305 Daniel Kleinman: Authors' interview, 28.09.2016

306 Daniel Kleinman: Authors' interview, 28.09.2016

307 Sam Mendes: Authors' interview, 29.09.2016

308 Sam Mendes: Authors' interview, 29.09.2016

309 Daniel Kleinman: Authors' interview, 28.09.2016

310 Sam Mendes: Authors' interview, 29.09.2016

311 Sam Mendes: Authors' interview, 29.09.2016

312 Jany Temime: Authors' interview, 05.09.2016

Chapter 32 The Road to Bond 25

1 'New Sony Chief Tom Rothman on His Plan to Get the Studio Back in the Game' by Brent Lang and James Rainey, *Variety*, 02.06.2015

2 'Spectre' Producer Expects Daniel Craig to Return for Another Bond Movie' by Stephen Galloway, 06.11.2015, www.hollywood reporter.com

3 'Spectre' Producer Expects Daniel Craig to Return for Another Bond Movie' by Stephen Galloway, 06.11.2015, www.hollywood reporter.com

4 'Spectre' Producer Expects Daniel Craig to Return for Another Bond Movie' by Stephen Galloway, 06.11.2015, www.hollywood reporter.com

5 'Spectre' Producer Expects Daniel Craig to Return for Another Bond Movie' by Stephen Galloway, 06.11.2015, www.hollywood reporter.com

6 'New Sony Chief Tom Rothman on His Plan to Get the Studio Back in the Game' by Brent Lang and James Rainey, *Variety*, 02.06.2015

7 'Spectre' Producer Expects Daniel Craig to Return for Another Bond Movie' by Stephen Galloway, 06.11.2015, www.hollywood reporter.com

8 Company number 09577149, www.companieshouse.gov.uk

9 Albert R Broccoli with Donald Zec, *When The Snow Melts*, Boxtree Ltd 1998, p. 169

10 'Paramount Lands Blake Lively Spy Thriller *The Rhythm Section* By 007 Producers & IM Global' by Mike Fleming Jr, Deadline.com, 16.08.2018

11 Barbara Broccoli: *Woman's Hour*, BBC Radio 4 04.12.2013

12 Barbara Broccoli appointed BAFTA's Vice President for Film, BAFTA Press Release, 04.04.2016

13 *The Silent Storm* official production notes, 2014

14 Barbara Broccoli appointed BAFTA's Vice President for Film, BAFTA Press Release, 04.04.2016

15 Barbara Broccoli appointed BAFTA's Vice President for Film, BAFTA Press Release, 04.04.2016

16 'Of Course I'm Getting My Kit Off! I've Been Working Out For Six Months' by Dave Calhoun, *Time Out* #2351, 20-25.10.2015

17 'Of Course I'm Getting My Kit Off! I've Been Working Out For Six Months' by Dave Calhoun, *Time Out* #2351, 20-25.10.2015

18 The Truth Behind That $150 Million Daniel Craig Bond Rumor by Christie Lee, www.vanityfair.com, 09.09.2016

19 Daniel Craig: Authors' interview 22.10.2015

20 'Daniel Craig "Absolutely First Choice"' for Bond Producers' by Leo Barraclough, *Variety*, 30.10.2016

21 'Spectre' Producer Expects Daniel Craig to Return for Another Bond Movie' by Stephen Galloway, 06.11.2015, www.hollywood reporter.com

22 Beyond Bond, Daniel Craig talks with Nicholas Schmidle, Beyond Bond, The New Yorker Festival, Mastercard Stage at SVA Theatre 1, 07.10.2016.

23   Press release, MGM, Eon Productions
      24.07.2017
24   *The Late Show*, CBS, 15.08.2017
25   Magic 106.7, Boston, 15.08.2015
26   *The Late Show*, CBS, 15.08.2017
27   *The Late Show*, CBS, 15.08.2017
28   'Britain Ruled by Nazis – What Would Bond
      do? 007 Writers Purvis and Wade Take on
      Len Deighton in *SS-GB*' by Rob Collins, *The
      Telegraph*, 19.02.2017
29   'Britain Ruled by Nazis – What Would Bond
      do? 007 Writers Purvis and Wade Take on
      Len Deighton in *SS-GB*' by Rob Collins, *The
      Telegraph*, 19.02.2017
30   Press release, MGM, Eon Productions
      24.07.2017
31   Neal Purvis: Authors' interview 23.09.2016
32   'Five Studios' Mission: Winning the
      Distribution Rights to James Bond' by Brookes
      Barnes *New York Times*, 20.04.2017
33   'Five Studios' Mission: Winning the
      Distribution Rights to James Bond' by Brookes
      Barnes, *New York Times*, 20.04.2017
34   'Gary Barber Ouster Came as MGM Board
      Pushed for Bigger Deals, More Strategic
      Moves' by Cynthia Littleton, *Variety*, 20.03.2018
35   'MGM Using James Bond Rights as Leverage
      for a Possible Sale' by Tatiana Siegel, *The
      Hollywood Reporter*, 04.04.2018
36   'Bond 25: Danny Boyle High on MGM's List
      to Direct (Exclusive)' by Justin Kroll, *Variety*,
      20.02.2018
37   'How A Danny Boyle-Directed James Bond
      Film Could Happen: Think *Trainspotting*
      Reunion' by Mike Fleming Jr, Deadline.com,
      21.02.2018

38   'Oscar-winning director Danny Boyle is set
      to take charge of the new Bond film by the
      end of the year' by Baz Bamigboye, *Daily Mail*,
      09.03.2018
39   'Danny Boyle Confirms He's Working on
      Bond 25' by Dave McNary, *Variety*, 15.03.2018
40   Eon Productions and Metro Goldwyn Mayer
      Studios Partner With Universal Pictures to
      Distribute *BOND 25*' Universal Pictures press
      release, 24.05.2018
41   Barbara Broccoli: Authors' interview
      21.10.2012
42   'The Name's Wilson, Michael Wilson,' by
      Liz Jobey, *Financial Times Weekend* magazine,
      13.10.2012
43   'Serious Bondage' by Gary Russell, *Starburst*,
      July 1989
44   Barbara Broccoli: Woman's Hour, BBC Radio
      4, 04.12.2013
45   'The Name's Wilson, Michael Wilson' by
      Liz Jobey, *Financial Times Weekend* magazine,
      13.10.2012
46   Helen De Winter *What I Really Want to Do Is
      Produce*, Faber & Faber, p. 44
47   'The Name's Wilson, Michael Wilson,' by
      Liz Jobey, *Financial Times Weekend* magazine,
      13.10.2012
48   Helen De Winter, *What I Really Want to Do Is
      Produce*,, Faber & Faber, p. 44
49   Michael Wilson: Authors' interview 21.10.2012
50   Barbara Broccoli: Authors' interview
      21.10.2012
51   'All in the family,' *MI6 Confidential*, issue 19,
      January 2013
52   Michael Wilson: Authors' interview 21.10.2012

Epilogue

1   Sean Connery: Authors' interview, 12.10.2016
2   Sean Connery: Authors' interview, 12.10.2016
3   Sean Connery: Authors' interview, 12.10.2016

4   Sean Connery: Authors' interview, 12.10.2016
5   Sean Connery: Authors' interview, 12.10.2016
6   Sean Connery: Authors' interview, 12.10.2016

Afterword

1   Moore family press statement 23.05.2017
2   Gareth Owen: Author's interview: 01.05.2018
3   Sean Connery press statement 23.05.2017
4   George Lazenby press statement 23.05.2017
5   Official James Bond Twitter account 24.05.2017
6   Official James Bond Twitter account 23.05.2017

7   'Pierce Brosnan writes tribute to Roger
     Moore: 'We fell in love with a magnificent
     actor' by Pierce Brosnan, www.variety.com,
     30.05.2017
8   Gareth Owen: Author's interview: 01.05.2018

INDEX

NOW PAY ATTENTION

SOME KIND OF HERO will return